FOUNDATIONS

of Restaurant Management & Culinary Arts

Level One

Teacher's Wraparound Edition

National Restaurant Association

Prentice Hall

Boston   Columbus   Indianapolis   New York   San Francisco   Upper Saddle River   Amsterdam

Cape Town   Dubai   London   Madrid   Milan   Munich   Paris   Montreal   Toronto

Delhi   Mexico City   Sao Paulo   Sydney   Hong Kong   Seoul   Singapore   Taipei   Tokyo

Editorial Director: Vernon Anthony
Executive Editor: Wendy Craven
Director of Marketing: David Gesell
Campaign Marketing Manager: Leigh Ann Sims
School Marketing Manager: Laura Cutone
Senior Marketing Assistant: Les Roberts
Associate Managing Editor: Alexandrina Benedicto Wolf
Project Manager: Kris Roach
Senior Operations Supervisor: Pat Tonneman
Operations Specialist: Deidra Skahill
Cover Designer: Jane Diane Ricciardi
Manager, Rights and Permissions: Zina Arabia

Cover Art: Kipling Swehla
NRAS Product Management Team: Janet Benoit, Megan Meyer, William Nolan, Rachel Peña, and Wendi Safstrom
Product Development and Project Management: Emergent Learning, LLC
Writing and Text Development: Kristine Westover, Michelle Graas, Michelle Somody, Tom Finn
Editorial and Composition: Claire Hunter and Abshier House
Printer/Binder: Courier Kendallville
Cover Printer: Phoenix Color

Credits and acknowledgments borrowed from other sources and reproduced, with permission, in this textbook appear on appropriate page within text (or on page 873).

2 3 4 5 6 7 8 9 10 V011 15 14 13 12 11 10

Prentice Hall
an imprint of

PearsonSchool.com/careertech

ISBN 13: 978-0-13-707053-4
ISBN 10: 0-13-707053-5

Brief Table of Contents

Level 1

This is the first book in a two-book series covering the Foundations of Restaurant Management & Culinary Arts.

Level 2

Table of Contents for the second book of this two-book series covering the Foundations of Restaurant Management & Culinary Arts. The ISBN for the Level 2 book is 0-13-138022-2.

Can students using this book receive recognition from the National Restaurant Association?

Yes!

The *Foundations of Restaurant Management & Culinary Arts*–Levels 1 and 2 curriculum teaches students the fundamental skills they will need to begin a career in the industry. What's more, after completing each level of this industry-driven curriculum, students can sit for the National Restaurant Association's exam for that level. Students who pass both the Level 1 and Level 2 exams receive certificates from the National Restaurant Association.

NATIONAL RESTAURANT ASSOCIATION®

FOUNDATIONS
of restaurant management & culinary arts

Certificate No.

CERTIFICATE OF RECOGNITION

For successfully completing the objectives set forth in Level One
of Foundations of Restaurant Management & Culinary Arts,
the National Restaurant Association awards this certificate to:

MARY SMITH

PRESIDENT & CEO, NATIONAL RESTAURANT ASSOCIATION /
NATIONAL RESTAURANT ASSOCIATION EDUCATIONAL FOUNDATION

EXAM DATE

LEVEL ONE

©2010 National Restaurant Association Educational Foundation. All rights reserved.
09101501   v.0910

NATIONAL RESTAURANT ASSOCIATION®

FOUNDATIONS
of restaurant management & culinary arts

Certificate No.

CERTIFICATE OF RECOGNITION

For successfully completing the objectives set forth in Level Two
of Foundations of Restaurant Management & Culinary Arts,
the National Restaurant Association awards this certificate to:

MARY SMITH

PRESIDENT & CEO, NATIONAL RESTAURANT ASSOCIATION /
NATIONAL RESTAURANT ASSOCIATION EDUCATIONAL FOUNDATION

EXAM DATE

LEVEL TWO

©2010 National Restaurant Association Educational Foundation. All rights reserved.
09101501   v.0910

Welcome Teachers!

Dear Teachers:

Thank you for choosing *Foundations of Restaurant Management & Culinary Arts* for your classroom!

We at the National Restaurant Association are thrilled to take this journey with you and your students as they learn more about the restaurant and foodservice industry. Restaurant and foodservice operations make up one of the most dynamic industries in the United States today. They are a shining example of the entrepreneurial spirit and a place where employees become owners every day.

Millions of opportunities: As the nation's second-largest private-sector employer, the restaurant and foodservice industry creates opportunity for millions of Americans. The industry employs nearly 13 million people today and is expected to add almost 2 million positions over the next decade.

This means there are many opportunities and career paths ahead for your students. Whether it's a quick-service restaurant, a family operation, or a multi-million-dollar company providing on-site foodservice at schools or hospitals, our industry is the place for them to build their career. Please encourage them to explore all that the industry has to offer.

Industry-backed learning materials matter: *Foundations of Restaurant Management & Culinary Arts* was developed with input from industry leaders. We believe that an industry-backed education is the best way to prepare your students to lead the industry into the future. Working with industry and academia, we have identified the management, operational, and culinary skills critical to success in the industry. The skills you teach in Level 1 and Level 2 will give your students a competitive advantage and solid foundation upon which to build their careers or further their educations.

We are proud that you have chosen to partner with the National Restaurant Association to prepare your students for their futures. As the leading business association for the restaurant industry, the Association works to lead America's restaurant industry into a new era of prosperity, prominence, and participation, enhancing the quality of life for all we serve. Our philanthropic foundation, the National Restaurant Association Educational Foundation, enhances the restaurant industry's service to the public through education, community engagement, and promotion of career opportunities.

We invite you to learn more about us at www.restaurant.org and www.nraef.org, and be sure to check out Overview of the ProStart® Program on page VI to learn more about the ProStart program and its benefits for students and educators.

Overview of the ProStart® Program

The National Restaurant Association Educational Foundation's (NRAEF) ProStart® program teaches high school students the management and culinary skills needed for a career in the restaurant and foodservice industry. Throughout an exciting two-year period, they study in the classroom, participate in mentored work experiences, and test their skills in local and national competitions. Whether students are looking to enter the job market directly after graduation or plan to attend college, a ProStart graduate makes a solid candidate for success.

The heart of the ProStart program is the connection with the restaurant and foodservice industry. The career-building program was developed by the National Restaurant Association Educational Foundation and is supported by partnerships with state restaurant associations across the United States. The program is designed to:

- Increase and strengthen industry involvement in high school classrooms

- Set the standard for restaurant and foodservice career education

- Improve the image of restaurant and foodservice management as a career

- Recruit and train students to become the next industry leaders

How the ProStart Program Works

Classroom Experience
The Foundations of Restaurant Management & Culinary Arts—Levels 1 and 2 curriculum teaches students the fundamental skills they will need to begin a career in the industry. After completing each level of the industry-driven curriculum, students sit for the National Restaurant Association's exam for that level.

Mentored Work Experience
ProStart students put classroom learning to work on the job in qualified industry operations. In their work experience, students receive mentor support, character development, and real-world skills that help launch their careers. Working with industry mentors, they demonstrate that they have mastered a series of competencies defined as critical to success by the industry.

ProStart National Certificate of Achievement
Students who pass both the Level 1 and Level 2 exams and complete the 400-hour mentored work experience are eligible to earn the ProStart National Certificate of Achievement. ProStart graduates who earn this prestigious certificate possess a solid foundation for their future careers, and are eligible to earn special scholarships and college credit from colleges and universities across the country. It also opens the door to our vibrant and growing industry.

National ProStart Invitational

During their two years in the program, students have the opportunity to put their skills to the ultimate test in the National ProStart Invitational. This demanding culinary and management competition invites top students to represent their state, with winning teams competing for scholarships. To compete at the National ProStart Invitational, teams must first win at the state level competition hosted by their state restaurant association.

How the ProStart Program Benefits Students

Students who earn the ProStart National Certificate of Achievement have access to numerous scholarship and articulation opportunities to put them on the fast track to a college degree. The NRAEF offers special scholarships to students who earn the certificate, as well as to winning teams at the National ProStart Invitational. Annually, more than $1.5 million in scholarships are awarded to competition winners at the state and national levels. In addition, many colleges and universities across the country have articulation agreements with ProStart that award students scholarships, class credits, or work hour credits when they enroll.

Students in the ProStart program have access to support and resources from the National Restaurant Association, the NRAEF, and their state restaurant association. They join a network of restaurateurs and chefs who recognize the students as the future of the industry and are committed to helping them succeed. The National Restaurant Association also offers a complimentary student membership to ProStart students.

How the ProStart Program Benefits Educators

ProStart program educators benefit from professional development opportunities, ranging from state-wide training hosted by state restaurant associations to national webinars. The NRAEF also sponsors the Educator Training & Development Awards. Recipients are hosted for a week of management training, alongside the company's own managers, by ProStart sponsor companies.

Each participating state restaurant association employs a ProStart Coordinator to work with ProStart educators in the state. The coordinator helps connect educators and classrooms with local industry. These connections can aid in securing mentored work experience for students, classroom supplies and equipment, and classroom demonstrations, among others. ProStart educators also have access to support and resources from the National Restaurant Association and NRAEF, including a complimentary Association membership.

How to Get Involved

To learn more about joining the ProStart program, contact your state restaurant association. For more information on the program or to locate your state ProStart Coordinator, visit www.prostart. restaurant.org.

Learning Objectives

Chapter 1: Welcome to the Restaurant and Foodservice Industry

Section 1.1
1.1 Identify the two segments of the restaurant and foodservice industry, and give examples of businesses in each of them.
1.2 Categorize the types of businesses that make up the travel and tourism industry.
1.3 Outline the growth of the hospitality industry throughout the history of the world, emphasizing growth in the United States.
1.4 List chefs who have made significant culinary contributions, and note their major accomplishments.
1.5 List entrepreneurs who have influenced foodservice in the United States.

Section 1.2
1.6 Identify foodservice opportunities provided by the travel and tourism industry.
1.7 Identify career opportunities offered by the travel and tourism industry.
1.8 Identify the two major categories of jobs in the restaurant and foodservice industry.

Section 1.3
1.9 Name reasons why people travel.
1.10 Describe the differences between leisure and business travelers.
1.11 Identify national organizations that rate commercial lodging and foodservice establishments, and list factors used in making their rating judgments.
1.12 List and describe the characteristic types of lodging operations.
1.13 List and describe activities associated with front-desk operations.

Chapter 2: Keeping Food Safe

Section 2.1
2.1 Define what a foodborne-illness outbreak is, and list the costs associated with one.
2.2 Recognize risks associated with high-risk populations.
2.3 Identify factors that affect the growth of pathogens (FAT TOM).

2.4 Identify characteristics of TCS food and list examples.
2.5 Identify methods for preventing biological contamination.
2.6 List guidelines for storing chemicals safely.
2.7 Recognize the need for food defense systems.
2.8 Identify the most common allergens and methods for preventing allergic reactions.
2.9 Identify government agencies that regulate the restaurant and foodservice industry.

Section 2.2
2.10 List personal behaviors that can contaminate food.
2.11 List the steps to proper handwashing, and identify when hands should be washed.
2.12 Identify proper personal cleanliness practices and appropriate work attire.
2.13 Identify ways to handle ready-to-eat food safely.
2.14 Identify when foodhandlers should be prevented from working around food or from working in the operation.

Section 2.3
2.15 Identify ways to prevent cross-contamination.
2.16 Identify ways to prevent time-temperature abuse.
2.17 List different temperature-measuring devices and their uses.
2.18 Identify characteristics of an approved food source.
2.19 Identify criteria for accepting or rejecting food during receiving.
2.20 Outline proper procedures for storing food.
2.21 Identify the minimum internal temperature requirements for cooking various TCS food.
2.22 Outline proper procedures for holding, cooling, and reheating TCS food.
2.23 Identify ways to handle food ready for service.
2.24 Outline proper procedures for preparing and serving food for off-site service.

Section 2.4
2.25 List the HACCP principles and explain their importance to food safety.

Section 2.5
2.26 Explain the difference between cleaning and sanitizing.
2.27 Outline proper procedures for cleaning and sanitizing tools and equipment.
2.28 Identify factors that affect the effectiveness of sanitizers.
2.29 List the elements of a master cleaning schedule.

Preface

Our objective with this program is simple yet significant:

Provide an industry-driven curriculum that prepares students for a career in restaurant and foodservice management.

To achieve that objective, *Foundations of Restaurant Management & Culinary Arts* was meticulously developed by the National Restaurant Association with input and contributions from countless representatives from both industry and education. That balanced perspective is important in helping students make the connection between classrooms and careers.

The visual tour that follows summarizes many of this textbook's most distinguishing and remarkable features. *Foundations of Restaurant Management & Culinary Arts*, Level 1 and Level 2, provide the following benefits:

- Comprehensive coverage of culinary and management topics
- An industry-infused approach
- Pedagogy that supports 21st Century Learning
- Relevant and timely topics from global cuisines to sustainability
- Content aligned to certificates and ProStart program opportunities
- Certificate opportunities that meet Carl Perkins funding requirements
- Supplements and technologies that help educators do more in less time

We offer a pedagogy that is fortified by 21st Century Learning themes and objectives:

Foundations of Restaurant Management & Culinary Arts provides teachers and students with tools carefully developed to reinforce 21st Century Learning:

- Critical thinking and problem solving
- Communication and collaboration
- Creativity and innovation
- Global awareness
- Health literacy

Thank you for considering *Foundations of Restaurant Management & Culinary Arts!*

Features of the Teacher's Wraparound Edition Include:

Chapter Overview–This includes summary information on the sections in each chapter. Teachers can use this material as an introduction to what students are about to learn.

Advance Preparation–A table is included on the opening page of each chapter, with suggestions for steps instructors may take to prepare for the class.

Customized Instruction Options–These list the pages where teachers can look for instructional materials customized for different levels of learning.

Chapter Tools–Directs teachers to activities that include 21st-Century Skills, Mathematics, Science, or Literacy.

ServSafe Connection–This points teachers to where this content is covered.

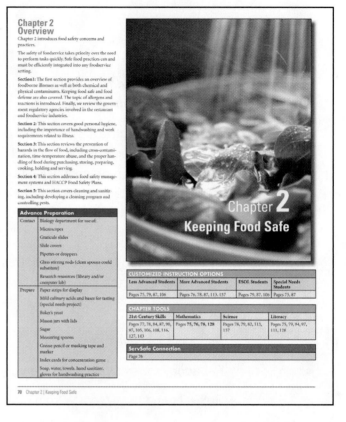

Focus and Engage–Introductory text helps teachers get the students introduced in what they are about to learn.

Introduce the Section–This includes a list of important facts covered in the chapter that can be used to introduce content to come.

Vocabulary Terms–Key terms and definitions introduced on the current page are supplied.

Discuss–These discussion topics relate directly and indirectly to the content on the current page.

Reinforce and Review–Topics covered in the previous section, or in previous chapters, that instructors may want to review before continuing are provided.

Teaching Tips–These items help explain the content and provide additional information for instructors to use in the classroom.

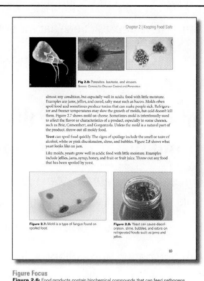

Customized Instruction Boxes–These include accommodations and additional activities for More Advanced, Less Advanced, ESOL, Special Needs, and At-Risk Students.

Figure Focus–Every figure in the student edition has a corresponding Figure Focus feature in the Teacher's Wraparound Edition, to provide additional information for discussion and instruction.

In-Class and Homework Activity Boxes–These original activities are not in the student edition textbook. They are designed to encourage students to use critical-thinking skill and to promote teamwork, cooperation, and leadership skills.

Feature Focuses–Every feature and box in the student edition has a corresponding feature in the Teacher's Wraparound Edition, to provide answers, discussion prompts, and additional teaching tips.

End-of-Section and Chapter Activities–Answers, additional teaching tips, discussion points, and supplemental activities relating to the end of chapter activities are provided.

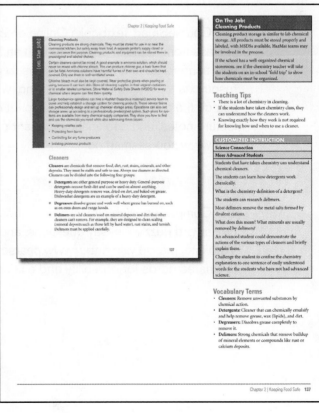

Supplements:

Activity Guide

The Activity Guide contains a wealth of additional lab and classroom activities to supplement the activities in the Student Edition. It includes critical-thinking activities that review and enhance the text learning, as well as hands-on application activities that give students more opportunities to experience the course content interactively. Separate books for Level 1 and Level 2.

Test Book with ExamView® Assessment Suite CD-ROM

The comprehensive test bank includes objective and short answer questions for both levels of the Student Text. Questions are provided in print format for duplication with separate answer keys, as well as on CD in ExamView® software for creating randomized and customized exams. Separate books for Level 1 and Level 2.

Teacher's Resource CD

A complete media CD supports the teaching package. It includes PowerPoint® presentations, videos, and interactive media for each chapter, as well as point-of-use teaching notes and tips, answers, and class/lab set-up information for the activities in the student Activity Guide. Separate CDs for Level 1 and Level 2.

CourseSmart Textbooks Online

The CourseSmart Textbooks Online enable students to access the textbook they use in class from home or anywhere with an Internet connection. CourseSmart eTextbooks give schools an affordable alternative to providing students with the essential learning resources they need to succeed. And, with a CourseSmart eTextbook, students can search the text, make notes online, print out reading assignments that incorporate lecture notes, and bookmark important passages for later review. For more information, visit www.coursesmart.com.

Additional Supplements

The Companion Web site includes student resources and additional activities such as crossword puzzles, essay questions, and self-grading quizzes. To access the Companion Web site, please visit http://www.pearsonhighered.com/nra. Recipe Cards are printed on laminated cards for durability and ease of use.

Acknowledgements

The development of Level 1 and Level 2 of *Foundations of Restaurant Management & Culinary Arts* would not have been possible without the expertise and guidance of our many advisors, contributors, and reviewers. We would like to thank the thousands of educators who have been involved in the ProStart program and given us invaluable support and feedback as they have taught the National Restaurant Association's curriculum. Additionally, we offer our thanks to the following individuals and organizations for their time, effort, and dedication in creating these first editions.

Curt Archambault
Jack in the Box, Inc.

Linda Bacin and the staff
of Bella Bacinos, Chicago, IL

Allen Bild
Hammond Area Career Center
Hammond, IN

Brian Bergquist
University of Wisconsin-Stout

Scott Brecher
Long Beach High School
Long Beach, NY

Barbara Jean Bruin
The Collins College of Hospitality Management

Nancy Caldarola
Concept Associates, Inc.

Jerald Chesser
The Collins College of Hospitality Management

Billie DeNunzio
Eastside High School
Gainesville, FL

Mary K. Drayer
Trotwood-Madison High School
Trotwood, OH

John A. Drysdale
Johnson County Community College, Emeritus

Therese Duffy
Warren High School
Downey, CA

Michael Edwards
EHOVE Career Center
Huron, OH

Annette Gabert
Ft. Bend ISD Technical Education Center
Sugar Land, TX

Lee Gray
Hospitality Education Foundation of Georgia

Elizabeth Hales
Compass Group North America

Abbie Hall
Lithia Springs High School
Douglasville, GA

Nancy Haney
Tri-County Regional Vocational High School
Medfield, MA

Lyle Hildahl
Washington Restaurant Association Education
Foundation

Tanya Hill
Golden Corral Corporation

Steven M. Hinnant, II
National Academy Foundation High School
Baltimore, MD

Nancy Iannacone
Capital Region BOCES Career and Technical
School
Schoharie, NY

Gary E. Jones
Walt Disney World

Mary June
Adams Twelve Five Star School District Magnet
Program
Thornton, CO

Betty Kaye
The Ohio State University

Thomas Kaltenecker
McHenry County College

Lauren Krzystofiak
Lake Park High School
Roselle, IL

Terri Kuebler
Eureka CUSD #140 High School
Goodfield, IL

Lettuce Entertain You Enterprises
and the staff of Wildfire, Chicago, IL

Michael Levin
Peabody Veterans Memorial High School
Peabody, MA

Paul Malcolm
Johnson & Wales University Charlotte

Edward Manville
Apex High School
Apex, NC

Victor Martinez
Hospitality Industry Education Foundation

Timothy Michitsch
Lorain County JVS
Oberlin, OH

Patricia A. Plavcan
Le Cordon Bleu College of Culinary Arts

Mark Molinaro
New England Culinary Institute

Scott Rudolph
The Collins College of Hospitality Management

Michael Santos
Micatrotto Restaurant Group

Greg Schaub
Aramark Corporation

Susan G. Seay
North Carolina Hospitality Education Foundation

Ed Sherwin
Sherwin Food Safety

Rudy Speckamp
Culinary Institute of America

John Stephens
Compass Group North America

Karl Titz
University of Houston

Laura Walsh
Walsh Nutrition Group, Inc.

Anthony Wietek
The Cooking and Hospitality Institute of Chicago

LaDeana Wentzel
Restaurant Association of Maryland Education
Foundation

Michael Yip
Tulsa Technology Center
Tulsa, OK

Michael Zema
Elgin Community College, Emeritus

Table of Contents

Emeril Lagasse

Chef / Restaurateur

Emeril Lagasse is the chef/proprietor of 13 restaurants including three in New Orleans (Emeril's, NOLA, and Emeril's Delmonico); four in Las Vegas (Emeril's New Orleans Fish House, Delmonico Steakhouse, Table 10, and Lagasse's Stadium); two in Orlando (Emeril's Orlando and Tchoup Chop); one in Miami (Emeril's Miami Beach), one in Gulfport, Mississippi (Emeril's Gulf Coast Fish House), and two in Bethlehem, Pennsylvania (Emeril's Chop House and Burgers And More by Emeril).

The recognition and awards he has garnered have made him known to food-loving Americans everywhere. His restaurants consistently win critical praise and top ratings, and he is the best-selling author of 13 cookbooks.

In September 2002, Emeril established the Emeril Lagasse Foundation to support and encourage culinary arts and education programs for children. As of May 2009, the foundation has contributed $3 million to organizations in New Orleans and on the Gulf Coast. The Foundation also extended its partnership with the New Orleans Center for the Creative Arts (NOCCA) to establish the city's first comprehensive 4-year professional training program in culinary arts for high school students, and has donated capital funds to develop the Emeril Lagasse Foundation Culinary Learning Center at Cafe Reconcile in New Orleans. Each fall, the Foundation hosts its annual Carnivale du Vin, a premiere wine and food event to benefit the children of the New Orleans region.

The Story Behind the Man

I became interested in cooking at a very early age, and it's something I've always been passionate about. My mom, Miss Hilda, who is Portuguese and French Canadian, and my dad, Mr. John, were a huge influence on my life. I learned a great deal from my mom—she taught me how to cook and that started my passion for the culinary arts. I also worked at a local Portuguese bakery while in school, where I learned the art of making breads, pastries, and cakes. I found out that there are no shortcuts when it comes to baking. Everything is so precise. It was an important lesson that paid off when I decided to pursue cooking as a career.

While in high school, music was another big passion for me. I was in a local band and played the drums, and it's something that continues to be a big part of my life. I was even offered a scholarship to music school, but I decided instead to enroll in culinary school at Johnson & Wales University. It was definitely one of the toughest decisions I've had to make, and I remember my mom cried!

After culinary school, I spent some time doing apprenticeships in France. Early in my career, I worked in some busy restaurant kitchens in New York City. At the time, being a chef was not a glamorous job. You started very early and ended very late at night. Seeing how much work went in to creating every dish is what really pushed me forward. A few years later, I was offered a job as chef at Commander's Palace in New Orleans. I found that Louisiana's rich food culture melded very well with my background, training, and travels. While cooking in New Orleans, I worked hard to honor the traditional foods that people have been eating for generations, and still find new ways to experiment and make them my own.

Eight years later, I opened Emeril's Restaurant, and I'm very proud to have put my own mark on the local scene.

As I mentioned earlier, I learned the art of baking at an early age. I was amazed by how labor intensive the process is...taking the raw ingredients and turning them into something delicious. What I learned from baking is one of the most important foundations of my restaurants. We make everything from scratch...bread, pasta, Andouille sausage, Worcestershire sauce, ice creams, dozen of sauces. It's all about choosing the best ingredients, paying attention to every small detail, creating each dish with skill and consistency. There are no shortcuts.

In the hospitality/restaurant industry, we are in the business of making people happier than they were before they walked in the door. It's one of the few careers where you can see an instant reaction to your hard work and is very gratifying. I enjoy cooking so much that I don't think of it as a job….I'm just doing what I love to do.

Keys to Success

Everyone needs a mentor—someone that you trust and admire who can show you the ropes and help you along the way with practical advice. Read as much as you can…cookbooks, culinary magazines, and industry publications. It will make you a better chef, a better professional, a better leader.

To run a successful restaurant, you must assemble a great team to help look after every detail. I rely on a very capable, talented team to help me oversee things; many of them have been working with me for over 15 years. Every night before our restaurants open for dinner we have what we call "family-meal," where we gather together to eat, we talk about the guests coming in that night, the daily specials, who's celebrating birthdays or anniversaries, and we review our service commandments. It really helps get everyone on the same page and excited about the night ahead. Communication and teamwork are the most important tools in the hospitality business.

❝ *Every day I wake up and try a little bit harder than the day before.* **❞**

One of the most popular dishes at Emeril's—and one that I still love to make—is gumbo. Gumbo is a dish that has a deep history with influences from the Creole, French, Spanish, and African cultures. A good gumbo takes a few hours to make. You start by making a roux, slowing stirring it, adding vegetables, adjusting the seasonings. You taste it again, add another layer of seasoning. There are so many different ways to make a gumbo—each chef has his or her own recipe and secrets—but every step and every ingredient counts.

A successful career in this industry is like making a gumbo. It takes patience, passion, experimentation, and a positive attitude. My advice to you is to work hard and bring your unique talents and personality in to the operation every day. If you respect the history and art of cooking, you're well on your way to becoming an industry leader.

So, to all of you interested in pursuing a career in this industry……"Kick it up a notch!"

Chapter 1 Overview

Chapter 1 introduces the student to the restaurant and foodservice industry by describing both its history and its current shape.

Section 1: The first section provides an overview of the restaurant and foodservice industry, covering its scope and history.

Section 2: This section discusses a wide range of career options in the restaurant and foodservice industry, addressing both job opportunities and types of establishments.

Section 3: The final section describes the lodging industry, covering everything from why people travel to career paths in the lodging field.

Advance Preparation	
Review	Chapter text for sections 1–3
	Local, state, and federal regulations addressing the restaurant and foodservice industry
Contact	Local leaders in the restaurant and foodservice industry
	State restaurant association
	Local and state chapters of other foodservice and hospitality organizations
Prepare	Collect magazine, newspaper, and Internet articles on topics involving restaurant, foodservice, and lodging for class discussion
	Develop a list of Web sites that address hospitality matters and prepare it for distribution

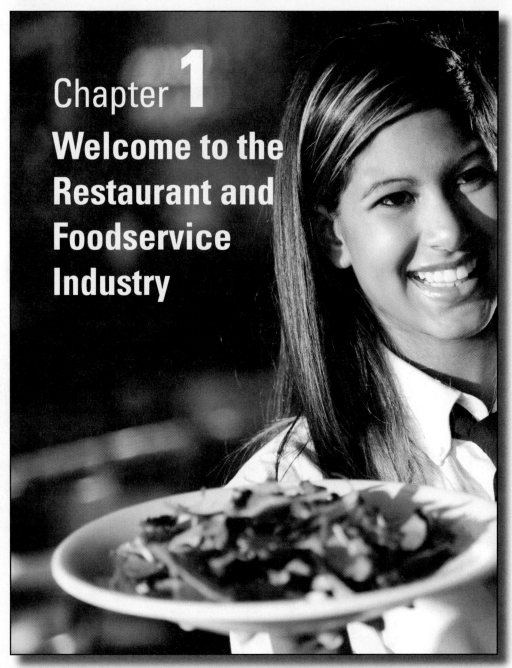

Chapter 1
Welcome to the Restaurant and Foodservice Industry

CUSTOMIZED INSTRUCTION OPTIONS			
Less Advanced Students	More Advanced Students	ESOL Students	Special Needs Students
Pages 18, 28, 37, 56	Pages 12, 16, 39	Pages 10, 17, 40, 55	Pages 8, 17, 40

CHAPTER TOOLS			
21st-Century Skills	Mathematics	Science	Literacy
Pages 5, 9, 10, 15, 16, 17, 18, 21, 22, 28, 29, 37, 39, 40, 44, 45, 53, 55, 56, 59	Pages 9, 12, 39, 53	Pages 22, 59	Pages 8, 10, 12, 16, 17, 18, 21, 28, 29, 36, 37, 39, 40, 44, 45, 55, 56

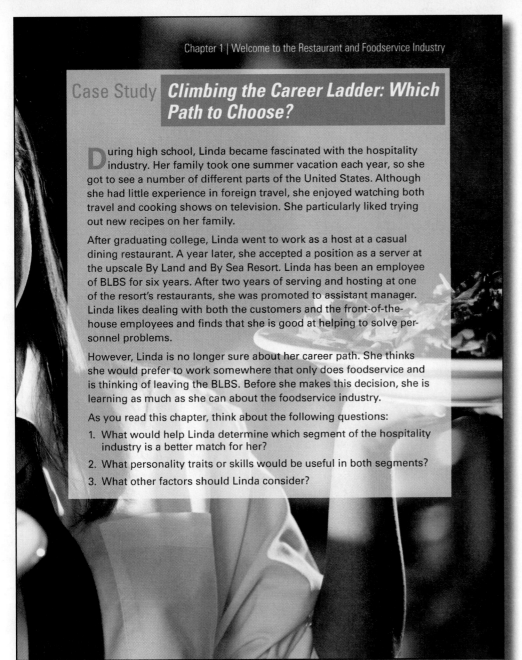

Case Study | *Climbing the Career Ladder: Which Path to Choose?*

During high school, Linda became fascinated with the hospitality industry. Her family took one summer vacation each year, so she got to see a number of different parts of the United States. Although she had little experience in foreign travel, she enjoyed watching both travel and cooking shows on television. She particularly liked trying out new recipes on her family.

After graduating college, Linda went to work as a host at a casual dining restaurant. A year later, she accepted a position as a server at the upscale By Land and By Sea Resort. Linda has been an employee of BLBS for six years. After two years of serving and hosting at one of the resort's restaurants, she was promoted to assistant manager. Linda likes dealing with both the customers and the front-of-the-house employees and finds that she is good at helping to solve personnel problems.

However, Linda is no longer sure about her career path. She thinks she would prefer to work somewhere that only does foodservice and is thinking of leaving the BLBS. Before she makes this decision, she is learning as much as she can about the foodservice industry.

As you read this chapter, think about the following questions:

1. What would help Linda determine which segment of the hospitality industry is a better match for her?
2. What personality traits or skills would be useful in both segments?
3. What other factors should Linda consider?

Case Study
Climbing the Career Ladder: Which Path to Choose?

- This case study (and those found throughout the textbook) are designed to help students think more deeply about common foodservice issues.
- Encourage students to make this activity personal —to put themselves in Linda's position as she considers her career options. Ask students about their own jobs or career goals. How does Linda's situation relate to their own?
- Note that there are follow-up questions about the case study at the end of the chapter.
- This activity could be done in groups, as a class, or as a homework assignment.

Professional Profile

Discuss	Review Michael Santos's career path with students. What lessons can be learned from it?
	Discuss the importance of having a passion. Encourage students to describe their own passions.
	Ask students why they feel it is or is not important to challenge themselves—in school, in extracurricular activities, at work, and elsewhere.
Reinforce and Review	Emphasize the importance of consistency and hard work—not just in the hospitality industry, but in any career path.
	Reinforce the qualities and characteristics that make a good employee.
Teaching Tips	Ask students to identify what they feel are the most important words and phrases in the profile.
	Emphasize that a career path is just that: a route that may have many stops along the way.
	Make sure students understand the roles of formal and informal education in a career path.

[professional profile]

Michael Santos VP of Operations and Human Resources; Partner

Micatrotto Restaurant Group; Raising Canes Chicken Fingers, Las Vegas

" *The pursuit of excellence is more important than the achievement.* **"**
— Joe Micatrotto Sr.

Growing up, I spent a lot of time with my mom and grandmother in the kitchen. For some reason pots, pans, and wooden spoons seemed to intrigue me slightly more than my GI-Joe figures and cap guns. Don't get me wrong, I enjoyed those toys (and still have my cap guns), but food always captured my attention. I just love to eat. So, I guess you could say my passion for this industry began in my mother's kitchen. Watching my mom and grandmother prepare meal after meal after meal with laughter and joy, well, it just seemed like a fun place to be. I love to prepare meals, bring people together, see them enjoy it, and then have them leave the table with a smile.

I wanted to work and earn my own money, so I chose to apply to a local restaurant at the age of 16. I was hired as a host, and that was the beginning. My goal was to make sure that I delivered to the guest what my mom and grandmother delivered to the family at every gathering: good food and an enjoyable atmosphere. I worked my way through the ranks as host, buser, cook, server, trainer, and manager.

In this industry, I've found that working hard and being consistent are the strongest forces moving you ahead. Have a goal in mind, and have your next goal ready and waiting. Never be afraid to reach higher. Mistakes will happen; you just learn from them and keep pushing forward. Challenge yourself!

I went on to work for a major Italian concept, also the recipient of Nation's Restaurant News Hot Concepts Award in 1998. Buca di Beppo had a critical impact on my career. I connected with several mentors there, two of whom I still work with today at the Micatrotto Restaurant Group.

Having a passion for something means having a strong belief in its need and results. As a server and restaurant manager, you quickly learn to serve guests. That's the job. But serving guests with sincerity and integrity makes a huge difference. At 21, I became an assistant general manager at Buca di Beppo, simultaneously working my way through college.

In 2004, I graduated from California State University, Long Beach with a B.S. in Finance and a B.S. in Human Resource Management. Focused on career growth, I decided to look into opportunities as a general manager of a restaurant. This proved harder than expected, so I made a decision to leave restaurants in 2005

4

and become a director of operations and human resources for a manufacturing company. Not my passion, but it aligned with what I had studied in college.

The harder I worked, the more I realized that I really belonged in foodservice in one way or another. Food was at the heart of my inner core. It's what drives me and brings me satisfaction. Fortunately, as I came to this realization, my former mentors from Buca di Beppo approached me. They had created a restaurant group and asked me to join as a partner, responsible to help with the growth of Raising Canes Chicken Fingers in Las Vegas.

I never forget that a guest will always want a good balance of great food and great service. Without mastering both, your operation will struggle.

So, for those of you interested in this industry, I say: "Always stay positive and believe in your abilities. Work hard to learn the proper way of doing a job and then become the best at it!"

Welcome to the Restaurant and Foodservice Industry

The hospitality industry is all about serving your guests. If your focus is not set on making a guest's experience the best it can be, then you are missing what this industry is about. Being passionate about your product and the service you provide is what will make you successful.

Both your image and that of your company will speak for you days after you have touched a guest. The simple things we take for granted often have the most impact on a guest dining out. The simple greeting as soon as the guest arrives, the sincere thank you, eye contact at the time of payment—all of these go a long way in making a guest feel appreciated and valued.

The hospitality industry is about connecting with your guests and giving them what they want and need once in your restaurant, hotel, or kitchen. It's not about you, not about the hours you work. It really is about the end result.

This takes some getting used to, and some people just find they aren't cut out for the industry. Others do not understand how important it is to WOW a guest. I was fortunate to be born into a family who loved to cook, bake, and eat. And my passion for service has allowed me to pursue my career. I will never stop seeking achievement and I will understand that achievement does not necessarily focus on you. The greatest achievements in this industry are often from those around you—your crew and fellow partners.

5

Focus and Engage

Discuss
- Why is the "end result" so important in the restaurant and foodservice industry?
- What if your guests create challenges for you and your coworkers?
- Suggest scenarios such as guests who are rude to the servers, guests who repeatedly send food back to the kitchen (whether or not it has been prepared properly), or guests with specific allergies or other food concerns that present a challenge to a busy kitchen. Ask students how these situations can be addressed to leave the guests feeling satisfied.

In-Class Activity: Solving Guest Problems

21st-Century Skills—Business Literacy, Work Creatively with Others, Solve Problems, Work Effectively in Diverse Teams
Divide students into groups and ask each group to come up with a customer service dilemma.
They should develop a brief skit demonstrating the wrong way to manage the situation, and then showing a better way to resolve matters.

Discuss

- Finish the rest of the introduction, relating "passion" to "achievement." Talk about how working closely with your colleagues can help achieve personal and team goals. Ask students to relate their own experiences with teamwork, both pro and con.

Section 1.1 Overview of the Restaurant and Foodservice Industry

Introduce the Section

a. Review the introductory paragraphs with students, emphasizing the broad basis of the restaurant and foodservice industry.
b. Connect the historical development of the foodservice industry to other courses students have taken to help contextualize the material.
c. Discuss the objectives for the section.

Vocabulary Review

a. Direct students to the key terms.
b. Pronounce each word, and have the students repeat the pronunciation out loud.
c. Discuss the definition of each word.

Teach

Discuss

- Why is the restaurant and foodservice industry so important to the American economy?
- Ask students how our society has shaped this industry. For example, home meal replacement is relatively new to the foodservice industry. Why?
- Ask students about their favorite restaurant experiences. What made the event so memorable—the food, the atmosphere, the service, the people who shared the experience?

Reinforce and Review

- Emphasize the sheer size of the hospitality industry (an estimated 13 million workers in the United States alone).
- Discuss the roles played by women and minorities in foodservice. Encourage students to discuss why these groups are so prominent in this industry.

1.1 Overview of the Restaurant and Foodservice Industry	1.2 Career Opportunities in the Industry	1.3 Overview of the Lodging Industry
• The restaurant and foodservice industry • The big picture: the hospitality industry • The history of hospitality and foodservice	• Types of establishments • Career pathways	• Why people travel • Types of lodging operations • Ratings organizations • Lodging careers

SECTION 1.1 OVERVIEW OF THE RESTAURANT AND FOODSERVICE INDUSTRY

Can you think of a special occasion that you celebrated at a restaurant? A party or event that was held at a hotel? A trip that introduced you to foods you didn't know existed? Those are all memorable events. And if you like food, like people, like celebrating, or just like going out, then the restaurant and foodservice industry offers exciting opportunities for you.

This industry has annual sales of over $550 billion dollars. There are more than 945,000 restaurant and foodservice operators. The industry employs more than 13 million people (9 percent of the workforce). That means it is one of the largest private-sector employers in the United States.

Over 57 percent of restaurant and foodservice managers are women. Approximately 25 percent of eating-drinking establishments are owned by women, 15 percent by Asians, 8 percent by Hispanics, and 4 percent by African-Americans. The industry expects to continue to grow over the next decade, with 14.8 million jobs by 2019.

Whether you like to cook, to work with people, to lead, or maybe do all three, this textbook will help you to develop an understanding of what it takes to succeed in this exciting industry. With focus and hard work, you can take the skills and knowledge you learn now and build a rewarding, exciting, and long-lasting career.

To introduce you to this dynamic industry, we will first take a look at the size and scope of the many restaurants and businesses that comprise it. Then, to understand how restaurants and foodservice businesses throughout the United States have evolved, we'll look at historical events that have affected how we do things today. You'll see that whether we're talking about the banquets of Rome or the quick-service explosion of the 1950s, the passion and commitment of restaurateurs and chefs to their customers and to the joy and comfort of food

6

have been the driving forces behind so many important advancements. Perhaps by the end of this textbook you'll discover that you have the same passion and drive to contribute to the industry's future.

Study Questions

After studying Section 1.1, you should be able to answer the following questions:

- What are the two segments of the foodservice industry?
- What are the types of businesses that make up the travel and tourism industry?
- Throughout the history of the United States, how has the hospitality industry grown?

The Restaurant and Foodservice Industry

Why is the restaurant and foodservice industry so successful? For one thing, it includes all of the places, institutions, and companies responsible for any meal prepared outside the home. That includes not only restaurants, but everything from catering to cruises as well.

Most people eat at restaurants and foodservice operations for enjoyment and entertainment. This means that the restaurant and foodservice industry is a service industry, one in which you provide a service to your customer. Do you like people? Do you like providing a positive experience? Then this could be the place for you.

There are many opportunities in this field. The industry can be divided into two major parts or segments: commercial and noncommercial.

Commercial Restaurant and Foodservice Segment

The commercial segment makes up almost 80 percent of the restaurant and foodservice industry. Types of foodservice within this segment include restaurants, catering and banquets, retail, stadium, and airline and cruise ships:

Restaurants: There are many types of restaurants, including quick-service, fine-dining, casual, theme restaurants, buffets, and cafeterias. See Table 1.1 for a description of restaurant segments.

7

Discuss

- Discuss why the commercial segment of foodservice is so much larger than the noncommercial segment.
- What exactly is a service industry? Ask students to identify other examples of service industries.

Reinforce and Review

- Reinforce the role of service and how it relates to both "image" and "end result."
- Review the differences between commercial and noncommercial foodservice.

Vocabulary Terms

- **Restaurant:** A business establishment serving meals to the public.

Table 1.1: Restaurant Segment Definitions

• Discuss the main restaurant segments and how they differ.

• Ask students to name some local or national restaurants in each category.

• Encourage students to describe their experiences with non-restaurant commercial foodservice businesses.

Reinforce and Review

• Review the definitions, services offered, and price ranges of each restaurant segment.
• Review the various types of commercial foodservice operations (see also pp. 10–11).

Teaching Tips

• Show Table 1.1 (Restaurant Segment Definitions) on an overhead projector.

In-Class Activity: Restaurant Segments

Literacy Connection

Ask students to create a chart with five columns, each headed by one of the five restaurant segments shown in Table 1.1.

Give students a five-minute period in which to list as many restaurants under each heading as possible. When time is up, ask students to share their lists with the class.

Discuss whether restaurants have been properly categorized.

CUSTOMIZED INSTRUCTION

Literacy Connection

Special Needs Students

What is your favorite food? What type of restaurant is most likely to serve it? Why?

Vocabulary Terms

• **Catering and banquets:** A set menu is selected by a host and then is prepared by and served to invited guests by a third party, either at the third party's (the caterer's) establishment or at some other facility, such as a park or a private home.
• **Retail:** A business establishment offering prepared meals to be consumed on-site or off-premises.
• **Stadiums (arenas):** Open-air or enclosed structures designed for spectators to watch live sporting events. Typically, a wide variety of foods are available.

Table 1.1: Restaurant Segment Definitions		
Restaurant Segment	**Services Offered**	**Average Per-Person Dinner Check**
Family Dining Full-Service Restaurant	Serving staff provides service, and the order is taken while the patron is seated. Patrons pay after they eat.	$10 or less
Casual Dining Full-Service Restaurant	Serving staff provides service at the table, and the order is taken while the patron is seated. Patrons pay after they eat.	$10–$25 range
Fine Dining Full-Service Restaurant	Serving staff provides service at the table, and the order is taken while the patron is seated. Patrons pay after they eat.	$25 or more
Quick Service (also known as Fast Food) Restaurant	Establishments primarily engaged in providing foodservice where patrons generally order or select items and pay before eating. Food and drink may be consumed on premises, taken out, or delivered. Also includes snack and nonalcoholic beverage bars.	$3–$6 range
Quick-Casual Restaurant	Quick casual restaurants are defined as attractive and comfortable establishments serving freshly prepared, wholesome quality, authentic foods in a reasonably fast service format.	$7–$9 range

Catering and banquets: In the catering and banquet segment, the menu is chosen by the host of an event for a specified number of people. Caterers may have their own facility or may also be located in another business, such as a hotel or a convention center, and provide foodservice to that business's customers. They may also do off-site catering, which involves preparing food at one location and delivering it to the guest's location.

Retail: Retail stores offer prepared meals that can be eaten in the store or taken home. These products can be found in supermarkets, convenience stores, and specialty shops selling limited items such as coffee, doughnuts, and candies. Vending is also included in retail. Vending machines are available to dispense various types of food, such as sodas, sandwiches, and candy.

Stadiums: The food offered at stadiums stretches from the peanuts in the stands to the fine dining in the luxury suites. Some stadiums have privately run

8

foodservice operations. However, most use large-scale contractors to handle the business. Figure 1.1 is an example of a quick service concession at a stadium.

Figure 1.1: Stadium foodservice ranges from peanuts and quick service to fine dining in luxury suites.

[trends]

Supper Selections and Dinner Decisions

Over the last two decades, the field of home meal replacement (HMR) has grown at a rapid rate. The balance of family, work, and social life is increasingly difficult to maintain. Many Americans would often prefer to spend money to purchase prepared food, rather than spend their time preparing the food themselves—time they could be spending with family or friends.

The convenience of picking up fully or partially prepared meals from a local supermarket or restaurant has a psychological component as well. Families can still sit down together for a "home-style" meal.

Many supermarkets have revamped their "to-go" options in recent years. Fried chicken and macaroni salad were once the typical takeout items. But groceries now offer everything from fresh pizzas (either baked or take-and-bake) to sushi prepared before customers' eyes. Some have even leased space to quick-service (also known as fast-food) restaurant concepts.

Fast-casual restaurants such as Applebee's have added separate takeout entrances, and many offer separate takeout menus, listing only the items which have been developed or adapted for home consumption. In a move away from their traditional base, fast-food restaurants are offering entire meals for families. For example, Pizza Hut now offers more entrees such as pans of lasagna and other pasta dishes.

Dinner outlets, where customers assemble the components of a week's worth of family meals in just a few hours, are on the rise. Even caterers are getting into the act, offering a variety of menu items for customer takeout. All things considered, options in family dining have greatly expanded in recent years.

9

Figure Focus

Figure 1.1: Ask students to suggest what types of food this concession stand might sell—expensive or inexpensive, "junk food" or "fancy food"?

**Trends:
Supper Selections and Dinner Decisions**

Divide students into small groups to discuss the following:

- How has the increased availability of fully or partially prepared meals from supermarkets, restaurants, and caterers changed American eating habits?

- How does spending time to prepare food differ from spending money to purchase prepared food?

- Is a "homemade" meal the same as a "home-style" meal? If not, what are the differences?

**Homework Activity:
What's the Real Cost?**

Mathematics Connection, 21st-Century Skills—Health Literacy, Information Literacy, Work Independently

Ask students to list the prepared foods that they or another family member purchase in a typical week for dinner (not including snack foods, soda, and the like).

Students should research the cost to purchase the prepared items and the time spent to obtain them.

Then students should list the ingredients that would be required to make each dish from scratch at home, research these costs, and estimate the time it would take to prepare each item (including time to purchase the ingredients).

Use this information as the basis for a class discussion.

**In-Class Activity:
HMR**

21st-Century Skills—Health Literacy, Think Creatively, Collaborate with Others

Divide students into small groups to discuss the following:

- How does the increase in home meal replacement affect American eating habits?

- What impact might this have on physical health?

- What about emotional health?

Encourage students to think as broadly as possible about these issues.

Trends:
Foodservice at Sporting Events

Divide students into small groups to discuss the following:

- Has the rise of "gourmet concessions" at sports events changed the way fans experience the games?

- Are there some foods that just aren't appropriate at sporting events? If so, which ones, and why?

CUSTOMIZED INSTRUCTION

Literacy Connection

ESOL Students

What types of concessions are available at sporting events in your country of origin?

Which foods from your home culture might be appropriate at U.S. sporting venues?

Share this information with the rest of your class.

Discuss

- Describe the dining options typically available on luxury cruises and airplanes (also see p. 11).
- Make sure students understand the difference between stadium contract feeders and having outright ownership of concessions (self-operating).

Reinforce and Review

- Review the various concession styles available at contemporary sporting events.

Teaching Tips

- If available, obtain menus or dining descriptions from various cruise ships. Make these into transparencies or handouts for class discussion.

Vocabulary Terms

- **Airlines:** Transport companies serving passengers traveling by air.
- **Cruise ships:** Large boats used less for transporting people from one place to another than for entertaining passengers during their travel.

[trends]

Foodservice at Sporting Events

At least since the first strains of "Take Me Out to the Ball Game" were played and probably long before, certain foods have been linked to sporting events. Peanuts, popcorn, and hot dogs have been part of American sports for decades. But contemporary athletic facilities—football and baseball stadiums, basketball arenas, and even track fields—are now providing contemporary foodservice options to their customers. No longer limited to the traditional concession stands, today's sports facilities offer a wide variety of foodservice outposts, including all-you-can-eat pavilions and luxury suites. Sure, fans can still get a bratwurst or a sack of peanuts, but today they can also get almost anything else. For example, the Kansas City Royals' Kauffman Stadium offers such diverse options as malt shop banana splits, smoked Kansas City strip loin, and almost anything in between.

Some major participants in this type of foodservice, known as stadium contract feeding, include Levy Restaurants, Aramark, Custom Food Services, and Compass North America. These companies often provide not only general concession services to their customers, but premium catering services as well. These categories are sometimes divided between two vendors. For instance, the Cleveland Browns contract with Sportservice for general concessions and with Levy Restaurants for premium foodservice in the stadium's luxury suites. But foodservice is not limited to game days. Many stadiums, arenas, and other facilities offer catering options to customers for weddings, birthday parties, or dances on days when no game is scheduled.

Although many national chains such as McDonald's, Quizno's, and Pizza Hut are frequently represented at sporting events, significant efforts are often made to involve local restaurants in concessions. Montgomery Inn barbecue is available to fans of both the Cincinnati Reds and the Cleveland Browns, while fans of the Washington Nationals can enjoy Ben's Chili. Teams receive a percentage of foodservice profits, typically ranging between 40-45 percent. Some teams, like the New England Patriots, control their own concessions outright, and others are taking this concept a step further. For example, the New York Yankees and the Dallas Cowboys recently established Legends Hospitality Management, a joint venture that will not only handle all foodservice for the two teams' stadiums, but will also solicit business from other athletic facilities nationwide.

Airlines and cruise ships: In 2007, over 12 million passengers worldwide took cruises. Anyone who has ever taken a cruise knows that food is available 24/7 on the ship. Options range from casual dining and buffets to elegant dinners to room service. Food selection varies as well, from steak to vegetarian to children's meals and pizza. Cruise ships may serve up to several thousand meals at each seating. Figure 1.2 shows the dining area on a cruise ship.

Figure 1.2: Cruise ships offer multiple dining options to passengers.

Figure Focus
Figure 1.2: What type of meal do students think the guests in this dining room will eat? What clues are there in the photograph?

Homework Activity:
Stadium Contract Feeders

Literacy Connection, 21st-Century Skills—Entrepreneurial Literacy, Use and Manage Information, Be Self-Directed Learners

Ask students to research a stadium contract feeder of their choice and write a brief essay describing its offerings, its customers, and its history.

Did You Know...?
Passengers and crew on the Royal Caribbean International ship Mariner of the Seas consume an average of 20,000 pounds (9,000 kg) of beef, 28,000 eggs, 8,000 gallons of ice cream, and 18,000 slices of pizza in a week.

Source: www.absoluteastronomy.com

Airlines, especially on transatlantic flights, will offer meals, sometimes more than one, to help passengers adjust to time differences. These range from a simple beverage in short-haul economy class to a seven-course gourmet meal using real dishes and glassware in long-haul first class. If customers notify airlines of specific dietary needs in advance, many options are available, including low-fat, diabetic, vegetarian, or Kosher meals. In the United States, many airlines no longer offer meals for travel within the United States, although they allow travelers to bring food purchased at the airport onto the plane.

Noncommercial Foodservice Segment

The noncommercial segment represents about 20 percent of the foodservice industry. This segment prepares and serves food in support of some other establishment's main function or purpose. For example, the cafeteria at a local university supports the school's goal of educating students by serving them meals so that they have the energy to participate in class and activities.

Categories in this segment include schools and universities, the military, health care, business and industry, and clubs:

- Schools and universities provide on-campus food services to students and staff.

- Military bases and ships provide food services to military personnel. Food is also offered at clubs, such as an officer's club.

- Health-care facilities such as hospitals and long-term care facilities (including nursing homes and independent living centers for seniors, known as assisted living) offer foodservice.

- Businesses and industries offer foodservice as a convenience to employers and benefit to employees in manufacturing or service industries. Examples include cafeterias, executive dining rooms, and vending machines.

- Clubs and member-based facilities—golf, city, alumni, athletic—also offer foodservice as a convenience to their members and sometimes as a way to help provide the organization with additional funds.

11

Discuss

- Discuss the importance of the noncommercial foodservice segment to today's society.
- Identify the various components of this segment. Encourage students who have experienced any of these facilities to share their experiences.
- Ask students why businesses and clubs might provide foodservice to their employees and members. How can this affect the organization's finances and operations?

Reinforce and Review

- Review the major difference between commercial and noncommercial foodservice: noncommercial foodservice establishments provide food in support of some other primary goal, while for commercial foodservice establishments, providing food is the primary goal.

Teaching Tips

- Give examples of local noncommercial foodservice establishments to enhance student understanding.
- If possible, organize a tour through the campus foodservice department so that students can learn more about large-scale foodservice.

Discuss

- Make sure students understand the differences
  between contract feeding and self-operating.
  Under what circumstances might one be
  preferable to the other?

Discuss

- Discuss the role of cultural attractions (museums,
  architecture, parks) in increasing demand for
  foodservice.
- Encourage students to give examples of travel
  and tourism services.
- How can travel and tourism contribute to the local
  economy? Is this always a positive development?
  Ask students to give examples of both positive and
  negative outcomes.

Reinforce and Review

- Review the difference between hospitality and
  travel and tourism.
- Review the relationships among travel and tourism, hospitality, and restaurants and foodservice.
- Point out the historical development of hospitality, restaurants, and foodservice as a reaction to
  increased travel and tourism.

Teaching Tips

- Help students develop a list of reasons why people
  spend money while traveling.

[fast fact]

Did You Know...?
The Fast Food: Global Industry Guide forecasts that the global quick-service market will
reach $130 billion by 2012. The United States generates 63 percent of global quick-
service market revenue.

Within the noncommercial segment, foodservice is typically handled in one of
two ways. In **contract feeding,** contractors are businesses that operate foodservice
for companies in the manufacturing or service industry. These contractors will
manage and operate the employee dining facilities. Some manufacturing and
service companies are **self-operators,** which means they hire their own staff to
operate foodservices.

The Big Picture: The Hospitality Industry

Restaurants and foodservice are a component of the hospitality industry. In
turn, hospitality falls under the umbrella of the travel and tourism industry.
Beginning in the 1700s, wealthy Europeans began to spend several months a
year traveling to major cities in Europe, Turkey, and North Africa to see famous
art, visit historic buildings, and eat local foods. In the 1800s, an increasing
number of people, especially Americans and Europeans, had money to spend
on traveling for pleasure. As a result, more and more hotels and restaurants were
built, and a variety of events were offered to attract tourists.

Travel and Tourism

Today, the U.S. travel and tourism industry averages annual sales of over $1
trillion. **Travel and tourism** is defined as the combination of all of the services
that people need and will pay for when they are away from home. This includes
all of the businesses that benefit from people traveling and spending their
money, such as transportation or restaurants. **Hospitality** refers to the services
that people use and receive when they are away from home. This includes,
among other services, restaurants and hotels.

12

Vocabulary Terms

- **Contract feeding:** Businesses that manage foodservice operations for other companies.
- **Self-operators:** Companies that manage their own foodservice operations.
- **Travel and tourism:** The combination of all services that people use when traveling and away
  from home, including transportation, lodging, and dining.
- **Hospitality:** The services that people use when away from home, including lodging and dining
  but not transportation.

Tourism

Tourism is travel for recreational, leisure, or business purposes, and it has become a popular global leisure activity. In fact, in 2005 tourism was the first, second, or third largest employer in 29 states, employing 7.3 million people to take care of the 1.19 billion trips tourists took in the United States.

Tourist attractions range from museums, theme parks, monuments, sporting events, zoos, and shopping malls to national and state parks, safaris, and adventure tours.

Transportation

Tourists travel in a variety of ways. Back in the 1800s, the development of the railroad helped people travel faster and to more places. In the 1920s, travelers began to journey by car. As Henry Ford and other industrialists began mass-producing more affordable cars, people started to travel more. In addition to the creation of major highway systems, the 1950s saw the growth of commercial airlines, with faster and bigger airplanes being developed after World War II.

Today, transportation includes the following categories:

- Airplanes
- Trains
- Charter services
- Buses
- Cars
- Ships

Hospitality

Everywhere tourists go, they need places to stay and places to eat. The people who work in the lodging business and serve customers need to know what's happening in town, what there is to do and see, where to eat, and how to get from one place to another.

Foodservice is a key sector in the hospitality industry. Other segments include lodging and event management. Table 1.2 depicts the segments of the hospitality industry and examples of each.

13

Discuss

- Emphasize the role of tourism as an agent of economic development. Ask students to give examples of jobs related to or affected by tourism.
- Discuss the relationship between transportation and tourism. Encourage students to relate changes in transportation (the growth of the interstate system, increases or decreases in fuel costs, etc.) to changes in tourism and the resulting effects on local economies.
- How has the use of cars influenced the way Americans travel? How has it affected the hospitality industry?

Reinforce and Review

- Review the definition of tourism and relate it to both transportation and hospitality.

Teaching Tips

- Display brochures from local and regional tourist attractions (often available from hotels or motels). Do these brochures mention hospitality or foodservice? How does a local economy benefit from the presence of such attractions?
- Divide students into groups and ask each to develop a list of tourism-related occupations. See which group can develop the longest list or the most unusual (yet still appropriate) jobs. Use this as a basis for a class discussion.
- Ask each student to identify a local tourist attraction, and then identify all hospitality-related establishments within one mile. Use this as a basis for class discussion about tourism as an economic engine.

Vocabulary Terms

- **Tourism:** Travel for recreation, leisure, or business.

Table 1.2: Hospitality Segments

- Review Table 1.2 with students. What other examples of each hospitality segment can they identify?

Table 1.2: Hospitality Segments	
Hospitality Segments	**Examples**
Foodservice	Hotels Restaurants Retail establishments
Lodging	Hotels Motels Resorts
Event management	Stadiums Expositions Trade shows

Discuss

- Describe the history of social dining in Greece. Encourage students to compare lesche and *phatnai* to contemporary hospitality establishments—for example, the trend toward "family-style" restaurant dining.
- Ask students to discuss the concept of nourishing the soul. Why was this concept considered important in ancient Greece?
- Common foods enjoyed at *phatnai* included grapes, olives, bread, and dried fish. Why were these foods selected? Ask students to relate Greek geography and agricultural practices to patterns of consumption, especially for travelers.

Reinforce and Review

- Review the distinction between lesche and *phatnai*.
- Reinforce with students that restaurants had not yet been developed. Discuss with them how that would have affected society.

Teaching Tips

- Many contemporary restaurants and other hospitality establishments commonly provide recorded or live music for their guests. Ask students to discuss how this practice relates to ancient Greek customs and beliefs.

Vocabulary Terms

- **Lesche:** In ancient Greece, private clubs that offered food to members.
- *Phatnai:* In ancient Greece, dining establishments catering to travelers, traders, and visiting diplomats, who brought their food with them to have it prepared on-site.

The History of Hospitality and Foodservice

So, how did this industry develop into what we know today? It was a complicated evolution, reflecting the social and physical environments of the time. The following is a condensed overview of the history of hospitality.

The Real Beginning: Ancient Greece and Rome

In 2004, the Summer Olympics were held in Greece. More than 10,000 athletes took part in the games. After practicing and competing in events, most of the athletes went to restaurants to eat. But back when the first Olympics were held in Ancient Greece, this wasn't possible because restaurants had not been invented yet.

Ancient Greeks rarely dined out, though they enjoyed the social aspect of dining and often got together for banquets. Private clubs, called **lesche** (LES-kee), offered food to members. Other establishments, called *phatnai* (FAAT-nay), catered to travelers, traders, and visiting diplomats. It is most likely that travelers brought standard fare like grapes, olives, bread made from barley, dried fish, cheese, and wine with them to these clubs. In ancient Greece, meals were considered a time to nourish the soul as well as the body. People ate while reclining on couches, enjoying music, poetry, and dancing to enhance the experience. Figure 1.3 depicts an ancient Roman banquet.

14

Figure 1.3: Common foods served at ancient Roman banquets included olives, figs, goat cheese, pork, fish, bread, and wine.

[fast fact]

Did You Know...?
Some Greeks believed that pleasure was the purpose of life and that it was achieved through self-control and balance. The leader of this movement was a man named Epicurus. Because of his ideas, we use the term **Epicurean** *(ep-ih-KUR-ee-an)* to refer to a person with a refined taste for food and wine.

In 282 B.C., Rome conquered the lands surrounding the Mediterranean Sea, formerly occupied by the Greeks. The Romans were very different from the discriminating Greeks. Meals were primarily served in the home.

Romans' desires for exotic foods and spices increased trade, stretching the Roman Empire farther east and north. They invaded the regions that are now France, Germany, and England, as well as moving west into Spain and Portugal. With their power came increased wealth, which they lavishly spent on banquets for their friends, clients, and those people of a lower social standing who depended on the aristocracy for financial aid in exchange for political support.

15

Figure Focus
Figure 1.3: Encourage students to discuss their impressions of this Roman banquet hall.

In-Class Activity: Trading Places
21st-Century Skills—Global Awareness, Reason Effectively, Collaborate with Others
How did the growth of the spice trade and affiliated activities change the global economy?
How were regional eating habits affected?
In what ways are these developments reflected in contemporary society?
Discuss these issues in small groups.

Discuss
- Identify Epicurus and describe his philosophy. Ask students to reflect upon how this set of beliefs may have shaped Greek eating habits.
- Point out to students that the Roman Empire superseded Greek rule. How would this have affected the people living in those areas? How might their eating patterns have changed?
- Analyze the relationship between exotic ingredients and increased trade. How does this relate to the earlier discussion about transportation and tourism?

Reinforce and Review
- Note the similarities in the foods enjoyed by both Greek and Roman banqueters, although their societies were very different. How do students account for that?
- Extravagant banquets were displays of power in Roman societies. Are there contemporary analogies?

Teaching Tips
- Epicurious.com is a popular culinary Web site. Show some of its pages to the class and ask them to consider whether the Web site would meet with Epicurus's approval. Why or why not?

Vocabulary Terms
- **Epicurean:** A person with a refined taste for food and wine; from the Greek philosopher Epicurus, who believed that pleasure, achieved through self-control and balance, was the ultimate purpose of life.

Divide students into small groups to discuss the following:

- Why would Marcus Apicius poison himself rather than simply make less exotic and extravagant food choices?

- What does this story say about the relationship between status and food in ancient Rome?

Discuss

- Discuss the effects of Christianity on Europe. How did this change affect regional eating patterns?
- Explain the relationship between agrarianism and feudalism. Encourage students to relate this to contemporary developments in agriculture in the United States.
- As trade sharply decreased, so did the use of exotic ingredients. Ask students how this affected eating habits.

Reinforce and Review

- Review the difference between ancient Greek and Roman banquets and medieval banquets.
- Reinforce the importance of Christianity as a factor in social and economic development during the Middle Ages.

Teaching Tips

- Pre-Christian religions effectively preserved natural resources, which were often believed to be inhabited or protected by gods or spirits.

Fast Fact:
Did You Know...?

Marco Polo and other explorers reopened trade routes between Europe and Asia. How did this expand Europeans' dining and fashion options? What effect might this have had on their political views?

Did You Know...?

One Roman in particular, Marcus Apicius, a gourmet and lover of luxury, made great efforts to obtain the most exotic foods for his feasts. He was so interested in cooking that he wrote one of the earliest known cookbooks, *De Re Coquinaria (On Cooking)*. Recipes from this book are still used today. The story goes that when he realized that he would soon go broke, Marcus Apicius poisoned himself rather than die from hunger.

300-400 B.C.
Ancient Greece and Rome

475-1300
The Middle Ages

The Middle Ages

The end of the Roman Empire was the beginning of a long, slow period of change in Europe. The victorious German tribes took Christianity back to Germany. The new faith led to two major changes in their way of life. First, it united Europe into one large church-state called Christendom. Second, it ended the view that gods and spirits inhabited the forest. The ancient Nordic myths included the belief that trees were sacred and could not be cut down and that diverting river water for agriculture would displease the gods of the rivers. With these fears dismissed, people began to clear large tracts of land, moving from a nomadic group dependent on hunting and foraging for food to an agrarian (farming) society.

A feudal society developed. Landowners lived in relative comfort, unless under attack or out attacking someone else. Large banquets were held almost every night. Unlike the banquets of the Greeks and Romans, a medieval dinner had only one purpose: to eat.

Travel in those times was extremely dangerous. Trade with the Far East and India was greatly reduced from when the Greeks and Romans dominated the landscape, and came to a stop completely when the Moors invaded Spain in 800 A.D. This blocked the shipment of spices and fine goods from reaching Europe. For the next 200 years, Europe remained isolated from the rest of the world. It wasn't until Pope Urban II called for the removal of the Moors from Spain and the Holy Lands in 1095 A.D. that Europeans looked beyond their borders once again.

Did You Know...?

Marco Polo (1254–1324), a trader and explorer from the Venetian Republic who gained fame for his worldwide travels, reintroduced foreign spices to Europe. His travels from Italy to China brought many Middle Eastern spices, such as curry and cardamom, to countries where they could not be grown successfully.

16

CUSTOMIZED INSTRUCTION

Literacy Connection, 21st-Century Skills—Critical Thinking and Problem Solving, Access and Evaluate Information, Be Self-Directed Learners

More Advanced Students

Have students research eating habits in the Middle Ages in greater depth.

How was an individual's diet determined by his or her place in the social structure?

What ingredients were most commonly used by what classes of people?

How did the spread of Christianity affect European diets?

How did Islam in regions with a strong Moorish presence affect local eating habits?

Students should research these or similar issues and write a paper describing their findings.

The Renaissance through the French Revolution

Partly to show off their wealth, noblemen instructed their cooks to use large amounts of exotic spices in their foods. It wasn't long before merchants in Venice controlled the spice trade. Because of their location on the Adriatic Sea, they could easily obtain spices from India and sell them at very high prices to distributors headed north. Venice prospered as a seaport and bought and sold spices and other goods for buyers bound for other destinations.

This expansion of world travel changed the mind-set of the artists and philosophers of that time. They adopted Epicurean lifestyles once again. While the majority of the population was unaffected by this renewed interest in all things Greek and Roman, it did much to create the food preparation system we now call **haute cuisine** (hote kwee-ZEEN), an elaborate and refined system of food preparation.

[fast fact]

Did You Know...?
Today, sitting down to dinner generally requires plates, cups, silverware, and napkins. But it wasn't until the Renaissance, with its ideas about life and art and a return to an Epicurean lifestyle, that a formal style of eating began. During the Middle Ages silverware was made of wood or horn, but often people used their hands. Only the wealthy could afford silverware. During the Renaissance period, artisans began making utensils from pewter, iron, and brass. The movement started in Italy and was carried into France by Catherine de Medici in 1533 when she married King Henry II of France. She brought her entire staff of cooks and their refined recipes for artichokes, spinach dishes, and ice cream to the French court. She also introduced the French to the fork. The use of silverware quickly caught on, and many aristrocrats began to carry personal silverware when dining out.

International trade greatly improved the European way of life. For instance, Europeans were introduced to coffee from Africa. The first coffeehouse, or **café**, opened in 1650 in Oxford, England. Unlike the dark and imposing taverns, pubs, and ale houses that catered only to men, the new coffeehouses were open, airy, and inviting. Smart bakers soon started offering pastries at these establishments. Women were welcome, and the coffee shop soon made it acceptable to eat in public. Figure 1.4 shows a café from the Renaissance period.

17

Discuss

- The Renaissance, or "rebirth," was a time of radical change in European society. Ask students to share what they know about this time period.
- Explain the increased growth in trade and other economic development during the Renaissance and how it relates to the increased interest in food—especially haute cuisine.
- How did the opening of coffee houses to women affect society? Ask students to consider the importance of creating a public space for both men and women.

Reinforce and Review

- Review the importance of trade and travel to economic development and to eating habits. Remind students of the earlier discussion of tourism.
- Make sure students understand that haute cuisine became the basis for contemporary Western fine dining and had a significant effect on everyday eating habits as well.

Teaching Tips

- Use a world map to show students typical trade routes used during the Renaissance.

CUSTOMIZED INSTRUCTION
Literacy Connection
ESOL Students
What flavors are characteristic of your culture of origin?
Present a brief report to the class.

CUSTOMIZED INSTRUCTION
Literacy Connection
Special Needs Students
Provide ingredients originating in different parts of the world and encourage students to taste them.
Talk about what flavors are representative of different cultures.

Vocabulary Terms

- **Haute cuisine:** An elaborate and refined system of food preparation.
- **Café:** During Renaissance times, a coffee house; this term has later been expanded to cover a variety of smaller restaurants.

Fast Fact: Did You Know...?

Divide students into small groups to discuss the following:

- How would the introduction of silverware affect the foods people consumed?
- Why might diners bring their own silverware with them when dining out?

Homework Activity: The Ingredient Connection

Literacy Connection, 21st-Century Skills—Global Awareness, Access and Evaluate Information, Create Media Products

Assign each student an ingredient—a spice, a vegetable, and so on—and ask him or her to research its history.

Each student should create a poster, handout, or oral report to share his or her findings with the class.

Discuss

- Explain the rise of guilds. How do they relate to contemporary labor unions? What role did they play in the French economy?
- Describe Boulanger and his *restorante*, the prototype of today's restaurant. Encourage students to speculate on the effects this had on society.
- Ask students to discuss the French Revolution and how it affected modern foodservice.

Reinforce and Review

- Review the rise of guilds and their effect on French society.
- Reiterate the importance of Boulanger and his *restorante* to the contemporary restaurant and foodservice industry.

Teaching Tips

- Boulanger was sued by the guilds, who believed he was infringing on their territory. Provide students with examples of contemporary lawsuits that have pivoted around foodservice.
- Divide students into groups and have each develop a culinary guild. They should define a specialty and establish standards of practice. One member of each group will be a spokesperson and describe the guild and its operations to the class.

Homework Activity: Poverty and Society
Literacy Connection, 21st-Century Skills—Civic Literacy, Access and Evaluate Information, Work Independently
Is poverty related to social unrest, as believed by the French government?
Research local poverty issues.
What effect do they have on your community?
Write a report on your findings.

Vocabulary Terms

- **Guilds:** Associations of people with similar interests or professions.
- ***Restorante:*** A café serving *restaurers*, or hot and revivifying soups; the origin of the contemporary restaurant.

Guilds, associations of people with similar interests or professions, were organized during the reign of Louis XIV in France in an attempt to increase the state's control over the economy. Each guild controlled the production of its specialties and could prevent others from making and selling the same items. Two of these guilds were the *Chaine de Rotissieres (roasters)* and the *Chaine de Traiteurs (caterers)*. Cooking guilds like these established many of the professional standards and traditions that exist today.

Figure 1.4: Cafés were open, airy, and inviting.

In 1765, a man named Boulanger began serving hot soups called *restaurers* (meaning restoratives) for their health-restoring properties. He called his café a ***restorante***, the origin of our modern word *restaurant*. His *restorante* became very popular. People enjoyed having a place to go to have a hot meal and good conversation with friends. The foodservice guilds believed that he was moving in on their businesses and took their case to court. But the government was under even stronger pressure to alleviate the poverty that was causing social unrest in Paris.

Despite the government's attempt to end the political unrest, the French Revolution began. When the French Revolution was over, large numbers of cooks and other guild members found themselves unemployed. They followed Boulanger's example and began opening restaurants of their own. Within 30 years Paris had over 500 restaurants serving meals. Dining out on a large scale was born.

18

Figure Focus

Figure 1.4: How did cafés provide a "social space"? How does this relate to modern coffee houses?

CUSTOMIZED INSTRUCTION
Literacy Connection, 21st-Century Skills—Information Literacy, Create Media Products, Work Independently, Produce Results
Less Advanced Students
Research the etymologies of "rest," "restore," and "restaurant."
What other words are associated with these?
Create a poster showing the relationships among these words.

Colonial North America

The first Europeans to settle in North America were city dwellers poorly equipped for farming. As more people immigrated to the New World to find their fortunes or to escape religious persecution, cities along the East Coast grew. Boston and New York became major centers of trade. As early as 1634, an inn in Boston called Cole's offered food and lodging to travelers.

Figure 1.5: Coaching inns provided coaching travelers with a place to rest.

However, very few early colonial Americans ever traveled or dined out. Once they settled down, they rarely traveled more than 25 miles from their homes. When people did travel, they stayed at inns, often sleeping together in the same large room and even sharing a single bed. Not much care was given to the preparation of meals, and if travelers arrived after dinner had been served, they would have to go without.

[fast fact]

Did You Know...?

As stagecoach routes were established in the mid-1600s, coaching inns became popular resting places where travelers could expect a meal and a bed for the evening. Although these inns resemble today's lodging facilities, it wasn't until the 1700s that American inns really began to combine food and beverage service with lodging. Figure 1.5 shows a coaching inn from the 1600s.

Industrial Revolution

Back on the other side of the Atlantic, Europe was importing silver and spices, and finding a large international market for its own goods, in particular cloth made from wool or linen. Turning raw fiber into cloth is a slow process that

19

Discuss

- Many early colonists came to America to practice religious freedom. Encourage students to discuss the relationship between religion and food.
- Early inns had few amenities and were often extremely uncomfortable. How does this fit with modern conceptions of hospitality?
- Developing urban areas were centers of trade, which meant that they were also centers for the exchange of ingredients and knowledge. Encourage students to discuss what this might have meant to the development of an American cuisine.

Reinforce and Review

- Relate the development of trade centers and inns to the earlier discussion of travel and tourism and to students' previous American history classes.
- The urban colonists had little experience producing their own food and gravitated toward the newly developing cities.

Teaching Tips

- Encourage students to imagine the strictures of colonial diets: many colonists had no agricultural experience, and many foods were in short supply or simply not available.
- For a homework project, have students research and design menus that the early colonists might have eaten. Use these as a basis for class discussion.

**Fast Fact:
Did You Know...?**

How might the lack of amenities available at coaching inns affect transportation? Would travelers wish to journey long distances under these conditions?

Figure Focus
Figure 1.5: Why were early coaching inns so inhospitable?

Discuss

- The socioeconomic results of the Industrial Revolution were widespread, including mass urbanization. What implications did these have for the developing foodservice industry?
- The invention of the railroad facilitated travel between urban and rural areas. Not only could tourists get places quickly, but so could ingredients. Encourage students to discuss how this could have changed the restaurant and foodservice industry.

Reinforce and Review

- Relate developments in urban transit, such as buggies and railroads, to travel, tourism, and hospitality.
- Mass migration to cities, a trademark of the Industrial Revolution, resulted in a rapid increase in the number of dining and lodging facilities.

requires a lot of different steps. In order to keep up with the demand, wool merchants developed a putting-out system of production that created cottage industries.

Cottage industries were made up of families that worked together in the home to produce goods. These cottage industries put cash in the hands of farm laborers and eventually led to the start of the Industrial Revolution.

Merchants soon found a better way to control production. They began to build factories near large towns where they could find lots of employees. These early factories were operated by children from local orphanages, but when the English government outlawed this practice, merchants again turned to the farming family. Realizing the opportunity to earn a better living, entire families moved to the city to find work in the emerging factories.

This mass migration put a heavy stress on cities. People needed to live close enough to the factory to walk to work, go home for lunch, and leave again for dinner. This packed the inexpensive areas of town with people, which led to unsanitary conditions. The problem became so intolerable that cities such as Paris began to run horse and buggy transit buses to help employees move out of the overcrowded areas. Figure 1.6 shows a horse and buggy. As the cities became business hubs, dining and lodging establishments opened up to serve the needs of workers and employers.

Figure 1.6: Horse and buggy transported people out of overcrowded areas.

With the invention of the railroad in 1825, inns, taverns, and foodservice facilities located near railway stations began to grow. Travelers could now reach remote areas from coast to coast by rail.

Figure Focus

Figure 1.5: Did the availability of horse-drawn buggies to transport workers to their homes outside the overcrowded cities actually increase mass migration by expanding the geographic boundaries of the city? How does this relate to the modern suburb or exurb?

Early Hotels, Coffee Houses, and Diners

(1) In 1794, The City Hotel in New York City opened, the first building in the United States designed specifically as a hotel. The property inspired the construction of other establishments, and American innkeepers continued to build bigger and better-equipped lodging properties throughout the 1800s. The Tremont House, the first of the grand hotels, was built in Boston in 1828. It was the first hotel to offer private rooms with locking doors.

(2) By 1800, European-style coffee shops appeared. Figure 1.7 offers an example of a coffee shop.

(3) The classic American diner began in this time period. Factory workers who were unable to go home for lunch needed to be fed. To meet this need, cooks designed diners, horse-drawn kitchens on wheels, and drove them to factory entrances to sell food. The practice caught on, and soon there were a number of these traveling diners competing for business. To increase sales, some began adding chairs to provide their customers a place to sit down and enjoy their meal. By 1912, there were more than 50 roaming diners clogging the streets of Providence, Rhode Island. The city passed an ordinance that forced the diner carts off the streets after 10 a.m. To stay in business, some owners found permanent places in which to park their carts. Diners are still popular today.

Figure 1.7: 1800's European-style coffee shop.

Divide students into small groups to discuss the following:

- Why was the opening of the Tremont House, with its private rooms and locking doors, so significant for early travelers?

- Why have diners remained popular for 200 years, while other industries and types of establishment have come and gone?

**Homework Activity:
Food Carts**

Literacy Connection, 21st-Century Skills—Language Arts, Create Media Products, Work Independently

Food carts are popping up across the country, serving up everything from waffles to ribs.

Ask students to design their own food carts. Each student should develop a theme, plan a menu, and diagram the kitchen layout.

Each student should create a poster to share with the class.

Figure Focus

Figure 1.7: How does this coffee shop from over 200 years ago compare to today's coffee shop?

Divide students into small groups to discuss the following:

- How do both pasteurization and sanitary canning help make safe food available to a wider number of people?

- Florence Nightingale claimed 100 years ago that good health depended upon a combination of diet, surroundings, activity, and hygiene. If we know this, why are so many Americans following unhealthy habits?

Discuss

- Discuss the meaning of "progress" as posited by the Enlightenment. Ask students to relate this concept to food production.
- Elaborate restaurants, serving a small percentage of the population, offered extravagant meals with unusual and costly ingredients. Encourage students to link this to the tradition of expressing power through food, as established during Roman times.

Reinforce and Review

- The Enlightenment, with its emphasis on science and rationality, resulted from the Renaissance, which emphasized art and philosophy.
- Despite the term "Gilded Age," it was a time of agony for many workers, who were exploited by their employers.

Teaching Tips

- Obtain menus from Gilded Age restaurants like Delmonico's as well as menus from today's most opulent restaurants (often available online). Create transparencies or handouts so that students can compare the different menus. Encourage students to identify similarities and differences.

Chapter 1 | Foundations of Restaurant Management & Culinary Arts

[fast fact]

Did You Know...?
During this period, scientific advancements were made which impacted the foodservice and hospitality industries. Louis Pasteur (1822–1895), developed a process called pasteurization which made milk safer to drink by heating it to a certain temperature to destroy harmful bacteria. Another scientist, Nicolas Appert (1749–1841), discovered a way to can food to keep it fresh and safe to eat. He is known as "the father of canning." Nurse Florence Nightingale (1820–1910) argued that health was dependent on appropriate diet, surroundings, activity, and hygiene. Figure 1.8 is a photo of Louis Pasteur.

Figure 1.8: Louis Pasteur developed the process of pasteurization.

The Gilded Age

The Renaissance sparked the scientific revolution known as the Enlightenment, which changed the way knowledge was obtained and accepted. The new scientific method relied on information from direct observation and mathematical logic. This period of intellectual growth in the 18th century changed the way scientists looked at the world.

The Enlightenment's concept of progress, which was measured in production and profit, was adopted by America's industrial leaders. Workers were subjected to long hours at low wages while the profits for the owners continued to rise.

When high society dined out, they did so in style. Entrepreneurs opened fancy restaurants such as Delmonico's and the Astor House so that people could dine and be seen in elegant surroundings. Dinners of up to 18 courses were not uncommon. Figure 1.9 on the following page shows Delmonico's.

22

Figure Focus

Figure 1.8: Examine the photograph closely to observe the scientific equipment shown. What items do you recognize?

In-Class Activity: **The Science of Pasteurization**
Science Connection, 21st-Century Skills—Health Literacy, Critical Thinking and Problem Solving, Be Self-Directed Learners
Why is it important to pasteurize milk? What bacteria are removed by pasteurization? How does the pasteurization process work? Is it possible to do in the typical home or restaurant?
Is raw milk available in your area? What legal issues might be involved in its production?
If possible, obtain samples of raw and pasteurized milk. Compare the two under a microscope. How are they similar? How are they different? Now compare the two samples visually. Is there any readily detectable difference between the two?

In 1848, gold was discovered in California and people poured into the state to claim their fortunes. Some travelers hit the jackpot and, with their newfound wealth, wanted to enjoy the fine dining that they knew existed in New York. A number of fine restaurants quickly opened. Unfortunately, many of the new residents struggled to stay afloat. With such a sudden growth of people coming into Northern California, meeting the demand to feed them was nearly impossible. Clever restaurateurs developed the **cafeteria,** an assembly-line process of serving food quickly and cheaply without the need for servers.

Figure 1.9: Delmonico's during the Gilded Age.

[fast fact]

Did You Know…?
In the 1800s, Marie-Antoine Carême redesigned the chef's uniform. He believed that white would represent cleanliness. He also believed that there should be different sizes of hats to differentiate between the cooks and the chefs. Chefs wore tall hats and younger cooks wore shorter hats.

The 20th Century

By the turn of the century, employment in the United States was at an all-time high. More and more people went to work in new factories, stores, and office buildings. People were therefore eating out more, especially for lunch.

23

Discuss

- The Gold Rush of 1848 prompted thousands to move to California—only a few of whom struck it rich. Encourage students to discuss the logistics of feeding and lodging this rapidly enlarging population.
- Cafeterias were the foodservice industry's version of the Industrial Revolution. Ask students to think through the differences between cafeterias and luxurious restaurants like Delmonico's—staffing, ingredients, resources, and so on.
- With more Americans working than ever before, restaurants serving lunch were doing a booming business. What are some other implications that the rise in employment may have had for the restaurant and foodservice industry?

Reinforce and Review

- Review the relationship between the discovery of gold and the rise of the cafeteria.
- Increasing employment contributed to increased restaurant business, as more and more people had busier lives.

Teaching Tips

- Relate the development of the cafeteria to the modern-day school lunch system.

Fast Fact:
Did You Know…?

Carême chose white for the chef's uniform to symbolize cleanliness. But kitchens during his time were fueled with coal and were usually poorly ventilated, which made them dirty. Was white really the best choice, under these conditions?

Vocabulary Terms

- **Cafeteria:** An assembly-line process of serving food quickly and cheaply without the need for servers.

Figure Focus

Figure 1.9: Compare the Delmonico's dining room to the contemporary cruise ship seen in Figure 1.2 and the ancient banquet hall seen in Figure 1.3.

Table 1.3: Chefs in History

- Divide students into two teams—one to study Carême and one to study Escoffier. (In large classes, it may be advisable to divide the class into four or more teams.)

- Have each team research its chef in greater detail.

- Students should prepare some sort of group project. Team Carême, for instance, could make a *pièce montée*, while Team Escoffier could develop a presentation describing the structure of a traditional brigade system.

Discuss

- Discuss the importance of Marie-Antoine Carême and Georges-Auguste Escoffier to the restaurant and foodservice industry. Encourage students to discuss how these chefs are relevant to today's hospitality industry.
- Place these two chefs within the context of European history and French society. Why were they able to become so successful?

Reinforce and Review

- Review the highlights of each man's career.

Teaching Tips

- Many excellent biographies of both Carême and Escoffier exist, and copies of Escoffier's seminal cookbook, *Le Guide Culinaire*, are found in professional kitchens worldwide. If possible, obtain some of these for students to learn more about these figures and their times.
- Part of Escoffier's lingering fame results from his frequent publication of articles and books about the culinary arts—he may have been the first true "celebrity chef." Encourage students to discuss the role of publicity in creating a "celebrity chef."

Table 1.3: Chefs in History

Today, the term chef is a mark of respect and distinction that describes a professional cook who has reached the position through hard work and dedication to quality. Two important figures that helped the role of the chef earn the level of respect and admiration it has today are Carême and Escoffier.

In the late 18th century, dining in France was elevated to new heights. More and more restaurants were opening and serving food to a wide variety of people, from the very wealthy to the very poor. A few of these restaurants focused on serving grand cuisine, or fancy meals with many courses of complex food.

Marie-Antoine Carême (1784–1833)	Georges August Escoffier (1846–1935)
Accomplishment: Defined the art of **grand cuisine**	**Accomplishment:** Credited with refining Carême's grand cuisine into the more contemporary **classical cuisine**
History: Carême was born just before the French Revolution into a large and very poor family. He was abandoned as a child and found work as a kitchen boy, then became an apprentice to a pastry chef. Carême soon developed a reputation for excellence. He opened his own shop, and worked for some of the most famous people of his time.	**History:** In 1898, along with Cesar Ritz, he opened London's Savoy Hotel. He simplified the flavors, dishes, and garnishes of Carême. He believed that fewer ingredients in a meal maintained balance and perfection. For example, he simplified Carême's system of categorizing sauces by identifying five grand sauces. He was also renowned for creating dishes named for famous individuals or events, and he wrote a number of influential articles and books, some of which are still in use today.
Contribution to Foodservice: Carême believed that cuisine was simply a branch of architecture, as demonstrated by his **elaborate pièces montées,** which were masterpieces of decorative art. Figure 1.10 is an example of one of Carême's pièces montées. He also perfected the recipes for many fine French sauces, codifying them into four categories. Many would agree that Carême's greatest claim to fame was training many famous chefs who became his followers and continued his tradition in many fine hotels and restaurants.	**Contribution to Foodservice:** Escoffier not only took great care in his food preparation, he also established **exact rules of conduct and dress for his chefs.** In the kitchen, Escoffier's staff always dressed neatly and worked quietly. He also organized and defined the role of workers in the professional kitchen, developing the kitchen brigade system, which assigns certain responsibilities to kitchen staff. For example, Escoffier introduced the *aboyeur*, or expediter, who takes orders from servers and calls out the orders to the various production areas in the kitchen. This system has been adapted to fit the modern restaurant and is still widely used. Figure 1.11 is a photo of Escoffier, known as the "King of the Kitchen."

Figure 1.10: One of Carême's pièces montées.

Figure 1.11: Escoffier refined the grand cuisine of Carême into classical theme.

24

Figure Focus

Figure 1.10: *Piéces montées* were beautiful to look at, but were they practical to make or to eat?

Figure 1.11: Escoffier "simplified" the work of his predecessor Carême, but in what sense was his cuisine actually "simple"?

[fast fact]

Did You Know...?
In the 1900s:

(1) Restaurants opened that specialized in serving lunch, like Child's, Schrafft's, and Savarin. These were among the first lunchtime restaurants and coffee shops, a foodservice trend which has continued to grow.

(2) The discovery of vitamins in 1919 provided additional benefits to public health. Widespread commercial use of refrigeration kept food from spoiling quickly and helped to feed larger numbers of people.

Later, during the Depression in the 1930s, hotels and fine restaurants started to close. But the 1930s brought an important advancement in the foodservice industry.

[trends]

The Birth of Quick-Service Restaurants
The first White Castle restaurant opened in 1921 in Wichita, Kansas, serving food that could be prepared and eaten quickly. This was the birth of the fast-food operation, or quick-service restaurant. Figure 1.12 shows the first White Castle restaurant.

Figure 1.12: The first White Castle restaurant, circa 1921.

**Fast Fact:
Did You Know...?**

Encourage students to discuss how these three topics—the rise of lunchtime restaurants, the discovery of vitamins, and the introduction of refrigeration—are all related. What effect did these have on society?

**Trends:
The Birth of Quick-Service Restaurants**

The first quick-service restaurants opened less than 100 years ago, but in that time they have transformed the American culinary landscape. Encourage students to discuss ways in which the presence of QSRs has affected society as a whole or the students in particular.

Teaching Tips

- Foods containing certain vitamins were widely popularized in the 1920s and later. How might this relate to contemporary nutritional trends such as the government Food Pyramid or the Atkins and South Beach diets?
- Ask students to imagine a society without quick-service restaurants. What positive and negative aspects might there be?

Figure Focus
Figure 1.12: How does this resemble a contemporary quick-service restaurant? How is it different?

Discuss

- Compare the Gold Rush of 1848 and the Second World War in terms of their effects on population mobility and the hospitality industry. Encourage students to relate information learned in other courses to this concept.
- Ask students why they believe that quick-service restaurants became so popular in the postwar era.
- How does the presence or absence of public or private transportation affect dietary choices?
- Describe how the concept of "eating out" has changed over time. Encourage students to discuss how this change has affected their own lives.

Reinforce and Review

- Review the relationship between transportation and the restaurant and foodservice industry.
- Note the importance of consistency in the success of quick-service restaurants and relate this to the Professional Profile (pp. 4-5).

Teaching Tips

- Obtain local or state maps: one showing the area's current population distribution, the other showing the population distribution during an earlier period (ideally, somewhere between 1940 and 1980). Ask students to discuss how transportation and foodservice have played roles in changing where people prefer to live.
- Ask students to describe the ideal neighborhood in terms of access to transportation and food.

Fast Fact: Did You Know...?

Why is consistency considered so important in contemporary foodservice?

Fast Fact: Did You Know...?

How do twentieth century motels differ from seventeenth century coaching inns? How are they similar?

During World War II in the 1940s, the lodging industry prospered. Many people were traveling for war-related reasons. No new hotels were being built because all construction materials and labor were devoted to the war efforts. Finding an empty hotel room was difficult for travelers.

After World War II, in the 1940s and 1950s, the quick-service restaurant segment of the industry grew quickly.

[fast fact]

Did You Know...?
Some of the early restaurants, like KFC and McDonald's, are still serving food today. Consistency was a major factor in the success of these establishments. Patrons were guaranteed a specific level of quality, taste, food safety, and price. The high volume of fast-food restaurants offset the low prices, so profits could be quite high.

The increased availability and popularity of the automobile, together with a new interstate freeway system, made cross-country vacations a popular option for many American families during this time period.

[fast fact]

Did You Know...?
The first motels developed along highways across America, offering travelers a convenient place to bathe, sleep, and eat before getting back on the road.

In 1958, transportation technology advanced and commercial airlines became a popular and increasingly economical way of traveling. Builders turned their eyes toward land near airports as the next new place to situate hotels, motels, and foodservice facilities.

The rapid growth of national chains from the 1970s to today has changed the face of the foodservice industry. It has caused a major shift in how people look at food and the social context of food. "Eating out" has become almost as commonplace as eating at home, not just for special occasions or as a convenience. In the last few decades, lifestyles have moved steadily toward busier households that no longer have a dedicated daily food preparer. Large restaurant chains

26

such as Red Lobster, Pizza Hut, and Denny's lead the way for full-service, casual dining chain restaurants. Growth in this area has been matched only by the growth in the quick-service sector.

[fast fact]

Did You Know...?
The Food Network was launched in November 1993 with a show called *Food News and Views* followed by *Talking Food*, a call-in show. Today, the Food Network offers more than 140 hours of programming weekly. The Food Network is distributed to more than 96 million U.S. households.

[trends]

The Growth of Home Meal Replacements
In the 1990s, there was major growth in the home meal replacement sector. Food-service outlets were created to serve a growing customer base: those who did not want to cook, but wanted to eat at home. Development in this area led to expansion of the restaurant as an integrated part of the grocery industry. Grocery stores sell salads and main dishes that are ready to take home and serve. There is also the take-home option for ordering food and bringing a dinner home to eat, such as at KFC, Boston Market, and Applebee's.

In addition, the 1990s also saw the return to the coffeehouse type of establishment that began in Oxford, England, in 1650. The "Starbucks movement" delivers the same feelings of community and comfort to the guest that made the coffeehouse so popular earlier in history. Figure 1.13 shows customers at a coffee house.

Figure 1.13: People enjoy passing time at a coffee house.

27

Discuss
- Discuss the importance of The Food Network to the hospitality industry, in particular linking it to the growing population of "foodies" and the "celebrity chef" phenomenon. Encourage students to discuss how this has affected them.
- How has the presence of home meal replacements at groceries and supermarkets affected the sales of raw ingredients?
- Ask students to discuss the roles played by coffee houses in their own lives. Why are these establishments so popular, and what effect do they have on society?

Reinforce and Review
- Review the importance of The Food Network to the hospitality industry.
- Discuss the relevance of home meal replacements to the restaurant and foodservice industry.

Fast Fact:
Did You Know...?

Why are people so interested in watching other people cook and eat? Ask students if they enjoy watching cooking shows on TV.

Trends:
The Growth of Home Meal Replacements

Why are takeout and precooked meals so important in the modern foodservice industry? How do both they and modern coffee houses contribute to a sense of community and comfort?

Figure Focus
Figure 1.13: Compare this coffee house to the one shown in Figure 1.7.

The creativity of chefs has resulted in major developments in culinary style and form. Table 1.4 lists the famous chefs from the 20th century.

Table 1.4: Chefs of the 20th Century	
Name	**Contribution**
Fernand Point (1897–1955)	Known as the father of modern French cuisine, or nouvelle cuisine. He **created lighter sauces and used regional ingredients** to great effect. He mentored many other renowned chefs, including Paul Bocuse.
Julia Child (1912–2004)	Responsible for **popularizing French cuisine and techniques** with the American public. She starred in many television series and wrote bestselling cookbooks, including *Mastering the Art of French Cooking*. Her engaging personality was as much a part of her success as her practical recipes.
Paul Bocuse (1926–)	Built on the principles he learned from Fernand Point, **creating lighter, healthier dishes that still reflected classical French flavors** and traditions. He is one of the first chefs to be widely known, partly because of his dedication to educating young chefs. L'Auberge du Pont de Collognes is his most famous restaurant in Lyon, France.
Alice Waters (1944–)	Opened her award-winning restaurant, Chez Panisse, in Berkeley, California, in 1971. Her goal was to **provide dishes that used only seasonal, local products at the height of freshness** and quality. Even today, the menu changes every day. Her success placed her at the forefront of sustainable agriculture in foodservice and has influenced countless chefs.
Ferdinand Metz (1941–)	A Certified Master Chef who served as the president of the Culinary Institute of America. Leader of the U.S. Culinary Olympic Team, winning unprecedented back-to-back gold medals in the prestigious Hot Foods category, each for almost 20 years. His contributions to the education of American chefs have helped to **foster professionalism and innovation** and strengthen the system for chef apprentices and certification.

Throughout history, entrepreneurs have made great contributions to the food-service industry by developing restaurant chains, diners, and franchising operations. Table 1.5 describes some of these developments.

Table 1.5: Contributions from Entrepreneurs

Gilded Age	(1837) The **Delmonico brothers** open additional restaurants in Manhattan, beginning the **first restaurant chain,** or group of restaurants owned by the same business organization. (1876) **Fred Harvey** opens Harvey House Restaurant in Topeka, Kansas, which becomes one of the most popular restaurants serving the needs of people riding the new transcontinental railroad. Harvey opened multiple locations at train stations across the country, **building one of the earliest nationwide chain restaurants.** (1872) **Walter Scott** of Providence, Rhode Island, begins selling dinners from a horse-drawn wagon to workers outside their factories, a **precursor to the diner.**
20th Century	(1921) **Roy Allen and Frank Wright** begin selling rights allowing people to sell their root beer (A&W), creating the **first franchise company.** (1921) **Walter Anderson and E.W. Ingram** open the first **White Castle** in Wichita, Kansas. It becomes the **first chain of quick-service hamburger restaurants,** providing a consistent product from unit to unit. (1935) **Howard Johnson begins franchising restaurants,** using a standardized design and menu intended to make traveling customers feel comfortable in familiar surroundings. (1954) **Ray Kroc partners with the McDonald brothers** to franchise their small hamburger restaurants. He eventually buys his partners out, and by 1963 over 500 **McDonald's** restaurants are open. His marketing techniques and emphasis on building consistent, family-centric operations are keys to his success. (1957) **Joe Baum** opens The Forum of the Twelve Caesars in New York City. It becomes the city's **first sophisticated theme restaurant.** In 1959, he opens The Four Seasons, which becomes one of the most expensive culinary establishments in Manhattan. (1958) **Frank Carney creates the Pizza Hut franchise,** one of the first quick-service franchises to focus on a menu other than hamburgers. (1966) **Norman Brinker opens the first Steak and Ale,** a full-service restaurant designed for middle-class customers. (1968) **Bill Darden** opens the **first Red Lobster, focusing on affordable prices and full service.** Eventually, Darden Restaurants includes the Olive Garden and Bahama Breeze chains, becoming one of the largest casual-dining companies in the United States. It recently added The Capital Grille, a high-end steak house, to its group. (1971) **Zev Siegel, Jerry Baldwin, and Gordon Bowker open Starbucks** in Seattle, Washington. Starbucks has grown to the largest coffeehouse company in the world, with more than 16,000 stores in 49 countries. (1971) **Richard Melman** founds Lettuce Entertain You Enterprises, a **multifaceted restaurant group.** LEYE has quick-service, casual-dining, and fine-dining restaurants under its umbrella. Innovative and creative concepts help to build both the brand of the group and the brand of several restaurants, including Wildfire, Café Ba-Ba-Reeba!, and Big Bowl. (1977) **Ruth Fertel** opens a second **Ruth's Chris Steak House,** starting one of the first **national fine-dining chains.** Fertel insists on consistent product and very high quality. Each restaurant offers the same menu, but has a unique building design.

Table 1.5: Contributions from Entrepreneurs

- Discuss the similarities and differences in entrepreneurial behavior from the Gilded Age to the twentieth century. Ask students to comment on how these behaviors reflect larger societal trends.

- Compare the diners and chain restaurants of the Gilded Age to those of the twentieth century. How have these basic concepts changed or remained the same?

- Review the time line with students. They should understand the broader picture of entrepreneurial contributions to society, as opposed to simply memorizing all the names and dates.

- Ask students to identify other notable entrepreneurs, chains, or restaurants. How has each contributed to society? For instance, Trader Vic's was part of a midcentury craze for all things Polynesian.

Homework Activity: Entrepreneurial Enterprises

Literacy Connection, 21st-Century Skills— Entrepreneurial Literacy, Reason Effectively, Create Media Products

Students should each select one of the entrepreneurs on this list (or another) and research his or her career.

What factors are responsible for the individual's success?

Make a poster describing these elements.

Discuss

- Discuss prospects for future change in the food-service industry. What are the students' predictions?
- Is it true that "The more things change, the more they stay the same"? How important is the role of tradition in contemporary foodservice? Which is more important, tradition or innovation?

Summary

- Remind students to review the following:
  1. The two segments of the foodservice industry

The Future

The spread of civilization, growth of international trade, and improvements in science and technology all played a part in making foodservice the successful industry it is today.

The foodservice industry is one that is often bound by tradition, but it must also be responsive to changes in the society it serves. It provides the familiar and comfortable, while also working to deliver innovation and adventure. The restaurant of the 21st century does not differ from Boulanger's 1765 *restorante* in that they both "restore" guests' comfort. The goal is to provide guests with an opportunity to reenergize.

Summary

In this section, you learned the following:

- The foodservice industry is divided into two segments. The commercial segment makes up 80 percent of the industry and includes operations in restaurants, catering and banquets, retail, stadium, airlines, and cruise ships. The noncommercial segment includes schools and universities, the military, health care, business and industry, and clubs. There are five restaurant segments in the foodservice industry:

  - Family dining full-service restaurants provide serving staff and orders are taken while the patron is seated. The average per-person dinner is $10 or less.

  - Casual dining full-service restaurants provide serving staff and the order is taken while the patron is seated. The average per-person dinner is $10-$25.

  - Fine dining full-service restaurants provide serving staff and the order is taken while the patron is seated. The average per-person dinner is $25 or more.

  - Quick-service (fast food) restaurants provide foodservice where patrons generally order or select items and pay before eating. Food and drink can be eaten on premises, taken out, or delivered. The average per-person dinner is $3-$6.

  - Quick-casual restaurants serve freshly prepared, wholesome quality, authentic foods in a reasonably fast service format. The average per-person dinner is $7-$9.

30

- The travel and tourism industry is comprised of transportation and hospitality services.

- Throughout history, social and political events have impacted the hospitality and foodservice industry:

  - In Ancient Greece and Rome, the desire for exotic foods and spices increased trade and contributed to the Roman Empire's expansion further east and north.

  - During the Middle Ages, the German tribes brought Christianity to Germany, which ended the view that gods and spirits inhabit forests, which led in turn to Europeans eventually developing a farming society. The need to develop land led to feudalism. Trade to the Far East and India was reduced when the Moors invaded Spain and blocked shipment of spices and fine goods from reaching Europe.

  - During the Renaissance, Catherine de Medici brought haute cuisine, sweet foods, and the use of silverware from Italy to France. The first café opened in which women were welcome, and eating in public became acceptable. Guilds formed, establishing many of the professional standards and traditions that exist today.

  - Settlers moving across the wide expanse of North America led to a need for food and lodging for travelers. Stagecoach routes were established, which included staging inns where travelers could expect a meal and place to sleep.

  - The Industrial Revolution resulted in mass migration to cities so that workers (who often used to be farmers) could be close to new factories. This led to the development of horse-and-buggy transit buses. The invention of the railroad allowed many more travelers to reach remote locations. Many famous hotels were built during this time.

  - Scientific advancements in the 19th century included the discovery of pasteurization by Louis Pasteur and development of the process of canning by Nicolas Appert.

  - During the 20th century, the Depression caused many hotel properties to close. The first fast-food restaurant, White Castle, opened. During World War II, the lodging industry prospered. After World War II, other quick-service restaurants were opened. The 1950s and '60s saw growth in chain restaurants.

31

Summary (cont.)

2. The types of businesses that make up the travel and tourism industry
3. How the hospitality industry has grown throughout the history of the United States

Section 1.1 Review Questions

1. **Family dining full-service restaurant:** Serving staff provides service, and the order is taken while the patron is seated. Patrons pay after they eat. Average per-person check is $10 or less.

   Casual dining full-service restaurant: Serving staff provides service at the table, and the order is taken while the patron is seated. Patrons pay after they eat. Average per-person check is $10–$25.

   Fine dining full-service restaurant: Serving staff provides service at the table, and the order is taken while the patron is seated. Patrons pay after they eat. Average per-person check is $25 or more.

   Quick-service (also known as fast food) restaurant: Establishments primarily engaged in providing foodservice where patrons generally order or select items and pay before eating. Food and drink may be consumed on premises, taken out, or delivered. Also includes snack and nonalcoholic beverage bars. Average per-person check is $3–$6.

   Quick-casual restaurant: Attractive and comfortable establishments serving freshly prepared, wholesome quality, authentic foods in a reasonably fast-service format. Average per-person check is $7–$9.

2. Louis Pasteur (1822–1895) developed a process called pasteurization, which made milk safer to drink by heating it to a certain temperature to destroy harmful bacteria. Nicolas Appert (1749–1841) discovered a way to can food to keep it fresh and safe to eat; he is known as "the father of canning."

3. Many historical events have impacted the food-service industry:

   a. Rome conquered the lands surrounding the Mediterranean Sea, formerly occupied by the Greeks, in 282 B.C. The Roman Empire subsequently expanded to the west, east, and north, coinciding with popular desires for exotic foods and spices.

   b. The end of the Roman Empire united and Christianized much of Europe: societies based on hunting and gathering food now became agrarian, and a feudal society developed. Trade decreased sharply, and Europe remained isolated until 1095 A.D., when Pope Urban II called for the expulsion of Moors from Spain and the Holy Land.

   c. World trade and travel increased, and Venice was the center of the lucrative spice trade. Haute cuisine developed during this period as international trade exposed Europeans to such innovations as drinking coffee and enjoying cafés. Guilds protecting various industries arose, establishing professional standards and traditions in foodservice that exist today, and

Section 1.1 Review Questions

1. Describe the different restaurant segments, the services offered, and the average price per person for dinner.

2. What were the significant contributions made to foodservice by Pasteur and Appert?

3. Describe the historical events that impacted the foodservice industry in the following time periods:

   a. Ancient Greece and Rome

   b. The Middle Ages

   c. The Renaissance

   d. Colonial North America

   e. The Industrial Revolution

   f. The Gilded Age

   g. The 20th Century

4. Why was the Industrial Revolution important to the foodservice industry?

5. Michael Santos says that the hospitality industry is all about serving your guests. Historically, when do you think that the concept of serving guests became really important? Why?

6. Linda has to analyze her strengths and weaknesses to determine her career path. Why do you think you might be interested in a career in the foodservice industry rather than remaining in the broader resort industry?

7. How did the Germanic conquest of Rome affect the development of European eating patterns?

8. Describe three changes in foodservice during the 20th century.

9. How did the development of the railroad system in the United States cause the foodservice industry to grow?

32

the first restaurant was established in 1765. The French Revolution paved the way for more restaurants, and "dining out" was born.

d. North America was colonized by European city dwellers, who brought urban ideals and lifestyles with them. As more immigrants arrived, cities grew, and Boston and New York became major trading centers. By 1634, an inn in Boston had opened to offer travelers food and lodging.

e. Cottage industries and the subsequent Industrial Revolution resulted in mass migration from farms to cities, causing crowded and unsanitary conditions and encouraging the rise of dining and lodging operations. The invention of the railroad in 1825 enabled these operations to thrive as the number of travelers increased. The first building in the United States designed specifically as a hotel opened in 1794, and European-style coffee shops had opened by 1800. The now-classic American diner also arose during this time period.

f. The Enlightenment concept of progress, measured in production and profit, meant long hours and low wages for workers along with increased profits for owners. This enabled the rich to dine stylishly in such elegant restaurants as Delmonico's and the Astor House. The 1848 gold rush also contributed to the spread of fine restaurants as well as to the cafeterias, which catered to the less wealthy.

g. Increased employment initially led to the spread of dining out, especially as restaurants specializing in lunch service (including the first quick-service restaurants) developed.

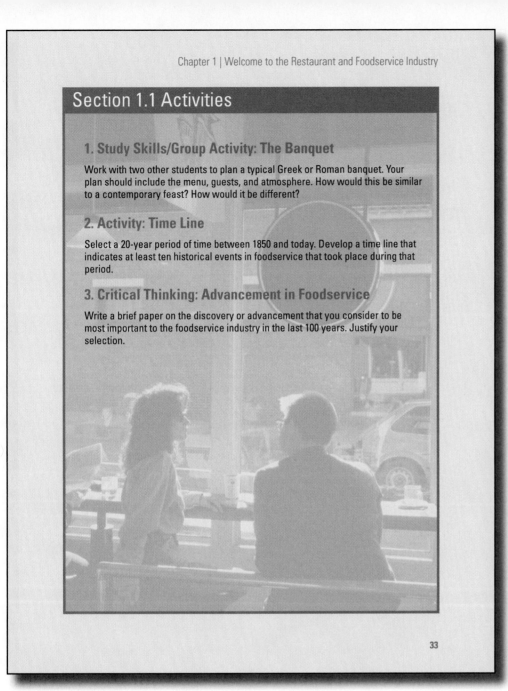

Section 1.1 Activities

1. Study Skills/Group Activity: The Banquet

Work with two other students to plan a typical Greek or Roman banquet. Your plan should include the menu, guests, and atmosphere. How would this be similar to a contemporary feast? How would it be different?

2. Activity: Time Line

Select a 20-year period of time between 1850 and today. Develop a time line that indicates at least ten historical events in foodservice that took place during that period.

3. Critical Thinking: Advancement in Foodservice

Write a brief paper on the discovery or advancement that you consider to be most important to the foodservice industry in the last 100 years. Justify your selection.

33

Section 1.1 Activities

Students' answers will vary.

Section 1.1 Review Questions (continued)

The discovery of vitamins also increased popular interest in healthy eating habits. Although the Depression closed many restaurants, the lodging and foodservice industries prospered during World War II. Later, developments in transportation, including a new interstate freeway system, improved access to automobiles, and the emergent airline industry, contributed to the continued success of lodging and foodservice establishments—particularly for quick-service restaurants and national chains. Toward the end of the century, viewership of the Food Network and popularity of home meal replacements emerged as significant trends.

4. The Industrial Revolution caused mass migration to cities, and dining and lodging establishments opened to serve the needs of both workers and employers. Operations near railway service flourished as travel increased.

5. Students may choose any era as long as they provide solid arguments. For example, during the Gilded Age, a number of fine-dining restaurants arose to serve the wealthy, who might otherwise have simply enjoyed opulent meals at home. These new restaurants had to meet and even anticipate their diners' every request or face desertion.

6. Students should consider their own strengths and weaknesses in answering this question.

7. The Germanic conquest of Rome contributed to a new feudal economy, one based on agrarian principles rather than on hunting and foraging. Forests were methodically cleared and waters diverted for agricultural needs. Travel and trade slowed dramatically, limiting available ingredients.

8. Changes in foodservice during the twentieth century include the opening of restaurants specializing in lunch, the discovery of vitamins, the widespread use of commercial refrigeration, the rise of quick-service and casual-dining chain restaurants, the success of lodging and foodservice establishments catering to travelers, the introduction of the Food Network, and growth in the home meal replacement sector.

9. Travelers on the newly-developed railroad system required lodging and dining options along the way. Fred Harvey's popular chain of Harvey House Restaurants was at the forefront of these establishments.

Section 1.2
Career Opportunities in the Industry

Introduce the Section

a. Describe the variety of career paths and working environments available in the restaurant and foodservice industry.

b. Discuss the skills needed to succeed in this industry. Why are they important? What other skills are important to have? How do all these skills apply to other career paths? Relate this to both the Case Study and the Professional Profile.

c. Discuss the various rating systems that have developed to evaluate restaurants.

d. Discuss the objectives for the section.

Vocabulary Review

a. Direct students to the key terms.

b. Pronounce each word, and have the students repeat the pronunciation out loud.

c. Discuss the definition of each word.

Teach

Discuss

- Talk with students about the nature of restaurant and foodservice careers. Encourage students who have worked in the industry to share their experiences with the class.
- Describe the characteristics of successful foodservice employees. Ask students to suggest other fields in which these skills are valuable.

Reinforce and Review

- The restaurant and foodservice industry continues to grow, offering a wide variety of career options to ambitious students.

Teaching Tips

- Consider asking the school career counselor to give a presentation to the class on careers in foodservice, including information about postsecondary schools offering relevant diplomas or degrees. Alternately, if there is such a school in your area, consider asking the placement counselor to share student experiences with the class.
- Ask whether any students are interested in a career in the restaurant and foodservice industry. Ask them what attracts them to the industry and why.

1.1 Overview of the Restaurant and Foodservice Industry	1.2 Career Opportunities in the Industry	1.3 Overview of the Lodging Industry
• The restaurant and foodservice industry	• Types of establishments	• Why people travel
• The big picture: the hospitality industry	• Career pathways	• Types of lodging operations
• The history of hospitality and foodservice		• Ratings organizations
		• Lodging careers

SECTION 1.2 CAREER OPPORTUNITIES IN THE INDUSTRY

It's never too early to begin thinking about a career in the restaurant and foodservice industry. Even though you're in school, you can still be thinking about how your interest in food could someday lead to a career in this thriving industry. More new restaurants are opening each year. Many restaurant chains are ranked among the nation's top corporations. Many jobs and opportunities exist in the foodservice industry for people who possess the right combination of interests, skills, education, and training.

The restaurant and foodservice industry employs an estimated thirteen million people, 9 percent of the U.S. workforce. On a typical day in the United States, more than 130 million individuals will be patrons of foodservice operations.

When you work in the restaurant and foodservice industry, you have daily contact with guests and often receive immediate feedback about the quality of food and service. So quality must be right the first time! More than anything else, people who work in this industry must love to serve others. They must enjoy working with food; be efficient, flexible, and able to work cooperatively; and remain calm under pressure in a fast-paced environment. Does this describe you?

Note: Specific career opportunities will be discussed in greater depth in Chapter 12. This is simply an overview of the many types of opportunities and businesses that make up the restaurant and foodservice industry.

34

Study Questions

After studying Section 1.2, you should be able to answer the following questions:

- What types of establishments offer foodservice opportunities within the travel and tourism industry?
- What are the two categories of career opportunities in the foodservice industry?
- What are the entry-level jobs in this field? What types of opportunities exist in the lodging and transportation areas?

Types of Establishments

There are many establishments providing foodservice opportunities within the travel and tourism industry.

Restaurants

Restaurants prepare and serve meals to customers. The following types of business opportunities are available in restaurants:

- **Corporate restaurant groups:** Companies with multiple concepts
- **Chains:** Multiple units of the same concept
- **Franchisee/franchisor:** A company that allows another to use its name, sell products, and receive services
- **Independents/entrepreneurs:** Single restaurants, as well as individuals who take risks to open a concept or a restaurant, build it to success, and then move on to the other projects

There are so many restaurants available that people sometimes need help in deciding whether or not to patronize a specific establishment. There are several organizations that describe and rate restaurants and foodservice organizations.

Foodservice Ratings

Many customers look to organizations that review establishments and post ratings to decide where to dine. Two popular resources are the *Zagat Survey* and the *Michelin Guide*.

35

Discuss

- What are the differences between chains and franchises? Ask students to name some examples of each and encourage them to identify distinguishing characteristics.
- Why might individuals choose to become either franchisees or entrepreneurs? Encourage students to discuss issues of individuality, security, and consistency.

Reinforce and Review

- There are a variety of different business opportunities available in the travel and tourism industry: restaurants, foodservice ratings, catering, retails, stadiums, convention centers, national and state parks, theme parks, shopping centers, monuments, museums, zoos, health services, schools, universities, the military, corrections, and lodging, for instance.
- The four categories of restaurant business operations are corporate restaurant groups, chains, franchises, and independents/entrepreneurs.

Teaching Tips

- Consider asking a local entrepreneur, franchisee, or manager within either a chain or corporate restaurant group to speak with your class.
- Ask students to pick out their favorite restaurant and identify what type of business it is.

Discuss

- What are the differences between *The Zagat Survey* and the *Michelin Guide*? Encourage students to discuss which rating system might be more effective and why.
- How can individual critics and writers shape public opinions about restaurants? Why might their words be more or less valid than a broad-based rating organization?
- What strengths should caterers have to do their jobs well? Compare these entrepreneurs to those who own their their own restaurants. How are the two groups similar and different?

Reinforce and Review

- Make sure that students understand the distinctions between *The Zagat Survey* and the *Michelin Guide*.
- Students should understand the roles played by individual food critics and Internet writers.
- Explain how catering differs from restaurant business.

Teaching Tips

- Ask students to relate details of any experiences they have had with catered events.
- Each year, the *Michelin Guide* issues new restaurant ratings. Obtain the current year's ratings (available online) and share them with the class.

Vocabulary Terms

- ***The Zagat Survey:*** A consumer-based guide that rates restaurants on four qualities (food, décor, service, and cost) according to customer surveys.
- ***Michelin Guide:*** A somewhat secretive rating system that judges restaurants according to the reports made by company inspectors; restaurants may be granted one to three stars, but obtaining a single star is considered a sign of a very good restaurant.

The Zagat Survey is a consumer-based guide that rates restaurants on four qualities: food, décor, service, and cost. Each area is rated on a 30-point scale. The ratings are based on the input of many people, which is why it's called a survey. *The Zagat Survey* is available in book form and on the Internet. It has been reviewing restaurants for over 30 years.

The ***Michelin Guide*** is a rating system better known in Europe, but it has recently begun rating organizations in the United States and elsewhere. Restaurants are rated from one to three stars. The criteria include the considerations below:

- Quality of product
- Mastery of flavors
- Cooking mastery
- Personality of the cuisine
- Value for the price
- Consistency

One-star restaurants are considered "very good" establishments. Two-star restaurants are described as "excellent." Three-star restaurants are the pinnacle of "exceptional cuisine." The highest rating is difficult to achieve. For example, in 2010 only five restaurants in New York City (in which there are thousands of restaurants) received the honor.

In recent years, the Internet has become a powerful tool for consumer-based reviewing of both restaurants and lodging properties. Some online sites are devoted entirely to consumer reviews, while others that sell travel and tourism services have incorporated reviewing into their selling pages to help consumers make choices. The sites themselves set the reviewing criteria. Some have specific categories, while others simply allow users to write whatever they want. Some local markets have their own sites of reviews.

Finally, food critics working for newspapers, local magazines, and local television can have an effect on how potential customers view a restaurant.

Catering

Catering provides opportunity for creativity in menu selection and style of service. Caterers provide foodservice for everything from special events in private homes to large-scale events such as golf tournaments, weddings, or corporate dinners. Caterers can be found in catering departments within hotels, independent catering companies, and restaurants. Restaurants can cater on-site or off-site. Personal chefs also cater by working in private homes. In catering,

36

In-Class Activity:
Internet Restaurant Reviews

Literacy Connection

Divide students into small groups and ask them to debate the pros and cons of Internet restaurant reviews, the shield of anonymity, the presence or absence of advertising support, and the effect that a particular Web site's user criteria might have on the writer's outspokenness.

The students should list the highlights of their discussions on the blackboard or a poster so that they can be readily shared with the class.

After 10 minutes, ask the groups to share their results to stimulate a larger discussion.

no two customers are the same and each event is different. Figure 1.14 shows a catered event.

Retail

Retail foodservice opportunities are found in businesses that offer home meal replacements and ready-made dishes. Restaurants in department stores or take-out sections in grocery stores are good examples. Figure 1.15 is a photo of the Food Hall at Harrod's department store located in London, England.

Stadiums

A stadium is a sports arena that is usually oval or horseshoe-shaped, with tiers of

Figure 1.14: Catered events included both hot and cold foods.

Figure 1.15: Harrods, a luxury department store, offers many dining choices for shoppers.

seating for spectators. At any given stadium, there are up to 8,000 people with foodservice needs that must be addressed in a small period of time, usually up to four hours. Spectators sitting in tiered seating often drink beer and eat hotdogs. Foodservice is provided by servers, walking vendors, cooks, and cashiers. These facilities also have corporate suites that offer superior service and food. Stadiums typically have contract feeders, a unique venue with managers who specialize in managing stadium events.

37

Figure Focus

Figure 1.14: Why should culinary staff monitor the food at catered events?

Figure 1.15: How is Harrods similar to and different from American department stores that also sell food?

Discuss

- How have retail foodservice options changed in recent years? Ask students to share their individual experiences with these changes. Link the conversation to the material in Section 1.1.
- Why have the foodservice options at stadiums and sports arenas changed so much in recent years? Again, ask students to share their experiences, linking the conversation to the material in Section 1.1.
- Relate the developments in both of these areas to shifts in the U.S. economy and society. This may include economic growth and contraction, public health, or any other subject you deem appropriate.

Reinforce and Review

- Both retail foodservice and stadium foodservice have dramatically expanded their offerings in recent years.
- Independent restaurants are often found in both retail establishments and athletic stadiums.

Teaching Tips

- Encourage students to visit the Harrods Food Hall online (www.harrods.com) to see what a major department store offers in the foodservice arena.

CUSTOMIZED INSTRUCTION
Literacy Connection, 21st-Century Skills— Think Creatively, Communicate Clearly, Produce Results
Less Advanced Students
Working alone or in pairs, list some retail outlets in your community that offer home meal replacements and ready-made dishes. Consider the dishes that each offers, then select a theme describing that outlet. For instance, a large supermarket specializing in deli-style salads and prepared chickens could be described as having "Comfort Food," and a health food store with a salad bar and vegetarian options could be considered "Healthy Convenience." Compare your results with your classmates. Whose themes are the best?

Discuss

- Why might an industry choose to sponsor an exposition, convention, or trade show? How might these events affect the economy of the hosting site as well as the health of the industry itself? Link this discussion to the material in Section 1.1.
- What if a community builds a convention center but cannot attract any special events? What other elements does a city need to appeal to potential clients?

Reinforce and Review

- Conventions, expositions, and trade shows are all large-scale special events, but they differ in important ways.
- Expositions and trade shows are similar, but expositions are open to the public and trade shows are not.

Teaching Tips

- If there is a convention center in your community, consider asking the booking manager or another employee to speak to the class.
- Ask students to suggest conventions or expositions that they have attended or would like to attend—use this information to showcase the wide variety of these events.

Vocabulary Terms

- **Convention center:** A facility specifically designed to house large-scale special events.
- **Convention:** A gathering of people, all of whom have something in common.
- **Exposition:** A large show, open to the public, which highlights a particular type of product or service.
- **Trade show:** A large show that highlights a particular type of product or service but which is not open to the public.

Convention Centers

Many cities have built facilities specifically designed to house large-scale special events, which include conventions, expositions, and trade shows. These facilities are commonly known as **convention centers**. A few large, well-known convention centers include the Jacob K. Javits Convention Center in New York, Las Vegas Convention Center, and the Dallas Convention Center.

A **convention** is a gathering of people, all of whom have something in common. They are often all members of a particular organization, or they may simply be individuals who share a hobby. Although many conventions are held annually, the convention sites can change from year to year for the convenience of attendees. Examples of conventions include the New York International Restaurant and Foodservice convention and Comic-Con International, San Diego.

Expositions are large shows, open to the public, that highlight a particular type of product or service. Such shows give manufacturers and service providers a chance to display their offerings to many people at a single event. Expositions include auto shows, garden shows, and computer product shows. The Chicago Auto Show, Black Expo, Macworld Expo, and Northwest Flower and Garden show are a few examples of expositions.

Figure 1.16: Trade shows allow companies in a specific industry to showcase and demonstrate their latest products or service.

While expositions are open to the general public, **trade shows** are restricted to those involved in the industry being featured. Figure 1.16 is a photo of a trade show. Producers or manufacturers rent space at trade shows to exhibit, advertise, and demonstrate their products or services to people interested in that specific field. Trade shows may also feature presentations, seminars, and other educational programs relating to current industry issues. For example, The Worldwide Food Expo is the largest food and beverage technology event in North America. And the National Restaurant Association Restaurant, Hotel-Motel Show is the largest single gathering of restaurant, foodservice, and lodg-

38

Figure Focus

Figure 1.16: Who is the audience for an industry's trade show since the public is not invited?

ing professionals in the world, attracting more than 1,800 exhibiting companies. The National Restaurant Association show is one of the largest conventions in the world in any profession.

Depending on the size of the event, a convention, exposition, or trade show can have a major impact on the local economy of its host city. Some large events can bring 100,000 people or more to a city for three or four days. Those people will eat in the city's restaurants, shop in its stores, and use its hotels for lodging. These events are good sources of jobs in catering, customer service, and contract foodservice.

National and State Parks

Many people make national or state parks their travel destinations. The national park system is operated by the National Park Service, which is part of the U.S. Department of the Interior. Some of the best-known national parks include Yellowstone, Glacier, Sequoia, the Everglades, Yosemite, and the Grand Canyon. In addition to parks, the system includes recreation areas, former battlefields, and other historic sites, monuments, and memorials.

Figure 1.17: Foodservice at national parks range from quick-service to fine-dining.

National and state parks offer a variety of attractions. Some people come mainly to see natural wonders, like the Grand Canyon. Others are more interested in studying plant and animal life. Still others visit parks to camp, ski, hike, boat, fish, and swim. Many parks offer high-quality accommodations, ranging from campgrounds to hotels, as well as a wide variety of restaurants, including fine dining, quick-service restaurants, cafeterias, lounges, and recreational facilities. While National Park Service operations are federally managed, most of the guest facilities in national parks are managed by private companies. Figure 1.17 shows foodservice at a national park.

39

Discuss

- Why might hospitality-related trade shows, like the National Restaurant Association Restaurant, Hotel-Motel Show and the Worldwide Food Expo, attract so many exhibitors and guests?
- The National Park Service operates the national park system, but it contracts with private companies to manage foodservice operations at most sites. Is this a good idea? Why or why not? In what other ways is the federal government involved with foodservice?

Reinforce and Review

- Hosting a major event such as an exposition or trade show can have significant financial benefits for a community.
- National and state parks offer a wide variety of hospitality services, although most guest facilities are privately managed by outside companies.

Teaching Tips

- If there is a national or state park in your vicinity, obtain information about the hospitality services available and share it with the class. Encourage students to envision improvements to these services and the effects these might have on the local economy.

Figure Focus

Figure 1.17: At what sort of national park do students think this photograph was taken, and why?

CUSTOMIZED INSTRUCTION

Mathematics Connection, Literacy Connection, 21st-Century Skills—Economic Literacy, Critical Thinking, Problem Solving

More Advanced Students

The multiplier effect describes the chain reaction of economic expansion that begins when a bank lends money to a customer. In basic terms, money is used to create more money.

For instance, a customer deposits $100 in a bank. The bank is required to keep 15 percent ($15) of this deposit on hand as reserves, but it loans out the remaining $85 to another customer, who in turn deposits the $85 into another bank. This second bank is also required to keep a 15 percent reserve ($12.75), but it loans out the remaining $72.25 to a third customer. If this cycle continues, ultimately that original $100 deposit will have created $666.67 in deposits ($100 / 15 percent). Develop a hypothetical situation in which a community hosts a major event, such as a convention or exposition. Include the number of people in attendance and the amount of money they spend—lodging, dining, shopping, sightseeing, and so forth. Then apply the multiplier effect, using whatever percentage of reserves you choose, to determine the total financial benefit to the local economy. Present your information in a one-page essay.

Discuss

- What role do theme parks play in the hospitality industry? Compare their effects to those of one-off or annual events, such as conventions and expositions.
- How can food choices reinforce overall themes at a theme park? What other restaurant and foodservice establishments have themes?

Reinforce and Review

- Theme parks offer an array of entertainment options, including foodservice, that all combine to reinforce a central concept.
- Although theme parks are largely casual environments, maintaining a consistent level of quality remains important.

Theme parks

Modern theme parks offer a full array of entertainment features that create an overall atmosphere of fun. A typical theme park includes exhibits, rides, and other attractions focusing on one unifying idea, such as Sea World's theme of ocean life. The popularity of theme parks as tourist destinations has had a major impact on all

Figure 1.18: Foodservice at a theme park.

hospitality industries, including foodservice, lodging, and transportation. Theme parks have also impacted the local economies and job markets of the areas in which the parks are located. Figure 1.18 shows foodservice at a theme park.

Quality of food and service is no less important in this setting than it is in a free-standing restaurant. Food is a major part of the guests' experience. Dishes can be matched to the theme of the park, and the venue's design might also contribute to the larger theme. For example, barbecued meat and beans might be served in a saloon-style restaurant in a Wild West–themed park.

40

What is the connection between a farmstand selling fresh berries *and* fried-chicken dinners?

[fast fact]

Did You Know...?
Back in the 1920s, Knott's Berry Farm was just that, a roadside stand selling fresh-picked berries. But once the owners began to offer fried chicken dinners, the crowds rolled in. To accommodate the lengthy wait times, in 1940 owner Walter Knott built a ghost town to entertain his customers. This later became America's first theme park, which now has roller coasters, a Boardwalk, and Camp Snoopy among its attractions.

High-quality food was originally an essential part of the theme park experience. Over time, it developed into an uninspiring and overpriced hodgepodge; sno-cones, cotton candy, and waffle fries were among the highlights. Today, however, many theme parks worldwide offer a variety of foodservice options to the hungry guest. National quick-service chains, like McDonald's and Cinnabon, are common sights, and many theme parks coordinate restaurants and concession stands to the theme itself. This enhances the overall impression that the guest has truly left daily life behind to enter an exciting new world.

For instance, The Brown Derby at Disney's Hollywood Studios, named for a famous see-and-be-seen restaurant that gave the world the Cobb Salad, is a full-service, fine-dining restaurant with a 1930s theme. Reservations are required. EPCOT's Tutto Italia Restorante also features fine dining with classic Italian specialties. Tokyo Dining at the same park provides sushi and bento boxes. Sea-World offers Sharks Underwater Grill, showcasing both elegant seafood dishes and an exhibit of live sharks. Mythos at Universal's Islands of Adventure has been named best theme park eatery in the world for six continuous years by Theme Park Insider. Other restaurants at the park include Green Eggs and Ham in Seuss Landing, Pizza Predattoria in Jurassic Park, and the Captain America Diner.

[trends]

Amusement Park Food
According to the International Association of Amusement Parks and Attractions (IAAPA), 94 percent of people that visit amusement parks have a favorite amusement park food. Of those surveyed, 28 percent prefer funnel cake, 17 percent prefer ice cream, 14 percent prefer pizza, 13 percent prefer hot dogs, and 12 percent prefer cotton candy.

Shopping

In recent years, shopping areas have become a major destination for travelers in the United States and other countries. With the growth of automobile travel over the last half century, traditional downtown shopping areas have been

41

Discuss

- Theme parks originally offered high-quality food, but over time foodservice options deteriorated (although they have now returned in full force). Ask students why high-quality food might have been an attraction in the early days of theme parks. Are the reasons they suggest valid today? If so, why was there a period of time in which theme parks offered relatively poor food?
- How have improvements in transportation affected retail shopping? How does this in turn affect local economies?

Reinforce and Review

- Theme parks reinforce their motifs by coordinating restaurants and other foodservice outlets, enhancing the overall guest experience.
- Despite the importance of maintaining a consistent theme throughout a single park, national quick-service chains are common sights at many theme parks.

Teaching Tips

- Invite students to suggest possible theme parks and appropriate foodservice outlets that would enhance the experience.
- Explain how to make a cobb salad—a bed of mixed greens topped with cooked sliced chicken, avocado, bacon, Roquefort cheese, hard-boiled eggs, and tomatoes, dressed with a vinaigrette made with dry mustard and red wine vinegar. Encourage students to discuss why a salad would gain such renown, especially as the dish seems so standard now.

Trends:
Amusement Park Food

Divide students into small groups to discuss the following:

- The text notes the many themed foodservice options available at theme parks and highlights some fine-dining options. How does this square with the IAAPA's findings about individual amusement-park preferences for traditional foods like hot dogs and funnel cakes?

- Under what other circumstances do people typically eat dishes like funnel cakes and cotton candy? Are there simply foods that we associate with some activities and not others?

Discuss

- Providing foodservice for shoppers has become big business with the growth of larger malls and outlet centers. How is this related to changes in theme park foodservice, as previously discussed?
- Encourage students to discuss their own spending patterns at malls. Do they see food courts and mall restaurants as natural gathering places? How are these quasi-public spaces related to the increase in coffeehouses?

Reinforce and Review

- Shopping malls, plazas, and outlets provide a wide variety of foodservice options to meet the needs of a diverse population of shoppers.
- Large malls and outlet centers can attract guests from across the country, contributing significantly to the local economy.

Teaching Tips

- Ask students to expound upon the socialization aspect of shopping, as mentioned in the text. Do students spend time "shopping" without actually buying anything? What does "shopping" really mean in this context?
- Relate this socialization to food consumption. What are "social" foods? Are they foods we share under certain circumstances but not others? For instance, we would probably share an entire ham with other people, often at a holiday event, but we might not share a ham sandwich at lunchtime.

**Fast Fact:
Did You Know...?**

Why do students think that such an enormous retail establishment might be based in Minnesota? Why not New York, Chicago, Las Vegas, or another major city?

---

replaced by big shopping centers located outside larger cities. The rise of large retail chains has helped to continue this trend.

Malls and outlet malls attract millions of tourists who choose shopping as a recreational activity. While many people flock to shopping centers simply to look for bargains, others find shopping itself an enjoyable activity. They value the socialization and relaxation as much as the act of buying. Shopping malls and plazas offer a variety of foodservice opportunities that include quick-service and casual-dining restaurants.

The largest fully enclosed retail and family entertainment complex in the United States is the Mall of America in Bloomington, Minnesota. It employs about 12,000 people and attracts over 40 million visitors a year, with dozens of restaurants representing many styles.

[fast fact]

Did You Know...?
The Mall of America opened in 1992 in Bloomington, Minnesota. Since then, more than a half billion people have visited. It is the largest fully enclosed retail and family entertainment complex in the U.S. Tourists spend an average of $162 per visit.

The Mall of America has more than 500 stores. There are 20 sit-down restaurants, 30 fast-food restaurants, 36 specialty food stores, 14 movie screens, and 12,550 parking spaces. Figure 1.19 shows dining choices at the Mall of America.

Big outlet centers attract travelers from hundreds or even thousands of miles away, particularly

Figure 1.19: The Mall of America has generated $800 million in total taxes, including state, regional, and local taxes through 2007.

from areas where desirable name-brand merchandise is hard to come by. This generates income for the restaurants, hotels, and other businesses in the surrounding community.

42

Figure Focus

Figure 1.19: Compare the food-court photograph to the picture of Delmonico's found in Figure 1.9.

Department stores are a major segment of the retail industry. The biggest advantage to shopping at a department store is that the shopper can purchase all sorts of items during a single visit to just one store. Examples of department stores include JCPenney, Macy's, and Bloomingdale's. While some department stores are part of large national chains, others are independent. Foodservice opportunities vary in these stores. Some have cafés while others have cafeterias or even full-service restaurants in the building.

[fast fact]

Did You Know...?

Some large retail establishments offer a variety of dining options to meet different needs. This is just good business. It keeps people in the store rather than making them leave when they get hungry. It also makes the shop a destination and encourages spontaneous purchases.

At Macy's on State Street, there are five in-store restaurants. These range from the fast and convenient food court (The Market Place) to pub fare (Infield) to an upscale food court (Seven on State) featuring renowned chefs such as Rick Bayless, to The Walnut Room, which is one of Chicago's oldest and most famous restaurants.

Another segment of the retail industry consists of large discount chains, such as Wal-Mart, Kmart, and Target. Discount chains offer a large variety of products at lower prices. They often have an edge over department stores because of national advertising campaigns, larger-volume purchasing, and sophisticated ordering and distri-

Figure 1.20: An example of foodservice operations inside Target.

bution networks. Cafeteria-style and quick-service operations are popular additions to these stores, as shown in Figure 1.20.

43

Discuss

- Department stores and discount chains often attract overlapping demographics. Why might some people choose to shop at one type of outlet and not at another? Why might some people choose to shop at both? What is the role of independent stores in this mix?
- Department stores often offer restaurants with table service, while discount stores often offer restaurants with counter service. How does this difference reflect the differing goals of the two types of store?

Reinforce and Review

- Both department stores and discount chains typically offer dining options to their customers, although the options available differ depending on the type of establishment.
- Department stores allow shoppers to purchase a variety of items during a single visit.
- Discount chains also allow shoppers to purchase a variety of items during a single visit, but they are often less expensive than department stores.

**Fast Fact:
Did You Know...?**

Divide students into small groups to discuss the following:

- What messages do retailers hope to convey by the restaurants they provide? How does the choice of foodservice offered reinforce the identity and image of the hosting store?

- Why would The Walnut Room, one of Chicago's oldest and most famous restaurants, choose to be part of a department-store food court?

Figure Focus

Figure 1.20: What other national foodservice chains are commonly located inside retail establishments?

Discuss

- Visitors to monuments, museums, and the like often expect foodservice options to be available. Why do we associate visiting these places with eating? Why would we be disappointed if no dining options were available?
- Career opportunities in healthcare foodservice are expected to increase over the next several years. What might be some pros and cons to these jobs? What skills might be required?

Reinforce and Review

- Concessions can range from cotton-candy stands to full-service restaurants.
- Knowledge of nutritional issues is essential for foodservice workers in the healthcare industry—an area expected to grow significantly as the baby-boomer generation ages.

Teaching Tips

- Consider inviting the foodservice director of a local hospital or long-term care facility to speak to the class about careers in this field.

Homework Activity: Healthcare and Foodservice

Literacy Connection, 21st-Century Skills—Civic Literacy, Health Literacy, Access and Evaluate Information, Be Self-Directed Learners

What are your state's requirements governing foodservice operations in healthcare facilities, and why are they important?

Research these regulations and describe your findings in a one-page report.

Vocabulary Terms

- **Monument:** Typically, either a structure built to memorialize something or someone or a structure recognized for its historical significance.
- **Concession:** The right for one retail establishment to operate within another; here, a restaurant or other foodservice outlet which has permission to operate at a venue like a museum or a zoo.

Monuments, Museums, and Zoos

Monuments are typically either structures built to memorialize something or someone, or structures recognized for their historical significance. Examples of monuments include the Statue of Liberty, the Eiffel Tower, Mount Rushmore, and the Pyramids. **Concessions**, restaurants within the monuments or associated with them, are common foodservice opportunities. The Statue of Liberty has basic concessions such as hot dogs, ice cream, and beverages.

Museums provide fine-dining restaurants, banquets, or casual concessions, such as kiosks and cafeterias. Approximately 22 percent of museums have foodservice in-house. More than half of all art museums have a full-service restaurant.

Zoos offer a wide range of foodservice options including concession, fine, and casual dining. For example, the San Diego Zoo offers everything from quick-service food to top-quality dining with attentive service. Food choices range from full meals to snacks, healthy food choices, and delicious treats. Throughout the zoo, there are food carts and stands. In addition, there are casual dining restaurants that offer hamburgers, sandwiches, hot dogs, chicken, and pizza. Finally, there is a full-service, fine-dining restaurant that offers fresh fish and grilled meats.

Health Services

With the baby boomer generation moving into retirement, analysts expect growth in foodservice opportunities in hospitals, long-term care facilities, and assisted living facilities. Some states require that menus be approved by state officials to ensure that the specific nutritional needs of patients and clients are met. Foodservice in healthcare requires special attention to the dietary needs of patients. Figure 1.21 shows a commercial kitchen in a hospital.

Figure 1.21: Foodservice employees in hospitals work to provide healthy, nutritious meals.

Figure Focus

Figure 1.21: Foodservice employees who work in a healthcare setting must be especially careful to observe proper sanitation principles.

Schools and Universities

Schools and universities often use **satellite/commissary feeding**: one kitchen prepares food that is then shipped to other locations to be served. Schools and universities have different business cycles from most other types of establishments. Cycles are based on the academic year. During off-times, staff is reduced. Student workers are used through the year to help with foodservice in schools and universities.

Federal regulations determine the requirements for the food that K-12 schools provide to students. Some K-12 schools offer one or two meals a day in cafeterias or through kiosks. Universities and colleges provide much more variety and large institutions generally have multiple contract feeders present at the same school.

Military

Foodservice opportunities in the military are greater now than in the past. You do not need to be a member of the military to work in military foodservice as long as you meet security requirements. More than one million meals are prepared in military kitchens each day, as shown in Figure 1.22. Cafeterias must focus on nutrition.

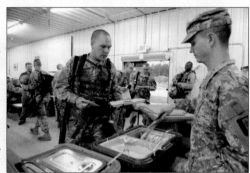

Figure 1.22: The military serves food to hundreds of thousands of service members each day.

Corrections

Food is critical to maintaining a positive and peaceful atmosphere in correctional facilities. Well-prepared food at minimal cost is the challenge. There are both contract feeding and staff employed directly by the institutions, which often offer competitive wages at the management level. Any potential employees must meet security requirements.

45

Figure Focus
Figure 1.22: Like healthcare operations, military foodservice outlets must focus on nutrition.

Discuss
- Schools, the military, and correctional institutions are all charged with providing nutritional meals to individuals who typically have few or no other dining options. Encourage students to explore the similarities and differences in such institutional foodservice operations.
- What are some pros and cons of a foodservice career in one of these institutions? What challenges and opportunities might they offer?

Reinforce and Review
- Satellite/commissary feeding is common in many large institutions such as schools and the military.
- Educational, military, and correctional institutions must provide well-balanced, nutritional meals for a relatively small cost.

Teaching Tips
- If your campus uses a commissary or contract feeder, use these as illustrations.

Homework Activity: Government Regulations

Literacy Connection, 21st-Century Skills—Civic Literacy, Access and Evaluate Information, Work Independently

Research the federal, state, and local regulations that affect the foods available in your school. For instance, although federal regulations determine the requirements for the foods served in your school, state or local measures might regulate the presence of vending machines or the use of fruits and vegetables grown on campus.

Write a brief essay summarizing your findings.

Vocabulary Terms
- **Satellite/commissary feeding:** A central kitchen prepares a large amount of food, portions of which are subsequently shipped to other locations to be served.

Discuss

- Front-of-the-house and back-of-the-house employees are all service professionals, although some serve guests directly and others indirectly. What does it mean to be a service professional? What characteristics are required?
- Now that "chef's tables" are common and celebrity chefs are everywhere, what new skills do back-of-the-house employees need that would have been unnecessary a few decades ago?

Reinforce and Review

- As noted in Section 1.1, there is enormous variety in both types of lodging and types of foodservice available at lodging establishments.
- Front-of-the-house employees serve guests directly, while back-of-the-house employees serve guests indirectly—by serving the "internal customers" who then serve the guests.

Teaching Tips

- Encourage students who have worked in the foodservice industry to share what they have learned about service and professionalism.
- Make sure students understand the concept of "internal customers." A flowchart on the board might help. The server is the intermediary between the dining room and the kitchen.

Vocabulary Terms

- **Front-of-the-house:** This term covers those foodservice employees who directly interact with guests. Foodservice establishments are often referred to as "houses," and the dining area is typically in the front part of the building, hence the term.
- **Back-of-the-house:** Similarly, this term covers those foodservice employees who do not work directly with the public, although they do indirectly serve guests. They typically work in kitchens, bake shops, and offices, traditionally in the rear of the "house."

Lodging

The range of opportunities is as widespread as the types of properties. Many luxury hotels have award-winning, fine-dining operations. Other properties have everything from coffee carts to buffets to full-service operations. Even inexpensive hotels and motels now offer on-premises breakfasts to travelers.

Career Pathways

There are many career opportunities in the hospitality industry, including positions for both front-of-the-house and back-of-the house.

Foodservice Careers

For organizational purposes, jobs in the foodservice industry are divided into two categories: front-of-the-house and back-of-the-house.

Front-of-the-house employees serve guests directly. Front-of-the-house positions include managers, assistant managers, banquet managers, dining room managers, maître d's, hosts/hostesses, cashiers, bar staff, serving staff, and busers. Figure 1.23 shows a hostess greeting guests.

Figure 1.23: A hostess in a restaurant discusses the menu with customers.

Back-of-the-house employees work outside the public space. Back-of-the-house positions include chefs, line cooks, pastry chefs, dishwashers, bookkeepers, storeroom clerks, purchasers, dietitians, and menu planners. While these employees don't ordinarily serve guests directly, they are service professionals because they serve the people—the "internal customers"—who serve the guests.

In recent years, chefs have become more involved with their guests, especially through visits to the dining room and "kitchen" tables that allow guests a closer

46

Figure Focus

Figure 1.23: Why is it so important for the guest's first impression of the restaurant staff—usually, the host or hostess—to be positive?

view of the operation's inner workings. Exhibition kitchens are also popular with diners. The kitchens become part of the dining experience, meaning the back-of-the-house staff is more directly involved with customers. In environments like these, the back-of-the-house staff benefit from some customer service training. Figure 1.24 is an example of an exhibition kitchen.

Entry-Level Jobs

Whether your interest is in a job in the front or the back of the house, you can expect to begin your career in an entry-level position. An **entry-level job** is one that requires little or no previous experience. Such jobs are an important starting point in any career. Entry-level jobs usually lead to other positions with more responsibility. The foodservice industry offers many entry-level positions, and the industry as a whole is expected to generate more new jobs than any other service industry over the next decade.

Entry-level jobs in the foodservice industry include host/hostess, buser, assistant cook, server, expediter, and dishwasher. It is easy to see why these jobs are important to the foodservice operation. Each role is important to the success of the operation as a whole. The operation can only be as good as its team. Figure 1.25 shows a buser clearing a table.

Jobs in foodservice can be varied and unique. Higher-level jobs include planning menus, developing recipes, managing a foodservice operation, writing about food, developing marketing and advertising strategies, teaching others about food and nutrition, and supplying food to restaurants. Some specific examples of positions are included in Table 1.6.

Figure 1.24: Exhibition kitchens allow customers to watch chefs prepare their meals.

Figure 1.25: A buser clears and cleans tables and sets up tables for the next customers.

47

- Entry-level jobs are the starting point for most careers in the restaurant and foodservice industry. Although these jobs are not always exciting, the tasks these employees perform are crucial to the guest's experience. Ask students to identify entry-level jobs in other industries.
- Higher-level foodservice jobs often require additional formal education and training. How might this be obtained? For instance, why might someone choose to attend culinary school rather than learn on the job, or vice versa?

Reinforce and Review

- Entry-level jobs are an important part of the foodservice industry, introducing ambitious employees to the industry while performing tasks that are vital to a positive guest experience.
- Higher-level jobs usually require more education and training. They can either be stops along the career path or ends in themselves.
- The restaurant and foodservice industry is expected to create more jobs than any other service industry in coming years.

Vocabulary Terms

- **Entry-level job:** A job that requires little or no experience.

Figure Focus

Figure 1.24: At what types of restaurant can guests commonly watch their food being prepared?

Figure 1.25: From a public-health perspective, why is a buser's job so important?

Table 1.6: Examples of Jobs in the Restaurant and Foodservice Industry

- Ask students to evaluate the various jobs on these two pages. What skills unite both front-of-the-house and back-of-the-house employees? Which of the jobs listed is the most important in a restaurant?

- Why must the executive chef command the kitchen's respect and loyalty? Do managers in other industries require their employees to behave in this way, or is this unique to the foodservice industry?

- Restaurant and foodservice employees all play different roles, but they coordinate with one another to ensure proper guest service.

- Typically, front-of-the-house employees should enjoy working with people and back-of-the-house employees should enjoy working with food. But everyone's job comes down to service.

- Ask students to consider whether they would prefer front-of-the-house or back-of-the-house positions and why.

Table 1.6: Examples of Jobs in the Restaurant and Foodservice Industry	
FRONT OF THE HOUSE	Do you really like to deal with people? Consider some of these opportunities.
Restaurant and Foodservice Managers	Restaurant and foodservice managers are **responsible for both front-of-the-house and back-of-the-house operations.** They are responsible for service, staff training, maintaining the operation and its property, keeping food safe, keeping guests and employees safe, marketing and promoting the operation, ensuring profits, keeping costs down, purchasing and storing food, and supervising employees. The most difficult tasks faced by managers include dealing with dissatisfied customers and uncooperative employees.
Servers	Servers spend more time with guests than any other employees. The server's attitude and performance has a huge **impact on the guest's enjoyment** of the dining experience. In a full-service operation, servers greet customers, take orders, serve beverages and food, check on customers' needs during their meals, present the bill, collect the payment, and continue to provide service until customers have left the table.
Host/Hostess	The host/hostess stands near the front of the establishment. The host/hostess **makes the first impression** in any restaurant or foodservice operation. If that impression is friendly, hospitable, and gracious, guests will feel relaxed and ready to enjoy themselves. In addition to greeting customers, hosts/hostesses assist guests with coats or other things they wish to check; take reservations; seat customers; ask whether departing customers enjoyed their meals; thank customers for their visits; and answer customers' questions about hours of operation, types of credit cards accepted, and what menu items are available.
BACK OF THE HOUSE	Do you really like working with food? Then think about these positions.
Executive Chef	An executive chef is the **highest-ranking member of a culinary team,** responsible for all aspects of kitchen management. From a small bistro to a prestigious resort, the executive chef is in charge of all things food related throughout the establishment.
	The executive chef's **responsibilities are not limited to cooking.** The chef must also possess exceptional managerial and organizational skills. The chef is responsible for hiring and supervising kitchen staff as well as directing their work and training them in their duties. Although this work can be—and often is—delegated to a sous chef (the chef's assistant) the chef remains the **ultimate authority** and must therefore command the kitchen's respect and loyalty. The executive chef is also responsible for ensuring that all dishes are prepared properly, that sanitation and hygienic standards are met, and that financial targets are achieved. Other duties may include handling marketing and publicity efforts, developing business plans; and creating menus. In short, the executive chef is the problem solver and role model for the kitchen.
	To become an executive chef, aspirants must typically have worked in the industry for a number of years, gradually moving up in the kitchen hierarchy. Some establishments require their executive chefs to possess culinary degrees or to engage in ongoing professional education. The American Culinary Federation offers certification for executive chefs and for many other positions in the back of the house, as well as many continuing education opportunities. To see these requirements go to www.acfchefs.org.

48

Table 1.6: Examples of Jobs in the Restaurant and Foodservice Industry *continued*

Sous Chef	Sous chefs are responsible for the kitchen team in the executive chef's absence. Sous chefs **create recipes and prepare meals.** Sous chefs are responsible for directing the work of other kitchen workers, estimating food requirements, and ordering food supplies. Sous chefs are under pressure to prepare safe, delicious meals. They should be able to communicate clearly to ensure orders are completed correctly.
Line Cook	The most common title in the kitchen is that of line cook. A line cook (also known as *chef de paetie*) is **any cook working a particular station in the kitchen.** The number of line cooks in a kitchen depends on the type of establishment. Examples include grill cook, sauté cook, or fry cook. All food that comes out of the kitchen is the responsibility of the line cooks. Generally, the line cooks work alone at their stations, but they must coordinate with each other to make sure food for an order comes out at the same time and in a timely manner. Line cooks are also responsible for stocking their stations with proper food and tools prior to the start of their shifts. The line cook reports to the head cook or the executive chef.

Careers in Travel and Tourism

There are many other types of transportation and tourism service careers in addition to the restaurant and foodservice careers that are related to this industry. Transportation focuses on all aspects and methods of traveling, so many of these companies must employ drivers, ticket agents, mechanics, engineers, managers, and other administrators.

Tourism focuses on the many ways in which people spend their time and money away from home. Careers in this field include positions such as tour guides, convention planners, travel writers, amusement park employees, or park rangers.

Discuss
- Why are employees like mechanics and travel writers considered to be part of the travel and tourism industry? Is this category too broad, or not broad enough—for instance, should city bus drivers be included?
- What employees do students think should be included in the travel and tourism industry?

Reinforce and Review
- Transportation involves all aspects and methods of traveling.
- Tourism involves all the ways in which people spend time and money when away from home.

Teaching Tips
- At the beginning of Section 1.2, it was suggested that the instructor ask whether any students were drawn to careers in the restaurant and foodservice industry. Now that the section has been completed, repeat the question. Have more students developed an interest in this industry, or have some of the students who were originally interested changed their minds? Why?

49

Summary

- Remind students to review the following:
  1. The types of establishments that offer foodservice opportunities within the travel and tourism industry
  2. The two categories of career opportunities in the foodservice industry
  3. The entry-level jobs in this field

Summary

In this section, you learned the following:

- Restaurant and foodservice opportunities include restaurants, banquets/catering, retail, stadiums, convention centers, national and state parks, theme parks, shopping areas, monuments, health services, schools and universities, the military, corrections, and lodging.

- The front-of-the-house employees serve guests directly. Positions include managers, assistant managers, hosts/hostesses, cashiers, bar staff, serving staff, and busers. The back-of-the-house employees work outside the public space. Positions include chefs, line cooks, pastry chefs, dishwashers, bookkeepers, storeroom clerks, purchasers, dieticians, and menu planners. Back-of-the-house employees serve the servers and front-of-the-house employees.

- Entry-level positions require little or no previous experience and usually lead to other positions with more responsibility. Entry-level positions in the foodservice industry include host/hostess, server, quick-service counter server, buser, prep cook, and dishwasher.

Section 1.2 Review Questions

1. List the foodservice opportunities in the travel and tourism industry.

2. What is a front-of-the-house employee? Provide some examples.

3. What is an entry-level position?

4. What is the difference between the *Zagat Survey* and *Michelin Guide*?

5. Do you think that Michael Santos's career path is a typical one? Why or why not?

6. What would you recommend Linda choose as the next step in her career? Why?

7. Research a career path in the hospitality industry, starting with a typical entry-level position.

8. Think of an experience you had as a customer within the hospitality industry that was particularly positive or negative. What happened? What did you do about it? With whom did you speak? If there was a problem, how was it resolved?

9. Go online and research the statistics for the types of foodservice opportunities available. Where do analysts anticipate growth in this market?

51

Section 1.2 Review Questions

1. Foodservice opportunities in the travel and tourism industry include restaurants, foodservice ratings organizations, catering establishments, retail establishments, stadiums, convention centers, national and state parks, theme parks, shopping centers, monuments, museums, zoos, health services, schools and universities, the military, correctional institutions, and lodging establishments.

2. Front-of-the-house employees serve guests directly. Examples include managers, assistant managers, banquet managers, dining room managers, maître d's, hosts, hostesses, cashiers, bar staff, serving staff, and busers.

3. An entry-level position is one which requires little or no experience.

4. *The Zagat Survey* is based on consumer input and rates restaurants on food, décor, service, and cost, using a 30-point scale. The *Michelin Guide* employs professional inspectors and rate restaurants from one to three stars, based on quality of product, mastery of flavors, and other criteria.

5. Working one's way up through the ranks, as Michael Santos has done, is a fairly typical career path, although students may argue that a VP of Operations and Human Resources for a restaurant group could develop the necessary skills and experience while working in another industry.

6. Students may choose creatively so long as they give good reasons for their answers. Typical selections might include dining-room manager, banquet manager, or restaurant manager.

7. Students may choose from a variety of common entry-level positions, including buser, host, and assistant cook.

8. Students should describe the experience and its resolution.

9. Growth opportunities may include quick-service restaurants, home meal replacement, and health services.

Section 1.2 Activities

1. Students may choose from virtually any relevant establishment but should thoroughly research each. Pros might include specific information about amenities, while cons might include location or lack of cleanliness.

2. Students should research local businesses to learn more about how each relates to the community. Questions to consider may include the following: How many workers are employed? Is the business locally owned? What are annual sales figures? Does it participate in local charity fundraisers?

3. This activity is intended to encourage students to consider the broad range of career opportunities in the hospitality industry and the appropriate qualifications needed for each.

Section 1.2 Activities

1. Study Skills/Group Activity: Foodservice and Tourism

Work with two other students to research three specific foodservice establishments in the travel and tourism field. Compare and contrast the pros and cons of each type of establishment. Prepare and present a brief oral report on your findings.

2. Activity: Foodservice Opportunities in Your Community

The travel and tourism industry offers a number of foodservice opportunities. List three opportunities that might be available in your area, and describe the role each plays in the community.

3. Critical Thinking: How to Begin Job Hunting

Select a local employer in the hospitality industry (in foodservice, travel and tourism, or lodging) and interview a manager about career opportunities in the field. What qualifications are needed for entry-level or advanced positions?

52

1.1 Overview of the Restaurant and Foodservice Industry	1.2 Career Opportunities in the Industry	1.3 Overview of the Lodging Industry
• The restaurant and foodservice industry	• Types of establishments	• Why people travel
• The big picture: the hospitality industry	• Career pathways	• Types of lodging operations
• The history of hospitality and foodservice		• Ratings organizations
		• Lodging careers

SECTION 1.3 OVERVIEW OF THE LODGING INDUSTRY

Have you ever been a tourist? Most likely you have. If you've ever visited a museum, flown on an airplane, or stayed overnight in a hotel or motel, you've experienced the travel and tourism industry firsthand. People travel for many reasons, including vacations, business, and visits with friends and family. When traveling, people need a variety of services including foodservice and lodging. This section provides an introduction to travel and lodging operations and careers.

Study Questions

After studying Section 1.3, you should be able to answer the following questions:

- Why do people travel?
- What are the differences between leisure and business travel?
- What national organizations rate commercial lodging and foodservice establishments?
- What factors are listed in rating judgments?
- What are the characteristics of lodging operations?
- What are the activities associated with front-desk operations?

Why People Travel

People travel for a variety of reasons. Some might be attending out-of-town conventions, while others are visiting relatives or traveling abroad to experience a foreign culture. Business travelers might go to a specific place for the purposes of sales, negotiations, training, or other types of business related to their jobs.

53

Section 1.3 Overview of the Lodging Industry

Introduce the Section

a. Discuss the various reasons people travel and the various types of transportation and lodging available to them.
b. Talk about the different rating systems used to assess lodging and how these relate to the rating systems used to assess restaurants, as discussed in Section 1.2.
c. Discuss the objectives for the section.

Vocabulary Review

a. Direct students to the key terms.
b. Pronounce each word, and have the students repeat the pronunciation out loud.
c. Discuss the definition of each word.

In-Class Activity: Travel Time

Mathematics Connection, 21st-Century Skills—Reason Effectively, Communicate Clearly, Work Independently

How often do you travel more than 50 miles away from home in a year, and for what reasons? How do you get there? Create a bar graph showing the number of miles you annually travel on such trips, the reasons you travel, and the types of transportation you use. For instance, if last year you flew 2,000 miles to visit your grandparents, drove a total of 400 miles to visit outlet malls, and took a bus 600 miles to attend a youth convention, your bar graph would look like this:

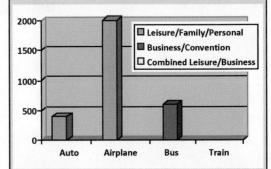

Compare your results with your classmates. Talk about the different reasons high school students may travel, as opposed to adults. How might these different reasons affect your choice of lodging and discretionary spending?

Teach

Discuss

- Discuss the various reasons people travel: education, family, business, leisure, and so on. Why might people traveling for different reasons have different lodging or transportation needs?
- Many lodging facilities offer a variety of services calculated to attract specific demographic groups. Suggest a few categories, such as middle-aged parents with young children, and encourage students to come up with services that might attract each group.

Reinforce and Review

- Although people travel for many reasons, they all want clean, comfortable, safe, and secure accommodations.
- Travelers also want convenience. A lodging's location as well as the amenities it may offer are part of this calculation.
- Business travelers represent the majority of guests for most lodging establishments.

Teaching Tips

- Name some lodging options in your community and ask students why certain types of guests might be more or less attracted to each.
- If possible, obtain some brochures about local hotels, motels, and other lodging facilities to distribute among students.

Leisure travelers go to a place for relaxation, entertainment, education, adventure and sport, and social and family events. Figure 1.26 illustrates the percentages of why people travel and the modes of transportation used.

All guests seek clean, comfortable, safe, and secure accommodations. They want knowledgeable, helpful staff who are familiar with the facilities and the local area. However, business and leisure travelers also require and expect different things when they travel.

Leisure travelers often want to "get away from it all." They're on vacation, eager to do fun things like shopping, fine dining, sightseeing, attending sports events, or simply finding the time to relax. Leisure travelers want a location that's convenient to the things they want to enjoy—for example, near a beach or the theatre district of a city. Some leisure travelers also want family services, such as babysitting services, children's menus, high chairs, and play areas. Spa services, fine-dining opportunities, and social activities such as nightclubs and casinos are typically attractive to leisure travelers without children. Many hospitality operations cater to specific leisure travelers by offering services or activities designed especially for them. Some facilities, for example, sponsor programs for children; others provide guests with social activities or on-site recreational or health facilities. Figure 1.27 shows leisure travelers on the beach.

Business travelers want the same convenience, directed to the business district or convention center they plan to visit. They represent the majority of guests for most lodging establishments.

Total Domestic U.S. Person-trips, 2004	1,163.9 Million
Purpose of Trip	
Leisure Travel *	81%
Business/Convention **	12%
Combined Business and Pleasure	7%
Modes of Transportation Used	
Auto, Truck, RV	73%
Airplane	16%
Bus/Motorcoach	2%
Train/Ship/Other	4%
Rental Car (Primary Mode)	3%
Top Activities for Domestic Travelers	
Shopping	First
Attend a social/family event	Second
Outdoor Activities	Third

A person-trip is one person traveling 50 miles (one way) or more away from home and/or overnight. A trip is one or more persons from the same household traveling together.

*Travel for visiting friends/relatives, outdoor recreation, entertainment/sightseeing, or other pleasure/personal reasons.

**Travel for business - either general reasons (e.g., consulting, service) or to attend a convention/conference/seminar.

Source: Travel Industry Association of America; Travelscope ®

Figure 1.26: Percentages of why people travel and the modes of transportations used.

Figure 1.27: Leisure travel is for fun and gives people a chance to be free from work or duty.

Figure Focus

Figure 1.26: Why do students think leisure plays such a major role in travel?

Figure 1.27: Beachfront locations are particularly popular with many leisure travelers, although physical surroundings are less important for many business travelers.

Recognizing and catering to their needs is essential to the success of many properties. Typical business travelers spend most of their time working. In addition to well-lit work spaces and telephones, they often need computer workstations, Internet access, copiers, and fax machines as well as meeting and banquet facilities. Many business travelers expect 24-hour room service and valet parking, and place a high priority on comfortable beds and amenities such as mini bars and large bathrooms. Consistency is an important factor. Business travelers want efficient and consistent service, fast, affordable food, and opportunities to socialize over a drink or a meal. See Figure 1.28.

Figure 1.28: Business travelers spend most of their time working.

To meet the needs of both leisure and business travelers, marketers classify tourism according to the type of travel experience that people desire.

Cultural and Historic Tourism

In addition to visiting places of historical interest and importance, cultural travelers visit other lands to observe, learn about, and live among people whose cultures are different from their own. Cultural and historic tours are often organized for groups of travelers, although many people plan their own trips. Examples include visiting Paris to learn how the French live; going to Washington, D.C., to see famous monuments; traveling to Williamsburg, Virginia, to walk along colonial streets; and traveling to Beijing to meet Chinese people and see the Great Wall. Figure 1.29 shows tourists visiting the Eiffel Tower.

Figure 1.29: Tourism increases the wealth and job opportunities in an area.

55

Discuss

- Page 55 mentions a number of amenities business travelers often seek while on the road and cites the importance of consistency. Encourage students to relate this information to the discussion of "service professionals" in Section 1.2.
- Cultural and historic tourism are important sources of revenue for many communities. Ask students to suggest reasons why such tourists might visit your area. What elements might attract them? How might they spend their money?

Reinforce and Review

- Business travelers often spend most of their time working, so lodging operations catering to these individuals must provide appropriate and attractive facilities.
- As in all other components of the travel and tourism industry, consistency is a critical factor in ensuring guest satisfaction.
- Cultural and historic tours can help travelers learn more about their own history and culture as well as those of other peoples.

Teaching Tips

- Ask students to describe the services that would be provided at their ideal lodging facility. How might these differ from those typically offered to business travelers?

CUSTOMIZED INSTRUCTION
Literacy Connection, 21st-Century Skills— Information Literacy, Communicate Clearly, Work Independently
ESOL Students
What important historic and cultural sites do you think that travelers to your country of origin should visit and why?
Alternately, what historic or cultural sites would you like to visit in the United States?
Prepare a brief oral presentation on either option.

Figure Focus

Figure 1.28: Since business travelers spend so much of their time working, should hotels and motels even bother providing any nonwork amenities to them?

Figure 1.29: What tourism opportunities exist in Paris, besides the Eiffel Tower?

Discuss

- What are the differences between environmental tourism and recreational tourism? How might they overlap? What options for either sort of tourism are available in or near your community that might attract travelers?

- Lodging amenities add value and increase traveler satisfaction by making it more convenient for travelers to receive services. However, it may be more expensive to receive the service at the lodging operation than at a nearby business—convenience can be costly. Why might it be wiser to patronize services such as a haircut or a fax transmission either at the lodging property or at another establishment? Should you always use either one or the other?

Reinforce and Review

- Environmental tourists visit places to enjoy their natural beauty, while recreational tourists visit places to participate in some activity.

- Lodging properties may be classified by the level of service provided, the rates charged, the amenities offered, or any combination of these or other factors.

Vocabulary Terms

- **Amenity:** A service or product provided to guests for their convenience, either with or without an additional fee.

Environmental Tourism

Some travelers visit places in order to enjoy their natural beauty. These tourists often enjoy photography, hiking, biking, mountain climbing, camping, and canoeing. Examples of environmental destinations include the Grand Canyon and Niagara Falls. Figure 1.30 shows a Grand Canyon restaurant's dining area.

Recreational Tourism

Travelers on recreational vacations usually look for places where they can swim, lie in the sun, ski, play golf or tennis, see shows, or gamble. Examples include Vail, Colorado; Las Vegas, Nevada; and Ft. Lauderdale, Florida. See Figure 1.31.

Figure 1.30: The Grand Canyon offers a wide range of dining options.

Types of Lodging Operations

Lodging properties can be classified by the level of service provided, the rates charged, the amenities offered, or any combination of these or other factors.

Figure 1.31: Vail is a popular recreational skiing place.

An **amenity** (a-MEN-i-tee) is a service or product provided to guests for their convenience, either with or without an additional fee.

Lodging amenities range from restaurants, lounges, and parking garages to newsstands, boutiques, hair stylists, dry cleaners, and florists. Amenities add value to guests' experiences by satisfying their needs in a convenient manner. By putting these facilities within easy reach of their guests, lodging operators can increase customer satisfaction.

56

Figure Focus

Figure 1.30: Does hiking the Grand Canyon seem compatible with a luxury meal?

Figure 1.31: Does skiing, which is often considered a relatively expensive sport, seem to be more compatible than hiking with enjoying a fine-dining meal?

Luxury properties are hotels that offer top-of-the-line comfort and elegance. While often defined as part of the full-service sector, luxury hotels take service and amenities to new heights of excellence. The rooms are spacious and well-decorated and may feature luxurious extras, like bathrobes. Other amenities found at luxury properties include

Figure 1.32: Luxury hotel rooms are spacious and offer guests many amenities.

gift shops, boutiques, and a variety of restaurants and lounges. These establishments are often aimed at wealthy travelers and corporate executives. The Ritz-Carlton and the Four Seasons are examples of luxury hotels. See Figure 1.32.

Full-service properties cater to travelers in search of a wide range of conveniences. They offer larger rooms and well-trained staff, and feature amenities such as swimming pools, room service, fitness centers, or services for business travelers. They commonly also have meeting and banquet rooms available for client use. A variety of foodservice options may be present, including quick, casual, and fine dining. The Hyatt and Westin are examples of full-service properties.

Mid-priced facilities fall somewhere between the full-service and economy sectors. They are designed for travelers who want comfortable, moderately priced accommodations. Also known as tourist-class properties, these facilities provide on-premises food and beverage service and simple decor. The Holiday Inn and the Radisson are examples of mid-priced hotels.

Economy lodging offers clean, low-priced accommodations primarily to traveling salespeople, senior citizens, and families with modest incomes. To maintain low rates, these properties employ small staffs and provide limited amenities. Guest rooms usually have one or two double beds, as well as a bathroom with clean towels and soap. In return for doing without the extras offered at full-service or luxury properties, guests enjoy sanitary, fully furnished accommodations at budget prices. Motel 6 and Travelodge are examples of economy lodging. Figure 1.33 on the following page is an example of a economy lodging room.

57

Figure Focus

Figure 1.32: What about this room do students consider luxurious?

Discuss

- The four types of lodging properties discussed on this page represent similar types of operations—except for the amenities and prices. Why would people choose to stay at one category rather than another? Should you conserve your money with an economy room or splurge because you're on vacation? Are different selections appropriate under different circumstances?
- Of the four categories of lodging properties listed on this page, which do students think would attract the most guests each year and why? Which might earn the highest revenues?

Reinforce and Review

- Luxury properties and full-service properties are similar, but luxury properties offer a wider and more elegant range of options.
- Mid-priced lodging operations are popular with leisure travelers who do not need many in-house services.
- Economy lodging provides few extra services, specializing in clean and low-priced accommodations for the traveler on a budget.

Teaching Tips

- Ask students to name local establishments that fit into one of these categories. Include the categories that appear on the next page.

Vocabulary Terms

- **Luxury property:** A hotel offering top-of-the-line comfort and elegance.
- **Full-service property:** A hotel offering a wide range of conveniences, though without the level of excellence offered by a luxury property.
- **Mid-priced facility:** A hotel offering comfortable, moderately-priced accommodations.
- **Economy lodging:** Typically a motel offering clean and inexpensive accommodations with few extras.

Discuss

- All-suite properties, resorts, and bed and breakfasts represent three very different types of lodging. Why might these appeal to some travelers more than the types of properties discussed on the previous page?
- How can seasonality affect the lodging industry? For instance, the text notes that resorts often have well-defined tourism seasons. Encourage students to discuss how the time of year relates to the "busy season" at various types of lodging properties.

Reinforce and Review

- All-suite properties are similar to mid-priced facilities, except they offer apartment-style arrangements rather than simply a bedroom with a bathroom.
- Resorts provide a wide variety of on-site services for those who choose to stay at one location throughout their vacation and are particularly popular with recreational travelers.
- Bed and breakfasts provide quiet, home-like accommodations that often encourage guests to mingle.

Vocabulary Terms

- **All-suite property:** A lodging operation that offers apartment-style facilities at midmarket prices.
- **Resort:** A property that provides extensive facilities for vacationers seeking recreational activities and entertainment.
- **Bed and breakfast:** An operation with relatively simple amenities, including a communal breakfast and often shared bathrooms and common events.

All-suite properties offer apartment-style facilities at midmarket prices. They have larger spaces that include a sitting area, often with dining space, and small kitchen or bar area in addition to a bedroom and bath. While all-suite establishments appeal to different people for different reasons, all guests enjoy the at-home atmosphere and the extra space that these properties provide for

Figure 1.33: Economy lodging rooms are modestly priced with limited amenities.

both work and relaxation. The roominess is often a draw for traveling families, since parents and children can spread out as if they are staying in an apartment instead of a hotel room. Marriott Suites and Comfort Suites are examples of all-suite properties.

Resorts feature extensive facilities for vacationers who are looking for recreational activities and entertainment. Appealing to specific types of guests, some resorts provide programs for singles only, families with children, couples only, or senior citizens. Other establishments focus on a particular area of interest, such as golf, tennis, scuba diving, or health. They are often specific to a destination (such as skiing or beaches) with amenities to match such as ski rentals and lifts or scuba diving and boating excursions. Often located in beautiful vacation areas, resorts usually have distinct tourism seasons. While resorts cater primarily to vacationers, many rely on conventions to keep vacancy rates low year-round.

Resorts, however, enjoy only a small part of the business travel market. Club Med and Disney World Resorts are examples of resorts. Figure 1.34 is an example of a resort.

Bed and breakfasts cater to guests looking for quaint, quiet accommodations with simple amenities. Bed and breakfasts are usually privately owned homes converted to have several

Figure 1.34: Resorts provide vacationers with recreation and relaxation.

58

Figure Focus

Figure 1.33: How does this bedroom compare with the one shown in Figure 1.32?

Figure 1.34: What about this photograph signals relaxation?

guest rooms. Often guests may share bathrooms with other guests staying at the bed and breakfast. At bed and breakfasts, guests are served breakfast during a specified time in a small dining room. The operations usually do not serve lunch or dinner, but may offer special hours for tea or cocktails in the afternoon. Bed and breakfasts are different from other lodging properties because the owner usually lives on

Figure 1.35: Bed and breakfasts are small establishments that offer overnight accommodations and breakfast.

the property and manages its day-to-day operations. Figure 1.35 shows a bed and breakfast.

[what's new]

The Greening of the Lodging Industry

As consumers across the United States and elsewhere become increasingly drawn to "green" (that is, environmentally sound) business practices and everyday behaviors, hotels, motels, and resorts are joining the trend. A number of green activities are emerging within the lodging industry in response both to customer demand and economic pressures. Many behaviors, such as lowering thermostats and reducing water overuse, are excellent ways of saving money.

Hotels and motels can take a number of steps to become "greener." Installing low-flow showerheads and toilets can help eliminate water waste. Defrosting frozen items in advance rather than thawing them under running water is another step. Facility-wide recycling programs can cut down on the overall waste stream, which can lower garbage costs. Using tried-and-true cleaning materials, such as baking soda, is both cheaper and less toxic than using more common cleaning chemicals. Creating personalized Web sites for each event to be held at a property, rather than accumulating stacks of paper that will soon be unnecessary, not only conserves resources but can also make a hotel or motel stand out from its competitors. Even landscaping can have a big effect on the amount of energy and water required to keep a property looking and running its best.

Customer response to such innovations has generally been positive, and management interest in "going green" continues to increase. Overall, it is safe to say that upward trends in green practices throughout this important industry—according to the American Hotel and Lodging Association, total lodging industry revenue for 2007 reached $139.4 billion—will likely continue for years to come.

59

Figure Focus

Figure 1.35: Why are so many bed and breakfasts, like the one in this picture, housed in older buildings?

Discuss

- The *AAA TourBook* rates lodging properties on overall quality. How do its criteria match those used by *The Zagat Survey* or the *Michelin Guide*?
- Why would soundproofing be a factor in assessing a property's quality? What other factors do students think should be included in the assessment? Note that the list continues onto p. 61.
- The AAA rating system judges properties in relationship to others, not just on their own merits. This is analogous to "grading on a curve." Encourage students to discuss the pros and cons of this system.

Reinforce and Review

- The *AAA TourBook* uses a diamond system to judge the overall quality of lodging establishments.
- Factors include management and staff, housekeeping, maintenance, room décor and furnishings, bathrooms, guest services and facilities, soundproofing, security, parking, and exterior appearance.

Teaching Tips

- Engage students in a discussion of the distinction between an "excellent property" and an "exceptional establishment."

Vocabulary Terms

- **The American Automobile Association's *AAA TourBook:*** The most widely recognized rating service for lodging properties in the United States.

Ratings Organizations

To distinguish one lodging property from another, several organizations rate the quality of lodging establishments. The **American Automobile Association's *AAA TourBook*** is the most widely recognized rating service in the United States. Figure 1.36 shows the AAA logo. Distributed to members of the AAA, the guide uses a diamond system in judging overall quality:

1. Functional accommodations that comply with minimum standards; meet basic needs of comfort, privacy, cleanliness, and safety
2. Noticeable enhancements in terms of decor and/or quality of furnishings
3. Marked upgrade in services and comfort, with additional amenities and/or facilities
4. Excellent properties offering a high level of service and a wide variety of amenities and upscale facilities
5. Exceptional establishments providing the highest level of luxury and service

The AAA looks at many factors when judging properties:

- Management and staff
- Housekeeping
- Maintenance
- Room decor and furnishings
- Bathrooms
- Guest services and facilities
- Soundproofing

Figure 1.36: AAA uses a diamond system in judging overall quality.

60

Figure Focus

Figure 1.36: Does it make a difference to prospective guests to see the AAA's logo outside the hotel or motel where they hope to stay for the night?

- Security
- Parking
- Exterior appearance

The **Mobil Travel Guides** are another major American rating resource. The *Mobil Travel Guides* rate thousands of properties with a five-star system:

1. Good, better than average
2. Very good
3. Excellent
4. Outstanding—worth a special trip
5. One of the best in the country

The *Mobil Travel Guides* rate a facility by looking at the quality of the building and its furnishings inside, maintenance, housekeeping, and overall service. The top rating is very difficult to achieve, with fewer than 100 properties across the United States receiving five stars each year.

Lodging Careers

Careers in the lodging industry are typically divided into those with customer contact and those that support the running of the operation.

Customer contact positions include front office, food and beverage, or concierge. The front office is the heart of all lodging properties. It has four main responsibilities:

1. Check-in
2. Reservations
3. Information
4. Checkout

Behind-the-scenes positions may include housekeeping, accounting and financial, security, or engineering and facility management.

Discuss

- The format of the *Mobil Travel Guide* resembles the *Michelin Guide* in several ways. The backing companies of each are related, too: Mobil is an international oil and gas company, while Michelin is a tire manufacturer. Why might companies like this choose to support lodging and restaurant guides?
- Careers in the lodging industry, as in the restaurant and foodservice industry, can be readily divided into "front-of-the-house" and "back-of-the-house" positions. What skills are common to both industries?

Reinforce and Review

- The *Mobil Travel Guide* uses a star system to judge the overall quality of lodging properties, with fewer than 100 properties receiving top marks each year.
- The four main responsibilities of the front office at a lodging property are check-in, reservations, information, and checkout.

Vocabulary Terms

- **Mobil Travel Guide:** A ratings system that assesses thousands of lodging properties annually.

Divide students into small groups and ask them to discuss the following:

- Can the increase in guest information available to a lodging property using PMS increase the potential for error or liability? For instance, what if a hotel employee mistakenly types that a guest is "allergic to deer" instead of "allergic to dairy," and the guest is served a smoothie containing yogurt—what is the hotel's liability?

- What about identity theft? If criminals can gain access to the hotel's software, they can obtain very personal information about guests, which could be used to impersonate or even blackmail these people.

- Can the benefits of PMS software overshadow traditional customer-relations skills? Discuss some ways that people and technology can work together to create positive guest outcomes.

[what's new]

Property Management Systems

You have probably heard the phrase POS system, in which "POS" means "point of sale" or "point of service." POS refers to the place where some sort of transaction occurs. Although POS could be a retail shop or restaurant, a POS system generally indicates a computer terminal or linked group of terminals. These terminals process a customer's purchase: anything from a roll of paper towels to a three-course meal. Figure 1.37 shows a POS system.

Figure 1.37: A POS system is the place where transactions occur.

But what happens when the situation becomes more complex? For instance, a hotel guest may wish to have a king-size bedroom with a balcony overlooking the mountains, a massage at 2 p.m., and a tee-time at 9:30 a.m. The guest is also allergic to pineapple, prefers a window table in the on-site restaurant, and would love tickets to a particular concert. And, by the way, she is booking her reservation online. Now what?

For these and other reasons, many hotels and motels have adopted Property Management System (PMS) software. This technology can serve a variety of functions by which managers and staff can improve guest experiences. Common attributes of PMS software include the following:

- Scheduling: Rooms, spa services, restaurant reservations, and event planning

- Database maintenance: Guest preferences, vendor information, and maintenance and housekeeping records

- Accounting and sales: All financial transactions, including mini bar and Internet fees

Often, this software works jointly with online travel sites, such as Expedia and Orbitz. These travel sites improve both the guest's access to an expedited booking process and the hotel's ability to self promote.

PMS software can significantly enhance a guest's experience with a hotel or motel by enabling the management to provide a wide variety of amenities in a seamless manner. Although final responsibility resides with humans—after all, people not only provide the services desired, but enter the information into the computer in the first place—this software can help provide a smooth, trouble-free stay.

62

Figure Focus

Figure 1.37: In what sort of establishment is this POS transaction probably taking place?

Summary

In this section, you learned the following:

- People travel for a variety of reasons including vacations, business, visiting relatives/friends, or experiencing a foreign culture.

- Leisure travelers want to get away from it all. They may require special services or activities, like programs or activities for children, social activities, and spas. Business travelers spend most of their time working and often need access to office equipment such as computers, copiers, faxes, wireless networks, and meeting facilities.

- The American Automobile Association's *AAA TourBook®* uses a diamond system in judging overall quality. It is the most widely recognized rating system in the United States.

- The AAA judges management and staff, housekeeping, maintenance, room décor and furnishings, bathrooms, guest services and facilities, soundproofing, security, parking, and exterior appearance.

- The *Mobil Travel Guide* rates thousands of properties using a five-star rating. It looks at quality of the building and its furnishings inside, maintenance, housekeeping, and overall services. Fewer than 100 properties receive a five-star rating each year.

- Lodging properties differ greatly depending on the needs of the travelers:
  - Luxury properties are top of the line full-service operations that offer comfort and elegance at a premium price.
  - Full-service properties offer large rooms, well-trained staff, and amenities (pools, room service, fitness center, services for business travelers, banquet rooms).
  - Mid-priced facilities provide comfortable, moderately priced accommodations.
  - Economy lodging provides clean, fully furnished rooms at budget prices. They have smaller staff and provide limited amenities.
  - All-suite properties offer apartment-style facilities with an "at-home" atmosphere.
  - Resorts feature extensive facilities for vacationers looking for recreational activities and entertainment.
  - Bed and breakfasts provide quiet accommodations with simple amenities. They are usually privately owned homes converted to have several guest rooms.

- The front office is the heart of all lodging properties. It has four main responsibilities: check-in, reservation, information, and checkout.

63

Summary

- Remind students to review the following:
  1. Why people travel
  2. The differences between leisure and business travel
  3. The national organizations that rate commercial lodging and foodservice opportunities
  4. The factors listed in rating judgments
  5. The characteristics of lodging operations
  6. The activities associated with front-desk operations

Section 1.3 Review Questions

1. Leisure travelers go to a place for relaxation, entertainment, education, adventure and sport, and social and family events. Business travelers look for convenience, well-lit and properly-equipped workstations, Internet access, meeting and banquet facilities, valet parking, 24-hour room service, comfort, in-room amenities, and consistency.

2. Luxury properties are hotels offering top-of-the-line comfort and elegance, aimed at wealthy travelers and corporate executives. Full-service properties cater to travelers in search of a wide range of conveniences. Mid-priced facilities are designed for travelers who want comfortable, moderately priced accommodations. Economy lodging offers clean, low-priced accommodations primarily to traveling salespeople, senior citizens, and families with modest incomes. All-suite properties offer apartment-style facilities at midmarket prices, popular with traveling families. Resorts feature extensive facilities to vacationers looking for recreational activities and entertainment. Bed and breakfasts cater to guests looking for quaint, quiet accommodations with simple amenities. They differ from most other lodging properties because the owner typically lives on-site and manages daily operations.

3. Cultural and historic tourists seek educational opportunities, whether learning about historic events or about different cultures and societies. Environmental tourists visit places to enjoy natural beauty. Recreational tourists look for places to enjoy specific activities, such as swimming, golfing, or seeing shows.

4. The AAA judges lodging establishments with a diamond system, examining factors like management and staff, housekeeping, maintenance, room décor and furnishings, bathrooms, guest services and facilities, soundproofing, security, parking, and exterior appearance.

5. Students may answer this question in a variety of ways, so long as they justify their responses. For instance, they could argue that business travelers and leisure travelers have different needs and therefore should be treated in different ways, or they could argue that all travelers are fundamentally the same and should be treated in the same manner.

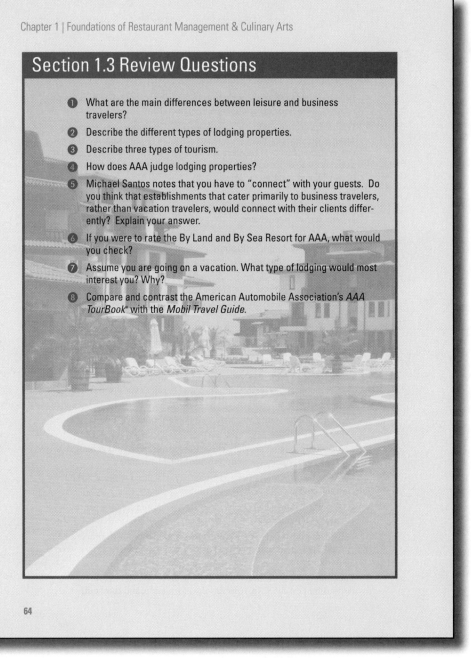

Section 1.3 Review Questions

1. What are the main differences between leisure and business travelers?
2. Describe the different types of lodging properties.
3. Describe three types of tourism.
4. How does AAA judge lodging properties?
5. Michael Santos notes that you have to "connect" with your guests. Do you think that establishments that cater primarily to business travelers, rather than vacation travelers, would connect with their clients differently? Explain your answer.
6. If you were to rate the By Land and By Sea Resort for AAA, what would you check?
7. Assume you are going on a vacation. What type of lodging would most interest you? Why?
8. Compare and contrast the American Automobile Association's *AAA TourBook* with the *Mobil Travel Guide*.

64

6. Important factors to inspect include management and staff, housekeeping, maintenance, room décor and furnishings, bathrooms, guest services and facilities, soundproofing, security, parking, and exterior appearance.

7. Students may answer this question in a variety of ways, so long as they justify their responses.

8. The *AAA TourBook* is the most widely recognized rating service in the United States and uses a diamond system to judge overall quality. Similarly, the *Mobil Travel Guide* judges overall quality, but it uses a star system to rate lodging properties. It is very difficult for a property to achieve top marks in either system.

Section 1.3 Activities

1. Study Skills/Group Activity: Going Green at School

Hotels, motels, and resorts are increasingly turning to "green" practices, both to meet customer needs and to lower energy costs. What about schools? Work with two or three other students to identify some ways in which your school practices green behaviors as well as some areas for improvement.

2. Activity: AAA Ratings

Analyze the ratings assigned by AAA. What are the differentiating factors?

3. Critical Thinking: Comparing Facilities

Imagine that you are a new hotel guest. What do you notice upon arriving, checking in, and reaching your room that suggests that you are in a well-run facility? What suggests a poorly run facility?

65

Section 1.3 Activities

1. Answers will vary from school to school. Students should research both current practices and opportunities for improvement in a respectful manner.

2. Students should consider each level of the diamond system. For instance, in what ways do "noticeable enhancements" differ from "marked upgrades"? How do "excellent" and "exceptional" differ?

3. Students should identify specific elements—the cleanliness of the bathroom, the friendliness of the employees, the maintenance of the parking lot—in their responses.

Case Study Follow-Up

1. Linda's strengths, weaknesses, and interests should determine her career path.

2. Students may answer this question in a variety of ways, so long as they justify their responses.

3. Students may answer this question in a variety of ways. Possible responses include perseverance, honesty, willingness to work hard, intelligence, and professionalism.

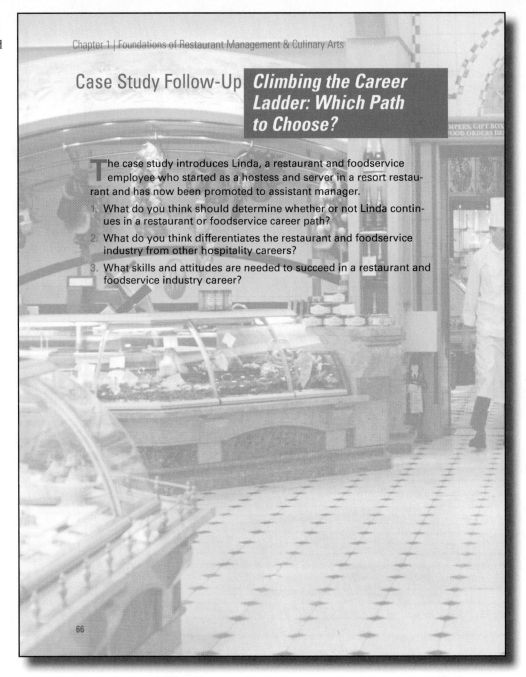

Case Study Follow-Up Climbing the Career Ladder: Which Path to Choose?

The case study introduces Linda, a restaurant and foodservice employee who started as a hostess and server in a resort restaurant and has now been promoted to assistant manager.

1. What do you think should determine whether or not Linda continues in a restaurant or foodservice career path?

2. What do you think differentiates the restaurant and foodservice industry from other hospitality careers?

3. What skills and attitudes are needed to succeed in a restaurant and foodservice industry career?

66

Apply Your Learning

Your Hotel's Budget

Larger hotels and resorts can be quite complex, with a number of income sources and necessary expenses. Create an imaginary hotel or resort, describing it in a paragraph or two, and develop its annual budget. Be creative. Does your facility have outdoor recreation? Is it renowned for any particular reason? In your budget, include as many income and expense categories as is realistic, showing how much money your facility expects to earn or spend in each category. Although this is a creative exercise, you should cover such typical budget items as payroll, restaurant income, room rentals, spa fees, utilities, and so on.

Contemporary Events in Foodservice

This chapter has introduced you to the history of the foodservice industry, but what about contemporary events? Research recent developments in local foodservice and write two paragraphs about foodservice developments in your community during the last 10 years.

Can It!

Among Georges Auguste Escoffier's other notable achievements, he developed canned tomatoes. How does the canning process work, and how has it changed since Escoffier's time? What health and safety issues might be involved? What about nutrition?

Critical Thinking   Career Investigation

Visit the dining room of a local restaurant to learn about the division of labor, customer service, and first impressions. Which employees perform which tasks? What is the restaurant's philosophy on customer service? What is your first impression upon entering the dining room, and what is the impression the restaurant wishes to convey? Talk with the manager about practical applications of the material discussed in the text, and present your findings in an oral report.

67

Apply Your Learning

Your Hotel's Budget

Students should be both realistic and creative in their responses. They should include all appropriate income and expense categories for the facility they describe, and all mathematic calculations should be correct.

Contemporary Events in Foodstuffs

Students may complete this exercise in a variety of ways, so long as they provide clear and accurate information about local foodservice developments.

Can It!

Students should provide an accurate explanation of the contemporary commercial canning process, identify the biological organisms destroyed and the problems they might otherwise cause, and discuss the relationship between properly canned foods and public nutrition.

Critical Thinking   Career Investigation

Students should clearly identify the tasks performed by different employees and describe the facility's customer-service policies and philosophy. They should demonstrate understanding of the relationship between the image a restaurant wishes to project and its own policies and practices. Finally, they should have a brief, professional conversation with a manager about basic hospitality principles and how the restaurant seeks to achieve them.

Exam Prep Answers

1. B
2. B
3. A
4. C
5. D
6. D
7. A
8. C
9. A
10. C

Exam Prep Questions

1 Pasteurization is the process of

A. boiling water to eliminate germs.

B. heating milk to remove harmful bacteria.

C. canning foods to keep them fresh and safe to eat.

D. cleaning cooking utensils to make sure they are safe and sanitary.

2 One of the first cookbooks, *De Re Coquinaria (On Cooking)* was written by

A. King Henry II.

B. Marcus Apicius.

C. Emperor Lucullus.

D. Catherine de Medici.

3 Which culinary advancement cuisine did Catherine de Medici bring to France?

A. Haute

B. Grand

C. Classic

D. Noveau

4 The first impression of an operation that guests receive is from the

A. chef.

B. server.

C. host/hostess.

D. general manager.

5 Tourists who visit places in order to enjoy their natural beauty are _____ tourists.

A. historic

B. cultural

C. recreational

D. environmental

6 Which type of lodging is most likely to rely on business travelers and typically experiences low occupancy rates on weekends?

A. Downtown

B. Luxury rural

C. Economy suburban

D. International airport

7 As part of the full-service segment, which properties cater to wealthy travelers and corporate executives?

A. Luxury

B. All-suite

C. Economy

D. Bed and breakfast

8 What type of restaurant provides serving staff that takes orders while patrons are seated and the average per-person dinner is $10-$25?

A. Fine dining full-service

B. Quick-casual restaurant

C. Casual dining full-service

D. Family dining full-service

9 A service or product provided to guests for their convenience, either with or without an additional fee, is a(n)

A. amenity.

B. donation.

C. endowment.

D. catering service.

10 Boulanger affected the growth of the foodservice industry by

A. opening the first café.

B. developing pasteurization.

C. opening the first restaurant.

D. inventing the cooking guilds.

69

Chapter 2 Overview

Chapter 2 introduces food safety concerns and practices.

The safety of foodservice takes priority over the need to perform tasks quickly. Safe food practices can and must be efficiently integrated into any foodservice setting.

Section1: The first section provides an overview of foodborne illnesses as well as both chemical and physical contaminants. Keeping food safe and food defense are also covered. The topic of allergens and reactions is introduced. Finally, we review the government regulatory agencies involved in the restaurant and foodservice industries.

Section 2: This section covers good personal hygiene, including the importance of handwashing and work requirements related to illness.

Section 3: This section reviews the prevention of hazards in the flow of food, including cross-contamination, time-temperature abuse, and the proper handling of food during purchasing, storing, preparing, cooking, holding, and serving.

Section 4: This section addresses food safety management systems and HACCP Food Safety Plans.

Section 5: This section covers cleaning and sanitizing, including developing a cleaning program and controlling pests.

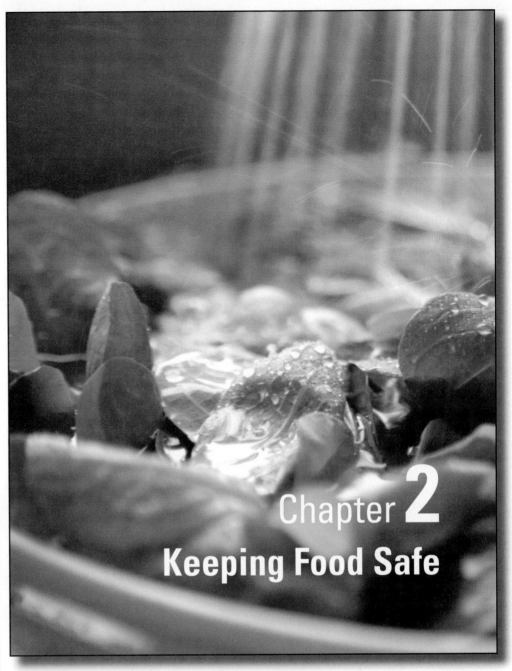

Chapter 2
Keeping Food Safe

Advance Preparation	
Contact	Biology department for use of:
	Microscopes
	Graticule slides
	Slide covers
	Pipettes or droppers
	Glass stirring rods (clean spoons could substitute)
	Research resources (library and/or computer lab)
Prepare	Paper strips for display
	Mild culinary acids and bases for tasting (special needs project)
	Baker's yeast
	Mason jars with lids
	Sugar
	Measuring spoons
	Grease pencil or masking tape and marker
	Index cards for concentration game
	Soap, water, towels, hand sanitizer, gloves for handwashing practice

CUSTOMIZED INSTRUCTION OPTIONS

Less Advanced Students	More Advanced Students	ESOL Students	Special Needs Students
Pages 75, 79, 87, 106	Pages 76, 78, 87, 113, 137	Pages 79, 87, 106	Pages 75, 87

CHAPTER TOOLS

21st-Century Skills	Mathematics	Science	Literacy
Pages 77, 78, 84, 87, 90, 97, 105, 106, 108, 116, 127, 143	Pages **75, 76, 78,** 128	Pages 78, 79, 82, 113, 137	Pages 75, 79, 94, 97, 111, 128

ServSafe Connection

Page 76

Case Study *It's All Wrong*

Linda recently left her position at the By Land and By Sea Resort. She had been looking for an opportunity to be a manager at an independent restaurant where she would have more control, so she has accepted the position of manager at the Uptown Grille.

This position involves handling a lot of public relations and meetings with local groups in addition to her restaurant responsibilities. Today, she and Chef Jean have a meeting scheduled with the local Chamber of Commerce.

While Linda and Chef Jean are at their meeting, FoodCorp International makes its weekly delivery. The delivery includes cases of canned vegetables, fresh lettuce, fresh tomatoes, sour cream, frozen shrimp, and fresh chicken. Brian, the line cook, is responsible for receiving, inspecting, and storing deliveries.

Brian is in the middle of prepping raw chicken and carrots for a stew when the delivery arrives. He pushes them over, inadvertently leaving them on the same cutting surface. Then, he wipes his hands on his apron, and attends to the delivery.

Brian proceeds to check the order. He puts the frozen shrimp in the freezer and the fresh chicken in the refrigerator. He puts the fresh tomatoes, lettuce, and canned vegetables in dry storage. Then he loads a case of sour cream into the tightly packed refrigerator. When he is finished, he goes back to his work area to prep the remaining vegetables. It takes Brian about 45 minutes to receive, inspect, and store the delivery.

At the time of receiving, the shrimp are frozen solid and the packages are sealed, but they contain a large amount of ice crystals. The boxes with the fresh tomatoes and lettuce have some holes and wet marks.

Linda and Chef Jean return from their meeting and find that they are behind schedule for tonight's dinner service. Michael, a line cook who had an upset stomach earlier today, is feeling better, so he grabs the same uniform he wore yesterday when prepping turkey. As soon as Michael arrives at work, Linda puts him to work on prepping the vegetables for dinner service. During prep, Michael's stomach starts to bother him, but since they are behind schedule, Linda asks him to stick it out as long as possible. Michael agrees to stay, but within a few

Focus and Engage

Discuss

- This chapter encourages students to relate food safety to foodservice.
- The student's assumptions will be challenged, as they realize that some practices they use at home may be wrong for foodservice.
- This chapter will cover several scientific principles.

Case Study
It's All Wrong

- Managers play an important role in ensuring food is safe. For example, managers take care of equipment, handle deliveries, coach and monitor employees, and develop cleaning processes.
- If food is not safe, speed and efficiency do not matter. Safe practices must be in place first, and then efficiency can be developed within that framework.
- Use established processes and reminders like "FAT TOM" in addition to checklists and reports to collect and maintain data.
- Managers could teach the importance of food safety during employee meetings. Also, job responsibilities must include safe foodhandling practices, and there must be a self-inspection or other form of accountability.

Case Study (Cont.)

- The case study scenario is full of bad examples. There are several unsafe foodhandling practices, and a few correct ones.

- The students can probably identify and name several of the bad ones:

  - Brian prepped raw chicken and carrots at the same time. They were on the same cutting surface.

  - Brian put fresh tomatoes and lettuce into dry storage at room temperature. They were in boxes with some holes and wet marks. Perhaps a tomato was overripe, or some other problem was present. The produce should have been properly inspected, processed, and stored under refrigeration.

  - The refrigerator is tightly packed, which reduces air circulation.

  - The inspection of the frozen shrimp delivery should have alerted Brian to the possibility that it might have thawed and refrozen, due to the ice crystals.

  - Michael should not work while ill.

  - When Michael returns to work, he should wear a freshly laundered uniform. His dirty uniforms should be laundered after use.

  - Michael should be excused to go home when he shows symptoms.

  - Michael should more thoroughly wash his hands after using the restroom.

  - Michael should get a new apron after using the restroom.

  - Brian does not hold the chicken hot enough for safe service.

Teaching Tips

- The case study could be a role play at the beginning of the chapter, with the students in the "audience" jotting down as many things as they think might be a problem.

- At the end of the chapter, repeat the very same role play of the case study. The students will again write down the errors.

- Compare the two lists of errors.

Case Study | *It's All Wrong* (continued)

minutes he heads to the restroom in the hopes of relieving his symptoms. He quickly rinses his hands, wipes his hands on his apron, and heads back to prep work.

Brian cooks the chicken he prepped earlier. He checks the temperature of the chicken with an infrared thermometer for five seconds and finds that it is 165°F. Brian removes the chicken from the oven and holds the chicken for dinner service, which is starting shortly. After an hour, Brian checks the held chicken, and the internal temperature is 130°F. Brian serves the held chicken as orders come in.

As you read this chapter, think about the following questions:

1. What role do managers play in ensuring safe food?

2. How can you balance the need to move quickly with the need to keep food safe?

3. What techniques can you use to remind yourself to put food safety first?

4. What could managers do to help employees focus on handling food safely?

[professional profile]

Melisa Bouchard

Quality Assurance Coordinator

Brinker International (parent company of Chili's, Maggiano's, and On the Border)

❝ *I began working in the restaurant industry when I was in college at Sam Houston State, from which I received a bachelor of science degree. At the time, I thought it was just going to be a job to pay bills. However, 12 years later, it's become much more than that. I can honestly say that a big factor in choosing this career path is the dedication and loyalty I have for Brinker.* ❞

I wanted to stay and grow with them, so I continued on with Brinker as a server and then bartender, which led to a restaurant management position. I remember that, as a restaurant manager, I spent much of my time in the dining room visiting with our guests. As I would walk through the room, I saw families visiting with each other as they enjoyed the food prepared by our team members. These were people's mothers and grandmothers; fathers and grandfathers; parents' precious children. I felt honored they chose to dine with us…knowing they were in good hands where the service would be great and the food would be excellent and most importantly, safe.

72

Eventually, I made my way to our corporate office as a member of our food safety team. In this position, I have been able learn more about the "behind-the-scenes" planning of the programs that are in place in our restaurants to keep our guests safe while maintaining our high quality standards.

Foodservice operators impact a large population on a daily basis, so it is very important they have all the tools necessary to serve safe food. And cooking is the last step in the foodservice process, so it is very important that the staff is properly trained in all areas of food safety. Cooking to proper temperatures, avoiding cross-contamination, and holding product at the proper temperature are all major components. Discussing these topics on a daily basis, as well as establishing habits that build food safety into what you do every day, helps to ensure safe food is being served to our guests.

For those of you interested in entering this field, remember that understanding and getting involved in the many steps of the food-chain process will be very beneficial when developing and implementing food safety programs and procedures. There are so many key players, and they all have different roles that play a huge part in serving safe food. As an operator, you do not always see all the work that goes on away from the restaurant, and from a corporate standpoint, you do not always see what goes on in operations. Therefore, understanding both worlds helps establish a "big picture" of food safety.

Remember, "There is no sincerer love than the love of food."---George Bernard Shaw

About Food Safety

And when it comes to food safety, knowledge, communication, and a passion for serving safe food are most important.

Illness caused by eating unsafe food can cost money, jobs, and even lives. The reputation of a restaurant or foodservice operation can be destroyed by a single case of food-related illness. All operations, from four-star restaurants to school cafeterias, must keep food safe. Every person in the operation must work toward this goal—managers and employees both share this responsibility.

2.1 Introduction to Food Safety	2.2 Good Personal Hygiene	2.3 Preventing Hazards in the Flow of Food	2.4 Food Safety Management Systems	2.5 Cleaning and Sanitizing
• What is a foodborne illness? • Forms of contamination • Biological contamination • Chemical contamination • Physical contamination • Food defense • Allergens • U.S. regulation of food safety	• How foodhandlers can contaminate food • Personal cleanliness and work attire • Handwashing • Bare-hand contact with ready-to-eat food • Work requirements related to illness	• Cross-contamination • Time-temperature abuse • Purchasing • Receiving • Storage • Preparation • Cooking • Holding, storing, and reheating • Serving	• The HACCP plan	• How to clean effectively • Sanitizing • Developing a cleaning program • Controlling pests

73

Professional Profile

Discuss	The restaurant as a safe and important venue for family interaction.
Reinforce and Review	Why do you think cooking can be viewed as an art, a science, and a way of sharing? Review the separate worlds of on-the-scene restaurant operations and off-site corporate decision-making. How can these worlds connect for the good of the operation?
Teaching Tips	Remind students why it is helpful to have a broad perspective of the steps in the food-chain process.

Section 2.1 Introduction to Food Safety

Introduce the Section

a. Find out if any students have worked in a foodservice operation.

b. Review any real or virtual experiences the students may have already had with food safety.

c. Help the students to identify and discuss food safety practices and principles.

Vocabulary Review

a. Direct students to the key terms.

b. Pronounce each word, and have the students repeat the pronunciation out loud.

c. Discuss the definition of each word.

Teach

Discuss

- An understanding of food safety precedes a workable understanding of cooking.
- Food safety involves many factors, including kitchen design, food purchasing, personal hygiene, cleaning and sanitizing, food preparation, cooking, and table service.
- Food safety problems can lead to illness or even the death of a guest.
- A serious food safety problem can put an establishment out of business.
- All staff must be trained in proper food-handling techniques.
- Vendors must be reputable.
- An establishment must be able to trace foods to their sources.
- Restroom facilities must be clean and safe both in the back of the house and for the guests.
- A reputation may take years to build, but may be lost in a day if guests become ill.

Vocabulary Terms

- **Foodborne illness:** A disease transmitted to a person by food.
- **Foodborne-illness outbreak:** When two or more people get the same illness after eating the same food.

SECTION 2.1 INTRODUCTION TO FOOD SAFETY

Dining out is an experience that most people enjoy. Restaurants offer more than good food. They can be the perfect place for talking to friends, celebrating, conducting business, or relaxing. When people dine out, they expect to have a good time. But even more importantly, they expect to eat tasty, wholesome, safe food in a clean environment, served by a pleasant staff.

Study Questions

After studying Section 2.1, you should be able to answer the following questions:

- What is a foodborne-illness outbreak?
- What are the costs associated with a foodborne-illness outbreak?
- Who is at high risk for contracting foodborne illness?
- What is FAT TOM?
- What are the characteristics of TCS food?
- What methods can prevent biological contamination?
- What are the guidelines for storing chemicals safely?
- Why is a food defense system needed?
- What are the most common allergens, and what are the methods for preventing allergic reactions?
- What government agencies regulate the restaurant and foodservice industry?

What Is a Foodborne Illness?

A **foodborne illness** is a disease transmitted to people by food. A **foodborne-illness outbreak** is when two or more people get the same illness after eating the same food. Overall, the restaurant and foodservice industry does an excellent job of providing safe food to the public. But foodborne illness still costs the United States billions of dollars each year. National Restaurant Association figures show that one outbreak can cost an operation thousands of dollars and might even force it to close.

74

Costs of a Foodborne Illness to an Establishment

Loss of customers and sales	Loss of reputation
Negative media exposure	Lowered employee morale
Lawsuits and legal fees	Employee absenteeism
Increased insurance premiums	Staff retraining

Figure 2.1: Foodborne illnesses can seriously affect any restaurant or foodservice operation.

Consider the following cases:

- At an East Coast school, over 400 children became ill after they were served lunch. Later, it was discovered that the source of the illness was contaminated egg salad sandwiches that the students ate.

- A nationwide *Salmonella* spp. outbreak traced to peanut butter sickened more than 400 people in 43 states, and three elderly people died from the outbreak. The peanut butter was distributed to schools, hospitals, and long-term care facilities.

- An elderly woman died and several hundred other people became sick after eating food served at a state fair. Most of the people who became sick were tourists. Health departments across the country received reports of illness, and many people were hospitalized.

The Centers for Disease Control and Prevention (CDC) estimates that there will be 76 million cases of foodborne illness in the United States each year. Of these, approximately 325,000 require hospitalization and 5,000 end in death. Figure 2.1 shows the many ways in which foodborne illness can impact an operation.

75

Figure Focus

Figure 2.1: This graphic details the various types of damage that can be done to a restaurant or foodservice operation if it experiences a foodborne-illness outbreak.

ServSafe Connection: The ServSafe® Food Safety Training and Certification Program

ServSafe is a program for food safety training. Certification is available to help operations meet state and local laws regarding safe foodhandling.

Fast Fact: Did You Know...?

Legal issues surrounding food safety should not be discounted or underplayed.

Reinforce and Review

- Food safety is a public health concern for everyone in the foodservice industry.
- Each person in the foodservice industry plays a role in food safety.

Fast Fact: Did You Know...?

The cost calculator may be demonstrated on a computer projector.

CUSTOMIZED INSTRUCTION

Mathematics

More Advanced Students

Choose one of the cases on the previous page. Construct a hypothetical scenario to illustrate the case. Create the specifics necessary to calculate the cost of the case. Use the USDA Economic Research Services foodborne–illness cost calculator to complete this task.

[ServSafe Connection]

The ServSafe® Food Safety Training and Certification Program

Help advance your career in food safety! The ServSafe® program is the most widely recognized training and certification program for food protection managers in the industry, and is approved in all 50 states. Over the last 30 years, this program has awarded more than 3.5 million ServSafe Food Protection Manager Certifications.

Although many of the people who achieve the certification are managers in their operations, the ServSafe certification examination is open to anyone, including students and aspiring restaurant and foodservice managers.

Most people take a ServSafe food safety training class or a ServSafe online course. The second step is taking the exam to achieve the certification, which is known as a Food Protection Manager Certification.

The information in this chapter is a portion of what you would need to know to become a certified food protection manager. You'll also see sidebars in other chapters called "ServSafe Connection" that highlight critical food safety guidelines. If you can master the food safety content throughout this book, then you are well on your way to preparing for a ServSafe certification. For more information on the ServSafe program or to find a class in your area, visit www.ServSafe.com.

[fast fact]

Did You Know...?

A restaurant or foodservice operation can be held legally responsible for the food it serves. A court might order an operation to pay money to the person(s) who suffered illness caused by its food. Depending upon the laws in the state where the incident happened, the state might require an operation to prove that it has done everything that could be reasonably expected to prevent foodborne illness by ensuring that it serves safe food.

Most important are the human costs. Victims of foodborne illnesses may experience loss of time at work, medical costs, long-term disability, and possibly death.

As you can see, you will play an important role in keeping food safe. If you know and understand the basics of food safety, then you can do your share in preventing food-related problems.

[fast fact]

Did You Know...?

The U.S. Department of Agriculture Economic Research Services has developed a foodborne illness cost calculator as a way to estimate the annual cost of foodborne illness. The cost calculator allows you to estimate medical costs, costs associated with time lost from work, and costs of premature death for most foodborne pathogens.

Try this at www.ers.usda.gov/Data/FoodborneIllness/.

76

High-Risk Populations for Foodborne Illnesses

Certain groups of people have a higher risk of getting a foodborne illness than others. These groups are known as **high-risk populations**. Operations that serve these groups must sometimes follow special rules.

The **immune system** is the body's defense against illness. When the system is weak, it cannot fight off illness as easily as a healthy system. There are a variety of reasons why someone's immune system might be weakened:

- Elderly people's immune systems weaken with age.

- Infants and preschool-age children have not yet built strong immune systems.

- Pregnant women's immune systems are weaker during pregnancy.

- People with cancer or on chemotherapy, people with HIV/AIDS, and transplant recipients all have immune systems weakened by illness or treatment.

These people are all considered high-risk populations for foodborne illness.

Forms of Contamination

To prevent foodborne illness, it is important to recognize the hazards that can make food unsafe. A **hazard** is something with the potential to cause harm. In the preparation of food, hazards are divided into three categories: biological, chemical, and physical.

Many hazards contaminate food because someone has handled the food incorrectly. **Contamination** means that harmful things are present in food, making it unsafe to eat. Food can become unsafe through any of the following practices:

- Poor personal hygiene transfers **pathogens**, the microorganisms that cause illness, from your body to food.

- Time-temperature abuse allows food to stay too long at temperatures that are good for pathogen growth.

- Cross-contamination transfers pathogens from one surface or food to another.

- Poor cleaning and sanitizing allows contaminated surfaces to touch food.

- Purchasing from unapproved suppliers brings food from companies that aren't following food safety practices into the operation.

77

Teaching Tips

- Operations that serve high-risk populations must keep these customers' status in mind when serving food. They also must sometimes follow special rules as determined by law.
- It is important to consider every aspect of potential contaminations.
- Hazards can be reduced or eliminated.
- Various unsafe practices can increase the chance of foodborne illness.
- Monitor all processes and practices for food safety procedures.

In-Class Activity: Unsafe Practices Awareness Team Jigsaw Display

21st-Century Skills—Health Literacy, Collaboration with Others, Create Media Product

Assign the students to five teams.

Each team creates and prepares a statement of awareness about a particular food-safety problem.

The teams each write their statement on a strip of paper for display.

The problems are the five points outlined in the text:

- Poor personal hygiene
- Time-temperature abuse
- Cross-contamination
- Poor cleaning and sanitizing
- Purchasing from unapproved suppliers

The statements can be written in the form of information, a pledge, a mnemonic or rhyme, acronym, or any other expression they choose.

As each team presents its statement, it adds its paper strip to a poster or bulletin board display for the classroom.

Vocabulary Terms

- **High-risk populations:** Groups of people who are especially vulnerable to foodborne illness. Usually included are infants, very young children, pregnant women, the elderly, and those with compromised immune systems from cancer, HIV/AIDS, chemotherapy, or transplant surgery.
- **Immune system:** The human body's defense system to prevent and fight disease.
- **Hazard:** Something potentially dangerous or harmful.
- **Contamination:** The introduction of a harmful entity to a food item, beverage, or water.
- **Pathogens:** Disease-causing microorganisms.

Mathematics Connection, Science Connection, 21st-Century Skills—Be Self-Directed Learners

More Advanced Students

pH is the negative log of the hydrogen ion concentration in a solution. What does this mean? Have students research and explain very briefly to the class how the number is derived and what it means. Have the students express it in a graphic or a written form, or with a demonstration.

The pH scale ranges from 1 to 14. 7 is neutral like water. Less than 7 is an acid. Greater than 7 is a base.

Since pH is a logarithmic expression, it means that a concentration of hydrogen ion (acid) in a solution increases or decreases by multiples of 10.

The concentration of hydrogen ion in any solution is always less than 1, because 1 represents 100% of the solution. Therefore, since the portion of the concentration is a fraction and is less than 1, it can be expressed as a number with a negative exponent.

The greater the concentration of hydrogen, as in an acid, the larger the fraction. This will be expressed with a "less negative" number for the exponent, such as -4.

The smaller the concentration of hydrogen, as in a base, the smaller the fraction. This will be expressed as a "more negative" number for the exponent, such as -11.

Since pH is defined as the "negative log," the negative exponent number becomes a positive number, such as pH 4 for an acid, or pH 11 for a base.

It is important to realize that pH is not an arbitrary scale, but is a real scale of measure that is simplified to be expressed in a more convenient way.

An understanding of acids and bases is very helpful in culinary arts and foodservice. It will be addressed throughout the text.

Vocabulary Terms

- **Microorganisms:** Living species that can be seen only through a microscope.
- **FAT TOM:** The conditions that foodborne pathogens need to grow in food.
- **TCS:** Acronym for Time and Temperature Control for Safety, a designation of foods that are vulnerable for pathogen growth.

Biological Contamination

Microorganisms are small, living organisms that can be seen only through a microscope. Most living things, including humans, carry microorganisms on, or in, their bodies. Microorganisms that cause illness are called pathogens. They can be transferred from surfaces and hands to food and other surfaces. Pathogens are the greatest threat to food safety in a restaurant or foodservice operation.

There are four types of pathogens that can contaminate food, causing food-borne illness:

- Viruses
- Bacteria
- Parasites
- Fungi

Biological toxins can also be present in food. These toxins may be produced by pathogens contaminating the food, or they may occur naturally in certain plants and animals. Biological toxins can also cause foodborne illness.

Many viruses, bacteria, and parasites cause illness, but cannot be seen, smelled, or tasted. On the other hand, some fungi, like mold, change the appearance, taste, or smell of food—but they might not cause illness.

Pathogens need six conditions to grow. An easy way to remember these conditions is by remembering the phrase **FAT TOM**. Table 2.1 shows what FAT TOM stands for: food, acidity, temperature, time, oxygen, and moisture.

Any type of food can be contaminated, but some types actually encourage the growth of pathogens. Table 2.2 lists the foods that are most likely to become unsafe.

All these types of food have the FAT TOM conditions needed for pathogen growth. Not surprisingly, they are also commonly involved in foodborne-illness outbreaks.

Foodhandlers can help to keep food safe by controlling FAT TOM. Most of the time, however, a restaurant or foodservice operation is only going to be able to control time and temperature. Food that is most vulnerable for pathogen growth is also referred to as food that needs time and temperature control for safety—**TCS food** for short.

78

Teaching Tips

- Biological contamination is a topic that includes concepts the students have learned in science classes in middle school and high school.
- The students' health classes will also have connections to this.
- Help the students to review the information they have learned in the past, and connect it to the foodservice realm.

Discuss

- Talk about the difference between a living pathogenic organism and a pathogenic toxin.
- Toxins can be produced by organisms.

Table 2.1: FAT TOM

	Food	To grow, pathogens need an energy source. Carbohydrates, such as baked potatoes, and proteins, such as beef, are some examples.
	Acidity	Pathogens grow best in food that contains little or no acid. An example of food with a lot of acid is lemons. Food items with little acid include chicken and cooked corn. Figure 2.2 shows the acidity of common food types.
	Temperature	Pathogens grow well in food that has a temperature between 41°F and 135°F. This range is known as the temperature danger zone. Figure 2.3 shows the temperature danger zone.
	Time	Pathogens need time to grow. When food is in the temperature danger zone, pathogens grow. After four hours, they will grow to levels high enough to make someone sick.
	Oxygen	Some pathogens need oxygen to grow. Others grow when oxygen isn't there. For example, some pathogens that grow without oxygen would grow quickly in cooked rice.
	Moisture	Pathogens need moisture in food to grow. For example, tomatoes and melons have a large amount of water in them, which means they can easily support the growth of pathogens.

Acidic

pH		
0		
1	1.8–2.4	Lemons and limes
2		
3	3.7–4.0	Tomatoes
	3.8–4.0	Mayonnaise
4		
5	5.0–6.0	Bread
	5.5–6.0	Raw chicken
	6.1–6.5	Cantaloupe
6	6.4–6.8	Milk
7	7.3–7.6	Cooked corn
8+		

4.6–7.5 Ideal for pathogen growth

Alkaline

Figure 2.2: pH level of common foods.

Figure 2.3: The temperature danger zone.

°F / °C — The Temperature Danger Zone — 135°F (57°C) ... 41°F (5°C)

Discuss

- Have the students think of examples of food-borne pathogen organisms that can alter the appearance or odor of a food.
- Help the students to understand and realize that some foodborne pathogens cannot be detected by human senses.
- Can the students contribute examples of food-borne pathogen problems they have experienced or heard about?
- Could these problems have been detected by the human senses before the food was eaten?
- How could these problems have been prevented?

Table 2.1: FAT TOM

- This table includes photos and statements about the food safety acronym.

Figure Focus

Figure 2.2: The pH scale shows the acid or base (alkaline) content of foods and other substances. pH means "parts hydrogen" and is an expression of concentration of the ion that makes something an "acid." The lower the pH number, the greater the acid content.

Figure 2.3: The safe zone for storing or holding cold food is below 41°F. The safe zone for cooking or holding hot foods is above 135°F.

Teaching Tips

- Ask the students for ideas about why these foods are vulnerable.
- Ask the students what these foods have in common.
- Ask the students about the differences between these various foods.
- See if the students can suggest foodhandling methods that might improve the safety of these foods.
- Have them store their answers as a preassessment tool.

Table 2.2:
Food Most Likely to Become Unsafe

- Why? See if the students have ideas about this.

Table 2.2: Food Most Likely to Become Unsafe

	Milk and dairy products
	Meat: beef, pork, and lamb
	Eggs (except those treated to eliminate *Salmonella* spp.)
	Poultry
	Fish
	Shellfish and crustaceans
	Baked potatoes
	Heat-treated plant food, such as cooked rice, beans, and vegetables
	Tofu or other soy protein; synthetic ingredients, such as textured soy protein in meat alternatives
	Sprouts and sprout seeds
	Sliced melons and cut tomatoes
	Untreated garlic-and-oil mixtures

To control temperature, foodhandlers must keep TCS food out of the temperature danger zone. But the reality is that TCS food is most likely going to spend some time in this range. Restaurant and foodservice workers must limit how long the TCS food actually spends in the temperature danger zone.

Like TCS food, ready-to-eat food also needs careful handling to prevent contamination. **Ready-to-eat food** is exactly what it sounds like: food that can be eaten without further preparation, washing, or cooking. Some examples of ready-to-eat foods include washed fruit and vegetables both whole and cut, deli meat, bakery items, sugar, spices, seasonings, and cooked food.

Viruses

Viruses are the leading cause of foodborne illness. Restaurant and foodservice managers must understand what viruses are and how they can make people sick. Most importantly, managers must know how to prevent viruses from making customers sick.

Viruses can survive refrigerator and freezer temperatures. They can't grow in food, but once they are eaten, they grow inside a person's intestines. Viruses can be transferred from person to person, from people to food, and from people to food-contact surfaces. Examples of viruses that can cause foodborne illness include hepatitis A and Norovirus.

People carry viruses in their feces and can transfer them to their hands after using the restroom. Food can become contaminated if hands are not washed the right way. The best ways to prevent the spread of viruses are to stay home if you've been vomiting or have diarrhea or jaundice (yellowing of skin and eyes), to wash your hands at the right times and in the right way, and to avoid using bare hands to handle ready-to-eat food.

Bacteria

Bacteria also cause many foodborne illnesses. Figure 2.4 depicts a microscopic view of bacteria.

Figure 2.4: Bacteria cause many foodborne illnesses.

81

Teaching Tips

- All foods must be kept out of the danger zone of 41°F to 135°F.
- Foods that are to be served at room temperature must be evaluated for potential vulnerability to pathogens. They must be held at safe temperatures.
- Viruses require a living host to survive, but may be carried in a food product from one person to another. Once inside, a virus can grow and reproduce.
- Viruses can survive refrigeration and freezing.
- Viruses are best avoided through very careful handwashing and hygiene.
- Workers who are ill with diarrhea, vomiting, or jaundice should not come to work until they are better.
- Bacteria reproduce rapidly in moist plant and animal tissue in the temperature danger zone.
- Some bacteria are safe to consume, but others are pathogenic. Some can be fatal.
- Keeping food out of the temperature danger zone as much as possible helps to prevent the growth of bacteria.

Vocabulary Terms

- **Ready-to-eat food:** Foods that may be eaten and enjoyed without additional preparation.
- **Viruses:** Pathogenic organisms that are smaller than a single cell, and can survive in foods even under refrigeration.
- **Bacteria:** Single-cell organisms that can proliferate, some of which are pathogenic.

Materials for each group:

Microscope

4 Glass graticule slides (microscope slides with gridlines)

4 Slide covers

1 Envelope active dry baker's yeast

2 8 oz. mason jars with lids

3 Tbsp. sugar in a container

Measuring spoons

8 oz. Warm (100°F) water

8 oz. Cold (40°F) water

2 Disposable pipettes (eyedroppers will do)

2 Glass stirring rods (clean spoons will do)

Pencil

Paper

Grease pencil (masking tape and marker will do)

Procedure:

Divide the students into pairs or small groups. Have the students read the experiment procedure aloud together. As a group, have them write down and date a hypothesis of the outcome.

Fill a mason jar with 8 oz. warm water.

Add 1 ½ tbsp. sugar to the water.

Stir.

Add 1 tsp. yeast to the sugar/water solution.

Stir.

Repeat the same procedure with 8 oz. cold water.

Place two drops of the warm water solution onto the center of a glass slide, and place a coverslip over the sample.

Repeat the same process to make a slide of the cold-water solution.

Under the microscope at lowest power, focus on the warm-water slide. Increase the power until the yeast cells are easily countable. Have the students draw the grids on paper. Have the students count the number of cells in three grid squares. The student makes a mark with a pencil dot in the grid square to represent each cell counted.

Repeat for the cold water slide. Make sure the students label the data accordingly.

Screw the lids on the jars. Label the jars with the group names, date, time, and whether it's a cold-water or warm-water yeast solution.

Refrigerate the cold-water solution.

Place the warm-water solution in the warmest overnight place available in the classroom.

The next day, have the students make new slides

Figure 2.5: Bacteria growth at 20-minute intervals.

Knowing what bacteria are and how they grow can help you to control them. If FAT TOM conditions are right, bacteria will grow rapidly, doubling their number as often as every 20 minutes, as shown in Figure 2.5. Some bacteria, as they grow and die, create toxins (poisons) in food. Cooking may not destroy these toxins, and people who eat them can become sick. Examples of foodborne bacteria include *Salmonella* spp., shiga toxin-producing *E. coli,* and *Clostridium botulinum.*

You can control most bacteria by keeping food out of the temperature danger zone.

Parasites

In the United States, illnesses from **parasites** are not as common as those from viruses and bacteria. However, it is still important to understand what parasites are and how to prevent contamination. Figure 2.6 shows images of parasites, bacteria, and viruses.

Parasites cannot grow in food. They need to live in a host organism to grow. A **host** is a person, animal, or plant on which another organism lives and feeds. Parasites can live in cows, chickens, pigs, and fish—many types of food that humans like to eat. They also can contaminate water. Examples of parasites that can cause illness include *Cryptosporidium parvum* and *Giardia duodenalis.*

The most important measure that restaurant and foodservice managers can take to prevent parasites is to purchase food from approved, reputable suppliers.

Fungi

Fungi can cause illness, but most commonly they are responsible for spoiling food. Fungi are found in air, soil, plants, water, and some food. Mold and yeast are two examples of fungi.

Mold that is visible to the human eye is actually a tangled mass of thousands of tiny mold plants. Molds share some basic characteristics. They grow under

82

with their cold-water and warm-water solutions. Have them repeat the process of viewing and counting the cells in the samples.

Compare the data from both viewings of both samples.

Data Analysis:

Have the students determine the percentage of colony growth or decline between the two samples of "before" and "after." For example, with the cold-water solution, if the students counted 25 cells in the grid in the first sample and 30 cells in the second sample, the increase would be 5 cells, or 20 percent. The colony grew by 20 percent in a 24-hour period.

They should compare the before and after growth of each temperature solution.

They should also compare the colony growth between the two temperature solutions. For example, if there were 30 cells counted in the grid in the refrigerated sample after 24 hours, and 300 cells counted in the grid in the warm-water sample, then the refrigerated sample had only 10 percent of the growth compared to the warm sample.

Conclusions:

Have the students compare their results to their hypothesis. Have the students draw conclusions about the growth of microorganisms under various temperature conditions.

Fig 2.6: Parasites, bacteria, and viruses.
Source: Centers for Disease Control and Prevention

almost any condition, but especially well in acidic food with little moisture. Examples are jams, jellies, and cured, salty meat such as bacon. Molds often spoil food and sometimes produce toxins that can make people sick. Refrigerator and freezer temperatures may slow the growth of molds, but cold doesn't kill them. Figure 2.7 shows mold on cheese. Sometimes mold is intentionally used to affect the flavor or characteristics of a product, especially in some cheeses, such as Brie, Camembert, and Gorgonzola. Unless the mold is a natural part of the product, throw out all moldy food.

Yeast can spoil food quickly. The signs of spoilage include the smell or taste of alcohol, white or pink discoloration, slime, and bubbles. Figure 2.8 shows what yeast looks like on jam.

Like molds, yeasts grow well in acidic food with little moisture. Examples include jellies, jams, syrup, honey, and fruit or fruit juice. Throw out any food that has been spoiled by yeast.

Figure 2.7: Mold is a type of fungus found on spoiled food.

Figure 2.8: Yeast can cause discoloration, slime, bubbles, and odors on refrigerated foods such as jams and jellies.

83

Figure Focus

Figure 2.6: Food products contain biochemical compounds that can feed pathogens. These photos show several types of pathogens. The furthest left is Giardia, which is a two-nucleus parasite that can cause gastrointestinal illness to a host for years. Bacteria are varied single-celled organisms and can cause numerous problems from mild to deadly. Viruses are not complete cells and may cause mild to serious illness in a host organism.

Figure 2.7: Mold in cheeses can indicate spoilage unless a safe mold is carefully introduced to the cheese during processing.

Figure 2.8: Yeast digests carbohydrate, giving off carbon dioxide gas as a waste product. This can cause a can or lid to bulge or pop when opened. As yeast proliferate, they appear like a growth or slime layer.

Teaching Tips

- The experiment on the previous page uses yeast, which is actually a fungus.
- Yeast is easy to use in the kitchen laboratory, nontoxic, and demonstrates microbial growth.
- The results may be discussed and applied to the growth of bacteria, mold, and fungi.
- This experiment will help the students grasp the concept of pathogen growth.
- Baker's yeast is a fungus microbe that grows in a colony. It is used for leavening bread.
- Bread rises as the yeast reproduces. The growing colony of yeast metabolizes sugar and gives off carbon dioxide gas as a waste product. This gas production creates bubbles that safely expand bread dough.

Discuss

- Guide students in a discussion about yeasts and molds in food.
- How can you tell if a variety of yeast is useful or bad?
- How can you tell if a mold is harmful or beneficial to the food?
- How can you tell if food has spoiled?

Reinforce and Review

- It is not always possible to see a parasite in food. Unlike yeast, bacteria, or mold, a parasite does not alter the color, texture, or smell of the food product. In fact, there may be only one two-celled parasite specimen in an entire batch of food. No one will be affected except the one person who ingests the live parasite.
- Usually, parasites are present in foods where the hygiene of the water, kitchen, or foodservice personnel is poor.

Vocabulary Terms

- **Parasites:** Organisms that live off of a living host's metabolism, contributing nothing and often robbing the host of health and well-being.
- **Host:** The organism that unwittingly provides home and food to a parasite, often at the expense of its health.
- **Fungi:** Microorganisms that grow by spore, like yeast, mold, or mushrooms.
- **Mold:** A type of fungus that can be beneficial or harmful.
- **Yeast:** A type of fungus that can be beneficial or damaging to food, depending upon the type of yeast.

The five-second rule is meant as a humorous joke, not a scientific principle. Any food dropped on the floor should be discarded. Floors have pathogens that have been tracked in on shoes, among other things.

Teaching Tips

- There are many steps along the way from a food's initial ingredient production to the finished product on your fork.
- Help the students to brainstorm about the various steps.
- What food safety problems could arise at each step?

In-Class Activity:
The Human Flow Chart

21st-Century Skills —Financial, Economic, Business, and Entrepreneurial Literacy

Have students assemble themselves into a line of steps that represents a food item, beginning with the production of the raw ingredients and ending with the item being eaten by the customer.

These steps will consider food production problems that include biological, chemical, and physical contamination.

Each student will represent a step.

Each student will describe the step.

Each student will point out what food safety problems could arise at that step.

Each student will mention how a problem at his or her step could impact public health.

Each student will form and verbalize an opinion about how a problem at this step would impact the profitability of the food item.

Each student will indicate what measures taken at this step will ensure the safety of the food.

As the students verbally identify the various potential sources of trouble, they will also be able to verbalize the connectivity between various trades, sources, and vendors.

Did You Know...?
Ever heard of the five-second rule? It implies that if food drops on the floor and is picked up within five seconds, it won't get contaminated with bacteria. Next time you drop food on the floor, remember that a clean-looking floor isn't necessarily clean. Any food that makes contact with the floor can pick up pathogens.

Biological Toxins

Pathogens make biological toxins, or poisons. Sometimes certain kinds of plants or animals contain toxins naturally or because that plant or animal has been contaminated itself somewhere in the food chain. Toxins can make people sick, so restaurant and foodservice managers must be aware of them.

Seafood toxins, which can contaminate fish or shellfish, make seafood unsafe. Seafood toxins may be a natural part of the food, made by pathogens on the seafood, or form when toxic algae are eaten by the fish or shellfish. When people eat contaminated seafood, they cannot taste or smell these toxins. Food-handlers cannot destroy toxins by freezing or cooking, either, once they form in food. The best way to prevent illness from this source is to purchase seafood from approved, reputable suppliers.

Most people who get sick from mushroom toxins have eaten poisonous wild mushrooms collected by amateur hunters. Many types of mushrooms look alike, and it is easy to mistake toxic varieties for edible ones. Mushroom toxins can't be destroyed by cooking or freezing. Buying mushrooms from approved, reputable suppliers is the best way to prevent illness from this source.

Illnesses from plant toxins usually happen because products were purchased from an unapproved supplier or because items weren't cooked correctly. For example, undercooking kidney beans may cause toxins to form in the beans. Purchasing from approved, reputable suppliers and then cooking and holding dishes correctly are the best prevention methods.

Chemical Contamination

Chemicals have caused many cases of foodborne illnesses. These contaminants come from everyday items that may be found in many restaurant and food-service operations.

Restaurant and foodservice chemicals can contaminate food if they are used or stored in the wrong ways. This includes cleaners, sanitizers, polishes, and machine lubricants. Store chemicals in a separate area away from food, utensils, and equipment used for food. Always follow the manufacturers' directions when

84

using chemicals, and be careful when using them while food is being prepared. Figure 2.9 shows an example of inappropriate chemical storage.

Figure 2.9: These chemicals are not stored properly, which can cause contamination of food.

Some utensils and equipment contain toxic metals that can contaminate acidic food. A person who then eats this food gets toxic-metal poisoning. This illness is frequently caused by using equipment with lead, copper, or zinc. When an acidic food, such as tomato sauce, comes in contact with the metal, the acid may dissolve some of the metal into the food. To prevent toxic-metal poisoning, you should only use utensils and equipment, including kettles, pots, serving ware and pans, that are made for handling food.

Physical Contamination

Physical contamination happens when objects get into food. These objects can be naturally occurring, such as the bones in fish. Others result from accidents and mistakes. Figure 2.10 shows examples of physical contaminants. Physical contaminants include the following:

- Metal shavings from cans
- Glass from broken lightbulbs
- Fingernails, hair, and bandages
- Jewelry
- Fruit pits

Most physical contamination can be prevented by inspecting food closely, practicing good personal hygiene, and following preparation procedures.

85

Teaching Tips

- Galvanizing is a very thin covering of zinc.
- If zinc items are used with an acid food, the zinc can leech out into the food and become toxic.
- For example, lemonade made in a zinc container (such as a new, clean, galvanized can or bin) may cause the zinc to go into the solution in the beverage and sicken people who drink the lemonade.

Discuss

- How can you prevent physical contaminants from entering food for service?
- How can you inspect foods for foreign items?
- If a guest finds a foreign object in a food item and brings it to the attention of the staff, what should be done?
- What legal responsibilities does a foodservice establishment have in such a case?
- How and where should this type of problem be reported?
- Who should be held responsible?

Figure Focus

Figure 2.9: Food and chemicals should not be stored in the same area.

Discuss

- Ask the students, "Have you ever heard of deliberate contamination of food at a foodservice operation?"
- Perhaps the students have heard or read about such things. They may be aware of other sorts of deliberate poisoning, such as anthrax-laden white powder on mailed letters or packages.
- Discuss the various ways that they can defend the food supply of their establishment.

Reinforce and Review

- If the students are not aware of real cases of food terrorism, they could research past incidents.
- One would be the 1984 bioterrorism attack of salad bars in The Dalles, Oregon.
- Allergic reactions occur when a protein or other unique chemical of a food enters the gut and bloodstream of a person with antibodies or other sensitivities to that unique molecule.
- The body begins to fight the molecule as if it were a disease, and produces histamine in defense.
- Histamine can cause swelling. Severe swelling can block off the airway of an allergic person, causing death.
- Immediate medical attention is necessary. Call 911, give anti-histamines and epinephrine (Epi-Pen). If an allergic attack is severe, there is no time to lose.
- Some allergies are thought to be caused by too-early introduction of foods during infancy.
- Other allergies are "idiopathic," or of unknown cause.
- There is thought today that some allergies are increasing due to food-processing methods (such as peanut processing).

Figure 2.10: Foodservice employees must be careful to avoid physical contamination of food from metal can shavings and fruit pits.

Food Defense

The prevention measures discussed throughout this section will help prevent accidental contamination of food. But restaurant and foodservice employees also must take steps to prevent people from purposely contaminating food. Competitors, vendors, former employees, or terrorists may try to tamper with the food in your operation. Attacks might occur anywhere from the farm to the restaurant. They are usually focused on a specific food item, a manufacturing process, or a business. For example, someone might choose to target the manufacturing of a common food product, like peanut butter, because so many people would be affected.

One important way to prevent tampering is to control access to the operation's food storage and preparation areas. Uniforms and nametags help identify staff and vendors. Security badges also help ensure that only the people who belong there are in the specific food area. All employees in an operation, from buser to executive chef, should report anything that seems suspicious. As the saying goes, "If you see something, say something."

Allergens

The number of people in the United States with food allergies is increasing. A **food allergy** is the body's negative reaction to a food protein. People with food allergies can become sick or even die from eating even the smallest amount of a triggering allergen. In a restaurant or foodservice operation, managers, servers, and kitchen staff must each do their part to keep customers with food allergies safe.

The following is a list of the major allergens in the United States. They account for 90 percent of all food-allergic reactions:

- Milk and dairy products
- Eggs and egg products
- Fish

86

Figure Focus

Figure 2.10: Even if a product arrives from a supplier with a problem (such as a cherry pit in the pie filling pictured on the right) it is the responsibility of the restaurant to check it before serving it.

Figure 2.11: Have the students identify the various types of nuts shown in the photo on the next page: From top left, clockwise: chestnuts, pistachio nuts (not a true tree nut, but a seed), walnut, hazelnuts, pecans, almonds, and in the center, peanuts (not a true nut, but a legume).

- Shellfish (crab, shrimp, lobster)
- Wheat
- Soy and soy products
- Peanuts
- Tree nuts, such as pecans and walnuts (see Figure 2.11)

Employees should be aware of these food items and the menu items that contain them.

Figure 2.11: Tree nuts and peanuts are a common allergen.

When serving customers with food allergies, servers must be ready to answer customers' questions about any menu item. Specifically, they should be able to do the following:

- Tell the customer how each dish is made.
- Tell the customer about any "secret" ingredients that may contain allergens. While you might not want to share these recipes with the public, you still must be able to tell the "secret" items when asked.
- Suggest alternative menu items that don't have the food allergen.

Servers should never take a guess about what a menu item contains. If they don't know, they should ask someone who does, such as the manager or kitchen staff.

When preparing food for customers with food allergies, kitchen employees must make sure that allergens are not transferred from food containing an allergen to the food served to the customer. This is called **cross-contact.** Figure 2.12 illustrates the steps that kitchen staff must take to avoid cross-contact.

[fast fact]

Did You Know...?
Food allergies vary from irritating to life threatening. Each year in the United States, approximately 30,000 people go to the emergency room to get treated for severe allergies. It is estimated that 150–200 Americans die because of allergic reactions to food each year.

Allergies affect 2 percent of adults and 4–8 percent of people in the United States. While there are treatments for the reactions caused by allergies, there is no cure for food allergies themselves. Signs of a food allergy reaction include hives, itching in and around the mouth, swelling of body parts, fainting, and difficulty breathing.

A severe reaction, known as anaphylaxis, is life threatening and requires immediate attention. Signs of a severe reaction include swelling of the throat, extreme difficulty breathing, shock with a drop in blood pressure, and loss of consciousness.

87

Teaching Tips

- An allergy to tree nuts may include various kinds of nuts. Walnuts, pecans, hazelnuts, and almonds are the most commonly used tree nuts.
- Peanuts are not really nuts, but legumes.
- Peanut allergies are not the same thing as tree nut allergies. Someone may be allergic to one and not allergic to the other.
- However, if someone is allergic to tree nuts, it may include several varieties of nuts.
- It is possible to have both a peanut allergy and a tree nut allergy.
- The symptoms of either type of allergy may be so severe as to be quickly life-threatening.
- Menu disclosure and adherence to a recipe are necessary when using nuts in a restaurant.

Fast Fact:
Did You Know...?

Death from a food allergy can occur at any age. Individuals may be in otherwise perfect health. Diagnosis of a food allergy at the first sign of a troubling symptom is important. This will help the individual identify problem foods and avoid them. It will also give the individual a chance to carry anti-histimine and epinephrine in case of emergency.

21st-Century Skills—Reason Effectively, Critical Thinking, and Problem Solving

More Advanced Students

Research peanut allergies in the United States.

Is the incidence rising or falling?

What might be the cause of the change?

What can be done?

What are the risks of a peanut allergy?

Who is affected?

What is the treatment?

What does this mean for the restaurant industry?

There may be other facts or questions that can be addressed.

Have the student or group of students present their findings to the class.

Less Advanced Students

Research various cuisines that rely heavily on peanuts.

Are there specific foods, such as Thai dishes, that contain peanuts, but might not appear to?

How would you disclose the presence of peanuts in a menu item?

Present findings to the class.

Special Needs Students (Adapt to suit the needs)

What is the difference between "peanut" and "tree nut"?

How did each get its name?

Are there any nuts that are neither "peanuts" nor "tree nuts"? Cashews, Brazil nuts, and pistachios are three good examples.

Present findings to the class.

ESOL Students

Name the various nuts and identify them or photos of them.

Verbalize the difference between a "peanut" and a "tree nut."

Help the student overcome any confusion with pronunciation or the concept of "nuts" that are not actually nuts.

The student will present his or her findings to the class. English-speaking students might not be aware of potential confusions.

Vocabulary Terms

- **Cross-contact:** To introduce an allergen to a food via equipment that was previously used with a food item containing an allergen.

Discuss the various opportunities and risks associated with peanut allergies in a college dormitory or cafeteria kitchen. Peanut butter has long been a snack staple for students on a budget.

How about the same issues as they relate to foodservice in military deployment situations?

How would this relate to hospital foodservice operations?

How can the risk of exposure for allergic individuals be reduced where individuals are living in close quarters, eating the same food prepared in the same kitchen?

1. Make sure the allergen doesn't touch anything that is going to be served to or used by these customers, including food, beverages, and utensils, or anything that is used in preparing food for them, such as equipment and gloves.

2. Wash, rinse, and sanitize cookware, utensils, and equipment before preparing their food.

3. Wash your hands and change gloves before preparing their food.

4. Use equipment assigned only for preparing their food.

Figure 2.12: Kitchen staff must follow specific steps to avoid cross-contact.

[on the job]

Peanut Allergy and Kitchen Equipment

Food often makes a long journey before it arrives on a customer's table, from the farm or ocean to the fork. For a person with a peanut allergy, a long process presents many opportunities for food or equipment to come into contact with peanuts. More children and adults are allergic to peanuts now than at any previous time in recorded history. It is important for restaurant and foodservice operations to be aware of any peanuts in recipes and of equipment contact with peanuts. If a customer has an allergy and asks about peanuts in a menu item, the server must give accurate information. If a peanut-allergic person is exposed and has an anaphylactic response, it will be immediate and life threatening.

In the event of a peanut or other allergy problem, call 911 immediately, and get help from the people in the area. The victim should be given an injection of epinephrine (EpiPen is a very common brand of auto-injector) and an antihistamine (Benadryl) as soon as possible to help keep airways open. Some individuals carry their own and can self-administer. Do not wait or delay. Do not try to drive the person to the ER, but have an ambulance come to you. The paramedics have epinephrine in case more is needed.

Prevention of food-allergy problems is especially critical in dormitories or schools where young people eat meals daily in a foodservice facility away from home.

88

Figure Focus

Figure 2.12: These steps can help ensure that menu items are safe from cross-contact. Always use a clean and sanitized utensil or piece of equipment. Always use fresh towels, and even be careful of aprons and jackets.

U.S. Regulation of Food Safety

Today, many government departments monitor food safety. In the United States, most regulations that affect restaurant and foodservice operations are written at the state level. However, federal, state, and local governments are all involved.

The Food and Drug Administration (FDA) writes the *FDA Food Code*, which recommends specific food safety regulations for the restaurant and foodservice industry. But the code is not actual law. Each state decides whether to adopt the *FDA Food Code* or some form of it as law. The laws passed at the state level are then enforced by state or local (city or county) health departments. Health inspectors from city, county, or state health departments conduct inspections in most states.

[fast fact]

Did You Know...?
According to Gallup, 71 percent of Americans have a fair amount or great deal of confidence in the federal government to ensure the safety of the food supply in the United States.

Figure 2.13: Health inspectors ensure that an operation is following all food safety laws.

89

Teaching Tips

- The Food and Drug Administration oversees food production businesses.
- It is part of the Department of Health and Human Services.
- This is a different agency than the United States Department of Agriculture, which also oversees food production and distribution.
- Another separate government entity is the Centers for Disease Control, which oversees food safety issues.
- The Department of Commerce helps regulate fish and seafood.
- The Department of Justice has the Bureau of Alcohol, Tobacco, and Firearms, which oversees alcoholic beverages in the United States.
- There are many, many different government entities involved in the restaurant industry.
- The first agency to satisfy would be the local (city, county) health department.

Discuss

- What are the standards of the local health department?
- Does anyone in the class already have a local foodhandler's permit?
- If so, have the student (or students) explain the process of obtaining one.

Fast Fact:
Did You Know...?

The United States has the safest, most vast, most varied, most diverse, most nutritious, and most widely available food supply of any civilization in the history of the world to this point.

Figure Focus

Figure 2.13: A visit from a health inspector should be welcomed and not dreaded. Always keep the foodservice operation ready for a surprise inspection.

Teaching Tips

- The importance of compliance with regulations cannot be overstated to the students.
- The students might not yet be used to accountability and responsibility.
- In a foodservice operation, lack of compliance has serious and expensive consequences.

On The Job:
Public Health Inspector

The job of a public health inspector serves the greater public good by keeping citizens safe.

Discuss

- Self-inspection is a form of accountability.
- Have the students experienced this in their own lives?
- How would it harm a fine restaurant to disregard the local public health regulations?
- In the interest of being successful in business, is it a good idea to self-inspect?
- Can this principle be applied to other areas of students' lives?
- Explore some of these real-life skills with the students in the activity at the bottom of the page.

Vocabulary Terms

- **Inspection:** An overseeing agency's representative visits and examines a foodservice operation for safety, cleanliness, and proper foodhandling practices to ensure the safety of the customer and employees.

An **inspection** is a formal review or examination conducted to see if an operation is following food safety laws. All operations serving food to the public, from quick-service restaurants to hospitals, nursing homes, and schools, are inspected. The most important reason for inspections is that failing to keep food safe can put the health of customers at risk. Failing an inspection could also result in an operation going out of business. Figure 2.13 on the previous page shows an inspector during an inspection.

[on the job]

Public Health Inspector

Public health inspectors play different roles, but their goal is always the same: to improve public safety. Some inspectors investigate restaurants and other foodservice facilities to make sure that all health and safety rules within the jurisdiction are being observed. Most facilities inspected fare well; the inspector identifies any concerns and educates management and employees. However, occasionally kitchens don't do well on the inspection, and the inspector finds major errors in day-to-day operations. In these instances, the health inspector has the authority to fine the business or even, if the problems are severe, close the facility. After the inspection, the inspector will write a report so that both management and the local government know the results.

Some health inspectors investigate wells and septic systems to prevent threats to the public water supply. Others may focus on environmental concerns, like air or soil pollution. And still others may investigate processing plants, such as slaughterhouses.

To become a public health inspector, a four-year degree in public health, food science, or a related field is usually required, as are a strong interest in science and good communication skills. Local governments often require prospective inspectors to pass additional examinations before they can be hired.

Successful restaurant and foodservice managers understand local food safety requirements and design policies that address them. They also conduct their own self-inspections. A self-inspection should check for the same things that a health inspector would, so that an operation is always prepared and functioning appropriately.

90

In-Class Activity:
Chalk Talk

21st-Century Skills—Use Systems Thinking; Make Judgments and Decisions

On a chalkboard, white board, or document camera, have students volunteer to discuss the principle of self-inspection.

Have them create the following organizer on the board or paper:

Quest	What Teachers and Parents Tell Us	Self-Inspection Tactics

Help the students to verbalize their own empowerment in creating positive outcomes for their own lives and interests.

Summary

In this section, you learned the following:

- A foodborne illness is a disease transmitted to people by food. A foodborne-illness outbreak is when two or more people get the same illness after eating the same food.

- The costs of a foodborne-illness outbreak include financial costs to the restaurant or foodservice operation and human costs: loss of time at work, medical expenses, long-term disability, and possibly death.

- High-risk populations include people with weakened immune systems: the elderly, infants, preschool-age children, pregnant women, and people with HIV/AIDS or cancer, as well as people on chemotherapy and transplant recipients. They have a higher risk of getting a foodborne illness.

- Pathogens need six conditions to grow. These conditions can be remembered by FAT TOM: food, acidity, temperature, time, oxygen, and moisture.

- Those foods that need time and temperature control for safety, such as milk or fish, are called TCS foods. Ready-to-eat food also needs careful handling to prevent contamination.

- Contamination from biological toxins can be prevented by purchasing from approved, reputable suppliers and then cooking and holding dishes correctly.

- To store chemicals properly, you must keep them in a separate area away from food, utensils, and equipment used for food. Then follow safe storage rules.

- A food defense system helps to prevent people from purposely contaminating food. One important way to prevent tampering is to make sure access to an operation's food is controlled through use of uniforms and name tags.

- The most common allergens include milk and dairy products, eggs and egg products, fish, shellfish, wheat, soy, peanuts, and tree nuts. To prevent allergic reactions, servers must be able to answer questions about any ingredients in menu items. In addition, kitchen employees must be sure that allergens are not transferred by cross-contact.

- The restaurant and foodservice industry is monitored by many agencies. The FDA writes the *FDA Food Code,* and each state adopts the code as it sees fit. State and local health departments then enforce these laws.

91

Summary

- Remind students to review the following:
  1. Foodborne-illness outbreaks
  2. The costs associated with a foodborne-illness outbreak
  3. Who is at high risk for contracting a foodborne illness
  4. FAT TOM
  5. The characteristics of TCS food
  6. The methods that can prevent biological contamination
  7. The guidelines for storing chemicals safely
  8. Why you need a food defense system
  9. The most common allergens and the methods for preventing allergic reactions
  10. The government agencies that regulate the restaurant and foodservice industry

Section 2.1 Review Questions

1. Four types of pathogens:
   Viruses—Live in human waste, can survive freezing, and can make people ill.
   Bacteria—Toxic microorganisms that proliferate in the temperature danger zone.
   Parasites—Organisms that live in a host, usually in the intestines, often acquired through bad drinking water or poor sanitation in food preparation.
   Fungi—Molds, yeasts, and other fungi growths that spoil food.

2. Children, pregnant women, the elderly, people with cancer or on chemotherapy, people with HIV/AIDS, and transplant recipients are all at a higher risk for getting a foodborne illness. These groups are susceptible to illness because their immune systems are weak, underdeveloped, or somehow compromised.

3. Food can be made unsafe by biological contamination, physical contamination, and chemical contamination.

4. All ingredients that are potential allergens should be disclosed on the menu. Servers should be able to correctly answer questions about allergens in menu items.

5. Student responses will vary.

6. They should focus their attention on personnel. They need to add personnel and properly train everyone. They do not have enough personnel to properly receive food, and Brian does not follow accepted guidelines. Perhaps he also needs more training. Also, since they do not have enough personnel, they are behind after the meeting and the food receiving. They also have a sick worker in the kitchen who should go home. Also, he is not adequately trained in safety and poses many risks.

7. There are many agencies involved in food safety from the farm to the table. Student responses will vary.

8. The manager should replace the menu item immediately with some sort of apology, perhaps in the form of a complimentary dinner. The kitchen should discover the source of the problem and make sure that safe procedures will be followed to prevent this from happening in the future.

Section 2.1 Review Questions

1. Describe the four types of pathogens that can contaminate food and cause foodborne illness.

2. Which populations have a higher risk of getting a foodborne illness and why?

3. List the three types of hazards that make food unsafe.

4. How can servers prepare to address the needs of customers with food allergies?

5. Melisa Bouchard indicates that guests expect their food to be safe. Is this something that you think about when you go out to eat? Why or why not?

6. Linda and Chef Jean are setting up a self-inspection for Uptown Grille. Given the situation that they faced today, where should they focus their attention?

7. How are the federal, state, and local governments each involved in food safety? Do you think this system works well? If not, what would you change?

8. A diner was eating at a restaurant. In a plate of noodles was a rather large shard of broken, off-white ceramic. Upon finding this physical hazard, the diner showed the problem to the server and requested a replacement plate of noodles. What should the manager of the restaurant do for the customer? What should the manager do to make sure this situation doesn't happen again?

92

Section 2.1 Activities

1. Study Skills/Group Activity: How to Work Safely

Brainstorm as a group about the various ways in which viruses cause foodborne illness. How can you prevent viruses from making customers sick? Create a poster called Personal Hygiene Rules for the Uptown Grille.

2. Activity: How to Handle an Outbreak

In recent years, there have been numerous incidents of foodborne illness making national and international headlines. Select one episode, and write two paragraphs on it, describing the source of the problem, the identity of the pathogen, the number of people affected, and the steps taken to rectify the situation.

3. Critical Thinking: Keeping Food Safe

Most restaurants go to great lengths to ensure that they serve safe food. However, this activity usually stays behind the scenes. How can foodservice establishments highlight all this effort for customers? Is keeping food safe a marketing opportunity? If you were designing a marketing campaign based on food safety, what would your focus be?

93

Section 2.1 Activities

1. The students will have unique solutions to this problem, and each will have a poster. The solutions should all comply with the information in the text.

2. The students can research this online or through other resources.

3. Each student or group will have a unique solution to this problem, but all marketing efforts should be appetizing and inviting. Nothing should be suggestive in a way that would ruin the appetite.

Section 2.2
Good Personal Hygiene

Introduce the Section

a. Help the students define personal hygiene.
b. Encourage the students to verbalize the significance of personal hygiene to foodservice personnel.
c. Assist the students to view hygiene as a process, not just a habit or philosophy.
d. Determine some real-world strategies for keeping food and individuals safe through hygiene practices.

Vocabulary Review

a. Direct students to the key terms.
b. Pronounce each word, and have the students repeat the pronunciation out loud.
c. Discuss the definition of each word.

Teach

Discuss

- Foodhandling personnel are all employees who work in a restaurant, whether or not they directly touch or handle food.
- Proper personal hygiene practices can prevent pathogens from spreading.
- Handwashing is an essential skill that requires attention and practice.
- Foodservice operations need clearly defined requirements concerning ill personnel.

Teaching Tips

- Early in grade school, students probably learned about covering their mouths when they sneeze.
- That is a beginning.

In-Class Activity:
Personal Hygiene—KWL Chart to
Guide Learning

Literacy Connection
Have the students fold a clean sheet of paper into thirds.
Have them label the first column "K" for Know.
Have them label the second column "W" for Want to Learn.
Have them label the third column "L" for Learned.

2.1 Introduction to Food Safety	2.2 Good Personal Hygiene	2.3 Preventing Hazards in the Flow of Food	2.4 Food Safety Management Systems	2.5 Cleaning and Sanitizing
• What is a foodborne illness? • Forms of contamination • Biological contamination • Chemical contamination • Physical contamination • Food defense • Allergens • U.S. regulation of food safety	• How foodhandlers can contaminate food • Personal cleanliness and work attire • Handwashing • Bare-hand contact with ready-to-eat food • Work requirements related to illness	• Cross-contamination • Time-temperature abuse • Purchasing • Receiving • Storage • Preparation • Cooking • Holding, storing, and reheating • Serving	• The HACCP plan	• How to clean effectively • Sanitizing • Developing a cleaning program • Controlling pests

SECTION 2.2 GOOD PERSONAL HYGIENE

Good personal hygiene is a key factor in the prevention of foodborne illnesses. Any employee in a restaurant or foodservice operation can accidentally contaminate food. He or she might not even realize it when it happens. Successful managers help to make personal hygiene a priority.

Study Questions

After studying Section 2.2, you should be able to answer the following questions:

- What personal behaviors contaminate food?
- What are the steps to proper handwashing, and when should hands be washed?
- What are proper personal cleanliness practices?
- What is proper work attire?
- How should ready-to-eat food be handled?
- When should foodhandlers be prevented from working with or around food?

How Foodhandlers Can Contaminate Food

As you have learned, foodhandlers can contaminate food in a variety of situations:

- Having a foodborne illness
- Having wounds that contain a pathogen

94

The students will write what they already know about personal hygiene in the "K" column.

The students will write what they expect and hope to learn about hygiene in foodservice in the "W" column.

The students will leave the "L" column blank until the end of the section.

Discuss

- The students can brainstorm ideas about good personal hygiene.
- Have the students share what they have in the "K" column of their paper.
- Have them also share what they have in the "W" column.
- Assure the students that all (or most) of the items in the "W" column will be presented in this section of useful information.
- The students may find it interesting to realize that personal hygiene helps them in all areas of life, not just on the job in foodservice.

- Having contact with a person who is ill

- Touching their hair, faces, or bodies and then not washing their hands

- Touching anything that may contaminate their hands and then not washing them

- Having symptoms such as diarrhea, vomiting, or jaundice (a yellowing of the eyes or skin)

- Eating, drinking, smoking, or chewing gum or tobacco while preparing or serving food

Foodhandlers are not just the people who prepare food. Servers and even dishwashers are considered foodhandlers, because they either handle food directly or work with the surfaces that food will touch. To prevent foodhandlers from contaminating food, managers must create **personal hygiene** policies. These policies must address personal cleanliness, clothing, hand care, and health.

Personal Cleanliness and Work Attire

Personal cleanliness is an important part of personal hygiene. Pathogens can be found on hair and skin that aren't kept clean. These pathogens can be transferred to food and food equipment. All foodhandlers must bathe or shower before work and keep their hair clean.

Staff who wear dirty clothes at work make a bad impression on customers. More importantly, dirty clothing may carry pathogens that can cause foodborne illnesses. The following are guidelines designed to prevent foodhandlers from spreading foodborne illnesses:

- Foodhandlers should always cover their hair. Tie long hair back. Wear a clean hat or other hair covering. Figure 2.14 shows a foodhandler wearing a hat.

- Wear clean clothing every day. This includes chef coats and uniforms.

- Remove aprons and store them in the right place when leaving prep areas, for example, when taking out garbage or using the restroom. Change any apron that becomes dirty.

- Remove jewelry from hands and arms before preparing food or when working around prep areas. Do not wear watches, bracelets (including medical bracelets), or rings, except for a plain metal band. Figure 2.15 on page 97 is a photo of a foodhandler removing a watch.

95

Teaching Tips

- There are many ways to neglect personal cleanliness.
- There are also many ways to spread illness and infection to another person.
- The students can verbalize many of these from past experience.
- The list in the text can be expounded upon in discussion with the class.

Discuss

- Students may realize that current styles and trends may be a challenge for foodservice managers and customers.
- Ask the students how they feel about visible tattoos on wait staff and those working directly with the public.
- Ask the students how they feel about facial hair and mouth or ear piercing on wait staff and those working with the public.
- Can the students think of other styles, perhaps more current since the publication of this text, that might send a hygiene message to customers?
- Are there hairstyles that impact the impression of good hygiene?
- There are hairstyles that may be created by keeping hair matted and infrequently washed.
- Should such hairstyles influence a foodservice manager's hiring practices?
- Can the students think of clothing that might be inappropriate for work?

Vocabulary Terms

- **Foodhandler:** Any employee who handles food directly or works with the surfaces that food will touch.
- **Personal hygiene:** Practices and strategies for maintaining physical cleanliness and not spreading disease to others.

Individuals have a desire and a right to project their personal style and image. A foodservice operation also has the same desire and right.

An owner of an operation can choose how to present the business through the look of the personnel.

It is not a violation of rights to offer employment opportunities contingent upon having the appropriate look. If an employer does not want the public to see piercings or tattoos on employees, he or she may choose not to hire someone who has them.

Figure 2.14: Hairnets or covered hair is required by most restaurant and foodservice operations.

[on the job]

Making a Personal Statement

Many people like making a personal statement at school, at work, or out with friends. This often means favoring a particular hairstyle, wearing intricate jewelry, or applying detailed makeup. For people desiring a more permanent change, there are also facial piercings and tattoos.

These choices might not translate well into a professional environment, though, especially one in which there is the potential to contaminate food. Moreover, the ambiance of a particular restaurant, hotel, or other hospitality business might not mesh well with a less traditional "look."

A basic rule for foodhandlers is that they should never wear anything that could harm food. Jewelry could carry pathogens; it's even possible that a small bit of jewelry, such as an earring back, could fall into the food and be lost. Facial piercings, including earrings, should be removed. Hair restraints should always be worn, especially for long hair. Wearing too much makeup can be a problem, too. When the kitchen becomes hot, sweat can cause particles of makeup to contaminate food, so be moderate when considering cosmetic choices.

The rules are somewhat different for front-of-house employees, who primarily interact with customers. It is often acceptable for such employees to wear more jewelry than their coworkers in the kitchen; the same goes for makeup, and there is sometimes more flexibility with hairstyles as well. On the other hand, tattoos that might go unnoticed in kitchens might raise eyebrows in the dining room and must often be covered; in fact, some organizations do not hire employees with tattoos in particular places, such as necks and hands. Facial piercings, depending on their size and placement, might also be forbidden. Much depends on the style of the particular operation.

Handwashing

Handwashing is the most important part of personal hygiene. It may seem like an obvious thing to do, but many foodhandlers do not wash their hands correctly or as often as they should.

96

Figure Focus

Figure 2.14: It is important and customary for foodservice employees to keep their hair restrained and covered. Even beards are covered. Do the students understand why?

Figure 2.15: Foodservice workers should take off any jewelry before working with food.

Foodhandlers must wash their hands before they start work. They must also do it after the following activities:

- Using the restroom
- Handling raw meat, poultry, or seafood
- Touching the hair, face, or body
- Sneezing, coughing, or using a tissue
- Eating, drinking, smoking, or chewing gum or tobacco
- Handling chemicals that might affect food safety
- Taking out garbage
- Clearing tables or busing dirty dishes
- Touching clothing or aprons
- Handling money
- Touching anything else that may contaminate hands, such as dirty equipment, work surfaces, or towels

Figure 2.16 shows the steps for proper handwashing. The whole process should take about 20 seconds. Foodhandlers should wash their hands only in a designated handwashing sink. If they are not careful, they can contaminate their hands again after washing them. Using a paper towel to turn off the faucet and to open the door when leaving the restroom can prevent this.

97

Figure Focus

Figure 2.15: Jewelry should be removed for the protection of the food. Additionally, the individual may be protected from irritation from wearing wet rings, bracelets, or wristwatches next to the skin.

	1. Wet hands and arms with running water as hot as you can comfortably stand (at least 100°F).
	2. Apply soap. Apply enough to build up a good lather.
	3. Scrub hands and arms vigorously for 10 to 15 seconds. Clean under fingernails and between fingers.
	4. Rinse hands and arms thoroughly under running water.
	5. Dry hands and arms with a single-use paper towel or warm-air hand dryer.

Figure 2.16: Steps for proper handwashing.

Hand Sanitizers: You Can Even Carry It in Your Pocket

Hand sanitizers are now commonplace. They were a bright new idea not that long ago. Isopropyl alcohol is a good skin sanitizer, but it is a very thin and runny liquid, so product-development chemists mixed alcohol with some glycerin to thicken it.

Now you can pump it into your hands through a dispenser and easily rub it onto your skin. Brilliant! A new foam version is now available, that comes in an upside-down dispenser that does not require you to touch a pump with a freshly washed hand. Even more brilliant!

The most important thing to keep in mind with sanitizers is that they do not clean away dirt or anything else. They should never take the place of handwashing in a restaurant or foodservice operation. They kill most germs, but not all. Nothing replaces the need for you to completely wash your hands before applying a hand sanitizer. If you choose to use sanitizers after washing your hands, wait until the sanitizer is completely dry before handling food or equipment.

Did You Know...?

Handwashing is very important to good hygiene. Everyone knows how to wash his or her hands, right? WRONG. Most people do not wash long enough or carefully enough. Experts say you should scrub your hands long enough to sing "Happy Birthday" twice.

Hand Maintenance

Besides handwashing, hands need additional care to prevent spreading pathogens. Figure 2.17 illustrates hand care guidelines for foodhandlers.

98

Discuss

- Hands are very personal, very individual, and unique in their purpose.
- The students might have strong feelings about the upcoming portion of the text dealing with hand maintenance and appearance.
- Do the students have feelings about fingers, fingernails, and their decorations?

Teaching Tips

- Students might not realize how frequently they handle their cell phones or other digital devices.
- Discuss text messages, cell calls, and MP3 players.
- These trends will change over the years. Discuss whatever is current.

Figure Focus

Figure 2.16: There is skill and technique involved in properly performing a seemingly simple task like handwashing.

	Keep fingernails short and clean. Long fingernails can be difficult to keep clean.
	Do not wear false nails. They can break off into food and are difficult to keep clean.
	Do not wear nail polish. It can disguise dirt under nails and flake off into food.
	Wear a bandage over wounds on hands and arms. Make sure it keeps the wound from leaking. Also wear a single-use glove or a finger cot (a finger cover) over bandages on hands or fingers. These will protect the bandage and keep it from falling off into food.

Figure 2.17: Hand care for foodhandlers.

[fast fact]

Did You Know...?
80 percent of infectious diseases are transmitted by touching surfaces that have germs on them.

Source: WebMD

Bare-Hand Contact with Ready-to-Eat Food

Using bare hands to handle ready-to-eat food can increase the risk of contaminating it. Gloves, tongs, and deli tissue can help keep food safe by creating a barrier between hands and food. Figure 2.18 shows how to use gloves correctly.

Work Requirements Related to Illness

Restaurants and foodservice operations have a responsibility to ensure that their employees do not spread foodborne illnesses. Foodhandlers who are sick can spread pathogens to food. Depending on the illness, they might not be able to work with food until they recover.

Table 2.3 explains how managers should handle employees with illnesses.

99

**Fast Fact:
Did You Know...?**

How would germs get on surfaces? What surfaces could these be? Does a human face count as a surface?

Teaching Tips
- Bare-hand contact could be used in some settings, such as handling bakery items or serving on a hospital tray line.
- Even loading a vending machine could involve bare-hand contact with food products.
- Perhaps the students are aware of using gloves for these contacts.
- Tongs are often used at buffets and salad bars.
- Do the students have experience picking up food items with deli tissue? Where?

Discuss
- Do you ever feel obligated to go to work or school even when you are sick?
- How could this impact a foodservice establishment?
- What if there are not enough employees to run the operation?
- What if an employee who is contagious works that day?
- If you were a manager, what would be your policy?

Figure Focus
Figure 2.17: These guidelines are not limited to foodhandlers. Healthcare providers follow the same guidelines. Gloved hands are often recommended as well.

Figure 2.18: How to use gloves correctly.
- Never use gloves in place of handwashing.
- Wash hands before putting on gloves and when changing to a new pair. Otherwise, dirty hands might contaminate the clean gloves.
- Make sure the gloves fit. They shouldn't be too loose or too tight.
- Never rinse, wash, or reuse gloves.
- Gloves should be changed as soon as they become dirty or torn. They should also be changed before beginning a different task; at least every four hours during continual use; and after handling raw meat, seafood, or poultry, and before handling ready-to-eat food.

Table 2.3: Handling Employee Illnesses	
Situation	**Procedure**
The foodhandler has a sore throat with a fever.	The foodhandler cannot work with or around food. If the operation serves mostly high-risk customers (such as a nursing home), then the foodhandler shouldn't be in the operation.
The foodhandler has at least one of these symptoms: Vomiting Diarrhea Jaundice	The foodhandler shouldn't be in the operation.
The foodhandler has been diagnosed with a foodborne illness.	The foodhandler shouldn't be in the operation.

Summary

In this section, you learned the following:

- The following personal behaviors of foodhandlers can contaminate food:
  - Having a foodborne illness
  - Having wounds that contain a pathogen
  - Having contact with a person who is ill
  - Touching the hair, face, or body and then not washing their hands
  - Touching anything that may contaminate their hands and not washing them

100

Figure Focus

Figure 2.18: Latex-based gloves may be allergenic to some individuals. Disposable plastic gloves are convenient to use and usually have a loose fit. They require some getting used to. Nitrile gloves fit more tightly and allow for better dexterity, but take longer to put on and remove.

- Having symptoms such as diarrhea, vomiting, or jaundice
- Eating, drinking, smoking, or chewing gum or tobacco while preparing or serving food

■ The steps to proper handwashing are as follows:

1. Wet hands and arms with running water as hot as you can comfortably stand (at least 100°F).
2. Apply enough soap to build up a good lather.
3. Scrub hands and arms vigorously for 10 to 15 seconds. Clean under fingernails and between fingers.
4. Rinse hands and arms thoroughly under running water.
5. Dry hands and arms completely with a single-use paper towel or warm-air hand dryer.

■ Hands should be washed before starting work. They also must be washed after these activities: using the restroom; handling raw meat, poultry, or seafood; touching the hair, face, or body; sneezing, coughing, or using a tissue; eating, drinking, smoking, or chewing gum or tobacco; handling chemicals that might affect food safety; taking out garbage; clearing tables or busing dirty dishes; touching clothing or aprons; handling money; and touching anything else that may contaminate hands.

■ Personal cleanliness practices include bathing or showering before work, keeping hair clean, wearing clean clothes, removing jewelry from hands and arms, and keeping nails clean.

■ Proper work attire includes always covering hair, wearing clean clothes, removing aprons and storing them in the right place after leaving the prep area, and removing jewelry from hands and arms.

■ Using bare hands to handle ready-to-eat food can increase the risk of contaminating it. Use gloves, tongs, or deli tissue when handling ready-to-eat food.

■ Employees shouldn't work with or around food when they have a sore throat with a fever. They should be prevented from being in the operation when they are vomiting, have diarrhea or jaundice, or have a foodborne illness.

101

Summary

- Remind students to review the following:
  1. Personal behaviors that contaminate food
  2. The steps and timing of proper handwashing
  3. Proper personal cleanliness practices
  4. Proper work attire
  5. Handling ready-to-eat food
  6. When to prevent foodhandlers from working with or around food

Section 2.2 Review Questions

1. Contamination can be caused by improper wound care; touching the face, nose, hair, mouth, or body and then not washing again; touching contaminated clothing, objects or surfaces; and eating, drinking, chewing gum, smoking, or chewing tobacco while working.

2. Properly clean and bandage the wound. If the employee can continue working, the hands should be completely washed again and the employee should wear a clean pair of gloves or a finger cot. If the wound continues to bleed or ooze, the employee should not continue to work with food.

3. Proper handwashing technique includes the following steps:
   - Remove jewelry and watch.
   - Wet hands and arms with hot running water.
   - Apply soap and lather.
   - Scrub hands and arms vigorously for 10 to 15 seconds. Clean between fingers and under fingernails.
   - Rinse hands and arms under hot running water.
   - Dry hands completely with clean single-use towels or an air dryer.

4. Hands should be washed before working in a kitchen. They should also be washed after any of the following:
   - Using the restroom
   - Handling raw meat, poultry, or seafood
   - Touching face, hair, or body
   - Sneezing, coughing, wiping nose, or using a tissue
   - Eating, drinking, chewing gum, smoking, or chewing tobacco
   - Handling unsafe chemicals
   - Handling or removing garbage
   - Clearing or busing tables or dirty dishes
   - Touching aprons or clothing
   - Handling money
   - Touching anything potentially contaminating

5. Student responses will vary. Responses should address the flow of communication and mention accountability.

6. Michael should have been prevented from working with food the day after an illness. If he worked on tasks that didn't involve food or food-contact surfaces, it would not place the operation at risk when he discovers that he is not well yet. However, if he worked with food, it might be necessary to discard the food he has prepared thus far when he discovers that he is not yet better.

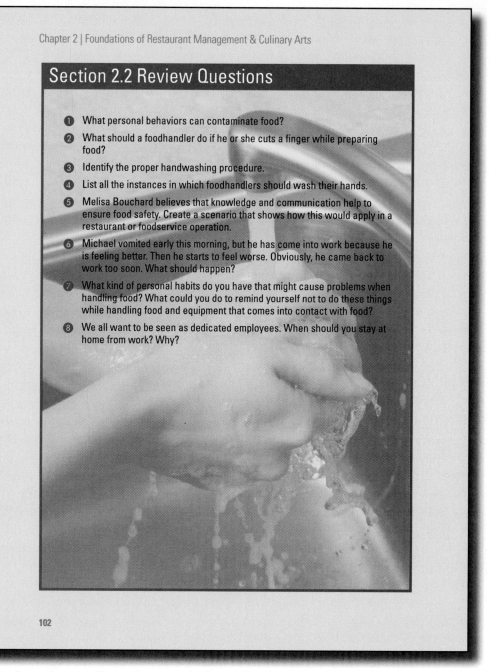

Section 2.2 Review Questions

1. What personal behaviors can contaminate food?
2. What should a foodhandler do if he or she cuts a finger while preparing food?
3. Identify the proper handwashing procedure.
4. List all the instances in which foodhandlers should wash their hands.
5. Melisa Bouchard believes that knowledge and communication help to ensure food safety. Create a scenario that shows how this would apply in a restaurant or foodservice operation.
6. Michael vomited early this morning, but he has come into work because he is feeling better. Then he starts to feel worse. Obviously, he came back to work too soon. What should happen?
7. What kind of personal habits do you have that might cause problems when handling food? What could you do to remind yourself not to do these things while handling food and equipment that comes into contact with food?
8. We all want to be seen as dedicated employees. When should you stay at home from work? Why?

102

7. Student responses will vary. Encourage students to be self-analytical and candid.

8. Any illness that could spread to others is a good reason to call in sick. It is the responsibility of the establishment to have enough personnel to reasonably cover sick leaves and not place the food at risk.

Section 2.2 Activities

1. Study Skills/Group Activity: What's Your Style?

Brainstorm as a group about the balance between personal choice and professional appearance. Assuming you are investing in a restaurant, what type of "look" do you want your employees to portray? Do you foresee any food safety problems with this look? Create an ad for the positions of manager, server, and line cook for your restaurant. Include information on the ambience and environment that you wish to portray.

2. Activity: Hygiene Policy

What are the personal hygiene requirements for foodhandlers in your community? Contact your local health department or other authority to learn more. Develop a poster to share this information with the rest of the class, including the name of the local authority. Based on this information, create a hygiene policy for your restaurant employees.

3. Critical Thinking: What Should I Do?

You are the manager of a local restaurant. One of your employees arrives at work complaining of a stomachache. Today will be a busy day; another staff member is on vacation, and there are already many dinner reservations. What do you do? Write two paragraphs describing your response and why.

103

Section 2.2 Activities

1. Group responses will vary. However, each group should address the current issues of tattoos, piercings, hairstyles, clothing and jewelry hazards, modesty, and other issues.

2. Answers will vary. If the students are to work in local foodservice, they will require a local foodhandler's permit. This activity will help them prepare.

3. Student responses will vary. The answer should address personnel and staffing issues. Allowing for illness of an employee should be part of any personnel management strategy.

Section 2.3
Preventing Hazards in the Flow of Food

Introduce the Section
a. The flow of food begins when an operation buys food.
b. The flow of food ends with the guest being served.
c. There are many steps along the way that involve many people.
d. The safety of the food supply should be guarded at each step.

Vocabulary Review
a. Direct students to the key terms.
b. Pronounce each word, and have the students repeat the pronunciation out loud.
c. Discuss the definition of each word.

Teach

Discuss
- Students can begin to reason with their knowledge of foodservice.
- Students may find it interesting to think about the sources of their own food.
- Students can begin to appreciate the safety of the current food supply in most areas.
- Students might want to verbalize their understanding and appreciation.

Teaching Tips
- The students may consider these concepts to be repetitive of those covered earlier.
- Not only are they worthwhile to review, many are also new.
- Concepts they have already learned are reinforced and seen in a new light.
- Students will be interested to see how so many aspects of commerce and production come together in the flow of food from the source to service.
- Help the students to begin to feel familiar with all the layers of sources and resources.

2.1 Introduction to Food Safety
- What is a foodborne illness?
- Forms of contamination
- Biological contamination
- Chemical contamination
- Physical contamination
- Food defense
- Allergens
- U.S. regulation of food safety

2.2 Good Personal Hygiene
- How foodhandlers can contaminate food
- Personal cleanliness and work attire
- Handwashing
- Bare-hand contact with ready-to-eat food
- Work requirements related to illness

2.3 Preventing Hazards in the Flow of Food
- Cross-contamination
- Time-temperature abuse
- Purchasing
- Receiving
- Storage
- Preparation
- Cooking
- Holding, storing, and reheating
- Serving

2.4 Food Safety Management Systems
- The HACCP plan

2.5 Cleaning and Sanitizing
- How to clean effectively
- Sanitizing
- Developing a cleaning program
- Controlling pests

SECTION 2.3 PREVENTING HAZARDS IN THE FLOW OF FOOD

The flow of food begins well before the food is prepared for service. Responsibility for keeping food safe begins before a finished plate is presented to a customer. The steps that an operation takes to buy, store, prepare, cook, and serve food all pose risks to food safety. Understanding where contamination can happen in these steps and how to prevent it are critical tasks for restaurant and foodservice professionals.

Study Questions

After studying Section 2.3, you should be able to answer the following questions:

- What are the ways to prevent cross-contamination?
- How can time-temperature abuse be prevented?
- What are the different temperature measuring devices and their uses?
- What are the characteristics of an approved food source?
- What are the criteria for accepting or rejecting food during receiving?
- What are the proper procedures for storing food?
- What are the minimum internal temperature requirements for cooking various TCS foods?
- What are the proper procedures for holding, cooling, and reheating TCS food?
- How should food be handled for service?
- What are the proper procedures for preparing and serving food for off-site service?

104

Cross-Contamination

Think about the foodservice kitchens you have seen at school or in restaurants: lots of people and lots of food, all moving quickly. Pathogens can move around just as quickly in an operation. They can be spread from food or unwashed hands to prep areas, equipment, utensils, or other food. The spread of pathogens from one surface or food to another is called **cross-contamination**. It can happen at almost any point in the path that food takes in an operation. This path is known as the **flow of food**. It begins when you buy the food and ends when you serve it, as shown in Figure 2.19.

purchasing   receiving   storing   preparing   cooking   holding   cooling   reheating   serving

Figure 2.19: The flow of food.

When foodhandlers know how and when cross-contamination can happen in the flow of food, then they can prevent it. The most basic way to prevent cross-contamination is to separate raw food and ready-to-eat food. To do this, follow these guidelines:

- Make sure workstations, cutting boards, and utensils are clean and sanitized.

- Do not allow ready-to-eat food to touch surfaces that have come in contact with raw meat, seafood, or poultry.

- If using the same table to prepare many kinds of food, prepare raw meat, seafood, and poultry at a different time than ready-to-eat food. Be sure to clean and sanitize work surfaces and utensils between each product.

Time-Temperature Abuse

Most foodborne illnesses happen because TCS food has been **time-temperature abused**. Food has been time-temperature abused any time it remains at 41°F to 135°F. This is called the **temperature danger zone** because pathogens grow in this range. They grow especially fast in the middle of the range, between 70°F and 125°F.

Food is time-temperature abused any time it is cooked to the wrong internal temperature, held at the wrong temperature, or cooled or reheated incorrectly. Figure 2.20 shows food being measured for the correct temperature.

The longer food stays in the temperature danger zone, the more time pathogens have to grow. To keep food safe, reduce the time it spends in this temperature range. If food is held in this range for four or more hours, throw it out.

105

Homework Activity: Authentic Experience

21st-Century Skills—Health Literacy, Implement Innovations

The students learn about cross-contamination and the flow of food.

These processes provide challenges in the home as well as in foodservice.

Have the students evaluate their home kitchen for the flow of food and for potential cross-contamination problems. Other foodhandling practices that they can observe, good or bad, may be included in this activity as well.

Have the students make a list of possible problems with their home food systems.

The students will determine a workable solution to the problem.

The students implement the solution and report on the results.

Vocabulary Terms

Cross-contamination: The transfer of pathogens from one surface or food to another.

Flow of food: The path food takes in foodservice, usually from purchase to service.

Time-temperature abused: A food item that has been held in the temperature danger zone too long to remain safe.

Temperature danger zone: 41°F to 135°F.

Figure Focus

Figure 2.19: The icons represent the various steps in the flow of food. The nonverbal presentation can help all students, including ESOL students, to identify what is happening.

As the twentieth century advances, fewer and fewer analog round dials are being used. Children born in the late twentieth and early twenty-first centuries may have very limited experience with them.

Digital displays are becoming standard on most instrumentation. However, a round dial can be very accurate, usually through a mechanical or chemical process that may not require electricity.

Have the students list the various round dials they have seen or used.

This list may include clocks, thermometers, speedometers, odometers, bathroom scales, etc.

Discuss together how the dials work and how they are read.

If necessary, create a simple visual with a paper plate and a brad fastener, showing a dial with a needle that can move.

Have the students demonstrate the ability to read a round dial visual aid, clock, thermometer, or other dial device.

Complete the activity by having the students demonstrate the ability to read and interpret a bimetallic stemmed thermometer.

Vocabulary Terms

Calibrate: To standardize the accuracy of a measuring device.

Bimetallic stemmed thermometer: Can check temperatures from 0°F to 220°F. This makes it useful for checking both hot and cold types of food.

Thermocouples: A probe thermometer with a heat-sensitive tip and a digital display which measures heat by variations of voltage passing between two different metals.

Thermistor: A probe thermometer with a heat-sensitive tip and a digital display which measure heat by variations in the flow of current in wire resistors at varying temperatures.

Figure 2.20: Food temperatures must be checked often. Food held in the temperature danger zone will grow pathogens.

Thermometers

The most important tool used to monitor temperature is the thermometer. Three types of thermometers are commonly used in operations—bimetallic-stemmed thermometers, thermocouples, and thermistors. The infrared thermometer, while not as common, is becoming more popular.

All of these tools will be effective only if foodhandlers follow specific guidelines for using them. Tools also have to be adjusted regularly, or **calibrated**, to keep them accurate.

Bimetallic Stemmed Thermometers

A **bimetallic stemmed thermometer** can check temperatures from 0°F to 220°F. This makes it useful for checking both hot and cold types of food. It measures temperature through its metal stem. When checking a temperature, insert the stem into the food up to the dimple, because the sensing area of the thermometer goes from the tip of the stem to the dimple. This trait makes the thermometer particularly useful for checking the temperature of large or thick food. It is usually not practical for thin food such as hamburger patties. Adjust this thermometer by using its calibration nut. Figure 2.21 shows a bimetallic stemmed thermometer.

Figure 2.21: Bimetallic stemmed thermometers are used to check both hot and cold foods.

Thermocouples and Thermistors

Thermocouples and **thermistors** are also common in restaurant and foodservice operations. They measure temperatures through a metal probe and display them digitally. The sensing area on

106

Figure Focus

Figure 2.20: A food thermometer should always be within easy reach. Use it often!

Figure 2.21: Some bimetallic stemmed thermometers have a notch on the probe that indicates how far to submerge the probe in the food item. They are read with a round dial.

Teaching Tips

- It is important when using a bimetallic stemmed thermometer to insert the long probe nearly to the dial.
- It is useful for measuring the temperature of thick cuts of meat.
- Thermocouples and thermistors are easier to use for measuring liquid or soft or thin food items.
- Having a thermometer handy allows food to be checked periodically.
- The probe should be completely clean and sanitized before being used in food.

thermocouples and thermistors is on the tip of the probe. This means they don't have to be inserted into the food as far as bimetallic stemmed thermometers to get a correct reading, making them good for checking the temperature of both thick and thin foods.

Thermocouples and thermistors come in several styles and sizes, with different types of probes. Figure 2.22 shows the types of temperature probes:

- Immersion probes check the temperature of liquids.
- Surface probes check the temperature of flat cooking equipment, such as a griddle.
- Penetration probes are useful for checking the internal temperature of thin food.
- Air probes check the temperature inside refrigerators and ovens.

1) Immersion probe checking the temperature of soup.

3) Penetration probe checking the temperature of a hamburger.

2) Surface probe checking the temperature of a griddle.

4) Air probe checking the temperature of a cooler.

Figure 2.22: The four types of temperature probes.

107

- Why is it important to accurately read a food thermometer?
- Why is it important to accurately measure the temperature of foods?
- Should the temperatures of foods be recorded or noted?
- Why would this be beneficial to a foodservice operation?

Figure Focus
Figure 2.22: The students can learn to read the various thermometers and understand that they are measuring heat. They can also be aware of the units used (Fahrenheit, Celsius).

In-Class Activity: Calibration and Agreement of Thermometers

ICT Literacy

Materials:

A small Rock Cornish Game Hen

An oven

A roasting pan

A bimetallic stemmed thermometer

An immersion probe thermometer

A surface probe thermometer

A penetration probe thermometer

An air probe thermometer

An infrared thermometer

As a class, perform the following tests. Break into groups or perform the tests as a demonstration for the whole class. Students may function as demonstrators. Start the activity at the very beginning of the class period.

Set an oven to 350°F and preheat. When the oven indicates that it has reached temperature, check the temperature agreement with the air thermometer. Also check with the infrared thermometer. Do they all agree?

Using the formula: 1 hour per 1 pound of hen at 350°F, determine the proper cooking time for the hen.

Roast a whole hen to an internal temperature of 165°F. Measure the temperature of the bird with a bimetallic stemmed thermometer (in the breast or leg), a penetration probe thermometer (in the same location on the other side of the chicken), and an immersion probe thermometer (in the cavity). Do they all agree?

The surface of the oven or the surface of the hen can be measured using the surface probe thermometer (keep the surface probe clean) and the infrared thermometer.

Record all findings in a table.

How much agreement is there with the recipe and the time required to cook to 165°F?

Is there variation between the different temperature measuring devices?

Which devices would need to be calibrated?

Vocabulary Terms

Infrared thermometers: A thermometer that measures waves of heat coming from the surface of the food and displays the temperature digitally.

Infrared Thermometers

Infrared thermometers measure the temperatures of food and equipment surfaces. These thermometers are quick and easy to use. Infrared thermometers do not need to touch a surface to check its temperature, so there is less chance for cross-contamination and damage to food. However, these thermometers cannot measure air temperature or the internal temperature of food. Figure 2.23 shows an infrared thermometer.

Figure 2.23: Infrared thermometers measure the temperatures of both food and equipment.

Purchasing

All the food used in a restaurant or foodservice operation should come from approved, reputable suppliers. An approved food supplier is one that has been inspected by appropriate agencies and meets all applicable local, state, and federal laws. Restaurant and foodservice purchasers must make sure that their suppliers use good food safety practices. This applies to all suppliers along the supply chain, whether a local farmer or a large-sized corporation. An operation's supply chain can include growers, shippers, packers, manufacturers, distributors (trucking fleets and warehouses), and/or local markets.

Receiving

To keep food safe during receiving, an operation needs to have enough trained staff available to receive, inspect, and store the food. Deliveries should be carefully

108

Figure Focus

Figure 2.23: The heat waves given off of a surface include infrared radiation, which can be digitally measured and displayed.

Teaching Tips

- Cutting corners in purchasing may be more costly in the long run.
- Be especially careful to only purchase from reputable vendors.
- Make sure that vendors are well-identified and keep careful records.
- Vendors should be resources for information on how to best store and prepare the foods they sell.
- Learn to rely on good vendors with strong local track records.

and immediately inspected and then put away quickly. Follow the guidelines reviewed below when deciding if an item should be accepted or rejected.

Temperatures

Use thermometers to check food temperatures during receiving. Figure 2.24 shows how to check the temperature of various foods.

Deliveries of cold TCS food should be 41°F or lower, unless otherwise specified by the manufacturer. Deliveries of hot TCS food should be 135°F or higher. Frozen food should be frozen. Reject any frozen food that has ice crystals on the product or packaging. (This means the product may have thawed and refrozen.) You should also reject the food if any fluids or frozen liquids appear in the bottom of its case.

Figure 2.24: Checking the temperature of various types of food.

Packaging

The packaging of food and nonfood items should be intact and clean. Reject any items with packaging problems, such as tears, holes, punctures, leaks, dampness, or water stains. You should also reject any items with signs of pest damage or expired use-by dates.

Meat, poultry, and eggs should also have an inspection stamp on their packaging. See Figure 2.25. The stamps prove that the items meet the safety standards of the U.S. Department of Agriculture (USDA) or a state department of agriculture.

109

Teaching Tips

- Receiving and processing deliveries are specific tasks.
- Time must be dedicated to carefully fulfilling these functions.
- Food must be properly stored for safety and quality.
- Improperly stored food causes very expensive waste, and may be dangerous.
- Intake records document the arrival conditions and procedures for receiving food.

Discuss

- Why is it important that deliveries be measured for temperature?
- At what temperatures should foods be delivered? Discuss both hot and cold foods.
- If a TCS food is arriving at a temperature within the danger zone, what should the foodservice operation do with the delivery?
- What aspects of a package should be inspected?
- When should a package be rejected?

Reinforce and Review

- The "sell-by" date is different from the expiration, or "use-by" date.
- A food product will not be fresh after the expiration date.

Figure Focus

Figure 2.24: It is recommended to periodically check the storage temperature of vulnerable food items, not just the preparation or serving temperatures.

- Students may benefit from role-playing the situation of inspecting and refusing a delivery.
- It may help the students to feel empowered to act correctly should the situation arise.

Discuss

- Shellfish must be traceable in case of a toxin or problem.
- Shellfish can be traced back to the date and place they were caught.
- Eggs are cold enough at 45°F. When they are refrigerated, they will drop to 41°F or colder.
- The grade of the egg is different from the inspection.
- The inspection makes sure the eggs are safe and comply with the grading standards.
- Milk and dairy should always be refrigerated at or below 41°F.

Figure 2.25: Checking for inspection stamps is a way to make sure food is coming from an approved source. The inspection stamps for meat and poultry are mandatory.

Inspection and Grading Stamps for Meat	Inspection and Grading Stamps for Poultry
USDA Inspection Stamp	USDA Inspection Stamp

USDA Grading Stamp USDA Grading Stamp

Product Quality

Poor food quality is sometimes a sign of time-temperature abuse. Reject food if it has any of these problems:

- Abnormal color (for example, fresh fish should not have dark spots or discoloration)
- Slimy, sticky, or dry texture
- Soft flesh that leaves an imprint when you touch it
- Abnormal or unpleasant odor (for example, fish that smells like ammonia)

Some products have additional specific guidelines for receiving.

Shellfish

Shellfish can be received either shucked or live. Make sure that raw shucked shellfish are packaged in containers for one-time use only. Containers must be labeled with the packer's name, address, and certification number. Containers one-half gallon (1.9 L) or smaller must have either a "best if used by" or "sell by" date. Containers larger than one-half gallon (1.9 L) must have the date the shellfish were shucked.

110

Figure Focus

Figure 2.25: Grading and passing inspection are not the same thing. Inspections are mandatory, while grading is voluntary for meat, poultry, and eggs.

Live shellfish must be received with shellstock identification tags. These tags must remain attached to the delivery container until all of the shellfish have been used. Employees must write on the tags the date that the last shellfish was sold or served from the container. Operators must keep these tags on file for 90 days from the date written on them. Reject shellfish if they are very muddy, have broken shells, or are dead.

Eggs

Eggs must be clean and unbroken when you receive them. Reject eggs if they do not meet the following guidelines:

- Shell eggs must be received at an air temperature of 45°F or lower.
- Liquid, frozen, and dehydrated egg products must be pasteurized and have a USDA inspection mark.
- Eggs also must meet USDA grade standards. See Figure 2.26.

Milk and Dairy Products

Milk and dairy products must be received at 41°F or lower unless otherwise specified by law. They also must be pasteurized and meet FDA Grade A standards.

Storage

Food can become unsafe if stored improperly. Store all TCS food at 41°F or lower, or at 135°F or higher. Monitor food temperatures regularly.

Label all ready-to-eat TCS food that is prepped in-house if it will be held for longer than 24 hours. The label must include the name of the food and the date by which it should be sold, eaten, or thrown out. Store ready-to-eat TCS food that has been prepped in-house for a maximum of seven days at 41°F or lower. Throw it out after seven days.

Rotate food in storage to use the oldest inventory first. Many operations use the **first-in, first-out (FIFO) method** to rotate refrigerated, frozen, and dry food

Grading and Inspection Stamps for Eggs

USDA Inspection Stamp

USDA Grading Stamp

Figure 2.26: These are grading and inspection stamps for eggs.

Teaching Tips

- First in, first out, or FIFO, is a system of rotation that makes the most economical sense. It uses food efficiently.
- All foods should be evaluated by date and observation for quality and freshness before using.
- Last in, last out, or LILO, is the same system.
- Poor management of food rotation will result in a first in, last out, or FILO system.
- Last in, first out, or LIFO, is the same as FILO, and wastes the food that was stored first.

Figure Focus

Figure 2.26: The U.S. Department of Agriculture has standards for all eggs, meat, and poultry. Fish is under the Department of Commerce.

Discuss

- In a previous activity, the students were to evaluate their home kitchens for safe foodhandling practices.
- They can refine their improvements through what they will learn about cross-contamination.
- Storing raw foods below ready-to-eat foods is a simple strategy to use at home.
- Students who already work in foodservice can make sure that these strategies are implemented where they work.
- Cross-contamination may be avoided by having plenty of high-quality equipment so that there is always something clean to use.
- Cutting boards may be a source of cross-contamination. They must be cared for and cleaned and sanitized correctly.

during storage. Here is one way to use the FIFO method:

1. Identify the food item's use-by or expiration date, which is usually somewhere on the packaging, as shown in Figure 2.27.

2. Store items with the earliest use-by or expiration dates in front of items with later dates.

3. Once shelved, use those items stored in front first.

Figure 2.27: Rotate food using the FIFO method: first-in, first-out.

Preventing Cross-Contamination

Always store food to prevent cross-contamination. Wrap or cover food. Store refrigerated raw meat, poultry, and seafood separately from ready-to-eat food. If raw and ready-to-eat food cannot be stored separately, store ready-to-eat food above raw meat, poultry, and seafood. This will prevent juices from raw food from dripping onto ready-to-eat food.

Store raw meat, poultry, and seafood in coolers in the following top-to-bottom order:

1. Seafood (top)

2. Whole cuts of beef and pork

3. Ground meat and ground fish

4. Whole and ground poultry (bottom)

Figure 2.28: Store food in coolers in the correct top-to-bottom order.

112

Figure Focus

Figure 2.27: This potato salad is clearly labeled. It will be easy to have it in rotation.

Figure 2.28: Do not overfill coolers or freezers. Airflow is needed for the equipment to work.

This order is based on the minimum internal cooking temperature of each food. Meat cooked to higher temperatures is always stored beneath meat cooked to lower temperatures. Figure 2.28 on the previous page shows how to properly store foods in a cooler.

Do not overload coolers or freezers. Storing too many food items prevents good airflow and makes the units work harder to stay cold. Similarly, do not line cooler or freezer shelves with aluminum foil. This blocks the circulation of cold air.

Preparation

Time-temperature abuse can easily happen during preparation. To avoid time-temperature abuse, remove from the refrigerator only as much food as can be prepared in a short period of time. Prepare food in small batches so that ingredients don't sit out for too long in the temperature danger zone.

When thawing food before preparation, it's important to remember that freezing doesn't kill pathogens. When frozen food is thawed and exposed to the temperature danger zone, any pathogens in the food will begin to grow. To reduce this growth, never thaw food at room temperature. Thaw TCS food in one of these ways:

▪ Thaw food in a cooler, at a product temperature of 41°F or lower.

▪ Submerge food under running water at 70°F or lower. Make sure the water is potable—safe to drink.

▪ Thaw food in a microwave oven if it will be cooked immediately after thawing.

▪ Thaw food as part of the cooking process.

Figure 2.29 illustrates the acceptable methods for thawing food.

Refrigerator   Potable running water   Microwave oven   Cooking

Figure 2.29: Acceptable methods for thawing food.

113

Teaching Tips

- Help the students understand that frozen pathogens will not reproduce, but they can again after they thaw.
- Think of always keeping TCS foods out of the danger zone.
- Remind the students that thawing in a microwave will warm the food, perhaps into the danger zone, from the interior to the exterior. It's fine if the food is going to be cooked right away.

CUSTOMIZED INSTRUCTION
Science Connection
More Advanced Students
Research pathogens and freezing.
How can they reproduce after being frozen?
Why are human cells destroyed by freezing?
Why can microbes survive?
Prepare an explanation for the class in three sentences.

Figure Focus
Figure 2.29: There are several safe and reliable ways to thaw frozen foods.

Discuss

- What are the common cooking methods?
- How can temperatures of food items be checked when using these methods?
- What type of thermometer is best for checking the temperature of the inner part of a food item?
- What is the ideal internal temperature reading?

Fast Fact:
Did You Know...?

Sprouts always sound like a healthy alternative.

The sprouts themselves did not cause the health problems, but rather pathogenic microbes present with the sprouts.

Cooking

Cooking food to the correct temperature is critical for keeping it safe. Each type of food has a minimum internal temperature that it must reach. Once food reaches its minimum internal temperature, make sure that it stays at that temperature for a specific amount of time. Figure 2.30 shows the correct way to check temperature.

Table 2.4 identifies the minimum internal temperatures and times for specific types of food.

Operations that primarily serve high-risk populations, such as nursing homes and day-care centers, cannot serve certain items—for example, raw seed sprouts, raw or undercooked eggs (such as over-easy eggs), raw or undercooked meat (such as rare hamburgers), or seafood.

[fast fact]

Did You Know...?
Since 1995, 13 foodborne-illness outbreaks worldwide have been linked to sprouts. These outbreaks sickened 956 people and resulted in one death.

Source: www.healthnews.com

Figure 2.30: To check food temperature correctly: 1) Pick a thermometer with a probe that is the right size for the food. 2) Check the temperature in the thickest part of the food. Take at least two readings in different locations.

114

Figure Focus

Figure 2.30: It is important to take two readings to verify internal temperature throughout the item.

Table 2.4: Cooking Requirements for Specific Types of Food

Minimum Internal Temperature	Type of Food
165°F for 15 seconds	Poultry—including whole or ground chicken, turkey, or duck Stuffing made with TCS ingredients Stuffed meat, seafood, poultry, or pasta Dishes that include previously cooked TCS ingredients (raw ingredients should be cooked to their minimum internal temperatures)
155°F for 15 seconds	Ground meat—including beef, pork, and other meat Injected meat—including brined ham and flavor-injected roasts Ground seafood—including chopped or minced seafood Eggs that will be hot-held for service
145°F for 15 seconds	Seafood—including fish, shellfish, and crustaceans Steaks/chops of pork, beef, veal, and lamb Eggs that will be served immediately
145°F for 4 minutes	Roasts of pork, beef, veal, and lamb
135°F	Commercially processed, ready-to-eat-food that will be hot-held for service (cheese sticks, deep-fried vegetables)
135°F	Fruit, vegetables, grains (rice, pasta, etc.), and legumes (such as beans, refried beans) that will be hot-held for service

[nutrition]

Start the Water Boiling Before You Harvest the Corn!

Careless food-handling can actually decrease the nutrient content of food. Nutrient profiles can be affected by staleness or improper storage. Farm-fresh corn on the cob is one example. The sooner it is cooked and eaten, the higher the sugar content. As the corn ages in transport and storage, sugar converts to starch.

This alters not only the flavor, but also the way a body metabolizes the corn after it is eaten. Sweet-tasting, simple CHO (carbohydrate) molecules are rather quickly cleaved and enter the bloodstream as glucose, raising blood sugar. They are then transported into the cells via insulin. Not-so-sweet starch is a complex CHO, which cleaves more slowly and distributes the glucose to the blood and cells over a longer time frame. The increase in blood sugar is not as dramatic.

Both simple and complex carbohydrates definitely play a role in healthy eating, and you need some of both. Too many simple CHOs are bad, of course. But that doesn't mean you want to eat bland, starchy corn instead of fresh, sweet corn. Get simple CHOs through yummy high-fiber corn, rather than through something with fewer additional nutritional benefits.

115

Nutrition:
Start the Water Boiling Before You Harvest the Corn

Careful foodhandling, fresh foods, and informed decisions help consumers choose a nutritious diet.

The example of corn is only one of many.

Table 2.4:
Cooking Requirements for Specific Types of Food

- This table specifies the internal temperature a food should achieve during cooking. It also specifies the time required at the temperature to ensure the safety of the item. Please note the length of time for cooking poultry, ground meat, and seafood. Now note the time required for roasts of pork, beef, veal, and lamb.

Teaching Tips

- Perhaps the students realize that in a foodservice operation, discarding food is very expensive.
- Loss of inventory with no chance to make a sale loses money in two ways.
- Help the students discuss the costs of lost food due to improper temperature handling.
- The food has already been purchased, delivered, received, stored, and prepared.
- How much has this cost the operation?
- Now the food must be discarded and cannot be sold.
- This is another loss of revenue.
- The students can realize that mismanagement of time and temperature is costly.
- If food is sold anyway, customers might become ill.
- Ask the students how this might impact the revenues of the restaurant.

Essential Skills:
Holding Foods

This information should be committed to memory by each student.

Each student should be able to say the danger zone temperatures and time frames.

Each student should be aware of the handling rules for TCS foods.

In-Class Activity:
TCS Mnemonics

21st-Century Skills—Creativity and Innovation, Communication and Collaboration

Working in pairs or teams, have the students develop mnemonic devices (memory clues) to help them recite the information in the Essential Skills box.

These can include acronyms, poems, songs, skits, picture clues, nonverbal cues, or anything that will assist.

Have the students present their work to one another in class.

Holding, Cooling, and Reheating

If foodhandlers aren't serving cooked food immediately, they must keep it out of the temperature danger zone. This means cooling the food quickly, reheating it correctly, and/or holding it correctly.

Holding

To hold TCS food safely, hold hot food at 135°F or higher and hold cold food at 41°F or lower. Be sure to check temperatures at least every four hours. Throw out any food that's in the temperature danger zone. Figure 2.31 shows the proper way to hold hot food.

Essential Skills
Holding Foods

- Hold hot food at 135°F or higher.
- Hold cold food at 41°F or lower.
- Check temperatures at least every four hours. Throw out any food that's in the temperature danger zone.
- Do not use hot-holding equipment to reheat food if it is not designed to do so.

Figure 2.31: Hold hot food at 135°F or higher.

Figure Focus
Figure 2.31: Hot TCS foods must be held hot, and cold TCS foods must be held cold. Whether the refrigerator is an enormous warehouse or a small cooler, the temperature must remain below 41°F for cold TCS foods.

[what's new]

Infrared Technology

Infrared is a frequency of radiation waves of the electromagnetic spectrum, and **radiation** is simply the transfer of energy without physical contact. Infrared is just beyond the wavelength of the visible color red. This means that the waves are always all around you, whether you can detect them or not. Infrared waves play a role in culinary technology. One example is the culinary laser thermometer that uses infrared technology to quickly measure the surface temperature of hot pans.

The transfer of heat from something hot to something cold is really the flow of energy from a source of high energy to a lower energy material. When ice melts, waves of energy bombard the surface of the ice and cause the water molecules to move faster, which makes them liquid again. Temperature is really just molecular speed. When hot food is quickly cooled for storage, the hot food is actually transferring energy in the form of heat away from the product to something else (like a cooling paddle). You don't add cold, you remove heat. Thanks to radiation, materials do not have to be touching to transfer heat.

Figure 2.32 shows dishes under an infrared light, waiting to be served.

Figure 2.32: The chef is holding food under an infrared light until it is served.

Cooling

Remember, pathogens grow well in the temperature danger zone. And they grow much faster at temperatures between 125°F and 70°F.

Cool TCS food from 135°F to 41°F or lower within six hours. First, cool food from 135°F to 70°F within two hours. Then cool it to 41°F or lower in the next four hours. Figure 2.33 explains how to properly cool TCS foods.

117

Perhaps the students can think of examples of radiation in their world. These might include microwave ovens, radios, satellite transmissions, cell phones, sunburns, and all the light and colors they see.

Even though radios are an example of radiation, sound waves are not part of the electromagnetic spectrum. Please help the students to avoid this common misconception.

Discuss

- Ask the students why 70°F up to 125°F would be a range for fast growth of pathogens.
- What is the temperature of the human body?
- It might interest the students to realize that pathogens are adapted to certain temperature zones.
- Ask the students how an item would be cooled quickly, within two hours.
- Do the students think that hot foods should be placed directly into the refrigerator?
- What have they learned about heat transfer?

Figure Focus

Figure 2.32: The infrared light is sending waves of energy into the food to keep it hot. Also in this photo are light tubes in the hood, and in the back a microwave oven with the door open. These also use electromagnetic radiation to transfer energy.

Teaching Tips

- Foods can be reheated and then recooled, if necessary, to salvage the inventory.
- If foods do not cool quite quickly enough, this may be a safe and necessary strategy.
- Food that may have been destroyed by microbial growth (such as a yeast bloom) cannot be "fixed" by reheating.
- The quality of the food should be carefully evaluated before using the reheating strategy.
- The food should be properly and completely cooled with the second try.
- The quality of the food item should be carefully evaluated after reheating to see if it has lost flavor, texture, or appearance.

Discuss

- Reheating from chilled is another skill that requires time and equipment.
- The proper strategy for this step may be noted on the recipe.

Table 2.5:
Cooling Food Quickly and Safely

- These are recommended techniques for careful and safe cooling of foods.
- The cooling time, method, and equipment required may be noted on the recipe.
- Plan adequate time and personnel for this step.

First, cool food from 135°F to 70°F within two hours.

2 hours

Then cool it to 41°F or lower in the next four hours.

4 hours

Figure 2.33: Cool TCS foods from 135°F to 41°F or lower within six hours.

If food hasn't reached 70°F within two hours, it must be either thrown out or reheated and then cooled again. Table 2.5 outlines how to cool food quickly and safely.

Table 2.5: Cooling Food Quickly and Safely	
	Reduce the size of food into smaller amounts by either cutting large food items into smaller pieces or dividing large containers of food into smaller containers or shallow containers.
	Place small containers into a prep sink or a large pot filled with ice water. This is called an ice-water bath. Stir the food frequently to cool it faster and more evenly.
	Use ice paddles to stir food. Ice paddles are plastic paddles that can be filled with ice or with water and then frozen. Food stirred with these paddles cools quickly.

Reheating

If foodhandlers plan to reheat leftover or previously prepared TCS food so that it can be held for service, they must heat the food to an internal temperature of 165°F. The food needs to go from storage temperature to 165°F within two hours and then stay at that temperature for 15 seconds. If it doesn't reach this temperature, throw the food out.

If the food is going to be reheated for immediate service, just reheat it to an appropriate serving temperature.

118

Figure Focus

Figure 2.33: Cooling involves two phases. The first phase is essential for safe cooling. If it isn't completed properly, the food must either be thrown out or reheated and then cooled again.

Did You Know...?
Doggy bags are containers of food that are left over from a meal that the customer has chosen to take home. Most of the time, the food is taken away while it is in the temperature danger zone, where bacteria that causes foodborne illnesses grows well. To minimize risk of foodborne illness, restaurant staff should transfer the food (leftovers) into a new, unused, food-grade container, and they should remind the customer to store the food according to food safety guidelines.

Serving

The biggest threat to food that is ready to be served is contamination. Kitchen and service employees must know how to serve food in ways that keep it safe.

The kitchen staff must follow the guidelines below:

- Handle ready-to-eat food with tongs, deli sheets, or gloves.

- Use separate utensils for each food item. Clean and sanitize them after each serving task.

- Store serving utensils in the food with the handle extended above the rim of the container, to prevent anyone accidentally touching the food while they try to retrieve the utensil, which might contaminate the food. Alternatively, place utensils on a clean and sanitized food-contact surface.

The service staff needs to be just as careful as the kitchen staff. They can contaminate food by handling the food-contact areas of glasses, utensils, and dishes. Figure 2.34 shows guidelines for service staff when serving food.

Off-Site Foodservice

Any delay between preparation and service increases the threat to food safety. Food that will be served off-site has a greater risk of time-temperature abuse and contamination. Figure 2.35 shows an example of an insulated food container that keeps food at the proper temperature during holding, transporting, and catering.

There are specific procedures to keep food for off-site service safe:

- Pack food in insulated food containers that can keep food out of the temperature danger zone. Use only food-grade containers that won't mix, leak, or spill food.

- Check internal food temperatures regularly.

- Clean the inside of delivery vehicles regularly.

119

Fast Fact: Did You Know...?

A "doggy bag" used to be a little paper bag for leftover bones that actually would be given to a dog.

Currently, the menu items a customer has purchased but not finished may be packaged for the customer to enjoy at home later.

The food should be packaged for refrigeration and, if hot, for reheating in a microwave.

Wait staff should mention the temperature recommendations to the customer, or have them printed and included with the leftovers. These could be printed on the guest check.

Teaching Tips

- Students probably realize that food served in restaurants in the United States is usually safe.
- Contamination is a potential problem.
- Help the students to realize that potential problems are problems that can be completely avoided and never happen.
- Assure the students that safe practices avoid problems.

In-Class Activity: Practice with Tongs

Have students pick up various items of various shapes and sizes.

Discuss

- Ask the students to list the various circumstances where food might be served off-site.
- Have the students discuss the demands of a catering operation for food safety.
- Are any of the students planning a career in off-site catering?

Hold dishes by the bottom or edge.

Hold glasses by the middle, bottom, or stem.

Do **NOT** touch the food-contact areas of dishes or glassware.

Carry glasses in a rack or on a tray to avoid touching the food-contact surfaces.

Stacking china and glassware can cause them to chip and break.

Do **NOT** stack glasses when carrying them.

Hold flatware by the handle.

Store flatware so servers grasp handles, not food-contact surfaces.

Do **NOT** hold flatware by food-contact surfaces.

Minimize bare-hand contact with food that is ready to eat.

Use ice scoops or tongs to get ice.

NEVER scoop ice with your bare hands or a glass. A glass may chip or break.

Figure 2.34: Service staff should use these guidelines when serving food.

120

Figure Focus

Figure 2.34: Students can identify the differences between the correct and incorrect method photos. They can practice the various strategies. Even small maneuvers should be practiced.

Figure 2.35: Food should be held and transported at the proper temperature using insulated equipment.

Summary

In this section, you learned the following:

- Cross-contamination can be prevented by making sure workstations, cutting boards, and utensils are clean and sanitized; not allowing ready-to-eat food to touch surfaces that have come in contact with raw meat, seafood, or poultry; preparing different kinds of foods at different times; and cleaning and sanitizing work surfaces and utensils between each product.

- To prevent time-temperature abuse, minimize the amount of time that food spends in the temperature danger zone.

- Three types of thermometers commonly used in operations are bimetallic stemmed thermometers, thermocouples, and thermistors. In addition, infrared thermometers use infrared technology to produce accurate external temperature readings of food and equipment surfaces.

- An approved food source (supplier) is one that has been inspected and meets all applicable local, state, and federal laws.

121

Summary

- Remind students to review the following:
  1. Preventing cross-contamination
  2. Preventing time-temperature abuse
  3. The different temperature measuring devices and their uses
  4. The characteristics of an approved food source

Figure Focus

Figure 2.35: An investment in proper equipment is important for off-site service.

Summary (cont.)

5. The criteria of accepting or rejecting food during receiving
6. Proper procedures for storing food
7. Minimum internal temperature requirements for cooking various TCS foods
8. Proper procedures for holding, cooling, and reheating TCS foods
9. Handling food for service
10. Proper procedures for preparing and serving food for off-site service

- The criteria for accepting or rejecting food during receiving are as follows:
  - **Temperature:** Cold TCS should be 41°F or lower, hot TCS should be 135°F or higher, and frozen food should be frozen. Reject any frozen food that has ice crystals on the product or packaging or if any fluids or frozen liquids appear in the bottom of its case.
  - **Packaging:** For both food and nonfood items, packaging should be intact and clean. Reject any item that has a package with tears, holes, punctures, leaks, dampness, water stains, signs of pest damage, or an expired use-by date.
  - **Product quality:** Reject any food that has an abnormal color, slimy or sticky texture, soft flesh that leaves an imprint when you touch it, or abnormal or unpleasant odor.
  - **Shellfish:** Raw, shucked shellfish are packaged in containers for one-time use only. Containers must be labeled with the packer's name, address, and certification number. Live shellfish must be received with identification tags. Employees must write on the tags the date that the last shellfish was sold or served from the container, and keep the tags as records. Reject shellfish if they are muddy, have broken shells, or are dead.
  - **Eggs:** Shell eggs must be clean and unbroken. Reject shell eggs received at an air temperature higher than 45°F.
  - **Milk and dairy products:** These products must be received at 41°F or lower unless otherwise specified. They must be pasteurized and meet FDA Grade A standards.

- All TCS foods must be stored at 41°F or lower or at 135°F or higher. Label all ready-to-eat TCS food prepped in-house that will be held for more than 24 hours. These foods can be stored in-house for a maximum of seven days at 41°F or lower. Rotate food to use the oldest inventory first, and wrap or cover food. Refrigerate raw meat, poultry, and seafood separately from ready-to-eat food. Store raw meat, poultry, and seafood in coolers in the following top-to-bottom order: seafood on top, then whole cuts of beef and pork, then ground meat and ground fish, and at the bottom, whole and ground poultry.

- The following are minimum internal temperature requirements for cooking TCS foods:
  - **165°F for 15 seconds:** Poultry, stuffing made with TCS ingredients, stuffed meat/seafood/poultry/pasta, dishes that include previously cooked TCS ingredients
  - **155°F for 15 seconds:** Ground meat, injected meat, ground seafood, eggs that will be hot-held for service

122

- **145°F for 15 seconds:** Seafood, including fish, shellfish, and crustaceans; steaks/chops of pork, veal, and lamb; eggs that will be served immediately

- **145°F for 4 minutes:** Roasts of pork, beef, veal, and lamb

- **135°F:** Commercially processed ready-to-eat food that will be hot-held for service; fruits, vegetables, grains, and legumes that will be hot-held for service

■ Hold hot TCS food at 135°F or higher, and hold cold TCS food at 41°F or lower. Cool TCS food from 135°F to 41°F or lower within six hours—135°F to 70°F within the first two hours, and then to 41°F or lower in the next four hours.

■ Reheat TCS food for hot-holding by heating it from storage temperature to an internal temperature of 165°F in less than two hours. Then make sure that the food stays at that temperature for 15 seconds.

■ Kitchen staff should handle ready-to-eat food with tongs, deli sheets, or gloves; use separate utensils for each item; clean and sanitize after each serving task; and store serving utensils in the food with the handle extended above the rim of the container. The service staff should hold dishes by the bottom or edge; hold glasses by the middle, bottom, or stem; carry glasses in a rack or on a tray; hold flatware by the handle; store flatware so servers grasp handles; minimize bare-hand contact with ready-to-eat food; and use ice scoops or tongs to get ice.

■ Food prepared and served off-site must be packed in insulated food containers and checked for internal food temperature regularly. The vehicle used to transport food must be clean.

123

Section 2.3
Review Questions

1. The oldest product rotates to the front and is used before newer product. This keeps the storage fresh and in motion so nothing is neglected in the back until it is too old to use and wasted.

2. a. 145°F b. 135°F c. 145°F d. 155°F e. 165°F

3. Divide food into smaller containers for refrigeration. Use frozen cooling paddles. Cool the entire container in an ice-water bath.

4. Several types of thermometers were discussed in this section. Bimetallic stemmed thermometers are used to test the temperatures of thick foods, like meats. Thermocouples and thermistors have stems that must be pushed into foods in order to get a reading. They can be used on thin or thick foods. Infrared thermometers are used to measure the surface temperatures of foods or equipment.

5. She cooks to proper temperatures, works to avoid cross-contamination, and holds the finished product at the proper temperature.

6. There were many things Brian overlooked or mishandled, including:
   - Raw chicken and carrots on the same cutting board
   - Wipes hands on apron without rewashing
   - Fresh tomatoes and lettuce into dry storage
   - Refrigerator too full
   - Doesn't rewash hands
   - Shrimp show ice crystals and should have been refused for improper freezing
   - Ignored evidence of problems with the tomatoes and lettuce freshness/ripeness

7. Student responses will vary. They might include having a power generator or propane backup, emergency procedures for maintaining food temperatures, and time frames for various equipment, such as refrigerators without power.

8. Cutting boards, utensils, and equipment may cause cross-contamination if not properly used or cleaned between uses.

Section 2.3 Review Questions

1. Explain the FIFO method of stock rotation.

2. What is the minimum internal temperature for the following foods?
   a. Veal
   b. Rice that will be hot-held for service
   c. Seafood
   d. Ground meat
   e. Poultry

3. Describe the process for cooling food quickly and safely. Identify ways you can help to cool food more quickly.

4. Compare the different types of thermometers used to measure the temperature of food.

5. What factors are most important to Melisa Bouchard as she works to improve safety in the flow of food?

6. At the Uptown Grille, Brian received the order from FoodCorp International. As he stored the food, what should he have checked? Did you notice any "red flags"?

7. What would happen if there were a major power outage in your area? Could this be a threat to a restaurant or foodservice operation? How? What could be done to protect the operation?

8. Where in the flow of food do you think cross-contamination is most likely to occur? Why?

124

Section 2.3 Activities

1. Study Skills/Group Activity: Safeguarding the Flow of Food

As a group, brainstorm three types of off-site foodservice—for example, catering an event at a banquet hall versus catering a beachside clambake versus catering a summer luncheon in a garden. For each type/site, what steps would you have to take to keep food safe?

2. Activity: The Flow of Protein

Select a protein, such as meat or eggs, and diagram its flow through a kitchen. Where do you think the risks to the proteins' safety are? How would you prevent the protein from becoming contaminated?

3. Critical Thinking: Storing Food

You are responsible for receiving food at the restaurant where you work. One supplier brings you a large order consisting of fresh vegetables; whole, fresh chickens; sacks of flour; and live oysters. How do you properly receive and store these items? Describe your actions.

125

Section 2.3 Activities

1. Group ideas will vary. Make sure each allows for adequate and proper temperature controls, time controls, and sanitation in the setting.

2. Student responses will vary depending upon the kitchen the students choose. The classroom kitchen might be a good place to start. Pay special attention to the storing and handling of the protein when it is raw. The internal cooking temperature should be noted. Also, any and all holding procedures should keep protein out of the temperature danger zone for that specific protein.

3. First, tend to the oysters and chicken. Immediately refrigerate the chicken properly. The oysters must have the paperwork completed properly for record keeping. Then process the fresh vegetables for safe and optimal storage. Finally, the flour must be stored in a FIFO system that is safe from insects or rodents.

Section 2.4
Food Safety Management Systems

Introduce the Section

a. This section teaches HACCP, which is an integral management tool and strategy for all foodservice operations.

b. HACCP principles are sound operations and process analyses.

Vocabulary Review

a. Direct students to the key terms.

b. Pronounce each word, and have the students repeat the pronunciation out loud.

c. Discuss the definition of each word.

Teach

Discuss

- Sometimes problems only show up after they have happened and the bad consequences have begun.
- HACCP is a system of analyzing a process for potential problems so that they can be avoided before they occur.
- A HACCP "way of thinking" can be beneficial in foodservice, and in any area of life.

Vocabulary Terms

- **Food safety management system:** Formal procedures an operation uses to ensure safe food-handling.
- **HACCP or hazard analysis critical control point:** Pronounced "HA-sip," a widely used food safety management system that includes identification of areas where problems could occur and strategies to decrease or eliminate risks.

2.1 Introduction to Food Safety	2.2 Good Personal Hygiene	2.3 Preventing Hazards in the Flow of Food	2.4 Food Safety Management Systems	2.5 Cleaning and Sanitizing
• What is a foodborne illness? • Forms of contamination • Biological contamination • Chemical contamination • Physical contamination • Food defense • Allergens • U.S. regulation of food safety	• How foodhandlers can contaminate food • Personal cleanliness and work attire • Handwashing • Bare-hand contact with ready-to-eat food • Work requirements related to illness	• Cross-contamination • Time-temperature abuse • Purchasing • Receiving • Storage • Preparation • Cooking • Holding, storing, and reheating • Serving	• The HACCP plan	• How to clean effectively • Sanitizing • Developing a cleaning program • Controlling pests

SECTION 2.4 FOOD SAFETY MANAGEMENT SYSTEMS

In the earlier sections, you learned how to handle food safely throughout the flow of food. The next step in preventing foodborne illness is the development of a food safety management system. One such system is a Hazard Analysis Critical Control Point system, or HACCP.

Study Questions

After studying Section 2.4, you should be able to answer the following questions:

- What are the HACCP principles?
- Why are the HACCP principles important?

The HACCP Plan

One of the best ways for restaurant and foodservice managers to prevent foodborne illness is to develop and follow a food safety management system. A **food safety management system** is a group of procedures and practices that work together to prevent foodborne illness. Combined, these procedures and practices control risks and hazards throughout the flow of food in an operation.

A **Hazard Analysis Critical Control Point,** or **HACCP** (HASS-ip), system is an example of a food safety management system. HACCP identifies major hazards at specific points within a food's flow through the operation. The idea is that if managers can figure out where a biological, chemical, or physical hazard might happen, then they can prevent, eliminate, or reduce it.

126

An effective HACCP system is based upon a written plan that considers an operation's menu, customers, equipment, processes, and operations. Because there are so many variables, each HACCP plan is unique. A plan that works for one operation might not work for another.

HACCP Principles

A HACCP plan is based on seven basic principles. Each HACCP principle builds on the information gained from the previous principle. Consider all seven principles, in order, when developing a plan:

1. Conduct a hazard analysis.
2. Determine critical control points (CCPs).
3. Establish critical limits.
4. Establish monitoring procedures.
5. Identify corrective actions.
6. Verify that the system works.
7. Establish procedures for record keeping and documentation.

In general terms, the principles break into three groups:

- Principles 1 and 2 help identify and evaluate hazards.
- Principles 3, 4, and 5 help establish ways for controlling those hazards.
- Principles 6 and 7 help maintain the HACCP plan and system, and verify its effectiveness.

Principle 1: Conduct a Hazard Analysis

First, look for the potential hazards in the food an operation serves. These hazards might be physical, chemical, or biological.

A good place to begin looking for hazards is to see how food on the menu is processed in the operation. Many types of food are processed in similar ways. For example, both salads and cold sandwiches are usually prepared and served without any cooking. Next, identify any TCS food in these items. Then determine where any food safety hazards are most likely to happen for each TCS food. Figure 2.36 on page 129 shows Principles 1, 2, and 3 in action.

Principle in Action

The management team at Enrico's Italian Restaurant decides to create a HACCP program. They begin by analyzing their hazards.

127

Teaching Tips
- HACCP plans are written and may be viewed by management, employees, inspectors, etc.
- Each foodservice operation has a unique HACCP plan because each site and menu is different.
- The HACCP principles are briefly outlined here, but are addressed in depth in the text of the section.

Discuss
- Why do you think that HACCP and safety procedures are written down?
- Why might records need to be kept?
- Isn't common sense good enough?

Reinforce and Review
- Each aspect will be addressed in depth. If the students don't fully grasp a phrase, such as "critical control points," they will be able to after reading the text.

Teaching Tips
- A hazard analysis requires broad perspective.
- It also requires knowing the starting point and the desired outcome.
- The students may require help seeing the beginning, the intermediate steps, and the outcome.
- Each hazard analysis must be definable.

In-Class Activity: Personalized HACCP

21st-Century Skills—Life and Career Skills

Perform a HACCP inspection of an aspect of home or student life, such as grade performance in a class.

Implement all of the steps.

Identify the critical control points where things could go wrong.

Consider remedies and corrective actions.

Monitor the progress of the improvements.

Reevaluate by HACCP one month later.

Teaching Tips

- Help the students understand the "Principle In Action" examples.
- Perhaps the students can think of some real-life experiences or examples.
- Can HACCP be instituted in this classroom?
- Can the students develop a HACCP plan for the classroom?
- The classroom plan may be limited to one menu or one recipe for the purposes of this lesson.

The team members note that many of the ingredients for their dishes are received, stored, prepared, cooked, and served the same day. The most popular of these items is the spicy charbroiled chicken breast.

The team determines that bacteria are the most likely hazard for food prepared this way.

Principle 2: Determine Critical Control Points (CCPs)

Find the points in the process where the identified hazard(s) can be prevented, eliminated, or reduced to safe levels. These are the **critical control points (CCPs).** Depending on the menu item, there may be more than one CCP.

Principle in Action

Enrico's management identifies cooking as the CCP for food that is prepared and cooked for immediate service. This includes the chicken breasts.

These food items must be handled safely throughout the flow of food. However, proper cooking is the only step that will eliminate or reduce bacteria to safe levels.

Because the chicken breasts are prepared for immediate service, cooking was the only CCP identified.

Principle 3: Establish Critical Limits

For each CCP you have identified, determine its critical limit. A critical limit is a requirement, such as a temperature requirement, that must be met to prevent, eliminate, or reduce a hazard. Make sure a critical limit is very specific and clearly written. Ideally, the limit should state a requirement and a preferred method for achieving that requirement. Figure 2.37 on page 130 illustrates Principles 4, 5, and 6.

Principle in Action

A critical limit is needed for the cooking CCP for the chicken breasts. Management decides that the critical limit will be cooking the chicken to a minimum internal temperature of 165°F for 15 seconds.

Team members determine that the critical limit can be met by cooking the chicken breasts in the broiler for 16 minutes.

Principle 4: Establish Monitoring Procedures

Determine the best way for your operation to check to make sure critical limits are being met. Make sure the limits are consistently met. Identify who will monitor them and how often.

128

Purchasing $

Receiving — Storing

Preparing

Chicken's Flow of Food — Cooking

Serving

16 minutes

Figure 2.36: Enrico's managers put HACCP principles in action by 1) analyzing their menu; 2) identifying the critical control point for their popular chicken sandwich; and then 3) establishing the critical limit for the CCP.

129

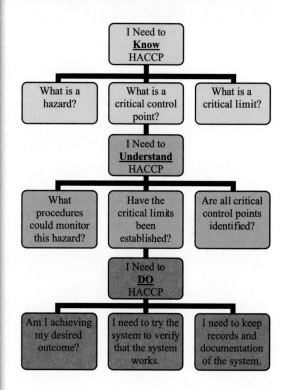

Figure Focus

Figure 2.36: The illustration shows the following principles:

1. **Conducting a hazard analysis:** The menu is being evaluated for a potential hazard, which is a chicken dish. Chicken is a TCS food that can become contaminated with bacteria if mishandled.

2. **Determining critical control points:** The chicken must be cooked in a way that keeps it out of the danger zone and cooks it to an adequate internal temperature. The other aspects of food flow are important, but cooking is the critical one for eliminating a hazard from bacteria.

3. **Establishing critical limits:** This chicken dish must be cooked at least 16 minutes in this establishment for the internal temperature to be adequate for safety.

Invite a chef or foodservice manager from a local establishment (even the school cafeteria) to visit the class.

Have this professional discuss the real-world application of HACCP principles in the workplace.

Invite the students to write questions for the guest to answer concerning HACCP.

Figure 2.37: Enrico's managers then decided that 4) grill cooks would check the temperature of each chicken after cooking; 5) that the grill cook would continue to cook the chicken if it didn't meet the right temperature; and that 6) managers would check the temperature logs that grill cooks complete to make sure the system was working.

Principle in Action

At Enrico's, each chicken breast is cooked to order. So the team decides to check the critical limit by inserting a clean and sanitized thermocouple probe into the thickest part of each chicken breast.

The grill cook must check the temperature of every chicken breast after cooking. Each chicken breast must reach the minimum internal temperature of 165°F for 15 seconds.

Principle 5: Identify Corrective Actions

What do you do if a critical limit hasn't been met? You must take a **corrective action**, a step to fix the problem. Corrective actions should be determined in advance so everyone knows what to do when critical limits aren't met.

130

Figure Focus
Figure 2.37

1. A way to evaluate the critical control point is chosen. In this case, a thermometer will measure the internal temperature of the chicken after the 16 minutes of cooking.

2. The employee has a corrective action identified. If the chicken is not hot enough, the chicken must cook longer until it is hot enough.

3. The employee has recorded the temperature reading and the corrective action taken in the log. This will help the manager see if there is a pattern, which might reveal another critical control point.

Principle in Action

If the chicken breast hasn't reached its critical limit within the 16-minute cook time, then the grill cook at Enrico's must keep cooking the chicken breast until it has reached it for the required 15 seconds.

This and all other corrective actions are noted in the temperature log.

Principle 6: Verify That the System Works

Determine if the plan is working as intended. Evaluate it on a regular basis. Good record keeping will help you to identify patterns. Use your monitoring charts, records, and hazard analysis to determine if your plan prevents, reduces, or eliminates identified hazards.

Principle in Action

Enrico's management team performs HACCP checks once per shift. They make sure that critical limits have been met and that appropriate corrective actions have been taken when needed.

They also check the temperature logs on a weekly basis to identify patterns. This helps to determine if processes or procedures need to be changed. For example, over several weeks they notice problems toward the end of each week. The chicken breasts often fail to meet the critical limit. Appropriate corrective action is being taken.

Management discovered that Enrico's receives chicken shipments from a different supplier on Thursdays. This supplier provides a 6-ounce chicken breast. Enrico's chicken specifications list a 4-ounce chicken breast. Management works with the supplier to make sure they receive 4-ounce breasts. The receiving procedures are changed to include a weight check.

Principle 7: Establish Procedures for Record Keeping and Documentation

Maintain the HACCP plan and keep all documentation created when developing it. Keep records for the following actions:

- Monitoring activities
- Taking corrective action
- Validating equipment (such as records of inspections or repairs)
- Working with suppliers (such as invoices and purchase specifications)

131

- Help the students to see the flow of HACCP from beginning to end.
- The students may realize that this is a very logical, common-sense process.
- Perhaps some of the students may think it is overstated. For example, do they really need to be told in writing to cook the chicken longer if it is not hot enough?
- Explain to the students the liability protections that come from complete procedure guidelines and record keeping.
- The health inspector may ask to review HACCP records during a visit.
- The success or failure of an establishment may rest upon proper HACCP records.

Summary

- Remind students to review the following:
  1. HACCP principles
  2. Why HACCP principles are important

Principle in Action

Enrico's management team determines that time-temperature logs should be kept for three months. Receiving invoices will be kept for 60 days. The team uses this documentation to support and revise the HACCP plan.

[fast fact]

Did You Know...?
The Center for Food Safety and Applied Nutrition (CFSAN) is one of six centers within the Food and Drug Administration (FDA). Its major responsibility is to ensure that food is safe, nutritious and wholesome. The Center regulates approximately $240 billion worth of domestic food and $15 billion worth of imported foods.

Summary

In this section, you learned the following:

- The HACCP principles are as follows:
  - Principle 1: Conduct a hazard analysis
  - Principle 2: Determine critical control points (CCPs)
  - Principle 3: Establish critical limits
  - Principle 4: Establish monitoring procedures
  - Principle 5: Identify corrective action
  - Principle 6: Establish verification procedures
  - Principle 7: Establish procedures for record keeping and documentation
- A HACCP system is important because it focuses on identifying specific points within a food item's flow through the operation that are essential to prevent, eliminate, or reduce hazards to safe levels.

Section 2.4 Review Questions

❶ Describe what happens in each of the seven principles of a HACCP system.

❷ What is a critical control point (CCP)?

❸ What is the purpose of a food safety management system?

❹ What is a critical limit?

❺ What might Melisa Bouchard do to ensure that all employees understand the importance of a HACCP system?

❻ Linda and Chef Jean need to update their HACCP system. They are adding a new menu item, Texas Chili. Identify the hazards for this dish, and then determine the CCP(s), critical limits, and monitoring procedures that the staff should use to keep the chili safe.

❼ Suppose you are in a restaurant or foodservice organization with a higher-than-average turnover in the kitchen. How would you ensure adequate monitoring procedures and corrective actions?

133

Section 2.4
Review Questions

1. The HACCP principles are valuable to all students in all areas of life, not just foodservice. They will benefit from thoroughly learning this process.

   Principle 1: Conduct a hazard analysis. What are the risks? What could go wrong in this particular situation?

   Principle 2: Determine critical control points. If something could go wrong, where and how would this happen? What are the specific risks?

2. Critical control points are the aspects of any process that could create a problem if improperly handled.

3. A food safety management system verifies, quantifies, justifies, and communicates the procedures and practices that keep guests safe.

4. A critical limit is a parameter for safety.

5. Ms. Bouchard can correlate the activities and training of the front-of-the-house staff and the back-of-the-house staff to all understand and comply with the same programs for the safety of the guests and the establishment.

6. They need to analyze the recipe from food receiving to table service. They need to address the safety precautions required for every single ingredient and process involved in the menu item. They also need to coordinate this menu item with the food safety procedures of the other menu items and of the kitchen as a whole. This would begin by conducting a complete hazard analysis and identifying the critical control points for this particular item. It would progress from there.

7. Each student will have different answers, but should include something about training, HACCP training, record keeping and accountability, monitoring, etc.

Section 2.4 Activities

1. Each group will develop a slightly different system. Each group should address:
   - Handling the raw chicken
   - Preventing cross-contamination
   - Cooking the soup at the correct temperature
   - Holding the soup at the correct temperature
   - Properly cooling the soup in the shortest possible amount of time
   - Storing the soup under proper refrigeration
   - Reheating the soup quickly enough for safety
   - Reaching and maintaining a safe temperature when reheating

2. Each student will have a different report. They could compare commonalities in class, and critique their findings.

3. The students will come up with various ideas. All procedures for preventing foodborne illness should address:
   - Receiving and storage
   - Personal hygiene
   - Cross-contamination risks
   - Time-temperature controls
   - HACCP

Section 2.4 Activities

1. Study Skills/Group Activity: Develop a HACCP Plan

In a group, develop a HACCP system for chicken noodle soup that will be cooked, held, cooled, and reheated.

2. Activity: HACCP in Your Community

HACCP systems are often found in chain restaurants and franchises. Call or visit a local chain or franchise restaurant, and ask the manager how HACCP is implemented in the operation. Write a one-page report on the system you learn about, including examples of how HACCP is implemented.

3. Critical Thinking: Making a Food Safety Management System Work

Think about what you have learned so far about preventing foodborne illnesses. What types of policies or procedures do you think should be in place to support a food safety management system?

2.1 Introduction to Food Safety	2.2 Good Personal Hygiene	2.3 Preventing Hazards in the Flow of Food	2.4 Food Safety Management Systems	2.5 Cleaning and Sanitizing
• What is a foodborne illness?	• How foodhandlers can contaminate food	• Cross-contamination	• The HACCP plan	• How to clean effectively
• Forms of contamination	• Personal cleanliness and work attire	• Time-temperature abuse		• Sanitizing
• Biological contamination	• Handwashing	• Purchasing		• Developing a cleaning program
• Chemical contamination	• Bare-hand contact with ready-to-eat food	• Receiving		• Controlling pests
• Physical contamination	• Work requirements related to illness	• Storage		
• Food defense		• Preparation		
• Allergens		• Cooking		
• U.S. regulation of food safety		• Holding, storing, and reheating		
		• Serving		

SECTION 2.5 CLEANING AND SANITIZING

In the previous section, you learned that a good food safety management system depends on food safety programs. A cleaning program is one of the most important of these programs.

Food is less likely to become contaminated in a clean and sanitary kitchen. However, if not done correctly, cleaning and sanitizing can be just as harmful to customers and employees as the illnesses it helps prevent.

Study Questions

After studying Section 2.5, you should be able to answer the following questions:

- What is the difference between cleaning and sanitizing?
- What are the proper procedures for cleaning and sanitizing surfaces?
- What factors affect the effectiveness of sanitizers?
- What are the elements of a master cleaning schedule?
- What organizations certify that equipment meets sanitation standards?
- What is the proper procedure for managing pests?

How to Clean Effectively

Food can be contaminated easily if equipment and kitchen surfaces aren't kept clean and sanitized. **Cleaning** removes food and other dirt from a surface. **Sanitizing** reduces pathogens on a surface to safe levels.

135

Section 2.5
Cleaning and Sanitizing

Introduce the Section

a. The difference between cleaning and sanitizing will be presented.

b. Both chemical cleaners and sanitizers are used, and must be cared for properly.

c. Cleaning and sanitizing are skills with proper techniques and procedures.

d. Cleaning is done routinely according to a schedule.

e. Insects, rodents, or other pests must be controlled to keep them out of the kitchen and the food.

Vocabulary Review

a. Direct students to the key terms.

b. Pronounce each word, and have the students repeat the pronunciation out loud.

c. Discuss the definition of each word.

Teach

Discuss

- The students can describe the difference between cleaning and sanitizing.
- If the students are not aware of the difference, help them to understand.
- Ask the students about "scheduled cleaning." Are they already familiar with the concept?

Vocabulary Terms

Cleaning: Removing dirt and debris from a surface.

Sanitizing: Reducing pathogens on a surface to safe levels.

Discuss

- Help the student to identify which areas of the kitchen would need to be cleaned and rinsed.
- Have them also identify the areas that would need to be sanitized after cleaning.
- Can sanitizing be dangerous? How?

Essential Skills: Cleaning and Sanitizing a Surface

The basic four steps to cleaning and sanitizing are outlined.

Help the students understand that cleaning requires time and effort that must be planned for.

Teaching Tips

- Help the students understand how and why cleaning supplies need to be kept separate.
- The cloths for cleaning and the cloths for cooking uses must be completely different.
- Cleaning equipment, cloths, and chemicals must be stored away from the food.
- The orange bullets are the times to clean.
- Ask the students if this seems like too much cleaning.
- Help the students to verbalize a possible reason why the cleaning must be done at each of these times.

All surfaces must be cleaned and rinsed, including walls, storage shelves, and garbage containers. However, any equipment or surface that touches food, such as knives, stockpots, preparation tables, and cutting boards, must be cleaned and sanitized.

Essential Skills
Cleaning and Sanitizing a Surface

1. Clean the surface. See Figure 2.38a.
2. Rinse the surface.
3. Sanitize the surface. See Figure 2.38b.
4. Let the surface air-dry.

Figure 2.38a: Step 1—Clean the surface.   **Figure 2.38b:** Step 3—Sanitize the surface.

All food-contact surfaces need to be cleaned and sanitized at the following times:

- After they are used
- Before foodhandlers start working with a different type of food
- Any time foodhandlers are interrupted during a task and the items being used may have been contaminated
- After four hours, if items are in constant use

Whatever you are cleaning, never use cloths or towels meant for cleaning food spills. Store cloths or towels for general cleaning in a sanitizer solution between uses. Keep towels that come in contact with raw meat, seafood, or poultry separate from other cleaning towels.

136

Figure Focus

Figure 2.38a: The surface is being cleaned with a dedicated rag and bucket.

Figure 2.38b: After the surface is clean, it is sanitized with a separate and dedicated rag and bucket.

Cleaning Products

Cleaning products are strong chemicals. They must be stored for use in or near the commercial kitchen, but safely away from food. A separate janitor's supply closet or room can serve this purpose. Cleaning products and equipment can be stored there in preassigned and labeled shelves.

Certain cleaners cannot be mixed. A good example is ammonia solution, which should never be mixed with chlorine bleach. This can produce chlorine gas, a toxic fume that can be fatal. Ammonia solutions have harmful fumes of their own and should be kept covered. Only use them in well-ventilated areas.

Chlorine bleach must also be kept covered. Wear protective gloves when pouring or using, because it can burn skin. Store all cleaning supplies in their original containers or in smaller labeled containers. Store Material Safety Data Sheets (MSDS) for every chemical where anyone can find them quickly.

Large foodservice operations can hire a HazMat (hazardous materials) service team to come and help establish a storage system for cleaning products. These service teams can professionally design and set up chemical-storage areas. Operations can also set storage areas up according to a professionally predesigned system. Such plans for systems are available from many chemical-supply companies. They show you how to find and use the chemicals you need while also addressing these issues:

- Keeping volatiles safe
- Protecting from burns
- Controlling for any fume-producers
- Isolating poisonous products

Cleaners

Cleaners are chemicals that remove food, dirt, rust, stains, minerals, and other deposits. They must be stable and safe to use. Always use cleaners as directed. Cleaners can be divided into the following four groups:

- **Detergents** are either general purpose or heavy duty. General-purpose detergents remove fresh dirt and can be used on almost anything. Heavy-duty detergents remove wax, dried-on dirt, and baked-on grease. Dishwasher detergents are an example of a heavy-duty detergent.

- **Degreasers** dissolve grease and work well where grease has burned on, such as on oven doors and range hoods.

- **Delimers** are acid cleaners used on mineral deposits and dirt that other cleaners can't remove. For example, they are designed to clean scaling (mineral deposits such as those left by hard water), rust stains, and tarnish. Delimers must be applied carefully.

137

On The Job: Cleaning Products

Cleaning product storage is similar to lab chemical storage. All products must be stored properly and labeled, with MSDSs available. HazMat teams may be involved in the process.

If the school has a well-organized chemical storeroom, see if the chemistry teacher will take the students on an in-school "field trip" to show how chemicals must be organized.

Teaching Tips

- There is a lot of chemistry in cleaning.
- If the students have taken chemistry class, they can understand how the cleaners work.
- Knowing exactly how they work is not required for knowing how and when to use a cleaner.

CUSTOMIZED INSTRUCTION

Science Connection

More Advanced Students

Students that have taken chemistry can understand chemical cleaners.

The students can learn how detergents work chemically.

What is the chemistry definition of a detergent?

The students can research delimers.

Most delimers remove the metal salts formed by divalent cations.

What does this mean? What minerals are usually removed by delimers?

An advanced student could demonstrate the actions of the various types of cleaners and briefly explain them.

Challenge the student to confine the chemistry explanation to one sentence of easily understood words for the students who have not had advanced science.

Vocabulary Terms

- **Cleaners:** Remove unwanted substances by chemical action.
- **Detergents:** Cleaner that can chemically emulsify and help remove grease, wax (lipids), and dirt.
- **Degreasers:** Dissolves grease completely to remove it.
- **Delimers:** Strong chemicals that remove buildup of mineral elements or compounds like rust or calcium deposits.

Teaching Tips

- Another use for the thermometer is to check the temperature of cleaning water.
- To eliminate pathogens and kill them, cleaning water must be at least 171°F.
- Time is also required at this temperature, usually at least 30 seconds.
- This is very hot water, so protect the safety of employees.
- Chemicals like chlorine alter the metabolism or habitat of pathogens, making it impossible for them to survive.
- These chemicals are strong and must be used according to manufacturer's instructions.
- Do not mix two chemical cleaners. For example, mixing chlorine and ammonia can create a deadly gas.
- Chemicals usually do not need to be hot to sanitize.
- However, follow the instructions.
- There must be adequate time for the chemical to work, so time the amount of contact time a sanitizer has with a surface.
- Contact time is different for different sanitizers.

Vocabulary Terms

- **Abrasive cleaners:** Cleaners that contain a very fine grit that helps clean surfaces.
- **Contact time:** The amount of time a sanitizer must be in contact with the surface being sanitized.

- **Abrasive cleaners** have a scouring agent that helps scrub hard-to-remove dirt. Dishwashers often use abrasive cleaners to remove baked-on foods in pots and pans. They must be applied carefully to avoid damaging smooth surfaces.

Sanitizing

Food-contact surfaces must be sanitized after they have been cleaned and rinsed. Sanitizing can be done either by using chemicals or heat. Both methods have specific requirements that must be followed for the sanitizing to be effective.

Heat Sanitizing

One way to sanitize items, such as tableware, utensils, or equipment, is to soak them in hot water. For this method to work, the water must be at least 171°F and items must be soaked for at least 30 seconds. Be sure to check the water with a thermometer.

Chemical Sanitizing

Tableware, utensils, and equipment can be sanitized by soaking them in a sanitizing solution. Employees can also rinse, swab, or spray items with the solution. Different types of sanitizer have different requirements for how long an item must be in contact with the solution. Be sure to read the manufacturer's directions.

Three common types of chemical sanitizers are chlorine, iodine, and quaternary ammonium compounds (or quats). Each type has to be mixed with water to create a sanitizer solution. Make sure to follow the manufacturer's directions when creating the solution. The concentration must be correct, or the sanitizer won't work. To make sure the concentration is right, use a test kit. These are usually available from the sanitizer manufacturer or supplier. Figure 2.39 is an example of a sanitizer test kit.

Factors That Influence the Effectiveness of Sanitizers

Several factors influence the effectiveness of chemical sanitizers:

- **Contact time:** Objects being sanitized must be immersed in the solution for a specific period of time. This is called **contact time.** The contact time depends on the type of sanitizer being used.

138

- **Temperature:** The water in sanitizing solutions must be the correct temperature.

- **Concentration:** Mixing sanitizer with the proper amount of water is important. The concentration of this mix (the amount of sanitizer to water) is critical. Concentrations that are too high can be unsafe and leave an odor or bad taste on objects. Concentrations that are too low may not be effective in killing pathogens.

Figure 2.39: Sanitizer test kit.

Cleaning and Sanitizing in a Three-Compartment Sink

Dishwashing staff clean and sanitize tableware and utensils in a dishwashing machine. They often clean larger items, such as pots and pans, by hand in a three-compartment sink. They must be sure to clean and sanitize each sink and drain board before washing any items. Figure 2.40 shows the steps for cleaning and sanitizing items in a three-compartment sink.

Essential Skills
Washing Kitchen Equipment in a Three-Compartment Sink

Start with carefully cleaned and sanitized drain boards and sink compartments. Then fill each compartment with the appropriate liquid—detergent solution, rinse water, and sanitizing solution or hot water.

❶ Rinse, scrape, or soak items before washing them.

❷ Clean items in the first sink. Wash them in a detergent solution at least 110°F. Use a brush, cloth, or nylon scrub pad to loosen dirt. Change the detergent solution when the suds are gone or the water is dirty.

❸ Rinse items in the second sink. Spray them with water or dip them in it. Make sure you remove all traces of food and detergent. If dipping the items, change the rinse water when it becomes dirty or full of suds.

139

Teaching Tips

- In a kitchen, a "dishwasher" is a person, not an appliance.
- The dishwasher uses a dishwashing machine.
- Large pots and pans must be cleaned by hand.
- The three-compartment sink allows for three-step cleaning.
- Three-compartment sinks allow for a sanitizing step.

Essential Skills: Washing Kitchen Equipment in a Three-Compartment Sink

There are actually five steps to cleaning in the three-compartment sink:

- Removing food from dishes
- Washing in hot water and dish detergent
- Rinsing
- Sanitizing in hot water or a solution
- Air dry

There must be spaces on each side of the three-compartment sink to allow for the first and last steps.

Vocabulary Terms

- **Temperature:** For cleaning purposes, a correct temperature for water or a sanitizer to effectively and safely kill pathogens without harming employees or customers.
- **Concentration:** The level of dilution of a chemical and water solution.

Figure Focus
Figure 2.39: A test kit may be purchased or provided by the manufacturer of cleaning supplies. It can test the concentration and/or effectiveness of a cleaning solution.

- The students would benefit from seeing a commercial dishwashing machine, as it looks very different from a home dishwasher.
- Show pictures, or if possible, take students to the school cafeteria or a foodservice establishment where they can see the equipment and processes in action.
- The bullets on this page define the various steps in caring for the dishwashing machine, and in using it properly.

❹ Sanitize items in the third sink. Soak them in hot water or a sanitizer solution. If using heat, remember to check the temperature of the water. If using chemicals, remember to use a test kit.

❺ Air-dry items. Place items upside down so they will drain.

Figure 2.40: Steps 1–5—Washing kitchen equipment in a three-compartment sink.

Cleaning and Maintaining a Dishwasher

It is important to clean and maintain dishwashers frequently throughout the day:

- Clear spray nozzles and food traps of food and other objects.
- Fill tanks with clean water as needed.
- Make sure detergent and sanitizer dispensers are filled.
- Use a delimer to remove mineral deposits when needed.

Always use dishwashers according to the manufacturer's directions. Also, follow these guidelines:

- Scrape, rinse, or soak items before washing.
- Presoak items with dried-on food.
- Never overload the dish racks. See Figure 2.41.
- Use the right rack for the items you are washing.
- Load racks so the water spray will reach all surfaces.
- As each rack comes out of the machine, check for dirty items.
- Rewash dirty items.

140

Figure Focus

Figure 2.40: This drawing shows how to establish a dishwashing system for pots, pans, and other large items that will not fit in the dishwashing machine.

Figure 2.41: Overloaded rack (left) and properly loaded rack (right).

- Air-dry all items; never use a towel to dry items.
- Frequently check water temperature and pressure; change the water when necessary.

Equipment

Equipment must meet certain standards, depending on whether the equipment's surfaces come in direct contact with food.

Fortunately, there are organizations to help with the task of choosing equipment. NSF International develops and publishes standards for sanitary equipment design. Underwriters Laboratories (UL) provides listings of equipment that meet NSF and other public health-related standards. Look for the NSF mark or the UL Classified or UL EPH Listed marks on restaurant and foodservice equipment. Only use equipment designed for use in a restaurant or foodservice operation:

- NSF creates standards for restaurant and foodservice equipment. It also certifies equipment. The NSF mark means an item has been evaluated, tested, and certified by NSF as meeting its food-equipment standards.

- UL provides classification listings for equipment that meets ANSI/NSF standards.

- UL also certifies items that meet its own standards for environmental and public health (EPH). Equipment that meets UL EPH standards is also acceptable for restaurant and foodservice use. This equipment has the UL EPH Listed mark.

[fast fact]

Did You Know...?

Stainless steel sinks are most commonly used in commercial kitchens. Stainless steel offers a good trade-off between cost, usability, durability, and ease of cleaning. They will not be damaged by hot or cold objects and resist damage from impacts. One disadvantage of stainless steel is that, being made of thin metal, it tends to be noisier than most other sink materials. Some of the better sinks include a heavy coating of vibration-damping material to the underside of the sink.

141

Discuss
- Ask the students why dishes and equipment should be air-dried and not towel-dried.

Teaching Tips
- Have some examples of electric devices and other items with the UL or NSF marks on them.
- Have the students find the marks.
- Ask them what the significance of the marks might be for the safety of the employees.

Fast Fact:
Did You Know...?

Why would noise be a concern in choosing a sink?

Figure Focus
Figure 2.41: The students can see the differences between the loads in the racks. Can they verbalize the reason the right photo is better?

Teaching Tips

- Help the students understand that a regular cleaning schedule will keep equipment clean and ready.
- Waiting until things are dirty and then cleaning them while waiting to use them is unsafe and inefficient.
- The growth of pathogens should be considered when forming a cleaning plan.
- Equipment is vulnerable to time and temperature pathogen growth.

Vocabulary Terms

- **Master cleaning schedule:** A plan for properly cleaning and maintaining all aspects of the operation, to be implemented and followed by employees.
- **Integrated pest management program:** A system to prevent, control, and/or eliminate insects and rodents from a foodservice operation.

Developing a Cleaning Program

A cleaning program is a system that organizes all of the cleaning and sanitizing tasks in the kitchen. A clean and sanitary operation is critical to a successful food safety management system.

Restaurant and foodservice managers with the most effective cleaning programs focus on three things:

1. Creating a master cleaning schedule
2. Training employees to follow it
3. Monitoring the program to make sure it works

To create a **master cleaning schedule**, you must walk through the facility and look at the way cleaning is done. Then figure out how things need to be cleaned and the ways in which to improve these processes. Next, make a master cleaning schedule. The schedule should have the following information:

- What should be cleaned
- Who should clean it
- When it should be cleaned
- How it should be cleaned

Figure 2.42 is a sample master cleaning schedule.

Once the schedule is created, employees must be trained to follow it. Then managers must make sure the schedule is working by checking that the cleaning is being done. Review and update the schedule as needed, for example, when the menu changes or when new equipment is purchased.

The importance of making sure the schedule is followed cannot be overstated. Effective cleaning helps to keep an operation free of smells, noise, pests, and messiness. It also helps prevent the transfer of pathogens from dirty surfaces to food or to clean surfaces. In addition, it helps customers to feel comfortable and safe in your operation.

Controlling Pests

How do restaurants and foodservice operations prevent pests, such as rodents and insects, from getting in? Good cleaning and sanitizing will help, but probably won't go far enough. So they need an **integrated pest management program** (IPM). An IPM program is a system that will prevent, control, or eliminate pest infestations in an operation.

142

Item	What	When	Use	Who
Floors	Wipe up spills	As soon as possible	Cloth, mop and bucket, broom and dustpan	
	Damp mop	Once per shift, between rushes	Mop, bucket	
	Scrub	Daily, closing	Brushes, squeegee, bucket, detergent (brand)	
	Strip, reseal	January, June	See procedure	
Walls and ceilings	Wipe up splashes	As soon as possible	Clean cloth, detergent (brand)	
	Wash walls	February, August		
Work tables	Clean and sanitize tops	Between uses and at end of day	See cleaning procedure for each table	
	Empty, clean, and sanitize drawers, clean frame, shelf	Weekly, Sat. closing	See cleaning procedure for each table	
Hoods and filters	Empty grease traps	When necessary	Container for grease	
	Clean inside and out	Daily, closing	See cleaning procedure	
	Clean filters	Weekly, Wed. closing	Dishwashing machine	
Broiler	Empty drip pan; wipe down	When necessary	Container for grease; clean cloth	
	Clean grid tray, inside, outside, top	After each use	See cleaning procedure for each broiler	

Figure 2.42: A sample master cleaning schedule.

Discuss

- Do you think that cleaning enhances safety?
- What types of safety are improved by a master cleaning schedule?
- Is the safety only for the health of the customers?
- Ask the students if they are aware of the fire hazard of grease in grease traps, hoods, filters, broilers, and grills.
- Even a layer of cooked-on old grease that seems benign can also be a fire hazard.

In-Class Activity: Cleaning the Restaurant

21st-Century Skills—Create Media Products, Apply Technology Effectively, Collaborate with Others

Form teams of students.

The students will seek permission to visit one or more foodservice establishments. They will photograph (with permission) the various cleaning processes, equipment, and storage of a commercial kitchen.

Students will create a PowerPoint presentation or posters for the class. They will describe the cleaning processes.

They can reflect upon their experiences.

Did the cleaning appear to be difficult?

Was it done according to a master schedule?

Was there adequate time to get the cleaning completed?

Figure Focus

Figure 2.42: The master cleaning schedule allows for regular maintenance cleaning and for immediate cleaning of spills and other problems.

Teaching Tips

- Managing pests may be critical to the reputation of the restaurant.
- If customers see a rodent or a cockroach in the dining room, they will probably tell friends about it.
- The students can think of ways rodents might have access to a restaurant.
- How would insects have access to a restaurant?
- If ants were crawling on the table, would you want to eat at that establishment?
- Keeping the kitchen and dining room extremely clean will deny the food to the pest.
- Trash should be removed frequently. Pests love it.
- If pests can nest, they can breed. This makes it worse.

An IPM program has two parts. First, it uses prevention measures to keep pests from entering the operation. Second, it uses control measures to eliminate any pests that do manage to get inside. There are three basic rules for an IPM program:

1. Deny pests access to the operation.
2. Deny pests food, water, and a hiding or nesting place.
3. Work with a licensed pest control operator to get rid of pests that do enter the operation.

Pests can enter an operation in one of two ways. Sometimes they are brought inside with deliveries. They can also enter through openings in the building. Prevent pests from entering by paying attention to the following areas:

- Check all deliveries before they enter the operation. Refuse shipments that have pests or signs of pests, such as wings or egg cases.
- Screen all windows and vents, and check the screens regularly for holes and dirt.
- Keep all exterior openings closed tightly. For example, drive-thru windows should be closed when not in use.
- Cover floor drains with hinged grates.
- Seal all cracks in floors and walls with a permanent sealant.
- Use concrete to fill holes or sheet metal to cover openings around pipes, as shown in Figure 2.43.

Pests are usually attracted to damp, dark, and dirty places. A clean operation offers them little access to food and shelter. The stray pest that might get in cannot survive or breed in a clean kitchen. In addition to adhering to the master cleaning schedule, follow these guidelines:

- Throw out garbage quickly and correctly. Don't let it pile up.
- Keep garbage containers clean and in good condition. Keep outdoor containers tightly covered.

Concrete

Sheet Metal

Fill openings or holes around pipes with concrete, or cover them with sheet metal.

Figure 2.43: Denying pests entry.

Figure Focus

Figure 2.43: Small openings, pipes, and joints are access points for pests. Cover or block them. If you can look into a space or an opening or split, block that access. If you can see daylight through any wall or opening besides a locked glass window, block the opening. Inspect the facility for access holes, even in the roof or foundation.

- Clean up spills immediately, including those around garbage containers.

- When possible, use dehumidifiers to keep humidity at 50 percent or lower. Low humidity helps prevent roach eggs from hatching.

- Keep food and supplies away from walls and at least six inches off the floor.

- Store all food and supplies right away.

- Use FIFO for products in storage, so pests don't have time to settle into them and breed.

Even after an operation has made every effort, some pests may still get in. If this happens, work with a **pest control operator**, or **PCO**, to get rid of them. PCOs have access to the most current and safe methods for eliminating pests. They are trained to determine the best methods for eliminating specific pests, are knowledgeable about local regulations, and are experts at applying, storing, and throwing out pesticides.

See Appendix C for additional information on food safety and pest control.

Summary

In this section, you learned the following:

- Cleaning removes food and other dirt from a surface. Sanitizing reduces pathogens on a surface to safe levels.

- All surfaces must be cleaned and rinsed; food-contact surfaces must be cleaned and sanitized. To clean and sanitize a surface, clean, rinse, and sanitize it, and then let the surface air-dry.

- Cleaners can be divided into the following groups: detergents, degreasers, delimers, and abrasive cleaners.

- Contact time, temperature, and concentration affect the effectiveness of sanitizers.

- A master cleaning schedule should identify what should be cleaned, who should clean it, when it should be cleaned, and how it should be cleaned.

- NSF and Underwriters Laboratories (UL) certify that equipment meets sanitation standards.

- To prevent pests from getting into an operation, an operation needs an integrated pest management program (IPM).

Teaching Tips

- It is well worth the expense of hiring a PCO to maintain the clean reputation of a restaurant.

Vocabulary Terms

- **Pest control operator (PCO):** A professional that rids a place of pests.

Summary

- Remind students to review the following:
  1. The difference between cleaning and sanitizing
  2. Proper procedures for cleaning and sanitizing surfaces
  3. The factors that affect the effectiveness of sanitizers
  4. The elements of a master cleaning schedule
  5. Which organizations certify that equipment meets sanitation standards
  6. The proper procedure for managing pests

Section 2.5 Review Questions

1. Cleaning removes food and dirt from a surface. Sanitizing reduces pathogens to a safe level.

2. An integrated pest management program (IPM) must be developed (perhaps with professional help) and carefully maintained to keep pests out.

3. A master cleaning schedule identifies the various things that must be cleaned and provides a time-table and strategy and procedure for cleaning.

4. Ms. Bouchard knows that a clean and sanitary environment will be safer for the guests and the employees. The cooking is the last step; the clean and sanitary environment must come first.

5. Linda can make sure that no foods, scraps, improperly stored foods, or garbage are available as food for pests. She can look for and block any access to the inside. She can also develop and implement an IPM.

6. Safety, philosophy, budget, equipment, and availability will impact this decision. All products must adequately do the job. All must be used according to manufacturer's instructions.

7. Contact time is the time required for the chemical to kill pathogens it contacts. If a product requires a certain contact time, reducing this time will be less efficient and more dangerous. The product will not be effective.

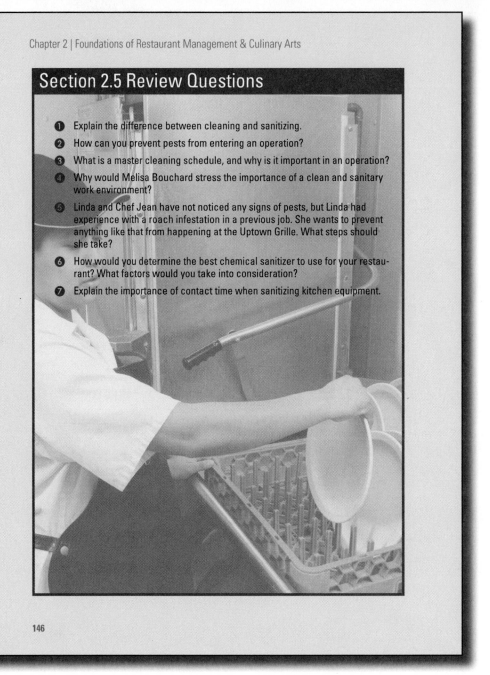

Section 2.5 Review Questions

1. Explain the difference between cleaning and sanitizing.
2. How can you prevent pests from entering an operation?
3. What is a master cleaning schedule, and why is it important in an operation?
4. Why would Melisa Bouchard stress the importance of a clean and sanitary work environment?
5. Linda and Chef Jean have not noticed any signs of pests, but Linda had experience with a roach infestation in a previous job. She wants to prevent anything like that from happening at the Uptown Grille. What steps should she take?
6. How would you determine the best chemical sanitizer to use for your restaurant? What factors would you take into consideration?
7. Explain the importance of contact time when sanitizing kitchen equipment.

146

Section 2.5 Activities

1. Study Skills/Group Activity: Master Cleaning Schedule

Pretend you own a small restaurant. Work in groups of two or three other students to develop a master cleaning schedule for the whole restaurant (kitchen, dining room, and restrooms).

2. Activity: No Pests Allowed!

You manage the foodservice operations for a large nursing home. How do you prevent pests from entering your facility? Develop an action plan.

3. Critical Thinking: How Clean Is It?

Observe cleaning practices at your school's cafeteria. Do they interfere with the students and faculty who are eating? Do they eliminate hazards?

147

Section 2.5 Activities

1. Each group will have a different plan and schedule. Keep food safety principles in mind while developing the cleaning schedule for the restroom and dining room, in addition to the kitchen.

2. There are many access points in a kitchen that is part of a much larger facility. The access to the kitchen must be carefully monitored and kept in good repair. All of these issues should be addressed, along with the basics of a foodservice IPM plan.

3. If students learn things about their school cafeteria that might not comply with what they are learning in this course, help them develop a positive approach to making suggested corrections.

Case Study Follow-Up

1. Linda and Chef Jean have not adequately staffed their establishment to allow them time away for various community activities, even if they promote the restaurant. They need more personnel if they are going to be away.

   There were many things Brian overlooked or mishandled and many red flags, including:
   - Raw chicken and carrots on the same cutting board
   - Wipes hands on apron without rewashing
   - Fresh tomatoes and lettuce into dry storage
   - Refrigerator too full
   - Doesn't rewash hands
   - Shrimp show ice crystals and should have been refused for improper freezing
   - There is evidence of problems with the tomatoes and lettuce freshness/ripeness

   Michael has not been adequately trained if he is putting on a dirty uniform. Also, there should be some staffing backup to cover for a sick employee. Linda should not put a potentially ill employee on food preparation.

   Brian does not hold the chicken at a hot-enough temperature. It is good that he checked it. Both Brian and Michael should have training or review of food safety procedures. There should be more documentation and accountability of following procedures.

2. An outbreak of foodborne illness could cost Uptown Grille many customers and much of its reputation. It could also cost a great deal of money to try to settle any claims, pay increased insurance costs, or other associated problems. In addition, the restaurant might actually have to close if inspection finds too many problems, or if the reputation drops off so far that guests stop coming.

3. Linda needs to retrain her staff. She also needs to hire more personnel, or have a better system in place for covering for ill employees. Linda needs to set time at the restaurant as her first priority for the workday, not meetings off-site. Promoting the restaurant will not make up for loss of reputation if guests become ill.

4. Chef Jean should discard any food that is spoiled or contaminated. HACCP principles will help prevent improper storage or handling, and help prevent future problems with spoilage or contamination.

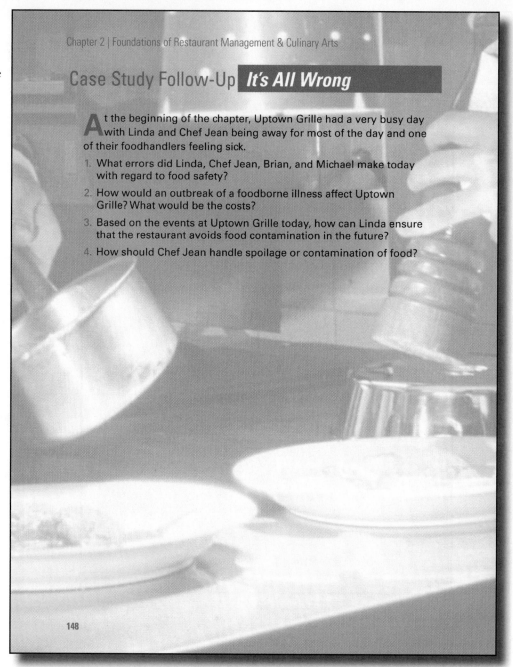

Case Study Follow-Up It's All Wrong

At the beginning of the chapter, Uptown Grille had a very busy day with Linda and Chef Jean being away for most of the day and one of their foodhandlers feeling sick.

1. What errors did Linda, Chef Jean, Brian, and Michael make today with regard to food safety?
2. How would an outbreak of a foodborne illness affect Uptown Grille? What would be the costs?
3. Based on the events at Uptown Grille today, how can Linda ensure that the restaurant avoids food contamination in the future?
4. How should Chef Jean handle spoilage or contamination of food?

148

Discuss
- Ask the class the questions concerning the case study.
- Do the students have enough information to form opinions after studying the chapter?

Apply Your Learning

The Danger Zone

In this chapter you have learned about the temperature danger zone for food. You know the boiling temperature at sea level. You know the freezing temperature at sea level. What is the temperature range in which you can safely hold hot foods without boiling them? What is the range for safely holding cold food without freezing?

Public Record

The reports made by public health inspectors are public records in many states. Select a local restaurant and obtain its three most recent inspection reports from your local health department. How has the restaurant improved or declined over time? Give a three-minute oral report on your findings.

The Transformation of Meat

Using a calibrated thermometer, cook three pieces of beef to three different internal temperatures: 145°F, 155°F, and 165°F. Allow the meat to rest for five minutes after removing it from the heat, and then cut each piece open in the center. How does the appearance of the meat change depending on the cooking temperature of each piece? How do the flavor and texture differ from piece to piece? Write two paragraphs summarizing your findings.

Critical Thinking Beware of Danger

There are living things besides microbes that can harm the food supply. What living things can you think of that could be a problem for a restaurant or foodservice operation? For example, perhaps your establishment is in an old building with a pipe stump from an old system still in an exterior wall. This pipe is open on both ends, from the inside to the outside world. Why could this be a problem? What should be done about it? Select one potential problem and one possible solution, and create a poster about it for the class.

149

Activities for Learning

The Danger Zone

This involves simple arithmetic: The safety zone is 41°F to 135°F. Freezing is 32°F. Boiling is 212°F. Set up simple ranges: Foods can be held without boiling from 135°F–211°F. Foods can be held without freezing from 33°F–41°F.

Public Record

These reports may be available online, at the county health department, or through another local agency.

The Transformation of Meat

Safety is not the only consideration with thermometers. Quality and doneness may be monitored as well.

Critical Thinking Beware of Danger

The students should come up with a solution to deny rodents and insects access through the pipe stump. A screen will keep out the rodents. There must be a more solid barrier or vent cover to keep out insects. Pest control operators might be able to treat any vent access chemically.

Exam Prep Answers

1. B
2. C
3. A
4. B
5. A
6. B
7. D
8. A
9. C
10. C
11. C
12. D
13. A

Exam Prep Questions

1 What is the temperature range for the temperature danger zone?

   A. 0°F to 32°F

   B. 41°F to 135°F

   C. 50°F to 140°F

   D. 70°F to 125°F

2 A critical control point (CCP) is a point

   A. in a recipe when ingredients are added.

   B. when chemically contaminated food is identified.

   C. where measures can be applied to prevent hazards.

   D. in the cooking process where food is tasted.

3 The temperature of a roast is checked to see if it has met its critical limit of 145°F for 4 minutes. This is an example of which HACCP principle?

   A. Verification

   B. Monitoring

   C. Record keeping

   D. Hazard analysis

4 First in, first out (FIFO) is a method of

   A. pest control.

   B. stock rotation.

   C. record keeping.

   D. temperature control.

5 How should food be labeled if stored out of its original container?

   A. Contents and date

   B. Foodhandler's name and title

   C. Foodhandler's name and the date

   D. Date and temperature at the time of storage

6 If food-contact surfaces are in constant use, they must be cleaned and sanitized every _____ hours.

   A. 2

   B. 4

   C. 5

   D. 6

7 To prevent food allergens from being transferred to food,

   A. avoid pewter tableware and copper cookware.

   B. store cold food at 41°F or lower.

   C. buy food from an approved, reputable supplier.

   D. clean and sanitize utensils before use.

8 Foodhandlers should keep their fingernails

   A. short and unpolished.

   B. long and unpolished.

   C. long and painted with nail polish.

   D. short and painted with nail polish.

9 To measure the temperature of equipment surfaces, use a(n)

   A. thermistor.

   B. thermocouple.

   C. infrared thermometer.

   D. bimetallic stemmed thermometer.

10 What is the maximum acceptable receiving temperature for fresh beef?

   A. 50°F

   B. 45°F

   C. 41°F

   D. 35°F

11 Where should raw poultry be placed in a cooler that includes raw and ready-to-eat food?

   A. On the top shelf

   B. Next to the produce

   C. On the bottom shelf

   D. Above the ready-to-eat food

12 Thawing food at room temperature could lead to

   A. cross-contamination.

   B. poor personal hygiene.

   C. physical contamination.

   D. time-temperature abuse.

13 The purpose of a food safety management system is to

   A. identify and control possible hazards.

   B. keep all areas of the facility clean and pest free.

   C. identify, document, and use the correct methods for receiving food.

   D. identify, tag, and repair faulty equipment within the operation.

151

Chapter 3 Overview

Chapter 3 introduces the student to the concept of workplace safety, including hazard detection, removal, and avoidance, legal issues, and caring for on-the-job injuries.

Section 1: The first section discusses laws and regulations that affect workplace safety and describes steps employers can take to provide safe working conditions.

Section 2: This section goes into greater detail about workplace hazards, including burns, falls, and cuts.

Section 3: Finally, this section addresses appropriate first-aid measures and describes potential external threats.

Advance Preparation	
Review	Chapter text for sections 1–3
	OSHA's Web site at www.osha.gov
	The National Sanitation Foundation's Web site at www.nsf.org
	The Underwriters Laboratories' Web site at www.ul.com
	District or campus safety policies, especially those involving fires and first-aid treatment
	Workplace smoking policies in your community
Contact	The local fire department to request a guest speaker
	The school nurse or another healthcare professional
	The local branch of the American Red Cross
Prepare	Copies of a sample Material Safety Data Sheet
	Bottles of common household cleansers
	A sheet of cardboard measuring 3 feet by 3 feet
	Photographs of first-, second-, and third-degree burns
	A variety of knives, with sharpening materials and storage devices

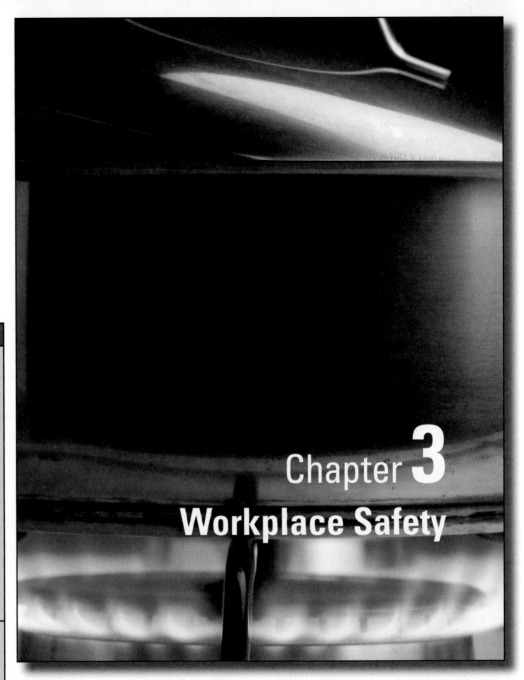

Chapter 3
Workplace Safety

CUSTOMIZED INSTRUCTION OPTIONS			
Less Advanced Students	More Advanced Students	ESOL Students	Special Needs Students
Pages 166, 178	Pages 157, 164	Pages 158, 166, 178	Pages 167, 170

CHAPTER TOOLS			
21st-Century Skills	Mathematics	Science	Literacy
Pages 157, 158, 159, 164, 166, 175, 177, 179, 180, 191, 201, 204	Pages 190, 204	Pages 175, 179, 191	Pages 157, 158, 159, 164, 166, 167, 170, 175, 177, 178, 179, 180, 191, 201, 204

Case Study *Safety First*

A local restaurant caught fire last night. Luckily, the restaurant was empty at the time, and no one was hurt. Upon hearing this news, Linda decides to move up the time for Uptown Grille's annual general safety audit. This includes an audit of the operation's facilities, equipment, employee practices, and management practices. After completing the audit, Linda meets with Chef Jean and the inspector to go over the findings.

The inspector finds a number of workplace safety violations:

- Boxes in front of the kitchen exit door.
- Backdoor exit gets stuck.
- The ice scoop is not in its dedicated holder next to the ice machine.
- Brian, the line cook, is seen carrying a large box, which obstructs his view, from the freezer to the kitchen.
- A waiter spills a drink and the spill is not cleaned up immediately. When the spill is finally cleaned, no sign is placed indicating that the surface is wet.
- Huge crack in a step leading into the restaurant.
- The guard on the electric slicer is off because the machine is being cleaned.
- Brian doesn't know where the MSDSs are kept.
- Chef Jean's apron is too baggy and comes below the knee.
- There is no Class C fire extinguisher in the restaurant.
- A cleaning agent's lid is unsealed and the cleaning agent is stored on an upper shelf.
- The food processor's electrical cord is frayed.
- The first aid kit is tucked away in Linda's office.
- The emergency evacuation plan has not been updated or discussed with employees in more than two years.
- The inspector is coming back in 30 days to check that all violations have been corrected and that any unsafe employee practices have been addressed.

As you read this chapter, think about the following questions:

1. Why is maintaining a safe work environment important?
2. How can falls/slips, cuts, burns, and fires be prevented in the workplace?

Case Study
Safety First

- Discuss the importance of safety in the workplace and how it can affect employees, guests, and the establishment's reputation.
- Ask students to explain why each of the violations noted in the case study are potential hazards.
- How can Linda and Chef Jean rectify all these problems before the inspector returns? Encourage students to discuss possible remedies, including employee training.
- Note that there are follow-up questions about the case study at the end of the chapter.
- This activity could be done in groups, as a class, or as a homework assignment.

Professional Profile

Discuss	What is a "safety-conscious culture"? Ask students to identify elements of this culture and how both managers and employees can foster it.

Why might it help to have an outside consultant perform a safety inspection? |
| Reinforce and Review | Reinforcing employee awareness about on-the-job safety is critical to operational well-being.

Problem-solving and communication skills are important tools for success in the restaurant and foodservice industry. |
| Teaching Tips | Explain the "lean-clean" quote and its application both in the foodservice industry and in other careers.

Point out that Flory Doyle's educational background isn't in workplace safety. Remind students of the breadth of career options in this industry. |

[professional profile]

Flory Doyle

Registered Dietitian and Field Specialist for EcoSure

I initially chose this profession because I wanted to understand the physiology of how our bodies process food and help others obtain good nutritional habits. As a Registered Dietitian with a B.S. degree in consumer sciences from Harding University, I completed my internship and did some graduate studies at Texas A&M University.

However, as I worked in both the clinical and the foodservice components, I found myself more drawn to the foodservice industry, so I decided to focus on foodservice management. As a foodservice manager, I learned the importance of practicing good sanitation and food safety to ensure that the safest food was being served to the public within a safe environment. I then decided to take my current position, which involves performing food safety and workplace safety evaluations for numerous clients.

I believe that continual and integrated education is a key factor in the success of an operation. If you invest time and effort in providing a good food safety/workplace safety knowledge base and back it up by integrating continual education throughout your daily operations, the dividends will pay off with a sound foodservice operation within a safety conscious culture.

You will never be bored in the foodservice industry. This field is full of challenges; every day is different. However, you need to love what you do, enjoy even the possible problems that it brings, and be willing to work hard to overcome these challenges. Problem solving and communication skills are important requirements for succeeding in this industry.

I perform different types of workplace safety evaluations, but my favorite ones are the play place safety evaluations in which I get to revert back to my childhood and climb through the play equipment. Among other things, I get to bang on windows as well as carefully inspect for missing hardware and broken equipment. And I really have a blast coming down slides. However, my favorite part is when kids that are in the play place ask me what I am doing and then offer to help me. I get guided tours all the time! When the kids are present it reminds me that what I am doing is very important in helping to keep them safe. That is very fulfilling. Remember:

❝ If you have time to lean, you have time to clean. **❞**

154

About Workplace Safety

Workplace Safety is very important and should not be taken lightly. It isn't something you do to prevent insurance claims and or keep the insurance rates low. One of the biggest investments and assets a foodservice operation has are its employees. Therefore, providing a safe environment with adequate lighting, floor mats in key areas, good upkeep on fire suppression systems, functional electrical systems/equipment in good condition, easily accessible personal protective equipment, etc., helps to send the message to your employees that you care about their safety. You acknowledge that they are important to your operation.

Workplace safety also helps employees to be efficient in their workspace. Along with providing a safe environment, provide your employees with a sound knowledge base (the why) of the importance of safe work practices and how to properly use personal protective equipment. All this should be followed up by daily reminders and positive feedback on good practices observed during daily tasks.

3.1 Introduction to Workplace Safety
• Safety and the law
• Government regulations
• The safety audit
• Personal protective equipment (PPE)
• Emergency plans

3.2 Preventing Accidents and Injuries
• Fire hazards
• Classes of fires and fire extinguishers
• Preventing burns
• Preventing slips, trips, and falls
• Lifting and carrying safely
• Preventing cuts

3.3 First Aid and External Threats
• First aid
• External threats

SECTION 3.1 INTRODUCTION TO WORKPLACE SAFETY

Just as food safety is vital to an operation's success, so is workplace safety. The need to protect guests and employees from harm cannot be emphasized enough. With the right training and tools, you can help to keep everyone safe, including yourself.

155

Focus and Engage

Discuss

- Why is it important to acknowledge the importance of employees to an operation? Shouldn't that go without saying?
- Why should employees understand why it's important to practice workplace safety, as opposed to simply observing safe habits because they're told to do so?

Section 3.1 Introduction to Workplace Safety

Introduce the Section

a. Address the importance of keeping both employees and guests safe.
b. Point out the importance of safety to everything that takes place at work, and relate this to maintaining a safe classroom environment.
c. Discuss the objectives for the section.

Vocabulary Review

a. Direct students to the key terms.
b. Pronounce each word, and have the students repeat the pronunciation out loud.
c. Discuss the definition of each word.

Teach

Discuss

- What are the legal ramifications of accidentally injuring or sickening an employee? How does that differ from accidentally injuring or sickening a guest?

Discuss

- Why do guests have a legal right to expect safety? Why isn't it "buyer beware"?
- Similarly, if employees don't feel safe in their workplace, why isn't it their responsibility to take a job elsewhere? Aren't they being paid to work under specific conditions?

Reinforce and Review

- Guests have a legal right to expect safe food served in a safe environment on safe premises.
- Employees have a legal right to work in a safe environment that is free of hazards.
- Liabilities are enforceable by law in court.

Teaching Tips

- Discuss the importance of maintaining a good reputation in the foodservice industry. Refer back to Chapter 1 and the discussion of the "rule of 10." Ask students to relate this to the spread of rumors and gossip.

Vocabulary Terms

- **Premises:** The establishment and all the property that surrounds it.
- **Liability:** The legal responsibility that one person has to another.

Study Questions

After studying Section 3.1, you should be able to answer the following questions:

- Who is legally responsible for providing a safe environment and ensuring safe practices?
- What is the role of Occupational Safety and Health Administration (OSHA) regulations?
- What are the Hazard Communication Standard (HCS) requirements for employers?
- What are the requirements for storing hazardous chemicals in an operation?
- What is the importance of general safety audits and safety training?
- Why is it important to complete accident reports?
- What is the purpose of an emergency plan?
- How can protective clothing and equipment prevent injuries?

Safety and the Law

Every restaurant and foodservice operation is responsible for the safety of all guests and employees. Guests have a legal right to expect safe food served in a safe environment on safe **premises.** Premises refers to all the property around the restaurant. Employees also have a legal right to work in a safe environment that is free of hazards. Restaurants that fail to provide this safe environment for their guests or employees can be sued and can lose their good reputations, as well as large amounts of money.

Restaurant and foodservice operators are now more aware of their responsibilities—and possible liabilities—for their guests and employees. **Liability** means the legal responsibility that one person has to another. These responsibilities, or liabilities, are serious because they are enforceable by law in court.

Restaurant managers should be knowledgeable about the following things:

- What hazards are

- The necessary steps to correct hazards

- How to display proper warnings where everyone can see them

Remember, if an accident does happen, a restaurant may be held legally responsible by the court.

[fast fact]

Did You Know...?

According to the Occupational Safety and Health Administration (OSHA), approximately 160,000 American children suffer occupation injuries each year; 54,800 are serious enough to require emergency room treatment.

Some of this information may seem complicated, but safety for guests and employees is very important to the success of any restaurant or foodservice operation. An effective safety program helps managers provide reasonable care. **Reasonable care** is a legal term that means that an ordinary person would think that the operation takes thoughtful, careful precautions. It is impossible to eliminate every possible risk in a public space, and very expensive to attempt. However, restaurants and foodservice operations have to make their premises as safe as they can though. A safety program that is written down and made part of the operation's employee training program and daily procedures can be used as evidence that the operation took reasonable care if a legal situation ever arose. A safety program can raise the overall quality of the dining experience, lower operating costs, and increase profitability.

One aspect of reasonable care for the safety of guests as well as the health and safety of employees is how a business treats its youngest employees. Table 3.1 outlines The Fair Labor Standards Act.

157

CUSTOMIZED INSTRUCTION

Literacy Connection, 21st-Century Skills—Critical Thinking and Problem Solving, Information Literacy, Be Self-Directed Learners

More Advanced Students

Research the standard of "reasonable care." What are its origins?

What is its role in the foodservice industry? How can it help or harm restaurants?

Write a brief essay on your findings.

Discuss

- Restaurant managers are expected to know about and respond to hazards in a timely manner, but they can't see everything. What if someone is injured due to a workplace situation that employees knew about but had failed to report to management?

- Alternately, what if managers fail to correct a hazard and someone is injured? Leaving aside the legal implications, what will this do to workplace morale?

Reinforce and Review

- Restaurant managers are expected to know about hazards, do whatever is necessary to correct them, and be sure there are proper warnings where everyone can see them.

- Restaurants and foodservice operators must make their premises as safe as possible, but it is impossible to eliminate every possible risk.

- A workplace safety program can raise the overall quality of the guest's dining experience, lower operating costs, and increase profitability.

Teaching Tips

- The restaurant and foodservice industry employs a large number of minors. Talk with students about the importance of reasonable care. From a safety perspective, why might employers be more or less likely to hire minors?

- Consider requiring students to design and implement a classroom safety program if none exists. How would it function? For instance, students could take turns serving as safety monitor, reminding their peers to follow certain practices.

Fast Fact:
Did You Know...?

Ask students to discuss why so many minors experience on-the-job injuries each year. What steps can be taken to reduce this number? Have any students in the class been affected by a workplace injury?

Vocabulary Terms

- **Reasonable care:** A legal term meaning that an ordinary person would think that an operation takes thoughtful, careful precautions.

Table 3.1: The Fair Labor Standards Act

- Why are younger employees excluded from performing certain tasks? Is the age cutoff arbitrary or sensible?

- Overall, are the restrictions on what work minors can perform and the hours during which they can do it a good idea? Do they protect younger, more vulnerable employees, or do they prevent ambitious workers from gaining necessary experience and earning a steady paycheck?

Discuss

- Are all workplace injuries, accidents, and illnesses documented, as OSHA requires? Ask students to identify situations in which employees or managers might choose not to report an incident. Note: don't give the impression that failing to report is a good idea.

Reinforce and Review

- OSHA is responsible for overseeing all workplace health and safety issues in the United States.
- When workplace accidents, injuries, or illnesses occur, forms detailing the incidents must be completed and submitted to OSHA, and investigations may take place.

Teaching Tips

- OSHA's Web site (www.osha.gov) has a number of resources for teen workers and their families, employers, and educators.

CUSTOMIZED INSTRUCTION

Literacy Connection, 21st-Century Skills— Information Literacy, Communicate Clearly, Work Independently

ESOL Students

What government safety administrations or nonprofit organizations are there in your country of origin? How do they work?

Write a brief essay describing these groups and their operations.

Vocabulary Terms

- **Occupational Safety and Health Administration (OSHA):** The federal agency that creates and enforces safety-related standards and regulations in the workplace.

Table 3.1: The Fair Labor Standards Act	
The Fair Labor Standards Act (FLSA) ensures that young people—those under the age of 18—do not risk their health, well-being, or educational opportunities.	
16 and 17 years of age:	They can work **unlimited hours** except in situations that are declared hazardous. Hazardous equipment includes power-driven meat processing machines, meat slicers, meat saws, patty forming machines, meat grinders, meat choppers, commercial mixers, and power-driven bakery machines. They are not allowed to operate, feed, set up, adjust, repair, or clean any of these machines.
14 and 15 years of age:	There are **restrictions on the number of hours they can work** and what they can do. They can **work in food preparation,** but cannot perform any baking activities and only limited cooking duties. They **cannot engage in cooking,** except with gas or electric grills that do not involve cooking over an open flame, and with deep-fat fryers that are equipped with and utilize devices that automatically lower and raise the baskets in and out of the hot grease or oil. They can prepare and serve beverages and use machines appropriate for performing this and other work such as dishwashers, coffee grinders, milkshake blenders, popcorn poppers, and microwaves that do not warm above 140°F. They may clean kitchen surfaces and non-power-driven kitchen equipment only when temperatures of surfaces do not exceed 100°F. They can filter, transport, and dispose of oil and grease only if the temperature does not exceed 100°F. They cannot perform any duties hazardous for 16-17-year-olds. They cannot use power-driven food slicers, grinders, choppers, cutters, and bakery-type machines in any capacity. They cannot use NEICO broilers, fryolators, rotisseries, or pressure cookers. They cannot perform work in a freezer or meat cooler.

Government Regulations

The **Occupational Safety and Health Administration (OSHA)** is the federal agency that creates and enforces safety-related standards and regulations in the workplace. OSHA has specific standards and forms for investigating and reporting accidents, injuries, and illnesses. Employers are required by law to

158

inform employees of job safety and health protection provided under the *Occupational Safety and Health Act of 1970*. Every restaurant and food-service operation must display an up-to-date copy of OSHA poster No. 2203 or No. 3165, "Job Safety and Health Protection" (or the state equivalent), where employees can easily see it when they report to work. This poster is so important that employers cannot post photocopies or versions that are smaller than the original or changed in any other way. Figure 3.1 shows the OSHA poster No. 2203, "Job Safety and Health Protection."

A restaurant or foodservice operation is required to report to OSHA any accident resulting in death or the hospitalization of three or more employees within eight hours of the occurrence. Other employee injuries and illnesses are recorded within six working days. In addition, each operation maintains a yearlong log of occupational injuries and illnesses, known as **OSHA Form No. 300.** A summary of these work-related injuries and illnesses, OSHA Form 300A, must be posted from February 1 to April 30 of the following year and easily accessible to employees. Figure 3.2 shows OSHA form No. 300.

Figure 3.1: The OSHA poster explains employee rights as related to workplace safety.

159

Figure Focus

Figure 3.1: Have any students seen this or a similar poster in their own workplaces or in other establishments?

Discuss

- The OSHA poster "Job Safety and Health Protection" must be posted—the original, not a photocopy, with no changes either in content or size—in a spot where employees can readily see it upon reporting to work. Is the government placing unnecessary restrictions on owners and managers, or does this regulation protect workers from potentially dangerous management practices? What benefits or disadvantages can students envision if this rule did not exist?
- Why must employers report all workplace-related illnesses and injuries to OSHA? How can this affect employees, either the healthy ones or the ones that are ill or injured?

Reinforce and Review

- Employers are required by law to inform employees of job safety and health protections provided under the Occupational Safety and Health Act of 1970.
- Employers may not post photocopies of the OSHA poster "Job Safety and Health Protection" or versions that are smaller than the original or have been changed in any other way.

Teaching Tips

- Review the content of the OSHA poster "Job Safety and Health Protection" with the class, asking students to explain each feature of the poster.
- Ask students to create their own version of this poster for classroom use. Additionally, create a classroom version of OSHA Form No. 300 for students to track any injuries that occur in the classroom or kitchen.

Homework Activity: Workplace Health and Safety Policies

Literacy Connection, 21st-Century Skills— Civic Literacy, Information Literacy, Work Independently

Each student should research a policy or regulation regarding workplace health and safety issues. Good places to start are OSHA's own Web site (www. osha.gov) and your state and local governments.

Write a one-page essay on the policy—what it states, who it affects, and how it might affect your own current or future employment.

Vocabulary Terms

- **OSHA Form No. 300:** A yearlong log of occupational illnesses and injuries, maintained by every operation to track workplace safety issues.

Discuss

- Ask students to discuss what chemical hazards are present in the classroom and kitchen. How can students protect themselves?
- What should the elements of a hazard communication program be? How should employers train employees on the proper use of chemicals?

Reinforce and Review

- OSHA requires employers to maintain a hazard communication program, through which employees are notified about chemical hazards present on the job and are trained to use chemicals safely.

Teaching Tips

- Make sure students know how to use any cleaning materials or other potentially hazardous materials available in the classroom in a safe and efficient manner.

[fast fact]

Did You Know...?
In 2008, OSHA inspectors inspected approximately 1,500 eating and drinking operations for workplace safety violations.

A hazard communication program is another critical OSHA requirement. The Hazard Communication Standard (HCS) is also called Right-to-Know and HAZCOM. This safety standard requires that all employers notify their employees about chemical hazards present on the job and train employees to use these materials safely.

Figure 3.2: The OSHA poster explains employee rights as related to workplace safety.

160

Figure Focus
Figure 3.2: All work-related injuries and illnesses should be recorded—but are they?

Chemicals can be considered physical hazards, health hazards, or both. Physical hazards are chemicals that can cause damage to property and immediate injury (most commonly burns). These chemicals can be flammable, explosive, highly reactive to air or water, or stored under pressure. Health hazards are chemicals that cause short- or long-term injuries or illnesses. They include chemicals that are toxic (poisonous), carcinogenic (cause cancer), irritating, or corrosive (cause a material to be eaten away or dissolved). Table 3.2 lists some common foodservice chemicals.

Table 3.2: Common Foodservice Chemicals

Chemical Cleaners	Fuels	Others
Ammonia (Quats)	Propane	Carbon dioxide
Brass and silver cleaners	Butane	Nitrogen dioxide
Chlorine bleach		Fire extinguishers
Degreasing agents		Herbicides and fungicides
Disinfectants		Pesticides
Drain cleaners		
Floor cleaners		
Dishwashing machine detergent		

[fast fact]

Did You Know...?
Nonlatex gloves are recommended to protect skin from hazardous chemicals. Latex gloves should not be worn because some workers may be allergic to latex. In fact, between 1 and 6 percent of the general population is allergic to latex.

OSHA establishes requirements for using chemicals. OSHA requires chemical manufacturers and suppliers to provide a Material Safety Data Sheet (MSDS) for each hazardous chemical they sell. Listed below is the information about the chemical that is contained in the MSDS:

- Safe use and handling
- Physical, health, fire, and reactivity hazards

161

Discuss

- OSHA oversees all use of chemicals in the workplace, from industrial lubricants used in factories to the glass-cleaning spray used in office buildings. How effective do you think OSHA can be, given the huge number of businesses in the United States and the vast number and variety of chemicals in use?

Reinforce and Review

- Chemicals can be considered physical hazards, health hazards, or both.
- Health hazards are chemicals that cause injuries or illnesses.
- Physical hazards are chemicals that can cause property damage or immediate injury.

Teaching Tips

- Explain how toxins, poisons, irritators, and corroders differ.
- Make sure students understand how seemingly innocuous chemicals like carbon dioxide or fire extinguishers can be hazardous.

Table 3.2: Common Foodservice Chemicals

- Are any of the chemicals listed in Table 3.2 available in the classroom? Have students explain how to use each safely.

Fast Fact: Did You Know...?

Nonlatex gloves are considered disposable protective equipment since they are discarded after a single use. What other examples of DPE might be used in the foodservice workplace? What other industries might also use DPE?

Discuss

- The MSDS for every chemical used at a workplace should be available to employees. Is it realistic to think that employees actually read these documents? Why or why not?

Reinforce and Review

- OSHA requires chemical manufacturers and suppliers to provide a Material Safety Data Sheet for each hazardous chemical they sell.
- Employees have the right to see the MSDS for any hazardous chemicals they use.

Teaching Tips

- Provide copies of a sample MSDS for students to view and discuss. What positive and negative aspects do they observe? How could the document be improved?
- Pass around bottles of various household cleansers. Ask students to write MSDSs for these cleansers, using the guidelines on pp. 161–162.
- Relate the information to the discussion in Chapter 1 of "green" cleaning products.

- Precautions
- Appropriate personal protective equipment (PPE) to wear when using the chemical
- First-aid information and steps to take in an emergency
- Manufacturer's name, address, and phone number
- Preparation date of MSDS
- Hazardous ingredients and identity information
- MSDSs are often sent with the chemical shipment. Purchasers can also request them from suppliers or manufacturers. Employees have a right to see the MSDS for any hazardous chemical they work with, so keep the sheets where employees can access them. Figure 3.3 is an example of an MSDSs binder.

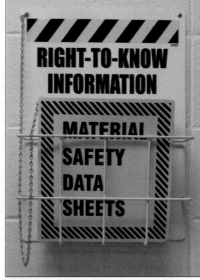

Figure 3.3: Material Safety Data Sheets describe the hazards of chemicals in a restaurant or foodservice operation. Employees should be trained to check the MSDS for each of the products they use.

162

Figure Focus

Figure 3.3: All employees should be aware of the ingredients found in any chemicals they may use. What potential hazards may occur when employees do not know the makeup of the chemicals they are using?

Safety and Occupational Health Specialist

A Safety and Occupational Health Specialist (SOH) for the Occupational Safety and Health Administration conducts safety inspections at work sites like restaurants or factories. These inspections look at how well businesses are obeying federal regulations about employee health and safety.

The inspector leads training sessions on health and safety for both employers and employees; looks at statistics and records that relate to safety issues; and investigates possible violations of the regulations and other employee health concerns. SOH specialists may be able to fine companies, depending on the kinds of violations they find. In many ways, SOH specialists have the same goal as food safety inspectors: to help employers provide safe workplaces and help employees protect themselves.

Being a Safety and Occupational Health Specialist requires a great deal of education and experience. Most jobs require a master's degree or more, with a major in occupational safety and health or a related field. People working toward becoming SOH specialists often look for jobs that include training employers and employees on workplace safety issues, developing policies on hazards and hazard prevention, and otherwise working with information involving employee health and safety. Although the Occupational Safety and Health Administration is the biggest employer of SOH specialists, many other governmental agencies and large businesses hire these professionals, too.

The Safety Audit

Is a particular operation safe? **Safety program guidelines** are based on existing safety practices and the insurance carrier's requirements. A safety program is designed to meet the specific needs of the operation. It also includes specific guidelines that are based on the geographic location, such as snow and ice removal, flood water drainage, or earthquake response plans.

The purpose of a **general safety audit** is to judge the level of safety in the operation. It is a safety inspection of facilities, equipment, employee practices, and management practices. A general safety audit identifies any areas or practices that might be hazardous to employees and guests.

The completed audit is in the form of a checklist. Any "no response" or blank space, which means that the inspector could not find the information, requires follow up. Regular safety self inspections can help make sure all employees are using correct safety practices throughout the operation. Figure 3.4 shows an example of a general safety audit. There are four general areas covered in a safety audit:

- **Facilities:** The building (exterior and interior) and major systems, such as electricity and plumbing. This includes outside areas, such as drive-thru windows, parking lots, and outdoor eating areas. Furnishings (such as booths, tables, and chairs) and fixtures (such as sinks, lights, and doors) are also considered to be part of the facility.

163

Discuss
- How can the presence of a safety program empower employees? Alternately, how can it create problems for workers?

Reinforce and Review
- A safety program is designed to meet the specific needs of a business establishment.
- A general safety audit identifies any potentially hazardous areas or practices.
- Regular safety self-inspections can help ensure all employees are maintaining appropriate safety practices.

On the Job: Safety and Occupational Health Specialist

Students will be learning about many kinds of job opportunities, some of which they have not been exposed to previously:
- Ask students what kinds of education and experience they think an SOH specialist needs.
- In what skill sets pertinent to this job might students most like to be involved? Training? Fines? Inspections? Why? Which of these skill sets do they think are most important? Why?
- What other agencies, besides OSHA, might use SOH specialists? Would they need additional training for these agencies?

Vocabulary Terms
- **Safety program guidelines:** The parameters of a workplace safety program, based on existing safety practices and the insurance carrier's requirements.
- **General safety audit:** An inspection that judges the level of safety in the operation; an assessment of facilities, equipment, employee practices, and management practices.
- **Facilities:** The building (interior and exterior) and major systems, such as electricity and plumbing.

Discuss

- What management practices could affect employee and guest safety?
- There is often a gap between what is taught and what is learned. If a manager has trained an employee on the proper use of a piece of equipment, and the employee makes an error and is injured, whose fault is it? Why?

Reinforce and Review

- Two organizations that label appropriate equipment for foodservice establishments are the National Sanitation Foundation and the Underwriters Laboratories.
- The four areas assessed during a general safety audit are facilities, equipment, employee practices, and management practices.

Teaching Tips

- Use the NSF and UL Web sites (www.nsf.org; www.ul.com) as resources for classroom discussions.

CUSTOMIZED INSTRUCTION

Literacy Connection, 21st-Century Skills— Critical Thinking and Problem Solving, Communicate Clearly, Information Literacy, Be Self-Directed Learners

More Advanced Students

Select and research a workplace health or safety issue.

Design an employee training session to address it, including any materials you think appropriate.

Present your training to the class.

Vocabulary Terms

- **Equipment:** Everything employees use to perform their jobs—refrigerators, vehicles, cooking equipment, etc.
- **Employee practices:** The methods and techniques employees use to perform their jobs.
- **Management practices:** The methods and techniques managers use to perform their jobs.

Yes	No	
FACILITIES		
☐	☐	Do all exit doors open from the inside—without keys—to allow rapid escape when necessary?
☐	☐	Are ground fault circuit interrupters (GFCI) installed wherever equipment and floors may become damp from cleaning?
☐	☐	Does the cooling system in the kitchen achieve the industry standard of 85°F (29.4°C) or lower?
EQUIPMENT		
☐	☐	Are machines properly guarded with covers, lids, and other devices?
☐	☐	Are hot pads, spatulas, and other equipment provided for use with ovens, stoves, and other heat-generating equipment?
EMPLOYEE PRACTICES		
☐	☐	Do employees make use of goggles, hair restraints, gloves, tampers, hot pads, safe knife storage devices, machine guards, and other personal protective equipment?
☐	☐	Do employees lift boxes and equipment properly?
MANAGEMENT PRACTICES		
☐	☐	Do managers follow all safety rules that apply to employees?
☐	☐	Do managers introduce new employees to the safety program?
☐	☐	Is senior management involved in creating safety policies?

Figure 3.4: The general safety audit is in the form of a checklist and covers facilities, equipment, employee practices, and management practices.

- **Equipment**: All equipment (cooking and cutting equipment, refrigerators, tools, vehicles, fire extinguishers, alarms, etc.) must meet legal standards for foodservice equipment. Two organizations that label appropriate equipment include the National Sanitation Foundation (NSF) and Underwriters Laboratories (UL). Equipment must be maintained in acceptable working condition. If equipment needs repair, the employees who use the machine must tell the team and their supervisor. If the equipment poses a hazard, then the machine itself should be turned off. A certified technician is the only person qualified to repair equipment and decide that it is ready to be used again.

- **Employee practices**: Managers must train employees in safe practices, and then supervise them to make sure they use these practices on the job. Training includes proper use of work equipment. Employees using equipment incorrectly will lead to equipment problems and potential injuries.

- **Management practices**: The inspector evaluates how committed management is to protecting employees and guests.

Figure Focus

Figure 3.4: What other questions do students think belong on a general safety audit?

Personal Protective Equipment (PPE)

Supplying good-quality tools, utensils, equipment, and protective clothing shows management's commitment to employee safety. Personal protective equipment, such as gloves and goggles, protects employees from potential hazards on the job. In addition, employees should not wear clothing or other items that can increase risk:

- Loose or baggy shirts that can get caught on machinery, catch on fire, or interfere with lifting
- Jewelry, especially necklaces and bracelets, that can get caught in machinery
- Scarves or neckties that can get caught in machinery or catch on fire

Cooks and other kitchen employees who work around heat can wear long sleeves to protect their arms and an apron or chef's jacket for added protection from burns. Dish-machine operators can wear water-resistant aprons and rubber gloves.

Employees can wear goggles or safety glasses to protect themselves from splashing chemicals or from food flying out of grinders, choppers, or mixers. In some states, safety glasses are required when deep-fat frying.

Shoes are an important part of personal protective equipment. Well-designed footwear helps prevent employees from slipping, tripping, or falling and protects their feet from falling objects or spills from hot water or food. Shoes should have the following qualities:

- Skid-resistant soles
- Low, sturdy heels
- Either no laces or laces that tie tightly
- Water, heat, and grease resistance
- Closed toes
- Nonporous material to prevent hot liquids or caustic chemicals from soaking through

Some employees, such as dishwashers and porters, can wear heat-resistant, knee-length protective aprons and snug-fitting gloves made from nonflammable materials. Others, such as cooks or bakers, wear standard aprons and use disposable gloves, side towels, and mitts, as needed. Some additional guidelines for chefs are listed below:

- They should never wear rubber or disposable plastic gloves when handling hot items as these can melt and burn hands.

165

Discuss

- Supplying good-quality equipment, including personal protective equipment, demonstrates a management's commitment to employee safety and well-being. What other management practices reinforce that commitment? Are there ways management practices can show a lack of concern toward employees?
- Employees should never wear disposable gloves when handling hot items to prevent burns. But employees should also keep bandages covered. How can an employee with a hand injury maintain his or her own safety as well as protect the food?
- What are some other ways that food safety and employee safety may appear to come into conflict? How can these situations be resolved?

Reinforce and Review

- Personal protective equipment protects employees from potential hazards on the job.
- Well-designed footwear helps prevent employees from slipping, tripping, or falling and protects their feet from falling objects or dangerous spills.

Reinforce and Review

- All mitts, gloves, and towels should be kept dry to prevent steam from causing injury.
- Protective clothing and equipment should be regularly checked for damage and wear.

Teaching Tips

- Present all types of personal protective equipment available for student use to the class. Explain how and when to use each article and how each piece should be maintained.

Fast Fact: Did You Know...?

How might flying particles or chemicals cause eye injuries in the foodservice industry?

CUSTOMIZED INSTRUCTION

Literacy Connection, 21st-Century Skills—Think Creatively, Communicate Clearly, Create Media Products

Less Advanced Students

Create a poster of employee "dos" and "don'ts." "Dos" could include hair pulled back from the face or the use of nonskid shoes, while "don'ts" could include wearing dangling jewelry or baggy clothing.

Present your poster to the class.

CUSTOMIZED INSTRUCTION

Literacy Connection, 21st-Century Skills—Think Creatively, Communicate Clearly, Create Media Products

ESOL Students

Create a poster translating common safety-related phrases from English into your dominant language. These could include "Be careful," "Watch out," "This is hot," "The floor is slippery," and "This knife is sharp."

Present your poster to the class.

- All mitts and gloves should be kept dry because wet materials can conduct heat quickly and cause steam burns.

- They should wear disposable gloves to handle food that is not too hot. Disposable gloves should never be washed or reused. Gloves that are too big will not stay on the hand, while those that are too small will tear and rip easily.

- Protective clothing and equipment should be checked frequently for worn spots, defects, or any damage that would make them less effective. Any damaged items should be replaced as soon as possible.

Figure 3.5 shows employees wearing correct and incorrect personal protective equipment.

[fast fact]

Did You Know...?

Each year in the United States, 2,000 workers have job-related eye injuries that require medical treatment. Flying particles account for 70 percent of eye injuries, and contact with chemicals accounts for 20 percent of eye injuries.

Figure 3.5: Employees wear personal protective equipment like gloves to protect themselves from potential hazards.

166

Figure Focus

Figure 3.5: Using personal protective equipment helps employees stay safe, but it also benefits employers—can students identify how?

Finally, employees are responsible for using the equipment properly and wearing the protective clothing that management recommends or provides. In the most successful safety programs, employees recognize and deal with safety hazards themselves.

Emergency Plans

The purpose of an **emergency plan** is to protect workers, guests and property in the case of an emergency or disaster. For an emergency plan to work, all employees must understand it *before* there is an emergency. Good planning can prevent confusion, reduce fear, and minimize injury and loss during an incident.

Emergency plans are specific to each operation and should be posted in highly visible areas. The following considerations should all be part of your plan:

- Floor plans of the facility, noting first-aid stations, alarms, sprinklers, and fire extinguishers

- Evacuation routes

- Emergency telephone numbers for each type of emergency

The main parts of a safety plan are installing fire safety equipment, developing and posting evacuation routes, keeping exit routes clear, and training and drilling employees.

Encouragement and incentives motivate people much more strongly than punishment and criticism. Praise employees for following the right procedures. A recognition or award system, such as thanking them for offering safety suggestions, is another good way to encourage safety practices.

When violations or accidents occur, it can mean that the safety program needs improvement. People should only do jobs they have been trained for and are physically able to do. Update and retrain employees whenever major aspects of the operation change or when new pieces of equipment are purchased.

Accident Investigation

An **accident** is an unplanned, undesirable event that can cause property damage, injuries or fatalities, time lost from work, or disruptions of work. A **near miss** is an event in which property damage or injury is narrowly avoided. Any event that makes guests or employees less safe should be investigated and recorded—even if an actual injury did not occur.

167

Discuss

- If employees choose not to use available and appropriate personal protective equipment and are injured, who is at fault? Why might an employee choose not to follow an established safety practice, especially when working in a potentially hazardous situation?
- Why might employees choose not to report near misses to management? Are these the same reasons that employees might choose not to report injuries or illnesses?

Reinforce and Review

- For an emergency plan to work, all employees must understand it before an emergency occurs.
- The main components of a safety plan include installing appropriate fire safety equipment, developing and posting evacuation routes, keeping exit routes clear, and training and drilling employees.
- Praise, gratitude, and awards are all appropriate incentives for encouraging employees to follow good safety practices.

CUSTOMIZED INSTRUCTION
Literacy Connection
Special Needs Students
What emergency phone numbers do you know? Which ones should a restaurant have on hand? Which ones does a school need?

Vocabulary Terms

- **Emergency plan:** A method of protecting workers, guests, and property in the case of an emergency or disaster.
- **Accident:** An unplanned, undesirable event that can cause property damage, injuries or fatalities, time lost from work, or disruptions of work.
- **Near miss:** An event in which property damage or injury is narrowly avoided.

Discuss

- Restaurants and other foodservice establishments are busy places. How can a thorough and appropriate accident investigation be performed in such a setting? What obstacles could arise?
- So far, several examples of OSHA forms have been discussed in the text. Do students think that OSHA requires too much paperwork? Are these forms a burden on already-overworked managers, or a method of preserving accurate records and tracking both short- and long-term employee health and safety issues?

Reinforce and Review

- Each restaurant and foodservice establishment must have forms for reporting any injuries or illnesses affecting either guests or employees.
- Emergency phone numbers should always be posted by every telephone, not simply in management offices.

Vocabulary Terms

- **Accident investigation:** A method of establishing the facts about any accident occurring in the workplace.

In addition, each operation needs to have forms for reporting injuries or illnesses involving both guests and employees. **Accident investigation** involves eight steps:

1. Record information as soon as possible after the event occurs, ideally within one hour. Use OSHA-required forms as well as appropriate corporate or company forms.

2. Include a description of the event, the date, and two signatures on accident report forms.

3. Collect physical evidence or take pictures at the site.

4. Interview all people involved and any witnesses.

5. Determine as clearly as possible the sequence of events, the causes and effects, and the actions taken.

6. Submit reports to OSHA, the insurance carrier, lawyer, and corporate headquarters, as appropriate. Keep copies of all reports and photographs for your files.

7. Keep all employees informed of procedures and hazards that arise from the situation.

8. If they aren't already available, post emergency phone numbers in public places.

Figure 3.6 shows samples from OSHA of an employee injury and illness form.

Figure 3.6: OSHA's Form 301 is one of the first forms you must fill out when a recordable work-related injury or illness has occurred.

168

Figure Focus

Figure 3.6: OSHA's Form 301 requires information about the injured or ill employee, the healthcare professional(s) the employee has consulted, and the incident in question.

Evacuation

A variety of emergencies, both man-made and natural, may require the evacuation of the workplace. These emergencies include fires, explosions, floods, earthquakes, hurricanes, tornadoes, toxic-material releases, civil disturbances, and workplace violence. Employers may want their employees to respond in different ways to different threats. An evacuation plan must identify when and how employees are to respond to different types of emergencies. A disorganized evacuation can result in injury, confusion, or property damage.

To protect employees and guests if there is an emergency, a well-designed emergency plan should be ready in advance, and employees should have training and practice with it. Place fire, police, and emergency rescue team telephone numbers on every phone, and post copies of the floor plan marking escape routes, exits, and assembly points in a variety of locations.

Plan **evacuation routes** to give everyone at least two ways out of the building to a safe meeting place. Make sure everyone knows the routes, exits, and meeting points. Keep routes and exits clear and unlocked. Do not use them for storage or trash. Knowing and practicing emergency safety procedures will help everyone remain calm if an incident should occur. Figure 3.7 is of an example of an evacuation route.

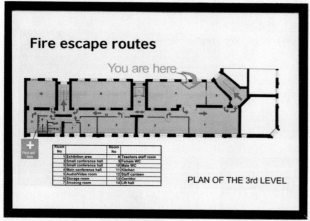

Figure 3.7: Fire escape routes depict all appropriate paths and exits.

Discuss

- Why is it important to have two separate evacuation routes in any workplace? Why should there be an established meeting place for all employees in the event of a workplace emergency?

Reinforce and Review

- An evacuation plan must identify when and how employees are to respond in different ways to different threats.
- Copies of the establishment's floor plan, clearly showing both evacuation routes as well as exits and assembly points, should be posted throughout the building.

Vocabulary Terms

- **Evacuation route:** An efficient path through and outside the building, terminating in an established meeting place.

Figure Focus

Figure 3.7: Evacuation plans illustrate not only the paths to safety, but also the locations of first-aid kits and assembly places.

Discuss

- No matter how well employees have been trained on how to behave in case of emergency, most foodservice establishments don't have the opportunity to train their guests on appropriate responses. How can guests be kept calm and orderly during an evacuation?
- What arrangements should be made to assist guests with special needs?

Reinforce and Review

- Evacuation routes should be planned to help get people out of the building as quickly as possible.
- These routes should be well-marked with lights and signs.

Teaching Tips

- Review the school's policy on emergency evacuation routes.

Table 3.3: Five Basic Steps to Maintaining Evacuation Routes

- Employees who fully understand their workplace's evacuation routes are more likely to remain calm in an emergency, encouraging guests to remain calm as well.
- A poorly maintained evacuation route can turn a minor emergency into a major disaster, including loss of life.

CUSTOMIZED INSTRUCTION

Literacy Connection

Special Needs Students

What is the best way to behave during an evacuation if you are an employee of the establishment?

How should you behave during an evacuation if you are a guest enjoying a meal or other entertainment?

An effective plan for evacuation does several things:

- Marks each route with signs and lights
- Provides emergency lighting (battery-powered)
- Makes sure that all exit doors open outward without keys
- Confirms that exit steps and ramps are marked, kept clear, and repaired as needed
- Selects one person responsible for checking remote areas (such as walk-in refrigerators, dry storage, and janitorial closets) to make sure everyone is evacuated

Developing and Maintaining an Evacuation Route

When planning evacuation routes, make sure there are at least two routes, using separate exit doors. Take into account where employees and guests will be and how big the facility is. This will help design a plan that moves people along the evacuation route and out of the building as quickly as possible. Consider anything that might slow the evacuation. For instance, guests with strollers or wheelchairs may need more time to leave the building. Plan a meeting place away from the building where staff can gather once evacuated. Table 3.3 outlines the five basic steps to maintaining evacuation routes.

Table 3.3: Five Basic Steps to Maintaining Evacuation Routes
1. Mark each route clearly with signs and lights. See Figure 3.8.
2. Provide additional battery-operated lights along the way; these will work in the event of a power outage.
3. Make sure that keys are not required to open any exit doors from inside the building; replace any locks that do require keys.
4. Keep all doors, staircases, pathways, and ramps that will be used in an evacuation clear of obstructions. See Figure 3.9.
5. Assign a staff member (one person for each shift, accounting for days off) to ensure that no other employees or guests are in out-of-the-way areas, like basement kitchens, storerooms, and bathrooms.

Figure 3.8: Mark each evacuation route with signs and lights.

Figure 3.9: All doors, staircases, pathways, and ramps that will be used in an evacuation must be clear of obstructions.

Figure Focus

Figure 3.8: Regularly inspect evacuation routes to make sure signs are present and lights are working.

Figure 3.9: Efficient, effective evacuation routes not only move employees and guests through and from a building quickly, but they help protect the owner and the business from liability.

Remember that no matter how well planned an evacuation route may seem on paper, it is worthless unless all employees know the plan. Make sure to train all staff on how to evacuate the building, and consider conducting practice drills to confirm that everyone knows and understands what to do in an emergency.

OSHA has an *Evacuation Plans and Procedures* tool available online that covers evacuation suggestions and recommendations for most emergencies.

Each employee should be trained in emergency plans and procedures during employment orientation. In addition, the company should run both scheduled and surprise emergency drills during the year.

Summary

In this section, you learned the following:

- Restaurants and foodservice operations are responsible for providing a safe environment and ensuring safe practices for their guests and employees.

- The Occupational Safety and Health Administration (OSHA) is the federal agency that creates and enforces safety-related standards and regulations in the workplace.

- The Hazard Communication Standard (HCS) requires that all employers notify their employees about chemical hazards present on the job and train employees to use these materials safely.

- Material Safety Data Sheets (MSDSs) describe hazards of the chemicals in a restaurant or foodservice operation. Each product has its own MSDS.

- General safety audits give an overview of the levels of safety in a restaurant or foodservice operation. Safety audits cover facilities, equipment, employee practices, and management practices.

- Accident reports are important because they signal that the safety program may need improvement.

- An emergency plan in a restaurant or foodservice operation protects property, workers, and guests in the case of an emergency or disaster.

- Protective clothing and equipment protect employees from potential hazards on the job.

171

Discuss

- All establishments, not just foodservice outlets, should spend an appropriate amount of time training employees on safety issues. But what is an appropriate amount of time? And how can training and reinforcement be effective in a busy and often stressful workplace?

Reinforce and Review

- No matter how well an evacuation route or safety plan may have been developed, it is worthless unless all employees have been properly trained to follow it.
- Each employee should be trained on emergency plans both during orientation and throughout the year.

Teaching Tips

- OSHA's "Evacuation Plans and Procedures" tool is a resource for helping students think about how to plan for and respond to workplace emergencies.

Summary

- Remind students to review the following:
  1. Who is legally responsible for providing a safe environment and ensuring safe work practices
  2. The role of OSHA regulations
  3. HCS requirements for employers
  4. Requirements for storing hazardous chemicals in an operation
  5. Importance of general safety audits and safety training
  6. Importance of completing accident reports
  7. Purpose of an emergency plan
  8. How protective clothing and equipment can prevent injuries

Section 3.1 Review Questions

1. A liability is a legal responsibility that one person has to another and is enforceable by law in a court.

2. The purpose of an MSDS is to provide managers and workers with all relevant information about a hazardous chemical, including its safe use and handling, appropriate personal protective equipment to wear when handling the chemical, and important precautions to take when using the chemical.

3. The best way for managers to get employees to comply with safety standards is to train them properly and reinforce these standards every day.

4. A general safety audit is a safety inspection of facilities, equipment, employee practices, and management practices that judges the level of safety in an operation. It is important because it can identify any areas or practices that might be hazardous to employees or guests.

5. A general safety audit protects a company's investment in its employees by identifying ways in which the workplace can be made safer and employees can improve their use of correct safety practices.

6. Linda should update the restaurant's emergency evacuation plan, which has not been adapted or discussed with employees in over two years, to ensure that any changes in restaurant or staff practices are covered in the plan.

7. When an on-the-job injury occurs, a restaurant or foodservice operation must report all relevant information—such as the nature and severity of the injury, the time of the injury, and the events leading up to the injury—to OSHA. This is done to help both the employer and OSHA develop a picture of the extent and severity of work-related incidents.

8. Students should list the items they think should be investigated during a safety inspection. For instance, are food safety regulations being observed? Does all equipment function properly? Are facilities properly maintained to prevent injury?

Section 3.1 Review Questions

1. What is a liability?
2. What is the purpose of an MSDS?
3. What is the best way for managers to get employees to comply with safety standards?
4. What is a general safety audit and why is it important?
5. Flory Doyle of EcoSure believes that one of the biggest investments and assets a foodservice operation has are its employees. How does a general safety audit help to protect that investment?
6. Why should Linda update the restaurant's emergency evacuation plan?
7. When an on-the-job injury occurs, what information must a restaurant or foodservice operation report to OSHA? Why is this information necessary?
8. Take a look around your school's kitchen. Does it appear to meet the basic safety requirements? Create a list reflecting your idea of a complete safety inspection. If possible, conduct the inspection.

172

Section 3.1 Activities

1. Study Skills/Group Activity: Classroom Audit

Work with two other students to conduct a general safety audit of your classroom, your home, or another part of your school, as permitted. Present a brief oral report on your findings to the class.

2. Activity: Classroom Emergency Plan

Develop an emergency plan for your classroom. During a class discussion, compare your ideas with those of your classmates.

3. Critical Thinking: Employee Safety and Risk Training

You are the general manager for a small restaurant with about 75 seats and 15 employees. Develop a plan for employee safety and risk training. Your plan should include at least six steps.

173

Section 3.1 Activities

1. Students should list the items they think should be part of a general safety audit, then conduct the audit itself.

2. Students should include floor plans (including locations of safety equipment, like fire extinguishers), evacuation routes, and emergency telephone numbers in their emergency plans.

3. Student answers may vary but should include components such as personal protective equipment, an emergency plan, a hazard communication program, training on relevant OSHA regulations, a procedure for accident investigation, proper use of hazardous equipment, and so forth.

Section 3.2
Preventing Accidents and Injuries

Introduce the Section
a. Address the importance of preventing fires and burns.
b. Explain how to protect against other workplace injuries, such as slips and cuts.
c. Discuss the objectives for the section.

Vocabulary Review
a. Direct students to the key terms.
b. Pronounce each word, and have the students repeat the pronunciation out loud.
c. Discuss the definition of each word.

Teach

Discuss
• Fire awareness is one of the most important concepts in the restaurant and foodservice industry due to the great potential for burns and fires. Encourage students to point out fire awareness tips.
• Is there any way to make the work of the foodservice industry absolutely risk-free? Is it possible to make any industry risk-free? If so, which ones?

Reinforce and Review
• There are four important aspects to fire safety: prevention, detection, extinguishing, and training.
• Other potential hazards in the foodservice industry include slips, trips, falls, cuts, sprains, and strains.

Teaching Tips
• Review relevant campus safety policies with the class.

3.1 Introduction to Workplace Safety	3.2 Preventing Accidents and Injuries	3.3 First Aid and External Threats
• Safety and the law • Government regulations • The safety audit • Personal protective equipment (PPE) • Emergency plans	• Fire hazards • Classes of fires and fire extinguishers • Preventing burns • Preventing slips, trips, and falls • Lifting and carrying safely • Preventing cuts	• First aid • External threats

SECTION 3.2 PREVENTING ACCIDENTS AND INJURIES

Restaurant and foodservice managers and employees should know how to protect themselves and their guests from a variety of sources of accidents. Fire, of course, is a major hazard. A large number of accidental fires in restaurants are caused by faulty electrical wiring and equipment, candles on guest tables, and fireplaces in the dining room and kitchen. Other sources of fire are heat lamps, heating equipment, hot-holding equipment, coffeemakers, teapots, hot oil, cooking surfaces with open flames, and water splashing into an outlet. There are four important aspects to fire safety: prevention, detection, extinguishing, and training.

Other sources of accidents and injuries in foodservice are cuts, sprains, strains, and falls. These are preventable if you take the steps to avoid or prevent them.

Study Questions

After studying Section 3.2, you should be able to answer the following questions:

■ What electrical hazards contribute to accidental fires?

■ What are the different classifications of fires and fire extinguishers?

■ With what frequency should equipment be cleaned in order to help prevent fires?

■ What actions should be taken in the event of a fire at a foodservice operation?

■ How do you clean up spills on the floor?

■ What are the steps to use ladders safely?

■ What are the steps to proper lifting and carrying procedures to avoid injuries?

■ What are the correct and safe uses of knives?

174

[fast fact]

Did You Know...?
According to OSHA, restaurant and foodservice operations report almost 13,000 injuries involving at least one missed day of work each year.

Fire Hazards

One-third of all accidental fires in restaurants are due to either faulty electrical wiring and equipment or improper use of equipment. Always check for hazards before using any electrical appliance. See Figure 3.10.

Employees can take other precautions to prevent fires. Prevent grease fires, for example, by scheduling regular cleaning for walls and work surfaces; ranges, fryers, broilers, and microwave and convection ovens; heating, air-conditioning, and ventilation units; and hoods and filters. Some health departments require that restaurant and foodservice operations use a professional company specializing in cleaning equipment. Inspect hoods and ducts weekly and clean them as often as necessary to remove grease buildup. In addition, a qualified contractor should professionally clean this equipment every six months. Figure 3.11 shows a hood ventilation system.

Figure 3.10: Electrical fires can be caused by having too many plugs in an outlet or extension cord.

**Fast Fact:
Did You Know...?**

Why do students think these injuries occur in the foodservice industry each year? Are 13,000 incidents a lot or a little?

Reinforce and Review

- One-third of all restaurant fires result from faulty electrical wiring and equipment or from improper use of equipment.
- Employees can take a number of precautions to prevent fires, such as regularly cleaning ranges, hoods, and ventilation systems.

**Homework Activity:
Grease Fires**

Science Connection, Literacy Connection, 21st-Century Skills—Communicate Clearly, Information Literacy, Be Self-Directed Learners
Research how grease and grease buildup are related to fires in the foodservice industry.
Why do grease fires occur, and how can they be prevented?
How much damage do grease fires cause annually?
How much can it cost to clean up after a fire (including any loss of business due to temporary closure)?
Write a one-page essay describing your findings.

Figure Focus
Figure 3.10: What might be a better solution than plugging all these cords into a single outlet?

Discuss

- Are there any potential fire hazards in the class-room? How can they be prevented?

Reinforce and Review

- Keep all flammable items and materials away from heat sources.
- Different types of fires require different types of fire extinguishers. Using the incorrect type of extinguisher can create a greater hazard.

Fast Fact: Did You Know...?

Why shouldn't water be used to put out small grease fires?

Vocabulary Terms

- **Class A fire:** Fire that usually involves wood, paper, cloth, or cardboard and typically occurs in dry-storage areas, dining areas, restrooms, or garbage areas.
- **Class B fire:** Fire that usually involves flammable liquids or grease and typically occurs in kitchens or maintenance areas.
- **Class C fire:** Fire that usually involves live electrical equipment and typically occurs inside equipment or walls.

Figure 3.11: A hood ventilation system is installed over cooking equipment to remove vapors, heat, and smoke.

To maintain safe conditions, keep all flammable items and materials away from heat sources, such as ranges and hot-water heaters. In addition, store all linens and food in dry storage boxes, and store paper goods away from corrosive materials, such as acid cleaners or bleaches.

[fast fact]

Did You Know...?
If a small grease fire starts on a grill, in the oven, or over the stovetop, sprinkle it liberally with baking soda.

Classes of Fires and Fire Extinguishers

All restaurant fires are classified as A, B, or C. **Class A fires** usually involve wood, paper, cloth, or cardboard and typically happen in dry-storage areas, dining areas, garbage areas, and restrooms. **Class B fires** usually involve flammable liquids and grease and usually start in kitchens and maintenance areas. **Class C fires** usually involve live electrical equipment and typically occur in motors, switches, cords, circuits, and wiring. Different types of fires require different types of fire extinguishers. Table 3.4 provides examples of the three classes of fires and the extinguishers that should be used on them.

176

Figure Focus

Figure 3.11: Why do the ventilation hoods completely cover the cooking surfaces?

Table 3.4: The Three Classes of Fires and the Appropriate Type of Extinguisher for Each

Ordinary Combustibles *Figure 3.12: Class A extinguisher.*	**Class A (Ordinary combustibles)** • Wood, paper, cloth, and cardboard • Most often occur in food storage rooms, dining areas, restrooms, and refuse storage areas • Type A, or A/B/C extinguishers may be used on a class A fire • Examples: Fire in trash can; cigarette igniting a tablecloth; plastic container that comes in contact with a range burner or hot griddle. See Figure 3.12.
Flammable Liquids *Figure 3.13: Class B extinguisher.*	**Class B (Flammable liquids)** • Flammable liquids, gases, grease, oil, shortening, pressurized cans • May occur in kitchens (deep-fat fryers) and maintenance areas • Only B/C extinguishers containing the dry chemicals sodium bicarbonate or potassium bicarbonate should be used on deep-fat fryer fires • If a class B fire does not occur in a deep-fat fryer, any A/B or B/C extinguisher can be used • Examples: Flames from a grill igniting grease deposits on a hood filter in the kitchen; aerosol cans stored near a heat source exploding. See Figure 3.13.
Electrical Equipment *Figure 3.14: Class C extinguisher.*	**Class C (Electrical equipment)** • Live electrical equipment, cords, circuits, motors, switches, wiring • Only those B/C and A/B/C extinguishers containing nonconductive materials, such as carbon dioxide, should be used on electrical fires • Examples: Fire in a toaster; frayed cord igniting while a machine is operating; fire in the motor of a grinder. See Figure 3.14.

A fire safety expert can help identify the right types of fire extinguishers for a restaurant or foodservice establishment. All types of extinguishing systems work by using one or more of four ways to put out a fire:

1. Remove the fire's fuel supply.
2. Deny it oxygen.
3. Cool the fire's fuel below its combustion point.
4. Disrupt the flame's chain reaction by using a dry chemical extinguisher.

177

Table 3.4: The Three Classes of Fires and the Appropriate Type of Extinguisher for Each

• A fire safety expert can help restaurants identify appropriate extinguishing systems.

• Why might a foodservice establishment choose to have all three types of extinguisher on hand?

• All extinguishing systems work the same way, but they are used for different types of fire.

Reinforce and Review

• The four steps to putting out a fire are: remove its fuel supply; eliminate its oxygen supply; cool the burning fuel below its combustion point; and use a dry chemical extinguisher.

In-Class Activity: Designing Logos

Literacy Connection, 21st-Century Skills— Health Literacy, Work Creatively with Others, Create Media Products

Table 3.4 on page 177 depicts logos associated with each of the three classes of fire extinguisher—A, B, and C. Working in groups of three or four, design new logos that you think accurately illustrate the appropriate use for each type of fire extinguisher.

Create a poster showing your proposals and present them to the class.

After all the presentations have been completed, the class should vote on which logos are the best and why.

Figure Focus

Figure 3.12: Class A fires are the most common and are often the most straightforward to extinguish.

Figure 3.13: Class B fires, caused by flammable liquids, can often lead to explosions.

Figure 3.14: Class C fires, or electrical fires, can occur without anyone realizing it.

Ask students to discuss the following:

- Why might restaurant and foodservice establishments choose to install closed-system frying technology? Why might they choose not to install this equipment?

- Closed-system frying technology represents a significant advance in foodservice safety. Suggest other common cooking processes that could benefit from such developments.

CUSTOMIZED INSTRUCTION

Literacy Connection

Less Advanced Students

List some popular deep-fried items. What types of restaurants specialize in these items?

CUSTOMIZED INSTRUCTION

Literacy Connection

ESOL Students

List and describe some common deep-fried dishes that are popular in your country of origin. Are there comparable dishes available here? List some examples.

[what's new]

Dangers of Deep Fryers

Deep fryers can create several challenges for employee safety. They can cause burns, as the hot fat can splatter onto an arm or face. They may also contribute to other hazards as well. For instance, tiny particles of oil often land on the floor surrounding the fryer, making it slippery. Even smaller particles of oil can build up in hoods which can lead to grease fires if the hoods are not properly cleaned. However, many guests love deep-fried food. How can operations protect employees while meeting customer demand?

Some restaurants and foodservice establishments are making deep fryers safer by installing closed-system frying technology. See Figure 3.15. These systems can automatically clean out deep fryers when the computer senses that they have become too dirty. Of course, employees can also trigger these cleanings. In either case, employees do not actually have to touch the hot oil, because the system filters the oil inside the body of the fryer. Some systems take this a step further and pump discarded oil directly out to a storage tank outside the building, where it can be picked up, usually by a waste-oil removal company. Then the system pumps clean, fresh oil into the fryers from a separate tank. A few systems can even use the old oil to supply some of the operation's power needs.

In terms of employee safety, there are a number of benefits to closed-system fryers. Workers are less likely to slip on spilled oil or to injure themselves carrying heavy containers of fresh oil in to refill fryers. Employees also do not have to filter hot oil, which reduces the risk of major burns. Other benefits include less wasted oil, fewer materials to recycle or throw away, and reduced labor costs.

Figure 3.15: Closed-system deep fryers are safer than regular fryers.

Figure Focus
Figure 3.15: Are closed-system fryers still dangerous in any way?

Handheld portable fire extinguishers can be used for small fires—those smaller than 3 feet tall and/or wide—but the person using the extinguisher must know the correct way to handle it. Larger fires are a job for the fire department. Portable fire extinguishers are marked with the type of fire they fight. A good practice is to identify the specific areas of the kitchen and facility where different types of fire extinguishers should be located. Table 3.5 lists the types of material in various portable extinguishers.

Table 3.5: Types of Portable Extinguisher Materials	
Water-Based Extinguishers	• Rechargeable from a clean water source. All recharging and testing should be done by an approved fire extinguisher servicing company. • Use them on class A fires only.
Aqueous Film-Forming Foam Extinguishers	• Reduce temperature and supply of oxygen to the fire. • They must be protected from freezing. • Use on class A or A/B fires. • Do not use on deep-fat fryer fires.
Carbon Dioxide Extinguishers	• These contain a gas-based mixture that leaves no residue. • They are limited in range. • They may deplete the user's oxygen supply. • Use them on class B or C fires.
Dry Chemical Extinguishers	• They interrupt the chemical action that sustains fire. • They are available in A/B/C and B/C. • Only B/C types should be used on deep-fat fryer fires.

All employees should know where extinguishers are located in an operation and what types they are. It is important that all fire extinguishers be clearly and properly labeled so the user can quickly identify the class of fire for which the equipment will be used. Train employees on safe use of portable fire extinguishers. A simple way to remember how to use a fire extinguisher is the PASS system. Figure 3.16 illustrates the PASS system.

179

Reinforce and Review

- Handheld portable fire extinguishers can be successfully used to combat small fires if used properly.
- All employees should be trained on the proper use of fire extinguishers and should know where each fire extinguisher in the facility is located.

Teaching Tips

- Ask students to identify where the classroom fire extinguishers are located.
- Hold up a piece of cardboard that measures 3 feet by 3 feet, or draw a 3-foot by 3-foot fire on the chalkboard, so that students have a visual aid to understand the difference between fires that can be battled with a portable fire extinguisher and fires that cannot.

Table 3.5: Types of Portable Extinguisher Materials

- What are the pros and cons of each extinguisher type?
- If the establishment only has one type of fire extinguisher on site, which should it be and why?

Homework Activity: Types of Extinguishers

Science Connection, Literacy Connection, 21st-Century Skills—Reason Effectively, Communicate Clearly, Information Literacy, Work Independently

Each classification of fire extinguisher is intended for use on a different type of fire. What chemicals does each extinguisher contain?

How does that specific chemical or combination of chemicals work to extinguish a particular type of fire? What are the other major uses for these chemicals?

What might happen if the wrong extinguisher is used on a particular fire?

Write a one-page essay on your research, focusing on the chemicals themselves rather than on the fire.

Reinforce and Review

- The four steps to the PASS system are: pull the pin, aim at the base of the fire, squeeze the trigger, and sweep from side to side.
- Employees should only use portable fire extinguishers if trained to do so.

Teaching Tips

- Consider asking the local fire department to speak to the class about the proper use of portable fire extinguishers, automatic sprinkler systems, and other fire-fighting techniques used in professional kitchens.

In-Class Activity: Remembering Safety Information

Literacy Connection, 21st-Century Skills—Work Creatively with Others, Create Media Products, Work Effectively in Diverse Teams

"PASS" is the acronym used to remember the four steps in properly using a portable fire extinguisher. Such mnemonics, or memory devices, help people retain information. Another common example is "Stop, Drop, and Roll," which is used to remind people of the steps to take to extinguish fire on their hair or clothing.

Working in small groups, develop other original mnemonics to help retain important safety information. Create a poster displaying your results.

Note: Several Web sites offer information about the use of mnemonics in healthcare and first aid.

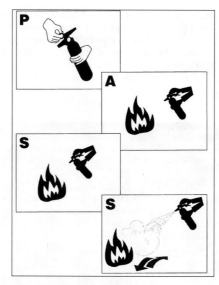

Figure 3.16: Use the pass system.
P = Pull the pin
A = Aim at the base of the fire
S = Squeeze the trigger
S = Sweep from side to side—stand 6 to 8 feet away from the fire when spraying

When fighting a fire, always leave a way to escape.

Make sure employees only use an extinguisher after they have been trained and always follow the instructions on the extinguisher. Many local fire departments will come out and provide demonstrations and training in the correct ways to use fire extinguishers.

Routinely check for discharged or damaged fire extinguishers. Replace any that are not working properly. Make sure that each fire extinguisher has a current, dated inspection tag. A fire extinguisher inspection checklist and calendar are helpful.

Any fire extinguisher that has been used or that has discharged any material must be serviced and recharged. Any fire extinguisher that shows any visible damage, has a missing pin or seal, or has a blocked nozzle should be completely replaced.

180

Figure Focus

Figure 3.16: Ask students to demonstrate the PASS system.

Automatic systems operate even when no one is in the facility. Automatic sprinklers provide an early and effective response to fire. Special kitchen sprinkler systems are required by the National Fire Protection Association (NFPA) for deep-fat fryers, ranges, griddles, and broilers. These systems usually include a type of heat detector that releases dry or wet chemicals, carbon dioxide, or inert gases.

An operation's fire extinguishing systems must be kept fully charged and inspected regularly. This includes automatic, mechanical, and portable extinguishers, sprinklers, and alarms. Any product that is found to be in unsatisfactory condition should be replaced immediately.

Fire Detection Devices

Smoke and heat detectors require a dependable source of electricity (either from batteries or from being connected to the wiring), a loud alarm, and a test button. Most detectors work by reacting to heat, smoke, or flame. **Smoke detectors** require a flow of air in order to work well, so they should not be located in "dead" spaces, such as the end of a hall or between ceiling beams. Smoke detectors should not be used in food preparation areas. **Heat detectors** detect fires where there is no smoke. They are activated by the significant increase of temperature associated with fire. **Flame detectors** react to the movement of flames. A fire safety expert should install and maintain all fire detection devices. Table 3.6 provides a description of common fire detection devices.

Table 3.6: Common Fire Detection Devices

Smoke Detectors	
Ionization detectors	This uses a small electric current to detect combustion particles from smoke, heat, or flames.
Photoelectric detectors	This uses a beam of light located inside the device to react to smoke or flame.
Heat and Flame Detectors	
Thermostats	This contains a metal strip or disk that closes against an electric contact and starts the alarm when a preset temperature is reached.
Rate of rise detectors	This triggers an alarm when the temperature rises faster than a preset number of degrees per minute.
Flame detectors	This uses infrared and ultraviolet sensors that respond to the movement of flame, or to its radiant energy.

181

Reinforce and Review

- Automatic sprinklers provide an early and effective response to fire, even when no one is on the premises.
- Smoke and heat detectors require a dependable source of electricity and should be regularly tested to ensure that they are working properly.

Vocabulary Terms

- **Automatic system:** A fire-fighting device that operates even when no one is in the facility.
- **Smoke detector:** A fire-detection device that operates by sensing the presence of smoke and therefore should not be used in the immediate food-preparation area.
- **Heat detector:** A fire-detection device that operates by sensing significant increases in temperature.
- **Flame detector:** A fire-detection device that operates by sensing the movement of flames.

Reinforce and Review

- Small fires, such as those in garbage cans or in pans, can often be successfully smothered.
- When in doubt, employees should engage an alarm and evacuate all guests and employees immediately.

Teaching Tips

- Reinforce with students that the fire-fighting techniques discussed in this chapter are for the use of employees in professional workspaces, not for students in classrooms.
- Review the district or campus protocol for handling classroom fires.

Should You Fight a Fire?

The most important rule for fighting a fire is to **ask yourself if you are in danger.** The only fires that employees of restaurants or foodservice operations ought to tackle are small ones, such as a fire in a single pan or a fire in a trash can. It is possible to smother a fire in a pan or use a fire extinguisher to put out a fire in a trash can.

[fast fact]

Did You Know...?

In the event of a fire or flames in a pan:

1. Slide a lid over the pan—that will smother the flames.
2. Turn off the heat source.
3. Leave the lid on the pan until the pan is cool.

Remember: If there is any doubt that you can fight a fire safely, the best response is to set off an alarm and evacuate immediately. If the fire is electrical or from an unknown source, notify the fire department even if the fire appears to be out.

While sometimes you can successfully fight a small fire alone, you should never put yourself or others at risk. According to the National Fire Protection Association (NFPA), do not attempt to fight a fire if the following events occur:

- The smoke is extremely thick.
- The fire is too hot for you to get close enough to fight it effectively.
- The fire is greater than 3 feet across.
- There are potentially hazardous substances near the fire.
- You do not have the correct type of fire extinguisher for the fire at hand.
- You do not know how to use the fire extinguisher.

When you make the decision that you cannot fight the fire alone, take the following steps:

1. Call the fire department.
2. Begin evacuating staff and guests.
3. Turn off the gas valve to prevent escalation. (Most restaurant and foodservice operations have a large valve that turns off all gas to the kitchen.)
4. Meet other employees at the preassigned meeting place.

182

5. Make sure that all persons have safely escaped.

6. When the fire department arrives, inform a firefighter if anyone is missing; do not reenter the building yourself.

No More Smoking in the Workplace

A major trend in the foodservice industry has been the increase in state and local laws banning smoking in workplaces, including restaurants and bars. In 2009, Wisconsin became the 26th state to pass such a law. A 2007 poll found that 54 percent of Americans favored banning indoor smoking in restaurants, while 29 percent favored bans for bars as well.

Arizona first enacted indoor air laws in 1973, and San Luis Obispo in California became the first city in the world to ban all indoor smoking in public places in 1990. However, until the last decade, many cities with smoking bans exempted restaurants and bars, requiring them to offer separate smoking and nonsmoking sections. Today bans are more likely to include restaurants and foodservice operations, even bars.

So far, it is hard to tell whether the bans have affected the health of workers and customers. Advocates on both sides point to different research. Since a ban on smoking in restaurants and bars was enacted in New York City in 2004, restaurant incomes and numbers of employees have increased, and hospital admissions for heart attacks have decreased. On the other hand, some researchers have found that there is no statistical relationship between workplace smoking bans and rates of death or hospital admissions. Another aspect to consider is that operations that can prove that they had experienced "significant economic hardship" from smoking bans have sometimes been allowed to permit smoking again.

What will be the effect of smoking bans on employee safety and the restaurant and foodservice industry? For now, it seems too early to know. Fortunately, researchers will continue to do their best to answer the question.

Preventing Burns

A burn is a type of injury. In the restaurant and foodservice industry, most burns are caused by heat. Burns are classified as being first, second, or third degree. The degree refers to the severity of the burn. Table 3.7 describes each degree of burn and the treatment for it.

Trends: No More Smoking in the Workplace

Engage students in a discussion about local policies and laws that affect smoking in the workplace.

Why might some states and communities regulate or ban smoking, while others do not?

What effects might these policies have on employees?

What effects might they have on a foodservice establishment's revenues or its ambiance?

Reinforce and Review

- In the foodservice industry, most burns are caused by heat.
- Burns are classified as first, second, or third degree, depending upon severity.

Teaching Tips

- Provide photographs of first-, second-, and third-degree burns to help students identify the differences.
- Make sure that students understand how to care for burns.

- All burns require immediate care, although only second- and third-degree burns require prompt medical attention.

- Since burns are common workplace injuries, what materials should restaurants have in their first-aid kits to care for them?

Discuss

- Many small establishments have little room to provide the safety measures described here, such as one-way traffic patterns. Encourage students to discuss whether more burns would be expected under these circumstances or whether the employees adjust to working together in a confined environment and therefore burn themselves and one another less frequently.

Reinforce and Review

- When carrying hot items (as well as sharp items), always inform any coworkers who are present, especially if you are heading toward a doorway or a corner.
- Always respect heat and assume that any heat source is turned on and is hot.

Teaching Tips

- Although deep-frying will not be covered in detail until Chapter 5, make sure students understand that all food to be fried should be dry and should not contain excessive ice crystals. The introduction of water to the hot oil can cause the fryer to overflow and cause injuries. For the same reason, fryer baskets should not be filled more than halfway.

Table 3.7: Degrees of Burn

Degree	Description	Treatment
First-Degree Burn	This is the least serious degree of burn. The skin turns red, feels sensitive, and may become swollen.	Run cool running water over the burn or cover with wet cool towels. Do not apply ice.
Second-Degree Burn	This burn is more serious and painful than a first-degree burn. Blisters form and may ooze. This degree causes intense pain and swelling.	Cool the skin in the same manner as for a first degree burn. Do not apply ice, ointments, or bandages. Seek medical attention immediately.
Third-Degree Burn	This is the most serious burn, but it is painless because damage to the nerves means the burned area does not have feeling. Skin may turn white and become soft, or it may turn black and hard.	Cover the burn with cool, moist, sterile gauze. Do not remove burnt clothing. Do not apply ointments, a cold compress, or cold water. Seek medical attention immediately.

Traffic patterns are an especially important consideration in preventing burns in the kitchen and serving areas. When carrying hot food or other hot items (such as a hot pot, pan, or utensil), warn others that you are coming through. It is also important to inform those working near you that a pot, pan, or utensil is hot.

Do the following things to prevent accidents from traffic patterns:

- Set one-way traffic patterns wherever possible.
- Maintain adequate travel and working space around heating and cooking equipment.
- Keep all aisles and doorways clear of obstacles. Doors should swing freely and not be in the way of work areas.

The best way for employees to avoid burns is to respect heat and to always assume that a heat source is on and hot. Be sure the kitchen is well equipped with hot pads or side towels. See Figure 3.17.

When using deep-fat fryers, it's important to remember some basic precautions:

- Before placing food in the fryer basket, dry it off or brush excess ice crystals off with a clean paper towel.
- Fill fryer baskets no more than half full.

184

Figure 3.17: Always assume surfaces are hot and use a hot pad to be safe.

- Follow manufacturer's directions for cleaning, filtering, and adding new fat or oil.

- Stand away from and never lean over the fryer when working.

- Lower and raise baskets gently.

- Place draining receptacle as close to the fryer as possible to avoid spills.

- Use long-handled tongs or another appropriate utensil when removing products from the deep-fat fryer.

[fast fact]

Did You Know...?
The restaurant and foodservice industry experiences the highest number of burns of any employment sector.

When using steam equipment, check the steamer and steam table contents carefully. In addition, check the pressure gauges in the steamers and make sure that pressure is released before opening. Always keep your face away from escaping steam. If steam tables are used in the dining area, post signs as necessary, and provide long-handled serving utensils so that guests do not have to get close to hot equipment. Table 3.8 lists ten steps for avoiding burns.

185

Reinforce and Review

- Always be extremely careful when working with deep fryers. Although they are valuable pieces of equipment, they have the potential to cause serious harm.
- Also, be extremely careful when using steam equipment, especially devices that use pressure.

Teaching Tips

- Steam equipment is covered in greater detail in Chapter 5, but describing it here might help students more clearly envision the potential hazards.

Figure Focus
Figure 3.17: Using a dry hot pad or folded towel can prevent serious injury.

Discuss

- Guests should always be warned if anything served to them is excessively hot, and dining-room employees should take great care to avoid causing injury. Are these gestures simply a way of being polite to guests, or do they presume that guests are too foolish to know that food served to them is likely to be hot? Or is all this just a good practice for avoiding lawsuits resulting from guest injuries?

Reinforce and Review

- Most common slips, trips, and falls occur on steps, floors, and pavement.
- The best way to protect guests and employees against falling—or against any other potential injury—is to anticipate what might happen.

Table 3.8: Steps for Avoiding Burns

- Make sure that students understand why following each of these ten steps is important, especially in a classroom full of novices.

Warn guests if plates, food, or beverages are hot. Always let guests know if the interior filling of a food is hot. For coffee service, servers should hold the cup themselves while filling the cup or set it on the table to avoid spills and splashes. For the same reason, cups with hot beverages and cups or bowls of hot soup should not be filled to the rim.

Table 3.8: Steps for Avoiding Burns

1.	Be sure equipment is in good working condition.
2.	Avoid overcrowding the range top.
3.	Set pot handles away from burners, and make sure they don't stick out over the edge of the range top.
4.	Adjust burner flames to cover only the bottom of a pan.
5.	Check hot foods on stoves carefully by standing to one side of the pot or kettle and lifting the edge of the lid farthest from you.
6.	Place sealed pouch bags in boiling water carefully to avoid splashing.
7.	Never leave hot fat unattended.
8.	Ask for help when moving or carrying a heavy pot of simmering liquid from the burners to storage or hot-holding areas.
9.	Metal containers, foil, or utensils should never be used in microwave ovens.
10.	Use hot pads and be careful when removing food and food containers from the microwave.

Finally, dishwashers should be careful when removing dishes from hot water or from a dishwashing unit that releases steam. Just-washed dishes are often too hot to handle. Always inform the dishwashing staff of dirty hot pots, pans, and utensils brought to the dish station.

Preventing Slips, Trips, and Falls

There are many ways to help prevent common slips, trips, and falls. Most occur on three types of surfaces: steps, floors, and pavement outside the building. These types of accidents usually occur while people are paying attention to something else as they walk—talking to companions, carrying objects, or simply daydreaming. The best way to safeguard guests and coworkers is to anticipate what might happen. While prompt service is important, hurrying can cause accidents. Watch for chairs or tables sticking into aisles. All aisles in serving and dining areas should be at least 4 feet wide.

[fast fact]

Did You Know…?
The National Restaurant Association stats show that slip, trip, and fall accidents are the greatest source of general liability claims in the industry.

Check exterior areas for weather hazards, such as snow, ice, flooding, standing puddles, or oil slicks. Remove debris, such as garbage or tree branches, especially after storms or high winds. Repair potholes or other damage to the pavement as soon as possible. Be sure there is adequate lighting in the parking lot and outdoor walkways, so that people can avoid possible hazards. If any bulbs are burned out, replace them immediately. Schedule routine maintenance to ensure parking lot safety. Sidewalks and ramps leading to the entrances of the restaurant should be clean and free of trash and brush. Keep stairways clear of boxes, bags, and equipment, and repair them immediately if any problem occurs.

Grease and oil on floors is a major cause of slips and falls and can occur anywhere. To prevent grease buildup, clean floors thoroughly at least once a day, usually after closing. Keep floor coverings (carpets, rugs, mats, and runners) in good repair and clean them regularly. Make sure that these coverings fit smoothly and are tight to the floor. Rug and runner edges should be unfrayed, securely bound, and free of holes or tears, especially at the seams. Use non-skid floor mats in areas that often get wet or slippery, such as entrances, aisles, and food-preparation and serving areas. Clean floors and carpets immediately whenever a spill occurs. The following is a list of the ways to safeguard guests and coworkers from trips and falls:

1. Check for places where guests and employees might run into equipment, furniture, or each other.

2. Watch for tables or chairs protruding into aisles, and for food or standing water on the floor or on mats in front of salad bars, buffets, and beverage areas.

3. Remind guests to step up or down for raised dining areas, and help those who may have difficulty walking, have poor eyesight, or are talking to their friends and not paying attention.

4. Be careful during rush-hour periods to avoid running into coworkers or guests.

5. Never run or become involved in horseplay with other employees. Safety must be one of the most important responsibilities of every employee.

187

**Fast Fact:
Did You Know…?**
Encourage students to discuss why, despite the prevalence of burn injuries, slip/trip/fall accidents are the largest generator of general liability claims in the foodservice industry.

Discuss

- A list of ways to prevent slips and falls appears on p. 187. Are most of these items just common sense? If so, why do employees and guests still become injured?
- Why might employees and guests become distracted and fail to observe good safety practices?

Reinforce and Review

- Performing routine maintenance of the facility's entire physical plant is an important way to protect against employee or guest injury.
- The presence of grease or oil on floors is a major cause of injury, so care should be taken to maintain clean floors.

Discuss

- Some of the safety guidelines described in this chapter, such as involving two staff members to handle grease spills or use ladders, may appear impractical for smaller or particularly busy operations. What is more important: guest service or employee safety? Do student answers to this question vary depending on circumstances?

Reinforce and Review

- All spills, especially of grease or oil, should be promptly cleaned.
- Employees should always use a ladder or step stool to reach items stored above shoulder level.

Teaching Tips

- If any ladders or step stools are available in the classroom for student use, ask volunteers to demonstrate the correct techniques for using these tools.

6. Report any conditions that could cause guests or staff to trip or fall.

7. Post signs, if necessary, to point out any problem areas and to reinforce overall safety.

Clean up spills immediately. While one employee is in charge of the cleanup, another employee should take the following steps:

- Verbally warn nearby guests and employees.

- Block the area. Post a sign, such as "Caution—Wet Floor," while cleanup is happening.

- Leave the sign in place until the area is safe. If the spill is liquid and can't be cleaned immediately, use an absorbent compound to soak up the liquid.

- Direct people around the spill.

Stairs, ramps, and raised dining areas often take people by surprise, causing them to trip. Tell employees to remind guests of steps and raised dining areas and to help those guests who may need assistance. There are some basic things an operation can do to prevent slips and falls in these areas:

- Provide adequate lighting.

- Clearly mark stairs and ramps.

- Be sure that handrails are sturdy and secure.

- Check stair coverings for tears or ragged edges.

- Keep stairs clear of obstacles. Never use them as storage areas.

- Post signs wherever hazards might occur for both workers and guests.

Using Ladders Safely

Employees should always use a ladder or step stool to reach racks and shelves that are higher than shoulder level. Three common ladders used in storage areas are straight ladders, step ladders, and step stools. A straight ladder should reach 3 feet above the spot where the top of the ladder rests against the support. Step ladders and step stools should be tall enough so that an employee will not have to stand on the top step or reach above his or her shoulder to place a load on a rack or shelf. Figure 3.18 shows different types of ladders employees of a restaurant or foodservice operation might use.

Inspect ladders to see that they are right for the job and are in good condition. Ladders are rated by the weight they can safely carry. Each ladder should be labeled with this information. Make sure that all parts of the ladder are in good condition. They should have nonskid feet and be long enough for safe support.

188

Figure 3.18: Ladders commonly used in restaurant or foodservice operations include a straight ladder, step ladder, and step stool.

The safest way to use a ladder is for two employees to work together. One person can hold the bottom of the ladder, and the other can climb up and pass or receive items. Here are a number of important tips for using ladders safely:

- Always work with someone who can hold the bottom of the ladder and pass or receive items. Be very careful if you must work alone.

- Set the ladder away from overhead obstacles. If you are working outside, keep the ladder firmly lodged, so that a strong gust of wind will not knock it over.

- Rest the ladder feet on a firm, flat, clean surface. Do not try to make it taller by placing it on a box or other object.

- The ladder should be within easy reach of the items needed or the place where items will be stored.

- Lock the folding bar of a step ladder or step stool in place.

- Test the ladder's balance before climbing.

- Never put a metal ladder on or near electrical wiring, service boxes, or equipment.

- Lock doors near the ladder or do not use the ladder near doors that someone may open.

- Use at least one hand to steady yourself while climbing. If an object cannot be carried easily in one hand, get help from someone, or leave the object where it is until help is available.

189

Reinforce and Review
- Ladders and step stools are valuable tools in the workplace, but they can be hazardous. Employees should always be aware of their environments before beginning to climb.

Teaching Tips
- Remind students that ladders should always be properly stored: folded shut and placed in a designated niche, where no one is likely to trip over them.
- Also, make sure students understand that they cannot climb on desks, chairs, counters, or other objects in the classroom, just as they would not as professional foodservice employees.
- If there are step stools or ladders in the classroom, consider designating a student (either on a permanent or a rotating basis) to inspect them each week for slippery substances, rust, and any mechanical problems.

Figure Focus
Figure 3.18: Which ladders have students used before? What other types of ladders can they identify?

Discuss

- Back injuries are common among foodservice employees. Safe lifting and carrying practices might eliminate many of these injuries, if observed. Why, then, do so many injuries still occur? Relate this to the earlier discussions on pp. 185, 186, and 187.

Reinforce and Review

- Performing warm-up exercises before beginning a shift or before lifting and carrying items may help employees protect themselves from injury.
- Heavy loads should be stored at waist level. If an item is particularly heavy, it should be labeled accordingly.

Teaching Tips

- Review proper classroom storage techniques with students.

In-Class Activity: Heavy Lifting

Mathematics Connection

Jerry is a new storeroom employee at a small grocery. He works a 40-hour week in his full-time position.

Company policies restrict the amount of weight that people can carry at once: 30 pounds for a single individual, 60 pounds for two-person lifting.

On a typical day, Jerry moves 142 boxes that weigh an average of 28 pounds apiece and team-carries another 18 loads that weigh an average of 56 pounds apiece. By the end of the day, how much has Jerry carried?

If this is a typical day, how much does he carry in a typical five-day week? How much will he carry in a typical year, minus two weeks of vacations and holidays?

- Be careful not to lean too far to one side to reach an item. Instead, move the ladder closer.
- Do not stand on the top two rungs of a straight ladder or the top step of a step ladder or step stool. When the job is completed, put the ladder back in its proper storage location, and chain or secure it to prevent it from falling on anyone.

Lifting and Carrying Safely

Some of the strongest muscles in the body are located in the back. However, use them carefully when lifting. Athletes do warm-up exercises to protect their muscles and backs from injury. That's a good idea for everyone; do some warm-up exercises for a few minutes to prepare muscles for lifting. As always, check with a doctor for exercises that are appropriate.

Good storage practices and special lifting techniques prevent back injuries. Store heavy loads on waist-level shelves and racks. Put lighter items on the top shelves. Mark extra-heavy loads.

Safe Lifting Practices

Before lifting anything, think out the process from beginning to end. Never take a risk with the back. Follow these precautions before lifting:

- Wear sturdy, nonskid shoes and be sure the laces don't trail on the ground.
- Don't wear loose clothes that might catch on the load or on a nearby object and throw off balance.
- Check the weight of the load. If the weight of the load is unknown, test it carefully while it is still on the floor or shelf by lifting a corner and setting it down again.
- Look for handholds that can be gripped with the whole hand. Wear gloves if the load is slippery or has sharp edges.
- Check the balance of the load. The contents of a box might have moved to one side, or a piece of equipment may be much heavier at one end. Surprise shifts in weight during the lift can be trouble.
- Ask for help if the load seems too heavy or hard to move.
- Use hand trucks, dollies, or carts to move heavy loads.
- Use proper lifting techniques.

190

Essential Skills
Steps in Safe Lifting

➊ Establish solid footing. Check the conditions of the floor. Stand close to the load, with feet shoulder width apart. Put one foot slightly in front of the other.

➋ Align the body. Stand straight. Face the load. Bend at the knees—not at the waist—and lower the body with the leg muscles to reach the load.

➌ Make the lift. Grip the load with the whole hand, not just the fingers. Keep the wrists as straight as possible. Tighten the stomach muscles and align the back. Arch the lower back by pulling the shoulders back and sticking out the chest. When getting a load off a lower rack, set the grip and check the weight before pulling the load off a rack. Transfer the weight immediately to the legs. Lift with the legs taking the weight. Smoothly and slowly take the load up. Do not twist while standing up. If the load is too heavy, slowly bend the knees and carefully set the load down on the floor. See Figure 3.19.

Figure 3.19: Step 3—Make the lift.

➍ Set down the load. Keep the lower back pulled in by tightening the stomach muscles. Keep the weight of the load on the legs. Bend at the knees and smoothly go down. Set down a corner of the load, slide the hand out from under it, and settle the rest of the load.

191

Figure Focus
Figure 3.19: What safe lifting behaviors can students identify in this photograph?

Reinforce and Review

- When carrying any item, such as a service tray or a large food container, first prepare a clean and clear space where you will place the object.
- Plan your route in advance to keep yourself safe and balanced and keep surprises to a minimum.

Carrying Safely

The principles of safe lifting hold true for safe carrying. In restaurant and food-service operations, people with heavy objects always have the right of way. Have servers and busers plan their routes so that they can keep their bodies and loads in balance while they are moving. The proper way to carry a tray is with one hand in front of the tray, and one hand in the middle, under a balanced load. It is helpful to have a tray stand already set up, or to have another employee set it up for the one carrying the tray.

Essential Skills
Steps for Carrying Loads

❶ Look for any hazards: slippery floors, pieces of furniture or equipment that may be out of place, spills, sharp corners, carpeting tears, narrow hallways, stairs, even people. Check for safe places to set the load down along the way, if necessary.

Figure 3.20: Step 3—Keep the load close to the body for good balance.

192

Figure Focus

Figure 3.20: What safe carrying practices can students identify in this photograph?

❷ Use the whole hand to grip the load, not just the fingers.

❸ Keep the load close to the body for good balance. Keep elbows against sides of the body to prevent bumping into anything. See Figure 3.20.

❹ Keep stomach muscles firm and tuck in the lower back. The load should be carried by the legs, not the back.

❺ When turning, move your feet instead of twisting at the waist.

Preventing Cuts

Cuts tend to happen most often to kitchen employees, but other staff and guests can be hurt from broken glass or sharp tableware. Some sharp hazards include can lids, cutting strips on aluminum foil and plastic wrap, box openers, knives, broken glasses, choppers, blenders, and slicers.

To avoid cuts, follow these kitchen safety tips:

- Use gloves or a towel to protect hands while removing lids from glass bottles or jars.
- Use proper openers on bottles or jars.
- Use plastic or metal scoops and ladles to handle food and ice; never use drinking glasses for these tasks.
- Cover food with plastic wraps or lids instead of glass.
- Never cool glasses, bottles, or carafes in ice intended for food or beverages.
- Throw out nearby food or ice when glass is broken.
- Wash sharp utensils separately and do not leave in a sink.
- Do not throw broken glass in the trash can. Take it out to the Dumpster.

193

Discuss

- Encourage students to discuss each kitchen safety tip and why each is important. Where appropriate, students should connect these tips to the material covered in Chapter 2.
- How can following these safety tips save money as well as protect employees?

Reinforce and Review

- Although cuts may occur more frequently to kitchen employees, other employees and guests are also vulnerable.
- Care should be taken to prevent breakage near anything that might be served to a guest, such as a pot of soup or an open ice machine.

Reinforce and Review

- No breakable items, such as dishes or glassware, should be stored above or near ice machines or food-preparation areas.
- Sharp knives are safer than dull ones, as they will cut cleanly and provide the employee with more control.

Teaching Tips

- A variety of knives will be discussed in Chapter 5, but presenting a few of the more common types now might help students understand how to use each type safely.
- Demonstrate safe knife passing and safe knife storage to students—again, this will be covered in Chapter 5 as well, but it is relevant here.

Fast Fact:
Did You Know...?

Encourage students to suggest ways of minimizing the incidence of cuts and burns in addition to the techniques the text has covered.

Essential Skills:
Safe Knife Handling Practices

Encourage students to discuss each of these practices. What is the reasoning behind each guideline? Do all of these make sense?

Why or why not?

- Glasses, bottles, and dishware should not be stored above or near ice machines or food preparation areas. If something breaks, glass can get into the ice or food that will be served to guests.

[fast fact]

Did You Know...?
Cuts and burns to hands on the job cost an estimated $300 million a year, according to *Nation's Restaurant News*.

Using Knives Safely

Knives are a standard tool in the kitchen, but they can be very dangerous if not handled properly. Each type of knife has a specific use. Sharp knives are much safer than dull ones. They cut more evenly, with less work, and provide more control. While walking through the kitchen, always hold the knife with the tip pointing down and close to your side. Verbally alert others when carrying a knife through the kitchen or foodservice facility. Knife skills will be covered in more detail in *Chapter 4: Kitchen Essentials*.

Essential Skills
Safe Knife Handling Practices

1. Keep knives sharpened. A sharp blade cuts more evenly and with less force than a dull blade. See Figure 3.21a.
2. Never touch sharp edges of knife blades.
3. Use a knife only for its intended purpose.
4. Place a damp cloth (or nonskid mat designed for this purpose) under a cutting board to help prevent the board from slipping.

Figure 3.21a: Step 1—Use a sharpening stone to keep knives sharp.

194

Figure Focus
Figure 3.21a: Freshly sharpened knives, combined with properly secured cutting boards, can eliminate much of the risk of injury.

⑤ Stop cutting and place the knife down on a flat and secure surface if an interruption occurs.

⑥ Never leave knives soaking under water.

⑦ Never try to catch a falling knife; step out of its way.

⑧ Carry knives with the cutting edge angled slightly away from your body. See Figure 3.21b.

Figure 3.21b: Step 8—Carry knives properly, with the cutting edge away from your body.

⑨ To pass a knife, place it down on a sanitized surface, and let the other person pick it up by the handle.

⑩ Store knives properly in racks, scabbards, or sheaths. See Figure 3.21c.

Figure 3.21c: Step 10—Store knives in racks.

Steel-mesh gloves protect hands from blades and knives, just as rubber work gloves can protect hands from hot dishwashing water and cleaning chemicals.

195

Figure Focus

Figure 3.21b: Point the knife toward yourself when passing it or when putting it down on a work space.

Figure 3.21c: What other knife storage devices might be appropriate besides this table-side unit?

Summary

- Remind students to review the following:
  1. The electrical hazards that contribute to accidental fires
  2. The different classifications of fires and fire extinguishers
  3. The frequency with which equipment should be cleaned in order to help prevent fires
  4. The actions that should be taken in the event of a fire at a foodservice operation
  5. How to clean up spills on the floor
  6. How to use ladders safely
  7. The steps for proper lifting and carrying procedures to avoid injuries
  8. The correct and safe use of knives

Chapter 3 | Foundations of Restaurant Management & Culinary Arts

Summary

In this section, you learned the following:

- Frayed cords, plugs with same-size prongs, too many plugs in an outlet, cracked switchplates, cracked receptacle plates, ungrounded plugs, and ungrounded outlets are electrical hazards that contribute to accidental fires.

- The different classifications of fires and fire extinguishers are class A (wood, paper, cloth), class B (flammable liquids, greases, gases), and class C (live electrical equipment) fires.

- Clean hoods and ducts at least every six months using a qualified cleaning contractor. Clean more often depending on use and grease buildup.

- In the event of a fire, remain calm and start evacuating people immediately, call the fire department, shut off the gas valve, meet at the designated assembly point, and inform a firefighter if someone is missing.

- When cleaning up spills on the floor, verbally warn guests and employees, block the area, post a "Caution–Wet Floor" sign, and direct people around the spill.

- The safest way to use a ladder is for two employees to work together. One person should hold the bottom of the ladder and the other should climb up and pass or receive items.

- Proper lifting steps include establishing a solid footing, aligning the body, making the lift, and setting down the load. Proper carrying procedures include looking for any hazards, using the whole hand to grip the load, keeping the load close to the body, keeping stomach muscles firm and tucking in the lower back, and moving the feet instead of twisting at the waist when turning.

- The correct and safe use of knives includes the following:
  - Keep knives sharpened.
  - Never touch the sharp edges of knife blades.
  - Use the knife for its intended purpose.
  - Place a damp cloth under a cutting board to prevent slipping.
  - Stop cutting and place the knife on a flat, secure surface if interrupted.
  - Never leave knives soaking under water.
  - Never try to catch a falling knife.
  - Carry knives with the cutting edge angled slightly away from the body.
  - Store knives in proper racks, scabbards, or sheaths.

196

196 Chapter 3 | Workplace Safety

Section 3.2 Review Questions

1. List the three classes of fires. What type of extinguisher should be used on each?

2. What can you do to prevent slips, trips, and falls in a restaurant or food-service establishment?

3. Describe the proper way to lift heavy objects.

4. Name three sharp hazards you are likely to find in a kitchen.

5. Flory Doyle of EcoSure notes that workplace safety helps employees to be more efficient in their workspace. Do you think that this is true? Provide two examples that show how workplace safety helps employees to be more efficient.

6. If Chef Jean hires two novice chef's assistants, what should he do to minimize the possibility of cuts in the kitchen?

7. How can burns be prevented in a professional kitchen?

8. Create four scenarios in which a fire breaks out in a restaurant or food-service establishment. For each, determine the course of action and type of fire equipment to be used. How could you have prevented each fire?

197

Section 3.2 Review Questions

1. Class A fires (ordinary combustibles) usually involve wood, paper, cloth, or cardboard and typically happen in dry-storage areas, dining areas, garbage areas, and restrooms. Class B fires (flammable liquids) usually involve flammable liquids and grease and usually start in kitchens and maintenance areas. Class C fires (electrical equipment) usually involve live electrical equipment and typically occur in motors, switches, cords, circuits, and wiring. Water-based extinguishers can be used on class A fires. Aqueous film-forming foam extinguishers can be used on class A or A/B fires. Carbon dioxide extinguishers can be used on class B or C fires. Dry chemical extinguishers can be used on class A/B/C or B/C fires.

2. To avoid slips, trips, and falls, anticipate what might happen. Provide adequate lighting, clearly mark stairs and ramps, be sure that handrails are sturdy and secure, check stair coverings for tears or ragged edges, keep stairs clear of obstacles, and post signs wherever hazards might occur for both workers and guests.

3. The proper way to lift heavy objects is to establish a solid footing, align the body, make the lift, and set down the load. Use leg and stomach muscles to take some strain off the back.

4. Sharp objects you are likely to find in a kitchen include broken glass, sharp tableware, can lids, cutting strips on aluminum foil and plastic wrap, box openers, knives, choppers, blenders, and slicers.

5. Students may answer this question in a variety of ways, so long as they justify their responses.

6. Chef Jean should train the new employees to use all knives and sharp equipment to follow proper safety procedures.

7. To prevent burns, respect heat and always assume that heat sources are on and hot. Be especially careful when traveling through a kitchen area and when using deep-fat fryers and steam equipment. Be sure equipment is in good working condition. Avoid overcrowding the range top. Set pot handles away from burners, and make sure they don't stick out over the edge of the range top. Adjust burner flames to cover only the bottom of a pan. Check hot food on stoves carefully by standing to one edge of the pot or kettle and lifting the edge of the lid farthest from you. Place sealed pouch bags in boiling water carefully to avoid splashing. Never leave hot fat unattended. Ask for help when moving or carrying a heavy pot of simmering liquid from the burners to storage or hotholding areas. Metal containers, foil, or utensils should never be used in microwave ovens. Use hot pads and be careful when removing food and food containers from the microwave.

8. Students may answer this question in a variety of ways, so long as they justify their responses.

Section 3.2 Activities

1. Students may choose from a variety of safety methods, so long as they present correct information in a clear and logical manner.

2. Students may complete this activity in a variety of ways, so long as they justify their responses. For instance, students may suggest that guests be reminded to step up or down for raised dining areas. Appropriate training might include how to phrase this reminder appropriately.

3. Students have some options when answering this question. For instance, they could choose to issue dishwashers heat-resistant, knee-length protective aprons or smocks. Students could also choose to require employees to wear nonskid shoes.

Section 3.2 Activities

1. Study Skills/Group Activity: Workplace Safety Poster

Work with two other classmates to create a poster about workplace safety. The poster could cover how to handle knives, how to carry heavy loads, or other potential hazards.

2. Activity: Preventing Injuries

Identify six ways you can help prevent customer injuries in your restaurant. What training will your employees need to protect guests?

3. Critical Thinking: Employee PPE

You manage a large cafeteria. What personal protective equipment (PPE) should you distribute to which employees? What PPE do you require them to have?

198

SECTION 3.3 FIRST AID AND EXTERNAL THREATS

First aid refers to medical treatment given to an injured person either for light injuries or until more complete treatment can be provided by emergency service or other health-care providers. Effective first aid meets the injured person's emotional and medical needs. It also helps to diffuse the shock, anger, and resentment an injured person may feel toward your operation.

Study Questions

After studying Section 3.3, you should be able to answer the following questions:

- What is first aid?
- What is CPR?
- What is the Heimlich maneuver?
- What are some external threats to an operation?

First Aid

A good **first-aid** program requires equipment, training, a concerned attitude for the injured, and a thorough follow-up. To ensure employee and customer safety, always remember the following points:

- Accidents can be prevented.
- Accidents have serious results.
- You have a responsibility to keep yourself safe.
- You have a responsibility to keep your guests and other employees safe.

199

Section 3.3
First Aid and External Threats

Introduce the Section

a. Explain the importance of knowing important first-aid tips, including CPR and the Heimlich maneuver.
b. Point out some external threats and how they can affect a foodservice operation.
c. Discuss the objectives for the section.

Vocabulary Review

a. Direct students to the key terms.
b. Pronounce each word, and have the students repeat the pronunciation out loud.
c. Discuss the definition of each word.

Teach

Discuss

- Part of an effective first-aid program includes an attitude of concern for the injured person. However, employees and managers should be cautious not to say anything that might later create legal issues for the establishment. Ask students to role-play situations in which employees care for injured guests.

Reinforce and Review

- First aid may consist of care for light injuries or treatment given until medical professionals can provide more extensive services.
- Effective first-aid treatment includes treating a person's physical and emotional needs.
- Employees have a responsibility for keeping themselves, their colleagues, and their guests safe.

Vocabulary Terms

- **First-aid:** The medical treatment given to an injured person.
- **First-aid program:** A program for providing emergency medical treatment that includes equipment training, a concerned attitude for the injured person, and a thorough follow-up.

Discuss

- Unfortunately, sometimes guests may become ill or injured at a foodservice establishment. How should employees and managers behave in such a situation? How might employee and management response to such an event affect the establishment's reputation?
- Sometimes employees are injured on the job. Is it more important to get the job done, or to take care of an injury? Does this depend on the situation? When an employee chooses one response or another, how might an employer or manager react?

Reinforce and Review

- First-aid kits should be readily accessible throughout the establishment and in any service vehicles.
- Generally, employees should not attempt to administer first aid to another person unless they have been trained to do so. If employees must render service in an emergency situation, they should tell healthcare professionals exactly what aid they have performed.

Teaching Tips

- If there is a first-aid kit available in the classroom, make sure students know where it is and how each item in it should be used. Also, make sure students know the quickest way from the classroom to the nurse's office.
- Review district and campus policy regarding first-aid treatment for students.

Some state and local agencies require restaurant and foodservice establishments to have first-aid kits. Kits should be located within easy reach of possible accident sites inside the restaurant and also placed in delivery or catering vehicles if employees often work away from the establishment. Figure 3.22 shows a standard first-aid kit.

Most operations have specific policies for handling injuries. Typically, managers should be notified as soon as possible about any situation involving an injury. Employees should be trained to offer assistance when possible (locate a first-aid kit, call 911, etc.). Most operations also have a formal incident report form for accidents and injuries to be completed and kept on file. Be sure to complete and process full documentation following any accident or first-aid procedure. Include the accounts of witnesses if possible.

Common restaurant and foodservice injuries requiring first aid include minor heat burns, chemical burns, cuts, sprains, and muscle cramps. Table 3.9 lists the steps to care for these common minor injuries.

NOTE: The information below is intended for self-care. Do not attempt to administer first aid on someone else if you are not qualified and/or certified to do so. In a serious emergency, you may need to provide assistance while waiting for paramedics to arrive. For example, a person reacting to a food allergy may need an EpiPen administered immediately or risk death. If you provide assistance in this type of situation, tell health-care professionals about what you have done after they arrive.

Figure 3.22: First-aid kits should be located within easy reach of potential accident sites inside a restaurant or foodservice operation.

200

Figure Focus
Figure 3.22: Can students identify each article in the photograph and how each is used?

Table 3.9: First Aid for Common Minor Injuries

Minor Burns

1. Cool the burn by running the burned area under cold running water for 5 minutes or until the pain subsides.
2. Cover the burn with a sterile gauze bandage. Gauze should be wrapped loosely to avoid pressure to the burn area. Do not apply ointment to the burn, as it could prevent proper healing.
3. Take an over-the-counter pain reliever.

Chemical Burns

1. Remove the cause of the burn by flushing the chemicals off the skin surface with cool, running water for 20 minutes.
2. Remove items such as clothing or jewelry that have been contaminated.
3. Apply a cool, wet cloth to relieve pain.
4. Wrap the burned area loosely with a dry, sterile dressing.
5. Rewash the burned area.

Cuts and Scrapes

1. Stop the bleeding by applying pressure to the cut with a clean cloth.
2. Clean the wound with clean water.
3. Apply antibiotic cream or ointment to keep the wound moist.
4. Cover the wound with a bandage to prevent bacteria from getting in.
5. Change the bandage once a day, or when it becomes wet or dirty.
6. Watch for signs of infection—redness, pain, drainage, warmth, or swelling.

Sprains and Strains

First aid for sprains and strains includes rest, ice, compression, and elevation (RICE).

1. **R**est the injured part of the body.
2. Apply **I**ce or a cold compress for 10–15 minutes at a time every few hours for the first 48 hours to prevent swelling.
3. Wear an elastic **C**ompression bandage for at least 48 hours to reduce swelling.
4. Keep the injured part **E**levated above the level of the heart to reduce swelling.

Muscle Cramps

1. Massage the muscle.
2. Apply cold or heat.
3. Take an over-the-counter pain reliever, if required.

201

Table 3.9: First Aid for Common Minor Injuries

- These injuries are relatively common in the foodservice workplace. What injuries do students think are the most common in a school?
- Why do sprains, strains, and muscle cramps occur? What can students do to prevent them from happening in the first place?

In-Class Activity: First-Aid Techniques

Literacy Connection, 21st-Century Skills— Health Literacy, Apply Technology Effectively, Produce Results

Working in small groups, create computer slide shows illustrating a first-aid technique of your choice (although not one described in Table 3.9).

The slide show should contain at least five distinct visuals, describing the problem (for instance, a minor burn) and how and by whom it should be addressed.

Present your work to the class.

Reinforce and Review

- No one should attempt to perform either CPR or the Heimlich maneuver unless he or she has received specific, current training and certification.
- Training and certification for both CPR and the Heimlich maneuver should be repeated annually.
- Managers should schedule at least one person on each shift who is trained and certified for both CPR and the Heimlich maneuver.

Teaching Tips

- Provide students with information on CPR and Heimlich maneuver training and certification in your community.

Vocabulary Terms

- **Cardiopulmonary resuscitation (CPR):** A technique that attempts to restore breathing and heartbeat to injured people with no signs of breathing and no pulse.
- **Heimlich maneuver:** A technique that attempts to remove obstacles from a choking person's airway.

Additional needs, such as cardiopulmonary resuscitation (CPR) and Heimlich maneuver training, can be carefully assessed by each operation. **Cardiopulmonary resuscitation (CPR)** (CAR-dee-oh PULL-man-air-ee ree-SUHS-i-TAY-shun) restores breathing and heartbeat to injured persons who show no signs of breathing or pulse. **Do not attempt to perform CPR or the Heimlich maneuver unless you have had specific, current training and certification.** Figure 3.23 diagrams the steps in cardiopulmonary resuscitation.

The **Heimlich maneuver** (HIME-lick mah-NOO-ver) removes food or other obstacles from the airway of a choking person. Some states require either employee training in the Heimlich maneuver or posters to be displayed in the restaurant to describe the steps of the procedure. Figure 3.24 illustrates the Heimlich maneuver.

Training and certification for both CPR and the Heimlich maneuver must be renewed every year from a recognized provider of first-aid training. Managers should schedule at least one trained and certified person on every shift. In addition to knowing first-aid medical procedures, remember to show concern for the injured person. Proper training includes instruction on staying calm in emergencies and dealing with the shock and disorientation felt by those who are injured.

Step 1

Step 2

Step 3

Figure 3.23: Step 1—Check for breathing. Step 2—Give mouth-to-mouth resuscitation. Step 3—Perform chest compression to restart heartbeat. (Proper training is required to administer CPR.)

202

Figure Focus

Figure 3.23: Checking for airway, breathing, and circulation (ABC) is a standard practice in assessing whether a person might need cardiopulmonary resuscitation.

Figure 3.24: Steps for performing the Heimlich maneuver: Step 1—Place thumbside of fist against middle of abdomen just above the navel. Grasp fist with other hand. Step 2— Give quick, upward thrusts.

All employees should be trained in handling the emergencies that can happen at an operation. These emergencies might include any of the following situations:

- Foodborne-illness outbreaks
- Employees with contagious illnesses
- Customer or employee injuries on site
- Accidents involving restaurant vehicles
- Loss of power, water, or other utilities
- Fires
- Floods, storms, earthquakes, and other dangerous weather conditions
- Armed robberies and other criminal assaults

203

Reinforce and Review
- All employees should be trained on handling potential emergencies, including outbreaks of foodborne illness and injuries to guests.

Teaching Tips
- Consider asking the school nurse or another healthcare professional to speak with the class about common first-aid techniques.
- Make sure students understand that performing the Heimlich maneuver or cardiopulmonary resuscitation on fragile people (such as elderly people or infants) is itself dangerous and must be performed carefully to avoid injury.
- Explain to students how they could perform the Heimlich maneuver on themselves with a chair if no other help is forthcoming.

Figure Focus
Figure 3.24: Placing one's hands over one's throat is a universal sign of choking.

Discuss

- What costs are involved in providing a safe working and dining environment? Is there such a thing as being too safe? How can managers and owners develop a balance between safety and efficiency?

Reinforce and Review

- All employees should be properly trained on basic first-aid techniques and concerns, including the threats posed by blood-borne pathogens.
- Back doors should be kept locked and alarmed at all times to reduce or eliminate the risk of theft or other intruders.

What's New:
First-Aid Training and Your Staff

Why is it important for students to understand the role of managers at this stage of their careers? What information can students take from this sidebar that will be important in the short term?

Homework Activity:
Costs and Benefits

Mathematics Connection, Literacy Connection, 21st-Century Skills—Information Literacy, Work Independently, Critical Thinking and Problem Solving, Communicate Clearly

How much money does the foodservice industry lose each year in pilferage and other types of theft? How much is lost to arson, vandalism, workplace violence, and other external threats?

Make a chart illustrating how much each category of threat costs the industry annually.

Next, research how much the foodservice industry spends annually on insurance, security, and other precautions to protect against these threats.

Make a chart of these costs as well.

Compare your two charts. If you were a restaurant owner, where would you spend your security-related money so that it would have the greatest impact?

Vocabulary Terms

- **Arson:** The deliberate and malicious burning of property.

Remember, **do not attempt to perform CPR or the Heimlich maneuver unless you have had specific, current training and certification.** You can cause harm to the injured person if the procedures are not done properly, as well as place yourself and your operation at risk. CPR and the Heimlich maneuver can save lives, but they are difficult to do. For example, both CPR and the Heimlich maneuver are handled differently for infants and small children than for adults.

[what's new]

First-Aid Training and Your Staff

As a manager, ensure that all your employees have a basic knowledge of first-aid techniques for the most common injuries suffered in a restaurant or foodservice establishment: cuts, heat burns, chemical burns, and muscle pain (such as cramps or sprains). State and local agencies may have resources available to assist you with educating your employees, but you should have sufficient knowledge to teach your staff what injuries can be safely handled in-house and which require immediate professional attention. Encourage employees to attend cardiopulmonary resuscitation (CPR) training. In fact, consider reimbursing employees for the certification fees.

Make sure that your employees understand the threats posed by bloodborne pathogens. All employees should be trained on proper care for a wound as well as appropriate protocol for cleaning up safely. Hopefully, your staff will never need to know any first-aid information more sophisticated than how to apply their own bandages, but it is important to be prepared.

First-aid kits should be properly stocked at all times. Various sizes of bandages, antibiotic creams, and burn gels or sprays are basic components, but also consider including gauze, surgical tape, cold packs, antacids, and pain-relieving tablets. Gloves, tweezers, and scissors are valuable tools as well. Consider having one first-aid kit for each dining area and each food-preparation area at your facility, and check supplies at least weekly.

External Threats

An often overlooked workplace safety issue involves external threats, such as arson and theft. **Arson,** the deliberate and malicious burning of property, is very difficult to stop, but good overall fire safety and building security can eliminate many opportunities for an arsonist.

It is important that employees keep back doors locked and alarmed at all times to prevent the occurrence of pilferage and to reduce the risk of robbery. Locking and alarming all doors and windows while the facility is closed for business reduces the risk of intruders, limits loss from robbery, and helps prevent property damage from vandalism. Develop and implement security policies and procedures to combat these risks. Have all employees review these procedures and policies and actively practice the security measures.

204

Chapter 2: Keeping Food Safe discussed in detail how to prevent purposeful food contamination and tampering. To make sure that food is safe, control access to an operation's food supplies. Uniforms and name tags are a good way to identify staff and vendors. Safety badges also ensure that people in the food area belong there. Remember, "If you see something, say something."

Summary

In this section, you learned the following:

- First aid is medical treatment given to an injured person either for light injuries or until more complete treatment can be provided by emergency services.

- CPR stands for cardiopulmonary resuscitation. CPR restores breathing and heartbeat to injured persons who show no signs of breathing or pulse.

- The Heimlich maneuver removes food or other obstacles from the airway of a choking person.

- External threats to an operation include arson, theft, and food tampering.

205

Summary

- Remind students to review the following:
  1. First aid
  2. CPR
  3. The Heimlich maneuver
  4. External threats to an operation

Section 3.3
Review Questions

1. The most common foodservice injuries include minor burns, chemical burns, cuts and scrapes, sprains and strains, and muscle cramps.

2. Emergencies that employees might have to handle in a foodservice operation include foodborne-illness outbreaks; employees with contagious diseases: customer or employee injuries on-site; accidents involving restaurant vehicles; loss of power, water, or other utilities; fires; dangerous weather conditions; and criminal assaults.

3. External threats may include arson and theft.

4. CPR, or cardiopulmonary resuscitation, restores breathing and heartbeat to injured persons who show no signs of breathing or pulse.

5. Students may answer this question in a variety of ways. For instance, staff members may react to an accident involving a restaurant vehicle by contacting the insurance company and the establishment's lawyer; interviewing the employee involved in the accident; communicating information about the accident to all employees, along with any company-approved message to provide to inquisitive guests or vendors; and preparing a press release about the incident, if necessary.

6. Linda should provide appropriate first-aid training to all employees, even those who have had some prior training or experience, to ensure that all employees understand appropriate procedures. To meet the restaurant's needs without burdening individuals, this training can be administered in brief sessions scheduled during the restaurant's slow periods. Employees could also be encouraged to enroll in more formal training sessions off-site, with the restaurant agreeing to pay some or all of the costs.

7. A system of identification badges should be put into place to prevent non-employees from wandering into staff areas. This can prevent both intentional and accidental food tampering as well as pilferage. Signs can be posted reminding guests that they may not enter staff areas, and employees can be trained on polite ways to ensure that only staff and vendors are permitted in these areas. For instance, employees can ask any non-uniformed persons in work areas if they need help.

8. Students may answer this question in a variety of ways, so long as they justify their answers.

Section 3.3 Review Questions

1. Describe the most common foodservice injuries.
2. List four of the emergencies that employees might have to handle in a food-service operation.
3. What are two external threats that might occur at an operation?
4. What is CPR and when is it used?
5. Flory Doyle emphasizes the importance of all aspects of workplace safety. Provide examples of two possible emergencies. How would a properly prepared and safety-conscious staff member deal with each situation?
6. Linda has found that many of her employees do not have adequate first-aid training or experience. What steps should she take to correct this situation? How can she address the restaurant's overall needs without burdening individual employees?
7. Assume that you are managing the kitchen staff of a senior center. It's a fairly casual environment, and people tend to come in and out constantly, whether they should or not. What overall steps can you take to ensure employee and customer safety?
8. Assume you are running a small restaurant with minimal staff. How much first-aid training would you want employees to have?

Section 3.3 Activities

1. Study Skills/Group Activity: Slip Up

You are part of the management team at a local coffee bar. A customer slips and falls on some spilled coffee. What do you do? Working with two or three other students, develop an appropriate response.

2. Activity: First-Aid Kit

You own a large restaurant that appeals to families. What should your first-aid kit contain in case of employee injuries? What about customer injuries?

3. Critical Thinking: CPR Training

Being trained and certified in cardiopulmonary resuscitation (CPR) is extremely important—you could save someone's life. Research the availability of CPR training in your area. Do you plan to undertake this training? Why or why not?

207

Section 3.3 Activities

1. The students' response should include the following elements: retraining employees on the prompt handling of spills; treating the injured guest with appropriate care and concern; notifying management promptly; notifying emergency personnel if necessary; and completing a formal incident report form, including witness statements.

2. Students may suggest a variety of items to be included in a first-aid kit for employees or for guests. The employee kit should include various sizes of bandages, antibiotic creams, burn gels or sprays, gauze, surgical tape, gloves, tweezers, cold packs, antacids, pain-relieving tablets, and scissors. The guest kit should include these items as well as items specifically intended to treat children: bandages depicting cartoon characters, child-safe pain relievers and other medications, and lollipops might all be included.

3. Students should independently research the availability of local CPR training. Whether or not they plan to obtain the training is immaterial as long as they justify their responses.

Case Study Follow-Up

1. Linda and Chef Jean should retrain staff on the importance of reporting physical hazards to management, stressing the responsibility each staff member bears. To prevent over-reporting, Linda and Chef Jean may consider having staff apply stickers to any physical hazards, noting the date and time at which the hazards were reported to management, or instituting a hazard log, where employees reporting hazards could describe the problems and note the dates and times at which they were reported to management.

2. The best way for Linda to ensure that staff members are following established safety procedures is to watch them working, issuing reminders as necessary.

3. If employees do not follow proper safety procedures, they should be reminded of the correct method and retrained if necessary. If employees persist in following unsafe procedures, discipline or even termination may be appropriate responses.

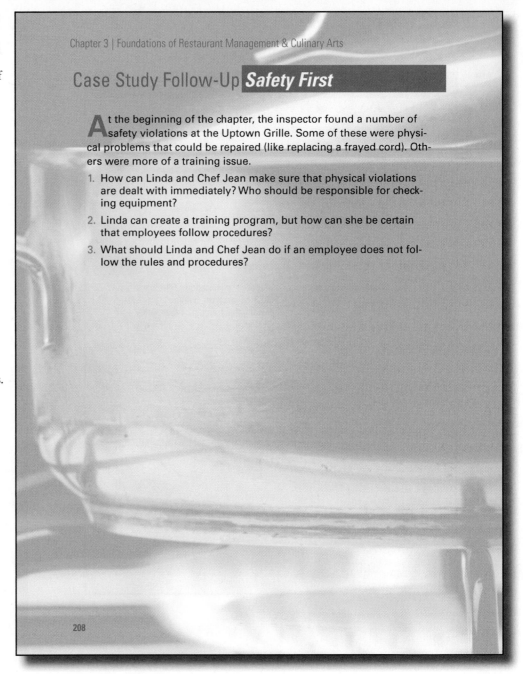

Case Study Follow-Up *Safety First*

At the beginning of the chapter, the inspector found a number of safety violations at the Uptown Grille. Some of these were physical problems that could be repaired (like replacing a frayed cord). Others were more of a training issue.

1. How can Linda and Chef Jean make sure that physical violations are dealt with immediately? Who should be responsible for checking equipment?

2. Linda can create a training program, but how can she be certain that employees follow procedures?

3. What should Linda and Chef Jean do if an employee does not follow the rules and procedures?

208

Apply Your Learning

Employee Injuries

A catering business has 427 employees. Last year, 114 separate employees were injured on the job: 42 suffered first-degree burns, 37 suffered knife cuts, 24 slipped or fell while working, and 11 contracted a foodborne illness while working. What percent of employees were injured last year? Create a pie chart that shows the percentage of each type of injury.

History of OSHA

The Occupational Safety and Health Administration (OSHA) was established in 1970 to develop and enforce safety-related guidelines and directives for the workplace. Write three paragraphs on OSHA's history and scope. What does it do, and how does it or will it affect your working life?

Keeping Chemicals Safe

Many chemicals are used to keep a foodservice establishment clean and safe and to avoid the outbreak of foodborne illness. However, these chemicals can themselves be hazardous. For instance, mixing bleach and ammonia, two common cleaning agents, can result in toxic fumes, and oven cleaners can cause chemical burns. Identify two chemicals frequently used in restaurants or foodservice establishments (such as your school cafeteria) and describe their uses, side effects, and potential for harm. How can you use these products safely? Write two paragraphs discussing each chemical you select.

Critical Thinking Safety Plan

As the food and beverage manager for a large convention center, you are responsible for the safety and well-being of a number of people—foodhandlers, serving staff, housekeeping personnel, maintenance staff, and administrators, plus thousands of guests using your facilities every day. What elements of a comprehensive workplace safety plan must you develop?

Apply Your Learning

Employee Injuries

Students should be able to perform all calculations correctly and draw an accurate pie chart.

History of OSHA

In addition to discussing OSHA's history and mission in a factual manner, students should determine accurate relationships between OSHA's responsibilities and the students' own professional lives.

Keeping Chemicals Safe

Students can select from a variety of chemicals but must be able to discuss their uses, side effects, and potentials for harm in a clear and factual way. Obtaining Material Safety Data Sheets for each chemical chosen will facilitate this process but is not necessary.

Critical Thinking Safety Plan

Broadly speaking, students should discuss training programs and emergency plans, describing ways to keep both staff and guests safe. This discussion should be as comprehensive as possible, addressing everything from proper lifting of heavy items to accident investigation to external threats.

Exam Prep Answers

1. B
2. A
3. D
4. D
5. D
6. C
7. C
8. D
9. A
10. C

Exam Prep Questions

1 Which federal agency creates and enforces safety-related standards and regulations in the workplace?

A. HCS

B. OSHA

C. NOAA

D. HAZCOM

2 A safety inspection of an operation's facility, equipment, employee practices, and management practices is called a(n) _____ audit.

A. general safety

B. emergency plan

C. material safety data

D. accident investigation

3 A choking person can be helped by the use of

A. CPR.

B. first aid.

C. defibrillation.

D. the Heimlich maneuver.

4 The best way to carry a knife in a kitchen is to hold the blade pointing

A. inward and above your head.

B. upward and to your stomach.

C. outward and close to your side.

D. downward and close to your side.

5 A class B fire extinguisher should be used for which types of fires?

A. Hot griddles

B. Electrical equipment

C. Paper, cloth, wood, and plastic

D. Grease, oil, or liquid stored under pressure

6 Which class of fire extinguisher should an employee use to put out an electrical fire?

A. Class A

B. Class B

C. Class C

D. Class A/B/C

7 What is the most serious degree of burn?

A. First

B. Second

C. Third

D. Fourth

8 An event in which property damage or injury is narrowly avoided is a(n)

A. hazard.

B. liability.

C. accident.

D. near miss.

9 What type of heat detector uses infrared and ultraviolet sensors that respond to the movement of flame or to its radiant energy?

A. Flame detector

B. Ionization detector

C. Rate of rise detector

D. Thermostat detector

10 Heat detectors are activated by a significant

A. increase in oxygen.

B. decrease in oxygen.

C. increase in temperature.

D. decrease in temperature.

Chapter 4 Overview

Chapter 4 introduces the student to the concepts of professionalism and recipe standardization—both essential to an ambitious foodservice employee.

Section 1: The first section discusses the role of professionalism in the workplace, identifying six key attributes of a culinary professional.

Section 2: This section explains the role of mathematics in the foodservice industry, covering the gamut from basic mathematic principles and measurement to standardizing recipes.

Advance Preparation	
Review	The National Restaurant Association (www.restaurant.org), the National Restaurant Association Educational Foundation (www.nraef.org), and the American Culinary Federation (www.acfchefs.org) Web sites
	Campus and district policies regarding respect, diversity, and harassment
Contact	Representative from the state restaurant association or a professional chef
Prepare	Information about degree- and diploma-granting culinary and foodservice programs
	Information about continuing education options for foodservice professionals
	Examples of tasting menus from local or national restaurants
	Sample math problems to accompany classroom discussion and for in-class assignments

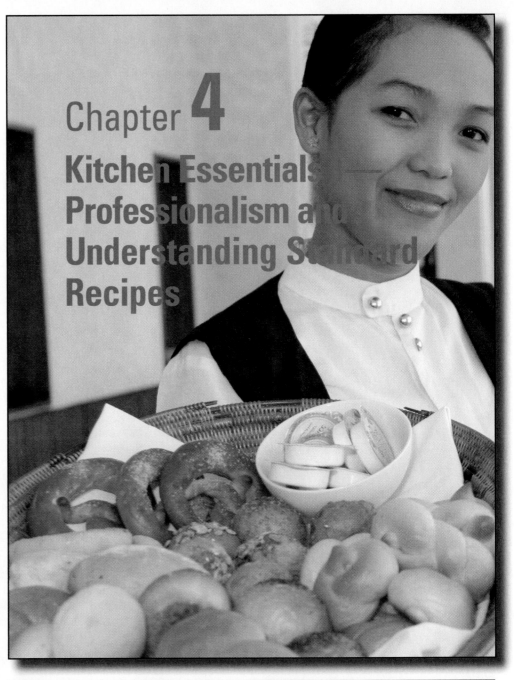

Chapter 4
Kitchen Essentials 1— Professionalism and Understanding Standard Recipes

CUSTOMIZED INSTRUCTION OPTIONS			
Less Advanced Students	**More Advanced Students**	**ESOL Students**	**Special Needs Students**
Pages 217, 236, 257	Pages 215, 235, 255	Pages 220, 224	Pages 222, 228, 251

CHAPTER TOOLS			
21st-Century Skills	**Mathematics**	**Science**	**Literacy**
Pages 214, 215, 216, 218, 219, 221, 224, 226, 230, 235, 255	Pages 230, 236, 242, 244, 251, 255, 257	Pages 219, 221, 244	Pages 214, 215, 216, 217, 218, 219, 220, 221, 222, 224, 226, 228, 230, 235, 236, 242, 244, 251, 255, 257

Case Study *The Art of Professionalism*

Chef Jean hired Alex, a culinary student, for a prep cook position to help with catering jobs. Alex is an aspiring chef. He knows that he will gain invaluable experience as a prep cook and that this will help him move to the next level.

Chef Jean is teaching Alex about professionalism including providing courteous, friendly, and efficient customer service. Chef Jean also stresses the importance of being a team player. Chef Jean says, "A good prep cook is always aware of what is going on in the kitchen and is always willing to help others get the job done."

Chef Jean is pleased with Alex's work ethic and his good people skills. He thinks that Alex will progress rapidly. So, he decides to ask Alex to help with menu planning and execution for several functions. Some of the menu items will be the same, but the numbers of people attending ranges from a small dinner party of 18 to large celebrations of 150. Alex will need to understand how to read a recipe, measure ingredients, convert recipes, and calculate yields. However, Alex admits that he is a bit math-phobic and is afraid of making a mistake that will cost the restaurant.

As you read this chapter, think about the following questions:

1. Does Alex appear to be a professional employee?
2. What can be done to address Alex's math phobia?
3. What skills does Alex need to possess to be able to complete his assignment properly?

Case Study
Climbing the Career Ladder

- Discuss the role of professionalism in the food-service industry. Do students see it as important? Link professionalism to the classroom.
- Why might helping with catering jobs be a good place for Alex to start working?
- Why are math skills so important? How can having poor math skills affect a restaurant or foodservice establishment?
- Note that there are follow-up questions about the case study at the end of the chapter.
- This activity could be done in groups, as a class, or as a homework assignment.

Professional Profile

Discuss	What is a profession? Discuss what it means to be a professional.
	Is it always possible to "give to the absolute best of your ability"?
	What are some ways to keep learning throughout a career?
Reinforce and Review	The foodservice industry, although once deemed menial, has become far more professional and has developed a higher profile in recent years.
Teaching Tips	Relate the profile on Dr. Jerald Chesser to the foregoing professional profiles.

Homework Activity: Culinary Educators

Literacy Connection, 21st-Century Skills—Work Independently, Information Literacy, Reason Effectively, Communicate Clearly

What education and experience is required to work as a culinary educator in a high school? What about in a college?

What other workplaces might hire a culinary educator and why?

Write a one-page report on your findings.

[professional profile]

Dr. Jerald Chesser, CEC, FMP, CCE, AAC

Professor (Educator)

The Collins College of Hospitality Management

California State Polytechnic University, Pomona

Author of:

The Art and Science of Culinary Preparation

The World of Culinary Supervision, Training and Management

I grew up in the restaurant business, working with my father in the kitchen and my mother in the dining room. I saw the pleasure they created for themselves and others. I wanted to be able to bring that same enjoyment to other people, so going into the restaurant business and becoming both a chef and owner was a natural fit.

When I was in high school and began to think about college, I decided I wanted to become a chef like my father. I can remember telling dad and still recall his answer: "No! You are going to go to college and make something of yourself." My parents were entrepreneurs, accomplished business professionals, and highly successful, but they were not considered to be (and did not perceive themselves to be) at the same level as other professionals—bankers, doctors, professors, or lawyers.

In fact, I still remember the day that my father apologized to me for coming to my school to get me in his chef's uniform because he was afraid he had embarrassed me! I have spent my life working to ensure that no father or mother ever again has to worry about embarrassing his or her child by being seen in a chef's uniform or because they are a restaurateur. And I ask that you carry on this challenge.

After getting a bachelor's and master's degree in history, I got a doctorate in education. I then went into education because I saw an opportunity to impact both individual lives and the industry that is so important to me. The match between the culinary/restaurant industry and education was a natural fit. I think that there is no greater achievement than to assist others in reaching their goals.

So, being able to help people to succeed in the restaurant industry, while helping to generate a sense of pride in what they do—well, it doesn't get any better than that.

The key to quality food and service is a sincere desire to feed both the body and the spirit. This is accomplished by doing everything to the absolute best of your ability.

Constant pursuit of knowledge, training, and experience is necessary to be the best you can be and deliver the best possible product and experience to the guest. Success without personal growth and development is not success—it is resting on your laurels.

214

Always remember that what we do in the restaurant industry goes beyond just feeding people. We have the opportunity to impact lives in small and large ways, both individually and as an industry.

Remember,

" *We are ladies and gentlemen serving ladies and gentlemen.* "

—Hermann G. Rusch

And another favorite quote:

" *If you would not want to eat it, then why would you ask your guest to eat it.* "

—William "Bill" Chesser, CEC, AAC

About Kitchen Essentials 1—Professionalism and Standardized Recipes

Professionalism is defined as the conduct, aims, or qualities that characterize or mark a profession. A profession is defined as a calling requiring specialized knowledge. To be a professional is to have more than just the specialized knowledge of the calling. It is to conduct yourself in a manner that always reflects positively on the profession.

Professionalism is not an option; it is a requirement. Integrity, attention to detail, concern for the welfare of others, seeking knowledge, mentoring and working constantly to advance others—all of these are part of being a professional. Your attire should be crisp, your shoes shined, your body clean and well-groomed. Begin to be the model of professionalism now.

Remember, to paraphrase the words of Aristotle, excellence is not an act, it is a habit. You do not get up one day and decide to be excellent…and then take a day off from being excellent. The same is true for professionalism because professionalism is part of being excellent. If you start to make this part of your norm, your standard, you will be successful.

Professional Profile

| Discuss | Ask students to explain the quotes Dr. Chesser cites at the end of his profile. How do they relate to professionalism? |

Focus and Engage

Discuss
- Why is professionalism the first "kitchen essential" discussed in the textbook? How does it relate to cooking techniques, guest service, or management skills?
- It is commonly said that "first impressions are everything." What are some ways people can determine whether or not an employee is "professional" at first glance?

CUSTOMIZED INSTRUCTION

Literacy Connection, 21st-Century Skills—Work Independently, Information Literacy, Reason Effectively, Communicate Clearly

More Advanced Students

Research the roots of the word "profession." What are its origins? What other contemporary words are etymologically related to it?

Invent and define three new words, based on the same roots as "profession." Use each in a sentence.

Section 4.1
Professionalism

Introduce the Section

a. Review the concept of professionalism and introduce the term "culinarian."
b. Describe the relationship between workstations and brigades, referring to the discussion of Georges-Auguste Escoffier in Chapter 1.
c. Discuss the objectives for the section.

Vocabulary Review

a. Direct students to the key terms.
b. Pronounce each word, and have the students repeat the pronunciation out loud.
c. Discuss the definition of each word.

Teach

Discuss

- Discuss the standards for work and behavior in the culinary classroom. Should they be the same standards used in "real" kitchens? Why or why not?

Reinforce and Review

- There are six ingredients of professionalism: knowledge, skill, taste, judgment, dedication, and pride.
- Professionals are honest, courteous, and responsible in their dealings with guests and colleagues.
- The foundations of the culinary profession include handling ingredients and equipment as well as traditional techniques and recipes.

**Homework Activity:
Six Ingredients of Professionalism**

**Literacy Connection, 21st-Century Skills—
Arts, Think Creatively, Create Media Products,
Communicate Clearly**

Working alone or in small groups, students should develop a creative product illustrating the "six ingredients of professionalism." This can be done in a variety of ways: a painting, a song, or a skit, for instance. The final product should be presented to the class.

Vocabulary Terms

- **Culinarian:** One who has studied and continues to study the art of cooking.

4.1 Professionalism	4.2 Using Standardized Recipes
• What does it mean to be a culinary professional?	• Business math
• Workstations	• U.S. and metric measurement systems
	• Standardized recipes
	• Converting recipes
	• Measuring
	• EP/AP amounts
	• Costing recipes

SECTION 4.1 PROFESSIONALISM

Wouldn't it be easy if there were a recipe for producing a good culinary professional? Well, at least we know the basic ingredients: knowledge, skill, taste, judgment, dedication, and pride. As you begin your career, these basics are the building blocks that will last throughout your professional life.

Study Questions

After studying Section 4.1, you should be able to answer the following questions:

- What is professionalism?
- What does it mean to be a professional culinarian?
- What is the kitchen brigade?
- What is the dining-room brigade?

What Does It Mean To Be a Culinary Professional?

To be professional is to be courteous, honest, and responsible in your dealings with customers and co-workers. Professionals maintain standards for their work and behavior, for instance, by being concerned with the following:

- A working environment that does not discriminate against other coworkers because of the way they look.
- Using products and equipment safely and avoid waste.
- Being fair with others and direct in their communications.

A **culinarian** is one who has studied and continues to study the art of cooking. All professional culinarians must first learn the foundations of their profession—handling ingredients and equipment as well as traditional techniques and recipes. Next, they must apply those skills in order to advance their profession as well as their own careers.

216

Most professions require a person to have a diverse range of skills and interests, and the culinary vocation is no different. A culinary professional is an artist, a business-person, a scientist, and a culinary explorer, among other things. Acquiring the skills and knowledge necessary to succeed in this profession is a lifelong journey.

A professional's responsibility is four-fold: to themselves, to coworkers, to the business, and to the guest. Waste, recklessness, disregard for others, or abuse are unacceptable. Abusive language, harassment, ethnic slurs, and profanity do not have a place in the professional kitchen. Courtesy, respect, discipline, and team-work build self-esteem and pride. See Figure 4.1 for the Culinarian's Code.

Culinarian's Code

I pledge my professional knowledge and skill to the advancement of our profession, and I pledge to pass it on to those who are to follow.

I shall foster a spirit of courteous consideration and cooperation within our profession.

I shall place honor and the standing of our profession before personal advancement.

I shall not use unfair means to affect my professional advancement or to injure the chances of another colleague to secure and hold employment.

I shall be fair, courteous, and considerate in my dealings with fellow colleagues.

I shall conduct any necessary comment on, or criticism of, the work of a fellow colleague with careful regard to the good name and dignity of the culinary profession, and will scrupulously refrain from using criticism to gain personal advantage.

I shall never expect anyone to subject themselves to risks which I would not be willing to assume myself.

I shall help to protect all members against one another from within our profession.

I shall be just as enthusiastic about the success of others as I am about my own.

I shall be too big for worry, too noble for anger, too strong for fear, and too happy to permit pressure of business to hurt anyone, within or without the profession.

Adopted by the American Culinary Federation, Inc., at its Convention in Chicago, August 1957

Figure 4.1: The Culinarian's Code.

Professionals are committed to providing excellent service. Service implies more than bringing food to a paying customer. Everyone, from the executive chef to the dishwasher, has a stake in keeping the customer happy. Open communication between the chef and staff, as shown in Figure 4.2, is an important aspect of good service. Good service includes (but is not limited to) providing the following:

Figure 4.2: Open communication among staff is an important aspect of good service.

217

- A professional has four sets of responsibilities: to himself or herself, to coworkers, to the business, and to the guests.
- Courtesy, respect, discipline, and teamwork build self-esteem and pride.
- Good service includes, but is not limited to, providing quality items that are properly and safely prepared, foods that are appropriately flavored, and foods that are attractively presented.

CUSTOMIZED INSTRUCTION
Literacy Connection
Less Advanced Students
Think about the Culinarian's Code. What are three specific things you can do each day to abide by it? List them and prepare for an in-class discussion.

Figure Focus

Figure 4.1: The Culinarian's Code has been recited by chefs for over 50 years.

Figure 4.2: Why does the person talking have a white hat, while the people listening have hairnets and/or short black caps? Is all kitchen communication one way?

Discuss

- Compare the effectiveness of formal versus informal education in the restaurant and foodservice industry. How might they complement or contradict one another?

Reinforce and Review

- Culinarians must be able to identify, purchase, utilize, and prepare a wide variety of foods as well as train and supervise an effective and professional staff.
- To stay abreast of industry advances, culinary professionals should read, travel, and taste new foods and dishes as much as possible.
- Professional organizations can help culinarians interact with one another.

Homework Activity: Professional Organizations

Literacy Connection, 21st-Century Skills— Communicate Clearly, Information Literacy, Initiative and Self-Direction

Select a professional organization of your choice. It does not have to be related to the restaurant and foodservice industry. Research who its members are and what its goals are, as well as other material that you find interesting.

Present a brief report to the class.

- Quality items that are properly and safely prepared
- Food that is appropriately flavored
- Foods that is attractively presented

Attributes of a Culinary Professional

Knowledge

Culinary professionals have to identify, purchase, utilize, and prepare a wide variety of foods. They are required to train and supervise a safe, skilled, efficient staff. In order to do this successfully, culinarians need to understand and apply certain scientific and business principles. A professional culinary program provides the culinary student with a basic knowledge of foods, food styles, and the methods used to prepare foods. In addition, students will learn about sanitation, nutrition, and business procedures, such as food costing.

As with any profession, an education does not stop at commencement. After culinary students join the ranks of the employed, they will continue to learn and grow. The culinary profession is constantly evolving, and additional classes, workshops, and seminars help culinarians perfect skills in specialized areas and keep up with new methods and styles of cooking. Culinary professionals should do the following:

- Regularly review periodicals and books devoted to cooking
- Travel as much as possible
- Try new dishes

It is also helpful to become involved in professional organizations in order to meet peers, gain insight, and exchange ideas. There are a number of professional organizations a culinarian can join:

- **National Restaurant Association Educational Foundation:** www.nraef.org
- **National Restaurant Association:** www.restaurant.org
- **American Culinary Federation (ACF):** www.acfchefs.org
- **International Council of Hotel, Restaurant & Institutional Educators (I-CHRIE):** www.chrie.org
- **Research Chefs Association (RCA):** www.culinology.com
- **American Hotel Motel Association (AHMA):** www.ahma.com

218

Figure 4.3 shows a chef giving a demonstration to students.

Skill

Culinary schooling alone does not make a student a culinary professional. Practice and hands-on experience provide the skills necessary to produce quality foods consistently and efficiently, to organize, train, motivate, and supervise a staff.

Almost all foodservice operations recognize that new workers, even those who have graduated from culinary programs, need time and experience to develop and improve their skills. Most graduates start in entry-level positions. Don't be discouraged; advancements will come, and the training pays off in the long run. Today, culinary styles and fashions change frequently. What does not go out of fashion are well-trained, skilled, and knowledgeable culinary professionals.

Flavor, Aroma, and Taste

Culinary professionals must produce foods that taste great, or the customer will not return. Professional chefs are judged on the ability to produce the finest flavors, manipulating tastes and aromas to achieve the desired results. It is critical that culinary professionals understand how flavor, aroma, and taste work. Figure 4.4 shows a culinary professional tasting a dish.

Flavor refers to all the sensations produced by whatever is in the mouth, but mostly the food's aroma and taste. Think about the last time you had a stuffy nose and nothing seemed to taste right. When people lose the ability to smell, they lose the ability to perceive flavors, even though the foods themselves don't

Figure 4.3: Demonstrations help culinary professionals perfect their skills and learn new methods or styles of cooking.

Figure 4.4: Before a dish is sent out of the kitchen, a culinary professional tastes the dish to check the flavor.

219

Figure Focus

Figure 4.3: Do demonstrations like this help students learn? What other learning methods can be successful?

Figure 4.4: What food safety precautions is the cook in this photograph taking?

Reinforce and Review

- Practice and hands-on experience help culinary professionals establish a solid base of skills.
- Most culinary professionals, even those who have graduated from culinary programs, will still start at entry-level industry positions.
- Professional chefs are judged according to their ability to produce particular flavors and must therefore understand how flavor, taste, and aroma interact.

In-Class Activity: Flavors and Aroma

Science Connection, 21st-Century Skills—Information Literacy, Communicate Clearly, Be Self-Directed Learners

Flavor cups of water with a variety of additives—sugar, salt, vanilla, lemon, almond, etc.—but do not tell students what the flavorings are. Each student volunteer should taste each flavored drink twice: once with his or her nose pinched shut, once with the nose open. After each taste, ask students to record what they think each flavor is. Ask students to compare their ability to determine flavors both with and without aroma.

Homework Activity: Flavor Profiles

Science Connection, 21st-Century Skills—Information Literacy, Communicate Clearly, Be Self-Directed Learners

What is a "flavor profile"? The "flavor profile" combines all the sensory impressions created by ingesting a substance by mouth, such as taste, odor, and texture.

Research this concept and its relevance to the foodservice industry.

Write a one-page essay on your findings.

Vocabulary Terms

- **Flavor:** All the sensations produced by whatever is in the mouth, but mostly the food's aroma and taste.

Discuss

- Psychological experiments have demonstrated that smell is the most evocative of the five senses. Why do smells remind us of our previous experiences and emotions? How can professional chefs use this to enhance their guests' experiences?

Reinforce and Review

- Many things create aroma: fermentation, the ripening (aging) process, and other chemical reactions.
- The five basic tastes are salt, sour, bitter, sweet, and umami. Umami refers to savoriness.
- The tongue and mouth can identify a number of other sensations besides taste, such as astringency and temperature.

On the Job:
Testing Tastes

Encourage students to discuss how a person can develop a taste memory. In what career paths outside the restaurant and foodservice industry might this skill be helpful?

How might the subjectivity of taste affect a budding chef's career? Are there some people who simply can't develop a "proper" palate?

CUSTOMIZED INSTRUCTION

Literacy Connection

ESOL Students

Umami, the "savory" taste, is found in almost every culture's cuisine. What umami-containing foods are popular in your culture of origin? Are these available in your community?

Give a brief presentation about this to the class.

Vocabulary Terms

- **Umami:** The savory, "meaty" taste, commonly identified with tomatoes, shiitake mushrooms, and soybean products.

change. The relationship between aroma and taste is so strong that if a cook changes how a food smells, but *doesn't* change how it tastes, then the food's flavor changes.

Many things create aroma: fermentation, the ripening process, other chemical reactions. People perceive aromas, or smells, when they trigger the receptors in the nose. These receptors then send messages to the part of the brain responsible for emotional responses. For many people, smells connect to emotions. For example, most people don't notice all the ingredients in a pot of spaghetti sauce, but a lot of people might remember the way they felt when they sat down to a home-style dinner with families and friends. This is why aromatherapy has become so popular. Humans can pick up very tiny amounts of the chemical compounds that make up smells and identify thousands of aromas. In fact, people can even recognize their blood relatives just by smelling them. Building on this ability, some fine-dining chefs now include elements in their tasting menus, such as smoking wood or fragrant blossoms, that contribute aroma, not taste, to a particular course.

Taste refers to our ability to identify substances like foods, minerals, and even poisons. Some bad-tasting substances are commonly added to dangerous chemicals to warn people away. There are five basic tastes: salt, sour, bitter, sweet, and **umami** (or savory). Educators used to believe there was a "tongue map" that could show where on the tongue each type of taste is experienced. That map is no longer used. Now researchers recognize that a single human taste bud can identify a number of different tastes. The tongue and mouth can also recognize other sensations besides taste: fattiness, astringency, calcium, metal, spicy-hot, minty-cool, numbness, mouthfeel, and temperature. While none of these is actually a taste, they affect people's perceptions of what they do taste, and experienced chefs use all of these effects to create specific dishes.

[on the job]

Testing Tastes

Most food or beverage companies use professional taste-testers to get feedback on their developing products. Other associations, such as the American Academy of Taste, conduct taste tests to decide which products to endorse. The tasting conditions must be as neutral as possible. For example, there should be no external odors in the tasting area, and the cups, plates, and cooking utensils must not have any odors or tastes of their own. Professional taste-testers evaluate products by using "taste memory," which is the ability to recognize and categorize flavors that they have previously experienced. They also rely on a prearranged set of standards and vocabulary so that when one taste-tester uses a word, the others all know exactly what that person means. Chefs often hold "cuttings" with their staff to decide which product—olive oil or hamburgers, for example—are best for their kitchens. These don't involve professional taste-testers, but these opportunities help young cooks develop their own taste memories.

220

Taste, however, is highly subjective: everyone's physical and cultural characteristics are different, so everyone has different personal preferences. Age, vitamin deficiencies, and genetic variations are just some of the reasons why a food won't taste the same to any two eaters. Although diners and circumstances can affect the way tastes are perceived, foods do have essential, characteristic tastes regardless of the situation. That is, if two people are eating bananas, and one person likes the taste and the other doesn't, well, the banana still tastes like a banana.

Flavor and its different components can remind people of loved ones, warn them away from poisons, help determine the best possible recipe—it's a long list. Professional chefs use all the tools in their arsenals to create the ideal experience for their guests, whether it's a quick burger and fries or an 18-course tasting menu.

The total perception of eating is a complex combination of smell, taste, sight, sound, and texture. Humans involve all senses in the pleasure of eating; therefore, all senses must be considered in creating and preparing a dish. Culinary professionals have to develop a taste memory by sampling foods, both familiar and unfamiliar. They think about what they taste, making notes and experimenting with flavor combinations and cooking methods. Culinarians are not inventive simply for the sake of invention. Rather, they consider how the flavors, appearances, textures, and aromas of various foods will interact to create a total taste experience.

Judgment

Culinary professionals must use discretion and appropriate behavior with coworkers, supervisors, and employees. Selecting menu items, determining how much of what item to order, deciding whether and how to combine ingredients, and approving finished items for service are all matters of judgment. Although knowledge and skill play a role in developing judgment, sound judgment comes only with experience. Of course, real experience is often accompanied by failure. Do not be upset or surprised if a dish does not turn out as expected. Learn from mistakes as well as from successes. That is how everyone develops sound judgment.

Dedication

Becoming a culinary professional is hard work. The work is physically and mentally taxing, the hours are usually long, and the pace is frequently hectic. Despite these pressures, the culinarian is expected to efficiently produce consistently fine foods that are properly prepared, seasoned, garnished, and presented. To do so, he or she must be dedicated.

The foodservice industry is competitive and depends on the continuing goodwill of a demanding public. One bad dish or one off night can result in a disgruntled diner and lost business. The culinary professional is always mindful of the food prepared and the customer served.

221

Discuss

- Becoming a culinary professional can be a grueling experience. Long hours and difficult work are part and parcel of the job. If this profession is so demanding—physically, mentally, and even emotionally—why has there been such an explosion of interest in the restaurant and foodservice industry in recent years?

Reinforce and Review

- The total perception of eating is a complex combination of smell, taste, sight, sound, and texture.
- Not every dish will turn out a success, which is why it is important to practice dishes before serving them to guests. This is an important part of the learning process and helps young cooks develop sound judgment.
- Despite a variety of pressures, cooks and chefs must be dedicated enough to their profession to work efficiently and consistently.

Teaching Tips

- Explain the concept of a "tasting menu," presenting examples from locally and nationally renowned restaurants.

Homework Activity: The Science of Supertasting

Science Connection, Literacy Connection, 21st-Century Skills—Health Literacy, Information Literacy, Work Independently

People don't all taste the same thing in the same way. In fact, about 25 percent of people with European heritage are "supertasters"—they experience tastes with a much greater intensity than people who are not supertasters.

Research this concept, explaining the scientific basis for supertasting. How does this phenomena affect people's eating habits and overall health? Is there such a thing as a "non-taster"? What types of food are enjoyed by supertasters and regular tasters?

Write a one-page essay on your findings.

Discuss

- In recent years, many restaurants have switched from traditional chef attire to colorful uniforms, bandannas, and even T-shirts. Does wearing such clothing diminish a cook's/chef's professionalism?

Reinforce and Review

- Culinary professionals must be dedicated to their colleagues, with all staff members working toward a shared goal.
- Having a sense of pride in one's work and appearance is a necessary component of professionalism.

CUSTOMIZED INSTRUCTION
Literacy Connection
Special Needs Students
Culinary professionals all work toward a common, shared goal. What are your goals? How can teamwork and dedication help you achieve them?

The culinarian is also dedicated to his or her staff and coworkers. Virtually all foodservice operations rely on teamwork to get the job done well. Teamwork requires a positive attitude and dedication to a shared goal. These are as impressive to a prospective employer as well-polished technical skills. Teamwork is discussed in more detail in Chapter 8: *Management Essentials.*

Pride

It is important to have a sense of pride about a job well done. Pride extends to personal appearance and behavior in and around the kitchen. Professionals are well-groomed and dress in clean, well-maintained, ironed uniforms when working.

For example, the traditional professional chef's uniform consists of the following:

- Comfortable leather shoes that are polished and kitchen safe (with nonskid soles and closed toes)
- Trousers (either solid white, solid black, black-and-white checked, or black-and-white striped) that are hemmed and fit appropriately, possibly with a belt
- Clean, pressed, white double-breasted jacket
- Clean, ironed apron
- Clean neckerchief, usually knotted or tied cravat style
- Hat or toque

The uniform reflects the clothing worn by professional cooks and chefs and provides some operational advantages:

- Checked trousers disguise stains.
- The double-breasted white jacket can be rebuttoned to hide dirt, and the double layer of fabric protects from scalds and burns.
- The neckerchief absorbs facial perspiration.
- The apron protects the uniform and insulates the body.
- The toque's wide brim absorbs perspiration, and the high hat lets the chef be easily spotted.

Wear this uniform with pride. Keep shoes polished, and trousers and jacket pressed as shown in Figure 4.5.

Figure 4.5: Culinary professionals must be well-groomed and professional.

222

Figure Focus

Figure 4.5: In what ways does this person present a professional demeanor? Is there anything unprofessional about him?

The crowning element of the uniform is the toque. A toque is the tall, white hat traditionally worn by chefs. Most chefs now wear a standard 6- or 9-inch high toque, but as you learned in *Chapter 1: Welcome to the Restaurant and Foodservice Industry*, a cook's rank in the kitchen often dictates the type of hat he or she wears. Beginners wear flat-topped calottes; cooks with more advanced skills wear low toques; and the master chefs wear high toques.

[fast fact]

Did You Know...?

The 101 pleats on a traditional hat represent the number of ways the wearer of the toque should be able to use eggs in a preparation.

Respect

Respect is having consideration for oneself and others. In order to respect others, a person must first respect him- or herself. Respect includes consideration of other people's privacy, their physical space and belongings, and different viewpoints, abilities, and beliefs. Disrespect hurts people. It devalues the person and their ideas, excludes them from the team, lowers morale, and creates an atmosphere of negativity.

Respect in a foodservice operation is threefold:

- **Respecting ingredients**: Be sure to use as much of an ingredient as possible (minimizing waste), and paying careful attention to product (don't let it burn or rot).

- **Respecting guests**: Make sure every plate maintains a consistently high standard, not being offended or angered by special requests, and accepting criticism of a dish or experience with grace.

- **Respecting coworkers**: Treat people with dignity, honoring their personal lives, and offering constructive criticism.

Remember the Golden Rule: Treat others as you want to be treated.

Personal Responsibility

Personal responsibility means that a person is responsible for the choices he or she makes. People are responsible for the way they think and feel. Personal responsibility means that a person accepts accountability and is in control.

223

Discuss

- How does personal responsibility change throughout life? Are there some elements that remain relevant despite one's age and status in life?

Reinforce and Review

- Respect involves having consideration for both oneself and others.
- Culinary professionals must respect ingredients, guests, and coworkers, treating both people and products with attention and care.
- Personal responsibility means that a person is responsible for the choices he or she makes, both at work and in one's private life.

Teaching Tips

- Review with the students district and campus policies on diversity, respect, and harassment.

**Fast Fact:
Did You Know...?**

Are there really 101 different ways to prepare eggs? Have students list as many as they can, either as a class or in small groups.

Note: Be prepared to suggest preparations that your students do not know. Escoffier's *Le Guide Culinaire* or Louis Saulnier's *Le Repetoire de la Cuisine* both include a wide variety of classical egg dishes, as do numerous Web sites.

Discuss

- The restaurant and foodservice industry is the largest private-sector employer in the country. Encourage students to discuss why this is the case.

Reinforce and Review

- Culinary professionals do their work efficiently and responsibly without making excuses for poor performance.
- Employers increasingly seek workers with culinary degrees.

Teaching Tips

- Make information about culinary programs available for interested students.

Fast Fact: Did You Know...?

What effects do students think a poor economy might have on employment in the restaurant and foodservice industry? What effects might a good economy have?

CUSTOMIZED INSTRUCTION

Literacy Connection, 21st-Century Skills— Information Literacy, Communicate Clearly, Be Self-Directed Learners, Create Media Products

ESOL Students

Describe the restaurant and foodservice industry in your country of origin.

How many workers does it employ? What are its annual revenues? What types of restaurants are popular?

Create a poster illustrating this information, plus anything else you think is important to say about your country's foodservice industry.

Examples of personal responsibility in a foodservice operation include the following:

- Doing the work without making excuses for why it's not being done more quickly or better
- Taking responsibility for your mistakes and being willing to correct them and learn from them
- Asking for help if it's necessary
- Being punctual for work
- Taking extra steps to learn and see what needs to be done, so you can be as big an asset to the kitchen as possible

[fast fact]

Did You Know...?
The National Restaurant Association reports that the restaurant and foodservice industry employs an estimated 12.8 million people, making it the second largest employer in the U.S. after the government. By 2019, an estimated 14.8 million will be employed by the restaurant and foodservice industry.

Education and the Culinary Professional

In the past years, there has been an increasing trend toward employers valuing a formal culinary education over on-the-job training. On-the-job training only exposes a student to one type of cuisine—the cuisine offered at the restaurant. It is also slower; it will take the student much longer to learn various techniques.

A formal culinary education allows the student to learn varieties of cuisine, theories, and techniques about food. Increasingly, employers are looking for applicants who have culinary degrees. There are more than 800 schools in the United States that offer some form of postsecondary culinary education. These schools offer programs that can result in an associate's degree, bachelor's degree, or a certificate that says you attended the program. The best culinary schools incorporate plenty of hands-on application in their curriculum, as shown in Figure 4.6 on the following page.

224

Figure 4.6: Hands-on training allows students to perform skills that they will use in their careers.

Chef de Cuisine

In large establishments, the chef de cuisine is responsible for handling all daily operations in a professional kitchen: everything from training and supervising staff to ordering supplies. Typically, the chef de cuisine creates menus, oversees a budget, and serves as a mentor to employees. The job is very similar to what an executive chef would do in a stand-alone restaurant, except that a chef de cuisine is typically responsible for only one kitchen of several at a particular location (for instance, at a resort, hotel, or convention center). The chef de cuisine reports to the executive chef of the facility.

Certifications are available for this position. Applicants must have either a high school diploma/GED and 100 hours of continuing education or 200 hours of continuing education. They must also have taken extensive classes in nutrition, food safety, and management and spent at least three years as a sous chef with responsibility for two or more full-time employees. Finally, applicants must pass both a written and a practical examination before certification.

Other qualifications for the position of chef de cuisine may include a degree from a culinary school, familiarity with foodservice computer software, and excellent communication and management skills.

Workstations

A foodservice kitchen has multiple workstations. A workstation is a work area in the kitchen dedicated to a particular task, such as broiling or salad-making. Workstations using the same or similar equipment for related tasks are grouped together into a work section. Workstations help keep a kitchen running smoothly. Budget and space are the two major issues in determining the number of workstations. Table 4.1 on the following page shows the different workstations typically found in kitchens.

225

Reinforce and Review

- A foodservice kitchen has several workstations, or areas devoted to a particular task or group of tasks.
- Budget and space are the two major determinants of the number of workstations a kitchen will have.

Figure Focus

Figure 4.6: Compare this photo to Figure 4.3; ask students to identify which situation might help them learn more quickly and thoroughly.

Table 4.1:
Work Sections and Their Stations

- What types of workers are involved with each work section?
- How is a work section different from a workstation?

Reinforce and Review

- A good kitchen design maximizes the flow of goods and staff from one area to the next as well as within areas.
- Food flows from receiving through storage, food preparation, holding, and service areas until it reaches its ultimate destination: the guest.

Homework Activity:
Flow of Food

Literacy Connection, 21st-Century Skills— Arts, Think Creatively, Create Media Products, Communicate Clearly

Chapter 2 discussed the flow of food from a safety perspective, and this chapter discusses it from a professionalism perspective.

Create a poster or a computer document in which you diagram the flow of food as it moves from receiving to the guest, and then trace the path of the empty plate back through cleaning and to storage.

Share your diagram with the class.

Table 4.1: Work Sections and Their Stations

Sections	Stations
Hot-foods section	Broiler station Fry station Griddle station Sauté/sauce station Holding
Garde-manger section	Salad greens cleaning Salad preparation Cold foods preparation Sandwich station Showpiece preparation
Bakery section	Mixing station Dough holding and proofing Dough rolling and forming Baking and cooling Dessert preparation Frozen dessert preparation Plating desserts
Banquet section	Steam cooking Dry-heat cooking (roasting, broiling)
Short-order section	Holding and plating Griddle station Fry station Broiler station
Beverage section	Hot beverage station Cold beverage station Alcoholic beverage station

The guiding principle behind a good kitchen design is to maximize the flow of goods and staff from one area to the next and within each area itself. Maximizing flow creates an efficient work environment, keeps food safe, and helps reduce preparation and service time.

Figure 4.7 on the following page shows the several sections of a professional kitchen. It includes an area for front-of-the-house staff to circulate, drop off orders, retrieve finished dishes, and return dirty dishes. The design accounts for the flow of foods from receiving, to storage, to the food preparation area,

226

to holding and service areas, and then to the dining room. The workstations are arranged to take advantage of shared equipment. For example, when the bakeshop is placed next to the hot-foods section, they can share ovens. The beverage station is located near the dining-room entrance so that food servers do not have to walk through food preparation areas to fill beverage orders.

Figure 4.7: Food is received, stored, prepared, and plated for service in the professional kitchen.

Kitchen Brigade System

In Chapter 1: *Welcome to the Restaurant and Foodservice Industry*, we noted that Escoffier is credited with developing the kitchen brigade system. A brigade is a system of staffing a kitchen so that each worker is assigned a set of specific tasks. These tasks are often related by cooking method, equipment, or the types of foods being produced. Escoffier created a distinct hierarchy of responsibilities and functions for commercial foodservice operations. Table 4.2 on the following page outlines Escoffier's kitchen brigade system.

227

Discuss
- Encourage students to envision what restaurant kitchens might have been like before the brigade system was introduced. What potential problems can students identify?

Reinforce and Review
- Kitchen workstations are arranged to take advantage of shared equipment, which lowers costs and increases efficiency.
- A brigade is a system of staffing a kitchen so that each worker is assigned a particular role and corresponding set of tasks.
- Brigades are hierarchical in nature, with the executive chef at the top of the "pyramid."

Figure Focus
Figure 4.7: What activities do students think happen in each of the work areas photographed? Why?

Table 4.2:
Escoffier's Kitchen Brigade System

- Encourage students to discuss the extent to which this system is practical today. Is it realistic to have so many staff members doing different things?

- What types of contemporary foodservice establishment might have employees in each of these categories? Which positions could be combined?

- According to Table 4.2, the executive chef is responsible for all kitchen operations. But exactly what does he or she do all day? Encourage students to discuss some activities that fall under the purview of the executive chef.

CUSTOMIZED INSTRUCTION

Literacy Connection

Special Needs Students

If you could have any job you wanted in a restaurant or other foodservice establishment, what would it be and why?

Table 4.2: Escoffier's Kitchen Brigade System

Kitchen Staff	Responsibility
Chef	Responsible for all kitchen operations.
Sous chef	Also known as the second chef. Responsible for scheduling personnel, and covering the chef or stations chefs' work as necessary. Also accepts orders from the dining room and relays them to various stations chefs, and reviews the dishes before service.
Stations chefs	Produce the menu items under the supervision of the chef or sous chef. Under Escoffier's system, each station chef is assigned a specific task based on either the cooking method and equipment or the category of items to be produced. They include the following: * Sauté station chef, *Saucier* * Fish station chef, *Poissonier* * Grill station chef, *Grillardin* * Fry station chef, *Friturier* * Roast station chef, *Rôtisseur* * Soup station chef, *Potager* * Vegetable station chef, *Legumier* * Pantry chef, *Garde-Manger* * Swing cook (works where needed), *Tournant,* * Pastry chef, *Pâtissier* * Demi-chefs (assistants), *Demi-Chef* * Commis (apprentices), *Commis* * Hot appetizer chef, *Entremetier* * Butcher, *Coucher* * Expediter, *Aboyeur* * Candy chef, *Confiseur* * Bread baker, *Boulanger* * Frozen-dessert chef, *Glacier* * Showpiece baker, *Décorateur*

228

Today, most foodservice operations use a simplified version of Escoffier's kitchen brigade. Figure 4.8 is an example of the kitchen brigade in action.

Figure 4.8: The kitchen brigade is a system of staffing a kitchen. Each worker is assigned a set of specific tasks.

Dining-Room Brigade System

Like the back-of-the-house staff, the front-of-the-house staff is also organized into a brigade. A traditional dining-room brigade is led by the dining-room manager (maître d') who generally trains all service personnel, oversees wine selections, works with the chef to develop the menu, organizes the seating chart, and seats the guests. The positions noted on Table 4.3 report to this manager.

Table 4.3: Dining Brigade System	
Staff	**Responsibility**
Wine steward	This person is responsible for the wine service, including purchasing wines, assisting guests in selecting wines, and serving the wines.
Headwaiter	This person is responsible for service throughout the dining room or a section of it.
Captains	This person is responsible for explaining the menu to guests and taking their orders. They are also responsible for any tableside preparations.
Front waiter	This person is responsible for assuring that the tables are set properly for each course, foods are delivered properly to the proper tables, and the needs of the guests are met.
Back waiter	This person is responsible for clearing plates, refilling water glasses, and other general tasks appropriate for new dining-room workers.

229

Reinforce and Review

- Most contemporary foodservice operations use a modified form of the brigade system.
- The dining-room brigade is led by the maître d', who trains service staff, oversees guest services, and coordinates dining-room activity with the chef.

Table 4.3:
Dining Brigade System

- Why are there so many fewer positions in the dining room than in the kitchen?

- Do most restaurants use all of these positions, or how might some be combined?

- What might the dining room have been like before the brigade system was introduced?

Figure Focus
Figure 4.8: What members of the kitchen brigade appear in this photograph?

Essential Skills: Scheduling Employees

Scheduling staff can be a difficult and time-consuming experience. What are some possible obstacles? How can the process be expedited?

Why is communication the most important part of scheduling staff? How can communication increase or decrease the potential for scheduling-related conflict

How do the six attributes of culinary professionalism relate to scheduling staff?

Homework Activity: Schedule, Schmedule

Mathematics Connection, Literacy Connection, 21st Century Skills—Critical Thinking and Problem Solving, Flexibility and Adaptability, Leadership and Responsibility

You own a restaurant that seats 100, usually serves 250 guests per service, and is open 5 days each week, Wednesday through Sunday. Prep time begins at 1:00 p.m., and the dinner service is 5:00–10:00 p.m. All cooking staff should have left the building by 11:00 p.m.

Your seven cooks, all of whom have very similar abilities and experiences, are named Amanda, Bruno, Cristina, Darryl, Eli, Fan, and Gary. They can each work a maximum of 40 hours and should each work all 5 days—except Eli, who needs Wednesday off this week for an excused absence. These are the only staff members who cook.

Draw up a weekly schedule for these seven cooks, either by hand or by using a computer program. Is it possible to give each cook 40 hours in this week, without overtime, while ensuring that all necessary work is completed?

After completing your schedule, write one to two paragraphs describing your staffing choices.

Depending on the nature and size of the restaurant or foodservice operation and the type of service provided, an operation may employ some or all of these positions. Figure 4.9 shows the dining-room brigade in action.

Figure 4.9: Most dining-room brigades are led by the dining-room manager.

Essential Skills
Scheduling Employees

Scheduling employees is an important part of a manager's job. But it can be difficult, especially in a large operation or in an operation open more than five days each week. You must respect individual employee's needs while making the right business decisions. A variety of software packages and Web sites can help, but you can also succeed by following these steps:

❶ Make a chart showing each day of the week you are open and each hour you need staff for prep work, deliveries, and cleaning. (Remember, you need staff even when the business is closed.)

❷ Figure out your busiest times and the number of employees doing each job that you will need to meet customer demands.

230

Figure Focus
Figure 4.9: Which members of the dining brigade are visible in this photograph?

❸ Anticipate any holidays or other events that may affect your normal patterns of work.

❹ Schedule full-time and part-time employees so that everyone works the appropriate number of hours and has scheduled breaks.

❺ Establish a policy requiring employees to request time off several days in advance to avoid last-minute surprises.

❻ Post the schedule several days in advance so employees know what to expect.

❼ Communicate with your employees so everyone understands the schedule and business policies.

This last step may be the most important one. Communicating with your employees shows that you respect them as individual human beings, not just workers. Treating them with dignity, while simultaneously requiring them to practice personal responsibility, will boost levels of professionalism throughout the operation.

Summary

In this section, you learned the following:

- Professionalism means being courteous, honest, and responsible in one's dealings with customers and coworkers. It also indicates that a person is maintaining standards for his or her work and behavior.

- Professional culinarians have knowledge, skill, taste, judgment, dedication, pride, respect, and personal responsibility.

- A kitchen brigade is a system of staffing a kitchen so that each worker is assigned a set of specific tasks. These tasks are often related by cooking method, equipment, or the types of foods being produced.

- A traditional dining-room brigade is led by the dining-room manager (maître d') who generally trains all service personnel, oversees wine selections, works with the chef to develop the menu, organizes the seating chart, and seats the guests.

231

Summary

- Remind students to review the following:
  1. Professionalism
  2. What it means to be a professional culinarian
  3. The kitchen brigade
  4. The dining room brigade

Section 4.1 Review Questions

1. To be professional is to be courteous, honest, and responsible in your dealings with customers and coworkers. Professionals have a four-fold responsibility: to themselves, to coworkers, to the business, and to the guest.

2. The eight attributes of a culinary professional are knowledge, skill, taste, judgment, dedication, pride, respect, and education.

3. The kitchen brigade system is a method of staffing a kitchen by assigning each worker specific tasks, often related by cooking method, equipment, or the types of food being produced. This distinct hierarchy often runs from the chef to the sous chef and then to the station chefs.

4. A workstation is a work area in the kitchen dedicated to a particular task. Workstations using the same or similar equipment for related tasks are grouped together into a work section.

5. Students may answer this question in a variety of ways, so long as they justify their responses.

6. Students may answer this question in a variety of ways, so long as they justify their responses.

7. Foodservice employees should be professional because professionals are committed to providing excellent service, essential to the success of any foodservice operation. Moreover, professionals treat themselves and one another with respect and courtesy, setting standards for their work and their behavior.

8. The benefits of the brigade system are that each employees knows his or her place in the kitchen hierarchy and his or her specific responsibilities, helping the kitchen run smoothly. Most contemporary foodservice operations use a simplified version of Escoffier's original brigade system.

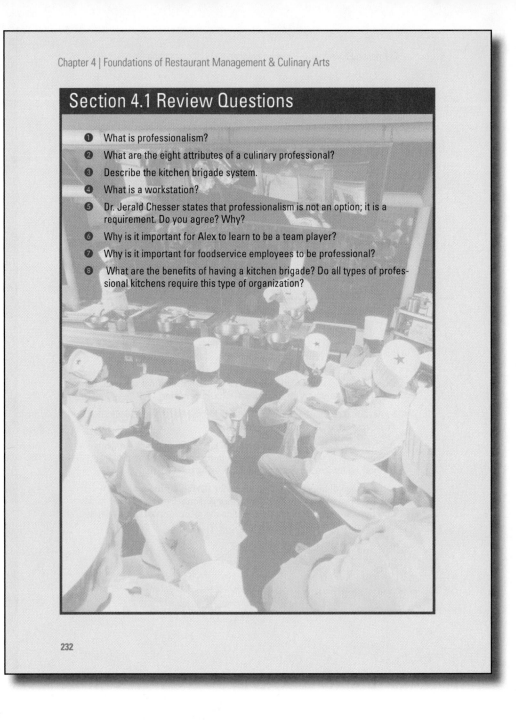

Section 4.1 Review Questions

1. What is professionalism?
2. What are the eight attributes of a culinary professional?
3. Describe the kitchen brigade system.
4. What is a workstation?
5. Dr. Jerald Chesser states that professionalism is not an option; it is a requirement. Do you agree? Why?
6. Why is it important for Alex to learn to be a team player?
7. Why is it important for foodservice employees to be professional?
8. What are the benefits of having a kitchen brigade? Do all types of professional kitchens require this type of organization?

232

Section 4.1 Activities

1. Study Skills/Group Activity: Skit About Culinary Professionalism

Work with two other students and select one of the eight attributes of a culinary professional. Discuss this attribute and create a brief skit illustrating its role in a professional kitchen.

2. Activity: Culinarian's Code

Consider the Culinarian's Code. What does it mean to you? Why do you think it is or is not relevant in today's kitchens? Write two paragraphs describing your opinion.

3. Critical Thinking: Position in the Kitchen or Dining-Room Brigade

Research one of the positions described in either the kitchen or the dining-room brigade. Write two paragraphs on what the job entails and what qualifications it requires.

233

Section 4.1 Activities

1. Students may choose from among the eight attributes of culinary professionals. The skit should clearly demonstrate the importance of the selected attribute to a professional kitchen.

2. Students should explain the importance or unimportance of the Culinarian's Code to both themselves and to the culinary profession using clear, well-written arguments.

3. Students may select from among the positions listed in the two brigades. Their responses should include information about the position's responsibilities, where it falls in the hierarchy, and what skills or qualifications are needed to obtain the positions, as well as any other relevant material.

Section 4.2
Using Standardized Recipes

Introduce the Section

a. Review the role of basic math skills in the restaurant and foodservice industry.
b. Explain the different types of measuring systems and devices.
c. Discuss the importance of standardizing recipes.
d. Discuss the objectives for the section.

Vocabulary Review

a. Direct students to the key terms.
b. Pronounce each word, and have the students repeat the pronunciation out loud.
c. Discuss the definition of each word.

Teach

Discuss

- A recipe is one of the most versatile and hard-working tools in the repertoire of the culinary professional.
- Foodservice professionals of all stripes must have a basic understanding of mathematical principles.

4.1 Professionalism
• What does it mean to be a culinary professional?
• Workstations

4.2 Using Standardized Recipes
• Business math
• U.S. and metric measurement systems
• Standardized recipes
• Converting recipes
• Measuring
• EP/AP amounts
• Costing recipes

SECTION 4.2 USING STANDARDIZED RECIPES

A recipe is one of the most versatile and hardworking tools in the professional kitchen. The ability to read a recipe correctly and to use it as the basis of a variety of calculations is critical to a chef's success. Strong math skills and careful attention to the details of a recipe will help you to create accurate and tasty items.

Study Questions

After studying Section 4.2, you should be able to answer the following questions:

- What are the basic math calculations using numbers and fractions?
- What are the components and functions of a standardized recipe?
- How do you convert recipes to yield smaller and larger quantities based on operational needs?
- What is the difference between customary and metric measurement units?
- How do you convert between customary and metric measurements?
- Which smallware and utensils are used for measuring and portioning?
- How do you calculate amounts for a purchased (AP) and edible portion (EP)?
- How do you calculate the cost and portion cost of a standardized recipe?

Business Math

Math skills are extremely important in foodservice settings. Foodservice managers are expected to have a basic understanding of math and know how to apply mathematical principles to business situations. Math skills are also essential in the professional kitchen. Chefs and managers need to know how to

234

determine recipe yields, convert recipes from customary to metric measure, and change the yields of recipes.

Technology has improved efficiency and productivity in foodservice operations. Many restaurants use software for recipe and menu costing, inventory control, purchasing, and nutritional analysis. Despite this fact, it is important for students to understand how to perform these tasks by hand. What happens if the computer freezes or if a program doesn't function properly?

[what's new]

Foodservice Software

Recent advances in technology have made it easier for chefs and foodservice managers to track costs, maintain inventories, and manage recipes. Although the initial time commitment to enter data, such as ingredient costs, original recipes, and portion sizes, can be significant, the time saved later can be used for many other, more important functions, such as mentoring employees, planning new menu items, and maybe even cooking.

Today's restaurant and foodservice software can help with a variety of functions:

- Costing recipes and convert them for various yields
- Managing inventory, including the date an item was purchased, the amount of it needed for each recipe, its cost, and when it should be reordered, and even make an automated shopping list
- Determining nutritional information for each ingredient and recipe and print out individual labels for portion sales
- Maintaining sales figures by menu item, ingredient, day part, day of week, and fiscal quarter
- Calculating labor cost per recipe or per service period
- Performing a wide variety of other tasks

Having this information so easily available helps chefs and managers make smarter decisions and build stronger, more profitable organizations.

[fast fact]

Did You Know...?

Math is known as the universal language because the principles and foundations of math are the same throughout the world. For example, adding up a grocery bill uses the same mathematical process regardless of where you are in the world.

235

What's New: Foodservice Software

Why is it important for a chef or other foodservice manager to know how to perform all the functions listed in this sidebar, such as calculating labor costs and managing inventory? Does having access to computer software mean that the chef or manager is no longer responsible for this information?

Are all of these functions really important to a foodservice establishment? Encourage students to discuss why each may or may not be necessary.

Fast Fact: Did You Know...?

Math is considered the "universal language" because the same processes are used to obtain the same results, no matter what languages the user speaks.

What is the difference between a "universal" language and a "common" language? What other languages do students think of as "universal"?

CUSTOMIZED INSTRUCTION

Literacy Connection, 21st-Century Skills— Reason Effectively, Information Literacy, Be Self-Directed Learners

More Advanced Students

Mathematics is one universal language; Esperanto is another. Esperanto was developed as a universal spoken language in the late nineteenth century.

Research Esperanto: its origins, its linguistic patterns, its similarities to and differences from other languages, and so on. Why was it developed? How many speak it today? What political and cultural implications has it had?

Write a one-page report on your findings, including a sentence or two translated into Esperanto.

Reinforce and Review

- Numbers can be added, subtracted, multiplied, divided, or expressed as fractions.
- To add numbers, line them up in a column, assigning each column a value—ones, tens, hundreds, etc.
- To check your work when subtracting, simply add the answer to the subtracted number. The result should be the first number.

CUSTOMIZED INSTRUCTION
Mathematics Connection, Literacy Connection
Less Advanced Students
Practice addition, subtraction, multiplication, and division operations now so that you will be prepared for the conversion and costing problems later in this chapter. Use examples from your other math classes.

Vocabulary Terms

- **Borrowing:** A subtraction technique in which if a digit in one column is too large to be subtracted from the digit above it, then 10 is borrowed from the column immediately to the left.

Mathematical Operators

As you may have learned in math classes, there are several operations that can be performed on numbers, and each corresponds to a familiar symbol:

- Addition ($10 + 2 = 12$)
- Subtraction ($10 - 2 = 8$)
- Multiplication ($10 \times 2 = 20$)
- Division ($10 \div 2 = 5$)

They can also be expressed as fractions, which is the same as dividing them: ($10/2 = 10 \div 2 = 5$)

These four basic math operations are the foundation for all other mathematical functions.

Addition

Numbers are added by lining them up in columns and then assigning each column of digits a value of 1, 10, 100, 1,000, and so on, beginning with the right-most column. In the number 372, for example, 2 is in the *ones* column, 7 is in the *tens* column, and 3 is in the *hundreds* column.

$$\begin{array}{r} {}^{1} \\ 24 \\ +\ 17 \\ \hline 41 \end{array}$$

When adding a column, if the sum of a column contains two digits, then the right digit is written below the sum line, and the left digit is added to the next column as you move from right to left.

Subtraction

When subtracting large numbers, a technique known as **borrowing** is often used. If a digit in one column is too large to be subtracted from the digit above it, then 10 is borrowed from the column immediately to the left.

$$\begin{array}{r} {}^{7}{}^{1} \\ \cancel{8}2 \\ -\ 17 \\ \hline 65 \end{array}$$

To check the work on a subtraction problem, simply add the answer to the subtracted number. The result should be the first number.

$$\begin{array}{r} {}^{1} \\ 65\ \text{(answer)} \\ +\ 17\ \text{(subtracted number)} \\ \hline 82 \end{array}$$

236

Multiplication

To multiply large numbers, the digit in the ones column of the second number is first multiplied by the digits above it, going from right to left. For example, to solve 32 × 4:

$$\begin{array}{r} 32 \\ \times\, 4 \\ \hline 8 \end{array}$$

Step 1: Multiply 4 by 2

Result is 8

Step 2: Multiply 4 by 3

Result is 12

The final result is 128.

$$\begin{array}{r} 32 \\ \times\, 4 \\ \hline 128 \end{array}$$

Figure 4.10 will help you review multiplication for the numbers 1 through 12.

Multiplication Table

	1	2	3	4	5	6	7	8	9	10	11	12
1	1	2	3	4	5	6	7	8	9	10	11	12
2	2	4	6	8	10	12	14	16	18	20	22	24
3	3	6	9	12	15	18	21	24	27	30	33	36
4	4	8	12	16	20	24	28	32	36	40	44	48
5	5	10	15	20	25	30	35	40	45	50	55	60
6	6	12	18	24	30	36	42	48	54	60	66	72
7	7	14	21	28	35	42	49	56	63	70	77	84
8	8	16	24	32	40	48	56	64	72	80	88	96
9	9	18	27	36	45	54	63	72	81	90	99	108
10	10	20	30	40	50	60	70	80	90	100	110	120
11	11	22	33	44	55	66	77	88	99	110	121	132
12	12	24	36	48	60	72	84	96	108	120	132	144

Figure 4.10: The multiplication table.

237

Reinforce and Review

- Understanding basic mathematic operations is the key to successfully following and standardizing recipes.
- To multiply large numbers, first multiply the digit in the ones column of the second number by the digits above it, moving from right to left.

Teaching Tips

- Provide as many examples of basic mathematic operations as you think necessary in whichever formats are most appropriate for the class. Some examples:

Addition

$18 + 32 = 50 \qquad 41 + 23 = 64 \qquad 12 + 29 = 41$
$106 + 16 = 122 \quad 417 + 89 = 506 \quad 1{,}020 + 17 = 1{,}037$

Subtraction

$79 - 16 = 63 \qquad 86 - 59 = 27 \qquad 91 - 34 = 57$
$720 - 89 = 631 \quad 400 - 201 = 199 \quad 2{,}323 - 54 = 2{,}269$

Multiplication

$16 \times 19 = 304 \qquad 79 \times 5 = 395 \qquad 74 \times 84 = 6{,}216$
$323 \times 4 = 1{,}292 \quad 922 \times 15 = 13{,}830$
$1{,}189 \times 17 = 20{,}213$

Reinforce and Review

- Larger numbers are divided using a combination of division and subtraction.
- When adding and subtracting fractions, numerators are added and subtracted the same way as whole numbers, while denominators must be translated into equivalent units.
- The first step in dividing fractions with different denominators is to determine the lowest common denominator.

Teaching Tips

- Provide as many examples of these operations as you think necessary in whichever formats are most appropriate for the class. Some examples:

Division

$160 \div 4 = 40$	$69 \div 23 = 3$	$102 \div 17 = 6$
$796 \div 4 = 199$	$1{,}550 \div 5 = 310$	$2{,}700 \div 90 = 30$

Fractions

$\frac{1}{3} + \frac{1}{2} = \frac{5}{6}$	$\frac{5}{9} + \frac{5}{18} = \frac{15}{18}$
$\frac{3}{4} + \frac{2}{3} = 1\frac{11}{12}$	$\frac{3}{2} - \frac{4}{5} = \frac{7}{10}$
$\frac{8}{9} - \frac{2}{3} = \frac{2}{9}$	$\frac{4}{7} - \frac{1}{2} = \frac{1}{14}$

Vocabulary Terms

- **Dividend:** The number being divided, which is placed inside the long division sign.
- **Divisor:** The number dividing the first number, which is placed outside the long division sign.
- **Numerator:** The upper part of a fraction.
- **Denominator:** The lower part of a fraction.
- **Like fractions:** When the denominators of fractions to be added or subtracted are the same, they are known as "like fractions."
- **Lowest common denominator:** The smallest number that both denominators can be divided into evenly.

Division

Larger numbers are divided using a combination of division and subtraction. The **dividend** is placed inside the long division sign, and the **divisor** is placed outside. For example, in the problem $728 \div 14$, 728 is the dividend, and 14 is the divisor.

$$14 \overline{)728} \quad \begin{array}{r} 5 \\ -70 \\ \hline 2 \end{array}$$

To solve $728 \div 14$:

Step 1: Divide 14 into 72

Result is 5

$14 \times 5 = 70$

Subtract from 72

Step 2: Bring down 8

Divide 14 into 28

Result is 2

$14 \times 2 = 28$

Subtract from 28

$$14 \overline{)728} \quad \begin{array}{r} 52 \\ -70 \\ \hline 28 \\ -28 \\ \hline 0 \end{array}$$

The final result is 52.

Fractions, Decimals, and Percentages

Culinary professionals need to understand the concepts of fractions, decimals, and percentages. They need to know how to use and apply these math functions in the kitchen.

Fractions

In adding and subtracting fractions, **numerators**, the upper portion of a fraction, are added and subtracted the same way as whole numbers (for example $\frac{1}{3} + \frac{1}{3} = \frac{2}{3}$). **Denominators**, the lower portion of a fraction, are not. If the denominators to be added or subtracted are the same (called **like fractions**), the denominators remain unchanged.

$$\frac{2}{3} + \frac{3}{4} =$$
$$\frac{8}{12} + \frac{9}{12} = \frac{17}{12}$$
$$\frac{17}{12} = 1\frac{5}{12}$$

If the denominators to be added or subtracted are different from each other, then the first step is to determine the **lowest common denominator**, which is the smallest number that both denominators can be divided into evenly. The next step is to multiply each numerator by the number that the corresponding denominator was multiplied by when

238

---

calculating the lowest common denominator. For example, in the next problem, both the numerator and the denominator in ⅔ are multiplied by 4, giving us the new, equivalent fraction ⁸⁄₁₂.

Fractions are often expressed as decimals. All decimals are based on one-tenth, one-hundredth, one-thousandth, etc. For example, 1.4 is 1 and 4-tenths, and 6.21 is 6 and 21-hundreths. Industry calculations are typically converted to decimals, not fractions.

Decimals

Decimals are added, subtracted, multiplied, and divided just like nondecimal numbers. When adding or subtracting decimals, the key is to line up the decimal points. Figure 4.11 shows some common fractions and their decimal equivalents.

When multiplying decimals, determine where to place the decimal point after calculating the final total answer. To do this, count the total number of digits to the right of all decimal points in the numbers that are being multiplied together and then place the decimal point in the final answer by counting that many places from the right. For example, there are a total of four digits to the right of the decimal points in 8.46 and 4.23. Therefore, the decimal point goes four places from the right in the answer, 35.7858.

Common fractions and their decimal equivalents	
$\frac{1}{8}$ = 0.125	$\frac{5}{8}$ = 0.625
$\frac{1}{6}$ = 0.1667	$\frac{2}{3}$ = 0.6667
$\frac{1}{4}$ = 0.25	$\frac{3}{4}$ = 0.75
$\frac{3}{8}$ = 0.375	$\frac{5}{6}$ = 0.8333
$\frac{1}{2}$ = 0.50	

Figure 4.11: Common fractions and their decimal equivalents.

```
  8.46      8.46       8.46
+ 4.23    - 4.23     x 4.23
-------   -------    -------
 12.69      4.23       2538
                      16920
                     338400
                    --------
                    35.7858
```

Reinforce and Review

- Fractions are often expressed as decimals, especially in the foodservice industry.
- Decimals are added, subtracted, multiplied, and divided in the same ways that nondecimal numbers are. When adding and subtracting, the key is to line up the decimal points.
- When multiplying decimals, don't add the decimal point until the final answer. Sum up the number of digits after the decimal points in all the numbers being multiplied and then count that many spaces from the right in the answer. That's where the decimal point belongs.

Teaching Tips

- Provide as many examples of these operations as you think necessary in whichever formats are most appropriate for the class. Some examples:

Decimals

3.25 + 4.78 = 8.03	5.64 + 1.98 = 7.62
6.23 + 2.75 = 8.98	8.44 − 2.39 = 6.05
5.22 − 4.5 = 0.72	1.27 − 1.1 = 0.17
4.6 × 5.2 = 23.92	6.22 × 4.5 = 27.99
3.3 × 2.4 = 7.92	9.4 ÷ 5.0 = 1.88
2.5 ÷ 1.25 = 2.0	7.2 ÷ 6 = 1.2

Figure Focus

Figure 4.11: These are common fractions in the foodservice industry.

Reinforce and Review

- To convert a decimal to a percentage, move the decimal point two places to the right and add a percent sign.
- When rounding numbers, if the next digit to the right is less than 5, the number is rounded down; if the next digit to the right is 5 or greater, the number is rounded up.
- When converting fractions to percents, first convert the fraction to a decimal.
- To determine that one number is a percent of another number, divide the portion by the whole.

Teaching Tips

- Provide as many examples of these operations as you think necessary in whichever formats are most appropriate for the class. Some examples:

Percentage

$5.0 \times 20\% = 1.0$ $4.0 \times 75\% = 3.0$
$2.5 \times 25\% = 0.625$ $50 \div 200 = 25\%$
$16 \div 40 = 40\%$ $60 \div 75 = 80\%$

Vocabulary Terms

- **Percent:** Part per 100.

To convert a decimal to a percentage, move the decimal point two places to the right and add a percent (%) sign. If necessary, add a zero on the back to get the second decimal place. For example, .123 = 12.3%.

$$4.23 \overline{)8.46} = 2.00$$

When dividing decimals, simply bring the decimal point up directly above the long division sign.

When calculators or computers do the math, numbers often have more digits to the right of the decimal point than are practical or useful. In these cases, numbers are rounded to the nearest tenth, hundredth, or thousandth. Numbers are sometimes rounded to the nearest whole number in order to eliminate the decimal point.

In business math rounding, if the next digit to the right is less than 5, then the number is usually rounded down (5.12 is rounded to 5.1). If the number to the right is 5 or above, then the number is rounded up (both 5.15 and 5.19 are rounded to 5.2). The number 5.192635 can be rounded to the nearest thousandth (5.193), hundredth (5.19), tenth (5.2), or whole number (5.).

Percentages

Percentages are a particularly important mathematical operation in foodservice operations. Managers and employees often express numbers as **percents**, or parts per 100. When working with a fraction that should be a percent, the first step is to convert the fraction into a decimal. For example, to express ½ as a decimal, the numerator (1) is divided by the denominator (2) for an answer of 0.5. Then add a zero (0) in the hundreds place (0.50), and the two digits to the right of the decimal point are expressed as 50 percent, or 50%.

$$\begin{array}{r} 60 \\ \times\, 0.20 \\ \hline 00 \\ 1200 \\ \hline 12.00 \end{array}$$

To determine a certain percent of a given number, the percent is first expressed as a decimal and then multiplied. For instance, to find 20 percent of 60, multiply 60 by 0.20.

In other words, 20 percent of 60 is 12.

It is also possible to determine that one number is a percent of another number. For instance, if 60 customers out of a total of 300 are ordering the house special, the percentage of customers ordering the special is found by dividing the portion (60) by the total (300). Remember that dividing is the same as making a fraction. The total will be the denominator of the fraction: $^{60}/_{300}$. The portion is the numerator, or the part that gives the number. When the numerator is smaller than the denominator, the answer will always be a decimal.

$$\frac{60}{300} = 0.20 = 20\%$$

240

Therefore, 60 is 20 percent of 300. Twenty percent of the customers are ordering the special.

Do the Math

Let's assume that you work at a restaurant. Your restaurant is having a special; 15 percent off of the entire check. If the check total is $75, what will the check total be after the discount?

Math influences every decision that a manager makes in a foodservice operation. It is the foundation of the kitchen and the back office.

U.S. and Metric Measurement Systems

The most commonly used system of measurement in the United States is based on customary units. Some examples of these customary units are ounces, teaspoons, tablespoons, cups, pints, and gallons. Most American recipes are written using this customary system. Often they are abbreviated, as shown in parenthesis in Table 4.4, which lists customary units used in recipes.

Table 4.4: Customary (U.S.) Units of Measure

Volume	Weight	Temperature	Length
teaspoon (tsp) tablespoon (tbsp) cup (cup) fluid ounce (fl oz) pint (pt) quart (qt) gallon (gal)	ounce (oz) pound (lb)	degrees Fahrenheit (°F)	inches (in)

Cooking and baking require exact weighing and measuring of ingredients to ensure consistent quality and minimal waste. It's important to understand that the same amount can be expressed in different ways by using different units of measure. This is called an *equivalent*. For example, 4 tbsp of flour is equivalent to $1/4$ cup of flour. Table 4.5 shows the customary units of measure commonly used in the United States and their equivalence to each other.

241

On the Job: Do the Math

Once the students understand how to solve this problem (75 × .15 = 11.25; 75 − 11.25 = $63.75), try them with variations:

- The special is 15% off beverages. The check total is $75, and the beverage total is $10. What is the check total after the discount? [10 × .15 = 1.50; 75 − 1.50 = $73.50]

- The special is 15% off all food. The check total is $75, and the food total is $65. What is the check total after the discount? [65 × .15 = 9.75; 75 − 9.75 = $65.25]

Discuss

- Accurate measuring is fundamental to following recipes, and therefore to determining the establishment's food costs. Encourage students to come up with examples of why accurate measuring is so important.

Reinforce and Review

- Math influences every decision a manager makes in a foodservice operation, whether in a kitchen or at a desk.
- Most American recipes are written using these customary units: ounces, teaspoons, tablespoons, cups, pints, and gallons.
- Fluid ounces, which measure volume, are not the same as ounces, which measure weight.

Table 4.4: Customary (U.S.) Units of Measure

- Display and explain customary measuring equipment for volume, weight, temperature, and length.

- Make sure that students understand which piece of measuring equipment is which and when each should be used.

Fast Fact: Did You Know...?

Encourage students to discuss why the Earth might have been chosen as a measuring stick. How else could the Earth be used to measure things?

Reinforce and Review

- The metric system of measurement is commonly used in other parts of the world and often appears in recipes, especially in baking.
- Important metric units of measurement in the foodservice industry include milliliters, liters, milligrams, grams, and kilograms.

In-Class Activity: Know Your Numbers

Mathematics Connection, Literacy Connection

Copy the units of measure equivalencies onto a notecard for easy access when working in the kitchen.

Vocabulary Terms

- **Metric unit:** A unit of measurement based on multiples of 10.

Table 4.5: Units of Measure (U.S): Equivalencies

Weight
1 pound = 16 ounces

Volume

16 cups	= 1 gallon	= 128 fluid ounces	= 4 quarts	= 256 tablespoons	= 768 teaspoons
1 quart	= 32 fluid ounces	= 2 pints	= 4 cups	= 64 tablespoons	=192 teaspoons
1 pint	=16 fluid ounces	= 2 cups	= 32 tablespoons		= 96 teaspoons
1 cup	= 8 fluid ounces	= 16 tablespoons	= 48 teaspoons		
1 fluid ounce	= 2 tablespoons				
1 tablespoon	= 3 teaspoons				

Length
1 foot = 12 inches

[fast fact]

Did You Know...?

The metric system was created approximately 200 years ago by a group of French scientists. It was created so that there would be a standard system for accurate and consistent measurement.

Metric units were defined in a way different from traditional units of measure. The Earth itself was selected as the measuring stick. For example, the meter was defined to be one ten-millionth of the distance from the equator to the north pole. It didn't turn out quite like this, because the scientific methods of the time were not quite up to the task of measuring these quantities precisely, but the actual metric units come very close to the design.

The metric system is the standard system used in many other parts of the world. It is also used by scientists and health professionals. **Metric units** are based on multiples of 10 and include milliliters, liters, milligrams, grams, and kilograms. For example, just as there are 100 pennies in one dollar, there are 100 milligrams in one gram. Often they are abbreviated, as shown in the parenthesis below. Table 4.6 on the following page lists the most common metric units used in recipes.

Table 4.5: Units of Measure (U.S.): Equivalencies

- Using a transparency or slide show presentation to illustrate equivalencies can help increase student understanding. For example:

Three teaspoons equal one tablespoon.

Two tablespoons equal one fluid ounce.

Table 4.6: Metric Units of Measure

Volume	Temperature	Weight	Length
milliliter (ml) liter (l)	degrees Celsius (°C) (or centigrade)	milligram (mg) gram (g) kilogram (kg)	millimeter (mm) centimeter (cm) meter (m)

It is important to be very familiar with both systems of measurement. As long as the correct measuring equipment is available, it's not necessary to convert measurements from one system to the other. If a recipe is written using metric units, use metric measuring tools. It is helpful, however, to understand some common equivalencies. For example, 4 tablespoons of flour is equivalent to ¼ cup of flour, or about 60 milliliters. Table 4.7 lists some common equivalents between customary and metric units of measure.

Table 4.7: Equivalent Measure

Volume			Weight		
Customary Measure	Customary Equivalent	Metric Equivalent	Customary Measure	Customary Equivalent	Metric Equivalent
1 tsp		5 ml	1 oz		28 g
1 tbsp	3 tsp	15 ml	1 lb	16 oz	450 g
1 fl oz	2 tbsp	30 ml	2 lb	32 oz	900 g
¼ cup	4 tbsp	60 ml			0.9 kg
⅓ cup	5 ⅓ tbsp	80 ml	2.2 lb		1 kg
½ cup		120 ml			
⅔ cup		160 ml	**Temperature**		
¾ cup		180 ml	Customary Measure	Customary Equivalent	Metric Equivalent
1 cup	8 fl oz 16 tbsp	240 ml 0.24 l	0°F		-17.8°C
1 pt	2 cup 16 fl oz	470 ml 0.47 l	32°F	(freezing point)	0°C
1 qt	2 pt 4 cup 32 fl oz	950 ml 0.95 l	212°F	(boiling point)	100°C
1 gal	4 qt	3.8 l			

Table 4.6:
Metric Units of Measure

- How do metric units of measurement differ from customary units of measurement?

- Which are easier to use and why?

Table 4.7:
Equivalent Measure

- Encourage students to compare metric and customary equipment.

Discuss

- Having two measurement systems in a single kitchen can give rise to confusion. What if an employee adds a kilogram of rice to the pot instead of a pound? Should a single measurement system be used? If so, which one? Encourage students to discuss potential pros and cons of each.

Reinforce and Review

- If the correct measurement equipment is available, recipes do not need to be converted from one system to another. Simply use metric equipment for metric recipes and customary equipment for customary recipes.
- Understanding common metric-customary equivalencies can make kitchen work easier.

Teaching Tips

- Display and explain metric measuring equipment for volume, weight, temperature, and length.

Discuss

• Using both Fahrenheit and Celsius measurements in the same kitchen can lead to errors. Mistaking 39°C for 39°F, for instance, means the difference between a safe holding temperature and a potentially dangerous one—39°C is the equivalent of 102.2°F! Why should a kitchen use one system of measurement over the other?

Reinforce and Review

• Thermometers measure degrees of temperature in either Fahrenheit (°F), which is customary in the United States, or Celsius (°C), which is the metric measure.

Table 4.8:
Temperature Conversion
• Provide students with additional problems so they can practice converting numbers between Fahrenheit and Celsius.

Homework Activity:
Altitude and Boiling Water
Mathematics Connection, Literacy Connection, Science Connection
The degree at which water boils varies depending upon the water's altitude. Find out your school's altitude and determine the boiling point at that level.
What is the boiling point at sea level? At 1,000 feet? At 5,000 feet? At 10,000 feet?
Is the freezing point affected by changes in altitude? If so, how?
Write a report on your findings.

Figure 4.12 shows a set of measuring tools.

Figure 4.12: Measuring carefully is important in the kitchen.

Measuring Temperature

Chapter 2, *Food Safety*, described how a thermometer is used to measure food's internal temperature. Thermometers measure degrees of temperature in either Fahrenheit (°F), which is the customary measure, or Celsius (°C), which is the metric measure. Convert between the two measurements easily by following the formulas outlined in Table 4.8.

Table 4.8: Temperature Conversion
Fahrenheit (°F) to Celsius (°C): Subtract 32 from the Fahrenheit number, multiply by 5, and then divide by 9.
Celsius (°C) to Fahrenheit (°F): Multiply the Celsius number by 9, divide by 5, and then add 32.
Temperature at which water boils: 212°F (100°C)
Temperature at which water freezes: 32°F (0°C)

Figure Focus

Figure 4.12: Ask students to identify some measuring equipment that is not shown in this picture. What pieces of measuring equipment do students think are most likely to be used in a foodservice establishment and why?

Standardized Recipes

A **recipe** is a written record of the ingredients and preparation steps needed to make a particular dish. Recipes used at home can follow any format that helps the cook prepare the dish. But recipes for institutional use, or **standardized recipes,** must follow a format that is clear to anyone who uses them. A standardized recipe lists the ingredients first, in the order they are to be used, followed by assembly directions or the method for putting the ingredients together.

Standardized recipes are critical tools that play an important part in a successful professional kitchen. Control of costs, quality, and consistency of product are no less important to the success of a restaurant than the preparation and service of great looking and tasting food. Consistent production of good food is the result of following a clear standardized recipe.

A standardized recipe includes the following information:

- **Name:** This is the title of the recipe.

- **Ingredients:** This is the food needed to make the recipe, usually listed in the order in which they are used. This makes it easier to follow the recipe and not forget any ingredient. Each ingredient must be clearly defined. For example, stating "onion" provides many choices such as yellow, red, white, green, or pearl.

Amounts of each ingredient are also given. Avoiding terms such as "to taste" and "as needed," makes it more likely the finished product will be what was intended by the creator of the recipe.

In commercial recipes, weight is generally the preferred method for measuring ingredients, rather than using other customary measurements such as cups or quarts or stating "one onion" or "a large apple," because weight is more accurate:

- **Yield**: This is the number of servings or the amount the recipe makes. This information is used to determine how much of the recipe quantity is needed. **Yield** is critical to understanding how much it will cost to produce the recipe.

- **Portion size**: This is the individual amount that serves a person.

- **Temperature, time, and equipment:** This includes size and type of pans and other equipment needed, the oven temperature, cooking time, and any preheating instructions.

- **Step-by-step directions**: This is how and when to combine the ingredients.

- **Nutrition information:** This is not essential, but useful. Nutrition information may include amounts of fat (saturated and unsaturated), carbohydrates, protein, fiber, sodium, vitamins, and minerals.

245

Reinforce and Review

- Recipes for institutional use must follow a clear, easy-to-understand format.
- A standardized recipe includes the recipe's name, ingredients, amounts required of each ingredient, recipe yield, portion size, temperatures required, time needed to prepare the recipe, equipment required, clear and easy-to-follow directions, and sometimes nutritional information.
- In commercial recipes, weight is generally the preferred unit of measurement.

Vocabulary Terms

- **Recipe:** A written record of the ingredients and preparation steps needed to make a particular dish.
- **Standardized recipe:** A recipe written according to an established format that helps the facility maintain consistency of product quality as well as control costs.
- **Ingredient:** An item of food needed to make a recipe.
- **Yield:** The number of servings or amount that a recipe makes.
- **Portion size:** The individual amount that serves a person.

Discuss

- Consistency, which includes using standardized recipes, is important to maintaining the restaurant's quality as well as to controlling costs. Does this mean that cooks and chefs must always measure each ingredient in a recipe, even if they have made the recipe multiple times before? Is "close enough" acceptable? What about the scope for personal creativity?
- How does the use of standardized recipes benefit the "front-of-the-house" employees and the guests they serve? What service-related problems can stem from failure to follow standardized recipes?

Reinforce and Review

- Recipes are road maps for cooks and should therefore be followed carefully.
- After a recipe has been followed exactly, evaluate the finished dish for ways to improve it. Remember that any change will affect the final product.

Vocabulary Terms

- *Mise en place*: The preparation and assembly of ingredients and equipment needed for a particular dish or for a service period.

The recipe is a road map for the cook. To get good results, follow it carefully:

- Read the recipe completely.
- Gather and "*mise en place*" all ingredients as specified. *Mise en place* is French for "to put in place." It means the preparation and assembly of ingredients, pans, utensils, and equipment or serving pieces needed for a particular dish or service.
- Measure carefully.
- Follow the instructions for preparation.

Once the recipe has been made as written, then the cook can decide if the end product is of the right quality and taste. Follow the recipe, and when it is clear what the recipe produces, evaluate the result and make changes if desired. In a recipe, each ingredient and method of preparation affects the final product.

The standardized recipe is a critical tool in the restaurant. The functions of standardized recipes include the following:

- Ensuring consistency of quality and portion size
- Helping purchasers to understand what to purchase
- Allowing cooks to understand what to prepare and how much of each ingredient is necessary
- Reducing waste, because no one is guessing amounts
- Helping servers to communicate accurate information to guests, such as dishes with potential allergens
- Meeting customer expectations for consistent dishes
- Helping managers to determine a dish's costs, which helps to control these costs

246

[trends]

Big or Small Portions

Surprisingly, food can be the least expensive part of a restaurant's costs, so serving big portions can help a restaurant stand out from the competition and attract new and returning diners. This has been key to the success of restaurants throughout the United States. But not only do many restaurants pride themselves on hefty portions, many customers associate "good value" with "lots of food." So why are so many nationally known restaurants beginning to offer smaller portions of their most popular dishes?

Diners are increasingly drawn to healthier eating habits, with mounting concerns over obesity. But as the saying goes, "People eat with their eyes." In other words, new research suggests that people will eat what is put in front of them—no matter how big the portion! Accordingly, offering smaller portions of popular items can attract consumers who want to eat less but still enjoy a satisfying meal, without alienating long-term diners who seek comfort in the familiar. This benefits restaurants because customers ordering these smaller items often spend more money overall. Guests perceiving that they have "saved" calories are more likely to order dessert!

Converting Recipes

Convert a recipe when the yield of the recipe (the amount it provides) is not the same as the amount of product needed. For example, suppose a recipe produces 96 portions, but a chef needs 250 portions for a function. It is necessary to convert the recipe from a recipe for 96 portions to one for 250 portions, as shown in Table 4.9.

Table 4.9: Converting the Yield from 96 Brownies to 250 Brownies

Figuring the Conversion Factor

Desired Yield = 250
Original Yield = 96
Conversion Factor: 250 ÷ 96 = 2.6

Ingredients	Amount for 96 pieces		Conversion Factor		Amount for 250 pieces
Unsweetened chocolate	1 lb = 16 oz	×	2.6	=	41.6 oz = 2 lb 10 oz
Butter	1 lb 8 oz = 24 oz	×	2.6	=	62.4 oz = 3 lb 14 oz
Eggs	1 lb 8 oz = 24 oz	×	2.6	=	62.4 oz = 3 lb 14 oz
Sugar	3 lb = 48 oz	×	2.6	=	124.8 oz = 7 lb 13 oz
Vanilla	2 tbsp	×	2.6	=	5.2 tbsp
Cake flour	1 lb = 16 oz	×	2.6	=	41.6 oz = 2 lb 10 oz
Baking soda	1.5 tsp	×	2.6	=	4 tsp
Chopped walnuts/pecans	1 lb = 16 oz	×	2.6	=	41.6 oz = 2 lb 10 oz

247

Divide students into small groups to discuss the following:

- How might the ambiance or menu prices at a restaurant affect the portion sizes it serves?

- Does eating less of one dish, as opposed to eating more of another dish, automatically qualify as "healthier" behavior?

- Why might guests find comfort in larger portions of food? What could that indicate about a society's physical and emotional well-being?

Reinforce and Review

- Recipes must be converted when the yield of the normal recipe is not the same (either larger or smaller) as the amount of product actually needed.
- To calculate a recipe's conversion factor, divide the amount of food desired by the amount of food yielded by the original recipe. This is discussed in greater detail on p. 248.

Table 4.9: Converting the Yield from 96 Brownies to 250 Brownies

- Why would the chef choose to convert the recipe from 96 to 250 servings, instead of simply baking three batches of the brownies (96 × 3 = 288) and cutting slightly larger portions, or saving the extra 38 brownies for another use, such as a dessert special?

Essential Skills:
Formula for Increasing or Decreasing Recipe Yields

Encourage students to bring recipes from home, so that the class can together practice converting recipes. Alternately, use the recipes in the chapters throughout this book.

Reinforce and Review

- If properly converted and prepared, a converted recipe should produce a finished product that is the same quality that the original recipe produces.
- The key to converting recipes is knowing both the recipe's original yield and the new desired yield.
- Multiplying each ingredient in a recipe by the same conversion factor keeps them all in the same proportions that they had in the original recipe.

Teaching Tips

- Provide as many examples of these operations as you think necessary in whichever formats are most appropriate for the class. Some examples:

Conversion Factor: Desired Yield / Original Yield

If a recipe serving 10 should serve 5:
$5 \div 10 = 0.5$ The conversion factor is 0.5

If a recipe serving 16 should serve 20:
$20 \div 16 = 1.25$ The conversion factor is 1.25

If a recipe serving 100 should serve 150:
$150 \div 100 = 1.5$ The conversion factor is 1.5

Vocabulary Terms

- **Conversion factor:** The number by which to multiply ingredients when converting a recipe, calculated by dividing the desired yield by the original yield.

The conversion of the recipe will impact the cost of the recipe, but not necessarily the cost of the portion. In other words, if a recipe for 24 cost $5.25 per portion, then increasing the recipe for 36 (of the same size portions) would not necessarily change that price. When properly converted and prepared, the quality of the product produced from the recipe should not vary from the original, no matter how many portions it yields.

Professional foodservice recipes have a large yield. Sometimes you have to change (or convert) a recipe if the yield is not the amount you need. Using basic math skills, it's easy to increase or decrease many recipes. Most recipes, even those for baked goods, can be doubled successfully.

Essential Skills
Formula for increasing or decreasing recipe yields

❶ Decide how many servings you need (or the desired yield).

❷ Use the following formula:

Desired yield ÷ Original yield = **Conversion factor**, which is the number by which to multiply the ingredients.

For example, if a chili recipe serves 8, and you need to serve 4, then 4/8 or $4 \div 8 = 0.5$. The conversion factor is 0.5.

❸ Multiply each ingredient amount by the conversion factor. This keeps all the ingredients in the same proportion to each other as they were in the original recipe. Be aware that weights and volumes are not interchangeable, so when converting a recipe, do not change volume measurement for weight.

For example, 1 cup of flour does not weigh 8 ounces.

❹ As needed, convert answers to logical, measurable amounts. Think about the equipment you will use for measuring.

For example: ¾ cup flour = 1 and ½ cup; 12 tbsp brown sugar = ¾ cup

❺ Make any necessary adjustments to equipment, temperature, and time. The depth of food in a pan affects how fast it will cook. Use pans that are the right size for the amount of food—neither too large nor too small.

Now, if a change is needed in the portion size, then the calculation requires an additional step. Suppose the cook wants to convert the yield of 250 brownies to small brownies? If 96 big brownies equals 125 small brownies, divide 250 by 125 (the desired yield divided by actual yield)—to get a conversion factor of 2.

The conversion of a recipe to produce more or less product can affect the equipment needed to produce the recipe. The adjustments will include measuring equipment and cooking/service equipment. For example, if a recipe that produces 24 portions and requires the use of 1 hotel pan to do final pan-up of the product is converted to produce 48 portions, 2 hotel pans will be needed. Another example is a recipe that calls for 1 tablespoon of an ingredient. If the recipe is increased by a multiplier of 16, then the item measure would be 1 cup. The cook needs a cup measure rather than a tablespoon measure. The failure to take equipment changes into consideration when converting a recipe can cause problems in preparation. Keep in mind that larger equipment might be needed for mixing and cooking larger amounts of food. Cooking times will often need adjustment as well.

Measuring

The term **measurement** refers to how much of something is being used in a recipe. Ingredients can be measured in several ways. Most ingredients are measured by volume. **Volume** is the amount of space an ingredient takes up. A salad recipe might list 1 cup cooked pasta or ½ teaspoon of pepper. Some ingredients are measured by weight or heaviness, such as 1 pound of fish filets or 2 ounces of butter. Other ingredients may be measured by the count, or number, of items, such as one medium banana or three egg whites. No matter how an ingredient is measured, careful, accurate measurement is necessary for quality and quantity control.

Measuring by Volume

Volume is not as accurate a measure as weight, particularly for solids because the character of the item creates major variations in the amount of space an item occupies. For example, 1 cup of water weighs 8 ounces, but 1 cup of flour weighs approximately 3.5-4 ounces, depending on whether or not it has been "packed." Volume is often used for amounts of dry ingredients such as herbs and spices that are too small to easily and accurately weigh.

Volume measurement is best used for liquids, but remember that even liquids can vary in weight in relation to volume. Always remember that the term fluid ounce is a volume measurement, not a weight. Only with water or a water-like substance is 1 cup (volume measurement) equal to 8 fluid ounces (volume measurement) and to 8 ounces (weight measurement). Examples of water-like liquids in the kitchen include milk, oils, thin liquids such as vinegar, and melted butter.

249

Reinforce and Review

- Converting a recipe to yield a greater or lesser amount will often affect the equipment used and the cooking time.
- No matter what method is used to measure an ingredient, the measurement itself must be performed carefully and accurately.
- Volume measurement is less accurate than weight measurement for solid items and is best used for liquids.
- For water and water-like substances, 1 cup is equal to both 8 fluid ounces and 8 ounces, although this is not true of other liquids.

Vocabulary Terms

- **Measurement:** Determining how much of something is used in a recipe.
- **Volume:** The amount of space an ingredient takes up.

Reinforce and Review

- Dry ingredients are usually measured by leveling them off evenly at the edge of the measuring utensil, although sometimes a recipe may call for a "heaping measure."
- Ingredients like spices are commonly measured as "pinches"—the amount that can be held between thumb and forefinger.

Teaching Tips

- Demonstrate ways of measuring dry ingredients.

Essential Skills: Measuring Dry Ingredients

Divide students into small groups to practice measuring dry ingredients by baking a simple cookie or brownie recipe.

After each batch has cooled, the class should determine which group produced the best-looking and best-tasting results.

What flaws in the batches do students think are attributable to poor measuring? What else might have affected the outcomes?

Dry ingredients are usually measured by leveling them off evenly at the rim of the spoon or cup using a straight-edged utensil. Sometimes, however, a recipe calls for a heaping measure: scoop up the ingredient with a utensil, but do not level it off. A heaping measure can give almost twice the amount of a leveled-off measure. Figure 4.13 shows the proper measure of dry ingredients.

Figure 4.13: To measure dry ingredients, take the straight edge of a knife and level off the ingredient.

Dry ingredient measuring tools usually come in a set of several sizes. A typical customary set of measuring cups includes $1/4$ cup, $1/3$ cup, $1/2$ cup, and 1 cup measures. A metric set includes 50 milliliter, 125 milliliter, and 250 milliliter measures. Even smaller amounts of dry ingredients can be measured as a dash or a pinch—the amount that can be held between the thumb and forefinger. Herbs and spices are often measured this way.

Essential Skills
Measuring Dry Ingredients

❶ Fill the cup with the ingredient. Some ingredients, such as flour and sugar, must be spooned into the cup lightly. Other ingredients, like brown sugar, must be packed down, but only if specified in the recipe.

❷ Level off the top of the cup using a straight-edge spatula. See Figure 4.14.

Figure 4.14: Step 2—Use a straight-edge spatula to measure off dry ingredients.

❸ Pour the ingredients into the mixture. If needed, use a rubber scraper to make sure all of the ingredient has been emptied out of the cup.

250

Figure Focus

Figure 4.13: How much does it matter to a recipe's success if the measurements are off by just a little?

Figure 4.14: How can proper measurement affect a restaurant's financial bottom line?

Liquid measuring cups are see-through and have measurement markings on the side. They are typically marked in fractions of a cup, fluid ounces, and milliliters. Customary sizes for measuring cups are 1 cup, 1 pint, 1 quart, and 1 gallon. Metric cups usually come in 250 milliliter and 500 milliliter sizes.

Measuring spoons generally come in a set of four or five. Most customary sets include these sizes: $1/4$ teaspoon, $1/2$ teaspoon, 1 teaspoon, and 1 tablespoon. Metric sets include 1 milliliter, 2 milliliter, 5 milliliter, 15 milliliter, and 25 milliliter measures.

Essential Skills
Measuring Liquids

When measuring liquid ingredients:

1. Set the measuring cup on a level surface.
2. Carefully pour the liquid into the cup.
3. Bend down to check the measurement at eye level for an accurate reading. See Figure 4.15.

Figure 4.15: Step 3—Check measurement at eye level.

4. Add more liquid, or pour off excess, until the top of the liquid is at the desired measurement mark.
5. Pour the ingredient into the mixing container. If needed, use a rubber scraper to empty the cup completely.
6. For small amounts of liquids, use measuring spoons.

251

Reinforce and Review
- Liquid measuring cups are see-through and are marked along the side with various measurements, often both customary and metric.

Teaching Tips
- Demonstrate ways of measuring liquid ingredients.

Essential Skills: Measuring Liquids

Why should students measure liquids by placing the measuring cup on a level surface, and then bending down to check the amount poured at eye level? Wouldn't it be easier to hold the measuring cup, or to pick it up to check the amount poured?

CUSTOMIZED INSTRUCTION

Mathematics Connection, Literacy Connection

Special Needs Students

Practice using different liquid and solid measuring cups, working with milk and flour.

What kinds of ingredients are easy to measure with this equipment? List as many as possible.

Figure Focus
Figure 4.15: The measuring cup contains 1½ cups of liquid. How many fluid ounces is this? How many teaspoons? How many gallons?

Discuss
- Why are both ounce/gram and pound/kilo scales necessary to have in a foodservice establishment?
- Besides following standardized recipes and controlling portion sizes, what other roles do scales play?

Reinforce and Review
- Weight is often measured in ounces, while volume is often measured in fluid ounces.
- Always correctly weigh an item and account for the weight of the container in which the item is being stored.

Teaching Tips
- Demonstrate the proper use of all scales available in the classroom.

Vocabulary Terms
- **Weight:** The measurement of an item's resistance to gravity.
- **Taring:** The process of accounting for the weight of the container holding the item to be weighed.
- **Spring scale:** A scale that measures the amount of pressure put on a spring.
- **Balance beam scale:** Also known as a baker's scale, the desired weight of an ingredient is placed on one end of the scale and the proper amount of the ingredient is placed on the other end.
- **Electronic scale:** A scale that measures resistance electronically.

Measuring by Weight

Weight is the measurement of an item's resistance to gravity. Weight is expressed in ounces and pounds. Think of the difference between a cup of popcorn and a cup of water. Both take up the same amount of space, but they do not weigh the same. The water is heavier. To find out how much each cup weighs, use a kitchen scale, not a measuring cup. Weight is often measured in ounces, while volume—as discussed earlier in this section—is measured in fluid ounces.

A food scale is helpful for measuring ingredients by weight. Scales are used to weigh ingredients for preparation and portion control. Both ounce/gram and pound/kilo scales are necessary.

When using a food scale, do the following:

- Decide in what container to weigh the food.
- Place the empty container on the scale.
- Adjust the scale until it reads zero.
- Add the food to the container until the scale shows the desired amount.

Remember to correctly weigh an item and account for the weight of the container in which the item is located. This is known as **taring** the scale. To do this properly, you should do the following:

1. On a movable-face scale (a spring scale or portion control scale) place the container on the scale. Then adjust the face back to zero.

2. On a balance-beam scale, place the container on one end of the scale. Then place the tare weight on the other end until the beam balances.

There are a few different types of scales available for weighing food:

- **Spring scale:** The scale measures the pressure placed on the spring.
- **Balance beam**, also called a **Baker's scale:** The weight of the item is placed on one end and then product is placed on the other end until the beam balances.

- **Electronic scale:** This measures resistance electronically.

Figure 4.16 shows different types of scales.

Figure 4.16: Types of scales include a spring scale (top), baker's scale (middle), and electronic scale (bottom).

252

Figure Focus
Figure 4.16: When might each type of scale be used?

Measuring Fat

Fat, such as butter, margarine, or shortening, can be measured in several ways:

- **Stick method:** This method is used for fat that comes in $1/4$-pound sticks, such as butter or margarine. The wrapper is marked in tablespoons and in fractions of a cup. Simply cut off the amount needed.

- **Dry measuring cup method:** Pack the fat down into the cup, pressing firmly to remove air bubbles. Level off the top. When adding to the recipe, use a rubber scraper to empty as much of the fat as possible from the cup. Apply the same technique when using measuring spoons to measure fat.

- **Water displacement method:** This method involves combining fat with water in a liquid measuring cup. First, do some math: subtract the amount of fat to be measured from one cup. The difference is the amount of water to pour into the measuring cup. For example, to measure $2/3$ cup of shortening, start with $1/3$ cup of water in a measuring cup. Next, spoon the fat into the cup, making sure it

Figure 4.17: To measure irregularly shaped objects such as fat, use the water displacement method.

all falls completely below the level of the water. When the water reaches the 1-cup level, you have the right amount of fat. Pour off the water and remove the fat with a rubber scraper. Although this method may seem complicated, it is the most accurate when measuring solid fats. Figure 4.17 shows the water displacement method of measuring fats.

It is sometimes difficult to be exact with the dry measuring cup method because air bubbles can make the measurement inaccurate. Using the water displacement method also makes the fat easier to scrape out of the measuring cup because it isn't packed tightly.

253

Reinforce and Review

- Fats can be measured by using the stick method for fats in stick form (like butter or margarine), the dry measuring cup method, or the water displacement method.
- The dry measuring cup method can be less accurate than the other methods because of the presence of air bubbles.
- The water displacement method is the most accurate way to measure solid fats.

Teaching Tips

- Demonstrate the three methods for measuring fats.
- Divide students into groups and provide them with measuring equipment and solid fats so that they can determine for themselves which methods are easiest and most accurate.

Vocabulary Terms

- **Stick method:** Cutting a stick of fat at the desired measurement to obtain the correct amount.
- **Dry measuring cup method:** Pressing fat into a measuring cup to displace air bubbles and then scraping it out.
- **Water displacement method:** Measuring method where the chef subtracts the amount of fat from one cup and then adds that amount of water to a measuring cup; scoops the fat into the measuring cup, keeping it below the water line, until the water reaches the one-cup level; pours off the water; and then removes the fat.

Figure Focus

Figure 4.17: This method is very accurate, but it is time consuming. In a busy kitchen, which is more important: accuracy or speed?

Reinforce and Review

- Sifting helps give dry ingredients a smoother consistency so that they more readily combine with other ingredients in a recipe.
- Never measure ingredients by holding the measuring cup over the mixing bowl or other container being used to make the recipe.
- Most vegetables must be trimmed and cut before using, so the edible portion must be calculated.

Teaching Tips

- Demonstrate a variety of sifters and sieves.
- Show how a given volume of unsifted flour changes when sifted.

Vocabulary Terms

- **Sifting:** A process that removes lumps from a dry ingredient, giving it a smoother consistency.
- **Edible portion (EP):** The part of an ingredient that is commonly eaten.
- **As purchased (AP):** The whole ingredient, as it is purchased from a purveyor.

Measuring Tips

Some recipes call for sifting ingredients; for example, flour, powdered sugar, and granulated sugar might need to be sifted together. **Sifting** is a process that removes lumps from an ingredient and gives it a smoother consistency. Be sure to sift dry powdery ingredients before measuring them. See Figure 4.18.

Never measure an ingredient while holding the measuring cup over the mixing bowl. Overpour and the entire recipe may be ruined.

Figure 4.18: Sifting removes lumps from ingredients such as flour to give them a smoother consistency.

If a recipe calls for ⅛ teaspoon of a dry ingredient but there is no ⅛ teaspoon measuring spoon, fill the ¼ teaspoon measure and level it off. Then, using the tip of a straight-edged spatula or table knife, remove half the ingredient.

EP/AP Amounts

Most vegetables have to be trimmed and cut before being used in recipes. As a result, cooks must calculate the correct **edible portion (EP)** amount from the untrimmed **as purchased (AP)** amount. Table 4.10 on the following page indicates the percentage yields for a variety of produce items.

Figure Focus

Figure 4.18: Why does using a sifter make the finished product (like flour or powdered sugar) fluffier?

Table 4.10: Percentage Yields of Various Produce Items

Produce Item	Yield
Artichoke, globe	80% (whole, trimmed); 30% (bottoms only)
Artichoke, Jerusalem	80%
Asparagus	55%
Bean, green or wax	88%
Bean, lima	40%
Beet	40–45% (75% purchased without tops)
Broccoli	65–75%
Brussels sprout	80%
Cabbage (white, green, or red)	80%
Carrot	75–80%
Cauliflower	55%
Celery	75%
Celery root (knob celery or celeriac)	75%
Corn (on the cob)	28% (after husking and cutting from cob)
Cucumber (slicing type)	75–95% (depending on peeling)
Eggplant	90% (75% if peeled)
Garlic	88%
Kohlrabi	55%
Leek	50%
Lettuce	75%
Mushroom	90%
Okra	82%
Onion, dry	90%
Onion, green (scallion)	60–70%
Parsley	85%
Parsnip	70–75%
Peas (green and black-eyed)	40%
Peas, edible pod	90%
Pepper, sweet (green or red)	82%
Potatoes, white	80%

continued

- Divide students into groups to practice working with some of these ingredients.
- They should weigh each ingredient in both AP and EP forms and calculate the amount of waste for each.
- Encourage students to discuss the following:
  - Why do some vegetables have a greater yield than others?
  - Does the size of the edible portion affect the item's price? For instance, at the grocery store, artichokes and asparagus tend to be more expensive than carrots and onions. Is this related to the amount of waste for each vegetable?
  - Is any of the material trimmed away from vegetables usable in other ways? If so, how and why?

CUSTOMIZED INSTRUCTION

Mathematics Connection, Literacy Connection, 21st-Century Skills—Reason Effectively, Information Literacy, Be Self-Directed Learners

More Advanced Students

Select a vegetable that is not on this list, such as Belgian endive, mustard greens, or turnips. Using at least three of the vegetables you select, perform a yield test on this vegetable to compare its AP and EP weights and thereby determine its yield percentage.

Reinforce and Review

- To determine how much of an item is needed to yield an AP amount, divide the EP amount by the yield percentage.
- A conversion chart is a useful tool for managers, as it estimates shrinkage from AP to EP amounts.
- A butcher's test measures the amount of shrinkage that occurs when a meat product is trimmed.
- A cooking loss test measures the amount of shrinkage during the cooking process.
- If the product is both expensive to purchase and sold in high volume, then the product can be especially important to the food cost percentage, so the butcher's test and cooking loss test should be performed regularly.

Teaching Tips

- Provide as many examples of these operations as you think necessary in whichever formats are most appropriate for the class. Some examples:

Determining the Desired AP Amount

3 lb trimmed celery ÷ .75 = 4 lb untrimmed celery

5.5 lb trimmed broccoli ÷ .65 = 8.46 lb untrimmed broccoli

10 lb trimmed potato ÷ .80 = 12.5 lb untrimmed potato

Determining the Desired EP Amount

4 lb untrimmed asparagus × .55 = 2.2 lb trimmed asparagus

9 lb untrimmed okra × .82 = 7.38 lb trimmed okra

5 lb untrimmed watercress × .90 = 4.5 lb trimmed watercress

Vocabulary Terms

- **Conversion chart:** A list of food items showing the average shrinkage from AP amount to EP amount.

Table 4.10: Percentage Yields of Various Produce Items *continued*

Produce Item	Yield
Potatoes, sweet (including yams)	80%
Radish	90%
Spinach and other greens	50–70%
Squash, summer (including zucchini)	90%
Squash, winter	65–85%
Tomato	90% (peeled)
Watercress	90%

To determine how much of an item is needed to yield an AP amount, simply divide the edible portion amount needed by the yield percentage. For example, a recipe for pasta salad calls for 4 pounds of cauliflower. The conversion chart shows that cauliflower has a 55 percent yield. To calculate how much will be needed to prepare 4 pounds of trimmed cauliflower, divide the desired EP amount by the yield percentage:

4 pounds trimmed cauliflower ÷ 0.55 = 7.27 pounds untrimmed

The chef needs to purchase 7.27 pounds of untrimmed cauliflower.

The formula can also be used in reverse. For example, the chef has 10 pounds of untrimmed cauliflower, which has a 55 percent yield:

10 pounds untrimmed cauliflower × 0.55 = 5.5 pounds trimmed cauliflower

In order to determine the AP quantity needed to result in a given EP quantity, it is also important to know the cooking loss for the item. Many quantity cookbooks, purchasing textbooks, and yield books include charts of average cooking loss for common food items. A **conversion chart** is a list of food items showing the expected, or average, shrinkage from AP amount to EP amount. These charts are tools that a manager can use, and they work well in most cases.

However, it is wise to conduct your own tests periodically to get the exact AP amount for your operation. A butcher test is used to measure the amount of shrinkage that occurs during the trimming of a meat product. This trimming includes deboning and removing fat and gristle. A cooking loss test is a way to measure the amount of product shrinkage during the cooking or roasting process. The amount of shrinkage due to trimming and cooking is usually expressed in terms of a percentage.

These tests are particularly important if the product is a high-cost item and if it is sold in high volume at the operation. If these two things are true, then the item can have a major effect on the operation's food cost percentage. So nothing should be left to chance. For example, if prime rib is a house specialty, a conver-

256

sion chart might not be accurate. There are many variables that determine the amount of shrinkage, such as the length of time the product is cooked and at what temperature.

Products today can frequently be purchased in an "as edible portion," usually known as a convenience item. This is something that is purchased trimmed and cut, such as precut fries. The price of the item is higher, but prep time and labor cost may ultimately be lower. For example, a manager should weigh the amount of time saved peeling and cutting potatoes for fries versus the cost of buying a product that comes already in that form. Figure 4.19 shows the selection of AP fruits and vegetables and then the EP version with their trim beside each item.

Figure 4.19: An edible portion (EP) is the amount of product that remains after it has been trimmed and cut.

Discuss

• How might restaurants decide whether to purchase convenience items, with a higher price, or more labor-intensive products, with a lower price but a higher labor cost? What types of restaurants might choose one or the other? What about combining the two?

Reinforce and Review

• Some products can be purchased in EP form, especially "convenience items."
• Prep time is typically lower for products purchased in EP form, but prices are often higher.

CUSTOMIZED INSTRUCTION
Mathematics Connection, Literacy Connection
Less Advanced Students
For some food items, AP amount equals EP amount. Besides convenience items, for what ingredients might this be the case? List as many as you can.

Figure Focus

Figure 4.19: These photographs illustrate the process of converting AP amounts into EP amounts. Why is this process necessary?

Reinforce and Review

- Standard recipe cost and standard portion cost are both important components in quantity food production.
- To find the total cost of a standardized recipe, a manager must know both the ingredient amounts needed and the market price for each one.
- Calculate the standard portion cost by dividing the total recipe cost by the recipe yield.

Table 4.11:
Standard Recipe Cost Calculation for the Brownie Recipe in Table 4.9

- The guiding principle is that the amount of the ingredient, multiplied by the cost of the ingredient, yields an ingredient cost. All the ingredient costs of a recipe are summed to yield the recipe cost.
- Use this brownie recipe, which yields 96 portions, to help students practice both recipe conversion and recipe cost calculation:
  - Convert the original recipe to yield 200 portions, and then calculate the new recipe cost.
  - Convert the original recipe to yield 300 portions, and then calculate the new recipe cost.
  - Convert the original recipe to yield 20 portions, and then calculate the new recipe cost.
  - Convert the original recipe to yield 50 portions, and then calculate the new recipe cost.
- Alternately, use the chili recipe on p. 261, which yields 26 servings:
  - Convert the original recipe to yield 50 portions, and then calculate the new recipe cost.
  - Convert the original recipe to yield 120 portions, and then calculate the new recipe cost.
  - Convert the original recipe to yield 15 portions, and then calculate the new recipe cost.
  - Convert the original recipe to yield 8 portions, and then calculate the new recipe cost.

Costing Recipes

Other factors that are essential in quantity food production are standard recipe cost and cost per serving, or standard portion cost. To find the total cost of a standard recipe, a manager must know both the ingredient amounts needed and the market price of each one. Then multiply or divide the ingredient amounts by the prices and add it all up to get the recipe cost. Divide the total cost by the yield to get the standard portion cost. Table 4.11 demonstrates how to calculate a standard recipe cost, using the ingredients for the brownie recipe in Table 4.9.

Table 4.11: Standard Recipe Cost Calculation for the Brownie Recipe in Table 4.9

Ingredient	Amount	Unit Cost
Unsweetened chocolate	1 lb	$5.50/lb
Butter	1 lb 8 oz	$2.50/lb
Eggs	1 lb 8 oz	$5.50/lb
Sugar	3 lb	$2.50/lb
Vanilla	2 tbsp	$6.50/lb
Cake flour	1 lb	$3.50/lb
Baking soda	1 ½ tsp	$2.75/lb
Chopped walnuts/pecans	1 lb	$1.49/lb

Ingredient	Amount × Unit Cost	Ingredient Cost
Unsweetened chocolate	1 lb × $5.50 =	$5.50
Butter	1.5 lb × $2.50 =	$3.75
Eggs	1.5 lb × $5.50 =	$8.25
Sugar	3 lb × $2.50 =	$7.50
Vanilla	$6.50 ÷ 32 tbsp = 0.203 × 2 tbsp=	$0.41
Cake flour	1 lb × $3.50 =	$3.50
Baking soda	$2.75 ÷ 96 tsp = 0.029 × 1.5 tsp =	$0.04
Chopped walnuts/pecans	1 lb × $1.49 =	$1.49
Total Cost of Recipe:		**$30.44**

258

Ingredient costs are usually rounded to the nearest cent. Portion costs are ordinarily carried out to **one-tenth** of a cent.

Many operations price out all recipes and then check them every six months to see if they are still accurate. Some establishments compare standard recipe costs to the national price index twice a year. If the index rises or drops a specific percentage, the total recipe cost is raised or lowered by this percentage, and the portion or yield cost is recalculated. While this method simplifies the recalculation process, foodservice operations should really do a complete revision every year.

Sometimes it's necessary to combine portion costs. A steak, for example, may cost $6.50 served by itself, but the cost increases to $10.99 when the steak is served with a salad, French fries, a roll, and butter. Some operators calculate the exact cost of each food item and then add the figures together to determine the total cost of a meal. Others simply calculate the average cost of all such extras and add this figure to appropriate items.

When patrons help themselves at a salad bar, there may be an extra calculation necessary to cost out a meal. The usual procedure is to keep an account of the cost of foods in the salad bar and track the number of salad bar patrons served from it. Dividing the number of patrons into the total cost of the salad bar will result in the average cost per serving. This figure can be added to the basic entrée cost. For example, if an operation spends $95.68 per day to keep its salad bar stocked and an average of 84 guests eat from the salad bar each day, the average cost per serving is:

$95.68 ÷ 84 = $1.14 per serving

Costing can be somewhat complicated. However, the success of a profitable restaurant or foodservice operation depends on balancing costs and prices.

Summary

In this section, you learned the following:

- The basic math calculations using numbers and fractions are addition, subtraction, multiplication, and division.

- A standardized recipe includes details such as the list and amounts of ingredients, yield, equipment, and cooking time and temperature. This information will help to ensure that cooks prepare the recipe the same way each time they make it.

Reinforce and Review

- To ensure that menu prices are appropriate, recipes should be recalculated for cost regularly to maintain accuracy.
- Some restaurants may choose to consider the exact cost of each "add-on" to the meal, such as rolls or pats of butter, while others combine these costs into a single "Q factor," which is then added to each recipe cost.
- To determine standard portion costs for salad bars and similar situations, divide the total cost of preparing the salad bar for a given service by the number of guests who patronize it.

Vocabulary Terms

- **One-tenth:** Portion costs are ordinarily carried out to one-tenth of a cent, or $0.000, to help maintain accuracy.

Summary

- Remind students to review the following:
  1. Basic math calculations using numbers and fractions
  2. The components and functions of a standardized recipe

Summary (cont.)

3. Converting recipes to yield smaller or larger quantities
4. Difference between customary and metric units of measurement
5. Converting between customary and metric units of measurement
6. The smallware and utensils used for measuring and portions
7. Calculating purchase (AP) and edible (EP) portion amounts
8. Calculating the cost and portion cost of a standardized recipe

- To increase or decrease recipe yields, do the following:
    1. Decide how many servings are needed or the desired yield.
    2. Determine the conversion factor, the number that each ingredient amount is multiplied by in order to adjust the yield of the recipe.
    3. Multiply each ingredient amount by the conversion factor.
    4. Convert ingredient amounts into logical, measurable quantities.
    5. Make any necessary adjustments to equipment, temperature, and time.

- Customary units include ounces, teaspoons, tablespoons, cups, pints, and gallons. Metric units are based on multiples of 10 and include milligrams, grams, kilograms, milliliters, and liters.

- It isn't necessary to convert between customary and metric measurements if a prep area has the correct measuring equipment.

- To measure temperature, use a thermometer; to measure fat, use the stick, dry measuring cup, or water displacement method; and to measure by weight, use a scale.

- To determine how much of an item is needed (the as purchased or AP amount) to yield an edible portion (EP) amount, divide the EP amount needed by the yield percentage. Get the yield percentage from a conversion table.

- To find the total cost of a standard recipe, a manager must know both the ingredient amounts needed and the market price of each one. Then he or she must multiply or divide the ingredient amounts by the prices.

Section 4.2 Review Questions

1 Determine the total cost and the cost per serving for the following recipe. The yield is 26 servings.

Chili

Ingredient	Unit Cost
4 lb ground beef	$3.39/lb
3 lb tomatoes	$1.69/lb
2 lb onions	$1.09/lb
1 lb green pepper	$1.59/lb
4 oz garlic	$2.59/lb
8 oz tomato paste	$1.79/pt

2 Describe the difference between the EP amount of broccoli and the AP amount of broccoli.

3 Convert the following recipe ingredients from customary units to metric units of measurements.

a. 1 c milk

b. 1 lb butter

c. 1 oz oregano

d. 2 tbsp olive oil

4 Convert the following recipe for 12 portions so that it yields 60 portions.

Stir-Fried Chicken

3 lb chicken	6 oz soy sauce	1 lb green peppers
1 ½ lb scallions	2 oz ginger	2 c water

5 What is the formula for increasing or decreasing recipe yield?

6 Dr. Jerald Chesser comments that a profession is defined as a calling requiring specialized knowledge. Why does a foodservice manager need to know details such as ingredient amounts and market price?

7 How would Alex change a recipe that serves 18 into one that serves 150?

8 How is math used in foodservice operations, both in front of the house and back of the house?

9 What is the difference between AP and EP and why is it important?

261

Section 4.2 Review Questions

1. The total cost is $23.95 and the cost per serving is $0.93.

2. The EP amount, or portion of an item which is edible, is generally smaller than the AP amount, or the item "as purchased." For instance, 65–75% of a given head of broccoli is usually edible. In this case, the EP amount would be 65–75% of the AP amount.

3. The converted amounts are
   a. 240 ml   b. 450 g   c. 28 g   d. 30 ml

4. The converted amounts are 15 lb chicken, 7.5 lb scallions, 1 pt 14 fl oz soy sauce, 10 oz ginger, 5 lb green pepper, and 2.5 qts water.

5. Determine the desired yield. Divide the desired yield by the original yield to obtain the conversion factor. Multiply each ingredient amount by the conversion factor. Convert to logical, measureable amounts as needed. Make any necessary adjustments to equipment, temperature, and time.

6. Foodservice managers need to know details such as ingredient amounts and market price to be sure that they are obtaining the best ingredients at the best prices for their establishment's needs. This will also help ensure consistency of quality and help meet customer expectations. Perhaps most importantly, this information helps managers determine the cost to produce each dish, which in turn helps to control costs.

7. Divide the desired yield by the original yield to obtain the conversion factor, or $150 \div 18 = 8.33$. Now multiply the amount of each ingredient by the conversion factor to obtain the correct amount needed to produce the larger recipe.

8. Managers in both the front and back of the house need to understand basic math in order to perform the basic functions of their jobs, such as purchasing inventory items, scheduling staff, and making the best use of resources. Student answers may vary so long as their responses indicate they understand the question being asked.

9. AP refers to an item, often produce, in its "as-purchased" state, before it has been trimmed or portioned. EP refers to the amount of that item which is edible, and is therefore usually smaller than the AP amount. It is important to understand the difference between the two so that enough of each ingredient can be purchased to prepare food for guests.

Section 4.2 Activities

1. Student responses should follow the guidelines expressed in the activity. The recipe cards should clearly demonstrate not only the original and the converted recipes but any changes in technique, timing, or equipment needed to prepare the larger recipe.

2. The conversion factors are as follows: salad dressing, 37.5; barbecue sauce, 9; bun, 3.75; strawberry tart filling, 18.75; and marinated vegetables, 11.25.

3. Students may choose from among the items listed in the AP/EP list, following the directions given in the activity. They should explain why they obtained their results, whether corresponding to the table or not.

Section 4.2 Activities

1. Study Skills/Group Activity: Recipe Cards

Work with two other students to find three appetizer recipes, each to serve between six and eight people, and each containing at least eight ingredients. Now convert each recipe to serve 20 people. Make a recipe card for each, showing both versions.

2. Activity: Recipe Conversion

Your restaurant will cater an outdoor picnic for 450 people.

- Salad dressing recipe serves 12
- Barbecue sauce recipe serves 50
- Bun recipe serves 120
- Strawberry tart filling recipe serves 24
- Marinated vegetable recipe serves 40

Calculate the conversion factor for each recipe.

3. Critical Thinking: AP/EP in Action

Select three items from the AP/EP list on pages 245 and 246, and go purchase them. Weigh the AP item, clean and trim it, then weigh the EP item. Do your results correspond to the percentages shown in the chart? Why or why not?

Case Study Follow-Up   *The Art of Professionalism*

At the beginning of the chapter, Chef Jean hired Alex as prep cook.

1. How are Alex's "people skills" relevant to his work as a prep cook?
2. Explain how Alex provides customer service. Who are his customers?
3. How can Chef Jean reinforce the lessons in professionalism he is teaching Alex, other than just telling him how to behave?
4. Chef Jean is ultimately responsible for Alex's work. How can he help Alex succeed in his assignment to help convert recipes?

263

Case Study Follow-Up

1. Alex needs to work well with other people as part of a team in order to perform his work as a prep cook. He must treat himself, others, and his work with respect; he should strive to become more proficient; he should increase his knowledge of the professional kitchen; and so forth.

2. Alex provides customer service to his colleagues in the kitchen by preparing the ingredients they will later use to create completed dishes, which will then be passed on to their guests.

3. Chef Jean can model the eight attributes of professional behavior to help Alex understand how to act in the workplace.

4. Chef Jean can assign Alex some math projects, ranging from basic mathematic operations to more complicated work, to help him become more comfortable with recipe conversion. It may also help to assure Alex that his math assignments, like his other tasks in the kitchen, will be overseen by management staff. If Alex miscalculates the recipe conversions, the errors will be corrected and Alex will receive extra assistance.

Apply Your Learning

Calculating Recipe Cost

The original recipe cost is $5.03. The converted recipe cost is $12.53. The new recipe cost is $0.51.

Culinary Education

Students should research a variety of culinary schools and apprenticeship programs to determine and describe the similarities and differences as well as the positive and negative aspects of each.

Volume vs. Weight

Students should calculate the weights of each ingredient and discuss why the volume and weight are or are not equivalent.

Chapter 4 | Foundations of Restaurant Management & Culinary Arts

Apply Your Learning

Calculating Recipe Cost

A ratatouille recipe serves ten. The EP amounts required to make the recipe are:

- 2 lb tomatoes ($0.95/lb)
- 2 lb summer squash ($0.79/lb)
- 1 lb eggplant ($1.19/lb)
- 8 oz onion ($0.25/lb)
- ½ oz garlic ($0.35/lb)
- 1 fl oz olive oil ($25/gallon)
- ⅛ oz kosher salt ($1/lb)

Using the AP/EP list on pages 255-256, calculate the recipe cost. Now convert the recipe to yield 25 portions. What is the new recipe cost? Calculate the portion cost.

Culinary Education

Today there are more options for culinary education than ever before. In addition to the time-honored practice of on-the-job training, two other paths are available: attending an accredited culinary school or participating in a formal apprenticeship program. Research both culinary schools and apprenticeship programs. How are they similar and different? What pros and cons do you see for each? Write three paragraphs on your findings.

Volume vs. Weight

Volume and weight are both ways to measure, but they measure very different things. Volume measures the space an object occupies, while weight measures how resistant the object is to gravity.

Using the wrong measurement can have a significant effect on the finished product.

264

Collect a dry cup measure and a liquid cup measure, plus a precise scale. Measure out the volume given for each ingredient below, then weigh it. Be sure to tare the scale first! Compare the weights for each item. What did you learn? Write two paragraphs on your findings.

- 1 c water
- 1 c heavy cream
- 1 c vegetable oil
- 1 c simple syrup (1:1 water : sugar)
- 1 c all-purpose flour
- 1 c granulated sugar
- 1 c dark brown sugar
- 1 c kosher salt

Critical Thinking | **The Importance of Professionalism**

Professionalism means many things, as you have learned. What do you personally think is the most important part of being a culinary professional and why? Prepare a brief oral report on your selection.

265

Critical Thinking **The Importance of Professionalism**

Students may respond in a variety of ways as long as they can speak clearly and logically about some aspect of culinary professionalism.

Exam Prep Answers

1. C
2. D
3. A
4. C
5. C
6. C
7. A
8. B
9. D
10. D

Exam Prep Questions

1 If you use 1 pound of mirepoix in a recipe that yields 1 gallon of soup, how much mirepoix do you need to make 3½ gallons of soup?

A. 2¾ pounds

B. 3 pounds

C. 3½ pounds

D. 4 pounds

2 At what temperature does water boil?

A. 32°F

B. 100°F

C. 172°F

D. 212°F

3 The number of servings a recipe makes is called the

A. yield.

B. portion.

C. dividend.

D. quantity.

4 The amount of space an item occupies is called

A. yield.

B. weight.

C. volume.

D. measurement.

5 The measurement of an item's resistance to gravity is called

A. yield.

B. length.

C. weight.

D. volume.

6 How many ounces does 1 cup of water weigh?

A. 4

B. 6

C. 8

D. 10

7 The process that removes lumps from a dry, powdered ingredient and gives it a smoother consistency is called

A. sifting.

B. mixing.

C. blending.

D. flattening.

8 The stick and water displacement methods are used to measure

A. liquids.

B. solid fats.

C. dry ingredients.

D. sifted ingredients.

9 To determine how much of an item is needed to yield an AP amount,

A. multiply the edible portion amount needed by the yield percentage.

B. divide the yield percentage by the edible portion amount.

C. add the yield percentage to the edible portion amount.

D. divide the edible portion amount needed by the yield percentage.

266

10 Fractions can be added once they have a

A. decimal.

B. dividend.

C. common numerator.

D. common denominator.

Chapter 5 Overview

Chapter 5 introduces the student to the cooking skills required in contemporary foodservice establishments.

Section 1: The first section describes a wide variety of equipment used in the professional kitchen, including receiving and storage equipment as well as items used to prepare, cook, and serve food.

Section 2: Essential pre-preparation skills are discussed, such as knife basics and seasoning.

Section 3: This section details basic dry- and moist-heat cooking methods.

Section 4: Finally, this section explores the relationship between cooking and nutrition.

Chapter 5
Kitchen Essentials 2—Equipment and Techniques

Advance Preparation	
Review	Material in Sections 5.1–5.4
	Relevant material in Chapters 2–4
	The U.S. Department of Agriculture's resources, such as the Dietary Guidelines for Americans 2005 and MyPyramid
Contact	Local registered dietician (ADA) or school nurse
Prepare	Blank index cards, a scale (for weighing humans), and a measuring tape
	Sample Dietary Reference Intakes
	Dietary Guidelines for Americans 2005
	Equipment for sharpening knives
	A variety of salts
	A recipe to accompany the activity on p. 303
	Batter and breading recipes to accompany the activity on p. 328

ServSafe Connection
Pages 313, 327, 338

CUSTOMIZED INSTRUCTION OPTIONS

Less Advanced Students	More Advanced Students	ESOL Students	Special Needs Students
Pages 277, 282, 314	Pages 278, 282, 315	Pages 277, 282, 340	Pages 282, 310, 354

CHAPTER TOOLS

21st-Century Skills	Mathematics	Science	Literacy
Pages 277, 278, 282, 286, 288, 291, 294, 303, 309, 310, 315, 319, 320, 331, 337, 340, 341, 345, 349, 350, 351, 352, 354, 355, 357, 358	Pages 283, 287, 314, 345, 357	Pages 278, 287, 288, 291, 294, 310, 314, 315, 320, 331, 349, 350, 351, 354, 355, 357, 358	Pages 277, 278, 282, 286, 288, 291, 294, 303, 309, 310, 314, 315, 319, 320, 331, 337, 340, 341, 345, 349, 350, 351, 352, 354, 355, 357, 358

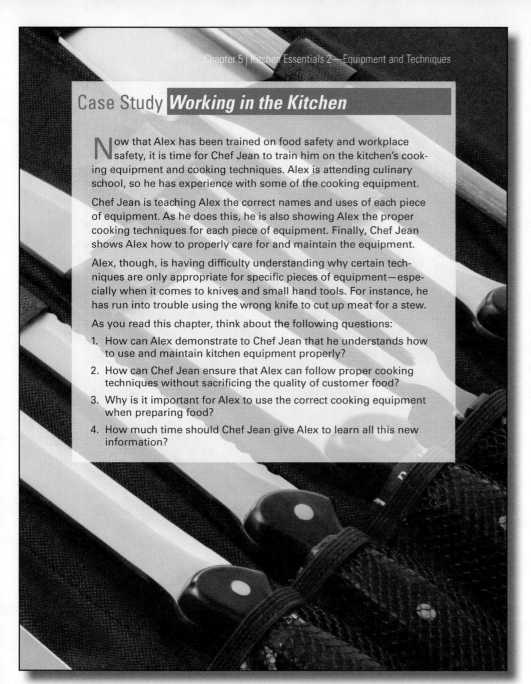

Case Study *Working in the Kitchen*

Now that Alex has been trained on food safety and workplace safety, it is time for Chef Jean to train him on the kitchen's cooking equipment and cooking techniques. Alex is attending culinary school, so he has experience with some of the cooking equipment.

Chef Jean is teaching Alex the correct names and uses of each piece of equipment. As he does this, he is also showing Alex the proper cooking techniques for each piece of equipment. Finally, Chef Jean shows Alex how to properly care for and maintain the equipment.

Alex, though, is having difficulty understanding why certain techniques are only appropriate for specific pieces of equipment—especially when it comes to knives and small hand tools. For instance, he has run into trouble using the wrong knife to cut up meat for a stew.

As you read this chapter, think about the following questions:

1. How can Alex demonstrate to Chef Jean that he understands how to use and maintain kitchen equipment properly?

2. How can Chef Jean ensure that Alex can follow proper cooking techniques without sacrificing the quality of customer food?

3. Why is it important for Alex to use the correct cooking equipment when preparing food?

4. How much time should Chef Jean give Alex to learn all this new information?

Case Study
Working in the Kitchen

- Although Alex, as a culinary student, has a certain amount of kitchen knowledge and experience, he still needs a lot of training to reach his potential value as a member of the Uptown Grille's team. But Chef Jean is a busy man, with many demands on his time each day. How much time is it realistic for him to spend training Alex? What can he delegate to others?

- What cooking techniques should Alex be taught? How might these be the same as or different from what he is learning at school?

- How can Alex remember which equipment is appropriate for which task?

- Note that there are follow-up questions about the case study at the end of the chapter.

- This activity could be done in groups, as a class, or as a homework assignment.

Professional Profile

Discuss	How is being an executive chef different from owning a restaurant? What skills are needed in each capacity? Why might "giving back" to the community be so important to many chefs, including Chef Benny? When Chef Benny says, "Keep your *mise en place* in order," what does he mean?
Reinforce and Review	Goal-oriented professionals can achieve a wide array of accomplishments. Being a chef is more than just being a good cook.
Teaching Tips	Discuss the importance of overcoming personal and professional obstacles and why perseverance plays an essential role in the foodservice industry.

[professional profile]

Benjamin Gordon Jr.

"Chef Benny"

Chef and Owner of Gordon Foods

With two parents who loved to cook, it was natural for me to develop an affinity for food at an early age. As a teenager, I was already working in restaurants—washing dishes or cleaning the floors—just to be near a professional kitchen. It didn't take long before I decided that not only did I want to cook, but I also wanted to own a restaurant.

After completing high school, I attended the Baltimore International Culinary Arts Institute (now the Baltimore International College), graduating in 1983.

With the help of my parents, I opened my first restaurant at the age of 21. Restaurant 2110, serving country French cuisine, soon became the talk of the town, frequently being featured in local and national publications. In addition to my local clientele, I prepared meals for celebrities such as Oprah Winfrey, Patti LaBelle, Martha Stewart, Ruby Dee, Tina Turner, Richard Dreyfuss, Charles "Rock" Dutton, Rachelle Ferrell, Will and Jada Pinkett-Smith, and Baltimore's former Governor, William Donald Schaefer. I later opened Chez Charles, which offered nouvelle French cuisine, and Benny's Jazz Club, a Cajun restaurant.

I became the Chef of the Baltimore Convention Center, teaching and cooking for thousands of guests from all over the country. And I was the youngest chef and restaurateur to be nominated and accepted to membership of the Chaine Des Rotisseurs, an international gourmet society. Currently, I serve as the official Chef for the Black Professional Men, Inc., in Baltimore.

As a former national spokesperson for Lawry's Seasonings, I have gone from local chef to a media celebrity. Now, I own Gordon Foods, which provides catering services, consulting services, systems development, and classes.

But it's most important to give back. I now spend a great deal of time mentoring high school students who are interested in the hospitality industry. In fact, I chose this industry because of my passion for food and the ability it has given me to help people. Food has been my window to the world. I believe that proper *mise en place* is the basis for all areas of life, not just cooking. It enables you to achieve a higher level of success.

Remember:

❝ *Keep your* mise en place *in order.* ❞

In July of 2004, Benny was cutting down a tree for a member of his family when the chain saw kicked back and severed his left arm. The chances of living, much less saving his arm, were slim. He was blessed to have skilled

270

doctors who saved his arm and his life. Benny notes that this "blessing" helped him to look at life in a different way. He still has his "dream," but now it has more purpose. The phrase "I can do that with one hand tied behind my back" has a newfound meaning for him. Benny says that he has raised the level of what he does, because he lives that blessing every day.

About Kitchen Essentials 2—Equipment and Techniques

You can't be the best at what you do without understanding the tools and techniques of your trade. So be sure you understand the following:

- Knife skills are the foundation of cooking.

- *Mise en place* is the most important element of cooking.

- Part of *mise en place* is determining which cooking method to use for each food. Choosing the correct or incorrect method can greatly impact a meal.

- Nutrition is the foundation of life. If you don't have proper nutrition, you cannot learn, think, heal, love, or enjoy life to the fullest.

5.1 Foodservice Equipment	5.2 Getting Ready to Cook	5.3 Cooking Methods	5.4 Cooking and Nutrition
• Receiving and storage equipment	• *Mise en place*	• Heat transfer	• Healthy diets
• Pre-preparation equipment	• Knife basics	• Dry-heat cooking methods	• Dietary guidelines for Americans
• Food-preparation equipment	• Seasoning and flavoring	• Moist-heat cooking methods	• MyPyramid
• Holding and serving equipment	• Pre-preparation techniques	• Combination-cooking methods	• Nutrition labels
		• Other cooking methods	• The problem of obesity
		• Determining doneness	

SECTION 5.1 FOODSERVICE EQUIPMENT

Of course, every restaurant and foodservice operation requires equipment. Some of the equipment is common to most kitchens, while some is unique to the operation. Equipment needs depend on many elements, such as the size of the kitchen, number of customers served, food items offered on the menu, and style of service.

This section introduces many of the tools and equipment typically found in a professional kitchen. Items are divided into categories according to their function: knives, smallwares, measuring and portioning devices, cookware, strainers and sieves, food prep, and storage containers.

271

Focus and Engage

Discuss

- *Mise en place* is the most important element of cooking. Without a thorough preparation, even the best cook cannot succeed. How can students develop strong *mise en place* skills?
- The text states that "Nutrition is the foundation of life." Taken literally, what does this mean to students? Can it be seen as a metaphor, too? If so, how?

Section 5.1 Foodservice Equipment

Introduce the Section

a. Review the importance of using the right tool for the job.
b. Introduce students to the equipment commonly found in the professional kitchen.
c. Discuss the objectives for the section.

Vocabulary Review

a. Direct students to the key terms.
b. Pronounce each word, and have the students repeat the pronunciation out loud.
c. Discuss the definition of each word.

Teach

Discuss

- The classroom kitchen is different in some ways from a professional kitchen. In particular, the equipment used may vary. Ask students to identify equipment that might be present in the school cafeteria or in a restaurant kitchen that is not available (either at all, or in the same dimensions) in the classroom kitchen. Encourage them to explain these differences.

Discuss
- Why is the receiving process so important in the scheme of the kitchen?

Reinforce and Review
- The receiving area is the first stop in the flow of food, and therefore the first opportunity an establishment has to check the quality of the goods it has ordered.
- Using a scale to double-check an item's weight, even if the weight is listed on the box, is one way to reduce mistakes in ordering and receiving.

Teaching Tips
- Review the material in Chapter 2 related to the flow of food.
- Point out which pieces of receiving equipment are available in the classroom, if any.
- Explain the classroom procedure for receiving goods.

Vocabulary Terms
- **Receiving table/area:** The site where goods are inspected upon delivery.
- **Scale:** The tool used to weigh goods.
- **Utility cart:** The piece of equipment used to move goods from one part of the facility to another.

Study Questions

After studying Section 5.1, you should be able to answer the following questions:

- What equipment is needed for receiving and storing food and supplies?
- What equipment is needed for pre-preparation?
- What are the basic types of pots and pans and their common uses?
- What types of preparation equipment are used in the foodservice kitchen?
- What equipment is needed for holding and serving food and beverages?

Receiving and Storage Equipment

Receiving Food

The receiving area is the first stop in the flow of food. It is here that all food deliveries enter the restaurant or foodservice operation. Before accepting the product, an employee checks the quality and quantity of the items ordered against those being delivered. This can be accomplished using several pieces of equipment found in the receiving area:

Figure 5.1: When deliveries are received, they are inspected for quality and quantity.

- **Receiving table/area:** Employees weigh, inspect, and check delivered items on a receiving table or in a receiving area. See Figure 5.1.

- **Scales:** Employees weigh items using a scale to confirm that what was ordered matches what is delivered.

- **Utility carts:** Carts of durable injection, molded shelving, or heavy steel are used to carry food cases to storage areas. Chutes, conveyors, dollies, dumbwaiters, and elevators are all used to move food and supplies from one area of the operation to another.

272

Figure Focus
Figure 5.1: What is this receiver doing correctly? What else must she do to check the produce order properly?

Storing Food

After food is delivered and received into the receiving area, it must be stored properly. Dry goods such as flour, sugar, and grains must be stored at least 6 inches off the floor on stainless steel shelving. Figure 5.2 shows refrigeration equipment. Perishable goods such as dairy products, meat, and fresh fruits and vegetables are stored in refrigerators and freezers:

Figure 5.2: Reach-in refrigerators and freezers have full-sized doors or half doors.

- **Shelving:** Shelving in storage areas should be made of stainless steel. Operations use stainless steel instead of wood because wood is difficult to keep clean and is not acceptable to many local health departments. Stainless steel shelves are very strong and easy to clean.

- **Refrigerators and freezers:** There are two basic types of refrigerators and freezers. A **walk-in refrigerator** or **walk-in freezer** (often called a "walk-in") is built right into the foodservice facility itself. A **reach-in refrigerator** or **reach-in freezer** can have one, two, or three internal compartments. A reach-in might have full-sized doors or half doors, windows in the doors, or doors on both sides of the freezer. Some have wheels so that they can be used in different areas of the kitchen. There are also roll-in, display, on-site, and portable refrigerators and freezers. All refrigerators must maintain temperatures between 32°F and 41°F. Freezers should maintain temperatures of 10°F to -10°F.

Pre-preparation Equipment

There are many types of pre-preparation equipment used in restaurant and foodservice operations, including those in the following categories:

- Knives
- Hand tools and small equipment
- Measuring utensils
- Pots and pans

273

Figure Focus

Figure 5.2: What benefits do reach-in refrigerators and freezers have? What are some inconveniences?

Discuss

- Why is it important to use good-quality kitchen knives?

Reinforce and Review

- Foodhandlers use knives in most cooking preparations, choosing from a variety of knives according to their needs.
- The two main parts of a knife are the blade, or cutting surface, and the handle, or holding surface.
- Most knives have tapered cutting edges; other options include serrated, Granton, and single-side.

Teaching Tips

- Display both forged and stamped knives for students, identifying the differences.

Vocabulary Terms

- **Blade:** The cutting surface of a knife.
- **Tip:** The forward part of the knife blade, including its point.
- **Cutting edge:** The sharp surface along the bottom of the blade, running from tip to heel.

Knives

Knives are the most widely used pieces of kitchen equipment. Foodhandlers use knives in most cooking preparations, from slicing to chopping to shredding. Each knife is designed for a specific purpose, such as paring a vegetable or cutting meat from the bone. A good knife is made of stainless steel because it is very durable and stays sharp for a long time.

The Parts of a Knife

A knife has two main parts, the blade and the handle. The **blade** is the cutting surface of the knife. The blade is made of metal and is either forged or stamped. A **forged blade** is made from a single piece of heated metal that is dropped into a mold and then struck with a hammer and pounded into the correct shape. A **stamped blade** is made by cutting blade-shaped pieces from sheets of milled steel. Figure 5.3 identifies the different parts of a knife.

The blade of the knife has several parts:

- **Tip**: Cooks use the tip for detailed work such as paring, trimming, and peeling.
- **Cutting edge**: The cutting edge is located along the bottom of the blade between the tip and the heel. Use it for slicing, carving, and making precision cuts. The cutting edge can be **flat ground** and **tapered** (both sides of the blade taper smoothly to a narrow V-shape), **serrated** (shaped into a row of teeth that can be set very closely or widely apart), **hollow ground** (sides of the blade near the edge are ground away to form a hollow, making the blade extremely sharp), *granton* (ovals are ground into the sides of the blade, which helps food to release easily), and **single side** (edge is on just one side).

Figure 5.3: Parts of a knife.

274

Figure Focus

Figure 5.3: Do all types of knives have all of these parts? Why or why not? What makes a "good" knife?

- **Spine**: The top of the blade is the spine and is the noncutting edge of the blade.

- **Heel:** The heel is the widest and thickest part of the blade. Use the heel to cut through large, tough, or hard foods.

- **Bolster**: The bolster is located at the heel of the blade. It is where the blade meets the handle.

- **Tang**: The tang is the metal that continues from the blade through the handle. A full tang is as long as the whole knife handle. Chef's knives and cleavers have full tangs. Some knives have partial tangs and are used for lighter work such as paring or bread knives.

- **Scales**: The scales are the part of the knife that creates the handle.

- **Rivets**: The rivets hold the handle to the tang.

- **Handle**: The handle is made with various materials, including hardwoods or textured metal.

- **Butt**: The butt is the end of the handle.

Types of Knives

There are many types of knives:

- **Boning knife**: Foodhandlers and cooks in the butchering area use this 6-inch knife to separate raw meat from the bone. The blade is thin, flexible, and shorter than the blade of a chef's knife.

- **Butcher knife**: Also known as a scimitar, cooks use the butcher knife to fabricate raw meat. It is available with 6- to 14-inch blades.

- **Butter knife**: Use this small knife with a blunt-edge blade to spread butter, peanut butter, and cream cheese on bread or dinner rolls.

- **Chef's (French) knife**: This is an all-purpose knife for chopping, slicing, and mincing all types of foods. Its blade is normally 8 to 14 inches long and tapers to a point at the tip.

- **Cheese knife**: Cooks use this thinly shaped utensil to cut through hard or soft-textured cheese.

- **Clam knife**: Use this short, blunt-point knife to shuck, or open, clams. Unlike the oyster knife, it has a very sharp edge.

- **Cleaver**: Use this heavy, rectangular knife to chop all kinds of food, from vegetables to meat. It is also able to cut through bones.

275

Discuss

- Which knives do students perceive as the most useful and why?
- Why are knives with partial tangs used for lighter work? They are not sturdy enough to hold up to the rigors of chopping and slicing in a professional kitchen. Introduce the concept of a "rat-tail" tang. The tang on these knives is not attached to the handle with rivets, but instead consists of a narrow piece of metal attached within the handle—like a foot in a sock. These knives tend to be weak and are easily broken.

Reinforce and Review

- The heel of the blade is used to cut through large, hard, or tough foods, while the tip is used for more delicate work.
- Some knives, such as clam or oyster knives, are used to pry rather than cut, although the blades can still be quite sharp.

Discuss

- Which knives would students expect to find in a classical French restaurant? A seafood restaurant? A steakhouse? A sandwich shop? A butcher shop?

Reinforce and Review

- This list covers most knives used in professional foodservice establishments. Restaurants specializing in specific cuisines or items, such as sushi, will usually have specialty knives on hand.

Teaching Tips

- Display a variety of knives for students so that they can better understand how "form follows function."

- **Deli knife**: Use the deli knife for thick sandwiches. The blade is serrated, which allows the knife to easily release. The most common deli knife is 8 inches.

- **Fillet knife**: A fillet knife is a thin, flexible blade for cutting fish fillets. It is a short knife, about 6 inches long.

- **Lettuce knife:** This is a plastic serrated knife designed to cut lettuce without causing the edges of the lettuce to turn brown.

- **Oyster knife**: An oyster knife is a short, stubby knife with a pointed tip for shucking oysters.

- **Paring knife**: Use the paring knife to trim and pare vegetables and fruits. It is a small knife with a sharp blade, only 2 to 4 inches long.

- **Santoku**: A santoku is a general-purpose kitchen knife with a 5- to 7-inch blade length. The santoku knife is designed for a comfortable, well-balanced grip, while allowing for full blade use.

- **Scimitar** (SIM-ah-tahr): A scimitar, also known as a butcher knife, is a long, curved blade; use it for cutting through large cuts of raw meat.

- **Serrated slicer**: Use this knife with a long, thin serrated blade to slice breads and cakes.

- **Slicer**: Cooks use this knife for slicing cooked meats; its blade can be as long as 14 inches.

- **Steak knife**: Use this curved knife for cutting beef steaks from the loin.

- **Tourné** (tour-NAY): Similar to a paring knife, this knife has a curved blade for cutting the curved surfaces of vegetables.

- **Utility knife**: An all-purpose knife used for cutting fruits, vegetables, and some meats, this knife's blade ranges from 6 to 8 inches long.

- **Vegetable peeler**: This is not technically a knife, but it has sharp edges for peeling potatoes, carrots, and other vegetables.

Figure 5.4 shows the different types of knives.

276

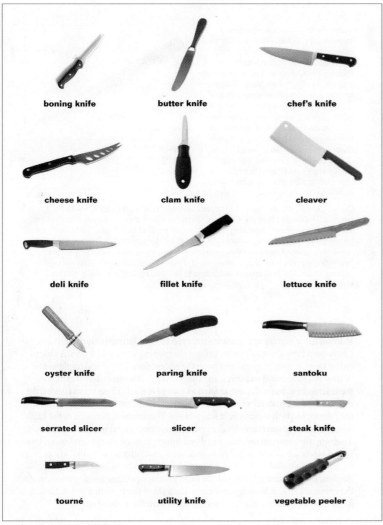

boning knife butter knife chef's knife

cheese knife clam knife cleaver

deli knife fillet knife lettuce knife

oyster knife paring knife santoku

serrated slicer slicer steak knife

tourné utility knife vegetable peeler

Figure 5.4: Types of knives.

277

Figure Focus

Figure 5.4: Do all of these items resemble what you think of as a "knife"? Why or why not? Ask students to point out which knives they have used or have seen used.

What's New: New Knives

Encourage students to discuss the following:

- Why might cooks in a Western restaurant choose Japanese-style knives?

- Are ceramic knives appropriate for foodservice? Why or why not? Note: Despite their fragility, ceramic knives are appropriate in restaurant and foodservice establishments since they are excellent for most tasks requiring a high degree of precision. However, care must be taken so that they are not used on items that are too hard for them to cut or knocked against hard surfaces.

Discuss

- What is the difference between steeling and sharpening?

Reinforce and Review

- Chefs use a sharpening stone and a steel to keep their knives sharp.
- Diamond steels and ceramic steels can produce extremely sharp edges if used properly.

Teaching Tips

- Demonstrate the honing process—both sharpening and steeling—for students.

Vocabulary Terms

- **Honing:** The regular maintenance required to keep knives in the best shape.
- **Sharpening stone:** A coarse- or fine-grained rectangular stone used to grind and hone the edge of a knife or another sharp object.
- **Steel:** A long rod—made of magnetized metal, ceramic, or impregnated with diamond dust—that is used to remove the microscopic burrs that form when knives are used.

[what's new]

New Knives

Japanese-style knives are becoming increasingly popular in American kitchens, both for home cooks and professional chefs. See Figure 5.5. Unlike the typical Western knife, which is sharpened on both sides of the edge of the blade, a Japanese knife is often sharpened along only one side. Japanese knives are sharpened at a more acute angle than are Western knives. They have a very hard temper, meaning that the cutting edge will stay extremely sharp for a long period of time. Usually, Japanese knives are made from high-carbon steel or from a mixture of high-carbon steel and iron. A number of brands are now available in the United States.

Figure 5.5: A Japanese knife is often sharpened along only one side.

Ceramic knives are also gaining in popularity. These knives are actually made of ceramic. This means they are extremely sharp, but also extremely fragile. Dropping the knife or using it to cut something hard can cause the blade to shatter. While they cannot be sharpened at home, most manufacturers will sharpen ceramic knives for a fee. The knives do not need to be sharpened often; once every year or two may suffice, depending on how vigorously they are used. These knives are excellent for slicing, peeling, and cutting, but are not well suited to heavy chopping or working with hard foods.

Knife Care

Honing is the regular maintenance required to keep knives in the best shape. Chefs keep their knives sharp by using a sharpening stone and a steel. A **sharpening stone** is used to grind and hone the edges of steel tools and implements. A **steel** is a long metal rod that is lightly grooved and magnetized. It removes the microscopic burrs that are created as a knife is used. These burrs create drag, dulling the slicing ability of the knife. The steel also helps to return the blade to the convex shape that exists on a sharp blade. This shape is flattened as the knife is used. **Ceramic steels** are slender ceramic rods embedded in a wooden handle. They are used both on ceramic and metal knives to hone sharpened knives. **Diamond steels** are slender metal rods, or sometimes flattened rods, that are impregnated with diamond dust. They should not be used to hone ceramic knives. Because of the diamond material, they can produce extremely sharp edges, as do the ceramic steels. A **honing steel** looks like a short sword with a round blade that helps remove broken pieces and realign the remaining ground edges.

Sharpening removes metal from the blade. It is only done when a knife is so dull that it cannot be brought back to a sharp edge with the steel. The knife

278

Figure Focus

Figure 5.5: How does this Japanese knife differ from a typical chef's knife?

blade is held at a 20-degree angle to a sharpening stone. The blade is then passed across the oiled or watered stone an equal number of times on each side until the desired sharpness is achieved. Often sharpening stone units hold three stones. These range from coarse to very fine and allow the blade to be smoothed as the process is finished.

To properly care for knives, follow these guidelines:

- Keep knives sharpened. A sharp blade cuts more evenly and with less force than a dull blade, so it is safer.

- Use a knife only for its intended purpose.

- Keep the handle of the knife clean and dry.

- Never leave knives soaking under water. Clean the knife immediately and return it to its proper storage place.

- Never talk or point with a knife.

- Never distract others who are using knives.

- If a knife is dropped, jump back and allow it to fall. Do not try to catch it.

- Store knives in knife kits, racks, or sheaths.

- Never hand someone a knife. Put the knife on the counter and let the other person pick it up.

Essential Skills
Knife Sharpening and Steeling

A sharp knife is a safe knife, so it's critical to sharpen your knives regularly. Follow this process to ensure that knives stay as sharp as possible.

❶ Collect the knives to be sharpened, a sharpening stone, mineral oil or water, a damp cloth or rubber mat, and a steel.

❷ Place your stone on the cloth or mat so it does not slip.

❸ Carefully lubricate the entire surface of the stone with either mineral oil or cool water (always use the same lubricant on a stone).

❹ Holding the knife at a 20-degree angle, carefully run the blade across the coarsest surface of the stone; repeat as necessary, with an equal number of strokes on each side of the blade. See Figure 5.6a.

Figure 5.6a: Step 4—Hold the knife at a 20-degree angle, and run the blade across the stone.

279

Figure Focus
Figure 5.6a: When learning to sharpen a knife, always place the sharpening stone atop a flat work surface. When you have more experience, you may find it easier to hold the stone in your hand, but be aware that this technique is more dangerous.

Discuss
- When a new cook arrives for the first day in the kitchen, other cooks will often drift by his or her station to introduce themselves—and examine the newcomer's knives. How can proper knife selection and maintenance be components of professionalism?

Reinforce and Review
- Sharpening units may include a number of faces, from coarse to very fine, to smooth the blade.
- Knives should be used only for their intended purposes and should be carefully stored (clean and dry) when not in use.

Essential Skills:
Knife Sharpening and Steeling

As students learn the process of sharpening knives, make sure they understand the importance of following each step in the process and why each step matters.

- Knives to be sharpened, as well as other necessary equipment, should be gathered at the beginning so that each item is ready when needed.

- Using a damp cloth or rubber mat underneath the stone can prevent it from slipping.

- Using either mineral oil or cool water to lubricate the stone will prevent friction and therefore heat buildup, which could damage the knife. Either oil or water is fine to use, but only use one or the other on any given sharpening stone.

- One way to ensure a 20-degree angle is to place the cutting edge of the knife on the stone, and then stack two pennies on the stone. Lower the side of the blade until it rests atop the pennies, but the cutting edge is still in contact with the stone. This is approximately a 20-degree angle. Alternately, use a protractor to mark a 20-degree angle on a piece of paper, which can then be held against the knife as a template.

Essential Skills: Knife Sharpening and Steeling (continued)

- Putting too much pressure on the blade while sharpening both increases friction and decreases the angle of contact.

- Knives should be carefully cleaned between sharpening and steeling to eliminate metal fragments from the blade. If these are left on the blade, they can damage both the steel and the knife.

- A common and safe way to steel a knife is to hold the steel vertically, with the tip placed on the work table and the handle upright. Grip the knife handle firmly, with the cutting edge facing downward. Steel at the same 20-degree angle used to sharpen.

- Using an equal number of strokes on each side of the blade when sharpening and steeling prevents misalignment.

- Wipe away any metal fragments from the knife and steel to prevent potential contamination.

⑤ Move to a finer surface of the stone and repeat the process, making sure not to put too much pressure on the knife.

⑥ Carefully wash and dry your knife.

⑦ Hold the steel vertically, with fingers clear of the working surface to prevent injury.

⑧ Holding the knife at a 20-degree angle, carefully run the edge of the blade along the steel, making sure that the entire edge is honed. See Figure 5.6b.

⑨ Repeat as needed, with an equal number of strokes on each side of the blade and using light pressure.

⑩ Wipe away any metal fragments on the knife or on the steel.

Figure 5.6b: Step 8—Run the edge of the blade along the steel.

[nutrition]

Loss of Moisture and Nutrients

When fruits and vegetables are sliced, they can lose moisture and nutrients, especially vitamin C, very quickly. In fact, any type of processing can cause nutrient deterioration. When more surface area is exposed to the air, the loss is quicker.

When preparing fruits and vegetables in advance, be sure to keep them refrigerated and carefully covered. Some vegetables, such as carrots and potatoes, should be stored in water. This prevents carrots from drying out and potatoes from discoloring.

Hand Tools and Small Equipment

Every restaurant and foodservice kitchen has small hand tools and small equipment called **smallware**. Hand tools are designed to aid in cutting, shaping, moving, or combining foods. Similar to knives, many hand tools are designed for specific tasks. Figure 5.7 shows a sample of small hand tools and small equipment used in restaurants and foodservice kitchens. Hand tools are easy to use and are an essential part of food pre-preparation:

- **Bench scraper**: A bench scraper is a rigid, small sheet of stainless steel with a metal blade. Use it to scrape material off a work surface or "bench" or to cut or portion soft, semifirm items (like bread dough or cookie dough).

- **Bowl scraper**: A bowl scraper is a flexible piece of rubber or plastic. Use it to combine ingredients in a bowl and then scrape them out again, to cut and

280

Discuss

- What items of smallware should be in every kitchen and why?

Reinforce and Review

- Hand tools, like knives, are designed to perform specific tasks in the kitchen, such as cutting, shaping, and combining foods.

Teaching Tips

- Peel three carrots and three potatoes. Submerge one of each item in water and refrigerate. Place one of each item on a plate and refrigerate. Finally, place one of each item on a plate and leave at room temperature. At the beginning of the next class period, compare the appearance (size, color, wrinkling, cracking, etc.) and aroma of each set of vegetables.

- Display the smallware available for use in the classroom and make sure students understand how to use each item.

Vocabulary Terms

- **Smallware:** Small equipment items and hand tools found in kitchens.

Figure Focus

Figure 5.6b: This cook is holding the steel horizontally and bringing the cutting edge toward his hand, but note that there is a guard separating the steel itself from its handle, protecting the cook's hand. As you become more proficient steeling your knives, you may find this technique is easier for you.

Nutrition: Loss of Moisture and Nutrients

Encourage students to discuss the following:

- How can a restaurant make sure that enough vegetables are prepared for service without preparing excessive vegetables that will continue to lose moisture and nutrients until the next service period?

separate dough, and to scrape extra dough and flour from wooden work tables.

- **Can opener**: In restaurant and foodservice kitchens, can openers are mounted onto metal utility tables because they are used to open large cans. A small handheld can opener, like those for home use, may be used in a restaurant or foodservice kitchen to open small cans of food.

- **Channel knife**: Use a channel knife to cut grooves lengthwise in a vegetable such as a carrot.

- **Cheesecloth**: A cheesecloth is a light, fine mesh gauze for straining liquids such as stocks or custards, for bundling herbs, or for thickening yogurt.

- **China cap**: A China cap is a pierced, metal, cone-shaped strainer; use it to strain soups, stocks, and other liquids to remove all solid ingredients. A very fine China cap made of metal mesh strains out very small solid ingredients. This is called a *chinois* (chin-WAH).

- **Colander** (CAH-len-der): A colander drains liquid from cooked pasta and vegetables. Colanders stand on metal feet, while strainers are usually handheld.

- **Cook's fork (kitchen fork)**: Use a cook's fork with two long, pointed tines to test the doneness of braised meats and vegetables, to lift items to the plate, and to steady an item being cut. Do not use a cook's fork to turn meats that are being dry-cooked because the tines may pierce the meat and release the juices.

- **Corer**: Use a corer to remove the core of an apple or pear in one long, round piece.

- **Fish scaler**: A fish scaler removes scales from a fish.

- **Food mill**: A food mill is a machine that comes with several detachable parts. Cooks use it to purée foods to different consistencies.

china cap

zester

funnel

sieve

strainer

wire whip

grater

Figure 5.7: A sample of small hand tools and small equipment.

281

Discuss

- This list of smallware includes items found in the typical foodservice establishment. Ask students to consider the expense of supplying all this equipment in addition to large items like ovens and refrigeration. Since these items are ultimately paid for through food sales, encourage students to imagine how much food, at what prices, must be sold to cover all the costs associated with operating a foodservice establishment.

Reinforce and Review

- Small hand tools are used for a variety of purposes, such as holding, straining, shaping, mixing, and cutting.

In-Class Activity: Name That Smallware!

Students should close their books and store their notes. Have ready a table laden with different hand tools, covered with a sheet or dropcloth. Divide the class into two teams. Hold up an item of smallware. The first team to identify the item correctly gets 1 point, and the first team to identify an appropriate use of the item gets 2 points. Keep going until all the items have been identified. The losing team must store the equipment.

Figure Focus

Figure 5.7: Strainers, sieves, and China caps all have similar functions, but they are used for different purposes. Why? Similarly, how does a grater differ from a zester?

CUSTOMIZED INSTRUCTION

Literacy Connection, 21st-Century Skills—Communicate Clearly, Information Literacy, Produce Results

Less Advanced Students

Select an item of equipment from the list on pp. 280–283. How and when is it used?

Either produce a brief oral report to the class or create a poster demonstrating the equipment and its uses.

More Advanced Students

Select an item of equipment from a different culture's cuisine—for instance, a tortilla press or spaetzle maker. How and when is it used?

Either produce a brief oral report to the class or create a poster demonstrating the equipment and its uses.

ESOL Students

What are some common hand tools in your culture of origin? Which items on the list on pp. 280–283 are commonly used there?

Either produce a brief oral report on a common hand tool in your culture of origin or create a poster demonstrating the equipment and its uses.

CUSTOMIZED INSTRUCTION

Literacy Connection, 21st-Century Skills—Communicate Clearly, Interact Effectively with Others, Work Effectively in Diverse Teams

Special Needs Students

Examine a variety of smallware. How is each used? How useful do you think each item is?

Discuss these hand tools in a small group.

- **Funnel**: Use a funnel to pour liquid from a larger to a smaller container.
- **Grater**: A grater grates hard cheeses, vegetables, potatoes, and other foods.
- **Kitchen shears**: Shears are strong scissors; use them to cut string and butcher's twine and to cut grapes into small clusters.
- **Offset spatula** (SPACH-e-la): An offset spatula turns foods on a griddle or broiler. It has a wide, chisel-edged blade and a short handle.
- **Parisienne** (pah-REE-see-en) **scoop**: A parisienne scoop, or melon baller, cuts ball shapes out of soft fruits and vegetables.
- **Pastry bag**: A pastry bag is a bag made of canvas, plastic, or nylon; use it to pipe out frostings, creams, and puréed foods. Different pastry tips create a variety of decorations.
- **Pastry brush**: Use a pastry brush to brush egg wash, melted butter, glazes, and other liquids on items such as baked goods, raw pasta, or glazes on meats.
- **Peeler**: A peeler cuts a thick layer from vegetables and fruits more efficiently than a paring knife.
- **Pie server**: A pie server is a specially shaped spatula made for lifting out and serving pieces of pie.
- **Piping tools**: Piping tools include piping bags (canvas, plastic, disposable), decorative tips (metal, plastic, of varying shapes), and presses (cylinders with a handle on one end that force dough through a metal cutout).
- **Pizza cutter**: Use a pizza cutter to cut pizza and rolled-out dough.
- **Ricer**: Use a ricer to create rice-like pieces of cooked food by pressing the food through a pierced hopper (small basket-shaped container that holds the material) by means of a plate on the end of a lever.
- **Rolling pin**: A rolling pin is a cylinder that cooks use to roll over pastry to flatten or shape it.
- **Rubber spatula**: A rubber spatula is a spatula with a long handle, often called a scraper, used to fold ingredients together and scrape the sides of bowls.
- **Sandwich spreader**: A sandwich spreader is a short, stubby spatula that cooks use to spread sandwich fillings and condiments.
- **Skimmer**: A skimmer has a larger round, flat head with holes. Use it to remove foam from stock or soup and to remove solid ingredients from liquids. Mesh skimmers are also available.

282

- **Sieve** (SIV): A sieve has a mesh screen to sift flour and other dry baking ingredients and to remove any large impurities.

- **Spoons**: Cooking spoons for quantity cooking are solid, perforated, or slotted. They are made of stainless steel and hold about 3 ounces. Solid spoons are serving spoons without holes in them. Use them to spoon out both liquid and solid ingredients. Perforated and slotted spoons have holes that allow liquid to drain while holding the solid items on the spoon.

- **Straight spatula**: A straight spatula is a flexible, round-tipped tool used for icing cakes, spreading fillings and glazes, leveling dry ingredients when measuring, and even turning pancakes and other foods.

- **Strainer**: A strainer is made of mesh-like material or metal with holes in it. Strainers come in different sizes and are often shaped like a bowl. Strainers strain pasta, vegetables, and other larger foods cooked in liquid.

- **Tamis** (TA mee)/**drum sieve**: A tamis is a screen that stretches across a metal or wood base that is shaped like a drum, and food is forced through it. It's used to purée very soft foods and to remove solids from purées.

- **Tongs**: Tongs are a scissor-like utensil that foodhandlers use to pick up and handle all kinds of solid food. To keep food safe, foodhandlers should never use their hands to pick up food.

- **Wire whip** (whisk): Wire whips of different sizes and heaviness are used to mix, beat, and stir foods.

- **Zester**: A zester shreds small pieces of the outer peel of citrus fruits such as oranges, lemons, and limes.

Measuring Utensils

Measuring utensils come in all shapes and sizes. They are widely used in restaurant and foodservice kitchens to measure everything from spices to liquids to dry goods like oats, grains, sugar, and flour. They can also measure temperature.

Figure 5.8 shows common measuring utensils used in restaurant and foodservice kitchens. Following are just some of the types of measuring utensils found in the restaurant and foodservice kitchen:

- **Balance scale/baker's scale**: A balance scale weighs dry ingredients in the bakeshop.

- **Bimetallic stemmed thermometer:** These thermometers are useful for checking large or thick food.

283

Discuss

- Why do so many items in this list appear to have French names? How does this relate to the discussion about the development of the restaurant and foodservice industry in Chapter 1?

Reinforce and Review

- Measuring equipment, as discussed in Chapter 4, is used widely in professional kitchens.
- This section describes some other common measuring equipment that students might not consider "traditional."

In-Class Activity: Yields and Peels

Mathematics Connection

How do yield percentages differ depending on what tools are used and who is using them?

Each student should receive two potatoes. Weigh each potato, and then peel one with a peeler and one with a paring knife, keeping the two piles of peels separate.

Weigh each peeled potato, and weigh each pile of peel. Calculate the yield percentage for each potato.

As a class, create two columns on the board, one labeled "Peeler" and one labeled "Paring Knife."

Each student should provide his or her results for each potato.

Students should calculate the class yield percentage for each category.

Discuss the results as a group.

Reinforce and Review
- Review the measurements and equivalencies.

Teaching Tips
- Labels are sized according to the volume they hold. Typically, they are labeled along the handle.
- Portion scoops are assigned a color, depending on how many scoops of that size can be obtained from a container holding a given amount of product.

Figure 5.8: Common measuring items used in professional kitchens.

- **Digital (electric) scale:** This is a precise scale used to measure weight. It provides a digital readout in both U.S. and metric systems.

- **Ladle:** Ladles come in various sizes, measured in fluid ounces and milliliters so they can be used to portion out liquids.

- **Measuring cup:** Measuring cups measure varying quantities of both dry goods and liquids. Measuring cups with spouts measure liquids, and those without spouts measure dry ingredients.

- **Measuring spoon:** Cooks use measuring spoons to measure small quantities of spices or liquids. The spoons measure in the amounts of ⅛ teaspoon (not all sets include this smallest size), ¼ teaspoon, ½ teaspoon, 1 teaspoon, and 1 tablespoon.

- **Portion scale:** Use this scale to measure recipe ingredients, from ¼ ounce to 1 pound to 2 pounds.

- **Scoop:** This short-handled measuring utensil scoops out soft foods, such as ice cream, butter, and sour cream. Portion scoops come in various sizes.

- **Thermocouple:** This thermometer measures temperature in thick or thin foods almost instantly. Do not leave this kind of thermometer in foods as they cook.

- **Volume measures:** Volume measures are similar to liquid measuring cups but bigger, usually available in sizes of 1 pint, 1 quart, ½ gallon, and 1 gallon.

Figure Focus
Figure 5.8: Which of these measuring tools were not discussed in Chapter 4? Does that mean that they are less important than the others?

Pots and Pans

Pots and pans are essential tools in the professional kitchen. Pots and pans are often called **cookware**. They are available in many shapes and sizes and are made of a variety of materials, such as copper, cast iron, chrome, stainless steel, and aluminum, with or without nonstick coating. In general, pots are larger vessels with straight sides and two loop handles. Pans, on the other hand, tend to be shallower, with one long handle and either straight or sloped sides.

Pots

Pots are available in a range of sizes based on volume. Use them on the stove top for making stocks or soups, or for boiling or simmering food. Figure 5.9 shows commonly used pots in the professional kitchen.

brazier   double broiler   fondue pot   stock pot

Figure 5.9: Commonly used pots in the professional kitchen.

- **Brazier**: This medium to large pot, more shallow than sauce pots, has straight sides and two handles for lifting. This is typically made of heavy-weight material with a thick bottom for good heat distribution. Use it to braise meat and vegetables. (This pan is also called a *rondeau*.)

- **Double boiler**: A pot that has an upper pot and a lower pot. The lower pot holds boiling or simmering water that gently cooks the food in the upper pot. Use it for melting chocolate or heating milk, cream, or butter.

- **Fondue pot**: A fondue pot is a pot with a heat source placed directly below the pot. Use it for a food-preparation process known as fondue. When eating fondue, guests use forks to dip bits of food or bread into the warm semi-liquid sauce (such as a cheese mix or chocolate).

- **Sauce pot**: Use to prepare sauces, soups, and other liquids. Sauce pots are more shallow than stock pots, with straight sides and two loop handles for lifting.

- **Stock pot**: A stock pot is a large pot for preparing stocks. Stock pots with spigots allow the liquid to be poured out easily without losing any of the solid ingredients.

285

Discuss

- Why would a cook choose one piece of equipment over another? For instance, when would a sauce pot be used instead of a stockpot, and vice versa?
- In general, why would a pot be chosen over a pan, and vice versa? What are some hazards of using the wrong equipment?

Reinforce and Review

- Pots and pans, collectively known as cookware, are essential to most preparations in the professional foodservice establishment, and a wide range of equipment is available.
- In general, pots tend to be deeper than pans and typically have straight or slightly slanted sides, while pans are usually shallow and broad.

Teaching Tips

- Display each pot and pan available in the classroom. Encourage students to suggest dishes that might be prepared using each one.
- The term *batterie de cuisine* is sometimes used to refer to all the cooking equipment (utensils, pots, and pans, and unfixed equipment like ranges) available in a professional kitchen. In French, this term has a military connotation, as if going into a restaurant's service period were equivalent to entering a war. Encourage students to discuss other connections between professional foodservice and the military—for instance, the term "brigade."

Vocabulary Terms

- **Cookware:** The all-inclusive term used to describe pots and pans.
- **Pot:** A large cooking vessel, usually metal but sometimes ceramic or glass, typically used to boil or simmer ingredients.

Figure Focus

Figure 5.9: Stockpots are usually the largest pots in the professional kitchen.

Reinforce and Review

- Pans are usually shallow, which allows reduction to occur more quickly than in a taller pot.

Vocabulary Terms

- **Pan:** A shallow cooking or baking vessel, usually made of metal.

Pans

Pans are usually smaller and shallower than pots. Pans are used for general stove-top cooking, especially sautéing, frying, or reducing liquids rapidly, for baking, and for holding food. Figure 5.10 shows pans commonly used in the professional kitchen.

set of pans

braising pan

cake pan

cast-iron skillet

crêpe pan

fish poacher

hotel pans

muffin tin

roasting pan

sauce pan

sauté pan

sautoir

sheet pan

spring form pans

wok

Figure 5.10: Pans commonly used in the professional kitchen.

286

Figure Focus

Figure 5.10: Why do students think different shapes of pots and pans have evolved?

- **Braising pan**: A high-sided, flat-bottomed cooking pan, this is used to braise, stew, and brown meat. The pan is also called a *brazier* or a *rondeau*.

- **Cake pan**: These baking pans have straight sides. They are available in a variety of sizes and shapes, including round, rectangular, square, and specialty (such as heart-shaped).

- **Cast-iron skillet**: This is a heavy, thick pan made of cast iron. Use it to pan grill, pan-fry, and braise foods like meat or vegetables.

- **Crêpe pan** (KRAYP): This is a shallow skillet with very short, slightly sloping sides. It is used to create crêpes, a specialty pancake.

- **Fish poacher**: This is a long, narrow, metal pan with a perforated rack that cooks use to raise or lower the fish so it doesn't break apart.

- **Hotel pan**: Use this pan to hold prepared food in a steam table, hot-holding cabinet, or refrigerator. These are sometimes used for baking, roasting, or poaching meats and vegetables, but the pan is really too thin and does not distribute heat well.

- **Muffin tin**: Small, round cups or molds are used to make muffins, cupcakes, or other small baked goods.

- **Roasting pan**: A shallow, rectangular pan with medium-high sides and two handles, cooks use it to roast and bake foods, such as meat and poultry.

- **Saucepan**: This is a pan with medium height, straight sides, and a single long handle. Use it for general cooking, in particular liquid or liquid-based mixtures, on ranges.

- **Sauté** (saw-TAY) **pan**: The original French sauté pan is slope-sided and made of thin metal for quick heating. It is used strictly to sauté items. In the United States, the "fry pan" is generally referred to as a sauté pan. A fry pan has curved sides and a long handle and is generally made of slightly thicker metal. It is used both to sauté and to pan fry.

- **Sautoir** (saw-TWAHR): The classic sautoir shape is called a sauté pan in the United States. It has a wide bottom and straight sides. Some typical tasks include pan-frying, stir-frying, and shallow poaching.

- **Sheet pan**: Cooks use this very shallow pan, about 1-inch deep, for just about anything, from baking cookies to roasting vegetables.

- **Spring form pan**: This is a two-part, spring-loaded baking pan. The bottom piece and ring secure with a spring to hold the bottom in place. Once an item is baked, the pastry chef can release the spring to make it easy to remove the cake from the pan.

287

Discuss

- Which pans on this list are primarily used for baking? What physical characteristics do they share?
- Similarly, which pans are primarily used for non-baking food preparation and why? How do these relate to the pots discussed on p. 286?
- Which pans on this list appear to have a wide general application and which appear to have very narrow functions?

Reinforce and Review

- Hotel pans are some of the most versatile items in the professional kitchen, as they can be used for cooking, baking, holding, and storage.
- Although sauté pans and woks evolved in different cultures and have different shapes, they can be used interchangeably for many preparations in the contemporary foodservice establishment.

In-Class Activity: Reduction Relationships

Science Connection, Mathematics Connection

Students should pour one cup of liquid (water is fine) into a shallow pan and one cup of liquid into a deep pot. Use a ruler to measure how deep the liquid is in each vessel.

Each vessel should then be placed on the stovetop, using the same amount of heat under each. Time how long it takes to reduce the liquid in each pan by half, again using the ruler.

Encourage students to discuss why the liquid in the shallow container reduces more quickly than the liquid in the deep container.

Discuss

- Why might a cook or a chef choose a pan made of one material over another?
- Why do pots and pans made of different materials require different cleaning methods?
- Why is it important for cooks (as opposed to dishwashing staff) to know how equipment made of different materials should be maintained?

Reinforce and Review

- Care should always be taken to use the correct cleaning methods for any pots or pans. In particular, cookware with nonstick coating should be treated gently to avoid scratches.
- Food-preparation equipment involves such important items as cutting and mixing equipment and cooking appliances, such as ranges and ovens.
- Always be extremely careful when using cutting and mixing machines, which can be extremely dangerous. In fact, minors are not permitted to use these devices in the workplace.

Teaching Tips

- Review appropriate cleaning methods for each type of cookware used in the classroom.
- Discuss the cleaning procedures to be followed in the classroom. Consider creating (or requiring students to create) a job list to ensure that the kitchen is clean at the end of each class period.

Homework Activity: Mental Metal

Science Connection, Literacy Connection, 21st-Century Skills—Information Literacy, Initiative and Self-Direction, Productivity and Accountability

A variety of metals are commonly used in cookware, such as aluminum and copper. Select one of these metals and research its uses in the foodservice industry and elsewhere.

Pay special attention to the concept of "heat transfer," and why the metal you select may be better suited for certain types of cooking than for others.

Discuss your findings in a one-page paper.

- **Wok**: This is a metal pan with a rounded bottom and curved sides. The curved sides make it easy to toss or stir food. Cooks use woks especially for frying and steaming in Asian cooking.

Care of Pots and Pans

Pots and pans are available in a variety of materials, each with specific instructions for care and cleaning. Always wait for pots and pans to cool before washing or rinsing to avoid warping. Follow these guidelines:

- **Aluminum**: Hand wash in soapy water. Use a nonabrasive cleaner to remove stains.
- **Cast iron**: Wash in warm, sudsy water. Keep properly conditioned and dry to prevent rust and pitting.
- **Chrome**: Wash in warm water with soap or detergent. Do not use abrasive cleaners.
- **Copper**: Use commercial cleaners to remove discoloration before regular washing.
- **Stainless steel**: Wash in hot, soapy water or warm ammonia and water solution. Rinse thoroughly and dry immediately to avoid water spots.
- **Nonstick coating**: Use a plastic mesh scrubber to scrub inside of the nonstick pan to avoid scratches. Remove all residue from the bottom of the pan or food may burn.

Food-Preparation Equipment

In addition to knives, hand tools, and pots and pans, other items are necessary to prepare food for cooking:

- Cutters and mixers
- Steamers
- Broilers
- Ranges, griddles, and fryers
- Ovens

Processing Equipment: Cutters and Mixers

Always use safety guards when using cutting machines. Make sure that employees are properly trained and informed of all precautionary measures that should be taken when operating the equipment. If they are not sure how to use the

288

machine, offer them assistance. Remember, it is illegal for minors to use, clean, or maintain cutters or mixers.

In the professional restaurant or foodservice kitchen, cutters and mixers are used to cut meats and vegetables and to mix sauces and batters. Figure 5.11 shows commonly used cutters and mixers in the professional kitchen.

countertop blender   food processor   vertical cutter mixer

meat grinder   meat slicer   mixer   wing whip

Figure 5.11: Commonly used cutters and mixers in professional kitchens.

■ **Countertop blender**: Blenders purée, liquefy, and blend foods. The blender consists of a base that houses the motor and a removable, lidded jar with a propeller-like blade in the bottom. Speed settings for the motor are in the base. Jars for the blender are made of stainless steel, plastic, or glass.

■ **Immersion blender**: An immersion blender is also known as a hand blender, stick blender, or burr mixer. It is a long, stick-like machine that houses a motor on one end of the machine with a blade on the other end. This operates in the same manner as a countertop blender to purée and blend foods except that a cook holds it manually in a container of food, whereas a countertop blender contains the food itself.

■ **Food chopper**: A food chopper chops vegetables, meats, and other foods using a vertical rotating blade and a bowl that rotates the food under the blade. This unit is often called a buffalo chopper. Never push food under the cover of the bowl, because your fingers could be caught by the moving blades. To clean the food chopper, first unplug the unit. Remove the blades carefully, and handle with the same care given a knife.

289

Discuss

- Minors aren't allowed to use certain pieces of equipment in the professional kitchen. However, the work still needs to get done. How can students perform the following tasks without using prohibited machinery?
  - Whipping egg whites
  - Slicing bread
  - Puréeing cooked vegetables
- Why is it important to unplug electrical equipment before cleaning and sanitizing it?

Reinforce and Review

- Cutting and mixing equipment is used to slice, chop, or purée ingredients and to whip or beat mixtures.
- Immersion blenders and countertop blenders essentially perform the same function, although one uses a self-contained vessel and the other is simply a mixing blade with a handle and motor.

Figure Focus

Figure 5.11: Link this graphic to the material in Chapter 3. Which of these machines can minors legally operate in a professional environment? Note: None of them.

Discuss

- Why is it important for students to know how to operate and maintain equipment that they can't legally use in the workplace?

Reinforce and Review

- A horizontal cutter mixer combines elements of a food processor and a mixer.
- Mandolines and meat slicers can both be used to slice a variety of ingredients in a variety of widths, using fixed blades that are extremely sharp. The mandolin blade does not move, while the meat slicer blade spins in place.

- **Food processors**: This is a processing machine that houses the motor separately from the bowl, blades, and lid. Food processors grind, purée, blend, crush, and knead foods.

- **Horizontal cutter mixer (HCM)**: The horizontal cutter mixer (HCM) cuts, mixes, and blends foods quickly with a high-speed, horizontal, rotating blade that is housed in a large bowl with a tight cover. To vary from coarse to fine or actual purée, control the length of time the blade runs through the product. Always count to ten before opening the lid after stopping the blade. The force created in the bowl moves the food rapidly. Allow time for food to stop moving, or it may fly out when the lid is opened. Unplug the unit before cleaning it. Handle the blades with the same care as a knife. The mixer will not operate if the hinged lid is not locked.

- **Mandoline**: This is a manually operated slicer made of stainless steel with adjustable slicing blades to slice and julienne. Its narrow, rectangular body sits on the work counter at a 45-degree angle. It is useful for slicing small quantities of fruit or vegetables, situations where a large electric slicer isn't necessary. There are also extremely popular plastic models, which may have fixed or adjustable blades. Typically, these do not stand on counters but are held over a bowl or work surface. Always use a hand guard or steel gloves to avoid injury.

- **Meat grinder**: This is a free-standing machine or an attachment for a standing mixer. Drop foods in through a feed tube, where they are pulled along by a metal worm, and then cut by blades as the food is forced out through the grinder plate. To avoid cross-contamination, clean all areas of a meat grinder thoroughly after use.

- **Meat slicer**: Most meat slicers have a slanted, circular blade. Food either passes through the machine automatically or a cook pushes a hopper that holds the product along a carriage into the blade. The thickness of the slicer is set by increasing and decreasing the distance between the guide plate and the blade. The guard on the hopper must always be used to move the hopper. This protects the hands. During cleaning, the machine must be unplugged and the blade set at 0 (no distance between the guide plate and blade). Remember that the blade is a knife and can cut even when it is not turning. Because slicer blades are very sharp, it is important to pay close attention when using them.

- **Mixer**: Mixers come in 5-quart, 20-quart, 60-quart, and 80-quart sizes. Cooks use them to mix and process large amounts of food with any number of specialized attachments, including paddles, wire whips, dough hooks, meat grinders, shredders, slicers, and juicers.

290

- **Flat beater paddle**: Use to mix, mash, and cream soft foods.
- **Wire whip**: Use to beat and add air to light foods, such as egg whites and cake frosting.
- **Wing whip**: A heavier version of the wire whip, use it to whip, cream, and mash heavier foods.
- **Pastry knife (paddle)**: Use to mix shortening into dough.
- **Dough arm (hook)**: Use to mix heavy, thick dough.

Always start the mixer on slow speed and then move to higher speeds as required to prevent splash over. Always scrape the bowl to ensure that even mixing takes place. Never place a scraper or any other object in the mixing bowl while the machine is running.

Steamers

Steamers are used in restaurants and foodservice operations to cook vegetables and grains. A steamer allows the food to come into direct contact with the steam, heating the food very quickly. Cooking with steam is a very efficient method of cooking. There are different types of steamers in use at restaurants and foodservice operations. Figure 5.12 shows the types of steamers used in professional kitchens.

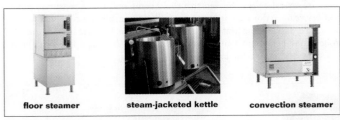

floor steamer   **steam-jacketed kettle**   **convection steamer**

Figure 5.12: Steamers used in the professional kitchen.

- **Steamer**: Use a steamer to steam foods such as vegetables and grains. It uses low or high steam pressure. A steamer often consists of a set of stacked pots. The lower pot holds boiling water. The upper pot has a perforated bottom that allows the steam to enter through and cook the food in the pot above. All types of steamers cook foods quickly in very hot (212°F) water vapor.
- **Convection steamers**: In a convection steamer, the steam is generated in a boiler and then piped to the cooking chamber, where it is vented over the food. Pressure does not build up in the unit. Rather, it is continually

291

Reinforce and Review

- To make sure that ingredients in a mixer (or food processor) are thoroughly combined, turn off the machine on a regular basis to scrape down the sides and bottom of the mixing bowl.
- Steaming food is a very efficient cooking method, as well as a nutritious one. Unlike many other cooking techniques, it requires no fat to produce a flavorful product.
- Since steamers cook food at 212°F, the temperature at which water boils to become steam, care must be taken when uncovering the food to avoid a serious burn.

Homework Activity: Under Pressure
Science Connection, Literacy Connection, 21st-Century Skills—Information Literacy, Initiative and Self-Direction, Productivity and Accountability
Pressure plays an important role in the steaming process. But how does it work? Research the relationship between pressure and steam, paying special attention to cooking processes. Discuss your findings in a one-page paper.

Figure Focus
Figure 5.12: Why might one type of steamer be preferable to another?

Discuss

- Compare the process of broiling versus the process of steaming. Encourage students to discuss differences in flavor, nutritional value, final appearance, and ingredients suited to one or the other technique.

Reinforce and Review

- Steam-jacketed kettles can hold up to 100 gallons, making them ideal for large batches of stocks or soups. Some models tilt or have spigots to facilitate the removal of the finished product.
- Tilting fry pans, or tilt skillets, often have a 30- to 40-gallon capacity and can be used for a variety of techniques and recipes—anything from steaming vegetables to scrambling eggs to braising meat.
- Broilers use very intense heat to cook food from above. Grills—including charbroilers—cook food from below.

exhausted, which means the door may be opened at any time without danger of scalding or burning as with a pressure steamer. Cooks use convection steamers to cook large quantities of food.

- **Pressure steamer**: A pressure steamer cooks foods with high-pressure steam. Water is heated under pressure in a sealed compartment, allowing it to reach temperatures greater than 212°F. It's very important to release the pressure before opening the door on a pressure steamer. The cooking time is controlled by automatic timers, which open the exhaust valves at the end of the cooking time to vent the steamer.

- **Steam-jacketed kettle**: These kettles come in free-standing and tabletop versions and in a very wide range of sizes. The kettle's bottom and sides have two layers, and steam circulates between the layers, heating liquid foods like soups and stews quickly and evenly. Because the circulating steam evenly heats all sides of the kettle instead of just the bottom, food cooks faster and more evenly and is less likely to burn.

- **Tilting fry pan**: Although this piece of equipment is often called a fry pan or skillet, cooks use it to grill, steam, braise, sauté, and stew many different kinds of food. Most tilting fry pans have lids that allow the unit to function as a steamer. They are very easy to clean.

Broilers

There are several types of broilers that cooks commonly use in restaurant and foodservice operations. Using very intense direct heat, broilers cook food quickly. For broilers, the heat source is above the food. Here are a few of the broilers most commonly found in restaurant and foodservice operations. Figure 5.13 shows the broilers used in a professional kitchen.

charbroiler   countertop broilers

Figure 5.13: Broilers used in professional kitchens.

Figure Focus

Figure 5.13: Why might one type of broiler be preferable to another?

- **Charbroiler**: Charbroilers use gas or electricity to mimic the effects of charcoal in a grill. Food juices drip onto the heat source to create flames and smoke, which adds flavor to broiled foods.

- **Countertop broiler**: This is a small broiler that sits on top of a work table. Primarily quick-service restaurants use these. The heat source is located above the food and produces an intense radiant heat.

- **Hotel broiler**: Use this large radiant broiler to broil large amounts of food quickly.

- **Rotisserie** (roe-TIS-er-ee): In a rotisserie, cooks place food on a stick, or spit, and roast it over or under a heat source. The unit may be open or enclosed like an oven. Cooks use it most often for cooking chicken, turkey, and other types of poultry.

- **Salamander**: This is a small radiant broiler usually attached to the back of a range. Use it to brown, finish, and melt foods to order.

Ranges, Griddles, and Fryers

In restaurant and foodservice kitchens, the range is usually the most frequently utilized piece of equipment. **Ranges** are cooking units with open heat sources. Like much of the restaurant and foodservice equipment mentioned earlier, ranges come in multiple sizes and variations suitable to the specific needs of an individual operation. Figure 5.14 shows the different types of ranges used in a professional kitchen.

deep-fat fryer   open burner   griddle   wok burner

Figure 5.14: Ranges used in professional kitchens.

Discuss

- Rotisserie chickens have been popular takeout items in groceries and supermarkets for two decades. Relate this to the discussion of home meal replacement in Chapter 1. Why would rotisserie chicken be a good option for retail outlets?

Reinforce and Review

- Salamanders are a popular equipment choice in a variety of foodservice establishments. Despite their small size, they are very efficient and can be used to finish dishes or even heat plates.
- Ranges are the most commonly used cooking appliances in the professional kitchen. Pots and pans are placed over open flames or heated metal plates or coils.

Vocabulary Terms

- **Range:** Cooking appliances, usually heated by natural gas or electricity, topped with open-flame burners or heated metal plates or coils on which cooking vessels are placed.

Figure Focus

Figure 5.14: What are the similarities between an open burner and a wok burner? How are they different?

Reinforce and Review

- Ranges are available with a number of different cooking surfaces, including open burners, flat-top burners, griddles, and ring-top burners.
- Induction burners work by means of magnetic attraction. The cooking vessel and the food inside it heat, but the cooking surface itself remains cool.

Homework Activity: Induced? Gadzooks!

Science Connection, Literacy Connection, 21st-Century Skills—Information Literacy, Initiative and Self-Direction, Productivity and Accountability

Induction burners use magnetic attraction between the cooking surface and the cooking vessel to create heat.

Research this process. How does magnetic attraction create heat? What types of cooking vessels are appropriate for use with induction burners? Will the cooking vessel still be hot after it is removed from the cooking surface?

Discuss your findings in a one-page paper.

- **Deep-fat fryer**: Gas and electric fryers cook foods in oil at temperatures between 300°F and 400°F. Some computerized fryers lower and raise the food baskets automatically.

- **Flat-top burner (also called a French top)**: A flat-top burner cooks food on a thick slate of cast iron or a steel plate that covers the heat source. A flat-top burner provides even and consistent heat.

- **Griddle**: Similar to a flat-top range, a griddle has a heat source located beneath a thick plate of metal. Cook foods directly on this surface, which is usually designed with edges to contain the food and a drain to collect waste.

- **Induction burner**: An induction burner generates heat by means of magnetic attraction between the cooktop and a steel or cast-iron pot or pan. The cooktop itself remains cool. Reaction time is significantly faster with the induction cooktop than with traditional burners. Do not use copper or aluminum pans on this burner. They will not work.

- **Open burner**: A grate-style gas burner supplies direct heat by way of an open flame to the item being cooked. The heat can be easily controlled.

- **Ring-top burner**: With a ring-top burner, cooks add or remove different-sized rings or plates to allow more or less heat to cook the food item. A ring-top burner provides direct, controllable heat. It can be either gas or electric.

- **Wok burner**: This is a gas burner (or propane for home use) with multiple jets, designed to cradle a rounded wok pan in extremely intense heat. The high heat of a wok burner produces the *wok hey,* which is a particularly savory, charred flavor associated with the best wok-cooked dishes.

Ovens

There are many types of ovens available to suit a variety of restaurant and foodservice operations. They vary in size and method of operation. Following are just a few of the kinds of ovens you might find in an operation. Figure 5.15 shows the different types of ovens used in a professional kitchen.

convection oven   combi oven   single oven   conveyor oven   microwave oven

Figure 5.15: Ovens used in professional kitchens.

Figure Focus
Figure 5.15: How does each of these ovens differ? How is a microwave oven different from the others?

- **Convection oven**: Convection ovens have a fan that circulates heated air around the food as it cooks. This shortens cooking times and uses energy efficiently. Reduce recipe temperatures designed for conventional ovens by 25 to 50 degrees, because the circulating air is so much more efficient.

- **Combi-oven**: This unit combines a convection oven with a steamer. Using a combi-oven, cooks can work with convective steam, with convective dry hot air, or with a combination of both. These are very efficient, flexible units, but they are relatively expensive.

- **Conventional (standard) oven**: In a conventional oven, the heat source is located on the floor of the oven. Heat rises into the cavity, or open space in the oven, which contains racks for the food to sit on as it cooks. These ovens are usually located below a range-top burner. Conventional ovens are inexpensive and easy to integrate with other pieces of cooking equipment.

- **Conveyor** (con-VAY-er) **oven**: In this type of oven, a conveyor belt moves the food along a belt in one direction. It cooks with heat sources on both top and bottom.

- **Deck oven**: A deck oven is a type of conventional oven in which two to four shelves are stacked on top of each other. Cook food directly on these shelves, or decks.

- **Microwave oven**: Microwave ovens heat food not with heat, but with microwaves of energy that cause a food's molecules to move rapidly and create heat inside the food. In restaurant and foodservice kitchens, cooks use microwaves mainly to thaw and reheat foods.

- **Rotary oven**: A rotary oven has three to five circular shelves on which food cooks as the shelves move around a central rod.

- **Slow-roasting oven**: Use this oven to roast meats at low temperatures. This helps preserve the meat's moisture, reduce shrinkage, and brown its surfaces.

- **Smoker**: Use a smoker for smoking and slow-cooking foods. A true smoker treats foods with smoke and operates at either cool or hot temperatures. Smokers generally have racks or hooks, allowing food to smoke evenly.

- **Tandoori oven**: This is a cylindrical or barrel-shaped oven, often made of clay, with a wood or charcoal fire inside at the base and an open top. Food can be thrust inside the oven on long metal spikes (famously, chicken), or portions of thin dough can be slapped against the inside of the oven to develop characteristic bubbling and charring. These ovens easily reach 800°–900°F.

295

Discuss

- Encourage students to discuss the similarities and differences among the ovens on this list. Which might be better options for some foodservice operations than others?

Reinforce and Review

- Combi-ovens combine convection ovens, which contain fans to help circulate hot air with steamers. These machines can be used for a wide range of kitchen needs and are very efficient.
- Conventional ovens, as the name implies, are the most common ovens in most foodservice establishments. Although they have certain limitations, they are flexible and efficient.
- Specialty items, like tandoori ovens, smokers, and deck ovens, are usually found in specific environments.

Reinforce and Review

- All relevant safety precautions should always be taken when working with large kitchen equipment.
- Electrical equipment should always be turned off and unplugged before cleaning or otherwise maintaining it.
- Any malfunctions should be promptly reported to managers and coworkers.

On the Job: Child Labor

Although high school students likely do not think of themselves as children, federal and state child labor laws apply to them and are enforced by the U.S. Department of Labor as well as OSHA. As discussed in Chapter 3, minors are prohibited from using "hazardous" equipment in the workplace, and further restrictions apply to younger employees. Encourage students to discuss the following:

- Why are minors allowed to use slicing, mixing, and cutting machinery in school, when they may not use it in the workplace?

- Why are minors prohibited from using this machinery in the workplace, even when their parents give permission?

- A variety of laws apply to the employment of minors. Which types of employers might be more or less likely to employ minors, given these restrictions?

Safety Precautions

When working with large equipment, observe safety precautions. It is important to perform proper and consistent maintenance and cleaning. Follow these guidelines when working with large equipment:

1. Learn to use the machines safely by getting proper instruction and reading the manufacturer's instructions.

2. Use all safety features—make sure that lids are secure, use hand guards, and make sure machines are stable.

3. Turn off and unplug electrical equipment completely after each use.

4. Clean and sanitize the equipment thoroughly after each use.

5. Reassemble all pieces of equipment properly, and leave machines unplugged after each use.

6. Report any problems or malfunctions promptly, and alert coworkers to the problem.

[on the job]

Child Labor

Child labor laws, enforced by the U.S. Department of Labor and the Occupational Safety and Health Administration, govern the working conditions of minors (people under the age of 18). Where these employees are concerned, an important safety regulation in restaurant and foodservice establishments involves some common kitchen equipment.

The Fair Labor Standards Act prohibits minors from using or cleaning any power-driven slicing, mixing, or cutting machines in the workplace. These include meat slicers, vertical choppers, and power mixers. Using this equipment is considered hazardous work. Even with a parent's or guardian's permission, minors may not operate these machines, and employers and supervisors may not allow minors to use them. Typically, prohibited machines will bear stickers or other warnings as a reminder of the potential hazard.

Additional rules apply to 14- and 15-year-olds. These employees are prohibited from certain classes of work, including baking, cooking (unless no open flame is used and, in the case of deep-fryers, the frying baskets are mechanically raised and lowered into the hot oil), and working in freezers or meat coolers.

Holding and Serving Equipment

Once the food arrives in the holding and service area, it is usually ready to be presented to the guest. Everyone in the kitchen has taken all care and precautions to ensure that the meals served to guests have been prepared accurately and with care.

Though most of the hard work in preparing a meal has already been done, the final touches made in the holding and service areas are important to delivering a quality meal. Figure 5.16 shows the different types of holding and serving equipment.

bain-marie   **chafing dishes**   **espresso machine**   **hot-holding cabinet (open and closed)**

Figure 5.16: Holding and serving equipment used in professional kitchens.

- **Bain-marie** (bayn mah-REE): A bain-marie is any type of hot-water bath meant to keep foods warm. Place food in stainless steel inserts, such as hotel pans, and then place the inserts in a container holding hot water. Inserts come in many sizes, ranging from 1 quart to 36 quarts. A bain-marie, when set properly, holds food at 135°F. Never use it to cook or reheat foods.

- **Carbonated beverage machine**: This machine is attached to tanks that hold the premixed blends for selected soft drinks and to a tank that contains CO_2. When a cook or server presses the switch on the unit, it automatically mixes the blend and gas to make the completed beverage. The unit contains a refrigeration unit to chill the lines to reduce foaming in the dispensed beverage.

- **Chafing dishes**: Use chafing dishes to keep food items hot on a buffet table. Typically, the heat source for chafers are Sternos, which are placed underneath the chafers filled with hot water.

- **Coffee maker**: A coffee maker is a machine that automatically makes coffee. The operator adds coffee and, because the unit is usually connected to a water supply, simply pushes a button to make the coffee. The units come in a variety of sizes, from ones that make a single 12-cup pot to the large banquet-size urns that make 100+ cups.

297

Discuss

- How can the appropriate use of holding and serving equipment improve a guest's experience? Likewise, how can inappropriate use worsen the experience?
- Which holding and serving equipment might be more or less suited to particular types of food-service establishments? For instance, buffet-style equipment like chafing dishes might be found in a country club but not in a quick-service restaurant.

Reinforce and Review

- Proper use of holding and serving equipment plays a role in ensuring high-quality guest service.
- Bain-maries and chafing dishes both use pans of heated water to keep food warm.
- Carbonated beverage machines, coffeemakers, espresso machines, and tea makers are popular in a variety of foodservice establishments.

Figure Focus

Figure 5.16: Are any of the holding and service items shown in this figure familiar to you? What holding and service items are available in your classroom or used in your school's cafeteria?

Why is coffee so popular? Encourage students to link the contemporary coffee shop with the material on early coffee houses discussed in Chapter 1.

Discuss

• How can the use of holding and service equipment facilitate a kitchen's prep work? Note: Prepared or partially prepared food can be stored on speed racks, coffeemakers and tea makers keep beverages warm to serve multiple guests, and bain-maries keep prepared food hot throughout a service period.

Reinforce and Review

• Hot-holding cabinets and hot boxes keep containers of prepared food hot, often for use in banquets or catering operations.
• Steam tables differ from bain-maries in that they are only used with hotel pans as inserts and they may not require hot water to keep food warm.

Teaching Tips

• Display and demonstrate any holding or service equipment available in the classroom.

[fast fact]

Did You Know...?

Coffee is the world's most popular stimulant. The United States consumes more than 400 million cups of coffee daily. Four out of five Americans drink coffee. Some sources note that green coffee is the second-most-traded commodity in the world. And crude oil is the first!

■ **Espresso machine**: This machine produces the traditional Italian coffee beverage called espresso. Espresso is a concentrated cofee beverage brewed by forcing hot water under pressure through finely ground coffee.

■ **Food warmer or steam table**: This unit differs from the bain-marie in two ways. The unit is designed to hold hotel pans, either one full-size pan or multiple smaller pans per slot. Different types of units are designed to work with water in the holding unit, without water, or either way. A food warmer/steam table, when set properly, holds food at 135°F. Never use it to cook or reheat foods.

■ **Hot box**: This is an insulated piece of equipment designed to hold sheet pans and hotel pans.

■ **Hot-holding cabinet:** The hot-holding cabinet is a heavily insulated cabinet designed to hold either hotel pans or sheet pans on racks in the interior. A thermostat controls the temperature, so that the cabinet holds food at the desired temperature. Often these units also have controls for humidity to prevent stored foods from drying out. Some units have wheels to make it easy to move them to the service area.

■ **Ice machine**: Ice machines make ice cubes, flakes, and chips, and crushed ice. Always scoop ice with a proper ice scoop.

■ **Tea maker**: This works the same as the coffee maker, but it makes tea for iced tea.

■ **Speed racks**: These racks are generally made of metal and have slots that foodhandlers can slide sheet pans into. This can create shelves of various heights, depending on need. Speed racks, equipped with wheels, are suitable for kitchens, bakeshops, dry storage, refrigerators, and freezers. A wider variant is made to hold large serving trays for banquets, so that cooks can make plates up in advance and store them (for instance, composed salads can be assembled and stored without dressing).

Summary

In this section, you learned the following:

- Receiving equipment includes receiving tables/area, scales, and utility carts. After food is received, it is stored on shelving or in refrigerators and freezers (walk-in or reach-in).

- Pre-preparation equipment includes knives, measuring utensils, hand tools and small equipment, and pots and pans.

- Pots come in many shapes and sizes and are made of copper, cast iron, stainless steel, and aluminum, with or without nonstick coating. The most common pots include the following:
  - Stock pot, used for preparing stock
  - Sauce pot, used to prepare sauces, soups, and other liquids
  - Double broiler, used to gently cook the food in an upper pot, over a lower pot that holds boiling or simmering water
  - Brazier, used to braise meat and vegetables

- Pans come in many shapes and sizes:
  - Saucepan, used for general cooking, particularly liquid or liquid-based mixtures
  - Sauté pan, used to sauté items
  - Cast-iron skillet, used for pan grilling, pan-frying, and braising foods such as meat and vegetables
  - Sheet pan, used for many things, but most commonly to bake cookies, rolls, and cakes
  - Hotel pan, used for baking, roasting, or poaching meat and vegetables
  - Roasting pan, used to roast and bake foods such as poultry and meat
  - Braising pan, used to braise, stew, and brown meat

- Preparation equipment includes cutters and mixers, steamers, broilers, ranges, griddles, fryers, and ovens.

- Holding and serving equipment can include the bain-marie, food warmer/steam table, hot-holding cabinet, coffee maker, tea maker, ice machine, hot box, chafing dishes, and espresso machines.

299

Summary

- Remind students to review the following:
  1. The equipment needed for receiving and storing food and supplies
  2. The equipment needed for preparation
  3. The basic types of pots and pans and their common uses
  4. The types of preparation equipment used in the foodservice kitchen
  5. The equipment needed for holding and serving food and beverages

Section 5.1 Review Questions

1. The uses are as follows:
   a. Boning knife: A 6-inch knife with a thin, flexible blade used to separate raw meat from the bone
   b. Cleaver: A heavy, rectangular knife used to chop a variety of foods and to cut through bones
   c. Paring knife: A small knife with a sharp blade, 2 to 4 inches long, used to trim and pare vegetables and fruits
   d. Serrated slicer: A knife with a long, thin, serrated blade, used to slice breads and cakes
   e. Utility knife: An all-purpose knife with a 6- to 8-inch blade used to cut fruits, vegetables, and some meats

2. Students may select and describe any tools from the list appearing on pp. 283–284.

3. Safety guidelines for using large equipment include the following:
   - Learn to use the machines safely by getting proper instruction and reading the manufacturer's instructions.
   - Use all safety features, making sure that lids are secure, using hand guards, and making sure machines are stable.
   - Turn off and unplug electrical equipment completely after each use.
   - Clean and sanitize the equipment thoroughly after each use.
   - Reassemble all pieces of equipment properly, and leave machines unplugged after each use.
   - Report any problems or malfunctions promptly, and alert coworkers to the problem.

4. Students should identify similarities and differences among the ovens described on p. 295.

5. Students should describe the importance of knife skills in the professional kitchen, using information from Benny Gordon's career path as relevant.

6. Students may respond in a variety of ways. However, answers should include the following basic equipment: chef's knife, paring knife, steel, vegetable peeler, kitchen shears, rubber spatula, tongs, whisk, measuring spoons, and a thermometer.

7. A convection steamer continuously releases steam (and pressure) from the unit, so the door may be safely opened without fear of scalding. These are used to cook large quantities of food for banquets or in institutional kitchens. A pressure steamer uses pressurized steam, which builds up within the unit. If pressure is not relieved before the door is opened, serious burns may result. These may be used in either large- or small-scale cooking operations.

8. Students should explain why a restaurant's specialty or theme might require specialized cooking equipment. For instance, a restaurant specializing in Chinese food might cook much of its food with woks and wok burners to provide specific flavors. Students should also describe a variety of equipment found in a casual-dining restaurant, from receiving and storage equipment through holding and serving equipment, but should not be expected to provide an exhaustive list.

Section 5.1 Review Questions

1. Identify the use(s) for the following knives:
   a. Boning
   b. Cleaver
   c. Paring
   d. Serrated slicer
   e. Utility

2. List and describe five common measuring tools.

3. List the safety guidelines for using large preparation equipment.

4. Compare the different types of ovens used in the restaurant or foodservice kitchen.

5. Why would Benny Gordon state that knife skills are the foundation of cooking?

6. What knives and hand tools should Alex carry with him as an entry-level cook?

7. What is the difference between a pressure steamer and a convection steamer? When would you use each one?

8. Why might a restaurant or foodservice operation want to use specialized equipment? What equipment would you expect to find at a casual-dining restaurant?

300

Section 5.1 Activities

1. Study Skills/Group Activity: Knife Safety Poster

Work with two other students to develop a poster about knife safety, including how to pass and transport knives. Use graphics to depict proper handling.

2. Activity: Preparation Tools

What preparation tools would you need to prepare and serve a pizza? Mashed potatoes? A beef stew?

3. Critical Thinking: It Can Only Be One

If you could have only one piece of major cooking equipment (for instance, a range or a steamer) in your professional kitchen, what would it be? Write two paragraphs defending your selection.

301

Section 5.1 Activities

1. Students may be as creative as they like provided they accurately describe safe knife techniques.

2. A pizza may be baked in a convection oven, a combi-oven, a conventional oven, a conveyor oven, a deck oven, or even a wood-burning oven. Mashed potatoes may be cooked atop a flat-top burner, an induction burner, an open burner, or a ring-top burner. They might also be cooked in a steamer, a convection steamer, a pressure steamer, a steam-jacketed kettle, or a tilting fry pan, and sometimes a mixer fitted with a paddle is used to mash the cooked potatoes. Beef stew may be made inside a convection oven, a combi-oven, a conventional oven, a conveyor oven, or a deck oven; atop a flat-top burner, an induction burner, an open burner, or a ring-top burner. It may also be cooked within a steamer, a convection steamer, a pressure steamer, a steam-jacketed kettle, or a tilting fry pan.

3. Students may choose from a variety of equipment so long as they adequately defend their responses.

Section 5.2
Getting Ready to Cook

Introduce the Section
a. Discuss the importance of *mise en place* and how it relates to culinary success.
b. Clarify the differences between seasoning and flavoring.
c. Discuss the objectives for the section.

Vocabulary Review
a. Direct students to the key terms.
b. Pronounce each word, and have the students repeat the pronunciation out loud.
c. Discuss the definition of each word.

Teach

Discuss
- Why is it important to plan ahead to ensure high-quality service for guests?
- Preparing to cook is said to be as important as the cooking process itself. How are both mental preparation and physical preparation essential components of success in the professional kitchen?

Reinforce and Review
- Getting ready to cook can mean the difference between success and failure.
- *Mise en place* refers to all aspects of the preparation and assembly of a dish or for a service period.
- The two problems facing the professional chef are that some work must be done in advance, but most foods begin to deteriorate immediately after preparation.

Teaching Tips
- Ask students to volunteer their own experiences with planning ahead—cooking a meal at home, taking a test, or participating in a sporting event, for example.
- In particular, relate planning for a meal service to studying for a test. In both, the individual must be ready to work at a given time, with no further opportunity for additional work, and no ability to change the outcome after the period has ended.

Vocabulary Terms
- *Mise en place:* The total preparation and assembly of all ingredients and equipment needed to produce a particular dish or to complete a successful meal service.

5.1 Foodservice Equipment	5.2 Getting Ready to Cook	5.3 Cooking Methods	5.4 Cooking and Nutrition
• Receiving and storage equipment • Pre-preparation equipment • Food-preparation equipment • Holding and serving equipment	• *Mise en place* • Knife basics • Seasoning and flavoring • Pre-preparation techniques	• Heat transfer • Dry-heat cooking methods • Moist-heat cooking methods • Combination-cooking methods • Other cooking methods • Determining doneness	• Healthy diets • Dietary guidelines for Americans • MyPyramid • Nutrition labels • The problem of obesity

SECTION 5.2 GETTING READY TO COOK

You may have heard the phrase, "Well begun is half done." This saying represents a widely shared philosophy of all good chefs. Before you can begin to cook, you must know how to prepare to cook. Getting ready to cook plays a major part in the success of your recipe. Even if you prepare only one short recipe, you must first do *pre*-preparation. Only then are you ready to begin the actual cooking.

Study Questions

After studying Section 5.2, you should be able to answer the following questions:

- What is *mise en place*?
- How do you use knives properly?
- What is the difference between seasoning and flavoring?
- What are the basic pre-preparation techniques?

Mise En Place

In the restaurant and foodservice industry, getting ready to cook is called ***mise en place***. *Mise en place* (MEEZ ehn plahs) is French for "to put in place." It refers to the preparation and assembly of ingredients, pans, utensils, equipment, or serving pieces needed for a particular dish or service.

Mise en place solves two basic problems facing the professional chef:

- **Problem #1:** There is too much work to do in a kitchen to leave everything until the last minute. Some work must be done ahead of time.
- **Problem #2:** Most foods are at their best quality immediately after preparation. They deteriorate as they are held, and they begin to lose their nutritional value.

302

There is only one way to solve these problems—plan ahead. Table 5.1 lists guidelines for proper *mise en place*.

Table 5.1: Planning Ahead

1. Identify each ingredient and piece of equipment needed to prepare, finish, and hold each menu item for service. Do this the night before when possible.

2. Write a time line showing which activities should be done in which order (for instance, peel carrots before cooking them). See Figure 5.17. Make sure to note any critical times—for example, if the beef roast takes 90 minutes to cook and requires 15 minutes of rest time, note those times. Do this the night before when possible as well.

3. Assemble the workstation (cutting board, containers, etc.), tools, and ingredients.

4. Perform advance preparation consistent with providing the best possible product to customers. As each item is finished, store it appropriately to prevent time-temperature abuse, nutrient loss, and moisture loss.

5. Once service begins, balance the need to work quickly with the need to prepare safe, delicious, and high-quality food for guests.

6. After service, clean the station and store any leftover food as quickly as possible, observing food safety rules.

7. Consider what went well during preparation and service. What could have been done better? How could the work have been streamlined? Think about these issues when preparing for the next day's work.

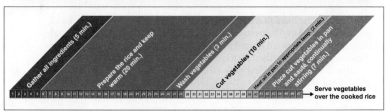

Figure 5.17: Step 2—Planning ahead.

The goal of pre-preparation is to do as much of the work as possible in advance without any loss in ingredient quality. The steps to pre-preparation include the following:

- Assemble the tools.
- Assemble the ingredients.
- Wash, trim, cut, prepare, and measure the ingredients.
- Prepare the equipment (preheat oven, line backing sheets, etc.)

The basic elements of *mise en place*—knife cuts, flavorings, herbs and spices, and basic preparations—are the building blocks of a professional chef's training. These methods and techniques will be essential throughout a professional career in restaurants and foodservice.

303

Figure Focus

Figure 5.17: Make sure students understand that most of the work required in the last four steps of the time line can be performed while the rice is cooking; this will both increase efficiency and maintain the quality of the cooked rice.

Reinforce and Review

- The only way to solve the two problems facing the professional chef is to plan ahead—to *mise en place* successfully.
- The goal of pre-preparation is to do as much advance work as possible while allowing the food to lose as little quality as possible.
- The four basic elements of *mise en place* are the building blocks of a professional chef's training.

Table 5.1: Planning Ahead

- Select a recipe in this textbook or from another source and present it to students. Also, give each student four index cards.

- On the first index card, students should identify each ingredient used to make the dish as well as the quantity required.

- On the second index card, students should identify each piece of kitchen equipment used to make the dish. This should include items like cutting boards, sanitation buckets, and anything else needed to set up a professional workstation.

- On the third index card, students should draw the workstation that will be used to make the dish.

- On the final index card, students should create a time line for creating the dish from start to finish, marked at fifteen-minute intervals. If you choose, you can make this more challenging for students by requiring this timeline to cover both the pre-preparation period and the service period itself.

- Divide students into two-person groups. Have them exchange cards and discuss one another's responses.

In-Class Activity: Creative Planning

Literacy Connection, 21st-Century Skills—Creativity and Innovation, Communication and Collaboration, Social and Cultural Skills, Productivity and Accountability

Working in groups of two or three, plan a creative way to demonstrate either the four steps of pre-preparation or the four building blocks of *mise en place*.

Skits, songs, oral reports, videos, slide shows, posters, and artwork are some options available.

Discuss

- Learning to use knives properly is fundamental to a successful career in the culinary arts. What other skills do students think are equally or more important?

Reinforce and Review

- Most raw ingredients, aside from dry goods, require some sort of trimming or cutting before they can be cooked.
- Most knives are used in conjunction with cutting boards. One hand holds down the ingredient and guides the knife, while the other hand grips the knife.

Teaching Tips

- Demonstrate the three basic knife grips for students and have them try each method.
- The easiest and safest way for most students to use their guiding hand is by forming it into a "claw," tucking the thumb behind the other fingers, and angling the fingernails back toward the thumb; this protects the fingers against injury. This is seen in the third photo in Figure 5.19.

Vocabulary Terms

- **Guiding hand:** The hand that holds the food during the cutting process.

Knife Basics

Usually, cleaning and cutting raw foods is one of the first steps of *mise en place.* Fresh vegetables, fruit, and meat often require trimming and cutting. Review Figure 5.4: Types of Knives and their most common uses on page 277.

To use most knives, hold the food on the cutting board with one hand and hold the knife by its handle with the other. There are three basic knife grips. Figure 5.18 illustrates the three basic knife grips.

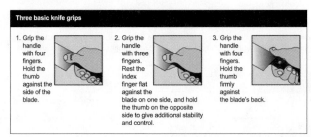

Three basic knife grips

1. Grip the handle with four fingers. Hold the thumb against the side of the blade.

2. Grip the handle with three fingers. Rest the index finger flat against the blade on one side, and hold the thumb on the opposite side to give additional stability and control.

3. Grip the handle with four fingers. Hold the thumb firmly against the blade's back.

Figure 5.18: Basic knife grips.

In every grip, the hand that is not holding the knife, called the **guiding hand,** prevents slippage and helps to control the size of the cut. Bend the fingers of the guiding hand inward toward the palm, and hold the thumb well back. One finger should be the farthest forward with the other fingers and thumb behind that finger. This allows a clear view while cutting. Figure 5.19 shows the proper place of the guiding hand.

Figure 5.19: Proper placement of the guiding hand.

Figure Focus

Figure 5.18: Most professional kitchens use the second knife grip, since holding the blade itself between finger and thumb provides greater stability and control.

Figure 5.19: The second picture and the third picture show the guiding hand in very different positions. Ask the students which appears to be safer and why.

When using a knife, move the knife in a smooth downward and forward slicing motion. With practice, a cook is able to cut food in many different ways, increase knife speed, and become more accurate with cuts. Figure 5.20 shows basic knife cuts.

Figure 5.20: Basic knife cuts, including dicing, mincing, and julienning.

Essential Skills
Peeling Technique

Follow these guidelines to peel a vegetable such as a potato or a carrot.

With a peeler:

❶ Hold the item to be peeled in the left hand (if right-handed), and push the peeler across the skin of the item away from the body with long, smooth strokes. In a commercial kitchen, chefs tend to use a back-and-forth method to save time and energy. See Figure 5.21a.

With a paring knife:

❶ If peeling using a paring knife, whether fruit or vegetable, hold the item in the left hand (again, if right-handed).

❷ Grip the paring knife with the last three fingers on the right hand.

❸ Place the thumb lightly on the upper portion of the item being peeled and glide the blade just below the skin of the item toward the stabilizing thumb using the index finger as a guide. See Figure 5.21b. The goal is to remove only the skin or rind.

Figure 5.21a: Step 1—Push the peeler across the skin of the item away from the body.

Figure 5.21b: Step 3—Glide the blade just below the skin of the item.

Reinforce and Review

- When slicing with a knife, push smoothly down and forward in a gliding motion. The width of the slice is determined by the size of the desired cut.
- Large dice are ¾" cubes, medium dice are ½" cubes, and small dice are ¼" cubes. Other common cuts include brunoise (⅛" cubes), brunoisette (¹⁄₁₆" cubes), batonnet (¼" × ¼" × 2" sticks), julienne (⅛" × ⅛" × 1"–2" strips), and chiffonade (very thin strips, used for leafy vegetables and herbs).

Essential Skills: Peeling Technique

Encourage students to practice peeling a variety of fruits and vegetables. Encourage them to consider the following:

- There are two common techniques for controlling mess while peeling: holding an ingredient in the air while peeling it, so that the peels fall directly into a waste container, and pressing an ingredient down onto a paper-covered cutting board so that the peels can be efficiently scooped up and discarded.

- What other uses are there for peels? How can these and other edible trim be incorporated into dishes, thereby helping to control food costs?

Figure Focus

Figure 5.20: Students should practice these and other knife cuts using a ruler to help with precision.

Figure 5.21a: What other ingredients should be peeled with a vegetable peeler?

Figure 5.21b: What other ingredients should be peeled with a paring knife?

Encourage students to discuss the following:

- From a historical perspective, why have butchers been so important to society?

- What sanitation issues are particularly important in butcher shops and other meat-handling facilities?

- Why do cooks and chefs need to be familiar with meat fabrication?

Reinforce and Review

- Proper seasoning makes an ingredient or dish taste more of itself, not more like the seasoning ingredient.
- Seasonings should be added at the beginning of the cooking process to create a depth of flavor, although additional seasoning can be added just before serving if needed.
- The four basic types of seasoning ingredients are salts, peppers, sugars, and acids.

Teaching Tips

- Conduct a salt cutting by providing a variety of salts and encouraging students to identify differences in appearance, aroma, and taste. Ask students which salts are suited for which purposes.
- Encourage students to taste all the seasoning ingredients available in the classroom. What other seasonings can students identify?

**Fast Fact:
Did You Know...?**

How is salt used as a preservative? Note: It inhibits the growth of bacteria by removing water from the item via osmosis, effectively preventing certain forms of biological activity from occurring.

[on the job]

The Butcher

Butchers are responsible for everything involving meat—from the living animal to a neatly trussed roast in a display counter. However, most butchers in the United States are either primal butchers or secondary butchers. Primal butchers select either carcasses or large portions of animals, make primal cuts, and prepare primal cuts for subsequent fabrication. Secondary butchers turn the primal cuts into portions usable by ordinary consumers. Many secondary butchers also produce sausages and other cured or smoked meats. Both types of butchers are responsible for maintaining high levels of hygiene and food safety.

Knives are of critical importance to butchery, especially boning knives. Other tools include meat hooks (for hanging carcasses and sides of meat), band saws, and personal protective gear such as safety gloves and belly guards. Butchers often work in grocery stores, processing plants, or butcher shops. They often work in chilly conditions to maintain the freshness of the meat. At other times, butchers work in open areas, where consumers can ask them questions about various cuts of meat.

No formal education is required to become a butcher, although some choose to attend culinary school. Apprenticeship programs are available in some areas. On-the-job training is also an option. Prospective butchers can start preparing themselves for their careers by improving their physical strength, practicing eye-hand coordination skills, and reading about various meats and how they are processed. Important traits include excellent interpersonal skills, a high level of personal hygiene, and tolerance for cold and damp conditions.

Seasoning and Flavoring

A **seasoning** is something that enhances the flavor of an item without changing the primary flavor of the dish. Basic seasonings include salt and pepper. They must be used with care to prevent overuse, but seasoning generally should be added at the start of the dish to create a depth of flavor.

There are four basic types of seasoning ingredients:

- Salts
- Peppers
- Sugars
- Acids

[fast fact]

Did You Know...?

The United States produces over 40 million tons of salt each year. Only 6 percent of the salt produced in the United States is used in food. Salt is an important preservative, as well as one of the most basic tastes.

Flavor refers to the way a food tastes, as well as its texture, appearance, doneness, and temperature. A **flavoring** should enhance the base ingredients of the dish, or it can also bring another flavor to the product. For example, the addition of a small amount of onion to a consommé enhances the flavor of the stock without changing it. The addition of a large quantity of onion introduces an onion flavor to the dish.

There are many types of flavorings that have the capability to change the taste of the original food product:

- Herbs
- Spices
- Extracts
- Fruits and vegetables
- Aromatic liquids
- Cured foods

So what is the difference between seasoning and flavoring? If a cook adds a small amount of salt to the water used to cook pasta, the pasta will simply taste like cooked pasta. That means it has been properly seasoned. However, if the cook adds a lot of salt, the cooked pasta will take on the distinct and easy-to-identify flavor of salt. Salt has become a flavoring in the dish, not a seasoning.

[nutrition]

Too Much Sodium

Seasoning generally involves the addition of salt and pepper. However, many people choose to limit their sodium intake for health reasons. Nothing can truly replace salt, an essential component of the human diet. However, other flavorings can be used to mask its absence and contribute other elements to a meal. Adding an acid, like fruit juice or vinegar, can punch up a dull dish, as can spicy peppers. A variety of herbs and spices can also contribute to the taste. When using prepared mixes, blends, or condiments, always check the label to ensure that the substitution won't add even more sodium to a dish.

Herbs and Spices

Herbs and spices are important ingredients used to enhance and add to the flavor of food. **Herbs** (URBS) are the leaves, stems, or flowers of an aromatic plant. **Spices** are the bark, roots, seeds, buds, or berries of an aromatic plant.

Herbs are available fresh or dried. Dried herbs are much stronger than fresh herbs because the herbs' flavorful oils are concentrated during the drying process. When using dried herbs, lightly crumble or grind them before adding

307

Reinforce and Review

- A major difference between seasoning and flavoring is the amount of the ingredient added.
- Flavorings change the taste of the original food item, while seasonings enhance the taste of the original food item.
- Herbs and spices are common plant-based flavorings. Herbs are usually derived from the more delicate parts of the plant, while spices are usually derived from the plant's sturdier components.
- Herbs are available fresh or dried. Dried herbs are stronger and therefore impart more flavor.

Teaching Tips

- Encourage students to taste all the flavorings available in the classroom. What other flavorings can they identify?
- Mix up a variety of salt-water solutions, each with a different concentration of salt. Encourage students to taste each mixture. At what concentration can each student recognize the taste of salt?

Nutrition:
Too Much Sodium

Salt is not only essential to the human diet, but an essential seasoning agent in the professional kitchen. Can other flavorings replicate the role of salt? Encourage a discussion.

Vocabulary Terms

- **Flavor:** All the sensations produced by whatever is in the mouth, but mostly the food's aroma and taste.
- **Flavoring:** An ingredient used to enhance the main ingredients of a dish by adding some quality of its own.
- **Herb:** The leaf, stem, or flower of an aromatic plant, used to flavor other ingredients.
- **Spice:** The bark, root, seed, bud, or berry of an aromatic plant, used to flavor other ingredients.

Discuss

- Both herbs and spices can be used either fresh or dry, sometimes in the same dish. Encourage students to suggest dishes that use multiple herbs and/or spices, fresh and/or dried.

Reinforce and Review

- Fresh herbs should be added at the end of the cooking process to preserve their delicate qualities.
- Whole spices can be used whole or ground. Whole spices should be added at the beginning of the cooking process, while ground spices should be added later in the process.
- Herbs and spices can be used in combination to create new flavors.

Teaching Tips

- Pass around the herbs and spices that are available in the classroom so that students can smell and taste them. Encourage students to imagine how the flavors might change when cooked.

Table 5.2:
Common Herbs and Spices
(continued on pp. 309–311)

- Ask students to link herbs and spices to various dishes and cuisines.
- Can students identify any herbs and spices that do not appear in this list?

them to a dish. This releases their flavor. When using fresh herbs in place of dry, use two to three times the amount called for in the recipe. Always add fresh herbs toward the end of the cooking process to retain their delicate flavors. It is common to use both dried and fresh herbs in the same dish.

Cooks use spices most often in their dried form. They can be purchased whole or ground. Whole spices should be added early during cooking to allow their flavors to carry throughout the food. Cut or ground spices can be toasted to enhance their natural flavors and then added later in the cooking process.

Each herb or spice used in a recipe contributes its own distinct flavor to a finished dish, and several of them can be used together to create new and exciting flavor combinations. Strong, flavorful spices and herbs such as pepper, cumin, basil, and oregano, or spice blends like curry powder, fines herbes, and Chinese five-spice, can often be used to reduce the amount of salt in recipes. Table 5.2 lists some of the herbs and spices most commonly used in restaurant and foodservice operations.

Table 5.2: Common Herbs and Spices			
Herbs		**Spices**	
	Basil		Allspice
	Bay leaves		Anise
	Chives		Capers
	Cilantro		Caraway

continued

Table 5.2: Common Herbs and Spices *continued*

Herbs			Spices	
	Dill			Cardamom
	Lavender			Cayenne
	Lemon grass			Chile pepper
	Marjoram			Cinnamon
	Mint leaves			Cloves
	Oregano			Coriander
	Parsley			Cumin
	Rosemary			Fennel

continued

309

Discuss

- Which plants have parts that can be used as both herbs and spices? For instance, cilantro leaves and coriander seeds come from the same plant. What other examples can students suggest?

Homework Activity: Spicy Stuff

Literacy Connection, 21st-Century Skills— Information Literacy, Initiative and Self-Direction, Productivity and Accountability

The spice trade has played a critical role in the development of various cuisines, but it has also had a major effect on history, culture, economics, and society.

Select a spice, either one from the table on pp. 308–311 or another. Research its history and the effects that its production and trade may have had on society. Why is this spice important, either as a cultural footnote or in modern cuisine?

Discuss your findings in a one-page paper.

Discuss

• Herbs are often associated with cooking, while spices are associated with both baking and cooking. Encourage students to identify some herbs and spices that are used in baked goods. For instance, poppy seeds are used in muffins, bagels, and pastries, while mint leaves appear in cookies and candies.

CUSTOMIZED INSTRUCTION

Science Connection, Literacy Connection, 21st-Century Skills—Information Literacy, Initiative and Self-Direction, Productivity and Accountability

Special Needs Students

Smell the different spices and herbs that are available in the classroom. Do they remind you of any particular dishes?

Now, using multiple pans, heat small amounts of vegetable oil, adding one type of spice or herb to each pan and allowing the aromas to develop. Note: This can be done by the students' aides or another adult, depending on your classroom situation.

Smell the warmed herbs and spices. Did the aromas change? Do they make you think of anything different now?

Which do you think is responsible for any changes you noticed—the heat or the oil?

Table 5.2: Common Herbs and Spices *continued*

Herbs		Spices	
	Sage		Ginger
	Savory		Mace
	Tarragon		Mustard seeds
	Thyme		Nutmeg
			Paprika
			Peppercorns
			Poppy seeds
			Saffron

continued

Table 5.2: Common Herbs and Spices *continued*

Herbs		Spices
		Sesame seeds
		Turmeric
		Vanilla bean

[fast fact]

Did You Know...?

Curry powder is made by blending up to 20 herbs and spices, including cinnamon, fennel, coriander, ginger, cumin, and peppers. In the late 1960s and early '70s, Indian food became much more popular. So outside of India, there has been some standardization of curry powder.

Storing spices and herbs properly helps to keep them fresh and flavorful. Heat, light, and air all speed the loss of flavor and color. A tight glass jar in a covered cabinet, drawer, or pantry away from any heat or light source is the best protection for dried herbs and spices. Avoid storing them close to stoves, dishwashers, sinks, or air ducts. If the spice rack is open, make sure to locate it away from direct sunlight.

Add volatile spices and herbs, such as vanilla and cardamom, toward the end of cooking to provide the full benefit of their aromas and flavors. These types of spices and herbs blossom with heat. Don't add them too early in the cooking process, or they will blossom and disperse before the dish is served.

Garlic and onion are both oil-soluble flavors. This means they impart their flavors best in oil. They should be added to the dish with oil, when possible, to gain the greatest distribution of their flavors throughout the dish.

311

Fast Fact: Did You Know...?

Curry powder blends were popularized in Britain during the nineteenth century when Britain governed India. Returning Britons wanted to bring the familiar tastes back to their homeland. Encourage students to discuss what other ingredients or dishes result from cross-cultural interactions.

Reinforce and Review

- Herbs and spices should be stored away from heat, light, and air to preserve their quality.

- Many spices and herbs blossom when exposed to heat. Although cooking is important to extract their flavors, cooking them too long can cause these flavors to dissipate entirely.

- Oil-soluble ingredients, like onions and garlic, should be cooked with oil to help their flavors permeate the final dish.

Essential Skills:
Peeling and Dicing an Onion

Encourage students to discuss the following:

- Why are uniform, precise cuts so important in the professional kitchen?

- Peeling and dicing an onion is an essential skill. What other vegetable-preparation techniques do students consider essential?

Students should practice peeling and dicing onions.

[fast fact]

Did You Know...?

Garlic belongs to the onion family. Its strong odor comes from the oils found in the bulb. To get rid of the smell of garlic from your hands, place your hands under cold running water while rubbing a stainless steel object.

Essential Skills
Peeling and Dicing an Onion

One of the most common tasks in a kitchen is preparing onions. Peeling and dicing an onion can be laborious work, but it is simplified by using the following steps. See Figure 5.22.

1. Holding the onion on its side, slice off its top and bottom, taking care not to remove too much of the root end, otherwise, the onion will fall apart.

2. Stand the onion upright (root end down) and slice it in half vertically.

3. Peel each half, discarding the peels.

4. With the curved side of the onion half half up, carefully make a number of horizontal cuts in the onion, taking care not to slice completely through the onion's root end; the number of cuts depends upon the size of the dice required.

5. Make a number of vertical cuts through the onion at right angles to the original cuts, again depending on the size of the dice required and without cutting through the onion's root end.

6. Slice across the onion to form dice.

Figure 5.22: Peeling and dicing an onion.

312

Figure Focus

Figure 5.22: The first time students peel and dice onions in the classroom, ask each student to time himself or herself. Calculate the class average, while encouraging students to keep records of their own performances. How quickly do students think they will be able to perform this task by the end of the year?

There are herbs and spices that must be used carefully because their dominant flavors can overpower the flavor of the dish. Rosemary, cinnamon, cardamom, and paprika are examples of herbs and spices that must be used with caution.

The key to using herbs and spices well is to build layers of flavor by adding items at various stages of cooking so that they are at their peak when the dish is served. Seasoning should always be checked and adjusted as the final step in completing the dish.

Use salt and pepper at the beginning of the cooking process. This will ensure that sauces, butter, or other liquids will not wash off the seasoning. It will also ensure that if a cook uses the sauté technique for a dish and **deglazes** the pan with a liquid to dissolve the remaining bits of sautéed food, the salt used will be incorporated into the sauce, and the cook won't need to add more.

[ServSafe Connection]

Preserving Herbs
Raw herbs are not TCS food. However, fresh herbs such as tarragon, basil, chervil, etc., may deteriorate very quickly. Keep them under refrigeration to preserve quality and flavor, especially because they're expensive and can be very labor intensive to prepare.

Pre-preparation Techniques

Mise en place also involves pre-preparing certain ingredients that need to be refined before they are ready for use at the time of preparation. Basic cooking techniques in pre-preparation include separating eggs, whipping egg whites, setting up a bain-marie, and making parchment liners for pans.

313

Discuss
- Encourage students to consider their favorite dishes. Do these contain a single predominant flavor or a combination of layered flavors?
- The remainder of this section focuses on basic pre-preparation techniques. Can students identify any others, besides the ones listed on this page?

Reinforce and Review
- Be cautious using herbs and spices with powerful flavors, as they can easily dominate the dish. Until students have more practice, they should follow recipes as written to avoid error.
- Adding herbs and spices at different cooking stages enables the cook to layer flavors, resulting in a more nuanced dish.
- *Mise en place* also includes basic pre-preparation techniques, such as separating eggs, whipping egg whites, setting up a bain-marie, and making pan liners.

ServSafe Connection: Preserving Herbs

Review the relevant material from Chapter 2 with the class. What does "TCS" mean, and why is it important?

Vocabulary Terms
- **Deglaze:** To add a liquid to a hot sauté pan, usually after the main ingredient has been removed, stirring to incorporate the flavorful bits stuck to the pan into the liquid to form the basis of a flavorful pan sauce.

Essential Skills: Separating Eggs

Encourage students to discuss the following:

- What food-safety issues are involved in separating eggs?

- Why should the separated whites be entirely free of yolks?

Students should practice separating eggs.

Essential Skills: Whipping Egg Whites

Encourage students to discuss the following:

- Why is cleaning the equipment the first step of this process? Shouldn't it already be clean?

- What can happen when whites are overbeaten?

- Why should the equipment used to whip cream be chilled before using?

Students should practice whipping egg whites.

CUSTOMIZED INSTRUCTION

Science Connection, Math Connection, Literacy Connection

Less Advanced Students

Measure one cup of cream and heat it to room temperature, using a thermometer. In the meantime, place a bowl and a whisk in the refrigerator.

Pour all of the cream into a room-temperature bowl. Timing yourself with a clock or stopwatch, use a room-temperature whisk to whip the cream. How long does it take to achieve soft peaks? Medium peaks? Stiff peaks? Write down your results.

Now measure one cup of cream and pour it into the bowl you have previously chilled. Timing yourself, use the chilled whisk to whip the cream. How long does it take to achieve soft peaks? Medium peaks? Stiff peaks?

Compare your results with other students. How do you explain your results?

Essential Skills
Separating Eggs

Note: It is necessary to separate eggs when a recipe calls for only raw egg yolks or egg whites.

1. Use two containers and a small bowl.
2. Crack open the egg over the bowl.
3. Transfer the egg back and forth between the halves of the shell, letting the white drop into the bowl. See Figure 5.23.
4. Place the yolk in one of the containers.
5. Inspect the egg white. If there are any traces of yolk present, reserve it for use in other preparations. If the white is clean, transfer it to the container for egg whites.

Figure 5.23: Step 3—Transfer the egg back and forth between the shells.

Essential Skills
Whipping Egg Whites

1. Thoroughly clean the mixing bowl and whisk. Oil residue will reduce the volume of the whipped egg white.
2. For the greatest volume in whipped egg whites, start with the egg whites at room temperature.
3. Begin whipping the egg whites by hand or machine at a moderate speed. Tilt the bowl to make whipping by hand easier, resting the bowl on a folded towel to prevent it from slipping. To add more volume and give the foam greater stability, add a small amount of lemon juice or cream of tartar. See Figure 5.24.

Figure 5.24: Step 3—Tilt the bowl to whip the egg whites.

When the whites are quite foamy, increase the speed of the mixer.

314

Figure Focus

Figure 5.23: Can students identify any dishes for which eggs should be separated?

Figure 5.24: When whisking by hand, be sure to incorporate all of the egg whites into the mixture—scrape the sides of the bowl with the whisk if necessary.

❹ Whip to the appropriate stage. Never overbeat egg whites. Overbeaten egg whites may still resemble those at the stiff peak stage, but their surface looks dry.

- Soft peak has a droopy, rounded peak.
- Medium peak has a moist surface and forms a rounded, but fairly stable, peak.
- Stiff peak has stiff, stable peaks. Stop beating while the surface is still moist and glossy.

Note: The method for whipping cream is the same as that for whipping egg whites. The cream should be cold when whipped. Clean and chill both the bowl and beaters in advance to give the whipped cream more volume.

Essential Skills
Setting Up a Bain-Marie

A **bain-marie** is a hot-water bath used to hold hot food and keep it at safe temperatures.

❶ Set up a deep pan large enough to hold containers of food comfortably.

❷ Carefully add enough hot water to fill one-half to two-thirds of the pan.

❸ Add food containers. See Figure 5.25.

Figure 5.25:
Step 3—Add food containers.

315

Figure Focus
Figure 5.25: The cook is setting up a bain-marie for a terrine mold, which will be baked in the oven; the steam created by the hot water will create a moist, gentle cooking environment.

Vocabulary Terms
- **Bain-marie:** A hot-water bath used to hold hot food or to cook delicate foods like custards and terrines in a moist environment.

Reinforce and Review

- Blanching and shocking are two pre-preparation techniques that often go together. In particular, these techniques are used to prepare green vegetables or pasta in advance of busy service periods.

Vocabulary Terms

- **Blanching:** Usually, plunging vegetables, pasta, or another ingredient into boiling water to par-cook ("partially cook") the item to decrease subsequent cooking time. It can also refer to the process of preparing bones for stock by cooking them to remove superficial proteins.
- **Shocking:** Plunging cooked or par-cooked foods into ice water to stop the cooking process.

Summary

- Remind students to review the following:
  1. *Mise en place*
  2. Proper use of knives
  3. The difference between seasoning and flavoring
  4. Basic pre-preparation techniques

Essential Skills
Making a Parchment Liner for a Round Pan

Parchment paper is often used to line pans to prevent food from sticking to them. In addition, it is also used to make a cartouche, which covers the surface of a stew, soup, stock, or sauce to reduce evaporation, to prevent a skin from forming, and/or to keep components submerged.

1. Cut a square of parchment paper a little larger than the pan's diameter.

2. Fold the square in half to form a triangle.

3. Continue folding in half until a long, thin triangle is formed. See Figure 5.26.

4. Position the triangle's narrow end above the pan's center and cut away the part that extends beyond the edge of the pan.

5. Unfold the triangle and flatten it into the pan.

Figure 5.26: Step 3—Fold the square until a long triangle is formed.

Blanching is another pre-preparation technique that will be discussed in greater detail in Section 5.3. This is the moist-heat method of cooking that involves cooking in a liquid or with steam just long enough to cook the outer portion of the food. The food is immediately placed in ice water to stop carryover cooking, also referred to as shocking.

Summary

In this section, you learned the following:

- *Mise en place* is French for "to put in place." It refers to the preparation and assembly of ingredients, pans, utensils, equipment, and serving pieces needed for a particular dish or service.

- To use knives properly, hold the food on the cutting board with one hand and hold the knife by its handle with the other. In every grip, the hand that is not holding the knife prevents slippage and helps to control the size of the cut. The fingers of the guiding hand are bent inward toward the palm, and the thumb is held well back. One finger should be the farthest forward, with the other fingers and thumb behind that finger. This allows a clear view when cutting.

- A seasoning is something that enhances the flavor of an item without changing the primary flavor of the dish. Flavor refers to the way a food tastes, as well as its texture, appearance, doneness, and temperature.

- Basic cooking techniques in pre-preparation include separating eggs, whipping egg whites, setting up a bain-marie, making parchment liners for pans, and blanching and shocking.

316

Figure Focus
Figure 5.26: When lining a square or rectangular pan with parchment, simply cut out the desired shape, saving any large scraps of paper for future use.

Section 5.2 Review Questions

1. Name and explain three types of basic cooking techniques.

2. Explain *mise en place*.

3. Describe how to use a knife properly.

4. What is the difference between seasoning and flavoring?

5. Why does Benny Gordon say that *mise en place* is the most important element of cooking?

6. Why is it important for Alex to execute basic *mise en place* skills properly?

7. Give an example of a dish in which many different flavorings are used. How does the cook make sure that one flavor does not overwhelm the others?

8. Explain how creating time lines can streamline your work.

317

Section 5.2 Review Questions

1. Students can choose among any of the cooking techniques used in pre-preparation and discussed in this section: separating eggs, whipping egg whites, setting up a bain-marie, making parchment liners for pans, and blanching and shocking.

2. *Mise en place* refers to the preparation and assembly of ingredients, pans, utensils, equipment, or serving pieces needed for a particular dish or service.

3. To use most knives, hold the food on the cutting board with one hand and hold the knife by its handle with the other, using one of the three basic knife grips. In every grip, the guiding hand prevents slippage and helps to control the size of the cut. Move the knife in a smooth downward and forward slicing motion.

4. A seasoning is something which enhances the flavor of an item without changing the primary flavor of the dish. A flavoring may enhance the base ingredients of the dish, or it may provide a different flavor to the dish.

5. Students should discuss the importance of *mise en place*, using information from Benny Gordon's career path as relevant.

6. Alex must properly execute basic *mise en place* techniques as part of learning the fundamentals of his chosen profession. By learning how to perform these tasks correctly, he is developing the basic skills he will need as a culinary professional as well as contributing to the success of his colleagues and the restaurant as a whole.

7. Students may choose any dish that contains a number of distinct flavoring ingredients. It is important to use flavorings, especially strong ones like rosemary and cinnamon, with caution, so that no single flavor overwhelms the others. Building layers of flavor by adding different herbs and spices at different times so as to maximize their contributions is an important part of culinary education.

8. Creating a time line forces the cook or chef to plan his or her work in advance, thinking through the steps of the preparation in a logical order. This planning helps the actual work proceed more quickly because the cook has already identified the necessary steps in the process as well as the ingredients and equipment needed and therefore will not waste time in figuring out what will be needed.

Section 5.2 Activities

1. Students do not need to obtain actual recipes for these dishes, although that might be a useful task. The goal is to create a functional plan of work, so students should include all steps they think are relevant to the cooking processes.

2. Students should present their knife cuts to the teacher for evaluation.

3. Students may answer in a variety of ways, so long as they address the questions.

Section 5.2 Activities

1. Study Skills/Group Activity: Planning Ahead

A popular menu item at your bistro is a seared duck breast, served with roasted potatoes and sautéed carrots. Work with two other students to follow the "Planning Ahead" rules on p. 303 to determine what steps are involved in creating and serving this dish. What work can be done in advance? In what order should the work be done?

2. Activity: Practice Basic Knife Cuts

Practice the basic knife cuts on p. 305, using a ruler to check sizes. Work on perfecting the correct size and shape for each cut.

3. Critical Thinking: Flavorings

What are some common flavorings you enjoy, and in what dishes do you especially enjoy them? How does that reflect your family's heritage or your community's nature?

318

5.1 Foodservice Equipment	5.2 Getting Ready to Cook	5.3 Cooking Methods	5.4 Cooking and Nutrition
• Receiving and storage equipment • Pre-preparation equipment • Food-preparation equipment • Holding and serving equipment	• *Mise en place* • Knife basics • Seasoning and flavoring • Pre-preparation techniques	• Heat transfer • Dry-heat cooking methods • Moist-heat cooking methods • Combination-cooking methods • Other cooking methods • Determining doneness	• Healthy diets • Dietary guidelines for Americans • MyPyramid • Nutrition labels • The problem of obesity

SECTION 5.3 COOKING METHODS

Cooking is—simply put—the process of preparing food for eating. What is your favorite way to prepare potatoes, fish, or beef? There are a variety of cooking methods, each producing different results. To be a good chef, you must master the skill of choosing an appropriate method for each specific food.

The three general types of cooking methods are dry-heat cooking, moist-heat cooking, and combination cooking. Each method can be used to bring out the flavor and tenderness of specific dishes. In addition, these methods can reflect cultural and regional preferences.

Study Questions

After studying Section 5.3, you should be able to answer the following questions:

- How is heat transferred to food through conduction, convection, and radiation?

- What are the types of cooking methods?

- What is dry-heat cooking, and which foods are best suited for it?

- What is moist-heat cooking, and which foods are best suited for it?

- What is combination-heat cooking, and which foods are best suited for it?

- How do you determine when food is done cooking?

- What are the guidelines for plating and storing food that has finished cooking?

319

Section 5.3 Cooking Methods

Introduce the Section

a. Describe the major cooking methods that will be discussed in the section.

b. Explain how dry-heat, moist-heat, and combination cooking methods differ.

c. Discuss the objectives for the section.

Vocabulary Review

a. Direct students to the key terms.

b. Pronounce each word, and have the students repeat the pronunciation out loud.

c. Discuss the definition of each word.

Teach

Discuss

- According to the text, "Cooking is… the process of preparing food for eating." Ask students to consider this statement. Does it imply that cooking does not require heat? Does it suggest that factories engaged in canning vegetables and fruit are cooking? Are gardeners considered cooks, since they are growing and thereby preparing food?

- What cultural and regional preferences do students associate with different cooking methods?

Reinforce and Review

- Each cooking method produces different results.
- The three basic categories of cooking methods are dry-heat, moist-heat, and combination cooking.

Homework Activity: Historical Dishes

Literacy Connection, 21st-Century Skills— Information Literacy, Initiative and Self-Direction, Produce Results

Select a dish you enjoy eating and research its history. Examine the culture with which it's associated, the ingredients it contains, and the techniques used to produce it.

Why is it important to understand the relationship between food and history?

Describe your findings in a one-page report.

Reinforce and Review

- Heat is a type of energy. The primary ways in which heat travels in a professional kitchen are through convection, conduction, and radiation.
- Conduction uses direct contact to transfer heat from one item to another, while convection uses indirect contact to transfer heat between items, mediated by air, water, or fat.
- Radiation does not involve direct contact. Microwaves agitate the water molecules inside the food to heat the item, while infrared waves are created when a heat source warms an intermediary object, which subsequently heats the food item.
- Infrared waves cook from the outside in, while microwaves work from the inside out.

Teaching Tips

- Demonstrate each of the three ways in which heat travels. For conduction, pour hot water into a cold pan. For convection, place a pan containing cold water into a hot oven. For radiation, place a pan containing cold water under a hot broiler.

Homework Activity: Heating up the Place

Science Connection, Literacy Connection, 21st-Century Skills—Information Literacy, Initiative and Self-Direction, Produce Results

Select one of the three methods of heat transfer commonly used in kitchens: convection, conduction, and radiation.

Explain how your selected method works and how it applies not only to foodservice but to other industries. Include any other information you believe to be relevant.

Produce a one-page report.

Vocabulary Terms

- **Conduction:** The transfer of heat from one item to another through direct contact between the items.
- **Convection:** The transfer of heat from one area to another.
- **Radiation:** The transfer of energy through space, often by microwaves or infrared heat.
- **Infrared heat:** A form of radiation created when the heat from a source is absorbed by another material and radiated outward to heat another object.

Heat Transfer

Heat is a type of energy. When two items of different temperatures have contact, energy, in the form of heat, transfers from the warmer item to the cooler until they both reach the same temperature. Heat travels in items in three ways, as shown in Figure 5.27.

Conduction is the transfer of heat from one item to another when the items come into direct contact with each other. Sometimes the heat is transferred to the air or from surface to surface. An example is when a cold plate begins to warm when covered with hot food. The heat of the food is conducted into the surface of the plate.

Convection is the transfer of heat caused by the movement of molecules (in the air, water, or fat) from a warmer area to a cooler one. When heating water, natural convection occurs. As water heats at the bottom of the pan, it travels upward. In the process, it transfers energy to the cooler water higher in the pot. This is a continuous process, with the hot water constantly rising and replacing the cooling water. It also occurs as mechanical convection in a convection oven when hot air is forced into the chamber.

Radiation does not require physical contact between the heat source and the food being cooked. Instead, heat moves by way of microwave and infrared waves. **Infrared heat** is created when the heat from a source is absorbed by one material and then radiated out to the food. The flame in a broiler heats the tiles in the broiler, which radiate the heat to the food. Microwaves agitate the water molecules in the food, creating a form of friction that heats the water and thereby the food.

It is important to remember that infrared waves affect the exterior of the food. Heat on the outside of the food then spreads inward through conduction. The result is that the outside of the food browns. Microwaves penetrate the item and cook it from the inside out, so browning does not take place. Microwaving is good for some recipes, but many foods can quickly become tough and rubbery or dried out if microwaved too long.

Figure 5.27: Heat patterns during conduction, convection, and radiation.

320

Figure Focus

Figure 5.27: What other examples of each kind of heat transfer can students suggest?

Dry-Heat Cooking Methods

In dry-heat cooking, food is cooked either by direct heat, like on a grill, or by indirect heat in a closed environment, like in an oven. Some food may lose moisture and become dry when cooked using dry heat. Any food prepared using dry heat must be naturally tender or prepared by adding moisture. There are several ways to add moisture:

- **Barding**: Wrapping an item (usually a naturally lean piece of meat, such as a pork tenderloin) with strips of fat before cooking to baste the meat, making it more moist

- **Larding**: Inserting long, thin strips of fat into a large, naturally lean piece of meat with a special needle before cooking to baste the meat from the inside

- **Marinating**: Soaking an item in a combination of wet and dry ingredients to provide flavor and moisture

Dry-heat cooking methods without fat include the following:

- Broiling
- Grilling
- Roasting
- Baking

Another way to prepare food is to use dry-heat cooking methods with fat and oil. These methods include the following:

- Sautéing
- Pan-frying
- Stir-frying
- Deep-frying

Broiling

Broiling is a rapid cooking method that uses high heat from a source located above the food. Broiled food becomes browned on the top. Foods that can be broiled include tender cuts of meat, young poultry, fish, and some fruits and vegetables.

321

Discuss

- Encourage students to discuss when and why to add moisture to items that are being cooked with the dry-heat method. If moisture is being added, does it still count as a dry-heat method?
- Which foods are good candidates to be cooked with dry-heat methods? Which foods might not be good options?
- Encourage students to describe their favorite dishes made with dry-heat cooking methods.

Reinforce and Review

- All foods prepared with dry-heat methods should be naturally tender or prepared with additional moisture.
- Adding moisture to items to be cooked with dry-heat methods is done in one of three ways: barding, larding, and marinating.
- Dry-heat methods that do not require fat include broiling, grilling, roasting, and baking. Any of these may have fat added, but it is not necessary.
- Dry-heat methods that do require the use of fat include sautéing, pan-frying, stir-frying, and deep-frying.
- Broiling cooks tender items rapidly, using a heat source above the item.

Vocabulary Terms

- **Barding:** Wrapping an item with strips of fat before cooking it to add moisture from the outside.
- **Larding:** Inserting long, thin strips of fat into an item before cooking it to add moisture from the inside.
- **Marinating:** Soaking an item in a combination of wet and dry ingredients to add flavor and moisture from the outside.
- **Broiling:** A dry-heat cooking method that rapidly cooks an item with high heat from a source above the food, typically browning the item on top.

Discuss

- Grilling and broiling can produce similar results and can be used to cook similar items. How do these cooking methods differ?

Reinforce and Review

- Grilling cooks small, tender items rapidly, using a heat source located below the item.

Vocabulary Terms

- **Grilling:** A dry-heat cooking method that rapidly cooks small, tender items with high heat from a source below the item.

Essential Skills
Broiling Food

1. Preheat the broiler.

2. Oil the broiler grill lightly or oil item lightly, if necessary.

3. Place the item on the broiler grid and move it into broiler cavity. See Figure 5.28a.

4. Adjust the distance between the item and the heat as needed to control the rate of cooking. Place the food farther away and cook it a little longer to reach a higher internal temperature in the finished product, and move it closer for less time for a lower internal temperature in the finished product. To cook red meat to a rare level, use shorter cooking times with more heat; for well-done use longer cooking times with less heat. Both should have a well-browned, flavorful crust on the outside and a juicy interior when finished. See Figure 5.28b.

5. Turn the item over halfway through the cooking process to achieve even cooking on both sides of the product. See Figure 5.28c.

Figure 5.28a: Step 3— Move the item into the broiler cavity.

Figure 5.28b: Step 4— Place the food farther away.

Figure 5.28c: Step 5—Turn the item halfway through the cooking process.

Grilling

Grilling is a very simple dry-heat method that is excellent for cooking smaller pieces of food. The food is cooked on a grill rack above the heat source. No liquid is added to the food during cooking. A cook might add small amounts of fat or oil during the cooking process simply to add flavor to the finished dish.

The result of grilling is food with a highly flavored outside and a moist inside. Grilled food has a smoky, slightly charred flavor because the fat melts and drips down into the heat source, along with some of the meat's juices. As the fat and

322

Figure Focus

Figure 5.28a: A common way of oiling the broiler grid is by adding a small amount of oil to a clean towel, which has been tied into a neat roll, and using a pair of tongs to rub the towel over the broiler grid.

Figure 5.28b: The final internal temperature of the item being cooked depends partly upon where the item is located on the broiler grid.

Figure 5.28c: Flipping the item over halfway during the cooking time helps ensure that the item will be cooked evenly.

juices burn, the smoke helps provide the charred flavor. The crosshatching "look" common to grilled food comes from the hot metal grill rack that the food sits on. Special woods, such as mesquite, hickory, or apple, can be used in the heat source to flavor the grilled food. Using a marinade can give the food a unique flavor as well as make it more moist.

Essential Skills
Grilling Food

❶ Thoroughly clean and preheat the grill.

❷ Season the main item. Marinate or brush it with oil, if necessary, to prevent it from sticking to the grill. See Figure 5.29a.

❸ Place the item on the grill.

❹ Turn the item about 60 degrees to produce crosshatch marks. See Figure 5.29b.

❺ Flip the item over to complete cooking to the desired doneness.

❻ The finished product should be cooked to the desired doneness, golden brown with no burning or charring. Achieving this requires control of the heat source.

Figure 5.29a: Step 2—Season the item.

Figure 5.29b: Step 4—Turn the item 60 degrees to produce crosshatch marks.

Roasting

Roasting and **baking** are techniques that cook food by surrounding the items with hot, dry air in the oven. As the outer layers of the food become heated, the food's natural juices turn to steam and are absorbed into the food. These juices create a natural sauce.

Bake food covered or uncovered, depending on the recipe. Food that is baked uncovered, such as cookies and casseroles, develop a golden brown color on top.

Roasting generally requires longer cooking times and is most often used with large cuts of meat, whole birds (poultry), or fish. Roasted food should have a golden brown exterior and moist, tender interior. Foods that can be baked or roasted include fish, tender meats and poultry, and some fruits and vegetables.

323

Discuss

- How does roasting differ from baking, and are these differences really important?

Reinforce and Review

- Flavor can be added to grilled items using aromatic woods and savory marinades.
- Roasting and baking both cook food by surrounding it with hot, dry air, causing the item's outer layers to heat and create steam within the food.
- Foods can be roasted or baked with or without a cover. Using a cover will help retain moisture, but foods cooked without a cover will develop a golden brown color.

Vocabulary Terms

- **Roasting:** A dry-heat cooking method that slowly cooks larger, often intact items in an oven with hot, dry air.
- **Baking:** A dry-heat cooking method that slowly cooks items in an oven with hot, dry air.

Figure Focus
Figure 5.29: What makes this steak a good candidate for grilling? Why do people expect that grilled items will have a cross-hatched appearance?

Discuss

- What are some characteristic of griddled items? What items are commonly cooked this way?

Reinforce and Review

- Griddled items can be cooked directly on a hot, flat surface or inside heavy pans.
- A high level of browning and a unique taste are two important characteristics of griddled foods.

Teaching Tips

- Students should practice griddling items.

Vocabulary Terms

- **Carryover cooking:** Foods continuing to cook even after they are removed from the heat source, thanks to the heat they retain.
- **Rest:** Allowing cooked items, especially meats, to sit briefly (often upon a rack) before they are cut into or served, enabling the recirculation of internal juices as well as the process of carryover cooking.

Essential Skills
Roasting Meat

1. Season, stuff, or marinate the main item, and sear, or quickly brown, its surface over direct heat.

2. Place the food on a rack in a roasting pan so that hot air can touch it on all sides. See Figure 5.30a.

Figure 5.30a: Step 2—Place food on a rack in a roasting pan.

3. Roast the item uncovered or covered, as the recipe calls for, until the desired temperature is reached. Allow for carryover cooking. **Carryover cooking** describes what happens to food after it has been removed from the oven. The roasted item holds a certain amount of heat that continues to cook the food.

4. Allow the roasted item to sit or **rest** before carving. Doing this allows the juices, which are being drawn out to the edges of the meat during roasting, to return to the center of the item and make it juicier.

Figure 5.30b: Step 6—Carve the roasted item.

5. Prepare pan gravy in the roasting pan.

6. Carve the roasted item, and serve it with the appropriate gravy or sauce. See Figure 5.30b.

Griddling

Griddling is cooking a food item on a hot, flat surface (known as a griddle) or in a relatively dry, heavy-bottomed fry pan or cast-iron skillet. The goal is to give the product an even, golden brown finish and a slightly crisp exterior texture. When cooking meats on a high-heat griddle or in a cast-iron pan, the result is a high level of browning that gives the finished product a unique taste and texture not achieved with other cooking methods. In particular, steaks, chops, and chicken breasts are often cooked on a griddle or in a hot cast-iron skillet.

The griddle is also used to prepare one of the most popular breakfast menu items: griddle cakes (pancakes). To produce a quality product, clean the griddle well and make sure the temperature of the griddle surface is appropriate to the item being cooked.

324

Figure Focus

Figure 5.30a: Why should a rack be used when roasting meat?

Figure 5.30b: What are some common flavorings for roasted poultry?

Sautéing

The **sautéing** (saw-TAY-ing) method cooks food rapidly in a small amount of fat over relatively high heat. The fat adds to the flavor. Meat strips, chicken, and fish are often prepared this way. The thinner and more delicate the piece of meat, the faster it will cook.

The literal translation of the French term sauté is "jump." To sauté is to cook the food quickly to keep water and vitamin loss at a low, while gaining a high degree of color and flavor. When sautéing, the pan is heated first, and just enough fat is added to coat the bottom of the pan.

Essential Skill
Sautéing

❶ Perform thorough *mise en place*.

❷ Cut food into appropriately sized pieces to allow maximum surface contact with the pan.

❸ Select the correct pan:

   a. Large enough to allow food to spread well in pan (overloading the pan does not allow rapid cooking)

   b. Sides that slant outward to allow moisture vapors to easily escape

   c. Made of a metal that provides good heat conductivity

❹ Use high to medium heat that can be easily controlled.

❺ Use minimal fat or clarified butter, just enough to prevent sticking and help conduct heat and flavor. See Figure 5.31a.

❻ Preheat the pan and fat to a high temperature (but not burning).

❼ Place a thin layer of food in the hot pan (overloading the pan drops the temperature of the pan too rapidly and items will not brown).

❽ Allow food to remain in contact with the surface long enough to brown, but move it often enough to prevent burning. See Figure 5.31b.

Figure 5.31a: Step 5—Use minimal fat to prevent sticking.

Figure 5.31b: Step 8—Keep food in contact with the surface of the pan to brown.

325

Figure Focus

Figure 5.31a: Relate the amount of food used in sautéing to the amount of fat used in broiling or grilling.

Figure 5.31b: Why is browning important to flavor development?

Discuss

- The literal meaning of "sauté" is "to jump." How does the sauté process resemble jumping? Do students think this name accurately reflects the cooking technique?

Reinforce and Review

- The thinner and more delicate the piece of meat, the more quickly it will cook. Careful attention must be paid to sautéing foods to prevent over-cooking.
- When sautéing, the pan should be heated first before any fat or other ingredients are added.

Essential Skills: Sautéing

Encourage students to discuss the following:

- Why should all *mise en place* be performed before the cooking process begins?
- Explain why certain pans are better or worse choices for sautéing foods.
- Why is it important not to overload the pan with raw food? What will be the effect on the food?
- What are the characteristics of a properly sautéed item?
- What are some common roasted items?

Students should practice sautéing food.

Vocabulary Terms

- **Sauté:** A dry-heat cooking method that cooks small, tender items quickly in a minimal amount of fat over relatively high heat, helping retain an item's inherent nutritional value while adding a significant amount of color and flavor.

Discuss

- How is stir-frying related to sautéing? Encourage students to compare and contrast the two cooking methods.
- How does the particular shape of a wok make it suitable for stir-frying?

Reinforce and Review

- Stir-frying uses high heat and minimal fat to cook small pieces of food very quickly.
- Sauces for stir-fried items are typically made directly in the cooking pan.

Fast Fact: Did You Know...?

What role have chopsticks played in the development of Chinese cuisines? What effects have they had on society?

Essential Skills: Steps for Stir-Frying

Encourage students to discuss the following:

- Why should all *mise en place* be performed before the cooking process begins?
- Why should the thickening agent used in a sauce for a stir-fried dish be added at the end of cooking?
- What are the characteristics of a properly stir-fried item?
- What are some common stir-fried items?

Students should practice stir-frying foods.

Vocabulary Terms

- **Stir-fry:** A dry-heat cooking method that uses very high heat and minimal fat to cook small pieces of food very quickly while being agitated.

Stir-Fry

Stir-fry is a cooking method closely related to sauté. Like sauté, it is a quick-cooking, dry-heat method. Food is cooked over a very high heat, generally in a wok with little fat, and stirred quickly. In this Asian style of cooking, sauce is usually created in the same pan after the product has been "sautéed."

In this method, a very small amount of oil is used in a pan over high heat. The items to be stir-fried, usually meats and fresh vegetables, are cut into bite-sized pieces. Figure 5.32 is an example of stir-fry cooking.

The wok, a bowl-shaped pan, makes stir-frying easy. A wok is usually made of rolled steel and is used for nearly all Chinese cooking methods.

Figure 5.32: Stir-frying vegetables.

[fast fact] Did You Know...?

Chopsticks are the second-most-popular eating tool in the world, after fingers. They originated in China sometime during the Shang Dynasty (1766–1122 BC). According to Confucius, knives represented aggression and therefore were not appropriate to use when dining. So, chopsticks became the utensil of choice.

Essential Skills
Steps for Stir-Frying

1. Perform thorough *mise en place*.
2. Heat a small amount of oil in a wok or large sauté pan. See Figure 5.33a.
3. Add the main item.
4. Stir-fry, keeping the food in constant motion with a wooden paddle or spoon. See Figure 5.33b.
5. Add additional ingredients, including seasonings, in the proper sequence (longest-cooking ingredient in first, shortest-cooking ingredient in last).
6. Add the liquid ingredients to the pan to create the sauce. Then add the thickener, as necessary.
7. Serve the food immediately.

Figure 5.33a: Step 2— Heat oil in a wok.

Figure 5.33b: Step 4— Stir-fry food.

326

Figure Focus

Figure 5.32: Why should food to be stir-fried be cut into bite-sized pieces?

Figure 5.33a: Relate the use of fat in stir-frying to the use of fat in sautéing.

Figure 5.33b: Why is it important to keep agitating the food during the stir-frying process?

Pan-Frying

Cooking techniques that use more fat than those discussed so far include pan-frying and deep-frying. To **pan-fry** food, cook it in an oil over less intense heat than that used for sautéing or stir-frying. Many recipes call for coating the food with batter, seasoned flour, or breading first. The hot oil seals the food's coated surface and locks the natural juices inside, instead of releasing them. The oil should be deep enough to come halfway up the side of the food being cooked. The object of pan-frying is to produce a flavorful exterior with a crisp, brown crust that helps retain the food's juices and flavor.

Only naturally tender food should be pan fried because this method of cooking brings out the food's distinct flavor and moistness. Even after cooking, the food should be tender and moist. Pan-fried food may be held for only a short time before being served. The outside of the food should be evenly golden brown, with a firm crust.

[ServSafe™ Connection]

Watch the Batter

Batters prepared with eggs or milk should be handled with care. There is a risk of time-temperature abuse and cross-contamination when batters are made with these products. Breading must also be handled with care because cross-contamination is a risk. If you make breaded or battered food from scratch, follow these guidelines:

- Prepare batters in small batches. Store what you do not need at 41°F or lower in a covered container.

- When breading food that will be cooked at a later time, store it in the refrigerator as soon as possible.

- Create a plan to throw out unused batter or breading after a set amount of time.

- Cook battered and breaded food thoroughly.

Discuss

- Pan-frying and deep-frying require more fat than other dry-heat methods to prepare. Does that mean that foods cooked with these methods are inherently poor nutritional choices? How can these cooking methods be used to create healthful dishes?

Reinforce and Review

- Most pan-fried items are cooked with some sort of crust, which protects the natural moisture within the food.
- Pan-frying produces items with a flavorful exterior, a moist interior, and a golden brown crust.
- Pan-fried items should be served as quickly as possible. Any delay will cause the crust to deteriorate and become soggy.

ServSafe Connection: Watch the Batter

What are the implications of undercooking battered or breaded foods? How can cross-contamination occur in the process of preparing these foods?

Vocabulary Terms

- **Pan-fry:** A dry-heat cooking method using a moderate amount of fat and a moderate amount of heat.

327

Essential Skills: Pan-Frying

Encourage students to discuss the following:

- Why should all *mise en place* be performed before the cooking process begins?

- Why should the pan contain so much cooking oil?

- What effect can oil that is too hot or too cool have on the finished product?

- What are the characteristics of a properly pan-fried item?

- What are some common pan-fried items?

Students should practice pan-frying foods.

Discuss

- How does deep-frying differ from pan-frying? How are they similar?
- What role do batters and breading play in fried foods?

Reinforce and Review

- Deep-frying cooks tender items that have been battered or breaded for protection by placing them in hot oil.
- Batters and breadings use similar ingredients, but batters blend the ingredients together.

In-Class Activity: Batter and Breading Cook-off

Prepare a number of batters and breadings as a class. Use them to coat and fry foods, and then perform a taste test as a group. Which coatings are the most visually appealing? Which have the best texture? Which has the best flavor?

Vocabulary Terms

- **Deep-fry:** A dry-heat cooking method that cooks tender, coated items by immersing them in hot fat.
- **Batter:** A combination of dry ingredients, liquid, and binder used to coat items that will be pan- or deep-fried.
- **Breading:** A coating for an item to be pan- or deep-fried made by dipping the item into successive pans of dry ingredient, liquid, and/or binder, and seasoned flour or crumbs.

Essential Skills
Pan-Frying

1. Perform thorough *mise en place*.

2. Fill a fry pan half to two-thirds full with appropriate oil or fat.

3. Heat the cooking oil to about 350°F. (Oil that is too cool will result in excess oil absorption by the item, and oil that is too hot will burn the outside coating before the item is cooked.)

4. Add the food item (usually breaded, coated with seasoned flour, or batter-coated) to the pan in a single layer.

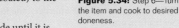

Figure 5.34: Step 6—Turn the item and cook to desired doneness.

5. Pan-fry the food on the first side until it is well browned.

6. Turn the item and cook it to the desired doneness. (If the item is extremely thick it can be finished in the oven to prevent burning the crust.) See Figure 5.34.

7. Drain the item on absorbent paper.

8. Season and serve it with the appropriate sauce and garnish.

To **deep-fry** food, bread or batter coat it, immerse (completely cover) it in hot fat, and fry it until it is done. The outside of the food item develops a crispy coating while the inside stays moist and tender. The coating on the food item can be a standard breading or a batter. A **batter** combines dry and wet ingredients. It is a mixture of the primary dry ingredient (wheat flour, all-purpose flour, corn meal, rice flour), the liquid (beer, milk, wine, water), and a binder (generally egg), which helps the mixture adhere to the product. Examples include the beer batter often used on fish, corn meal batter used on corn dogs, and tempura batter used on tempura vegetables and fish.

A **breading** has the same components as batter, but they are not blended together. A standard breading would be seasoned all-purpose flour and an egg and buttermilk dip. Place the product in the dip, remove, shake to remove excess dip, and then coat with the seasoned flour. For double-breading, repeat the process. If bread crumbs are an additional ingredient, submerge each item first in flour, then in egg and buttermilk, and then in crumbs.

328

Figure Focus

Figure 5.34: When turning a pan-frying item, be careful not to tear its fragile crust. Also, be very careful to avoid spattering yourself with hot fat.

Essential Skills
Standard Breading Procedure

Cooks often give fried foods a crisp coating through the standard breading procedure, which involves dredging the seasoned items in flour, egg wash, and finally a crunchy ingredient (such as breadcrumbs or grated cheese).

Figure 5.35: Step 2—One hand for wet food and one hand for dry food.

❶ Prepare an assembly line. Working from left to right (if you are right-handed), organize your seasoned, uncoated items, a pan of flour, a pan of egg wash, a pan of breadcrumbs or other crunchy substance, and a parchment-lined pan for the coated product.

❷ Keeping one hand for wet food and one hand for dry food, submerge each item first in flour, then in egg wash, and then in crumbs, removing any excess as you go. Make sure to coat the entire product. See Figure 5.35.

❸ Carefully arrange the coated items on the lined pan, separating layers with additional parchment paper as needed.

❹ Store the finished product in the refrigerator or freezer until needed.

❺ Discard all unused flour, egg wash, and crumbs to prevent cross-contamination.

Food that can be deep-fried must be naturally tender and of a shape and size that allows it to cook quickly without becoming tough or dry. As much as 35 percent of the flavor of a deep-fried food comes from the oil in which it is fried. Always use a good-quality oil.

The **"float"** of the item, the point when the item rises to the surface of the oil and appears golden brown, indicates doneness. To ensure doneness, be sure to check a piece of the item being cooked for the proper internal temperature. The crust should be crisp and delicate, surrounding a moist, tender piece of meat, fish, poultry, or vegetable. There are three slightly different methods for deep-frying food:

1. In the **swimming method**, gently drop a breaded or batter-coated food in hot oil, where it falls to the bottom of the fryer and then swims to the surface. Once the food items reach the surface, turn them over, if necessary, so they brown on both sides.

329

Figure Focus
Figure 5.35: Why is it important to keep one hand wet and one hand dry?

Discuss
- What are some common deep-fried items?

Reinforce and Review
- Foods that will be deep-fried should be naturally tender and cooked in clean, good-quality oil.
- To ensure doneness, be sure to check that the cooked foods reach the appropriate internal temperatures.
- The crust on a deep-fried item should be light and crunchy, not heavy, bready, or tough.

Teaching Tips
- Students should practice the standard breading procedure.
- Relate the discussion of deep-frying to the material in Chapter 3.

Vocabulary Terms
- **Float:** The point at which the cooking items rise to the surface of the oil and appear golden brown, typically (although not always) indicating doneness.
- **Swimming method:** A method of deep-frying food where a coated item is gently dropped into the hot oil, sinks to the bottom, and then swims to the surface.

Reinforce and Review

- The three techniques for deep-frying foods are the swimming method, the basket method, and the double-basket method.
- After adding food to hot oil, the recovery time is the time it takes the oil to regain its proper cooking temperature. Working in small batches will help lower recovery time and increase production efficiency.
- Use oil for deep-frying that has a neutral flavor and color with a high smoking point.

Teaching Tips

- To help students understand which items are better suited for each of the three deep-frying techniques, have them practice deep-frying a variety of foods to see which sink and which swim as well as which "swimming" foods need a longer cooking time.

Essential Skills: Deep-Frying

Encourage students to discuss the following:

- Why should the cooked food be blotted with absorbent paper toweling?
- What are some traditional garnishes for deep-fried foods?
- What are the characteristics of a properly deep-fried item?
- What are some common deep-fried items?

Students should practice deep-frying foods.

Vocabulary Terms

- **Basket method:** A method of deep-frying food where foods are placed into a basket and lowered into the hot oil.
- **Double-basket method:** A method of deep-frying food where coated foods are placed into a basket and then a second basket is placed directly atop the first, and the entire combination is lowered into the hot oil.
- **Recovery time:** The amount of time it takes oil to reheat to the correct cooking temperature once food is added.
- **Smoking point:** The temperature at which fats and oils begin to smoke, signaling that the fat has begun to deteriorate.

2. In the **basket method,** bread the food, place it in a basket, lower the basket and food into the hot oil, and then lift it all out with the basket when the food is done.

3. Use the **double-basket method** for certain food that needs to be fully submerged in hot oil for a longer period of time in order to develop a crisp crust. In this method, place the food item in a basket, and then fit another basket on top of the first. The top basket keeps the food from floating to the surface of the oil.

Recovery time is the amount of time it takes oil to reheat to the correct cooking temperature once food is added. The more food items dropped in the oil at one time, the longer the recovery time. The **smoking point** is the temperature at which fats and oils begin to smoke, which means that the fat has begun to break down. Use oil for deep-frying that has a neutral flavor and color and a high smoking point, around 425°F.

Essential Skills
Deep-Frying

❶ Heat the fat or oil to the proper temperature, usually 325°F to 375°F.

❷ Add the food item (usually breaded, floured, or batter-coated) to the hot oil, using the appropriate method (swimming, basket, or double-basket). See Figure 5.36a.

❸ Turn the item during frying, if necessary.

❹ If the item is too thick to cook fully in the oil, then crisp the item on the outside and finish it in the oven.

❺ Blot the food with absorbent paper toweling.

❻ Season and serve with the appropriate sauce and garnish. See Figure 5.36b.

Figure 5.36a: Step 2— Add the food item to hot oil using an appropriate method.

Figure 5.36b: Step 6— Season and serve.

Figure Focus

Figure 5.36a: Fill fryer baskets a maximum of halfway and lower them very carefully into the hot oil.

Figure 5.36b: Why should deep-fried items be seasoned after they are cooked?

Moist-Heat Cooking Methods

Moist-heat cooking techniques produce food that is delicately flavored and moist, sometimes with a rich broth, which can be served as a separate course or used as a sauce base. In fact, an entire dinner, complete with meat, fish, or poultry and vegetables, can be cooked in one pot. One example of this is the classic New England boiled dinner, consisting of corned beef, cabbage, and potatoes. Moist-heat cooking methods provide the opportunity to create nutritious, appealing dishes with a range of flavors and textures.

Moist-heat cooking methods include the following:

- Simmering
- Poaching and shallow poaching
- Blanching
- Steaming

Simmering

When **simmering**, completely submerge food in a liquid that is at a constant, moderate temperature. Use well-flavored liquid and cuts of meat that are less tender than those recommended for dry-heat cooking methods. Simmering less tender items cooks them at a slightly higher temperature than other moist-heat methods, 185°F to 205°F. Simmering differs from boiling in that bubbles in a simmering liquid rise gently and just begin to break the surface. Do not allow the water to come to a full boil, because the boiling motion will cause meat to become stringy and rubbery.

Poaching

When **poaching**, cook food between 160°F and 180°F. The surface of the poaching liquid should show some motion, but no air bubbles should break the surface. Use well-flavored liquid, and make sure the food is naturally tender. Cooks commonly poach chicken and seafood.

Cooks also often serve poached and simmered items with a flavorful sauce prepared from the poaching/simmering liquid to add zest to the dish's mild flavor. Be careful not to overcook poached and simmered food.

Shallow poaching cooks food using a combination of steam and a liquid bath. Shallow poaching is a last-minute cooking method best suited to food that is cut into portion-sized or smaller pieces. The food is partially covered by a liquid containing an acid (usually wine or lemon juice), herbs, and spices in a covered

331

Discuss

- Which foods are good candidates to be cooked with moist-heat methods? Which foods might not be good options?
- Encourage students to describe their favorite dishes made with moist-heat cooking methods.

Reinforce and Review

- Moist-heat cooking techniques produce food that is moist and delicately flavored.
- Common moist-heat cooking methods include simmering, poaching, shallow poaching, blanching, and steaming.
- Simmering cooks items at a slightly higher heat than poaching, but at a lower heat than boiling.
- Shallow poaching is similar to poaching, but the cooking food rests upon a bed of aromatic ingredients, is only partially submerged in liquid, and is covered by a lid (often by a cartouche—see Section 5.2).

Teaching Tips

- Heat three pots of water: one to poaching temperatures, one to simmering temperatures, and one to boiling temperature. Encourage students to identify how the water in each pan has a different appearance and to discuss the reasons.
- Students should practice poaching and simmering foods.

Vocabulary Terms

- **Simmering:** A moist-heat cooking method whereby less-tender foods are submerged in a liquid maintaining a constant temperature of 185°F–205°F.
- **Poaching:** A moist-heat cooking method whereby naturally tender foods are submerged in a liquid maintaining a constant temperature of 160°F–180°F.
- **Shallow poaching:** A moist-heat cooking method whereby naturally tender foods are placed on a bed of aromatic ingredients and partially submerged in liquid in a covered pan.

Homework Activity: Egg Proteins

Science Connection, Literacy Connection, 21st-Century Skills—Critical Thinking and Problem Solving, Work Independently, Produce Results

Demonstrate the egg-poaching process for the class so they can watch the albumen coagulate around the yolk. Note: Depending on the size of your class, you may want to do this in small groups or by creating a computer slide show of the various stages in the cooking process. You could also have each student, or pairs of students, practice poaching eggs after your demonstration.

Students should research the science behind egg poaching: what proteins are involved, the role of vinegar, and the temperatures at which various coagulations occur.

Each student should produce a one-page report on his or her findings.

Reinforce and Review

- Food that has been shallow-poached should be very tender and moist with a fragile texture. The cooking liquid serves as the base for a flavorful accompanying sauce.
- Blanching, a version of boiling, is commonly used to par-cook foods for later use. Shocking the items in ice water keeps the food from overcooking.

Teaching Tips

- Using green vegetables as an example, blanch and shock some items, and then boil some. Encourage students to compare the visual appeal of the two cooking methods, and then to taste them.

Essential Skills: Shallow Poaching

Encourage students to discuss the following:

- Why is a bed of aromatic ingredients added to the pan?
- Why are shallow-poached items so fragile?
- What are the characteristics of a properly shallow-poached item?
- What are some common shallow-poached items?

Students should practice shallow-poaching items.

Vocabulary Terms

- **Paupiette:** A thin fish fillet or slice of meat wrapped into a cylinder around a forcemeat filling.
- *Cuisson:* The cooking liquid used to shallow-poach an item and traditionally used as a base for the accompanying sauce.
- **Blanching:** Usually, plunging vegetables, pasta, or another ingredient into boiling water to par-cook ("partially cook") and to decrease subsequent cooking time; can also refer to the process of preparing bones for stock by cooking them to remove superficial proteins.
- **Par-cooking:** Partially cooking an item to shorten its subsequent finishing time during a meal service.

pan. The steam cooks the items that are not directly covered by the poaching liquid. Food that has been shallow poached should be very tender and moist, with a fragile texture. Cooks commonly shallow poach **paupiettes** of sole and other white fishes. Shallow poaching transfers much of the flavor of the food from the food item to the liquid. To keep this lost flavor, use the liquid as a sauce base. This liquid is called a *cuisson.*

Essential Skills
Shallow Poaching

1. Heat butter in a saucepan.
2. Add the seasonings to the pan, and make a level bed.
3. Add the food item and the poaching liquid. The liquid should come partway up the food item. See Figure 5.37a.
4. Bring the liquid to a proper cooking temperature, usually 160°–180°F.
5. Cover the saucepan with buttered parchment paper or a lid.
6. Finish the food in the saucepan, either over direct heat or in an oven.
7. Remove the food item from the poaching pan, and keep it warm and moist.
8. Reduce the poaching liquid, and prepare a sauce as desired.
9. Serve the food item with the sauce and appropriate garnish. See Figure 5.37b.

Figure 5.37a:
Step 3—Add a food item and the poaching liquid.

Figure 5.37b:
Step 9—Serve the food item with sauce and garnish.

Blanching

Blanching is a variation of boiling. When **blanching**, partially cook food (also called **par-cooking**), and then finish it later. Cooks frequently use blanching to pre-prepare vegetables.

An example of blanching is the preparation of green beans. Blanch the beans, and then give them a quick toss with seasoned butter in a hot pan at service. The result is a green bean cooked to perfection, with bright color, but prepared fresh and quickly at service. Many times, cooks blanch food that takes too long to cook thoroughly before they deep-fry it.

332

Figure Focus

Figure 5.37a: Carefully place the raw item atop the ingredient bed.

Figure 5.37b: A flavorful sauce is made from the reduced *cuisson.*

Essential Culinary Skill
Blanching

❶ Bring water to a boil, and then place items in the boiling water.

❷ Boil the food for a short time, not cooking it all the way.

❸ Remove the item from the pot, and then shock it by placing it in ice water. This immediately stops the cooking. See Figure 5.38.

❹ Drain and dry the item, and then hold it until it is time for finishing.

Figure 5.38: Step 3—Shock the item by placing it in ice water.

Steaming

Steaming is cooking food by surrounding it in steam in a confined space such as a steamer basket, steam cabinet, or combi-oven. Direct contact with the steam cooks the food.

Steaming can take place with or without pressure. Placing food in a steamer basket on top of a pot of boiling water directly exposes the food to steam, which is 212°F. Placing food in a commercial steam cabinet or combi-oven also cooks food through direct contact with the steam, but the temperature is generally higher because the steam is under pressure. It cannot escape the cabinet or oven. Both methods cook in the same way, but one cooks faster than the other. Take this into consideration when preparing a dish.

Enhance the flavor of food steamed over, but not directly in, boiling liquid by using broth instead of water as the liquid. Use naturally tender food, cut it into small sizes, and place it on a rack above the boiling liquid within a closed cooking pot. As the liquid comes to a boil, the steam created surrounds the food, heating it evenly and keeping it moist. Once all the ingredients are in the steamer and the cover is in place, do not remove the lid because the steam will escape, slowing down the cooking process.

333

Figure Focus
Figure 5.38: Resting the blanched item in the shocking water for too long can cause a loss of flavor and nutrients.

Discuss

- What are some similarities between steamed foods and poached or shallow-poached foods? Consider appearance, texture, flavor, and nutritional value.
- What ingredients are best suited for combination cooking techniques? Which are not?
- Encourage students to discuss their favorite foods cooked with combination techniques.

Reinforce and Review

- Steamed items typically have mild, delicate flavors with a fresh color and appearance.
- Combination-cooking methods include braising and stewing, both of which incorporate dry-heat and moist-heat methods.
- Combination-cooking methods are suited for less-tender items.

Vocabulary Terms

- **Combination cooking:** The use of both dry-heat and moist-heat cooking methods to produce a single dish.
- **Braising:** A combination-cooking method that is primarily used for larger pieces of meat.
- **Stewing:** A combination-cooking method that is primarily used for smaller pieces of food.

With steam, no browning can occur, so food appears pale. Items cooked with steam have mild, delicate flavors and often have a fresher taste, color, and appearance. Cooking time is longer with steaming than with boiling or simmering. Cook steamed food until it is just done but not overcooked. Steamed food should be moist and plump, not rubbery or chewy.

Essential Skills
Steaming Food on Top of the Range

1. Bring the liquid to a boil.
2. Add the food item to the pot in a single layer on a rack raised above the boiling liquid.
3. Cover the pot. See Figure 5.39.
4. Steam the food to the correct doneness.
5. Serve the food immediately with the appropriate sauce and garnish.

Figure 5.39: Step 3—Cover the pot.

Combination-Cooking Methods

Sometimes the best method for preparing certain food is a combination of both dry-heat and moist-heat cooking methods. Such cooking is called **combination cooking.** For example, braising and stewing use both dry and moist heat to cook food that is less tender. Combination-cooking techniques are useful because they can transform the less tender and less expensive main ingredients into delicious and tender finished products.

Combination-cooking methods include the following:

- **Braising**: Primarily used for larger cuts of meat
- **Stewing**: For smaller pieces of food

334

Figure Focus

Figure 5.39: If the steaming vessel is left uncovered, how might the flavor, texture, and appearance of the food be affected? How might this be similar to cooking delicate foods like custards and terrines without a hot-water bath?

Molecular Gastronomy

The term "molecular gastronomy" has recently become popular in the culinary world. Food writers use it as a catch-all term to describe a variety of unusual culinary techniques and the chefs who are associated with them. Once limited to a few high-end restaurants in Europe and the United States, many of these techniques have been adopted by restaurants worldwide, and some methods are even suitable for home use. Here is a quick survey of some common trends in molecular gastronomy:

- **Spherification:** Mixing juices or other liquids with calcium chloride and then dripping the mixture into an alginate solution causes "pearls" or "caviar" to form. These balls are liquid inside and gel outside, so when you bite into them, a burst of liquid, such as apple juice or chicken consommé, explodes in your mouth.

- **Foams:** Liquids are made foamy with carbon dioxide or by buzzing with an immersion blender (sometimes with lecithin or another stabilizer added first). The resulting froth, for instance, a delicate froth made of pan juices, is spooned directly onto a dish or frozen for later use.

- **Flash-freezing:** Immersing a food into liquid nitrogen or placing it on an Anti-Griddle™ can instantly freeze a sauce, cream, or purée, making anything from an ice cream to a liquid-filled ice pop.

- **Meat glue:** More correctly known as **transglutaminase**, this chemical "glues" proteins to one another to create a solid piece from fragments; for instance, bonding bacon to a rabbit loin or making "pasta" from finely ground meat pastes.

This is just the tip of the iceberg! New technologies and techniques are being pioneered daily. Since some of these can be tried at home, consider investigating further to see what novel concepts you can create.

Braising

In **braising**, first sear the food item in hot oil, and then partially cover it in enough liquid to come halfway up the food item. Then cover the pot or pan tightly, and finish the food slowly in the oven or on the stovetop until it is tender. A bed of seasonings adds moisture and flavor to the food. If the recipe calls for them, add vegetables to braised meat or poultry near the end of the cooking time. As the meat cooks, its flavor is released into the cooking liquid, which becomes the accompanying sauce. The key to quality braising is long, slow cooking. In an item such as coq au vin, the meat should slide from the bone in the final product, and the meat itself should fall apart with a gentle touch.

335

Encourage students to discuss the following:

- When and why should these techniques be used?

- How can they be applied in the classroom?

- Is the application of scientific techniques to culinary arts really anything new? After all, doesn't all cooking involve science?

Reinforce and Review

- To braise an item, first sear it in hot oil, and then add enough liquid to the cooking vessel to come halfway up the sides of the item.
- The key to quality braising is long, slow cooking, which breaks down the connective tissue in the meat, making it tender and delectable.

Teaching Tips

- Using an immersion blender, as well as lecithin or another stabilizer if available, foam a flavorful liquid (such as broth or flavored milk). Carefully spoon off the foam, place it on a parchment-covered surface, and immediately freeze it. Encourage students to consider ways in which a frozen foam could add value to a dish.

Vocabulary Terms

- **Spherification:** The use of calcium chloride and sodium alginate to produce spheres of a flavorful liquid.
- **Foam:** An airy substance produced by frothing a liquid, sometimes with an added stabilizer.
- **Flash-freezing:** The technique of instantly freezing a food, enabling it to be served in an unusual manner.
- **Transglutaminase:** An enzyme that "glues" proteins to one another.

Essential Skills:
Braising

Encourage students to discuss the following:

- Why should the main item be seared?

- Why is it important to add vegetables to the braising item? Note: Mirepoix typically refers to a mixture of diced onions, carrots, and celery, in a 2:1:1 ratio, used to flavor all manner of items from stocks to stews. It will be discussed further in Chapter 6.

- What are the characteristics of a properly braised item?

- What are some common braised items?

Students should practice braising foods.

Reinforce and Review

- Properly braised items are generally considered fork-tender, and well-done. The meat should be easily pulled apart with a fork, but should not be overcooked to the point that it is falling apart.
- Braised foods are both nutritious (since they preserve most of the nutrients in the cooking liquid) and inexpensive (since they utilize less-expensive cuts of meat and require little labor to produce).
- Common braising techniques include daube, *estouffade*, and pot roasting.

Vocabulary Terms

- **Daube:** A braised dish, typically made with beef, vegetables, red wine, and seasoning, with a main item that has been marinated before cooking, often in additional red wine.
- **Estouffade:** A brown braised dish, usually made with beef but sometimes with veal, made with red wine; alternately, the French term for braising.
- **Pot roasting:** A braised dish, less likely to contain wine than other braises; alternately, an American term for braising.

Essential Skills
Braising

1. Preheat both the pan and the oil.
2. Sear on all sides. See Figure 5.40a.
3. Add mirepoix and tomato.
4. Stir a small amount of liquid into the mirepoix to deglaze the pan.
5. Add the appropriate amount of liquid.
6. Cover the pot and finish the braise.
7. Check to see if the braised foods are done. See Figure 5.40b.
8. Place the pot over the direct heat, and continue to reduce the sauce to develop its flavor, body, and consistency. See Figure 5.40c.

Figure 5.40a: Step 2—Sear on all sides.

Figure 5.40b: Step 7— Check to see if the braised food is done.

Figure 5.40c: Step 8—Continue to reduce the sauce.

Slow, gentle braising causes the tougher connective tissue of lean meat to become fork tender and well done. More tender food requires less cooking fluid and can be heated at lower temperatures for a shorter time. Few nutrients are lost with braising. Braised food that is finished in the oven is less likely to be scorched than food that is finished on the stovetop. Braised food should be extremely tender, but should not fall into shreds.

Braising techniques include daube, *estouffade*, and pot roasting:

- **Daube** (DAWB): A braised dish usually made with red meat, often beef, vegetables, red wine, and seasoning. The main item is often marinated before braising.

- **Estouffade** (ess-too-FAHD): The French term refers to both the braising method and the dish itself (a beef stew made with red wine).

- **Pot roasting**: A common American term for braising as well as the name of a traditional dish.

336

Figure Focus

Figure 5.40a: A rich brown color should be developed on all sides of the meat to be braised.

Figure 5.40b: How should a braised item be checked for doneness? Is using a meat thermometer sufficient to ensure a high-quality dish?

Figure 5.40c: After the main item has finished cooking, it is often removed and rested while the cooking liquid is strained, degreased, and reduced to provide a sauce.

Stewing

Stewing techniques are similar to braising, but the pre-preparation is a little different. First, cut the main food item into bite-sized pieces, and either blanch or sear them. As with braising, cook the food in oil first, and then add liquid. Stewing requires more liquid than braising. Cover the food completely while it is simmering.

There are many kinds of stews. Here are some types that are popular in classical European cooking:

- **Blanquette** (blahn-KETT): A white stew made traditionally from veal, chicken, or lamb, blanquette is garnished with mushrooms and pearl onions, and served in a white sauce.

- **Bouillabaisse** (BOO-yuh-base): This is a Mediterranean fish stew combining a variety of fish and shellfish.

- **Fricassée** (frick-uh-SAY): This is a white stew, often made from veal, poultry, or small game.

- **Goulash** (GOO-losh): This stew originated in Hungary and is made from beef, veal, or poultry, seasoned with paprika, and generally served with potatoes or dumplings. See Figure 5.41.

- **Navarin** (nav-ah-RAHN): This stew is usually prepared from mutton or lamb, with a garnish of root vegetables, onions, and peas. The name probably comes from the French word for turnips (*navets*), which are used as the principal garnish.

- **Ragout** (ra-GOO): This is a French term for stew that means "restores the appetite." See Figure 5.41.

- **Matelote** (ma-tuh-LOAT): A special type of fish stew, matelote is usually prepared with eel.

Figure 5.41: Goulash and ragout.

337

Discuss

- How are stews and braises different? In which cultures are they found? Why are so many stewed and braised items so similar?
- Can students identify examples of stews and braises popular in non-European cultures? Note: For instance, moles are popular in Mexico, and adobo is popular in the Philippines.

Reinforce and Review

- Stews are similar to braises, except the meat is typically cut into smaller pieces in a stew; the stew meat may be blanched before cooking; and stewing may require more liquid than braising.

Teaching Tips

- Students should practice stewing items.

Homework Activity: Comparisons Are Odorous

Literacy Connection, 21st-Century Skills— Communicate Clearly, Information Literacy, Be Self-Directed Learners

Select a dish from the list on p. 337.

Find two recipes for the dish. Compare and contrast them, looking at ingredients, amounts, cooking time, and other relevant factors.

Now research the history of the dish. What ingredients "should" it contain? Is there debate about the ingredients to be used? Do the two examples you have match the ingredients of the "real thing?"

Discuss your findings in a one-page report, appending the recipes you consulted.

Figure Focus
Figure 5.41: How are these dishes similar? How are they different?

Nutrition: Nutritious Cooking

According to the text, "Fat helps carry flavor." What do students think this means? Note: Many flavoring ingredients, such as onions, are fat-soluble, so the molecules that give them their distinct flavors are readily transmitted through the medium of fat.

Why is fat-free and low-fat food often considered flavorless? What are some nutritious ways to combat this, while still obtaining the desired flavor in a dish?

ServSafe Connection: Safe Cooking Guidelines

Encourage students to discuss how following safe cooking practices is related to excellent guest service.

Reinforce and Review

- *Sous vide* cooking uses precise temperature control to cook vacuum-sealed foods in a water bath for a specific time.
- Some items take as little as a minute or two to prepare, while others may cook for over 24 hours.

Vocabulary Terms

- **Sous vide:** French for "under vacuum," a cooking method for sealed foods under rigorously controlled conditions.

[nutrition]

Nutritious Cooking

Some cooking techniques are naturally more nutritious than others. Sautéing and grilling, for instance, use a minimal amount of fat, while steaming and poaching require none at all. Deep-frying and pan-frying, on the other hand, increase the fat content of the final product. However, fat can help carry flavor. Foods cooked with fat often taste better than those cooked without it. For most people, it is possible to find a balance between more and less healthy cooking methods. Practicing moderation is the key. The well-thought-out use of herbs, spices, and other flavoring ingredients can also help people lower their fat intake without sacrificing great taste.

[ServSafe™ Connection]

Safe Cooking Guidelines

When cooking, follow these general guidelines:

- Specify cooking time and the required minimum internal cooking temperature in all recipes.
- Use a thermometer with a probe that is the right size for the food.
- Avoid overloading ovens, fryers, and other cooking equipment.
- Let the cooking equipment's temperature recover between batches.
- Use utensils or gloves to handle food after cooking.
- Taste food correctly to avoid cross-contamination.

Other Cooking Methods

Two other cooking methods include *sous vide* and microwave cooking.

Sous Vide Cooking

Sous vide is a method in which food is cooked for a long time, sometimes well over 24 hours. *Sous vide* is French for "under vacuum." Rather than placing food in a slow cooker, the *sous vide* method places food in airtight plastic bags in water that is hot but well below boiling point. This cooks the food using precisely controlled heating, at the temperature at which it should be served.

The water might feel about as hot as a bathtub, but feeling is not enough. For safety and quality reasons, *sous vide* water-bath temperatures are measured in tenths of a degree. The exact range is narrow and precise.

338

The aroma of food cooking actually means that precious molecules of flavor are escaping from the food. *Sous vide* locks all of those flavor molecules in with the vacuum seal. *Sous vide* foods do not lose flavor. In fact, in some cases, the flavors actually intensify and improve.

Microwave Cooking

Many foods can be baked or roasted in a microwave oven. However, microwave ovens do not give the same results as convection or conventional ovens because they cook food with waves of energy or radiation—microwaves—rather than with heat. Microwaving is good for some recipes, but many foods can quickly become tough and rubbery if microwaved too long.

Microwave cooking alters and denatures protein, causing it to toughen. This can be a problem in breads, eggs, and meats. Cooks can use special techniques with specific microwave recipes to maintain the quality of the finished recipe. Because there is no external heat source, there is no browning. Food cooks because microwave radiation increases molecular activity inside the food. It begins at the center, so the surface does not turn a crispy golden brown while the inside slowly cooks, as in a conventional oven.

Figure 5.42: Microwaves are used in restaurant and foodservice operations primarily to thaw and reheat foods.

Glass and ceramic cookware and plastics that are labeled microwave safe can be used in the microwave oven. Never use brown grocery bags, newspaper, metal, or foil in the microwave oven. Figure 5.42 shows a microwave oven.

Determining Doneness

There are two important qualities that cooks look for to determine a product's doneness:

- Has it achieved the desired texture?
- Has it reached the minimum internal temperature it needs to be safe?

For products that are made in large quantities, many restaurant and foodservice operations will test the products to determine the standardized cooking temperature and the length of cooking time that will produce the same doneness every time. This type of control depends on cooking the same size or quantity of product every time.

339

Reinforce and Review

- Cooking food in a vacuum-sealed environment retains all the flavor and nutritional components that might otherwise be lost when using more traditional cooking methods.
- Microwave cooking is more suitable for some ingredients and dishes than others. Using recipes designed for microwave ovens can help maintain a high level of quality.
- Like steaming or poaching, microwave cookery prevents browning on the item's exterior. Unlike those moist-heat techniques, though, the microwave cooks from the inside of the food toward the exterior.
- The two most important qualities in determining a dish's doneness are the desired texture and the necessary internal temperature. Taste is not a factor.

Teaching Tips

- If a microwave oven is available in the classroom, review the appropriate cooking equipment with the class.
- Break an egg into each of two ramekins and prick each yolk with a fork. Place one ramekin in a conventional oven to bake, while cooking the other one in the microwave. Encourage the students to predict the outcome of each dish. Note: You may wish to test this activity in advance, since results may differ widely based on the microwave oven used as well as the temperature of the conventional oven. Relate this discussion to the egg-poaching project earlier in this section.

Figure Focus

Figure 5.42: Ask students how home microwaves are different from those used in restaurant and foodservice operations.

Reinforce and Review

- Checking the temperature of an item is always necessary. Just because the item has completed its standardized cooking time does not mean that it is "done."
- The more done a high-protein item is, the more resistant to pressure it will be. Heat denatures and coagulates proteins, causing them to stiffen.
- The more done a vegetable is, the less resistant to pressure it will usually be. Plant fibers weaken and deteriorate with the application of heat.
- The plating, portioning, and garnishing of a finished product will determine the guest's satisfaction as well as the establishment's profitability.

CUSTOMIZED INSTRUCTION

Literacy Connection, 21st-Century Skills—Communicate Clearly, Create Media Products, Work Independently

ESOL Students

How are foods presented to guests in your culture of origin? In what ways is this process similar to and different from the plating process described here?

Select a dish from your culture of origin that you particularly enjoy. Create a poster with two pictures. First, illustrate how the dish would be properly presented to guests in your culture of origin. Second, show the dish might be presented to guests in this culture, following the guidelines in the text.

Vocabulary Terms

- **Portioning:** Determining the amount of an item that will be served to the guest, with special care taken to ensure that this predetermined amount is the amount that is actually served.
- **Overportioning:** Serving more than the predetermined amount of food, or failing to determine the appropriate amount of food per serving, which result in increased cost and lower profit.
- **Plating:** The decision, generally made at the time the menu is written, about what serving vessel will be used to present the product as well as how and where the product and its accompaniments will be placed on that vessel.

It is important to check the temperature of the item both in the tests that lead to standardized cooking times and temperatures and in the determination of doneness in smaller quantities and individual items such as a steak or chicken breast. Never assume that an item is at the right temperature because it has finished its standardized cooking time. Figure 5.43 shows a thermometer in a golden brown turkey.

Figure 5.43: To determine doneness, insert a thermometer to check temperature.

An experienced chef can estimate the degree of doneness in items like meat and fish by pressing the surface of the item. The more done the item is, the more resistance it has. The reverse is generally true for vegetables. As the fruit or vegetable cooks, its fibers break down and the item becomes softer.

The plating, portioning, and garnishing of a finished product will determine the guest's satisfaction and the profitability of the restaurant. **Portioning** is the amount of an item that is served to the guest. **Overportioning** results in increased cost and lower profit from an item. **Plating** is the decision about what serving vessel will be used to present the product, as well as the layout of the item on the plate or in the bowl and the garnishing of the item. Figure 5.44 shows a comparison of two plated dishes.

Figure 5.44: Contrasting plates: one plated neatly and one plated badly.

Figure Focus

Figure 5.43: Note that the thermometer is placed deep into the thickest part of the bird, avoiding both bones and the interior cavity—each of which will produce inaccurate temperature readings.

Figure 5.44: What is visually appealing about each plate? What is unappealing?

Garnish enhances the food being served. A garnish should be something that will be eaten with the item, functioning as a flavor component while visually adding to the appearance of the item. Simple garnishes are the best. Garnishes can be mixed with the other components of an item or added at the very end to enhance presentation. The addition of diced sun-dried tomato to rice pilaf brings both color and flavor, whether it is cooked into the rice or sautéed and used to top the rice at plating.

[fast fact]

Did You Know...?

When selecting a garnish, consider color. The color of the garnish affects the mood or tone of the dish.

- Green: Freshness and vitality
- Brown or gold: Warmth, comfort, richness
- Orange or red: Intensity, hunger

There are several things to consider when arranging the plate:

- Look at the plate or bowl as a picture frame. Select the right dish for the portion size. Keep the food off the rim of the dish.
- Maintain a good balance of colors. Remember, three colors are usually enough. Too many colors are unappetizing.
- Height makes any plate more attractive. Placing ingredients to bring height to a plate presentation is more interesting and appealing than simply spreading everything flat. Attractively prop the protein on the starch to bring height and interest. Do not hide the starch.
- Always cut the ingredients neatly and uniformly.
- Keep the arrangement of ingredients simple. Remember, the customer should want to eat the food, not just look at it.

The proper storage of food, both prepared and unprepared, affects the quality of the food prepared and served. Follow these storage guidelines:

- Wrap food properly to prevent drying and cross-contamination.
- Cool and store food properly to prevent pathogen growth.
- Store food in the correct type of container to prevent contamination and to protect flavor.
- Label and date containers to allow identification and rotation.

341

Fast Fact: Did You Know...?

Encourage students to discuss the following questions:

- Why is it important from a visual perspective to present a variety of colors on a single plate?
- From a nutritional standpoint, how might adding colors add nutrients?
- Should garnishes be added to a dish just to give it more color? For instance, a plate containing properly sautéed pork chop with caramelized apples, roasted cauliflower, and potato gratin might taste delicious but look dull. Will a simple sprinkle of chopped parsley improve the dish?

Reinforce and Review

- Maintaining a good balance of colors, textures, and height improves the appearance and enjoyment of a dish.
- While creating a visually appealing plate is important, remember that a server must safely deliver the dish to the table, and a guest must not feel awkward trying to eat it.
- Always cool and store any remaining food properly to avoid waste caused by spoilage or contamination, and label all food containers properly and promptly.

In-Class Activity: Designing a Plate

Literacy Connection, 21st-Century Skills— Create Media Products, Work Independently, Manage Projects, Think Creatively

Envision a menu item that would have at least five different items on the plate. Now design the plate and create a poster illustrating it, making sure to label each item clearly.

Is your plate visually appealing? Will it enthrall the guests, or will it intimidate them? Is there too much or too little food on the plate? Are there too many or too few colors? Is there anything else you should do to make your plate more effective?

Vocabulary Terms

- **Garnish:** The foods that accompany and enhance the main product, and are appropriate from both a flavor perspective and a visual perspective.

Summary

- Remind students to review the following:
  1. Heat transfers to food through conduction, convection, and radiation
  2. The types of cooking methods
  3. Dry-heat cooking and the foods best suited for it
  4. Moist-heat cooking and the foods best suited for it
  5. Combination-heat cooking and the foods best suited for it
  6. How to determine that food is done cooking
  7. Guidelines for plating and storing food that has finished cooking

Summary

In this section, you learned the following:

- Heat is transferred to food in three ways:
  - **Conduction**: Heat is transfered from one item to another when the items come into direct contact with each other.
  - **Convection**: Heat transfer is caused by the movement of molecules from a warmer area to a cooler one.
  - **Radiation**: This method does not require contact between the heat source and the food being cooked.

- Types of cooking methods include dry-heat cooking, moist-heat cooking, and combination-cooking methods.

- In dry-heat cooking, cook food with or without a fat, either by direct heat or by indirect heat in a closed environment. Broiling, grilling, roasting, baking, sautéing, pan-frying, stir-frying, and deep-frying are kinds of dry-heat cooking.

- Moist-heat cooking produces food that is delicately flavored and moist. Serve it as a separate course or used as a sauce base. Simmering, poaching, blanching, and steaming are techniques used in moist-heat cooking.

- Combination cooking uses techniques from both dry-heat and moist-heat cooking. Braising and stewing are types of combination cooking.

- To determine when food is done cooking, identify if the product has its desired texture and required minimum internal temperature.

- There are a number of guidelines for plating food that has finished cooking, such as selecting the right dish, maintaining a good balance of colors, adding some height to the plate, cutting the ingredients uniformly, and keeping the arrangement of food simple.

- The guidelines for storing food include the following:
  - Wrap food properly to prevent drying and cross-contamination.
  - Cool and store it properly to prevent pathogen growth.
  - Store it in the correct type of container to prevent contamination and to protect flavor.
  - Label and date food to allow identification and rotation.

Section 5.3 Review Questions

1. Explain the differences among conduction, convection, and radiation.

2. How do dry-heat and moist-heat cooking methods differ?

3. What is combination cooking?

4. What is carryover cooking?

5. Benny Gordon says that part of *mise en place* is determining which cooking method to use for each food. In a Cajun restaurant, which types of cooking might be most common? Provide an example of a dish prepared using each cooking method.

6. Why is it important for Alex to recognize doneness in different foods?

7. Which type of cooking would take longer, poaching or simmering? Why? Describe each process.

8. Why are braising and stewing called combination-cooking methods?

343

Section 5.3 Review Questions

1. These three heating methods differ in the way heat is transferred from one area to another. Conduction is the transfer of heat caused by direct contact between two surfaces, while convection is the transfer of heat caused by the movement of warm molecules to a cooler place. Radiation is the transfer of heat caused by either microwaves of infrared waves.

2. In dry-heat cooking methods, food is cooked either by direct heat or by indirect heat in a closed environment. These foods must be naturally tender or prepared by adding moisture to them. In moist-heat cooking methods, food is cooked in hot liquid. Naturally tender items are appropriate for certain cooking methods, like poaching, but naturally tough items are appropriate for other cooking methods, like simmering.

3. Combination-cooking methods combine elements of dry- and moist-heat cooking techniques to cook naturally tough items. Common combination-cooking methods include stewing and braising.

4. Carryover cooking is what happens to food after it has been removed from the oven, when the roasted item holds a certain amount of heat that continues to cook the food.

5. Students should research common Cajun dishes or Cajun restaurants to answer this question. Typical Cajun cooking methods include stewing, as for jambalaya and gumbo; boiling, as for crayfish and other crustaceans; and simmering, as for maque choux and bisque.

6. Alex needs to recognize doneness in different foods so that he can properly cook these foods, thereby avoiding waste. Also, knowing how long different foods take to reach doneness will help him learn when to begin cooking each food for a guest's meal.

7. Simmering, the submerged cooking of a relatively tough item at 185°F–205°F, takes longer than poaching because less tender ingredients are used. Poaching cooks relatively tender foods at 160°F-180°F for a shorter period of time.

8. Braising and stewing are considered combination-cooking methods because they combine elements of dry-heat cooking (cooking the meat in hot oil) with elements of moist-heat cooking (adding liquid to the meat and cooking it until tender).

Section 5.3 Activities

1. Students may choose from among a broad range of proteins. The cooking techniques they suggest must be compatible for the ingredient chosen, and the recipes they develop should be original, not plagiarized from another source.

2. Generally speaking, students should identify appropriate cooking methods for each item based on the item's size and degree of tenderness. They should be able to defend their answers.

3. Students should select one of these classic dishes and research its origins and ingredients, reporting their findings.

Section 5.3 Activities

1. Study Skills/Group Activity: Pick a Protein

Work with two other students to select a protein (not one used in the activity below), and identify three appropriate techniques for cooking it. For each technique, develop a recipe for the protein.

2. Activity: Cooking Methods

Which of the cooking methods discussed in the text are appropriate or inappropriate ways to cook the following items and why?

- Cod fillet
- Chicken thigh
- T-bone steak
- Chunks of lamb shoulder
- Duck breast

3. Critical Thinking: Combination Cooking

Several classical dishes, such as fricassées and daubes, are made with combination-cooking techniques. Select a dish from the braising or stewing categories on pp. 335–337, and write two paragraphs on its history, ingredients, and cooking method.

344

5.1 Foodservice Equipment	5.2 Getting Ready to Cook	5.3 Cooking Methods	5.4 Cooking and Nutrition
• Receiving and storage equipment	• *Mise en place*	• Heat transfer	• Healthy diets
• Pre-preparation equipment	• Knife basics	• Dry-heat cooking methods	• Dietary guidelines for Americans
• Food-preparation equipment	• Seasoning and flavoring	• Moist-heat cooking methods	• MyPyramid
• Holding and serving equipment	• Pre-preparation techniques	• Combination-cooking methods	• Nutrition labels
		• Other cooking methods	• The problem of obesity
		• Determining doneness	

SECTION 5.4 COOKING AND NUTRITION

Of course, cooking is all about providing a pleasurable experience for your customers. One of the critical factors in this experience is balancing wonderful food and nutrition. To accomplish this, you must understand what makes a healthy diet and what nutrients the body really needs.

Everyone has heard stories about the child who will only eat grilled-cheese sandwiches and tomato soup, or the toddler who only wants chicken nuggets, fries, and crackers. But as people grow up, their tastes expand.

Study Questions

After studying Section 5.4, you should be able to answer the following questions:

- What is a healthy diet?
- How can you use the Dietary Guidelines for Americans to plan meals?
- What is MyPyramid?
- What is a nutritional label, and how is it used?
- What is obesity, and how can it be prevented?

Healthy Diets

What is a healthy diet? According to the Dietary Guidelines for Americans, a healthy diet does the following:

- Emphasizes fruits, vegetables, whole grains, and fat-free or low-fat milk and milk products

345

Section 5.4
Cooking and Nutrition

Introduce the Section

a. Describe what makes a diet healthy and dietary guidelines for Americans.
b. Explain the federal government's role in public nutrition and dietary health.
c. Discuss the objectives for the section.

Vocabulary Review

a. Direct students to the key terms.
b. Pronounce each word, and have the students repeat the pronunciation out loud.
c. Discuss the definition of each word.

Teach

Discuss

- What makes a balanced diet? How does that differ from one person to another?
- How can gustatory pleasure be combined with proper nutrition? Does healthy food always have to taste bad?
- Why is the government involved in nutrition and public health? Should it be?

Reinforce and Review

- A healthy diet emphasizes produce and low-fat dairy and protein foods, while de-emphasizing saturated fats, trans fats, cholesterol, salt, and added sugars.

Homework Activity:
You Are What You Eat

Mathematics Connection, Literacy Connection, 21st-Century Skills—Use and Manage Information, Apply Technology Effectively, Work Independently

For three days, keep a log of everything you eat and drink. Track what it is, what ingredients it contains, and how much of it you eat. Use a conversion tool (available online and in book form) to determine how many calories you consume each day, as well as how many grams of protein, carbohydrate, and fat you eat.

Without doing any further research, do you think that this diet adequately met your nutritional needs for the three days? What do you think you could be doing better or worse? Were these three days representative of your normal eating habits, or was there a significant change in your diet?

Keep your results for reference later in the chapter.

Discuss

- Why do Dietary Reference Intakes provide nutrition guides for healthy people only? How does one's physical condition affect one's dietary needs?

Reinforce and Review

- Nutrition professionals teach people about and help them maintain a healthy diet using Dietary Reference Intakes as guides for nutrition and food selection.
- Two important Dietary Reference Intakes are the Recommended Daily Allowances and Adequate Intakes, both of which are established by the federal government.

Teaching Tips

- Obtain some sample DRIs. Ask students how much they think of a particular nutrient is required each day for an individual of a particular age and gender. Use the samples as part of a discussion on what populations need more or less of particular nutrients and why.

Nutrition:
Do You Need Everything Every Day?

Encourage students to discuss the following questions:

- Do most people eat too much to ensure that they receive enough nutrients, or for some other reason?
- Why is overnutrition expensive?
- Is it more important to eat the "right" foods or the right amount of food?

Vocabulary Terms

- **Dietary Reference Intake (DRI):** The recommended daily amount of nutrients and energy that healthy people of a particular age range and gender should consume.
- **Recommended Dietary Allowance (RDA):** The average daily intake that meets the nutrient requirements of nearly all healthy individuals of a particular age, gender, and physical group.
- **Adequate Intake (AI):** The average daily intake of a particular nutrient for a healthy person, assigned when insufficient scientific evidence is available to set an RDA.

- Includes lean meats, poultry, fish, beans, eggs, and nuts
- Is low in saturated fats, trans fats, cholesterol, salt (sodium), and added sugars

In the United States, nutrition professionals use standards and guidelines to teach people about and help them achieve a healthy diet. **Dietary Reference Intakes (DRIs)** are recommended daily amounts of nutrients and energy that healthy people of a particular age range and gender should consume. They are the guides for nutrition and food selection.

Two important Dietary Reference Intakes are Recommended Dietary Allowances (RDAs) and Adequate Intakes (AIs). **Recommended Dietary Allowances** are daily nutrient standards established by the U.S. government. They are the average daily intakes that meet the nutrient requirement of nearly all healthy individuals of a particular age and gender group. Different RDAs exist for men and women and for different age, height, and weight groups. The guidelines recommend specific amounts of protein, 11 vitamins, and 7 minerals. **Adequate Intakes** are similar to RDAs. They also identify daily intake levels for healthy people, but AIs are typically assigned when scientists don't have enough information to set an RDA.

[nutrition]

Do You Need Everything Every Day?

In nutrition, there are lots of nutrients to keep track of. Did I get enough pyridoxine (B_6) today? Have I eaten too much eicosanoic acid, a saturated fatty acid commonly found in peanut oil and butter? Will my body be able to handle the glucose load while I sleep? And what is my potassium status? Yikes! Too much to remember. Too many things to wonder over.

Relax! If you eat a varied diet in the United States, chances are you are doing fine. Vitamins and minerals are found in many foods. Include lots of fruits and vegetables and maybe a multivitamin in your diet, and you are probably covered. In fact, "overnutrition" is more of a problem in the United States than undernourishment.

Overnutrition usually means eating too many calories, too much sugar, and too much fat. This portioning aspect of nutrition needs daily attention. Every day you consume energy, and every day you burn energy. If you consume more than you burn, you will store the extra. You store extra energy as fat. Eating more than you use makes a body fat.

Rather than worrying about getting enough, plan to not get too much. Limit the number of high-fat and high-sugar foods you eat in a day. If you are gaining weight, you need to cut back. If you are losing weight, you could use a bit more.

Vegetarian Diets

People choose to eat vegetarian diets for many reasons:

- Religious beliefs
- Concern for the environment
- Economics
- Health considerations
- Animal-welfare factors
- Ethical considerations related to world hunger issues

A **vegetarian** is a person who consumes no meat, fish, or poultry products. There are different types of vegetarians:

- A **vegan** follows the strictest diet of all and will consume no dairy, eggs, meat, poultry, fish, or anything containing an animal product or byproduct, including honey. They consume only grains, legumes, vegetables, fruit, nuts, and seeds.
- A **lacto-vegetarian** consumes all the vegan items plus dairy products.
- An **ovo-vegetarian** consumes all vegan foods plus eggs.
- A **lacto-ovo-vegetarian** consumes all the vegan items plus dairy products and eggs.

A vegetarian diet can easily meet a person's nutrient requirements. Vegetarians need to eat a varied diet that includes enough calories to maintain weight. Vegetarians meet nutrient requirements by eating plant-based foods, such as fruits and vegetables, and beans, grains, nuts, and seeds. Most vegetarian diets have less fat, less cholesterol, and more fiber than a traditional American diet because they don't include meat in their diets.

Vegans need to be aware of their food choices. Because vegans do not eat any animal-based foods and there are no natural plant sources of vitamin B_{12}, vegans need to supplement their diet with a source of this vitamin. One option is to supplement their diets with multivitamin mineral supplements and include fortified and enriched foods. Vitamin B_{12} is key for good health. Nutritionists recommend a vegan diet rich in nuts, canola oil, flax, and other seeds and soy products to increase vegans' intake of fatty acids and linolenic acid.

Overall, a well-planned and carefully followed vegetarian diet can give a person the needed nutrients.

The wide availability of meat substitutes, including vegetable- and soy-based burgers, nondairy milk such as soy milk, and convenience vegetar-

347

Discuss

- Are any students in the class vegetarians or vegans? How might this affect their nutritional needs? How can it affect a teen's social life?
- Is following a healthy vegetarian or vegan diet more or less expensive than eating a diet that contains animal products? Is it more time-consuming?
- Does maintaining a vegetarian or vegan diet relate to environmental issues, such as climate change? What economic, societal, or environmental effects would result if the global population adopted a vegan diet?

Reinforce and Review

- People choose to eat vegetarian diets for a number of reasons, including religious and ethical beliefs, concern for the environment or for animals, economic factors, and health considerations.
- A vegetarian consumes no meat, fish, or poultry products. Subcategories include vegans, lacto-vegetarians, ovo-vegetarians, and lacto-ovo-vegetarians.
- Most vegetarian diets tend to be healthier than the traditional American diet, since plant-based foods can meet almost all nutritional requirements.
- Vegans must be careful to consume enough protein each day. Since there are no plant-based sources of vitamin B_{12}, which is essential for good health, taking a vitamin supplement is often encouraged.

Vocabulary Terms

- **Vegetarian:** A person who consumes no meat, fish, or poultry products.
- **Vegan:** A person who consumes (or uses) no animal products or byproducts.
- **Lacto-vegetarian:** A person who follows a vegan diet, with the addition of dairy products.
- **Ovo-vegetarian:** A person who follows a vegan diet, with the addition of eggs.
- **Lacto-ovo-vegetarian:** A person who follows a vegan diet, with the addition of dairy products and eggs.

Discuss

- Why might cultures from other parts of the world be more likely to emphasize vegetarian dishes and diets? Are these dishes inherently healthier or not? Encourage students to relate this to the U.S. "obesity epidemic."

Reinforce and Review

- Eighty percents of table-service restaurants offer vegetarian entrees to address changing consumer demands. Similarly, collegiate foodservice operations offer a variety of vegetarian options.
- The Dietary Guidelines for Americans 2005 presents dietary recommendations for healthy people and establishes the basis for federal food and nutrition programs.
- Updated every five years, the Dietary Guidelines for Americans reflect evolving scientific knowledge.

Teaching Tip

- Obtain copies of the Dietary Guidelines for Americans for student reference.

Vocabulary Terms

- **Dietary Guidelines for Americans 2005:** A report, jointly published by the USDA and the HHS, that suggests science-based advice about food choices to promote health and reduce risk for major chronic diseases.

ian entrées helps meet the needs of vegetarians. In addition, more ethnic foods are available that place emphasis on vegetarian dishes, such as Indian, African, Mexican, and Middle Eastern cuisines.

These products are also available to restaurant and foodservice menu planners. The National Restaurant Association reports that 80 percent of table-service restaurants offer vegetarian entrées to meet the needs of these consumers. Also, because many college students classify themselves as vegetarians, they are demanding such offerings from restaurant and dormitory foodservice operations at colleges.

Dietary Guidelines for Americans

The Dietary Guidelines for Americans 2005 is a document published jointly by the Department of Health and Human Services and the USDA. Figure 5.45 is a picture of the Dietary Guidelines for Americans 2005. This report offers science-based advice for healthy people over the age of two about food choices to promote health and reduce risk for major chronic diseases. Like the recommended dietary allowances, these dietary guidelines apply to diets eaten over several days, not to single food items or meals. These guidelines are updated every five years to reflect the latest Dietary Reference Intakes and other research. They also form the basis for federal food and nutrition programs. Table 5.3 highlights the key recommendations presented in the Dietary Guidelines for Americans 2005.

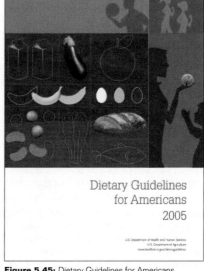

Figure 5.45: Dietary Guidelines for Americans.

Figure Focus

Figure 5.45: The USDA is the co-producer of the Dietary Guidelines for Americans. What else does it do?

[fast fact]

Did You Know...?
The Dietary Guidelines for Americans are periodically updated.

Table 5.3: Dietary Guidelines for Americans 2005

Adequate Nutrients within Calorie Needs	The human body requires more than 40 nutrients for good health. These nutrients should come from a variety of foods. One way to ensure variety is to choose foods each day from the five major food groups. Any food that supplies calories or nutrients can be part of a nutritious diet.
Weight Management	To maintain body weight in a healthy range, balance calories taken in with calories expended. People who are either overweight or underweight have increased chances of developing health problems. Being overweight is linked with shorter life expectancy, high blood pressure, heart disease, stroke, diabetes, certain cancers, and other types of illness. Being underweight is sometimes accompanied by malnutrition, eating disorders, and dehydration, and is linked to osteoporosis in women and a greater risk of early death in both women and men.
Physical Activity	Engage in regular physical activity and reduce sedentary activities to promote health, mental well-being, and a healthy body weight.
Fats	Limit intake of fat, saturated fat, and cholesterol. High levels of saturated fat and cholesterol in diets are linked to increased risk for heart disease. A diet lower in fat makes it easier to include the variety of foods needed for nutrients without exceeding calorie needs, because fat contains more than twice the calories of an equal amount of carbohydrate or protein. Here are some suggested limits for fats: • Total fat: An amount that provides less than 30 percent of total calories • Saturated fat: An amount that provides less than 10 percent of total calories • Cholesterol: Consume less than 300 mg per day; eating less fat from animal sources will help lower cholesterol (as well as total fat and saturated fat) in your diet These limits apply to the diet over several days, and not to a single meal or food. Some foods that contain fat, saturated fat, and cholesterol, such as meats, milk, cheese, and eggs, also contain high-quality protein and are excellent sources of certain vitamins and minerals.

continued

349

**Fast Fact:
Did You Know...?**

Why are the Dietary Guidelines for Americans updated frequently? Does scientific knowledge really change that quickly?

**Table 5.3:
Dietary Guidelines for Americans 2005 (continued on p. 350)**

- This document makes dietary recommendations for healthy people over the age of two. What specific health needs might specific individuals have that would affect their dietary needs?

- Why should fat consumption be limited?

- What factors are related to weight management besides the consumption of dietary fat?

**Homework Activity:
Fat City**

Science Connection, Literacy Connection, 21st-Century Skills—Information Literacy, Work Independently, Be Self-Directed Learners, Health Literacy

Fat has a bad reputation, but it is actually a nutrient that is required for your body to function properly.

Research the pros and cons of fat consumption. What health benefits does it offer? What are the effects of not consuming fat? On the other hand, how can consuming fat adversely affect your health? What problems can overconsumption cause?

Describe your findings in a one-page report.

Table 5.3 (continued)

- Why is it important to eat a variety of foods each day? Relate this to the discussion in Section 5.3 about the number of colors that should be on a plate.
- Why do students think that Americans consume so much dietary sodium?

Discuss

- Doughnuts, chocolate, mashed potatoes and gravy—even the healthiest eater will often have a dietary downfall. How can fatty or sugary foods fit within a healthy diet? How can recipes be altered to improve a dish's nutritional value?
- How do our emotions relate to our food choices? Are students familiar with terms like "stress eating" or "comfort eating"?
- Is it a restaurateur's responsibility to promote healthy food? What about the guest's personal responsibility?

Reinforce and Review

- Restaurants and other foodservice establishments can help their guests make healthier dietary choices by emphasizing plant foods and lean animal foods in their menus.
- Moderating the amounts of fat, sugar, and salt used to prepare dishes is another way foodservice operations can provide healthier choices to their guests.
- There are no bad food items. The key is moderating the intake of foods with lower nutritional value and replacing them with nutrient-rich choices.

Homework Activity: Potassium

Science Connection, Literacy Connection, 21st-Century Skills—Health Literacy, Information Literacy, Work Independently

What is potassium, and why is it important to the diet?

In what foods is it found? What effects might overconsumption and underconsumption of potassium have on the body?

Describe your findings in a one-page report.

Table 5.3: Dietary Guidelines for Americans 2005 *continued*

Food Groups to Encourage	Choose a variety of fruits and vegetables each day. Consume 2 cups of fruit and 2½ cups of vegetables per day. Consume 6-ounce equivalents of grains, with 3- or more ounce equivalents coming from whole grain products per day. Consume 3 cups per day of fat-free or low-fat milk or equivalent milk products. Children should also be encouraged to eat plenty of these foods. Eating suggested amounts of these foods will help increase carbohydrates and dietary fiber, and decrease fats in your diet.
Carbohydrates	Choose fiber-rich fruits, vegetables, and whole grains often. Use sugars in moderation. High-sugar foods supply calories and energy, but are limited in nutrients.
Sodium and Potassium	Consume less than 2300 mg (approximately 1 teaspoon) of sodium per day. Most people consume much more salt and sodium than they need, especially from packaged, canned, snack, and fast foods. Consume potassium-rich foods, such as fruits and vegetables.
Alcoholic Beverages	Drink in moderation, if at all—no more than one drink per day for women and no more than two drinks per day for men. People engaging in activities that require skill, attention, and coordination should not consume alcoholic beverages. Women who are pregnant, planning to become pregnant, or lactating; children; adolescents; and people with specific medical conditions should also avoid alcohol.

Restaurant and foodservice operations can help their customers meet dietary guidelines by providing menu items that focus on the kinds of food mentioned in the guidelines:

- Fruit
- Vegetables from each of the vegetable subgroups of dark green, orange, legumes, starchy vegetables, and other vegetables
- Whole grains
- Lean meat and fish
- Fat-free or low-fat milk and dairy products

The ways menu items are prepared can also support the dietary guidelines. The guidelines recommend minimizing and monitoring the amounts of fat, sugar, and sodium that food-preparation techniques add. When planning and preparing menu items, it is important to remember that while there are no bad food items, there are individual needs and limits. If a variety of nutritious items is on the menu, customers will be able to select menu items that meet their specific dietary needs.

350

Homework Activity: Considering Nutritional Value

Science Connection, Literacy Connection, 21st-Century Skills—Health Literacy, Information Literacy, Work Independently, Communicate Effectively

Select a favorite recipe and consider its nutritional value. How does it compare to the guidelines described in Table 5.3? Research individual ingredients as needed to determine their nutritional value.

What are some ways you could make this dish healthier?

Present a brief oral report to the class on your results.

MyPyramid

The USDA's MyPyramid food guide and the Nutrition Facts panel serve as tools to help people put dietary guidelines into practice. **MyPyramid** translates the RDAs and dietary guidelines into the kinds and amounts of food to eat each day. **Nutrition Facts** panels help people select the appropriate packaged food products to meet their nutritional needs.

Individual needs regarding food combinations and portions vary based on age, activity level, and gender. MyPyramid, a tool developed by the USDA, has two educational purposes:

- It teaches people how to eat a balanced diet from a variety of food groups without counting calories.

- It teaches people how to include physical activity in their daily lives and adjust food intake for the amount of activity.

MyPyramid replaces the 1992 Food Guide Pyramid and incorporates the recommendations of the Dietary Guidelines for Americans 2005. Figure 5.46 is a graphic of MyPyramid.

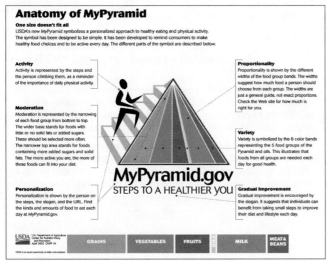

Figure 5.46: MyPyramid.

351

Discuss
- How can using MyPyramid help students and others make healthier lifestyle choices?
- How do the text and graphics associated with MyPyramid act as subtle marketing tools, calculated to appeal to younger Americans? Why might this be a goal?

Reinforce and Review
- The USDA also develops the MyPyramid food guide, which makes suggestions for specific food choices based on RDAs and other dietary guidelines, and the Nutrition Facts panels that describe the nutritional values of packaged foods.
- MyPyramid has two educational purposes: it teaches people to eat balanced diets without counting calories and it teaches people to incorporate physical activity into their daily lives.

Teaching Tips
- Use the MyPyramid Web site to start a discussion about its six themes and the roles they play in student lifestyles.

Vocabulary Terms
- **MyPyramid:** A customizable tool created by the USDA that translates RDAs and dietary guidelines into the kinds and amounts of food to eat each day, as well as the incorporation of physical activity.
- **Nutrition Facts:** An informational label that provides data about the nutritional value of packaged foods.

Figure Focus
Figure 5.46: Why is this information presented as a pyramid? What other shapes might also be good for conveying this data?

Homework Activity:
Evaluating the Self-Evaluation

Science Connection, Literacy Connection, 21st-Century Skills—Health Literacy, Information Literacy, Work Independently

Use MyPyramid to learn more about your specific dietary needs. Compare these to your three-day dietary records (p. 345). How are you doing? Are you on target to consume the appropriate amounts of each nutrient? Was your self-evaluation accurate? What could you be doing differently to maintain the best possible health?

Now you are ready for a bigger challenge. Using the Dietary Guidelines for Americans, track your performance in each of these categories for one week. Evaluate your performance. How similar are these results to your three-day log? Have you considered making any changes in your diet or exercise routine?

Why do you think activities like this might be worthwhile from time to time? Do you perceive any benefits from having this information, or does it seem unnecessary?

Discuss

- Which of the six MyPyramid themes do students perceive as most important and why?
- Is the notion of gradual improvement still relevant in the twenty-first century, when instant gratification is often perceived as a right?

Reinforce and Review

- The food groups represented in MyPyramid include grains, vegetables, fruits, milk and dairy products, and meat and beans. The category of fats and oils is shown, but is not considered its own food group.
- The discretionary calorie allowance is the amount of calories left over after nutritional needs have been satisfied that are available to "spend" on additional food consumption.
- MyPyramid has six key themes: proportionality, variety, physical activity, moderation, gradual improvement, and personalization.

In-Class Activity: Variations on a Theme

Literacy Connection, 21st-Century Skills—Health Literacy, Creativity and Innovation, Communication and Collaboration, Social and Cultural Skills

Working in groups of two or three, plan a creative way to illustrate one of the six MyPyramid themes.

Skits, songs, oral reports, videos, slide shows, posters, and artwork are some options available.

Vocabulary Terms

- **Discretionary calorie allowance:** The remaining amount of calories in a food intake pattern after accounting for the calories needed from all food groups.
- **Proportionality:** MyPyramid theme that suggests that people should include more servings of vegetables than fruit in their daily diets.
- **Variety:** MyPyramid theme that illustrates that food from all food groups is needed each day for god health.
- **Physical Activity:** MyPyramid theme that reminds people of the importance of daily physical motion.
- **Moderation:** MyPyramid theme that reminds people that no foods are bad, but that food items containing more added sugar and fat should represent fewer of an individual's food choices.

The food groups represented in MyPyramid are the following:

- Grains
- Vegetables
- Fruit
- Milk and dairy products
- Meat and beans

Fats and oils contain essential fatty acids and are also shown on MyPyramid, but are not considered a food group. There are calories allocated for these oils that are not part of the discretionary calorie allowance. The **discretionary calorie allowance** is the remaining amount of calories in a food intake pattern after accounting for the calories needed from all food groups. These calories should come from forms of food that are fat-free or low-fat and with no added sugars.

The MyPyramid symbol emphasizes six key themes:

1. **Proportionality:** The width of each colored band on the pyramid suggests how much food a person should choose from each food category. For example, the green band, which represents vegetables, is wider than the red band, which represents fruit. This suggests that people should include more servings of vegetables than fruit in their daily diets.

2. **Variety:** The color bands differentiate the six food categories representing the five food groups—grains, vegetables, fruit, milk, meat, and beans—plus fats and oils. This illustrates that food from all food groups is needed each day for good health.

3. **Physical activity:** In MyPyramid, a person's activity level is represented by the steps and the person climbing them. This is a reminder of the importance of daily physical activity. Nearly all Americans should be more active, because physical activity helps to maintain health.

4. **Moderation:** The narrowing of each food group from the bottom to the top represents moderation. The wider base represents food with little or no solid fats or added sugar. The USDA recommends choosing these food items more often. The narrower top represents food containing more added sugar and fat. The more active a person is, the more often these food items will fit his or her diet.

352

---

5. **Gradual improvement:** The MyPyramid slogan, "Steps to a Healthier You," suggests that people can benefit from taking small steps to improve their diet and lifestyle.

6. **Personalization:** The slogan, the person on the steps, and the Web site all suggest personalization of food intake. Caloric needs vary by age and activity level. Most older adults need less food, in part due to decreased activity. Individuals who are trying to lose weight and eat smaller amounts of food may need to select more nutrient-dense food to meet their nutrient needs.

For specific guidelines or recommendations, visit www.MyPyramid.gov.

Using MyPyramid for Menu Planning

Many suggestions for applying the dietary guidelines to menu planning also apply to using MyPyramid. There are three ways restaurant and foodservice professionals can use MyPyramid for specific guidance:

- **As a guide to the appropriate serving sizes for the various food groups:** Proportion the serving sizes as the pyramid is proportioned: very little oil, smaller amounts of meat, and more vegetables, fruit, and whole grains.

- **To evaluate portion sizes:** Evaluate the portion sizes offered by an operation in light of the serving sizes and number; revise them as needed, or expand current menu offerings with additional portion sizes.

- **To provide a more balanced menu:** Use MyPyramid as a quick guide to what constitutes a healthful diet, and plan menus that help customers get the most nutrition for their calories when eating at an establishment.

Restaurant and foodservice professionals can offer a variety of food items to cover all food groups, select lean meat, and reduce the amount of fats and oils used in cooking. By doing this, an operation can offer a wide variety of healthful meals that customers can enjoy in good conscience.

Figure 5.47 shows the MyPyramid food categories represented by each color and gives examples of daily recommendations for female and male adults ages 19 to 30.

353

Reinforce and Review

- Foodservice establishments can use MyPyramid as a guide to appropriate portion sizes for each food group as well as to evaluate their current menu choices and plan future dishes.
- Culinary professionals can offer a wide range of healthful meals without sacrificing flavor or quality.

Teaching Tips

- Encourage students to discuss what components of their diets they consider to be healthful.
- Consider asking the school nurse or a registered dietician to speak to the class about proper nutrition.

Vocabulary Terms

- **Gradual Improvement:** MyPyramid theme that suggests that people can benefit from taking small steps to improve their diet and lifestyle.
- **Personalization:** MyPyramid theme that illustrates the principle that all individuals have specific nutritional needs.

Science Connection, Literacy Connection, 21st-Century Skills—Health Literacy, Creativity and Innovation, Communication and Collaboration, Social and Cultural Skills

Using the MyPyramid recommendations, plan three days of meals that are appropriate for your age and activity level.

How difficult would it be to follow this plan? How different is it from your normal diet, both in foods eaten and amounts of food consumed?

Consider following this plan for three days. Do you think your body would feel any different? What changes might you expect?

CUSTOMIZED INSTRUCTION

Science Connection, Literacy Connection, 21st-Century Skills—Health Literacy, Communication and Collaboration, Social and Cultural Skills

Special Needs Students

What are some of your favorite foods? What health benefits does each provide? How can each one be part of a balanced diet?

Discuss your answers in a small group.

MyPyramid Food Categories

Grains	Vegetables	Fruits	Oils	Milk	Meat and Beans
Examples of Food					
Bread	Dark green vegetables	Apricots	Vegetable oil	Milk	Meat
Cereal	Orange vegetables	Apples	Animal fats	Cheese	Fish
Rice	Starchy vegetables	Bananas	Nuts	Yogurt	Fowl
Pasta	Dry beans and peas	Grapes	Olives	Ice cream	Eggs
	Other vegetables	Raisins	Avocados	Cottage cheese	Dry beans and peas
					Nuts and seeds
Daily Recommendations for females (F) and males (M), ages 19 to 30					
F 6 ounces	**F** 2½ cups	**F** 2 cups	**F** 6 teaspoons	**F** 3 cups	**F** 5½ ounces
M 8 ounces	**M** 3 cups	**M** 2 cups	**M** 7 teaspoons	**M** 3 cups	**M** 6½ ounces
At least one-half of the servings should be whole grain.	Eat more dark green and orange vegetables and dry beans and peas.	Eat a variety. Choose fresh, frozen, canned, or dried fruit. Limit daily intake of fruit juices.	Make most of fat sources from fish, nuts, and vegetable oils. Select fats with zero trans fat. Limit solid fats.	Choose low-fat or fat-free milk products.	Select lean or low-fat meat and poultry. Select fish high in omega-3 fatty acids more often.
Serving Equivalents					
One ounce equivalent:	**One cup equivalent:**	**One cup equivalent:**	**One teaspoon equivalent:**	**One cup equivalent:**	**One ounce equivalent:**
1 slice bread	1 cup cooked or raw vegetables	1 cup fruit	1 teaspoon oil, liquid or solid	1 cup milk or yogurt	1 ounce meat, fish, or poultry
1 cup cereal	2 cups leafy greens	½ cup dried fruit	Some food, such as peanut butter, counts toward oil servings. Refer to the MyPyramid Web site on how to count oils.	1½ ounces natural cheese	¼ cup cooked dry beans or peas
½ cup cooked rice or pasta				2 ounces processed cheese	1 egg
					1 tablespoon peanut butter
					½ ounce nuts or seeds

Adapted from the U.S. Department of Agriculture's MyPyramid

Figure 5.47: Daily recommendation for females and males ages 19 to 30.

Figure Focus

Figure 5.47: Do these serving sizes seem like an appropriate amount of food in a given day? Why or why not?

Registered Dietitian

Registered dietitians plan healthy meals and menus for individuals and restaurant or foodservice operations. Their educational route includes college, required internships, and often graduate programs in the biochemistry of food and human physiology. They must also pass a national registration exam, meet state licensure requirements, and complete 75 hours of continuing education training every five years to remain an RD.

Originally, they were employed by hospitals to help doctors feed patients with dietary restrictions. Their role has expanded into consumer information, preventive medicine, and professional menu planning to meet specific nutrition goals. In hospitals, they still treat nutrition-based disorders, especially since more illnesses seem to be tied to nutrition. Restaurateurs can find consulting dietitians who perform recipe analysis, menu planning, and nutrition guidance. This is especially important (and often required) for the food-services operations of nursing homes, retirement centers, colleges, and schools.

Local listings and the local chapter of the American Dietetic Association are excellent places to start looking for a licensed registered dietitian: www.eatright.org

Nutrition Labels

The Nutrition Facts panel can be a useful tool in selecting food for a healthy diet. In addition, learning how to read and use nutrition information can help people for a number of reasons:

- Avoid food allergens
- Plan special diets
- Limit fat, sodium, cholesterol, or calories
- Identify food items that are good sources of vitamins, minerals, and other nutrients such as fiber

Each nutrient on the panel is reported as a percentage of Daily Values (DV). The DVs are provided in percentages based on a 2,000-calorie diet. Providing percentages of DV on the panel helps people see how different types of food contribute to their overall daily diets. It is important to remember that because there is no bad food, people can use the nutritional information listed on food labels to make healthy diet choices. Figure 5.48 is an example of a nutrition facts label.

Nutrition Facts

Serving Size 1 Cake (43g)
Servings Per Container 5

Amount Per Serving

Calories 200 Calories from Fat 90

	% Daily Value*
Total Fat 10g	15%
Saturated Fat 5g	25%
Trans Fat 0g	
Cholesterol 0mg	0%
Sodium 100mg	4%
Total Carbohydrate 26g	9%
Dietary Fiber 0g	0%
Sugars 19g	
Protein 1g	

Vitamin A 0%	•	Vitamin C 0%
Calcium 0%	•	Iron 2%

* Percent Daily Values are based on a 2,000 calorie diet. Your daily values may be higher or lower depending on your calorie needs:

	Calories:	2,000	2,500
Total Fat	Less than	65g	80g
Sat. Fat	Less than	20g	25g
Cholesterol	Less than	300mg	300mg
Sodium	Less than	2,400mg	2,400mg
Total Carbohydrate		300g	375g
Dietary Fiber		25g	30g

Figure 5.48: Nutrition facts label.

355

Figure Focus

Figure 5.48: Based on student knowledge, what health benefits does this food confer?

On the Job: Registered Dietitian

Encourage students to discuss the following:

- Why is the work of registered dietitian important to public and individual health?
- Why must registered dietitians continue their education throughout their careers?
- For what reasons might a foodservice establishment choose to hire a registered dietitian?

Discuss

- Why are some food items, such as fresh meats and vegetables, not required to bear nutritional information?
- How can nutritional data be used as part of a marketing campaign? For what types of foods and for what demographic groups might this be particularly successful?

Reinforce and Review

- The Nutrition Facts panel, found on packaged foods, helps consumers make healthy food choices, both in selecting a food item and in determining how much of that item to consume each day.
- Among other things, nutritional information can help consumers avoid food allergens, plan diets, limit cholesterol intake, and identify good sources of nutrients.
- Daily Values (DVs) of various nutrients are reported as percentages based on a 2,000-calorie diet. Providing this information on food labels helps people identify ways in which consuming particular foods affects their daily diets.

Teaching Tips

- Using Figure 5.48 as an example, encourage students to identify how frequently or infrequently a given food should be consumed, based on its Nutrition Facts panel.

In-Class Activity: Reading the Label

Science Connection, Literacy Connection, 21st-Century Skills—Health Literacy, Analyze Media, Make Judgments and Decisions

Bring a Nutrition Facts label from some packaged food to class. Be careful to clip out only the panel itself, omitting any other packaging material that could give others a clue to the food that was in the package.

Exchange the panels with other students. Consider the information on the panel you receive and use it to determine whether you think the food should be consumed frequently, in moderation, or rarely.

Write a one-paragraph summary of your results, defending your assessment. Be sure to append the label.

Reinforce and Review

- The Food and Drug Administration requires a Nutrition Facts panel to contain certain nutrient information that is linked to current health concerns, listed in order of current priority.
- Information about the serving size of a particular food and the number of servings a package contains provides the basis for reporting that food's nutrient content.
- Nutrition Facts panels contain data about a food's fat content: the number of calories from fat per serving, the total grams of fat per serving, and the number of grams of saturated fat per serving.
- Dietary fiber is associated with decreasing cholesterol and facilitating food transport through the digestive tract.

Vocabulary Terms

- **Serving size:** The amount of food customarily eaten at one time for each food category.
- **Servings per container:** The number of servings contained within each package of food.
- **Total calories:** The caloric content of one serving.
- **Calories from fat:** The number of calories from fat in a single serving.
- **Total fat:** The total grams of fat in one serving.
- **Saturated fat:** The number of grams of saturated fat in one serving.
- **Trans fat:** Trans fatty acid, which has been shown to have a negative effect on cholesterol and heart health.
- **Cholesterol:** A waxy substance found in animal foods, used to build cell membranes; an elevated cholesterol level is related to coronary heart disease.
- **Sodium:** An essential element in the human diet, but too much can increase the risk of stroke or heart disease.
- **Total carbohydrate:** The total number of grams of carbohydrate, including dietary fiber and sugars.
- **Dietary fiber:** A complex carbohydrate associated with decreasing cholesterol and facilitating digestion.
- **Sugar:** A simple carbohydrate, more quickly used as an energy source than a complex carbohydrate.
- **Protein:** One of three main sources of energy, or calories, necessary for regulating and maintaining cells, organs, and tissues.
- **Vitamin A:** A vitamin that plays a significant role in vision.
- **Vitamin C:** A vitamin that plays a significant role as an antioxidant and in preventing certain diseases.
- **Calcium:** A mineral that plays a significant role in bone strength and development.
- **Iron:** A mineral that plays a significant role in oxygen storage and transport.

The FDA requires a nutrition facts panel to contain certain nutrient information because these nutrients address current health concerns. The order in which the nutrients must appear reflects the current priority of dietary recommendations. The mandatory components are as follows:

- **Serving size and servings per container:** The serving size is the basis for reporting each food's nutrient content and is defined as the amount of food customarily eaten at one time for each food category. The servings per container reflect how many servings are contained within the package. The size of the serving on the food package influences the number of calories and all the nutrient amounts listed on the top part of the label.
- **Total calories and calories from fat:** Caloric content of one serving, as well as the number of calories from fat in a single serving are listed.
- **Total fat and saturated fat:** Total grams of fat in one serving and the number of grams of saturated fat in one serving (included in grams of total fat per serving) are listed.
- **Trans fat:** All labels must list grams of trans fatty acid, also called trans fat, which has been shown to have a negative effect on cholesterol and heart health. Like the other fats, the amount of trans fat is listed as the number of grams in one serving.
- **Cholesterol:** Cholesterol is listed in milligrams, and the percentage of daily values is based not on calories, but on a daily recommendation of 300 milligrams or less.
- **Sodium:** Sodium is listed in milligrams with a percentage of daily values based on a daily recommendation of 2,400 milligrams or less. Figure 5.49 is an example of sodium percentages.
- **Total carbohydrate, dietary fiber, and sugars:** Dietary fiber and sugars are included in a food's total carbohydrate content. The percentage of dietary fiber is based on a daily recommendation of 25 grams. This has been associated with decreasing cholesterol and aiding in food transport through the digestive tract.
- **Protein:** The total grams of protein in one serving are listed.
- **Vitamin A, vitamin C, calcium, and iron:** The FDA requires the label to list vitamins A and C and the minerals calcium and

1/4 teaspoon salt = 575 mg sodium
1/2 teaspoon salt = 1,150 mg sodium
3/4 teaspoon salt = 1,725 mg sodium
1 teaspoon salt = 2,300 mg sodium
1 teaspoon baking = 1000 mg sodium soda

Figure 5.49: Sodium percentages.

Figure Focus

Figure 5.49: Baking soda is known as sodium bicarbonate, but it's not a salt.

iron because of their connection to health conditions like osteoporosis and anemia.

The Problem of Obesity

Overweight and obesity are health problems that individuals can overcome with an improved diet. A person who is overweight or **obese** has a weight that is greater than what is generally considered healthy. These terms also identify ranges of weight that have been shown to increase the likelihood of certain diseases and other health problems.

Teen and childhood obesity continues to grow at an alarming rate. According to the U.S. Centers for Disease Control and Prevention (CDC), about 16 percent of U.S. children and teens, aged 6 to 19, are obese.

Overweight and obesity ranges are determined by using weight and height to calculate a number called the body mass index (BMI). BMI is used because, for most people, it correlates with their amount of body fat. It is important to remember that although BMI correlates with the amount of body fat, it does not directly measure body fat. As a result, some people, such as athletes, may have a BMI that identifies them as overweight even though they do not have excess body fat. Figure 5.50 demonstrates how to compute BMI.

BMI can be calculated by:

$$BMI = \frac{weight \ in \ pounds \times 703}{height \ in \ inches^2}$$

Interpreting BMI:

Below 18.5...Underweight
18.5-24.9...Normal
25.0-29.9...Overweight
30 and above...Obese

BMI CALCULATOR

$$BMI = \frac{weight \ in \ pounds \times 703}{height \ in \ inches^2}$$

Below 18.5 - Underweight
18.5-24.9 - Normal
25.0-29.9 - Overweight
30 and above - Obese

Figure 5.50: How to calculate BMI.

According to the CDC, the following percentages of U.S. adults are overweight or obese:

- An estimated 65 percent of U.S. adults aged 20 years and older are either overweight or obese.

- An estimated 30 percent of U.S. adults aged 20 years and older, over 60 million people, are obese.

357

Figure Focus
Figure 5.50: Why is it important to know how to calculate one's BMI?

Reinforce and Review

- Overweight and obesity are health problems that can be resolved by improving one's diet. These terms also refer to ranges of weight associated with certain diseases and health conditions.

- About 16 percent of U.S. children and teens are obese, as are about 30 percent of U.S. adults. Accordingly, obesity is considered an epidemic.

- One's body mass index (BMI) is used to determine whether or not someone is overweight or obese, although BMI does not directly measure body fat.

- Being underweight is also a serious health problem, although it is less likely an occurrence in the United States than either overweight or obesity.

In-Class Activity: BMI Examples

Mathematics Connection, Science Connection, Literacy Connection, 21st-Century Skills—Health Literacy, Solve Problems, Produce Results

Where do you think you fit on the BMI scale? Calculate your own BMI and determine which category you fall into. Do you think that this accurately depicts you, or do you think other factors (such as greater than usual bone or muscle mass) might affect your score?

Now calculate the following BMIs: 5' 2", 100 pounds; 5' 10", 150 pounds; 5' 8", 200 pounds; and 6' 2", 250 pounds. Which of these belong in which BMI range?

Homework Activity: Trans Fatty Acids

Science Connection, Literacy Connection, 21st-Century Connection—Health Literacy, Information Literacy, Work Independently

What exactly is a "trans fat," or "trans fatty acid"? What is its role in the body? What positive and negative effects does it have on human health?

In what foods are trans fats usually found? How have these been spotlighted in discussions of public health?

Discuss these answers and anything else you think relevant in a one-page report.

Vocabulary Terms

- **Obesity:** A medical condition associated with lowered life expectancy and increased likelihood of major health problems.

Discuss

- Encourage students to discuss which of the causes of obesity might be more and less easy to resolve.
- Compare the information learned in Chapter 4 to the information learned in Chapter 5. Ask students to describe which chapter they perceive is more important to them and why.

Reinforce and Review

- The causes of obesity are interrelated and may include poverty and food insecurity, family history, lack of physical activity, and excessive caloric intake.
- The number of calories a person consumes should match the calories he or she needs in order to maintain his or her lifestyle.

In-Class Activity: Fighting the Good Fight
Science Connection, Literacy Connection, 21st-Century Connection—Health Literacy, Creativity and Innovation, Communication and Collaboration, Social and Cultural Skills, Analyze Media
Working in small groups, design a campaign to fight obesity, aiming it at children, teens, or adults. What is your core message? What types of media will be most effective at spreading this message? What are some ways to attract attention to your campaign?

Summary

- Remind students to review the following:
  1. What defines a healthy diet
  2. Using the Dietary Guidelines for Americans to plan meals
  3. MyPyramid
  4. Nutritional labels and how to use them
  5. Obesity and how it can be prevented

Several causes of obesity are known. It typically occurs because of a combination of these factors:

- **Poverty and food insecurity**: Psychological food issues may develop after any period of extreme hunger or starvation.
- **Family history**: Children of obese adults have a greater chance of becoming overweight or obese themselves. Reasons include genetics and family lifestyle.
- **Lack of physical activity**: Lack of physical activity in today's U.S. lifestyle also contributes to obesity because the excess calories consumed are not burned off. Today's activity levels have declined, but the human body's capabilities and needs have not changed.
- **Excessive caloric intake for their needs**: Some reasons for eating too much might include lack of nutrition knowledge, large portion sizes, emotional reasons, or enjoyment of food.

Obesity is the result of many connected factors. These factors must be managed so that the number of calories a person consumes matches the calories that person needs for his or her lifestyle. Generally, this means that people must reduce their caloric intake or increase their amount of physical activity, or both. Keeping these two balanced and part of a daily routine can help most individuals achieve weight control.

Summary

In this section, you learned the following:

- A healthy diet emphasizes fruits, vegetables, whole grains, and fat-free or low-fat milk and milk products. It includes lean meats, poultry, fish, beans, eggs, and nuts. And it is low in saturated fats, trans fats, cholesterol, salt, and added sugars.
- The Dietary Guidelines for Americans offer advice for healthy people over the age of two about food choices to promote health and reduce risk for major chronic diseases.
- MyPyramid teaches people how to eat a balanced diet from a variety of food groups without counting calories, how to include physical activity in their daily lives, and how to adjust food intake for the amount of activity.
- A nutritional label is useful in selecting food for a healthy diet. Nutrition labels are required to have serving size, servings per container, and total calories. They also list calories from fat, total fat and saturated fat, trans fat, cholesterol, sodium, total carbohydrates, total dietary fiber, total sugar, protein, vitamin A, vitamin C, calcium, and iron.
- Obesity is considered a major health problem. It can be prevented by eating a healthy diet, exercising, and eating fewer calories.

358

Section 5.4 Review Questions

1. Describe the key recommendations in the 2005 Dietary Guidelines for Americans.

2. Why is obesity a major health problem?

3. List the components required on nutritional labels.

4. What are the different types of vegetarian diets?

5. Why, as Benny Gordon states, is nutrition the "foundation of life?"

6. Are certain cooking techniques considered "healthier" than others? Provide an example and explain.

7. What can be done by food establishments to address the problem of obesity?

8. There is a lot of information available about MyPyramid. Use the material to design your own ideal nutrition program.

359

Section 5.4 Review Questions

1. The Dietary Guidelines for Americans 2005 recommends that healthy people over the age of two obtain adequate nutrients within calorie needs; balance calories consumed with calories expended to maintain a healthy weight; engage in regular physical activity and limit sedentary activity; limit intake of fat, saturated fat, and cholesterol; consume a variety of fruits and vegetables each day; choose fiber-rich foods, limiting sugar intake; consume under 2,300 mg of sodium daily; and drink alcohol in moderation, if at all.

2. Obesity is a major health problem because it increases the likelihood of certain diseases and other health problems.

3. The components required on nutritional labels are as follows: serving size and servings per container; total calories and calories from fat; total fat and saturated fat; trans fat; cholesterol; sodium; total carbohydrate, dietary fiber, and sugars; protein; and vitamin A, vitamin C, calcium, and iron.

4. Different types of vegetarian diets include vegetarian, vegan, lacto-vegetarian, ovo-vegetarian, and lacto-ovo-vegetarian.

5. Students should discuss the importance of proper nutrition, both from a consumer's perspective and from the perspective of a culinary professional caring for guests.

6. Students should identify a cooking technique that they consider to be healthy and explain why this is so. Any cooking technique can be selected, as long as the student provides a clear and logical argument in its defense.

7. Students can answer in a variety of ways. Some typical answers might include posting nutritional information about each dish, serving smaller portions, including more vegetables in each dish, using fewer fats and saturated fats when preparing food, and eliminating the use of trans fats.

8. Students should use MyPyramid to design a customized nutrition program.

Section 5.4 Activities

1. Students should research the selected diet to ensure that proposed menu options will provide adequate protein and iron.

2. Students may select whatever foods they choose so long as they provide accurate information about the foods' nutritional values.

3. The World Health Organization works globally to resolve nutritional deficiencies and other issues in malnutrition, including obesity, under the auspices of the United Nations. Students should research its programs in order to complete this activity.

Section 5.4 Activities

1. Study Skills/Group Activity: Vegetarian Menu

Work with two other students to develop a vegetarian menu that provides adequate protein and iron. Choose lacto-vegetarian, ovo-vegetarian, lacto-ovo-vegetarian, or vegan.

2. Activity: Database Research

Pick three foods. Research online databases to determine the nutrient content of these foods, including the amount of protein a person would receive and the number of calories from fat.

3. Critical Thinking: WHO?

What is the role of the World Health Organization (WHO) in nutrition? What are its services? How does it deliver its services?

Case Study Follow-Up | *Working in the Kitchen*

At the beginning of the chapter, Alex was beginning his training on kitchen equipment and cooking techniques.

1. Why did Chef Jean train Alex on professionalism before teaching him about kitchen equipment and cooking techniques?

2. Alex is working as a prep cook, and the kitchen employs skilled stewards and dishwashers. Why is it important for him to know how to care for and maintain kitchen equipment?

3. How will Alex's slowly improving math skills be used in his daily *mise en place*?

4. How much responsibility should a young cook like Alex be given in a professional kitchen?

361

Case Study Follow-Up

1. Professionalism, how one behaves toward oneself and toward others, is of fundamental importance in the foodservice industry, where all actions are directed toward providing the best possible guest service. If Alex can't learn to behave as a professional, then his other culinary skills won't matter.

2. Alex, like all culinary professionals, should know and understand the equipment used in the kitchen. For one thing, an emergency or sickness might require him to wash dishes or repair equipment. For another, if Alex comes to own his own establishment, he will need to know how to care for and maintain the equipment.

3. Each day, Alex will use math to determine how much of each ingredient to prepare for service, to follow or convert a recipe, or to prepare a time line.

4. Depending on their skill levels and character, cooks—even newer ones like Alex—should be given as much responsibility as is consistent with the kitchen's overall goals. Although Chef Jean and Linda will still oversee his activities, the more responsibilities Alex has, the more he will learn, both about himself and about the industry.

Apply Your Learning

Crack Some Eggs

Students should accurately perform the measurements and mathematic operations for this activity. This is also an opportunity to ensure that students understand the different stages in whipping separated eggs.

Time Line for Making a Reuben Panini

Students should consider all the ingredients used to create this dish. The time line for making a Reuben Panini should include every aspect of production, including curing the pastrami and slicing the potatoes for chips. Student responses may vary so long as the answers are consistent with producing the dish accurately.

Maillard Reaction

Students should research the Maillard Reaction and its role in dry-heat cooking methods. By cooking the chicken breasts in two different ways, they will have the opportunity to observe the characteristic browning found in dry-heat cookery. Student responses should include both what they learned from researching the Maillard reaction and their direct observations of the cooking chicken.

Apply Your Learning

Crack Some Eggs

Crack six eggs, separating the whites from the yolks. Measure the volume and weight of the six whites and the six yolks. What is the ratio between the volume of the whites and the yolks? What about the weight?

Then whip the whites, first to soft peaks, then to medium peaks, and then to stiff peaks. At each stage, measure the volume of the whipped whites. By what percentage has the volume increased at each stage? Next, whip the yolks until they are pale yellow and fluffy. Measure the volume. By what percentage has this increased over the original unwhipped volume? What is the ratio between the soft-peak whites and the whipped yolks; between the medium-peak whites and the yolks; and the stiff-peak whites and the yolks?

Time Line for Making a Reuben Panini

A popular menu item at your casual-dining restaurant is a Reuben panini: house-cured pastrami sliced thinly and piled onto rye bread, and then topped with Swiss cheese, house-made sauerkraut, and Russian dressing, before being pressed in a panini machine and served hot with freshly fried potato chips. What components of this dish can be made ahead? Write a time line for making this dish, along with lists of the ingredients and equipment you will need.

Maillard Reaction

Think about a steaming chunk of chicken in your favorite soup recipe. Now think about a piece of grilled chicken with perfect crosshatching. Both are delicious, but the flavors are very different. Why?

When certain foods containing both amino acids and sugars are cooked with dry-heat methods, a browning reaction occurs, resulting in savory, complex flavors and aromas. This is known as the Maillard reaction. The grilled chicken is affected by the Maillard reaction, but the chicken in the soup is not (unless, of course, the chicken was treated to a dry-heat cooking method before being added to the soup).

Research the Maillard reaction, and then cook two chicken breasts, one by a dry-heat method and one by a moist-heat method. What have you learned? Write three paragraphs on your findings.

362

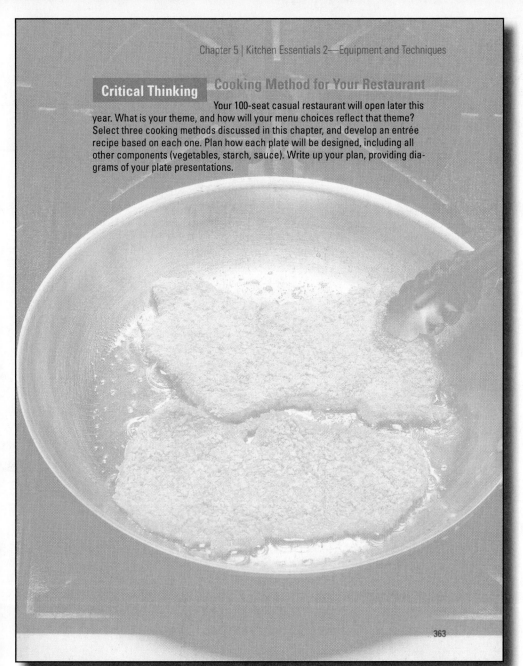

Critical Thinking Cooking Method for Your Restaurant

Your 100-seat casual restaurant will open later this year. What is your theme, and how will your menu choices reflect that theme? Select three cooking methods discussed in this chapter, and develop an entrée recipe based on each one. Plan how each plate will be designed, including all other components (vegetables, starch, sauce). Write up your plan, providing diagrams of your plate presentations.

363

Critical Thinking # Cooking Method for Your Restaurant

Students have wide latitude in completing this activity, but the Cooking Method for Your Restaurant and entrées selected should reinforce the restaurant's theme. Recipes and plate designs should be original. The plate diagrams may be simple or elaborate, but they should reflect the principles discussed on pp. 340–341.

Exam Prep Answers

1. B
2. A
3. D
4. B
5. B
6. B
7. B
8. D
9. B
10. A

Exam Prep Questions

1. A mandoline is used to
   A. hone knives.
   B. slice precisely.
   C. sharpen knives.
   D. make a turned cut.

2. A paring knife with a curved blade that makes cutting rounded surfaces easier is known as a(n)
   A. tourné.
   B. scimitar.
   C. chef's knife.
   D. boning knife.

3. A sautoir is a pan with
   A. straight sides and a long handle.
   B. high, sloped sides and no handle.
   C. the shape of a stockpot, but no handles.
   D. a wide, shallow bottom and a long handle.

4. What is the meaning of the French term *mise en place*?
   A. To work smart
   B. To put in place
   C. To listen carefully
   D. To place on a dish or plate

5. The leaves, stems, or flowers of an aromatic plant are
   A. spices.
   B. herbs.
   C. flavors.
   D. seasonings.

6. The cooking method that cooks food quickly, often uncovered, in a very small amount of fat over high heat is
   A. stewing.
   B. sautéing.
   C. pan-frying.
   D. simmering.

7. Poaching requires a cooking temperature of
   A. 200°F–210°F.
   B. 160°F–180°F.
   C. 250°F–260°F.
   D. 300°F–310°F.

8. The transfer of heat from one item to another when the items come into direct contact with each other is known as
   A. radiation.
   B. *sous vide*.
   C. convection.
   D. conduction.

9 Which cooking method requires longer cooking times and is most often used with large cuts of meat or poultry?

A. Grilling

B. Roasting

C. Poaching

D. Pan-frying

10 A braised dish usually made with red meat and vegetables that includes red wine and seasoning is called

A. daube.

B. *sous vide*.

C. *estouffade*.

D. pot roasting.

365

Chapter 6 Overview

Chapter 6 presents the preparation, selection, and uses of stocks, sauces, and soups.

Section 1: The first section describes how to make, use, and store stocks.

Section 2: This section presents the five grand sauces and their derivative sauces. The sauces are discussed with their culinary uses and applications.

Section 3: The final section discusses soups as menu items, as main dishes or accompaniments, and on lunch and dinner menus.

Advance Preparation	
Review	Review material in Sections 6.1–6.3
	Relevant material in previous chapters
Contact	Computer lab for Internet
	Cooking classroom if it is not your home classroom
	Local restaurants and foodservice operations, as needed
Prepare	Paper (students may provide their own)
	Photos of clear and thick soup examples for ESOL students
	Bulletin board, poster board, or long paper tape for activity
	Two colors of index cards
	8 lb or more of bones to prepare stock
	Eggs, lemon juice, and onion for making a raft
	Carrots, celery, and onion for making mirepoix
	Flour and butter for roux
	Butter and seasonings for compound butter
	Waxed paper or plastic wrap
	Ingredients for a soup or sauce of your choice (fish stock, velouté and clam chowder recipes at the end of the chapter)

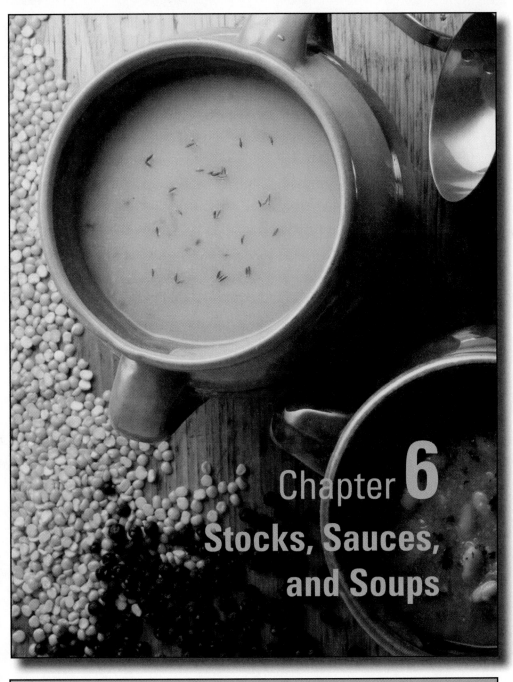

Chapter 6
Stocks, Sauces, and Soups

CUSTOMIZED INSTRUCTION OPTIONS

Less Advanced Students	More Advanced Students	ESOL Students	Special Needs Students
Pages 370, 394	Pages 370, 394	Pages 370, 394	Pages 370, 394

CHAPTER TOOLS

21st-Century Skills	Mathematics	Science	Literacy
Pages 370, 384, 387	Pages 370, 384	Page 376	Page 384

ServSafe Connection

Pages 383, 401

Case Study · *Want to Do Lunch?*

Uptown Grille has been open for dinner for two years. Linda thinks that if they offer a lunch menu, they might attract new clientele—people who might be hesitant to try them out for dinner, given their trendy, upscale reputation.

Linda has conducted research on the local lunch market and knows that there is an audience for this service—individuals, local volunteer groups, and business people. In addition, she has canvassed their "regulars" to see what might be an appealing menu format. Most were enthusiastic about the plan, suggesting that she offer a menu that draws attention to their fine dining, yet is relatively affordable.

Uptown Grille started to offer lunch in March on Wednesdays through Saturdays. Linda and Chef Jean have created a limited, yet reasonably priced menu, focusing on fine soups and assorted companion dishes, such as appetizers, breads, and seasonal salads. The five daily soups range from organic, low-fat vegetable to cream of asparagus to bouillabaisse. The appetizers are varied. Some include fish, some include meat, some are vegetarian. The salad dressings for the various salads range from oil and vinegar to spicy sesame. All in all, Linda thinks there is something for everyone.

Now, it is May...two months later. After an initial spurt, business has slowed down. The customers have mostly responded positively to the quality and flavor of the food, the service, and the prices. Linda is not sure why they aren't doing better.

As you read this chapter, think about the following questions:

1. What problems might Uptown Grille face with the menu selection?
2. What can Linda do to retain and bring in new customers?
3. Other than the menu, service, and price, what do you think might impact the volume of business?

Case Study
Want to Do Lunch?

- Is the restaurant conveniently located for a quick business lunch? Is there adequate parking? Is it possible to keep prices low enough to compete for lunch business while still offering fine dining? Are guests coming in for daily fare, or only when they have clients or a meeting? Is there outside seating in nice weather? What other considerations will the students in your class consider?

- Ask students to brainstorm in class. Issues that might be addressed include seasonal items in the spring and summer.

- The issues discussed in the first item might impact the business. Do guests like to eat lunch outdoors in good weather? Perhaps they need a take-out or delivery service for working folks.

- The case study represents real restaurant situations.

- How would the restaurant prepare these lunch options?

- What other menu items might attract lunchtime traffic?

- Ask students how they plan to draw customers when they have their own restaurants.

- How would the restaurant prepare these lunch options?

- What other menu items might attract lunchtime traffic?

Professional Profile

Discuss	How does Chef Sonnenschmidt's story about his youth affect you? Would you expect to be able to keep a job if you dissolved the stove? What sort of on-the-job behavior would you recommend for an apprentice?
Reinforce and Review	Discuss why you think cooking can be viewed as an art, a science, and a way of sharing.
Teaching Tips	Chef Sonnenschmidt emphasizes the 12 basic culinary skills. Discuss the basic skills that you consider most important.

Focus and Engage

Discuss

- Let the students know that soups are an integral part of cuisine the world over.
- The students may be aware that soups are a versatile and economical way to provide a main dish.
- Perhaps the students realize that soups are considered "comfort foods."
- Emphasize that finely made stocks, soups, and sauces demonstrate culinary skill.

[professional profile]

Frederic ("Fritz") H. Sonnenschmidt CMC, AAC, HOF

Certified Master Chef, Teacher, Author, TV Personality

❝ Cooking and baking is an art, a science, and a way of sharing. **❞**

I was always fascinated by the culinary arts. In 1947, a cook in the U.S. Army, which was using my school for a field kitchen, introduced me to the exciting possibilities of the cooking profession. I was 11 years old.

I started my career with an apprenticeship in Munich, Germany. After that, I had extensive experiences in hotel kitchens, including Executive Chef at the Sheraton Hotel in New York City. I became a teacher at the Culinary Institute of America in 1968, and retired from the institute as Culinary Dean in 2002.

By the way, in 2004, Chef Fritz was inducted into the American Academy of Chefs Culinary Hall of Fame, and he received a Lifetime Achievement Award from the Academy in 2007.

I believe in cooking using the 12 basic culinary fundamentals, focusing on their use in classical, modern, regional, global, eclectic, molecular, and fusion cuisine. When in doubt, fall back on these—they will save you!

For those of you interested in pursuing culinary arts, let me tell you a little story. When I started my apprenticeship, I worked for a top professional, Chef Anna Eichner. I wasn't terribly serious about my assignments. First, I had to clean the walls and floor of the meat refrigerator every day. Instead, I started a poker game. Of course, I got caught! After that, I was demoted to peeling potatoes and caring for the vegetable storeroom.

But when boredom set in, I started throwing eggs into a circle on the door. And yes, you guessed it. Caught again! My last chance was to clean the stove and start the fire every day, which meant going to work at 3 a.m. To do this, I used an acid chemical that is normally used to clean pipes. Well, you can imagine what the stove smelled like once I started the fire. Then, it started to corrode in front of my eyes. Chef Anna called me a very long list of unflattering names...but it made me realize that I had to change my behavior.

Many years later, I went back and visited Chef Anna. She referred to me as her star pupil. As we talked, she told me that: "Nobody's perfect. I had to shock you into changing your attitudes. Never regret your past mistakes. Change them, and help others to overcome theirs." It is the best advice I can pass on.

About Stocks, Sauces, and Soups

My favorite sauce is the demi-glace; it is the base of all sauces. And, my favorite soup is onion soup. It is simple, but needs all of the passion and cooking knowledge of a master chef.

368

6.1 Stocks	6.2 Sauces	6.3 Soups
• The essential parts of stock • Types of stock • Preparing bones for stock • Preparing ingredients for stock • Cooling stock • Degreasing stock	• Grand sauces • Basic ingredients in sauces • Preparing different kinds of sauces • Matching sauces to food	• Basic kinds of soup • Preparing soup

SECTION 6.1 STOCKS

Stocks are an important part of any professional kitchen. Stock is an essential ingredient in many soups and sauces. If you can make a great stock, you can make a great soup and sauce. When preparing stocks, flavor, clarity, and body are most important.

Study Questions

After studying Section 6.1, you should be able to answer the following questions:

- What are the four essential parts of a stock and the proper ingredients for each?

- What are the various types of stock and their specific ingredients?

- What are the three methods for preparing bones for stock?

- What are the ingredients for several types of stock?

- How and why do you degrease stock?

- What is the proper way in which to cool stock?

The Essential Parts of Stock

There are four essential parts to all stocks:

- A major flavoring ingredient

- A liquid, most often water

- Mirepoix (meer-PWAH)

- Aromatics

369

Section 6.1
Stocks

Introduce the Section

a. Stock is a flavorful liquid used as a foundational ingredient in many foods.
b. Stock extracts flavor from browned bones and/or vegetables.
c. Stock may be safely stored frozen or refrigerated for convenient use in the kitchen.
d. The study questions are topics that will be covered about stocks.
e. All stocks have some common ingredients.
f. There are several specific types of stocks.
g. The ingredients and the stock itself must be handled properly when cooking and storing.

Vocabulary Review

a. Direct students to the key terms.
b. Pronounce each word, and have the students repeat the pronunciation out loud.
c. Discuss the definition of each word.

Teach

Discuss

- The students may realize that a hearty soup is a full meal.
- The students may not realize that clear, broth-based soups can heighten the appetite.
- The students may consider a soup to be a side-dish item.
- Ask the students what they think rounds out a soup menu.
- Help direct the students to the study questions to direct their thinking as they read.

Teaching Tips

- Every stock has a flavoring component, such as bones or vegetables.
- Parts of food that might be discarded, like bones, are actually essential to use for stock.
- A good stock will enhance a savory dish with a fuller flavor spectrum.

Math Connection, 21st-Century Skills—Use Systems Thinking

The students can make a very simple pie graph of the proportions of vegetables for a basic mirepoix.

They can use colored paper, or color the paper accordingly: yellow for onions, orange for carrots, green for celery.

This seems very simple, but will cement the concept into their minds and help them understand the photo in figure 6.1.

Less Advanced Students

The concept of percentages may be difficult for some students. Help reinforce the correct math language and concept with this visual.

More Advanced Students

Have the more advanced math students determine the percentages that might be used with different ingredients for a white mirepoix. They can make a pie graph accordingly.

ESOL Students

Have real examples or photos of whole onions, carrots, and celery so the students are aware of what vegetables you are talking about.

Special Needs Students

If a student is visually impaired, cut a paper or styrofoam plate into 50 percent, 25 percent, and 25 percent sections as a manipulative for the student to handle.

Vocabulary Terms

- **Mirepoix:** A mixture of diced carrots, onions, and celery.
- **Aromatics:** A bundle of spices that usually includes parsley, bay leaves, peppercorns, and thyme.
- **Bouquet garni:** Whole, fresh aromatic herbs tied together to add flavor without adding leaves to the finished product.
- *Sachet d'épices*: A small fabric bag filled with aromatic spices and/or herbs. The bag keeps the aromatics contained so that leaves or powders do not get in the finished product.

Mirepoix is a French word that refers to the mixture of coarsely chopped onions, carrots, and celery that provide a flavor base for stock. The mixture is usually 50 percent onions, and 25 percent each of carrots and celery (see Figure 6.1). For pale or white sauces, such as fish fumet, chefs usually use white mirepoix, in which they substitute parsnips, additional onions, leeks, and even chopped mushrooms for carrots.

Aromatics, such as bouquet garni and *sachet d'épices*, are the herbs, spices, and flavorings that create a savory smell. **Bouquet garni** (boo-KAY gahr-NEE), French for "bag of herbs," is a bundle of fresh herbs, such as thyme, parsley stems, and a bay leaf tied together. *Sachet d'épices* (sah-SHAY day-PEESE) is similar to bouquet garni, except it really is a bag of herbs and spices. The chef places the spices, including parsley stems, dried thyme, bay leaf, and cracked peppercorns, together in a cheesecloth bag. If the stock is going to be strained, these ingredients do not need to be contained in a bag.

Figure 6.1: Mirepoix, a mixture of white onions, carrots, and pale green celery, enhances the flavor and aroma of stock.

Figure Focus

Figure 6.1: The piles of chopped vegetables represent the correct proportions for mirepoix.

In-Class Activity:
Assembly of Bouquet Garni and *Sachet d'Épices*

Assemble the necessary herbs, spices, strings, and cheesecloth bags.

Give students time to practice assembling these two packets, assisting as needed.

Types of Stocks

Stocks are often called the chef's "building blocks." They form the base for many soups and sauces. A **stock** is a flavorful liquid made by gently simmering bones and/or vegetables. This extracts the flavor, aroma, color, body, and nutrients of the ingredients. Some stocks may take up to 24 hours to properly cook, but stocks are one of the most cost-effective ways to use vegetable, meat, and fish trimmings.

There are many types of stock. Several are shown in Figure 6.2 below:

- **White stock:** This is a clear, pale liquid made by simmering poultry, beef, or fish bones.

- **Brown stock:** This is an amber liquid made by simmering poultry, beef, veal, or game bones that have been browned first.

- **Fumet** (foo-MAY): Very similar to fish stock, this is a highly flavored stock made with fish bones.

- **Court bouillon** (court boo-YON): This is an aromatic vegetable broth used for poaching fish or vegetables.

- **Glace** (glahs): Sometimes referred to as "glaze," this is a reduced stock with a jelly-like consistency, made from brown stock, chicken stock, or fish stock.

- *Remouillage* (ray-moo-LAJ): This is a weak stock made from bones that have already been used in another preparation, sometimes used to replace water as the liquid used in a stock; *remouillage* is the French word for "rewetting."

Figure 6.2: Stocks are made from a combination of vegetables, seasonings, bones, and liquids.

371

Discuss
- Stock adds a boost of flavor to a dish. Why?
- Is stock commonly used in the home kitchen?

Vocabulary Terms
- **Stock:** A water-based liquid flavored with bones or vegetables.
- **White stock:** A clear stock made from bones.
- **Brown stock:** A brown stock made from over-browned bones.
- **Fumet:** A stock made from fish bones, which can be concentrated or highly flavored.
- **Court bouillon:** Vegetable broth.
- **Glace:** Stock reduction used as a sauce or ingredient.
- *Remouillage*: A stock made from bones used in another dish.

Figure Focus

Figure 6.2: As shown, stocks are transparent and range in color from clear to amber to brown.

Approach a chef at a local restaurant that makes stock from scratch and ask if the restaurant will donate or sell a small sample of the stock for the students to taste.

Include this sample, along with samples of commercially prepared stocks of several varieties, including some low-sodium stock.

Prepare a blind taste test.

Have the bowls of stock labeled with a number.

Keep an unseen key identifying the various types of stock by number.

Use clean plastic spoons for each student and for each sample.

The students taste each sample and rate, rank, or note their opinions of it based on the rating, ranking, or sharing system chosen by the teacher.

Students should share their findings.

Teaching Tips

- Students could blanch bones in the classroom, preparing them for stock.
- They might also have time to brown bones for stock in the classroom.
- It may be difficult to simmer bones for stock within the constraints of the class period.
- Perhaps the students could brown bones in the class and take them home to make stock.
- Stock-making is an important skill for a chef. Try to include this opportunity if at all possible.

Vocabulary Terms

- **Bouillon:** A broth made by simmering a meat or vegetable.
- **Jus:** Flavorful, reduced stock.
- **Vegetable stock:** A stock made by simmering earthy vegetables for flavor.
- *Concassé*: A tomato that has been skinned, de-seeded, and chopped, so that it will not add debris.
- **Blanching:** Quickly boiling.
- **Brown:** Oven-roasted until golden brown.
- **Sweating:** Heating in fat until moisture is released and some softening occurs.

- **Bouillon** (BOO-yon)**:** This is the liquid that results from simmering meats or vegetables; also referred to as broth.
- **Jus:** This is a rich, lightly reduced stock used as a sauce for roasted meats.
- **Vegetable stock:** This is usually made from mirepoix, leeks, and turnips. Tomatoes, garlic, and seasonings may also be added to flavor or darken the stock, but tomatoes must be strained with a cheesecloth or filter so that no seeds or skins get into the stock. This is referred to as tomato *concassé* (kawn-ka-SAY). A chef might roast the vegetables or add a large amount of a particular vegetable, such as mushrooms for a mushroom stock.

Some kitchens use convenience items, such as prepared stocks, stock or sauce bases, and commercial concentrates to cut costs of food and labor in the kitchen. It's ideal to prepare all items from scratch, but it may not always be possible due to budget issues or staff skill levels. Fortunately, there are many quality convenience products available that can be used to good advantage in today's kitchen. The key to choosing any of these products is careful evaluation to make sure they provide a good level of quality. The quality of the stock affects the quality of all dishes prepared from it; if the prepared stock, base, or concentrate is high quality and has good flavor, then using it will not compromise quality. High-quality stock helps deliver high-quality product. Keep in mind, though, that commercially prepared stocks may contain a large amount of sodium (salt), depending on how they are produced.

Preparing Bones for Stock

To use bones for stock, they must first be cut to the right size and then prepared by blanching, browning, or sweating.

Blanching the bones rids them of some of the impurities that can cause cloudiness in a stock. In a stockpot, cover the bones with cold water and bring them to a slow boil. When the pot is at full boil, remove the floating waste or scum.

To **brown** bones, roast them in a hot (400°F) oven for about an hour, until they are golden brown. Once they are evenly browned, place in a stockpot, cover with cold water, and then bring to a simmer. This will give the stock a richer flavor and deeper color.

Sweating causes bone and mirepoix to release flavor more quickly when liquid is added. In the sweating process, cook the bones and/or vegetables in a small amount of fat over low heat until they soften and release moisture. For example, bones used for making fish fumet must be sweated with vegetables before adding the cooking liquid and seasoning.

372

Essential Skills
Blanching Bones

❶ Place at least 8 lbs of bones in a stockpot and cover with cold water. See Figure 6.3.

❷ Bring the water to a slow boil. Skim the surface if necessary.

❸ Once the water reaches full boil, drain the bones through a sieve or, if the stockpot has one, allow the water to drain away through a spigot.

❹ Once the water reaches full boil, drain the bones through a sieve or, if the stockpot has one, allow the water to drain away through a spigot. Discard the water.

❺ Now the bones are ready for any recipe that calls for blanched bones.

Figure 6.3: Step 1—Blanching bones.

Preparing Ingredients for Stock

Flavor, color, body, and clarity determine the quality of stock. A stock should be flavorful, but not so strong that it overpowers the other ingredients in the finished dish. In a chicken noodle soup, for example, you should taste the chicken, noodles, and vegetables as well as the broth. Fish, chicken, and beef stock have the strongest flavors, while white veal stock is considered neutral. With the exception of fumet, stocks should be almost crystal clear when they are hot. See Figure 6.4.

373

Figure Focus

Figure 6.3: The bones are being covered with water for blanching in a large stockpot.

Discuss

- Ask the students what they want to end up with.
- This is a question that should be asked in every aspect of cooking.
- In the case of stock, boiling hard or mishandling the components of the stock might decrease the effort or cooking time, but might yield a poor product. Is this really the goal?

Teaching Tips

- The bouquet garni and/or the *sachet d'épices* that the students made may be used in a demonstration of the final cooking time of a stock in the classroom.

Figure 6.4: Stock should be brought to a boil and then reduced to a simmer to bring out the full flavor. Rapid boiling of a stock causes impurities and fats to blend with the liquid.

Mirepoix should be trimmed and cut into a size suited for the type of stock. For stocks with short cooking times, like fish stock, the mirepoix should be sliced or chopped in small pieces. For stocks with cooking times of longer than one hour, such as beef stock, the vegetables may be cut into larger pieces. These can be 1 to 2 inches long, or even left whole.

Bouquet garni or *sachet d'épices* can be added to the simmering stock. Aromatics are usually added in the last hour for two reasons: to allow the heat to bring out their flavors and to prevent the loss of flavor (or development of unpleasant flavors) caused by overcooking. The flavors and aromas will be released from the herbs and spices as the stock cooks. Once the stock is flavored to taste, remove the aromatic.

To make stock, the ratio of liquid to flavoring ingredients is standard. To make one gallon of stock, use the following proportions:

- Chicken, beef, veal, and game stock: 8 lbs of bones to 6 qts of water, adding 1 lb of mirepoix

- Fish/shellfish stock or fumet: 11 lbs of bones or shells to 5 qts of water, adding 1 lb of mirepoix

- Vegetable stock: 4 lbs of vegetables to 4 qts of water, adding ¾ lb of mirepoix

374

Figure Focus

Figure 6.4: This stock with mirepoix is being simmered in a pot that is smaller than a commercial stockpot that might be available in a high school kitchen classroom.

Essential Skills
Preparing Stock

❶ Combine the major flavoring ingredient and the cold liquid.

❷ Bring to a simmer.

❸ Skim as necessary throughout the cooking time.

❹ Add the mirepoix and aromatics at the appropriate time, usually in the last hour of cooking.

❺ Simmer until the stock develops flavor, body, and color.

❻ Strain, then use immediately, or cool and store. Straining through cheese-cloth or a coffee filter helps to remove fat. See Figure 6.5.

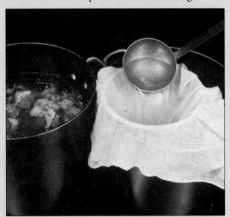

Figure 6.5: Step 6—Strain, then use immediately, or cool and store.

Cooling Stock

Foodborne pathogens need time and moisture to grow, but they won't grow when the temperature of the food is colder than 41°F or hotter than 135°F. The temperatures between 41°F and 135°F are in the temperature danger zone (also known as TDZ). Follow proper food safety practices when cooling stock. This will minimize the time the stock spends in the temperature danger zone.

375

Figure Focus
Figure 6.5: Straining stock through cheesecloth.

Essential Skills: Cooling Stock

Cooling stock safely can be done by observing safe foodhandling practices.

An ice-water bath is one such technique.

Discuss

- Heat transfer refers to the movement of energy from one source to another.
- For example, a hot pot of stock will have molecules in motion, perceived as heat.
- Air in a cooler will have slower molecules.
- Putting the hot pot in the cooler will transfer energy from the stock to the air in the cooler.
- The molecules in the cooler will speed up, and be warmer.
- This might put the contents of the refrigerator into the temperature danger zone.

In-Class Activity: Heat Transfer

Science Connection

Cool stock before putting it in the refrigerator for storage.

Why not just put it in the fridge hot?

The warmth of the soup will move into the refrigerator. The kinetic energy, or motion, of hot molecules imparts energy to the slower molecules in the cooler, heating them up. The hot soup pot will heat up items in the refrigerator.

One way to cool the pot of stock is to put some ice cubes into a zippered plastic storage bag, sealed. Put this in the pot. It will float.

Why will it float?

The solid phase of water has a lower density than liquid water. The solid form is a crystalline lattice structure that is more open than the flowing molecules in the liquid phase.

When the ice melts, remove the bag, empty the water in the sink, rinse the bag, fill it with more ice, and put it back in the stock.

How does the ice cool the stock?

Ice cools the soup the same way the stock warms the fridge. Actually, the stock warms the ice, and in so doing loses some of its heat. The kinetic energy of the molecules of stock transfers to the water molecules in the ice lattice, freeing them to move and flow. The ice melts and the water is warmer than the ice was. Some of the heat of the stock has moved into the bag.

Use scientific principles to answer all three questions.

Essential Skills
Cooling Stock

❶ Place hot stock into a clean, cool stockpot, and put that pot into an ice-water bath. See Figure 6.6.

❷ Stir stock often. When cooled, place the pot into the cooler.

❸ Alternatively, break down hot stock into smaller portions and place the smaller containers in the cooler.

❹ Stir occasionally so the contents of each container cool at the same rate.

Note: Be careful not to put a large stockpot of hot stock in the cooler. It will warm the cooler and its contents.

Figure 6.6: Step 1—Place stock into a stockpot, and then place the pot into an ice-water bath.

376

Figure Focus

Figure 6.6: Cooling a quantity of stock in an ice-water bath can be demonstrated in the classroom.

Management of Stocks

The stocks in a kitchen must be managed carefully. Stock is perishable, so keep it refrigerated or frozen. Only remove as much stock from the cooler as required for a particular task. Discard nonfrozen stock after four days.

Frozen stock may be held for three months. Freeze it in containers that best suit the way it will be used. Ice cube trays can work, or plastic airtight containers with lids. If the container has straight sides, or the bottom is smaller than the top, the block of frozen stock can slide out easily.

Chilled stock will set up and wiggle. This is due to a gelatin formed from specific types of proteins found in the tissues of the bones that were boiled. Vegetable stocks, of course, will not set up.

Once stock is clarified and degreased, it is a fat-free food. If no salt is added, it is fairly low in sodium, but very flavorful. Use stock for cooking vegetables or rice. This boosts the flavor of the dish without adding salt or fat. Keep in mind, though, that customers requiring a vegetarian diet will not be able to eat vegetables or grains cooked in meat or fish stock.

Degreasing Stock

After the stock has been stored, it must be degreased before it can be used. **Degreasing** is the process of removing fat that has cooled and hardened from the surface of the stock. Just lift or scrape away the fat before reheating the stock. Figure 6.7 shows stock being degreased.

Degreasing gives the stock a clearer and purer color. It also removes some of the fat content, making the stock more healthful. As the stock reheats, additional fat and impurities will rise to the top; skim these off to keep the stock clear.

Figure 6.7: Degreasing stock makes it healthier by reducing fat. Degrease stock by skimming, scraping, or lifting hard fat.

Discuss
- Fat floats, which makes degreasing stock possible.
- Fat molecules will not dissolve in water. They are hydrophobic and nonpolar.
- Stock is water-based.
- Fats and oils are less dense than water, which means they float in water.
- Since they float, and since they do not dissolve, they collect in a layer above the stock layer.
- Cooling fat to a solid is the same as freezing water to its solid state.
- A solid can be lifted off of gelled or liquid stock.
- Meat-based stocks will be gelled due to proteins from the connective tissues of the bones that form a gel structure when cooled.
- Vegetable-based stocks will remain liquid unless cooled below 32°F.
- There will be very little, if any, fat on vegetable-based stocks. But if there is, it will float.

Vocabulary Terms
- **Degreasing:** Gently scraping congealed fat from the top surface of gelled stock.

Figure Focus
Figure 6.7: Fat will float to the top above the stock. When chilled, the floating fat will congeal on the surface of the stock. This can be carefully removed.

It is important to address the issues of calorie, saturated fat, and trans fat consumption.

Carefully degreasing stock is an important strategy in eliminating fats where they are not needed or wanted.

Reinforce and Review

- Stocks have essential components that the students should be able to name.
- The students should also be familiar with the different types of stocks.
- Students should be able to discuss the procedure for correctly making a stock.
- The proper techniques for safely cooling stocks are important for the students to know.
- Improving the nutritional quality of foods by boosting their flavor with low-sodium, freshly made degreased stocks is important to understand.

Summary

- Remind students to review the following:
  1. The four essential parts of a stock and the proper ingredients for each
  2. The various types of stock and their specific ingredients
  3. The three methods of preparing bones for stock
  4. The ingredients for several types of stock
  5. How and why you degrease stock
  6. The proper way to cool stock

[nutrition]

Nutrition and the Fat Budget

Degreasing stock is an important step in creating an outstanding sauce or soup. It also helps improve the nutrition quality of recipes using that stock. The grease from the bones of animals is a saturated fat, which researchers have linked to coronary disease and certain types of cancer. People should limit the amount of fat they include in their diets.

Budgeting dietary fat intake to include some saturated fat is a reasonable approach. You might reserve part of your fat allowance for a special treat, such as a creamy, elaborate soup or sauce.

Summary

In this section, you learned the following:

- Stocks contain four essential parts: a major flavoring ingredient, liquid, aromatics, and mirepoix:

  - The major flavoring ingredient consists of bones and trimmings for meat and fish stocks and vegetables for vegetable stock.

  - The liquid most often used in making stock is water.

  - Aromatics are herbs, spices, and flavorings that create a savory smell; these include *sachet d'épices* or bouquet garni.

  - Mirepoix is a mixture of coarsely chopped onions, carrots, and celery that is used to flavor stocks, soups, and stews.

- There are many types of stock:

  - **White stock:** A clear, pale liquid made by simmering poultry, beef, or fish bones.

  - **Brown stock:** An amber liquid made by first browning/roasting poultry, beef, veal, or game bones.

  - **Fumet:** A highly flavored stock made with fish bones.

  - **Court bouillon:** An aromatic vegetable broth.

  - **Glace:** A reduced stock with a jelly-like consistency, made from brown stock, chicken stock, or fish stock.

  - *Remouillage:* A weak stock made from bones that have already been used in another preparation. It is sometimes used to replace water as the liquid used in a stock.

  - **Bouillon:** The liquid that results from simmering meats or vegetables; also referred to as broth.

- When using bones for stock, they must be cut to the right size and prepared by blanching, browning, or sweating.

- Degreasing is the process of removing fat that has cooled and hardened from the surface of the stock by lifting or scraping it away before the stock is reheated. Degreasing stock gives it a clearer look and removes some of the fat content.

- To cool stock, follow good food safety practices and limit the time the stock spends in the temperature danger zone (TDZ). To cool stock, place it in a clean stockpot, and then put that pot into an ice-water bath. Stir it often. When cooled, place the pot into the cooler. Another option is to break down the stock into smaller portions and place the smaller containers in the cooler. Stir occasionally so that the contents of each container cool at the same rate. Be careful not to put an entire large stockpot of hot stock in the cooler because it will warm the cooler and its contents.

379

Discuss

- Ask the students how they would cut bones to the right size for blanching, browning, and sweating.
- Who might they ask to help with this?

Section 6.1 Review Questions

1. The following are defined as:
   a. A small cheesecloth bag of aromatic herbs and spices

   b. Diced carrots, onions, and celery used as a flavoring

   c. Stock made from fish bones

   d. A small tied bundle of aromatic herbs and spices

   e. Brown stock, fish stock, or chicken stock, reduced to a gel

2. A major flavoring ingredient like bones or vegetables provides the flavor of the stock. A liquid, usually water, provides the volume. Aromatic herbs and spices as well as mirepoix help flavor the stock.

3. The stock may be divided into smaller containers for refrigeration. It can be cooled in a large container using frozen cooling paddles, causing the heat of the stock to transfer to the paddles as they warm. It can also be cooled by placing a container of stock in a bath of ice, which will also transfer heat away from the stock as it melts the ice.

4. Sweating allows the bones and the mirepoix to release flavor more easily when they are added to liquid. It breaks down connective tissue in bones and cellulose in mirepoix. Browning helps bones develop a richer, roasted flavor with a darker brown color. Blanching helps remove impurities from bones.

5. Stock carries the rich flavor of the bones into the sauce of the dish. As the bones and meat release fat, it liquefies and floats to the surface of the liquid portion. Once chilled in the refrigerator, the fat solidifies again, and can be skimmed off. Now the dish is less greasy and lower in fat content.

6. Soups and menu items that feature sauces can utilize the same stock. Stocks are the basis of grand sauces, which can be made into derivative sauces. One pot of stock can provide for several types of soups, stews, and sauces.

Section 6.1 Review Questions

1. Define the following:
   a. Sachet d'épices
   b. Mirepoix
   c. Fumet
   d. Bouquet garni
   e. Glace

2. Describe the four important parts of stock.

3. You are responsible for cooling a large amount of chicken stock. How will you do this?

4. Describe how and why bones, shells, and vegetables are
   a. sweated.
   b. browned.
   c. blanched.

5. In the *American Harvest* cookbook, Chef Sonnenschmidt notes that he likes to "make Braised Short Ribs on a cold day…letting it braise and perfume the air for much of the day. If time permits, and you can resist digging in immediately, cover, refrigerate, and skim off the surface fat the next day." Why is stock a key component of this flavorful dish? And why might you need to skim surface fat off of the dish the next day?

6. Stock is a staple in every restaurant. What kind of menu can Uptown Grille offer that uses stock at lunch and at dinner, while still offering a variety of selections?

7. How can a chef identify a potential food safety hazard with a stock? After identifying it, what should the chef do?

8. Why is it important to cool a soup or stock before storage? Why not just put it in the cooler while it is hot?

380

7. The chef can periodically check the temperature of the stock. It should not be held in the danger zone. It should be chilled to below 41°F for storage, and then quickly heated to above 135°F for preparation and service.

8. The principles of heat transfer are at work here. If hot stock is placed into a cooler, the heat from the stock will warm the air in the cooler. This will defeat the purpose of the cooler and may raise the temperature inside into the danger zone. At the very least, it will require much more energy to maintain the appropriate temperature within the refrigerator, adding expense and wasting resources.

Section 6.1 Activities

1. Study Skills/Group Activity: A Healthier Stock

Work with two other students to find the recipes for two stocks (either on the Internet or in a cookbook) and compare them for nutrition value. You should test each other by asking: "How can I make this recipe more nutritious?"

2. Activity: Pictogram

Draw a three-frame (or more) pictogram for each of the three methods of making stock from bones. It should look like a cartoon or diagram, showing the steps in each specific process.

3. Critical Thinking: Comparing Stocks

There are many types of stock. Pick two stocks, and write a short report comparing and contrasting the ingredients, cooking process, and nutrition value of each. Suggest three dishes for which each stock might be the base.

381

Section 6.1 Activities

1. Each student group will have a different set of choices. However, some common things to look for would include the things that boost nutrition such as vitamin C, beta carotene, or lycopene. These are antioxidant nutrients that are found in fresh vegetables, especially those of the cabbage family or those that are red or orange in color. To improve the nutrition, the students could reduce the salt content of the stock, and chill it to skim off the fat.

2. Below are simple examples of pictograms.

3. Student answers will vary. The information for this challenge is contained within the text.

Section 6.2
Sauces

Introduce the Section

a. There are grand sauces that are classic.

b. Most sauces are made using the same fundamentals.

c. Making sauces requires practice and skill.

d. Sauces should be matched to foods.

Vocabulary Review

a. Direct students to the key terms.

b. Pronounce each word, and have the students repeat the pronunciation out loud.

c. Discuss the definition of each word.

Teach

Discuss

• Begin with the grand sauces, which might be a new concept for some students.

• Ask, "Have you ever had food with so much sauce on it that you could not even taste the food?"

• The students may have favorite sauces.

• The students may not be aware of the grand sauces.

Vocabulary Terms

• **Sauce:** A flavorful liquid product added to food.

• **Saucier:** A cook who specializes in sauces.

• **Grand sauces:** Mother sauces, or foundation sauces.

• **Béchamel:** White milk sauce.

• **Velouté:** A pale sauce made with white meat, fish, or poultry.

6.1 Stocks	6.2 Sauces	6.3 Soups
• The essential parts of stock • Types of stock • Preparing bones for stock • Preparing ingredients for stock • Cooling stock • Degreasing stock	• Grand sauces • Basic ingredients in sauces • Preparing different kinds of sauces • Matching sauces to food	• Basic kinds of soup • Preparing soup

SECTION 6.2 SAUCES

The word *sauce* comes from the French word that means a relish to make food more appetizing. All types of sauces are important in cooking. A good sauce adds flavor, moisture, richness, and visual appeal. Sauces should complement food, not disguise it.

Study Questions

After studying Section 6.2, you should be able to answer the following questions:

■ What are the grand sauces? What other sauces are made from them?

■ What are the proper ingredients for sauces?

■ How do you prepare different kinds of sauces?

■ How do you match sauces to the appropriate type of food?

Grand Sauces

A **sauce** is a liquid or semisolid product that is used in preparing other foods. Sauces add flavor, moisture, and visual appeal to another dish. A **saucier** is a cook who specializes in making sauces.

There are five classical **grand sauces** that are the basis for most other sauces. These are sometimes called "mother sauces." They include the following:

■ **Béchamel** (BAY-shah-MELL): This is made from milk and white roux.

■ **Velouté** (veh-loo-TAY): This is made from veal, chicken, or fish stock and a white or blond roux.

- **Brown** or *Espagnole* **sauce** (ess-spah-NYOL): This is made from brown stock and brown roux.

- **Tomato sauce:** This is made from a stock and tomatoes (roux is optional).

- **Hollandaise** (HALL-en-daze): This is an emulsion made from eggs, butter, and lemon.

Figure 6.8: A saucier prepares a brown sauce.

Figure 6.8 shows a saucier preparing a brown sauce. Grand sauces are rarely used by themselves. They are often used to make derivative sauces. For example, **demi-glace** (deh-mee glahs), a rich brown sauce, is traditionally made by combining equal parts *espagnole* sauce and veal stock. Table 6.1 lists the grand sauces and their derivatives.

[fast fact]

Did you know...?
While there are many derivative sauces, the original grand sauces are works of art. Chefs use them to create outstanding dishes. One example is hollandaise sauce, featured in Eggs Benedict. Toast a crumpet or English muffin, and layer it with a warm slice of Canadian bacon or ham, a perfectly poached egg, and a generous spoonful of hollandaise sauce over all. Absolutely delicious!

[ServSafe Connection]

Holding Hollandaise
Hollandaise sauce is a delicate balance of warmth, egg/butter/lemon emulsion, and mild lemon butter flavor. Any abuse will break the sauce. Overheating or overcooling will destroy the balance. However, holding the sauce too long at a warm temperature in the danger zone is unacceptable, due to the egg content of the sauce.

The key is to make the right amount of hollandaise for the service, and use it immediately. Unfortunately, this is not always practical. Once a perfect hollandaise has been made, it can be held for up to an hour over a bath of lukewarm water (>135°F) on the stove. The stove should be at very low heat, not hot enough to boil the water bath.

Refrigerate unused hollandaise for one to two days, or freeze it to keep longer. When it's revived, it will be different, but it will still be a nice sauce.

For long holding, or to restore chilled hollandaise, maintain or reheat it over a double-boiler on low heat. Gently stir in some béchamel sauce. This new sauce is lovely for vegetables, fish, or chicken. However, it's not quite hollandaise any longer.

To attempt to restore the sauce to its original form as hollandaise, gently beat two tablespoons of the chilled sauce in a double boiler over hot water on low heat. When that portion has revived, add and gently beat in the rest one spoonful at a time.

383

Fast Fact
Did You Know...?

Eggs Benedict would be a good recipe for the classroom.

Hollandaise sauce is so delicious that it makes most anything enjoyable.

Hollandaise sauce is not a low-fat, low-cholesterol food.

ServSafe Connection:
Holding Hollandaise

Hollandaise is a fragile sauce to store. However, it can be stored and used again.

Perhaps the students could make enough hollandaise sauce for the Eggs Benedict to have some left over, which could be stored and restored as a classroom activity.

Perhaps the second time it is served, it could accompany steamed broccoli.

Vocabulary Terms

- **Brown sauce:** A sauce made from brown stock and browned roux.
- *Espagnole* **sauce:** The same as a brown sauce.
- **Tomato sauce:** Tomatoes and stock, with or without roux.
- **Hollandaise:** An egg, butter, and lemon sauce.
- **Demi-glace:** A sauce derived from brown sauce and veal stock.

Figure Focus
Figure 6.8: A brown sauce is being added to Brussels sprouts. Note that it is not a very dark brown.

- Help the students to understand what derivative means.

In-Class Activity:
Nested Recipes

Math Connection, Literacy Connection

Nested recipes are a data management name for classic recipes and their derivatives. When recipes are nested, they are used as an entity within another entity.

Whether the topic is nutrient analysis, cost analysis, equipment use, or time use, the basic recipe is quantified first. The next recipe that is derived is quantified using the first recipe as an ingredient.

The foodservice operation must understand the first recipe to understand all the recipes derived from it.

The nutrient ingredient value totals for the first recipe are plugged into the calculations for the values of the second, third, and so forth.

This may also be done for cost analysis, time analysis, ingredient analysis, or any other type of food analysis.

The following may be read verbatim to the students to help build their listening comprehension:

Let's do a time analysis.

A recipe of béchamel sauce will require a certain amount of time to make.

Once it is made, a cheddar cheese sauce may be derived from it.

Making a cheddar cheese sauce also requires time, and béchamel sauce will be one of its ingredients. Making baked macaroni and cheese with cheddar cheese sauce as an ingredient will also require a specific amount of time.

In order to know how much time baked macaroni and cheese really requires, you would have to add the time to make béchamel, plus the time to make cheddar cheese sauce, plus the time to make baked macaroni and cheese.

Using the above example, see if the students can understand this process when it is described verbally.

Gauge their understanding by having them verbalize the process in their own words. They could also verbally present other possible examples of nesting data.

Table 6.1: Grand Sauces and Their Derivatives

Grand Sauce	Derivative Sauce	Additional Ingredients
Béchamel	Cream	Cream (instead of milk)
	Cheddar cheese	Cheddar cheese
	Soubise (soo-BEEZ)	Puréed cooked onions
Veal velouté	*Allemande* (ah-leh-MAHND)	Egg yolks
	Hungarian	Egg yolks, Hungarian paprika
	Curry	Egg yolks, curry spices
Chicken velouté	Mushroom	Cream, mushrooms
	Supreme	Reduced with heavy cream
	Hungarian	Cream, Hungarian paprika
Fish velouté	White wine	White wine
	Bercy	White wine, shallots, butter, parsley
	Herb	White wine, herbs
Brown (espagnole)	Bordelaise (bohr-dl-AYZ)	Red wine, parsley
	Chasseur	Mushrooms, shallots, white wine and tomato *concassé*
	Lyonnaise (lee-oh-NEHZ)	Sautéed onions, butter, white wine, vinegar
	Madeira	Madeira wine
Tomato	Creole (KREE-ohl)	Sweet peppers, onions, chopped tomatoes
	Portuguese	Onions, chopped tomatoes, garlic, parsley
Hollandaise	Béarnaise (behr-NAYZ)	Tarragon, white wine, vinegar, shallots
	Maltaise	Blood orange juice and zest

Basic Ingredients in Sauces

Sauces need a liquid component, but some sauces, such as salsa, may contain more solid elements than liquid. A key ingredient in sauce is the thickener, which adds richness and body. Some examples of thickeners are roux, beurre manié, slurry, and liaison.

384

In-Class Activity:
Dishes That Use Derivative Sauces

21st-Century Skills—Access and Evaluate Information, Work Independently

Using the Internet, research classic dishes that use sauces derived from the grand sauces.

For example, a cheddar cheese sauce derived from béchamel is used in classic baked macaroni and cheese.

Challenge the students to work independently online to find at least one dish for each of the derivative sauces listed in Table 6.1

Have the students copy/scan Table 6.1 and add their own fourth column with the results of their research.

Have the students share their work with the class or turn it in for evaluation.

The students should keep this product for future reference.

Did you know...?

Roux can be cooked until it is white, blond, brown, or dark brown. The color depends on the temperature and time taken to cook the fat-flour mixture. None of these types of roux is better or worse than any other. The color you choose will depend on the flavor and color you want to give your sauce or soup.

Roux (ROO) is a thickener made of equal parts cooked flour and a fat, such as clarified butter, oil, or shortening. To make a roux, the fat is heated in a pan, and then the flour is added. The mixture is stirred until the flour and fat are fully blended. The color of the roux is determined by how long the mixture has been heated.

There are four commonly used types of roux:

- **White roux:** This is cooked for a very short period of time; used in sauces where little color is needed, like béchamel. White roux is bland and a little starchy and has the most thickening power.

- **Blond roux:** This is cooked longer than white roux, until the flour turns golden and has a nutty aroma; used in ivory-colored sauces like velouté. Blond roux has a little more flavor development. It is nutty tasting.

- **Brown/dark brown roux:** This sauce is cooked until it develops a dark brown color; used in dishes that require a dark brown color. Brown roux is nutty and a rich medium-brown color. Dark brown roux is quite dark, with a nutty, roasted flavor. It has the least thickening ability because the starch has been cooked the longest.

Beurre manié (byurr man-YAY) is a thickener made of equal parts flour and soft, whole butter. Mix flour and butter together, and then shape the mixture into small pea-sized balls and add to the cooking sauce. See Figure 6.9. Use beurre manié to thicken a sauce quickly at the end of the cooking process.

A **slurry**, cornstarch mixed with a cold liquid, can be used instead of roux. You cannot add cornstarch directly to a sauce; it will make the sauce lumpy. First, dissolve the cornstarch in a cold liquid.

Figure 6.9: Beurre manié is a paste made from flour and butter that is used as a sauce thickener.

385

Figure Focus

Figure 6.9: Small pieces of beurre manié are added to thicken a sauce.

In-Class Activity:
Roux Jigsaw

Supplies:

Butter

Flour

Milk

Light stock

Brown stock

Whisks

Pans

Bowls

Enough clean plastic spoons for each student to have three

Divide the students into pairs or teams, and assign them to a kitchen.

Refer students to the Essential Skills instructions for making roux which appears on p. 386. Then assign each team to make one of the following:

- White roux and béchamel sauce

- Blond roux and velouté sauce

- Brown roux and brown sauce

When each group's roux has reached the correct color and texture, have each group show it to the entire class. Encourage the students to look at and smell the aroma of the roux.

After each group has briefly displayed its roux, have each group make its assigned sauce.

Each group will serve the completed sauce in a bowl.

Each student can taste each sauce with a clean plastic spoon.

Vocabulary Terms

- **Roux:** A flour and fat thickener.
- **Beurre manié:** A flour and butter mixture that is rolled together into small balls of paste and used as a thickener.
- **Slurry:** A suspension of cornstarch in cold water, stirred to add as a thickener.

Demonstrate making roux for the students.

Show them the various color stages.

Teaching Tips

- As much as possible, have the students try the different types of thickening techniques.
- Emphasize that flour is added to a warm liquid, while cornstarch is added to a cold liquid.
- Adding the other way around (flour to cold or cornstarch to warm) will cause lumps of uncooked starch.

Vocabulary Terms

- **Liaison:** A mixture of egg yolk and cream to emulsify without thickening too much.
- **Temper:** Bringing a mixture slowly up to a warm temperature without cooking the liaison.

Essential Skills
Making Roux

❶ Heat clarified butter or other fat in a heavy saucepan.

❷ Add flour and stir together with the fat to form a paste. See Figure 6.10.

  Note: Most often, chefs use equal parts flour and fat (by weight), but some sources suggest 60 percent flour and 40 percent fat.

❸ Stir the roux continually to prevent burning.

❹ Cook the paste over medium heat until the desired color is reached.

Figure 6.10: Step 2—Add flour and stir with fat to form a paste.

Don't boil sauces thickened with cornstarch too long or the starch will break down, creating a watery sauce.

A **liaison** (lee-AY-zohn) is a mixture of egg yolks and heavy cream, often used to finish some sauces, such as *Allemande* sauce. Liaison adds a rich flavor and smoothness to the sauce without making it too thick. It is important to temper the liaison to prevent the egg yolks from curdling. To **temper** the sauce, slowly mix a little bit of the hot sauce with the eggs and cream mixture to raise the temperature, and then add the warmed-up egg mixture into the sauce.

Figure 6.11: *Boeuf Bourguignonne* is a well-known, traditional French recipe.

386

Figure Focus

Figure 6.10: It is important to constantly stir the roux to prevent burning.

Figure 6.11: The sauce for this dish is flavored with Bourgogne wine.

Red Wine

A lot is said about sauces being a lavish "extra" that weight-conscious individuals should have "on the side." A sauce is a beautiful, flavorful, integral part of a dish and its presentation. And some sauces even enhance the nutrition of an item. One is sauce *bourguignonne*, which uses the red wine *Bourgogne* to deglaze.

In the deglazing and gentle cooking, the alcohol content of the wine is decreased. The nutrient content of the wine remains, boosting the nutrition of the entire dish, be it *boeuf bourguignonne* (as seen in Figure 6.11) or coq au vin. Red wine provides antioxidants, flavonoids (like anthocyanins), procyanidids, and resveratrol. These long-name chemicals fight both cancer and heart disease.

Preparing Different Kinds of Sauces

There are various kinds of sauces besides grand sauces and derivative sauces. These include compound butters, cold or thick sauces like salsa and *coulis* (koo-LEE), and sauces made from the natural juices of meat.

Compound butter is a mixture of raw butter and various flavoring ingredients, such as herbs, nuts, citrus zest, shallots, ginger, and vegetables. Use compound butters to finish grilled or broiled meats, fish, poultry, game, pastas, and sauces, among other uses. Roll the butter into a long tube shape, then chill and slice for use as needed. See Figure 6.12. One blend is *maître d'hôtel* **butter** (MAY-tra doe-TEL), a softened butter flavored with lemon juice and chopped parsley. It is often used to garnish grilled meat or fish.

Figure 6.12: Compound butter is ordinary butter to which a flavor or additional ingredient, such as herbs, shallots, or lemon juice, has been added. The most common form is called beurre maître d'hotel.

Other miscellaneous sauces that add flavor, texture, and color to a dish include salsa and coulis. **Coulis** is a thick puréed sauce, such as the tomato coulis as pictured in Figure 6.13. **Salsa** is a cold mixture of fresh herbs, spices, fruits, and/ or vegetables. It can be used as a sauce for meat, poultry, fish, or shellfish. These sauces allow chefs to change a menu item by adding flavor, moisture, texture, and

387

**In-Class Activity:
Compound Butter Brainstorm**

21st-Century Skills—Think Creatively, Implement Innovation

Provide butter and various herbs, spices, and flavorings for the students to use.

Encourage the students to create their own mixture for compound butter, writing down their recipes as they work.

Wrap the butter in wax paper or plastic wrap and chill for later use.

Students should mark their work clearly with their names.

Vocabulary Terms

- **Compound butter:** A mixture of butter and other flavorful ingredients.
- *Maître d'hôtel* **butter:** A specific type of compound butter with lemon juice and parsley.
- **Coulis:** A thick puréed sauce made of tomatoes or fruits.
- **Salsa:** A cold, chunky sauce made of various combinations of vegetables and/or fruits and seasonings.

Figure Focus
Figure 6.12: Compound butter is wrapped for convenient storage and later use.

Discuss

- Salsas are extremely popular in the United States and other parts of the world.
- Salsas of various types are found throughout cuisines beyond Mexican food.
- Perhaps the students can think of various uses for salsa.
- Help the students to think creatively about the uses of salsa.
- Also help the students to think creatively about the ingredients in a salsa.
- Salsa is not limited to tomatoes, onions, chilies, and cilantro.

Teaching Tips

- Practice the correct pronunciations of jus-lié and au jus with the students.
- The students might have experience with a French dip sandwich served au jus.
- Encourage the students to always use the pronunciation guides for French culinary words.
- Chefs, cooks, and wait staff should pronounce culinary words correctly.

Vocabulary Terms

- **Jus-lié:** A sauce made with meat juice.
- **Au jus:** Meat juice served as-is with meat.
- **Wringing method:** Gently squeezing a sauce through a cheesecloth.

[fast fact]

Did you know...?
"Salsa" is the Spanish word for sauce. This food originated back in the time of the Incas and Aztecs. Today, when we think of salsa, we think of a fresh, uncooked sauce made of tomatoes, chiles, and a variety of other ingredients. The sauce can be smooth, semi-chunky, or evenly chopped. When we go to the grocery store, we can find spicy or mild salsa, with all sorts of ingredients added to it—corn, cilantro, garlic, black beans, guacamole or even mango or peach.

color to a dish. One advantage is that these sauces can provide a lower-fat alternative to the usually heavy grand or derivative sauces. Figure 6.14 shows salsa being used to add flavor to a fish dish.

Sauces are sometimes made with the natural juices of meat. **Jus-lié** (ZHEW-lee-AY) is a sauce made from the juices of cooked meat and brown stock. Meats served with their own juices are called **au jus** (oh ZHEW).

To finish a sauce, adjust the consistency. For example, it may be necessary to add stock to a sauce to thin it out. The added stock will also help flavor the sauce. Sometimes using a red or white wine can add a very distinctive taste to a sauce.

Once the flavor and consistency have been adjusted, the sauce may need to be strained to make sure it is smooth. The easiest way to strain sauce is the **wringing method**. In this method, place a clean cheesecloth over a bowl, and pour the sauce through the cheesecloth into the bowl. The cloth is then twisted at either end to squeeze out the strained

Figure 6.13: Coulis is a thick sauce made of puréed fruit or vegetables.

Figure 6.14: Salsa is a cold sauce made from a combination of vegetables, usually tomatoes, onions, and peppers. For example, pineapple papaya salsa is used as a topping on teriyaki salmon.

388

Figure Focus

Figure 6.13: This is a tomato coulis being strained through a *chinois*.

Figure 6.14: Discuss with students the different types of salsas that they've had.

sauce. The cheesecloth catches the unwanted lumps of roux, or herbs, spices, and other seasonings. Sauces may also be strained through a **China cap** lined with cheesecloth, a fine meshed strainer, or a *chinois* (chee-no-AH). Figure 6.15 shows sauce being strained using the wringing method.

As in all cooking, the final step in finishing a sauce is to adjust the seasonings. Salt, lemon juice, cayenne, and white pepper can all be used to bring out the flavor of the sauce.

Figure 6.15: For a velvety texture, use the wringing method to strain sauce through a piece of cheesecloth.

[what's new]

Chemists Measure Chili Sauce Hotness with Nanotubes

Perhaps you have seen domed buildings that look like a soccer ball. These are called geodesic domes. It's a shape that was designed by Buckminster Fuller.

In 1985, chemists discovered a carbon molecule shaped like one of these geodesic domes. They called the form carbon fullerene in honor of Mr. Fuller, but the nickname buckyball is the one that has been popularized in the news. Different sizes of buckyballs have different numbers of carbon atoms, but the most common one, the one that looks just like a soccer ball, has 60 interconnected carbon atoms.

As scientists experimented with fullerenes, they developed a new shape, one that is tube-shaped and looks like a straw made from a rolled-up mesh. It is called a nanotube because it is only a few nanometers in diameter. These straws are very useful, and have an interesting use in food science.

Hot chili sauce is hot because of chemicals called capsaicinoids that create a burning feeling. But just how hot is a hot sauce? Do you have to try it to know? The answer used to be "yes." Humans would taste and rate chili sauce hotness.

Using nanotubes as little molecular straws, these capsaicinoids can now be measured by chemists at Oxford University in Oxford, England. A rating can be assigned to a hot sauce before anyone has to taste it, burn his or her mouth, grab water, or do the tongue's-on-fire dance.

ScienceDaily (May 8, 2008)

Human taste testing is still a common practice in the food industry.

Tasting hot sauces can be impractical or inaccurate over time.

As the individual gets used to hotness, he or she may not rate a sauce as hot.

Reinforce and Review

- Adjusting seasonings is an art and a skill.
- Some individuals can tell when something will be appealing to many people.
- Other individuals need more salt or sour or other flavors than most people.
- It is a good idea to have at least two people sample a finished sauce.
- A perfectly textured and seasoned sauce is the sign of a good chef.

Vocabulary Terms

- **China cap:** Also called a *chinois*, a conical-shaped sieve.

Figure Focus

Figure 6.15: Straining a sauce through cheesecloth may seem labor intensive. Ask the students, "What do you want to end up with?" The extra effort can improve the finished product.

Use two colors of index cards.

On one color, make "sauce" cards. Write the name of a sauce on each card.

On the other color, make "dish" cards. Write some dish suggestions on each card. There should be twice as many dish cards as sauce cards.

Place the two types of cards face down on a table. Place the "sauce" cards on the left and the "dish" cards on the right.

Divide the class into two teams.

A player from team one can turn over a sauce card and then turn over a dish card.

If the two match well, the team gets a point and the dish card is removed.

If not, both the cards are turned over and remain in play.

The game is over when the dish cards are gone or a time limit has been reached.

The teacher is the final arbiter of the matches.

Reinforce and Review

- Students should be able to correctly spell the names of the five grand sauces.
- Students should be able to correctly pronounce the names of the five grand sauces.
- Students should be able to describe the five grand sauces.
- Students should be able to explain the procedure for making each of the five grand sauces.
- The students should be able to discuss and compare thickeners for sauces.
- The students should be able to name at least one derivative sauce from each of the five grand sauces.
- The students should be able to describe salsa, coulis, au jus, jus-lié, and compound butters.
- Sauces should be carefully matched to a dish. The students should be able to name one or two good combinations and one or two mismatched combinations.

Matching Sauces to Food

Several factors help to determine the right sauce for a dish:

- What will be the style of service? Some sauces are plated (put on the plate with the food). Others may be available self-serve on a buffet.
- How is the main ingredient of the dish being cooked? Bold sauces and garnishes work well for roasted meat. Lighter sauces are best for white meat and food cooked with light techniques, such as poaching or steaming.
- How does the sauce's flavor work with the dish's flavor? The sauce should complement, not clash with, the flavor and texture of the dish.

Summary

In this section, you learned the following:

- There are five classical grand sauces that are the basis for most other sauces. They are béchamel, velouté, brown or *espagnole* sauce, tomato sauce, and hollandaise:
  - Béchamel, the base for cream, cheddar cheese, soubise
  - Veal velouté, the base for *Allemande*, Hungarian, curry
  - Chicken velouté, the base for mushroom, supreme, Hungarian
  - Fish velouté, the base for white wine, bercy, herb
  - Brown or espagnole, the base for bordelaise, *chasseur*, lyonnaise, Madeira
  - Tomato, the base for Creole, Portuguese
  - Hollandaise, the base for béarnaise, *Maltaise*
- Thickeners, such as roux, beurre manié, slurry, and liaison, add richness and body to sauces.
- There are other sauces that are not classified as grand sauces or as derivatives of grand sauces. These include compound butters, salsa, and coulis. In addition, some sauces are made with the natural juices from meat, such as *jus-lié* or au jus.
- You should match sauces to the type of food you are serving. Consider factors such as the main ingredient of the dish and how the flavors will complement each other.

390

Summary

- Remind students to review the following:
  1. The grand sauces and the sauces derived from them
  2. The proper ingredients for sauces
  3. Preparing different kinds of sauces
  4. Matching sauces to the appropriate type of food

Section 6.2 Review Questions

1. Identify the primary ingredients in each of the five grand sauces.

2. Name three sauces that are not classified as grand sauces.

3. Why are thickeners important in preparing sauces? List some examples.

4. What is the most important factor to consider when matching a sauce with a meal?

5. Why do you think that Chef Sonnenschmidt calls the demi-glace sauce "the base of all sauces?"

5. Do you think it would help Uptown Grille to offer a menu with a wider variety of options at lunch? How would you incorporate sauces into the lighter, less expensive luncheon menu of a fine dining restaurant? What problems might arise?

6. Sauces are considered a foundation of French cuisine. Can you think of some sauces from other ethnic food styles and cuisines? What are they? How are they used?

7. Some sauces are built upon butter and/or cream with a high fat content. Can you suggest ways to decrease the fat content of soups and sauces?

391

Section 6.2 Review Questions

1. The five grand sauces are:
   Béchamel is a white sauce, roux-based with milk or cream.

   Velouté is made from a blond meat stock (veal, chicken, or fish) and is thickened with a white or blonde roux.

   Brown or *Espagnole* is made from a brown stock and a brown roux.

   Tomato sauce is made from stock and tomatoes, but not necessarily a roux.

   Hollandaise is made from butter and lemon juice, emulsified with egg yolk. There is no stock in this sauce.

2. Other sauces may include salsa, coulis, or au jus. Chili sauce is like a cooked salsa. The students might also mention gravy, which is really a brown sauce. They might mention soy sauce. Some might even mention salad dressings and dips.

3. Sauces are runny without thickeners. With too much thickener, the sauce is too stiff. If improperly handled, the sauce will be lumpy. Flour must be added to a warm liquid, but is best made first into a roux where the particles are coated with fat. Cornstarch thickener must be added to a cold liquid before being added to a hot liquid.

4. Student responses will vary. The sauce should not overpower the food it accompanies. The sauce should be flavorful, but not overpowering. The sauce should look nice on the plate. The sauce flavor should match the dish it accompanies. For example, a fish velouté should not accompany a beef dish.

5. A demi-glace is a stock that has been reduced. Reductions are very flavorful and rich. A nice demi-glace will add flavor, color, and richness to any derivative sauce.

6. Uptown Grille needs to offer a more diverse menu to stay current with trends as well as to prevent their customer base from becoming bored. Generally, people think of dishes with sauce as "heavier," but that is not always the case. Uptown Grille could offer luncheon pasta dishes with sauces that use light mayonnaise, mustard, and spices. Or, they could offer creative sandwich wraps with dressings made of a variety of mustards, onion, lemon juice, and olive oil. A large number of traditional sauces, such as barbecue sauce, can be made using "light" products. Uptown Grille should be careful to maintain a "fine dining" quality in their luncheon—emphasizing more unusual, non-traditional sandwiches and salads.

7. Student responses will vary. Possible answers include: Hungarian food may have a paprika sauce, Russian food uses sour cream sauces, and Asian foods use clear sauces often based upon soy sauce.

8. Substitute milk, low-fat, or skim milk for cream and thicken the sauce with flour and less butter. Skim all fat from stocks. Margarine has the same fat content as the same quantity of butter, so substituting margarine does not reduce the fat.

Section 6.2 Activities

1. All necessary information is found within the text. Encourage students to add photos or drawings of the sauce, including the correct color of the sauce.

2. Below is a sample Bones-to-Bordelaise flow chart. Other sauces would have different flow charts.

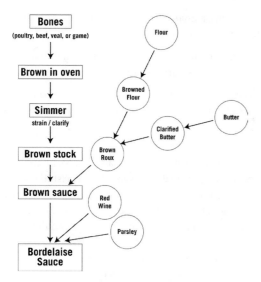

3. An example might be a family brunch, with Eggs Benedict as the dish. The accompanying sauce would be hollandaise. Student responses will vary.

Section 6.2 Activities

1. Study Skills/Group Activity: Flashcards

Create flash cards with each of the grand sauces or derivative sauces on one side, and the list of appropriate ingredients on the other side. With three other students, take turns holding up a list of ingredients and have them write down the name of the sauce (or vice versa).

2. Activity: Bones-to-Bordelaise

Make a flow chart of the various steps involved in making a specific derivative sauce, such as bordelaise sauce, Creole sauce, béarnaise sauce, etc. The chart should use arrows to indicate the direction and order of the process. Be sure to include the ingredients added at various steps. For example, you may start with beef bones. It is acceptable to use "flour" or "bones" or "butter" as starting points. Exhibit your flowchart, eliminating the name of the sauce. See how many of your classmates can guess the right sauce.

3. Critical Thinking: Which Sauce Should I Use?

Create a main dish with an accompanying sauce for a specific event as assigned by your teacher. Some examples might include a family brunch, a dinner at home, an open house, or a wedding. Create the recipe and then describe why you chose that specific dish for the event.

SECTION 6.3 SOUPS

Serving soup at the beginning of a meal provides an opportunity to make a good first impression. Preparing and serving soups helps you learn more about basic culinary techniques, seasonings, garnishing, and serving foods.

Study Questions

After studying Section 6.3, you should be able to answer the following questions:

- What are the two basic kinds of soup?
- How do you prepare the basic ingredients for broth, consommé, purée, clear, and cream soups?
- How do you prepare different kinds of soup?

Basic Kinds of Soup

There are two basic kinds of soup—clear soups and thick soups. **Clear soups** include flavored stocks, broths, and consommés. Examples include chicken noodle soup, minestrone (a tomato-based vegetable soup), and onion soup. **Thick soups** include cream soups and purée soups, such as bisques, chowders, cream of tomato, lentil, and split pea soup. Figure 6.16 shows a line chef preparing a clear soup.

Figure 6.16: Soup is a liquid food prepared from meat, fish, or vegetable stock combined with various other ingredients.

393

Figure Focus

Figure 6.16: Soup is an ancient liquid food that uses many types of ingredients.

Discuss

- The students may realize that there are two main categories of soup.
- The students may not realize that stock is the basis for both sauces and soups.
- The students can be made aware that there are specific techniques to making each type of soup.
- Inform the students that soups are versatile additions to any menu.

Vocabulary Terms

- **Clear soup:** A soup based on transparent broth.
- **Thick soup:** A soup that is opaque, more viscous than broth and perhaps chunky.

Section 6.3 Soups

Introduce the Section

a. There are specific kinds of soups.
b. There are two main soup categories: clear soup and thick soup.
c. There is a wide variety of soup recipes.

Vocabulary Review

a. Direct students to the key terms.
b. Pronounce each word, and have the students repeat the pronunciation out loud.
c. Discuss the definition of each word.

In-Class Activity: Soup/Stock/Grand Sauce Hierarchy

On a white board or projector, sketch the following:

Discuss whether or not this is the correct hierarchy. Make any necessary corrections.

In each of the boxes, have the students jot notes about the facts they have learned so far in the chapter about each topic.

In the Soup box, have the students use pencils to write ideas of what they think the connection of each box might be to the topic of soup. Also have them write down what they hope to learn about soups.

At the end of the chapter, have the students revisit this organizer and evaluate their original ideas.

Have them write their final facts in ink, and keep a copy of their work in their course notebook.

The top should be Stock with the Soup and Grand Sauce boxes underneath:

Trends: Go Local with Fruit Soup

Ask if any of the students have ever tried fruit soup.

Have they ever heard of it?

CUSTOMIZED INSTRUCTION

ESOL Students

Provide the student with a photo of clear soup labeled "Clear soup" and a photo of thick soup labeled "Thick soup."

Ask the student to fold one sheet of paper in half. Label one side "Clear Soup" and the other side "Thick Soup."

Provide the student with photos of various types of soups. Have the student assign them to the Clear or Thick side of the paper. Evaluate the student's comprehension of the words.

If the student does not have the language skills to continue, provide photos labeled with words that give the name of the soup and one characteristic of the type of soup. Have the student assign each to a side of the paper and write the new vocabulary in the correct column.

Have the student keep the organizer in the course notebook for future reference.

Special Needs Students

Since the class requirement calls for the use of sharp knives and open heat elements, it will be assumed that the special needs students can function at that level.

A less-advanced reader will proceed with the same differentiation as the ESOL student.

A hearing-impaired student may be able to join the More Advanced Student tier as well.

Have the student keep the organizer in the course notebook for future reference.

Less Advanced Students

Ask the student to please fold one sheet of paper in half. Label one side "Clear Soups" and the other side "Thick Soups."

On each section, write two characteristics of that type of soup.

Write two examples of each type of soup and a suggestion of how they would be served.

Have the student keep the organizer in the course notebook for future reference.

[trends]

Go Local with Fruit Soup

The restaurant industry continues to respond to consumers' demands for locally grown produce. Local production and delivery helps to ensure peak freshness, flavor, color, and nutrition for seasonal foods. Restaurants can capture this produce in menu items. Offering chilled fruit soups is one such strategy.

A cool, creamy greengage plum soup with a sprig of mint on a summer day is delightful. Another example is Swedish fruit soup, loaded with sour cherries, lemons, and tapioca, with a dollop of sour cream and a sprinkle of nutmeg. These soups can even be frozen for use later in the year. When considering local, fresh menu items, consider cool fruit soups for an appetizer or dessert.

There are many variations of these basic soups, including the following:

- Dessert soups, such as *Ginataan*, a Filipino soup made from coconut milk, milk, fruits, and tapioca pearls, and served hot or cold
- Fruit soups, such as winter melon or gazpacho, a savory soup with a tomato base
- Cold soups, such as borscht, a beet soup; or vichyssoise, a French-style soup made of puréed leeks, onions, potatoes, cream, and chicken stock
- Traditional regional soups, such as New England clam chowder or Manhattan clam chowder; or gumbo (a Creole soup made with okra)

Preparing Soups

Soups must be cooked properly. Most soups are cooked at a gentle simmer and stirred occasionally. If a soup is cooked for too long, the flavor can become flat and nutrients will be lost. Adding chopped fresh herbs, lemon juice, or a dash of hot pepper sauce to soup can brighten its flavor. Finishing techniques are important when preparing soup for service. For example, the line chef should remove the surface fat on the soup before service by blotting the soup with strips of unwaxed brown butcher paper. Soups should also be garnished just before service.

Clear Soups

Stock or broth is the basic ingredient in clear soups. Broth is made from a combination of water; vegetables; beef, fish, chicken, or veal; mirepoix; and bouquet garni. It should be clear to pale amber in color and have the flavor of the major ingredient.

One type of clear soup is consommé. This is a rich, flavorful broth or stock that has been clarified. A consommé is made by adding a mixture of ground meats

394

More Advanced Students

Fold a piece of paper in half. Label one side "Clear Soups" and the other "Thick Soups."

Contact or visit five restaurants or foodservice operations in your community. Learn about their soup offerings. Assign each to one of the two categories.

Note the following information:

- Name of soup
- Main dish or appetizer or other
- Base flavor
- Any other information that seems pertinent to the student or the restaurant

Be gracious and thank the chef or manager for his or her cooperation.

Have the student keep the organizer in the course notebook for future reference.

with mirepoix, tomatoes, egg whites, and ***oignon brûlé*** (oy-NYON broo-LAY) to bouillon or stock. This mixture is called clearmeat. *Oignon brûlé* is a "burnt onion." Cut an onion half across its hemisphere, then char the flat part either on a flattop or in a dry (fat-free) pan. This adds color and flavor to the consommé. Care must be taken to prevent too much burning.

Essential Skills
Preparing Basic Broth

❶ Combine the meat or vegetables and water.

❷ Bring to an even simmer.

❸ Add the mirepoix and bouquet garni. See Figure 6.17.

❹ Simmer for the appropriate cooking time depending on the main ingredient in the broth:

- Beef, veal, game, chicken: 2 to 3 hours

- Fish: 30 to 40 minutes

- Vegetables: 30 minutes to 1 hour

❺ Skim and strain. Cool and store, or finish and garnish for service.

Remember: A good broth should be clear, pale amber, with the distinct flavor of the major ingredient.

Figure 6.17: Step 3—Add mirepoix and bouquet garni.

The steps are similar to those for making a stock.

In-Class Activity:
100 Soups!

Prepare a bulletin board, blank poster, or long paper tape for the classroom.

As a class, compile a list of 100 soups. This may be adapted for smaller or larger classes. Divide 100 by the number of students that you have. The answer is the number of soups each student will have to identify and describe.

Assign the students to find and research their assigned number of soups.

As a class, compile a rough list allowing for some overlap and absent students. Determine the number of soups needed to reach one hundred. Assign that number to be researched and brought back.

When the list is ready, create the bulletin board, poster, or tape listing the 100 soups. They can be alphabetized, arranged as a spreadsheet, randomly arrayed, artistically presented or displayed in any other way that suits your classroom.

Display it in the room.

Vocabulary Terms

- ***Oignon brûlé:*** An onion that has caramelized, but that has not burned black.

Figure Focus
Figure 6.17: Note that mirepoix is added to the broth.

Essential Skills:
Preparing Basic Consommé

Tomatoes are added with mirepoix.

A raft is used to clarify the soup.

Reinforce and Review

- Can the students name the differences between stock, broth, and consommé?
- It might interest the students to see and taste the three in the same class period.

In-Class Activity:
Teacher Demonstration

The students should observe a raft clarification.

Make a very small batch of consommé and have it in the class for the students to see. It could be a very small saucepan or a large stockpot.

Make a raft with egg whites and the solid components that are simmering in the soup.

Show the students how it rises to the top.

Show the students how to gently and carefully break the hole in the raft.

If possible, let the students have some hands-on experience.

Vocabulary Terms

- **Raft:** A protein structure created to strain impurities from a clear broth.
- **Clarified:** Made clear.

Essential Skills
Preparing Basic Consommé

1. Combine the ground meat, mirepoix, seasonings, tomato product, *oignon brûlé*, and egg white. See Figure 6.18.
2. Blend in the stock.
3. Bring the mixture to a slow simmer, stirring frequently until the raft has formed.
4. Do not stir after the raft has formed.
5. Carefully break a hole in the raft and continue to simmer.
6. Strain, cool and store, or finish and garnish for service.

Remember: Good consommé should be crystal clear, aromatic, and emphasize the flavor of the major ingredient.

Figure 6.18: Step 1—Combine ingredients.

Slowly simmer the mixture until the impurities come to the surface, trapped in a **raft,** which is the floating layer of egg whites, meat and vegetable solids, and fats. Remove the raft, and the result is pure and clear, or **clarified**. Good consommé should be clear, aromatic, and emphasize the flavor of the major ingredient. If the consommé is too weak, a meat or poultry glaze may be added to enhance the flavor.

396

Figure Focus
Figure 6.18: Consommé is a clear, meat-based soup.

Essential Skills
Clarifying Stock

❶ Use egg whites, a mild acid (such as tomato or lemon juice), and a browned onion.

❷ Whip egg whites until the whites are foamy.

❷ Add these ingredients to the stock when stock is about 100°F.

❸ Simmer gently, at medium heat, for half an hour or more.

❹ When the raft of the egg structure and the scum has gathered, be careful not to stir the raft.

❺ Remove the raft by letting it settle completely to the bottom as it cools. Then, pour off the clarified stock, or carefully break a hole in the raft and gently ladle out the stock. See Figure 6.19.

❻ Discard the raft.

Figure 6.19: Step 5—Let raft settle to the bottom as it cooks.

Thick Soups

There are two kinds of thick soup—cream soups and purée soups. Both purée and cream soups are made with a liquid and either *sachet d'épices* or bouquet garni. Then a puréed main ingredient, to provide the main flavor, is blended into this base.

397

Essential Skills: Clarifying Stock

A raft is a unique thing in cooking.

The students should see one created, see how it strains the soup, and see how it is broken.

Teaching Tips

- Soups can be frozen. If you are not going to serve a soup immediately, freeze it.
- Leave head space in the freezer container to allow for the soup to expand as it freezes.
- Clear soups are appetizing because they increase the desire for additional food. Meat-flavored clear soups are one example. The aroma and flavor of meat will increase the flow of digestive juices. This boosts the appetite.
- Thick soups are satisfying because they quell hunger. A restaurant guest may be completely full after a serving. Thick soups can be a main dish item.
- Soup garnishes are added after the soup has been ladled into a serving bowl.
- Croutons can become soggy, so add them right before serving.

Figure Focus

Figure 6.19: A raft does not always appear appetizing. It is functional equipment, not food, even though it is made of food items.

Reinforce and Review

- Roux is not just used with sauces. Cream soups are also thickened with it.
- A purée soup will have thickness from the purée itself.
- Some of the purée ingredients will also have starch to add thickening.
- Careful handling maintains the quality of the soup.
- Overcooking and/or boiling damages or destroys the texture and body of a cream soup.

Teaching Tips

- The constraints of a school-based classroom might make it difficult to make a seafood bisque.
- If possible, involve the students in finding or creating a video or PowerPoint presentation about seafood bisque from online resources.

Vocabulary Terms

- **Purée soups:** Not every thick soup is flour or dairy based. This is another type of thick soup.
- **Bisque:** A creamy soup made from crustacean bones.

[nutrition]

Chili and MFP Factor

On a cold, wintry day, nothing tastes quite as good as a bowl of chili. Savory meat, warm kidney beans, and full-flavored tomatoes make it a classic American favorite. It is also a nutritional powerhouse where iron is concerned.

There are two types of iron in the diet: iron from animal sources (heme) and iron from vegetable sources (non-heme). The human body generally absorbs animal iron better than vegetable iron.

However, when a vegetable iron source is served with an animal source (heme and non-heme together in the same meal), there is a factor in the animal product that actually improves the absorption of the iron from all sources in that meal. It is called MFP Factor —you can remember it by thinking "Meat, Fish, Poultry." A little bit of an animal product greatly enhances the iron nutrition from all sources.

In chili, there is iron in the meat, iron in the beans, and MFP Factor. And there is even more good news: Vitamin C also enhances the absorption of iron from a meal by as much as three times. Tomatoes are a good source of vitamin C, so they get in the act as well. Savory meat, warm kidney beans, and full-flavored tomatoes: no wonder it's a classic.

The main difference between a purée and cream soup is that cream soups are usually thickened with an added starch, such as roux. **Purée soups** are thickened by the starch found in the puréed main ingredient, such as potatoes. Purée soups are coarser than cream soups, but should be liquid enough to pour easily from a ladle.

Cream soups must be thick with a smooth texture. They should never be boiled. Boiling can cause the milk fat to break down, making the soup too thin and watery. Try garnishing cream soups with a bit of the soup's main ingredient. For instance, place a few small blanched broccoli florets on a cream of broccoli soup.

Bisques are another kind of thick soup. Bisque (BISK) is a cream soup usually made from puréed shellfish shells, such as lobster, shrimp, or crab. The shells are puréed along with vegetables, making the texture slightly grainy. The bisque is then strained, garnished, and served. A properly prepared bisque should be pale pink or red, and have the flavor of the shellfish. Figure 6.20 shows a bisque soup—see Essential Skills, page 400.

Figure 6.20: Bisque is a rich, creamy soup that gets its color and flavor from lobster, shrimp, or crayfish.

Figure Focus
Figure 6.20: Gentle stirring and careful attention are needed to make a cream soup.

Essential Skills
How to Make Cream Soup

❶ Sauté the major flavoring, such as mushrooms for a cream of mushroom soup, in a little butter or oil.

❷ Add flour to make a roux and cook for a short time to remove any starchy taste.

❸ Add stock, *sachet d'épices*, and any vegetables, and then simmer until tender.

Note: Stock also includes aromatics, but these are separate aromatics being added to the finished stock and other ingredients.

❹ Purée and strain the mixture.

❺ Add additional stock to adjust the consistency as necessary.

❻ Add cream and garnish before serving. See Figure 6.21.

Figure 6.21: Step 6—How to make cream soup.

Chowders are hearty, thick soups made in much the same way as cream soups. Chowders are not puréed before the cream or milk is added. They are usually thickened with roux and typically include large pieces of the main ingredients (usually potatoes or seafood) and garnishes.

399

Essential Skills:
How to Make Cream Soup

Making a cream soup expands on the skill of making a sauce.

Vocabulary Terms

- **Chowder:** A chunky cream soup.

Figure Focus

Figure 6.21: The color of bisque comes partly from the pigment in crustacean shells and partly from tomatoes.

Crustacean shells have a carbohydrate compound called chitin that helps to thicken the soup.

Vocabulary Terms

- **Au sec:** Quite dry.

Essential Skills
Making Bisque

❶ Sear crustacean shells in a fat or sweat in stock. See Figure 6.22.

❷ Add mirepoix and sweat.

❸ Add tomato product.

❹ Reduce until the mixture is *au sec* (oh SEK). This means reduce it until it is very dry.

❺ Add stock and *sachet d'épices* or bouquet garni.

❻ Mix in the roux.

❼ Simmer and skim.

❽ Discard the *sachet d'épices* or bouquet garni when you have the desired flavor.

❾ Strain the soup and purée the solids.

Note: The solids that are puréed in this step include crustacean shells, which is why the soup must be strained in Step 11 below.

❿ Remix the liquid to the proper consistency.

Note: "Remix" refers to combining the reserved liquid that was strained out in Step 9 with the puréed solids. Not all of the liquid might be necessary to achieve the desired consistency in the finished soup.

⓫ Strain, then cool and store, or finish and garnish with the cooked, reserved meat from the crustacean.

Remember: A properly prepared bisque should have the flavor of the crustacean and a pale pink or red color.

Figure 6.22: Step 1—Sear shells in fat or sweat in stock.

400

Figure Focus

Figure 6.22: This photo shows sweating crustacean shells to extract flavor, color, and chitin.

[fast fact]

Did You Know...?

1. Americans sip over ten billion bowls of soup every year.

2. Ninety-nine percent of American homes buy soup each year, making it a $5 billion dollar business.

3. Women are more than twice as likely as men to eat soup as a typical lunch.

[ServSafe Connection]

Seafood Safety

Any menu item containing seafood, including soups or platter dishes with mollusks, such as bouillabaisse, cioppino, and paella, should be carefully constructed with seafood purchased only from approved, reputable suppliers.

The importance of the supplier's role in seafood purchasing cannot be overstated. Some species, including clams, mussels, and scallops, have been commonly linked to a variety of foodborne illnesses caused by toxins. The shellfish become contaminated as they filter toxic algae from the water. The toxins cannot be smelled or tasted—and they can't be destroyed by cooking or freezing. So the most important prevention measure for keeping contaminated shellfish out of an operation is buying the seafood from a safe source.

Shucked and live shellfish deliveries also require specific packaging and documentation that helps to track where the seafood came from. Operations are required to keep track of usage and file "shellstock identification tags" for certain products for three months from delivery.

With careful record keeping and strong attention to suppliers' practices, an operation can feature many complex and delicious seafood soups and dishes.

Summary

In this section, you learned the following:

- There are two basic kinds of soup—clear and thick. Clear soups include flavored stocks, broths, and consommés, and include soups such as chicken noodle soup and French onion soup. Thick soups include cream and purée soups, such as bisques or cream of tomato soup.

- Stock or broth is the basic ingredient in clear soups. **Consommé** is actually a rich, flavorful broth or stock that has been clarified. It should be clear, aromatic, and emphasize the flavor of the major ingredient.

- Cream soups are made with a thickener, such as roux. The main flavor in cream soups should be the major ingredient. For example, in a bisque, the main flavor should be shellfish.

- The main difference between a purée and cream soup is that cream soups are usually thickened with an added starch. **Purée soups** are thickened by the starch found in the puréed main ingredient (such as potatoes).

- There are many unusual kinds of soup, including cold soups, such as gazpacho; fruit soups, such as winter melon; and vegetable-based soups, such as minestrone, gumbo, or borscht.

401

Fast Fact
Did You Know...?

Soup is popular the world over and is found in every cuisine.

ServSafe Connection:
Seafood Safety

It is important to be able to track seafood purchases from the ocean all the way through to the dining guest.

Reinforce and Review

- The students should understand the two main types of soups.
- Stock is an essential ingredient in both sauces and soups.
- Cream soups should taste like their main ingredient.
- Cream soups use an added starch thickener.
- There are endless varieties of soups.

Summary

- Remind students to review the following:
  1. The two basic kinds of soup
  2. Preparing the basic ingredients for broth, consommé, purée, clear, and cream soups
  3. Preparing different kinds of soup

Section 6.3 Review Questions

1. Example of how these soups might be described include:

   Winter melon soup: This is an Asian soup with a clear broth made of chicken and ginger. There might be pieces of seafood or ham in the soup, along with scallions.

   Gumbo: A broth-based stew served over rice, thickened with either roux or filé powder. Gumbo may have various ingredients, but often contains trinity (a mirepoix-type mixture of onions, celery and green pepper), okra, andouille sausage, and shellfish.

   Borscht: An Eastern European beet soup that may also have beef or other meat and perhaps other vegetables like cabbage, onions, or carrots. Borscht has the characteristic deep red/magenta color of beets. Borscht may be served hot or chilled. Chilled borscht is usually a simple mixture of beets and broth, served with a dollop of sour cream. Sour cream may also garnish hot borscht, if desired.

   Minestrone: This is an Italian vegetable soup that typically includes white beans, pasta, tomatoes, zucchini, and perhaps some spinach, onions, or carrots. It is seasoned with basil and other mild savory spices, and is usually served hot, garnished with Parmesan cheese.

   Gazpacho: This is a Mexican chilled soup that is almost a salsa in a tomato-based broth. It may be chunky or puréed. It is usually quite spicy and piquant, flavored with chili peppers.

   Bisque: This is a creamy soup made with shellfish shells. The shells are simmered to soften them and to extract the flavor of the shellfish and the color of the shells. The softened shells are then forced through a sieve or *chinois*, and the debris is discarded. The soup is thickened with chitin, which is a complex carbohydrate that naturally occurs in the shells.

2. The two basic kinds of soup are clear soup and thick soup. Clear soup has a clear broth, no matter what other ingredients are included. Thick soups include cream soups and bisques.

3. Cream soups are thickened with cream or milk and a roux or other thickening agent. Purée soups are forced through a *chinois* or blenderized, and thickened with the main ingredient. Whatever the ingredients, they are now an opaque mixture.

4. Consommé is a clear soup that has been clarified.

5. The students may have a variety of ideas about this. Some common elements may be that onion soup is simple because it has very few elements. It requires great skill because the broth must be clear, amber-colored, flavorful, and well-balanced so that

Section 6.3 Review Questions

1. Describe each of the following types of soup, including the basic ingredients:

   a. Winter melon   d. Minestrone
   b. Gumbo   e. Gazpacho
   c. Borscht   f. Bisque

2. What are the two basic kinds of soup?

3. What is the main difference between cream and purée soups?

4. What is the name of a clear soup that has been clarified?

5. Chef Sonnenschmidt likes onion soup because while it is simple, it needs all of the passion and cooking knowledge of a master chef. Why would you find onion soup simple? In what aspects does it require the cooking knowledge of a master chef?

6. Soups are a critical offering on the Uptown Grille lunch menu. How can Linda balance the need to keep customers happy and interested while maintaining a lower price point?

7. When is a consommé served? Why?

8. How does a clarification work? What is a raft?

402

it is not overpowered by the onions. The bread must have a good crust that will be delicious even when soggy. It also must be served at a perfect temperature to melt the cheese without being too warm to eat and enjoy.

6. The students will have their own ideas about this. They may include something like the following: Linda can make soups that are not labor-intensive. A perfect consommé or seafood bisque would be more labor intensive than a gazpacho or minestrone. Also, certain ingredients, like shellfish, are more expensive than ingredients like beans.

7. A consommé may be served as an appetizer. This concept is based in human physiology. When a person smells or tastes a good cooked meat smell or flavor, it stimulates digestive juices, which boosts the appetite. It is an instinctive reaction. A beautifully made consommé is a work of art, and is served most often at the beginning of very formal meals.

8. Clarification works using the principles of the biochemistry of protein denaturation, although the students probably will not know this. In other words, protein from an egg will form a web or mesh type of structure. This web will gather debris in a clod. This material will float to the top of the broth as a mass that is called a raft.

Section 6.3 Activities

1. Study Skills/Group Activity: Alphabet Game

On a piece of paper, write each letter of the alphabet and place a line next to each letter. List the name of at least one type of soup for every letter of the alphabet, and note if the soup is clear or thick.

2. Activity: Soup to Soup

In reality, you would not serve multiple courses of soup at a meal. For this activity, create a soup appetizer, a soup main course, and a soup dessert. Make sure the flavors and textures are complementary.

3. Critical Thinking: Good Thick Soup

You have learned a lot about the creation of thick soups. Is it possible to create a nutritious, healthful thick soup? What substitutes might you have to make? Conduct some research and report back on a recipe for a healthful thick soup.

403

Section 6.3 Activities

1. Student might need to do some research to complete this. X and Z might be difficult.

2. Student responses will vary. Encourage students to be creative.

3. Thick soups can be very nutritious. Substitutions might include using milk instead of cream, starch thickener instead of butter, or lean meat instead of high-fat sausage or meat. Lots of vegetables, especially colorful ones, can add vitamins, minerals, anti-oxidants and fiber.

In-Class Activity: Good Thick Soup

The fat in the roux, plus the added cream, make thick soups a rather high-fat menu item.

How could the students create thick soups without as much fat?

Perhaps the students will come up with some innovative ideas.

Case Study Follow-Up

1. Students will present many ideas. One idea may be to have a variety of menu items made with fresh, local, seasonal ingredients.

2. The students will have a variety of strategies to suggest. One may be to have agreements with local farms, brokers, or greengrocers for direct purchase of fresh local items when possible. Another may be to limit lunch hours to reduce staff needs.

3. Student answers will vary. There are many things Linda can do. One might be to spend time getting acquainted with customers in the dining room. As she does, she may form relationships with guests and their businesses that may lead to further business.

4. Perhaps the students will debate this point. Perhaps limiting hours to only those during the busiest lunch rush would be wiser than limiting days. Guests would have to remember which days the restaurant is open, which might be inconvenient.

Case Study Follow-Up *Want to Do Lunch?*

According to the case study, Uptown Grille has been open for lunch for two months. After an initial spurt, business has slowed down. The customers have mostly responded positively to the quality and flavor of the food, the service, and the prices. Linda is not sure why the operation isn't doing better.

1. What can Uptown Grille do to make sure the menu is varied enough to appeal both to people who like fine dining and people who are very health conscious?

2. What steps can Linda take to keep costs within reason?

3. What can she do to ensure that customers will come back again?

4. Was opening only a few days a week a good way to start offering lunch? Why or why not?

404

Apply Your Learning

Math Makes a Good Soup

With a good recipe, you can make a good soup every time. However, a recipe makes a given amount of a dish, called the **yield**. If the recipe makes four cups of soup, the yield is four cups. This might be the perfect size batch to make if you are serving four people; each person would get one cup of soup. But if you have ten people to serve, how do you convert the recipe? Select a soup recipe and convert it to a ratio formula.

Soup Time Line

Research and create a history of soup, developing a time line. When was soup first created? What purpose did it serve? How did it become a popular and accepted standard fare? Is the original purpose still evident today?

Thickening Up

Starch thickeners provide structure and body to soups, sauces, pie fillings, and other liquids. The starch swells with water and forms a gel structure that gets thick. As the gel forms and heats it becomes clearer, so the product does not look as milky as the starch solution did at first. Thickening is a chemical reaction that cannot be reversed. Once a dry powdered starch becomes a thickened gel, it will not return to a dry powder on its own.

Wheat flour mixes best with fat. A thin coating of fat helps the flour distribute evenly in a hot liquid. This is why flour and butter are mixed to make a roux or beurre manié. The liquid must be hot to keep the fat melted so that lumps do not form.

Cornstarch mixes better in cold water. If the water is hot, the gel begins to form too soon. This will cause lumps with gel outside and powder inside. Once a cold-water slurry is made, the cornstarch can be mixed evenly into a liquid.

Create a reference chart about four thickeners: flour, cornstarch, arrowroot, and tapioca. Include all pertinent information in your table, such as mixing method, food uses, potential problems, benefits, and temperature range for best thickening.

Critical Thinking   Low-Fat Soup and Low-Fat Sauce

Restaurants often notify customers of menu items that are considered "Heart-Healthy" and low in fat. What are some low-fat soup choices? What are some low-fat sauce choices?

405

Apply Your Learning

Math Makes a Good Soup

Ten servings are desired. If the recipe makes four servings, how many batches do you need to make ten servings?
$10 \div 4 = 2.5$ The recipe conversion factor is 2.5 The quantity of each ingredient in the recipe will be multiplied by 2.5 in order to make ten servings.

Soup Time Line

Since this is not a history class, exhaustive research is not needed. The purpose of this activity is to help students realize that soup is an ancient food, common to nearly all cultures on Earth. The students will also be able to practice research reading and writing skills. The results do not need to be completely and exactly accurate to be valuable.

Thickening Up

This chart may be used for future reference. It can include various creative layouts. It should be something that the student could design, share with the class, and keep. Some research may be required.

Critical Thinking   Low-Fat Soup and Low-Fat Sauce

Student responses will vary. A low-fat sauce may be a glace or a tomato sauce. A low-fat soup may be a clear soup such as chicken noodle, or a purée soup like borscht. A cream soup is generally not low in fat.

Exam Prep Answers

1. A
2. A
3. B
4. A
5. D
6. B
7. D
8. B
9. A
10. B

Exam Prep Questions

1 The essential part of stock that is a mixture of coarsely chopped onions, carrots, and celery is called

A. mirepoix.

B. aromatics.

C. *sachet d'épices.*

D. bouquet garni.

2 What liquid is usually used for making stock?

A. Water

B. Boullion

C. Beef broth

D. Chicken broth

3 Roasting bones to enhance the flavor and color of stock is a process known as

A. sweating.

B. browning.

C. blanching.

D. par-boiling.

4 The ratio of liquid to flavoring ingredients in vegetable stock is

A. 1 lb of vegetables to 1 qt of water to yield 1 qt of stock.

B. 2 lbs of vegetables to 4 qts of water to yield 1 qt of stock.

C. 11 lbs of vegetables to 5 qts of water to yield 1 gal of stock.

D. 8 lbs of vegetables to 6 qts of water to yield 1 gal of stock.

5 After the stock has been stored, it must be degreased before it can be used. This is because

A. it is easier to heat up degreased stock.

B. the grease will ruin the flavor of the stock, turning it rancid.

C. all of the fat must be skimmed off in order for the stock to be healthful.

D. degreasing makes the stock clearer and purer, while removing some of the fat.

6 Béchamel, velouté, and hollandaise are all called

A. thickeners.

B. grand sauces.

C. derivative sauces.

D. compound butters.

7 A slurry, a liaison, and a roux are all considered to be

A. soups.

B. stocks.

C. aromatics.

D. thickeners.

8 What is a mixture of egg yolks and heavy cream that adds a rich flavor and velvety smoothness to the sauce without making it too thick?

A. Slurry

B. Liaison

C. Hollandaise

D. Compound butter

9 Stocks, broths, and consommés are all _____ soups.

A. clear

B. thick

C. puréed

D. bisque

10 Thick soups can be thickened with

A. cream.

B. cornstarch.

C. bouquet garni.

D. compound butter.

Fish stock

Cooking time: 60 minutes
Yield: 1 gal

Ingredients

1 lb	Mirepoix, small dice	Sachet:	
8 oz	Mushroom trimmings	2	Bay leaves
2 fl oz	Clarified butter	½ tsp	Dried thyme
10 lb	Fish bones or crustacean shells	¼ tsp	Peppercorns, crushed
5 qt	Water	8	Parsley stems

Directions

1. Sweat mirepoix and mushroom trimmings in butter until tender for 1 to 2 minutes.
2. Combine all ingredients except the sachet in a stockpot.
3. Bring to a simmer and skim impurities as necessary.
4. After 15 to 30 minutes into the cooking process, add the sachet and simmer uncovered for 30 to 45 minutes.
5. Strain, cool, and refrigerate.

Recipe Nutritional Content

Calories	25	Cholesterol	0 ng	Protein	4 g
Calories from fat	10	Sodium	240 mg	Vitamin A	0%
Total fat	1.5 g	Carbohydrates	0 g	Vitamin C	0%
Saturated fat	0 g	Dietary fiber	0 g	Calcium	0%
Trans fat	0 g	Sugars	0 g	Iron	0%

Nutritional analysis provided by FoodCalc®, www.foodcalc.com

407

Recipe

Fish Stock

- Fish stock can be used as a base for soups, sauces, gravies, rice and risotto dishes, and fish stews.
- To make fish stock, use bones from lean fish (such as cod), not fatty fish (such as salmon).
- Fish fumet is a strongly flavored fish stock, traditionally used as a poaching liquid.

Recipe

Velouté

- Velouté is one of the four mother sauces of French cuisine, as designated by Carême in the nineteenth century.
- Some sauces that may be derived from a velouté sauce include *sauce vin blanc*, *Allemande* sauce, and supreme sauce.
- Sauce velouté is most commonly served on poultry and seafood dishes.

Velouté

Cooking time: 45 minutes
Yield: 1 gal

Ingredients

8 fl oz	Clarified butter	5 qt	Chicken, veal, or fish stock
8 oz	Flour	To taste	Salt and white pepper

Directions

1. Heat the butter in a heavy saucepan. Add the flour and cook to make a blond roux.
2. Gradually add the stock to the roux, stirring constantly with a whisk to prevent lumps. Bring to a boil and reduce to a simmer. (Seasonings are optional; their use depends on the seasonings in the stock and the sauce's intended use.)
3. Simmer and reduce to 1 gallon (4 liters), approximately 30 minutes.
4. Strain through a china cap lined with cheesecloth.
5. Melted butter may be carefully ladled over the surface of the sauce to prevent a skin from forming. Hold for service or cool in a water bath.

Recipe Nutritional Content

Calories	4,180	Cholesterol	630 mg	Protein	146 g
Calories from fat	2,160	Sodium	8,470 mg	Vitamin A	120%
Total fat	244 g	Carbohydrates	343 g	Vitamin C	15%
Saturated fat	132 g	Dietary fiber	6 g	Calcium	20%
Trans fat	0 g	Sugars	77 g	Iron	115%

Nutritional analysis provided by FoodCalc®, www.foodcalc.com

408

New England–Style Clam Chowder

Cooking time: 45 minutes
Yield: 3½ qt

Ingredients

2 qt	Canned clams with juice	1 qt	Milk
Approx 1½ qt	Water or fish stock	8 fl oz	Heavy cream
1 lb 4 oz	Potatoes, small dice	To taste	Salt and pepper
8 oz	Salt pork, small dice	To taste	Tabasco sauce
2 oz	Whole butter	To taste	Worcestershire sauce
1 lb	Onions, small dice	To taste	Fresh thyme
8 oz	Celery, small dice	As needed for garnish	Fresh parsley
4 oz	Flour	As needed for garnish	Carrot, julienned

Directions

1. Drain the clams, reserving the clams and putting their liquid in the stockpot. Add enough water or stock to the clam liquid so that the total liquid equals 2 quarts.
2. Simmer the potatoes in the clam liquid until nearly cooked through. Strain and reserve the potatoes and the liquid.
3. Render the salt pork with the butter. To render fat, melt it over low heat until the fat is liquid. Strain the liquid fat to remove any particles of pork that remain.
4. Add the onions and celery to the rendered fat and sweat until tender but not brown.
5. Add the flour and cook to make a blond roux.
6. Add the clam liquid to the roux, whisking away any lumps.
7. Simmer for 30 minutes, skimming as necessary.
8. Bring the milk and cream to a boil and add to the soup.
9. Add the clams and potatoes, and season to taste with salt, pepper, Tabasco sauce, Worcestershire sauce, and thyme.
10. Garnish each serving with fresh parsley and julienned carrot as desired.

Recipe Nutritional Content

Calories	560	Cholesterol	120 mg	Protein	28 g
Calories from fat	280	Sodium	650 mg	Vitamin A	20%
Total fat	31 g	Carbohydrates	42 g	Vitamin C	50%
Saturated fat	15 g	Dietary fiber	5 g	Calcium	20%
Trans fat	0 g	Sugars	3 g	Iron	145%

Nutritional analysis provided by FoodCalc®, www.foodcalc.com

409

Recipe

New England-Style Clam Chowder

- The main difference between Manhattan and New England-style clam chowders is that Manhattan clam chowder uses a clear broth with tomato for coloring, while New England clam chowder is milk or cream-based.
- Other types of clam chowder include Rhode Island, Outer Banks, and Minorcan.
- Clam chowder is often served with oyster crackers.

Chapter 7 discusses the importance of developing sound communication skills as an element of success in the foodservice industry.

Section 1: The first section describes the process of communication, noting some common obstacles and barriers to understanding.

Section 2: This section focuses on specific communication skills, such as speaking and writing.

Section 3: The final section addresses two main categories of communication: organizational communication and interpersonal communication.

Advance Preparation	
Review	Material in Sections 7.1–7.3
	Relevant material in Chapter 4
Contact	A leader in the local foodservice community
Prepare	Sample food-related blogs from the Internet

Chapter 7
Communication

CUSTOMIZED INSTRUCTION OPTIONS			
Less Advanced Students	**More Advanced Students**	**ESOL Students**	**Special Needs Students**
Pages 421, 429	Pages 418, 434	Pages 417, 419, 428	Pages 417, 428

CHAPTER TOOLS			
21st-Century Skills	**Mathematics**	**Science**	**Literacy**
Pages 414, 416, 417, 418, 419, 420, 421, 425, 428, 429, 433, 434, 435, 437, 439, 444, 447, 448, 451	Pages 435, 439	Page 418	Pages 414, 416, 417, 418, 419, 420, 421, 425, 428, 429, 433, 434, 435, 437, 439, 444, 447, 448, 451

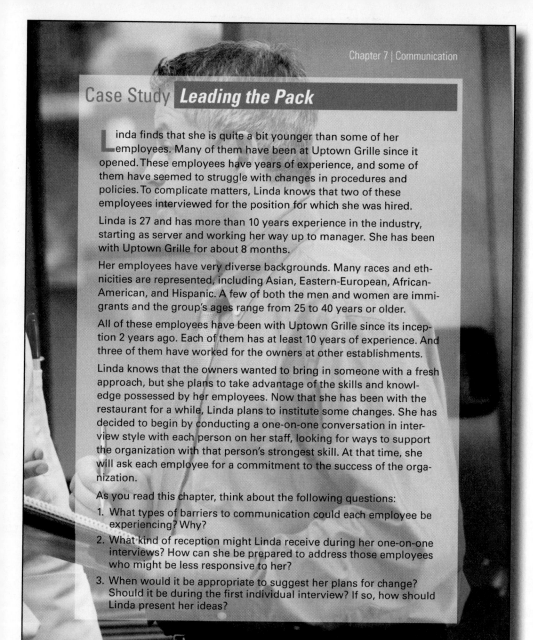

Case Study | *Leading the Pack*

Linda finds that she is quite a bit younger than some of her employees. Many of them have been at Uptown Grille since it opened. These employees have years of experience, and some of them have seemed to struggle with changes in procedures and policies. To complicate matters, Linda knows that two of these employees interviewed for the position for which she was hired.

Linda is 27 and has more than 10 years experience in the industry, starting as server and working her way up to manager. She has been with Uptown Grille for about 8 months.

Her employees have very diverse backgrounds. Many races and ethnicities are represented, including Asian, Eastern-European, African-American, and Hispanic. A few of both the men and women are immigrants and the group's ages range from 25 to 40 years or older.

All of these employees have been with Uptown Grille since its inception 2 years ago. Each of them has at least 10 years of experience. And three of them have worked for the owners at other establishments.

Linda knows that the owners wanted to bring in someone with a fresh approach, but she plans to take advantage of the skills and knowledge possessed by her employees. Now that she has been with the restaurant for a while, Linda plans to institute some changes. She has decided to begin by conducting a one-on-one conversation in interview style with each person on her staff, looking for ways to support the organization with that person's strongest skill. At that time, she will ask each employee for a commitment to the success of the organization.

As you read this chapter, think about the following questions:

1. What types of barriers to communication could each employee be experiencing? Why?

2. What kind of reception might Linda receive during her one-on-one interviews? How can she be prepared to address those employees who might be less responsive to her?

3. When would it be appropriate to suggest her plans for change? Should it be during the first individual interview? If so, how should Linda present her ideas?

Case Study
Leading the Pack

- How might students feel when working with a supervisor who is much older? How might they feel if the situation was reversed? What barriers to understanding one another do students perceive?

- Why might Linda's employees view her, and the changes she represents, with suspicion? How could she alleviate this?

- How can Linda develop a stronger trust relationship with her new colleagues? How can she overcome their concerns?

- Why will Linda ask each employee to make a formal commitment to organizational success? How can that make a difference in day-to-day work?

- Note that there are follow-up questions about the case study at the end of the chapter.

- This activity could be done in groups, as a class, or as a homework assignment.

Professional Profile

Discuss	Mary Fox earned her first job at Coca-Cola when she "wasn't even looking." Ask students to relate this to the discussion in Chapter 4 about the importance of professionalism and first impressions. How does the restaurant and foodservice industry "touch everyone"? Encourage students to provide examples. Knowing how to cook isn't really essential to achieving success in the restaurant and foodservice industry, since many career paths don't involve the kitchen at all. But what skills are important for all foodservice employees to share?
Reinforce and Review	The restaurant and foodservice industry touches everyone, since everyone must eat and drink. Within the restaurant and foodservice industry, there are huge opportunities for jobs and careers related to almost any set of skills and interests.
Teaching Tips	Ask students about their own passions. How can they communicate what they love to another person? How can they translate it into a successful career, within the foodservice industry or elsewhere?

[professional profile]

Mary Fox

Senior Sales Executive

Coca-Cola North America, Foodservice and Hospitality Division

I've always had what my dear mother likes to call "*the gift of gab*," and I learned at the young age of 16 that I was good at sales when I worked for a clothing store and received numerous national sales awards and recognition. In conjunction with that, I grew up in a "*Coca-Cola*" home, one that was brand loyal to Coca-Cola products, so I always loved the brand. I became even more interested in the company while studying about it in my business courses during college.

I graduated from the University of Illinois at Urbana/Champaign with a B.S. in business administration with a concentration in marketing. Amazingly enough, the opportunity to work for Coca-Cola came when I wasn't even looking. The woman that would eventually become my manager had been watching me sell to customers at the job I was working at in college and approached me about an open sales position that she had on her team. It was an incredibly valuable lesson to learn early in life...you never know who's watching you, so always be at your best.

Reflecting back on my career choice, I just love how the restaurant and foodservice industry touches everyone. No matter what walk of life you come from, no matter where you are at in the world, we all have our own unique stories about what and how we eat and drink. And let's face it, the foodservice industry is fun. It's an exciting field with endless possibilities. No matter what your talents are, you can find a place to call home in this industry...if you have entrepreneurial spirit, if you're technically savvy, or if you're a creative and brilliant innovator. All can be found in the restaurant and foodservice industry.

Cooking is one of my biggest passions, and I find it incredibly therapeutic. But it wasn't always that way. I couldn't make scrambled eggs 5 years ago. I believe truly good cooking comes from deep down in the soul, and once I made that connection, my true love affair with food and cooking began. While having the knowledge and skills to cook is very important, the greatest food comes from those who put their heart and soul into their cooking.

Be passionate about everything you do...from the most mundane tasks to the largest projects. Exuding passion is contagious, and ultimately, it's what will help you get through the good times and the bad times throughout your career.

Remember: **❝** *Food is our common ground, a universal experience.* **❞**
—James Beard, American chef and food writer

...and, another quote that is dear to my heart...

❝ *A billion hours ago, human life appeared on earth. A billion minutes ago, Christianity emerged. A billion Coca-Colas ago was yesterday morning.* **❞**
—1996 Coca-Cola annual report

412

About Communication

Communication is one of the most important of all skills. But you're only an effective communicator if you are able to engage your audience. So it's critical to (1) be aware of your surroundings and (2) be sensitive to who your audience is. Then you can adjust your communication style accordingly.

7.1 The Communication Process
• The process of communication
• Barriers to communication

7.2 Communication Skills
• Personal characteristics that affect communication skills
• Effective listening
• Effective speaking
• Effective telephone skills
• Effective writing

7.3 Types of Communication
• Organizational communication
• Interpersonal communication

SECTION 7.1 THE COMMUNICATION PROCESS

Communication is an important part of everyday life. It allows us to interact with each other and to share our knowledge, ideas, and experiences. Most people think communication is just speaking and listening, but it is so much more. We communicate through body language, gestures, writing, speaking, listening, and in many other ways. Of course, this means that just as many ways exist to miscommunicate. It is important to use positive communication by focusing and listening.

Study Questions

After studying Section 7.1, you should be able to answer the following questions:

- What is the communication process?
- What are the barriers to effective communication?

The Process of Communication

Communication is the process of sending and receiving information by talk, gestures, or writing for some type of response or action. Communication is a learned skill. Most people are born with the ability to express themselves, but need to learn how to effectively communicate. Communication includes both verbal (speaking and writing) and nonverbal communication (body language and gestures).

413

Teach

Discuss

- How does our audience affect our communication style?
- What is the difference between expressing ourselves and effectively communicating with other people?
- Which do students perceive as more important: verbal or nonverbal communication?

Reinforce and Review

- We communicate through body language, speaking, writing, gestures, listening, and many other ways. These are categorized as verbal and nonverbal communication.
- Communication is a learned skill, not an inherent talent.

Focus and Engage

Discuss

- Why is communication so important, both at work and in our personal lives?
- What does it mean to "engage your audience"? What are some techniques students can learn to hold people's attention?
- Being aware of and sensitive to the needs of others is a learned skill, but one that will be important throughout life.
- Divide students into small groups and ask them to discuss the following:
  - Do you know any bad communicators? What makes them bad at communicating?
  - Do you know any good communicators? What makes them good at communicating?
  - How do you feel after an interaction with either a bad or a good communicator?
- Reconvene the class and, as a group, list and discuss the characteristics of both good and bad communicators that students identified in the small groups.

Section 7.1 The Communication Process

Introduce the Section

a. Review the process of communication, identifying the different steps and participants.
b. Identify some common barriers to communication and discuss ways they can be overcome.
c. Discuss the objectives for the section.

Vocabulary Review

a. Direct students to the key terms.
b. Pronounce each word, and have the students repeat the pronunciation out loud.
c. Discuss the definition of each word.

Fast Fact: Did You Know...?

Encourage students to discuss the following:

- How much of this 75 percent is spent in effective communication, not just communication?
- If body language and other nonverbal activities are considered communication, does that mean we are communicating any time we are in the same room as another person?

Reinforce and Review

- Understanding how the communication process works is important for building strong relationships with employees and customers.
- Both what people say and how they say it help determine whether their message is effective.
- The five components of the communication process are the sender, receiver, message content, message channel, and context. Unfortunately, barriers often prevent the accurate transmission of the message from sender to receiver.

Teaching Tips

- Students should diagram the communication process, using the following situations:
  - A maître d' tells a hostess not to seat a recently arrived party. There is very little room in the waiting area, and it is raining outside.
  - A server asks the chef not to send a table's food yet because the woman in the party has just gotten up to make a telephone call. The delicate food is beginning to wilt under the heat lamps.
  - The health inspector tells the manager and chef that the restaurant must be closed for the evening due to a broken waste pipe. The restaurant is booked that evening for a private wedding reception.
- After diagramming the situations, discuss them as a class. How should each be handled?

[fast fact]

Did You Know...?
It is estimated that 75 percent of a person's day is spent communicating.

Understanding how the communication process works is important for building strong relationships with employees and customers. It isn't only what people say that is important. How they say it has a major impact on a message's success with the audience, too.

Barriers to Communication

1 Sender	**3** Message content	**5** Context
2 Receiver	**4** Message channel	**6** Barriers

Noise, environment, language, cultural differences, tone of message, nonverbal communication, and lack of comprehension can be barriers to communication.

Figure 7.1: Understanding the process of communication will help employees to communicate effectively with one another.

The communication process has five parts: sender, receiver, message content, message channel, and context. Figure 7.1 illustrates the communication process.

The following is an example of the communication process in the restaurant and foodservice industry:

- **Sender:** Chef
- **Receiver:** Line cook
- **Message content:** Fire three shrimp on table 10.
- **Message channel:** Downward
- **Context:** The line cook is "in the weeds," and the chef really needs that table out quickly.

414

Figure Focus

Figure 7.1: With so many potential barriers to communication, how can people ever truly communicate? Is it possible to understand exactly what someone is communicating to you?

Homework Activity: Barriers to Communication

Literacy Connection, 21st-Century Skills—Communicate Clearly, Use Systems Thinking, Produce Results

What barriers to communication have students experienced?

Each student should list the barriers to communication that he or she has directly experienced. Pick one particular instance and diagram the communication process that took place, including why it went wrong. How could the problem have been overcome? What lessons were learned for future interactions with that individual?

Write a one-page report addressing this information.

The person sending the message begins the communication process. Often, the sender wants something done as a result of the communication. Following are some of the things that the sender needs to think about before sending a message:

- Who will receive it?

- What message do I want to send?

- How should I send the message?

- What other factors do I need to consider as I deliver the message?

In most cases, the person who receives the message is not just a passive receptor of the information. Some things this person does are the following:

- Communicate understanding of the information

- Interpret the message

- Act on it

- Makes decisions along the way to complete the actions

The main connection between the people sending and receiving a message is the message content. The two kinds of messages are following:

1. **Historical information:** This is information that has already happened. Examples include company history and orientation information, status updates, and management decisions. Receivers don't usually need to do anything with these messages. They simply build receivers' knowledge for future situations.

2. **Action-required information:** People who send these types of messages expect something to happen because of the message. Some action must happen immediately or in the future. The person receiving the message is usually who must act on the information. One example is an order from a supervisor. It can be as simple as "Clean that table."

The sender must decide the best way for the message to be delivered. Which medium will help the message be as clear as possible for its intended audience? Messages can take many forms including the following:

- **Words:** This can mean verbal or written words.

- **Sounds:** For example, a siren is one way to send a message.

- **Graphic illustrations:** Some examples of this are pictures, diagrams, job aids.

- **Signs and symbols:** Gestures and nonverbal forms are two kinds of signs and symbols.

415

Discuss

- The two kinds of messages we convey are historical and action-required. What instances of each can students draw from daily life? What instances can they imagine occurring in the restaurant and foodservice industry?

Reinforce and Review

- Before sending a message, the sender should consider the recipient, the message itself, the means of transmitting the message, and any other factors that could affect the transmission.

- Similarly, when receiving a message, the receiver should communicate understanding of the message, interpret the message, act on the message, and make any necessary decisions that affect how the message is carried out.

- The two kinds of messages are historical information and action-required information.

- Messages can take a variety of forms. Words, sounds, graphic illustrations, and signs and symbols all carry information from sender to receiver.

Teaching Tips

- Divide students into small groups. Each group should pick a message and decide how, from whom, and to whom it should be conveyed. Students may want to incorporate barriers to communication as well. Each group should present a skit to the class clearly demonstrating the communication process.

Vocabulary Terms

- **Historical information:** Information that has already happened; it helps build receivers' knowledge for future situations.

- **Action-required information:** Information about something that needs to happen, either immediately or in the future; it tells the receiver what to do.

Discuss

- Developing a communication plan can help overcome barriers to communication. But is there always a way to develop a plan, or time to complete the process? How can students develop a "meta-plan," a general way of communicating with others that is flexible enough to adjust to any barriers that arise?
- Two common barriers to communication include lack of time and fear of confrontation. Encourage students to share their experiences with these barriers, as both senders and receivers of messages. What have the results been like?

Reinforce and Review

- Common barriers to communication include lack of time and fear of confrontation.
- Developing a plan for successful communication despite barriers includes preparation, delivery, and follow-up.

In-Class Activity: Barriers Both Ways

Literacy Connection, 21st-Century Skills— Self-Directed Learners, Use Systems Thinking, Reason Effectively

Develop a hypothetical situation in which you, the manager, must convey some information to a staff member. How do you choose to convey the message? What barriers might you perceive in the interaction?

Now, imagine that you are the staff member to whom that message is conveyed. What barriers might you perceive in the interaction? Why and how might these be different from the barriers you perceived as manager?

No one perceives the same situation in exactly the same way. Think about how you can be more aware of the barriers that might affect the people with whom you're communicating each day.

Barriers to Communication

Barriers to communication include anything that interferes or affects communication. Barriers to communication include lack of time and other pressing needs. Lack of time forces people to rush and doesn't allow them to think things out. It may also produce noncommunication. Some situations, particularly in a restaurant or foodservice operation, do not allow much time for complete communication. Follow up is required to make sure everyone is understood.

Another common barrier to communication is fear of confrontation. Younger people are often afraid to speak up when they notice something because they don't have as much experience. They are afraid of negative results such as punishment or retribution.

To prevent barriers in communication, make a plan:

1. Before sending a message, observe the audience. Hear what's happening. Look to see what's happening.

2. Decide the best way to get the message out with a chance of success.

3. Make sure the message was successfully received. In some cases, the barrier is not obvious until the message is already out there. Go back to the beginning of the process if the message wasn't a success and change the approach as needed.

Figure 7.2 shows a manager who may be having trouble overcoming a few barriers. What do you think they might be?

Lack of time (clock)

Fear of authority/ reprimand

Different cultural backgrounds

Figure 7.2: When communicating, it is important to be aware of potential barriers that might interfere with the communication.

Figure Focus

Figure 7.2: Is the manager doing anything correctly? If so, what? What are the employees communicating?

[on the job]

Nonverbal Communication Around the World

Nonverbal communication is an important part of communication. It includes touch, eye contact, gestures, posture, and facial expressions. Nonverbal communication is important because it repeats and complements a verbal message. However, in different cultures, nonverbal communication means different things:

United States: Greet each other with a firm, brief handshake. Make eye contact. Keep distance when communicating.

Japan: Eye contact and pointing the index finger are considered rude and aggressive.

India: Shake hands when meeting but seldom do men and women shake hands because of religious beliefs. Do not stand close; keep at least an arm's length between you and the person you are communicating with. The left hand is considered unclean, so use the right hand to touch or pass something.

China: Avoid body contact and pointing with the index finger. Winking is considered rude.

Be aware of the following obstacles to good communication before communicating any message. Table 7.1 describes the obstacles to good communication.

Table 7.1: Obstacles to Good Communication

Communication Obstacle	Description	Examples
Language differences	We all speak with accents and dialects that reflect where we live now and where we've lived in the past. A dialect is the variation of a language spoken by a particular group of people, such as Easterners, Southerners, or Bostonians. Even if everyone is speaking the same language, members of different groups must often work hard to understand what is being said. For many people, including those working in the restaurant and foodservice industry, English is a second language. It takes a lot of concentration and energy to master something new when someone is not completely familiar with the language. Be patient with people who are still learning. Don't let the way a person speaks affect you negatively.	This may be as easy as soda versus pop, or hoagie versus hero versus submarine versus grinder. It may also be something as easy as understanding the dialect. For example, in Boston: "Pahk the cah in Hahvuhd yahd" means "Park the car in Harvard yard."

continued

CUSTOMIZED INSTRUCTION

Literacy Connection, 21st-Century Skills—Communicate Clearly, Critical Thinking and Problem Solving, Social and Cultural Skills

ESOL Students

What are some obstacles to communication that you have experienced at school or in society? How did you react to these situations? What did you learn from them?

Write one paragraph describing these experiences.

Special Needs Students

What are some obstacles to communication that you have experienced at school or in society? How did you react to these situations? What did you learn from them?

Discuss these situations with a small group.

On the Job: Nonverbal Communication Around the World

Encourage students to discuss the following:

- What nonverbal communication have you experienced with supervisors or teachers? Is this different from the nonverbal communication you experience at home or with friends?

- In an increasingly multicultural society, how can nonverbal communication skills either help or hamper effective communication?

Table 7.1: Obstacles to Good Communication (continued on p. 418)

- How can language differences affect guest service? How do they relate to cultural differences?

- As a future leader in the foodservice industry, how can you work to eliminate language differences in the workplace?

In-Class Activity: Communication Barriers

Literacy Connection, 21st-Century Skills— Communication and Collaboration, Critical Thinking and Problem Solving, Social and Cultural Skills

Working in small groups, develop a skit about some barrier to communication and how it could be overcome. The story does not have to take place in the foodservice setting. The skit should be under five minutes.

Present two versions to the class. First, show them an incorrect way to overcome the barrier. Then, show them how to overcome the barrier in a positive way. Afterward, other classmates should be invited to give their feedback. How else could the situation have been addressed?

Table 7.1 (continued)

- How can using jargon, slang, or other specialized words cause message recipients to feel isolated, left out, or unwelcome? How can it make the speaker appear rude or poorly educated?

- How can the tone of someone's message have the same effects?

- Why is clarity so important in the restaurant and foodservice industry, especially when guests are directly involved in the conversation?

CUSTOMIZED INSTRUCTION

Science Connection, Literacy Connection, 21st-Century Skills—Communicate Clearly, Critical Thinking and Problem Solving, Social and Cultural Skills

More Advanced Students

Semantics is the study of meaning in language, including nonverbal and other types of communication. Research this branch of science to learn more about how and why language and its forms are studied and how this knowledge can facilitate communication.

For instance, do our words mean anything on their own, or do they simply refer to something else that has meaning? What role does memory play in our understanding of a message?

Write a one-page report on one of these or a similar topic to explore how semantics can be an obstacle to effective communication.

In-Class Activity: Clarity and Not-So-Clarity

Literacy Connection, 21st-Century Skills—Communicate Clearly, Critical Thinking and Problem Solving, Social and Cultural Skills

Develop three examples of unclear or ambiguous sentences and share them with the class.

For instance, "I can't recommend this dish too highly," could mean either that the speaker thinks the item is unworthy of praise or that the speaker has no words with which to express a sufficiently high opinion of the dish.

Use this exercise to think about the clarity of your day-to-day communications. How can you improve?

Table 7.1: Obstacles to Good Communication *continued*

Communication Obstacle	Description	Examples
Semantics (what words mean)	Not everyone understands words in the same way. Can the audience understand the message as you intended? Does the audience understand the actual words of the message as well as the speaker does? Do words or phrases mean one thing to the communicator and another thing to the audience? Consider replacing "common" phrases (or adages) or words that have multiple meanings with simpler terms. Make sure the intended meaning is clear.	The word "ill" means "to be sick" but also can mean "cool." The word mouse means "rodent" or "computer device." Cup of soup, cup of coffee, cup of flour all mean something different.
Jargon	Buzzwords, technical language, and slang usually shouldn't be used, unless the communicator is absolutely sure that the audience understands these words. It's better to avoid jargon altogether.	Use of "loop in" to mean "keep informed," or "heads-up" to mean "be aware" or "watch out."
Tone of message	Speakers can say something in a tone that differs from the meaning of what they're saying. People often judge the sincerity of a speaker by his or her tone. Is the tone one of open sharing and inclusion? Or does the speaker sound negative, snobby, or disapproving? Avoiding negativity and sarcasm is critical to sounding sincere.	"Turn in your time card by the end of the day." "Time cards should be turned in at the end of the day."
Clarity	Bad writing, such as not being direct or using too many tangents, can cause confusion and/or leave room for interpretation. Check the structure of the message to make sure that the message is as clear as possible. Follow good business writing guidelines.	"I can't recommend this dish too highly."
Assumptions	Do you assume someone knows how to solve a problem when it happens? Have you provided enough instruction to get the problem fixed? Or are you providing too much basic information? Make sure you understand what your audience knows before you deliver a message.	"We have too many people waiting to be seated."

continued

Table 7.1: Obstacles to Good Communication *continued*

Communication Obstacle	Description	Examples
Cultural differences	Consider any cultural differences.	If someone orders scones in most of the United States, he or she expects a biscuit-like quick bread item, perhaps with fruit in it. If they order scones in the Intermountain West of the United States (Idaho, Utah, Arizona), they expect a yeast-leavened deep-fried bread served with powdered sugar, butter and jam, or honey butter.
Prejudices and biases	A prejudice or bias is a preconceived idea about something that could affect a message, usually negatively. They come from many factors, including experiences, upbringing, and cultural beliefs. People can be biased against a group, a particular person, or even a situation. Do you carry certain biases based on experiences you have had? Do you think certain groups of people have a tendency to do something or not do something? Do you have attitudes that influence the way you send your message? Are you afraid to talk to certain people? Answer these questions honestly for yourself. Then reexamine your communications to make sure your messages don't include any bias.	"Teenagers are lazy." "Older people are computer illiterate."
Noise	Noise is any sound that interferes with clear reception. Will machinery, loud-talking people, or blaring radios interfere with the clear reception of the message? Is the noise associated with a specific time or location? Try to find a place to either get rid of or reduce this noise.	Should you try to talk to an employee in the entryway of your restaurant or foodservice establishment, or move to a quieter location?

continued

419

Table 7.1 (continued)

- How can cultural differences be used to improve communication in the workplace? How can they affect guest services as well as employee relationships?

- Can biases ever operate in a positive manner? That is, can your preconceived ideas ever help you learn or achieve something?

- How can negative biases be overcome? How can they affect workplace relationships and professional behaviors?

- What about emotional noise? For instance, if your intended receiver is angry, upset, or elated, he or she may not be able to hear your message. How else can emotional noise function as an obstacle to communication?

Teaching Tips

- Play the telephone game with your class, whereby you whisper a statement into a student's ear, and then each student whispers it to the next until the final student speaks it aloud. How has the message changed during the transmission process? What obstacles to communication might have occurred?

CUSTOMIZED INSTRUCTION

Literacy Connection, 21st-Century Skills—Communicate Clearly, Critical Thinking and Problem Solving, Social and Cultural Skills

ESOL Students

What types of nonverbal communication are considered appropriate in your culture of origin? Are the same actions used in the same ways in the United States? How can you effectively use nonverbal communication in either culture?

Table 7.1 (continued)

- Paying close attention to other people's gestures and nonverbal behaviors can help you be a better communicator. But what about your own? What nonverbal messages do you convey, intentionally or unintentionally? How could these behaviors and messages affect how other people see you?

- Can students think of other barriers to effective communication? How might these be overcome?

- Is it possible to be an effective communicator with everyone you meet? What about their responsibilities to you? How can both parties to a conversation improve their chances of having a successful interaction on all levels?

In-Class Activity: Is the Personal Professional?

Literacy Connection, 21st-Century Skills— Communicate Clearly, Critical Thinking and Problem Solving, Social and Cultural Skills

Divide into small groups. Discuss whether, how, and when one should keep one's personal life from entering into the workplace.

Is it ever appropriate to display how you "really" feel? Does this hold if you become sick or injured on the job, or if you had a bad day and just really need to vent? Does it matter who the audience is—your supervisor, your human-resources representative, or your best friend?

What about discussing personal information? Is it acceptable to tell your colleagues about life-changing events, such as a pregnancy or a death in the family? What about less-important affairs, such as attending a sporting event or meeting an old friend? Again, does the audience matter?

Based on this discussion, what aspects of your personal life do you now think are appropriate to share in the workplace, if any?

Table 7.1: Obstacles to Good Communication *continued*

Communication Obstacle	Description	Examples
Nonverbal boundaries	Face-to-face meetings can be difficult for people who need a lot of personal space. The amount needed can vary based on people's upbringing and experiences. Give the other person space before beginning communication.	North Americans usually feel comfortable with greater personal space, whereas Europeans prefer to be closer to their companions. While this may seem unimportant, the opinions associated with them can become a problem. Moving too close to a North American could appear insolent or even threatening. Moving too far from a European could appear disdainful or aloof.
Gestures	Does your body movement interfere with listening? Do your gestures help send the right message? You should avoid using gestures that might appear to be in conflict with the message.	An example might be smiling while shaking a fist.
Other distractions	Many other things can affect how successful communication is. For example, personal life and mood might have an impact. Sometimes, what is acting as a barrier to communication is not obvious until the communicator tries to deliver a message.	Be more careful with how you communicate with other people if you wake up "on the wrong side of the bed."

420

Essential Skills
Planning Your Message

Before delivering an important message, it's important to spend some time planning not only what you want to communicate but how you will communicate. It's also important to consider your audience and how your message might be received, as well as follow up after you deliver the message. Here are some steps in the process:

- Observe your audience over time and consider how people interact with you and with others, how they listen, what gets their attention.

- Be aware of any potential obstacles to communication; i.e., ways in which your words could be misunderstood or ways in which you could be misinterpreting other people's actions.

- Decide which medium is most appropriate for delivering your message; for example, a memo posted by the time clock, a quick group meeting, a one-on-one talk.

- Taking all these into account, create and communicate your message.

- Be aware of feedback, both spoken and active, such as changed behaviors, positive or negative comments.

- Review your actions and consider whether or not you achieved your goal, how you could have performed better, what to do next time.

Of course, every communication, large or small, sends a message about your values and priorities. Take the time to consider what you want to communicate. Make sure that you are consistent; the message may differ, but the underlying values and priorities should remain the same. Otherwise, you run the risk of confusing and alienating your coworkers, who may think you are untrustworthy.

Summary

In this section, you learned the following:

- Communication is the process of sending and receiving information by talk, gestures, or writing for some type of response or action.

- Barriers to effective communication include language differences, semantics, jargon, tone of message, clarity, assumptions, cultural differences, prejudices and biases, noise, nonverbal communication, gestures, and other distractions such as lack of time and other pressing issues.

421

Essential Skills: Planning Your Message

Encourage students to discuss the following:

- Is what we communicate more important than how we communicate it? Why, or why not?

- Why is reviewing your actions such an important component of message planning?

- Earlier in the section, the concept of "meta-planning" arose. How can these steps be incorporated into an all-purpose plan that can help you through any communication obstacles?

CUSTOMIZED INSTRUCTION

Literacy Connection, 21st-Century Skills— Communicate Clearly, Critical Thinking and Problem Solving, Social and Cultural Skills

Less Advanced Students

Plan a message that you will transmit to someone else, following the guidelines discussed on p. 421. What is particularly easy or particularly difficult about this task?

Use this plan as a template for other messages you need to communicate. How might you need to adapt it over time or under changing circumstances?

Summary

- Remind students to review the following:
  1. The communication process
  2. The barriers to effective communication

Section 7.1 Review Questions

1. Communication is the process of sending and receiving information by talk, gestures, or writing.

2. Semantics refers to what words mean. Words can often mean very different things to the speaker and the listener, which can cause confusion. Good communicators strive to avoid commonly misunderstood words to make sure that what they intend to communicate is actually what they communicate.

3. The two types of messages are those conveying historical information, which has already happened, and those conveying action-required information, which requires something to happen.

4. Understanding how the communication process works—both what is said and how it is said—is important for building strong relationships with employees and customers.

5. Students should identify similarities and differences in their communication styles, based on the person with whom they are communicating.

6. Although Sung has lived in the United States for many years, the cultural differences between the United States and Japan may be difficult for her to transcend. Alternately, language differences may make it difficult for her to feel confident speaking with newly arrived guests. Linda should work with Sung to improve her greeting skills, which will make Sung feel more comfortable.

7. Failed messages prevent the transmission of important information. In a kitchen, this may cause food to be prepared incorrectly, sanitation precautions to be ignored, or even anger and distrust between colleagues.

8. Cultural bias can prevent one employee from recognizing the valuable contributions another has made or can potentially make to the business. It devalues employees, resulting in a negative and tension-filled work environment.

Section 7.1 Review Questions

1. What is communication?

2. Explain semantics.

3. What are the two types of messages that can be sent?

4. Why is it important to understand the process of communication?

5. Mary Fox says that it's critical to be sensitive to who your audience is. Assume you have a problem with a friend and a situation with a teacher. Would you approach these people in the same way? If not, what would differ?

6. One of Linda's hostesses, Sung, appears to be a little formal and reserved with guests. Linda explains that patrons have to feel welcome as soon as they enter Uptown Grille. Sung grew up in Japan, but she has lived in this country for more than 20 years. What do you think the problem might be? How should Linda handle this situation?

7. How can failed messages create problems in the workplace?

8. How can cultural bias detract from a positive work environment?

Section 7.1 Activities

1. Study Skills/Group Activity: Miscommunication

Work with two other students and discuss a problem that you have experienced that was caused by miscommunication. Role play some of these situations to consider some other possible outcomes.

2. Activity: How to Handle Miscommunication

Read your local newspaper to identify a problem that, in your judgment, resulted from miscommunication. How would you have handled the situation? Create a one-page report on how you would have handled the situation differently.

3. Critical Thinking: Learning From Communication Obstacles

Think about a time when a specific communication obstacle created a problem for you. What could have resolved the problem? What did you learn from the episode?

423

Section 7.1 Activities

1. Students have a variety of options, so long as they understand that miscommunication caused the initial problems and that effective communication could have changed the outcomes.

2. Students should analyze the communication problem presented in the newspaper and present clear and reasonable alternatives.

3. Students should consider how personal problems have resulted from poor communication and how understanding what went wrong may help in the future.

Section 7.2
Communication Skills

Introduce the Section
a. Explain the importance of excellent communication skills to the restaurant and foodservice industry.
b. Review the role of personal characteristics in communication as well as steps to becoming a more effective communicator.
c. Discuss the objectives for the section.

Vocabulary Review
a. Direct students to the key terms.
b. Pronounce each word, and have the students repeat the pronunciation out loud.
c. Discuss the definition of each word.

Teach

Discuss
- Does apologizing always resolve conflict? How many times ought we to forgive someone who has repeatedly made the same mistake? What other actions might be appropriate?
- How can tension and conflict arise in a school? How can they be resolved?
- If good communication leads to good relationships, as the text states, then are bad relationships always the result of bad communication? Encourage students to share their thoughts.

Reinforce and Review
- Communication involves a set of learned skills that should be practiced regularly.
- The skills needed for good communication include listening, speaking, telephone, and writing skills.
- Misunderstandings resulting from obstacles to communication can result in tension and conflict, so it is important to make sure that both sender and receiver understand the intended message.

7.1 The Communication Process • The process of communication • Barriers to communication	7.2 Communication Skills • Personal characteristics that affect communication skills • Effective listening • Effective speaking • Effective telephone skills • Effective writing	7.3 Types of Communication • Organizational communication • Interpersonal communication

SECTION 7.2 COMMUNICATION SKILLS

Good communication leads to good relationships. Remember, communication is learned, so continue to practice good communication skills. The skills needed for good communication include listening, speaking, telephone, and writing skills. The more someone practices communication, the better he or she becomes at communicating.

Study Questions

After studying Section 7.2, you should be able to answer the following questions:

- What are the personal characteristics that can affect communication?
- What is effective listening?
- What is effective speaking?
- What are business-appropriate telephone skills?
- What is effective writing?

Personal Characteristics That Affect Communication Skills

We communicate in a variety of ways. It's not just about writing or speaking. Personal characteristics, such as body language, eye contact, and credibility, have a major impact on communication between people.

Despite best efforts, conflict and tension can result if people misunderstand each other. If someone says something that is unclear, politely ask him to explain. If you mistakenly offend someone, don't insist that you're right. Apologize and try again. Situations can usually be smoothed over when the people involved say that they are sorry.

424

In addition to speaking, we also communicate through body language. But the way we walk, stand, or sit is affected by the practices and traditions of our culture.

Whenever communicating with supervisors, coworkers, classmates, or customers whose backgrounds are different, be aware of their reactions. Specifically, look for reactions that might show they have misunderstood something. See Figure 7.3. The following are guidelines to help people accept and understand others from all walks of life:

- Be aware that not everyone has the same behaviors.

- If misinterpreted behavior has offended someone, clarify and apologize. If offended by someone else's communication, let that person know.

- See and treat people as individuals, rather than members of a particular group.

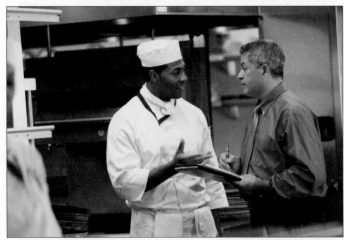

Figure 7.3: Avoiding miscommunication in the workplace results in happier and more productive employees.

In a restaurant or foodservice operation, it is also important that guests find the staff to be credible during communication. Credibility is the ability of a person to be believed. This quality is critical when the communication between two people centers on solving a problem.

425

Figure Focus
Figure 7.3: Do these coworkers look like they are communicating well or poorly? What are some indicators? What does this suggest about their professional relationship?

Discuss
- How can someone demonstrate credibility? How is it related to consistency?
- Why is it particularly important to avoid misunderstanding and conflict in the professional kitchen?

Reinforce and Review
- We communicate in part through body language, which is affected by the traditions and practices of our culture.
- Knowing how our culture affects our communication patterns can help us understand how other people's communication patterns are also affected by their cultures.
- Treating people as individuals, not as members of a group, can help clear obstacles to communication and improve relationships.
- Credibility is the ability of a person to be believed. It is critical when the communication between two people centers on solving a problem.

Teaching Tips
- Encourage students to visit a restaurant, business, or an area of town that is predominantly populated by a people of another race, culture, or ethnicity.

In-Class Activity: Minority Affairs

Literacy Connection, 21st-Century Skills—Communicate Clearly, Critical Thinking and Problem Solving, Social and Cultural Skills

Students should write an in-class essay describing an experience they had in which they were in the minority and their reactions to it. Students can discuss racial, cultural, ethnic, generational, or any other type of minority. If you choose, you can tie this activity to the Teaching Tips above and make this essay a follow-up report.

What assumptions did students bring with them to the experience, and how did they feel while there?

Did students experience any obstacles to communication? If so, what were they, and were they overcome?

What was the lasting impression students took with them from that experience?

Discuss

- How can students demonstrate credibility while listening? What about sincerity? Can these traits be faked? What might happen if someone was caught faking?

Reinforce and Review

- Product knowledge is an important part of credibility for servers since guests rely on them to provide accurate information and answer questions correctly.
- When handling complaints, both managers and servers must demonstrate credibility so that the guest can be confident that his or her problem has been clearly understood.
- Chefs must also demonstrate credibility when describing ingredients, cooking methods, and culinary history, both when speaking with guests and when training staff.
- Listening is the ability to focus closely on what another person is saying to summarize the true meaning of a message.
- An important point of effective listening is preparing to listen. Focus on the other person attentively and without interruption.

For servers, product knowledge is important to credibility. Servers must communicate accurate information to guests. At a minimum, servers should know the menu item descriptions, including specials. Great product knowledge includes preparation techniques, ingredients, allergens, substitutions, and the right combinations of food and drink. With this additional information, a server can present the menu accurately and answer guests' questions. A strong test of credibility occurs when a guest asks about the menu or specific items on it. The guest determines the server's credibility by the knowledge of his or her response. Imagine how a guest feels if a server does not know enough about the menu to answer the guest's question.

When a guest complains about something, the credibility of the server or manager who handles the complaint is critical to good communication. The server must know the operation's policies and procedures for managing complaints, including any allowed adjustments. If the guest senses the server is hesitant, lacks knowledge, or needs to check with someone higher up, the guest may think the server is not credible and may doubt his or her ability to resolve the complaint.

In another situation, chefs must have knowledge of processes and procedures to be credible. The level of knowledge depends on the type of cooking assignment. At a minimum, a chef should be able to describe the correct preparation process or procedure and know how to carry it out. Great cooking knowledge includes knowing the reasons for a process and every step in it, its history or development from earlier methods, and how to compare different, but related, processes.

Effective Listening

Listening is the ability to focus closely on what another person is saying to summarize the true meaning of a message. An effective listener actively participates in the communication process. See Figure 7.4 on page 428. To be an effective listener, follow these guidelines:

1. Prepare to listen. Stop talking and focus on the other person.

2. Show that you're paying attention. Body language is important for showing that you are listening:

   - Maintaining eye contact helps prevent the mind from wandering. In group communications, maintaining eye contact is not always possible, but try to stay focused. For example, in a preshift meeting, some might be tempted to ignore the parts that they think don't pertain to them, but it's important to understand what everyone in the operation is being asked to do (it also helps individuals to understand their roles better).

426

- Nodding means that the listener approves or recognizes what the person is saying.

- Leaning toward the person speaking shows that the listener is interested in the content of the message.

- Facial expressions can help show empathy for the person speaking, meaning that the listener understands the message without placing any judgment on it, or that he can relate to what the person is saying. (I know how you feel; I've felt that way, too.)

3. Don't interrupt and don't finish the other person's sentences in your mind or aloud. Listening to only the first few words of someone's sentence and then assuming they know the rest is a common mistake of poor listeners. Let the other person finish his or her ideas. That way, the reply addresses what the person actually said, not what the listener thought they said.

4. Ask questions to clarify. It's okay to ask the person to repeat something.

5. Occasionally rephrase and repeat what you have heard. Check listening skills by saying, "Here's what I think I hear you saying…" and then repeat the main message.

6. Listen between the lines. Often, it's not what someone says but how the person says it. Learn to read a person's body language. It will yield important clues to his or her true feelings on a subject.

7. Don't overreact. When someone says something that the listener strongly disagrees with, he shouldn't interrupt, become emotional, or answer rudely. Such reactions send out a strong signal that he's stopped listening and only wants to be heard. Would you listen to someone who doesn't want to listen to you?

8. Record key ideas and phrases. While most people probably don't need to take notes when talking to friends, note taking is a valuable way to improve listening skills in the classroom or workplace. Notes allow listeners to remember important points that they might otherwise forget. They can also then relay the message to others without losing its original meaning.

427

Discuss

- How can one be an effective listener in a hectic kitchen environment?
- Is it always possible to follow these steps to effective listening? Section 1 discussed the possibility of developing an overall plan for transmitting messages. How would a similar plan work for effective listening? Would anything suggesting a shortcut doom the listener's credibility?

Reinforce and Review

- When listening to others speak, don't interrupt them or finish their sentences—either aloud or to yourself. For one thing, you might be incorrect, and for another, the speaker might interpret your actions as a lack of interest in his or her words.
- Listen to everything a person communicates, not just what he or she says. Pay attention to tone, word choice, and body language to get the message.
- Try not to overreact to whatever someone tells you. While this may be difficult, focusing on your own emotions and your own responses means that you are no longer focusing on the speaker.

Teaching Tips

- Ask students to read back their notes from the last ten minutes of class. How much have they written down? How much are they likely to remember tomorrow?
- Ask students to store their books and notes, and then to write down everything they remember from the previous class session. Students should exchange their completed papers with one another. As you review the previous class material, students should grade one another based on how much they remembered correctly.

Discuss

- Why is it important to be brief and clear when delivering a message? How can you weigh brevity against accuracy? When do details matter?
- How can you tell what information is vital and what information is unimportant? What problems can failing to do this create?

Reinforce and Review

- Practice listening as often as you can. Like other professional attributes, it is a learned skill.
- When planning a message, be brief, clear, and to the point.
- Make sure to answer the five "W's" and "how" questions: Who? What? Where? When? Why? How?

CUSTOMIZED INSTRUCTION
Literacy Connection, 21st-Century Skills—Communicate Clearly, Critical Thinking and Problem Solving, Social and Cultural Skills
Special Needs Students
Practice developing the five "W's" and "how" questions. Interview a friend or classmate, using these six questions.
ESOL Students
Interview the person in your family who does most of the cooking. Ask the five "W's" and "how" questions about some food-related topic from your culture of origin. Share the results of the interview with your class, either as a poster or a presentation.

Figure 7.4: Effective communication includes good listening skills, making eye contact, and facial expressions.

Practice listening as often as you can. Listening is a learned skill, just like learning a knife skill or a cooking technique.

Effective Speaking

When planning a message, deliver the key points in a brief and clear manner. To ensure that the communication has covered all the vital information, answer the five "W's" and "how" questions. The five W's and how questions are the following:

- Who?
- When?
- What?
- Why?

Figure Focus

Figure 7.4: How do these staff members appear to be interacting? What does their body language suggest to you about their professional relationship?

- Where?
- How?

Develop the communication further and think about how the audience will respond to the message. Consider ways to personalize or customize it for them. Make sure the audience recognizes the importance of paying attention to the message. Table 7.2 shows the qualities of an effective speaker.

Table 7.2: Qualities of an Effective Speaker	
Interact with the audience.	Create a comfortable interpersonal and physical environment through tone and surroundings. Maintain eye contact.
Use suitable language.	Minimize jargon and buzzwords. Avoid slang. Eliminate sarcasm. Define technical terms.
Use appropriate nonverbal communication.	Use appropriate gestures, including postures that promote confidence. Use appropriate facial expressions. Show an appropriate demeanor (for example, enthusiastically deliver a motivating speech; don't deliver bad news with a smile).
Vary your speech patterns.	Vary the tone and pitch of the voice. Pronounce words clearly as best you can. Use complete sentences that are professional, not casual. Minimize any dialect in speech. Eliminate mumbling or swallowing word endings. Speak at a steady pace. Speak with confidence; be prepared for speaking.
Close the conversation.	Verify understanding. Repeat the message to ensure understanding. Thank listeners for listening. Present opportunities for follow up.

Effective Telephone Skills

A call receiver must be both an effective listener and an effective speaker. Telephone skills are an important tool in the restaurant and foodservice industry. All managers and employees need to know the steps for proper business phone answers. Figure 7.5 shows a manager using effective telephone skills:

429

Reinforce and Review

- Make sure your audience recognizes why your message is important for them. If your message isn't important to them, then consider either reworking it so that it becomes relevant or not sharing the information with that audience at all.
- A call receiver at a restaurant or foodservice establishment must be both an effective listener and an effective speaker.
- Regardless of who is actually responsible for answering the telephone, all employees should know and observe the proper techniques.

Table 7.2: Qualities of an Effective Speaker

- Relate this information to the material in Section 7.1 about obstacles to communication. How can successful speakers overcome these barriers?
- How can an effective speaker use body language to develop an audience's confidence? Alternately, what types of body language are often characteristic of ineffective speakers?
- Why should a speaker vary the tone and pitch of his or her voice while talking? What effect might that have on an audience?
- How can an effective speaker demonstrate that he or she is in charge of the conversation, without actually saying so?

CUSTOMIZED INSTRUCTION

Literacy Connection, 21st-Century Skills— Communicate Clearly, Critical Thinking and Problem Solving, Social and Cultural Skills

Less Advanced Students

Identify three ways in which you can improve your communication skills each day and write them on an index card or in a notebook. Practice these skills for one week.

Have these skills become easier and more natural, or have you become self-conscious and nervous? How have your communications with others changed as a result of this activity? Do you feel like a more effective speaker?

Discuss

- Why is it important for all staff members to understand and observe an establishment's telephone policies?
- Sometimes callers will be angry or even rude to foodservice staff. How should staff members respond? Is it ever appropriate to disagree with a caller?

Reinforce and Review

- When answering a ringing telephone, always provide the establishment's name, your name, and a pleasant and professional greeting as part of the opening process.
- Practicing effective listening and speaking skills is even more important on the telephone, where the parties cannot see one another's body language.
- Staff members should smile when speaking to guests on the telephone since it promotes a positive impression among guests.
- It's better to err on the side of caution when taking down guest information. Clarify any information you think necessary.

Teaching Tips

- Have student volunteers stand with their backs to the classroom. Ask them to smile or frown while they say commonplace sentences. Ask the other students in the class to identify whether the volunteers are smiling or frowning when they speak.

Figure 7.5: Effective telephone skills are necessary in a restaurant or foodservice operation.

1. State the name of the organization, followed by the call receiver's name and the question, "How may I assist you?"

2. Listen for the reason the caller has phoned the organization. Be sure to wait until the caller has finished before responding.

3. Maintain a positive, polite, and courteous attitude when speaking with the caller. Empathize with the caller and be enthusiastic. Remember that the person on the other end is hearing the information for the first time. The call receiver has one chance to make a good first impression. Even if you are tired of answering the same questions all day long, you should never let it show. Smile. This may seem like a strange thing to do for a phone conversation, but voices actually sound more pleasant when the speaker smiles. As a result, customers have a positive impression of the business before they even walk through the door.

4. If the caller has a large amount of information, take notes to be sure all the information is received. Be sure to ask the five W's and how questions when taking a message. Don't be afraid to ask the guest to repeat important information. It's better to be sure of the information than to make serious mistakes, such as booking the banquet on the wrong day or ordering the wrong type of wedding cake.

430

Figure Focus

Figure 7.5: Some especially popular restaurants hire dedicated reservationists, meaning that they spend the day taking reservations. Often, these staff members are not even located at the restaurant itself. Other restaurants contract with outside companies to handle reservations, and still others provide special VIP telephone numbers to special guests so that they don't have to wait on hold.

5. Paraphrase or repeat what the caller has stated. Speak loudly enough, but don't shout. Don't talk too fast, and don't slur words. Remember that some people have a difficult time hearing.

6. After listening to what the caller has to say, decide whether you can resolve the caller's problem. If not, know who the "right" person is to answer the caller's issues and transfer the call to provide a quick resolution. Before transferring the call, it is a good practice to get the caller's name and phone number in case the call is lost during the transfer process. This will allow the right person to call the caller back and help him or her resolve the problem.

7. If you can resolve the caller's concerns, explain to the caller any steps to be taken. Know the answers to frequently asked questions. Tape a list of important facts, figures, and phone extensions to the desk or to the phone itself so every employee can provide quick answers. This list simplifies things for other employees and controls the information they give out. But never make a guess. If you don't have the requested information, refer the person to the correct source or offer to find out and call back.

8. Close the conversation either by explaining to the caller that you'll be transferring him or asking whether there is anything else you can do to assist him.

9. Write messages down on a preprinted message form. Clearly note who called and the date and time of the call. Sign your name on the memo in case the person who receives it has any further questions about the message itself.

10. Always end the conversation on a positive note. Thank the person for choosing the restaurant and let him know that you look forward to his or her visit. End the call politely, perhaps by saying, "Thank you for calling (the name of the organization) and have a nice day."

Many restaurant and foodservice establishments have installed special telephone systems that provide useful messages to callers who are put on hold. Often these prerecorded messages inform customers of information they'll need after their call is picked up, such as account numbers or order numbers. Other messages alert callers to an establishment's latest promotion or new business hours. While these message systems help callers stay patient, don't expect customers to hold forever. Thirty seconds on hold seems like an eternity to many people.

When answering the phone, use these guidelines:

- Never put a caller on hold without first asking permission to do so.

- If a caller is on hold, get back to him as quickly as possible.

431

Discuss

- Compare the statement, "I don't know," to the statement, "I don't know, but I can certainly find out for you." How might a guest respond differently to one statement than to another?

Reinforce and Review

- Always take the caller's name and telephone number before transferring him or her to another line, and always tell the caller to whom you are transferring him or her and why. Never transfer a caller or put a caller on hold without permission.

- Remember that you cannot always handle the guest's problem, but you can always find someone who can.

- As in all other aspects of the foodservice industry, treating other people with care and concern is always a good idea. This is particularly important when dealing with callers who have complaints or problems.

- Never let a caller languish on hold. If he or she is awaiting a transfer, offer to have that person return the call. This demonstrates respect for the caller and his or her time.

Teaching Tips

- Have a student volunteer agree to start timing one minute when you give the signal. Pretend to call a local restaurant. After an initial greeting, you are placed on hold. Signal to the volunteer timekeeper to begin watch. Remain silent for several seconds. Over the next minute pretend to become increasingly angry with the length of time you have been on hold. Make side comments to the class, use body language, and do anything else you think will get their attention. When the student volunteer signals that one minute has passed, pretend that you have just been taken off hold. Scream into the phone that you have been waiting ten minutes, that you will never eat at that restaurant again, that you will tell all your friends how rudely you have been treated, and so on. Now talk with your students about the relativity of time. Encourage students to relate this concept to the restaurant and foodservice industry, highlighting its relevance to customer service.

Discuss

- Why are written messages typically more formal than spoken messages? How might people react differently to a written message than to a spoken message, even when the two say essentially the same thing?
- How is effective writing like other communication skills? How is it different? Which do students find the most challenging?

Reinforce and Review

- Written business communication includes everything from a letter of resignation to a new menu and may take the form of a memo, fax, email, letter, or report, among others.
- Written messages tend to be more formal than spoken messages and typically include three components: an introduction, a body, and a conclusion.
- To write a successful message, first plan the content and then plan the structure.

Vocabulary Terms

- **Introduction:** In a written document, the component that introduces the writer and his or her subject to the audience.
- **Body of the message:** In a written document, the component that presents the content or topics of the message.
- **Conclusion:** In a written document, the component that summarizes and closes the message.

- If the person whom the caller is trying to reach is still unavailable, ask the caller whether they wish to continue to hold and thank them for being patient.
- If a caller has waited longer than a minute, offer again to take a message.
- If possible, let the person for whom the caller is holding know that there is another call waiting. Try to find out how long the caller will have to hold.

Finally, be careful about side conversations with coworkers while talking to a customer on the phone. Putting a hand over the receiver doesn't completely block out the sound, and callers often hear what's being said in the background.

Effective Writing

Most of a manager's communication with staff, guests, and supervisors is done verbally, either in person or on the phone. However, written business communication is another means for a manager to share information. These types of messages include memos, faxes, emails, letters, and reports.

Written messages tend to have a more formal structure than spoken messages. Here are the common parts of most written messages:

- **Introduction:** This gets the audience's attention, gives the reason for the message, identifies the topics of the message, and establishes the writer's point of view.
- **Body of the message:** This portion presents the content or topics of the message.
- **Conclusion:** Here, the writer summarizes key points, calls for action, and identifies the benefits and value of the message.

To write a successful message, the communicator needs a strong process that helps him or her to plan what to say and builds the message's structure. A good process can also make writing feel less challenging and result in clear, concise messages. Table 7.3 lists the steps necessary to be an effective writer.

Table 7.3: Steps to Effective Writing

1. Think about the audience. The monthly financial update to the vice president of sales has a different audience than a training manual written for new servers. A memo to the kitchen staff summarizing new sanitation procedures has a different audience than a memo on the same subject sent to management. Some readers need thoroughness and detail. Others just want the bottom line, while some expect the written word to be a personal transaction between two people. The words and the sense these words convey are different in each case. Each piece of writing should be adapted to the particular audience. Write to each in a style they accept and expect.

2. Think about the purpose and what needs to be accomplished.

3. Think about the situation and details. Ask the five "W's" and "how" questions and write their answers. Who? Where? Why? What? When? How?

4. Record the action desired as a result of the written message.

5. Identify the benefits to the message. How will it help the company, the reader, the customers, and the communicator?

6. Identify the topics and group the details underneath it.

7. Order the topics in a logical sequence.

8. Write the main body first, then the introduction, and then the conclusion.

9. Read through the draft and edit and revise the content, grammar, spelling, flow, and readability. Ask someone else, such as a peer, to read the draft and make suggestions for improvement.

10. Write the final draft and distribute the communication.

While developing written communication, keep in mind these pointers that will make writing easier:

- Be brief. Write like the spoken word, simple and to-the-point. Long, drawn-out sentences are difficult to read. For example, don't use adverbs when the verb has already described the action. The best written messages get to the point quickly. Avoid stuffy sentences, too. They rarely impress a reader.

- Be clear and complete. Although being brief is important, be sure not to sacrifice clarity or completeness.

- Review writing to be sure ideas are understandable and comprehensive. Make sure to address the five W's and how questions. The reason for putting a message down on paper is to make it clear to the audience. One sentence should lead logically into the next sentence. It is the responsibility of a business writer to communicate ideas clearly. In most cases, restaurant and foodservice managers write to confirm oral agreements made over the phone with suppliers. In some cases, however, they will have an idea that differs from the ideas of the person to whom they are writing. It then becomes

433

Table 7.3: Steps to Effective Writing

- Once you have written and distributed a message, you have no control over the audience that will receive it. This is especially true in the Internet era. How can this affect your writing style or content?

- Be sure to ask the five "W's" and the "how" questions when you're planning the message and to answer them when you're writing it.

- You probably don't practice every word you say in front of a friend, so why is it important to have someone else review drafts of your written documents?

Discuss
- Why is clarity important in all forms of communication? How and why can words be used to obscure meaning?

Reinforce and Review
- The best written messages get to the point quickly, without extra words.
- Always review drafts of your work before distribution to make sure that your writing is clear, accurate, and informative.

In-Class Activity: Message About a Bottle (or a Plate or a Tablecloth...)

Literacy Connection, 21st-Century Skills— Communicate Clearly, Critical Thinking and Problem Solving, Social and Cultural Skills

Each student should write a message about some foodservice-related topic, following the guidelines shown in Table 7.3.

Exchange drafts with one another so that a peer can provide suggestions for improvement.

Revise the draft, incorporating peer suggestions as needed, and submit both draft and final copy.

Discuss

- How is a written message similar to a first impression? How do we present ourselves as we write?
- These days, it's quite possible that our written words can outlast our ideas and beliefs. How can people make sure that the words they write now do not cause embarrassment or worse later?

Reinforce and Review

- To guarantee clarity in writing, always keep the overall purpose for writing in mind.
- Write to express, not to impress.
- Always use a positive approach when writing. Even when conveying bad news, it is possible to demonstrate acceptance without demonstrating enthusiasm.
- By taking a break between writing a draft and writing the final version, your refreshed mind will be better able to note flaws in grammar and construction.

Homework Activity: Spreading the Good Word(s)

Literacy Connection, 21st-Century Skills— Communicate Clearly, Critical Thinking and Problem Solving, Social and Cultural Skills, Information Literacy

Select a topic (it does not have to be foodservice related) and write a letter to the editor of a local, regional, or national newspaper. Follow the guidelines described in Table 7.3.

Perform any necessary research to learn more about your topic or to learn the newspaper's mailing address. Ask a peer, instructor, or family member to review your letter before you send it.

necessary for them to carefully choose words and phrases that convey their opinions and persuade the reader to accept their ideas. At all times, writing is a reflection of the writer and the organization and must be free of errors to show a positive image. To guarantee clarity in writing, always keep the overall purpose for writing in mind. One way to do this is to write the purpose of the letter, report, or memo on a separate sheet of paper and keep it visible while writing. One of the most important points to remember is to write to express, not to impress.

- Keep it simple. Use short sentences and simple words where possible. Define jargon, acronyms, or technical terms so the reader understands the message.

- Check your work. Have someone else read materials to check for proper usage. If possible, use the grammar and spell check functions in a word-processing program.

- Always write with an upbeat attitude. Even if the message needs to deliver troubling news, make sure to include long-term benefits. No one likes to read negative messages.

- Take a time out. Set written messages down and come back to them later, even if it's only a few hours. It will be easier to spot and correct errors and awkward phrases.

- Read out loud to check grammar and punctuation. If a phrase or sentence is difficult to say, chances are a grammar or punctuation problem is present.

Figure 7.6 shows two sample workplace memos, both trying to convey the same material. One is well-written, answers the W's and how questions, and is properly organized, and the other is not.

CUSTOMIZED INSTRUCTION

Literacy Connection, 21st-Century Skills—Communicate Clearly, Critical Thinking and Problem Solving, Social and Cultural Skills, Information Literacy

More Advanced Students

How big is your vocabulary?

It's not an easy question to answer. In fact, there's no real consensus on how many words are even in the English language. As an example, the collected works of William Shakespeare are composed of 884,647 words, with 29,066 distinct forms. But because there is so much variation in how words are counted, estimates of Shakespeare's vocabulary vary from 18,000 to 25,000.

Using a dictionary, identify ten words that are not in either your speaking or reading vocabulary but that can be reasonably and logically used with reference to the foodservice industry. Practice using your ten words until they become a comfortable part of your vocabulary.

Write a brief essay describing this process. Was it difficult to select appropriate words? How did other people react to your using these words in conversation? Did you learn anything from this experience? Append a list of the ten words and their definitions, in your own words, to your essay.

Memorandum

TO: All Kitchen Staff

FROM: Al Bean, Manager

DATE: October 20, 2012

RE: Personal Hygiene

This memo is to clear up confusion expressed at the last staff meeting. As is posted in each of the restrooms, you must wash your hands before returning to work after going into the restroom for any reason.

Studies have shown that the spread of germs is minimized through appropriate and frequent hand washing. This includes applying soap to the hands, washing them for at least 20 seconds, then rinsing and drying thoroughly.

Throughout the day, should you sneeze, please cover your mouth and immediately use the soap dispensers located throughout the kitchen to clean your hands.

Should you have any questions, please feel free to contact me.

Memorandum

To: Staff

From: Management

Please make sure you follow all of the directions on personal hygiene that were discussed in the staff meeting.

Anyone not following the rules will be fired.

Figure 7.6: Written communication must be clear and complete.

Figure Focus

Figure 7.6: Which of these two memoranda is more effective and why?

In-Class Activity: Readin', 'Ritin', and 'Rithmetic

Mathematics Connection, Literacy Connection, 21st-Century Skills—Communicate Clearly, Critical Thinking and Problem Solving, Social and Cultural Skills

Many of the reports that foodservice managers generate have to do with numbers: profit and loss reports, food cost statements, accounts payable, and so on.

As a foodservice manager, you are responsible for calculating the labor cost each week. Unfortunately, the time clock is broken, and while you trust your employees to report the hours they worked accurately, you must calculate their wages and the overall labor cost by hand.

Kitchen Staff: The chef earned $1,000, the sous chef earned $700, the line cook earned $500, the prep cook earned $350, and the dishwasher earned $600.

Floor Staff: The manager earned $1,000, the lead server earned $400, the second server earned $300, the buser earned $250, and the bartender earned $700.

The total restaurant revenue for the week was $42,000. Workplace benefits, including taxes, total 33 percent of total wages. You do not have to include tips in your analysis.

Solve for:

a. Total kitchen wages plus benefits [$4,189.50]

b. Total floor wages plus benefits [$3,524.50]

c. Total labor cost (all wages plus all benefits) [$7,714.00]

d. Total kitchen labor cost as a percentage of total restaurant revenue [9.98%]

e. Total floor labor cost as a percentage of total restaurant revenue [8.39%]

f. Total labor cost as a percentage of total restaurant revenue [18.37%]

Based on this information only, how well is the restaurant performing? Write a brief but professional memo to the chef describing the restaurant's performance.

On the Job: Words in the Workplace

Encourage students to discuss the following:

- What is the difference between formal and informal language? How does it relate to the discussion of professionalism in Chapter 4?

- Think about the words you use each day. Which are appropriate and inappropriate in which settings? That is, how and why do we change our speech patterns depending on our audience?

Essential Skills: Writing Handwritten Notes

Encourage students to discuss the following:

- Have you ever received a handwritten note? What was your reaction? How did it affect your impression of the writer?

- At what times is it appropriate to send a handwritten note to someone you know in a strictly professional sense?

- How can sending a handwritten note demonstrate respect for the recipient? How can it demonstrate disrespect?

- Remember to follow the guidelines for effective writing in Table 7.3. Although you are writing instead of typing, this is still a piece of formal business communication.

[on the job]

Words in the Workplace

You may use a lot of slang or informal language when talking with friends and family. These might include words such as: "like," "y'all," "hey," "wassup," "totally," "guys," "buds," "y'know," "yo," "uh-huh," "uh-uh," and "see ya," or they might not. Informal language is fluid and changes nearly every day, so by the time you read this chapter, a whole new list of words might be part of your vocabulary!

However, these words are not appropriate in the workplace (neither is swearing, for that matter). These are casual expressions, used in your private life. The workplace, on the other hand, is a professional environment in which you need to use professional language. Using slang at work can hinder communication. Some people will pigeonhole you as unintelligent or sloppy based on your language, so they won't listen to you—or respect you.

Moreover, avoiding casual language can benefit you professionally. Proper speaking habits, like using good sentence structure and correct grammar, will help you stand out from your coworkers. They can also give you a better professional image, which can help you win future opportunities, such as management positions and visibility at public events.

Essential Skills
Writing Handwritten Notes

Why take the time to send a handwritten note? For a variety of reasons: the personal touch moves people, and it helps the communicator stand out from the crowd. It shows attention to detail and respect for others. It makes the recipient feel special, knowing that someone took the time to write a note. Like any other business communication, handwritten notes should be written professionally. Make sure handwriting is neat and no words are misspelled. Here are some tips to use when sending a professional handwritten note:

- Use appropriate notepaper. Plain white or ivory note cards are often best. If you are authorized to use company notepaper, do so.

- Write a rough draft on plain paper to help organize your thoughts. If you're not sure exactly what to say, ask a colleague for feedback.

- The salutation should be formal. For example, address it, "Dear Ms. Gonzales." If the communication is to someone with whom you are on a first-name basis, it's acceptable to write, "Dear Sam," but salutations such as "Hey, buddy" are not appropriate.

- The body of the note should refer specifically to the action for which you are thanking the recipient. "Thank you for donating a $100 gift certificate

436

to last week's charity auction," not "Thanks for the donation." Alternately, "I deeply appreciate all the support you have given my restaurant over the last five years," or "I wanted to invite you to our upcoming social event."

■ Use a professional closing, such as "Sincerely yours" or "Cordially."

Figure 7.7 is an example of a handwritten note.

Writing handwritten notes properly can help build stronger business relationships. Don't wait too long before sending thank you notes or invitations and always double-check the spelling of the recipient's name.

Dear Chef Jean,

Thank you for the wonderful dinner last night at Uptown Grille. The food was delicious. We enjoyed everything from the appetizers to the desserts.

We look forward to many more tasty dinners with you and your staff.

Sincerely yours,

Mike and Kelly Smith

Figure 7.7: Although handwritten notes are personable, they still must be professional.

One other factor to consider in writing is the growth and use of technology as a means to communicate. Emails, faxes, instant messaging, and text messaging are just some ways that technology has influenced the written word. Although these formats are more casual, it is important to apply the same principles to their use as with other forms of written communication. Make sure that the person receiving the message can understand and act upon it.

[fast fact]

Did You Know...?

Did you know that Barack Obama's text message announcing Joe Biden as his vice-presidential running mate reached 2.9 million U.S. mobile subscribers?

Reinforce and Review

- Many foodservice professionals use newer forms of communication, such as emails and instant messages, in their business. However, it's important to remember that any professional communication must still follow certain formal principles.
- When composing a message, always make sure that the receiver will be able to understand and act on it.

Fast Fact: Did You Know...?

Encourage students to discuss the following:

- How has the use of social media changed politics and society? What does "community" mean now?
- Is it appropriate to use jargon or informal language when texting or emailing your supervisor? What about a coworker, or a vendor? Is texting itself a professional form of communication?

In-Class Activity: Thank You So Much!

Literacy Connection, 21st-Century Skills—Communicate Clearly, Critical Thinking and Problem Solving, Social and Cultural Skills, Information Literacy

Write a formal, handwritten note to someone you know socially or professionally. Focus on clarity and be sure to answer the five "W's" and "how" questions. If necessary, practice your penmanship first.

Figure Focus

Figure 7.7: How does this thank-you note answer the five "W's" and "how" questions? Is this an example of effective writing?

Discuss

- Why do most people find writing so challenging? How can mastering effective writing skills advance a professional career?

Reinforce and Review

- Some common problems writers may encounter include failing to plan, writing without a purpose, forgetting the audience, and using incorrect style. These can all be addressed with some care and forethought.
- If your receiver doesn't see why he or she should be reading the message, he or she probably won't care about it and might even develop a poor opinion of you for wasting time.
- When you know your target audience, you know how to write a message that will meet their standards and expectations.

Despite every effort, all writers occasionally make mistakes. Beware of these common pitfalls:

- **Lack of planning:** Take a few minutes to think through the message's purpose and main points before writing. See Figure 7.8.

- **Lack of purpose:** If readers can't understand why they're reading a particular message, then they're probably not going to care about it.

- **Forgetting the audience:** Before writing, know who will be reading the words and whether they have any preference for how the message should be structured. Writing for an audience can make them understand the message better.

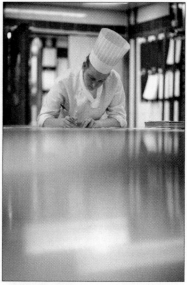

Figure 7.8: Before writing, plan out what you are trying to communicate.

- **Use of incorrect style:** Writing is usually more formal than speaking, but using some informal style can help an audience relate better to the message. Understanding the audience and purpose of the writing also influences the style choice.

Writing challenges most people. Understanding some of the writing issues that can work against any writer will help when revising messages. Thoughtfully use and master these concepts to capture the reader's attention and get the message across effectively.

438

Figure Focus

Figure 7.8: In business writing, like any other part of foodservice work, planning is critical to success. How does this relate to the concept of *mise en place*?

How Texting and IMs Can Affect Written Communication Skills

Texting and instant messaging (IM) are communication technologies that are very successful. Many teens have quickly adopted these tools, even texting or instant-messaging friends and family members instead of speaking directly with them. Texts and IMs are made up of very short and simple sentences, often using a limited vocabulary. Many teens use "text-ese" in their schoolwork, with poor grammar and spelling in their papers. Some even include emoticons and acronyms. Those who have trouble using formal English in their schoolwork may have trouble writing resumes, cover letters, and other professional documents in the future. This can create problems with getting and keeping jobs.

Some researchers believe that when a person doesn't use his brain's full capacity to think deeply when communicating, that person then risks losing the ability to think deeply at all. Using "text-ese" doesn't always require thought, just reaction; short and simple sentences based on a small vocabulary do not demand much. According to this school of thought, if the brain never has to work very hard to communicate, then the brain eventually will not *be able* to work very hard to communicate. Basically, it's the old "use it or lose it" argument.

Get in the habit now of using proper English in professional situations. Texting and instant messaging are often not allowed at work, and "text-ese" is never acceptable there. If you have questions or need more information, ask a language-arts instructor or guidance counselor for help.

English	Text-ese
How are you today?	HRU 2day?
I don't understand.	?
As I remember.	AIR
Please let me know.	PLMK
Parent in room.	PIR

What's New: How Texting and IMs Can Affect Written Communication Skills

Encourage students to discuss the following:

- How does "text-ese" differ from formal written English?

- Do students believe that texting can affect brain capacity? In what ways?

- How can students develop better habits of written communication?

In-Class Activity: "That's Not What I Meant!"

Mathematics Connection, Literacy Connection, 21st-Century Skills—Communicate Clearly, Critical Thinking and Problem Solving, Social and Cultural Skills

How many times have you heard this lament? Maybe you've said it a time or two yourself. Either way, this statement indicates that the speaker needs to practice his or her communication skills.

Think about how you interact with different people each day: family, friends, teachers, co-workers, and others. All these interactions mean more opportunities to practice your skills as an effective communicator. Most people, though, spend more time thinking about what they will say than how they will say it and don't spend much time actually thinking about what other people are communicating to them.

Create a communication log where you record as many of your interactions with other people as possible. Keep track of where and when each interaction took place, how long it lasted, and what you discussed. Maintain this log for one week to observe patterns.

Now add a new column to the log to record the time you think you spent listening to the other person during each interaction. You don't need to keep track with a watch, but do try to estimate the percentage of the conversation that you spend listening rather than talking. Maintain this log for a week as well.

What do you think you learned from this activity? How did knowing that you would have to estimate your listening time affect you during each conversation? With whom did you spend more of your time listening than talking, and vice versa?

Summary

- Remind students to review the following:
  1. The personal characteristics that can affect communication
  2. Effective listening
  3. Effective speaking
  4. Business-appropriate telephone skills
  5. Effective writing

Summary

In this section, you learned the following:

- Effective listening includes preparing to listen, showing attention, not interrupting the speaker, asking questions to clarify the message, rephrasing and repeating what was heard, listening between the lines, not overreacting, and recording key ideas and phrases.

- An effective speaker interacts with the audience, uses suitable language, uses appropriate nonverbal communication, varies speech patterns, and closes the conversation.

- The steps for proper business telephone answering are: state the name of the organization followed by the call receiver's name and the questions; listen for the reason the caller has phoned the operation; maintain a positive attitude when speaking with the caller; take notes to ensure all of the information is clear; paraphrase or repeat the message; try to resolve the caller's problems and explain any steps necessary; close the conversation; write the message down on paper, and then end the conversation on a positive note.

- Written communication must be clear, concise, and positive. Effective business writing answers the W's and how questions. Using professional language with proper grammar, spelling and punctuation will make memos, messages, emails, and personal notes easier to understand.

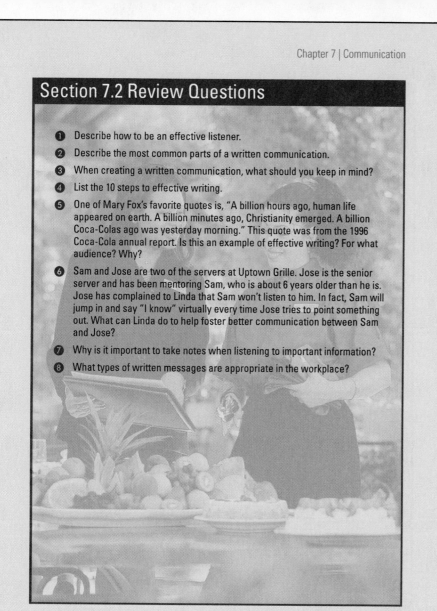

Section 7.2 Review Questions

❶ Describe how to be an effective listener.

❷ Describe the most common parts of a written communication.

❸ When creating a written communication, what should you keep in mind?

❹ List the 10 steps to effective writing.

❺ One of Mary Fox's favorite quotes is, "A billion hours ago, human life appeared on earth. A billion minutes ago, Christianity emerged. A billion Coca-Colas ago was yesterday morning." This quote was from the 1996 Coca-Cola annual report. Is this an example of effective writing? For what audience? Why?

❻ Sam and Jose are two of the servers at Uptown Grille. Jose is the senior server and has been mentoring Sam, who is about 6 years older than he is. Jose has complained to Linda that Sam won't listen to him. In fact, Sam will jump in and say "I know" virtually every time Jose tries to point something out. What can Linda do to help foster better communication between Sam and Jose?

❼ Why is it important to take notes when listening to important information?

❽ What types of written messages are appropriate in the workplace?

441

---

6. Linda should work with Sam to improve his communication skills, especially his tendency to interrupt. One way to do this might be to hold a training for all servers to reinforce and refine good communication skills. This would benefit a larger number of people and prevent Sam's embarrassment, although it's possible that Sam might not realize his own flaws in a group setting. If the problem persists, Linda should meet with Sam to discuss his performance, suggest ways to improve, and emphasize the importance of developing better communication skills.

7. It is important to take notes when listening to important information to remember salient points that might otherwise be forgotten.

8. Types of written messages that are appropriate in the workplace include memos, faxes, emails, letters, and reports.

Section 7.2
Review Questions

1. To be an effective listener, follow these guidelines:
   - Prepare to listen.
   - Show that you're paying attention.
   - Don't interrupt or finish the other person's sentences.
   - Ask questions to clarify.
   - Occasionally repeat and rephrase what you have heard.
   - Listen between the lines.
   - Don't overreact.
   - Record key ideas and phrases.

2. The most common parts of a written communication are the introduction, the body, and the conclusion. The introduction gets the attention of the audience, gives the reason for the message, identifies the topics of the message, and establishes the writer's point of view. The body presents contents and the topics of the message. The conclusion summarizes key points, calls for action, and identifies the benefits and the value of the message.

3. When creating a written communication, always keep these tips in mind:
   - Be brief.
   - Be clear and complete.
   - Review writing to be sure ideas are understandable and comprehensive.
   - Keep it simple
   - Check your work.
   - Always write with an upbeat attitude.
   - Take a timeout.
   - Read out loud to check grammar and punctuation.

4. The ten steps to effective writing are:
   - Think about the audience.
   - Think about the purpose and what needs to be accomplished.
   - Think about the situation and details.
   - Record the action desired as a result of the written message.
   - Identify the benefits of the message.
   - Identify the topics and group the details underneath it.
   - Order the topics in a logical sequence.
   - Write the main body first, then the introduction, and then the conclusion.
   - Read through the draft and revise the content, grammar, spelling, flow, and readability, asking a peer to comment.
   - Write the final draft and distribute the communication.

5. Students should explain why this statement is or is not effective and to whom it might be addressed.

Section 7.2 Activities

1. Students should consider their interactions with others, both positive and negative, and determine how they can be good communicators and colleagues in the workplace.

2. Students may choose from among a wide range of policy changes so long as their message is clear and professional and includes all the information needed to explain the new policy.

3. Students should consider their communication styles and how these may affect those around them, using the material in Section 7.2 for guidance. For instance, does one's communication style cause other people to find him or her credible? How does one's communication style cause a particular reaction in another person? Student responses should be at least two paragraphs in length.

Section 7.2 Activities

1. Study Skills/Group Activity: Interacting with Coworkers

Work with a partner to identify five ways you can interact well with your coworkers.

2. Activity: Communicating a Policy Change to Employees

You need to communicate some important policy changes to your employees. Write a message to them, containing all the relevant information and addressing the five W's and how questions.

3. Critical Thinking: Communication Style

How does your communication style affect how others perceive you at school or work? How do other people's communication styles affect how you perceive them?

442

7.1 The Communication Process	7.2 Communication Skills	7.3 Types of Communication
• The process of communication • Barriers to communication	• Personal characteristics that affect communication skills • Effective listening • Effective speaking • Effective telephone skills • Effective writing	• Organizational communication • Interpersonal communication

SECTION 7.3 TYPES OF COMMUNICATION

Communication involves the exchange of information through many different ways. The types of communication include organizational and interpersonal communication, focusing on sharing information and verbal messages.

Study Questions

After studying Section 7.3, you should be able to answer the following questions:

- What is organizational communication, and how might it be used in the restaurant and foodservice industry?

- What is interpersonal communication?

- How can relationships be built through interpersonal communication?

Organizational Communication

Managers must have strong communication skills to build credibility and a strong reputation. Similarly, a business must be able to communicate to build its identity and reputation with the public and even its own employees. **Organizational communication** is the numerous messages and information that convey operational procedures, policies, and announcements to a wide variety of audiences.

Organizational communication can be sent to people inside the organization or outside the organization. An example of a message sent inside an organization is an e-mail stating a change in the dress code. An example of a message sent outside an organization is a table tent for guests to read that outlines the new sustainable practices taking place in the operation.

Two important types of organizational communication are the **mission statements** and **vision statements** of an operation. A mission statement primarily serves an internal function. It describes the company's purpose and key

443

Section 7.3
Types of Communication

Introduce the Section

a. Explain the differences between interpersonal communication and organizational communication.

b. How can effective relationships be developed in the workplace?

c. Discuss the objectives for the section.

Vocabulary Review

a. Direct students to the key terms.

b. Pronounce each word, and have the students repeat the pronunciation out loud.

c. Discuss the definition of each word.

Teach

Discuss

- Encourage students to describe organizations they have joined or employers they have had. Have any had mission statements or vision statements? Which types of organizations do students associate with mission and vision statements?

- To what extent do students believe that an organization's or business's mission statements and vision statements reflect actual practice at that institution? In what tangible ways can an organization or business observe such a statement?

- What examples of organizational communication can students identify?

Reinforce and Review

- A business must be able to communicate effectively to build and maintain its brand identity as well as its reputation.

- Organizational communication can be sent to people either inside or outside the organization.

- The two most important types of organizational communication are mission statements and vision statements.

Vocabulary Terms

- **Organizational communication:** The numerous messages and information that convey operational procedures, policies, and announcements to a wide variety of audiences.

- **Mission statement:** A document that describes a company's purpose and key objectives to its team and owners.

Discuss

- How does a vision statement differ from a mission statement? Can the same organization have both?
- How can the quality of organizational communication affect both actual guest service and how guests perceive service?
- Should foodservice establishments get involved in community activities and politics? Why or why not? What civic issues might be particularly relevant to the foodservice industry?

Reinforce and Review

- High priorities for organizational communication include industrial, environmental, and community-related issues.
- Organizational communication is key to alerting the public about changes affecting the establishment.

Vocabulary Terms

- **Vision statement:** A document that defines the company's purpose and values to employees and customers.

On the Job:
Food Writer, Food Editor, and Food Critic

Encourage students to discuss the following:

- How have food writers contributed to the growth of the contemporary restaurant and foodservice industry, and vice versa?

- How has the Internet provided opportunities for novice food writers to gain access to a crowded field?

- What skills might be necessary for food writers to possess? How do these relate to the skills that culinary professionals are expected to have?

In-Class Activity:
You Gotta Have Vision

Literacy Connection, 21st-Century Skills—Communicate Clearly, Critical Thinking and Problem Solving, Social and Cultural Skills

Working in small groups, write a vision statement for the course.

Identify the course's purpose, values, and customers, as well as any other material you consider to be important.

As a class, vote on the best vision statement. Now decide what students can do each day to live up to this document.

objectives to its team and owners. A **vision statement** is directed both internally and externally. It defines the company's purpose and values to employees (so they know how they are expected to behave) and customers (so they understand why they should work with or patronize the company). These statements should be shared at orientation, discussed during employee meetings, and sometimes even posted or distributed in print.

Other high priorities for organizational communication include industrial, environmental, and community-related issues. Industrial and environmental issues impact every restaurant and foodservice organization. For example, parking lot construction or renovations to the building need to be communicated in a timely manner so the guest is not inconvenienced. Regulatory changes, such as pollution reduction (no-smoking ordinances) caused by consumer demands for better air quality, affect restaurant and foodservice establishments. Organizational communication is key to alerting the public about these changes and the restaurant's support of them.

[on the job]

Food Writer, Food Editor, and Food Critic

All these terms describe a writer who focuses on food in some way. Writers may concentrate on ingredients, restaurants, or anything else involving food and cooking. Some food writers research and write stories. Others will proofread, edit, and fact-check those stories, testing recipes as well. Still others assess food-related manuscripts for publication as periodical articles or books. And some food writers don't write for publication. Instead, they develop content for television, movies, and the radio.

Career opportunities are available in newspapers, television, radio, magazines, movies, and the Internet. Food writers who are further along in their careers may even contribute to books or write their own. However, food writers often begin as freelancers, pitching ideas or finished articles to editors for potential publication. Others start out on the Internet, as the number of food-related blogs and Web sites continues to increase.

There are no specific educational requirements for food writers, and they come from all walks of life. However, many do have a background in writing or communications, and more than a few have worked in restaurants and other foodservice establishments. It's essential to have strong writing skills and to work well independently. You must also be aware of industry and consumer trends, be knowledgeable about ingredients and cooking techniques, and, most importantly, have a real passion for food.

444

Interpersonal Communication

Part of a manager's role is to create a positive and respectful work environment. **Interpersonal communication** is one key to succeeding in these tasks. Interpersonal communication occurs in all types of relationships. However, it can vary depending on the relationship type. For example, the short interaction restaurant and food-service employees have with guests is different than the relationship they have with friends and family.

Interpersonal communication is any two-way communication that has immediate feedback. Basically, it is a conversation,

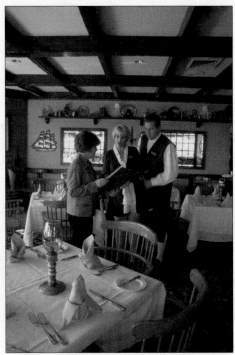

Figure 7.9: Interpersonal communication allows for immediate feedback.

although three people can sometimes be involved. The people in the conversation are trying to relate to each other at some level. The goals of interpersonal communication are to achieve a specific outcome, such as provide performance feedback, and to improve the relationships of the people involved. Figure 7.9 shows coworkers engaged in interpersonal communication.

Discuss

- How can interpersonal communication contribute to a positive and respectful work environment? Similarly, how can it contribute to a negative and hostile work environment?

Reinforce and Review

- Part of a manager's role is to create a positive and respectful work environment. The successful use of interpersonal communication is one piece of this puzzle.
- Interpersonal communication occurs in all types of relationships, but it can vary depending on the relationship type.
- Interpersonal communication consists of any two-way communication in which the people involved are trying to relate to one another.
- The goals of interpersonal communication are to achieve a specific outcome and to improve the relationships of the people involved.

Vocabulary Terms

- **Interpersonal communication:** Any two-way communication that has immediate feedback.

445

Figure Focus

Figure 7.9: How are these staff members communicating? What feedback is being received and by whom?

Encourage students to discuss the following:

- How does this information fit with the information on effective listening presented in Section 7.2?

- What are the best ways to practice listening skills?

- What happens when an employee wants to discuss something with a manager, but that person is brusque or nonresponsive? How can that affect an entire workplace?

- Similarly, what happens when an employee is rude or dismissive of a manager? What effects can that have on the workplace?

Essential Skills
Listening

Learning to listen to another person's point of view is a developed skill in most people. It is very easy to hear what other people are saying, all the while mentally preparing the next funny, clever, and witty reply. If only the speaker would hurry up!

That is not the best way. Truly listening to what another person says will encourage that person to continue talking and sharing. The more shared, the better acquainted two people become.

There are more parts to listening. The first is responding. It's important to quickly mention or repeat back something about the conversation, demonstrating an interest. The next part is confidence. If a person says something, keep it quiet unless it is necessary to share the information for someone's safety.

The listener should indicate that he or she is engaged. Listening with glazed and distracted eyes is not convincing. Look at the person's face and eyes. Periodically repeat back a bit of what the other has said to make sure the meaning is understood.

Employee: "I have an idea about scheduling that might save us money."

Manager: "Great! Would you please share it with me?"

Employee: "If we . . ., then . . . ."

Manager: So, you are saying that if we . . ., then . . . will happen for us?"

Employee: "Yes! I'm sure it would help."

Manager: "I appreciate your ideas. I will think about how we can try them."

People are the most important part of the restaurant, for without the staff there is no food on the tables. Learn to listen and work well with other people (see Figure 7.10).

Figure 7.10: To be successful, employees must learn to listen and work well with co-workers.

Figure Focus

Figure 7.10: According to the text, "People are the most important part of the restaurant." Does it really matter how well a cook can cook or how well a server can serve if they are good communicators? What skills are important in what roles, and why?

Sharing Information

In interpersonal communication, one person shares information that helps the other person relate back. Typically, a person shares information that the other person normally wouldn't know. By sharing, the two become closer and strengthen their relationship. For example, having a conversation about where one was raised and went to school, professional goals and aspirations, or what type of music each person likes can help two colleagues develop closer bonds that will in turn increase their trust in one another.

But this trust can't be based only on conversations. "Actions speak louder than words." The actions managers and employees take in the workplace show people a lot about who they are and what they value. Do they appreciate cultural differences? Are they humble? Do they praise others? Do they remain professional at all times? Often, fellow employees will make judgments about someone's personal integrity and effectiveness in a job based on how well they model positive attitudes and behavior in the organization. Employees who observe positive behavior are also more likely to set equally high standards for their own behavior.

Managers' actions also allow employees to better predict how they will react. For example, making the work environment a fun place by telling a funny story or having fun, friendly activities can lead employees to view the manager as more approachable. Additionally, showing humility has a huge impact on employee-manager relationships. No employee likes to work with a manager who feels solely responsible for why the organization is performing well and achieving its goals. Effective managers remain humble and give credit where credit is due. They look for every opportunity to build trust and respect among the staff.

[on the job]

Interpersonal Communication at Work: Leading Groups of Diverse Coworkers

Leading groups of diverse employees can be a challenge for even the most experienced supervisor. The restaurant and foodservice industry can be stressful, and bringing together workers of different ages, ethnicities, nationalities, religions, and cultures can increase the stress. But that doesn't have to be the case. Successful leaders know that capitalizing on the strengths each employee brings to the workplace can build a healthier, more effective environment. Here are some ways to accomplish this mission:

- Be a task-oriented leader. Focus on responsibilities, deadlines, and hierarchies, not emotions.
- Listen more than talk. Employees are more likely to offer suggestions when they haven't heard the manager's opinion. The manager might learn a new technique or piece of information.

447

Discuss
- What we say and what we do can often be very different things. It is often said that actions speak louder than words. Is this true? To what extent do students think actions matter more than words, and vice versa?
- How can someone encourage positive interactions in the workplace, either as a peer or as a manager?

Reinforce and Review
- When engaging in interpersonal communication, a person shares information that another person normally would not know. This sharing helps strengthen the relationship.
- The actions that both managers and employees take in the workplace demonstrate their personalities, beliefs, and values to their colleagues and guests.
- When employees see their peers engaging in positive behaviors, they become more likely to act positively themselves.

Teaching Tips
- Relate this material to the content on credibility in Section 7.2.
- Encourage a discussion on the potential for conflict between humility and ambition in the workplace.

On the Job: Interpersonal Communication at Work: Leading Groups of Diverse Coworkers (continued on p. 448)

Encourage students to discuss the following:
- What are some ways students can prepare to become strong members of diverse teams that value every member's contributions?
- What specific actions can students take as leaders to build a strong and positive team?
- In what ways can leading a diverse group of employees be both personally and professionally rewarding?

In-Class Activity: Chasing the Ideal

Literacy Connection, 21st-Century Skills— Communicate Clearly, Reason Effectively, Social and Cultural Skills

What communication skills would your ideal leader demonstrate?

How would this person interact with you and other colleagues and guests?

Write three paragraphs on the communication skills you would hope to find in an ideal leader.

Discuss

- Encourage students to describe experiences they've had in which someone has exhibited empathy toward them or toward another, or experiences in which they exhibited empathy themselves.
- Demonstrating empathy implies a nonjudgmental acceptance. What if you cannot accept the other person's behaviors, attitudes, or values in a particular situation? What if you feel compelled to judge that person's actions? Encourage students to discuss how to handle these incidents.

Reinforce and Review

- Whatever the intention of the message, both managers and employees must remember that how a person receives the message also affects the outcome and success of the communication.
- By using empathic statements in communication with staff, the manager conveys genuine concern about them and understanding of their situation.
- Positive perspective, even of negative events, brings positive results.
- Respecting the views and opinions of employees helps to strengthen interpersonal communications and relationships.

Teaching Tips

- Communication is a two-way relationship, and the message sent is not always the message received. Relate this to the material on obstacles to communications in Section 7.1.

Homework Activity: Picture This!

Literacy Connection, 21st-Century Skills— Communicate Clearly, Create Media Products, Social and Cultural Skills

Create a poster, artwork, or some other visual medium that illustrates some aspect of interpersonal communication. For instance, you could select sharing information or giving feedback.

The artworks should be exhibited so that students can examine them. As a class, discuss how these artworks not only display actions in interpersonal communication but are themselves demonstrations of interpersonal communication because the artist is communicating his or her values through the art. Discuss as a group.

Vocabulary Terms

- **Empathy:** The act of identifying with the feelings, thoughts, and attitudes of another person, demonstrating nonjudgmental acceptance.

- Research the cultures of coworkers. This can help uncover some important obstacles to communication, such as listening postures and facial expressions.
- Ask coworkers directly and respectfully about their cultures. This indicates that the manager sincerely wants to learn.
- Treat all colleagues with respect, and make sure everyone else does, too.

Is it easy to lead a diverse group? Not always. Is it rewarding? Yes. In fact, this opportunity may be one of the most rewarding.

Verbal Messages

Verbal messages also have a significant impact on interpersonal communication and therefore on the relationships a manager has with employees. Whatever the intention of their message, managers must remember that how a person receives the message also affects the outcome of the interpersonal communication. For example, showing **empathy** to employees who are having personal challenges creates a stronger bond with them. Empathy is the act of identifying with the feelings, thoughts, or attitudes of another person. Empathetic individuals may put others at ease with nonjudgmental acceptance. Often it is referred to as "standing in someone else's shoes." By using empathic statements in communications with staff, the manager conveys genuine concern about them and understanding of their situation.

The following is an example of how empathy can help diffuse a difficult situation:

> Employee to manager: "Chris called in sick again today. He's been out a lot lately, and it's been hard on all of us."

> Manager to employee: "I know that this has been a difficult situation, and I appreciate the fact that all of you have been pitching in to keep everything running smoothly. We are working to resolve this so that the situation won't continue to be a problem."

If a manager spoke this way of an employee, the rest of the employees would understand that they are being recognized for their extra effort and that management knows there's a problem. How would this make you feel about your manager?

Positive perspective, even of negative events, brings positive results.

Along with being empathic, respecting employees' views and opinions is another way of building stronger interpersonal communications with them. Displaying this type of acceptance conveys the message that the manager values their ideas and believes in collaboration. Additionally, employees

448

perceive managers' feedback as interest in their development and performance. Similarly, by receiving their feedback, the manager conveys to employees the message that they are open to improving themselves. In both situations, the message creates a long-lasting impression on the receiver, which improves the relationship.

Successful managers use all the available and appropriate ways to communicate with staff and coworkers. Interpersonal communication, in particular, allows managers to model an organization's values to employees. Here are examples of ways that managers use verbal messages to communicate positive values to employees:

- Chatting or having casual conversations with the staff can set the best tone. Managers want to build a friendly environment, which can increase their employees' trust. The nonverbal cues that accompany these types of chats, such as a pat on the back, a smile of thanks, or a "thumbs up," can also create an appreciation of positive values, resulting in a stronger bond between managers and coworkers. Figure 7.11 shows a manager using nonverbal cues to show his chef that he is pleased.

- Finding opportunities to coach, counsel, and provide feedback to an employee supports both the employee and the organization. The easiest and most immediate way to convey positive values and support by the organization is through feedback. Feedback is communication that helps a person understand how well he or she has done something and how to improve (think of it like a report card with comments from a teacher). Most manager feedback—whether positive or constructive—is related to an employee's performance. Employees prefer continuous feedback (letting people know how they're doing as they go) about how they are doing on the job, rather than once a year at a performance review. The manager provides employees with this information (see Figure 7.12). Likewise, the more feedback employees get, the more they will feel comfortable with it and look forward to the experience. Some initial ways to approach feedback with employees include the following:

  - Offer to provide clarification or help with tasks.

  - Invite them for coffee to put them more at ease.

  - Point out positive things they are doing along with constructive feedback.

  - Thank them for their efforts even when there is room for improvement.

  - Understanding the appropriate behavior in conducting one of these conversations is also essential for ensuring that an employee views the feedback as constructive and is willing to listen to it and then act upon it.

449

Discuss

- What are some appropriate ways to give and receive feedback? Is it appropriate for peers to give feedback to one another, or can this damage a relationship? As a manager, how is giving feedback a critical component of the job?

Reinforce and Review

- Managers should not only give employees appropriate feedback but should actively solicit feedback about their own work and the company's policies. This process helps to establish a relationship of trust and respect between managers and employees.
- Interpersonal communication provides a pathway for managers to model appropriate behaviors to their employees. Transmitting an organization's values to employees is particularly important.
- Nonverbal and verbal cues can convey appreciation of positive values and the employees who exhibit them.
- The easiest and most immediate way to convey positive values and support by an organization is through feedback.

Teaching Tips

- Encourage students to identify ways in which managers can approach feedback with their employees.
- Ask students to volunteer for a role-playing activity in which they portray managers giving feedback to employees. Situations could include demonstrating appreciation for a particular task, concern over a series of tardy appearances or any other interaction between a manager and an employee.

Discuss

• How do students perceive the coaching-doing balance? Are peer coaches a good idea, or can they create internal frustration and resentment in the workplace?

Reinforce and Review

• Coaching helps reinforce and improve performance on the job.

Teaching Tips

• Discuss the role of a mentor and how that person can help a student or employee develop personally and professionally throughout life.
• Obtain examples of food-related blogs to show students.

• Coaching helps reinforce and improve performance on the job. Coaching can be used when an employee needs more direction during on-the-job training, or when an employee needs support and encouragement to stick with a task. Coaches (who might include more experienced coworkers) provide additional guidance, clear directions, and more training. They also understand the delicate balance between coaching and doing.

Figure 7.11: Nonverbal communication is communication without words and includes facial expressions, gestures, and eye contact.

Figure 7.12: Most employees favor instant feedback.

Figure Focus

Figure 7.11: What do the physical appearances of these employees tell you?

Figure 7.12: What elements in this photograph suggest positive communication? What elements suggest negative communication?

Trends:
Food Blogs

Food Blogs

Just 10 years ago, no one knew what a "blog" was. Fast-forward to today, and worldwide there are more than 5,000 blogs about food. Writers across the world are turning to the Web to write accounts of their experiences with food. Subjects may include cookbooks, restaurants, ingredients, chefs, regional cuisines, the restaurant and foodservice industry, or farmers' markets. There is at least one blog for virtually anything and everything food-related.

Every blog is different. They vary widely as far as frequency of updates, quality of writing, and visual appearance. The common thread is a love of food. Blogs commonly contain recipes, photographs, and some personal information, such as a tale of culinary success or, more likely, failure on an epic scale. The best blogs combine good writing with a catchy "hook," high-quality photos, and a passion for food. There are even annual awards for the best food blogs, with categories such as best food blog for humor, for a particular city, and for writing. Figure 7.13 is an example of a food blog.

Like other blogs, food blogs often start slowly, but if they catch media attention, a single defining moment can cause radical growth in page views as well as financial attention. Some blogs have been criticized for poor writing or for unprofessional behavior, such as spreading baseless rumors about restaurants or chefs. As a result, a food blog code of ethics has been developed to help like-minded bloggers agree to certain standards of practice.

Note: To learn more about this code of ethics, look online at http://foodethics.wordpress.com.

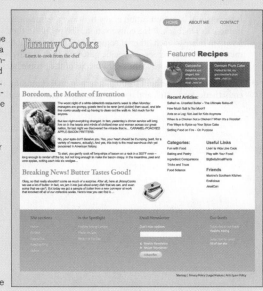

Figure 7.13: Food blogs are a great way to share ideas and thoughts with others.

Trends:
Food Blogs

Encourage students to discuss the following:

- How do food blogs affect the restaurant and foodservice industry? In what ways can this be positive or negative?

- Why should bloggers have a code of ethics or standards of practice? In what ways can this affect what they write and how they write it?

Homework Activity:
Blogging for Bucks

Literacy Connection, 21st-Century Skills—Communicate Clearly, Critical Thinking and Problem Solving, Social and Cultural Skills, Media Literacy, Create Media Products

Design a blog for an imaginary foodservice establishment.

What information do you think is important to include in your blog?

How can you attract readers and turn them into regular guests at your establishment?

What are some other ways to gain positive publicity for your establishment besides a blog?

451

Figure Focus
Figure 7.13: What positive and negative aspects are evident in this blogger's Web site?

Summary

- Remind students to review the following:
  1. The definition of organizational communication and how it is used in the restaurant and foodservice industry
  2. Interpersonal communication
  3. Building relationships through interpersonal communications

Summary

In this section, you learned the following:

- Organizational communication is the numerous messages and information that convey operational procedures, policies, and announcements to a wide variety of audiences. Send organizational communication to people inside the organization or outside the organization. Use organizational communication in the restaurant and foodservice industry with mission and vision statements.

- Interpersonal communication is any two-way communication that has immediate feedback. It is a conversation. The people in the conversation are trying to relate to each other at some level. The goals of interpersonal communication are to achieve a specific outcome, such as provide performance feedback, and to improve the relationships of the people involved.

- Relationships can be built through interpersonal communication by being empathetic, respectful, and open to sharing information with others.

Section 7.3 Review Questions

1. What is interpersonal communication? Provide an example of this that would be pertinent to the restaurant and foodservice environment.

2. Define organizational communication.

3. List three examples of appropriate information that employees can share to strengthen their relationships with their manager.

4. What are three ways in which managers use verbal messages to communicate positive values to employees?

5. Mary Fox believes that communication is one of the most important skills that you can possess. Do you think you can be an effective manager without having strong communication skills? Provide examples to support your answer.

6. Linda is having a difficult time explaining to her employees why they should commit to the success of Uptown Grill. What tools can she use to help build a team feeling?

7. What is the hardest part of engaging interpersonal communication with new coworkers? Why?

8. How can a manager's communication skills affect a restaurant's overall success?

453

Section 7.3 Review Questions

1. Interpersonal communication is any two-way communication that has immediate feedback. Its goals are to achieve a specific outcome and to improve the relationships of the people involved. An example might be a conversation between a senior cook and a newly hired cook about the contents of the walk-in refrigerator, or a conversation between two servers about an upcoming training seminar.

2. Organizational communication is the numerous messages and information that convey operational procedures, policies, and announcements to a wide variety of audiences.

3. Examples of appropriate information employees can share to strengthen their relationships with their manager include where each was raised and attended school, professional goals and aspirations, and musical tastes.

4. Three ways in which managers use verbal messages to communicate positive values to employees include chatting informally with staff, providing feedback on employee performance, and demonstrating empathy.

5. Students should explain why they do or do not believe that an effective manager might not also be an effective communicator. Either answer is acceptable as long as it is adequately supported.

6. Students can address this question in a variety of ways, but they should include both organizational and interpersonal communication in their answers.

7. Student answers may vary, so long as they are properly supported.

8. Students can respond in a variety of ways, citing organizational and interpersonal communication skills, but they should agree that a manager's communication skills play a significant role in the restaurant's overall welfare.

Section 7.3 Activities

1. Students may choose to model verbal or nonverbal interpersonal communication. The skit should be clear as to what communication is appropriate in the workplace and what is not.

2. Student answers will vary. To take this a step further, students could be encouraged to consider why and how the feedback that they find helpful differs from the feedback they tend to give others, or what types of feedback they tend to give to which populations.

3. Students should describe both the positive value and the method by which it was communicated and explain how it affected them.

Section 7.3 Activities

1. Study Skills/Group Activity: Appropriate Versus Inappropriate Behavior

Work with two other students and perform a skit modeling both appropriate and inappropriate interpersonal communication in the workplace.

2. Activity: Feedback

Create a list of the types of feedback that are most helpful to you and the types of feedback you are most likely to give others.

3. Critical Thinking: Positive Values

Consider a time when an instructor or supervisor communicated positive values to you. How did that make you feel and why?

454

Case Study Follow-Up | *Leading the Pack*

At the beginning of the chapter, Linda planned on conducting one-on-one interviews with her diverse staff and then asking each employee for a commitment. She really wants to move Uptown Grille in some new directions and now realizes that she needs her team to buy in.

1. What steps can Linda take to build a group commitment to her new vision?

2. Should she still conduct one-on-one interviews? Will the focus of those interviews change?

3. How can she best harness the experience of her employees—both their job experience and their experience with the owners?

455

Case Study Follow-Up

1. Students should suggest organizational and interpersonal communications that Linda can use when building a group commitment. They should also discuss potential barriers to good communication and steps Linda can take to overcome these obstacles.

2. Students may agree or disagree with conducting one-on-one interviews and whether the focus of such interviews should change, so long as they give logical reasons for their positions.

3. Although responses may vary, students should emphasize interpersonal communication skills. Linda needs to learn more about her new colleagues and how they relate to one another in order to achieve her goals.

Apply Your Learning

 ## Informal Language

Students should keep track of their ten words and how they are used. A simple chart, listing the word, with whom it was used, and the context in which it was used should suffice. They should submit the list of ten words and a bar chart showing the context or the conversers.

 ## Assess Communication

Students can select almost any document, as long as its content is appropriate for a classroom and a copy of it can be submitted. They should analyze the document as thoroughly as possible, according to the criteria given.

Apply Your Learning

 ### Informal Language

Do you often use informal language, "filler" words (like, totally, you know), and slang in conversation? Or how many times in a day? Make a list of ten words you commonly use that fall into one or another of these categories. Now keep track of how often you use each of these words in a day. Who are you with and where are you when you use these words most frequently?

Now divide your day up into categories based on where and how you spent your time that day: for example, "Class," "Lunch," and "Work" are all categories you can use. Create a bar chart showing where you are when you use these informal words the most. Alternately, create a bar chart using the people you spent the day with as categories ("Parents," "Teachers," and "Friends," for instance), and show who your companions are when you use these words the most.

An example: If you used the words from your list a total of seven times during dinner and a total of eighty times during work, then you would create a bar seven units high for the category "Dinner" and a bar eighty units high for the category "Work."

 ### Assess Communication

Pick out a written document, such as a memo, newspaper article, or advertisement, and assess it based on the following criteria:

- How well does it communicate its message?
- To whom is the message addressed?
- What barriers to communication could prevent the message from being heard?
- Does the document have an underlying message, and if so, what is it?
- How could the document be improved?
- What questions about the message do you still have after reading the document?

Create a report that answers these questions and attach a copy of the document to the report.

456

---

¹Ⓗ The Brain and Communication

When did language start? What did it originally look like, and why did it develop at all? Evolutionary linguistics studies these issues to learn more about how the human brain has evolved to support the complex communication abilities that we enjoy today. Research some aspect of the role that the brain plays in communication. For example, the way visual or auditory messages are transmitted to the brain, how we learn to speak as children, or how human brains differ from those of other primates. Write a two-page report on your findings.

Critical Thinking Enhancing Your Communication Skills

Communication is a big part of daily living that we are all good at, right? Wrong. There are always techniques we can use to develop better communication skills and enhance our relationships at home, school, and work.

How can you communicate more effectively with others at work and school? What can you do to present a professional image? Develop a personal plan for enhancing your communication skills and public image using the information you learned in this chapter. Practice it for one week. How have your interactions with others changed? Do you feel yourself to be a more effective communicator? Why or why not?

457

¹Ⓗ The Brain and Communication

Students may study any aspect of the role the brain plays in communication to complete this assignment, including the sample topics provided. All sources used to write the actual report should be cited.

Critical Thinking Enhancing Your Communication Skills

Students should consider their communication styles and habits before developing a plan of action. They should use the material included in this chapter as a starting point for making changes. Students should submit copies of their action plans, as well as an assessment of how following the plan affected their communications and interactions with others.

Exam Prep Answers

1. D
2. B
3. C
4. C
5. D
6. B
7. D
8. C
9. A
10. A

Exam Prep Questions

1 The process of sending and receiving information by talk, gestures, or writing for a response or action is

A. speaking.

B. messaging.

C. management.

D. communication.

2 Some researchers believe that _____ can impair your written communication skills.

A. emailing

B. texting

C. typing

D. audiotaping

3 A two-way communication that has immediate feedback is _____ communication.

A. verbal

B. nonverbal

C. interpersonal

D. organizational

4 Identifying with another person's feelings or thoughts is called

A. esteem.

B. respect.

C. empathy.

D. sympathy.

5 A letter sent to employees within an organization about a new health-care policy is an example of _____ communication.

A. verbal

B. written

C. interpersonal

D. organizational

6 Facial expressions are an example of what type of communication?

A. Verbal

B. Nonverbal

C. Interpersonal

D. Organizational

7 The numerous messages and information that convey operational procedures, policies, and announcements to a wide range of audiences is _____ communication.

A. verbal

B. written

C. interpersonal

D. organizational

8 The variation of a language spoken by a particular group of people is called

A. jargon.

B. accent.

C. dialect.

D. semantics.

9 Slang and buzzwords are known as:

A. jargon.

B. gestures.

C. prejudices.

D. semantics.

10 What part of a written message presents the content or topics of the message?

A. Body

B. Greeting

C. Summary

D. Introduction

459

Chapter 8 Overview

Chapter 8 introduces the student to some basic concepts in management, building on the material learned in Chapter 7 (Communication).

Section 1: The first section explains how colleagues can learn to work together more efficiently and respectfully.

Section 2: This section addresses some of the skills involved in successful leadership, including ethics, problem solving, and motivation.

Section 3: The third section discusses the processes involved in hiring new employees, such as interviewing, onboarding, and orientation.

Section 4: The final section explains some common methods for training and evaluating employees.

Advance Preparation	
Review	Sections 8.1–8.4
	Relevant material in Chapters 3, 4, and 7
	The U.S. Equal Employment Opportunity Commission's Web site (www.eeoc.gov)
Contact	A guest speaker who can discuss workplace diversity with students
Prepare	Obtain a copy or thorough description of the Fair Labor Standards Act
	Index cards
	District and campus policies regarding harassment and discrimination in the classroom

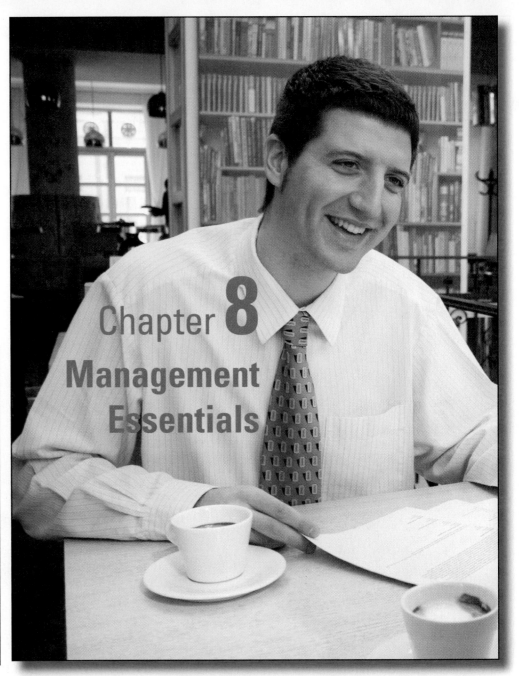

Chapter **8**
Management
Essentials

CUSTOMIZED INSTRUCTION OPTIONS			
Less Advanced Students	More Advanced Students	ESOL Students	Special Needs Students
Pages 512, 519	Pages 488, 512	Pages 471, 512	Pages 471, 512

CHAPTER TOOLS			
21st-Century Skills	Mathematics	Science	Literacy
Pages 465, 466, 467, 471, 473, 478, 480, 481, 485, 488, 489, 490, 494, 501, 506, 507, 509, 512, 514, 518, 519, 523, 529, 531	Pages 488, 502, 518	Pages 467, 488	Pages 465, 466, 467, 471, 473, 478, 480, 481, 485, 488, 489, 490, 494, 501, 502, 506, 507, 509, 512, 514, 518, 519, 523, 529, 531

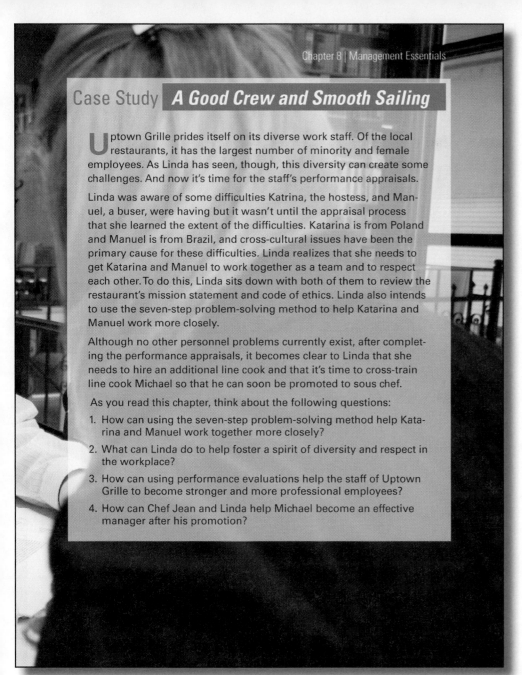

Case Study *A Good Crew and Smooth Sailing*

Uptown Grille prides itself on its diverse work staff. Of the local restaurants, it has the largest number of minority and female employees. As Linda has seen, though, this diversity can create some challenges. And now it's time for the staff's performance appraisals.

Linda was aware of some difficulties Katrina, the hostess, and Manuel, a buser, were having but it wasn't until the appraisal process that she learned the extent of the difficulties. Katarina is from Poland and Manuel is from Brazil, and cross-cultural issues have been the primary cause for these difficulties. Linda realizes that she needs to get Katarina and Manuel to work together as a team and to respect each other. To do this, Linda sits down with both of them to review the restaurant's mission statement and code of ethics. Linda also intends to use the seven-step problem-solving method to help Katarina and Manuel work more closely.

Although no other personnel problems currently exist, after completing the performance appraisals, it becomes clear to Linda that she needs to hire an additional line cook and that it's time to cross-train line cook Michael so that he can soon be promoted to sous chef.

As you read this chapter, think about the following questions:

1. How can using the seven-step problem-solving method help Katarina and Manuel work together more closely?

2. What can Linda do to help foster a spirit of diversity and respect in the workplace?

3. How can using performance evaluations help the staff of Uptown Grille to become stronger and more professional employees?

4. How can Chef Jean and Linda help Michael become an effective manager after his promotion?

Case Study
A Good Crew and Smooth Sailing

- In what ways can the restaurant's mission statement and code of ethics provide guidelines for appropriate workplace behavior and employee interactions?
- Encourage students to share experiences in which cross-cultural differences have caused difficulties in the workplace and elsewhere. Relate this to the discussion in 7.1 about barriers to communication.
- Relate management essentials to communication skills throughout the chapter. Ask students to consider whether communication is the most important skill set for a successful manager to have.
- Note that there are follow-up questions about the case study at the end of the chapter.
- This activity could be done in groups, as a class, or as a homework assignment.

Professional Profile

Discuss	Relate Jeff Cook's discussion of humility to the material covered in Chapter 7. How is this compatible with individual achievement? Should employees be recognized for their achievements?
	Encourage students to explore how this case study addresses professionalism and collegiality.
	Ask students to discuss how guest service skills are important in any industry.
Reinforce and Review	Good management skills are always in demand, even across industries.
	There is always room to improve one's performance.
	A team's performance is the real measure of a manager's ability.
Teaching Tips	Jeff Cook demonstrates clear passion for his job and career. Encourage students to identify how other Professional Profiles have also focused on passion.

Focus and Engage

Discuss

- The *Foundations of Restaurant Management & Culinary Arts* textbook assumes that interested students will go on to management careers in the restaurant and foodservice industry. Encourage students to explain why this assumption is made.
- Encourage students to share experiences they have had in which counseling has been used as either a disciplinary or a teaching tool.
- The goal of employee counseling is to change the action to the desired outcome in the future.
- All employee counseling should be done in private and in a manner that respects both the team member and the establishment.
- Most cooks aren't "chefs." That title is earned, as is the title of leader. In both cases, the individual is a manager who has earned the respect of his or her employees.

[professional profile]

Jeff Cook

Dream Dance Steak,
General Manager

Potawatomi Bingo Casino

My hospitality life started as a 16-year-old kid pushing 150 pounds of freshly ground beef from the butcher to the bar where I worked every weekend in the summer. That turned into six days a week to put myself through college. When it came time to choose between a nonpaying internship or managing the bar, my career path was finalized.

After seven years at the best burger bar in Wisconsin, I became part owner of a sports bar where I had the pleasure of seeing the Badgers win multiple Rose Bowls and the Packers win a Super Bowl. Everyone thinks the Super Bowl must have been the highlight of running a sports bar, but for me it was the NFC Championship the week prior. The game started at noon and the bar was slammed by 10:30 a.m. By 4 p.m., there was a conga line of fans going around the outside of the bar. If I could make guests that happy every day, I would probably be retired by now.

I joined Potawatomi Bingo Casino's Food & Beverage team in 2003 after 18 years in the family-owned bar business. Although my educational background isn't specifically related to the hospitality industry, the management skills I learned studying corporate fitness have been beneficial in the casino setting. During my six years in the department, I have overseen five of its six restaurants, including opening one of them during our expansion. In September 2009, I became the general manager of Dream Dance Steak, Potawatomi Bingo Casino's four-star, four-diamond steak house.

Whether I'm running a bar or an upscale restaurant such as Dream Dance Steak, there are a few missions I keep in mind.

❝ *First, hire the personality and then teach the skill.* **❞**

In this industry you must genuinely be a people person. The second is progress, not perfection. To the critical eye, there is always room for improvement, but if you are getting better every day you will be successful. Lastly, as managers we are not judged by our ability, but by the ability of our team. For example, when the casino expanded, my goal was to fill the new management positions with my team members. Two years later, my team had the most team members in management positions.

About Management Fundamentals

To be successful in business, you need knowledge of the basic fundamentals—in this case, the fundamentals of management. As managers, you will have to counsel team members. Some managers use counseling as a disciplinary tool, but

462

it should be used as a teaching tool. First, all counseling should be done in private, and if you have another manager in the restaurant, have that person in the room as a witness. Team members generally know what they've done incorrectly and will be defensive, so start by asking what they could have done differently. Then recite back to them what they did and how they should handle the situation the next time it occurs, so that they understand completely. Remember, you are teaching and the goal is to change the action to the desired outcome in the future. If your team members feel comfortable that you are trying to help them, not punish them, as they leave they will thank you. I've taught all my managers to listen for a thank-you after every counseling session.

Getting the thank-you is important because team members respect managers who are genuinely trying to help them improve. When your team members respect you, they view you as more than a manger—they view you as a leader. Manager is a title you are given, but when you become a leader, the title is earned.

8.1 Learning to Work Together	8.2 Being a Successful Leader	8.3 Interviewing and Orientation	8.4 Training and Evaluation
• Diversity • Respectful workplaces • Teamwork	• Leadership skills • Motivation • Ethics • Problem solving • Organizational skills	• Job descriptions • Interviewing job applicants • Lawful hiring practices • Onboarding • Orientation	• Training • Performance appraisals • Management equipment

SECTION 8.1 LEARNING TO WORK TOGETHER

The world of work is very different from the world of school. While you may not get a grade based on how well you do a job, your performance at work will determine whether or not you get a raise or promotion. Employers will be watching closely to see if you are the kind of employee they want to give additional responsibilities and money to.

Another difference between the classroom and the "real world" is that if your performance or attitude is poor, an employer can fire you. If this happens, you will need to find another job, but it will be difficult without a good reference from your last employer.

When you enter the world of work, even as a part-time employee, you are expected to follow guidelines of professional, adult behavior. These guidelines help all employees work well together and contribute to the success of the organization. Qualities that employers expect to find in successful employees are really a matter of common sense. Remember that, as part of a team, not only is your employer relying on you but so are your teammates.

463

Section 8.1
Learning to Work Together

Introduce the Section

a. Review the importance of workplace diversity and how it can strengthen a business establishment.

b. Point out the relationship between creating a respectful workplace and developing a healthy team.

c. Discuss the objectives for the section.

Vocabulary Review

a. Direct students to the key terms.

b. Pronounce each word, and have the students repeat the pronunciation out loud.

c. Discuss the definition of each word.

Teach

Discuss

- How can students find their first jobs? Who are some appropriate references they can use?

- Encourage students to identify some of the qualities employers expect to find in successful employees.

- Jeff Cook, the Professional Profile for this chapter, looks for personality when making hiring decisions. How can students successfully demonstrate appropriate personality traits during the hiring process?

Reinforce and Review

- Like teachers at school, employers provide feedback. Unlike school, however, your performance and the feedback it generates can have far more serious ramifications than a bad grade.

- Employers expect to find certain qualities in successful employees.

- The guidelines of professional, adult behavior help all employees to work together to support and develop the business.

- Employees are really team members. The employer and the other team members rely on one another to succeed.

Teaching Tips

- Relate the concept of learning to work together to the concept of professionalism, as discussed in Chapter 4.

Discuss

- How is the high school environment similar to and different from the workplace environment?
- What protections do students have that employees do not, and vice versa?
- How do students experience diversity in both the classroom and the workplace? What can be learned in each environment?

Reinforce and Review

- In a diverse environment, people must learn to value and respect others, regardless of their differences.

Teaching Tips

- Each student should write down three unusual or lesser-known facts about himself or herself on an index card. Make sure the students know that the facts will not be kept confidential. Collect and shuffle the cards. Read each card aloud to the class, asking students to guess who wrote each and why. Use this as a springboard to discuss the breadth of diversity.

Vocabulary Terms

- **Diversity:** The great variety of people and their backgrounds, experiences, opinions, religions, ages, talents, and abilities.

Study Questions

After studying Section 8.1, you should be able to answer the following questions:

- What is the difference between school and workplace environments?
- How do stereotypes and prejudices negatively affect people's ability to work together?
- What are the benefits of diversity to a workplace?
- How can diversity be promoted in the workplace?
- What is a harassment-free environment and mutually respectful workplace?
- What are the guidelines for handing harassment claims?
- What is teamwork?

Diversity

Diversity refers to the great variety of people and their backgrounds, experiences, opinions, religions, ages, talents, and abilities. In a diverse environment, people must learn to value and respect others, no matter how different they are. Figure 8.1 shows a diverse workplace.

This is a culturally diverse world, and everyone should expect to meet people who are different in many ways. People in high school now will be a part of the workforce in the 21st century—a century that will be characterized by greater diversity than ever before.

Figure 8.1: Diversity in the workplace is a reflection of the changing marketplace. Diversity in the workplace maximizes the potential of all employees.

464

Figure Focus

Figure 8.1: What does this photograph tell you about the workplace environment in which it was taken?

Stereotypes and Prejudice

Stereotypes are generalizations that individuals make about particular groups that assume that all members of that group are the same. Stereotypes are hard to change since they are usually not based on actual experience. Stereotypes take a lot of contrary experience to alter. All people are hurt by stereotyping—those who are inappropriately labeled by stereotypes, and those who think stereotypes are true. People who believe in stereotypes—either positive or negative—are cheated out of genuine relationships with people; this will cloud their personal and business judgment in untold ways.

Stereotypes produce prejudice or bias. **Prejudice** is a general attitude toward a person, group, or organization on the basis of judgments unrelated to abilities. Some people are brought up in an environment where they learn to like certain people and groups, and dislike others. Sometimes the prejudice comes from personal experience, and sometimes from the lessons taught by family members and other adult role models. **Bias** is a tendency toward a particular perspective or idea based on prejudice.

On the other hand, many groups of people do have common beliefs, such as religion, or share common ways of acting. These groups have **cultural tendencies** to do some things based on their beliefs and their habits. In contrast, stereotypes do not distinguish between what a group of people may tend to do or believe and what an individual does or believes.

Because there are many different groups of people employed in restaurant and foodservice operations, managers want to set a climate in which employees honor cultural tendencies and break down stereotypes. Building a team that works well together means helping everyone understand and value the strengths that each individual brings to work and exposing prejudice and stereotypes as the problems that they are. If a manager fails to do this, there will be many negative and, often, legal consequences. Allowing prejudiced and biased behaviors creates a hostile working environment for employees that can result in anger, distrust, frustration, violence, and possibly lawsuits.

In the restaurant and foodservice environment, prejudice and stereotyping have no place. Unfortunately, they are as alive and well here as they are in the broader society. People who do not want to work with a person from another culture, race, religious group, or specific gender are caught in habits and beliefs that run counter to honoring diversity and often are contrary to law. This is something that managers cannot tolerate. Managers need to expose prejudice and bias whenever they occur and set the expectation that they will not be tolerated in the workplace.

465

Discuss

- What are some legal problems that can result from prejudiced or biased behavior in the workplace? What ethical concerns can also arise?
- How do bias and prejudice function as barriers to communication? How can they be overcome?

Reinforce and Review

- Stereotypes are hard to change since they are rarely based on actual experience, but sufficient contrary experience can ultimately change them.
- Stereotypes do not distinguish between what a group of people may tend to do or believe and what an individual does or believes.
- Managers need to establish a climate in which all employees honor and respect cultural tendencies and work to demolish stereotypes.
- Allowing prejudiced or hostile behaviors in the workplace creates a hostile working environment for all employees.
- Managers should not tolerate prejudice and bias in the workplace.

Teaching Tips

- Consider inviting a guest speaker to discuss workplace diversity.

Homework Activity: Food in Diversity

Literacy Connection, 21st-Century Skills— Think Creatively, Communicate Clearly, Create Media Products

Design a menu that incorporates some dishes or concepts from your culture, religion, neighborhood, or another group to which you belong.

Develop a poster and an oral presentation to demonstrate your menu. Discuss how you selected each dish.

Vocabulary Terms

- **Stereotype:** A generalization that an individual makes about a particular group which assumes that all members of that group are the same.
- **Prejudice:** A general attitude toward a person, group, or organization based on judgments unrelated to abilities.
- **Bias:** A tendency toward a particular perspective or idea based on prejudice.
- **Cultural tendency:** The tendency of a group of people to do some things based on common beliefs and habits.

Discuss

- What are some elements of a hostile work environment? How can they be addressed?
- What are some elements of a positive work environment? How can they be built upon to improve the workplace?
- Page 466 lists a number of activities that can help break down stereotypes. How can these be effective? What have students learned about interpersonal communication that can help with this process?

Reinforce and Review

- The lower the employee morale, the higher the chances of conflict and turnover, which are both expensive for employers.
- It is important for employees to know that they are not being judged by personal characteristics, but by their relevant skills and abilities.
- Breaking down stereotypes can help managers promote a culture of mutual respect.

Fast Fact: Did You Know...?

Encourage students to discuss the following:

- Why does McDonald's have so many female and minority franchisee owner/operators? What experiences do you have from eating or working at a McDonald's, or even from watching commercials or reading print advertisements, that might explain this phenomenon?

- What professional opportunities exist in quick-service restaurants? What can employees learn there that can be used either in future foodservice positions or in another industry?

If managers allow harassment, employees will learn it is acceptable to treat each other as less than equals and colleagues. It also opens the door for the development of a culture of distrust and frustration—the opposite of what anyone wants in an operation. If employees do not feel trusted or welcome, they will not work hard, their productivity will fall, and their willingness to help each other will decrease dramatically. The lower the morale, the higher the chances for conflict and turnover.

Since discriminatory treatment in many cases is illegal, allowing it to happen in an operation opens the manager to the possibility of a complaint, investigation, or possible lawsuit.

Building a work environment in which people are honored for their contributions makes a real difference in an operation. It is important for employees to know that they are not being judged by personal characteristics—such as race or sex, their membership in some group, their similarity to the manager, or even to the majority of employees. To promote this culture of mutual respect and realize the benefits of diversity, a manager needs to help break down the stereotypes that people hold and manage activities that impact diversity. There are a number of activities that can help break down stereotypes:

- Recruit a diverse work group.
- Increase cross-cultural communication among employees by having employee events, where people share food from their cultures and have an opportunity to socialize.
- Provide world maps that show where people are from.
- Use workshops to increase communication skills .
- Educate employees about diversity and discrimination through diversity and sensitivity training.
- Set and communicate expectations for positive behavior from guests to vendors to other employees.
- Hold employees accountable.

[fast fact]

Did You Know...?

McDonald's has the largest number of minority and female franchisee owners/operators in the quick-service industry. The company estimates that 37 percent of all U.S. owners/operators are minorities or women.

Source: http://www.mcdonalds.com/usa/work/diversity.html?DCSext.destination=
http://www.mcdonalds.com/usa/work/diversity.html

466

Homework Activity: Design Your Own Culture

Literacy Connection, 21st-Century Skills—Think Creatively, Communicate Clearly, Design Media Products

Each student should envision an imaginary culture and the foods it eats. What are some typical ingredients? What dishes are consumed regularly, and which foods are reserved for more special occasions? What cooking equipment and techniques are used most often?

Students should design a poster illustrating their culture's food habits, explaining it to classmates during a "culture" expo.

As a class, discuss the similarities and differences among the imaginary cultures and the ways they deal with food. Discuss the ways in which cultures consist of learned behaviors, not innate characteristics.

Modeling

Assembling a diverse staff is not enough on its own to encourage positive cross-cultural interaction. Individual managers can do many things to help employees of all cultures feel comfortable in an operation. One of the most important is **modeling** the behavior expected from employees. When a manager participates in teasing, joke-telling, or other behaviors that show he or she tolerates or even encourages stereotyping and discrimination, it sends the message that these behaviors are acceptable. In contrast, demonstrating how to encourage and honor diversity goes a long way toward establishing a hospitable and welcoming environment for all employees.

Benefits of Diversity

Providing a welcoming environment for employees is a way to encourage each person to do his or her best. A manager has a commitment to all employees to value the quality of their work, to make their working situation hospitable, and to recognize the benefits of diversity. This welcoming environment also should extend to guests and vendors.

Creating an environment that values all people has many benefits beyond fulfilling legal obligations. Encouraging and honoring differences can mean a larger and higher-quality labor pool, a more enjoyable and productive environment, improved public relations, and ultimately, more guests. It is also the right thing to do in a cultural environment that increasingly recognizes the importance of protecting people from discriminatory treatment and honoring individual differences.

Creates a More Enjoyable and Productive Environment

A broad, diverse workforce means that employees with different backgrounds will look at the same situations and challenges from a variety of viewpoints. These diverse views can lead to a more productive work environment and more creative problem solving, an especially valuable service in the fast-paced environment of most restaurants.

Employees with different backgrounds can contribute their talents and be recognized for making a difference. In addition, all employees can learn from one another and appreciate the value of different ethnic, racial, and cultural backgrounds. Sometimes, this learning translates to helping with the dietary requirements of some guests. Sometimes, it means recognizing different ways of celebrating cultural beliefs, and sometimes it means just learning about the lives of coworkers so that everyone enjoys and respects each other more fully. All of these benefits contribute to creating a positive workplace.

467

Discuss

- In what ways besides diversity training can modeling be an effective management tool?
- How can diversity be economically valuable? Encourage students to explore ways in which creating a positive work environment can either save or generate money.

Reinforce and Review

- Demonstrating how to encourage and honor diversity can help establish a hospitable and welcoming environment for all employees.
- A manager has a commitment to all employees to value the quality of their work, to make their working situation hospitable, and to recognize the benefits of diversity.
- Creating a positive work environment has a variety of social and economic benefits.
- All employees can learn from one another and appreciate the value of their different backgrounds.

Teaching Tips

- Review the four benefits of diversity listed on pp. 467–468 and discuss how each can relate to a workplace or to a school.

Homework Activity: It's All Relative

Science Connection, Literacy Connection, 21st–Century Skills—Reason Effectively, Information Literacy, Be Self-Directed Learners

The study of human evolution continues to provide new information about how our species has developed and the connections between humans and other types of animals. In fact, all living cells share common characteristics and descend from a common gene pool.

Research the topic of human evolution to learn the origins of our ancestors. Why have so many distinct cultures and societies developed from a common starting point? How does studying the process of evolution and human histories help us to understand ourselves and our own societies? What can genetics tell us about who and what we are?

Write a two-page paper on these or related topics.

Vocabulary Terms

- **Model:** To behave in the manner in which others viewing the behaviors are expected to behave.

Discuss

- What does it mean to be an employer of choice?
- To what extent will potential employees trade tangible benefits, such as increased wages and other financial gains, for intangible benefits, such as a positive work environment and a harassment-free workplace? Encourage students to discuss where they might draw the line.
- In the restaurant and foodservice industry, high turnover and a small pool of skilled workers are common problems. Why might these situations occur? As employers, how might students reverse these trends? How can the industry itself reverse these trends?
- In what ways can students engage in cross-cultural interactions?

Reinforce and Review

- A staff that mirrors the community can encourage new business from local patrons and interest from local job applicants.
- When there are workers from a variety of backgrounds in an establishment, individuals often feel more valued and secure.
- When facing a claim of illegal discrimination, a manager who can demonstrate a history of positive policies, processes, and actions can present a strong defense.
- Positive cross-cultural interaction can enhance the workplace environment by breaking down stereotypes and prejudices.
- Diversity training can help people overcome their fears and concerns about other cultures that may be unfamiliar to them.

Teaching Tips

- Cross-cultural interaction is a form of interpersonal communication and may be verbal and nonverbal.
- Inform students about opportunities for cross-cultural interactions in the school and in the community.

Vocabulary Terms

- **Cross-cultural interaction:** Meaningful communication among employees from diverse cultures and backgrounds.

Attracts More Customers

Recruiting and hiring people from a range of areas, especially the local community, can help an operation build a staff that mirrors the community. This practice often builds new business from customers who feel more comfortable patronizing establishments where the staff is drawn from their community or who want to support diverse businesses.

Another benefit is the publicity about the operation. Word will get around quickly that it is an equal opportunity employer that hires from the community, and soon people will be asking for work.

Becomes an Employer of Choice

When an operation values diversity and demonstrates it by hiring a diverse staff, more people will likely seek employment in such a positive environment. When there are persons of many ethnic heritages working in and patronizing an operation, the person who comes from a relatively small minority will feel less unusual. Potential employees (and guests) will recognize diversity and will feel more comfortable about seeking employment in the operation. For all these reasons and other business benefits, promoting an environment in which diversity is encouraged and honored helps potential job seekers view an operation as a viable place of employment.

With a wider range of potential employees to consider, the labor pool increases, and so do the chances of finding good employees. Given the difficulty of finding qualified employees and the high rate of turnover in the industry, any program that improves the quality of the labor pool is worth pursuing.

Improves Legal Protection

Promoting diversity helps managers fulfill legal requirements and better positions an operation to defend against any claims of illegal discrimination. If a manager finds him- or herself with a complaint, a history of positive policies, processes, and actions can provide a strong defense.

Cross-Cultural Interaction

Encouraging positive **cross-cultural interaction,** or meaningful communication among employees from diverse cultures and backgrounds, helps break down stereotypes and prejudices and improves the workplace environment. There are many ways to develop cross-cultural diversity and communication skills:

- **Participate in diversity and sensitivity training:** Diversity training sessions help people overcome their fears and unfamiliarity of other cultures, especially if the training is a reward or enrichment rather than a punishment for

468

violating diversity policies. In some operations, the manager conducts ongoing diversity training by learning and then sharing facts about the customs, languages, and habits of the cultures of different employees. By doing this, managers can demonstrate that differences are fun to learn about and not something to be ashamed of, hidden, or feared.

- **Model behavior:** Managers must be a positive role model for employees when it comes to diversity. If a manager teases, tells jokes, or exhibits other behaviors that seem to tolerate or even encourage stereotyping and discrimination, employees will believe that these behaviors are acceptable. On the other hand, encouraging and honoring diversity helps to build a welcoming environment for all staff.

- **Integrate diversity into the mission statement:** Policies and procedures that promote cross-cultural interaction should be based on a mission statement that includes diversity goals. That way, everyone can see how important diversity is to the business.

- **Encourage studying and using different languages:** If employees speak different languages, especially in the kitchen, everyone has an opportunity to learn from each other. Learning at least a few key words of the languages spoken by other employees can be helpful to getting work done and building relationships. Additionally, many operations offer educational assistance to employees who want to study English.

- **Use multilingual materials:** Using posters and charts printed in the languages spoken by staff also improves communication, and offering training in relevant languages ensures that all employees learn important knowledge and skills. Orientation materials should also be provided in more than one language. These multilingual materials also show the value of diversity in an operation.

Respectful Workplaces

Two critical aspects of a positive work environment are respectfulness and equal treatment for all employees. Everyone in an operation must understand what a harassment-free environment means. In a **harassment-free environment**, complaints are handled appropriately and a workplace that respects all employees is supported on an ongoing basis.

Harassment happens when slurs or other verbal or physical conduct related to a person's race, gender, gender expression, color, ethnicity, religion, sexual orientation, or disability interferes with the person's work performance or creates an unhealthy work environment. Figure 8.2 is an example of one type of unwelcome physical contact between employees.

469

Discuss
- How can a manager encourage employees to leave their comfort zones and learn more about an unfamiliar culture?
- Many restaurants and foodservice establishments are small employers, with few staff members and managers. How feasible is it that these managers should spend a significant portion of their workday on diversity training and modeling? Is it important for them to do so?
- What is the difference between a joke and harassment? Does it differ based on context and the employees involved? Is it possible to have fun on the job without inviting legal problems?

Reinforce and Review
- Encouraging and honoring diversity helps to build a welcoming environment for all staff.
- An establishment's mission statement should include diversity goals to demonstrate its commitment to diversity.
- Learning other languages spoken in the workplace can help foster a positive work environment, as can providing training materials in all relevant languages.
- Two critical aspects of a positive work environment are respectfulness and equal treatment for all employees.

Vocabulary Terms
- **Harassment-free environment:** A workplace in which all employees are respected and complaints are handled appropriately.
- **Harassment:** Verbal or physical conduct related to gender, race, gender expression, color, ethnicity, religion, sexual orientation, or disability, which interferes with a person's work performance or creates a negative work environment.

- Have students experienced any instances of these or other types of harassment? Ask them to describe the setting. How did they respond to the situation?
- What is the difference between harassment and discrimination? Encourage students to identify examples of each.

Encourage students to discuss the following:

- What are some ways that sexual harassment can occur, either at work or at school?

- Is there always a relationship between harassment and power? What if the incident arises between peer coworkers or between an employee and a nonemployee?

- Why is it important to consider the context of the incident when investigating an allegation of sexual harassment?

- What are some ways in which employers, managers, and employees can help prevent sexual harassment in the workplace?

Harassment covers many categories, such as the following:

- Sexual
- Ethnic
- Age
- Religion
- Physical limitations

Figure 8.2: Harassment in the workplace is illegal and should never be tolerated.

[on the job]

Facts About Sexual Harassment from the EEOC

The U.S. Equal Employment Opportunity Commission says the following about sexual harassment in the workplace:

"Sexual harassment is a form of sex discrimination that violates Title VII of the Civil Rights Act of 1964.

"Unwelcome sexual advances, requests for sexual favors, and other verbal or physical conduct of a sexual nature constitutes sexual harassment when submission to or rejection of this conduct explicitly or implicitly affects an individual's employment, unreasonably interferes with an individual's work performance, or creates an intimidating, hostile, or offensive work environment.

"Sexual harassment can occur in a variety of circumstances, including but not limited to the following:

- The victim as well as the harasser may be a woman or a man. The victim does not have to be of the opposite sex.
- The harasser can be the victim's supervisor, an agent of the employer, a supervisor in another area, a coworker, or a nonemployee.
- The victim does not have to be the person harassed but could be anyone affected by the offensive conduct.
- Unlawful sexual harassment may occur without economic injury to or discharge of the victim.
- The harasser's conduct must be unwelcome.

"It is helpful for the victim to directly inform the harasser that the conduct is unwelcome and must stop. The victim should use any employer complaint mechanism or grievance system available.

Figure Focus

Figure 8.2: What is the man in this picture doing that constitutes harassment? What might be an appropriate form of corrective action?

"When investigating allegations of sexual harassment, EEOC looks at the whole record: the circumstances, such as the nature of the sexual advances, and the context in which the alleged incidents occurred. A determination on the allegations is made from the facts on a case-by-case basis.

"Prevention is the best tool to eliminate sexual harassment in the workplace. Employers are encouraged to take steps necessary to prevent sexual harassment from occurring. They should clearly communicate to employees that sexual harassment will not be tolerated. They can do so by establishing an effective complaint or grievance process and taking immediate and appropriate action when an employee complains."

In some cases, specific local laws also make discrimination based on sexual orientation illegal. Everyone has the responsibility to prevent harassment. Preventing discrimination is just as important as responding to it, for the welfare of everyone in the operation and the business itself.

Most companies have some type of harassment-free workplace policy that provides guidelines and procedures for how to behave in the workplace. Company policies need to adopt a prevention approach, acknowledging mutual respect as the goal for all who work in the environment.

The purpose of these policies is to provide a productive and pleasant work environment that protects all employees from harassment. Although the focus is on employee-related harassment, the policies should also cover harassment by nonemployees, because these situations—once they have been reported to a supervisor—also must be remedied.

Each organization will have its own statement regarding harassment, but in general, these statements should include some or all of the following aspects:

- Emphasize mutual respect for all.
- State the values of respect held by the organization.
- State that all staff are expected to adhere to the policy.
- Define the areas covered by the Civil Rights code.
- Address the covered situations as defined by its respective jurisdictions, but also consider expanding the areas based on other types of abuse not covered by civil rights laws.
- Alert managers to their responsibility for maintaining a harassment-free environment.
- Give employees options for help with dealing with harassment.
- Allow for informal resolution if the affected parties choose it.

471

Discuss

- What effect can harassment have on a restaurant or foodservice establishment's financial situation? Encourage students to identify ways in which harassment can cost money.
- Is a pleasant work experience the same as a fun one or an enjoyable one? Is work supposed to be pleasant?
- Why is it important for employers to establish harassment-free workplace policies?

Reinforce and Review

- Every person in a workplace has the responsibility to prevent harassment, not just respond to it.
- The purpose of a harassment-free workplace policy is to provide a productive and pleasant work environment that protects all employees from harassment by either employees or nonemployees.
- Mutual respect for all should be emphasized in every workplace.

CUSTOMIZED INSTRUCTION

Literacy Connection, 21st-Century Skills—Think Creatively, Reason Effectively, Communicate Clearly

Special Needs Students

What contributions to diversity can you make? In what ways are your experiences valuable in the workplace?

ESOL Students

What strengths does your background give you in today's workplace? How can your experiences be most appropriately valued on the job, and how do they empower you? How else do you think that your contributions can help build a stronger employee team?

Write a one-page essay on these questions or any related topics.

Discuss

- How can the presence of appropriate workplace policies related to diversity, discrimination, and harassment not only help resolve complaints but actually prevent them from arising in the first place?
- Why should investigations of alleged workplace harassment be conducted in confidence? How does this relate to an open-door policy?

Reinforce and Review

- Policies should ensure that any employee who feels that he or she has been harassed is encouraged to voice his or her objection to the offending person and to inform a manager of the situation.
- Policies that encourage communication, such as an open-door policy and anti-retaliation statements, should be enforced.
- All complaints should be investigated in confidence out of respect to all employees.
- Managers are legally liable for maintaining a harassment-free environment. To protect oneself and one's employees, uphold all applicable laws and promote all employer guidelines and policies.

Vocabulary Terms

- **Complainant:** The person with a complaint, usually in regards to harassment.

- Indicate the process for handling a complaint.
- Indicate that the organization has no tolerance for disrespectful behavior and misconduct, any of which may result in disciplinary action—including termination.

Policies must also ensure that any employee who feels that he or she has been harassed is encouraged to voice his or her objection to the offending person and bring the subject to the attention of a manager. The following guidelines can be used in a complaint resolution or management process:

- An open-door policy should be put into place, as well as policies that protect the person with the complaint, called the **complainant**, from retaliation.
- Complaints should be reported initially to the complainant's direct supervisor or manager, unless that supervisor or manager is the subject of the complaint. In that event, the next level of management or a human resources representative should receive the complaint.
- The complaint should be processed in accordance with any local or state law, and then following company policy.
- Complaints should be investigated thoroughly by the complainant's direct supervisor or manager, unless that supervisor or manager is the subject of the complaint. In that event, the next management level or a human resources representative should conduct the investigation. In all cases, investigations must be done in confidence.
- Employees should be prohibited from discussing the situation with other employees.
- Managers should communicate the information with only the appropriate parties.
- Managers need to document the complaint and collect statements from all involved parties.
- If the investigation reveals that an employee has harassed someone, the offender must be subject to appropriate disciplinary procedures, including termination.

Managers have significant responsibility for addressing harassment in the workplace. They are legally liable for maintaining a harassment-free environment. In fact, managers at all levels, including company presidents, have been cited and fined for not dealing with harassment effectively. It is therefore crucial that managers acknowledge and respond to complaints immediately, as well as act upon any type of harassment they see or become aware of. The best approach is a proactive one that upholds applicable laws and follows and promotes company guidelines and policies.

Teamwork

You've probably had plenty of chances to work on a **team**—maybe in class as a part of a project or as a member of a sports team. Do you remember a time when you tried to accomplish a task by yourself, only to realize you needed the help of a friend, classmate, or coworker? Chances are the two of you finished the task more efficiently than by doing it alone.

A team is a group of individuals with different skills and experience levels who are working to complete a task or meet a goal. **Teamwork** uses each member's strengths, so the group has more success working together than working alone. The most successful teams respect each other's opinions and find ways to work together to create positive results. Working in teams provides both advantages and disadvantages, as described in Table 8.1.

Table 8.1: Some Advantages and Disadvantages of Teamwork

Advantages	Disadvantages
Team members can learn from each other.	Conflict between team members can develop, and has to be handled.
People bring different skills and experiences to problem solving and can come up with solutions that one person would not have thought of.	Communication is more complicated.
Several people working together can get more done than individuals working on their own.	Some members of a team might let other members do more of the work.
Team members can support each other during difficult projects.	It can take longer to make decisions.

In the restaurant and foodservice industry, successful managers know that no one person can make an operation run well. They look to their employees for help with the challenges facing an operation. For example, the kitchen team works together to make the food. One person doesn't make each dish from prepping to garnishing. The servers work with the hosts and busers to keep things moving smoothly in the front of the house. Everyone has to trust that everyone else knows what they are doing and all the skills come together to make it possible.

Often, the people doing the work have a better understanding of where breakdowns might be and can help build a solution together. People on successful teams are also more likely to feel a responsibility to their team members to achieve the goals.

473

Discuss

- How can working in teams help provide better guest service? In what ways can teams be more, or less, efficient than individuals?
- Encourage students to discuss the similarities and differences between the restaurant and foodservice industry and the secondary-education system. In what ways do teams operate? How are successful managers important in each?

Reinforce and Review

- The most successful teams respect each other's opinions and find ways to work together to achieve positive results.
- Team members have to trust that all the other members know what they are doing to create successful outcomes.
- People on successful teams tend to feel a responsibility to one another as well as to the organization.

Teaching Tips

- Encourage students to share their experiences with both successful and unsuccessful teams. What have they learned, and how?
- Relate participation in a successful team to the interpersonal communication skills learned in Chapter 7.

Table 8.1: Some Advantages and Disadvantages of Teamwork

- How can the disadvantages of teamwork be mitigated? What can team members do to overcome these barriers?
- The free-rider problem occurs when team members do not participate appropriately in a team's work, instead "riding freely" on the backs of others. How can this situation be resolved?
- What are some ways teams can operate in the restaurant and foodservice industry?

Vocabulary Terms

- **Team:** A group of individuals with different skill and experience levels who are working to complete a task or meet a goal.
- **Teamwork:** Working as a group and using each member's strengths, so that the group can attain a higher level of success than working alone.

Essential Skills: Developing a Strong Team

Encourage students to discuss the following:

- How can team members decide what their goals will be?

- Many teams are composed of peers, without one clear leader. How can an individual act as a leader to ensure that the team's work is successfully completed without appearing arrogant or pushy?

- As a manager or team leader, what can you do to foster accountability among team members?

- Alternately, how can a manager stay a part of a team that he or she leads? Can the manager ever be "just one of the gang"?

Discuss

- After studying this section, what have students learned about communication and its role in the workplace that they had not previously learned in Chapter 7? How has their understanding of communication (especially interpersonal communication) changed?

Essential Skills
Developing a Strong Team

How can you lead a team that doesn't act like a team? Bringing your staff together to focus on common goals can be a difficult project, but developing true collaboration can be deeply meaningful and rewarding. Consider these guidelines when preparing to lead a team:

- **Define your goals:** What was the group established to accomplish? What is the time line for achieving these tasks? How will success be measured? Who or what will be served by the team's efforts? Does the team have the authority and ability to fulfill its mission?

- **Be clear with your coworkers:** Does everyone know why the team has been formed, or why he or she has been asked to participate? Do people understand the expectations that you and upper management have for the team's progress and success?

- **Make resources available:** Do team members have all the expertise they will need, or will some outside help be necessary? Are funds readily available for legitimate team-related activity?

- **Set positive examples:** Do you model appropriate pro-team behavior? Do you communicate openly with your team members, and do they communicate well with one another? Do team members feel that they can be honest with one another and offer their real opinions?

- **Create accountability:** Do team members feel that they are individually and jointly responsible for the success or failure of the team? Are members more likely to assign blame or to seek answers? Do members understand what the real outcomes of their work will be on the company or its guests?

- **Remember you're part of a team, not a group of individuals:** Do you assign too many individual tasks, or do team members collaborate to complete activities? Do you reward and recognize team achievements? Have all team members (as well as other company employees) bought into the team culture?

Even before you have the opportunity to lead a team, you can model team-friendly behaviors like congratulating colleagues on their successes or offering to help with tasks. Portraying these healthy attitudes will make you more likely to become a valued team member and a leader for tomorrow.

Summary

In this section, you learned the following:

- In a school environment, students are graded on their performance. In a workplace environment, employees' performance determines whether or not they get a raise or promotion. If a person's performance is poor, he or she runs the risk of being fired.

474

- Stereotypes are generalizations that individuals make about particular groups that assume that all members of that group are the same. Prejudice is a general attitude toward a person, group, or organization on the basis of judgments unrelated to abilities.

- Diversity in the workplace creates a more enjoyable and productive environment, encourages restaurants and foodservice operations to be an employer of choice, attracts new customers, improves legal protection, and encourages new ideas, talents, and perspectives.

- Diversity is promoted in the workplace by offering diversity and sensitivity training, modeling good behavior, integrating diversity into the mission statement, encouraging studying and using languages, and providing multilingual materials.

- In a harassment-free environment, complaints are handled appropriately, which results in a workplace that respects all employees on an ongoing basis.

- There are important guidelines for handling harassment claims:

  - Maintain an open-door policy.

  - Complaints should be reported initially to the complainant's direct supervisor or manager.

  - The complaint should be processed in accordance with any local or state law and company policy.

  - Complaints should be investigated thoroughly by the complainant's direct supervisor or manager.

  - Employees should be prohibited from discussing the situation with other employees.

  - Managers should communicate the information only with the appropriate parties.

  - Managers need to document the complaint and collect statements from all parties involved. If appropriate, the offender must be subject to appropriate disciplinary procedures.

- Teamwork uses each team member's strengths so the group has more success working together than an individual would have working alone.

475

Summary

- Remind students to review the following:
  1. The difference between school and workplace environments
  2. How stereotypes and prejudices negatively affect people's ability to work together
  3. The benefits of diversity in the workplace
  4. How to promote diversity in the workplace
  5. The definition of a harassment-free environment and mutually respectful workplace
  6. The guidelines for handling harassment claims
  7. The definition of teamwork

Section 8.1 Review Questions

1. The benefits of diversity to a workplace include creating a more enjoyable and productive environment, attracting more customers, becoming an employer of choice, and improving legal protection.

2. An environment is harassment-free when all employees are respected and all complaints are handled appropriately.

3. Teamwork uses each member's strengths so the group has more success working together than working alone. Although working in teams may have some disadvantages, successful teams respect each member's opinions and find ways to work together to create positive results.

4. Diversity can be promoted in the workplace by the following means:
   • Recruiting a diverse work group
   • Increasing cross-cultural communication among employees by having employee events
   • Providing world maps to show where employees are from
   • Using workshops to increase communication skills
   • Educating employees about diversity and discrimination
   • Setting and communicating expectations for positive behavior
   • Holding employees accountable for their actions

5. Jim Cook might recommend building a team by hiring people based on their personalities and training them so they can develop the tools and skills needed in that particular workplace.

6. Students should discuss how cross-cultural differences can complicate working relationships. The material in Chapter 7 on barriers to communication might prove helpful.

7. Stereotypes are generalizations that individuals make about particular groups that assume that all members of that group are the same. These generalizations produce prejudices, which are general attitudes toward a person, group, or organization on the basis of judgments unrelated to abilities.

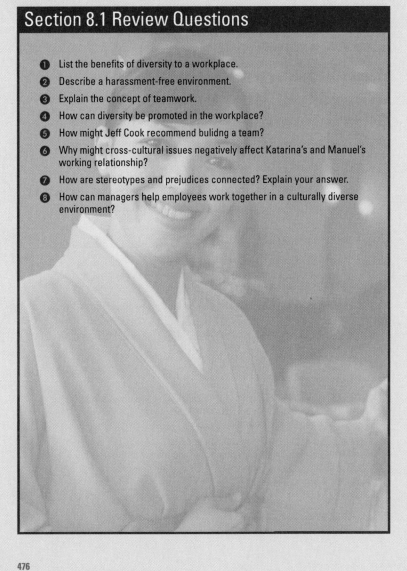

Section 8.1 Review Questions

1. List the benefits of diversity to a workplace.
2. Describe a harassment-free environment.
3. Explain the concept of teamwork.
4. How can diversity be promoted in the workplace?
5. How might Jeff Cook recommend bulidng a team?
6. Why might cross-cultural issues negatively affect Katarina's and Manuel's working relationship?
7. How are stereotypes and prejudices connected? Explain your answer.
8. How can managers help employees work together in a culturally diverse environment?

476

8. Managers can help employees work together in a culturally diverse environment by developing and adhering to a formal statement regarding harassment which protects all employees. Managers can also participate (and encourage employees to participate) in diversity and sensitivity training, model appropriate behavior, integrate diversity into the mission statement, encourage studying and using different languages, and use multilingual materials.

Section 8.1 Activities

1. Study Skills/Group Activity: Create a Harassment-Free Workplace Policy

Work with two other students to develop a harassment-free workplace policy for your restaurant. Include a training plan for your policy.

2. Activity: Workplace Diversity Report

Select a company you admire for its products, for its corporate ethics, or for some other reason. Research its workplace diversity, both its public statements and its actual employment practices. Create a one-page report that presents your findings.

3. Critical Thinking: Create Cross-Cultural Interaction

How do you think that being a member of a diverse team in the workplace is different from being a leader of a diverse team? How are the challenges and opportunities different in each case?

477

Section 8.1 Activities

1. Students should use the material on pp. 471–472 as they develop a harassment-free workplace policy and a training plan for that policy.

2. Students can choose any company they like, but it may be easier to obtain this information about larger businesses. Students should draw clear relationships between the company's public statements and actual practices.

3. Students should discuss the different roles played by managers and employees in diverse teams, using the material on pp. 473–474.

Section 8.2
Being a Successful Leader

Introduce the Section
a. Discuss the skills most effective managers share.
b. Explain the role of professional ethics and the workplace.
c. Discuss the objectives for the section.

Vocabulary Review
a. Direct students to the key terms.
b. Pronounce each word, and have the students repeat the pronunciation out loud.
c. Discuss the definition of each word.

Teach

Discuss
- Encourage students to discuss the best leaders they have encountered. What made these people so successful? How did they affect their employees, students, or members?

Reinforce and Review
- Good leaders must understand the goals, values, vision, and missions of an operation in order to successfully lead the team.
- Good leaders are made, not born.

In-Class Activity: Designing the Perfect Boss

Literacy Connection, 21st-Century Skills— Think Creatively, Communicate Clearly, Work Independently

What does your ideal supervisor look like? What goals and attributes would he or she have? How might he or she relate to other employees, and in what ways would he or she support your organization or establishment?

Write a job description for the perfect boss, identifying what you believe are the most important qualifications a supervisor should have.

Share your description with classmates as part of a group discussion.

8.1 Learning to Work Together	8.2 Being a Successful Leader	8.3 Interviewing and Orientation	8.4 Training and Evaluation
• Diversity • Respectful workplaces • Teamwork	• Leadership skills • Motivation • Ethics • Problem solving • Organizational skills	• Job descriptions • Interviewing job applicants • Lawful hiring practices • Onboarding • Orientation	• Training • Performance appraisals • Management equipment

SECTION 8.2 BEING A SUCCESSFUL LEADER

In order for restaurants and foodservice operations to be successful, they must have managers who have leadership skills and qualities. Remember, good leaders are made not born. Good leaders must understand the goals, values, vision, and mission of an operation in order to successfully lead the team.

Study Questions

After studying Section 8.2, you should be able to answer the following questions:

- What are ethics and what role do they play in the restaurant and foodservice industry?
- What are the characteristics of a leader?
- What are the common expectations that employees have about managers?
- What is motivation and what role does a manager play in motivating employees?
- What is an organizational goal and why should the goal be SMART?
- What are the purposes of vision statements and mission statements?
- How do employees' roles and jobs impact the mission and goals?
- What are the steps for solving a problem?

478

Leadership Skills

Leadership is the ability to inspire and motivate employees to behave in accordance with the vision of an organization and to accomplish the organization's goals. Figure 8.3 shows a leader directing his or her team.

Good leaders demonstrate the following behaviors:

Figure 8.3: Leaders need to inspire and motivate employees.

- **Provide direction:** Leaders communicate clearly and ensure that others know what is expected of them. One of the ways to accomplish this is to discuss roles and responsibilities, verifying that everyone understands the directions.

- **Lead consistently:** Using the organization's vision, mission, and values as checkpoints, leaders maintain the organization's standards by holding themselves and others accountable for their actions. Leaders must treat everyone fairly.

- **Influence others:** Leaders have the responsibility to earn the respect of others, which in turn enables them to encourage those they lead. Good performance, professionalism, and engaged, satisfied employees are all a result of leaders who influence through example. Leaders also build consensus through a give-and-take dialogue, considering other people's opinions to help form their own.

- **Motivate others:** The importance of communication cannot be overstated. Leaders give pep talks, ask for advice, and vocally praise people's work. They also must keep everyone informed, so that personnel know what they are supposed to be doing and how it contributes to the big picture. Finally, communication motivates people—instilling a sense of belonging by allowing them to contribute ideas.

- **Coach and develop others:** Leaders help others learn better ways to perform a task and take pride in others' success.

- **Anticipate change:** Leaders look for ways to continuously improve and for better ways to do things, understand the link between change and learning, and communicate the benefits of new processes and procedures. It is also crucial to help others to embrace the change if it is to be successful.

- **Foster teamwork:** A good team leader sees who is good at each task, helps team members improve their performances, and puts the team's goals ahead of his or her own. Ultimately, a successful team leader needs to listen, be consistent, and provide direction to bring the team together.

479

Discuss

- Page 479 describes a number of behaviors typically demonstrated by good leaders. Encourage students to discuss the qualities shared by good leaders. Which of these should also be shared by employees.

Reinforce and Review

- Leadership is the ability to inspire and motivate employees to behave in accordance with the vision of an organization and to accomplish the organization's goals.
- Leaders must consistently hold themselves and their employees accountable for their actions, treating all fairly.
- True leaders are respected by their employees, which gives them the necessary influence to lead by example.
- Keeping employees informed, involved, and motivated is important to leadership success, as is coaching.
- Leaders not only seek to create positive changes but to help others embrace those changes.
- Ultimately, a successful team leader needs to listen, be consistent, and provide direction.

Teaching Tips

- Relate this material to the discussion of modeling in Section 7.3.

Figure Focus

Figure 8.3: Motivating and inspiring employees is a day-to-day challenge, but it is also an opportunity.

Encourage students to discuss the following:

- How does each quote provide a different perspective on leadership?

- What do these quotes all have in common?

- What is the central difference between leadership and management?

Discuss

- Ask students to suggest techniques to turn first-time guests into regular patrons.
- Sometimes leaders must recognize that their employees have challenges in their personal lives that are affecting their work. How can true leaders acknowledge these situations without accepting the negative behaviors these challenges may generate in the workplace?

Reinforce and Review

- When welcoming or otherwise interacting with guests, be genuine and make eye contact. This helps guests feel truly welcomed and comfortable.
- Getting to know guests is part of the long-term success of any restaurant or foodservice establishment.
- Empathy is the act of showing understanding and sensitivity to someone else about a situation.

In-Class Activity: Quotable Notes

Literacy Connection, 21st-Century Skills—Think Creatively, Reason Effectively, Communicate Clearly

Each student should spend ten minutes devising his or her original quote about leadership or management.

As a class, discuss the similarities and differences among the quotes. How can each be used in the classroom or in the workplace?

Vocabulary Terms

- **Interpersonal skills:** People skills.

[fast fact]

Did You Know...?

"The most dangerous leadership myth is that leaders are born—that there is a genetic factor to leadership. This myth asserts that people simply either have certain charismatic qualities or not. That's nonsense; in fact, the opposite is true. Leaders are made rather than born." —Warren G. Bennis

"Leaders aren't born they are made. And they are made just like anything else—through hard work. And that's the price we'll have to pay to achieve that goal, or any goal." —Vince Lombardi

"Inventories can be managed, but people must be led." —H. Ross Perot

"Don't tell people how to do things, tell them what to do and let them surprise you with their results." —George S. Patton

Interpersonal Skills

People skills are also known as **interpersonal skills**. A person who possesses good interpersonal skills is a person who can generally relate to and work well with others. There are many ways to practice people skills in the workplace:

- **Acknowledge guests:** When guests enter the restaurant or foodservice operation, it is important that employees greet them as they would a personal friend who is coming for dinner at their home. Make eye contact with guests as they enter your area of service. Welcome guests with a great smile and a genuine, enthusiastic greeting. Doing so makes the guest feel important and wanted. It is important to pay attention to guests' concerns, questions, and body language. Getting to know guests is important to the long-term success of any restaurant. Figure 8.4 shows a hostess greeting guests as they arrive at a restaurant.

Figure 8.4: This hostess is showing good interpersonal skills by smiling and by welcoming incoming customers.

- **Show empathy:** Everyone from time to time will come up against issues and challenges in life. A person with strong people skills will demonstrate empathy for the life and work challenges that everyone faces. Empathy is the act of showing understanding and sensitivity to someone else about a situation.

Figure Focus

Figure 8.4: What nonverbal communication is this hostess demonstrating?

Successful managers know that showing understanding and sensitivity is not about accepting the issues or challenges the employee is facing, but about acknowledging that the employee is having these issues and challenges.

- **Praise others:** Think about how it feels to hear "Good job!" Everyone likes to be praised and appreciated for his or her efforts. Managers especially need to praise staff, because it helps employees feel motivated to provide the best service they can. Figure 8.5 shows a manager praising his kitchen staff for a job well done.

Figure 8.5: Praise and recognition motivate employees and create a good working environment.

- **Be aware of cultural differences:** As individuals in a diverse world, it is important that all employees and managers make themselves aware of the many cultural differences they may encounter with guests and coworkers. Every employee in the restaurant needs to understand that each person is unique and brings strengths and opportunities to the workforce. There may be different ways of doing things, looking at situations, levels of interaction, and appropriate behavior between cultures. Learning to accept these differences is beneficial to everyone.

- **Be ethical, approachable, and professional:** No matter what job a person holds in a restaurant or foodservice operation, every individual represents him- or herself, the team, and the image of the business. Acting with integrity and in an ethical way promotes great teamwork and encourages others to return the favor. As a manager or an employee, being open and approachable will create an operation that runs more smoothly and can head off more serious problems. For example, what seems like a small workplace complaint, for instance, "The floor in the back is a little slippery," can turn into a much bigger problem. If ignored, it might lead to someone falling and becoming seriously injured. All employees should be aware of their actions and the impact those actions have on others.

481

Discuss

- How are interpersonal skills and interpersonal communication similar? How are they different?
- All employees should be aware of how their actions affect one another. How is this also true in a high school setting? How can students' actions affect themselves and others?

Reinforce and Review

- Praising staff members helps motivate them to perform at even higher levels.
- Every employee in a foodservice establishment must understand one another's strengths and weaknesses.
- Employees represent themselves, the team, and the establishment, so it is always important to consider the possible effects of one's actions on each of these.
- Demonstrating professional integrity and ethical behavior in the workplace is essential to developing strong relationships with colleagues and guests.

In-Class Activity: Motivational Moments
Literacy Connection, 21st-Century Skills— Think Creatively, Reason Effectively, Collaborate with Others
Each student should spend ten minutes developing three concrete things that, as a manager, he or she could do each day to motivate employees.
Divide the class into small groups so that students can discuss which ideas might be more or less successful. The best ideas should be debated as a class.

Figure Focus
Figure 8.5: Ask students if praise and recognition from teachers help motivate them.

Discuss

- Motivation can help employees work harder to achieve particular goals. Encourage students to explain how either internal or external motivation relates to their willingness to achieve academic or athletic goals.
- How do students feel about internal motivation? What about external motivation? Which do they feel is more rewarding?

Reinforce and Review

- A leader motivates and influences others every day, with every decision.
- Leaders can use a judicious balance of internal and external motivations to encourage each employee to perform at his or her best each day.
- Just as managers have certain expectations of their employees, employees have certain expectations of their managers. These fall into the categories of professionalism, personal treatment, and work and task support.

Teaching Tips

- Praise and positive feedback are great in theory, but if the same comments are repeated each day, they may become less effective as employees come to view the repetition as mechanical and meaningless. With the class, discuss the idea that familiarity breeds contempt. In what ways is this relevant to the restaurant and foodservice industry?

Vocabulary Terms

- **Motivation:** The reasons a person takes action or behaves in a certain way.
- **Internal motivation:** The personal drive to do the best work possible whether or not there are rewards.
- **External motivation:** The personal drive to do the best work possible in exchange for a reward.

Motivation

Motivation is comprised of the reasons why a person takes action or behaves in a certain way. A big part of leadership is keeping team members motivated to do a good job and work hard toward the team's success. Continually giving employees constructive feedback is essential. Making employees feel valued and like important players on the team keeps them motivated, which in turn influences others to be the same. A leader motivates and influences other people through his or her own actions every day with every decision.

Internal motivation is the personal drive to do the best work possible whether there are rewards or not. People who are internally motivated are seeking satisfaction or maybe a feeling of accomplishment. External motivation is when the drive comes from the desire to receive something, such as a reward or recognition for achieving results. Examples of **external motivation** are paychecks, bonuses, and health benefits.

Leaders balance focus on both types. They train and coach. They encourage others to feel good about their performance and their jobs. They set goals for themselves and other people, as well as rewards for achieving those goals. Even the recognition of personal milestones, such as celebrating a birthday or graduating from a program, is part of motivating.

Employee Expectations of Managers

Employees respond to and are more easily motivated by managers whom they respect and trust. Employees come to the workplace with expectations and hopes of working with these kinds of managers. Their expectations fall into three groups: professionalism, personal treatment, and work and task support (refer to Table 8.2).

Table 8.2: Employee Expectations of Managers

Professionalism	Demonstrate knowledge.
	Demonstrate leadership.
	Practice honesty.
	Practice confidentiality.
	Practice respect.
	Practice moral behavior.
	Practice ethics.
Personal Treatment	Practice fairness.
	Practice consistency.
	Provide support.
	Practice empathy.
	Provide feedback.
Work and Task Support	Provide clear directions.
	Provide tools and resources.
	Encourage professional growth and development.
	Include employees in decision-making that affects them.
	Provide a safe environment.
	Practice reasonable and rational behavior.

Professionalism

Professionalism is the combination of the knowledge, skills, attitudes, and behaviors a person shows while performing a job. It includes interactions with other employees, vendors, and guests. People with high levels of professionalism are excellent performers, honest, and respectful, and they lead and serve others with integrity and fairness.

Personal Treatment

Personal treatment refers to the ways in which managers interact with staff and the value system that governs their daily conduct. Employees expect their managers to practice ethical behavior.

Work and Task Support

Employees expect to have the tools and resources they need to perform their duties. Employees also expect that a manager will provide coherent directions on what is required. An extension of these resources includes providing a safe and harassment-free work environment. Hazards and risks in the immediate workplace are always present in a restaurant or foodservice operation, and a manager needs to ensure that they are minimized for employee safety. Finally, employees need and want support for their own personal and professional

483

Table 8.2: Employee Expectations of Managers

- Students should relate Table 8.2 to the activity on p. 478.
- What are the most important expectations a manager should fulfill, and why?
- Why is this table entitled Employee Expectations of Managers, not Employee Expectations of Leaders? Does it matter?
- How can managers develop the skills they need to meet employee expectations?
- It has been said that a manager should be able to do every task that he or she requires his or her employees to do, only better. What do students think of this statement?

Reinforce and Review

- Professionals are excellent performers. They are honest, respectful, and can lead and serve others with integrity and fairness.
- Employees expect managers to exhibit ethical behavior in their relations with employees, other staff, vendors, and guests.
- Employees expect to be given the tools and resources they need to perform successfully.

Teaching Tips

- Relate the discussion to the material on professionalism in Chapter 4.
- Point out the relationship between employee expectations and manager modeling.

Vocabulary Terms

- **Professionalism:** The combination of the knowledge, skills, attitudes, and behavior a person shows while performing a job.
- **Personal treatment:** The ways in which managers interact with staff and the value system that governs their daily conduct.

Discuss

- Why is it important for employees to feel free to raise issues and concerns about workplace matters? Is it possible to feel too free? Where do students think boundaries should be drawn?
- Encourage students to give examples of times that they had to give a supervisor or teacher unwelcome information. How did the process make them feel? Were the results as unpleasant as predicted? What steps could have been taken to prevent the situation from arising in the first place?
- How can students and employees know which workplace concerns are significant enough to voice to management and which are not? Is there a foolproof way of deciding this?

Reinforce and Review

- The harder a manager works to meet employee expectations, the more likely it is that the desired results will ensue.
- Employees need to be able to express legitimate concerns without fear of retribution.
- Most managers want to know about relevant workplace issues, although few wish to be bothered with inconsequential matters.
- Restaurant and foodservice establishments that experience few problems typically solve emergent concerns quickly and appropriately, using good systems to recognize and resolve problems.

Teaching Tips

- Relate this material to Chapter 7.

Vocabulary Terms

- **Problem solving:** The determination of a solution to a workplace concern.
- **Problem-solving process:** The logical sequence of identifying and defining a problem through resolving and documenting a solution.

development. Creating a work environment that takes care of and meets these expectations is another critical task that managers face.

Effective managers discover ways to meet these expectations by devoting time to examining work conditions and developing strong relationships with their employees. The results that managers get from meeting these expectations are usually in direct proportion to the amount of time they allocate to them. If a manager devotes time to developing him- or herself and others and provides an encouraging work environment, motivational challenges are more likely to be minimized.

Communication with Employees

In general, most managers practice an open-door policy. Managers need to understand the importance of communication and how communication or lack thereof can affect an operation. So, they want to know what employees are thinking and feeling.

Employees need to understand that operational issues may arise that force them to communicate important information to a manager. There will be times that such information may put a manager or an employee in a position they do not want to be in, but the right decision should be made. Employees need to feel safe. They need to know that they will be able to voice their concerns without suffering any retribution.

Most of the time, managers want to have constructive and valid opinions about work tasks. They, just like the employee, want the job to be productive and fun. Managers want to hear about items that may be preventing employees from completing their daily tasks so that they can address those issues as needed. Managers must be sure to keep those lines of communication open.

Problem Solving

Successful managers recognize a problem when it occurs. Then they define it, come up with a solution, and implement that solution quickly. Problems happen in every business. Restaurants with a large number of problems are most likely having the same problems again and again because they were not solved correctly the first time. On the other hand, an operation with few problems probably solves any problems it does have accurately and quickly.

Problem solving depends on an intentional process followed in a logical sequence. Following the sequence leads to a reasonable conclusion. When management works through the **problem-solving process** correctly, the operation will not have to deal with the problem again once it has been solved. It is

484

therefore critical that managers follow a problem-solving model to explore all of a problem's potential causes. There are several models available. The process model presented here is a compilation of some of the most common versions. It is composed of seven major steps. Each step provides input to the next until the final phase, which calls for documenting the outcome of the process. Figure 8.6 illustrates this problem-solving model:

Figure 8.6: To explore all of a problem's potential causes, follow the problem-solving model.

1. **Define the problem:** Before beginning to solve a problem, the first step is to define the problem as precisely as possible. Misdiagnosing a problem will lead to a meaningless solution because it won't address the real problem. Ask numerous questions to find out exactly what is happening. Do not take a problem at its face value.

   • Identify who or what is affected. Once the problem has been defined, determine who or what is being affected by the problem. The answer to these questions could include one or more groups of people, including employees, management, owners, guests, or the public. It could also include one or more individuals within these groups and not necessarily the entire group. Asking these questions might also identify processes or systems within the restaurant that are not performing as well as they could, even though they may not be the source of, or even be affected by, the problem.

2. **Determine the root cause:** Normally, one or two sources will be the cause of a problem. The **root cause** is the action or situation that initiates the problem. Typically, root causes are system breakdowns or human errors. Restaurant and foodservice operations are made up of a series of systems, including those for purchasing, production, customer service, cash handling, cost control, scheduling, etc. Problems occur either when one of

485

Figure Focus

Figure 8.6: What happens if the solution to the problem is misidentified, or if the action plan is implemented unsuccessfully? What might the next steps be?

Discuss

• How is the problem-solving process discussed on pp. 484–488 useful in one's personal or academic life? Encourage students to discuss whether this might or might not be a valuable tool.

• Why is it so important to conduct a thorough investigation when attempting to identify and define a problem and who it affects?

• Ask students to explain why documenting a problem and the steps involved in its resolution can help prevent future problems from arising.

Reinforce and Review

• Each step of the problem-solving model provides input to the next, until documentation is reached.

• Misdiagnosing a problem prolongs the time until an appropriate resolution can be reached, so a thorough investigation is essential to uncovering the root cause of the problem.

• The process of determining the root cause of a problem can uncover other problems within the establishment that can in turn be resolved.

Homework Activity: Go with the Flow

Literacy Connection, 21st-Century Skills— Use Systems Thinking, Solve Problems, Create Media Products, Work Independently

Each student should select a problem he or she has experienced. Should they wish, students may also choose hypothetical situations for this exercise. through the seven steps of the problem-solving model to determine and document an appropriate resolution.

For each step in the plan, describe the appropriate action to be taken. For instance, step 3 requires students to "determine alternative solutions and consequences." Students should list all the solutions to the problem as well as the possible consequences of implementing each solution. Consult the material on pp. 484–488 to learn more about what each of the seven steps requires.

As part of this assignment, students should create a flowchart illustrating their use of the problem-solving model.

Vocabulary Terms

• **Root cause:** The action or situation that initiates a problem.

Discuss

- How can good interpersonal communication and interpersonal skills affect the outcome of an investigation into a problem's root cause? What roles can the barriers to communication discussed in Chapter 7 play in this outcome?
- Unfortunately, not all managers are true leaders, and some can initiate or worsen problems even through the best of intentions. When a manager's actions are the root cause of a workplace problem, how should the staff react?
- Section 8.1 discussed the role of bias in creating hostile work environments. How can bias cloud the investigation of a workplace problem, resulting in misdiagnosis of the problem or the application of an inappropriate solution?

Reinforce and Review

- When conducting or participating in the investigation of a problem, focus on systems, processes, and actions rather than on people or personalities.
- Doing nothing should always be considered as a possible solution to a workplace problem.
- Digging deeply to explore all the ramifications of a potential solution to the problem is critical to finding the correct resolution and implementing an action plan.

these systems breaks down or was not designed carefully in the first place. When human error is the cause of problems, question the people affected by the problem to determine its root cause. During the investigation, probe deeply to find the real root cause of the problem, rather than just one of the contributing factors or symptoms. Be sure, however, to avoid accusations and blame when asking staff these kinds of questions.

3. **Determine alternative solutions and consequences:** An alternative is a potential solution to a problem. The list of alternative solutions should be as long as necessary. At this point, do not think about whether a solution is reasonable or workable; if it is a potential answer, put it on the list. One alternative that should always be investigated is "do nothing." It's possible to come up with an elaborate resolution for what ultimately is a nonproblem. On the other hand, the action of "doing nothing" could have disastrous consequences. Now that the list of alternatives is complete, analyze it for the consequences that each solution might have. These key questions should be asked for each solution:

   - What are the consequences of this action? Who will be affected by this decision and how will they be affected? Will it be a positive or negative effect?

   - Is it cost effective? Will the solution cost more than the problem? If so, is there a more reasonable approach? Can the solution be reconstructed to cost less money? All too often, management chooses a costly solution that is financially worse than the problem.

   - Is it reasonable? Investigate the complexity of the solution. Does it have a chance to succeed, or is it so complex that people will ignore it, resulting in a reoccurrence of the problem?

   - Will it close the loop? In the case of a problem caused by a system loophole, be sure the solution will address both the problem and the loop.

   - Will it be effective? Will the solution work? Does it have a chance? Will everyone accept it as reasonable? Remember that a solution without acceptance will not be effective.

4. **Select the best solution:** Consider the consequences of the proposed alternatives and answer the questions in the previous step to narrow the list of possible solutions. Sometimes two or three alternatives are left. If so, put the remaining options through this same scrutiny again. The problem and solution must be looked at from all angles, as though examining all six sides of a cube. Ask the tough questions and dig deep to find the correct

486

solution. Do not rush the process. The correct solution will result in the problem going away. The incorrect solution will result in going through the entire process again.

5. **Develop an action plan:** After choosing a solution, the next step is to develop an action plan. An action plan is a strategy of steps to carry out so that a problem does not recur. It must describe exactly what should happen, step by step. The output from the action plan might take the form of a policy addition or change, an operational addition or change, or an employee handbook addition or change.

6. **Implement the action plan:** Communicate the action plan and its outcome to all individuals involved. Those who are involved in the problem and/or solution need to understand what the solution is, why it is needed, when it will be finalized, and how it will impact them. This group might include owners, other managers, employees, guests, suppliers, or the public. Acceptance depends in part on who is affected by the problem and/or by its solution. Conduct a follow-up to find out whether the affected parties received the action plan's message and accepted the solution.

7. **Document the problem and solution for future reference:** Every restaurant and foodservice operation should have a problem/solution file. It should contain documentation, such as a report written by management describing the problem and its solution. Prior to going through the problem-solving exercise, consult this file for similar events to get some insight into solving the current dilemma. Add the current situation's report and resolution to this file to assist future managers with their problem-solving encounters. This step isn't just about filing away a problem, and not learning from it or ever looking at it again, but using the solutions to make improvements so the operation doesn't just move from problem to problem.

Table 8.3 describes a problem using the problem-solving model.

Discuss

- Sometimes, the action plan needed to resolve a workplace concern can appear unpleasant to employees, especially if it involves changing established work patterns or even terminating colleagues. How can managers motivate employees to follow an action plan that will ultimately benefit both employer and employees when initial perceptions are negative or even hostile?
- Alternately, the new protocols required by an action plan may seem unnecessary or even ridiculous to employees if there is no perceived benefit to them. Will employees really follow these new policies when left unsupervised? Again, how can managers get cooperation with an action plan under these circumstances?
- How can a manager know when a problem is better left alone? Which workplace concerns should always be investigated? Is it possible that management bias can prevent the investigation of legitimate problems? How does this relate to interpersonal communication?

Reinforce and Review

- An action plan describes exactly what must happen to resolve a problem, step by step.
- Following up the implementation of an action plan with an investigation of employee cooperation is an essential component of the problem-solving process.
- Every step of the problem-solving process should be documented for future reference and education.

Vocabulary Terms

- **Action plan:** A strategy of steps to carry out so that a problem does not recur.

487

- Students should understand that sometimes multiple solutions can be combined into a single action plan.

- How can this action plan help servers and cooks work together more effectively? How can it improve guest service?

Discuss

- How can managers and employees, especially at smaller establishments, find the time to attend professional-development courses without it affecting their daily work?
- Should every employee have the opportunity or responsibility to engage in professional development? Why or why not? Should it be mandatory?

Reinforce and Review

- Continual learning is key to professional development, leadership growth, and goal setting.

CUSTOMIZED INSTRUCTION

Science Connection, Mathematics Connection, Literacy Connection, 21st-Century Skills—Think Creatively, Reason Effectively, Manage Goals and Time, Be Self-Directed Learners

More Advanced Students

In addition to the project outlined at right, students should research behavioral science, or the science of why humans and animals behave as they do. What can behavioral science teach you about your own habits and customs? Does knowing why you behave in the ways that you do affect your ability to change your behaviors?

Incorporate this material, along with other information you consider relevant, into your essay on changing your habits. The essay should be at least two pages in length.

Vocabulary Terms

- **Professional development:** The sum of the activities that a person performs to meet goals and/or to further his or her career.

Figure Focus

Figure 8.7: Why are ongoing training sessions important?

Table 8.3: Sample Problem Using the Problem-Solving Model

1. Define the problem.
"Guests are complaining that they are waiting too long to receive their entrées."

2. Determine the root cause.
The cooks preparing the entrée components are not cooking the food quickly enough.

3. Determine alternative solutions and consequences.
Do nothing; change the preparation of certain menu items so they can be cooked more quickly or so more preparation can be done in advance; remove certain items from the menu if they are too complicated to prepare or require too many pans; instruct the servers to put orders in for the entrées sooner; instruct the cooks to work more quickly.

4. Select the best solution.
Instruct the servers to put the orders in for the entrées sooner.

5. Develop an action plan.
Make a list of the steps that need to be taken to change the current policy.

6. Implement the action plan.
Talk with servers about putting in orders for entrées when diners have finished about one-third of their appetizers instead of waiting until each diner is nearly finished eating; codify this change by posting a memo about it near the time clock and by adding it to the employee manual.

7. Document the problem and solution for future reference.
Add a copy of the memo to the policy file and make sure that new servers are informed of the policy when being trained; observe the effects of the new policy to determine whether it has the desired effect of reducing guest complaints.

Professional Development

As daily tasks become more complex and a new manager gains more responsibility, he or she must also gain new knowledge to keep pace with these changes. Continuous learning is key to professional development. It is an integral part of a leader's growth.

Professional development is the sum of activities a person performs to meet goals and/or to further his or her career. Continuous learning is key to professional development and goal setting. Professional development and mentoring plans with specific career goals are critical to career development. But any development plan should include personal, educational, and professional goals. Figure 8.7 shows an example of a manager encouraging professional development.

Figure 8.7: Setting goals is part of professional development.

488

Homework Activity: Behave Yourself

Mathematics Connection, Literacy Connection, 21st-Century Skills—Think Creatively, Reason Effectively, Manage Goals and Time

It is often said that humans are creatures of habit. Many people like doing the same thing at the same time each day and can even become ill if they cannot follow their customary routines.

Pick out three habits that you have. These could include such habits as biting your nails, doing your homework in a certain place, or making your bed in a certain fashion. Ideally, identify a behavior that you think will be easy to change, a behavior that you think will be moderately difficult to change, and a behavior that you think will be difficult to change.

List ways you can change each habit. For instance, you could decide to do your homework in a different room or seated in a different position. Determine which changes you would like to implement and why.

For one week, do your best to implement these changes. Keep track of your successes and failures by recording your results, and rate your performance each day on a scale of 1 to 10 with a score of 1 meaning you did nothing to change the habit and a score of 10 meaning you completely changed the habit that day. Graph your results for the week, showing your performance with each habit.

What behaviors were easy to change? Which were more difficult? Why do you think that is the case?

Write a one-page essay on your experiences with this project to accompany your graph.

Essential Skills
Professional Development

Whenever you apply for a new job, whether it's your first or your fifth, you should think about how it fits into your long-term goals. That means you should determine some goals, as well as a time line for achieving them and a path for accomplishing them. None of this has to be set in stone. Like most people, you'll probably change your mind about your career several times throughout your life. But taking the time to plan for your professional development will give you more options and help you decide what you really want to do:

- Take some classes. Learn a language, work on your communication skills, or study a management technique: any of these can help you in a variety of career paths by making you more versatile and more valuable to current and prospective employers.

- Join a professional organization. Not only can networking help you add to your contact list, but it can help you find new career opportunities as well. If there is no chapter or group available in your area, consider participating online, or even starting your own!

- Get certified. Earning professional certification not only forces you to keep abreast of new developments in your field but makes you more attractive to employers.

Many classes are available free, including some online courses, and most professional associations provide free or low-cost membership to students. Devoting time and money to your professional growth is perhaps the soundest investment you can make: making wise choices can have enormous payoffs.

Design a workable plan and take action; without these, achieving goals is impossible. A good development plan includes the following:

- Written plan identifying two-year, five-year, and ten-year goals, and beyond
- Written assessment of professional goals
- Assessment of what is needed to meet these goals
- Time line establishing key milestones for achieving these goals

Ultimately, everyone is responsible for his or her own development and success.

Ethics

Ethics are a set of moral values that a society holds. They are typically based on the principles of honesty, integrity, and respect for others. They can be influenced by cultural backgrounds, religious beliefs, personal codes of conduct, and individual experiences. They help guide the decisions people make, sometimes whether they realize it or not.

489

In-Class Activity:
Ethics and Diversity

Literacy Connection, 21st-Century Skills—Communication and Collaboration, Reason Effectively, Social and Cross-Cultural Skills

Working in small groups, discuss the moral values that affect your behavior at school, at home, and in the workplace. Why might people with different backgrounds and characteristics have different values? What values do students share, and why might that be the case? How can understanding values help explain behaviors?

Essential Skills:
Professional Development

Encourage students to discuss the following:
- What steps can students take today to engage in professional development?
- How can professional development be important to each student?
- Explain how professional development can facilitate personal goals as well as professional ones.

Discuss
- Why is designing a development plan important to achieving career goals? How specific should it be? How often should it be evaluated?

Reinforce and Review
- Identifying and assessing goals is essential to achieving them.
- Ultimately, everyone is responsible for his or her own development and success.
- Ethics help guide a person's decisions, whether or not they realize it.

Homework Activity:
Prior Planning Prevents Poor Performance

Literacy Connection, 21st-Century Skills— Use Systems Thinking, Adapt to Change, Work Independently

Design a realistic development plan that identifies, evaluates, and assesses your professional and personal goals.

If you don't have a specific career path in mind yet, focus on more general goals. If you know the career path you want to take, you can be more specific. Chapter 12 focuses on building a career in the hospitality industry and can be a helpful resource.

What is your plan? Why do you think it will be effective as well as workable? Attach a two-paragraph explanation of how you devised your plan to the development plan itself.

Vocabulary Terms
- **Ethics:** The set of moral values a person holds.

Discuss

- Why would a business establish a code of ethics? How might this differ from a mission statement or a vision statement? When should it be established, and who should participate in writing it?

Reinforce and Review

- A written code of ethics helps remove any guesswork about what is acceptable or unacceptable behavior.
- An organization's code of ethics may include any issues that could affect workplace operations, from vendor relations to employee benefits.

Homework Activity: Ethical Workplaces

Literacy Connection, 21st-Century Skills— Think Creatively, Critical Thinking and Problem Solving, Work Independently

Imagine that you own a company of some kind, and imagine that your company needs a code of ethics. Draft a code of ethics in your own words, covering all workplace issues that you think are important.

Now envision some problem arising in the workplace. For instance, a guest is dissatisfied with his meal, or a server and a cook are having problems communicating professionally. How can your code of ethics help you and your employees know what to do?

Attach a discussion of the "problem" to your code of ethics.

Vocabulary Terms

- **Workplace ethics:** Guiding principles that effective leaders use in setting the professional tone and behavior in their operations.

In the business world, **workplace ethics** serve as guiding principles that effective leaders use in setting the professional tone and behavior in their operations. Many establishments have created written codes of ethics, which are designed to remove guesswork about what is acceptable or unacceptable behavior. Figure 8.8 is a sample code of ethics. These codes act as a safety check for evaluating decisions before applying them. An organization's code of ethics may include employee treatment, wages, benefits, working conditions, behavior of employees with reference to the use of company resources, acceptance of gifts from guests/vendors/suppliers, and other issues that impact organizational operations.

75 EAST PLEASANT STREET, FUNTOWN USA 50094

Code of Ethics

Purpose of Code of Ethics

The purpose is to ensure that all managers and employees work free of conflicts of interest, and in an ethical and proper manner. We strive for the highest standards in the delivery of safe food in a quality manner while also providing outstanding customer service.

In order to carry out the highest standards, Uptown Grille personnel will:

- Conduct themselves in a professional manner with integrity and respect.
- Promote a positive work environment for all employees to feel respected and treated with dignity.
- Be in compliance with laws, rules and regulations.
- Protect and properly use company assets.
- Provide equal opportunities.
- Not tolerate discrimination and harassment.
- Serve food in a safe and sanitary environment.
- Report illegal or unethical behavior.
- Allow no conflicts of interest with the company.
- Provide a healthy and safe environment while protecting the environment and natural resources.
- Provide knowledge, education, experience, and motivation for all the staff.
- Maintain the confidentiality of confidential information entrusted to them by the company or its customers.
- Resolve complaints and grievances in good faith through direct communication and negotiation and within reasonable timeframes.

Figure 8.8: A code of ethics is comprised of broad statements that help guide ethical decision making.

490

Figure Focus

Figure 8.8: Did the Uptown Grille cover all relevant practices in its code of ethics? Is there anything included that seems unnecessary or irrelevant to you?

To determine whether a decision or action is based on sound workplace ethics, managers and employees should ask the following questions:

- Is the decision/action legal?
- Will the decision/action hurt anyone?
- Does the decision/action represent the company?
- Does the decision/action make anyone uncomfortable?
- Does the decision/action convey respect for others?
- Have I involved others by asking for their perspective on the situation?
- Is this decision/action essentially fair given all the circumstances?
- Does this decision/action uphold the values of the organization?
- Could I tell my decision to my boss, family, or society as a whole?
- How would others regard the details of this decision/action if it were disclosed to the public?
- Am I confident that my decision/action will be as valid over a long period of time as it seems now?

Guests expect operations to act in ethical ways. The most obvious example is food safety and cleanliness. Guests expect operations to make decisions that protect people from harm. Ethical behavior also encourages repeat business and a loyal customer base.

It can be difficult to see an operation's ethics until something goes wrong. For example, replacing a poorly prepared food item at a guest's request, even if it affects food costs, is the right thing to do. It's possible that the dish might simply taste bad, or it could be that the dish has been contaminated. To keep everyone safe and maintain guests' trust, replace the dish.

Successful employees want to do their jobs well, which means they will follow the policies and procedures for their jobs. When operations build these policies and procedures with ethical values in mind, the employees see how important ethical behavior is to the operation. Knowing that their organization practices ethical decision-making helps them to make choices with integrity and honesty as well.

People also bring their personal values to their jobs. Employees may choose their employers based on how ethically the company does business and how well those values fit with their own.

491

Discuss

- In the workplace, transparency describes behaviors and decisions that are made openly, often with employee input, rather than in secret and behind closed doors. Transparency is a vital part of accountability.
- People cannot be held accountable for their actions if it is unclear who has actually performed the actions. Encourage students to discuss how transparency, accountability, and responsibility are related to workplace ethics.
- Why is the question of legality first on the list of questions managers and employees should consider in making decisions? Should employees or managers ever behave in an illegal manner in the workplace?
- Successful employees, who want to do their jobs properly, follow appropriate policies and procedures. But not every employee is successful, and some individuals may be skilled at hiding their inappropriate or unethical behaviors. How can a leader work to prevent these behaviors from occurring in the workplace? Can all employees who perform poorly be converted into successful employees?
- What problems can arise when employees bring their personal values to their jobs? How can this undermine diversity, respect for colleagues, and guest service?

Reinforce and Review

- It can be difficult to see an operation's ethics until things go wrong. It's easy to follow the rules when no problems arise.
- When operations use sound workplace ethics to establish policies and procedures, this models the importance of ethical behavior to employees.
- Employees may choose their employers based on how ethically the company does business and how well the company's values mesh with their own.

Encourage students to discuss the following:

- Why might companies choose to publicize their business transactions? How might this affect public perception?

- How can publicity affect a business? Is it true that there is no such thing as bad publicity?

- Why might employees choose to work for companies they consider to be ethical? What might this indicate about their internal and external motivations?

Discuss

- How are organizational goals related to an individual's development plan?
- Organizational goals are generally established at the top of a business's hierarchy, but the employees at the bottom of the hierarchy, such as servers and cooks, are typically the ones who must do the hard work to achieve the goals. How can organizational goals be made realistic and workable for all staff?

Reinforce and Review

- Being a leader means setting goals for employees.
- Goals are what people commit to do for an organization.
- Employees at all levels within a company achieve their goals through a combination of knowledge, skills, resources, attitudes, and tools.

Vocabulary Terms

- **Goals:** Statements of desired results, used to measure actual performance within an organization.
- **Organizational goals:** Overarching statements of desired goals which help maintain an establishment's structure and which aid in evaluating achievements.

[trends]

Corporate Ethics Code

A corporate ethics code is a policy that outlines a company's ethical standards, such as values, motivations, and guidelines. It describes a company's way of approaching the world. Such codes can be vague statements or explicit policies, depending upon the company and its level of commitment to the project. Companies often make their codes of ethics public so that guests and vendors alike can see how the company chooses to conduct business. This way, they can be excellent tools for marketing and recruitment, as well as principles for guiding internal decision-making.

Corporate ethics codes became prominent in the U.S. in the 1980s, although some firms had developed them much earlier. Today, almost all Fortune 1000 companies have established codes of ethics.

We can't see inside a company; we can only see some of its behaviors. For instance, if we see that a company makes a donation to a charitable organization that we think is deserving, then we'll be more likely to have a positive impression of the company's ethics. Like all of us, a company's credibility rests on the way in which it visibly matches its behavior to its words.

To help workers understand corporate policies, employers may offer seminars and other training opportunities, but management's good example is ultimately the most important factor in determining whether employees will behave ethically. In other words, if the top executives follow the corporate ethics code, then the middle managers will; if the middle managers follow the code, the frontline workers will.

Researching a company's ethics is more important than ever to prospective employees. Helpful resources include the company's own Web site and employees; news reports about the company, both print and online; government sources, such as the Federal Trade Commission or the local health authority; and consumer and industry groups, like the Better Business Bureau or the Chamber of Commerce.

Organizational Goals

Being a leader means setting goals for employees. For example, a chef may set a goal of lowering the food cost to 31 percent, or a lead baker may establish a goal of producing 600 baguettes each day. As a manager moves higher and higher through a company, he or she will set goals for more and more people. The highest level of goals is known as organizational goals.

Goals are statements of desired results. Management uses them to measure actual performance within an organization. In other words, goals are what people commit to do for an organization. Employees achieve them through a combination of knowledge, skills, resources, attitudes, and tools. See Figure 8.9. On a larger scale, **organizational goals** provide structure and a destination for an operation, and function like a yardstick to help evaluate the operation's progress.

492

Every business is composed of a series of levels that represent departments or functions within the organization. Each of these levels creates goals for the organization. Figure 8.10 shows the different levels of goals within an organization. At the highest level are organizational goals.

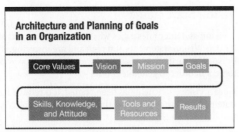

Architecture and Planning of Goals in an Organization

Core Values — Vision — Mission — Goals

Skills, Knowledge, and Attitude — Tools and Resources — Results

Figure 8.9: Goals should be specific and attainable.

These goals focus on broad statements of what the organization as a whole wants to achieve. They are aligned with the vision and mission of the organization. Organizational goals also lay the foundation for specific employee goals commonly found on performance plans.

Examples of typical organizational goals in restaurant and foodservice operations include sales goals (weekly, monthly, annual dollar goals); budget goals (such as amount of food costs or labor costs for a year); and customer service goals (speed of service, comment card scores).

An **objective** is a specific description or statement of what a manager wants to achieve. The most effective goals are SMART:

- **Specific:** Goals should be clearly stated and list exactly what is expected.

- **Measurable:** Management needs to be able to determine whether goals have succeeded or failed by some result.

- **Achievable:** Goals should be realistic and able to be met.

- **Relevant:** Goals should be connected to the vision and mission of the business.

- **Time bound:** Goals need to have a date for accomplishment.

Different Levels of Goals within an Organization

1. Organizational goals
2. Departmental/team goals
3. Individual performance goals

Figure 8.10: Every organization has overall goals, department goals, and individual goals.

SMART goals provide clear expectations for everyone in the operation. They're usually no longer than a sentence. An example of a SMART goal might be, "Staff will decrease guest complaints by 5 percent over the next 3 months."

493

Discuss

- How do organizational goals help define daily objectives? In other words, how can employees at lower levels work to achieve company-wide missions?
- How does communication play a role in establishing both organizational and individual goals? What barriers to communication may arise?

Reinforce and Review

- Organizational goals lay the foundation for specific employee goals, commonly found in performance plans.
- The most effective goals are SMART: specific, measurable, achievable, relevant, and time bound.
- SMART goals provide clear, concise expectations for all employees.

Teaching Tips

- Ask students to decide what a SMART goal might be for the class. How can the brief goal be translated into action?

Vocabulary Terms

- **Objective:** A specific description or statement of what a manager wants to achieve.

Figure Focus

Figure 8.9: Developing SMART goals gives employees both reasonable expectations and solid motivation.

Figure 8.10: Where would an employee's daily task list fit in this pyramid?

Discuss

- What do the sample vision statements on p. 494 tell students about the companies who wrote them? How does reading these statements affect student views of these companies?

Reinforce and Review

- Vision statements articulate what the organization will promote and deliver to customers in order to generate profits.
- Vision statements are refined into mission statements and goals, which assure that the vision is implemented throughout operational procedures.

Teaching Tips

- Refer to Chapter 7 for more information on mission statements and vision statements.

In-Class Activity: Competing Visions

Literacy Connection, 21st-Century Skills— Communication and Collaboration, Social and Cross-Cultural Skills, Work Creatively with Others

While studying Chapter 7 (p. 444), the class voted on the best vision statement for the course and discussed ways students could abide by it each day.

As a class, compare this vision statement to those shown on p. 494. What similarities and differences do you observe? Which do you prefer and why?

Vocabulary Terms

- **Vision statement:** A document that defines the company's purpose and values to employees and customers.
- **Mission statement:** A document that describes a company's purpose and key objectives to its team and owners.

Vision Statements

A **vision statement** describes what an organization wants to become and why it exists. Vision statements aim high and are inspiring, stimulating, and exceptional. They articulate what the organization will promote and deliver to customers in order to generate profits.

Once a vision statement has been crafted, it is refined further into a mission statement and goals to assure that the vision is implemented through operational procedures.

Here are some examples of real-life vision statements:

- Coca-Cola: Our vision serves as the framework for our Roadmap and guides every aspect of our business by describing what we need to accomplish in order to continue achieving sustainable, quality growth.
  - People: Be a great place to work where people are inspired to be the best they can be.
  - Portfolio: Bring to the world a portfolio of quality beverage brands that anticipate and satisfy people's desires and needs.
  - Partners: Nurture a winning network of customers and suppliers, together we create mutual, enduring value.
  - Planet: Be a responsible citizen that makes a difference by helping build and support sustainable communities.
  - Profit: Maximize long-term return to shareowners while being mindful of our overall responsibilities.
  - Productivity: Be a highly effective, lean and fast-moving organization.
- Heinz: "Our VISION, quite simply, is to be 'THE WORLD'S PREMIER FOOD COMPANY, OFFERING NUTRITIOUS, SUPERIOR-TASTING FOODS TO PEOPLE EVERYWHERE.' Being the premier food company does not mean being the biggest but it does mean being the best in terms of consumer value, customer service, employee talent, and consistent and predictable growth. We are well on our way to realizing this Vision but there is more we must do to fully achieve it."
- Kraft Foods: "Helping People Around the World Eat and Live Better"

Mission Statements

A **mission statement** refines the vision statement by stating the purpose of the organization to employees and customers. It should include what the

494

organization intends to sell or provide and to whom, and sometimes the geographic region as well. One of the main benefits of a mission statement is that it provides a source of accountability for the organization. It communicates what the organization is striving to do each day. It needs to be written clearly, concisely, and in an interesting manner.

Managers need to ensure that operational goals are directly linked to this statement. It is vital in today's competitive industry that everyone does his or her best to understand this connection.

Here are some examples of real-life mission statements:

- Coca-Cola: Our Roadmap starts with our mission, which is enduring. It declares our purpose as a company and serves as the standard against which we weigh our actions and decisions.

  - To refresh the world...

  - To inspire moments of optimism and happiness...

  - To create value and make a difference.

- Heinz: "As the trusted leader in nutrition and wellness, Heinz—the original Pure Food Company—is dedicated to the sustainable health of people, the planet, and our Company."

- McDonald's: "Our Plan to Win, with its strategic focus on 'being better, not just bigger,' has delivered even better restaurant experiences to customers and superior value to shareholders."

- Denny's: "Our Mission at Denny's is to establish beneficial business relationships with diverse suppliers who share our commitment to customer service, quality, and competitive pricing."

Managers also need to communicate and clarify to employees how their jobs support these statements and impact the success of the organization. Since employee performance drives business performance, employee roles and responsibilities need to be based on the vision, mission, and goals of the organization as well. For example, if the mission statement of a restaurant is to deliver high-quality service, then employees might be empowered to make decisions about how to resolve a guest's complaint themselves.

Job descriptions should specify standards and responsibilities that reflect the company values. When employees meet those responsibilities and live up to the standards, it directly impacts the goals of the organization.

Job descriptions should specify quality standards and responsibilities that reflect the company values. These are called employee operational behavior

495

Discuss

- How do mission statements, vision statements, and goals work together to explain a company's plans and behaviors?
- Encourage students to compare the mission statements and vision statements for Coca-Cola and Heinz, as seen on pp. 494–495. Which seems more guest-friendly, the mission or vision statements? What do they say about their companies' day-to-day activities?
- Based on their mission and/or vision statements, ask students to identify specific tasks or behaviors that employees might perform at each company described on pp. 494–495.

Reinforce and Review

- One of the main benefits of a mission statement is that it provides a source of accountability for the organization, communicating daily goals and objectives.
- Since employee performance drives business performance, employee roles and responsibilities need to be based on the vision, mission, and goals of the organization.
- The extent to which employees do or do not live up to the requirements of their job descriptions directly affects the company's well-being.
- Job descriptions should reflect company values and standards. They are another form of organizational communication.

Teaching Tips

- Refer to Chapter 7 for more information.

Discuss

- How can employees on the front lines with customers express corporate goals? What actions can employees take each day to reinforce the company's image, goals, and mission?
- What can managers do each day to reinforce appropriate behaviors and actions that employees should take to observe company policies? How can they help new employees to understand and support the company's mission?
- What if a company has no vision statement, mission statement, specified organizational goals, or even written job descriptions? What might this indicate about the role of communication in such workplaces? How might this affect employee performance as well as overall guest service?

Reinforce and Review

- Employees should directly demonstrate company values to one another and to guests each day and through each action.
- Managers should confirm that employees are practicing company values each day.
- The strongest mission and vision statements drive an operation's culture.

statements. When employees meet those responsibilities and live up to the standards, it directly impacts the goals of the organization. Not only should employees know the importance of their behavior, but each employee should also be able to take action to exemplify company values to customers. For example, if it is part of a restaurant's mission to provide excellent customer service, servers should be able to respond to guest complaints immediately, without needing a manager's approval before replacing an entrée, for instance.

This is just one way that employees understand how their jobs support the company mission and goals. Similarly, managers need ways to confirm that employees are practicing the values and missions of the company on a daily basis. The strongest mission and vision statements drive an operation's culture.

Managers need to identify ways to communicate the mission and goals to employees. Then the staff will understand the importance of these goals and the need for everyone to support the company mission. Some things that a manager can do include the following:

- During orientation, ensure that new hires get information about the vision, mission, and goals of the organization. Communicate the expectation that everyone in the organization supports these statements.
- Ensure that all training materials align with and emphasize the importance of these statements.
- Post the statements in a prominent place for staff to see.
- Document these statements in employee handbooks to be presented during orientation.
- Discuss at employee meetings how operations are faring in terms of the mission and goals.

Summary

In this section, you learned the following:

- Ethics are a set of moral values that a society holds. In the restaurant and foodservice industry ethics serve as guiding principles for effective leaders to use in setting professional tone and behavior in their operations.
- Good leaders provide direction, lead consistently, influence others, motivate others, coach and develop others, anticipate changes, and foster teamwork.

- The steps in problem solving: define the problem, determine the root cause, determine alternative solutions and consequences, select the best solution, develop an action plan, implement the action plan, and document the problem and solution for future reference.

- Professional development is important to help meet your goals and advance in your career.

- Employees expect managers to be professional; interact appropriately; practice ethical behavior; provide clear direction, tools, resources, and a safe environment; and encourage professional growth and development.

- Motivation is comprised of the reasons why a person takes action or behaves in a certain way. Leaders are expected to provide constructive feedback, make an employee feel valued, influence others through their own actions with everyday decisions, provide external motivation, and support internal motivation.

- Organizational goals are statements of desired results. The most effective goals are SMART: Specific, Measurable, Achievable, Relevant, and Time bound. SMART goals provide clear expectations to everyone in the operation.

- A vision statement describes what an organization wants to become and why it exists. Vision statements inspire. Mission statements refine the vision statement by stating the purpose of the organization to employees and customers.

- Employee roles and responsibilities are based on the vision, mission, and goals of the organization.

497

Summary

- Remind students to review the following:
  1. The definition of ethics and the role that ethics play in the restaurant and foodservice industry
  2. The characteristics of a leader
  3. The common expectations that employees have about managers
  4. Motivation and the role that managers play in motivating employees
  5. Organizational goals and why these goals should be SMART
  6. The purposes of vision statements and mission statements
  7. How employee roles and jobs impact the mission and goals
  8. The steps for solving a problem

Section 8.2 Review Questions

1. Workplace ethics serve as guiding principles that effective leaders use in setting the professional tone and behavior in their operations. Written codes of ethics help to eliminate any guesswork about what is acceptable and what is unacceptable, providing a safety check for evaluating decisions before applying them.

2. Managers can motivate employees by providing constructive feedback on their performance, making employees feel valued and important. Communicating relevant information to employees is also a key motivator. When employees understand why changes will occur or how their performance directly affects the workplace, they feel stronger attachments to the workplace.

3. The seven steps to solving a problem are:
   - Define the problem.
   - Determine the root cause.
   - Determine alternative solutions and consequences.
   - Select the best alternative solution.
   - Develop an action plan.
   - Implement the action plan.
   - Document the process for future reference.

4. Vision statements describe what an organization wants to become and why it exists. They aim high and inspire employees and customers alike. Mission statements, on the other hand, refine the vision statement by stating the purpose of the organization to employees and customers, providing a source of accountability for the organization.

5. Jeff Cook solves employee problems by counseling them and teaching them how to improve their behavior to create desired future outcomes.

6. Linda can use the mission statement to clarify to Katerina and Manuel how their jobs support one another as well as the Uptown Grille's ultimate success. She can also point to the standards the mission statement sets for employee performance and how their interpersonal problems keep them from meeting these standards.

7. Good leaders inspire and motivate employees by providing constructive verbal and nonverbal feedback, modeling appropriate conduct, coaching employees, fostering teamwork, providing direction, anticipating change, leading consistently, and influencing one another.

Section 8.2 Review Questions

1. What is the role of ethics in the workplace?
2. List ways a manager can motivate employees in the workplace.
3. Explain the steps for solving a problem.
4. What is the purpose of vision statements and mission statements?
5. What does Jeff Cook do to solve employee problems?
6. How can Linda use Uptown Grille's mission statement to help Katarina and Manuel improve their working relationship?
7. How do good leaders inspire and motivate employees?
8. Explain how SMART can help managers and employees provide better service to customers.

498

8. SMART goals are specific, measurable, achievable, relevant, and time bound. They can help managers and employees provide better service by providing clear expectations for all staff.

Section 8.2 Activities

1. Study Skills/Group Activity: Make a Statement!

Work with two other students to draft a vision statement, mission statement, and goals for your restaurant.

2. Activity: Problem Solving

Despite a strong economy, sales at your large, family-style restaurant have been down all summer, so employee morale is suffering as workers are bored and fear layoffs. Create a presentation using the seven-step problem-solving plan to improve the situation.

3. Critical Thinking: Leadership Skills

Think about an employer or instructor (without naming names) who has demonstrated positive or negative leadership skills. How did his or her behavior affect your attitude about the job or class?

499

Section 8.2 Activities

1. Students should model the vision statement and mission statement on the material given on pp. 494–496. Goals should be based on the vision and mission statement they create.

2. Students can use the example on p. 488 as a guide for completing this activity. Although their solutions to the problem will vary, they should reach these solutions in a clear and logical manner.

3. Students should prepare a brief oral or written report on how this demonstration of positive or negative leadership skills affected their own attitudes.

Section 8.3 Interviewing and Orientation

Introduce the Section

a. Explain how job descriptions are written.

b. Describe the interview process as well as lawful hiring practices.

c. Review the differences between onboarding and orientation.

d. Discuss the objectives for the section.

Vocabulary Review

a. Direct students to the key terms.

b. Pronounce each word, and have the students repeat the pronunciation out loud.

c. Discuss the definition of each word.

Teach

Discuss

- Encourage students to share any experiences they have had with job interviews. Do their descriptions have anything in common?

Reinforce and Review

- Interviews are the best way for employers to get to know an applicant's background and experience.

- Managers must know and understand all applicable laws governing hiring practices to avoid liability.

8.1 Learning to Work Together	8.2 Being a Successful Leader	8.3 Interviewing and Orientation	8.4 Training and Evaluation
• Diversity • Respectful workplaces • Teamwork	• Leadership skills • Motivation • Ethics • Problem solving • Organizational skills	• Job descriptions • Interviewing job applicants • Lawful hiring practices • Onboarding • Orientation	• Training • Performance appraisals • Management equipment

SECTION 8.3 INTERVIEWING AND ORIENTATION

No matter what career you choose, interviewing and being interviewed will be part of it. Interviews are the best way for employers to get to know an applicant's background and experience. It is critical for managers to know and understand lawful hiring practices and to be up-to-date on any changes made to these laws. Orientation is an important part of starting a job, and managers need to have the skills to conduct orientation.

Study Questions

After studying Section 8.3, you should be able to answer the following questions:

- What information is included in a job description and why is it important to a business?

- What is the difference between exempt and nonexempt employees?

- What are the manager's responsibilities for maintaining labor law knowledge?

- What are discriminatory language and practices in the hiring process?

- What methods ensure a fair and consistent hiring process?

- What is onboarding and why is it important to a business?

- What can employees expect during orientation?

- What items do employees receive during orientation?

- What topics are addressed in orientation sessions and employee manuals?

500

Job Descriptions

A **job description** is a document that defines the work involved in a particular assignment or position. A job description includes the position title and the responsibilities or duties of a position. Figure 8.11 is an example job description for an executive chef.

Job Title:	Executive Chef
Summary:	The executive chef is part of an operation's management team. An executive chef oversees the entire kitchen, from supervising all kitchen employees, to purchasing food supplies and making decisions about menu items.

Primary Responsibilities:

- Coordinate work of the kitchen staff and direct preparation of meals.
- Determine serving sizes and plan menus.
- Order food supplies.
- Hire and supervise kitchen staff, including training.
- Ensure all dishes are prepared properly and consistently.
- Ensure sanitation and hygienic standards are met.
- Ensure financial targets are achieved.
- Manage marketing and publicity efforts.
- Develop business plans.
- Create menus.
- Oversee customer relations.
- Oversee and direct all kitchen work, personnel, and activity.

Knowledge and Skills Requirements:

- Possess exceptional managerial and organizational skills and work well with a team.
- Possess a high level of manual dexterity and artistic ability, as well as a strong palate.
- Maintain a high degree of personal cleanliness.
- Knowledge of foreign language can improve communication with other staff, vendors, and customers.
- Possess broad and deep knowledge of ingredients, regional and national cuisines, the use and maintenance of common kitchen equipment, and management fundamentals

Working Conditions:

- Ability to work efficiently and cleanly in small working quarters.
- Ability to prepare meals quickly while ensuring quality, safety, and sanitation.
- Ability to stand for hours at a time
- Ability to lift weights of fifty pounds
- Ability to work under extremely hot conditions
- Ability to work long hours, often 12-hour work days including mornings, evenings, holidays, and weekends.

Education Requirements:

Experience in the industry for a number of years, gradually moving up in the kitchen hierarchy. Some establishments require their executive chefs to possess culinary degrees or to engage in ongoing professional education.

Figure 8.11: Sample job description of an executive chef.

501

Discuss

- Each member of the class works each day at the job of being a student. What would a job description for a student look like? What would be some of the primary responsibilities? What are the working conditions?

Reinforce and Review

- A job description includes the position title, the responsibilities of the person holding that position, any requirements the position might have, and a brief statement of the conditions under which the person holding the position is expected to work.

Homework Activity: Dream Jobs

Literacy Connection, 21st-Century Skills— Think Creatively, Communicate Clearly, Work Independently

Write a job description for your dream job, following the format shown in Figure 8.11. You may use any job except that of executive chef, and the work must be original.

If your dream job is in the restaurant and foodservice industry, information on these careers may be found in Chapter 12.

Vocabulary Terms

- **Job description:** A document that defines the work involved in a particular assignment or position.

Figure Focus

Figure 8.11: Does this sound like a realistic amount of work for an executive chef to handle? Did students realize how many noncooking responsibilities an executive chef might have each day?

Discuss

- How can a job description be used as a communication tool? What does it say about the employer's expectations as well as about the employer's culture?

Reinforce and Review

- The job description is a useful tool in recruiting and maintaining employees, since it clearly sets out the employer's expectations and the employee's responsibilities.
- Job descriptions define the scope of a job, as well as establish boundaries between positions.
- Positions covered by the FLSA are considered nonexempt. The law specifies the minimum wage and conditions under which overtime is paid.
- Positions not covered by the FLSA are considered exempt and are often salaried positions, whereas nonexempt positions are often paid hourly wages.

Teaching Tips

- Provide a copy of the Fair Labor Standards Act for students to examine.

Table 8.4: Exempt and Nonexempt Positions

- How do the levels of responsibility vary between these exempt and nonexempt positions?
- Why might management positions tend to be salaried and exempt, while employee positions tend to be hourly and nonexempt?

Vocabulary Terms

- **Exempt:** Not covered by the Fair Labor Standards Act.
- **Nonexempt:** Covered by the Fair Labor Standards Act.

The responsibilities include both essential and nonessential functions performed by the person holding that position. The job description is a helpful tool for human resources and management in recruiting and maintaining employees.

Many job descriptions also include educational and legal requirements for holding the position, such as a diploma or sanitation certificate, and organizational information, such as to whom the position reports. Other organizational information commonly included is the class or salary grade of the position.

Because a job description identifies the scope of a job, it helps set employees' expectations. Job descriptions also define the boundaries between positions so there is no confusion about who is responsible for doing what.

Job descriptions frequently distinguish between **exempt** employees and **nonexempt** employees. These categories are defined by the Fair Labor Standards Act (FLSA). Different rules apply for paying employees based on the duties of their jobs and other factors. For positions that are covered under this law, the FLSA specifies a minimum wage and when overtime pay is required.

Positions that are exempt—or not covered under this law—are not legally entitled to overtime pay or the minimum wage established by the FLSA. Exempt positions are often known as salaried positions, because their compensation is usually based on a set salary rather than an hourly wage. On the other hand, positions that are covered by the FLSA are known as nonexempt: these employees must be paid for every hour of overtime. Table 8.4 lists some typical exempt and nonexempt positions in restaurant and foodservice operations.

Table 8.4: Exempt and Nonexempt Positions

Exempt	Nonexempt
Dining room managers	Cooks
Executive chefs	Dishwashers
Banquet chefs	Serving staff
Pastry chefs	Busers
General managers	Janitors
	Catering staff and catering sales persons
	Clerical staff
	Receptionists
	Hosts

502

Homework Activity: Working for a Living

Mathematics Connection, Literacy Connection

Jimmy, a buser, earns $7.50 per hour and is a nonexempt employee. This week, he is scheduled to work 25 hours. How much will his gross pay be? Next week, he is scheduled to work 50 hours because a colleague will be away. Overtime pay, which is 1.5 times the regular hourly rate of pay, covers all work over 40 hours per week. How much will Jimmy's gross pay be next week?

On the other hand, Pat is a dining room manager. She is an exempt employee and earns $35,000 per year. What will her gross pay be this week?

Explain how the pay calculations for the two positions differ.

Interviewing Job Applicants

At some point in a manager's career, he or she will probably be expected to interview and hire prospective employees. Unlike being interviewed, the interviewer's job will be to ask questions and think about how well that person will fit in to the operation.

Sometimes it is difficult to know the right questions to ask an applicant during a job interview. Asking the wrong type of questions can make it hard to find the most qualified people. The wrong questions may also be illegal. The process of selecting and interviewing applicants is strictly regulated by laws that protect the civil rights of job applicants. An employer must have hiring and employment practices that protect these civil rights. In addition, employers must keep good records to prove they have observed the laws. Figure 8.12 shows a manager interviewing a job applicant.

Figure 8.12: A job interview allows applicants to show potential employers why they should hire you.

All hiring and interviewing practices must be fair and directly related to the job. To avoid charges of **discrimination**, or making a decision based on a prejudice, employers should use identical application forms and tests for everyone who applies for the same job. Job applicants should be asked the same kinds of questions in interviews, and each one should receive the same information about the job and the organization. Employers *cannot* ask about the following things:

- Race
- Age
- Religion
- Gender
- Sexual orientation
- Parents' names
- Birthplace (or birthplace of parents)
- National origin or ethnic background
- Former name or maiden name

503

Discuss

- To avoid charges of discrimination, interviewers may not ask potential employees about any of the items listed on pp. 503–504. Encourage students to explain how asking about each item on the list could open the establishment to charges of discrimination. Relate this to the material covered in Section 8.1 on prejudice and bias in the workplace.
- Chapter 12 of this text covers interviews from the interviewee's perspective, but Chapter 8 covers interviews from the interviewer's side of things. Why do students think that the management aspect is being prioritized here?

Reinforce and Review

- The interviewer's job is to ask questions and think about how well the candidate might fit into the organization.
- An employer must follow hiring and employment practices that protect the civil rights of current and potential employees.
- All hiring and employment practices must be fair and directly related to the job.
- To avoid charges of bias and discrimination, all job candidates should be given the same information about the job and the same application materials, and they should be asked the same kinds of questions during the interview itself.

Teaching Tips

- Relate this material to Section 8.1.

Vocabulary Terms

- **Discrimination:** Making a decision based on a prejudice.

Figure Focus

Figure 8.12: Why is this job interview being conducted over coffee?

Discuss

- How can following appropriate hiring and employment practices relate to building a positive and harassment-free work environment?
- Diversity is desirable in the workplace, but it is illegal to ask questions related to certain types of diversity during job interviews. Ask students to explain this apparent dichotomy.

Reinforce and Review

- Discussing certain topics, even those that may be legal, can result in discrimination charges against the interviewer and employer, as it may leave the impression that these issues factor into hiring decisions.
- Interviewers must keep all job requirements and interview questions directly related to the job.
- The Equal Employment Opportunity Commission (EEOC) and other government agencies enforce laws prohibiting discrimination in the workplace.

Teaching Tips

- The EEOC's Web site (www.eeoc.gov) has more information about legitimate interview topics, identifying discrimination and harassment, and other related topics.

Vocabulary Terms

- **Equal Employment Opportunity Commission (EEOC):** The agency of the federal government that enforces laws related to employment discrimination.

- Prior arrests (arrests are not convictions; there is no proof that the applicant is guilty of a crime)
- Marital status or any other information about a spouse
- Children, plans to have children, or childcare arrangements
- Disabilities an applicant might have unless it has a direct bearing on job performance
- Height, weight, hair color, or other questions about an applicant's physical characteristics, unless the information is directly relevant to doing the job

In addition, there are other topics that managers might want to avoid, such as personal finances, transportation, political affiliations, and union memberships. It is legal to ask about some of these topics. But bringing them up can leave an operation vulnerable to discrimination charges. Discussing these topics can give the impression that they factor into hiring decisions.

Interviewers need to keep all job requirements and interview questions directly related to the job.

Employers need to write the information in job postings and advertisements in a manner that not only provides clear information about the job, but avoids discriminatory language as well. The **Equal Employment Opportunity Commission (EEOC)** and other government agencies enforce laws that ensure everyone, regardless of race, age, gender, religion, national origin, color, or ability/disability, gets a fair chance at any job opening. This means employers should not write a notice or advertisement in any way that eliminates or discourages certain groups of people from applying.

The following are guidelines for avoiding discriminatory language in job postings and advertisements:

- Avoid gender-specific titles and other language: Instead, use gender-neutral language or gender-inclusive language. For example, for a position that involves waiting on tables, use "server," both "waiter" and "waitress," or "waitstaff." Don't use just "waiter" or just "waitress."

- Avoid references to groups of people that imply age, race, color, religion, gender, national origin, physical traits, disabilities, sexual orientation, or other traits that do not relate to job functions: For example, instead of advertising a position that is good for "homemakers," "retirees," or "students," advertise the hours or seasonality of the job.

- Focus on the actual skills, knowledge, and abilities needed on the job: For example, instead of advertising a position as a "man's job," state the actual requirement, such as "must be able to lift 50 pounds."

504

As in job descriptions, describing the duties a person might have to do on the job—so long as they are actually true—provides honest information and fair warning to each applicant and encourages the broadest range of qualified applicants. Including this information also helps protect you and your operation from possible claims of discrimination.

Throughout the hiring process, managers must use standardized tools and practices to make sure every applicant is treated fairly and consistently. This equal treatment is important for protecting the operation from charges of discrimination. The following are some of the tools and practices managers can use:

- **Job application:** A standard job application form should be filled out by anyone who wants a job in the operation. The form helps managers to get the same types of information from every interested person. Many application forms also include legal statements that allow businesses to check references and remind applicants that lying on the application is grounds for dismissal. Applications should be

Figure 8.13: Job applications give general information to a potential employer.

kept on file, even when people aren't hired for the jobs they applied for. They might be good candidates for future positions. Likewise, managers shouldn't write notes on these applications during interviews. That way, other managers reviewing the application aren't influenced by notes that might not apply to the job they are hiring people for. Figure 8.13 is an example of a job application.

- **Screening interviews:** These discussions come before a job interview. They are intended to find out if an applicant meets the basic requirements to be considered for the job. Screening helps save time and money on more extensive interviewing. They can happen in person or by phone.

- **Cover letters** and **résumés:** Some companies appreciate letters that show a person's interest in the job, accompanied by an outline of their experience and education. These are also screening tools. Figure 8.14 is a sample cover letter and Figure 8.15 is a sample résumé.

505

Figure Focus
Figure 8.13: How do job applications serve as screening tools for interviewers?

- Employee turnover is typically high in the restaurant and foodservice industry, so it is important to encourage the broadest possible range of qualified applicants. What can a manager do to attract the best possible candidates for the job? How does this relate to becoming an employer of choice, as discussed in Section 8.1?
- Encourage students to share how their job-seeking experiences have or have not mirrored the process described in the textbook. Have interviewers been formal or informal? Have they offered written job descriptions and other information about the position, or has all the information been given verbally? How can the use of written documents protect employers?

Reinforce and Review
- Describing the actual duties employees will be expected to perform helps potential applicants determine whether or not to seek employment with a particular establishment.
- Throughout the hiring process, interviewers must use standardized tools and practices to ensure that each applicant is treated fairly and consistently.
- Any notes taken about an applicant should be recorded on a separate sheet of paper, not the person's application or résumé.
- Cover letters and résumés not only provide additional information to the employer, but act as screening tools to eliminate potentially unsuccessful employees.

Vocabulary Terms
- **Job application:** A standardized form requesting relevant information about a job candidate, such as employment history and educational background.
- **Screening interview:** An interview that helps an interviewer decide whether the applicant is a good candidate for further interviews and potential employment.
- **Cover letter:** A document introducing the applicant to the employer, typically accompanying a résumé.
- **Résumé:** An outline of the applicant's employment history, educational background, and other relevant information.

Homework Activity: Cover Story

Literacy Connection, 21st-Century Skills—Reason Effectively, Communicate Clearly, Work Independently

Write a cover letter, using either a real or a hypothetical employer but describing yourself, your background, and your skills accurately. Express yourself as professionally as possible, but remember that the cover letter is a tool to get you noticed by a prospective employer.

Exchange your cover letter with a classmate. If you were a hiring manager, how would you evaluate that person's cover letter? Would you consider offering that person an interview? What is the overall impression that the cover letter makes on you?

Evaluate your classmate's comments on your own cover letter, asking for clarification as necessary.

In-Class Activity: Covering It All

Literacy Connection, 21st-Century Skills—Reason Effectively, Communicate Clearly, Work Independently

Working in small groups, students should assess the cover letter shown in Figure 8.14 at greater length. Topics to consider include, but shouldn't be limited to:

- How does this letter showcase the candidate's strengths? What about her weaknesses?

- The applicant is a senior in high school, writing in January. Does she plan to leave town in the fall for college? Even if she stays here, how might her schedule change?

- How much training will the applicant need to become an effective part-time server?

Each group should present a one-paragraph summation of the applicant to the class. Which groups would or would not schedule her for an interview? Why or why not?

Ms. Linda Brown
Manager
Uptown Grille
75 East Pleasant Street
Funtown, USA 50094

January 5, 2010

Dear Ms. Brown:

I am applying for the position of part-time server with the Uptown Grille that I read about in Sunday's *Anytown Daily.* This position offers a great opportunity for me to continue my career in foodservice. I am a senior at Anytown High School, where I'm enrolled in a new program that combines food preparation classes with health and safety procedures as well as business management courses. Currently, I work as a busperson at the Blue Bird Café, so I have learned some of the basics of customer service, possess a valid Food Handlers' Card, and have received eight hours of food safety training.

For your review, I am enclosing a copy of my résumé that shows my qualifications. I am hard-working, dependable, and honest, with a pleasant disposition and outgoing personality. My references can testify to these characteristics.

I am sure that once you have had a chance to review my résumé and meet with me, you will agree that my enthusiasm and willingness to learn will help me become an ideal server at Uptown Grille. You can reach me Monday through Friday after 3:30PM or at any time on Saturday and Sunday at 123-456-7890.

I look forward to hearing from you at your earliest convenience. Thank you for your consideration.

Sincerely,

Faith Fitzpatrick
110 West 84th Street
Funtown, USA 50094
Phone: 123-456-7890
Email: ffitz@notmail.net

Figure 8.14 A cover letter highlights an applicant's strengths and confirms interest in the position.

Figure Focus

Figure 8.14: If you were an interviewer or hiring manager, what sort of impression would this cover letter make on you?

Faith Fitzpatrick
110 West 84th Street
Funtown, USA 50094
Phone: 123-456-7890
Email: ffitz@notmail.net

Objective

> To work as a part-time server at Uptown Grille

Work Experience:

2009-present, Busperson, Blue Bird Café, Funtown, USA

- Clear tables quickly and set correctly
- Refill water and other beverages during dinner service
- Assist servers in serving food, as needed

Related Experience:

- Help serve food at high school café (sponsored by Foodservice Class)
- Organized junior class bake sale
- Developed new recipe for low-fat chocolate chip cookies sold at annual bake sale
- Used computer program to type recipes for class cookbook
- Volunteer kitchen worker at community Thanksgiving dinner

Related Skills and Abilities

- Strong customer service, teamwork, and interpersonal skills
- Ability to use word-processing and spreadsheet programs
- Dedicated to maintaining a clean dining area and adhering to all safety and health guidelines
- Work well with others

Education

- Senior at Funtown High School
- Currently taking food, management, and health and safety procedures classes in Foodservice school-to-career program.

References Available on Request

Figure 8.15 A résumé is a summary of your experience, skills, and achievements that relate to the job position.

507

Homework Activity: Résumés

Literacy Connection, 21st-Century Skills— Reason Effectively, Communicate Clearly, Work Independently, Guide and Lead Others

As a hiring manager, what do you hope to see on a candidate's résumé? Are you more interested in experience and skills learned, or do you look for personalities that can be easily integrated into your company's culture?

You need to hire an employee for your restaurant Design a résumé for a candidate you would be strongly interested in interviewing. Include the candidate's education, work experience, and related skills as well as a stated objective. The sample résumé in Figure 8.15 can give you some ideas.

You don't need to include extravagant desires. For instance, your buser candidate doesn't have to have attended Harvard or Yale. But do be realistic about the skills and attributes you want to hire. Think about people with whom you've worked and why you liked or disliked working with each one, as well as what they brought to the group. This may provide insight into the types of people you'd wish to hire.

Exchange your finished résumé with another student. Does that résumé impress you as well? Why or why not?

Figure Focus

Figure 8.15: As a hiring manager, are you favorably or unfavorably impressed with this résumé?

Encourage students to discuss the following:

- Why is it important to check the references job applicants provide?

- Why should a lawyer review all hiring and employment documents you create?

- How does requesting a signature attesting that the application form has been completed honestly actually ensure that the application is completed honestly?

Discuss

- How does the job search work, from the employer's perspective?

Essential Skills
Creating an Employee Application Form

An application form is one of the most important tools you have for gathering information about potential employees:

- **Remember what information you cannot request a candidate to provide:** You may not legally ask about an applicant's age, gender, marital status, parental status, race, religion, or nationality.

- **Ask for relevant personal information:** The candidate's legal name, mailing and permanent addresses, telephone numbers, email address, employment status, eligibility for employment in the United States, and Social Security number are all legitimate requests here. You may also ask whether the individual has ever been convicted of a felony and whether the individual, if hired, would be willing to undergo a pre-employment drug screening.

- **Request educational information:** You can ask what schools the applicant attended, the dates attended, and the degrees earned. You can also ask about courses of study or awards won.

- **Ask for an employment history:** You can ask where the candidate has worked, the dates worked, the positions filled, the tasks performed, and the salary earned. You can also ask for a supervisor's name and contact information.

- **Request references:** These "character witnesses" can provide more information about a potential employee.

- **Ask for any other relevant information:** The candidate can provide details of any professional certifications, awards, or other activities that might make him or her a more appealing employee.

- **Request a signature:** The potential employee should sign the application just below a statement attesting that the application form has been completed honestly. You should specify penalties for dishonesty.

Figure 8.16: To avoid asking potential employees questions that are protected under law, have a lawyer review your application form.

Most importantly, have the finished document examined by a lawyer before you give it to an applicant. See Figure 8.16. After all, much of the information that you're asking for is sensitive material, and you may have inadvertently asked applicants to provide material that is protected information. A lawyer's assistance can help you avoid uncomfortable moments—or even lawsuits.

508

Figure Focus
Figure 8.16: Remember the importance of shielding yourself and the company from any claims of discrimination during the hiring process.

Many other options are available. For example, other options are personality or ability tests, references, background checks, and medical records. Whichever methods are used, managers must make sure that every person is given a fair chance and that all laws are followed.

Managers should develop a standard list of questions that gets them the information they need while making sure all laws are being followed. The same list should be used for every applicant for the same position.

Some questions can be answered with a yes or no or with a brief factual statement and are appropriate for some information. However, most questions should ask the applicant to explain his or her experience and past performance. The following are examples of those questions:

- Discuss two skills you developed at your previous job.

- What area of your work skills do you most want to improve?

- How would your colleagues describe your work habits?

[fast fact]

Did You Know...?

The most common interview questions are:

"Tell me about yourself."

"Why did you leave your last job?"

"Why do you want this job?"

"Why should I hire you?"

"What would you like to be doing five years from now?"

Some applicants go through a series of interviews as part of the screening process for a job. This is known as **successive interviewing**. The interviews can be done by one person or by many people in the operation, such as the dining room manager and the general manager. This style of interviewing helps to provide various impressions of an applicant. Pooling the information from the interviews gives a better picture about the person and often lets managers share perspectives on the candidates.

Background checks, reference checks, and other investigations such as medical and drug tests, cost time and money. When these methods are used, they are often done after an operation has decided to hire a candidate—just before a job offer, after the job offer but before the new hire starts, or just after the new hire starts the job. If these checks provide information that contradicts information supplied by the candidate or new hire, the operation has grounds to withdraw the offer or terminate the new hire, assuming it has appropriate policies for handling such situations.

509

Discuss

- Why should interviewers use the same list of questions with each candidate? What if the applicant makes a comment that could open up a new area of information? Should the interviewer keep to the script?

- How might successive interviewing be better suited to larger establishments than to smaller ones?

Reinforce and Review

- Managers should develop a standard list of questions that gets them the information they need while ensuring that all relevant laws are followed.

- Interviewers should emphasize open-ended questions during the interview process in order to solicit more information about each candidate.

- Most questions should ask the applicant to explain his or her experience and past performance in the workplace.

- Pooling information from successive interviews helps give interviewers a better picture of the applicant.

- Employers should establish policies for terminating new hires or withdrawing job offers in case background checks, drug tests, or other sources of information indicate that a candidate should not be hired.

Fast Fact: Did You Know...?

Encourage students to discuss the following:

- What can these questions tell an employer about a candidate?

- Why are open-ended questions more appropriate than closed questions for job interviews?

- What can candidates learn about employers from the types of questions they ask?

Vocabulary Terms

- **Successive interviewing:** A process through which a single candidate undergoes a series of interviews as part of the screening process for a new job.

In-Class Activity: Question Time

Literacy Connection, 21st-Century Skills—Critical Thinking and Problem Solving, Communicate Clearly, Work Independently

Consider the three questions listed on p. 509. What do they tell you about the interviewer and the company's culture? Why would these particular answers be of interest to the interviewer?

Answer each of the three questions, as if for a potential interviewer. What do your answers tell the interviewer about you? Consider the words you chose, how you used those words, and what you left out of your answers.

Discuss

- Why might an applicant's prior employer be unwilling to talk with a potential employer about the applicant's performance? Does that always indicate that the applicant should be rejected?
- Why is it important to conduct interviews in a private place, free of interruptions and distractions?
- Should nonmanagement employees be involved in the hiring process? What strengths and weaknesses might they bring to the process?

What's New: Online Job Applications

Encourage students to discuss the following:

- How might using online application forms either encourage or discourage applicants?
- How can using a strictly online application process enhance the development of a positive work environment and lessen the opportunity for bias and prejudice to enter the hiring process?
- In what ways can employers save time, energy, and money by using online application systems?

In planning to conduct interviews, employers should remember to do the following:

- Prepare a list of legal and appropriate interview questions.
- Schedule interviews when there will be no distractions.
- Inform other employees and coworkers that they cannot be disturbed during interviews.
- Interview applicants in private areas.
- Make sure that all paperwork has been read and reviewed before the interview.
- Have any information about the operation available for applicants.
- Try to involve other appropriate supervisors, such as managers, chefs, and kitchen managers, in the interviewing process. This provides several opinions of job applicants.
- Check job applicants' references. The standard question to ask references is: "Would you hire this person again?" If references are willing to talk to you, ask about candidates' punctuality, dependability, and attitude toward work.

[what's new]

Online Job Applications

It used to be that if you wanted a job in a restaurant or other foodservice establishment, you would simply show up and ask to speak with a manager or to complete a job application. While this is a great way to check the place out, it's not necessarily the most efficient way to get a job. You have to go to the restaurant during a certain time of day, and the management has to take time to evaluate your application. It's no wonder that many large restaurant groups and franchises are turning to online job applications, either managed in-house or outsourced to another agency.

Online applications help prevent hiring biases by presenting all potential employees in the same way. Physical appearance is not an issue. Since each applicant must complete the entire application with no gaps, the manager doesn't have to spend valuable interview time obtaining information that the applicant should already have provided. The technology can sort applicants by different criteria. For instance, the system can eliminate from consideration all management applicants without a high-school degree or GED, or all potential cooks without foodhandling cards. Sometimes the online application form includes an assessment test so the employer can learn more about the applicant's actual experience or qualifications. Also, automated responses to applicants notifying them either that they will be considered for interviews or that they do not meet employer qualifications at that time prevent potential employees from falling into limbo.

Historically, the restaurant and foodservice industry has experienced high employee turnover. This contributes to the thousands of job applications that restaurants and other operations receive each year. That's a lot of paper to process. Using online application forms can help managers identify potential candidates for hire more efficiently as well as maintain a professional, organized image. Most importantly, managers can save time, money, and energy by switching to automated systems.

510

Lawful Hiring Practices

Managers for restaurant or foodservice operations need to know the legal and regulatory environment in which they operate. Knowing the applicable laws is important because managers must ensure that operations comply. Fortunately, the policies and procedures of most operations closely follow the laws. Managers may not need to understand the details of every law that affects the operation, but they do need to understand the intent of the laws and the details that directly affect their workplaces.

Managers also need to know what they do not know, so they can recognize when to get additional information or defer issues to specialists, such as a human resources or legal professionals. Not knowing or following the laws puts the manager and the operation at risk for complaints, fines, and lawsuits.

Since laws and regulations vary from state to state and may be amended, one responsibility of managers is to keep up-to-date on the changing laws. If an operation has a human resources professional, he or she can keep managers informed of applicable changes in the laws. These laws impact all areas of an operation, and understanding them is an important aspect of the manager's job. Some potential resources that managers can use to stay up-to-date include online resources and professional associations. Posters in the workplace, such as those required by OSHA, explain in detail many of the major laws that apply to employment. Some posters vary by state.

In the restaurant and foodservice industry, there are numerous laws and regulations governing what can and cannot happen and what should and should not happen in the workplace. Many of these laws protect employees from discriminatory, unsafe, unfair, or unethical treatment. Some of these laws also protect customers and the community from discriminatory practices. Regulations can outline guidelines, practices, policies, and procedures. They guide what an operation is required to do to be in compliance with the law.

Antidiscrimination laws can impact many aspects of daily operations, including job descriptions, recruiting, screening, hiring, employee development, training, and promotions. Most company policies enforce these laws and contain zero tolerance statements for discrimination of any kind. A **zero tolerance policy** means that no violation is forgiven—the offender is disciplined accordingly. The discipline goes up to and includes termination. For example, a zero tolerance policy might state that if an employee is caught stealing, the consequence will be immediate termination.

Other areas that are impacted by laws include the following:

- Food safety and alcohol service

- Scheduling and work assignments

511

- How can smaller restaurants and foodservice establishments ensure that they are obeying relevant hiring and employment laws if they do not have the ability to employ a human-resources department?

- In what ways can zero tolerance policies send a statement to employees about the company's ethics and values?

Reinforce and Review

- Managers must ensure that establishments comply with all applicable laws, so they must stay abreast of new developments.

- Failure to observe laws may result in complaints, fines, or lawsuits against the company.

- Many laws affecting the restaurant and foodservice industry protect employees from discriminatory, unsafe, unfair, or unethical treatment.

- Companies often employ zero tolerance policies for discriminatory and other inappropriate or illegal behaviors.

Vocabulary Terms

- **Zero tolerance policy:** A policy that states that no forgiveness is available for certain breaches of discipline.

Encourage students to discuss the following:

- Why is it important for managers to know about unions and union contracts?

- How can the presence of a union contract affect the workplace in either a positive or negative way?

- Why might employees at a particular worksite or in a particular industry choose to join a union? Why might they not?

Reinforce and Review

- Federal and local governments have enacted a variety of laws to protect working minors from unsafe or unfair conditions.

Teaching Tips

- The Fair Labor Standards Act addresses a variety of occupational protections, but it includes provisions aimed at protecting minors from physical harm in the workplace, as discussed in Chapter 3.

CUSTOMIZED INSTRUCTION

Literacy Connection, 21st-Century Skills—Reason Effectively, Use Systems Thinking, Communicate Clearly

Special Needs Students

Why are child labor laws important? What roles might they play in the restaurant and foodservice industry? Discuss in small groups.

ESOL Students

Describe the child labor laws in effect in your country of origin. How do they relate to those in the United States? Describe their similarities and differences in a brief essay.

Less Advanced Students

Select one provision of the Fair Labor Standards Act that applies to workers your age. How does it protect employed minors? Describe the provision and its effects in a brief essay.

More Advanced Students

Research the history of the Fair Labor Standards Act. Why does it address child labor? What historical circumstances might have made this portion of the act more or less likely to pass? How might the law be written differently in 1960? In 2012? Write a two-page report on your findings.

Vocabulary Terms

- **Child labor laws:** Special laws offering additional workplace protections for children and youth.

- Workplace safety
- Union relations
- Wages and payroll, including how overtime is paid and when breaks should occur
- Employee benefits, like health care and retirement savings

[fast fact]

Did You Know...?

Labor unions are organizations of workers who have joined together to work collectively to negotiate the wages, hours, and terms and conditions of their employment with their employer. Many unions also engage in political activity, either by directly supporting candidates for office or by supporting or opposing ballot initiatives. In the U.S., companies with union representation typically follow one of the following models:

- **Closed shop:** This means only union members are eligible for hire.

- **Union shop:** This means that anyone is eligible for hire, but new employees must join the union within a set amount of time after hire.

- **Agency shop:** This means that all employees are either union members or fair-share payers—the latter pay a fee, generally less than union members pay in dues, that entitles them to participation in union-negotiated benefits without actually joining the union.

- **Open shop:** This means that employees are either union members or nonmembers; unlike the agency-shop model, nonmembers pay no fees or dues, but are still entitled to receive union-negotiated benefits.

Workers in a wide variety of jobs belong to unions, including foodservice employees. The UFCW serves workers in retail food, meatpacking and poultry, food processing and manufacturing, and retail stores. The SEIU unites workers in three sectors—health care, property services, and public services. Unite Here represents workers in the hospitality, gaming, foodservice, manufacturing, textile, laundry, and airport industries.

While the federal government strives to protect all workers, special laws called **child labor laws** offer additional protections for children and youth. To protect minors from unsafe conditions in the workplace and from work schedules that may interfere with their education or affect their well-being, federal and local governments have enacted various child labor laws. The Fair Labor Standards Act (FLSA) of 1938, as amended, established various occupational protections primarily related to wages, but it also established provisions for child labor. Various state and local laws were built on this federal law to offer further protections for minors.

512

Generally, child labor laws restrict the hours young employees can work and the type of work they can do. According to the Department of Labor, 16- and 17-year-olds can work in front-of-the-house positions but are restricted in the back of the house. The laws impact these areas:

- **Hours worked:** Under the FLSA, 14- and 15-year-olds may work outside school hours for limited periods. The federal government does not limit the hours of 16- and 17-year-olds. They may even work overtime, and employers must pay them overtime wages the same as they would for anyone else. However, state and local laws may preempt the FLSA in these areas.

- **Operating hazardous equipment:** No one under the age of 18 can operate, feed, set up, adjust, repair, or clean any equipment declared hazardous, such as electric slicers.

- **Driving:** Federal law also prohibits minors from holding most driving jobs. Sixteen-year-olds cannot drive on the job at all, and 17-year-olds are severely restricted in this area. No employee under 18 years of age is allowed to drive on public roads unless it is only incidental to the job.

- **Work permits and/or age certificates:** Most states require that minors provide employers with a work permit or age certificate as a condition of employment. Depending on the state, these documents may be issued by the local school district or a government labor department.

For more information, check with your state and local departments of labor or seek professional advice.

Onboarding

Onboarding is the process that a company uses to integrate new employees into an organization. The goal of onboarding is to give companies a better chance at making sure the people they hire stay in their jobs. Many restaurants and foodservice operations lose most of their new employees within the first six months after hiring them. Onboarding isn't just a single event, like a training class. It is a process that lasts from a candidate's first contact with a company through up to a year on the job. Figure 8.17 is a sample agenda for an onboarding session.

Discuss

- How can the Fair Labor Standards Act and other state and local laws influence the hiring of minors in the restaurant and foodservice industry?
- How could onboarding take place in a high school setting? How could it ease the transition from middle school to high school? What are some specific elements it could include?
- Encourage students to describe any experiences they have had with onboarding. Why is the concept of onboarding particularly well suited to the restaurant and foodservice industry?

Reinforce and Review

- Child labor laws restrict the hours young employees can work and the type of work they can do.
- Most states require that minors provide employers with some proof of age, such as a work permit or an age certificate.
- Onboarding is a process that begins with a candidate's first interaction with a company and may continue through his or her first year of employment.
- A good onboarding program fulfills the needs of both the employer and the employee.

Vocabulary Terms

- **Onboarding:** The process a company uses to integrate new employees into the organization, improving employee retention rates.

513

Discuss

- How can onboarding help improve employee retention rates?
- How is onboarding related to a positive work environment? In what ways does it involve communication skills?
- How can onboarding save a company money in the long run?

Reinforce and Review

- Onboarding builds relationships among employees as well as between the new employee and the company itself.
- Companies that practice onboarding must consider how to integrate new employees into the workforce.
- Onboarding programs can protect companies in two important ways. First, onboarding teaches new employees to perform tasks safely and accurately. Second, a good onboarding program can satisfy certain legal needs.

In-Class Activity: New Hire Packets

Literacy Connection, 21st-Century Skills—Reason Effectively, Collaborate with Others, Guide and Lead Others

What documents and other items should be part of a new hire packet? As a hiring manager, what items do you think would not only make the new employee feel welcome but also give him or her all the tools necessary to do the job without feeling overwhelmed?

Make a list of the documents and other items that you think would be appropriate to include in a new hire packet. After ten minutes, exchange your list with another classmate. How are the two lists similar? How are they different? Discuss as a group.

Figure 8.17: Sample onboarding agenda.

A good onboarding program fulfills the needs of both the new employee and the company. There are many benefits to onboarding:

- Provides the company with a thought-out plan for new employees
- Helps job candidates and new employees understand the mission, vision, and culture of a company
- Builds relationships between new employees and other team members
- Avoids overwhelming new employees
- Boosts new employees' productivity and likelihood to stay
- Satisfies legal needs
- Ensures that new employees learn the correct, safe ways to perform tasks
- Gives the company feedback about what it can improve to help other new employees

514

Figure Focus

Figure 8.17: In your opinion, does this onboarding agenda cover all the essential information an employee should know? Why or why not?

Each company's onboarding process will be different. But most companies have a program that begins when a candidate for a job makes contact with the company and lasts upwards of a year. There are typically four phases of onboarding:

- **Hiring:** During hiring, companies stay connected with candidates and prepare for new hires. Examples include: providing Web sites with the company's history that potential employees can access, welcome letters, and checklists for supervisors to complete to prepare for a new hire's arrival.

- **Orientation:** New employees need to complete paperwork and learn about the company's policies. But they should also be introduced to team members and have an opportunity to interact with them. Orientation shouldn't be just a "dump" of forms and information onto the new employee. It can also last several days.

- **Training:** An onboarding program that includes many types of training has a better chance of success. For example, training might include role-plays, games, videos, and online activities. Finding ways to engage new employees helps to increase interest in learning.

- **Scheduled follow-up:** Good onboarding programs include contact with employees after orientation and training are over. Surveys, discussions, and quick chats at specific points, such as at sixty to ninety days on the job, helps keep everyone connected.

An onboarding program demonstrates the hospitality and customer service standards that all employees should meet. Employees should feel comfortable in their jobs, happy in their work, and geared toward customer needs. Onboarding programs should establish a culture of hospitality from the very beginning by welcoming new employees in a careful and thoughtful manner.

The lack of an onboarding program often contributes to more turnover (the number of people who leave a company during a given time period), because people do not feel comfortable in their new positions. If new employees do not feel they belong in an operation, they will find another place to work, or they will stay and be unhappy and unproductive. In the long run, a well-planned onboarding program reduces the time and costs needed to help an employee become productive and motivated.

Orientation

Orientation is the process that helps new employees learn about the procedures and policies of the operation and introduces them to their coworkers. The purpose of orientation is to make new employees feel comfortable in their new jobs, to let them know what their responsibilities are, and to make them feel part of the team.

515

Discuss

- Onboarding costs money. Wages and salaries of all the staff engaged in the onboarding process and not actually performing their regular duties can be expensive. In what tangible and intangible ways is onboarding valuable to a company? If you were an employer, would you onboard new staff? Why or why not?
- What is a culture of hospitality, and how can it be extended to coworkers as well as to guests? How is it related to the presence or absence of a positive work environment?
- How are onboarding and orientation different? As a manager, which would you prefer? As a newly hired employee, which would you prefer?

Reinforce and Review

- An onboarding program demonstrates the hospitality and customer service standards that all employees should meet.
- The four phases of onboarding are hiring, orientation, training, and scheduled follow-up.
- Employee turnover increases when employees do not feel comfortable in their jobs.
- A well-planned onboarding program reduces the time and cost of helping an employee become productive and motivated.
- The purpose of orientation is to make new employees feel comfortable in their new jobs, know what their responsibilities are, and feel like part of the team.

Vocabulary Terms

- **Orientation:** The process that helps new employees learn about the procedures and policies of the operation and introduces them to their coworkers.

Discuss

- The type of orientation a new employee receives typically depends on the size of the organization. How might the quality of the process differ based on the organization's size as well? How might turnover be affected?
- Why is reviewing the job description an important part of most orientation processes? How can this help a new employee feel more secure?
- How are onboarding and orientation essential components of organizational communication? Who is communicating with whom?

Reinforce and Review

- The type of training a new employee receives depends on the size of the organization and the job.
- The purpose of training is to be sure that employees know how to do a job on their own.
- Orientation programs both provide information about the company and provide information about the job.

The type of orientation employees receive depends on the size of the organization. In large operations, employees may complete some paperwork, hear lectures, and receive printed manuals or links to an online manual. Smaller operations might give new employees a photocopied employee manual, an individual tour of the operation, and introduce them to the company's mission and to coworkers.

The type of training employees receive depends on the job and the size of the organization. Some training may be accomplished by watching videos and reading workbooks, similar to a high school classroom experience. Many organizations also use computer-based training. Other training may be hands-on, similar to working in a classroom kitchen or cafeteria kitchen. The purpose of training is to be sure that employees know how to do the job on their own. New employees should remember to ask questions. It shows that they are serious about doing a good job.

Focus of Orientation

Orientation programs usually have two focuses: providing information about the company and providing information about the job. In large operations, employees learn about corporate culture. In an orientation program that includes many new employees, everyone can participate equally in the general orientation about the company.

This part of orientation includes the following:

- Review of the operation's mission, vision, history, and culture
- Identification of key managers and organizational structure
- Explanation of benefits and benefit schedules, when applicable
- Completion of any outstanding hiring-related paperwork
- Explanation of company policies and procedures
- Distribution of the employee handbook

After the general orientation, new employees need to learn about the specific demands of their jobs. Starting with a job description, the person learns what he or she is expected to do, when it must be done, and what materials are provided. Typically, the direct supervisor conducts this detailed job orientation and provides time for asking questions.

Job orientation should include the following aspects:

- Review and distribution of the job description
- Explanation of expectations for the employee's performance in training and on the job

516

- Training on how to do the job to standards
- Review of the employee's work schedule
- Distribution of contact numbers
- Introduction to coworkers and other staff
- Tour of the work area
- Distribution of any personal equipment or materials supplied by the operation, such as a uniform or a name tag

Supervisors give new employees whatever tools they need on their first day. These might include the following:

- Name tag and/or employee pass
- Locker or other personal space
- Uniform
- Office, cubicle, desk, or work area
- Telephone
- Employee manual containing general information concerning employment
- Training materials to help explain the work they will be doing
- First week's schedule

In addition to the job description and other hiring-related documents, additional documents used in orientation programs include organization charts, work schedules, copies of menus and promotional materials, and contact information. Of course, there are many other possibilities. To avoid overwhelming new employees, some operations spread out the orientation over a few days. New employees often receive an orientation packet that includes and organizes all the documents they need.

Orientation organizers should include all of the operation's policies and procedures in an **employee manual** handed out during orientation. An employee manual contains general information about employment, including company policies, rules and procedures, employee benefits, and other topics related to the company. When employees receive the employee manual, they should sign a form stating that they have received it. The employee's signature means that he or she has read the information and agrees to follow the rules and policies it contains. In some cases, a digital signature is created to show that employees have read the online version of the manual. Table 8.5 lists items commonly included in the employee manual.

517

Discuss

- How can a job description function as a teaching tool? How can it reinforce the prevailing company culture?
- Why is it common for employees to sign documents stating that they have received and read the employee manual?

Reinforce and Review

- Supervisors give employees whatever tools they need on the first day of work.
- Orientation packets commonly organize all the material a new employee needs.
- Employee manuals contain information about the company's policies and procedures.

Vocabulary Terms

- **Employee manual:** A booklet or binder containing all the operation's policies and procedures.

Table 8.5: Contents of a Typical Employee Manual

- What appear to be the most important items in the employee manual? Why?

- Why is it important to know and understand an employer's policies and procedures, especially if zero tolerance policies are in effect?

- How can the employee manual function as a teaching and communication tool? What messages can it convey about the employer?

In-Class Activity: Policy Planning

Mathematics Connection, Literacy Connection, 21st-Century Skills—Critical Thinking and Problem Solving, Analyze Media, Collaborate with Others

Working in small groups, review Table 8.5. The groups should select one item from each of the four main categories and draft a policy addressing each.

The policies that each group writes should be as comprehensive as possible. They should assume they are creating policies for their own businesses.

At least one of the policies needs to include a mathematic example of the policy's effects. For instance, if the group chooses to draft a policy on paid holidays, then the group would not only need to explain who is eligible for pay and what days would be considered paid holidays, but would need to include an example of how the process would work:

Sally is a full-time line cook, paid $12 per hour. She typically works a Wednesday-Sunday week. If a paid holiday falls during that Wednesday-Sunday week, then she will be paid her normal weekly pay despite working only four days, as follows:

$12 per hour, multiplied by 4 days worked at 8 hours per day

$12 × 4(8) = $384

$12 per hour, multiplied by 1 paid holiday covered at 8 hours per day

$12 × 1(8) = $96

Therefore Sally's gross pay for the week would remain $480 ($12 × 40 hours of work)

If the paid holiday falls on a Monday or Tuesday, Sally is not eligible for holiday pay and will work her normal Wednesday–Sunday schedule.

After each group has drafted its policies, join as a class to discuss the choices each group made.

Table 8.5: Contents of a Typical Employee Manual	
Employment Policies	Absence from work
	Schedule substitutions and trading work shifts
	Paid holidays
	Overtime
	Tips
	Pay periods
	Shift changes
	Time cards
	Performance appraisals
	Wage and salary reviews
	Work breaks
Rules and Procedures	Dress code
	Illegal activities (i.e., drinking alcohol, drugs)
	Grievances (complaints or problems at work)
	Disciplinary procedures
	Probationary policies
	Causes for dismissal
	Emergencies (i.e., injuries, fires, natural disasters, robberies)
	Safety rules
	Off-duty time at the operation
	Friends visiting the operation
	Personal telephone use
Employee Benefits	Medical and dental insurance coverage
	Sick leave and disability
	Meals
	Pension, retirement, and/or death benefits
	Profit sharing
	Retirement
Other Topics That May Be Included	Employee and locker areas
	History and mission of the organization
	How the company is organized (the chain of command)
	Job description
	Where to enter and leave the facility
	Smoking and nonsmoking areas
	Restrooms
	Breakage (accidents, broken dishes or equipment)
	Parking
	Training opportunities
	Employee assistance programs
	Job openings and postings

[on the job]

Human Resource Managers

People don't often think about the importance of human resource (HR) managers until they need one. Restaurant groups and franchises commonly employ regional human resource managers to ensure that management at each location is treating employees with respect and following all applicable laws. These HR managers develop standards, policies, and procedures to be observed by each restaurant, as well as providing professional advice and assistance to employees and managers on a daily basis. They work to improve employee relations and to develop new leaders. Regional human resource managers also serve as liaisons between each restaurant and the national office, making sure that communication lines stay fluid and helping to resolve any emergent problems quickly and appropriately.

Regional human resource managers typically have a bachelor's degree, often in business or management, and may hold advanced degrees. This position carries great responsibility, so several years' experience in this field is a must. In addition, strong communication, interpersonal, and computer skills are essential. HR managers should be excellent trainers, facilitators, educators, and listeners. They should be familiar with all applicable federal, state, and local laws affecting the restaurants in their assigned regions. Finally, they spend a great deal of time traveling among job sites, making sure that corporate rules are being followed and that appropriate standards are being maintained.

Summary

In this section, you learned the following:

- A job description is a document that defines the work involved in a particular assignment or position.

- Exempt employees are not legally entitled to overtime pay or the minimum wage established by the FLSA. Nonexempt employees are paid for every hour of overtime.

- Managers are responsible for knowing the laws to ensure that the operation complies with all laws.

- Managers must avoid discriminatory language and use the same application forms and tests for everyone who applies for the job. Everyone regardless of race, age, gender, religion, national origin, color, and ability gets a fair chance at a job opening. Managers should avoid gender-specific titles, avoid references to a specific group of people, and focus on the actual skills, knowledge, and abilities needed for the job.

- Tools used to ensure a fair and consistent hiring practice include job applications, screening interviews, cover letters and résumés, personality or ability tests, references, background checks, and medical records.

519

On the Job: Human Resource Managers

Encourage students to discuss the following:

- How can human resource managers affect an employee's daily work?

- How would interested parties begin to train for a human resource manager position?

- Why is the work of a human resource manager so important? How can they help facilitate employee and employer goals?

Discuss

- What have students learned about communication from a managerial standpoint during this section? How do they think they will be able to capitalize on this information in the next few years?

CUSTOMIZED EDUCATION

Literacy Connection, 21st-Century Skills— Critical Thinking and Problem Solving, Analyze Media, Work Independently

Less Advanced Students

Review Table 8.5. In each of the four categories, identify the item that seems the most important to a newly hired employee. Write two or three sentences about each of the four items, explaining your choices.

Summary

- Remind students to review the following:
  1. The information included in a job description and its importance to a business
  2. The difference between exempt and nonexempt employees
  3. The manager's responsibilities for maintaining labor law knowledge
  4. Discriminatory language and practices in the hiring process
  5. Methods that ensure a fair and consistent hiring process
  6. Onboarding and its importance to a business
  7. What employees can expect during orientation
  8. The items that employees receive during orientation
  9. The topics covered in orientation sessions and employee manuals

- Onboarding is the process that a company uses to integrate new employees into an organization. It gives companies a better chance at making sure the people they hire stay in their jobs.

- During orientation, employees can expect to fill out paperwork, hear lectures, and receive printed materials such as an employee manual.

- Employees may receive the following items during orientation: name tag/employee pass, locker or other personal space, uniform, office/desk, telephone, employee manual, training materials, first week's schedule.

- An employee manual generally includes employment policies, employee benefits, rules and procedures, and other information about the company such as mission of the company.

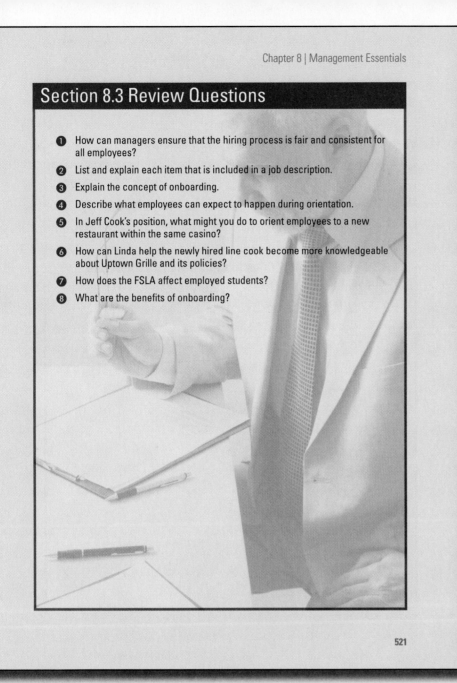

Section 8.3 Review Questions

1. How can managers ensure that the hiring process is fair and consistent for all employees?

2. List and explain each item that is included in a job description.

3. Explain the concept of onboarding.

4. Describe what employees can expect to happen during orientation.

5. In Jeff Cook's position, what might you do to orient employees to a new restaurant within the same casino?

6. How can Linda help the newly hired line cook become more knowledgeable about Uptown Grille and its policies?

7. How does the FSLA affect employed students?

8. What are the benefits of onboarding?

521

Section 8.3 Review Questions

1. Managers must use standardized tools and practices to make sure every applicant is treated fairly and consistently.

2. The six components of a job description include:
   - A job title, which gives the name of the position being described
   - A job summary, which briefly describes the position's responsibilities
   - The primary responsibilities, a list of the position's most important functions
   - The knowledge and skills requirements, which describes the performance background required to hold the position
   - Working conditions, the context in which the employee holding the position will be expected to work
   - Education requirements, the formal and informal education required to hold the position

3. Onboarding is the process that a company uses to integrate new employees into an organization, helping companies retain employees by fulfilling their needs and helping them feel connected to the organization.

4. During the orientation process, new employees typically learn general information about the company, including its personnel, its policies, and its culture. Employees also learn more specific information about the positions they will hold, including employee manuals as well as any tools they will need on their first day in the workplace.

5. Students should describe an orientation process for employees hired to work at a new restaurant within an existing casino, combining their understanding of Jeff Cook's philosophy of management and the material on orientation programs on pp. 516–517.

6. Students can suggest a variety of ways that Linda can help the new employee become more knowledgeable, but they should be sure to discuss onboarding and orientation in their answers.

7. The Fair Labor Standards Act established child labor laws that restrict the hours that 14- and 15-year-olds can work and prevent minors from operating hazardous equipment and from most driving jobs.

8. The benefits of onboarding include providing the company with a plan for new employees. Onboarding can help job candidates and new employees understand the vision, mission, and culture of the company. It can also help build relationships between new employees and other team members. A good plan can help avoid overwhelming new employees, and can boost productivity while improving retention rates. It can also satisfy legal needs, ensure that employees are properly trained to perform tasks, and help a company find out about ways it can improve to help other new employees.

Section 8.3 Activities

1. Students should use the six categories of information contained in a typical job description, as in the example on p. 501. To create the job descriptions, students in each group must agree on the theme, mission, and culture of the hypothetical restaurant.

2. Students should be sure to consult local laws, which may differ from the FSLA.

3. Students should build on the material learned in Section 8.2 to discuss how workplace ethics inform interviewing and hiring processes.

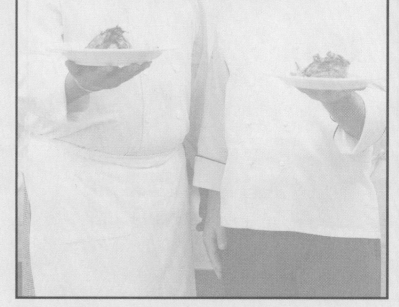

Section 8.3 Activities

1. Study Skills/Group Activity: Job Descriptions

Work with two other students to write job descriptions for three positions at your soon-to-open restaurant: entry-level prep cook, server, and executive chef.

2. Activity: Laws for Teenagers in the Workplace

Research federal, state, and county laws affecting teenagers in the workplace and write a one-page paper on your findings.

3. Critical Thinking: Ethics in the Hiring and Interview Process

Explain the role played by ethics in the hiring and interviewing processes.

522

8.1 Learning to Work Together	8.2 Being a Successful Leader	8.3 Interviewing and Orientation	8.4 Training and Evaluation
• Diversity • Respectful workplaces • Teamwork	• Leadership skills • Motivation • Ethics • Problem solving • Organizational skills	• Job descriptions • Interviewing job applicants • Lawful hiring practices • Onboarding • Orientation	• Training • Performance appraisals • Management equipment

SECTION 8.4 TRAINING AND EVALUATION

After an operation hires an employee, job training begins. Training encourages employees to work together as a team. There are different types of training.

Study Questions

After studying Section 8.4, you should be able to answer the following questions:

- What are the benefits of training?
- What skills should a trainer have?
- What are the key points of effective employee training?
- What are the benefits of cross-training?
- What is effective group training and on-the-job training?
- What is the employee evaluation process?

Training

Training improves the skill, knowledge, and attitude of employees for their jobs. Effective training is essential to the productive functioning of an operation. Effective training should accomplish the following:

- Improve the quality of employee work
- Promote employee growth
- Keep employees challenged and satisfied in the organization
- Create talent to help the organization grow

523

Section 8.4
Training and Evaluation

Introduce the Section

a. Explain how training can help employees and employers succeed.
b. Differentiate among cross-training, group training, and on-the-job training.
c. Discuss the objectives for the section.

Vocabulary Review

a. Direct students to the key terms.
b. Pronounce each word, and have the students repeat the pronunciation out loud.
c. Discuss the definition of each word.

Teach

Discuss

- All staff need training at some point, and all employees deserve a positive work environment. How can effective training be a part of a positive work environment?

Reinforce and Review

- Training encourages employees to work together as a team.
- Effective training is essential to the productive functioning of an operation.

Teaching Tips

- Relate the information in this section to the importance of communication skills and keeping staff onboard.

Vocabulary Terms

- **Training:** Activity that improves the skill, knowledge, and attitudes of employees for their jobs.

In-Class Activity: Training Agendas

Literacy Connection, 21st-Century Skills—Critical Thinking and Problem Solving, Manage Goals and Time, Guide and Lead Others

Plan a training seminar to teach "coworkers" how to perform a series of tasks or to develop a skill of your choosing. Design the agenda. What do you include, and what do you omit?

Review your agenda with another student to determine whether it is clear, logical, and effective. What improvements does he or she suggest?

Discuss

- According to the old saying, "You have to spend money to make money." How can spending money on employee training save money in employee turnover and increase sales?
- How do trainers themselves learn the important skills listed on p. 524? In what ways can they improve their skill sets?
- Another business saying is, "Invest in people, not in product." What are the ramifications of this statement? How can human resources be the most important resources a business can have?

Reinforce and Review

- Training helps employees do their jobs better by helping them feel confident that they are an effective and efficient part of a team.
- Training combats turnover by keeping current employees and helping new employees become productive faster.
- Training involves understanding what it takes to start with a novice and go through the steps to make that person proficient.
- Managers look for the ability to teach others in the people they promote.

When employees gain knowledge and skills, their morale and confidence increases. Training helps employees do their jobs better because they can be confident that they are an effective and efficient part of the team. As the performance of employees improves, the business reaps rewards, too: increased sales, fewer on-the-job accidents, improved customer satisfaction, and lower amounts of food waste.

Training combats turnover. When an operation replaces an employee, the new employee usually starts at a skill and knowledge level that is lower than a fully productive employee. Rather than waiting for the slow process of informal learning to show results, train new employees quickly and reap productivity benefits.

Qualified Trainers

For training to have the desired effect, the trainer must be a qualified expert in the subject, and should also be good at training others. Training is very different from simply giving a presentation. There is a tremendous difference between giving a presentation, lecture, or demonstration on a subject or skill and enabling other people to learn a subject or skill. The latter involves understanding what it takes to start with a novice (beginner) and go through the steps to make that person proficient. There are a number of important skills for training others:

- Identifying what the learner may already know
- Motivating the learner
- Setting the stage and providing advance organizers (previews of what is to come)
- Chunking the subject or skill into manageable pieces
- Letting the learner try and make mistakes without interference
- Having patience with the learner
- Giving constructive feedback
- Observing the extent of understanding and learning
- Adjusting or expanding on topics or procedures based on the extent of learning
- Helping the learner transfer the learning back to the job

Being a good trainer helps employees reach the next level in their careers. Managers look for the ability to teach others in the people they promote. Great trainers also understand that training employees to be more skilled workers

524

makes them better candidates for the next level. The ability to train replacements is a critical skill in the rapidly growing restaurant industry. Table 8.6 lists the six key points to effective employee training.

Table 8.6: Six Key Points of Effective Employee Training	
1.	Both the employee and trainer must be motivated.
2.	Training should be designed for the new employee and the task he or she needs to learn. All new employees do not learn at the same rate.
3.	Involve the new employee in the training by using hands-on practice and demonstration.
4.	Set realistic goals so that the trainer and new employee know what is to be accomplished.
5.	Feedback is essential to help the new employee remember each task. Always emphasize positive results, even when correcting the way an employee performs a task.
6.	Managers can use results to objectively evaluate employees' progress.

Cross-Training

Cross-training is when employees learn the functions of another job within the operation. Employees benefit from cross-training by becoming more skilled, which makes them more valuable to the company. It also sets them up for a promotion which can earn them more money. Many organizations are looking for employees that are eager to learn more than one area of the business.

Cross-training benefits the organization more than the individual, because employee absences and sudden surges in demand can be met with available staff. The benefits of cross-training to an operation include the following:

- Develops backups for operation
- Lets employees discover different interests and career goals
- Aids in scheduling by giving managers more options for who to schedule when
- Reduces overtime and turnover
- Boosts teamwork and morale

Cross-training is essential to productivity in the restaurant because it encourages more teamwork. Employees are more likely to help their coworkers if they know what that coworker will need. The business is very unpredictable at times and if one employee becomes overwhelmed, having another employee able to jump in helps keep the operation moving smoothly. Figure 8.18 illustrates six employees, all of whom have been cross-trained on certain jobs.

Table 8.6: Six Key Points of Effective Employee Training

- Why must both the trainer and the trainee be motivated to succeed? What if only one is motivated? Can the training itself succeed under these circumstances?
- Why is feedback critical throughout the training process? What other roles does communication play in this process?
- Why is an objective review of employee progress so important? What benchmarks can be used to evaluate employee progress?

Discuss

- Employers invest significant amounts of money in training their employees. Trained employees are very attractive to other employers, who may seek to hire them away. How can employers retain these skilled employees?
- How are flexibility and cross-training related? How can either affect the employer or the employee? What role does communication play in these matters?

Reinforce and Review

- The ability to train replacements is a critical skill in the rapidly growing restaurant industry.
- Employees benefit from cross-training by becoming more skilled, and thus, more valuable.
- Cross-training benefits the organization more than the individual in the immediate sense, because employee absences and sudden surges in demand can be readily accommodated.
- Cross-training is essential to productivity because it encourages teamwork and collegiality.

Vocabulary Terms

- **Cross-training:** An activity in which employees learn the functions of another job within the operation.

Fast Fact: Did You Know...?

Encourage students to discuss the following:
- How can managers keep staff from feeling demoted when they are asked to learn positions below their current job?

- What if staff members don't want to learn certain skills, positions, or tasks? Can they be required to learn these responsibilities anyway? How can they be kept motivated and successful employees under these circumstances?

Discuss

- Why do students think on-the-job training is so popular in the restaurant and foodservice industry? What makes it a particularly appropriate training method for this industry? Are there any downsides to on-the-job training?

Reinforce and Review

- On-the-job training allows employees to demonstrate skills and reinforce what they have been taught. It also allows the trainer to monitor performance and give feedback.
- Before they can train other employees, trainers must be up-to-date on all procedures and prepare all necessary teaching tools.

Vocabulary Terms

- **On-the-job training:** A process that helps teach skills that are easily demonstrated and practiced, popular in the restaurant and foodservice industry.

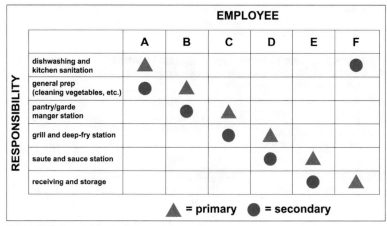

Figure 8.18: Cross-training employees.

[fast fact]

Did You Know...?

Cross-training isn't always sideways. It can also be up or down. Employees can be cross-trained on positions either above or below their current jobs in an effort to help work in the entire operation flow more smoothly.

On-the-Job Training

On-the-job training (OJT) is appropriate for teaching skills that are easily demonstrated and practiced, such as preparing menu items, operating cash registers, and using tools and equipment. It is a popular form of training. Employees receive this type of training as they work in the restaurant and foodservice industry. OJT allows employees to demonstrate skills and reinforce what they have been taught. It also allows the trainer to monitor employee progress, give feedback, comment about or correct an action or process, and correct tasks that are not being done properly. There are four steps to on-the-job training:

1. **Prepare:** This is when the trainer gets ready for teaching someone; the trainer needs to be up-to-date on procedures and have all the tools the trainee will need ready.

526

Figure Focus

Figure 8.18: How does cross-training employees affect a manager's ability to schedule staff?

2. **Present:** Give the learner the information he or she needs to know.

3. **Practice:** The learner performs the task with the trainer observing and providing feedback.

4. **Follow up:** The trainer verifies that the learner can perform the tasks.

Before on-the-job training can actually begin, the new employee's duties should be broken down into separate work steps. For example, if a new employee is learning how to take payment from a guest while working the cash register, he or she would practice several steps, including the following:

1. Repeat aloud the amount of money the guest hands over.

2. Lay the payment on top of the cash drawer until the entire transaction is complete.

3. Count the change given back to the guest.

4. Give the guest a receipt.

5. Thank the guest.

The trainer should make sure to explain to new employees why it is important to learn the skills being covered in training. In the example above, the cashier must take correct payments from guests in order for the operation to stay in business and ensure that employees get paid.

Before trainers can demonstrate a task, they themselves must be able to perform the task very well. Imagine how frustrating it would be if a math teacher wasn't able to explain a difficult math concept. A good trainer understands what needs to be learned and is comfortable with his or her own knowledge and ability to communicate that knowledge to new employees.

Group Training

Group training is usually the most practical choice when many employees need the same type of training. This method offers many benefits:

- It is cost effective.

- The training is uniform—all employees hear the same thing.

- Managers know exactly what employees have been taught.

- It encourages group discussion.

- New employees can offer input, get information, and work together to solve problems.

Discuss

- Why must trainers be sure to verify that employees can perform the tasks on which they have been trained? To what extent can the verification process also be one of self-reflection. What can the trainer learn from the employee about improving the training process for the next employee?

- Trainers play an important role in teaching the employees they train about the company's culture and values. How does this education play out during the on-the-job training process?

- Group training, although practical in many circumstances, is not always the most effective route in the restaurant and foodservice industry. What are the positive and negative aspects of this type of training?

Reinforce and Review

- To help employees learn new duties, their tasks must be broken down into separate work steps.

- Trainers must make sure to explain to new employees why it is important to learn the skills being taught.

- Good trainers thoroughly understand the subjects they will cover and feel confident in their ability to communicate this information to new employees.

- Group training is usually the most practical choice when many employees need the same type of training.

527

Discuss

- How is group training particularly suitable when a new restaurant is preparing to open? How can the skills learned in this type of training be most effectively verified? Similarly, how can students most effectively demonstrate the skills they have learned in this course?
- How can performance evaluations be used to communicate desires, goals, and expectations between employers and employees? Why should these evaluations focus on responsibilities and positions, not on personalities?
- How can a performance appraisal form help make the evaluation process more efficient?

Reinforce and Review

- Group training is ideal for training groups of new or temporary foodservice employees.
- Formal evaluations give managers and employees the opportunity to communicate, discuss performance, and establish goals.
- The evaluation process begins on the employee's first day of work, when managers begin keeping performance files and monitoring progress and professional development.
- Employees should protect themselves by keeping their own personnel files, containing information about their accomplishments, activities, new skills learned, and anything else professionally relevant.
- The focus of a performance appraisal should be on the employee's responsibilities, not any mistakes he or she may have made during the year.

Vocabulary Terms

- **Employee performance appraisal:** A formal evaluation of a person's work performance over a specific period of time.
- **Performance appraisal form:** A document that helps a manager evaluate an employee's performance.

Group training is also ideal for training a group of new employees or many temporary employees who must begin working right away. For example, organizations frequently use this method during new restaurant openings. Much of the learning in high school is also accomplished through group training—this class is an example of this method.

Performance Appraisals

Employee performance evaluation is similar to school grades or report cards. Just as a report card lets students know how well they are doing in school, a performance evaluation shows the progress of employees on the job.

An **employee performance appraisal** is a formal evaluation of a person's work performance over a specific period of time. All employees want to receive good evaluations because in many workplaces, promotions and salary increases (raises) are based on these evaluations. Formal evaluations give the manager and employee an opportunity to communicate, discuss how well the employee is doing, and set performance goals. The evaluations become part of the employee's permanent record at the particular company, just as grades are part of a student's permanent academic record.

A good evaluation program begins on the employee's first day on the job, with employee progress reviewed regularly throughout his or her employment with the operation. Managers and employers should keep files on each employee and record any important information, including pay raises, special projects completed, achievements, problems with coworkers, excessive lateness, or absenteeism. Employees also have a responsibility to the evaluation process to keep their own records of their accomplishments.

When a manager meets with an employee about workplace performance, the focus should be on the employee's responsibilities, not on his or her mistakes. If an employee is not performing well, the manager and employee must set goals in order to improve the situation. If employee performance does not change, the manager must document problems, counsel the employee, and give verbal and written warnings. If problems continue, the employee might be fired. All conversations about performance should be private between the employee and the manager.

The most effective way to rate employee performance is through the use of a **performance appraisal form**. A manager uses a performance appraisal form to help evaluate an employee's performance. Figure 8.19 shows a sample performance appraisal form. After discussing each area on the form, the manager and employee must agree on measurable goals for the future.

528

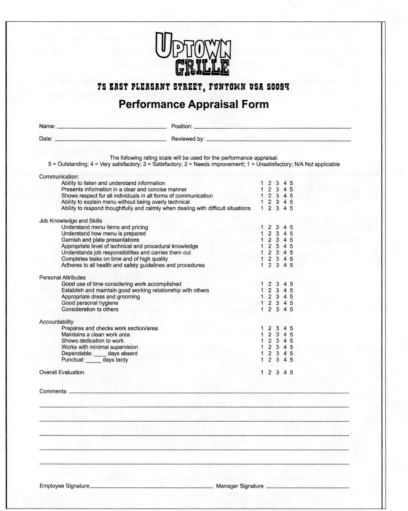

UPTOWN GRILLE

75 EAST PLEASANT STREET, FUNTOWN USA 50094

Performance Appraisal Form

Name: _____ Position: _____

Date: _____ Reviewed by: _____

The following rating scale will be used for the performance appraisal:
5 = Outstanding; 4 = Very satisfactory; 3 = Satisfactory; 2 = Needs improvement; 1 = Unsatisfactory; N/A Not applicable

Communication:
Ability to listen and understand information	1 2 3 4 5
Presents information in a clear and concise manner	1 2 3 4 5
Shows respect for all individuals in all forms of communication	1 2 3 4 5
Ability to explain menu without being overly technical	1 2 3 4 5
Ability to respond thoughtfully and calmly when dealing with difficult situations	1 2 3 4 5

Job Knowledge and Skills
Understand menu items and pricing	1 2 3 4 5
Understand how menu is prepared	1 2 3 4 5
Garnish and plate presentations	1 2 3 4 5
Appropriate level of technical and procedural knowledge	1 2 3 4 5
Understands job responsibilities and carries them out	1 2 3 4 5
Completes tasks on time and of high quality	1 2 3 4 5
Adheres to all health and safety guidelines and procedures	1 2 3 4 5

Personal Attributes
Good use of time considering work accomplished	1 2 3 4 5
Establish and maintain good working relationship with others	1 2 3 4 5
Appropriate dress and grooming	1 2 3 4 5
Good personal hygiene	1 2 3 4 5
Consideration to others	1 2 3 4 5

Accountability
Prepares and checks work section/area	1 2 3 4 5
Maintains a clean work area	1 2 3 4 5
Shows dedication to work	1 2 3 4 5
Works with minimal supervision	1 2 3 4 5
Dependable: _____ days absent	1 2 3 4 5
Punctual: _____ days tardy	1 2 3 4 5

Overall Evaluation   1 2 3 4 5

Comments: _____
_____
_____
_____
_____
_____
_____

Employee Signature _____   Manager Signature _____

Figure 8.19: Performance appraisals help set goals, evaluate performance, motivate, coach, and provide ongoing feedback.

529

Working in small groups, students should select something other than a class that can be appraised objectively. Good choices might include a book, an event, or a restaurant.

Once the subject has been selected, students should adapt the Performance Appraisal Form in Figure 8.19 as needed. They should determine four main categories on which the subject can be assessed, and then identify at least three more specific characteristics.

For example, if a group chooses to rate a supermarket, then one category could be Variety of Goods Sold, and one characteristic within that category could be Quality of Fresh Produce.

The group should then evaluate the subject's performance in each category, using a scale similar to that used in Figure 8.19. Comments and suggestions for improvement could be included as well.

Each group should present an oral report on its subject, explaining how it was selected and appraised, as well as its performance.

Figure Focus

Figure 8.19: How would students react to being presented with a performance appraisal form? How accurately do students think that forms like these can reflect their actual performance? How can students use forms like these to learn more about themselves?

Discuss

- The compliment sandwich is a common management technique in which a piece of constructive criticism is bookended by compliments. How can this technique be applied in everyday life?

Reinforce and Review

- During a performance evaluation meeting, employees have the opportunity to ask questions and make statements regarding their progress.
- Managers should end all evaluation meetings on a positive note, with both parties looking forward to achieving future goals and accomplishments.

Essential Skills: Conducting Performance Evaluations

Encourage students to discuss the following:

- Why is it important for students to learn how to evaluate others?

- Explain why overall performance trends should be the focus of an evaluation, not a mistake or two.

- How can employee self-evaluation forms be useful tools, both during the formal evaluation process and at other points throughout the year?

- How might an employer require an employee to address particular needs and goals? Why might this be important in terms of management flexibility?

- Why is it important to treat others with respect, especially when delivering bad news?

Before the manager ends a performance evaluation meeting, employees are often asked to sign and date the written appraisal form indicating that they have seen it and agree with the evaluation. Employees are also given the chance to ask questions or make final comments about their progress.

The appraisal process should cover an entire year of job performance by the employee (although some operations evaluate hourly employees on a six-month basis).

No matter how employees are rated, managers should always end evaluation meetings on a positive note. Both manager and employee should walk out of these meetings looking forward to achieving future goals and accomplishments.

Essential Skills
Conducting Performance Evaluations

Waiting to receive your annual performance evaluation can be nerve-wracking. So can providing the evaluations. The following tips can help you evaluate your employees in a relatively painless manner that's fair to all:

- **Ask your employees to participate:** Develop a self-evaluation sheet that employees can use to rate their work during the previous year. See Figure 8.20. Provide plenty of space where they can describe any particular successes they have had or to explain any problems they may have encountered. Some employers ask their workers to complete these forms each week or each month to keep the process up-to-date: it can be difficult to remember all the details of an interaction that happened nearly a year ago. These sheets should be completed and submitted at least one week before the employee's scheduled evaluation date.

- **Give a heads-up:** When informing each employee of the time and date of the upcoming performance evaluation, you should tell each one about any particular issues you plan to discuss at that time. You can also ask whether the employee will have any specific issues to raise.

- **Talk about a year, not a day:** If the employee had one really bad day during the course of the year, and the event was not repeated, there's no need to harp on it now—appropriate discussion and punishment should have occurred at the time of the offense. Focus on the overall trend of the year. Has the employee's performance been steadily improving or declining? Now is the time to discuss that.

- **Don't surprise people:** An annual performance evaluation is no time to blindside an employee, and you shouldn't be storing up negative information. The evaluation should reinforce what you and the employee both already know.

- **Discuss future goals and plans:** If you have specific needs that the employee must address, say so, and give a time frame and potential penalties for failure to address these needs. Consider making this a formal document that both you and the employee must sign and date. Also, consider asking each employee about his or her short- and long-term goals. If there are ways you can help, say so, and then keep your word.

530

Finally, when it's your turn to evaluate others, remember how things felt on the other side: be clear and honest, and don't go out of your way to hurt someone's feelings. Respect the work that your employees do each day, and respect them as humans. You may have bad news to deliver, but there are no bad people.

UPTOWN GRILLE

75 EAST PLEASANT STREET, FUNTOWN USA 50094

Self-Evaluation Form

Employee Name: _____

Employee Title: _____

Review Date: _____

Instructions: Please complete the following information to help you prepare for your annual performance review.

1. Please provide a summary of your job responsibilities.
    _____
    _____

2. How do you feel about your performance as an employee this past year?
    _____
    _____

3. What are some of your major job-related achievements this past year?
    _____
    _____

4. What would you like to accomplish over the next year?
    _____
    _____

5. What other skills or experience do you have that you would like to be using in this job?
    _____
    _____

6. Based on the responsibilities of your current position, what additional skills, knowledge, equipment, working conditions, or education would help you more effectively perform your present job?
    _____
    _____
    _____

7. List any topics you would like to discuss with your supervisor during your performance appraisal conference.
    _____
    _____

8. On a scale of 1 to 10, with 10 being excellent, how would you rate your overall performance this past year?
    _____

Employee Signature _____ Date _____ Manager Signature _____ Date _____

Figure 8.20: Self-evaluations provide information from the employee and the manager so they can work together to create goals and plans.

531

Homework Activity: Self-Evaluation

Literacy Connection, 21st-Century Skills— Critical Thinking and Problem Solving, Analyze Media, Work Independently

Students should evaluate their academic performance, adapting Figure 8.20 as needed. What can students learn from this activity? How can this help them adjust their behaviors to help accomplish their goals?

Figure Focus

Figure 8.20: How can self-evaluation forms help an employee assess his or her own behavior?

Discuss

- What professional advantages does a point-of-sale (POS) system have over the traditional order book?
- Are all the items of management equipment listed on p. 532 essential to the restaurant and food-service workplace? Which items might be more appropriate for one establishment than another?
- Are communication skills the most important skill set a manager can have? Why or why not?

Reinforce and Review

- POS systems help managers track sales, employee activity, and other information, as well as facilitate guest orders.
- Understanding what equipment is important and how it is used is important for foodservice managers.
- As a manager's career progresses, he or she should take whatever opportunities arise to expand his or her knowledge of professional equipment.

Teaching Tips

- Relate the POS system to the property management systems described in Chapter 1.
- What special equipment should restaurants and foodservice establishments keep on hand in case of unusual nonemergency situations, such as power outages? Encourage students to list some emergency equipment. Examples might include such items as flashlights, battery-operated calculators or adding machines, manual credit-card machines with appropriate blanks, a telephone that does not require batteries, business cards, and plain paper.

Vocabulary Terms

- **Point-of-sale (POS) systems:** These systems allow servers to enter orders and prompts for other order information.

Management Equipment

Point-of-sale (POS) systems allow servers to enter orders and prompts for other order information (such as the temperature for a steak). They also allow managers to track employee activity, the number of menu items sold, and analyze worker productivity. POS systems can take different forms: touch-screen monitors, handheld electronic order pads, cash registers, and back-of-the-house monitors and printers. People who use this equipment must be trained on how to use it.

Advanced POS systems are networked to communicate with a central computer. They integrate with inventory tracking systems and automatically delete the standard amount of each ingredient used to make a menu item. They can draft purchase orders automatically and send them to the supplier based on sales and inventory information.

Understanding the purpose of restaurant and foodservice operation office equipment and how to operate it is key to effective restaurant management. In general, it consists of the following:

- Telephone
- Fax/scanner/printer
- Office computer
- POS server—all POS terminals operate off a central computer
- Calculators
- Camera system
- Safe
- Inventory control software
- Money counters
- Counterfeit bill identifiers
- Cash registers
- E-procurement system (buyers transmit orders directly to the supplier's distribution center or access the supplier's inventory on the Internet)

As a manager's career progresses, he or she should take whatever opportunities arise to increase knowledge and comfort level with the variety of equipment needed to run an operation. Large-scale operations, hotels, chains, bars, and fine-dining operations all use these systems. Smaller operations might still use pads and paper and a traditional cash register.

532

Summary

In this section, you learned the following:

- Training improves the skill, knowledge, and attitude of employees. It improves the quality of employee work, promotes employee growth, keeps employees challenged, and creates talent to help the organization grow.

- Trainers need to be able to identify what the learner may already know, motivate the learner, set the stage, group the subject or skill into manageable pieces, let the learner try and make mistakes without interference, have patience with the learner, give constructive feedback, observe the extent of understanding and learning, adjust or expand on topics or procedures, and help the learner transfer the learning back to the job.

- There are several key points to effective employee training: both the employee and trainer must be motivated; you must design training for the new employee and the task he or she needs to learn; involve new employees in the training by using hands-on practice and demonstration; set realistic goals so that the trainer and new employee know what is to be accomplished; provide feedback to help the new employee remember each task; and use results to evaluate employees' progress objectively.

- Cross-training provides backup for operations, lets employees discover different interests and career goals, aids in scheduling, reduces overtime and turnover, and boosts teamwork and morale.

- On-the-job training involves learning something new by doing it under the supervision and guidance of an experienced employee with training skills. Group training is most practical when many employees need the same type of training.

- Employees are evaluated by a performance appraisal. An employee performance appraisal is a formal evaluation of an employee's work performance over a specific period of time.

533

Summary

- Remind students to review the following:
  1. The benefits of training
  2. The skills that a trainer should possess
  3. The key points of effective employee training
  4. The benefits of cross-training
  5. Effective group training and on-the-job training
  6. The employee evaluation process

Section 8.4
Review Questions

1. A performance appraisal is a formal evaluation of a person's work performance over a specific period of time, often tied to promotions and pay increases.

2. If an employee is not performing well, the manager and employee should set goals during the formal performance appraisal in order to improve the situation. If improvement is not forthcoming, the manager must document problems, counsel the employee, and give verbal and written warnings. In some situations, the employee might be terminated.

3. Skills a trainer should have include identifying what the learner may already know, motivating the learner, setting the stage and providing advance organizers, chunking the subject or skill into manageable pieces, letting the learner try and make mistakes without interference, having patience with the learner, giving constructive feedback, observing the extent of understanding and learning, adjusting or expanding on topics or procedures based on the extent of learning, and helping the learner transfer the learning back to the job.

4. Cross-training is when employees learn the functions of another job within the operation, thereby becoming more skilled. On-the-job training is for teaching employees, typically newly hired employees, skills that are easily demonstrated and practiced.

5. Students should relate the information given in Jeff Cook's profile to the material about performance appraisals on pp. 528–531.

6. Chef Jean should make sure that Michael's trainer is qualified to cross-train him on his new responsibilities and should provide oversight and testing opportunities to ensure that Michael thoroughly understands his new role.

7. Properly training employees is critical to the success of any organization. It improves the quality of employee work, promotes employee growth, keeps employees challenged and satisfied in the organization, and creates talent to help the organization grow.

8. Cross-training benefits employees by giving them more skills and thereby making them more valuable. It also makes them more eligible for promotion and pay increases.

Section 8.4 Review Questions

1. What is a performance appraisal?
2. What should a manager do during an employee performance appraisal if the employee has not been performing well?
3. List the skills that a trainer should have.
4. What is the difference between on-the-job training and cross-training?
5. Given Jeff Cook's basic management philosophy, how might an employee be given a performance appraisal?
6. What can Chef Jean do to make sure that Michael is properly cross-trained?
7. Why is it important to train employees properly?
8. How does cross-training benefit employees?

534

Section 8.4 Activities

1. Study Skills/Group Activity: How to Train Employees Skit

Work with two other students to plan and perform a skit on training new or current employees. You can focus either on what to do or what not to do.

2. Activity: Evaluations

In what ways are you evaluated at school? By your peers? How do these relate to workplace performance evaluations? What would you change about this evaluation?

3. Critical Thinking: How to Train Someone to Perform Your Tasks

Identify some task that you perform regularly. How would you train someone else to do it? Explain the task in six steps.

535

Section 8.4 Activities

1. Students' skits should clearly demonstrate either proper or improper employee training. There should be no ambiguity.

2. Students should consider the relationships among the different types of evaluations and suggest improvements to formal workplace appraisals.

3. Students should clearly define the steps involved in performing the chosen task.

Case Study Follow-Up

1. Students should suggest some specific ways in which Linda and Chef Jean can take advantage of the challenges posed by diversity.

2. Students should identify at least three ways in which Manuel and Katarina can behave more professionally and create a stronger relationship.

3. Students should discuss onboarding, orientation, mentoring, and other ways in which Chef Jean can integrate the new employee.

4. Students should base their answers on the material on successful leadership in Section 8.2.

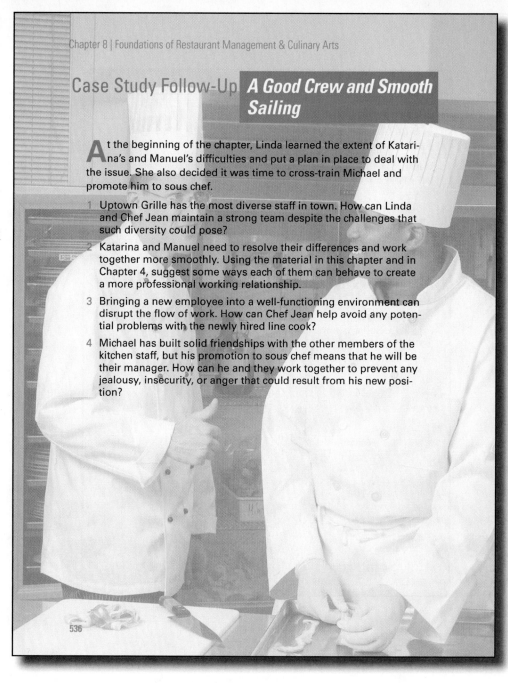

Case Study Follow-Up *A Good Crew and Smooth Sailing*

At the beginning of the chapter, Linda learned the extent of Katarina's and Manuel's difficulties and put a plan in place to deal with the issue. She also decided it was time to cross-train Michael and promote him to sous chef.

1 Uptown Grille has the most diverse staff in town. How can Linda and Chef Jean maintain a strong team despite the challenges that such diversity could pose?

2 Katarina and Manuel need to resolve their differences and work together more smoothly. Using the material in this chapter and in Chapter 4, suggest some ways each of them can behave to create a more professional working relationship.

3 Bringing a new employee into a well-functioning environment can disrupt the flow of work. How can Chef Jean help avoid any potential problems with the newly hired line cook?

4 Michael has built solid friendships with the other members of the kitchen staff, but his promotion to sous chef means that he will be their manager. How can he and they work together to prevent any jealousy, insecurity, or anger that could result from his new position?

536

Apply Your Learning

Payroll Taxes

Taxes—they're inevitable. If you are an employee, you pay payroll taxes. And if you're an employer, you pay payroll taxes, too. Employees pay federal and state income taxes, which are based on how much they earn and how many exemptions they take. An exemption, in this case, refers to the amount that an employee can deduct from his or her tax liability for the employee, the employee's spouse and children, and the employee's other relatives under certain circumstances. This has the practical effect of increasing an employee's take-home pay. Employees also pay Social Security tax (6.2 percent of employee pay, up to an established earnings amount, which changes annually), Medicare tax (1.45 percent of employee pay), and any other state and local taxes. Employees may also pay voluntary deductions, such as health insurance premiums, through their payroll.

Employers are responsible for withholding all this money from employee paychecks and submitting it to the proper authorities. They must also pay Social Security and Medicare taxes—they pay the same amount as each employee, so if buser Karen pays $18.60 each week in Social Security tax and $4.35 in Medicare tax, then her employer must also pay $18.60 and $4.35 each week—plus federal and state unemployment taxes. They also pay salary or wages, overtime, bonuses, and any other contracted amounts.

Assume you work as a sous chef and earn $43,000 per year. You are not eligible for overtime, and you have no voluntary deductions. You are not married and have no children, so you take no exemptions except one for yourself. What taxes must you pay in your current city and state? Current federal and state tax tables are available in your school library and online. What is your take-home pay?

Hamburger University

Ever heard of Hamburger University? It's not a joke, and it's not in Germany. Instead, it's McDonald's training center in Illinois. Each year, over 5,000 students from around the world attend training programs for managers and franchise-holders. Hamburger University helps develop leadership by encouraging innovative and original thinking while simultaneously immersing students in the McDonald's corporate culture. The success of the program, which has operated continuously since 1961, has brought it global recognition and prestige.

537

Apply Your Learning

Payroll Taxes

Students should research local and federal tax regulations to complete this exercise and should clearly identify each step in the mathematic operations used to calculate take-home pay.

Hamburger University

Students do not need to base their future businesses on McDonald's and Hamburger University, but they do need to research this program to understand how this leadership training contributes to the company's success. Then, students should clearly identify their businesses' characteristics and develop vision statements and training programs.

What is Management Science?

Students should research management science and determine how its principles can be applied to hypothetical situations. However, not all situations will readily lend themselves to simple equations, so students should not be graded on whether or not they can accurately perform this task.

Critical Thinking Ethics

Students should think deeply about their own ethics and situations which could compromise them, in the workplace and elsewhere.

Research Hamburger University and the role it plays in maintaining the company's success. Then think about a business you would like to own someday. First, identify the type of business you'll have, the number of employees you'll hire, and the services or products you will provide. Then develop a vision statement for your company. Now that you know what your company will do and why it will do it, plan a training program for your future employees. Will it be similar to the program at Hamburger University? Why or why not?

What is Management Science?

Management science, also known as operations research, is the field of using scientific techniques to reach management goals. Management science isn't simply "how to manage;" instead, it turns management problems into mathematical equations or abstract models so that the most efficient, rational decisions can be made.

Research management science, then pick out a situation that you could imagine arising in a restaurant or foodservice establishment, such as managing the flow of perishable supplies or scheduling staff for a catering event. How can management science help you resolve this problem? Can you write an equation to fit the situation?

Critical Thinking Ethics

It has been said that when an ethical dilemma arises in the workplace and an individual must determine what to do, his or her own ethics usually come in third: the employee will first look to the example set by a direct supervisor, and then to the company's own ethics, before examining his or her own principles. Why might this be true or false? What are your personal ethics? What happens if they come into conflict with an employer's ethics?

538

Exam Prep Questions

1 Generalizations that individuals make about particular groups that assume all members of that group are the same are called

A. diversity.

B. principles.

C. prejudices.

D. stereotypes.

2 The variety of people and their backgrounds, experiences, opinions, and abilities is known as

A. diversity.

B. principles.

C. prejudices.

D. modeling.

3 An operation's vision statement serves to communicate

A. why the organization exists.

B. who the organization is serving.

C. when the organization was created.

D. what key elements the organization has.

4 A set of moral values that a society holds is called

A. ethics.

B. values.

C. objectives.

D. motivation.

5 The ability to inspire and encourage employees to behave in agreement with the vision of an organization and to accomplish the organization's goals is

A. diversity.

B. teamwork.

C. leadership.

D. motivation.

6 What type of statement describes what an operation wants to become and why it exists?

A. Goal statement

B. Vision statement

C. Mission statement

D. Objective statement

7 The process that an operation uses to integrate new employees into an organization is called

A. training.

B. diversity.

C. orientation.

D. onboarding.

8 What type of training would you use if you needed to teach a new employee how to prepare menu items?

A. Role-playing

B. Cross-training

C. Group-training

D. On-the-job training

Exam Prep Answers

1. D
2. A
3. A
4. A
5. C
6. B
7. C
8. D
9. A
10. D

9. When an employee learns the functions of another job within the operation is it known as

   A. cross-training.

   B. group-training.

   C. on-the-job training.

   D. onboarding-training.

10. What is the most effective way to rate employee performance?

    A. Employer feedback

    B. Question and answer

    C. Group evaluation meetings

    D. Performance appraisal forms

Chapter 9 Overview

Fruits and vegetables are used throughout all cuisines. They are grown locally or shipped globally. They are used fresh, dried, frozen, or cooked. Using fruits and vegetables in cuisine depends upon proper selection and handling practices.

Section 1: The first section reviews the types and grades of fruit, as well as factors that impact purchasing decisions, proper storage, preparation, and cooking methods.

Section 2: The second section reviews the types and grades of vegetables, as well as factors that impact purchasing decisions, proper storage, preparation, and cooking methods.

Advance Preparation	
Review	Review Sections 9.1–9.2
	Relevant material in earlier chapters
Contact	Biology or chemistry teacher for litmus paper or pH test strips
	Computer lab for Internet
	Principal or other administrator for planter or section of greenhouse
Prepare	Costumes for Reader's Theater
	Apples and corers, peelers, knives, and other apple equipment
	Clear containers
	Kitchen acids (vinegar, lemon juice)
	Kitchen bases (baking soda, milk of magnesia)
	Paper towels
	Litmus paper or pH test strips
	Nasturtium seeds
	Red cabbage
	Broccoli
	Spinach
	Carrots
	Any other fruits or vegetables desired

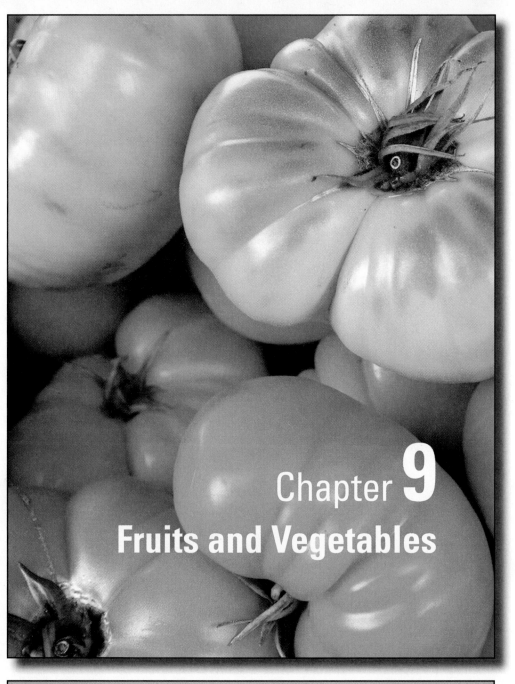

Chapter 9
Fruits and Vegetables

CUSTOMIZED INSTRUCTION OPTIONS

Less Advanced Students	More Advanced Students	ESOL Students	Special Needs Students
Pages 563, 591	Pages 563, 577, 602	Pages 561, 562, 563, 576	Page 563

CHAPTER TOOLS

21st-Century Skills	Mathematics	Science	Literacy
Pages 547, 554, 559, 564, 584	Page 580	Pages 560, 561, 572, 592	Pages 547, 551, 554, 574, 584

ServSafe Connection

Page 581

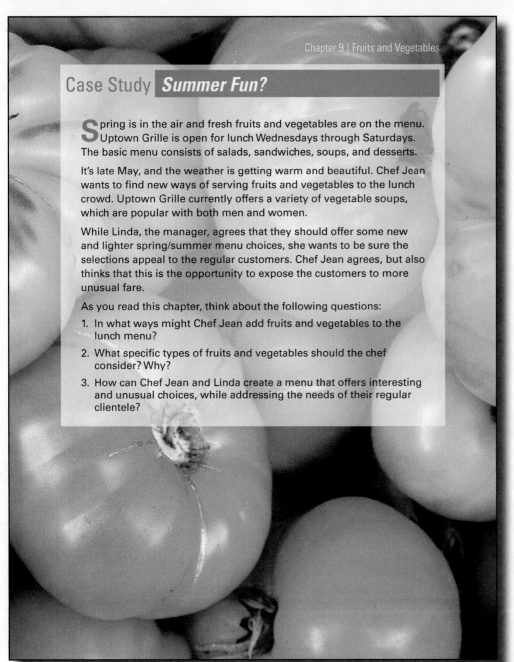

Case Study | *Summer Fun?*

Spring is in the air and fresh fruits and vegetables are on the menu. Uptown Grille is open for lunch Wednesdays through Saturdays. The basic menu consists of salads, sandwiches, soups, and desserts.

It's late May, and the weather is getting warm and beautiful. Chef Jean wants to find new ways of serving fruits and vegetables to the lunch crowd. Uptown Grille currently offers a variety of vegetable soups, which are popular with both men and women.

While Linda, the manager, agrees that they should offer some new and lighter spring/summer menu choices, she wants to be sure the selections appeal to the regular customers. Chef Jean agrees, but also thinks that this is the opportunity to expose the customers to more unusual fare.

As you read this chapter, think about the following questions:

1. In what ways might Chef Jean add fruits and vegetables to the lunch menu?

2. What specific types of fruits and vegetables should the chef consider? Why?

3. How can Chef Jean and Linda create a menu that offers interesting and unusual choices, while addressing the needs of their regular clientele?

Case Study
Summer Fun?

- Fruits and vegetables are seasonal items, especially if local crops are used.
- While the students may brainstorm from past restaurant experience, also encourage them to remember a few chapters back to fruit soups, coulis, salsa, and other foods made with fresh fruits and vegetables.
- Student responses will vary to how Chef Jean could add fruits and vegetables to the lunch menu. They could add some creative seasonal salads, some fruit-based desserts, and perhaps even chilled soups like gazpacho, Swedish cherry soup, or green gage plum cream soup.
- The chef should consider the fruits and vegetables that are grown locally. Not only will they be accessible when they are in season, but they will be more flavorful because they can be harvested and shipped closer to optimal ripeness.
- If the menu remains essentially the same, with one or two new or added items in each category, then the clients will be comfortable with the additions.

Professional Profile

Discuss	How does Chef Kinder's first point relate to students' careers? Ask students about Chef Kinder's second point. Do they consider themselves artists?
Reinforce and Review	Not only is the work environment like a family, but the restaurant itself can be as well. If dining guests feel warm and welcome, they will want to visit again. Ask students if they have ever thought of a restaurant experience as a mini-vacation. Cambaceres and Tallyrand were noted French bon vivants during the Napoleonic period. The food creations were dedicated to providing pleasure to the dining guest.
Teaching Tips	How can students share a successful dish over and over? Remember to standardize a recipe by keeping careful records. The results are then repeatable.

[professional profile]

Daron A. Kinder

Chef / Owner, The Porterhouse

I started working in the culinary field when I was 13 years old. The first restaurant job I had was a local family-style restaurant called Alize at the Elberta Inn Restaurant, located in Vermilion, OH. I worked as a dishwasher for one week and then, because an employee walked off the job, I was able to move up into the pantry position. During my time there I noticed two things:

1. Because of the long hours, you develop friendships that feel more like a second family. And, just like with a family, you want to go back and visit them the following day because you had such a great time.

2. Unlike an artist who creates one piece of art and sells it to one person, I can re-create the same art over and over again and let everyone share the same experience.

My career education started at EHOVE Career Center in Milan, OH. Our class used the ProStart curriculum as the fundamental basis for our advancement. We studied chapter by chapter. Along with the normal class routine, I had the option of participating in culinary competitions. And really ....the best competition I attended was the ProStart competition. In this competition, we had to prepare a three-course meal only using nonelectrical equipment and a butane burner. Along with the meal preparation, we had to design a menu, prepare food costings, project the sale price, and construct recipes for each dish and sauce we prepared.

I then went on to receive my associate's degree in culinary arts and bachelor's degree in culinary business management from the Culinary Institute of America in Hyde Park, NY. My college was very diverse; there were students from all over the world. One day, I was given the personal task of preparing guacamole for the day's service. Many of my fellow students had some experience and insight on how to prepare the "best" guacamole. So, we all stopped what we were doing and pulled up the classroom chairs around the prep table. We must have spent 30 minutes debating about how to prepare the perfect guacamole, while our other classmates finished their daily tasks. The chef was furious, until we explained what we were doing. Eventually, we all started preparing our unique recipes. And, to this day, I've never tasted a guacamole as fresh, diverse in flavors, and perfect as I did that very day.

You know, when guests come into your restaurant, there are three things they look for: self-fulfillment, entertainment, and relaxation. People consider a restaurant experience to be a sort of mini-vacation, a chance to get away from any stressful situation. In this profession, we work very hard to ensure that all of our customers leave their problems at the door and, for the next hour or two, have a wonderful, relaxing experience.

So, if you are interested in this field, plan on enjoying every single minute of it. There will be rough times, a lot of stress, and some long hours, but the self-satisfaction you can get makes it all worthwhile.

Remember:

" *The great sonatas of the stove were known by their dedication to Cambaceres or Talleyrand and not by their creators' names.* **"** —Pierre Hamp

About Fruits and Vegetables

Of course, you can get fruits and vegetables all year-round, but there is a noticeable difference in the quality and flavor when a particular product is in season. And I enjoy the many new gene-spliced fruits and vegetables coming out year after year to entice consumers into trying something new and educating their palates. A good example of this is the lematos—a cross between a tomato and a lemon. Not the best mix, but very creative!

So, my favorites? Well, I particularly like the Tomato Napoleon and the Delarobi Fruit Tart.

Tomato Napoleon: This dish alone, when all the products are in season, is just magnificent. A simple balsamic reduction smeared on the plate with layers and layers of fresh and vibrant flavors stacked next to it—just wonderful! I love to use red and yellow tomatoes with arugula and slices of red onion accompanied with slices of fresh-made mozzarella cheese and the best olive oil you can buy. This is a dish that people crave.

Delarobi Fruit Tart: This is a very simple dessert with a lasting impression. A flaky tart accompanied with pastry cream and seasonal berries—fabulous. And to make this simple dessert even better, you can prepare a fresh chutney, compote, or even a coulis to serve with it. This dessert, using seasonal produce, guarantees that your customers are tasting the season in its purest form.

545

Teaching Tip
- The dish he refers to as Tomato Napoleon, is sometimes called Caprese Salad.
- The season's freshest and most flavorful fruits and vegetables can help inform and inspire a menu.

Focus and Engage

Discuss

- Ask students what foods come to mind when they think about healthy eating. Students can reflect on the case study and the professional profile.
- Have the students already developed an idea in their minds about fruits and vegetables on the menu?

Section 9.1
Fruits

Introduce the Section

a. The students will become familiar with many types of fruit.
b. There are USDA grades for quality.
c. Fruit purchasing and storage require knowledge and skill.
d. Fruits may be prepared a variety of ways for the guest.
e. Fruits offer vast varieties of color, flavor, and texture.

Vocabulary Review

a. Direct students to the key terms.
b. Pronounce each word, and have the students repeat the pronunciation out loud.
c. Discuss the definition of each word.

Teach

Discuss

- Types of fruit include citrus, pommes, melons, berries, drupes, and tropical.
- The USDA quality grades are: U.S. Extra Fancy, U.S. Fancy, U.S. No. 1, U.S. No. 2, and U.S. No. 3.
- Purchasing decisions are based upon season, availability, quality, freshness, price, menu selection and nutrient profile.
- Store fruit with an awareness of ethylene gas and its effect on ripeness. Also, fruit needs to be cool and protected to maintain both freshness and moisture. To ripen, store at 65–70°F. To store ripe fruit, refrigerate at 41°F or lower. Do not chill bananas.

9.1 Fruits	9.2 Vegetables
• Types and market forms	• Types and market forms
• Purchasing fruits	• Purchasing vegetables
• Storing fruits	• Storing vegetables
• Preparing fruits	• Preparing vegetables
• Cooking fruits	• Cooking vegetables

SECTION 9.1 FRUITS

Fruit is one of the most healthy and natural foods, containing vitamins and minerals that we need. Our initial experience with fruit occurs during the first year of life when we eat baby food. As we grow, we are introduced to whole fruit like apples, bananas, pears, peaches, and berries. As our taste buds mature, we start to enjoy fruit in cooking.

Although fruit is commonly used in desserts, they are also part of other delicious dishes. Fruit can be grilled, broiled, poached, sautéed, baked, and microwaved. This section identifies the various types of fruit, cooking methods, and how to purchase and store fruit.

Study Questions

After studying Section 9.1, you should be able to answer the following questions:

- What are the various types of fruit?
- What are the USDA quality grades for fresh fruits and vegetables?
- What factors affect purchasing decisions?
- How do you properly store fruit?
- What are the steps in preparing fruit for service?
- What are the various methods for cooking fruit?

Types and Market Forms

Scientifically speaking, a **fruit** is an organ that develops from the ovary of a flowering plant and contains one or more seeds. From a culinary point of view, fruit can be the perfect snack food, or the basis of a dessert, colorful sauce or soup, or an addition to meat, fish, shellfish, or poultry. No food group offers a greater variety of colors, flavors, and textures than fruit.

546

- Fruits need to be evaluated for ripeness, and then washed carefully. Fruits are then dealt with according to variety. They may be peeled, cored, or sectioned, to remove inedible portions. Peeled fruits that will enzymatically brown should be treated with a mild acid like lemon juice to prevent browning during service.
- Fruits may be poached, boiled, baked, roasted, fried, sautéed, grilled, or broiled.

Vocabulary Terms

- **Fruit:** The seed-bearing ovary of a flowering plant.

Fruit is often used in sweet dishes, such as puddings, pies, and jellies. It can also be found in salads or appetizers. Fruit is used to cut the richness of meats like pork and duck, or brighten the delicate flavor of fish and veal.

Fruit is both delicious and nutritious. The sweetness of fruit comes from **fructose** (FROOK-tose), a natural form of sugar. Generally, people find fruit to be refreshing and an excellent source of dietary fiber.

Did You Know...?

Is fructose bad for you? Fructose is a monosaccharide, a simple sugar. It is a natural sugar. A small amount of fructose, such as the amount found in most vegetables and fruits, is not a bad thing. But it is difficult for the body to process too much fructose at once. Fructose provides empty calories.

In earlier times, diets contained only very small amounts of fructose. These days, nutrition researchers estimate that about 10 percent of the calories in our diets come from fructose.

Fruit can be purchased in a variety of market forms:

- Fresh—including whole and cut up
- Frozen
- Canned
- Dried

Fruits are grouped by growing season and location. The three main groups of fruit are summer, winter, and tropical.

Summer Fruits

Summer fruits include berries, cherries, grapes, melons, peaches, nectarines, plums, and pears. Most summer fruits are delicious when eaten raw. They are also popular baked or cooked in different foods.

Fruits that have a central pit enclosing a single seed are known as **drupes**. Cherries, plums, peaches, nectarines, and apricots are examples of drupes. Table 9.1 lists the characteristics of each type of summer fruit and provides a photo of each.

547

**Fast Fact:
Did You Know...?**

High-fructose corn syrup is used to sweeten soda pop and other foods.

**In-Class Activity:
Mnemonic Device**

Literacy Connection, 21st-Century Skills—Use Systems Thinking

Have the students think of a rhyme, song, or saying that begins with each of the first letters of the following words:

Fresh

Frozen

Canned

Dried

Have them share their creations.

Vocabulary Terms

- **Fructose:** Naturally occurring pentose sugar in plants.
- **Summer fruits:** Fruits that are in season only in the summer months.
- **Drupes:** Fruit with a central pit.

Why are green grapes called "white"?

What color is the juice of a white grape?

Table 9.1:
Summer Fruits (continued on p. 549)

- The students should be able to use personal experience or brief research to name one dish based on cherries and one on grapes.

[fast fact]

Did You Know...?

Did you know that grapes are 80 percent water? Grapes grow in clusters of 6 to 300. They can be many colors, including red, black, dark blue, yellow, green, and pink. What we call "white" grapes are really green in color. Grapes can be eaten raw or used to make jam, juice, jelly, vinegar, wine, raisins, and grape seed oil.

Table 9.1: Summer Fruits

Name	Characteristics	Sample varieties
Cherries	• Cherries are available in many colors. • They vary in texture from hard and crisp to soft and juicy. • Flavors run from very tart to very sweet. • Sweet red cherries are the most popular. • USES: Sweet cherries are usually used in cooking. Tart varieties are best used in baking and preserves.	• Queen Anne • Bing • Montmorence—used as maraschino cherries; can be candied or baked
Grapes	• Grapes grow in clusters on vines. • They are smooth skinned and available with or without seeds. The flavor and color are in the skin. • Technically, grapes are berries, but they are grouped separately because they have so many uses, including eating, cooking, and wine making. • USES: Wine grapes are tarter than the sweeter table grapes. Table grapes work well in salads and desserts.	• Thompson seedless • Napoleon • Concord

(continued)

Table 9.1: Summer Fruits *continued*

Name	Characteristics	Sample varieties
Melons	• Succulent and fragrant, these fruits are related to squash and cucumbers. They are categorized into two groups: sweet melons and watermelons. • Sweet melons have tan, green, or yellow skin. The rind is very tough, while the flesh is rich and flavorful. These melons have a network of seeds at the center. • Watermelons are much larger than sweet melons and have a smooth, thick green skin. Watermelon flesh is usually deep pink with a light, crisp texture. Seeds are found throughout the melon, although you can now buy seedless watermelons. • USES: Melons can be served as appetizers, salads, or desserts. Cantaloupe is a popular breakfast fruit. They are attractive when cut into decorative shapes for use in fruit trays, salads, and garnishes.	Sweet melons • Cantaloupe (muskmelon) • Crenshaw • Honeydew Watermelons • Jubilee • Crimson Sweet
Peaches, apricots, and nectarines	• Peaches are sweet and juicy, with a distinctive fuzzy skin. They come in two categories: freestone and clingstone. The flesh of freestone peaches separates easily from the pit, while clingstone peaches have flesh that clings to the pit. Peach flesh varies in color from white to creamy yellow to yellow-orange to red. • Apricots resemble peaches with their fuzzy skin, but are smaller and slightly drier. • Nectarines are similar to peaches in color, shape, and flavor. They have smooth skin, with flesh that resembles the texture of plums. • USES: All three fruits work well in salads and desserts (both hot and cold).	Peaches • Redhaven • Elberta • J.H. Hale Apricots • Hunter • Orange Red • Rival Nectarines • Redgold • Juneglo • Summer Beaut

(continued)

549

Table 9.1(continued)

• The students should be able to use personal experience or brief research to name a dish based on melons, and one based on peaches, apricots, or nectarines.

Table 9.1 (continued)

- The students should be able to use personal experience or brief research to name one dish based on plums, one based on pears, and one based on berries.

Fast Fact:
Did You Know...?

Pay for teachers was usually a place to live and food to eat, with few, if any, luxuries.

Table 9.1: Summer Fruits *continued*

Name	Characteristics	Sample varieties
Plums	• Plums range in size from as small as an apricot to as large as a peach. • They come in many shades of green, red, and purple. • There are two categories: dessert and cooking. Cooking plums are generally drier and more acidic than dessert plums. • Dried plums are called prunes. These are often eaten as a snack and can play an important role in promoting good digestive health. • USES: Both can be eaten raw or used in both sweet and savory dishes.	• Red Beauty • Black Beauty • Santa Rosa
Pears	• Pears have a sweet taste, with a smooth, juicy flesh. • They do not ripen entirely on the tree; they're usually picked and then allowed to continue to ripen. A ripened pear will have a good fragrance and be tender on the stem end. • USES: Firm pears should be used in cooking.	• Bartlett • Bosc • d'Anjou
Berries	• Of the summer fruits, berries are the most highly perishable, tender, and fragile. • The best way to work with berries is to handle them very little and serve them as soon as possible. • USES: They are often used in salads, jams, and desserts.	• Blueberries • Raspberries • Blackberries • Boysenberries • Strawberries

[fast fact]

Did You Know...?

Did you know that apples float because 25 percent of an apple's volume is air? And did you know that "an apple for the teacher" came from the time when teachers were so poorly paid that parents would also provide food?

550

Winter Fruits

Though summer fruits are plentiful, winter also offers a good selection of fruit that provides plenty of nutrition and great taste. Winter fruits include apples and citrus fruits, such as oranges, grapefruits, lemons, limes, and tangerines. Table 9.2 lists the characteristics of each type of **winter fruit**.

Table 9.2: Winter Fruits

Name	Characteristics	Sample varieties
Citrus fruits	• Citrus fruits are characterized by thick skins, aromatic oils, and segmented flesh. • They are also abundant in vitamin C. • The flavor of citrus fruits ranges from a very sweet orange to a very tart, sour lemon. • USES: All citrus fruits can be served fresh, candied, and as juice; as appetizers, garnishes, and desserts; or as part of salads or main dishes.	• Oranges • Grapefruits • Lemons • Limes • Tangelos • Tangerines
Apples	• Apples are among the most commonly used and available fruits. • They have smooth skin and firm flesh and can be tender or crisp. • The flavor of apples ranges from very tart, like the Granny Smith, to very sweet, like the Golden Delicious. • USES: Tart apples are used for cooking and baking. Sweet apples are best when eaten raw.	• Red Delicious • Golden Delicious • Rome • McIntosh • Granny Smith

[fast fact]

Did You Know...?

1. Each year, 68 million tons of apples are produced by apple growers.

2. China leads the word in apple production, followed by the United States.

3. Delicious, Golden Delicious, and Granny Smith account for about half of the apples produced in the United States.

551

In-Class Activity: A Misnomer?

Literacy Connection

Ask the students if they are familiar with the term misnomer. Ask them to look it up if they do not know it.

It means misnamed.

Apples do not produce in the cold winter months. They ripen in the fall. However, they store well through the winter.

Citrus fruits ripen during fall and early winter months, but not in cold places. A hard freeze can kill a citrus crop.

Is it a misnomer to call apples and citrus fruits winter fruits?

Have the students rename the category of fruits, and share what they come up with.

Table 9.2: Winter Fruits

- The students should be able to use personal experience or brief research to name one dish based on citrus fruits and one based on apples.

Fast Fact: Did You Know...?

Apples are very popular in the United States, but they are also eaten in other temperate climates.

Vocabulary Terms

- **Winter fruit:** Apples and citrus fruit.

- The students should be able to use personal experience or brief research to name one dish based on bananas, one based on figs, one on kiwis, and one on mangos.

Vocabulary Terms

- **Tropical fruit:** Fruit that grows in the zones between the 23rd parallels, which includes the equator.

Tropical Fruits

Tropical fruits are named for the climatic conditions under which they are grown. None of these fruits can tolerate frost. Tropical fruits include figs, dates, kiwis, mangos, bananas, papayas, pomegranates, guava, star fruit, and passion fruit. Table 9.3 lists the characteristics of each type of tropical fruit.

Table 9.3: Tropical Fruits		
Name	**Characteristics**	**Sample varieties**
Bananas	• Unlike most fruits, bananas are picked almost green and allowed to ripen as they travel from the farm to the buyer. • Flavors range from sweet to mild. • Bananas are rich in carbohydrates, fiber, vitamins, and minerals (such as potassium). • Some varieties of tree-ripened bananas are juicy. • USES: Fully ripe bananas are excellent for eating and baking. Green bananas can be used for cooking.	• Cavendish • Burro • Plantain
Figs	• A very versatile fruit, figs are green or black. • They are best when eaten raw. • Figs have a sweet, delicate flavor and edible seeds. • USES: They are often used in baking pies, cookies, and cakes.	• Mission • Kadota • Brown Turkey
Kiwis	• Kiwis are also known as Chinese gooseberries. • Kiwis have fuzzy skin and bright, green-colored flesh. Their insides have tiny edible seeds. • Their flavor is similar to that of strawberries. • USES: Kiwis are excellent as a garnish or for adding color and texture to fruit salads.	• Hayward • Chico • Golden
Mangos	• Mangos are medium-sized, thick-skinned fruits with a light-yellow flesh. • They have a spicy-sweet flavor. • USES: They are an excellent addition to fruit salads, and they go well with spices, such as curry.	• Tommy Atkins • Ataulfo • Keitt

(continued)

552

Table 9.3: Tropical Fruits *continued*

Name	Characteristics	Sample varieties
Papayas	• Papayas have a soft, juicy, pink-orange flesh with a central mass of black seeds. • They have a sweet-tart flavor. • Freezing them destroys their flavor and texture. • USES: Ripe papayas can be eaten raw, and unripe papayas can be cooked and served like vegetables.	• Solo • Rainbow • Maradol
Pineapples	• Pineapples have a diamond-pattern skin and golden flesh. • They are very juicy when ripe, with a tangy sweet-tart flavor. • USES: Pineapples are often used in baking, and can be puréed to make fresh juice.	• Red Spanish • Cayenne • Sugarloaf
Coconuts	• The coconut has several layers. Its outermost layer is a smooth, light brown covering that is usually removed before shipping. Next is the familiar dark brown, hairy shell. Beneath that is a thin, brown skin covering the bright, white meat. • A ripe coconut should be heavy and sound full of liquid when shaken. Mold at its eyes indicates poor quality. • USES: Coconut meat is eaten raw, cooked in many recipes, and pressed to make coconut oil. In the center is the juice, called coconut water. Coconut milk is not the juice from the center, but is a mixture of warm water and coconut meat.	• Dwarf and tall varieties, named after their place of origin, such as Fiji dwarf and Panama tall

Table 9.3 (continued)

• The students should be able to use personal experience or brief research to name one dish based on papayas, one on pineapples, and one on coconuts.

Discuss

• Have you ever bitten into a bad piece of fruit?
• How could you tell it was bad?
• Should freshness be evaluated?
• Would you serve fruit that wasn't fresh in a restaurant?
• What would happen to your job, or your restaurant, if you served bad fruit?

How do you know when fruits and vegetables are fresh and of a high quality? Characteristics of freshness vary from one item to another, but there are some common traits. See Table 9.4. Fruits and vegetables should be plump and free of bruises, mold, brown or soft spots, and pest damage. Any attached leaves should be firm and not wilted. Overall, the color and texture should be appropriate to the particular type of fruit or vegetable. Figure 9.1 shows an example of damaged fruit and good fruit.

Figure 9.1: Damaged fruit (left) has bruises and mold. Fresh fruit (right) has a clear appearance free of bruises, mold, or soft spots.

553

Figure Focus

Figure 9.1: Throw away any fruit that has mold. Bruises might be difficult to see but often can be felt.

Table 9.4:
Characteristics of Fresh Fruit
(continued on p. 555)

- The students should be able to evaluate the quality of any fruit listed in the table.

In-Class Activity:
Reader's Theater

Literacy Connection, 21st-Century Skills—Communicate Clearly

The students will participate in a reader's theater. Three students or three groups of students will appear.

The text of the script will be the information found in Table 9.4.

The first student or group will say, very dramatically, the name of the fruit.

The second student or group will describe, very dramatically, the qualities of freshness for that fruit.

The third student or group will describe, very dramatically, the signs of poor quality for that fruit when it goes bad.

Costumes should be encouraged.

Have fun with it!

Table 9.4: Characteristics of Fresh Fruits

Fruits	Signs of Good Quality	Signs of Poor Quality
Apples	Firmness; crispness; bright color	Softness; bruises (Irregularly shaped brown or tan areas do not usually affect quality).
Apricots	Bright, uniform color; plumpness	Dull color; shriveled appearance
Bananas	Firmness; brightness of color	Grayish or dull appearance (indicates exposure to cold and inability to ripen properly)
Blueberries	Dark blue color with silvery bloom	Moist berries
Cantaloupes	Stem should be gone; netting or veining should be coarse; skin should be yellow-gray or pale yellow	Bright yellow color; mold; large bruises
Cherries	Very dark color; plumpness	Dry stems; soft flesh; gray mold
Coconuts	Liquid inside when shaken; hard shell	Cracks; wet "eyes"
Figs	Plumpness	Soft areas; dull color
Grapefruit	Should be heavy for its size	Soft areas; dull color
Grapes	Should be firmly attached to stems; bright color and plumpness are good signs	Drying stems; leaking berries
Honeydew	Soft skin; faint aroma; yellowish white to creamy rind color	White or greenish color; bruises or water-soaked areas; cuts or punctures in rind
Lemons	Firmness; heaviness; rich yellow color	Dull color; shriveled skin
Limes	Glossy skin; heavy weight	Dry skin; molds
Mangos	Plumpness; firmness	Clear color; blemishes
Nectarines	Plumpness; firmness	Green skin; very hard or soft skin
Oranges	Firmness; heaviness; bright color	Dry skin; spongy texture; blue mold
Papayas	Firmness; symmetry	Dark green skin; bruises
Peaches	Slightly soft flesh	A pale tan spot (indicates beginning of decay); very hard or very soft flesh
Pears	Firmness	Dull skin; shriveling spots on the sides

(continued)

Table 9.4: Characteristics of Fresh Fruits *continued*

Fruits	Signs of Good Quality	Signs of Poor Quality
Pineapples	"Spike" at top should separate easily from flesh	Mold; large bruises; unpleasant odor; brown leaves
Plums	Fairly firm to slightly soft flesh	Leaking; brownish discoloration
Raspberries	Stem caps should be absent; flesh should be plump and tender	Mushiness; wet spots on containers (signs of possible decay of berries)
Strawberries	Stem cap should be attached; berries should have a rich red color	Gray mold; large uncolored areas
Tangerines	Bright orange or deep yellow color; loose skin	Punctured skin; mold
Watermelon	Smooth surface; creamy underside; bright red flesh	Stringy or mealy flesh (spoilage difficult to see on outside)

[nutrition]

Drupes, Anyone?

Drupes are a type of fruit with a center stone. Orange drupes have no relationship to oranges (citrus fruits) at all. Orange drupes are peaches, nectarines (which are actually a type of peach), and apricots. They are all good sources of beta-carotene, which gives them their orange color. Beta-carotene is present in both fresh and cooked fruit.

Beta-carotene is pro-vitamin A, which the body can convert to vitamin A. It is also an antioxidant. Antioxidants can prevent or slow the oxidative damage to our body. When our body cells use oxygen, they naturally produce free radicals (by-products) which can cause damage. Antioxidants can prevent and repair damage done by these free radicals.

In addition to beta-carotene, these fruits are rich in fiber and glucose. Apricots contain a whopping 2 grams of dietary fiber in every 100 grams of fruit, with peaches and nectarines close behind at 1.5 and 1.7 grams, respectively. And all three are very low in calories: per 100 grams of fruit, an apricot contains 50 calories, a peach 40 calories, and a nectarine 44 calories. They are naturally fat-free and cholesterol-free. Best of all, they taste great! They can be used in a variety of recipes—fresh, cooked, or dried.

Purchasing Fruits

Some fruits, such as bananas, apples, pears, and grapes, are available all year. The quality, degree of ripeness, and price vary with the season. Other fruits, such as peaches, plums, mangos, and berries, have a specific growing season. Knowing the growing season for a particular fruit is important. During its growing season, the fruit is plentiful, the quality is higher, and the price is usually lower. Some operations have seasonal menus that are based on what is fresh and

Table 9.4 (continued)

- The students should be able to evaluate the quality of any fruit listed in the table

Nutrition: Drupes, Anyone?

Orange drupes are an excellent source of beta-carotene, while orange oranges are not.

Teaching Tips

- Ask the students to tell you if they are in the Northern or Southern hemisphere. Then ask them what month it is.
- After they have correctly answered those simple questions, ask them to name local fruit that is in season.
- Ask them to name fruit that can be shipped in from other parts of the world.

555

Discuss

- How could a freeze in Brazil impact the price of a meal served in Denver?
- Help the students to realize that fruit is part of the global economy.
- Help them to also realize that weather impacts the crops.
- Can weather be controlled, at least in the short term?

Teaching Tips

- Purchasing decisions must be made wisely because fresh fruit can deteriorate if they are not used in time.
- Since fresh fruit tends to be expensive, deterioration and waste are expensive.
- Purchasing requirements are guided by the recipes you use.
- If a new member of the kitchen staff does not know proper and efficient techniques for preparing fresh fruit, time will be lost.
- The limitations of the restaurant, community, vendors, along with other factors, must be considered when making purchasing choices.

Reinforce and Review

- The way the fruit is to be used dictates the grade that can be used.
- Apples for applesauce do not have to look as beautiful as apples for a fruit basket.
- The lower grades may still be fresh, ripe, tasty, and perfectly safe to use.
- The upper grades still need timely and proper handling and care.
- The lowest grade may have poor texture and flavor, but still be safe to eat.

Vocabulary Terms

- **Quality grades:** Identifying categories of quality.

---

locally available. Many customers today have shown interest in eating local produce and supporting the restaurants that serve it.

Other factors that could affect the purchasing decisions an operation makes include the following:

- **Recipe requirements:** Many standardized recipes identify specific varieties and market forms needed.
- **Staff skills:** Highly skilled employees can handle natural, uncut produce efficiently. Employees with fewer skills in peeling and cutting will often need to use processed products.
- **Available equipment:** Operations must consider what types of equipment are available before choosing fruits.
- **Vendor limitations:** Purchasers must spend time to find the vendor that best meets an operation's needs.

Grading

The U.S. Department of Agriculture (USDA), has developed quality grades for fresh fruits and canned fruits. **Quality grades** are like a rating system based on quality standards—the better the quality, the higher the quality grade assigned to it. The quality is based on a combination of size, color, shape, texture, and defects. The price is also usually higher for the best grades.

Fresh fruits are graded before shipping. USDA grades (from highest to lowest) for fresh fruits include U.S. Extra Fancy, U.S. Fancy, U.S. No. 1, U.S. No. 2, and U.S. No. 3. Most fruits purchased for foodservice operations are U.S. Fancy. Fruit with lower grades can be used in dishes such as baked pies, puddings, jams, jellies, and cobblers, where their appearance is not important.

Canned products rated U.S. Grade A Fancy have the highest quality among canned goods. This means that the fruits' colors and flavors are excellent and their sizes and shapes are perfectly uniform. U.S. Grade B Choice are rated second best, which means that their overall colors and flavors are average. U.S. Grade C Standard means that the quality is poor. Some of the pieces may be bruised and mushy and have several imperfections.

[fast fact]

Did You Know...?

Sneezing from hay fever is not unusual, especially in the springtime. There are pollens in the air that cause allergy symptoms in many people. However, eating certain fruits can also cause an allergic reaction, even in a person who isn't truly "allergic" to the fruit. It can be worse during the pollen season. It's called oral allergy syndrome.

The body recognizes protein in the fruit as the pollen that causes hay fever. It's a mistake the body makes, but it causes symptoms just the same. The most obvious is itching in the mouth right after eating the fruit.

The most common culprits are melons, kiwi, and apples. The symptoms don't usually last a long time. If the fruit is cooked, there may be no symptoms at all. If a person was truly allergic to the food itself, cooked fruit would cause symptoms, too.

In rare cases, OAS may cause severe allergic symptoms including asthma and even anaphylaxis. Anaphylaxis is a life-threatening allergic reaction. Keeping an EpiPen on hand, especially during allergy season, may save a life. An EpiPen is an automatic injection device that administers epinephrine. It can help stop allergic reactions quickly and allow you to get the medical help necessary.

Storing Fruits

All fruits must be properly stored. Many ripe fruits, except for bananas, can be stored at 41°F or lower. Under the best circumstances, fruits should be stored in their own refrigerator, separate from vegetables.

Certain fruits (including apples, bananas, melons, and avocados) emit **ethylene** (ETH-el-leen) **gas,** which causes fruits to ripen. While this increases ripening in some unripe fruits, it also causes ripe fruits and vegetables to spoil. Ethylene-producing fruits should be stored in sealed containers if separate refrigeration or storage is not available. Another reason to store fruits and vegetables separately is because some produce, such as onions or garlic, give off odors that taint the natural, delicate flavors of dairy items. Most fruits need to be kept dry because excess moisture causes produce to spoil quickly. To keep moisture down, use the fruit bins in refrigerators, which have lower humidity than the rest of the refrigerator; don't wash fruit until just before using it; and don't store it in tightly closed plastic bags.

Fruit that needs to ripen should be stored at room temperatures of 65°F to 70°F. Some citrus fruits have a longer life, but most restaurants limit the storage of citrus produce items to three weeks.

557

Teaching Tips

- Bananas should not be refrigerated.
- Avocados and other ethylene gas emitters can ripen each other after purchase.
- Store fruit away from ethylene emitters.
- Storage should have good airflow.
- Plastic storage bags prevent airflow.
- Do not plan to store fruit for a long time.
- Enjoy them very fresh, at the height of their ripeness, texture, flavor, and nutrient value.
- Fruit may be safely stored out of the refrigerator under certain circumstances.
- Do not allow any stored fruit to become warm or hot, unless you are cooking it.

Vocabulary Terms

- **Ethylene gas:** A gas emitted by certain fruit that can cause other fruit to ripen.

Discuss

- Why is it important to wash fresh fruit before eating it?
- What if the fruit has a peel that will be removed? Does it still need to be washed?

Teaching Tips

- Fresh produce may be sprayed with insecticide. It is wise to remove this before serving.
- Anything on the skin can find its way to the flesh of the fruit on a knife blade or even a clean, gloved hand.
- Even organic fruit should be washed. Chemical insecticides may not be used, but manure might be.
- Some manure solutions are sprayed onto crops with pumps.
- Always wash fresh fruits and vegetables.
- There is a proper way to cut and prepare each type of fruit. Sometimes, there may be more than one way.

Preparing Fruits

Cleaning

Cleaning is the first step in preparing fruits. It is important to wash fruit for the following reasons:

- The skin on fruit can carry a number of pathogens.
- Fruits are exposed to chemicals, dirt, animals, and pests while growing and while being prepared for sale.

There are special solutions available for cleaning fruits. Wash fruits as close to preparation time as possible.

Use cold water and a gentle touch to avoid bruising fruits while handling them. Fragile berries such as blackberries and raspberries are not always washed. Use a brush on fruits with heavy rinds to scrub away any residue on the skin.

Peeling, Seeding, Trimming

Fruits often need to be prepared before they are served. Different fruits get prepared different ways. Preparation includes removing skins, removing cores, removing seeds and stones, zesting, and removing stems:

- **Remove skins:** Some fruits, such as berries and cherries, are not peeled. Others, such as oranges and bananas, can be peeled by hand: simply grasp an edge of the peel and pull. Still other fruits, such as papayas and apples, must be peeled with a paring knife: carefully cut into the fruit, just below the skin, and cut away long strips of peel. Sturdier fruits like pineapples are stood on end, and the peel is cut away with a utility or chef's knife. Figure 9.2 shows a prep cook using a paring knife to peel an apple.

Figure 9.2: Use a paring knife or peeler to remove skin.

- **Remove cores:** Most fruits do not have cores. Pineapples are halved lengthwise, and the core is cut out with a knife. To core apples and pears, scoop out the seeds with a parisienne scoop and use a paring knife to remove the slender core that runs from the stem end to the blossom end.

Figure Focus

Figure 9.2: Is this the only correct way to prepare an apple?

- **Remove seeds and stones:** To seed fruits with large cavities, like papayas or melons, cut the fruit in half and scoop out the seeds with a spoon, taking care to remove as little flesh as possible. To seed citrus fruits, such as oranges or lemons, cut the fruit horizontally and remove the seeds with the tip of a paring knife. To remove cherry stones, use a cherry pitter. Both hand tools and larger hopper-based devices are available. For other stone fruits, cut vertically through the fruit and twist the two sides of the fruit apart. The stone can then be pulled or cut from the flesh. To remove a pit from a mango, cut off each flat side on the fruit, and then cut away the remaining flesh from the pit.

Figure 9.3: Zest is the outermost layer of a citrus fruit.

- **Zest:** This technique is primarily used to obtain the aromatic oils in the skins of citrus fruits. Only the surface of the skin is removed, leaving behind the bitter, white pith. Use either a microplane or a zester to zest the fruit; alternately, cut and julienne strips of peel. Figure 9.3 shows an orange being zested using a zester.

- **Remove stems:** There are two common ways to remove stems. For harder fruits, twist the stem from the fruit; for softer items, pull the stem directly out of the fruit. A few fruits, like figs, demand that the stem be cut away from the fruit.

Cutting Fruits

Use a sharp knife to cut fruit to ensure that your cuts are clean. This gives the fruit a nice, clean appearance and maintains the fruit's quality because you lose fewer juices. Fruits are often cut into wedges, slices, chunks, or cubes for service. Figure 9.4 shows lemon wedges.

Figure 9.4: For service, fruits are cut into wedges, slices, chunks, or cubes.

559

In-Class Activity: Apple Olympics

21st-Century Skills—Work Effectively in Diverse Teams

Apples are not expensive, and are available year-round throughout the United States. However, another fruit may be substituted to better suit the needs of the classroom.

Review knife safety skills and practices with the students.

Set up several stations for preparing apples. Each station should offer a different method for washing, peeling, coring, slicing, and/or dicing an apple.

Ideas include:

- Peeling first, and then coring and slicing
- Coring before peeling
- Cutting up the apple and then peeling and coring each piece
- Using special equipment for peeling, coring, and slicing
- Using a special coring tool and a knife for peeling and slicing
- Any other variant the teacher wants to include

Have students work in pairs and time each other at each station. Record the times.

Which method was the most efficient for the majority of the students?

Were there some students who preferred a different method than the most popular or efficient one?

Award everyone with slices of apple, with Golden Delicious slices for the winners.

Figure Focus

Figure 9.3: Be sure to wash citrus fruit before zesting.

Figure 9.4: How many lemons do you think a seafood establishment would use in an evening?

Teaching Tips

- As a class, discuss the various methods outlined for preparing fruit.
- Perhaps the students can research other methods used in foodservice.
- Caution the students about using home-based methods without further research.
- Home-based methods may be traditional and comfortable, but may not be the most efficient in a commercial kitchen.

Figure Focus

Figure 9.5: Dried fruits have the same nutritional quality as the fresh versions, but they have less water.

In-Class Activity:
Apples and Enzymatic Browning

Science Connection

Have students test to see if apples can be treated with an edible substance to prevent browning.

Equipment:

One apple, cut into five wedges
Ten clear containers
White vinegar
Lemon juice
Baking soda
Milk of Magnesia
Water
Measuring cups
Litmus paper (pH indicator test strips)
Paper towels

Mix ¼ cup baking soda with ½ cup water in a clear container and stir to dissolve. Label it Baking Soda.

Mix ½ cup Milk of Magnesia with ½ cup water in a clear container and stir to dissolve. Label it Milk of Magnesia.

Put 1 cup water in a clear container and label it Water.

Put 1 cup vinegar in a clear container and label it Vinegar.

Put 1 cup lemon juice in a clear container and label it Lemon Juice.

Test the pH of each cup with litmus paper or other pH indicator test strips and add the pH level to the label.

Students should find that the lemon juice and vinegar are acids, or have a pH below 7. They should find that the baking soda and Milk of Magnesia are bases, and have a pH above 7. Water should have a pH at or near 7.0, which is neutral. Note that all of the liquids are solutions, except water, which is a compound.

Dip a separate apple wedge into each cup, coating the apple completely. Place the apple on a piece of clean paper towel in front of the cup. Students should observe the apples after 30 minutes and record their observations.

Leave the apples out overnight. The next day, ask students to look at the apples and record their observations again. Be sure that they note the time.

Juicing and Puréeing

Fresh fruits can be juiced and puréed. Handheld juicers can be used to juice citrus fruits. Fruit purée is made by putting prepared fruit (peeled, trimmed, or seeded as necessary) into a blender or food processor. If the fruit is soft and juicy, you can make the purée without adding more liquid.

Preparing Dried Fruits

Dried fruit can be served as is, without any advance preparation. However, when it is an ingredient in a dish or baked item, rehydrate or soften dried fruit before adding it. Put dried fruit in a bowl, cover it with warm or hot liquid, and let it sit until it is ready to use. Be sure to drain all liquid before using the fruit. Figure 9.5 shows a bowl of dried fruit.

Figure 9.5: Popular dried fruits include raisins, apples, and figs.

[ServSafe Connection]

Fruit and Cross-Contamination
Wash fruit before using it, and use standard food safety practices to avoid cross-contamination from fruit to the cutting board, knives, or your own hands.

Be particularly careful with melons. Scrub the rind with a sanitized brush under running water before cutting. Melons are considered TCS foods once the rind has been penetrated. Pathogens can enter through the stem end, other openings, or bruises.

Cooking Fruits

Although restaurant and foodservice operations commonly serve fruit raw, many varieties can be cooked. These varieties of fruit can be served hot or cold,

560

In-Class Activity (continued)

Present data in a chart similar to this one:

Apple Slice Treatment	Baking Soda	Milk of Magnesia	Water	Lemon Juice	Vinegar
pH reading					
Appearance of apple at 30 minutes					
Appearance of apple at 24 hours					

Help the students to draw data-based conclusions.

Polyphenol oxidase is an enzyme. What is an enzyme?

Enzymes can accelerate a chemical reaction, but they do not enter into or cause the actual reaction.

The apples turn brown in the presence of oxygen. Do the treatments remove oxygen? Or do they slow down the reaction by deactivating the enzyme?

Oxygen remains, and the enzyme is deactivated with treatment, which slows the process.

Do acids and bases have different effects upon the apple slices?

Acids work better and are more palatable.

Formulate an opinion about apple handling based upon these results.

as part of the main entrée, as a snack, or as a dessert.

Preparing fruits for cooking involves washing them with water and then peeling, slicing, and cutting them. Some fruits, such as citrus fruit, melons, pineapples, and kiwi, keep their attractive appearance after they have been cut. Others, such as apples, pears, bananas, and peaches, turn an unappetizing dark color when their flesh has been exposed to air.

Figure 9.6: Enzymatic browning can be seen in fruits such as bananas, apricots, pears, and grapes.

A chemical process called **enzymatic** (en-zi-MAT-ick) **browning** occurs when the oxygen in the air comes in contact with the flesh of cut fruit. This is what causes the fruit to turn brown. Figure 9.6 shows a photo of enzymatic browning. The reaction occurs more quickly in fruits that contain the enzyme **polyphenol oxidase** (pol-lee-feen-nole OX-ee-days), also referred to as PPO. Enzymatic browning is a fruit's survival technique to protect it from the environment.

[fast fact]

Did You Know...?

Enzymatic browning actually develops the color and flavor in dried fruits, such as figs and raisins. This is a chemical process involving polyphenol oxidase or other enzymes that create melanins, resulting in a brown color.

To keep cut fresh fruits from discoloring, coat them with some form of acid, such as lemon juice, as soon as they are cut. These acids lower the pH on the surface of the fruit, which helps to slow down discoloration.

It is always important to avoid overcooking fruit. Even minimal cooking can make fruit overly soft or mushy. When fruit is cooked with sugar, the sugar is absorbed slowly into the cells, firming the fruit. **Acids,** such as lemon juice, help fruit to retain its structure. **Alkalis,** such as baking soda, cause the cells to break down more quickly, making the fruit soft.

While every recipe and method is slightly different, most cooked fruit is done when its is tender and easily pierced with a fork. The following are just some of the methods used to cook fruit:

- Grilling and broiling
- Poaching
- Sautéing

561

Discuss

- Help students to realize that prunes are a variety of plums.
- Make sure they also understand that raisins are dried grapes.
- Assure them that dry fruits are not a source of iron unless the fruit is fresh shortly before drying.

Fast Fact:
Did You Know...?

Melanins are brown pigments.

CUSTOMIZED INSTRUCTION

Literacy Connection, Science Connection

ESOL Students

Help the students to realize that "melon" and "melanin" are not the same thing. The words sound similar, but are not actually related.

The primary pigment in orange melons is beta-carotene. Green melons have chlorophyll. Watermelon has lycopene.

Vocabulary Terms

- **Enzymatic browning:** Brown color triggered by conditions of ripeness and storage and caused by pigments in the fruit.
- **Polyphenol oxidase:** A compound that enhances enzymatic browning in fruit.
- **Acid:** Hydrogen ions in solution which, in mild culinary acids, creates a sour taste like vinegar or lemon juice.
- **Alkali:** Hydroxide ions in solution which, in mild culinary terms, creates a bitter taste like baking soda or soap residue.

Figure Focus

Figure 9.6: Enzymes are naturally occurring chemical catalysts. They speed up reactions.

If possible, have a quince in the classroom for the students to see and taste.

ESOL Students

Quince ("kwince") is spelled the same way as the Spanish word for 15, which is pronounced "keen-say."

Perhaps native Spanish speakers can practice the context differences between the two words.

Teaching Tips

- Cooking fruit breaks down and softens the cellulose in the cell walls of the fruit.
- Some of this is desired.
- Too much cooking makes fruit very soft and saucy, which works well for jam.
- For a fruit to hold its shape, it must not be overcooked.

Vocabulary Terms

- **Caramelization:** A browning caused by heating carbohydrates in the presence of oxygen.
- **Poached:** Simmered in water or another liquid.

- Baking
- Frying (with or without batter)
- Microwaving

> **[trends]**
>
> **Quince**
>
> Quince? No, this isn't the number 15 in Spanish, but a fruit, pronounced "kwince".
>
> Quince is a type of pome fruit (the same family as apples and pears). It is very sour, so it is not eaten raw. It is yellow when ripe and looks like a squatty pear. Quince grows on trees, and is fairly common in Mediterranean Europe and Asia Minor. See Figure 9.7.
>
> When sweetened and cooked, quince is a flavorful and aromatic fruit for jams and jellies. Interestingly, when cooked, it turns from yellow to rosy pink.
>
> The landmark restaurant Chez Panisse in Berkeley, California, has used quince sauce as a glaze for apple or pear tarts. Stewed quince has a unique flavor that blends nicely with cinnamon and allspice in a winter fruit compote or as an accompaniment to pork.

When grilling or broiling fruits, you must cook them quickly to avoid breaking down the fruit's structure. Pineapples, grapefruits, bananas, and peaches are all good fruits to grill or broil. Cut the fruits into slices, chunks, or halves, and coat with sugar or honey to add flavor and **caramelization** (a browning process). Place fruits to be grilled or broiled on an oiled sheet pan or broiling platter. Only thick fruit slices need to be turned or rotated to heat fully. Figure 9.8 shows grilled pineapple.

Fruits that are poached are cooked in simmering liquid. Therefore, use fruits that are firm enough to hold their shape during **poaching**. This includes plums, apples, peaches, and pears. Apples and pears can be cut in large pieces, but other small fruit should remain whole. Some famous poached fruit dishes include Peach Melba and Pears Belle Hélène. Poached fruits are also often used in other desserts as fillings or toppings.

Figure 9.7: The quince is one the earliest known fruits.

Figure 9.8: Fruits such as apples, pears, and pineapples are great to grill for dessert.

Figure Focus

Figure 9.7: There are ancient stories in several cultures featuring quince.

Figure 9.8: Grilled fruits carmelize, which makes both the flavor and the color more rich.

Essential Skills
Poaching Fruit

❶ Prepare the fruit as necessary (seed, peel, etc.). The peel can be included with the fruit as it poaches to add flavor.

❷ Combine the fruit with enough poaching liquid to cover the fruit and bring it just to a simmer. See Figure 9.9a.

❸ Reduce the heat and gently poach the fruit until it is tender. Test the doneness by piercing the fruit with a sharp knife. There should be little or no resistance. See Figure 9.9b.

❹ Let the fruit cool in the poaching liquid, or serve immediately.

Figure 9.9a: Step 2—Combine fruit with poaching liquid.

Figure 9.9b: Step 3—Poach the fruit until tender.

Fruit has a rich, syrupy flavor when sautéed in butter, sugar, and spices. Cherries, bananas, pears, and pineapples are ideal for sautéing. When sautéing fruit, peel, core, and seed the fruit and then cut it into uniform sizes. Dessert fruits can be sautéed with sugar to create a caramelized glaze or syrup. It can be used to fill crêpes or as toppings for sponge cakes. Recipes for sautéed fruit that accompany main entrées usually add onions, shallots, or garlic to the mixture. Figure 9.10 shows sautéed fruit as a dessert dish.

Figure 9.10: Fruits like cherries, bananas, pears, and pineapples are good for sautéing.

563

Essential Skills:
Poaching Fruit

Poached fruit is more tender than raw fruit and is best served hot or warm.

CUSTOMIZED INSTRUCTION

More Advanced Students

Have the students research Auguste Escoffier and present their findings. They should address at least three major contributions he made to the modern foodservice industry.

Less Advanced Students

The students should research the connection between Peach Melba and Auguste Escoffier and present their findings.

Special Needs Students

The students should make a piece of artwork depicting a Peach Melba ready to be served.

ESOL Students

If the student does not speak French, help with the correct pronunciation of Auguste Escoffier.

If the student is a French speaker, have the student help non-French speakers with pronunciation.

Teaching Tips

- Be careful not to burn the added sugar.
- Burned sugar is black and will ruin the product.

Figure Focus

Figure 9.9a: This figure shows peeled pears being carefully placed in poaching liquid, so as not to damage them.

Figure 9.9b: This figure shows peeled poached pears being carefully removed from the poaching liquid to serve them.

Figure 9.10: Sautéed fruits are usually done in butter, giving a buttery flavor to the carmelized sugar.

Essential Skills:
Strawberry Coulis

A coulis should be a flavorful, colorful, artistic sauce that stands up in a bead.

In-Class Activity:
Fruit Dessert Jigsaw PowerPoint

21st-Century Skills—Create Media Products

Have the students locate photographs or take photographs of various fruit desserts, including some non-fruit desserts served with a fruit coulis or sauce.

Each student should contribute at least one photograph.

Assemble the photos into a PowerPoint presentation. Include music, quotes, video, or anything else that would make the project interesting and meaningful.

Vocabulary Terms

- **Coulis:** A fresh purée sauce made of a fruit or vegetable.

Fruit sauces can be made from a variety of fruits. Some of the most popular fruit sauces include applesauce, fresh berry **coulis** (cool-LEE), and compotes. Coulis is a sauce made from a purée of vegetables or fruits that can be served hot or cold. Fruit coulis is most often used on desserts. Raspberry coulis, for example, is especially popular with poached apples. Compotes can be made by simmering dried fruits, such as apricots, currants, and raisins. They are often served either warm or chilled, topped with whipped cream, cinnamon, or vanilla sugar. Fresh berry sauces can be made of cooked or raw fruit. They can also be used as a base for dessert soufflés or as flavoring for Bavarian creams, buttercreams, and other fillings and icings. Ideally, sauce should be made from fresh fruits, but a good-quality sauce can be made by using unsweetened, frozen fruits.

Essential Skills
Strawberry Coulis

You may have seen a drizzle of a puréed, sweetened, and reduced fruit sauce (usually made of berries) called coulis on dessert plates. Chefs like it because it can be drizzled directly onto the plate to add excitement to the presentation. It can also garnish the dessert itself.

Make the coulis a consistency that flows through a squirt-bottle tip with only a little squeezing. It should be about as thick as ketchup, and should stand up in a bead. It should not be so thick that it clogs the bottle's tip or comes out in a clump. Also, if it is too runny it will be a mess. Coulis requires practice, especially if it is to be presented in swirls or other artistic shapes.

A bit of warning: A coulis can also be a distraction from the dessert itself. Coulis should be an artistic way to apply an important ingredient of the dish. Salvaging a less-than-perfect dessert or presentation with a squirt of berry sauce is not the idea.

Use the coulis to create delicious and flavorful beauty on the blank canvas of the dessert plate, in harmony with a high-quality dessert.

Ingredients for Strawberry Coulis

½ pint fresh strawberries, stemmed and rinsed, or 10 ounces frozen strawberries

¼ cup granulated sugar

Juice of ½ lemon, or to taste

564

Directions

In a blender or food processor, purée strawberries with sugar and lemon juice. See Figure 9.11. Taste and add more sugar or lemon juice as needed. Strain seeds from strawberries, if desired. Cover and refrigerate the coulis until ready to serve. Makes 10 servings.

Figure 9.11: Strawberry coulis can be used as a base for souffles, as a filling, or icing.

Fruit sauces are made by cooking the fruit in liquid until the fruit has been broken down. Then a sweetener, such as sugar, honey, or syrup, is added. Once the sauce has cooled, spices and other flavorings are added to give it the finishing touch.

Essential Skills
Making a Fruit Sauce

❶ Peel the fruit and cut it into small pieces for faster cooking. *Alternative:* Purée the fruit in a blender, food processor, food mill, or through a drum sieve. See Figure 9.12a.

❷ Add the appropriate amount of liquid, and heat the purée in a saucepan until it is almost boiling. Lower the heat to a simmer, and cover the pan.

❸ Cook, stirring occasionally, until the fruit has broken down. See Figure 9.12b.

❹ Sweeten as desired with sugar, honey, or syrup.

565

Essential Skills:
Strawberry Coulis (continued)

The presence of dissolved sugar will increase the viscosity and translucence of the fruit for the coulis.

Teaching Tips

- Fruit sauces may be thickened with a starch.
- Some chefs use cornstarch, while others prefer arrowroot, which is more expensive.
- Flour is not used because it is opaque.

Essential Skills:
Making a Fruit Sauce

A fruit sauce is cooked, while a coulis may be uncooked.

A fruit sauce may be refrigerated and used cold, or used warm.

Figure Focus

Figure 9.11: There are many uses for a strawberry coulis. The best part is the flavor of fresh berries!

- Why are Rome Beauty apples considered ideal for baked apples?
- What characteristics would you want in an apple for baking?
- Are there other apples that would work well?
- Are Rome Beauty apples also recommended for apple pie?

Essential Skills: Baking Apples

When coring the apple for baking, be sure to remove the core out to the edge of the core line, not just the seeds and center. Apples may be baked whole or in halves.

---

❺ Add any additional spices or other flavorings, such as vanilla, once the sauce has cooled slightly.

Figure 9.12a: Step 1—Peel fruit or use a blender to purée.

Figure 9.12b: Step 3—Break down fruit by cooking, stirring occasionally.

Figure 9.13: Firm fruits like apples, pears, and bananas are good for baking.

Fruits can also be baked or prepared in a microwave oven. When *baking* fruits, you should choose firm fruits that are whole or cut into large pieces, such as apples, pears, and bananas. Apples, especially the Rome Beauty variety, are the most popular baked fruit because they are easy to prepare. Baked fruits are a healthy and nutritious dessert. Figure 9.13 shows baked pears.

Essential Skills
Baking Apples

❶ Core apples from the top by removing the stem with a parisienne scoop and scooping out the center of the fruit until all seeds are removed and the cavity is large enough to accommodate the desired amount of stuffing. See Figure 9.14a.

566

Figure Focus

Figure 9.12a: The fresh fruit is prepared by purée.

Figure 9.12b: The fruit should not remain in big raw clumps, but should break down a bit as cooked.

Figure 9.13: Baked Rome apples served warm are comfort food.

❷ Cut a thin strip of skin from around the middle of each apple to prevent them from splitting during baking.

❸ Fill each apple's core cavity with cinnamon, nutmeg, raisins, or dates for variety and flavor. See Figure 9.14b.

❹ Place the apples in ¼ inch of hot water in a baking dish.

❺ Bake at 350°F until tender, or about 45 to 60 minutes. See Figure 9.14c.

Figure 9.14a: Step 1—Core apples from the top.

Figure 9.14b: Step 3—Fill the cavity of the apple.

Figure 9.14c: Step 5—Bake at 350°F until tender.

When microwaving fruits, watch the cooking time carefully. It's easy to overcook fresh fruits because they are so tender. Always cover fruits when microwaving them, but leave a small opening from which excess steam can escape. When cooking whole fruits, such as plums or pears, in the microwave, puncture them with a fork in several places to keep them from bursting.

Serving Fruits

Fruit plates and salads are a popular way to serve fruit. Serve fruit at room temperature to make sure it has the best flavor. Fresh fruit can be served as a garnish with entrées and desserts. For example, use fresh fruit to top cereal or yogurt, add fresh berries on a chocolate cake, or add a slice of melon with an omelet at breakfast. Figure 9.15 shows pound cake being served with fresh fruit.

Figure 9.15: Fruit is used as a garnish on dessert.

567

Teaching Tips

- There are many Essential Skills in the Fruits section of this chapter.
- Have the students try as many of these methods as possible in the classroom.
- Include microwave cooking and raw purée.
- Fresh fruit can be expensive.
- In order to use fresh fruit in the classroom, it might be possible to arrange a donation or discount from a local grower.
- Try to use fruit that is either in season locally or available off-season at a reasonable price.
- Apples may be reasonable and available throughout the year.
- Apples are versatile, and apple recipes are plentiful.
- Tropical fruit, berries, and melons may be expensive.

Figure Focus

Figure 9.14a: Apples for baking may be cored down through the top or halved and cored.

Figure 9.14b: The cavities are filled with brown sugar, butter, spices, nuts, or other fillings that will enhance the dessert.

Figure 9.14c: Do not overbake an apple. Baked apples should remain moist and tender.

Figure 9.15: When fruit is used as a garnish, it should be clean, fresh, ripe, and edible.

Summary

- Remind students to review the following:
  1. The various types of fruit
  2. The USDA quality grades for fresh fruit
  3. Factors that affect purchasing decisions
  4. How to properly store fruit
  5. The steps needed to prepare fruit for service
  6. Various methods for cooking fruit

Summary

In this section, you learned the following:

- The three main groups of fruit are summer, winter, and tropical:
  - Summer fruits include berries, cherries, grapes, melons, peaches, nectarines, plums, and pears.
  - Winter fruits include citrus fruits and apples.
  - Tropical fruits include bananas, figs, kiwis, mangos, papayas, pineapple, and coconut.
- The USDA grades for fresh fruit include U.S. Extra Fancy, U.S. Fancy, U.S. No. 1, U.S. No.2, and U.S. No 3. Canned fruit is rated U.S. Grade A Fancy (highest quality), U.S. Grade B Choice (second best), and U.S. Grade C standard (poor quality).
- The factors that affect purchasing decisions of fruit include recipe requirements, staff skills, available equipment, and vendor limitations.
- Fruit needs to be kept dry to avoid spoiling. Fruit that needs to ripen should be stored at room temperatures of 65°F to 70°F.
- Preparing fruit for service may include any combination of cleaning, peeling, seeding, trimming, cutting, juicing, and puréeing.
- Fruit can be grilled, broiled, poached, sautéed, baked, or microwaved:
  - Some fruits, such as apples, pears, bananas, and peaches, undergo enzymatic browning when the oxygen in the air comes in contact with the flesh of cut fruit.
  - Avoid overcooking fruits, as they will become soft or mushy.
  - Pineapples, apples, and bananas are good fruits to grill or broil.
  - Plums, apples, peaches, and pears are good fruits to poach.

Section 9.1 Review Questions

1. List the appropriate cooking method for each type of fruit. Some fruits may be suitable for more than one cooking method.

   a. Raspberries   e. Pears

   b. Pineapples   f. Grapefruits

   c. Peaches   g. Bananas

   d. Apples

2. What are the different quality grades given to fresh fruit and canned produce by the USDA?

3. For each fruit, identify whether it is a tropical, summer, or winter fruit.

   a. Apple   f. Grapefruit

   b. Cherry   g. Kiwi

   c. Coconut   h. Papaya

   d. Fig   i. Peach

   e. Grape   j. Tangerine

4. If you cut up an apple and leave it on the counter for 30 minutes, it will probably look brown. Why does this happen?

5. Daron Kinder remarks that there is a noticeable difference in quality and flavor when a particular product is in season. Can you provide examples of a dessert for each season that uses a seasonal fruit?

6. What fresh fruits can Chef Jean add to the menu that are in season?

7. Is dried fruit more nutritious than fresh fruit? Why or why not?

8. What is enzymatic browning, and how can it affect fresh fruit?

Section 9.1 Review Questions

1. Appropriate cooking methods include:
   a. Boiled, sautéed
   b. Grilled, baked, broiled
   c. Sautéed, boiled, baked
   d. Baked, boiled, fried, sautéed
   e. Poached, sautéed
   f. Boiled, broiled
   g. Baked, roasted, fried, sautéed

2. USDA quality grades are U.S. Extra Fancy, U.S. Fancy, U.S. No. 1, U.S. No. 2, and U.S. No. 3.

3. The fruits on the list are of the following types:
   a. Winter
   b. Summer
   c. Tropical
   d. Tropical
   e. Summer
   f. Winter
   g. Tropical
   h. Tropical
   i. Summer
   j. Winter

4. It turns brown because of enzymatic browning due to the production of polyphenol oxidase.

5. Examples of seasonal desserts include:
   Summer—fresh Peach Melba
   Fall—fresh apple pie
   Winter—broiled grapefruit
   Spring—banana fritters

6. He might add stone fruits like plums, peaches, apricots, and cherries, or some melons and berries.

7. The fruit itself does not gain nutrients as it dries, unless nutrients are added in the processing technique. If a person eats a larger quantity of dry fruit than fresh fruits, then more nutrients would be consumed. Some nutrients, like vitamin C, are easily destroyed during drying. Other nutrients, such as minerals, remain.

8. An enzyme called polyphenol oxidase protects the outer surface of the cut fruit. It looks brown and can actually keep moisture in and impurities out. If browned fruit is to be eaten when it is still fresh, remove the browned portions. The color is unappealing and the flavor becomes dull.

Section 9.1
Activities

1. Use Tables 9.1, 9.2, and 9.3 for answer keys.

2. Each student's work will be unique.

3. Each student's work will be unique.

Section 9.1 Activities

1. Study Skills/Group Activity: Name That Fruit

In a small group, play "Name That Fruit," beginning with citrus fruit. Race to make a list of all the citrus fruit you can think of in one minute. Compare the lists with the other members of your group. The group member with the longest accurate list wins 10 points. For round two, try varieties of apples; for round three, types of drupes. Continue with melons, berries, tropical fruit, and any other category you choose.

2. Activity: Dessert Anyone?

Put together a dessert menu that consists of recipes using at least three fruits from each of the summer, winter, and tropical fruit categories. Below each recipe, include a "fun fact" about one of the fruits used in the recipe.

3. Critical Thinking: Watermelon

How many creative things can you think to do with a whole watermelon? List 10 menu or buffet items that use watermelon as part of the ingredients and/or presentation. Describe each on paper using words and/or sketches.

SECTION 9.2 VEGETABLES

Like fruits, vegetables are becoming more important and popular as more focus is being put on healthy living and healthy diets. There has also been an increase in people following vegetarian diets, which has led to restaurant and food-service operations increasing the variety of vegetables they offer. From quick service to fine dining, more vegetables are being incorporated into meals and being put on menus. Vegetables provide nutrition as well as flavor, texture, color, and variety to a meal. Vegetables are not only a side dish but are also main courses themselves.

Study Questions

After studying Section 9.2, you should be able to answer the following questions:

- What are the various types of vegetables?
- What is hydroponic farming?
- How do you store produce?
- What are the various methods for cooking vegetables?
- How do you maintain the quality of vegetables?

Types and Market Forms

A **vegetable** is an edible, herb-like plant. The parts of vegetables that people eat include the leaves, fruit, stems, roots, tubers, seeds, and flowers. Vegetables can be purchased whole or cut in fresh, frozen, canned, and dried forms. Unlike fruits, vegetables are eaten cooked more often than raw.

Vegetables are often categorized by their botanical origins or by their edible parts. They may be classified as a flower, fruit, green leafy, seed, root/tuber, or stem vegetable.

571

Section 9.2 Vegetables

Introduce the Section

a. There are many categories of vegetables on the market.

b. Purchasing and storing vegetables affects quality and needs skill.

c. Preparing and cooking vegetables also take skill.

Vocabulary Review

a. Direct students to the key terms.

b. Pronounce each word, and have the students repeat the pronunciation out loud.

c. Discuss the definition of each word.

Discuss

- Ask students if they like to eat vegetables. Have them say why or why not.
- Vegetables are playing an increasing role in cuisine.
- There are many culinary and even artistic principles to learn about vegetables in foodservice.
- Types of vegetables include fruit vegetables, flower vegetables, green leafy vegetables, seed vegetables, root and tuber vegetables, and stem vegetables.
- Hydroponic farming is farming in a nutrient medium and controlled environment rather than farming in dirt and open air.
- Tubers and roots should be stored dry, unpeeled, and in a cool dark place. Vegetables that need to ripen should be stored at 65°F–70°F. Ripe vegetables should be stored at 41°F or lower.
- Vegetables may be simmered, steamed, poached, boiled, baked, roasted, fried, sautéed, stir-fried, grilled, broiled, microwaved or *sous vide*.
- Vegetables should be eaten soon after harvest. Local and seasonal choices can help ensure this. Vegetables should be optimally cooked and not overcooked.

Vocabulary Terms

- **Vegetable:** An edible plant.

Teaching Tips

- Many of the flower vegetables come from the botanical familia brassica.
- Vegetables that come from the cabbage family are called cruciferous vegetables. Cruciferous is another word for cross, because the flower petals on these plants may appear in fours.
- Flower vegetables even include some flower blossoms, like Nasturtium Tropaeolum.
- These flowers are actually part of the mustard family and taste peppery.
- They are part of the greater brassica family, too.

Table 9.5:
Types of Flower Vegetables

- These are also called cruciferous vegetables.

In-Class Activity:
Plant Cultivation

If there is a planting bed, a pot area with good light, or a greenhouse at your school, ask to use it.

During good weather, plant edible nasturtium seeds. Water them, and make sure they have adequate light. Nasturtiums grow quickly and are prolific.

Harvest the flowers. Carefully remove any insects and dirt, and wash the flowers. Taste them in a tossed green salad.

The use of nasturtium flowers in salad was popularized in the 1970s by Alice Waters of Chez Panisse in Berkeley, CA.

Vocabulary Terms

- **Flower vegetable:** An edible flower portion of a plant, such as broccoli.

Flower Vegetables

Flower vegetables include broccoli, cauliflower, Brussels sprouts, and cabbage. When we think of cooking these products, we focus on the "head" of the vegetable. Table 9.5 lists the characteristics of each type of flower vegetable.

Table 9.5: Types of Flower Vegetables		
Name	**Characteristics**	**Sample Varieties**
Broccoli	• Broccoli has a deep green color, tiny clustered buds (florets), and crisp leaves. • To prepare broccoli, cut the stems lengthwise and cook them with the heads attached. This ensures that the cooking times for both the stems and the florets are the same. • USES: Broccoli can be served raw or cooked and is often used in salads or as crudités.	• Green Goliath • Green Comet • Waltham
Cauliflower	• Cauliflower is available in three colors: white, green, and purple. • It has firm stalks and florets, with leaves at its base. The florets and the leaves are edible. • USES: Cauliflower can be served cooked or raw, often used in salads or as **crudités.** It is often cooked by steaming, stir-frying, or as an ingredient in stews and tempura (tem-POO-rah). **Tempura** is Japanese-style breaded and deep-fried vegetables.	• Snowdrift • Danish Giant • Romanesco
Cabbage	• Cabbage has thick, waxy leaves that lay tight together and form a large, round head. • Some varieties have curly leaves and a looser form. • Flavors run from sweet to mild to strong. • USES: Cabbage is used often in coleslaw or stir-fried.	• Savoy • Red • Napa
Brussels sprouts	• Brussels sprouts resemble miniature cabbage and grow on a thick stalk. • Flavors tend to be milder than cabbage. • USES: Brussels sprouts are best roasted or steamed.	• Wellington • Brilliant • Millennium

[fast fact]

Did You Know...?
The name "broccoli" comes from the Latin word *brachium*, which means "branch" or "arm." Broccolini is another green vegetable similar to broccoli with small florets and long, thin stalks. It is sometimes called "young broccoli", even though it is really a cross between broccoli and *kai-lan*, Chinese broccoli.

Fruit Vegetables

Fruit vegetables include avocados, cucumbers, eggplants, peppers, squash, and tomatoes. These products come from flowering plants and have seeds, which technically make them fruits. But when we think of how we eat them, we eat them as vegetables. Table 9.6 lists the characteristics of each type of fruit vegetable.

Table 9.6: Types of Fruit Vegetables

Name	Characteristics	Sample Varieties
Avocados	• Avocados have green or black leathery skin. • Their flavor is rich and buttery. They have rich, mild flavor and a smooth, buttery, dense texture. • USES: They are usually served with lime or lemon juice to prevent the flesh from turning brown. **Guacamole** (gwak-ah-MOE-lee), a favorite traditional Mexican dip, uses mashed avocados as the main ingredient.	• Hass • Bacon • Gwen
Eggplants	• Eggplants are glossy, firm vegetables. Eggplant varieties come in shades of purple from light violet to almost black. They also come in a wide range of sizes and shapes. The most common variety is dark purple-black and ranges from 10 to 12 inches long. • USES: Eggplant is always served cooked, never raw. **Babaganoush** (BAH-bah-gahn-OOSH), a Middle Eastern dip, uses eggplant as the main ingredient. Eggplant is also used in Italian and Greek cooking.	• Black Beauty • Japanese • White
Bell peppers	• Bell (or sweet) peppers are named for their shape. • All varieties start out green, but as they ripen, their colors change to red, green, yellow, cream, or purple. • Ripe green peppers are not as sweet as the other colors. • USES: Bell peppers can be served raw, as a seasoning in other dishes, or as a main entrée.	• Holland • Bell Boy • Lady Bell

(continued)

Fast Fact: Did You Know...?

Broccoli looks almost like a tree with branches.

Broccoli, branch, and the Latin word for arm, brachium, are all similar.

Table 9.6: Types of Fruit Vegetables (continued on p. 574)

• Most fruit vegetables are not sweet tasting like fruits.

Discuss

• How do avocados vary from most vegetables?
• The students might be aware that avocados have a greater fat content than other vegetables.
• How do avocados vary from most fruits?
• Would you call an avocado a fruit or a vegetable?

Vocabulary Terms

• **Fruit vegetable:** A seed-bearing ovary from a flowering plant.

Table 9.6 (continued)

- This list includes many commonly enjoyed vegetables.

In-Class Activity: Taste-Testing Peppers

Literacy Connection

Peppers of various varieties range in hotness from the mild bell pepper to the very hot habañero.

Assemble a nonblind taste test with labeled samples of various peppers. Also have a whole pepper of each variety for the students to see and handle.

Some to consider including might be:

- Green Bell
- Red, Orange, Yellow Bell
- Anaheim
- Serrano
- Habañero
- Jalapeño
- Green Chili
- Other locally available varieties

Students should keep records of their findings, and should rate each pepper for hotness, flavor, and texture.

Have the students suggest dishes that would call for each variety of pepper.

Have the students create a table, chart, cards, or other tool for remembering the qualities of peppers. This will be for their future use. Make sure they spell the names of the peppers correctly. They should also draw or photograph each pepper as part of their tool.

For a more in-depth activity, fire roast a pepper to show the students a new possibility.

How does fire-roasting change the flavor of a pepper?

Table 9.6: Types of Fruit Vegetables *continued*

Name	Characteristics	Sample Varieties
Chili peppers	• Chili peppers are in the same family as bell peppers, but they are smaller and much hotter. Flavors can run from mild to painfully hot. Most of the hot, spicy flavor is in both the seeds and the membranes, so seeded chili peppers are not quite as hot as whole chili peppers. • Like bell peppers, chili peppers also range in colors, including yellow, red, black, and even purple. • USES: Chili peppers are often used to make sauces and to add flavorful heat to a dish.	• Habanero • Cayenne • Poblano • Jalapeño
Winter squash	• Winter squash have hard shells and large seeds. • Flavors range from sweet to mild to bitter. Some also have a nutty flavor. • USES: They are often baked, steamed, or sautéed.	• Butternut • Acorn • Spaghetti • Banana
Summer squash	• Unlike winter squash, summer squash is much smaller, with soft skin and small seeds that are eaten. • Their flavors are generally mild. • USES: Though summer squash is good raw, it can also be grilled, sautéed, steamed, or baked.	• Yellow Crookneck • Pattypan • Zucchini
Cucumbers	• Cucumbers have a thin skin that is sometimes waxed and an inner core of seeds. • USES: Because of their fresh, mild flavor, cucumbers are excellent in salads or when served with a dip. Cucumbers are an especially popular vegetable used in Middle Eastern cooking. Cucumbers are almost never served cooked outside of Asian cuisine.	• Garden • Japanese • Kirby
Tomato	• The tomato is really a type of berry and is grown in hundreds of varieties. • Tomatoes range in colors from green to yellow to bright red. Tomatoes are at their best when they are vine-ripened. • USES: The versatile tomato is a colorful and nutritious addition to many dishes and a popular ingredient in salads. Sliced tomatoes are also commonly served alone, seasoned with a dash of salt or pepper. Tomatoes may be stewed, fried, grilled, baked, pickled, boiled, or made into sauce or juice. • The size of a tomato determines how it is used. • Large green tomatoes are best for frying. • Jumbo red tomatoes are good plain, stuffed, or baked. • Medium-sized tomatoes are good for slicing. • Overripe tomatoes are excellent in stews, sauces, and casseroles.	• Cherry • Beefsteak • Grape

Did You Know...?
Ever wonder why people use the phrase "cool as cucumber?" The inner temperature of a cucumber is 20 degrees cooler than the outside air.

Tomatoes and Lycopene
Pigments in fresh fruits and vegetables are sometimes nutrients as well as colors. Lycopene is an example. It is the red pigment of tomatoes (and watermelon, red peppers, etc.). It is a chemical relative of the orange beta-carotene found in carrots. Lycopene is an antioxidant. Antioxidants stop the chain reactions caused by "free-radicals," or highly reactive oxidative (destructive) changes that can occur in body tissues.

There is more research to be done in the area of lycopene nutrition. There is no such thing as lycopene-deficiency disease as far as researchers know at this point, so it is not considered a necessary vitamin. But the effect of antioxidants on the body looks very promising, as nutritionists consider the big picture of good health.

Raw tomatoes are not as rich in lycopene as cooked tomatoes. The body can use it better from a cooked tomato, and even better if there is some oil or fat in the same meal.

Green Leafy Vegetables

Green leafy vegetables include various types of lettuce, mustard greens, spinach, and Swiss chard. Green leafy vegetables are very high in vitamins A and C, iron, and magnesium. Table 9.7 lists the characteristics of each type of green leafy vegetable.

Fast Fact:
Did You Know...?

Cucumbers are very refreshing in the hot summer.

Nutrition:
Tomatoes and Lycopene

Italian cuisine is rich in lycopene.

Vocabulary Terms

- **Green leafy vegetables:** Edible green plant leaves.

575

Table 9.7: Types of Green Leafy Vegetables		
Name	**Characteristics**	**Sample varieties**
Lettuce	• There are hundreds of varieties of lettuce, with varying flavors, colors, and shapes. • In the United States, there are four main categories of lettuce: butterhead, crisphead, leaf, and romaine. • Crisphead lettuce, such as iceberg lettuce, has light-green leaves that are tightly packed together. Its mild flavor makes it good to use in salads and as a garnish for sandwiches. • Butterhead has small, round, loosely formed heads with a soft, buttery texture. • Unlike iceberg lettuce, both romaine and leaf lettuce are loosely packed. Their leaves grow upward in bunches, and their edges are slightly ruffled. Leaf lettuce has a milder flavor than romaine lettuce, and is also good in salads. The crisp, more flavorful romaine lettuce is often used in Caesar salad. • USES: Lettuce is used in salads or as garnish on a sandwich or entrée.	• Iceberg • Romaine • Bibb
Mustard greens	• Mustard greens have a bitter, strong flavor. • The leaves are usually dark green. • USES: Mustard is served raw, in salads, or lightly sautéed with vinegar and herbs.	• Curled • Asian
Spinach	• Spinach is one of the most adaptable greens used in cooking. • It has dark green leaves that can be smooth or curly. • USES: With a slightly bitter flavor, spinach is often used in soups, salads, and casseroles.	• Baby • Savoy • Smooth Leaf
Swiss chard	• Swiss chard is actually a type of beet that does not have a root. • The flavor of chard is rich and similar to spinach. • USES: It produces dark green, wide leaves that are often steamed, sautéed, and used in soups.	• Red • White • Multicolor

Spring Greens and Field Mixes

Not too long ago, a little iceberg lettuce with mayonnaise dressing was considered a dinner salad. Consumers today are interested in more flavorful and nutritious salad greens. Variety lettuce mixes have gained popularity in recent years, both in restaurants and grocery stores.

Spring greens, field greens, field mixes, and other terms are used to describe a mix of assorted salad greens. Some greens are lettuces; some are related to cabbage; others, like radicchio, are chicory. Even leafy herbs like cilantro find their way into flavorful salads.

Spring greens are the new leaves of leafy vegetables that had been harvested the previous season. Some **brassica** (cabbage family) and chicories are strong enough to survive the winter. When they begin to send up new growth in March or early April, the leaves are tender, bright, and flavorful. They are often found in fresh, spring salads.

Field mixes may be more tender and can be planted in the spring for harvest a few weeks later. **Mesclun mix** is a seed blend that includes a variety of leafy lettuce and other greens. Other single greens may be added to blends at harvest. These assorted leaves may have a bold flavor like arugula, be peppery like watercress, savory like chive, or tangy like sorrel. Others are milder, like romaine or frisée.

Combine these mixes with nuts, dried fruit, and goat cheese. When served with bread, they make a nutritious meal. Or toss them with ripe tomatoes, olive oil and wine vinegar, balsamic vinegar, or lemon juice. Then they make a colorful and interesting side dish.

Seed Vegetables

Seed vegetables include corn, peas, and beans. In this category, the edible portions of the vegetable (kernels, peas) are actually seeds. Table 9.8 lists the characteristics of each type of seed vegetable.

Table 9.8: Types of Seed Vegetables

Name	Characteristics	Sample varieties
Corn	• Flavors vary among the white, yellow, and bicolored varieties. • Popcorn is a variety of corn grown especially for its small ears and pointed kernels that explode when heated. • USES: Sweet corn, served on the cob, can be grilled or boiled. It should be served very soon after it is picked. If not, its natural sugars will begin to turn to starch, making the corn less sweet and much chewier.	• Butter and Sugar • Bantam • Silver Queen
Peas	• The most common peas are green garden peas. They have a sweet, delicate flavor. • Peas are a colorful addition to salads, soups, and garnishes. • USES: Some peas can be eaten in their pods. Snow peas, for example, are often used in Asian cooking and have firm skin and a light flavor.	• English • Snow • Sugar Snap

(continued)

577

Table 9.8:
Types of Seed Vegetables
(continued on p. 578)

- There is a lot of category crossover between seed vegetables and grains.

CUSTOMIZED INSTRUCTION

More Advanced Students

Mesclun is a catch-all word for a mix of green leafy lettuce-type vegetables.

Have the student investigate the various types of leaves that feature in mesclun mixes.

Do all the greens in the mix mature at the same time? What does this mean for harvest and use?

Vocabulary Terms

- **Brassica:** Cabbage family and chicory family vegetables.
- **Field mix:** Tender baby greens, assorted in a salad mix.
- **Mesclun mix:** Tender baby greens and lettuces, perhaps mixed with baby chicories or sorrel.
- **Seed vegetables:** The edible soft seeds of plants.

Table 9.8 (continued)

- There is also a lot of category crossover between seed vegetables and legumes.

Fast Fact: Did You Know...?

Is corn a grain or a vegetable?

How does it function in cuisine?

Is the nutrient profile of corn similar to other vegetables or to other grains?

Vocabulary Terms

- **Root vegetable:** An edible plant root.

Table 9.8: Types of Seed Vegetables *continued*		
Name	**Characteristics**	**Sample varieties**
Beans	• Fresh beans include green beans, yellow wax beans, and French **haricot verts** (HAIR-ee-ko VAIR). These beans are small and are most often eaten while still in the pod, its long, outer shell. • Lima beans and fava beans are examples of beans that are shelled, or removed from the pod. They are larger and more firm than green beans. They stand up well to cooking. • USES: Fresh beans are very good sautéed, steamed, or microwaved. Dried, shelled beans usually need to be soaked or boiled first, and are best in soups, stews, and curries. All beans add flavor and color to soups and salads and are nutritious side dishes.	• Green • Yellow Wax • Lima • Fava

[fast fact]

Did You Know...?

1. The United States is the leading producer and exporter of corn.
2. The United States produces two-fifths of the world's supply of corn.
3. Corn is also called maize.

Root and Tuber Vegetables

Root vegetables and tubers are grouped together because part, or all, of the part people eat grows underground. **Root vegetables** are rich in sugars, starches, vitamins, and minerals. These plants exist both above and below ground. A single root extends into the ground and provides nutrients to the leafy green part of the vegetable that is above the ground. Some common root vegetables include carrots, beets, radishes, turnips, and onions.

[nutrition]

Sweet Onions

About 100 years ago, a farmer brought onion seeds from the island of Corsica (near Italy) to his home in Walla Walla, Washington. He planted them and thus began Walla Walla Sweet Onions. Similar varieties were farmed in Vidalia, Georgia, on the Hawaiian Island of Maui, and in Nevada.

These onions are very popular, especially for dishes that call for raw onions. They contain a respectable amount of vitamin C. They have a greater water content than regular onions. They will last in a cool, dark, ventilated storage place for four to six weeks without refrigeration. Yellow onions can be kept longer, but they are more pungent.

The thought of an onion actually being sweet might seem odd. They have a fairly high sugar content, so they taste a little bit sweet, especially after being sautéed in butter.

Perhaps the best thing about sweet onions is their low sulfur content, which reduces stomach upset. Onions can cause stomachaches in some people. The lower sulfur also makes it easier to slice a sweet onion without crying.

Tuber vegetables include potatoes, sweet potatoes, and yams. Tubers are enlarged, bulbous roots capable of generating a new plant. Tubers are actually fat, underground stems. Table 9.9 lists the characteristics of each type of root and tuber vegetable.

Table 9.9: Types of Root and Tuber Vegetables		
Name	**Characteristics**	**Sample varieties**
Carrots	• Carrots contain a large amount of carotene, a pigment easily convertible to vitamin A. • USES: Carrots can be served raw, as crudités, as a garnish, or as an ingredient in salads. Carrots are fundamental to mirepoix. Cooked carrots make excellent side dishes and additions to soups. Carrots are even used in desserts, cooked or raw.	• Imperator • Baby • Rainbow
Beets	• Beets were originally grown for their tops, not their roots; today, however, the roots are far more commonly used. • Colors run from red to yellow to white. • Cooks prefer smaller beets to larger ones for two reasons: their appearance is better, and they cook faster than larger beets. • USES: Beets are popular in salads. Pickled beets add spice and zest to salads or to a side dish. They may also be steamed, baked, or roasted.	• Red Ace • Chioggia • Golden
Radishes	• Radishes are small, round roots that are available in many colors, from deep red to pale cream. • USES: Their crisp texture and peppery flavor make them a flavorful and colorful addition to salads. They can be decoratively cut as a garnish or served as an appetizer with vegetable dip.	• Cherry Belle • Snow Belle • Icicle Short Top

(continued)

579

Nutrition: Sweet Onions

Sulfur is a harsh element, also called brimstone.

Low-sulfur onions are easy to enjoy and digest.

Table 9.9: Types of Root and Tuber Vegetables (continued on p. 580)

• Brightly colored vegetables are nutritious, especially if they are purple, orange, or red.

Teaching Tips

• Potatoes do not need to be discussed in depth at this point. They are discussed in detail in Chapter 11.

Vocabulary Terms

• **Tuber vegetable:** An edible underground stem of a plant.

Table 9.9 (continued)

- When a tuber like a potato shows a green color, it is no longer good to eat.

Discuss

- Onions are a good topic for a discussion.
- How do onions function in cuisine?
- Do people eat onions alone?
- Can the students think of some dishes that feature onions?
- What qualities do onions add to other dishes?
- If possible, have a few different types of onions, including a leek, to show students.

In-Class Activity: Onion Layers and Fibonacci Number Systems

Math Connection

In nature, many things are represented by a recurring number system that follows a pattern.

A mathematician from the Middle Ages called Leonardo de Pisa (nicknamed Fibonacci), lived in the twelfth and thirteenth centuries.

Fibonacci noticed that plants and other things in nature have features with predictable mathematical patterns. Things like leaves on a branch, petals on a flower, chambers in a nautilus shell, and layers of an onion all have a pattern to their design.

The Fibonacci system starts with 1.

The given number is added to the number that precedes it to derive the next number. For example, if 1 is the start, then the number preceding 1 is 0.

The equation is 1 + 0 = 1, so the sequence is now 1, 1.

Add the new 1 to the number that precedes it: 1 + 1 = 2. The sequence is now 1, 1, 2.

Add the new 2 to the number that precedes it: 2 + 1 = 3. The sequence is now 1, 1, 2, 3.

And so forth.

Continue building the sequence with a few more equations.

Take apart an onion. See if you can observe the natural occurrence of a Fibonacci number system in the anatomy of the onion.

Do you observe Fibonacci systems in other fruits and vegetables?

Table 9.9: Types of Root and Tuber Vegetables *continued*

Name	Characteristics	Sample varieties
Turnips	• Like radishes, turnips have a hot, peppery flavor that is best when baked. • They are larger than radishes and usually have a rose-colored skin and bright white flesh. • USES: Turnips may be baked, boiled, steamed, or mashed.	• Baby • White • Yellow
Onions	• All varieties of onions have a strong flavor and aroma, and can be used as seasonings. • USES: Common, or bulb onions, like white, yellow, or red, are best when sliced or chopped for use in stuffing or casseroles. Small onions, like pearl onions, are best for boiling or cooking with roasts and stews. They can also be prepared whole and served as a side dish.	• Bermuda • Vidalia • Pearl
Scallions and shallots	• Green onions, or scallions, are actually common onions that are pulled before they are mature. • The slender, dark green leaves of green onions are attached to the thick white bulb. • Shallots are shaped like small bulb onions. They separate into small cloves when broken apart. • USES: The mild flavor of green onions and shallots makes them a great addition to meat dishes and sauces, or for use in salads.	• Gray • Dutch Yellow • French Red
Leeks	• Leeks resemble large green onions. They have the mildest flavor in the onion family. • USES: They are best when baked or grilled, and are often used in stocks, sauces, and soups.	• Musselburgh • Edison • Oarsman
Potatoes	• Potatoes are available in many varieties, with different flavors, sizes, textures, and colors. • Potatoes should all be firm, free of marks, and well shaped. • USES: Moist potatoes are well suited to boiling. Drier potatoes are better for baking.	• Russet • Red • New • Fingerling
Sweet potatoes	• The sweet potato's color comes from beta-carotene. • Its thick skin is not usually eaten. • Colors can range from light yellow to deep orange. • Sweet potatoes and potatoes actually come from different botanical families. Both are root tubers. • USES: Sweet potatoes are best when boiled, baked, or puréed for soups.	• Goldrush • Georgia Red • Velvet

(continued)

580

Table 9.9: Types of Root and Tuber Vegetables *continued*

Name	Characteristics	Sample varieties
Yams	• Yams are often confused with sweet potatoes. They have more natural sugar and moisture than sweet potatoes. • Colors range from deep red to creamy white. • They can be substituted for sweet potatoes in most recipes. • USES: Yams are best when boiled, baked, or puréed for soups.	• Purple Ube • Japanese Mountain • White Guinea

[fast fact]

Did You Know...?
On average, an American consumes around 21 pounds of fresh and processed onions every year.

[ServSafe Connection]

Do You Know Your Chanterelles from Your False Morels?
Some mushrooms are edible and delicious. Others are poisonous. Different kinds of mushrooms can cause a variety of symptoms, from mild, such as swollen lips, to severe gastrointestinal upset or even death.

Foodborne illnesses linked with mushrooms are almost always caused by people eating toxic, wild mushrooms collected by amateur hunters. Most cases happen because toxic mushrooms are mistaken for edible ones.

If you want to use mushrooms or mushroom products in a dish, make sure to buy them from an approved, reputable supplier.

Stem Vegetables

Stem vegetables include asparagus, celery, artichokes, and mushrooms. In this category, the vegetables that we eat are the stems of plants. Table 9.10 lists the characteristics of each type of stem vegetable.

Table 9.9 (continued)

• Yams and sweet potatoes are often mistaken for each other. What are the differences?

**Fast Fact
Did You Know...?**

Onions are popular in cuisines around the globe.

**ServSafe Connection:
Do You Know Your Chanterelles from Your False Morels?**

Restaurateurs should not hunt for and harvest wild mushrooms for their dining guests.

Do wild mushrooms grow in your locale?

Are they safe or poisonous?

Vocabulary Terms

• **Stem vegetables:** Edible plant stems, like celery.

- The flower of the artichoke is not eaten, except for a tiny fleshy part at the end of the petal or leaf. The stem is the heart.

Teaching Tips

- Perhaps the students are not aware of hydroponic farming.
- See if the students realize how much of their produce comes from hydroponic operations.
- Show them photographs of a hydroponic system.

Vocabulary Terms

- **Hydroponic farming:** Farming without dirt in a nutrient-rich watery medium.

Table 9.10: Types of Stem Vegetables

Name	Characteristics	Sample varieties
Asparagus	• Asparagus has tender stalks and tips. • Thicker stalks mean that the plant is older. • USES: Asparagus can be steamed while standing upright in a pot, with the tips on top, roasted, or sautéed.	• White • Green • Viola
Celery	• Green, leafy stalks of celery are familiar ingredients. • USES: They are commonly used in salads, soups, stews, and as a garnish in tomato juice. In addition, the crisp, sturdy stalks make celery an excellent appetizer, either stuffed or served with dip.	• Ventura • Giant Red • Giant Pascal
Artichokes	• Artichokes are the immature flowers of a thistle plant brought to America by Italian and Spanish settlers. • Whole artichokes can be simmered, steamed, or micro-waved. Often they are served with lemon juice, garlic butter, or hollandaise sauce. • The artichoke heart may be cooked separately and then served in salads, puréed as a filling, or served as a side dish. • USES: Young, tender globe artichokes can be cooked whole. Mature artichokes need to have the fuzzy center (known as the choke) removed first.	• Green Globe • Emerald • Imperial Star
Mushrooms	• Mushrooms are a family of fungi, many of which are edible. • **Fungi** (FUN-ghee) are a large group of plants ranging from single-celled organisms to giant mushrooms. • The flavor of mushrooms ranges from delicate and fruity to pungent and garlicky. • Mushrooms come in many shapes, sizes, and colors. Though many varieties are perfectly safe to eat, there are some that can cause severe illness or even death. • USES: They are served raw with dips and in salads, deep-fried, and cooked in a variety of sauces, soups, stews, and stir-fry recipes.	• White • Crimini • Portabella

Purchasing Vegetables

Improved shipping methods and new ways of farming have made most produce available all year. The use of hydroponic farming is popular. In **hydroponic (hi-dro-PON-ick) farming**, vegetables are grown indoors year-round, under regulated temperatures and light, in nutrient-enriched water. To reduce cost and promote freshness, some restaurants grow their own fresh herbs on the premises. Figure 9.16 shows vegetables being grown using hydroponic farming.

582

Hydroponic carrots grow especially straight.

Figure 9.16: Hydroponic farming allows vegetables to be grown indoors year-round, under regulated temperatures and light in nutrient-enriched water.

Some vegetables, such as spinach, potatoes, and broccoli, are available all year. The quality, degree of ripeness, and price vary with the season. Others, such as asparagus, summer squashes, tomatoes, and green beans, have a specific growing season. Knowing the growing season for a particular vegetable is important. As with fruit, during their growing seasons vegetables are plentiful, the quality is higher, and the prices are usually lower. Some operations have seasonal menus that are based on what is fresh and locally available. Many customers today have shown interest in eating local produce and supporting the restaurants that serve it.

The same factors that could affect the purchasing decisions that operations make for fruit apply for vegetables. See page 556.

[what's new]

A Lettuce Farm on a Rooftop

Hydroponic gardening is done without soil, in a water-and-nutrient solution. The word "hydroponic" means "water work," and that is exactly what happens. The water does all the work! Well, the hydroponic farmers work hard, too. Plants are supported in a rack or frame, the correct fertilizing nutrients are added to the water, and that's all there is to it! It involves more chemistry than weed-pulling.

Many of the carrots, lettuces, and other vegetables that you eat, especially during the winter months, are produced hydroponically.

583

Figure Focus

Figure 9.16: A small hydroponic space may be very productive, as plant growth systems can be layered.

This business is an example of a micro-enterprise.

In-Class Activity:
The Nutrients of Lettuce

**Literacy Connection, 21st-Century Skills—
Health Literacy**

Have the students reflect upon the What's New piece about the rooftop farm in Peru.

The article mentions that the diets of the families are improved by the addition of the lettuce.

They eat the dark green leafy lettuce. They also have more money to purchase other foods.

How do the lettuce and other foods mentioned in the article improve the diets of the families?

What nutrients are contained in dark green leafy lettuce and the other foods mentioned in the piece? Have students write up what they learn.

In Lima, Peru, Alfredo Rodriguez Delfin, professor of biology at the Universidad Agraria La Molina, has helped a group of mothers improve their families' lives by teaching them hydroponic gardening techniques. Low-income women in a section of Lima called Villa el Salvador banded together to start a hydroponic lettuce farm on their apartment-building rooftop. Their system allows for nearly three times the harvest yield of the same square-footage of dirt using traditional methods. A small rooftop becomes a big farm. The women of Villa el Salvador produce about 30,000 lettuce plants each month.

They raise dark green leafy lettuce in a nutrient-boosted solution, sterile from foodborne pathogens. Their lettuce is ready to harvest in two months. They sell it in sealed, clean containers to local grocers. This is a source of income. It's also a major nutritional boost for their families and community members who buy it. With the proceeds of sales, they can afford to add eggs, potatoes, and a few other staples to their otherwise meager diet. They are improving their families' health, their economic status, and their community.

Quality Grades

The same quality grades that the USDA applies to fruit apply to vegetables as well.

Storing Vegetables

All produce must be properly stored. Roots and tubers should be stored dry and unpeeled in a cool, dark area. Many of the other ripe vegetables can be stored at 41°F or lower, but not all will be stored at these temperatures. For example, potatoes should never be stored in the refrigerator. They should be in a cool, dark place, because the low temperatures of a refrigerator convert the starch to sugars. Remember, if possible, vegetables should be stored separately in one refrigerator and fruit in another refrigerator. As with some fruit, certain vegetables emit ethylene gas, which causes fruit to ripen.

Most vegetables need to be kept dry because excess moisture causes produce to spoil quickly. For this reason, produce should not be peeled, washed, or trimmed until just before it is used. For example, outer leaves on lettuce should be left on the head, and carrots should be unpeeled. Leafy tops on root vegetables (beets, turnips, carrots, radishes) should be removed and either discarded or used immediately. These tops can be used for stock, since they contain flavor and nutrients. The leaves on these green vegetables absorb nutrients from the root and increase moisture loss.

Vegetables that need to ripen, such as tomatoes and avocados, should be stored at room temperatures of 65°F to 70°F. Once produce is ripe, refrigerate it immediately or it will become overripe. Even with proper storage, most foodservice operations do not keep produce for more than four days. Some vegetables, such as onions and beets, have a longer life, but most restaurants limit the storage of these items to three weeks. Figure 9.17 shows the proper storage of produce.

584

Figure 9.17: Proper storage of vegetables keeps them fresher longer.

Green vegetables must be placed carefully in a refrigerator. A refrigerator has cold and warm spots, and vegetables can be sensitive to temperature variations of a few degrees, so it is important to know the temperatures in your refrigerator.

Preparing Vegetables

Vegetables must be properly prepared before they are cooked. Preliminary preparations might include cleaning, peeling, slicing, dicing, chopping, and mincing.

Cleaning

All fresh vegetables, even if they will be peeled before cutting, must be cleaned thoroughly. Washing removes surface dirt as well as bacteria and other contaminants. Leafy vegetables contain sand and dirt, and even bugs. Celery and leeks are always dirty at the root. To clean vegetables, run them under water that is a little warmer than the produce. When cleaning leafy greens, such as lettuce and spinach, remove the outer leaves, and pull the lettuce and spinach completely apart and rinse thoroughly. As with fruit, special solutions are available for cleaning vegetables. Wash vegetables as close to preparation time as possible.

Chopping, Dicing, Mincing

The cutting surface should be at a comfortable height so that the elbows are in a natural position. It is best to set up a cutting station with a container to hold

585

Teaching Tips
- Celery and lettuces usually carry some field dirt that needs to be rinsed off.
- Manure might also be present if it was used as a fertilizer.
- Spinach may have dirt on any part of the leaf.
- Perhaps the best way to teach vegetable cleaning is to have the students clean some.

Figure Focus
Figure 9.17: Cool air circulates around the vegetables.

Teaching Tips

- The students can learn best through hands-on practice.
- Help the students to understand the value of a good sharp knife and a good cutting board.

Essential Skills: Dicing Onions

The final vertical strokes of the knife produce a pile of diced onions.

---

any peelings and another container to hold the cut vegetables as you cut them. This allows you to safely cut on a clear cutting board. It should be large enough to accommodate piles of chopped material while the cook is still chopping. It should be securely in place, and not move as the cook chops. Placing a damp towel or rubber mat underneath a cutting board can anchor it on the counter. For safety, foods such as meat, fish, and poultry require a different cutting board from that used for fruits and vegetables. Make sure the vegetables do not touch surfaces exposed to raw meat, seafood, or poultry.

Essential Skills
Dicing Onions

1. Start by cutting off the root end.
2. Slice off the stem end.
3. Peel the onion. See Figure 9.18a.
4. Cut the onion in half from the stem end to the root end and lay one half on the cutting board.
5. Make a series of horizontal cuts, evenly spaced, from one end of the onion to the other. See Figure 9.18b. Make sure not to cut through the end so the onion will hold together as you continue to cut.
6. Hold the onion together and slice vertical cuts in the opposite direction in the desired width to finish the cut.

Figure 9.18a: Step 3—Peel the onion.

Figure 9.18b: Step 5—Make a series of horizontal cuts.

Essential Skills
Mincing Carrots

1. Peel the carrot.
2. Cut off the ends and slightly flatten one side.

Figure Focus

Figure 9.18a: Peeling the onion is not the first step.

Figure 9.18b: The horizontal cuts do the dicing so the onion is not just sliced.

❸ Now it will sit on the board while you slice it into lengthwise slices. See Figure 9.19a.

❹ Lay the slices flat and slice them again into julienne strips. See Figure 9.19b.

❺ Collect the strips together and chop across them, using the rocking motion of the blade. The free hand can hold the carrot. Keep the fingertips tucked back to protect them from the blade. The knuckles can help guide the size of the chop. Go very slowly at first, so that your guiding hand does not come in contact with the sharp edge of the blade. See Figure 9.19c.

Figure 9.19a: Slice lengthwise.

Figure 9.19b: Step 4—Lay slices flat and slice again.

Figure 9.19c: Step 5—Chop strips using a rocking motion.

Dicing is cutting a product into cubes with a chef's knife. Normally, dicing refers to about a half-inch cube—the same size as dice. This is a common technique for use with vegetables.

Essential Skills
Dicing Vegetables

❶ Determine the size of cube that is needed.

❷ Prepare the vegetable by washing and peeling.

❸ Trim the vegetable so that the sides are straight and at right angles. It is often helpful to cut vegetables in half first so that you are working with a flat surface. See Figure 9.20a.

❹ Cut into panels. Before something can be diced, it needs to be cut into logs or sticks, such as a julienne. Always begin by cutting off one side to make it flat. Next, make rectangular slices or panels. See Figure 9.20b.

587

Teaching Tips

- There are many Essential Skills in this section.
- The students will benefit from trying as many of them as possible.

Vocabulary Terms

- **Dicing:** Cutting into small cubes.

Figure Focus

Figure 9.19a: Remember to peel the carrot and slice off the ends before you begin to slice it.

Figure 9.19b: It would be very difficult to dice carrots if you initially cut them into round circles, rather than julienne strips. Why?

Figure 9.19c: A rocking motion allows you to keep cutting, rather than picking the knife up after each cut and "resetting" it.

- Show the students a mezzaluna.
- If one is not available, perhaps there is an ulu handy. It's like a one-handed mezzaluna from Alaska.

Essential Skills:
Mincing Garlic

Mincing fresh garlic is time consuming. It's more than just holding and cutting. You have to peel the garlic, separate the cloves, and prevent the minced pieces from sticking to the knife. Garlic needs to be loosened and slightly crushed to release it.

Vocabulary Terms

- **Mincing:** A fine chop cut made using a chef's knife or mezzaluna.
- **Mezzaluna:** A half-moon shaped blade with two handles.

---

❺ Cut into logs. Stack a number of the rectangles or panels on top of each other and then slice lengthwise, making uniform logs or sticks. See Figure 9.20c.

❻ Line up the logs or sticks and cut across them again, creating perfect cubes. See Figure 9.20d.

Figure 9.20a: Step 3—Trim the vegetables.

Figure 9.20b: Step 4—Cut into panels.

Figure 9.20c: Step 5—Cut into logs.

Figure 9.20d: Step 6—Line up logs and cut into cubes.

Mincing is a fine chop cut made by using a chef's knife or mezzaluna. This cut is commonly used on smaller foods, such as garlic, fresh herbs, and ginger.

Essential Skills
Mincing Garlic

❶ Separate garlic cloves by wrapping an entire head of garlic in a towel and pressing down on the top. See Figure 9.21a.

❷ Loosen the skin from each clove by placing a clove on the cutting board, placing the flat side of the blade on top, and hitting the blade with a fist or the heel of your hand. See Figure 9.21b.

Figure Focus

Figure 9.20a: You need to peel and wash the vegetable before trimming it.

Figure 9.20b: Cutting panels (with a flat side) will help to keep the vegetable stable as you slice them.

Figure 9.20c: Cutting the vegetable into logs makes it easier and more efficient to begin dicing. It helps to ensure an even cut.

Figure 9.20d: When dicing vegetables, it's important to have the cubes be of an even size, so that they cook uniformly.

❸ Peel off the skin and remove the root end and any brown spots. See Figure 9.21c.

❹ Crush the cloves by laying them on the cutting board and using the same technique as for loosening the skin, but this time apply more force. See Figure 9.21d.

❺ Mince the cloves using a rocking motion.

❻ Sprinkling a garlic clove with a dash of salt before mincing will allow the salt to absorb a little of the liquid so it won't stick to the knife and will be easy to mince.

Figure 9.21a: Step 1—Separate the cloves.

Figure 9.21b: Step 2—Loosen the skin.

Figure 9.21c: Step 3—Peel the skin and remove the root end.

Figure 9.21d: Step 4—Crush the cloves.

Essential Skills
Slicing Celery

❶ Chop off the ends and quickly string the stalks, removing the major strings.

589

Teaching Tips

- Garlic is a member of the onion family.
- Garlic minces and crushes well, which releases the flavoring agents.

Essential Skills: Slicing Celery

Celery must be handled properly when preparing it for mirepoix. Stringing the celery makes it more palatable.

Figure Focus

Figure 9.21a: There are several cloves in a garlic bulb.

Figure 9.21b: Garlic skin needs to be loosened from the flesh.

Figure 9.21c: There is a little stub end to cut off.

Figure 9.21d: The heel of the hand on the side of the blade of the knife can push down to crush garlic.

- The students now have the necessary skills to make mirepoix.

Trends:
Organic vs. Organic

Food science and nutrition are specialties of biochemistry, which is based in organic chemistry.

---

❷ Place the stalk curved-side up, and use the tip of the knife to cut the stalk into strips.

❸ Once in strips, proceed to chop the same as a carrot.

Figure 9.22a: Step 1—Chop off the ends.

Figure 9.22b: Step 2—Cut the stalk into strips.

[trends]

Organic vs. Organic

Organic food is grown or produced using methods that are free of chemicals that could be harmful to humans. This includes pesticides, fertilizers, added hormones, and antibiotics. Sustainable, meaning the product can be grown without damaging the environment, is not the same as organic, but they often go hand-in-hand.

"Organic" also refers to any chemical compound that is carbon-based. This would include most pesticides, fertilizers, hormones, and antibiotics. Some of the permissible chemicals used in organic farming include some mineral fertilizers that are not organic molecules.

Organic material that is used for fertilizer is often based on manure. For this reason, it is essential for safety to thoroughly wash any and all organic fruits and vegetables, just as you would all produce in the kitchen. Manure, even though it is usually thoroughly composted and treated for safety before being used to fertilize plants, may harbor harmful pathogens.

Chemistry terms aside, consumers seeking organic foods want safe, simple, wholesome products free of toxic additions. The consumer wants to feel confident that the product will promote good health and nutrition, without being harmful.

Cooking Vegetables

Prepare vegetables for cooking as close to the actual cooking time as possible. This will ensure the vegetables' freshness and add to the overall quality and flavor of the finished dish. Here are some other factors essential to well-cooked vegetables:

- Purchase vegetables that are at the peak of quality.
- Maintain proper storage and handling standards.
- Select a cooking process that is best suited to the vegetable.

Figure Focus

Figure 9.22a: You can do an entire bunch at a time.

Figure 9.22b: Stringing celery is recommended before cutting the stalk into strips.

Vegetables must be cooked in a way that protects their texture, flavor, color, and nutrients. Overcooking vegetables will reduce their quality, nutrient value, and appearance.

Maintaining the quality and flavor of the vegetable depends on both the type of vegetable and the cooking method used. There are many cooking methods for vegetables:

- Boiling (blanching, parboiling)
- Steaming
- Microwaving
- Roasting and baking
- Sautéing and stir-frying
- Pan-frying
- Deep-frying
- Grilling
- Stewing and braising
- *Sous vide*
- Puréeing

See Table 9.11 for the appropriate cooking method for different vegetables.

Table 9.11: Vegetable Cooking Guide

Cooking Method	Appropriate for:
Baking	Carrots, eggplant, mushrooms, onions, potatoes, squash, tomatoes
Boiling	Dried beans and legumes, cabbage, carrots, corn on the cob, potatoes
Braising	Cabbage, celery, mushrooms, potatoes, squash, zucchini
Broiling	Eggplant, mushrooms, onions, tomatoes
Deep-frying	Brussels sprouts, carrots, cauliflower, eggplant, potatoes, squash, zucchini
Steaming	Artichokes, asparagus, green beans, beets, broccoli, Brussels sprouts, cabbage, carrots, cauliflower, celery, onions, potatoes

Cooks use both appearance and texture to test whether or not a vegetable is cooked. Green vegetables show a visible difference from one stage of doneness to another. White and orange vegetables show very little change in their color,

591

- It can be interesting to experiment with cooking methods.

**In-Class Activity:
Vegetable Memory Buzz**

The students should memorize the various cooking methods for vegetables using any mnemonic device that suits them, including acronyms, poetry, first initials, or songs.

Have the students compete to see who can name them all. The first student will attempt to recite all the cooking methods, in order. If the student makes a mistake, the next student may try.

Continue down the line until every student has had a turn. It may take several rounds before any single student recites them all in order.

The first to get them all correct, in order, should get a prize, like an apple or a carrot.

The restaurant industry is competitive, so some competitive activities for high school students are appropriate.

CUSTOMIZED INSTRUCTION

Less Advanced and Special Needs Students

If the teacher feels that a particular student will not be able to participate and compete in the activity above, the teacher can have that student be the keeper of the answer key.

This student can also be the one to present the award at the end.

Table 9.12:
Vegetable Color Changes During Cooking

- Some colors are very appetizing, while others are drab and lifeless.

In-Class Activity:
Demonstration of Acids and Bases on Vegetable Colors

Science Connection

This activity can be completed by students, though a teacher demonstration also works well.

The students have already learned that vinegar is an acid and baking soda is a base. Reinforce this and have new vinegar and baking soda solutions for the demonstration.

You will also need red cabbage, broccoli, spinach, and carrots to complete this activity.

Slightly shred or cut and parboil each of the vegetables on the list.

In clear bowls, put a sample of each vegetable in acid and a sample of each in base.

Let them sit and observe the color changes over the course of the class period.

Allow the vegetables to sit overnight and observe the colors the next day.

Discuss

- What colors in the demonstration appear the most palatable?
- Would you want to eat a blue vegetable?

so cooks check their texture to determine doneness. Table 9.12 illustrates the different color changes in vegetables and shows whether cooking vegetables in acid or alkali is necessary to keep the natural color.

Table 9.12: Vegetable Color Changes During Cooking					
Color	Examples of Vegetables	Cooked with Acid	Cooked with Alkali	Overcooked	Reason for Its Color
White	Potatoes, turnips, cauliflower, onions, white cabbage	Yellow	Yellowish, gray		No coloring compounds
Red	Beets, red cabbage (but not tomatoes; their pigment is like that in yellow vegetables)	Red	Blue/blue green	Greenish blue, faded	Anthocyanins that respond to pH changes
Green	Asparagus, green beans, lima beans, broccoli, Brussels sprouts, peas, spinach, okra, green peppers, artichokes	Olive green	Bright green	Olive green	Chlorophyll that responds to pH changes
Yellow and orange	Carrots, tomatoes, rutabagas, sweet potatoes, squash, corn	Little change	Little change	Slightly faded	Beta-carotene, which has no noticeable color response to pH changes

Boiling is best for hard, starchy vegetables, such as corn and potatoes. Blanch vegetables by quickly and partially cooking them in hot water or oil. This cooking method has some important effects:

- Makes the skin easy to remove
- Sets the color of vegetables that are served cold
- Eliminates or reduces strong flavors
- Is the first step in other cooking methods

592

Parboiling, like blanching, partially cooks vegetables in boiling water.

Steaming is an excellent way to prepare vegetables for to-order service. It is the best way to retain vitamins and minerals because the vegetables are cooked gently in a vapor, or steam bath, not in direct contact with water.

Essential Skills
Steaming Vegetables

❶ Bring the liquid to a full boil, and add the seasonings and aromatics.

❷ Add the vegetables to the steamer in a single layer. See Figure 9.23a.

❸ Steam the vegetables to the desired doneness.

❹ Serve the vegetables, or plunge them in an ice bath and then refresh and hold. See Figure 9.23b.

Figure 9.23a: Step 2—Add the items to the steamer in a single layer.

Figure 9.23b: Step 4—Serve or plunge the items in an ice bath.

Microwaves cause food molecules to vibrate, and the friction from that vibration generates heat. This causes the food's natural liquids to steam the item. Cook vegetables in a microwave-safe container, covered, in a small amount of liquid. Or leave the vegetable whole, with the skin or peel intact, and steam it with its own moisture.

Essential Skills
Microwaving Vegetables

❶ Place the vegetable in a suitable dish or plate, and cover it.

❷ Place it in a microwave oven, and cook it to the desired doneness.

593

Figure Focus
Figure 9.23a: Do not overfill a steamer.

Figure 9.23b: An ice-water bath will stop the cooking.

- Vegetables may be brushed with olive oil before grilling or roasting.
- Vegetables may be marinated a few hours before grilling or roasting.
- A marinade that contains some oil is a good idea for roasting vegetables.

❸ Serve the vegetables, or refresh and hold. See Figure 9.24.

Figure 9.24: Step 4—Serve the vegetables.

Roasting and baking are two very popular ways to cook vegetables. Roast or bake vegetables in a hot or moderate oven. Leave them whole or cut them into large pieces without adding liquid. This cooking method is best suited to vegetables with thick skins that protect the interior from drying or scorching, such as winter squash, potatoes, and eggplant. Figure 9.25 is a photo of roasted crab apple with pork.

Figure 9.25: Adding roasted vegetables to a dish is a way to make a healthy and hearty dish.

594

Figure Focus

Figure 9.24: Serve vegetables hot and fresh.

Figure 9.25: Vegetables may be roasted on a grill or in the oven.

Essential Skills
Roasting Vegetables

❶ Place the vegetables onto a preheated, hot pan and into a hot or moderate oven.

❷ Roast them to the desired doneness. See Figure 9.26.

❸ Serve, hold, or use them in a secondary technique.

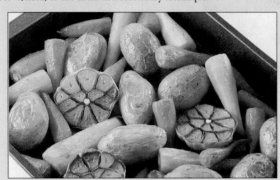

Figure 9.26: Step 2—Roast to desired doneness.

Essential Skills:
Sautéing and Stir-Frying Vegetables

Sauté using butter, olive oil, or another type of fat. Stir-frying is done quickly with a light oil or stock.

Teaching Tips

- Stir-frying is a typical Asian technique.
- The color of stir-fried vegetables should be bright and true.
- Overcooking stir-fry will make the color dull.
- Stir-fried vegetables should also remain crisp.
- Overcooking stir-fry will also make vegetables too soft.
- Proper stir-frying yields a crisp, bright, hot, freshly sweet vegetable.

While thick-skinned vegetables are well suited for roasting, vegetables with little or no skin are best when sautéed. Sautéing gives vegetables a crisp texture. Some vegetables are suitable for sautéing in their raw state, such as mushrooms and onions. Partially cook denser vegetables, such as green beans and carrots, before they are sautéed.

Essential Skills
Sautéing and Stir-Frying Vegetables

❶ Heat the pan; add the cooking medium, and heat it.

❷ Add the vegetables.

❸ Sauté the vegetables, keeping it in motion. See Figure 9.27a.

❹ Add the aromatics, seasonings, or glaze, and heat thoroughly.

595

Figure Focus

Figure 9.26: Watch the vegetables. Try to roast vegetables that will be done at the same time.

Essential Skills: Glazing Vegetables

A glaze is especially good on carrots.

Teaching Tips

- Glazing recipes frequently call for some butter and sugar. The combination forms a unified and flavorful glaze.

Vocabulary Terms

- **Glazing:** A shiny finishing technique.

❺ Serve the vegetables immediately. Figure 9.27b.

Figure 9.27a: Step 3—Keep vegetables in motion.

Figure 9.27b: Step 5—Serve immediately.

Glazing is a finishing technique that gives vegetables a glossy appearance. Add a small amount of honey, sugar, or maple syrup to the vegetable to coat it and give it a sheen as the vegetable reheats. For example, cooks often glaze small pearl onions and baby carrots.

Essential Skills
Glazing Vegetables

❶ Bring the liquid to a simmer and season or flavor as the recipe instructs.

❷ Sweat or smother the vegetables and any aromatics in a cooking fat or in the cooking liquid, if desired. See Figure 9.28a.

❸ Pour or ladle enough cooking liquid into the pan to properly cook the vegetables.

❹ Cover the pan and cook until the vegetables are done.

❺ Remove the vegetables and drain. See Figure 9.28b.

❻ Reserve the cooking liquid. Add honey, brown sugar, or maple syrup and continue to reduce to make the glaze.

❼ Gently toss the vegetables in the glaze.

596

Figure Focus

Figure 9.27a: The wok and a bamboo tool can help toss the vegetables.

Figure 9.27b: Vegetables can lose color and crispness if held.

Figure 9.28a: Step 2—Sweat or smother the vegetables.

Figure 9.28b: Step 5—Remove the vegetables and drain.

Unlike the cooking methods covered so far, cooks often coat pan-fried vegetables with breading or batter. The amount of oil used in pan-frying is greater than that for sautéing. Cook batter-dipped vegetables in oil or butter until their exteriors are lightly browned and crisp.

Essential Skills
Pan-Frying Vegetables

❶ Heat the pan.

❷ Add the cooking oil and heat. See Figure 9.29a.

❸ Add the vegetables.

❹ Cook until their exteriors are slightly browned and crisp. See Figure 9.29b.

❺ Blot them on absorbent paper toweling.

❻ Season and serve immediately.

Figure 9.29a: Step 2—Add cooking oil and heat.

Figure 9.29b: Step 4—Cook until slightly browned and crisp.

597

**Essential Skills:
Pan-Frying Vegetables**

The crispness of the browning will soften if the vegetable is held.

Discuss
- Stir-frying is done in a wok.
- Pan frying is done in a frying pan.
- Similar techniques apply to both.
- Perhaps the students would like to discuss the similarities and differences between the two.

Figure Focus
Figure 9.28a: These are pearl onions.

Figure 9.28b: When draining, reserve the cooking liquid to use for glazing.

Figure 9.29a: Melt the fat in the pan before the vegetables are added.

Figure 9.29b: Paper towels will absorb the excess fat from the frying pan.

- Can the students think of examples of deep-fried vegetables?
- Deep-fried potatoes are French fries, which will be discussed in more depth in a later chapter.

Essential Skills: Deep-Frying Vegetables

Coating provides a medium for the crispy deep-frying.

Essential Skills: Grilling Vegetables

Marinating a vegetable should begin a few hours before grilling.

As in pan-frying, coat vegetables to be deep-fried with breading or batter just before cooking. Instead of a shallow pan, use a deep fryer or large, heavy pot. Blanch slow-cooking vegetables, like broccoli and cauliflower, before they are deep-fried to speed the cooking process.

Essential Skills
Deep-Frying Vegetables

1. Coat the vegetables with breading or batter.
2. Heat the oil in a deep-fryer and add the vegetable. See Figure 9.30a.
3. Fry the vegetable until they are evenly browned or golden.
4. Remove from the oil and blot them on absorbent paper towels.
5. Adjust the seasoning and serve the vegetables immediately. See Figure 9.30b.

Figure 9.30a: Step 2—Heat the oil and add the vegetables.

Figure 9.30b: Step 5—Adjust seasoning and serve immediately.

Grilling is a popular method for cooking vegetables. Some vegetables can be grilled in the raw state, while others must be marinated. To marinate vegetables, soak them in oil or vinegar, herbs, and spices. This gives them added flavor and helps to tenderize the vegetable. The vegetable must be able to withstand the grill's intense heat. Some vegetables well suited for grilling are bell peppers, potatoes, zucchini, and onions.

Essential Skills
Grilling Vegetables

1. Heat the grill or broiler.
2. Marinate the vegetables or brush them with oil. See Figure 9.31.
3. Grill or broil until the vegetables are tender and properly cooked through.

598

Figure Focus

Figure 9.30a: Make sure there are no water droplets going into the fat.

Figure 9.30b: Hot, crispy fried foods will become soggy and oily if held. If they cool, the fat will congeal.

❹ Season to taste and serve the vegetables immediately.

Figure 9.31: Step 2—Marinate or brush with oil.

Vegetable stews and braises are good ways to retain the vitamins and minerals that are transferred to the cooking liquid. For either method, cook vegetables in oil or stock and then season them. Add broth or another cooking liquid, then cook the vegetables until tender. In these methods, serve the liquid as part of the dish. Cut stewed vegetables into small pieces; cut braised vegetables into large pieces or leave whole.

Essential Skills
Stewing and Braising Vegetables

❶ Heat the pan.

❷ Heat the oil or stock.

❸ Add vegetables, and cover with seasonings or aromatics.

❹ Add the liquid, bring it to a simmer, and cook the vegetable. See Figure 9.32a.

❺ Add the remaining vegetables and aromatics. See Figure 9.32b.

❻ Cook the stew or braise until the vegetables are tender.

❼ Adjust the seasoning, and finish the dish according to the recipe. See Figure 9.32c.

599

**Essential Skills:
Stewing and Braising Vegetables**

Stewing may require a long cooking time. Not every ingredient stews in the same amount of time.

Teaching Tips

- Some vitamins and minerals are water-soluble. What does this mean for vegetables that have been boiled in water?
- Some vitamins are fat-soluble. What does that mean for vegetables that have been boiled in water?
- Some vitamins are destroyed by high heat. What would be the result of boiling vegetables which contain those vitamins?
- Some vitamins are more available after cooking than before.
- The best solution is to eat a varied diet that uses a variety of foods and cooking methods.

Figure Focus
Figure 9.31: Oil helps the vegetables to grill and taste slightly smoked without burning.

- Discuss *sous vide* cooking with the students.
- *Sous vide* prevents aromatic molecules from leaving the food.
- Aroma and flavor contain the same molecules. If they remain in the food, there is more flavor.

Essential Skills: Puréeing Vegetables

First, cook the vegetables until they are soft. Puréed vegetables are often used as an ingredient in other recipes.

Vocabulary Terms

- *Sous vide:* A slow, low-heat, airtight water bath method that preserves aroma, flavor, and moisture.
- **Puréed:** Finely mashed or strained.

---

❽ Serve the vegetables or hold.

Figure 9.32a: Step 4—Add liquid, simmer, and cook.

Figure 9.32b: Step 5—Add remaining vegetables.

Figure 9.32c: Step 7—Adjust seasoning.

Sous vide is a method in which food is cooked for a long time, sometimes well over 24 hours. Rather than placing food in a slow cooker, the *sous vide* method uses airtight plastic bags placed in hot water well below boiling point. Food is cooked using precisely controlled heating, at the temperature at which it should be served.

Serve **puréed (PYOO-rayed)** vegetables as individual dishes or use them in other preparations, custards, and soufflés. Cook the vegetable until it is tender enough to purée easily by pushing it through a sieve or food mill, or using a vertical chopping machine or blender. Some vegetables, such as tomatoes, spinach, and cucumbers, can be puréed from the raw state.

Essential Skills
Puréeing Vegetables

❶ Cook the vegetable until it is very tender. See Figure 9.33a.

❷ Drain it and remove any excess moisture.

❸ Purée the vegetable using a sieve, a heavy-duty blender, or an immersion blender. See Figure 9.33b.

Figure Focus

Figure 9.32a: Simmer ingredients that need the most cooking time first.

Figure 9.32b: Later, add vegetables or other ingredients that might not need as much stewing time.

Figure 9.32c: Correct the seasonings before serving.

❹ Adjust the seasoning, finish, and serve, or use in a secondary preparation. See Figure 9.33c.

Figure 9.33a: Step 1—Cook until tender.

Figure 9.33b: Step 3—Purée using a sieve or blender.

Figure 9.33c: Step 4—Adjust seasoning.

Holding Vegetables

The best way to maintain overall quality is to cook vegetables soon after purchase and then serve them as quickly as possible. If vegetables must be held for a period of time before being served, here are some techniques to maintain their quality:

- Boiled or steamed vegetables can be refreshed in cold water.

- Starchy vegetables should be well drained and spread out to dry.

- Baked or roasted vegetables should be held uncovered in a holding drawer if they are to be served within four hours of their preparation. If not, spread them on sheet pans, cool completely, and then wrap them.

- Braised or stewed vegetables can be held in a steam table.

- Various methods of reheating vegetables include simmering them in stock or water, microwaving, sautéing them in butter or cream, or dry-sautéing using a cooking spray in the pan.

- Avoid holding vegetables either in steam tables or directly in water for extended periods of time.

Discuss

- Encourage the students to think of ways to hold vegetables.
- What qualities might be lost with long holding?
- What holding methods might damage the quality of vegetables?
- What holding methods would protect color, texture, and flavor?
- If at all possible, have the students cook and hold vegetables using various methods.
- Have them evaluate the product.

Figure Focus

Figure 9.33a: Peel tomatoes before cooking them for purée.

Figure 9.33b: The sieve or blender breaks down the cooked structure to a soft mash.

Figure 9.33c: Always check the seasoning with a clean spoon.

Reinforce and Review

- There are various categories of fruits and vegetables.
- Students should be able to distinguish between the different types.
- Not all fresh produce comes from a commercial acreage farm. Some is hydroponic. Organic is also available.

Teaching Tips

- Students may be interested to learn about various vegetable and fruit condiments, including the following:
  - **Chutney**—A fresh or pickled fruit or vegetable and spice sauce from India. An example of chutney could be a sauce of tomatoes, cinnamon, and raisins.
  - **Compote**—Fresh fruit in a light sugar syrup, perhaps lightly cooked, perhaps raw.
  - **Confit** – Candied fruit.
  - **Conserve**—A fresh fruit sugar jam-like preparation with whole pieces of small fruits.
  - **Coulis**—A puréed fruit sauce made glossy and viscous with dissolved sugar and a bit of cooking, then thickened with cornstarch or arrowroot. There are also uncooked versions of coulis.
  - **Jam**—A cooked or frozen mixture of crushed fruit and sugar, thickened with pectin.
  - **Jelly**—A boiled and cooled mixture of fruit juice and sugar, thickened with pectin.
  - **Marmalade**—A slightly sour and bitter yet very sweet jam or conserve made with citrus juice, sugar, and bits of citrus peel.

Summary

In this section, you learned the following:

- Flower, fruit, green leafy, seed, root/tuber, and stem are categories of vegetables:
  - Flower vegetables include broccoli, cauliflower, Brussels sprouts, and cabbage.
  - Fruit vegetables include avocados, cucumbers, eggplants, peppers, squash, and tomatoes.
  - Green leafy vegetables include various types of lettuce, mustard greens, spinach, and Swiss chard.
  - Seed vegetables include corn, peas, and beans.
  - Root vegetables include carrots, beets, radishes, turnips, and onion.
  - Tuber vegetables include potatoes, sweet potatoes, and yams.
  - Stem vegetables include asparagus, celery, artichokes, and mushrooms.
- Hydroponic farming allows vegetables to be grown indoors year-round under regulated temperatures and light in nutrient-enriched water.

602

- **Preserves**—Another name for jams, jellies, and marmalades. However, preserves may also be their own category with larger chunks of fruits than jam usually contains.
- **Relish**—Chopped mixture of fruits and vegetables, pickled.
- **Salsa**—Chopped mixture of vegetables and sometimes fruits with spices. Usually tomatoes are included.

■ Roots and tubers should be stored dry and unpeeled in a cool, dark area. Many of the other ripe vegetables can be stored at 41°F or lower. Most vegetables need to be kept dry because excess moisture causes produce to spoil quickly. Vegetables that need to ripen should be stored at room temperatures of 65°F to 70°F. Once produce is ripe, refrigerate it immediately or it will become overripe. Green vegetables must be placed carefully in a cooler.

■ There are many ways to cook vegetables, including boiling (blanching, parboiling), steaming, microwaving, roasting and baking, sautéing and stir-frying, pan-frying, deep-frying, *sous vide*, stewing and braising, grilling, and puréeing.

■ The best way to maintain overall quality is to cook vegetables rapidly and then serve them as soon as possible.

603

Summary

- Remind students to review the following:
  1. The various types of vegetables
  2. Hydroponic farming
  3. How to properly store produce
  4. The steps needed to prepare vegetables for service
  5. Maintaining the quality of vegetables

Section 9.2 Review Questions

1. Appropriate cooking methods for each include:
   a. Simmer, steam, microwave
   b. Simmer, steam, microwave, boil
   c. Simmer, steam, microwave, boil, stir-fry
   d. Simmer, steam, microwave, boil, sauté, roast
   e. Boil, bake
   f. Bake, grill, roast
   g. Bake, boil, microwave, fry, roast, sauté
   h. Simmer, steam, boil, roast, fry, *sous vide*

2. One way to hold vegetables without losing quality is to stop the cooking process using cold water. Draining, holding uncovered, using a steam table, and simmering in stock can all help keep the quality high. Do not hold vegetables for a long time or they will lose color, texture, flavor, and quality.

3. The classifications of the vegetable are:
   a. Stem
   b. Fruit
   c. Flower
   d. Root
   f. Fruit
   g. Stem (fungi)
   h. Green leafy
   i. Root
   j. Seed
   k. Green leafy
   l. Tuber

4. Both grow underground and are part of the root system of the plant. Roots can be above and below the ground and are part of a single root. Tubers are fat underground stems that can reproduce a single new plant.

5. Each student's work will be unique.

6. Field greens and baby greens, plus tender new stem vegetables are a great way to celebrate summer. Very light, minimal cooking may be used, like steaming, sautéing, or stir frying.

7. Vegetables can be used in many main-dish salads. They can be used as meat substitutes as well, such as Portobello mushrooms for a hamburger patty. Vegetables can be used in sauces, dressings, pasta dishes, and even in breads and pasta doughs.

8. Mature means it is full-sized and the appropriate color for harvest. Ripe means it is optimal for eating. Mature fruit is sometimes harvested and shipped before it is fully ripe.

Section 9.2 Review Questions

1. Identify the appropriate cooking method for each type of vegetable.
   a. Artichokes
   b. Brussels sprouts
   c. Cabbage
   d. Carrots
   e. Dried beans and legumes
   f. Eggplant
   g. Potatoes
   h. Tomatoes

2. If you have to hold vegetables before serving, what should you do to maintain their quality?

3. Vegetables may be classified as a flower, fruit, green leafy, seed, root/tuber, or stem vegetable. Identify the appropriate classification for each of the vegetables below.
   a. Asparagus
   b. Avocado
   c. Broccoli
   d. Brussels sprout
   e. Carrot
   f. Eggplant
   g. Mushroom
   h. Mustard green
   i. Onion
   j. Peas
   k. Spinach
   l. Sweet potato

4. How are roots and tubers alike? How are they different? Give some examples of each.

5. Daron Kinder specifically likes to try new gene-spliced vegetables. Research two gene-spliced vegetables and identify a recipe in which each is used.

6. What vegetables can Chef Jean use on the lighter spring/summer menu, and what are some appropriate cooking techniques?

7. In addition to being a side dish, how else can vegetables be used?

8. What is the difference between a mature piece of fruit and a ripe piece of fruit?

Section 9.2 Activities

1. Study Skills/Group Activity: Vegetable Cookbook

Work with three other classmates to find two recipes that use a vegetable as an appetizer, two recipes that use a vegetable as the main ingredient of a salad, two recipes that use a vegetable in an entrée, and two recipes that use a vegetable as a dessert. Put the recipes together and create a vegetable cookbook.

2. Activity: The Most Interesting Vegetable

Pick an interesting or unusual vegetable, and then create a presentation on why this vegetable is unique. Include information on the history of the vegetable and how it is cultivated. Make a creative presentation to the class using PowerPoint, charts, and/or props. After all class members have made their presentations, the class votes on the best one.

3. Critical Thinking: Vegetable Condiments

Have you ever noticed how many fruit and vegetable condiments there are? Relishes, jams, compotes, salsa—it's a long and sometimes confusing list. Create a chart of the similarities and differences between chutney, compote, confit, conserve, coulis, jam, jelly, marmalade, preserve, relish, and salsa.

605

Section 9.2 Activities

1. Each student's work will be unique.

2. Each student's work will be unique.

3. Each student's work will be unique.

Case Study Follow-Up

1. The chef can add salads, desserts, cold soups, and main dish items that feature seasonal offerings. Recipes could range from pasta sauce to berry coulis. The students will have their own ideas.

2. One idea would be a cold, creamy sweet fruit soup.

3. He should use locally grown produce, harvested and transported for optimal ripeness.

4. Exotic produce may be used at various times of the year. Some are available year-round, for a price, so they could be permanent menu items. Local produce will be flavorful and not require shipping great distances.

5. There will need to be space in coolers, preferably a fruit cooler and a vegetable cooler. Also, there will need to be dry dark storage for tubers, plus 65°F–70°F storage for fruits and vegetables that need to ripen.

Discuss

- See if the students understand why fruit and vegetable menu items could be a draw to a restaurant.
- Students should realize that fruits and vegetables require a financial commitment.
- See if the students can verbalize the impact of fresh produce on the Uptown Grille's menu.
- Ask the students for menu item suggestions.

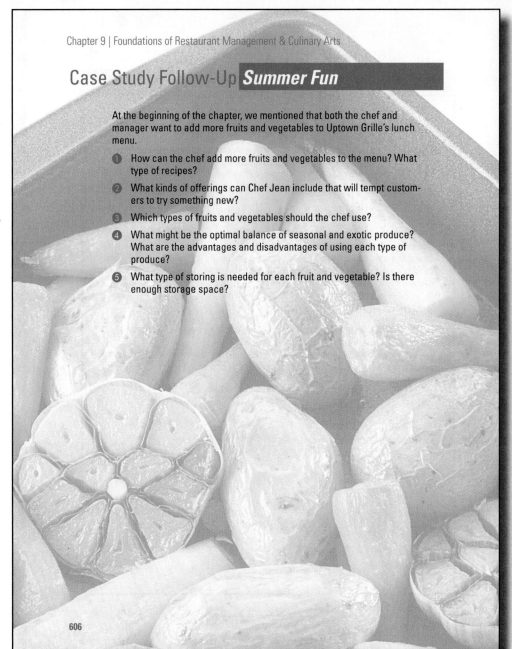

Case Study Follow-Up *Summer Fun*

At the beginning of the chapter, we mentioned that both the chef and manager want to add more fruits and vegetables to Uptown Grille's lunch menu.

1. How can the chef add more fruits and vegetables to the menu? What type of recipes?

2. What kinds of offerings can Chef Jean include that will tempt customers to try something new?

3. Which types of fruits and vegetables should the chef use?

4. What might be the optimal balance of seasonal and exotic produce? What are the advantages and disadvantages of using each type of produce?

5. What type of storing is needed for each fruit and vegetable? Is there enough storage space?

606

Apply Your Learning

Apply Your Learning

Timing and Preparation

Develop a dinner menu that includes a fresh vegetable or fruit salad, a roasted vegetable as part of the main dish, a steamed side vegetable, and a fruit-based dessert. Each recipe has time requirements. Make note of all time-related aspects, including time to prepare *mise en place*, time to tend various steps, baking or cooking time, cooling or holding time (which is best for the success of the menu), and time to plate each recipe for service.

After all of the recipes have been considered, determine the time you would like to serve the meal. Make a time line on paper, with the service point at the end. Mark the time line in increments of time, minutes, quarter hours, hours, days, etc.

Working backward from the end point, subtract the time required for each step of each recipe. Mark on the time line when to begin each step. This will not only tell you when to begin, it will also give you an idea of how well the various recipe preparations will coordinate. Having too much to do at any given point—especially toward the end—will be frustrating.

As you work on the timing, also consider the geometry of your kitchen and workspaces. There must be a place to perform each step. Include preparation of *mise en place*, preheating equipment, and parboiling items in the planning. Consider the space required. Consider personnel and who will do what, when, and where.

Once the time line has been established, see if your calculations have been realistic. Is everything ready on time? Make adjustments to the time line as necessary.

Kiwi Fruit

Kiwi fruit is a large green berry with a rough and fuzzy brown skin. The skin should always be removed before serving. The kiwi is often considered to be a tropical fruit. However, it can grow well in temperate zones, not just in the tropics.

Investigate the origin of the name "kiwi fruit" and the fruit's home. Write a paragraph about it. Investigate the difference between a temperate climate zone and a tropical climate zone. Include information about this in a second paragraph about the kiwi's homeland.

607

Timing and Preparation

Students should begin the time line on the far-right side with the desired serving time. Students should work backwards, moving left, through the time requirements to determine when preparations for each dish should begin.

If several recipes need to be made for meal service, a time line will help plan when to begin each dish and how to dovetail the preparations of all the dishes that must be ready at once.

See the sample time line at the bottom of the page.

Kiwi Fruit

Kiwi fruit is really a large berry from New Zealand. The Kiwi is a wingless, flightless bird indigenous to New Zealand. Kiwi has also become a nickname for all things New Zealand. The name was given to the fruit to help market it internationally as a New Zealand product.

New Zealand is an island nation located in the Southern Hemisphere, south of the tropical zone, in the temperate zone. It is cooler than a tropical climate.

Sample Time Line

desserts final	roll dough		prep carrots		prep potatoes	salad greens	prep meat	roast all	bake rolls	salad	serve
8	9	10	11	12	1	2	3	4	5	5:50	6

Go Bananas!

In the twentieth century, bananas became available worldwide outside the tropics. They were mass produced on plantations in South America and shipped everywhere.

In the twenty-first century, the Philippines, India, Southeast Asia, and other tropical regions will be more involved in banana production and trade.

The current situation for bananas is precarious, and they are vulnerable to a pandemic that could destroy the crop. There is not enough genetic diversity in the bananas that are cultivated for trade. Genetic engineering may be able to correct or improve this situation, but without intervention, the varieties of bananas worldwide consumers enjoy may become virtually extinct.

Gros Michel bananas were the commonly exported variety early in the twentieth century. There was not enough genetic diversity in the crops and they all fell prey to Panama Disease and almost completely died out. The Cavendish variety was substituted for export, but it faces the same potential problem unless new varieties are developed.

Critical Thinking Rhubarb

Each student's work will be unique. They may include various elements, such as something about seed pods, varied uses for sweet or savory fruits, comparisons, or similarity of flavors.

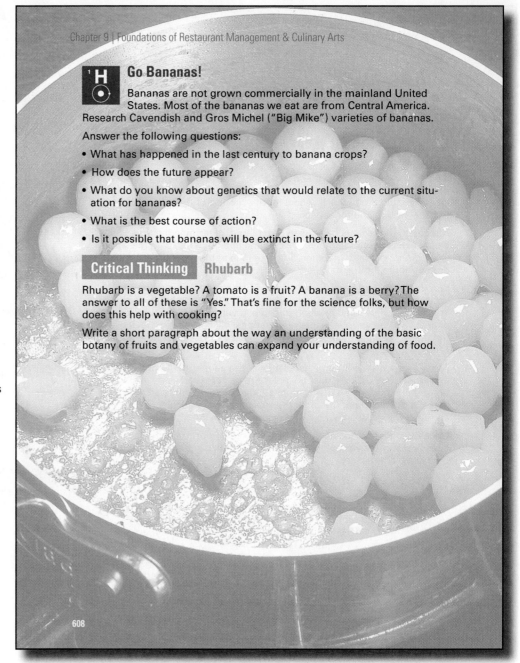

Go Bananas!

Bananas are not grown commercially in the mainland United States. Most of the bananas we eat are from Central America. Research Cavendish and Gros Michel ("Big Mike") varieties of bananas.

Answer the following questions:

- What has happened in the last century to banana crops?
- How does the future appear?
- What do you know about genetics that would relate to the current situation for bananas?
- What is the best course of action?
- Is it possible that bananas will be extinct in the future?

Critical Thinking Rhubarb

Rhubarb is a vegetable? A tomato is a fruit? A banana is a berry? The answer to all of these is "Yes." That's fine for the science folks, but how does this help with cooking?

Write a short paragraph about the way an understanding of the basic botany of fruits and vegetables can expand your understanding of food.

608

Exam Prep Questions

1 Fruits that have a central pit enclosing a single seed are known as

A. drupes.

B. winter fruits.

C. tropical fruits.

D. summer fruits.

2 Rome and Granny Smith are types of

A. pears.

B. apples.

C. bananas.

D. oranges.

3 What type of vegetable form is rich in sugars, starches, vitamins, and minerals, and exists both above and below ground?

A. Root

B. Stem

C. Flower

D. Tuber

4 Chili peppers, avocados, and squash are what type of vegetables?

A. Seed

B. Fruit

C. Tuber

D. Flower

5 Canned fruit that is bruised and mushy would be given a USDA rating of

A. U.S. Grade A Fancy.

B. U.S. Grade. B Choice.

C. U.S. Grade C Standard.

D. U.S. Grade D Poor.

6 At what temperature should you store vegetables and fruits that need to ripen?

A. 41°F or lower

B. 51°F to 56°F

C. 60°F to 65°F

D. 70°F or higher

7 Fruits that are cooked in simmering water are

A. broiled.

B. poached.

C. sautéed.

D. roasted.

8 The form of cooking in which a vegetable is quickly and partially cooked in hot water or oil is known as

A. poaching.

B. parboiling.

C. *sous vide.*

D. blanching.

609

Exam Prep Answers

1. A
2. B
3. A
4. B
5. D
6. C
7. B
8. B
9. B
10. D

9 What is the most appropriate cooking method for cabbage and celery?

A. Baking

B. Braising

C. Broiling

D. Steaming

10 The chemical process that occurs when oxygen in the air comes in contact with the flesh of cut fruit and turns it brown is called

A. seeding.

B. glazing.

C. caramelizing.

D. enzymatic browning.

610

Brussels Sprouts in Pecan Butter

Cooking time: 45 minutes
Yield: 6 servings, 3 ounces

1 pound	Brussels sprouts	4 ounces	Pecans, chopped
2 ounces	Whole butter	To taste	Salt and pepper

Directions

1. Trim the Brussels sprouts, and mark an X in the bottom of each with a paring knife to promote even cooking.
2. Boil the sprouts in salted water until tender, approximately 10 minutes.
3. Drain and hold the sprouts in a warm place.
4. Heat the butter in a sauté pan until noisette. Add the pecans and toss to brown them.
5. Add the Brussels sprouts, and toss to reheat and blend flavors. Adjust the seasonings and serve.

Recipe Nutritional Content

Calories	370	Cholesterol	20 mg	Protein	13 g
Calories from fat	200	Sodium	1350 mg	Vitamin A	70%
Total fat	23 g	Carbohydrates	40 g	Vitamin C	440%
Saturated fat	6 g	Dietary fiber	13 g	Calcium	20%
Trans fat	0 g	Sugars	8 g	Iron	30%

Nutritional analysis provided by FoodCalc®, www.foodcalc.com

611

Recipe

Brussels Sprouts in Pecan Butter

- Brussels sprouts are a form of wild cabbage.
- Production in the United States began around 1800, when the French settlers brought them to Louisiana.
- They contain essentials vitamins and minerals. Some think they have cancer-inhibiting potential because they contain nitrogen compounds called indoles and vitamin C, which acts as an antioxidant.

Recipe

Spinach Au Gratin

- Spinach used to be known as Popeye's secret weapon.
- Spinach originated in Persia, modern-day Iran.
- In 1533, Catherine de' Medici, Queen of France, decided she liked spinach so much that she had it served at every meal. As a matter of fact, many spinach dishes are called "Florentine" because Catherine originally came from Florence, Italy.
- There are four main types of spinach—savoy, flat (smooth-leaf), semi-savoy, and baby spinach.

Spinach Au Gratin (Ruth's Chris Steak House, Phoenix, AZ)

Cooking time: 45 minutes
Yield: 8 servings, 8 ounces each

1 fluid ounce	Clarified butter	To taste	Salt and pepper
1 ounce	Flour	1 pound, 8 ounces	Cheddar cheese, shredded
1 pint	Half-and-half		
2 pounds, 8 ounces	Frozen chopped spinach, thawed		

Directions

1. Heat the butter in a saucepan. Add the flour, and cook to make a blond roux.
2. Add the half-and-half, whisking to remove any lumps of roux. Bring to a simmer, and cook for 15 minutes.
3. Drop the spinach into boiling salted water, and cook for 2 minutes. Remove from the heat and drain well.
4. Combine the hot spinach with the cream sauce, and adjust the seasonings.
5. Fill eight 10-ounce gratin dishes with the creamed spinach. Top each with 3 ounces of cheese, and place under the broiler until the cheese is melted and browned and the spinach is very hot. Serve immediately.

Recipe Nutritional Content

Calories	510	Cholesterol	120 mg	Protein	29 g
Calories from fat	340	Sodium	860 mg	Vitamin A	370%
Total fat	39 g	Carbohydrates	14 g	Vitamin C	6%
Saturated fat	24 g	Dietary fiber	5 g	Calcium	90%
Trans fat	0 g	Sugars	1 g	Iron	20%

Nutritional analysis provided by FoodCalc®, www.foodcalc.com

612

Banana Fritters
Cooking time: 45 minutes
Yield: 40 fritters

1	Egg, beaten		1	Banana, large
8 ounces	Milk		12 ounces	Pastry flour, sifted
2 ounces	Unsalted butter, melted		4 ounces	Granulated sugar
1 teaspoon	Vanilla extract		1 tablespoon	Baking powder
2 tablespoon	Finely grated orange zest		½ teaspoon	Salt
2 fluid ounces	Orange juice		As needed	Powdered sugar

Directions

1. Whisk together the egg, milk, butter, and vanilla. Add the orange zest and orange juice.
2. Peel and dice the banana, and add to the egg mixture.
3. Sift together the flour, sugar, baking powder, and salt. Gently stir in the banana-egg mixture to form a thick batter.
4. Heat deep-fryer oil to 350°F. Fry 1 tablespoon portions of the batter until the fritters are brown and crisp, approximately 5 minutes.
5. Drain on paper towels, dust with confectioners' sugar, and serve hot.

Recipe Nutritional Content

Calories	230		Cholesterol	10 mg		Protein	1 g
Calories from fat	170		Sodium	70 mg		Vitamin A	2%
Total fat	20 g		Carbohydrates	12 g		Vitamin C	2%
Saturated fat	3.5 g		Dietary fiber	0 g		Calcium	4%
Trans fat	0 g		Sugars	5 g		Iron	2%

Nutritional analysis provided by FoodCalc®, www.foodcalc.com

613

Recipe

Banana Fritters

- Fritters can refer to any type of food that is coated in batter and fried or sautéed. There can be potato fritters, apple fritters, corn fritters, conch fritters, etc.
- Fritters are very popular snacks in South Asia. They are often cooked roadside in deep woks.

Chapter 10 Overview

Chapter 10 provides an overview of service and hospitality before delving into the specific details of tending to guest needs in a professional manner.

Section 1: The first section discusses why proper guest service is essential to any business and describes some ways in which staff can identify and address needs.

Section 2: This section explains some particular service activities, such as taking orders and processing payments.

Section 3: The final section describes some service styles, typical staff responsibilities, and service tools.

Advance Preparation	
Review	Sections 10.1–10.3
	Chapters 1, 2, 3, 4, 7
Contact	The state liquor authority
Prepare	Copies of local restaurant reviews
	Copy of an older etiquette guide

ServSafe Connection
Page 663

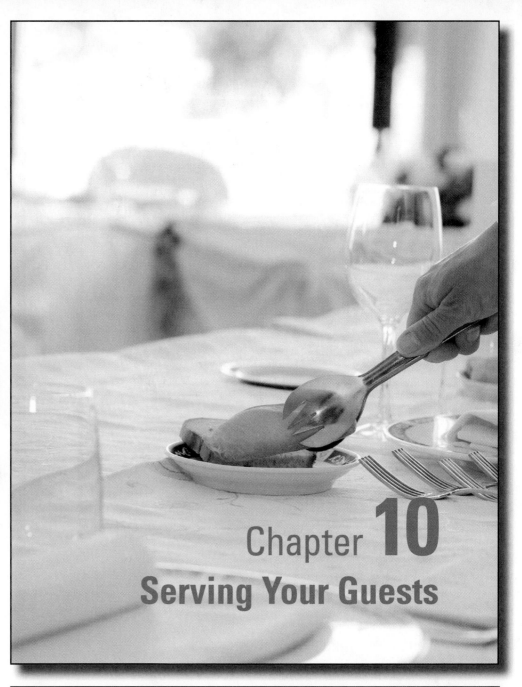

Chapter 10
Serving Your Guests

CUSTOMIZED INSTRUCTION OPTIONS			
Less Advanced Students	**More Advanced Students**	**ESOL Students**	**Special Needs Students**
Pages 639, 655	Pages 639, 655	Pages 624, 639	Pages 624, 643

CHAPTER TOOLS			
21st-Century Skills	**Mathematics**	**Science**	**Literacy**
Pages 618, 619, 620, 624, 630, 634, 636, 637, 639, 640, 643, 655, 658, 660, 664	Pages 631, 638	Pages 619, 634, 640	Pages 618, 619, 620, 624, 630, 631, 634, 636, 637, 638, 639, 640, 643, 655, 658, 660, 664

Case Study · *Wanted: Customer Service*

Uptown Grille has decided to offer gourmet versions of deli standards for a take-out menu. Customers can either purchase takeout items, such as cheeses and cured meats, or can order a snack or casual meal to enjoy in the adjacent seating area. The establishment is known for both its exceptional customer service and for its unusual food offerings.

Uptown Grille has been a popular destination for casual dining. Recently, however, management has seen a change. Business has slowed dramatically, and the word around town is that the customer service is to blame. Linda and Chef Jean are really concerned about the situation, but they're not sure how to handle it. Recently, they had to replace a number of seasoned employees, but it has been difficult to find qualified staff to fill these positions. Most of their new employees are inexperienced, but they all seem friendly and eager to learn.

As you read this chapter, think about the following questions:

1. What should Linda and Chef Jean do to ensure their employees provide excellent customer service? What would you do?

2. Complaints often arise when inexperienced staff members serve customers. How can Linda and Chef Jean work with their employees to resolve any problems?

3. How can Linda and Chef Jean win back community support?

4. Once they achieve a high level of quality customer service, how can Linda and Chef Jean maintain this standard?

Case Study
Wanted: Customer Service

- What do students envision when they consider excellent customer service? Encourage them to describe their most positive or negative experiences as guests.
- How can poor customer service sink an otherwise strong restaurant or foodservice establishment?
- Is good food more important than good service? Why or why not?
- How does good guest service relate to communication? What skills did students learn in Chapter 7 that can help them provide better service?
- Note that there are follow-up questions about the case study at the end of the chapter.
- This activity could be done in groups, as a class, or as a homework assignment.

Professional Profile

Discuss	What does the quote at the beginning of Danny Meyer's Professional Profile mean? How is it relevant to either guest service or the restaurant and foodservice industry as a whole?
	How can students know themselves? What can they do to learn more about themselves and what makes them happy?
Reinforce and Review	People remember how they feel about an experience long after they've forgotten everything else.
	Passion for guest service should be a primary motivating factor for anyone considering a career in the restaurant and foodservice industry.
Teaching Tips	Engage students in a discussion about emotions versus experiences.

[professional profile]

Danny Meyer, Restaurateur

CEO of Union Square Hospitality Group

This includes Union Square Cafe, Gramercy Tavern, Eleven Madison Park, Tabla, Blue Smoke, Jazz Standard, Shake Shack, The Modern, Cafe 2 and Terrace 5 at the Museum of Modern Art, and El Verano Taqueria and Box Frites (both at Citi Field), as well as Hudson Yards.

Remember:

❝*You can shear a sheep many times, but you can only skin it once.*❞

I grew up in a family that relished great food, cooking, get-togethers, travel, and hospitality. Thanks to my father's travel business, I spent much of my childhood eating and traveling to near and far-off places.

So, while I studied political science at Trinity College, I found that I couldn't stop thinking about food and wine. It was then I knew that I had to follow my passion. My first restaurant experience in 1984 was as an assistant manager at Pesca, an Italian seafood restaurant in the Flatiron District of New York City. Then, I returned to Europe to study cooking as a culinary *stagière* in both Italy and Bordeaux.

I opened my first restaurant, Union Square Cafe, in 1985, when I was 27 years old. Since then, USC has pioneered a new breed of American eatery, pairing imaginative food and wine with caring hospitality, comfortable surroundings, and outstanding value. Of course, other restaurants have followed, with varied themes—French-American, rustic Italian, Indian, Barbecue and jazz, Indian, burgers. However, as different as these venues may be, they share a common emphasis on hospitality.

By the way, Danny Meyer's bestseller, Setting the Table, *examines the power of hospitality in restaurants, business, and life (HarperCollins, October 2006).*

You know, long after people forget what you do and say, they will remember how you made them feel. And that's hospitality...you have the wine, the food and the setting. But what people will remember is how you made them feel.

If you are considering this industry, be sure you know yourself. Be emotionally self-aware so that you understand why you're getting into this business. Make sure you're at your happiest when you're making other people feel happy. Know that you're naturally enthusiastic about your subject—food and drink. And, finally, know that you have the stamina, persistence, and competitive skills to stay ahead in a business that will always provide you with lots of competition.

About Serving Your Guests

To truly serve your guests, you must understand the difference between service and hospitality. We always hear about the importance of service, but this only describes the degree to which a business does what it says it will...the degree to which it lives up to promises. It doesn't say anything about how a person *feels*. Hospitality is about the attitude with which we serve people. It's all about how they feel.

10.1 The Importance of Customer Service	10.2 Ensuring a Positive Dining Experience	10.3 Service Styles, Set-ups, and Staff
• Definition of service and hospitality • First impressions • Identifying customer's needs	• Reservations and requests • Greeting and taking orders • Suggestive selling • Alcohol service • Processing payments • Getting feedback on customer satisfaction • Resolving customer complaints	• Contemporary service • Traditional service • Traditional service set-ups • Traditional service staff responsibilities • Service tools and stations

SECTION 10.1 THE IMPORTANCE OF CUSTOMER SERVICE

Make no mistake: every employee in a restaurant or foodservice operation, from the front to the back of the house, is responsible for providing good service. The host's attitude, the server's tableside personality, and the responsiveness of the busers all contribute to the dining experience. And customers notice all of it. Competition for customers has never been greater. They have high expectations, especially about the way they want to be treated. Even if the food is great, guests will be disappointed if the service is poor, and then they probably won't be back. But if an operation gets it right, they could be rewarded with repeat business, again and again.

This section discusses customer service and how it affects an operation's success. This section also discusses identifying and addressing customers' needs, two critical aspects of providing good customer service.

617

Focus and Engage

Discuss

- How do students define service and hospitality? How does this relate to their earlier discussion of positive and negative experiences as guests?
- Professionals are commonly expected to keep their emotions out of the workplace. Is this always possible for foodservice professionals, who are tasked with engaging and, to a certain extent, manipulating their guests' emotions?

Section 10.1 The Importance of Customer Service

Introduce the Section

a. Point out the differences between service and hospitality.
b. Explain the importance of first impressions to guests.
c. Discuss the objectives for the section.

Vocabulary Review

a. Direct students to the key terms.
b. Pronounce each word, and have the students repeat the pronunciation out loud.
c. Discuss the definition of each word.

Teach

Discuss

- How are customer service and hospitality important in terms of good business decisions? How are they important in terms of a service professional's self-esteem?

Reinforce and Review

- Every foodservice employee is responsible for providing good service.

Discuss

- Which is more important, service or hospitality? Why?
- How can hospitality be measured so that an establishment can tell how well it and its employees are performing?

Reinforce and Review

- Both hospitality and service are critical to high-quality customer service.
- The benefits of excellent guest service can include increased customer satisfaction and loyalty, an enhanced business reputation, and a positive work environment.
- Customer service often makes the difference between positive and negative guest experiences.
- To stand out from the competition, restaurants and foodservice establishments should provide the best possible guest service.

In-Class Activity: Competitive Advantage

Literacy Connection, 21st-Century Skills— Collaborating with Others, Use Systems Thinking, Initiative and Self-Direction

A competitive advantage makes one restaurant more appealing than another. This advantage can take many forms. Location, quality of service, menu options, and price range are just a few.

Working with another student, interview a local foodservice owner or manager and ask what he or she believes are the company's competitive advantages over another restaurant. Why do people choose to visit their restaurant. How does the restaurant capitalize on or publicize these advantages?

Together, prepare a brief oral report for the class on your interview.

Vocabulary Terms

- **Service:** The benefits restaurant and foodservice employees provide to guests.
- **Hospitality:** The feeling guests take with them from their experience with an operation.
- **Competitive advantage:** The element that attracts a customer to one establishment over another.

Study Questions

After studying Section 10.1, you should be able to answer the following questions:

- What exactly are *service* and *hospitality*, and how do they affect an operation's success?
- What is the importance of first impressions?
- What is the best way to identify the customer's needs, and what types of special needs should staff be aware of?

Definition of Service and Hospitality

Service is what restaurant and foodservice employees provide. It is measured by how well everyone in the operation is doing their jobs. **Hospitality** is the *feeling* that guests take with them from their experience with the operation. It refers to the interaction between a guest and host: the service, care, and attention. The physical environment—the décor, the lighting, the readability of menu—all add to the hospitality experience. Hospitality and service are critical to high-quality customer service.

Many benefits are gained by providing good customer service, including the following:

- Increased customer satisfaction
- Increased customer loyalty
- Decreased marketing costs (as customers share by "word of mouth" how good an operation is)
- Enhanced business reputation
- Positive work environment (which keeps employees loyal)
- Increased profits

Customer service often makes the difference between positive or excellent dining experiences and negative or ordinary ones. In fact, products served by similar competitive restaurants are usually very much alike. These offerings do not add much of a **competitive advantage,** the thing that attracts a customer to one operation over another. So, when the offerings of competitors are similar, the competitive advantage often comes from the nature and quality of customer service. It is important to provide the best possible level of customer service to stand out from the competition.

618

Before beginning a career in the restaurant and foodservice industry, it is important to understand what service is all about. Working in a service industry means serving people directly. This is the single most important aspect of the job. Good service comes from a natural desire to serve, but it can be improved through training, effort, and commitment.

First Impressions

First impressions are often the strongest impression we have of a person, place, or event. A positive first impression goes a long way in setting the tone of a guest's experience. It accomplishes a number of different goals, such as the following:

- Makes the customer feel welcome
- Helps the customer feel confident about the decision to come to the operation
- Sets the stage for a good dining experience
- Makes customers more likely to forgive minor errors

A strong first impression is one of the least expensive and most effective forms of advertising. If the impression is followed with a high level of service, as well as good food or a good product, the operation will probably have a return customer. Making a positive first impression is not hard. Restaurant and foodservice employees have to be conscientious. Figure 10.1 is an example of a positive greeting by a hostess.

Figure 10.1: The host/hostess greets guests, escorts them to tables, and provides menus.

The initial **customer interaction** is one of the best ways in which to make a strong first impression. This initial interaction can come in many different

619

Figure Focus
Figure 10.1: What can students observe about the establishment from this photograph?

Discuss

- What if an employee loves the physical work involved in the restaurant and foodservice industry, but dislikes or is ambiguous toward the concept of service? For instance, a cook may love the stress and challenge of producing excellent food for its own sake, not for the guests who will ultimately enjoy it. What advice would students give such a person?
- Besides a positive first impression, what are some other ways a restaurant can advertise itself? How can the first impression be part of a restaurant's overall brand?

Reinforce and Review

- The single most important aspect of working in the service industry is serving people directly.
- Good service requires a natural desire to serve but can be enhanced through training, commitment, and effort.
- A strong first impression is one of the least expensive and most effective forms of advertising. It sets the tone for the guest's overall experience.
- Foodservice staff must be conscientious about their work in order to make a positive first impression on guests.

Homework Activity: The Science of First Impressions

Science Connection, Literacy Connection, 21st-Century Skills—Access and Evaluate Information, Work Independently, Reason Effectively

According to recent psychological research, it takes only one-tenth of a second to form a first impression of a stranger's face. Longer exposures may not significantly change that impression.

Research the science underlying first impressions. Write a one-page paper on how this relates to the restaurant and foodservice industry.

Vocabulary Terms

- **First impression:** The guest's initial experience with the establishment and often the strongest impression they have of the overall experience.
- **Customer interaction:** Any engagement between guests and employees.

Reinforce and Review

- Some ways to make a positive first impression on a guest include using proper telephone skills, making guests feel welcome and comfortable in the establishment, and displaying courtesy and respect in every interaction.
- The facility's cleanliness and appearance, both inside and out, are important components of a guest's first impression.

Teaching Tips

- Relate this material to the discussion of proper telephone skills in Chapter 7.

Homework Activity: Match It Up

Literacy Connection, 21st-Century Skills— Think Creatively, Create Media Products, Communicate Clearly

A restaurant's exterior should relate somehow to the establishment's overall "brand," or identity. For instance, restaurants that serve traditional Mexican food may have roofs of red tile and walls of adobe or stucco, whereas quick-service restaurants may have drive-thru windows. In essence, a potential guest should be able to ascertain some idea of a restaurant's menu simply by looking at the restaurant's exterior.

Identify three separate restaurant concepts and design a building exterior for each that helps to extend and reinforce the restaurant's identity. Create a single poster showcasing each building and describing the food served within it. Be prepared to discuss why you feel that the designs you have selected are appropriate to the type of food each establishment sells.

settings, and a good customer service plan accounts for them all. Following are a few ways to generate positive first, and lasting, impressions:

- Begin customer service from the moment a customer calls. This includes using good telephone skills, such as standard greetings, when answering the phone.

- Greet customers immediately upon their arrival to make them feel comfortable and welcome. This includes thanking them for coming and inviting them inside.

- Display courtesy, respect, and friendliness in every customer interaction—smile, make eye contact, and make friendly conversation.

- Learn guests' names and recognize "regulars."

The facility's cleanliness and appearance are also very important to first impressions. The outside of the facility is frequently the first thing a guest sees, as shown in Figure 10.2. Maintain exterior facilities, such as the parking areas, sidewalks, and entranceways, so that they look clean and inviting. Maintain interior facilities so that they look and smell clean and fresh; this includes clean floors, tables, utensils, menus, and counters, as well as well-stocked and spotless restrooms.

Figure 10.2: The exterior of a restaurant or foodservice operation is as important as the interior. The exterior is the first impression guests see. Compare these two photos. Where would you prefer to eat?

Figure Focus

Figure 10.2: What do these exteriors suggest to students about the menus, service styles, and customer base of the restaurants within them?

The **appearance** of all restaurant and foodservice employees also impacts the first impression. Employees make a good impression on guests by presenting themselves professionally. They should make sure to do the following:

- **Dress appropriately:** Wear clean, wrinkle-free uniforms or clothing that is in good condition.
- **Practice good hygiene:** This includes clean hands, nails, face, and hair (held back or put up).
- **Wear minimal jewelry:** This will depend on the policy of management.

In addition, employees should not do the following:

- Drink, eat, smoke, or chew gum in front of guests.
- Wear strong fragrances.

Identifying Customers' Needs

It is up to all employees to ensure prompt, friendly, and professional service from a customer's arrival to departure. To start, identify the customer's needs. Although all customers share some basic needs, such as friendly efficient service and a high quality product, some have special needs. The quality of a customer's experience will be affected by how well the service staff identifies these needs:

- **Age:** Older customers may need additional help. Some have difficulty seeing, hearing, walking, carrying food to a table, or counting money. Always be respectful and have patience when serving older customers. This group may have dietary restrictions and concerns to which employees should be attentive.
- **Families with young children:** This group may also have special needs. They may need high chairs or booster seats, entertainment (such as paper and crayons) to keep the children happy, and a children's menu. See Figure 10.3 for examples of what might help families with children. Servers should know how to locate these items quickly. Children often get restless when they are hungry, so providing a quick snack (such as crackers or rolls) or

Figure 10.3: Servers need to be aware of the needs of guests with young children.

621

Discuss

- How can any special needs that guests might have be accommodated without affecting the quality of other guests' experiences?
- Almost every person will have some sort of special need at some point in his or her lifetime. How do service professionals learn to look past these needs to see their guests as people, not problems?
- Sometimes, guests do not mention their needs or desires outright. How can a service professional intuit and accommodate these needs?

Reinforce and Review

- Employees make good first impressions on their guests by presenting themselves professionally.
- Employees should accurately identify a guest's needs, both spoken and implicit.
- Always be respectful and patient when addressing and serving older customers.
- Families with children may require more frequent attention than other guests, as the needs of small children may change abruptly. Servers in particular should know where items to accommodate these younger guests can be found.

Teaching Tips

- Relate making a good impression on customers to making a good impression on a potential employer. Encourage students to discuss similarities and differences.
- Remind students that proper appearance is related to both food safety (Chapter 2) and professionalism (Chapter 4).
- Service professionals should never comment adversely on their guests and their needs, either publicly or privately. To do so suggests that the individual does not sincerely care about providing guest service.

Vocabulary Terms

- **Appearance:** How people look.

Figure Focus

Figure 10.3: These items typically accommodate small children and their families. What service items may be necessary to assist guests with other special needs?

Discuss

- Do true service professionals ever take risks with their guests' dietary needs? How can both front-of-the-house and back-of-the-house employees ensure that all guests with food sensitivities or allergies are properly accommodated?
- How can accommodating guests' special needs be a component in assessing a restaurant's or staff member's credibility, as discussed in Chapter 7?

Reinforce and Review

- Customers may have special dietary needs, so servers must know exactly what ingredients are used in each dish.
- Employees should accommodate guest requests for specially prepared dishes whenever possible, but servers should always check with the kitchen to make sure that the needs can be met before the table's order is finalized.

Teaching Tips

- Many establishments keep copies of current recipes in the service area so servers can check to see whether any ingredients might pose problems for specific guests. This is one way in which consistency in preparing food is critical. If a cook unwittingly substitutes peanut oil for canola, many guests with peanut sensitivities and allergies could be imperiled.
- Servers should also be aware of every ingredient used in each of the day's specials. If there is any doubt, they should check with the kitchen to ensure guest safety.

---

sending the children's order to the kitchen right away will be greatly appreciated by the customer. Children may also have dietary restrictions, such as allergies, of which servers need to be aware.

- **Dietary needs:** Customers may have special dietary needs, so server knowledge of the menu is critical. Servers must know exactly what is in every menu item. Disclaimers on the menu—for high-risk populations—are not enough. See an example of a disclaimer in Figure 10.4.

Food allergies can be severe and, sometimes, fatal. If the server doesn't know the answer to a customer's specific question about menu ingredients, he or she should ask someone who does know. Don't ever take the chance of serving something that may cause an allergic reaction. Take the time to find out for sure.

Guests on special diets often ask that menu items be changed in some way. Even if the request seems strange or picky, employees should provide customers with exactly what they order.

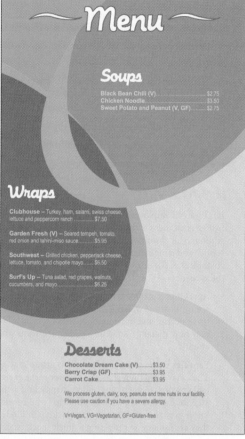

Figure 10.4: Sample menu with dietary disclaimer.

Figure Focus

Figure 10.4: How can printing a dietary disclaimer on a menu help protect a restaurant from legal trouble?

- **First-time guests**: First-time customers might be unfamiliar with the menu or any special touches that a particular operation offers. These customers might enjoy a brief introduction to the facility and its menu. Servers can easily identify a first-time customer simply by asking. They should plan to spend some extra time with these clients.

- **Special occasions**: Special occasions usually mean that the customer has specific needs. Large groups, for example, might require special menus or a special location within the operation (separated from other guests) and additional dedicated servers.

- **Foreign-language customers**: Language differences present challenges to efficient and responsive service. Depending on where the facility is located, dual-language menus might help make all customers feel more comfortable and welcome. Having a server on staff who speaks another language is also helpful. Finally, including pictures of menu items can help bridge any language gaps.

- **People with disabilities**: Without calling special attention to customers with disabilities, employees need to accommodate them in every way possible, such as seating a guest in a wheelchair in an area with plenty of space. The staff has to address the needs of customers with temporary disabilities as well, such as a broken arm or leg. The physical facility should be equipped to effectively accommodate these needs—for example, having ramps for wheelchairs or hand railings in restrooms.

[fast fact]

Did You Know...?

According to the U.S. Census Bureau, more than 51 million Americans have some form of disability. That's almost 20 percent of the country's population.

- **People dining alone**: Some people who are dining alone may have work to do or may simply be trying to get away from it all for awhile. Consequently, such guests may want to be seated in a quiet corner or at a brightly lit table. The best policy is to ask these individuals what they prefer. Make sure that single diners receive the same level of service and attention as a larger party.

  Try to anticipate guests' needs and accommodate them before being asked. This requires watching and listening to guests carefully. Employees should do their best to please guests and think creatively when serving them.

623

Discuss

- Some of the positive effects of a diverse workplace were discussed in Chapter 8. How can having a diverse staff help a restaurant prepare for and meet the needs of a diverse customer base?
- Besides cleanliness and appearance, what other physical aspects of a foodservice facility signal a welcoming atmosphere to all types of guests? What can the lack of a ramp or of a booster seat indicate to guests who require them?

Reinforce and Review

- Guests with special needs of any variety often require extra time and attention from the server.
- Both single diners and large parties should be treated with the same levels of courtesy, dignity, and respect as any other guests.
- Restaurants should be physically equipped to accommodate guests with temporary or permanent disabilities.
- All employees should do their best to please guests and think creatively while serving them.

Teaching Tips

- Students should remember that a service professional's goal should always be to make guests feel as comfortable as possible.
- Bring in copies of local restaurant reviews. Encourage students to discuss why service quality is usually mentioned in these articles. Relate this to the material in Chapter 1 about restaurant rating systems.

Fast Fact:
Did You Know...?

Encourage students to discuss the following:

- How can a restaurant plan to accommodate guests with disabilities?
- Nearly 20 percent of Americans have disabilities. How can a restaurant market itself to capture these patrons' business?
- How can employing staff members with disabilities help restaurants be more mindful of guests' needs?

Fast Fact: Did You Know...?

Encourage students to discuss the following:

- How can the information discussed in this article be reframed to address all guests, not just single diners? Is serving a single guest fundamentally different from serving any other table?

- Why is it important for a host or hostess not to assume that a single guest will be dining alone?

- Why can single diners sometimes require more attention than other parties?

CUSTOMIZED INSTRUCTION

Literacy Connection, 21st-Century Skills— Reason Effectively, Communicate Clearly, Use Systems Thinking

Special Needs Students

Discuss any particularly positive or negative experiences you have had when dining at a restaurant. How have these experiences altered your perception of the establishment?

CUSTOMIZED INSTRUCTION

Literacy Connection, 21st-Century Skills— Reason Effectively, Communicate Clearly, Work Independently

ESOL Students

Consider any particularly positive or negative experiences you have had when dining at a restaurant. How have these experiences altered your perception of the establishment? How have they affected your perception of the restaurant industry as a whole?

Respond to these questions in a brief essay.

[fast fact]

Did You Know...?

Not all restaurant customers arrive in couples or groups. Single diners, such as business travelers, students, singles, or people who just want a quiet lunch or evening out, are an important part of your business. Think of them as scouts for future customers. If their experience is positive, they will likely return with family or friends.

Single diners can sometimes be perfectly comfortable dining alone; others might feel self-conscious. It's important to treat these customers with sensitivity and to give them the same level of service that you would to other tables.

To be a single-diner service star, follow these tips:

1. Don't automatically assume the guest will be dining alone by saying, "Party of one?" or "One for dinner?" Instead, ask, "How many will be in your party?" or "Will anyone else be joining you this evening?"

2. Ask the customer where he or she wishes to sit, if choices are available. Some single diners prefer bar seating, whereas others enjoy spreading out at a table or banquette. Sometimes the guest will be reading or reviewing paperwork, which requires good lighting. Other times, the guest may simply want to eat, so muted lighting may be more appropriate.

3. Be attentive without hovering, just like with any other guests. Since single diners won't be having lengthy conversations, they may finish each course more quickly. On the other hand, if reading or working, they may take more time. It's your responsibility to gauge this and communicate with the kitchen as needed.

4. Follow your management's service policies—again, just like with any other guests. Avoid making comments such as, "All alone tonight, huh?" You don't know the other person's circumstances. Be courteous and friendly without becoming overbearing.

Summary

In this section, you learned the following:

- Service is what restaurant and foodservice employees provide. It is measured by how well everyone in the operation is doing their jobs. Hospitality is the feeling that guests take with them from the experience they had in the operation. Together, these elements make up customer service, and good customer service can lead to increased customer satisfaction, increased customer loyalty, decreased marketing costs, enhanced business reputation, positive work environment, and, ultimately, increased profits. Often customer service gives an operation a competitive edge when food quality within the market is the same.

624

- First impressions are often the strongest impressions we have of a person, place, or event. A positive first impression goes a long way in setting the tone and influencing a guest's experience. The many benefits to making a strong first impression include making the guest feel welcome, helping the guest feel confident about the decision to come to the operation, and making the guest more likely to forgive minor errors.

- All employees should try to anticipate customers' needs and accommodate them before being asked. This requires watching and listening to customers carefully for clues about their needs. Employees should do their best to please customers and think creatively when serving them. They should be mindful of such factors as age, dietary needs, parental needs for children, solo diners, disabilities, foreign-language customers, and the fact that special occasions will often require special service.

625

Summary

- Remind students to review the following:
  1. The meanings of service and hospitality, and how they affect an operation's success
  2. The importance of first impressions
  3. The best way to identify a customer's needs, and the types of special needs that the staff should be aware of

Section 10.1 Review Questions

1. Many benefits are gained by providing good customer service, including increased customer satisfaction, increased customer loyalty, decreased marketing costs, enhanced business reputation, positive work environment, and increased profits.

2. Positive first impressions are important to an operation's success because they make the customer feel welcome, help the customer feel confident, set the stage for a good dining experience, make customers more likely to forgive minor errors, provide effective and low-cost advertising, and help ensure return visits.

3. Foodservice employees can make good first impressions by beginning customer service from the moment a customer calls; greeting customers immediately upon their arrival to make them feel comfortable and welcome; displaying courtesy, respect, and friendliness in every customer interaction; and learning guests' names and recognizing "regulars."

4. Special needs that an employee might notice include:

   Age: Employees should be respectful and patient, offering assistance where needed.

   Families with young children: Employees should provide quick snacks, entertainment materials, high chairs or booster seats, and children's menus as needed.

   Dietary needs: Employees should be attentive to food allergies and sensitivities and should be knowledgeable about the ingredients used to prepare each dish.

   First-time guests: Employees should provide an introduction to the facility and menu and should plan to spend extra time with these guests.

   Special occasions: Employees should be aware of special requests, such as particular menus or seating arrangements.

   Foreign-language customers: Dual-language menus or menus with pictures may be helpful, as may bilingual employees.

   People with disabilities: Employees should accommodate these guests' needs in every way possible, without calling special attention to the circumstance.

   People dining alone: Employees should be sensitive to these guests' seating and dining preferences.

5. Hosts and hostesses can greet customers immediately upon their arrival, making the guests feel welcome and appreciated. A friendly, respectful attitude is important.

Section 10.1 Review Questions

1. List three reasons why customer service is important to an operation's success.

2. List three reasons why making a good first impression is important to an operation's success.

3. What are two things a foodservice employee can do to make a good first impression?

4. List three special needs that an employee might notice, and provide an example of each situation.

5. Danny Meyer states that "...long after people forget what you do and say, they will remember how you made them feel." What can a host or hostess do to make guests feel welcome?

6. Given the need to regain ground, what steps can Linda and Chef Jean take to create a positive first impression? Make a list of five steps, and describe how they should go about each one.

7. Think of two restaurant experiences you've had: one in which you came away very happy with your overall experience and one in which you came away disappointed. Walk through each experience, listing your impressions from start to finish. How much did first impressions relate to your overall dining experience?

8. Of the groups with potential special needs noted in the chapter, which ones would you be particularly concerned about in your business? Pick two groups, and explain your choices.

626

6. Students may answer this question in a variety of ways, so long as they provide five logical steps Linda and Chef Jean can take to recover their losses and provide excellent customer service.

7. Students should clearly link their first impressions of each dining experience with their impressions of the overall event.

8. Students should identify two special-needs groups and discuss why they would be given particular care and attention in the students' businesses.

Section 10.1 Activities

1. Study Skills/Group Activity: Restaurant Wars!

As a group, come up with two restaurants that compete in a similar market, offer a similar menu, and have similar food quality. Then, examine in detail how each tries to gain a competitive advantage through their customer service. List their similarities and differences, as well as the pros and cons of each. As a group, which one would you be more likely to patronize? Why?

2. Activity: "Hello, and Welcome to…"

You're in charge of first impressions at your establishment. Write scripts for each of the following service staff:

a. Greeter

b. Server

c. Bartender

d. Buser

How exactly should each of these staff members greet the guests? What should they say and ask? How should they respond to guests' initial questions and orders? How would you like the initial interaction between guest and staff to play out?

3. Critical Thinking: I Spy…A First Impression!

Visit a local restaurant and observe what you see in the dining room during the first three minutes you spend there. You do not have to dine at the restaurant to complete this assignment. What is your first impression? Based on this impression, what would you expect of the dining experience? Discuss your findings in two paragraphs.

627

Section 10.1 Activities

1. Students should identify similar restaurants competing locally and determine how each attempts to gain a competitive advantage over the other in terms of customer service, as well as noting similarities and differences between the two and their positive and negative aspects.

2. These scripts should be brief and to the point. Students should also describe how they would like their employees to communicate nonverbally with their guests.

3. Students should describe their first impression of the selected restaurant and how it affects their ideas about what the dining experience might be like. Students may relate this to question 7 on the previous page as they draw inferences between first impressions and overall encounters.

Section 10.2
Ensuring a Positive Dining Experience

Introduce the Section

a. Explain how dining-room staff members play a major role in determining a guest's experience.
b. Point out ways that standard transactions, such as taking guest orders or processing payments, can be opportunities to demonstrate high levels of customer service.
c. Discuss the objectives for the section.

Vocabulary Review

a. Direct students to the key terms.
b. Pronounce each word, and have the students repeat the pronunciation out loud.
c. Discuss the definition of each word.

Teach

Discuss

- What are the elements that influence a guest's experience at a restaurant? Which do students perceive as the most important of these, and why?
- How can the relationships between managers and employees affect the quality of customer service? In other words, what role can a positive or negative work environment have on guests?
- Ultimately, what is the fundamental relationship between guest service and an establishment's bottom line?

Reinforce and Review

- Often, people dine out to save themselves from having to cook and clean. Instead of serving, they wish to be served.
- Any successful restaurant must be dedicated to quality customer service.
- Guest service is an ongoing process that is rooted in respect and care.

10.1 The Importance of Customer Service	10.2 Ensuring a Positive Dining Experience	10.3 Service Styles, Set-ups, and Staff
• Definition of service and hospitality • First impressions • Identifying customer's needs	• Reservations and requests • Greeting and taking orders • Suggestive selling • Alcohol service • Processing payments • Getting feedback on customer satisfaction • Resolving customer complaints	• Contemporary service • Traditional service • Traditional service set-ups • Traditional service staff responsibilities • Service tools and stations

SECTION 10.2 ENSURING A POSITIVE DINING EXPERIENCE

One of the main reasons people go out to eat is so they don't have to do the hard work of cooking and cleaning themselves. In short, they want to be served instead. Therefore, the importance of customer service can't be stressed enough. Any successful restaurant and foodservice operation must be dedicated to quality customer service. And to be successful at serving customers well means understanding all of the factors that go into the process.

Good service starts with the very first customer interaction, sometimes as early as a phone call for a reservation. But it never really ends. Quality customer service isn't something that personnel commit to once. Rather, it's an ongoing process of always making guests feel welcome, treating them with care and respect while they are in an establishment, and continually following up with them in an effort to keep serving them better.

Study Questions

After studying Section 10.2, you should be able to answer the following questions:

- What is the proper way to handle reservations and special requests?
- What is the importance of customer greetings?
- How should a server interact with guests, and what information should be included in an order?
- What is suggestive selling, and why is it important?

- How should alcohol service be handled?
- How are payments processed?
- What is the importance of customer feedback, and what are some methods to collect such feedback?
- What is the best way to resolve customer complaints?

Reservations and Requests

A lost or incorrect reservation or a mishandled special request can be extremely frustrating for customers. If a customer's visit starts with this kind of problem, it can be difficult to turn the visit into a positive experience. That is why it is extremely important to have an accurate system to record reservations and special requests and implement them at the right time.

An effective procedure begins with a specific place to record reservations and special requests. The type, speed, and complexity of the restaurant determines how sophisticated the procedure is and what technology is used. For example, a fine-dining restaurant with table service may record reservations and special orders in a book or computer at the greeter's station. Reservations and requests should be saved in one place and include standard information, including when and by whom the information was recorded. As shown in Figure 10.5, the information recorded should contain the following:

Figure 10.5: Reservation information includes customer name, customer contact information, date and time of arrival, number of people in the party, and any special needs or requests made by the customer.

629

- How does the reservation process set the tone for the guest's actual visit? How can the process reinforce and reflect the restaurant's identity?

Reinforce and Review
- Problems with the reservation process can disrupt a guest's entire experience with a restaurant, so using an accurate system to record reservations and related information is essential.
- An effective reservation procedure begins with having a specific place to record reservations and special requests.
- A restaurant's service style and menu help determine the manner in which reservations are taken.

Teaching Tips
- Guest service never ends. It is a continuous chain of interactions.

Figure Focus
Figure 10.5: What other information might be important for the restaurant's staff to know prior to a guest's arrival?
Note: This information could include the following: whether the guests are first-time diners or regular patrons; where the guests would like to sit; any specific dining preferences or requirements—for instance, if a guest loves trout or is allergic to peanuts; whether the guests tend to linger over their meals or dine quickly; birthdays, anniversaries, or other important dates; whether the guest is a "friend of the house" and requires special treatment; and any information recorded from a guest's previous visits to the restaurant.

Discuss

- Many restaurants either call guests before their visit (or require their guests to call them) to confirm that the guests' plans have not changed. What are the financial benefits to confirming reservations?
- Managers typically schedule employees to work based on the predicted number of diners. How can unexpected events, such as multiple no-shows or unusual levels of walk-in traffic, affect a restaurant's finances? How can these events affect employees?

Reinforce and Review

- Confirming all reservations and special requests is good customer service, as it both makes the guests feel important and it helps the restaurant control its costs.
- Flags alert service professionals to special requests and ensure communication among staff members to meet the guests' needs.
- With proper procedures in place, restaurants can avoid problems with the reservation process, which helps satisfy guests.

- Customer name
- Customer contact information
- Date and time of arrival
- Number of people in the party
- Any special needs or requests the customer may have

Confirming all reservations and special requests is good customer service. It makes the guests feel important and protects the establishment against no-shows. It also helps management to plan food and labor needs and control the flow of customers and food orders throughout the shift.

Some operations ask for credit card numbers to confirm the reservation when it's placed. This is done frequently for special events. Some places charge customers for "no-shows," when customers do not honor the reservations they've made.

With special requests, it is important to have a way to "flag" or call attention to the special request. This ensures that cooks, servers, and other staff will be more attentive to the request, communicate better with each other to fulfill the request, and avoid errors.

Taking reservations and completing special requests may seem like simple tasks, but they actually take planning and organization. With proper procedures, establishments can avoid making mistakes in these situations and so avoid disappointing guests.

630

Homework Activity: Designing a "Flag"

Literacy Connection, 21st-Century Skills—Create Media Products, Reason Effectively, Communicate Effectively

Flags are devices used to alert staff members to special guest needs. For instance, a diner celebrating a birthday might have pre-ordered a specialty cake to be cut and served as dessert, so both kitchen and dining-room staff need to be aware of this. Flags aren't actual flags. They can be slips of paper, notes in a computer, or anything else that accurately communicates the special need.

Design a flag for your restaurant and illustrate it on a sheet of paper. Be prepared to discuss why you selected the particular design, how you decided what information it contains, and how the message is conveyed to all necessary staff members.

[trends]

Reservations Online or Off

At one time, there was only one way to get a reservation at a restaurant. Whether the restaurant was hot and new or stately and old, customers had to call the restaurant and were often placed on hold. This process usually took a few minutes. Frequently, after waiting, customers learned that a table would not be available for the date or time requested.

With the advent of online reservation systems, however, things have changed a lot; making a reservation is easier. The diner enters the Web site, selects a restaurant, and types in the number of diners and the date desired. Often, the service will promptly inform the prospective guest of the seating times available for that date, so the guest can either select a time or choose from other options. Some establishments offer discounts for diners reserving tables at off-peak hours or "points" that can be used toward future meals. Consumers pay no fee for any of these services. So, online reservation systems have become very popular. Thousands of restaurants now participate in OpenTable, RestaurantReservations, and similar services, while countless other restaurants have their own reservation Web sites. See Figure 10.6 for an example of what these reservation pages look like.

As helpful as this is for the consumer, it is equally advantageous for the restaurant. Not only are reservations managed with less effort, but thousands of details about frequent users of the reservation systems are available—everything from birthdays to email addresses to drink preferences to frequent dining companions. This provides restaurants with a wealth of useful information about their guests that can be used to enhance customer service. Restaurants can develop a database with customers' email addresses, allowing establishments to email customers directly to inform them of particular events and promotions.

Figure 10.6: Online reservations allow guests to make reservations quickly.

Figure Focus

Figure 10.6: What other benefits can guests experience through the use of online reservation systems?

Discuss

- What can a greeter do to make or break a guest's experience?
- Why is it important for the greeter and the server to communicate?
- How can taking a guest's order be an opportunity to learn more about the guest? How is it an opportunity to reinforce the restaurant's identity?

Reinforce and Review

- In addition to welcoming guests, greeters must also evaluate and determine the customers' specific needs for the current visit.
- Servers inform guests about the menu, take orders, and make sure that any special requests are accurately understood by the kitchen staff.

Teaching Tips

- Recruit volunteers to role-play a greeter welcoming a party of diners.

Vocabulary Terms

- **Greeter:** Provides the first impression in appearance, friendliness, and attentiveness. To do this, the greeter evaluates and determines the customer's specific needs for the current visit.

Greeting and Taking Orders

The **greeter** provides the first impression in appearance, friendliness, and attentiveness. To do this, the greeter evaluates and determines the customer's specific needs for the current visit. The greeter is responsible for the following:

- Asking whether the customer has reservations, and, if so, checking the reservation log for all information pertaining to the customer's visit

- Noting any special dietary needs, seating arrangements, celebrations, and so on, and passing the information along to the rest of the staff

- Arranging for the customers to be escorted to their seats

In an operation without a greeter, these tasks fall to the server or dining room manager.

After the guests are seated, the server takes over. As each guest at the table selects their meal, the server notes guest orders on pre-printed guest checks or small note pads. These written orders may be entered into an electronic Point of Sale (POS) machine at the wait station or the guest ticket may be handed directly to the chefs to start the meal preparation.

Some guests will ask the server whether certain ingredients can be removed from dishes due to food allergies or other special needs. Servers need to correctly note any special requirements in the preparation of a guest's food item and ensure that the chef understands the request. Double-checking written receipt of special requests with the chefs is always a good idea.

632

Essential Skills
Taking a Table-Side Order

Writing down orders needs to be done carefully, using the same method each time. A server should always do the following when writing their table check:

❶ Include proper seat and table numbers where appropriate. The seat numbers of a table start at the server's left, no matter what the shape of the table. The server approaches each table at the specific place determined by the floor plan. See Figure 10.7 for an example.

Figure 10.7: Step 1—Sample floor plan.

❷ Use a grid to write down order in delivery sequence; for example, drink, appetizer, soup, salad, entrée, dessert. Remember, it is critical to keep everything organized and consistent for all checks. See Figure 10.8 for an example of an orderly table check.

❸ Use abbreviations, sometimes already made up by the servers. Examples can be temps (for temperatures), CB (for cheeseburger), BK (for blackened).

❹ Take and note temperatures as needed, along with any special requests by the guests.

❺ Finally, repeat the order back to the guests before leaving the table.

Guest Check

Table	Guests	Check Number	Server
17	5	074809	Alice

1	Caesar (1)
2	Asparagus (3) 5
1	Cuke 2 SOS
1	Roulade 4
1	Tartare 2
1	Soup d.j. (3)
1	Egg 4
2	Filet (1) MR 4 M
1	Salmon 2
1	Quail 3
1	Sweetbreads 5
	Total

Figure 10.8: Step 2—Table check.

Essential Skills: Taking a Table-Side Order

Encourage students to discuss the following:

- Some restaurants, especially fine-dining establishments, instruct their servers to memorize guest orders rather than writing them down or immediately entering them into an electronic device. Is this good or bad guest service? How would students react to this if they were the diners? What if they were the servers?

- Why is it essential for servers to record desired cooking temperatures and other requests accurately, in terms of both customer desires and kitchen needs?

Figure Focus

Figure 10.7: Where would servers stand when interacting with each table?
Note: For Section 1, servers would stand with their backs to the main dining room, between positions 1 and 2 or positions 1 and 4. For Section 2, they would stand between positions 1 and 2. For Section 3, the best place to stand would be between positions 1 and 4.

Figure 10.8: How will the kitchen interpret this guest check?
Note: Table 17 has five diners. The numbers in parentheses indicate female diners. Numbers in the left-hand column indicate how many orders of a particular dish are required. Numbers after the buzzwords indicate the seats that ordered the dishes, so the food can be put in front of the correct person. "SOS" indicates that the diner would like the item without dressing on it, or "sauce on the side." "MR" indicates that the guest would like her meat cooked medium rare, while "M" indicates that the guest would like his meat cooked medium. The soup of the day or du jour is indicated by the initials "d.j." Lines drawn between orders indicate the end of a course and the beginning of a new one, so this table has ordered three courses.

Fast Fact: Did You Know...?

Encourage students to discuss the following:

- What problems can miscommunication between the dining room and the kitchen or a mistake recording a guest's order cause?

- When a server knows that the kitchen has accurately received a table's order, he or she gains more confidence. How does this confidence affect a server's credibility and therefore a guest's dining experience?

- How can repeating back orders contribute to a positive work environment?

On the Job: Hot Tips: Gratuities and You

Encourage students to discuss the following:

- Why do guests tip their servers? Why should they tip at all? Are guests required to tip for poor service?

- How can knowing the tip amount in advance affect the quality of service? For instance, does a guest who regularly leaves large tips receive more attentive service than a guest who does not tip as highly?

- How does the tipping process act as feedback on the guest's overall experience and on the quality of service provided? How does it relate to professionalism?

- Since tips are taxed, what is the best way of recording tip income to avoid penalties?

Homework Activity: Float Like a Butterfly

Science Connection, Literacy Connection, 21st-Century Skills—Reason Effectively, Access and Evaluate Information, Work Independently

Have you ever had a day when everything went wrong? Perhaps something little went awry, and you didn't think much about it. But then more things started to go wrong, and everything snowballed to create a truly terrible day.

The butterfly effect is a concept in chaos theory that suggests that apparently insignificant events may trigger significant events. How can it relate to the restaurant and foodservice industry? Research this concept and write a one-page paper describing your findings.

[fast fact]

Did You Know...?

Use a very simple serving strategy to minimize errors in the kitchen, hold down an operation's food costs, and reduce customer wait times and customer complaints: Have all servers repeat orders back to guests after the initial order has been taken. It's simple to do and takes very little time, yet it can help the overall efficiency of the operation in many ways:

- First, repeating orders helps avoid potential miscommunications between guests and servers in the initial ordering:
  - This can help to reduce the food costs incurred by having to correct such mistakes.
  - The kitchen won't have to redo plates; this helps keep the kitchen running efficiently.
  - If the kitchen is running efficiently, food quality and plate presentation will be better, and the speed of service to the rest of the dining room will be faster.
  - When quality of food is high and speed of service to the whole of the dining room is fast, more guests leave happy and satisfied with their dining experience.
  - Happier guests lead to repeat customers.
  - Repeat customers lead to a higher and more regular income for the operation.

- Knowing that all orders are going into the kitchen exactly as they should be provides the server with added confidence. Therefore, he will be freer and more confident when serving other guests.

- Finally, it keeps the staff happier as a whole because mistakes and set-backs will be reduced, so everyone can better do their jobs.

[on the job]

Hot Tips: Gratuities and You

Everybody likes to get tips, and no wonder: many service employees earn far more through gratuities than from actual wages. Always remember that tips are a guest's way of thanking the server, chef, and perhaps even the hostess for providing excellent service, not a way to pad a paycheck. When service staff become too complacent and believe they are entitled to good tips regardless of the quality of service, guests suffer.

Whether serving a table or managing a crew of servers, keep the following in mind:

1. Never look at the signed credit-card slip in front of a seated guest. It gives the impression of greediness, as if the server can't wait to see the tip.

2. Sometimes, if a guest says, "Keep the change" or if the guest tips at a register, the server can't avoid knowing the amount of the gratuity. In these cases, it is extremely important that they not show any emotion. Visible happiness at a good tip is almost as bad as visible disappointment at a poor one.

3. Never make guests feel uncomfortable because of the amount of their tip (high or low). This won't always be easy. Any experienced server knows that terrible tips sometimes follow great service. But if the servers continue to treat guests with

634

respect, even when the servers know the amount of the gratuity, the guests will feel more at ease in the restaurant and will, therefore, be more likely to return for future meals. It's just good business.

The bottom line is that the exchange of all money between staff and guests must be professional. The transaction is a payment for services rendered by the operation. In the long run, the more professional the service, the better the tips will be.

Note: The IRS requires that employees report tips if they receive $20 or more per calendar month. The employee must provide written reports by the tenth of the following month.

[what's new]

POS and Pacing

Many restaurant and foodservice establishments use POS, "point-of-sales" systems, to track guest orders and checks, communicate information to back-of-house employees, maintain reservations and waiting lists, and track labor and sales figures. See Figure 10.9 for an example. In fact, these systems typically have a broad range of features. The POS saves time and money by increasing the efficiency of standard restaurant operations. It also plays an important role in customer service by helping the server to properly pace the meal.

"Pacing" is the speed at which a guest proceeds through a meal. If a single guest is in a hurry to reach another engagement, he will likely complete each course more quickly and may order fewer courses than the typical diner. On the other hand, a group of long-lost friends may spend more time talking than eating,

Figure 10.9: POS systems save time and money by increasing efficiency in restaurant and foodservice operations.

so each course takes longer. The server must communicate with the kitchen about each party's needs. By sending a quick message through the POS system, the server can explain that the next course should be brought out quickly or held back. This can be done without having to leave the dining area and other guests. The POS, therefore, saves time and improves the level of customer service available to all the customers.

What's New: POS and Pacing

Encourage students to discuss the following:

- How can pacing affect the kitchen? How can both kitchen and dining-room staff accommodate both patrons who eat quickly and those who choose to linger?

- Why is communication between front-of-the-house staff and back-of-the-house staff critical in the pacing process?

- What positive and negative experiences have students had with pacing? What are some possible explanations for either good or bad pacing?

635

Figure Focus

Figure 10.9: What can students observe about the foodservice establishment from this photograph?

Discuss

- How can professional staff members engage in suggestive selling without making guests feel uncomfortable? What issues of delicacy and discretion may arise?
- Encourage students to explain the role of both verbal and nonverbal communication in suggestive selling.

Reinforce and Review

- The success of suggestive selling depends on product knowledge, effective communication skills, and sales training.
- Suggestive selling maximizes guest satisfaction and increases the average check, resulting in more profits.
- Being pushy is not the same as suggestive selling. The goal is to maximize guest satisfaction, not to exploit diners.
- Discussing daily specials is an important part of suggestive selling and should be done at the beginning of the ordering process.

Teaching Tips

- Students should remember that the goal of suggestive selling is to make guests happy and thereby increase return business.
- Recruit volunteers to role-play suggestive selling.

Homework Activity: Suggestive Selling

Literacy Connection, 21st-Century Skills— Think Creatively, Reason Effectively, Communicate Clearly

Using the menu in Figure 10.4 (p. 622), pick out three items and write the dialogue you would use to sell each dish. What ingredients or preparation methods would you highlight? What descriptive terms could you use to make the dishes sound attractive?

Each student should present his or her dialogue to the class.

Vocabulary Terms

- **Suggestive selling:** Involves recommending additional or different items to a guest. It is one of the keys to the success of any retail business.

Suggestive Selling

Suggestive selling involves recommending additional or different items to a guest. It is one of the keys to the success of any retail business. In a restaurant, suggestive selling maximizes guest satisfaction and increases the average check, resulting in more profits. The success of suggestive selling depends on product knowledge, effective communication skills, and sales training.

Many employees are reluctant to suggestive sell because they are shy or uncomfortable with selling (feeling that they are acting "pushy"). Managers who train servers commonly point out that this will increase the guest's check and, therefore, the server's tip. A good suggestive selling program includes the following:

- Enhancing servers' communication skills, so they can be effective with customers
- Developing servers' product knowledge, so they can vividly and accurately describe items to customers. Servers need to be able to answer specific questions about the menu items, including ingredients, preparation techniques, and levels of seasoning.
- Learning which items complement one another
- Anticipating guest needs
- Suggesting add-on items such as drinks, appetizers, and desserts
- Identifying specific items based on guest preferences; for example, "If you like chocolate, you'll love our new molten lava cake"
- Suggesting items that servers themselves enjoy
- Suggesting core products and services that sell well
- Suggesting the establishment's "best" items, increasing the probability that the customer will be happy
- Using props, such as dessert trays
- Observing guest behavior to determine whether they want service or a product; for example, at the end of the meal, watching the guest to see whether he or she wants the check or dessert
- Recognizing the positive effect of suggestive selling on the financial position of the establishment

Talking about daily specials is a part of suggestive selling. It is acceptable, and recommended, to mention these "deals" right at the start of the ordering process. Most guests welcome recommendations and are more than willing to try specialties.

636

Using active and descriptive words to explain foods is a great way to suggestively sell menu items. Words such as *sweet, juicy, mouth-watering, prime,* and *rich* make foods sound appetizing. Other words provide an actual description of the item (*sashimi-grade, organic, heirloom*). If the server can legally make these claims, he or she should. For example, "Our Belgian waffles are made with fresh eggs, whole wheat flour, and milk, and are served hot from the griddle, topped with fresh strawberries and pure whipped cream or vanilla ice cream."

After guests place an order, let them know they've made a good decision by saying something like, "Excellent choice, sir. The salmon is very fresh today. I think you'll really enjoy it." This makes guests feel good about their decision, and they will look forward to the meal. Show enthusiasm for the items that guests suggest. Servers can also recommend menu items that they personally like. Management should establish a policy that staff be honest with guests when they ask for personal recommendations, as guests can often detect and appreciate sincerity.

Suggestive selling training is an ongoing effort. First, a manager or designated trainer can conduct training formally. Second, suggestive selling can be an occasional agenda item for staff meetings. Managers can set aside time at these meetings to discuss the best practices or problem experiences. Third, informal training can occur through observation and feedback. In all cases, practice is the key to successful suggestive selling.

Alcohol Service

The service of alcohol is frequently an integral part of a dining experience. Most customers expect alcohol at least to be available, so it's essential that alcohol service is conducted professionally and safely. Managers and staff must understand the effects of alcohol and become familiar with any and all laws that apply to their establishments.

Every state has its own liquor laws and oversees the sale and service of alcohol within its borders. Each state's liquor board or liquor authority develops and enforces its own regulations for alcohol service. These agencies also are responsible for issuing and monitoring liquor licenses, issuing citations for violations, and holding hearings for violators of the liquor code.

Laws vary considerably from state to state. Many states have dram shop laws, which create a special liability for establishments with liquor licenses and for the people employed by them. These laws allow an injured person, who may not even have been in the establishment, to sue the business, its owners, and its employees for injuries caused by a guest who was drinking there. In addition, many counties and towns have their own, often stricter, liquor laws.

637

Discuss

- Suggestive selling depends on good communication skills, but it also requires honest and accurate descriptions. Should managers write scripts for servers to use when telling customers about each dish? Or should servers write their own scripts, so that they can choose words and phrases that make them feel comfortable?
- How do local and state laws affect which staff members can serve what items to guests?
- In many restaurants, the term VIP doesn't mean Very Important Person. It means Visibly Intoxicated Person. Why is it critical for all employees to recognize VIPs?

Reinforce and Review

- Using active and descriptive words can facilitate suggestive selling, and if servers can legally make claims about the ingredients and their provenance, they should.
- Managers should allow staff members to be honest about their opinions when asked about particular dishes, even ones they may not personally enjoy.
- Managers and staff must understand the effects of alcohol and be familiar with all relevant laws.
- Each state's liquor board or liquor authority develops and enforces its own regulations for alcohol service, which vary widely from state to state.
- Dram shop laws allow an injured person, who may not have even entered the establishment, to sue the business, its owners, and its employees for injuries caused by a guest who was drinking there.

Teaching Tips

- Most restaurants require servers to taste any new dishes or special items so that they can accurately describe them to guests.

Homework Activity:
Legal Eagles

Literacy Connection, 21st-Century Skills—Access and Evaluate Information, Work Independently, Be Self-Directed Learners, Civic Literacy

What laws govern the sale and service of alcohol in your community? Who may serve or sell alcohol, and who may legally consume it? What laws affect restaurants that serve alcohol, and what penalties exist for over service to a customer or service to a minor?

Research local and state regulations to answer these questions, as well as any other information you think is relevant. Discuss your findings in a one-page report.

Discuss

- Why might sellers or servers of alcohol face criminal charges for certain activities, instead of civil penalties? What are the potential ramifications of these activities for one's career? What are the ramifications for one's life?
- How can laws restricting how and by whom alcohol is served affect hiring decisions in foodservice establishments? Encourage students to relate this to the discussions of the Fair Labor Standards Act in Chapter 8.
- How can employees tell who should and should not be asked to show identification before ordering alcohol? How might guests react when told they cannot be served?

Reinforce and Review

- The amount of alcohol absorbed into a person's bloodstream is called the blood alcohol content, or BAC. In all 50 states, it is illegal to drive with a BAC of .08 or higher.
- In all 50 states, the minimum age to purchase alcohol is 21, although some states allow minors to consume alcohol.
- Some states allow 18-year-olds to serve alcohol, but most states require those serving alcohol to be 21 years of age or older.
- Some areas prohibit minors from entering bars, taverns, or restaurant lounge areas, although they may be admitted to other parts of these establishments.
- The best way to ensure that customers are of legal age to drink is to check their identification.

Teaching Tips

- The more often that servers examine guest identification, the more adept they will be at recognizing valid and invalid identification.

Sellers or servers of alcohol may face criminal charges for the following actions:

- Serving alcohol to a minor
- Serving a guest who is, or appears to be, intoxicated
- Possessing, selling, or allowing the sale of drugs on the premises
- Allowing a minor to sell alcohol

In Illinois, for example, selling or serving alcohol to a minor is punishable by a fine of up to $2,500 and a jail sentence of up to one year.

The amount of alcohol absorbed into a person's bloodstream is called blood alcohol content (BAC). A BAC of .10 means that there is about one drop of alcohol present for every thousand drops of blood. In all 50 states, it is against the law to drive with a BAC of .08 or higher. A BAC of .30 or higher can lead to coma or death.

In all 50 states, you must be 21 years old to purchase alcohol. In some states, it is currently legal for a parent or legal guardian to purchase alcohol and serve it to a minor child. In general, a server must be 21 years old to serve alcohol, but this law varies. In some states, you can be 18 years old to serve alcohol.

For example, some states allow underage servers to bring alcohol to the table, but they cannot pour it. Other states allow underage servers to take the order and payment for the drink, but not to serve it. Some states require the underage server to apply to the liquor authority for permission to serve alcoholic beverages.

In some areas, the law does not allow minors to enter a tavern or restaurant bar area. Some establishments may require guests to be older than the age allowed by law to enter the bar.

If you sell or serve alcohol, you are responsible for ensuring that customers are of legal age to drink. The best way to do that is by checking each customer's identification. The proper procedure for checking IDs is the following:

1. Greet the guest politely
2. Politely ask the guest for ID
3. Verify the ID. Make sure it is valid, has not been issued to a minor, is genuine, and belongs to the guest. If you're unsure, ask for another form of ID, compare the guest's signature to the one on the ID, or ask questions only the ID's owner could answer. (For example, "How tall are you? What is your middle name?") Notify the manager of any suspicious forms of ID.
4. Serve or refuse the guest

638

In-Class Activity: BAC Levels

Mathematics Connection, Literacy Connection

Blood alcohol content, or BAC, is a measure of how much alcohol has been absorbed into a person's bloodstream. A BAC of 0.10 means that there is about one drop of alcohol present for every thousand drops of blood.

Calculate how many drops of alcohol are present per thousand drops of blood at the following concentrations:

- 0.05 [½ drop of alcohol per thousand drops of blood]
- 0.08 [⁴/₅ drop of alcohol per thousand drops of blood]
- 0.12 [1-¹/₅ drops of alcohol per thousand drops of blood]
- 0.15 [1½ drops of alcohol per thousand drops of blood]
- 0.20 [2 drops of alcohol per thousand drops of blood]
- 0.25 [2½ drops of alcohol per thousand drops of blood]
- 0.30 [3 drops of alcohol per thousand drops of blood]

To make sure an ID is genuine, look for signs of tampering, including bubbles and creases, improper thickness, and ink signatures. If you spot a fake ID, take several possible steps, depending on company policy and the laws in the area. This may include refusing service, refusing entry to the establishment, and/or confiscating the ID. Always check with the manager regarding suspicious or fake IDs. Follow company policy.

Some establishments use ID readers to check IDs with bar codes or magnetic stripes. Although these tools can help verify the age of a person, use them in conjunction with other checking procedures to make sure the ID is valid.

Acceptable forms of ID include the following:

- Driver's license
- State ID card
- Military ID
- Passport

Figure 10.10 shows sample identifications.

In most states, proper ID does not include a birth certificate, school ID, or voter's registration card. All states add special features on a minor's ID to make an underage guest easy to spot.

Figure 10.10: Sample driver's license and passport.

Check with the manager for the valid IDs issued by your state, or use an ID checking guide. These guides provide full-size samples of each state's drivers' licenses. They also provide a detailed description of minor IDs, state ID cards, and valid drivers' licenses in current circulation.

Because it is illegal to serve alcohol to a minor, card any guest who appears to be under 21 years of age. To take the guesswork out of carding, many

639

Reinforce and Review

- Always check with the manager when faced with a suspicious form of identification.
- Acceptable forms of identification include a driver's license, state ID card, military ID, and passport.
- All states add distinguishing features to minor identification cards so that sellers and servers of alcohol can immediately realize that the person is underage.
- Because it is illegal to serve a minor, check the identification of any guest who appears to be under 21 years of age.

Teaching Tips

- Ask students to examine their own identification cards for the elements that mark them as minors.
- Consider asking a representative from the state liquor authority to speak with students about the laws affecting them.

CUSTOMIZED INSTRUCTION

Literacy Connection, 21st-Century Skills— Civic Literacy, Access and Evaluate Information, Communicate Clearly

More Advanced Students

State and local liquor laws vary tremendously. Many areas, for instance, are "dry," which means liquor cannot be legally sold within their boundaries. Other areas regulate the types of alcohol that can be sold in different establishments at different times of day. Some states require the sale of "package" liquor, or alcohol sold in a bottle instead of as a drink, to be conducted only by state agencies.

Research the history of your state's liquor regulations. When were they first established, and by what entity? How have the laws changed since then? How and by whom are they enforced? What historical factors, such as Prohibition, may have played a role in your state's laws?

Write a one-page report on your findings.

Less Advanced Students

What was Prohibition? How did it affect the sale and consumption of alcohol in the United States? How did it affect restaurants, bars, and taverns?

Research the history of Prohibition in the United States, including the events that led to its enactment as well as to its repeal.

Write a one-page report on your findings.

Figure Focus

Figure 10.10: Would students serve alcohol to either of these people, based on these identifications? Why or why not? What factors would they consider?

CUSTOMIZED INSTRUCTION

Literacy Connection, 21st-Century Skills—Civic Literacy, Communicate Clearly, Use and Manage Information

ESOL Students

What policies govern the consumption of alcohol in your country of origin?

Prepare a brief oral report on the laws, the agency in charge of developing and enforcing the laws, and how these laws can affect restaurants and their employees.

Discuss

- How can documenting an alcohol-related incident and detailing the establishment's response protect a restaurant from financial hardship, legal burdens, and injury to its reputation?
- How do financial transactions between the guest and the restaurant differ from financial transactions between the guest and the server?
- How can the payment process reinforce or detract from the guest's overall experience in the restaurant? Is the last impression as important as the first impression? Why or why not?

Reinforce and Review

- When an alcohol-related incident occurs on the premises, managers typically file reports documenting the event and the actions that staff members took in response.
- Always follow management policies when deciding which guests should and should not be asked to present identification.

**Fast Fact:
Did You Know...?**

Encourage students to discuss the following:

- How can the restaurant and foodservice industry work to increase guest and public safety and to decrease the incidence of alcohol-related crashes?

**Homework Activity:
Alcohol's Effect on the Human Body**

Science Connection, Literacy Connection, 21st-Century Skills—Access and Evaluate Information, Health Literacy, Be Self-Directed Learners

How is the amount of alcohol in one's bloodstream directly connected to one's health? Research the physiological effects of alcohol on the human body, and write a one-page report on your findings.

---

establishments require staff to card guests who are clearly older than 21. Always follow house policies on when to card.

Filing Alcohol-Related Reports

When an alcohol-related incident occurs on an operation's premises, the manager often needs to file a report, which is used to document what happened and what actions were taken to address the situation. The manager should provide accurate information and fill out the report immediately so important facts aren't forgotten.

Reports are often completed for all of the following reasons:

- The operation stops alcohol service to a guest.
- The restaurant or foodservice operation arranges alternate transportation for a guest.
- The manager confiscates a guest's ID.
- An illegal activity or violent situation takes place.
- A guest becomes ill (requiring medical treatment).
- A guest becomes injured.

Remember, incidents involving alcohol use can be very serious. It's always best to be on the safe side if something happens in the establishment, which means it's better to have an incident report on file than not to have one.

[fast fact]

Did You Know...?

According to the CDC, 36 people in the United States die every day from motor vehicle crashes that involve an alcohol-impaired driver. Approximately 700 more are injured. The annual cost of alcohol-related crashes totals more than $51 billion.

Processing Payments

Processing payments is as vital a function as greeting the customers or serving the food. This is the time at which the guest gives back to the establishment in return for the service and food that they have received. Accept and process the payment with thanks and tact. The way in which the payment is processed can be the difference between a one-time and repeat guest.

Most establishments accept cash or credit. For cash transactions completed with a cashier, the cashier accepts the check and cash payment from the guest, restates the total to the guest, and then counts out the change.

Credit cards are used more and more frequently by customers, even for smaller transactions. It's essential to know how the process works. Credit card machines vary, but the procedures are fairly standard. Swipe credit cards through these machines to obtain authorization from a databank. The credit card machine displays an authorization response.

For credit card transactions completed with a cashier, the following steps should be taken:

- After authorization, the customer finalizes the total (noting any tip that they want to add) and signs the slip.

- The cashier keeps the credit card in his or her possession during this process.

- Before returning the credit card to the customer, the cashier compares the signature on the credit card with the signature on the slip to verify the customer's identity. If the signatures are different, the cashier politely asks the customer to provide additional identification, such as a driver's license or other valid government-issued ID.

- After confirming the customer's identity, the cashier returns the credit card to the customer along with a copy of the credit card slip.

Many operations now have credit card systems that do not require guests to sign for charged transactions under a certain dollar amount, or even at all.

The procedure for processing payment as part of table service is very similar to processing at a register. Process a payment when serving customers tableside by following these steps:

1. Present the check at the table.

2. Collect payment from the customers.

3. Process payment.

4. Return the change or credit card receipt and credit card.

When processing a cash payment, do not count out the change to the customer and repeat the totals. Simply make change away from the table and then return it to the customer.

For credit card payments, bring the credit card and receipt to the table together. It is helpful for servers to explain to customers which copy they should take. Collect the signed receipt and secure it immediately after the customer has left.

Finally, remember to *always* thank customers for their patronage.

641

Discuss

- How can the availability of credit and debit card machines in an establishment affect its guests? Why might guests choose to patronize or avoid such businesses? How does this relate to the earlier discussion of competitive advantage in Section 1?

- Why should servers and other staff members always thank guests for their patronage? If the visit was disastrous, might the guests interpret this as hypocrisy? How can professional staff members project a sincere, credible image?

Reinforce and Review

- For cash transactions, cashiers accept payment directly from the guest, restate the total owed, and count out the change. If servers are involved in this transaction, the payment and change to be returned are usually calculated behind the scenes, and the change is then returned to the guest's table.

- Credit card machines display authorization or rejection notices, so servers and cashiers can determine whether a legitimate payment has been made.

- If there is uncertainty about the legitimacy of a credit card, the guest may be asked politely to present an additional form of identification.

- When serving seated customers who have paid by credit card, be sure to secure the signed copy of the credit card receipt immediately after the customers have left the table to prevent identity theft.

Discuss

- How is obtaining feedback from guests similar to or different from receiving feedback from a manager or peer?
- Encourage students to discuss which feedback strategies might be useful in different types of establishments.
- How can guest service be measured? What are some useful benchmarks?

Reinforce and Review

- The simplest and most obvious way to obtain guest feedback is to ask the guest throughout the meal.
- Problems mentioned in comment cards should be taken seriously and resolved as quickly as possible.
- All staff members should be made aware of positive and negative feedback from customers. Those mentioned by name should be either praised or trained, depending upon the comment.
- Managers sometimes call individual guests after their meal to inquire about their experience and obtain more feedback.

Vocabulary Terms

- **Comment cards:** Quick surveys that guests complete that note their level of satisfaction with the food and service provided.
- **Surveys:** Similar to comment cards, these typically include open-ended questions intended to elicit more detailed information.

Getting Feedback on Customer Satisfaction

To determine how well the restaurant or foodservice operation meets guests' expectations, it is useful to measure their satisfaction. This will help to understand the quality of the operation's customer service.

Routinely ask whether the food, drink, service, and accommodations (seating, temperature, lighting, and so on) are satisfactory during a guest's visit. This is the simplest and most obvious way to get critical customer feedback. Additional ways include the following:

- Encouraging guests to complete comment cards at end of visit
- Assessing customer satisfaction through surveys after visit
- Holding focus groups with both customers and employees to get detailed feedback
- Starting a mystery-shopper program

Comment cards are quick surveys that customers complete noting their satisfaction with the food and service. These are short and simple. Place pencils on the tables to encourage guests to fill out the cards.

Take any problems mentioned in comment cards seriously and correct them whenever possible. Circulate the general results, so that every manager and employee is aware of customer concerns. Praise those employees who are complimented by customers. Instruct and train any employees who are mentioned as part of a complaint.

Surveys are similar to comment cards, but sometimes include more open-ended questions. For example, surveys might include questions such as "How can we improve our service?" and "What would make you come back?" rather than "How was your meal?"

In addition to written surveys, managers can call a sampling of guests the day after their visit to get feedback over the telephone. See Figure 10.11 for examples of questions on a customer feedback survey.

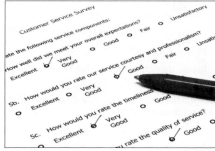

Figure 10.11: Surveys are an inexpensive way to gather customer feedback.

Figure Focus

Figure 10.11: How is good different from very good? Is there a meaningful distinction?

It takes time and effort for guests to provide feedback through the phone or a Web site. To encourage guests to respond, some operations offer a complimentary food item or discount. As with comment cards, a higher proportion of people with complaints are likely to provide feedback. Remember that offering a complimentary meal or discounted entrée may unintentionally discourage negative input.

Focus groups consist of customers that meet as a group to talk with managers about possible improvements in service or other areas. Many successful service managers use weekly or monthly focus groups to stay updated on any potential customer service improvements, as shown in Figure 10.12.

Figure 10.12: Focus groups are a good way to test new ideas such as menu items with a small group of people at the same time.

Focus groups can also be conducted with employees. Employee feedback is an important part of providing great customer service. Managers may want to hold focus groups with employees from each area of the restaurant and foodservice operation. At the focus group meeting, employees should feel free to make comments about the operation without fear of angering management and with the assurance that no one will repeat anything said outside the meeting. Varying the employees in the group gives everyone an opportunity to contribute and helps keep employees invested in the overall efficient functioning of the operation.

Mystery shoppers are hired by an operation to visit and report on their experiences and impressions of a particular foodservice operation. These shoppers provide more in-depth feedback than comment cards or surveys, especially if they have been trained on an establishment's systems and procedures.

When beginning a mystery shopper program, managers can present it as an opportunity for all employees to see how they are viewed by customers. Encourage everyone to take criticism constructively and be willing to improve performance based on mystery shopper reports. Some multi-unit companies reward single operations for positive mystery shopper feedback.

643

Figure Focus

Figure 10.12: Why might a focus group discussing snack foods take place in a casual environment?

Discuss

- Different people experience the same event or action in different ways. This is known as subjectivity. How can subjectivity affect a guest's response to the service provided? For instance, one guest may praise a server and another complain about her, both for the same actions. How does this relate to the barriers to communication discussed in Chapter 7?
- How can employee focus groups affect staff morale and the work environment? How might managers be affected?
- How can a mystery shopper program strengthen a restaurant or foodservice establishment? How can they expose problems?

Reinforce and Review

- Offering guests incentives to provide feedback can increase the response rate on surveys and comment cards, but this may unintentionally discourage negative input.
- Focus groups can be conducted with either guests or employees, as both groups are likely to have suggestions for improving customer service. Involving employees, without fear of retribution, can help cement their relationships with the workplace and contribute to a positive work environment.
- Managers should encourage staff members to take criticism constructively and use it to improve individual and team performance.

CUSTOMIZED INSTRUCTION
Literacy Connection, 21st-Century Skills— Think Creatively, Reason Effectively, Collaborate with Others
Special Needs Students
How are focus groups similar to discussion groups? How do each provide feedback? In what ways can each increase learning opportunities? Discuss these questions with a small group.

Vocabulary Terms

- **Focus groups:** Customers or employees that meet as a group to talk with managers about possible improvements in service or other areas.
- **Mystery shoppers:** Individuals hired by an establishment to visit and report on their experiences and impressions of the establishment.

What's New: The New "Word of Mouth": Customer Review Web Sites

Encourage students to discuss the following:

- Relate the information in this article to the discussion of blogging and ethics in Chapter 7.

- How can employees and managers determine whether feedback they receive on these sites is genuine or motivated by malice?

- How and when should a representative of a restaurant or foodservice establishment respond to online criticism?

Discuss

- How can customer complaints, whether online or in the establishment, have positive results? What role does communication play in addressing and assuaging guest concerns?
- Some establishments require the manager to resolve complaints, while some allow nonmanagerial staff to handle problems. How might the two types of workplace differ? How might employee relations with their managers and with the establishment itself differ from place to place?

Reinforce and Review

- Any unhappy customer is bad for business, so every operation needs an organized system for handling and resolving all guest complaints.
- It is important that managers support employees' decisions when they authorize them to resolve complaints. This reinforces the trust relationship between the two and helps establish a positive work environment.
- Every staff member must be trained on how to address customer complaints with respect and patience.

[what's new]

The New "Word of Mouth": Customer Review Web Sites

For the longest time, a "word of mouth" reputation meant just that: opinions about a restaurant's food or service spread from one person to another—in person! But the Internet has quickly changed all of that. With the ever-increasing number of Web sites dedicated to posting customer feedback, word of mouth can spread just as easily around the country as it can around a county. This poses both possibilities and risks for restaurant and foodservice establishments.

On the downside, any irate customer can post a negative review to a Web site for thousands of people to access and read with the click of a button. This means any mistake an operation makes, any bad night that an operation has, can come back to haunt it on the Web for years to come. There's definitely less room for error in a world where instant feedback has become the norm.

Web sites like TripAdvisor specialize in collecting customer feedback on restaurants around the world, but information on a local restaurant can just as easily be found in Google Maps where thousands of people submit their opinions about everything from restaurant décor to food to customer service. The iPhone offers the popular Urbanspoon application that allows customers to not only rate and give feedback, but encourages guests to take pictures of menus and food. The number of Web sites that offer such review forums is only increasing.

On the upside, operations can use all of this feedback constructively. They can examine the positive things customers are saying and try to capitalize on those elements, and they can also look to improve on the negative things people are saying. And the best part? Any operation can access and use this feedback without paying a penny. For better or worse, it's all totally free!

Resolving Customer Complaints

There will inevitably be occasions when things go wrong and a guest is not happy. Any unhappy customer is bad for business, so every operation needs an organized system for handling and resolving all guest complaints.

The person who first receives the complaint is responsible for making sure it gets resolved, even if that means deferring to someone else, such as a manager, to do so. Some operations choose the on-duty manager or shift supervisor to resolve complaints. Other operations allow employees to solve the problem without supervision. It is important that managers support employees' decisions when they authorize them to resolve complaints. This develops the trust necessary to have empowered employees. However an operation chooses to resolve customer complaints, management must train every staff member on how to handle these situations.

644

Handle guests' complaints in proven ways. These methods help to effectively resolve problems:

- Listen to the guest attentively, always looking for ways to solve the problem.

- Treat the guest with courtesy and respect.

- Don't become defensive. Don't take guests' complaints personally.

- Be patient.

- Empathize with the guest.

- Paraphrase the problem to confirm it with the guest. In other words, restate the problem and main details.

- Take responsibility for the situation as a manager or employee. Don't hide behind a job description. Never brush off a guest by saying, "Sorry, that's not my job."

- Don't pass the buck or blame other employees. Take ownership for resolving complaints unless the situation necessarily calls for additional help or authority, such as a supervisor or manager.

[fast fact]

Did You Know...?

Many restaurants conduct regular staff training exercises to ensure that everyone understands policies, procedures, and menu items. Some facilities take this a step further, using scheduled or random quizzes to test employee knowledge. These can be oral or written tests. Other establishments use role-playing activities to demonstrate proper server-customer interaction. All of these activities help to maintain a consistently high level of quality customer service, no matter which servers are working during a particular shift.

When are tests a good idea?

- When management changes the menu or beverage list

- When staff members need a refresher on management policies

- When customers complain

- When management hires a number of new employees

- When management implements new policies or procedures

- When servers need a refresher on suggestive selling methods

Testing can and should be used as a vital tool to maintain and improve business operations. Be sure to frame it in that light for staff, rather than as a way to "catch" employees.

Discuss

- Is the customer really always right? How far must foodservice staff go in order to resolve complaints? Are there some guests who can't be satisfied?
- How is the process for resolving guest complaints described on p. 645 related to the discussions of verbal and nonverbal communication and interpersonal communication in Chapter 7?

**Fast Fact:
Did You Know...?**

Encourage students to discuss the following:

- How can periodic tests of employee knowledge improve guest experiences as well as staff skills?

- How can conducting these tests strengthen employee morale and contribute to a positive work environment?

- How can the information in this article be related to professionalism?

645

Discuss

- Why might some guests choose not to complain to a restaurant or foodservice establishment about problems they have experienced?
- How does being specific when asking about guest experiences contribute to a server's credibility and the guest's perception of the quality of service?

Reinforce and Review

- The large majority of customers choose to leave unhappy rather than complain openly about their concerns.
- Irritated and unhappy guests often show signs, such as unconvincing responses about the meal and the service or not finishing a meal, that the professional server can identify and act upon.
- Proactively addressing complaints can turn dissatisfied customers into repeat guests.
- Staff should never ignore or avoid a dissatisfied guest, and they should notify managers of all guest complaints.

On the Job: Mirror, Mirror. . . Responding to Customer Complaints

Encourage students to discuss the following:

- How can the mirroring technique reduce conflict? Can it sometimes worsen a situation?
- Why is it important for servers and other staff to demonstrate empathy and effective listening skills when faced with a customer complaint?
- What is at the root of a customer complaint? Do guests want the problem resolved, do they want to be heard, or do they want to take advantage of the restaurant?

It is important to recognize when a guest is upset so that the problem can quickly be resolved. Some problems are easy to recognize, especially when a customer is visibly upset. However, most problems are more difficult to recognize because the large majority of customers simply go away unhappy.

Customers need to be asked whether everything was enjoyable. Rather than only asking, "Was everything OK?", ask "Did you enjoy the red snapper?" Actively look to see whether the guest is demonstrating signs of being unhappy with the service or meal, and then encourage the guest to explain the problem. Some of the more subtle signs of an irritated guest include looking annoyed, not finishing a meal, avoiding eye contact, or saying unconvincingly that everything was just "OK." Be aware of these signs and be ready to help solve any problems. In short, never ignore or avoid a dissatisfied guest. Problems occur and mistakes are made; customers understand this. Proactively addressing such occurrences with customers can turn a dissatisfied customer into a repeat guest.

[on the job]

Mirror, Mirror... Responding to Customer Complaints

Far too often, conflicts get out of control because people don't listen to each other, or don't act like they're listening to each other. A method of conflict resolution that tries to fix this common problem is mirroring, or paraphrasing language.

Mirroring language is very simple to do and helps clarify points of view when people are frustrated or angry. People mirror language when they simply repeat back what someone else has said before carrying on with their own thoughts or ideas. For example, if a customer is irate because they've waited over an hour for their entrée to come, first listen attentively to all they have to say and then begin a response by first repeating back what they said. For instance, "I understand that you've been waiting for over an hour, and that your kids are starving, and you feel your server has been avoiding you. I apologize for this, and I want to try to fix this situation for you."

By repeating back, or mirroring, all the grievances of the guest, the manager demonstrates two crucial things: 1) attentive listening and 2) empathy. This diminishes any chance for continued misunderstanding or miscommunication. If the manager simply starts by saying, "I apologize" without clearly stating they are apologizing for, the guest might not think that they are really listening.

Mirroring, then, is a simple tool to diffuse a potentially explosive situation. After all, often all a disgruntled guest wants is to be heard, and mirroring can resolve that issue simply by doing it.

Notify managers of all guest complaints. This helps the whole operation to take corrective action so the problem won't happen again. Customers appreciate it when managers apologize and show concern. In extreme cases, a follow-up written note of apology is appropriate.

When receiving complaints from guests over the phone, a manager or host may be trying to understand a situation in which they were not personally involved. Follow the same steps for resolving the complaint as if talking to the guest in person. Remember, the caller is probably not angry at the person to whom they are speaking, but at the situation.

It's a good idea to take notes when hearing a guest's complaint over the phone. The manager needs all the facts to work out a solution or pass along the information. Follow up on details that are unclear. This lets the caller know that someone is really listening to the complaint. Apologize for the problem so the caller knows they are understood. If the caller needs to be referred to someone else, be sure to give the customer the name of the person who will be handling the complaint. Most important, be sure the person who is responsible for dealing with the customer receives the message.

Managers also handle written letters and email complaints. Handling a customer complaint in writing requires additional care. Whenever an employee or manager is resolving a complaint, they should never accept responsibility (either verbal or written) for a customer's injury or damage to property unless a proper investigation and insurance inquiry has occurred. They should also never document any standard policy for reimbursing customers in writing. Each company has its own guidelines for how to respond to these situations, and most organizations want the flexibility to resolve complaints on a case-by-case basis. For more information, please see *Chapter 7: Communication*.

[on the job]

Responding to Customer Complaints

More than anything else, guests with complaints want to be heard. Take advantage of this important feedback from customers. It may be uncomfortable at the time, but use the information to improve the establishment's level of service. Moreover, if an unhappy guest feels that he or she is being ignored, it will make the situation worse. This will likely result in losing any future business from the customer.

Many customers will not complain in person; instead, they may simply never return to the establishment. So when a customer takes the time to present a complaint, treat both the person and the complaint with respect. Be sympathetic and take responsibility for problems that have occurred. When possible, offer a remedy that is consistent with the concern. Each situation is different.

For instance, a 30-minute delay between the clearing of the salads and the arrival of the entrées might infuriate a guest. An appropriate solution might be to offer a free dessert along with a sincere apology. But don't go overboard; an inappropriate solution might be to comp the entire meal. Sometimes the solution is simply allowing the guest to feel that someone else really understands the problem.

Discuss

- How can following up a problem with a dissatisfied customer improve a damaged relationship?
- Sometimes, guest complaints are more serious, especially when they are motivated by injury to themselves or damage to their property. How can professional employees learn to demonstrate empathy without accepting responsibility for the situation until after the conclusion of a formal investigation?
- Often, complaining guests are not actually angry with the staff member to whom they are complaining, but at the situation itself. How can professional foodservice employees learn to separate themselves from the situation so that they can look as objectively as possible at the customer's concerns?

Reinforce and Review

- When handling a complaint over the telephone, managers should always take notes and obtain as many facts as possible.
- When passing on a complaint for another staff member to resolve, make sure that the guest complaining knows who will be handling the situation and that the relevant staff member receives the message.
- Staff members should never accept responsibility for injury or property damage until a proper investigation has determined that the establishment is at fault.

On the Job:
Responding to Customer Complaints

Encourage students to discuss the following:
- How can employees respond to customer complaints in a respectful manner even if they are unhappy with what they are hearing?
- How can employees demonstrate appreciation for complaints, which are ultimately a way of improving service and business?

Summary

- Remind students to review the following:
  1. The proper way to handle reservations and special requests
  2. The importance of customer greetings
  3. How a server should interact with guests, and what information should be included for an order
  4. Suggestive selling and its importance to the operation
  5. Understanding the effects of alcohol and the specific legalities that apply to restaurant and foodservice establishments
  6. Customer payment options and processes
  7. The importance of customer feedback
  8. Resolving customer complaints effectively

Summary

In this section, you learned the following:

- Reservations should include the following information:
  - Customer's name
  - Customer's contact information
  - Date and time of arrival
  - Number of people in customer's party
  - Any special needs or requests the customer may have

- Greeters often present the first impression a guest will have of an establishment. They should be friendly, professional, and create a welcoming atmosphere for customers.

- Servers should be attentive and friendly when interacting with a table of guests. They should also be careful and organized when taking and placing orders. All table check information should include the following:
  - Proper seat and table numbers, where appropriate
  - Proper order in delivery sequence
  - Accepted abbreviations of operation that all staff can understand
  - Temperatures as needed, along with any special requests

- Suggestive selling involves recommending additional or different items to a customer. It is one of the keys to the success of any retail business. In a restaurant, maximize guest satisfaction and increase the average check with suggestive selling, resulting in more profits.

- All managers and staff must understand the effects of alcohol and become familiar with any and all laws that apply to their establishments. Every state has its own liquor laws and oversees the sale and service of alcohol within its borders. Laws vary considerably from state to state. Many counties and towns have their own, often stricter, liquor laws. Sellers or servers of alcohol may face criminal charges for the following actions: serving alcohol to a minor; serving a guest who is or appears to be intoxicated; or possessing, selling, or allowing the sale of drugs on the premises.

- Customer payment is usually processed with cash or credit. Accepting payment graciously and processing it efficiently is just as important to customer service as any other service task. When processing payment tableside, the following procedure is used:

- Present the check at the table.
- Collect payment from the customers.
- Process payment.
- Return change or credit card receipt and credit card.
- All staff must be sure to thank guests for their patronage when payment is processed.

▪ Customer feedback is important in keeping an operation running efficiently and profitably. Routinely ask whether the food, drink, service, and accommodations (seating, temperature, lighting, and so on) are satisfactory during a customer's visit. Additional ways to determine customer satisfaction include the following:

- Encouraging customers to complete comment cards at end of visit
- Assessing customer satisfaction through surveys after visit
- Holding focus groups with both customers and employees to get detailed feedback
- Starting a mystery-shopper program

▪ Resolving a customer complaint effectively can be the difference between gaining a repeat customer and gaining a bad reputation. The ways to effectively address customer complaints include the following:

- Listen to the guest attentively.
- Treat the guest with courtesy and respect.
- Don't become defensive.
- Don't take customers' complaints personally.
- Be patient.
- Empathize with the guest.
- Paraphrase the problem to confirm it with the guest.
- Take responsibility for the situation as a manager or employee.

649

Section 10.2 Review Questions

1. Information that should always be included when taking a reservation is the customer name, the customer's contact information, the date and time of arrival, the number of people in the party, and any special needs or requests the customer may have.

2. Employees can effectively execute suggestive selling by talking about daily specials, using active and descriptive words to explain menu items, and showing enthusiasm for the choices guests make.

3. Dram shop laws create special liabilities for establishments with liquor licenses and their employees. These laws allow an injured person, who may not even have been in the establishment, to sue the business, its owners, and its employees for injuries caused by a guest who had been drinking there. In states with dram shop laws, servers may be sued or even face criminal charges for serving alcohol to guests who are or appear to be intoxicated.

4. Operations can obtain customer feedback by asking customers about their visits, encouraging guests to complete comment cards, offering customer surveys, conducting focus groups, and starting a mystery-shopper program.

5. Servers can suggest specific items based on known guest preferences, recommend their own favorite dishes, offer dishes or beverages that complement one another, and suggest unusual items for special occasions. Student examples of these actions will vary.

6. The best way for Linda and Chef Jean to get feedback from customers about their new program is to ask customers directly for their opinions.

7. Students may answer this question in a variety of ways, such as consulting with a manager or asking for an additional form of identification.

8. Alcohol service policies should be:
   a. No alcohol should be served to this guest.
   b. Staff should follow house policies on whether to card anyone who appears to be under a particular age threshold.
   c. Staff should follow house policies on whether to card anyone who appears to be under a particular age threshold.

Section 10.2 Review Questions

1. List three bits of information that should be included in any reservation.

2. What are three ways in which an employee can effectively execute suggestive selling?

3. What is a dram shop law? Explain how it could affect the server of a restaurant.

4. List three ways in which an operation can collect customer feedback.

5. How can you make guests feel special and still pursue suggestive selling? Provide two examples.

6. Linda and Chef Jean have been running a new customer service program for six months. It seems like business is starting to pick up again, but they're not getting the response they had hoped for. They need to get customer feedback to identify what's working with the new program and what isn't. What would be the best method to gather feedback and why?

7. After an expensive meal, a guest hands you a credit card. It seems that the name you heard his friends calling him is different than the name on the card. Explain how you would handle this situation using the information you have learned in this chapter.

8. Given the importance of checking identification when providing alcohol service, what program would you implement for your staff to follow? Start with the request for alcohol from the three different people listed here. What would you do?
   a. A 15-year-old boy
   b. A 25-year-old woman
   c. A 35-year-old man

650

Section 10.2 Activities

1. Study Skills/Group Activity: The Service is the Thing!

Working with two or three other students, develop a skit demonstrating proper customer service, beginning with the customer's entrance and concluding with his departure. Perform your skit for the class.

2. Independent Activity: Sell! Sell! Sell!

You're the owner of a restaurant that is struggling to make money. You know that your service staff lack experience and need to improve their skills. You decide that you need to start a more aggressive suggestive selling training program with them. Knowing their limitations, you want to focus on a few basic points. What three suggestive selling points would you focus on with your staff and why?

3. Critical Thinking: Happy Anniversary?

Two guests of your restaurant had an unfortunate experience. The reservation they made for an anniversary dinner was lost, as were the special instructions they had included about their dessert. It was a busy night, so it took nearly an hour to seat the couple, and it was not possible to prepare the desired dessert. Obviously, they are very unhappy. As the manager on duty, how do you handle their complaint? What can you do to resolve the situation?

651

Section 10.2 Activities

1. Skits should demonstrate appropriate customer service throughout the "visit."

2. Student responses will vary but should include the information on suggestive selling found on pp. 636–637.

3. Student responses will vary but should include the information on resolving customer complaints found on pp. 644–647.

Section 10.3
Service Styles, Set-ups, and Staff

Introduce the Section

a. Identify prominent types of service style and equipment.

b. Describe the traditional responsibilities of service staff members.

c. Discuss the objectives for the section.

Vocabulary Review

a. Direct students to the key terms.

b. Pronounce each word, and have the students repeat the pronunciation out loud.

c. Discuss the definition of each word.

Teach

Discuss

- Encourage students to discuss service styles that they have experienced. What style seems appropriate for what type of environment? How can different service styles affect a guest's meal and his or her overall impression of a restaurant?

Reinforce and Review

- The service style is often a bigger factor in determining the identity of an operation than the food it serves.

10.1 The Importance of Customer Service	10.2 Ensuring a Positive Dining Experience	10.3 Service Styles, Set-ups, and Staff
• Definition of service and hospitality	• Reservations and requests	• Contemporary service
• First impressions	• Greeting and taking orders	• Traditional service
• Identifying customer's needs	• Suggestive selling	• Traditional service set-ups
	• Alcohol service	• Traditional service staff responsibilities
	• Processing payments	• Service tools and stations
	• Getting feedback on customer satisfaction	
	• Resolving customer complaints	

SECTION 10.3 SERVICE STYLES, SET-UPS, AND STAFF

The style an operation uses to serve its guests can very well define how people come to think of that operation as a whole. In fact, sometimes the service style is more of a factor in determining the identity of an operation than the food itself. For example, customers might be able to order a hamburger at a fine-dining establishment or a local diner, and although there might be a difference in the quality of the burger, their takeaway from the experience may well have more to do with the style in which they were served the burger than the burger itself. Was it on a plastic platter or a silver platter? Were they using linen or paper napkins? Was the server dressed in formal or casual attire? These are just a few of the many factors that work toward defining a restaurant and foodservice operation's service style.

This section discusses contemporary and traditional service styles and the various types of table set-ups used in traditional service styles, as well as the different roles and responsibilities service staff members have.

Study Questions

After studying Section 10.3, you should be able to answer the following questions:

- What is the contemporary style of service?
- What is the traditional style of service?
- What are the traditional utensils and table set-ups?
- What are traditional staff responsibilities?
- What are standard service tools and stations?

Contemporary Service

Quick-service is an easy and fast way to dine and typically involves no servers. Instead, guests help themselves to food set up in food bars or order at a counter. Other forms of quick-service include drive-through service, buffet service, carry-out service, vending service, and cafeteria service.

Traditional Service

Traditional service style reflects four main influences: American, French, English, and Russian. Each service style varies depending on the menu, theme, and décor. See Figure 10.13 for examples of table settings for each.

Figure 10.13: American, French, English, and Russian table settings.

Reinforce and Review

- Quick-service restaurants typically do not use servers. Instead, guests may help themselves to food or place an order through a cashier.
- Traditional service styles include American, Russian, French, and English, each of which may be used in an American restaurant.

Vocabulary Terms

- **Quick-service:** An easy and fast way to dine in which diners serve themselves or order from a cashier.
- **Traditional service:** One of four types of service, differing in level of elegance, used in sit-down restaurants.

Figure Focus

Figure 10.13: How do these settings differ? What elements do they have in common?

Discuss

- How do the four traditional service styles differ from one another in terms of guest perception and cost to provide?

Reinforce and Review

- American service is widely used, since it is easy and inexpensive to provide and requires few tools and utensils.
- French service is the most elegant style of service, but it is expensive to provide and therefore used less often.
- English service, also known as family-style dining, is the simplest and least expensive service style and is becoming more popular in the United States.
- Russian service is the most formal and is quite expensive, so it is used less often today.

Teaching Tips

- Make sure students understand that French service is not universally used in France, nor is it exclusive to France. The same is true for the other service styles.

Vocabulary Terms

- **American service:** Cooks arrange the food on plates, which are then delivered to guests by servers.
- **French service:** Servers present cooked food on tableside carts before arranging it on individual plates and delivering these to guests. Servers often cook some components of the food as well.
- **Guéridon:** A tableside cart that holds cooked and partially prepared food as well as serving dishes and cooking and serving utensils, used to cook and serve food.
- *Réchaud:* A warming unit or burner kept on or built into a guéridon.
- **English service:** Bowls and platters of food are placed on the table and either plates or food are passed around the table.
- **Family-style dining:** English service.
- **Russian service:** Bowls and platters of food are placed on a cart near the table and servers serve food onto the guests' plates from the bowls and platters while circling the table.

American service: Food is arranged on plates in the kitchen by cooks and brought directly to the guests' table by the server. The meal is complete on one plate. American service has quickly been adopted by many operations because it is one of the easiest service styles and uses the fewest tools and utensils.

French service: This style is typically considered the most elegant, but it is very expensive. Servers present the food to guests from a tableside cart, called a guéridon. A **guéridon** (gay-ree-DAHN) holds food or liquid items that will be served to guests, as well as serving dishes and other utensils the servers and guests may need. The food is kept hot by a warming unit in the cart, called a *rechaud* (ray-SHOW). The finishing touch to the food is done tableside to create a memorable moment for the customer. Tableside cooking is the art of showing great craftsmanship in both culinary arts and service skills. This type of service is expensive to implement because of the cost of the carts and the additional skills required of the servers

English service: Also known as **family-style dining**, English service is the simplest and least expensive. In English service, bowls and platters of food are placed on the table, and a seated host or hostess places the food onto plates. The host of the table then serves the meal on the plates for the other diners, or diners pass the dishes around the table so they can serve themselves. Although not as common as American service, family-style dining is gaining in popularity due to its simplicity.

Russian service: This style is the most formal service style. All food preparation is done in the kitchen. The bowls and platters of food are then brought on a cart to guests at the table. Servers hold the bowls and platters as they serve the food to each guest (see Figure 10.14). Service platters hold food for tables of up to eight guests but are very heavy (in previous times they were made of pure silver) and very hot. Servers need to go through

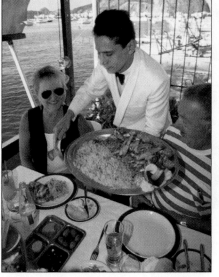

Figure 10.14: The server is illustrating the Russian style of service.

Figure Focus

Figure 10.14: What attributes must servers have to perform Russian service properly?

substantial training before being able to serve Russian style. The server is essentially in charge of making the plate look perfect. Not surprisingly, crowding customers during service is a problem in Russian service.

Table Settings

Every operation has its way of setting a table. However, virtually all the place settings mentioned in this section contain several items. In a traditional table setting, the server places the napkin in the middle of the setting; the dinner knife to the right of the setting with its sharp edge facing the middle of the setting; a spoon to the right of the knife; the dinner fork to the left of the setting; a water or wine glass above the knife point on the right side of the setting; and a bread plate to the left, next to the fork.

Although many restaurants use this traditional setting, other full-service operations use a specific place setting that matches its service style. For example, the French, Russian, and American service styles all have different place settings. Refer to Figure 10.13 to see the various settings.

Many of the utensils used in the more unique service styles and settings are also found in the traditional service setting. Though differences may be small, it is important to recognize the various table settings available and to use the most appropriate one.

Traditional Service Set-ups

Understanding the many types of silverware that an operation uses is very important. Use specific utensils for certain foods and set each table accordingly. The variety of knives, forks, and spoons used in any given operation can be huge. Some of the most necessary and widely-used utensils are discussed in this section.

The basic knives used most often when dining include the following:

- **Dinner knife:** This is used for all entrées and main courses.
- **Butter knife:** This is smaller than a dinner knife and used to butter bread or cut breakfast foods, fruit, and other softer foods.
- **Steak knife:** This is used to cut beef.
- **Fish knife:** This is used only to filet and cut fish.

Present fish and steak knives to guests who order those specific dishes.

See Figure 10.15 for pictures of various types of knives.

Figure 10.15: Various types of knives.

Figure Focus
Figure 10.15: Why are steak and fish knives not part of the traditional place setting?

Reinforce and Review

- The four basic knives used by diners are the dinner knife, butter knife, steak knife, and fish knife.
- Steak and fish knives are presented to those who order dishes requiring their use.

Teaching Tips

- Entrées is here used in the French sense, meaning introduction or appetizer.

CUSTOMIZED INSTRUCTION

Literacy Connection, 21st-Century Skills—Design Media Products, Communicate Clearly, Access and Manage Information

Less Advanced Students

Pick out a utensil used either to eat or to serve food. Research its history and uses.

Design a poster illustrating your chosen utensil and some interesting facts about it. Also, prepare a brief oral report to share this information with the class.

More Advanced Students

A popular trend in foodservice sustainability is providing biodegradable utensils and takeout containers instead of plastic ones. Research these items. What materials are used to make them? How long do they last? How sturdy are they? How much do they cost compared to plastic versions?

Write a one-page report on your findings.

Vocabulary Terms

- **Dinner knife:** Used for all entrées and main courses.
- **Butter knife:** Used to butter bread and cut soft items, especially at breakfast.
- **Fish knife:** Used to eat a portion of fish.
- **Steak knife:** Used to eat a portion of beef or lamb.

Discuss

- Do all restaurants need to have all these types of utensils? How does a menu determine which implements are required and thereby control costs?

Reinforce and Review

- Different utensils are used to eat different foods.

Vocabulary Terms

- **Dinner fork:** Used to eat main courses, vegetables, and pasta.
- **Salad fork:** Used to eat salads, appetizers, and delicate foods.
- **Fish fork:** Used to eat fish.
- **Snail fork:** Used to eat snails.
- **Lobster fork:** Used to eat lobsters.
- **Oyster fork:** Used to eat oysters.
- **Cake fork:** Used to eat pastries, cakes, and desserts.
- **Dessert forks:** Used to eat desserts.
- **Bouillon spoon:** Used to eat clear soups and broths.
- **Soup spoon:** Used to eat cream soups and some pastas.
- **Sauce spoon:** Used to eat dishes with sauce served on the side.
- **Coffee spoon:** Used for hot drinks, fruit cocktails, and ice cream.
- **Espresso spoon:** Used for espresso.
- **Demitasse spoon:** Espresso spoon.

Use a number of different forks when dining in a full-service operation, including the following:

- **Dinner fork:** This is used to eat main courses, vegetables, and pasta.
- **Salad fork:** This is smaller than the dinner fork and used for salads, appetizers, desserts, fruit, smoked fish, and other delicate foods.
- **Fish fork:** This is used only for eating fish.
- **Snail fork** and **lobster fork:** These are small, thin forks used only to eat those shellfish. A small, round **oyster fork** is served with both oysters and clams.
- **Cake fork:** This has only three tines and is used to eat cakes, tortes, pies, and pastries.
- **Dessert forks:** These often have a broader tine and can cut through a soft cake or other pastry like a knife.

See Figure 10.16 for pictures of various types of forks.

Figure 10.16: Various types of forks.

Just as with knives and forks, different spoons match different courses and foods:

- The two types of soup spoons are the bouillon spoon and soup spoon. Use a **bouillon spoon** for clear soups or broths. The bouillon spoon has a rounded spoon head. Use a larger **soup spoon**, with an oval spoon head, for cream soups and long strands of pasta.
- Use a **sauce spoon** with dishes served with sauce on the side.
- Use a **coffee spoon**, which is smaller than a soup or sauce spoon, not only with coffee, tea, and hot chocolate, but also for fruit cocktails and ice cream.
- An **espresso spoon**, or **demitasse spoon**, is much smaller than a coffee spoon and matches small espresso cups.

656

Figure Focus

Figure 10.16: How does the shape of each utensil reflect its purpose?

- The **sundae** or **iced tea spoon** has an especially long handle to dip into a deep sundae or stir large glasses of tea.

- A **grapefruit spoon** has jagged edges for carving into the grapefruit.

See Figure 10.17 for pictures of various types of spoons.

Figure 10.17: Various types of spoons.

Use other utensils for foods that are a bit more difficult to eat. For example, **snail tongs** are a specialized utensil for holding a snail shell so the snail can be removed. Since the shells of lobsters and crabs are hard and thick, use a **shell cracker** to crack them.

657

Discuss

- How can the use of uncommon service utensils add to a restaurant's ambiance or to guest perceptions of service? For instance, the presence of shell crackers usually signals that the restaurant has made a serious commitment to high-quality crustaceans. What does that indicate to guests?

Teaching Tips

- Older etiquette guides typically contain information on a wide variety of utensils, some of which are rarely used in contemporary dining. Obtain such a book and bring it in for students to see the range of utensils and the specificity of their uses.

Vocabulary Terms

- **Sundae spoon:** Used to eat sundaes or stir iced tea.
- **Iced tea spoon:** Sundae spoon.
- **Grapefruit spoon:** Used to eat grapefruit.
- **Snail tongs:** Used to hold snail shells so the cooked meat can be extracted.
- **Shell crackers:** Used to crack the shells of cooked crabs and lobsters.

Figure Focus

Figure 10.17: Ask students which of these spoons they use at home.

Reinforce and Review
- Drinking glasses come in an assortment of shapes, sizes, and materials.
- Mugs and cups are used to keep hot drinks hot.

Homework Activity: Form and Function

Literacy Connection, 21st-Century Skills— Reason Effectively, Work Independently, Access and Evaluate Information

Figure 10.18 displays a variety of glassware used in foodservice establishments. Select one and research its uses. How does its shape reflect its primary use?

Prepare a brief oral report on your findings.

Vocabulary Terms
- **Drinking glass:** Refers to a wide variety of shapes and sizes of drinking vessels, which may be made from a number of different materials.
- **Mug:** A thick, sturdy vessel used to keep hot drinks hot.

Drinking glasses (including mugs and cups) come in many shapes and sizes and often use either clear glass, plastic, or a thicker, solid ceramic. Generally, if a drink is cold, like soda, water, or iced tea, it will come in a clear glass. Serve hot drinks, like coffee, tea, and cocoa, in cups or **mugs** made from thick glass, or ceramic. This helps drinks stay hot. See Figure 10.18 for various types of drinking glasses.

Figure 10.18: Different types of glassware.

658

Figure Focus
Figure 10.18: How does the shape of a glassware item depend on what it is intended to contain?

Perhaps the most important part of the table setting is the **china**, which is also referred to as dinnerware. Like glasses, cups, and silverware, plates have adapted to fit the various types of food:

■ An **underliner plate**, or **charger**, is a larger decorative plate used underneath the plate on which food is served.

■ A **dinner plate** is 10 to 12 inches across. Use dinner plates for all kinds of main courses and meals and as a base plate for smaller plates and bowls.

■ A **salad plate** is much smaller than a dinner plate (7 or 8 inches across). Use it for desserts and appetizers as well as salads and as a base plate for gravy and sauce boats and sundae glasses that are served with a napkin or paper doily to prevent slipping.

■ Use a **bread and butter plate** for more than bread and butter. Use it as a base for jams and other condiments that may spill easily.

■ A **soup plate** is flat around the edge but has a dip in the center to hold soup, pastas, and even mussels, shrimp, and clams.

■ A **soup bowl** is smaller and deeper with no flat edge, and unlike the soup plate, is used only for soup. Soup bowls or cups are sometimes equipped with lids (individual tureen) or a single handle for easier service. Serve these bowls and cups on **chargers**, service plates that don't directly touch the food.

■ A **monkey dish** is a shallow bowl, often used for relishes or dipping sauces.

See Figure 10.19 for pictures of various types of plates.

Soup plate

Place setting consisting of a dinner plate, salad plate, and saucer

Standard soup bowl

Figure 10.19: Sample dinnerware.

659

Reinforce and Review
- China, or dinnerware, is the most important part of a table setting.

Vocabulary Terms
- **China:** The dishes from which food is served or consumed.
- **Underliner plate:** A larger decorative plate used below the plate on which food is actually served.
- **Charger:** Underliner plate.
- **Dinner plate:** Used for main courses and meals and as a base plate.
- **Salad plate:** Used for appetizers and desserts and as a base plate.
- **Bread and butter plate:** Used for bread and butter or as a base plate.
- **Soup plate:** Used for soup, pasta, and shellfish.
- **Soup bowl:** Used for soup.
- **Monkey dish:** Used for relishes or dipping sauces.

Figure Focus
Figure 10.19: How does the dish used to present a menu item affect the way it is enjoyed? For instance, what types of food would look attractive when served on black plates?

Fast Fact: Did You Know...?

Encourage students to discuss the following:

- What other utensils, glassware, or china can be traced back to particular cultures or civilizations?

- Why did utensils develop? How might cuisines have been different if they had not?

Homework Activity: Dish It Up

Literacy Connection, 21st-Century Skills—Think Creatively, Reason Effectively, Work Independently

Invent a new menu item that must be eaten on a particular dish or with a particular utensil.

The catch? You have to develop the dish or utensil yourself.

What would it look like? How would it be held, if necessary? What materials would be used to make it? What properties would it have? Why would it be the only dish or utensil suitable for consuming your newly invented menu item?

Design a prototype of your new invention using some visual medium. Present an oral report to the class, explaining your design and how it would be used.

Vocabulary Terms

- **Tureen:** A covered bowl used to serve soup to several diners.
- **Snail plate:** Used for holding a portion of snails.
- **Gravy boat:** A vessel used to hold and serve gravy.
- **Finger bowl:** Used to rinse one's hands after eating certain foods.

Though the pieces mentioned previously can be served with many foods, a number of china pieces are used for only one purpose. For example, use a **tureen**, a large covered bowl, to serve soup for up to eight people. The **snail plate** has six or twelve indentions for holding snails. A **gravy boat** has a special lip or spout to prevent spilling when pouring the sauce onto the plate. Use a **finger bowl**, a small bowl filled with water and often a citrus fruit slice (lemon or orange), to clean the fingers after eating, especially with messier meals such as shellfish and ribs. See Figure 10.20 for pictures of various types of one-purpose china.

| tureen | snail plate | gravy boat | finger bowl |

Figure 10.20: Various types of china.

[fast fact]

Did You Know...?

The fork has origins dating back to the ancient Greeks more than 2,000 years ago. They were larger than the forks we use today and had two tines rather than three or four tines, which are more common today.

Figure Focus

Figure 10.20: Is it cost effective to serve items such as snails, which require several pieces of specialized equipment?

Traditional Service Staff Responsibilities

Many large, traditional, full-service restaurants have a formal service organization—a group of servers who perform service-related tasks. Every one of the servers in the front of the house works together to ensure that guests enjoy themselves.

One of the people involved in the formal service organization is the **maître d'hotel** (MAY-tra doe-TEL), who is responsible for the overall management of service. The **headwaiter** is responsible for service in a particular area, such as a banquet room or dining room, while the **captain** is responsible for a server area of about 15 to 25 guests, and is assisted by the front waiter or an apprentice. Working with the captain, the **front waiter** has only 1 to 2 years of experience. An **apprentice** is a server in training.

In less formal service structures, a **floor manager** might run the dining room. The floor manager is in charge of the operation during a particular shift and supervises a team of servers. Each individual **server** is responsible for a specific section of the dining room. **Food runners** are sometimes employed to assist with bringing food from the kitchen to the tables. **Busers** assist with the cleaning up and resetting of tables.

No matter how an operation organizes its employees, it is important that each person know their roles and their specific tasks and responsibilities.

661

Discuss
- How can some of these positions be combined or eliminated in smaller restaurants without affecting the quality of guest service?

Reinforce and Review
- The formal service organization traditionally involves a number of front-of-the-house team members, such as the maître d'hotel and the captain, that are less commonly used in less formal service structures.
- No matter how an establishment organizes its staff, all team members must understand their roles and responsibilities.

Vocabulary Terms
- **Maître d'hotel:** Individual responsible for the overall management of service in a formal service organization. Also known as maître d'.
- **Headwaiter:** Individual responsible for service in a given area of a restaurant in a formal service organization.
- **Captain:** Individual responsible in a smaller service area in a formal service organization.
- **Front waiter:** Assists captain with service.
- **Apprentice:** A server in training.
- **Floor manager:** Individual running the dining room in a less formal service structure. Supervises the service team and is in charge of operations during a particular shift.
- **Server:** Individual responsible for a specific section of the dining room in a less formal service structure.
- **Food runner:** Brings food from the kitchen to the guests in a less formal service structure.
- **Buser:** Cleans and resets tables in a less formal service structure.

On the Job:
The Maître d'

Encourage students to discuss the following:

- What skills should a contemporary maître d' have? Is diplomacy as necessary today as in the past?

- What opportunities and challenges might face a maître d' each day?

- How is the maître d' ultimately responsible for a guest's experience at the restaurant?

Teaching Tips

- The formal service organization is a tightly run hierarchy.

[on the job]

The Maître d'

The maître d' in a restaurant, hotel, or cruise ship is responsible for ensuring that high standards of customer service are maintained for every diner. The full name, maître d'hôtel, is French and means "master of the hotel." This refers to the days when the maître d' worked for members of royalty or the aristocracy. Traditionally, they had to be masters of diplomacy and politics in order to provide the high levels of service for which they were known. See Figure 10.21 for a maître d' then and now.

Today, while the clients may have changed, the work is essentially the same. Maîtres d' are responsible for the smooth running of the establishment. They handle everything from customer complaints to straightening a buser's tie. Diplomacy is still a critical part of the job. After all, they have to negotiate the needs of *all* the guests at the same time—first-timers and regulars, happy and disgruntled. Like concierges, maîtres d' often find themselves called upon to address unusual requests. An experienced maître d' views these requests as opportunities to accommodate the guest, not as inconveniences.

Some maîtres d' work their way up through other front-of-house positions, while others come from different service industries. Some culinary schools offer related courses, and The Culinary Institute of America requires all students to serve as maîtres d' in its campus restaurants.

Figure 10.21: Maître d' then and now.

Figure Focus
Figure 10.21: How are the two images similar and different?

Service Staff Guidelines for Handling Food and Tableware

Just because service staff do not cook the food doesn't mean they don't have to be just as careful as the kitchen staff. Service staff can contaminate food simply by handling the food contact areas of glasses, dishes, and utensils, not to mention improper handling of ready-to-eat items. Following are guidelines all service staff should use when serving customers:

- Hold dishes by the bottom or very edge. Hold glasses by the middle, stem, or bottom. Do not touch the food contact areas of dishes or glassware.

- Hold flatware by the handle. Store flatware so servers grasp handles, not food contact surfaces.

- Use tongs or gloves when handling ready-to-eat items like bread or rolls. Do not use bare hands.

- Carry glasses on a tray to avoid touching the food contact surfaces. Stacking china and glassware can cause them to chip or break. Do not stack glasses when carrying them.

- Use ice scoops or tongs to put ice in a glass. Never scoop ice with bare hands because such contact can contaminate the ice. And never scoop ice with a glass because the glass could chip or break in the ice.

Service Tools and Stations

In full-service restaurants, servers usually carry many different **service tools** with them. They may carry a hand towel, a lighter, a corkscrew, change, a pen, an order pad, and sometimes a crumber, which is used to neatly gather and clear crumbs and debris from a table cloth. Figure 10.22 shows a crumber in use. These items are helpful to have on hand because servers use them so often.

Figure 10.22: Crumbers neatly gather and clear crumbs.

663

Figure Focus
Figure 10.22: How can the use of a crumber affect customer experience?

Discuss

- How can a properly managed service station improve a server's efficiency and the guests' experiences? How can a poorly managed one complicate the service period?

Reinforce and Review

- A service station prevents servers from having to leave the dining room to obtain necessary items during service.
- A variety of service utensils allow servers to distribute items like slices of desserts or individual rolls without touching the food with their hands.

Homework Activity: Banquet Business

Literacy Connection, 21st-Century Skills—Think Creatively, Reason Effectively, Work Independently

Figure 10.24 demonstrates a server preparing for a banquet. Banquet service is typically different from a restaurant's normal service period. One major difference is that people attending banquets often have little or no choice about what they will eat because there is one set menu for all guests. This is done to facilitate the flow of service to large parties and help banqueting organizations control their costs.

Design a three-course menu for an organization's banquet. What utensils would guests need to eat these dishes? What service style would be most appropriate?

Write a one-page paper, listing the dishes you have selected and explaining why each would be appropriate for a banquet, as well as identifying necessary utensils and the appropriate style of service.

Vocabulary Terms

- **Service station:** The area in which an operation keeps additional items such as napkins, silverware, condiments, menus, and other necessary items where they will be easy for staff to obtain during service.
- **Serving utensils:** Tools that servers use to give guests individual portions of food.

The **service station** is the area in which an operation keeps additional items such as napkins, silverware, cups and saucers, condiments, menus, and water glasses. A service station prevents servers from having to go to the back of the house to get them and is a good way to keep much needed utensils close by. Figure 10.23 shows an example of a service station.

Servers use different **serving utensils** when they serve food to guests. Use large serving spoons to serve many items, such as casseroles and vegetables. Use pastry tongs to serve individual pastries, such as cream puffs and small cakes. Cake and pie servers come in many shapes to match the size of the piece of cake, or pie. This keeps the dessert from breaking apart as it is served. Figure 10.24 shows how to properly serve ready-to-eat items such as bread or rolls.

Figure 10.23: Serving station.

Figure 10.24: Use tongs or gloves when handling ready-to-eat items like bread or rolls. Do not use bare hands.

664

Figure Focus

Figure 10.23: Why is it important to keep a service station neatly organized?

Figure 10.24: What can students observe about this establishment from the photograph?

Essential Skills

Left, Right, Left—Proper Placements for Table Service

Not only are servers responsible for properly setting the table and serving the guests, they must also know how to remove items from the table while guests are still seated. And they must know how to do this so that they do not get in the guests' way and interrupt their meals. To accomplish this, servers should conduct certain table tasks from specific places.

Perform these tasks at the guests' left side:

- Presenting and serving from platters
- Serving solid foods, including salad and bread
- Clearing the table of extra utensils and crumbs
- Setting and clearing bread and butter
- Removing anything served from the left

Perform these tasks at the guests' right side:

- Setting and clearing plates (except for bread and butter)
- Changing flatware
- Serving soup and beverages

However, some exceptions to the rule exist:

❶ At corner tables, serve guests so as to disturb them as little as possible. This means serving from whichever side is most convenient.

❷ At rectangular tables, servers should stand at the head of the table when opening wine, taking orders, and assisting guests with the menu. Do this so all seated guests can see the server.

Figure 10.25: Step 3—Servers should carry glasses on a tray.

❸ Servers should be careful in how they handle guests' plates and utensils in order to be as sanitary as possible. See Figure 10.25. Servers should carry glasses on a tray to avoid touching the food-contact surfaces.

665

Essential Skills:
Left, Right, Left—Proper Placements for Table Service

Encourage students to discuss the following:

- How does conducting table maintenance tasks from specific sides of a guest accommodate the guest's needs?

- Why is it important for servers to be able to adjust their performance of basic tasks as needed?

- How can clearing used dishes, glasses, and silverware be conducted in a sanitary manner?

Figure Focus

Figure 10.25: Where should this server hold the glasses as he transfers them to the table? Where should he stand as he serves each guest?

Summary

- Remind students to review the following:
  1. Contemporary style of service
  2. Traditional style of service
  3. Traditional utensils and table set-ups
  4. Traditional staff responsibilities
  5. Standard service tools and stations

Summary

In this section, you learned the following:

- Contemporary service, also known as quick-service, is an easy and fast way to dine and typically involves no servers. Instead, guests help themselves to food set up in food bars or order at a counter. Other forms of quick-service include drive-through service, buffet service, carry-out service, vending service, and cafeteria service.

- Traditional service style consists of four main influences: American, French, English, and Russian. Each service style varies depending on its menu, theme, and décor. American is one of the easiest and uses the fewest utensils. French is known as the most elegant, but is also the most expensive. English is the simplest and least expensive. Russian is the most complicated.

- Specific utensils are used for certain foods, and each table must be set accordingly. The variety of knives, forks, and spoons used in any given operation is huge.

- Many traditional, large, full-service restaurants have a formal service organization, or group of servers, to perform service-related tasks. Every one of the servers in the front of the house must work together to ensure that guests enjoy themselves. For formal service structures, the staff includes the maître d'hotel, the headwaiter, the captain, the front waiter, and an apprentice.

- For less formal services, the staff consists of the floor manager, server, food runners, and busers.

- Service tools can include a hand towel, a lighter, a corkscrew, change, a pen, an order pad, and a crumber. The service station is the area in the operation where additional items are kept, such as napkins, silverware, cups and saucers, condiments, menus, and water glasses. Servers use different serving utensils, which include large serving spoons, pastry tongs, and cake and pie servers.

Section 10.3 Review Questions

1. Define contemporary service.

2. What are the four styles of traditional service?

3. What are the different characteristics of each style of traditional service?

4. What is the traditional service hierarchy of a formal full-service establishment?

5. Would one service style be more likely to make guests feel welcome than another? If so, which one and why?

6. How would you describe Uptown Grille's service style? What are the pros and cons of such a style?

7. Look into the various service styles. What is the origin of each? How do these origins reflect the style of each service? That is, what does the style say about the culture from which it came? On a broader scale, how does service reflect the personality of the restaurant?

8. The efficiency of a restaurant's servers is integral to quality customer service. You're in charge of establishing what servers wear, the tools they are expected to carry, and the equipment stocked in their service station. Write a paragraph for each of these criteria describing your plan.

667

Section 10.3 Review Questions

1. Contemporary service is also known as "quick-service," an easy and fast way to dine that typically involves no servers; instead, guests help themselves to food or order from a counter or drive-thru window.

2. The four styles of traditional service are Russian, French, English, and American.

3. In American service, food is arranged on plates in the kitchen, and servers transport the food to the guests' table. It is one of the easiest service styles and requires the fewest tools and utensils. In French service, servers finish cooking the food in front of the guests, and then serve them; this style is very elegant, but is also very expensive, requiring both a great deal of equipment and a number of highly trained service staff. In English service, or family-style dining, food is placed on the guests' table in platters and bowls, and the guests serve themselves or are served by a member of the dining party. This method is simple and inexpensive, so it is gaining in popularity. Finally, in Russian service, food is arranged on platters in the kitchen, and servers arrange food on guests' plates; like French service, this style is expensive in terms of equipment and staff costs.

4. The traditional service hierarchy of a formal full-service establishment is as follows: the maître d' is responsible for the overall management of service, then the headwaiter is responsible for service in a particular room or dining area, and then the captain is responsible for an area of 15 to 25 guests. The captain is assisted by a front waiter or an apprentice.

5. Student answers may vary but should clearly state why they believe the chosen service style makes guests feel most welcome.

6. Students should identify the service style (a combination of quick-service and American) and describe its pros and cons; answers may vary.

7. Students should research each service style and consider how a restaurant's chosen style relates to the ambiance and menu.

8. Students should describe each of these categories, using the content in Section 10.3 for assistance.

Section 10.3 Activities

1. Silverware needed for each situation:
   a. Dinner knife, steak knife, dinner fork
   b. Dinner knife, salad fork
   c. Dinner knife, dinner fork, soup spoon
   d. Bouillon spoon
   e. Cake fork, coffee spoon

2. The diagrams do not need to be elaborate but should be explicit, with explanations below each describing the complexity, expense, and popularity of each service style.

3. Students should clearly identify why the chosen service style will be most appropriate for the new restaurant.

Section 10.3 Activities

1. Study Skills/Group Activity: Setting the Table

Working with two or three other students, identify the silverware needed to serve the following dishes properly:

- Grilled steak with baked potato and vegetables
- Garden salad with ranch dressing
- Chicken and dumpling stew
- Shellfish consommé
- Triple-layer mocha fudge cake with vanilla ice cream

2. Independent Activity: Making Sense of Style

Create a diagram (or diagrams) that present each of the four traditional service styles: American, French, Russian, and English. Be sure to take into account kitchen versus tableside plating, degree of complexity, expense, and popularity in the United States.

3. Critical Thinking: Service with a Style

You're starting up a new mid- to upscale restaurant and need to determine what service style to use. You can choose one of the four traditional styles or combine aspects of different ones to create your own. Write up a one-page description of the service style you would employ. Why did you choose this style?

668

Case Study Follow-Up | *Wanted: Customer Service*

At the beginning of the chapter, Uptown Grille was having trouble with customer service. Linda and Chef Jean were trying to figure out what to do.

1. As noted previously, Uptown Grille has recently lost some long-term employees. How can their absence affect customers? How can their absence affect the current staff?

2. Linda and Chef Jean are ultimately responsible for customer service, but obviously they can't be watching their staff all of the time. How can they ensure that their employees are providing good service even when they're not around?

3. What program can they employ to ensure that employees make a positive first impression, both on new customers and on customers who have previously had negative experiences at Uptown Grille?

669

Case Study Follow-Up

1. Students should describe the effects that losing long-time employees can have on a business.

2. Student answers may vary, but they should address the role of employee training and customer feedback.

3. Student answers may vary, but using mystery-shopper programs and training employees on the importance of first impressions is key.

Apply Your Learning

Training Service Staff

Students should be able to develop a rough estimate of the costs required to hire and train a new employee, based on information that is available on employment Web sites.

Mission Accomplished

Students can use information provided in other chapters of the text to write a mission statement for their restaurant. They should also explain specific ways in which they and their staff will provide customer service in keeping with the mission statement.

Allergies

Students should research a food allergy or sensitivity to learn more about how people are affected by certain ingredients.

Critical Thinking   A Selling Script

Students should refer to the information on suggestive selling on pp. 636–637 to help develop ideas on suggestive selling.

Apply Your Learning

Training Service Staff

Just how expensive is it for an operation to have a high turnover rate for service staff? To answer this question, you'll have to figure out how much it costs to train a new employee. Research the training costs involved in hiring a new staff member, from putting out help-wanted ads, to conducting the interview process, to teaching the new employee the operation's policies and procedures. It may be helpful to speak with the owners of one or two local operations to get a feel for the work and costs that are involved. When you've completed your research, propose an average cost for having to hire a new employee.

Mission Accomplished

It can sometimes be difficult to ensure that all the employees at a large restaurant or foodservice establishment are maintaining the same high levels of customer service. To make this task easier, restaurants often adopt mission statements, which define an establishment's overall goals and philosophy. Write a mission statement for a restaurant you want to start, making sure to address customer service. Then, write an additional paragraph identifying the specific steps you can take to make sure that you and your employees are treating your guests in ways that match your mission statement. For instance, if your mission statement asserts that you will provide friendly service, then you should explain specific ways in which you will provide such service.

Allergies

It is estimated that up to 2 percent of U.S. adults suffer from food allergies, some of which may be fatal. So, it is critical that servers be well-informed about the ingredients in each dish. Identify and research a food allergy or sensitivity, such as peanut, soy, or gluten, and prepare a two-paragraph summary of your findings. Identify some foods that contain these ingredients, particularly those that you might not suspect. One example might be the wheat in red licorice.

Critical Thinking   A Selling Script

You own a local restaurant. Prepare a three-minute oral script that will welcome guests to your establishment and suggestively sell an appetizer, entrée, and dessert to them. Once you and your classmates have completed your scripts, perform each, and vote on who did the best job of selling and why.

Exam Prep Questions

1. Quality customer service will most likely result in

   A. lower payroll.

   B. higher turnover.

   C. better customer loyalty.

   D. increased marketing costs.

2. When rival restaurants share similar menus and food quality, a competitive advantage can most easily be gained through

   A. creating a unique menu.

   B. moving to a better location.

   C. improving customer service.

   D. underselling other operations.

3. An operation ensures that the exterior of the facility is spotless and well-kept, and the staff frequently rehearses the restaurant's greeting script. What is the most likely outcome of this operation's efforts?

   A. Table service will become slower but more thorough.

   B. Staff turnover will increase due to the script requirements.

   C. Customers will have a positive first impression of the operation.

   D. Profits will decrease because of costs to maintain the exterior of facility.

4. For servers, wearing _____ will help to create a positive first impression.

   A. a clean, ironed uniform

   B. brightly polished jewelry

   C. expensive, strong perfume

   D. a hat or head-covering for sanitary purposes

5. What is a helpful service tip for addressing the needs of parents with small children?

   A. Treat the children the same as the adults.

   B. Avoid going to the table unless necessary.

   C. Bring out crayons and paper before service.

   D. Serve children's food in take-out containers.

6. What does a POS machine do?

   A. Compiles feedback from comment cards

   B. Creates weekly shift and cleaning schedules

   C. Lists acceptable substitutions for menu items

   D. Sends orders into the kitchen from service stations

7. When checking to see whether a guest is of legal age to drink alcohol, a _____ is an acceptable form of identification.

   A. passport

   B. college ID

   C. birth certificate

   D. credit card with signature

671

Exam Prep Answers

1. C
2. C
3. C
4. A
5. C
6. D
7. A
8. C
9. B
10. B

8 What are mystery shoppers?

A. Repeat guests who frequently complete comment cards

B. Guests who report a positive dining experience but never return

C. Anonymous diners hired by an operation to critique the service

D. Customer appreciation programs that are run during the holidays

9 What is the most immediate way to gather customer feedback?

A. Mailing surveys

B. Talking to diners

C. Holding focus groups

D. Distributing comment cards

10 Which service style is considered simple and inexpensive, but is not as frequently used as the others?

A. French

B. English

C. Russian

D. American

Chapter 11 presents the various types of potatoes, legumes, grains, and pastas. It also reviews the selection, storage, preparation, and appropriate cooking methods for each of these products.

Section 1: This section focuses on potatoes, including the types of potatoes, selection and storage of potatoes, and cooking methods.

Section 2: This section addresses legumes and grains, including the different types of these products, selection and storage of legumes and grains, and cooking methods.

Section 3: Finally, this section reviews pasta and dumplings and the cooking methods appropriate for each.

Advance Preparation	
Review	Sections 11.1–11.3 Chapters 2, 6, and 9
Contact	Computer lab for Internet
	Cooking classroom if it is not your home classroom
	Local restaurant and foodservice operations, as needed
	Local resources for specialty grains
Prepare	Idaho russet and Yukon gold potatoes (one each, uncooked)
	Purple Peruvian and Red Thumb potatoes (samples, cooked)
	Starch and styrofoam packing peanuts
	Acetone
	Water
	Clear glass containers
	Baking potatoes
	Foil
	Oil
	Varieties of pastas

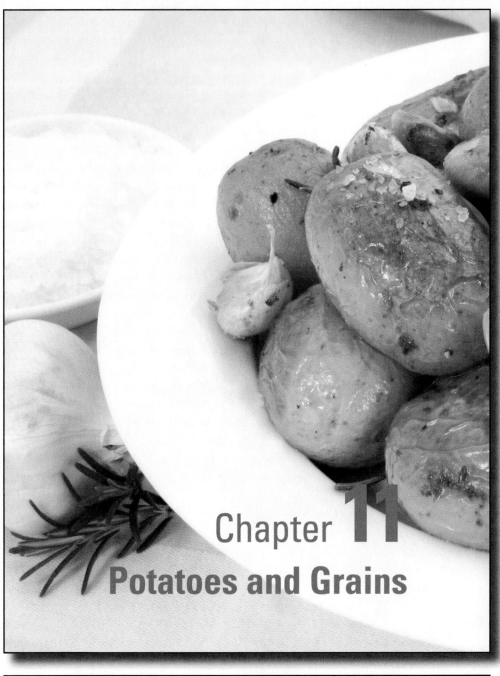

Chapter 11
Potatoes and Grains

CUSTOMIZED INSTRUCTION OPTIONS			
Less Advanced Students	**More Advanced Students**	**ESOL Students**	**Special Needs Students**
Pages 681, 713	Pages 681, 689, 694	Pages 681, 689	Pages 681, 712

CHAPTER TOOLS			
21st-Century Skills	**Mathematics**	**Science**	**Literacy**
Pages 681, 684, 685, 696, 698	Pages 698, 719	Pages 681, 688, 694	Pages 685, 720

ServSafe Connection
Pages 681, 718

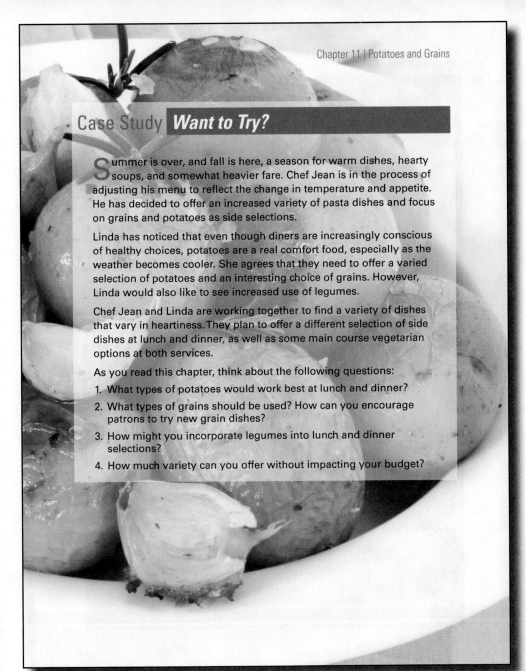

Case Study *Want to Try?*

Summer is over, and fall is here, a season for warm dishes, hearty soups, and somewhat heavier fare. Chef Jean is in the process of adjusting his menu to reflect the change in temperature and appetite. He has decided to offer an increased variety of pasta dishes and focus on grains and potatoes as side selections.

Linda has noticed that even though diners are increasingly conscious of healthy choices, potatoes are a real comfort food, especially as the weather becomes cooler. She agrees that they need to offer a varied selection of potatoes and an interesting choice of grains. However, Linda would also like to see increased use of legumes.

Chef Jean and Linda are working together to find a variety of dishes that vary in heartiness. They plan to offer a different selection of side dishes at lunch and dinner, as well as some main course vegetarian options at both services.

As you read this chapter, think about the following questions:

1. What types of potatoes would work best at lunch and dinner?

2. What types of grains should be used? How can you encourage patrons to try new grain dishes?

3. How might you incorporate legumes into lunch and dinner selections?

4. How much variety can you offer without impacting your budget?

Case Study
Want to Try?

- The case study involves taking a broad look at the menu.
- Chef Jean is looking for foods that are a bit more filling for the winter months.
- Linda is looking at the marketing aspects of non-meat options.
- Throughout the chapter, help the students to see things from both marketing and culinary perspectives.

Discuss	What does Chef Izard teach about commitment and the hours needed to successfully run a restaurant?
	Does food make people happy?
	Chef Izard's quote: "Make it happen." What does this mean to students?
Reinforce and Review	Chef Izard points out the health benefits of both potatoes and grains.
	Are students aware of these benefits?
Teaching Tips	Ask students if they are more interested in the culinary arts or in business. Is a restaurant both of these?

[professional profile]

Stephanie Izard, Restaurateur

The Drunken Goat/Stephanie Izard, Inc.

Although I didn't know it at the time, by the age of ten I had already figured out what I wanted to be when I grew up. At home, my favorite activity was to play "restaurant," offering friends and family a menu that I created from scratch. I was influenced by my parent's global cooking and the gourmet club they hosted each month, and my love affair with food took off.

As I grew older, I enjoyed cooking, but somehow thought my career should be business related.

In pursuit of a nonfood career, I attended the University of Michigan. But, there was no denying my interest in food, so after earning my degree in sociology, I entertained the idea of culinary school. I graduated in 1998 and left Michigan, heading west where I went on to earn my culinary degree at the Scottsdale Culinary Institute.

My culinary career began with a stint as a line cook at the French-inspired Christopher's Fermier Brasserie. Two years later, I left Arizona and returned to the Midwest, thrusting myself into the culinary capital of the region, Chicago. I again worked as a line cook for my first job in the Windy City, this time at Jean Georges' restaurant, Vong's Thai Kitchen. I next moved to the position of roundsman at Shawn McClain's award-winning new American/Asian restaurant Spring, and afterward became sous chef at the critically acclaimed French bistro, La Tache.

In 2004, I took a tremendous risk and opened my own restaurant, Scylla. Three years later, Scylla was named one of the 10 finest small restaurants in the country by *Bon Appetit* magazine. Soon after that, I did an extremely difficult thing: in order to allow time for travel, and a chance to give serious thought to my next venture, I closed Scylla.

In the fall of 2007, when I returned from my travels, I received a call from the producers of Bravo's Top Chef; they wanted me. An avid fan of the show (although I had to record and watch the program on my own schedule due to the nature of the long hours of a restaurant chef), I entered the competition telling myself, about the food, to "just make it taste good," and about the drama, to just avoid it. In the end, it worked, and I was not only named the Top Chef, but also voted fan favorite by the show's audience.

I love food! I love the people in this industry. I love the challenges. I love the excitement. And I really just love feeding people delicious food.

You have to really love food and cooking to last in this industry. You have to be ready to work harder than you ever have before. There's nothing easy about it. But at the end of the day (or rather, some time after midnight) you have the satisfaction that you just made a serious amount of people very, very happy. You'll most likely be working longer, harder hours than most of your friends, but you'll be going to work and doing what you love every day, which is a lot more than most people can say. And have fun in the kitchen because in the end, that's what it's all about. Excite the entire palate with every bite.

Remember:

❝ Make it happen. ❞

About Potatoes and Grains

I grew up loving potatoes in any shape or form. . . baked, twice baked, French fries, tater tots, hash browns, mashed. . . the list goes on. I still love all potatoes, and lately I've begun to explore all varieties from fingerlings to new potatoes to purple potatoes and others at the farmers' markets. It is important to know the difference in the starch content and flavor of each. I think that Idaho potatoes are best for fries; Yukons work better for mashed because they are creamier and less starchy; and new potatoes are perfect with the skins on because the skin is thin, beautiful, and delicious.

Grains have wonderful health benefits, as do potatoes. In vegetarian cooking, grains can be an essential way to get nutrients. I love "fun grains" like quinoa—they make great healthy salads.

11.1 Potatoes
- Types of potatoes
- Selecting and storing potatoes
- Cooking potatoes

11.2 Legumes and Grains
- Legumes
- Selecting and storing legumes
- Cooking legumes
- Grains
- Selecting and storing grains
- Cooking grains

11.3 Pasta
- Pasta and dumplings
- Cooking pasta
- Cooking dumplings

SECTION 11.1 POTATOES

Potatoes are native to North and South America. In the fifteenth century, the Spanish explorer Francisco Pizarro introduced them to Europe and sent them back to Spain. Potatoes became a staple in many countries, particularly in Ireland, because they were inexpensive and easy to grow. Today, the potato is the most important noncereal crop in the world.

677

Focus and Engage

Discuss

- Ask, "What do you like to eat in cold weather?"
- The chapter emphasizes foods that are often used as side dishes.
- Can non-meat options be used as main-dish items?
- Help the students to know the difference between a cereal and a non-cereal crop.
- It might help students to briefly review Pizarro and the other New World explorers and their impact on the world today.
- Various types of potatoes will work for lunch and dinner. However, heavier fare is less desirable for lunch during a workday, since it might contribute to drowsiness. Lighter options or smaller servings may make for better mid-day choices.
- The students might not yet know about various grains that will be addressed in the chapter.
- The students will become more aware of legumes as they study the chapter. Legumes may be added to soups and salads, in addition to legume dishes.
- Most potato, grain, and legume foods are not expensive when compared to meat or cheese. The students might be interested in knowing the prices of the foods.

Section 11.1 Potatoes

Introduce the Section

a. There are many varieties of potatoes.
b. Handling potatoes requires skill and knowledge.
c. There are many cooking methods used for potatoes.

Vocabulary Review

a. Direct students to the key terms.
b. Pronounce each word, and have the students repeat the pronunciation out loud.
c. Discuss the definition of each word.

Teach

Discuss

- Potatoes are found the world over.
- Potatoes are tubers that grow underground.
- Potatoes have unique and complex characteristics.

- The students might not be aware of so many considerations.
- Help the students to recall different potato dishes they have eaten.
- How does a potato salad differ from a baked potato?
- Ask the students if they have eaten Yukon potatoes or new potatoes.
- Have an Idaho and a Yukon gold or other variety potato for the students to see and compare.

Study Questions

After studying Section 11.1, you should be able to answer the following questions:

- What are the different types of potatoes?
- What are the methods to selecting, receiving, and storing potatoes?
- What types of cooking methods and recipes are there for preparing potatoes?

Types of Potatoes

All potatoes are not the same. Potato varieties differ in starch and moisture content, shape, and skin color. That's why different varieties produce a different end product. Potatoes are categorized by the potato's starch and moisture content. The starch content of any potato increases with age.

High-starch, low-moisture potatoes are dense because they have a high amount of dry starch. These potatoes swell and separate as they cook, which makes the potato fluffy. High-starch, low-moisture potatoes are best when baked, puréed, or fried. They include Idaho and russet potatoes.

Medium-starch, medium-moisture potatoes are versatile. The high moisture prevents the potato from swelling when cooked. These types of potatoes hold their shape, so they are good for potato salads and potato cakes. Medium-starch, medium-moisture potatoes are best for boiling, steaming, sautéing, oven roasting, stewing, mashing, and braising. They include chef's all-purpose, Yukon gold, and yellow-fleshed potatoes.

Low-starch, high-moisture potatoes are new potatoes. New potatoes are best for boiling, steaming, and oven roasting.

Sweet potatoes, yams, and russet potatoes are suited to baking, puréeing, and frying because they are high in starch and low in moisture. Table 11.1 lists the characteristics of the different types of potatoes.

Table 11.1: Characteristics of Potatoes

Name	Characteristics	Best Cooking Methods
Sweet potatoes	• Sweet potatoes (as other potatoes) are tubers. Tubers are fat, underground stems capable of growing a new plant. • Their thick skin ranges in color from light to brownish red. • They are high in starch and low in moisture. • They have an orange, mealy flesh that is very high in sugar. • Unlike the russet or chef's potato, sweet potatoes are available canned in a sweet, sugary sauce. • They are available year-round. • They are popular ingredients in breads, pies, puddings, soups, and casseroles.	Boiling Baking Puréeing Roasted
Yam	• Yams are not related to the sweet potato. • They originated in Asia. • They are less sweet than sweet potatoes. • They range in color from creamy white to deep red. • Yams have more natural sugar and a higher moisture content. • Yams and sweet potatoes are used interchangeably.	Baking Puréeing Frying
Russet	• They are referred to as Idaho potatoes, although many other states also produce these potatoes. • They are the standard white baking potato. • Their skin is generally a brownish-red color. • Their flesh is mealy and white. • They are available in many shapes and sizes. • Russett potatoes are good for baking, frying, mashing, roasting, and broiling. They are often used to make French fries.	Baking Frying
Chef's/All-purpose	• They are drier and less starchy than russet potatoes. • They are less expensive than russet potatoes. • Since they are irregularly shaped, they are most suited to preparation in which the final shape of the potato is not visually important, such as mashing, puréeing, in salads, scalloped or casserole dishes, soups, braising, and sautéing.	Mashing Puréeing Braising Sautéing

continued

Table 11.1: Characteristics of Potatoes (continued on p. 680)

- The nutrient profiles of sweet potatoes and yams are similar, yet both are quite different from other potatoes.

- Do the students know why? The dark yellow color comes from beta-carotene, which becomes vitamin A after being eaten.

- Are potatoes grown in your local area? What types?

Discuss

- How are these four potatoes used on restaurant menus?
- Just how red are russets?
- What does the word russet mean?
- Look again at the Idaho potato and see why it's called russet.

Table 11.1: Characteristics of Potatoes *continued*

Name	Characteristics	Best Cooking Methods
New potatoes	• These are small, immature red potatoes that are harvested when they are very small, less than 2 inches in diameter. • Unlike other baking potatoes, new potatoes are high in moisture and sugar, but have a low starch content. • Boiling and steaming brings out the natural sweetness and fresh flavor of new potatoes. • They are good to use in any preparation where the potato must keep its shape.	Boiling Steaming Roasting
Yellow-fleshed	• Yellow-fleshed have become increasingly popular in the United States in recent years. • They are common in other parts of the world, including Europe and South America. • They produce a golden color and a buttery flavor. • They are good, all-purpose potatoes. • Yukon gold is one well-known variety. • They are good for baking, mashing, frying, whipping, or roasting. They are especially good for potato pancakes.	Mashing

[fast fact]

Did You Know...?

The U.S. Census Bureau 2008 reports that 1.8 billion pounds of sweet potatoes were produced by major sweet potato-producing states in 2007. North Carolina produced the most sweet potatoes, with 667 million pounds. California was a distant second with 426 million pounds of sweet potatoes produced.

[ServSafe Connection]

One Bad Apple

There is an old expression: "One bad apple will spoil the whole bunch." Apples aside, this is true with potatoes. Soft bacterial rot in potatoes can begin with one infected tuber and spread to an entire pile. Some potato problems are carried in bacteria or mold spores in the dirt that clings to the potatoes. Store and clean them properly before preparation, and these potential problems will never develop into real problems.

However, if grown, harvested, or stored improperly, a potato can develop diseases with names like soft rot, pink rot, silver scurf, and pythium leak. Most of these ailments are discovered and treated on the farm level before the crop goes to market. However, improper storage of potatoes in the pantry can initiate growth of bacteria that can do great damage to an entire shipment.

Potatoes are amazing. They breathe and circulate and can even heal their own wounds. But if rot begins, they can no longer breathe and heal. This creates decay as the bacteria feed on the starch and sugar and proliferate throughout the spud. Once growing, the bacteria can take hold on neighboring tubers and block their respiration and otherwise wreak havoc. As the bacteria do their work, they generate heat, which increases the temperature of the storage pile of potatoes, moving them into the danger zone for more bacterial growth. A vicious cycle ensues, and before too long, the entire pantry is filled with rotting potato stench.

Store potatoes in a cool, dry, well-ventilated environment away from sunlight. Store them in an area that is too cool, and the potato will "stress," which reduces the cooking quality. The ideal temperature is 45°F to 55°F, with good airflow. Avoid storing potatoes in plastic. Store them in paper or cardboard, or in open crates. Remove excess dirt and clean the storage bins of dirt and debris between shipments.

If you notice small flying insects (fruit fly-type) or smell a musty, rotten, or ammonia odor near the potatoes, check all the potatoes immediately, especially toward the bottom of the pile. If one dark, soft, wrinkled, damp, or foul-smelling potato is found, immediately remove it from the pile. Check all the remaining potatoes, especially the neighbors to the bad one, and rotate them bottom to top. Remove and discard any suspicious potatoes.

If potatoes seem wholesome, but have begun to slightly wrinkle or shrink, clean and boil them for use in recipes. Only bake firm, fresh potatoes. And always purchase potatoes from approved, reputable farms, vendors, and suppliers.

681

ServSafe Connection: One Bad Apple

Potato science is an entire branch of agriculture.

In-Class Activity: Potato Hygiene Internet Research

Science Connection, 21st-Century Skills—Access and Evaluate Information

Potatoes are active plant crops and can be afflicted with various bacterial or fungal diseases.

Good hygiene, or storage and handling practices, can help potatoes retain their high quality and remain safe to eat.

More Advanced Students

Research two potato crop diseases. How can farmers prevent or arrest the growth of potato diseases?

Less Advanced Students

How can potatoes heal? Research this aspect of potato health. Does it apply to both growing and harvested potatoes?

Special Needs Students

Design a potato storage bin. Should you use plastic, or would brown paper or cardboard be a better choice? Why?

ESOL Students

Does the student's culture of origin use potato dishes?

The student can compare and contrast one or two potato dishes from their own culture with similar local dishes.

How do the names of the dishes compare?

Discuss

- Does potato storage require temperature control?
- Where would students find a suitable storage temperature in the school? Where would they find it at home?
- Why do the students think that yams may be stored longer than sweet potatoes?
- If temperature and time are both requirements, what about airflow and light?
- Ask the students what a restaurateur should do for potato storage.

Nutrition:
Peruvian Purples and Red Thumbs

If possible, have some colorful potatoes for the students to see and maybe even taste.

Selecting and Storing Potatoes

When selecting potatoes, choose potatoes that are firm and smooth. Do not accept potatoes with dark spots, green areas, mold, or large cuts. Store potatoes in a cool, dry place at temperatures ranging from 45°F to 55°F. The maximum storage period for russet and all-purpose potatoes is 30 days. Store yams for up to two weeks. Store sweet potatoes for up to one week. Store new potatoes—a small, immature red potato— no longer than one week. All potatoes are best stored in ventilated containers in indirect light. Figure 11.1 shows potatoes in a ventilated container.

Figure 11.1: Store potatoes in cool, dry places in ventilated containers to preserve freshness.

A wide variety of market options exists when purchasing potatoes. These forms include fresh, frozen, refrigerated, canned, and dried. Value-added forms are also available, such as potatoes cut into shapes.

[nutrition]

Peruvian Purples and Red Thumbs

Potatoes, just like other fresh produce, can be colorful. Although potatoes might not seem like the most colorful tuber, heritage varieties are filled with bright color. Fingerling potatoes are small, mature potatoes from delicious historic seed lines that come in yellow, orange, red, and even purple.

The naturally occurring colors come from pigment nutrients called flavonoids. The purple and red pigments are flavonoids called anthocyanins, which is the same pigment in blueberries or red cabbage. These are antioxidants that might even help fight off cancer.

Gorgeous color and great flavor aside, these foods are worth eating for the health-giving qualities of the pigments. As with all anthocyanin foods, a slightly acidic cooking medium keeps the color perky red, while a little alkaline causes a dull blue.

682

Figure Focus
Figure 11.1: Burlap bags allow for airflow. Plastic bags do not.

Cooking Potatoes

Potatoes that are exposed to light may develop a greenish color. Although the color is harmless, it means that the potato contains **solanine** (SOLE-ah-neen), a harmful, bitter-tasting substance. Potato sprouts can also contain **solanine**. Cut away and discard sprouts and any green portions before using potatoes. Always discard potatoes if you have any doubts about their freshness or safety. Figure 11.2 is a greenish potato with sprouts.

Figure 11.2: Green potatoes and potato sprouts contain solanine, which can be poisonous and cause gastrointestinal and neurological symptoms.

The potato is one of the most popular vegetables because it is inexpensive, adaptable, versatile, and tasty. Apply any cooking methods, including boiling, steaming, baking, sautéing, *en casserole*, deep-frying, and puréeing to produce a number of preparations with special flavors, textures, and appearances. Different potato varieties will produce different results.

The two categories for cooking potatoes are single-stage and multiple-stage techniques. In the **single-stage technique,** take potatoes directly from the raw state to the finished state by using one cooking method. Boiled and baked potatoes are examples of single-stage techniques.

In a **multiple-stage technique,** prepare potatoes using more than one cooking method before they are a finished dish. One example of potatoes prepared using the multiple-stage method is **lyonnaise** (LEE-on-AZE) potatoes. In this recipe, the potatoes are precooked, sliced, and then fried with onions, as shown in Figure 11.3.

Boiling is one of the easiest methods of cooking potatoes. In addition, boiling is often the first step for other preparations, such as puréed potatoes.

Figure 11.3: Lyonnaise potatoes is a delicious French dish.

683

Teaching Tips

- The students may not realize that potatoes are different than other vegetables and that green is a bad color for a potato.
- Green shoots and sprouts are not desirable or safe.
- Advise the students not to purchase potatoes that show green on the skins or have sprouted.
- Make sure that in-house storage does not promote sprouting or light exposure.

Discuss

- Can the students think of several different types of potatoes and potato dishes?
- Ask the students to categorize the dishes as single-stage or multiple-stage processes.
- Remind students that any dish that requires more than one cooking method, such as scalloped potatoes, would be multiple-stage.
- Help the students to realize that some complex processes might be single-stage, such as peeling and cutting potatoes for French fries, then deep-frying them. Even though there is a lot of preparation work there is only one cooking method used.

Vocabulary Terms

- **Solanine:** Harmful substance that can form in potatoes exposed to sunlight.
- **Single-stage technique:** One cooking method from raw potato to finished, like baking.
- **Mulitple-stage technique:** More than one cooking method required for a dish.
- **Lyonnaise:** Potatoes cooked, sliced, and then fried with onions.

Figure Focus

Figure 11.2: Watch for sprouting and green color in potatoes, as this could be a danger sign.

Figure 11.3: Lyonnaise potatoes are simple to make.

The pot should be large enough that the water will not boil over. Starchy potato water will burn.

Teaching Tips

- Help the students to realize that the mildness of potatoes can be a relief dish.
- The students may be aware that some foods produce flavor fatigue.
- This can be caused by strong spices, high fat content, intense natural flavors, or several other factors.
- Potato dishes can rest the taste buds with a warm, mild, soft food.

In-Class Activity:
Potato Bake-Off

21st-Century Skills—Make Judgments and Decisions

Bake several potatoes in the classroom.

Use the different methods suggested in the text, including wrapping in foil, oiling the skins, and leaving the skins simply washed. Baking a potato in the microwave would also be good for comparison.

If the class period is only 45 minutes, it might be necessary to preheat the oven before class and use very small potatoes for baking.

Be sure to pierce the skins before baking. Bake at 350°F until the potato is soft in the center.

Allow the students to taste-test the various types of potatoes.

Essential Skills
Boiling Potatoes

1 Place washed potatoes in a pot of cold, salted water with enough liquid to cover them.

2 Bring the water to a boil and simmer until they are done.

3 To test for doneness, pierce the potato with a fork or knife. If the fork slides easily through the potato, the potato is done. The boiled potato can then be served immediately or held for up to an hour. See Figure 11.4.

Figure 11.4: Step 3—Boiling potatoes.

Steaming is an especially good cooking method for new potatoes because of their high moisture content. Steam new potatoes until they are very tender. Like boiled potatoes, serve them right away or hold and use with another dish.

Unlike boiled and steamed potatoes, baked potatoes are always served in their skins. The best baking potatoes are Idahos or russets. There are a variety of ways to bake potatoes. Wrap potatoes in foil prior to baking to keep the skin soft, which makes the inside less fluffy. Rub the potato with oil to keep the skin soft while allowing the inside to get soft and fluffy. Bake with no foil or oil to leave the skin crisp. Figure 11.5 on the following page shows a baked potato.

684

Figure Focus

Figure 11.4: Boil potatoes until they are tender, not mushy.

Scrub all potatoes clean and pierce with a fork before placing in the oven, no matter the technique. Piercing the potato with a fork allows heat and steam to escape and prevents the potato from exploding. Cook baked potatoes directly on an oven rack or sheet pan and serve immediately.

Figure 11.5: Baking a potato with foil around it keeps the skin soft.

For *en casserole* potato dishes, combine peeled and sliced raw potatoes with heavy cream, sauce, or uncooked custard. See Figure 11.6. Slowly bake these dishes in a buttered pan. Toppings include bread crumbs, butter, and grated cheese, after which the food preparer broils the dish briefly to give it a golden a golden-brown color. These potatoes are excellent for banquet service because servers can divide them into individual portions very easily, and they can be held without losing quality.

Figure 11.6: Baking *en casserole* means that potatoes are sliced and baked in the oven in a creamy, tasty liquid.

Teaching Tips

- *En casserole* potatoes include scalloped potatoes, potatoes au gratin, etc.
- Adding the various cream sauces and ingredients makes these TCS dishes for food safety concerns.

In-Class Activity: Apples and Potatoes

Literacy Connection, 21st-Century Skills— Think Creatively

Potatoes are eaten the world over. They are actually compared to apples at times because of their versatility and availability.

In Austria, the potato is sometimes called an Erd Apfel or earth apple.

In the small town of Hatch, Utah, the term Hatch Apple refers to a small red potato that is eaten raw like an apple.

Can the students think of any dishes or recipes where potatoes could be exchanged for apples, or vice versa?

What would be the results of a potato/apple swap in a given dish?

Have the students write two paragraphs about any aspect of the potato/apple concept.

Humor is encouraged.

Figure Focus

Figure 11.5: Be sure the skins are completely clean. Many diners enjoy eating the skins.

Figure 11.6: Potatoes are extremely versatile.

The skin carries some minerals from the earth that are not distributed throughout the starchy flesh. However, the flesh is still very nutritious.

Discuss

- Why would Chef's potatoes be a better choice for sautéed potatoes than Idaho russets?
- Perhaps the students realize that the Idaho russet is fluffy and a bit dry, which makes it ideal for baking.
- But the fluffiness makes Idaho russets get a bit gummy or mushy and lose their shape when sautéed.
- Chef's potatoes maintain their shape better.

Teaching Tips

- Potatoes fried in oil become a golden brown color.
- The color of a fried potato is part of the appeal of French fries. The same gold color is desired for other fried foods.
- It is the "gold standard."
- The characteristics of a potato's starch create the golden brown color.
- The flavor is also ideal when fried properly.
- French fried potatoes of the perfect thickness become golden brown outside just as the inside becomes fluffy.
- Idaho russets are ideal for fries and yield the typical American French fries.
- French-fried Idaho russet potatoes are an American dish, not French.
- A French chef on President Jefferson's White House staff deep-fried small pieces of raw potato, calling them French Fried Potatoes.
- In France and Germany, long, skinny, deep-fried potatoes are called "pommes frites" (pom-fritts).
- British fries are called chips and may be sliced long like American french fries, or sliced in rounds.
- Our potato chips, the snack food in a bag, are called "potato crisps" by the British.
- Americans serve French fries with ketchup or fry sauce, a ketchup/mayonnaise-based condiment.
- British and Canadians serve chips with malt vinegar or with gravy.
- Germans serve theirs with sausages and mustard.

Chef's potatoes are the best for sautéing. Sautéed potatoes should have a crisp, evenly browned exterior with a tender interior. Sauté the potatoes in oil or butter, stirring or flipping them frequently until they are golden brown. For best results, serve immediately.

[fast fact]

Did You Know...?

Potatoes are 80% water and 20% solid.

Potatoes are more nutritious with their skin on.

The potato was the first vegetable grown in space in 1995.

Another popular method of cooking potatoes is deep-frying. Use this method to make French fries, cottage fries, steak fries, and many other fried potato dishes. Russet potatoes are best suited for deep-frying because of their low moisture content.

At service time, fry potatoes in fat heated to 350° to 375°F until golden brown. Deep-fry in two stages because of the long cooking time. When they are done, place the potatoes on a paper towel and season immediately. Do not hold deep-fried potatoes; serve immediately, as shown in Figure 11.7.

Figure 11.7: The average American eats more than 16 pounds of French fries each year.

Figure Focus

Figure 11.7: The statistic means that there are more than 16 pounds of French fries sold per American citizen, not that average Americans weigh their french fries. To put this in perspective, let the students know that the average American eats only 14 pounds of turkey a year.

On the Job:
Making the French Fries

Slicing potatoes for French fries by hand is labor intensive and not usually cost-effective.

[on the job]

Making the French Fries

The automatic potato peeler in a commercial kitchen can process up to 20 pounds of potatoes at a time. Whole washed potatoes are put into the drum. A rotating sharpened disc blade in the bottom removes the skin while the potato is tumbled to expose all sides to the blade. If you forget and leave the potatoes in there too long, there are no potatoes left at all.

In Idaho, the Spud Gun was invented to fire a potato. This is a fun idea that has its roots in the foodservice industry.

The Lamb Water Gun Knife is a long tube with a sharp slicing grid inside. A peeled potato is launched by a water jet through the tube. It is forced through the grid, making perfect French fries. Mr. Lamb first tested the invention in the parking lot of his potato processing operation. He shot potatoes through the tube with a fire hose.

Discuss

- Ask students to name their favorite potato dishes.
- There may be many answers given.
- Count the number of students who respond French fries.
- Are there any students in the class that do not know that French fries are made of potatoes?
- Be careful not to embarrass any students who are not aware of where their food comes from.

Vocabulary Terms

- **Latkes:** Pan-fried pancake made of shredded potatoes.

Make potato pancakes with grated potatoes and other ingredients. Pan-fry them to a crispy brown. They are traditional in many Eastern European cuisines, particularly in American-Jewish cooking, where they are called **latkes** (LAHT-keys). Latkes are traditionally served with apple sauce and sour cream. Figure 11.8 shows latkes.

Puréeing potatoes is another way to prepare potatoes. Puréed potatoes are important as the basis of many popular dishes, including mashed or whipped potatoes, duchesse potatoes, and potato croquettes.

Figure 11.8: Latkes, also known as potato pancakes, can be eaten plain, with a salad, or topped with apple sauce or sour cream.

For puréed, whipped, and mashed potatoes, first boil, steam, or bake the potatoes before combining them with other ingredients or mashing. Hold them for service in a bain-marie or a steam table. Refrigerate puréed potatoes that are to

687

Figure Focus

Figure 11.8: Latkes are a traditional Jewish dish, often served during Hanukkah. Potato dishes are found in many cuisines.

Fast Fact: Did You Know...?

In the early twentieth century, the term "French fried" was used for other fried foods, such as fried chicken or onion rings.

What's New: Bioplastic Quick-Service Packaging

Students might be interested in researching this technology.

What is the coating made of?

If possible, bring in two kinds of packing peanuts—styrofoam and bioplastic.

In-Class Activity: Polymer Chemistry

Science Connection

A polymer is a long chain molecule made up of smaller molecules that are either identical or quite similar. An example of a polymer is DNA. Other examples of polymers are the various forms of plastic that we use. Food examples include starches, proteins, and fatty acids.

Packing peanuts, whether they are styrofoam or starch, are made of a carbon-based polymer puffed up with air.

The students can observe the teacher perform the demonstration and record their observations.

Supplies:

- 4 clear glass containers
- Styrofoam packing peanuts
- Starch packing peanuts
- Acetone
- Water

Fill two clear glass containers with enough water that a packing peanut can be completely submerged.

Do the same with two more clear glass containers, but this time with acetone instead of water.

Use one container of acetone and one container of water for the styrofoam peanut test.

Drop styrofoam peanuts into the water. Have the students observe what happens to the peanuts and record their observations.

Then drop styrofoam peanuts into acetone. Have the students observe what happens to the peanuts. Again, have them record their observations.

Use the remaining containers of water and acetone to perform the same test on the starch peanuts. Again, have students record their observations.

What happens to make the peanuts dissolve?

be used in other dishes for several hours. Figure 11.9 shows mashed potatoes served with meat.

Whenever possible, cook potatoes in their skins to retain their nutrients. Cover the cut and peeled potatoes in a liquid to prevent discoloring.

Figure 11.9: Potatoes are a great accompaniment to meat dishes.

Did You Know...?

In 1802, President Thomas Jefferson served French fries at a White House dinner. Soon after, French fries became very popular. Today, French fries are one of the most profitable food items in restaurant and foodservice operations.

Bioplastic Quick-Service Packaging

Quick-service restaurants often package menu items in take-away containers. These have historically been made of polystyrene or other petroleum-based polymer plastic. A polymer is a long-chain molecule.

Potatoes, legumes, and grains can also be used for polymers. New technology has made it possible for food polymers called "bioplastics" to be used for disposable and take-away foodservice items.

Bioplastics are completely biodegradable and compostable. They are made from crops instead of petroleum, so they are renewable and sustainable.

The best part is they work. A water-resistant coating helps keep them from decomposing when filled with hot, steaming food. You might not even be able to tell the difference.

688

Figure Focus

Figure 11.9: Ask students what their favorite potato dishes are. In French restaurants, steak *frites* is a popular dish of steak served with French fries.

The polymer links separate, which dissolves the molecule.

Did all the peanuts dissolve in either kind of solution?

Which peanut dissolved in water the best?

Which peanut dissolved in acetone the best?

Which solution(s) dissolved styrofoam?

Which solution(s) dissolved starch?

Based upon your observations, which type of packing peanut would be the most biodegradable?

Which type of packing peanut would be best for the environment?

The peanuts made of styrofoam do not dissolve in water, so they are not biodegradable. They will dissolve in a solvent like acetone. The peanuts made of starch will dissolve in water, which means they are biodegradable.

Summary

In this section, you learned the following:

- Potato varieties differ in starch and moisture content. Types of potatoes include sweet potatoes, yams, russet potatoes, Idaho potatoes, all-purpose potatoes, and new potatoes. Sweet potatoes are tubers. Tubers are fat, underground stems capable of growing a new plant.

- Select potatoes that are firm and smooth without dark spots, green areas, mold, or large cuts. Store potatoes in a cool, dry place at a temperature ranging from 45°F to 55°F. It is best to store potatoes in ventilated containers in indirect light. Store russet and all-purpose potatoes for 30 days; store yams for two weeks; store sweet potatoes for one week. Potatoes are available fresh, frozen, refrigerated, or dried.

- The two categories for cooking potatoes are single-stage and multi-stage techniques. Take single-stage potatoes directly from the raw state to the finished state by using one cooking method. Boiled and baked potatoes are examples of single-stage techniques. When using a multiple-stage technique, prepare potatoes using more than one cooking method. Lyonnaise potatoes are precooked, sliced, and then fried with onions. *En casserole* potato dishes combine peeled and sliced raw potatoes with heavy cream, sauce, or uncooked custard. Boiling is the easiest method for cooking potatoes.

689

In-Class Activity: Polymer Chemistry (continued)

More Advanced Students

For students that have a further interest, research the answers to the following questions:

How much energy and resources are required to make a styrofoam peanut?

How much energy and resources are required to make a starch peanut?

Do these answers change your opinion about which peanut is better for the environment?

ESOL Students

The acetone is considered an organic solvent because it is a carbon-based molecule, even though acetone is a harsh chemical.

The term organic can mean carbon-based, polymer, and/or cyclic molecular chemistry. This type of chemistry includes plastics, petroleum products, and very harsh chemicals like acetone and benzene. Such products are considered harmful to the environment, but are still considered organic.

Organic can also mean chemical-free and benign to the environment.

The two uses of the word organic can have the opposite meaning. This may be confusing, so the meaning must be taken in context.

Help the ESOL student identify contextual clues for the meaning of the word organic.

Reinforce and Review

- Help the students to recall the many varieties of potatoes.
- Potatoes are best stored in a cool, dry, ventilated, dark place.
- Discuss the single-stage and multistage cooking of potato recipes.

Summary

- Remind students to review the following:
  1. The different types of potatoes
  2. The methods for selecting, receiving, and storing potatoes
  3. Types of cooking methods and recipes for preparing potatoes

Section 11.1
Review Questions

1. A tuber, as far as potatoes are concerned, is an underground stem growth that will reproduce another potato plant. It is a bulbous growth.

2. Single-stage techniques involve only one cooking technique to take the potato from raw to the table. Examples would be French fried potatoes and baked potatoes. Multiple-stage techniques involve more than one type of cooking and handling technique. Examples would be twice-baked potatoes and Lyonnaise potatoes.

3. *En casserole* potatoes are peeled, sliced raw potatoes cooked with a heavy cream sauce.

4. Some nutrients from the skins are lost if the skins are removed prior to cooking.

5. Student ideas will vary. Some ideas might include using potatoes in their skins, using smaller potatoes, mixing potatoes in salads, and offering a variety of colorful potatoes.

6. Student responses will vary.

7. Sweet potatoes are also tubers, but they are not true potatoes in spite of their name.

8. Students will present several concepts of their own. Potato varieties grow very well in the agricultural areas of the United States. They are nutritious and relatively inexpensive. They are easy to prepare in a variety of ways and have a mild yet full flavor. Potatoes deep-fried in fat can contribute many fat and carbohydrate calories to the diet. It is imperative to burn those calories with lifestyle choices.

Section 11.1 Review Questions

1. What is a tuber?

2. Explain the difference between single-stage and multiple-stage techniques for cooking potatoes.

3. What is an *en casserole* potato dish?

4. Why should you cook potatoes in their skins?

5. Chef Jean wants to try some unusual potato dishes while still focusing on the health benefits. He knows that people first think of potatoes as high in carbs and starches. What can he do to focus on the nutritional benefits of potatoes? What types of dishes might he try to create at lunch? At dinner?

6. Stephanie Izard says she has begun to explore all varieties (of potatoes) from fingerlings to new potatoes to purple potatoes and others at the farmers' markets. Research three "newer" varieties of potatoes, describe their properties, and describe how they are used in cooking.

7. Can you name any tubers that are not potatoes?

8. Why have potatoes become such an important part of the American diet? How does this choice affect our lifestyles?

690

Section 11.1 Activities

1. Study Skills/Group Activity: Potato Skit

Work with three other students and research the different names for French fries, potato chips, and potato skins that may be used in other English-speaking countries. Prepare a script for a skit. The script must use at least one of the new terms in every actor's line of the play. Rehearse and present your skit to the class.

2. Activity: Potato Matrix

Create a comparison matrix of the different types of potatoes.

Type of Potato	Origin	Nutritional Value	Appearance	Flavor	Cooking Method	Storage

3. Critical Thinking: Sweet Potatoes Versus Yams

Sweet potatoes and yams look similar and are interchangeable in most recipes. Why is that? What are the differences between the sweet potato and the yam? Where did they originate? How are they grown? What are the nutritional benefits of sweet potatoes compared to yams?

691

What are the nutritional benefits of yams?
True yams are not necessarily deep yellow. Those that are yellow or orange will have beta-carotene, which becomes vitamin A in the body. Yams of other colors will have other coloring compounds such as anthocyanin. Known as phytochemicals, natural color compounds have nutritional value as antioxidants, among other things. They also provide complex carbohydrate, fiber, vitamins C and B_6, potassium, and trace minerals such as manganese.

Section 11.1 Activities

1. The skits will all be different. The students should come up with the British terms chips and crisps, for French fries and potato chips, respectively. They may find other examples. These should be woven into the scripts.

2. This is a research project for the students to do. They can keep this matrix chart in their personal notes for future reference.

3. **What are the differences between a sweet potato and a yam?**
In the United States, a sweet potato has yellow flesh and a yam has deep orange flesh, but they are both from the same family of sweet potatoes. In Africa and Asia, a yam is a tuber from a different family and has flesh that is white, purple, yellow or pink.

What are the similarities between a sweet potato and a yam?
In the United States, a sweet potato is lighter in color and a bit pulpier than a yam, which is deeper orange and has a meatier, smoother flesh when cooked. The African and Asian yams are also starchy on the inside, and have very tough skins. They soften when cooked.

Where do sweet potatoes come from?
Sweet potatoes grow in South America, tropical islands, and the Southern United States.

Where do yams come from?
Yams come from Africa and Asia.

How are sweet potatoes grown?
They are grown on farms in warm, wet climates.

How are yams grown?
They grow in warm, wet climates like rainforests.

What are the nutritional benefits of sweet potatoes?
Sweet potatoes have complex carbohydrates, fiber, vitamins C and B_6, potassium, iron, and trace minerals (like zinc). Perhaps the most obvious and valuable nutritional aspect of sweet potatoes and U.S. yams is the deep yellow color. This comes from beta-carotene, which is converted to vitamin A in the body. Beta-carotene itself is also an antioxidant.

Section 11.2
Legumes and Grains

Introduce the Section
a. Different types of grains and legumes will be presented.
b. The skills and practices of proper selection and handling of grains and legumes will be detailed.
c. Cooking techniques, principles, and ideas will be introduced.

Vocabulary Review
a. Direct students to the key terms.
b. Pronounce each word, and have the students repeat the pronunciation out loud.
c. Discuss the definition of each word.

Teach

Discuss
- The term legume is technically part of the botanical legume family.
- However, since the increase in vegetarianism, sometimes legumes is a term used to define all nonanimal protein sources.
- Additionally, the original Food Guide Pyramid grouped nuts and beans in the same protein category as meat and eggs.
- The public, seeking vegetarianism, simply removed the animal products, leaving beans and nuts alone in the category.
- Help the students to differentiate between true legumes (beans, peas, and lentils), and nuts and seeds.
- This can be confusing, since peanuts are botanically legumes, not nuts.

Vocabulary Terms
- **Legumes:** Seeds from pod-producing plants of the Leguminosae family, usually a source of starch and protein.

11.1 Potatoes	11.2 Legumes and Grains	11.3 Pasta
• Types of potatoes	• Legumes	• Pasta and dumplings
• Selecting and storing potatoes	• Selecting and storing legumes	• Cooking pasta
• Cooking potatoes	• Cooking legumes	• Cooking dumplings
	• Grains	
	• Selecting and storing grains	
	• Cooking grains	

SECTION 11.2 LEGUMES AND GRAINS

Ever eat plant seeds? You eat seeds every time you eat a grain or bean product, like a bean burrito in a flour tortilla. Grains and legumes (beans, peas, and lentils) are actually the seeds of plants.

Grains and legumes are concentrated sources of nutrients—good tasting, inexpensive, and readily available. They are also full of protein, fiber, vitamins, and minerals.

Study Questions

After studying Section 11.2, you should be able to answer the following questions:

- What are the different types of grains and legumes?
- What are the methods to selecting, receiving, and storing grains and legumes?
- What types of cooking methods and recipes are there for preparing grains and legumes?

Legumes

Legumes (LEG-yooms) are seeds from pod-producing plants. Legumes include beans, peas, lentils, nuts, and seeds. Dried legumes have many uses in cooking, from salads and appetizers, to main courses and desserts. They are an excellent source of carbohydrates and fiber. Table 11.2 describes each legume and its common culinary uses.

692

Table 11.2: Legumes

	Type	Description	Common Culinary Uses
BEANS	Adzuki	Small; reddish-brown; available whole or powdered	Popular in Japanese cuisine, used in confections as a sweet paste or sugar-coated; savory dishes
	Black/Turtle	Large, black exterior; light creamy interior; sweet flavor	Soups, stews, salsas, salads, side dishes
	Canary	Slightly smaller than pinto beans; canary-yellow color	Popular in Peruvian dishes, specifically stews
	Cannellini/Italian Kidney	Medium; kidney-shaped; white; nutty flavor	Minestrone soup, salads, stews, side dishes
	Cranberry	Small; round; maroon markings; nutty flavor	Soups, stews, salads, side dishes
	Fava/Broad	Large; flat; oval; tan	Popular in Mediterranean and Middle Eastern cuisines; falafel, soups, stews, salads, side dishes
	Flageolets	Small; kidney-shaped; pale green to creamy white	Served with lamb; braised and puréed as a side dish
	Garbanzos/Chickpeas	Medium; acorn-shaped; beige; nutty flavor	Popular in many ethnic dishes; couscous, hummus, soups, stews, salads, side dishes
	Great Northern	Large; slightly rounded; white; mildly delicate flavor	Soups, stews, casseroles, side dishes
	Kidney	Medium; kidney-shaped; pink to maroon; full-bodied flavor	Chili con carne, refried beans, beans and rice, soups, stews, casseroles, side dishes
	Lentils	Small; round; varieties include French/European (grayish color with pale yellow interior), Egyptian, red, and yellow	Served as an accompaniment whole or puréed; soups, stews, salads, side dishes
	Lima/Butter	Medium; slightly kidney-shaped; white to pale green; buttery taste	Succotash, soups, stews, salads, side dishes
	Mung	Small; round; green	Sprouted for bean sprouts; ground into flour to make cellophane noodles and bean threads
	Navy/Yankee	Small; round; white	Baked beans, chili, soups, salads

continued

Table 11.2: Legumes (continued on pp. 694–696)

- The students can work as a class to find some or all of these beans.
- Photocopy an enlargement of this table and glue the real bean next to its name.
- Nuts and seeds are not botanically legumes.

Teaching Tips

- All of the types on this page are botanically legumes.
- Show the students as many of these legumes as possible, either by using photos or by bringing samples to class.
- Technically, legumes are the seeds from the pods of the Leguminosae family of plants.
- Nuts and seeds from other plant families are not true legumes.

Science Connection

More Advanced Students

Gregor Mendel was an Austrian priest who lived in a monastery during the 1800s. He spent his time observing and experimenting with plants, especially pea plants. He was a pioneer in the science of genetics and heredity. We have hybrids of grains, fruits, and vegetables partly because of Mendel's work.

Mendel observed that if he crossed yellow pea plants with green pea plants, certain traits carried into the new pea plants.

These days the observations seem simple and easy to explain. But in the 1860s it was not understood, and Mendel's work was innovative and not fully appreciated.

His approach can be practiced on paper using Punnett squares. These little charts demonstrate how parental traits combine and pass on to offspring. This way, traits that are dominant and traits that are recessive can be seen and predicted. Recessive traits still show up, and Punnett squares show how this can happen.

Have the more advanced student demonstrate a Punnett square with a single trait of a pea or bean.

Any biology textbook will have examples.

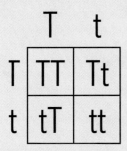

Table 11.2: Legumes *continued*

	Type	Description	Common Culinary Uses
	Pinto/Red Mexican	Medium; kidney-shaped; beige with brown streaks	Chili, refried beans, stews, soups
	Rice	Heirloom bean; plump grains resembling rice; slightly bitter taste; varieties include white, brown, Falcon, green, and Mocasin; related to kidney beans	Substitute for rice; soups, stews, casseroles, side dishes
	Soybeans	Small; pea- to cherry-shaped; bland flavor; colors include red, yellow, green, brown, and black; dried version is mature bean	Soups, stews, casseroles, side dishes
	Heirloom varieties (Calypso, Tongues of Fire, Jacob's Cattle, Madeira)	Range tremendously in size and color; many have stripes or speckles	Soups, stews, casseroles, side dishes, salads
PEAS	Black-eyed	Small; kidney-shaped; beige with black "eye"	Hoppin' John, soups, side dishes
	Pigeon/Gandoles	Heirloom bean; small; nearly round; beige with orange spotting	Popular in African, Caribbean, and Indian dishes
	Split	Small; round; split; dried; green or yellow; earthy flavor	Split pea soup, salads, side dishes
NUTS	Almond	Teardrop-shaped; pale tan, woody shell; sweet flavor; available whole in shell or shelled, blanched, slivered, sliced, split, chopped, ground; used to produce almond paste, almond butter, and almond oil	Raw, toasted, or cooked; in baked goods, confections, granola, curry dishes; eaten out of hand
	Brazil	Large, triangular nut; dark brown exterior, hard shell; white interior, rich nut	Raw, toasted, or cooked; eaten out of hand; baked goods
	Cashew	Kidney-shaped; tan; buttery, slightly sweet flavor; only sold hulled (its skin contains oils similar to those in poison ivy); used to produce cashew butter	Raw, toasted, or cooked; baked goods, confections; eaten out of hand

continued

694

Teaching Tips

- The rice bean is a type of bean that resembles the grain seed of wild rice.
- Peas are legumes. The peas that are used as a green vegetable are from the same family as dried peas.

Table 11.2: Legumes *continued*

	Type	Description	Common Culinary Uses
	Chestnut	Fairly large; round to teardrop-shaped; hard, glossy, dark-brown shell; off-white nut; sweet flavor; available whole in shell, canned in water or syrup, frozen, dried, or puréed	Raw or cooked; sweet and savory dishes, roasted, boiled, puréed
	Hazelnut/Filbert	Small; nearly round; smooth, hard shell; rich, sweet, delicate flavor; available whole in shell or shelled; blanched, whole, chopped	Raw, toasted, or cooked; sweet or savory dishes, baked goods, salads, cereals
	Macadamia	Nearly round; extremely hard shell; golden-yellow nut; rich, slightly sweet, buttery; available shelled only	Raw or roasted; baked goods, confections; eaten out of hand
	Peanut	Tan, pod-like shell; papery brown skin; off-white-colored nut; sweet flavor; available whole in shell or shelled, skinned; used to produce peanut butter and peanut oil	Raw or roasted; sweet or savory dishes, baked goods, confections, salads; eaten out of hand
	Pecan	Smooth, hard, thin, oval shell; two-lobed; brown nut, cream-colored interior; rich, buttery flavor; available whole in shell or shelled, halved, chopped	Raw or roasted; sweet or savory dishes, baked goods, pie, confections; salads; eaten out of hand
	Pine/Pignoli	Small, elongated kernel; about ½-inch long; light tan; buttery, mild flavor	Raw or roasted; sweet and savory dishes, baked goods, salads, pesto
	Pistachio	Tan; shell opens slightly when nut is mature; green nut; subtle, sweet flavor; available whole in shell; roasted, usually salted; shells sometimes dyed red; occasionally shelled, chopped	Raw or roasted; eaten out of hand; sweet and savory dishes
	Walnut	Light-brown shell; thick or thin; brown nuts; grown in gnarled segments; tender; oily; mild flavor; available whole in shell or shelled, halved, chopped; pickled; used to produce walnut oil	Raw or roasted; in sweet or savory dishes, baked goods, confections, salads; eaten out of hand

continued

695

Teaching Tips

- Nuts are not true legumes, but they contain protein like legumes do.
- Not all nuts are true nuts, either.
- For example, pistachio nuts are not really nuts. They are seeds.
- Peanuts are legumes that grow in a way similar to tubers.

Teaching Tips

- The lines between seeds and grains may seem blurred.
- Grains are the seeds of their plants.
- Flax seeds, for example, or often eaten with whole grains in cereals or breads.

Fast Fact:
Did You Know...?

Peanuts are legumes, not nuts.

In-Class Activity:
Legumes Table

21st-Century Skills—Use Systems Thinking; Use and Manage Information

Table 11.2 includes plant foods from various botanical families and categories.

The students can use Internet resources to botanically identify the various plant foods in the table.

The foods can then be rearranged by their actual botanical classification.

Table 11.2: Legumes *continued*

	Type	Description	Common Culinary Uses
SEEDS	Poppy	Very tiny; round; blue-black seeds; crunchy texture; rich, slightly musty flavor; available whole or ground	Filling and topping for baked goods; used in salad dressings; popular in cuisines of central Europe and the Middle East
	Pumpkin/ Pepitas	Small; flat; oval; soft; cream-colored hulls; greenish-brown, oily interior; delicate flavor; available whole or hulled, usually salted	Raw or roasted; sweet or savory dishes, baked goods; popular in Mexican cuisine
	Flax	Tiny, oval seeds; golden or dark brown; mildly nutty; used to produce linseed oil	Baked goods, hot and cold cereal
	Sesame	Tiny, flat, oval seeds; black, red, or tan; crunchy; sweet, nutty flavor; used to produce sesame oil and tahini (paste)	Raw or toasted; sweet and savory dishes, baked goods, confections, as garnish
	Sunflower	Small; somewhat flat; teardrop-shaped seeds; woody, black and white shell; light tan seed; mild flavor; available whole in shell or shelled, usually salted; used to make sunflower oil	Raw, dried, or roasted; baked goods, salads

© *The Professional Chef, 8th Edition*, The Culinary Institute of America, 2006

[fast fact]

Did You Know...?

Peanuts are actually a type of bean.

Selecting and Storing Legumes

Legumes' packaging should be intact with no rips or holes. Canned legumes should be dent free. Beans and peas are also available fresh, canned, dried, or frozen.

Store legumes in a cool, dry, well-ventilated area, away from light and excessive heat. Always discard any beans or peas that appear moldy, damp, or wrinkled. It is possible to keep dried beans for one to two years; however, they are best when they are used within six months of purchase.

Essential Skills
Softening Dry Beans

❶ Dry beans are not ready to eat, of course. They need some attention first.

❷ Rinse the dust off of them and sort out any pebbles or shriveled beans. This is best done on a white plate or surface, so you can see what you've got.

❸ Soaking dry beans softens them prior to cooking. Boiling dry beans in water for 2 minutes, then allowing them to soak for 1 hour prior to cooking will soften beans as well as an overnight soaking in cold water. Some beans and peas will actually soften better after this brief boiling.

❹ If salt is added to the soaking water, or the tap water used is very hard (high mineral content), the beans might not soften. Hard chemical complexes and hydrophobic bonds can form between molecules, preventing softening. Remember: Soft water, soft beans.

❺ Be sure to discard the soaking water, rinse the beans again, and cover with clean water. Then cook.

❻ Early in cooking, add salt for seasoning and to improve the flavor of the beans. Add an acid, like tomatoes, early in the cooking to lengthen the time required to soften the beans. Add a small amount of soda (no more than ⅛ teaspoon per cup of dry beans) to shorten the cooking time. Adding too much soda makes the beans bitter, dark, and mushy. Cook them until they are soft. Flavor the beans for recipes when they are fully cooked and softened.

Remember: The longer dry beans are stored, the longer they take to soften.

Teaching Tips

- Old potatoes cook more quickly than new potatoes, while beans are the opposite.
- Old beans soften more slowly than new beans.
- Rotate storage of dry beans in a FIFO system, so that older stock is used up.
- Do not overstore beans by purchasing more than you will use in a year.
- Beans can be held in dry, cool or room-temperature storage for up to two years.

Essential Skills:
Softening Dry Beans

Do not short-cut dry beans. If they are not soft, they are not palatable.

Teaching Tips

- Perhaps the students have sorted beans before.
- Help the students to realize that beans come from the farm unsorted.
- Alert the students to the fact that bulk dry beans may have small pebbles in them.
- Beans must be washed and sorted.

In-Class Activity: Soybean Table
Math Connection, 21st-Century Skills—Access and Evaluate Information
Soybeans are perhaps the most versatile legume. They are very nutritious and excellent to use.
Have the students design a table that displays the various uses of soybeans in foods.
The students can determine their own categories and divisions, as well as how to display their data.
The table should communicate the data clearly to others.

Vocabulary Terms

- **Colander:** A bowl with holes for water to pass through.
- **Sieve:** A bowl-shaped wire mesh with a handle used for rinsing.

Cooking Legumes

Rinse legumes before cooking. In some cases, soak legumes before cooking. Check dried legumes for dirt, stones, and other debris prior to washing by placing the product on a sheet pan. Place legumes in a large **colander** or **sieve** and rinse

Figure 11.10: Before cooking legumes, rinse or soak them.

well with cold running water to remove any dust or dirt particles. Then follow the procedure reviewed in the Essential Skills: Softening Dry Beans. Figure 11.10 shows legumes being rinsed.

Cook legumes before they are eaten to develop their flavor, to remove harmful substances, and to make them easy to chew and digest. Cook them so they are firm to the bite. Table 11.3 identifies the soaking and cooking times for various dried legumes.

You can serve legumes in many ways—soups, stews, salads or as side or main dishes. Red beans, for instance, are often served as a vegetarian dish in red beans and rice. Black beans are popular in Mexican cooking. Kidney beans are usually served in chili, bean salad, and Cajun dishes. Chickpeas are the basis for hummus. Soynuts are a popular snack and used as a garnish in salads.

698

Figure Focus

Figure 11.10: These split peas are being rinsed in a sieve.

Table 11.3: Soaking and Cooking Times for Dried Legumes

Type	Soaking Time	Cooking Time
Adzuki beans	4 hours	1 hour
Black beans	4 hours	1½ hours
Black-eyed beans	n/a	1 hour
Chickpeas	4 hours	2–2½ hours
Fava beans	12 hours	3 hours
Great Northern beans	4 hours	1 hour
Kidney beans	4 hours	1 hour
Lentils	n/a	30-40 minutes
Lima beans	4 hours	1–1½ hours
Mung beans	4 hours	1 hour
Navy beans	4 hours	2 hours
Peas, split	n/a	30 minutes
Peas, whole	4 hours	40 minutes
Pink peas	4 hours	30 minutes
Pinto beans	4 hours	1–1½ hours
Soybeans	12 hours	3–3½ hours

[nutrition]

Sprouts of Mung Beans, Chickpeas, and Alfalfa

"Sprouts" is a category for a legume or grain that has started to germinate and sprout into a plant, changing it to another type of food. Sprouts are great on salads, sandwiches, and in Asian dishes, boosting the total nutritional content of the meal.

Mung beans are used extensively in Asia and the Middle East for a variety of uses. When sprouted in water under limited daylight, these sprouts are pale, watery, crunchy, and mild. They are commonly referred to as "bean sprouts," and are readily available in the United States.

Chickpeas, also known as garbanzo beans, can also be sprouted. These sprouts have a bit more of the original starchy seed intact and recognizable. They are great in salads and are more filling than their lighter fellow sprouts.

Unlike mung bean or chickpea sprouts, alfalfa sprouts are bright green and a good source of vitamins, minerals, and colorful chlorophyll. Since alfalfa seeds are actually legumes, they provide a bit of protein in their sprouts, just like the other beans. They are very light and nutty, adding a crispy, leafy freshness to sandwiches and salads.

Many other grains and legumes can be sprouted. In reality, they are all seeds genetically coded to sprout. Some, including kidney beans, are toxic when sprouted, so investigate before any experimentation with sprouts.

699

Table 11.3: Soaking and Cooking Times for Dried Legumes

- If beans have been stored for longer than a year, the cooking time may increase.

Teaching Tips

- Split peas or lentils have a short cooking time and might be appropriate for cooking in the classroom.
- Once cooked, peas and lentils could be refrigerated and used in recipes during the next class period.

Nutrition: Sprouts of Mung Beans, Chickpeas, and Alfalfa

Warn the students about poisonous sprouts. Stick to the familiar ones for eating.

Teaching Tips

- Grains are technically seeds.
- Grains usually have a lot of starch in the endosperm.
- Grains do not usually have as great an oil content as other edible seeds, like sunflower seeds.
- The starch and protein in the endosperm can be used to make flour.
- Flour is a powdery grain derivative.
- Flour is useful and versatile.
- Making and using flour is an ancient skill.

Vocabulary Terms

- **Grains:** Edible grass seeds.
- **Whole grains:** Harvested but not milled.
- **Milling process:** Grinding and refining grains.
- **Hull:** Outside layer of a grain kernel.
- **Bran:** Fibrous layer of the grain kernel that surrounds the starchy center.
- **Endosperm:** The starchy interior part of the grain kernel.
- **Germ:** The fatty tip of a grain kernel.
- **Stone ground:** The process in which grains are ground and broken down; the grains retain more of their nutrients because the germ, bran, and hull are left intact.

Grains

Grains are grasses that grow edible seeds. Grains, along with **meals** and flours, are essential for everyday cooking. **Whole grains** are grains that have not been milled. In the **milling process,** the germ, bran, and **hull** of the grain are removed or polished. The **hull** of a whole grain is the protective coating, or husk, that surrounds the grain. **Bran,** a great source of fiber and B vitamins, is the tough layer surrounding the endosperm. The **endosperm** is the largest part of the grain and a major source of protein and carbohydrate. The smallest part of the whole grain is the **germ.** It is important because it provides a trace of fat and is rich in thiamin. Figure 11.11 shows the parts of a grain.

Grains that are ground and broken down are often referred to as **stone ground.** In this process, the grains retain more of their nutrients because the germ, bran, and hull are left intact.

Table 11.4 describes various grains, meals, flours, and starches and their common culinary uses.

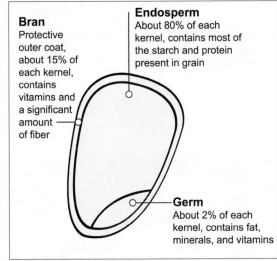

Bran
Protective outer coat, about 15% of each kernel, contains vitamins and a significant amount of fiber

Endosperm
About 80% of each kernel, contains most of the starch and protein present in grain

Germ
About 2% of each kernel, contains fat, minerals, and vitamins

Figure 11.11: Parts of a grain.

Figure Focus
Figure 11.11: Anatomy of a grain kernel.

Table 11.4: Grains, Meals, Flours, Starches

	Type	Description	Common Culinary Uses
WHEAT	Berries/ Whole	Unrefined or minimally processed whole kernels; light brown to reddish-brown; somewhat chewy texture; nutty flavor	Hot cereal, pilaf, salads, breads
	Cracked	Coarsely crushed, minimally processed kernels; light brown to reddish-brown; somewhat chewy texture; nutty flavor	Hot cereal, pilaf, salads, breads
	Bulgur	Steamed, dried, and crushed wheat; fine, medium, or coarse; light brown in color; tender; mild flavor	Hot cereal, pilaf, salads (Tabbouleh)
	Bran	Separated outer covering of wheat kernel; brown flakes; mildly nutty flavor	Hot and cold cereals, baked goods (bran muffins); used to increase dietary fiber
	Germ	Separated embryo of wheat kernel; small, brown, pellet-like; strong nutty flavor; available toasted and raw	Hot and cold cereals, baked goods; used to increase nutritional values in food
	Ebly®/ Tender	Soft, parboiled durum wheat; resembles plump grains of rice in raw state; resembles pearl barley when cooked; subtly mild flavor; available raw or cooked	Soups, salads, side dishes, entrées, desserts
	Farina	Polished, medium-grind wheat; white; flour-like; very mild flavor	Hot cereal
WHEAT FLOUR	Whole	Hard wheat; the entire kernel is finely milled; light-brown color; full, nutty flavor; graham flour is whole wheat flour with a coarser grind	Baked goods, pasta
	All-purpose	Blend of hard and soft wheat; the endosperm is finely milled; off-white color; usually enriched, may be bleached	Baked goods, pasta, thickening agent
	Bread	Hard wheat; the endosperm is finely milled; off-white color; usually enriched, may be bleached; also known as patent flour	Bread, soft rolls
	Cake	Soft wheat; the endosperm is very finely milled; pure white flour; polished soft wheat kernels; usually enriched and bleached	Cakes, cookies
	Pastry	Soft wheat; the endosperm is very finely milled; pure white flour; polished soft wheat kernels; usually enriched and bleached	Pie dough, muffins, biscuits, pastries

continued

701

Table 11.4: Grains, Meals, Flours, Starches

- Berry is another name for the whole kernel of a grain. There are many varities of grains, including amaranth and quinoa.

Discuss

- Help the students to come up with examples of foods made from each category.

- Durum wheat is used for semolina flour.
- It is sometimes called durum flour.
- There is a high protein content to the flour that gives it more gluten development.
- Durum products tend to be smooth, glossy, and elastic.
- Fresh durum bread is light and not mealy.
- It has a chewy, textured crust that most find appealing.
- Semolina flour is used in European breads and pastas.

Table 11.4: Grains, Meals, Flours, Starches *continued*

	Type	Description	Common Culinary Uses
	Durum	Hard wheat; the endosperm from a durum wheat kernel is finely milled	Bread
	Semolina	Durum wheat; the endosperm is coarsely milled; pale yellow	Pasta, gnocchi, puddings; used to make couscous
RICE	Brown	Whole grain, with the inedible husk removed; light brown; chewy texture; nutty flavor; available as short, medium, or long grain	Pilaf, salads
	White/ Polished	Husk, bran, and germ removed; white color; mild flavor; available as short, medium, or long grain	Pilaf, salads; short grain used to make rice pudding
	Converted/ Parboiled	Unhulled grain soaked and steamed before the husk, bran, and germ are removed; fluffy, separated grains when cooked; very light-brown color	Pilaf, salads
	Basmati	Extra-long grain; fine, delicate texture; aromatic, nutty flavor; aged to reduce moisture content; available as brown or white rice; popcorn rice is a variety of basmati	Pilaf, salads
	Jasmine	Aromatic, nutty flavor	Pilaf, steamed, rice pudding
	Arborio/ Italian	Very short, very fat grain; high starch content; off-white; creamy when cooked; also known as Italian rice; varieties include Carnaroli, Piedmontese, and Vialone Nano	Risotto, pudding
	Calaspara	Very short, very fat grain; high starch content; off-white; creamy when cooked	Paella
	Wild	Long, thin grain; dark brown; chewy texture; nutty flavor; marsh grass, unrelated to regular rice	Salads, stuffing; often combined with brown rice
	Sticky/ Pearl/ Glutinous/ Sushi	Round, short grain; very starchy; sticky when cooked; sweet, mild flavor	Sushi
	Rice flour	White rice that has been very finely milled; powdery, white; mild flavor	Thickening agent; baked goods

continued

Table 11.4: Grains, Meals, Flours, Starches *continued*

	Type	Description	Common Culinary Uses
	Heirloom	Varieties include Bhutanese Red, Forbidden Black, and Kalijira rice	Salads, stuffing; often combined with brown rice
CORN	Hominy	Dried kernels soaked in lye to remove the hull and germ; available canned or dried	Succotash, casseroles, soups, stews, side dishes
	Grits	Ground hominy; available in fine, medium, and coarse grinds	Hot cereal, baked goods, side dishes; popular in the southern United States
	Masa	Dried kernels; cooked and soaked in limewater, then ground into dough; pale yellow; moist; variation: masa harina, dried and ground to a fine flour; must be reconstituted to make a dough	Used to make tortillas, tamales, and other Mexican dishes; masa harina often used in baked goods
	Cornmeal	Dried kernels; ground to fine, medium, or coarse texture; colors: white, yellow, or blue; variations: corn flour (finely ground); polenta (coarse-ground)	Hot cereal, baked goods; coating items for sautéing or pan-frying
	Cornstarch	Dried kernels; hull and germ removed; ground to a powder; pure white	Thickening agent (slurry); baked goods; coatings
OATS	Groats	Hulled, usually crushed grain, especially oats, but can be wheat, buckwheat kasha, or other cereals	Hot cereal, salads, stuffing
	Rolled/ Old-fashioned	Groats, steamed and flattened; very pale brown, almost white; round, flake-like; tender; also available: "quick-cooking" and "instant"	Hot cereal (oatmeal), granola, baked goods
	Steel-cut/ Irish/ Scotch	Groats, cut into pieces; brown; chewy	Hot cereal, baked goods
	Bran	Outer covering of the oat	Hot and cold cereals, baked goods
	Flour	Groats, milled into a fine powder	Baked goods
OTHER GRAINS	Buckwheat	Whole or milled into flour; light brown; mildly nutty flavor	Hot cereal, pilafs; flour is used for pancakes, blinis, baked goods

continued

703

Teaching Tips
- Perhaps the students are unaware that corn is used in American cooking more than in European.
- The students may know that corn was introduced as a food to Europeans who had come to the New World.
- Native Americans have been cultivating corn crops since ancient times.
- Corn is used for animal feed in countries where humans still do not eat much corn.
- In parts of Europe, American canned corn is used as a pizza topping.

Discuss
- Specialty grains may be difficult to find.
- Some individuals need specialty grains for allergy reasons.
- This would be a medical need.
- Where could chefs or household consumers find variety grains locally?

Teaching Tips
- Most grains do not need to be refrigerated.
- Note the shelf life of grains and do not store them longer.
- Whole grains have a bit of oil in the germ of the kernel.
- This oil can become rancid.
- Keep whole grains out of direct sunlight because it accelerates the rancidity of oils.
- Sunlight is energy that can cause damage. Sunburn is one example. Rancid oil is another.
- Store grains in a cool, dry, shaded place.

Table 11.4: Grains, Meals, Flours, Starches *continued*

	Type	Description	Common Culinary Uses
	Kasha	Hulled, crushed kernels (buckwheat groats); roasted; reddish-brown; chewy texture; toasty, nutty flavor	Pilafs, salads
	Millet	Whole or milled into flour; bland flavor	Hot cereal, pilafs; flour is used for puddings, flatbreads, cakes
	Sorghum	Commonly boiled to a thick syrup	Porridge, flatbreads, beer, syrup,
	Rye	Whole, cracked, or milled into flour; ranges from light to dark brown; dense; pumpernickel flour is very dark, coarsely ground rye	Pilafs, salads; flour is used for baked goods
	Teff	Whole; extremely tiny; light to reddish-brown; sweet, chestnut-like flavor	Soups, casseroles; thickening agent
	Amaranth	Whole or milled into flour; greens are also eaten; color ranges from white to tan, gold, or pink; sweet flavor	Hot and cold cereals, pilafs, salads
	Spelt	Whole or milled into flour; moderately nutty flavor	Pilafs, salads; flour is used for baked goods; substituted for wheat flour for people with wheat allergies
	Job's Tears	Whole; small; white; slightly chewy texture; grass-like flavor	Pilafs, salads
	Quinoa	Whole or milled into flour; very tiny circles; off-white; mild flavor	Pilafs, salads, puddings, soups
	Barley	Hulled and Pearl (hull and bran removed); varieties: grits, flour; tan to white; nutty flavor	Pilafs, salads, soups; used to make whiskey and beer

© *The Professional Chef, 8ᵗʰ Edition*, The Culinary Institute of America, 2006

Selecting and Storing Grains

Whole grains have a shorter shelf life than milled grains. Purchase whole grains in quantities that can be used within three weeks. Carefully inspect grains when they are delivered. Check bags, boxes, and all containers to make sure they are intact, clean, and in no way below standard.

Store dry grains at least six inches above floor level on shelves in a dry, ventilated, and accessible area. Whole grains should be stored in the freezer. Brown rice and wild rice should be refrigerated. Figure 11.12 on the following page shows a grain product that should be rejected during receiving.

704

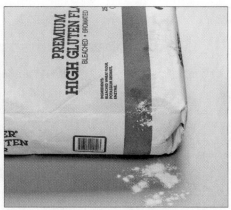

Figure 11.12: Reject grain products with packaging that has holes, tears, or signs of prior wetness.

Cooking Grains

Like legumes, soak grains before cooking them. For example, water softens the outer layer, or bran, of whole grains such as barley and buckwheat. This makes them easier to cook. Food preparers can select from several ways to cook grains, including steaming, pilaf, and risotto.

Cook steamed grains in a double boiler with a perforated bottom over simmering or boiling liquid. Properly steamed grains should be tender to the bite and have a good flavor.

Pilaf (PEEL-ahf) is a technique for cooking grains in which the food preparer sautés the grain briefly in oil or butter and then simmers it in stock or water with various seasonings. In the pilaf method, first heat the grain in a pan, either dry or with oil, and then combine it with hot liquid and cook in the oven or on the stove top. The grains will be tender, remain separate, and have a pleasing, nutty flavor. To give rice a particular flavor or color, add vegetable or fruit juice to the liquid. Use a soup base or replace the liquid with a flavored stock. Use an acid, such as tomato juice, to increase the cooking time up to 15 minutes. Figure 11.13 shows plated bulgur wheat pilaf as a side dish to lamb.

Figure 11.13: Plated bulgur wheat pilaf as a side dish to lamb.

705

Discuss
- It's a good idea to road test grains for menu items.
- Make sure the cooking time is accurate.
- Grains that are too hard or mushy are not desirable.
- Test time and cooking methods for the grains for local conditions.

Vocabulary Terms
- **Pilaf:** Grain that has been sautéed, then finished by simmering in water or stock.

Figure Focus
Figure 11.2: Rodents love finding flour and grains.

Figure 11.3: Pilaf may be made with bulgur wheat or rice. Pilaf is a technique.

Essential Skills
Making Pilaf

❶ Heat oil or butter in a pan.

❷ Add onions and sauté, stirring frequently until softened.

❸ Add grain all at once and sauté, stirring frequently until well coated with oil or butter. See Figure 11.14a.

❹ Add liquid to the grain and bring to a simmer. Stir the grain to keep it from clumping together or sticking to the pan. See Figure 11.14b.

❺ Add any remaining seasonings or flavors.

❻ Cover the pot and finish cooking the pilaf either on the stovetop over low to moderate heat or in the oven. Do not stir the pilaf as it cooks.

❼ The grains are done when they are tender but not mushy. See Figure 11.14c.

❽ Remove from heat. Let pilaf rest for 5 minutes.

❾ Serve while pilaf is still hot.

Figure 11.14a: Step 3—Adding grain.

Figure 11.14b: Step 4—Adding liquid to grain.

Figure 11.14c: Step 7—Grains are done.

706

Figure Focus

Figure 11.14a: Sauté first.

Figure 11.14b: Add liquid.

Figure 11.14c: Grains are separate and flavorful.

Most commonly, food preparers use the **risotto** (rih-ZO-to) method with one special medium-grain rice, **arborio** (ahr-BORE-ee-oh). Risotto has a very creamy consistency because of the starch that is released from the arborio rice as it cooks. This starch makes the finished product sticky and creamy. In the risotto method, the food preparer stirs the rice constantly as she adds small amounts of hot liquid, usually flavored broth or water, which are absorbed. The starch in the rice is released gradually during the cooking process, producing a creamy texture. The best risotto has a porridge-like consistency (sticky and creamy) and can be served as an appetizer or main entrée. The food preparer also can cool and shape it for later use. For example, use for deep-fried balls of risotto with cheese in the center.

Essential Skills
Risotto

❶ Heat oil or butter in a pot.

❷ Add onions and sauté, stirring frequently.

❸ Add rice and sauté, stirring frequently. See Figure 11.15a.

❹ Add one-fourth of the liquid to the grain and bring to a simmer. Continue stirring until rice has absorbed all the liquid. See Figure 11.15b.

❺ Add remaining liquid, stir, and simmer until grain absorbs the liquid.

Figure 11.15a: Step 3—Add rice and sauté.

Figure 11.15b: Step 4—Add liquid.

707

Discuss
- Ask the students if they have ever tried risotto.
- There may be students in the class who have never tried it.
- If there is a student familiar with it, ask that student to describe it.
- Discuss when it might be served.
- Osso buco, an Italian veal dish, is usually served with risotto.

Essential Skills:
Risotto

Take care to stir the risotto so that the starch does not stick or scald on the bottom. Risotto needs attention during preparation and is an excellent side dish.

Vocabulary Terms
- **Risotto:** Thick, creamy Italian rice dish.
- **Arborio:** The variety of rice used for risotto.

Figure Focus
Figure 11.15a: Sauté first.

Figure 11.15b: Add only a portion of the liquid to begin with.

Reinforce and Review

- Beans, peas, and lentils are botanically similar.
- Nuts are different and are not actually legumes.
- Peanuts and soynuts are legumes.
- Beans, peas, lentils, nuts, and seeds all provide vegetable protein.
- Uncooked legumes and grains do not require refrigeration.
- Uncooked legumes and grains do have a limited shelf life.
- Beans must be soaked for several hours or overnight before cooking to rehydrate.
- Grains must be soaked or cooked in liquid.

Summary

- Remind students to review the following:
  1. The different types of grains and legumes
  2. The methods for selecting, receiving, and storing grains and legumes
  3. Types of cooking methods and recipes for preparing grains and legumes

❻ Remove the pot from the heat and stir in butter. See Figure 11.15c.

❼ Serve risotto immediately. See Figure 11.15d.

Figure 11.15c: Step 6—Stir in the butter.

Figure 11.15d: Step 7—Serve the risotto.

Summary

In this section, you learned the following:

- Legumes are seeds from pod-producing plants. Beans, peas, and lentils are the three types of legumes. Grains are grasses that grow edible seeds. Wheat (including all-purpose white flour, soft wheat, hard wheat, and durum wheat), rice, oats, and barley are some common grains.

- Store legumes in a cool, dry, well-ventilated area, away from light and excessive heat. Discard any beans or peas that are moldy or wrinkled. Whole grains have a shorter shelf life than milled grains; use them within three weeks of purchase. Carefully inspect all grains when they are delivered. Do not accept packages that are ripped or that have holes. Canned products should be dent free.

- Soak legumes and grains before cooking. Techniques for cooking grains include pilaf and risotto. Pilaf is a technique for cooking grains in which the food preparer sautés the grain briefly in oil or butter and then simmers in stock or water with various seasonings. Food preparers usually use the risotto method with one special medium-grain rice, arborio. Risotto has a very creamy consistency because of the starch that is released from the arborio rice as it is cooked.

708

Figure Focus

Figure 11.15c: Add the remaining liquid.

Figure 11.15d: Stir butter into the risotto before serving.

Section 11.2 Review Questions

1. How should dried legumes be stored?

2. What happens to a grain when it is milled?

3. Explain the pilaf and risotto techniques for cooking grains.

4. What are the parts of a grain?

5. Chef Jean has traditionally used legumes primarily in soups and stews. He wants to experiment with beans and peas to create some interesting lunch options. Research two dishes that would use some form of bean or pea in a main course (other than a soup or a stew). Why would this be a suitable lunch option?

6. Stephanie Izard notes that grains are a basic component of many vegetarian dishes. Research two wheat grains and describe their properties and uses.

7. Grains such as quinoa and triticale are not only served, but sometimes are featured items at restaurants. What types of restaurants would feature these grains?

8. What grains have been most successful in the typical American home? Why?

709

Section 11.2 Review Questions

1. Dry legumes should be stored in a cool, dry, well-ventilated area away from light.

2. Milling removes or polishes the hull, the germ, and the bran of a grain. The starchy endosperm is ground into flour.

3. Pilaf is a method of cooking grains with first a sauté, then a simmer in stock or seasoned water. Each grain is separate and tender. Risotto is a rice dish that is thick and creamy, cooked in a broth or seasoned liquid and thickened with the starch from the rice. As it cooks, it is constantly stirred.

4. Grains are made of endosperm, germ, hull and bran. Refer the students to Figure 11.11.

5. Student ideas will vary. Some ideas might include three bean salad, green pea salad, or lima beans and bacon.

6. Two wheat grains would be any of those found in Table 11.4, such as bulgur or farina.

7. The students may find a variety of answers for this. Most answers will probably center on restaurants with a more rustic or natural flavor, perhaps vegan, or some ethnic.

8. Student responses will vary. Typically, corn, wheat, oats, and rice are the grains most often seen in American cuisine. There are many ways to use them and reasons for their appeal. One of these reasons is the use of grains in cold, prepared cereal products.

Section 11.2 Activities

1. At the time of publication, this is a controversial, hotly debated topic in U.S. agriculture policy. The student answers will vary.

2. Technically, legumes are the seeds from the pods of the Leguminosae family of plants. Nuts and seeds from other plant families are not true legumes.

3. This question is asking the students to think and work beyond the text. They might go to actual bakeries to glean information, rather than just relying on Internet or library resources. They should truly project themselves into the picture.

Section 11.2 Activities

1. Study Skills/Group Activity: Debate "America's Breadbasket"

The Midwest of the United States is called "America's Breadbasket." Team up with four other students to debate the following statement: "Resolved: United States corn production end use should be shifted from food to ethanol fuel." What are the pros and cons?

2. Activity: What is a legume?

What qualifies as a legume? Are fresh green pea pods legumes? Are alfalfa sprouts legumes? Research the definition of legume, list at least five different legumes, and suggest a menu item that could be created with each.

3. Critical Thinking: The Future of Flour

Project 15 years into the future and see yourself as the owner of a small bakery. How would you receive your deliveries of flour? How would you store your flour? How often would you have a delivery? How much flour would you order? Answer each question based upon research into the industry.

11.1 Potatoes	11.2 Legumes and Grains	11.3 Pasta
• Types of potatoes	• Legumes	• Pasta and dumplings
• Selecting and storing potatoes	• Selecting and storing legumes	• Cooking pasta
• Cooking potatoes	• Cooking legumes	• Cooking dumplings
	• Grains	
	• Selecting and storing grains	
	• Cooking grains	

SECTION 11.3 PASTA

The word pasta in Italian means paste, referring to a mixture of flour and water, and sometimes eggs. Yet, pasta appeals to virtually everyone, from toddlers to those with highly sophisticated palates. Pasta can be purchased at a store or made from scratch; then served easily at home or in the most elegant restaurant.

Study Questions

After studying Section 11.3, you should be able to answer the following questions:

- What are the different types of pasta?
- What types of cooking methods and recipes are there for preparing pasta?
- How do you prepare dumplings?

Pasta and Dumplings

Fast becoming a staple food item in America, pasta is one of the most versatile and convenient foods to prepare. Dried pasta and noodles are essential foods because they store well, cook quickly, and provide a base or accompaniment for many popular dishes. Many pasta varieties can also be purchased fresh or frozen. Colored and vegetable-flavored pastas can add color and nutrition to many entrées. Table 11.5 describes various dried pastas and their common culinary uses.

Dumplings are cooked balls of dough that often include a filling ingredient, such as pork, vegetables, or even sweets. Ravioli, which we refer to as pasta, really falls under the definition of dumpling. Virtually every type of cuisine has a dumpling dish from Chinese dumplings to Polish **pierogi** (pyeh-RRAW-ghee).

711

Section 11.3
Pasta

Introduce the Section

a. There are many different types of pasta, for many uses.

b. This section will feature cooking methods for pasta.

c. Dumplings are not the same as pasta, but there is a lot of overlap.

Vocabulary Review

a. Direct students to the key terms.

b. Pronounce each word, and have the students repeat the pronunciation out loud.

c. Discuss the definition of each word.

Teach

Discuss

- Pasta is made from a paste-like flour and water dough.
- There may be eggs, vegetables, or other ingredients added to the dough.
- Dumplings are also made from a simple dough.
- Ravioli is called pasta, but it's a dumpling.
- There are foods called dumplings that are not filled, so they might be better called pasta.

Vocabulary Terms

- **Pierogi:** Eastern European dumpling dish.

Table 11.5: Dried Pasta and Noodles

- Pasta is an Italian word, but not all noodles are Italian. How many of these varieties are the students familiar with?

CUSTOMIZED INSTRUCTION

Special Needs Students

Pasta comes in many shapes and sizes.

Each shape has a function in cuisine and most of the names are based upon the shape of the pasta.

Acini de pepe is a small, solid, round Italian pasta.

The name *acini de pepe* means peppercorn.

Acini de pepe is used in a sweet fruit salad to add bulk and substance. This salad is sometimes called Frog-Eye Salad because the pasta looks like a frog's eye.

Perhaps the special needs student would like to name or rename various shapes and sizes of pasta, according to what it looks like.

The names do not have to be serious.

Table 11.5: Dried Pasta and Noodles

	Type	Description	Common Culinary Uses
DRIED PASTA AND NOODLES	Bucatini	Hollow, long strands; spaghetti-shaped	Served with thicker sauces
	Bean thread noodles	Slender, gelatinous noodles; made from mung beans	Soups, stir-fries, salads, desserts, drinks; common to Asian-influenced dishes
	Capellini	Thin, long strands; thinner version: capelli d'angelo (angel hair)	Served with broth, oil, or very light sauces
	Fettuccine	Thick, long strands; flat, ribbon-shaped	Served with a variety of sauces, especially cream sauces
	Lasagne	Thick, long, flat, wide noodles; ruffled edges	Casseroles
	Linguine	Thin, long, flattened strands	Served with a variety of sauces, light to heavy
	Rice noodles	Various widths; long strands; made from rice flour	Common to Asian-influenced dishes
	Soba noodles	Fine, long strands; ribbon-shaped; Japanese buckwheat pasta	Soups, stir-fries; common to Asian-influenced dishes
	Spaghetti	Round, long strands; widths range in size	Served with a variety of sauces, light to heavy
	Udon noodles	Thick, long strands; Japanese noodles	Soups, stews, stir-fries; common to Asian-influenced dishes
	Vermicelli	Thin, long strands; similar to spaghetti	Broths, soups, light sauces
	Acini de pepe	Small; rice-shaped	Served with a variety of sauces; soups, salads, casseroles
	Casareccia	Short; rolled; twisted	Served with a variety of sauces; soups, salads, casseroles
	Elbow	Short; narrow, curved tubes	Served with a variety of sauces; soups, salads, casseroles
	Farfalle	Medium; bowtie-shaped	Served with a variety of sauces; soups, salads, casseroles
	Fusilli	Short; corkscrew-shaped	Served with a variety of sauces; soups, salads, casseroles

continued

Table 11.5: Dried Pasta and Noodles *continued*

	Type	Description	Common Culinary Uses
	Orecchiette	Flat; smooth; curved rounds	Served with a variety of sauces; soups, salads, casseroles
	Orzo	Small; grain-shaped	Served with a variety of sauces; soups, salads, casseroles
	Penne	Short tubes; smooth or ridged; diagonally cut	Served with a variety of sauces; soups, salads, casseroles
	Radiatore	Short; chunky shape with rippled edges	Served with a variety of sauces; soups, salads, casseroles
	Rigatoni	Thick; ridged tubes	Served with a variety of sauces; soups, salads, casseroles
	Shells	Small to large; resemble conch shells; larger shells stuffed	Served with a variety of sauces; soups, salads, casseroles
	Tubetti	Small to medium; tube-shaped	Served with a variety of sauces; soups, salads, casseroles
	Couscous	Small, irregular shape; grain-like; similar to coarse sand	Hot cereal, pilafs, salads
	Israeli couscous	Larger than traditional couscous; pearl-like, smooth, round balls; chewy texture; sometimes toasted	Pilafs, salads, soups
	Italian couscous	Larger than traditional couscous; irregular shape	Salads, fish- or tomato-based
	Fregola Sarda	Sun-baked; golden brown color; chewy texture; nutty flavor	Soups

© *The Professional Chef*, 8th Edition, The Culinary Institute of American, 2006

Discuss

- Orzo is shaped like a long grain of rice, and it often is used in soups or side dishes instead of rice.
- One example is using orzo in Greek avgo lemono soup, in place of rice, for a smoother texture.
- What is the difference between couscous, Israeli couscous, and Italian couscous?

CUSTOMIZED INSTRUCTION

Less Advanced Students

Some pastas are used commonly for certain dishes.

Radiatore, for example, is the classic pasta for a cold pasta salad.

Elbows are typical for baked macaroni and cheese.

Have the students identify pasta shapes that are strongly associated with particular dishes.

Nutrition:
Carbo-Loading with Pasta

Carbo-loading must be properly done to be of any real athletic benefit. The glycogen stored in the muscles must first be depleted and carbohydrate foods reintroduced on a timetable.

Simply eating a big spaghetti dinner before the big game is not true carbo-loading.

Teaching Tips

- While pasta and dumpling use a similar dough, they are not the same.
- The names are not interchangeable.
- However, they may be used interchangeably in some regions.
- Tortellini and ravioli are dumplings that are called pasta.
- In the Midwestern United States, dumplings are large, square, fresh noodles that boil in a chicken soup stock.
- In other regions, dumplings are puffy balls of dough that boil in a soup, often chicken.

Fast Fact:
Did You Know...?

Spaghetti is the pasta king.

[nutrition]

Carbo-Loading with Pasta

Carbo-loading, or carbohydrate loading, means to increase the carbohydrates athletes eat starting two days before a high-intensity endurance athletic event. During the same time, they reduce activity level. This encourages their bodies to store carbohydrates as glycogen, which is a form of starch energy stored in the muscles. It is believed that this energy will then be available to improve the performance of the athletes. And they won't get as tired as quickly.

Traditionally, a big spaghetti dinner has been the classic carbo-loading meal. Pasta is high in complex carbohydrates, easy to digest, mild, and does not promote gas or diarrhea. It also has some protein. Correctly done, carbo-loading can nearly double the muscle stores of glycogen in athletes! That translates into sustained energy and more endurance.

Pasta and dumplings are important elements of most cuisines because they are made from inexpensive, staple ingredients, and they can be used in many dishes. Pasta is used in appetizers, entrées, salads, and even desserts.

Prepare pasta and dumplings from a dough or batter that includes a starch, such as flour or potatoes, and a liquid. Use additional ingredients to add shape, color, texture, and flavor. The basic pasta dough recipe produces a stiff dough that can be stretched, rolled into thin sheets, and cut into desired shapes.

[fast fact]

Did You Know...?

According to the American Pasta Report, the most popular pasta dishes are spaghetti (40%) and lasagna (12%).

Source: American Pasta Report

Cooking Pasta

Many differences exist between fresh pasta and dried pasta. Fresh pasta cooks very quickly. The pasta is done when it feels firm to the bite, or **al dente** (ahl DAN-tay). Because fresh pasta cooks so quickly, food preparers have no reason to cook it in advance. However, they can hold cooked fresh pasta for short periods for banquet and buffet service, and then reheat it by placing it in a wire basket and dipping it briefly in a pot of boiling water. Figure 11.16 shows a variety of fresh pastas.

Figure 11.16: Fresh pasta is available in many shapes, colors, and sizes.

715

Discuss
- Fresh pasta is tender and flavorful.
- Dried pasta is used quite commonly in the United States.
- Have the students tasted the difference between the two?
- Which type of pasta would be simpler to use in a commercial kitchen?

Vocabulary Terms
- **Al dente:** Pasta that has a little resistance to the teeth.

Figure Focus
Figure 11.16: Fresh pasta has a uniquely delicious flavor and texture.

Teaching Tips

- The students may know that dry pasta comes in many shapes.
- Are the students also aware of the variety in colors?
- Do the students understand why pasta might be red, orange, or green?
- Help the students realize that some tomato purée added to pasta dough would make the pasta orange.
- Spinach purée added to pasta dough would make it green.
- The coloring nutrients from the vegetables are in colored pasta.
- Perhaps the students realize that fresh pasta may be in the same shapes as dried pasta.

In-Class Activity: Value-Added Pasta

Students may not be familiar with the term value-added. It means "an enhancement" that does not add significantly to the price. Some types of pasta are available for purchase with fillings such as meat, cheese, or vegetables already inside. The students might not be familiar with value-added pasta.

Reproduce the following for the students:

Types of Pasta

Circle the pasta types that are value-added.

spaghetti	agnolotti
lasagna	couscous
penne	fagottini
tortellini	macaroni
radiatore	farfalle
ravioli	tortelloni
bucatini	fettuccine
capellini	linguine

The value-added filled pastas are: tortellini, ravioli, agnolotti, fagottini, and tortelloni.

The students can research the various types of pasta and determine which are value-added.

The students might want to discuss whether or not spinach or tomato or herb flavored and colored pastas are value-added.

The students might also want to discuss manicotti, canneloni, and other stuffed pastas that are usually stuffed in-house as a specific menu item.

Cooking dry pasta takes longer than cooking fresh pasta. Like fresh pasta, the food preparer should cook it al dente and serve it as soon as possible. However, dried pasta can be held for a longer period of time. Figure 11.17 shows a variety of dried pastas.

Figure 11.17: Similar to fresh pasta, dried pasta comes in many shapes, sizes, and colors. Dried pasta takes longer to cook than fresh pasta.

716

Figure Focus
Figure 11.17: Pasta is beautiful in so many ways. It is visually exciting.

Essential Skills
Boiling Pasta

❶ Bring a large pot of water to a boil and add salt.

❷ Add pasta and stir until softened and separated.

❸ Cook until done, stirring occasionally.

❹ Drain pasta in colander. See Figure 11.18.

Figure 11.18: Step 4—Drain pasta.

❺ Serve pasta immediately. Pasta can be served with a sauce or tossed with oil.

717

**Essential Skills:
Boiling Pasta**

Pasta may sink to the bottom of the pot and stick. Stir the pasta and lift it off the bottom until the rolling boil carries it.

Teaching Tips

- It is a good idea to reserve a little bit of the cooking water for later use, if needed.
- Occasionally, the pasta and sauce are a bit dry.
- Adding more sauce might be too thick or too flavorful and overpower the pasta.
- Adding just a little of the starchy pasta cooking liquid can mildly add pasta essence to the dish.

Figure Focus

Figure 11.18: Drain pasta in a colander large enough to prevent the pasta from spilling out into the sink.

Freshly made and cooked pasta should be handled as TCS foods.

Teaching Tips

- The resting stage is not really rest at all.
- There are chemical reactions happening in the dough as the flour molecules hydrate.
- When all of the flour particles have fully hydrated, the dough will hold together.
- Rolling the dough acts a bit like kneading, developing some gluten linkages.
- The hydration, the rolling, and the gluten help give pasta a cohesive finish.
- Well-made pasta does not fall apart.

Vocabulary Terms

- **Resting stage:** The amount of time mixed pasta dough needs to sit.

[ServSafe Connection]

Safety Concerns with Fresh Pasta

Store freshly made pasta in the refrigerator up to two days. The ingredients are fresh and moist and must be held below the danger zone. If eggs are in the pasta, this is especially true.

Pasta can be made fresh in a pasta machine. Completely clean this machine after each use. The moist starchiness of pasta makes it a wonderful food and substrate for pathogens, including mold.

When cooking pasta, be sure that boiling water is properly managed to avoid any splashing when the pasta is added or removed.

For fresh pasta dough, use four simple ingredients: eggs, salt, olive oil, and flour (bread flour, all-purpose flour, or semolina flour). For flavor and color, add fresh herbs, spices, and vegetables. When adding vegetables to the mixture, the food preparer must ensure that they are as dry as possible before mixing into the dough. Chop or finely mince fresh herbs.

When mixing pasta dough, the most important stage is the **resting stage.** If the dough is not sufficiently relaxed, it will be difficult to roll the dough into thin sheets. Pasta dough should be smooth and elastic and slightly moist to the touch. When the dough has rested 15–30 minutes (depending on the specific recipe), it is ready to be rolled out into thin sheets. *Note:* Resting time depends on the type of flour and the type and amount of tenderizing agents used. Follow the resting time stated in the recipe.

Hold fresh, uncooked pasta under refrigeration for a day or two, or freeze it. If it is to be stored longer, dry the pasta and store in the same manner as commercially prepared dried pasta.

Any sauce served with pasta must be the right consistency to complement the type of pasta. For example long, flat pastas, such as fettuccine and linguine, are best served with smooth, light cream sauces. Pair tube and twisted pastas with heavier sauces, such as thick tomato and meat sauces, because they catch the sauce.

It's also important to pair the sauce with a pasta's particular flavor. For example, the delicate flavor of fresh pasta should be paired with a light cream or butter-based sauce, while heartier meat sauces are better for dried pastas. Filled pastas need only a very light sauce because a heavy sauce overpowers or conflicts with the flavor of the filling. Following are some rules of thumb for pasta:

- One pound dried pasta to one gallon of liquid.
- One pound dry pasta yields three pounds cooked pasta.
- One pound fresh uncooked pasta yields two to two and a half pounds cooked pasta.

718

Cooking Dumplings

Make **dumplings** from dough or batter, or even bread and potatoes as the main ingredients. Food preparers usually shape them into small, round balls. The only way to test the doneness of dumplings is to cut into one of them. Dumplings should never have a doughy, uncooked interior. Simmer dumplings in a flavorful sauce.

Figure 11.19: Chicken and dumplings.

Dumplings can be cooked in a variety of ways: simmered, steamed, poached, baked, panfried, deep fried, and broiled. Simmered or poached dumplings are quite popular. In fact, most dumplings are initially cooked by poaching. After poaching them, finish in any of the ways mentioned previously. Figure 11.19 is a photo of chicken and dumplings.

Slight additions or changes can transform pasta dough into a dumpling batter for **spaetzle** (SPAYT-z-el), small German dumplings, or breadlike dumplings that are tasty in stews. **Gnocchi** (nee-YO-key) are small potato dumplings served in Italian cuisine. Figure 11.20 shows a puffy dumpling, gnocchi, and spaetzle.

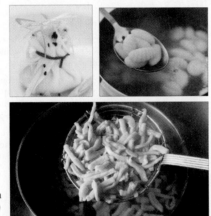

Figure 11.20: From top left, moving clockwise: puffy dumpling, gnocchi, and spaetzle.

719

In-Class Activity: Venn Diagram Dumplings

Math Connection

Some dumplings are boiled, some are baked, and some are fried.

Some are stuffed and some are not.

The students can use a Venn diagram to categorize dumplings.

Below is an example. There will be differences of opinion about how and where the foods and categories overlap.

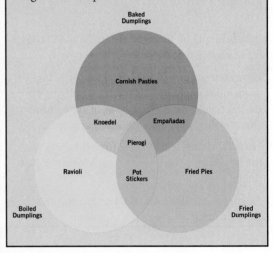

Vocabulary Terms

- **Dumplings:** Cooked balls of dough that may be solid or hollow with a filling.
- **Spaetzle:** Small German boiled dumplings used in soups, stews or as a side dish.
- **Gnocchi:** Small Italian potato dumplings.

Figure Focus

Figure 11.19: The dumplings in this dish are the broad, flat Midwestern style.

Figure 11.20: Dumplings come in various shapes and sizes.

Match the pasta to the sauce.

Literacy Connection

Ask the students to fold a piece of paper in half to make two columns.

In the column on the left, the students will write a list of the various types of pasta found in Table 11.5.

In the column on the right, the students will copy a list of various types of sauces.

Have them suggest various pasta sauces. Some suggestions might include marinara, alfredo, olive oil and cheese, meat sauce, *fruta de mare*, cheddar cheese sauce, salad dressing, and mayonnaise.

Have the students draw a line from the pasta to the type of sauce that would complement the pasta shape.

There is not necessarily a right or a wrong answer. Have the students discuss their reasoning.

Reinforce and Review

- Dried pasta may or may not contain eggs and is made from durum wheat.
- Pasta is boiled. Dumplings may be boiled or cooked by other methods.
- Pasta and dumplings have a simple starch dough in common.

Summary

- Remind students to review the following:
  1. The different types of pasta
  2. Types of cooking methods and recipes for preparing pasta
  3. Preparing dumplings

[trends] Pasta Sauces

While pasta is still making a strong showing in the restaurant and foodservice industry, the sauces have changed. Pasta used to be presented with a heavy tomato sauce, perhaps with meat. The other option was a white Alfredo sauce, or perhaps a clam sauce.

Lately, light tossings in olive oil, garlic, and herbs are appearing in restaurants. Menus feature lighter tomato sauces and thinner cheese sauces. Food preparers are tossing a variety of ingredients with the pasta as well: fresh cooked, or marinated vegetables; seafood; antipasto items; olives; capers; nuts; and meats. The result is a versatile array of possible menu offerings, all healthful and adventurous.

The main key is to match the sauce to the pasta. A heavy Alfredo sauce would completely overpower Capellini, while a sturdy Rigatoni can handle more than a little drizzle of olive oil and a sprinkling of grated cheese. Lasagna would not be enjoyable made into a pasta salad. American tuna casserole relies on egg noodles as a comfort food.

Summary

In this section, you learned the following:

- Fresh pasta uses four simple ingredients: eggs, salt, olive oil, and bread flour. Many varieties of dried pasta are available, including capellini, farfalle, linguine, penne, rigatoni, spaghetti, and ziti.
- Basic pasta dough recipes produce a stiff dough that can be stretched, rolled into thin sheets and cut into the desired shapes. Fresh pasta cooks quickly and should be cooked al dente. Food preparers can simmer, steam, poach, bake, pan fry, deep fry, or boil dumplings, depending on their type.
- Prepare pasta and dumplings from a dough or batter that always includes a starch—such as flour, meal, or potatoes—and a liquid. Add ingredients to change the dish's shape, color, texture, and flavor.

Section 11.3 Review Questions

① List the three rules of thumb for pasta.

② What is spaetzle?

③ How do you prepare a dumpling?

④ List and describe five dried pastas or noodles.

⑤ Chef Jean wants to offer a variety of pasta dishes on the fall menu. Research three pasta dishes that could be served for dinner. Make sure that each dish varies in terms of sauce or added components (meat, vegetables). Compare the nutrition values of the three dishes.

⑥ Research a vegetarian dish that would include both pasta and legumes. Submit the recipe for this dish. Is it something you would make at home? Why or why not?

⑦ What is the difference between durum and semolina? Which is best suited to pasta? Why?

⑧ What are the advantages and disadvantages of using fresh versus dried pasta in a restaurant or foodservice operation?

721

Section 11.3 Review Questions

1. The answers are found in the text, plus there may be others discovered by the students. The three listed in the text are:
   - One pound dried pasta to one gallon of liquid
   - One pound dry pasta yields three pounds cooked pasta
   - One pound fresh uncooked pasta yields two to two and a half pounds cooked pasta

2. Spaetzle is a German boiled dumpling. They are small, unfilled, and look like a free-form pasta. They are served as a side dish, usually with butter.

3. Dumplings are made from a simple dough that is usually filled with a meat, cheese, or vegetable mixture, then boiled or steamed. Some are also fried.

4. These may be found in Table 11.5 or elsewhere in the text. The students might like to use Table 11.5 to try to identify the various types of pasta in Figures 11.16 and 11.17.

5. Each student will have a unique approach to this question. As the students research the pasta dishes, they might use online resources that provide reliable nutrition information for each recipe.

6. Each student will have a different answer to this question.

7. Actually, durum is the type of wheat. Semolina is the flour made from durum wheat. The semolina flour is used for pasta. It is fine, smooth, and holds its shape and sheen when it dries.

8. Student responses will vary. The price of dry pasta is lower, and the shelf-life is longer. Dry pasta is purchased from a vendor. Fresh pasta may be purchased from a vendor or made in-house. It is softer, has an excellent texture and flavor and may be more popular with guests. However, it must be refrigerated and used within a couple of days, or it must be frozen for longer storage. It can also be dried completely like dry pasta. Fresh pasta made in-house is labor-intensive and therefore more expensive in that regard as well.

Section 11.3 Activities

1. Group responses will vary. There are many possibilities, including, but not limited to, tortellini salad or soup.

2. The students will need to do some studying about each type of pasta in order to compare and contrast them. This could be represented graphically or as a written or oral assignment.

3. Regular wheat-based pasta has gluten. Gluten naturally occurs in the wheat, and helps give pasta its texture. There are specially made rice, corn, and potato pastas for individuals on gluten-free diets.

Section 11.3 Activities

1. Study Skills/Group Activity: Value-Added Pasta

Pasta can be used as an ingredient in making related products, such as ravioli. These are value-added, which means they offer more than plain pasta and can command a higher price. Work with two other students to discuss value-added forms of pasta (cannelloni, tortellini, etc.). Brainstorm ways to use these pasta varieties in menu items.

2. Activity: Asian and Italian Pasta and Noodles

Asian cuisine uses pasta-type noodles extensively. Compare and contrast Asian and Italian pasta/noodle foods. Write two paragraphs about your conclusions.

3. Critical Thinking: Gluten

You have many requests for pasta and noodle dishes at the college dorm cafeteria that you manage. Some dorm residents cannot consume wheat gluten without problems. Are pasta dishes out of the question? Research an answer. Suggest a way to accommodate gluten-sensitive individuals.

722

Case Study Follow-Up **Want to Try?**

At the beginning of the chapter, we mentioned that Chef Jean wants to adjust his menu to reflect the change in temperature and appetite that seems to occur in the fall. He has decided to offer an increased variety of pasta dishes and focus on grains and potatoes as side selections.

1. What types of potatoes would work best at lunch and dinner?
2. How can you encourage patrons to try new grain dishes?
3. How might you incorporate legumes into menu selections?
4. How much variety can you offer without impacting your budget?
5. Should Chef Jean focus more on vegetarian plates?

723

Case Study Follow-Up

- Each of the five questions in this section relies upon the opinion and creativity of the individual students or groups.

- Question four is reality-based and should be approached with real numbers. This will help the students see that each idea must be feasible and justifiable for the establishment.

- Vegetarian offerings may be a good marketing tool.

Apply Your Learning

 Converting Pasta Quantities

Pasta conversions are different for each type of pasta.

Choose the type the students will use and determine the correct conversion. The students could do research on this.

Roughly, pasta tends to approximately double when cooked to al dente, but this is not accurate enough for a large-scale kitchen.

Ten pounds of cooked pasta will be three times the amount of dry pasta. Divide ten by three. You must start with 3.33 pounds of dry pasta to yield 10 pounds of cooked. The conversion factor is three, found in the pasta rules of thumb. You divide the conversion factor if you know the cooked yield you have or want. You multiply by the conversion factor if you know the amount of dry pasta you will start with and want to determine the cooked pasta yield.

However, according to some chefs, pasta only doubles when cooked al dente. To complicate things further, not all shapes of pasta cook at the same rate or yield. Choose a yield conversion factor that you are comfortable with.

 Potato: Poetry or Podium

The students can exercise their creativity with this activity. This will appeal very well to some students.

 Wheat Grass

The instructions provided may be followed to grow wheat grass in the classroom. First, check the school district policies concerning living things in the classroom.

Apply Your Learning

 Converting Pasta Quantities

If you want 10 pounds of cooked pasta, what quantity of dry pasta must you start with? What is the conversion factor? When do you multiply by the conversion factor? When do you divide by the conversion factor?

Use this same conversion factor to determine the quantity of cooked pasta you would have if you began with 32 pounds of dry pasta.

 Potato: Poetry or Podium

Choose one of the two activities:

Write a poem beginning with the line "The odor of one rotten potato..."

Share your creation with the class.

"The Power of the Potato Should Not Be Underestimated." —Alice Waters

Use this quoted statement as a theme for a two-minute talk about potatoes. Be prepared to present your speech to the class.

 Wheat Grass

Wheat grass, barley grass, and other sprouted grains have been popularized by health food proponents and designers alike. Small containers of dense, bright green wheat grass are beautiful to see and a good anchor for flower arrangements.

Beauty aside, sprouted grains such as wheat are filled with vitamins, minerals, antioxidants, and even amino acids. They are put through a juicer and added to smoothies or other healthful beverage-meals. They contribute a bright green color, so keep that in mind when tossing them in the blender with other colorful fruits!

Grow a sample of wheat grass. You can create a growth system in the classroom and have wheat grass in less than a week.

❶ Put clean potting soil in a clean drainage container, leaving 3 inches at the top.

❷ Spread a layer of wheat grass seed on top of the soil.

724

---

③ Cover with a thin layer of potting soil.

④ Spread a second layer of wheat grass seed.

⑤ Cover with another thin layer of potting soil.

⑥ Water well and keep the soil moist.

⑦ Position the wheat grass system in a bright part of the classroom.

⑧ The system may last up to two months.

Critical Thinking   A Delicate Problem. . .

While whole grains and legumes can be very nutritious, they are very high in fiber. This is a good thing. But not always at first.

Simply put, high fiber can cause gas and diarrhea. Diarrhea can cause you to lose nutrients by dumping them before they can be absorbed. Long-term diarrhea can cause a dangerous loss of nutrients and electrolytes.

It's safe to eat high fiber for most people. But phase it into the diet over a period of time. Adjust to it. No sense losing what you are hoping to gain.

Create a one week menu for a person who wants to increase dietary fiber. Assume that the current diet is low in fiber, and the goal is a high-fiber diet. Introduce the high fiber foods slowly over the week, distributed throughout the meals and the days. By the end of the week, half of the menu items served should be sources of fiber.

725

Critical Thinking   A Delicate Problem . . .

Any food with coarse bran should be added late in the week. Legumes could be added earlier, but they will produce intestinal gas. Roughly, a low-fiber diet is below 25 grams/day.

A high-fiber diet is above 35 grams/day; 25–35 grams/day is recommended for the average healthy adult.

When adding fiber to the diet, be sure to count the grams of fiber from fruits and vegetables.

Use USDA tables, available online, to find the grams of fiber for foods.

Exam Prep Answers

1. D
2. C
3. C
4. A
5. A
6. B
7. C
8. A
9. D
10. A

Exam Prep Questions

1 Potatoes exposed to light may develop a greenish color because they contain
- A. fiber.
- B. starch.
- C. chlorine.
- D. solanine.

2 Whole grains should be kept no more than _____ week(s).
- A. one
- B. two
- C. three
- D. four

3 Which type of potato is best to use for making sautéed potatoes?
- A. New
- B. Russet
- C. Chef's
- D. All-purpose

4 The term *al dente* describes pasta that is _____ to the bite.
- A. firm
- B. soft
- C. crisp
- D. mushy

5 Cooked pasta can be refreshed before serving by placing it in
- A. hot water.
- B. the cooler.
- C. the freezer.
- D. ice-cold water.

6 Spaetzle is a type of
- A. grain.
- B. pasta.
- C. potato.
- D. legume.

7 The edible seed of grain without its husk or hull is called the
- A. bran.
- B. germ.
- C. kernel.
- D. endosperm.

8 At what temperature range should potatoes be stored?
- A. 45°F to 55°F
- B. 55°F to 65°F
- C. 65°F to 75°F
- D. 75°F to 85°F

9 Seeds from pod-producing plants are called
- A. pilaf.
- B. beans
- C. grains.
- D. legumes.

10 The technique for cooking grains in which the grain is sautéed briefly in oil or butter is called
- A. pilaf.
- B. risotto.
- C. arborio.
- D. lyonnaise.

726

Garlic Mashed Potatoes

Cooking time: 45 minutes
Yield: 4 pounds

Ingredients

5 lbs	Potatoes, mealy	2 tsp	Salt
1 tbsp	Salt	¼ tsp	White pepper
4 oz	Whole butter, melted, hot	1 oz	Chopped garlic
8 fl oz	Milk, hot		

Directions

1. Wash and peel the potatoes. Cut each potato into four to six uniform-sized pieces.
2. Place the potatoes in a pot, cover them with water, and add 1 tablespoon salt to the water. Bring the water to a boil, reduce to a simmer, and cook until the potatoes are tender. Do not overcook the potatoes.
3. When the potatoes are cooked, drain them well in a colander. The potatoes must be very dry. Transfer them to the bowl of an electric mixer. Using the whip attachment, whip the potatoes for 30 to 45 seconds. Scrape the sides and bottom of the bowl and whip for another 15 seconds or until the potatoes are smooth and free of lumps. The potatoes must be smooth before adding any liquids, or they will remain lumpy.
4. Sweat chopped garlic in melted butter for 5 to 10 minutes without browning. Strain the butter if desired.
5. Add the garlic and butter, milk, and seasonings. Whip on low speed to incorporate all of the ingredients. Scrape the sides and bottom of the bowl and whip again for several seconds. Adjust consistency and seasoning.

Recipe Nutritional Content

Calories	220	Cholesterol	20 mg	Protein	8 g
Calories from fat	70	Sodium	660 mg	Vitamin A	4%
Total fat	8 g	Carbohydrates	33 g	Vitamin C	2%
Saturated fat	4 g	Dietary fiber	7 g	Calcium	2%
Trans fat	0 g	Sugars	3 g	Iron	8%

Nutritional analysis provided by FoodCalc®, www.foodcalc.com

727

Recipe

Garlic Mashed Potatoes

- Potatoes are a staple side dish in the United States. They are nutritious, versatile, and economical.
- According to the USPB (U.S. Potato Bureau), "Potatoes are consumed by 79 percent of U.S. households 1.8 times per week in-home."
- The russet potato has a higher starch content, so it is better for making fluffy mashed potatoes.

Recipe

Bulgur Pilaf

- Bulgur is a whole-grain cereal food made from several species of wheat.
- Bulgur is actually the oldest recorded "use" of wheat.
- It is used for pilaf, soups, stuffing, and bakery goods. Students may be familiar with tabbouleh and kibbeh; bulgur is the main ingredient in these dishes.

Bulgur Pilaf

Cooking time: 45 minutes
Yield: 8 servings, 4 ounces

Ingredients

2 oz	Whole butter		1	Bay leaf
4 oz	Onion, fine dice		1 qt	Chicken stock, hot
10 oz	Bulgur		1 tbsp	Salt and pepper

Directions

1. Melt the butter in a large, heavy saucepan over moderate heat. Add the onion and sauté until translucent.
2. Add the bulgur and bay leaf. Sauté until the grains are well coated with butter.
3. Add the stock and season to taste with salt and pepper. Reduce the heat until the liquid barely simmers.
4. Cover and continue cooking until all the liquid is absorbed and the grains are tender, approximately 18 to 20 minutes.
5. Fluff with a fork and adjust the seasonings before service.

Recipe Nutritional Content

Calories	250		Cholesterol	25 mg		Protein	4 g
Calories from fat	80		Sodium	910 mg		Vitamin A	6%
Total fat	9 g		Carbohydrates	40 g		Vitamin C	25%
Saturated fat	5 g		Dietary fiber	4 g		Calcium	4%
Trans fat	0 g		Sugars	2 g		Iron	4%

Nutritional analysis provided by FoodCalc®, www.foodcalc.com

728

White Bean Salad

Cooking time: (Approximately 15 minutes)
Yield: 3 pints

Ingredients

12 oz	White beans		3 tbsp	Red wine vinegar
As needed	Water		2 tsp	Fresh lemon juice
4 oz	Carrot, small dice		1 tbsp	Dijon mustard
2 oz	Celery, small dice		1 tbsp	Shallot, minced
2 oz	Leek, sliced		6 fl oz	Olive oil
2	Green onions, minced		To taste	Salt and pepper
1 tbsp	Parsley, chopped			
1 tbsp	Fresh thyme, chopped			

Directions

Day one: Sort and then soak beans overnight.
Day two: Cook beans one hour and then chill (overnight).
Day 3: Assemble.

1. Pick through the beans to remove any grit, pebbles, or debris. Place in a bowl of water and remove any skins or other items that float to the top. Drain and rinse the beans. Place in a clean bowl and soak them for at least 1 hour or overnight.

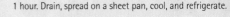

2. Drain the beans and place them in a saucepot with 6 cups of water. Bring to a boil, reduce to a simmer, and cook until tender, approximately 1 hour. Drain, spread on a sheet pan, cool, and refrigerate.

3. Blanch and refresh the carrot, celery, and leek. Drain and chill.

4. To make the dressing, combine the vinegar, lemon juice, and mustard. Add the shallot and whisk in the oil a little bit at a time. Season with salt and pepper.

5. Toss with blanched vegetables, green onions, parsley, and thyme. Add the dressing and toss together. Adjust the seasonings and serve chilled.

Recipe Nutritional Content

Calories	250		Cholesterol	0 mg		Protein	8 g
Calories from fat	70		Sodium	40 mg		Vitamin A	50%
Total fat	15 g		Carbohydrates	23 g		Vitamin C	10%
Saturated fat	2 g		Dietary fiber	10 g		Calcium	10%
Trans fat	0 g		Sugars	7 g		Iron	20%

Nutritional analysis provided by FoodCalc®, www.foodcalc.com

729

Recipe

White Bean Salad

- This is a particularly easy and nutritious picnic dish, and it can be made the day before and left to marinate.
- White beans may also be called cannellini, Great Northern beans, navy beans, and baby lima beans. They are used interchangeably in many recipes, but limas tend to be buttery and earthy while cannellinis are sweet and firm.
- Beans are a great source of fiber.

Chapter 12 introduces the student to ways that he or she can establish a successful career in the restaurant and foodservice industry.

Section 1: The first section describes what skills are necessary and how students can begin developing them, as well as creating tools to use in a job search.

Section 2: This section explains how to complete various types of applications, including employment and academic versions.

Section 3: The third section discusses how to prepare for and conduct a job interview.

Section 4: This section addresses personal and professional development.

Section 5: The final section describes a number of entry-level and career positions in the restaurant and foodservice industry.

Advance Preparation	
Review	Sections 12.1–12.5
	Relevant material from Chapters 1, 2, 4, 7, and 8
Contact	If available, a representative of the school's adult mentoring program
	School guidance or career counselor
Prepare	Sample publications from industry sources, such as magazines and weekly papers

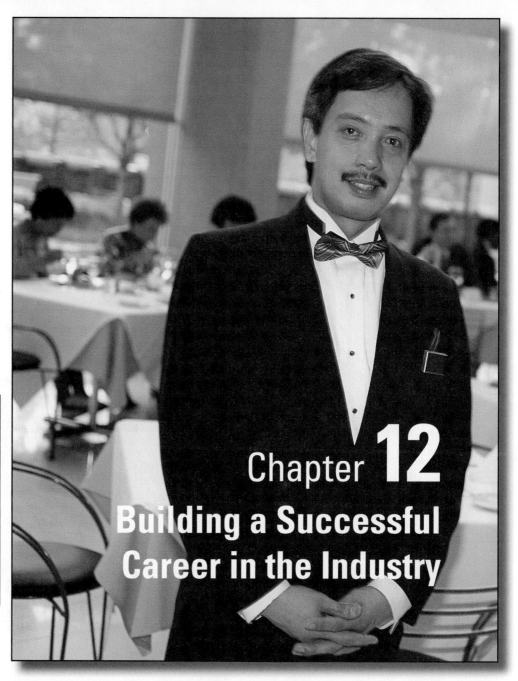

Chapter 12

Building a Successful Career in the Industry

CUSTOMIZED INSTRUCTION OPTIONS			
Less Advanced Students	More Advanced Students	ESOL Students	Special Needs Students
Pages 755, 756	Pages 755, 756	Pages 755, 767	Pages 755, 767

CHAPTER TOOLS			
21st-Century Skills	Mathematics	Science	Literacy
Pages 734, 735, 738, 742, 743, 744, 753, 755, 756, 757, 763, 765, 766, 767, 768, 772, 778, 780	Pages 744, 756, 757, 768, 778	Pages 772, 778, 780	Pages 734, 735, 738, 742, 743, 744, 753, 755, 756, 757, 763, 765, 766, 767, 768, 772, 778, 780

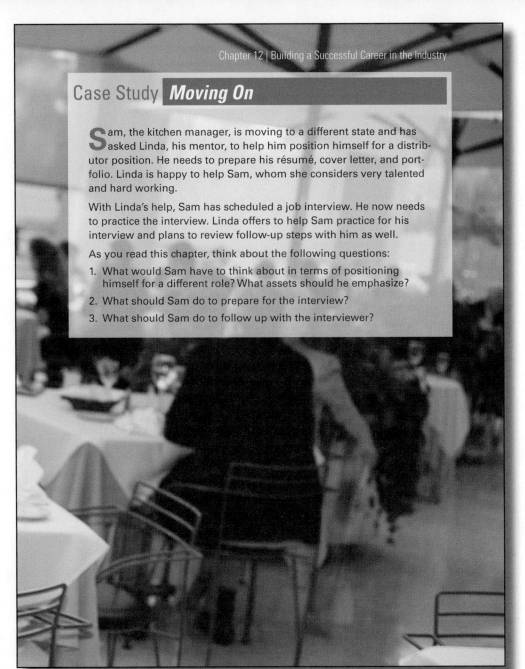

Case Study *Moving On*

Sam, the kitchen manager, is moving to a different state and has asked Linda, his mentor, to help him position himself for a distributor position. He needs to prepare his résumé, cover letter, and portfolio. Linda is happy to help Sam, whom she considers very talented and hard working.

With Linda's help, Sam has scheduled a job interview. He now needs to practice the interview. Linda offers to help Sam practice for his interview and plans to review follow-up steps with him as well.

As you read this chapter, think about the following questions:

1. What would Sam have to think about in terms of positioning himself for a different role? What assets should he emphasize?

2. What should Sam do to prepare for the interview?

3. What should Sam do to follow up with the interviewer?

Case Study
Moving On

- What skills will Sam need for his new job as a distributor? How are these related to the skills he uses in his present position as kitchen manager?

- How can Linda facilitate Sam's job search while keeping the focus on his merits and abilities rather than on her patronage?

- What other types of assistance can a mentor provide, in terms of career development?

- From a manager's perspective, losing a valued employee can be a challenge. What effect might Sam's resignation have on Linda and the other staff members at Uptown Grille?

- Note that there are follow-up questions about the case study at the end of the chapter.

- This activity could be done in groups, as a class, or as a homework assignment.

Professional Profile

Discuss	Explain how and when a recipe can be "just a guide." What about consistency? What about following orders? What about food costs? What about demonstrating respect for the chef who created the recipe?
	What is the relationship between service and honor? How does this relate to respect?
	Why is it important to reach back to help others in the industry? Is this important in every business, or just in the realm of hospitality?
Reinforce and Review	Preparing food is a measure of how much you care for others.
	Building a successful foodservice career requires hard work, personal determination, and willingness to learn new things.
Teaching Tips	Ron Yudd demonstrates a clear passion for his work. Relate this to other individuals appearing in Professional Profiles who have also emphasized the role of passion in their work.

[professional profile]

Ron Yudd
President/Points of Profit, Inc.
Founder: LeadershipCares

❝ *A recipe is just a guide.* ❞ —Jacque Pepin

I grew up in the restaurant business, working in Washington, D.C.-area restaurants during high school and college. I worked my way up from buser to area director, holding a variety of both back- and front-of-the-house positions, including kitchen manager, general manager, and training director.

After receiving a B.A. in English literature, I decided to remain in the restaurant industry. Simply put, I have a passion for food and serving others. And this career gave me a chance to be creative every day and to work with other creative people. It really provides more opportunities than any other industry I know.

As part of his extensive background, Ron held the position of Director of Food Service for the U.S. Senate in Washington, D.C. He served in the Senate for more than 21 years. His guests, associates, and employees still refer to Ron as "The Senator of Service." The Senate Restaurant serves more than 10,000 meals per day in ten restaurants. Fifty percent of the eight million dollars in annual sales is generated by special events and catering. Ron supervised more than 200 associates in the daily mission of delivering the highest quality food with a passion for personalized service.

Preparing food for others is the most honorable thing you can do. It is really a measure of how much you care for others. Prepping, cooking, and serving a meal is the ultimate gift you can give. After all, cooking at its most elemental level is all about giving yourself and sharing your gifts and talents with others.

So, if you want to enter this industry, dream big and always reach back to help others who are coming up behind you.

"Once you have mastered a technique, you barely have to look at a recipe again."
—Julia Child

About Your Career

Building a successful career in the restaurant and foodservice industry requires following a simple recipe. Combine hard work and personal determination with a willingness to learn new things, and you can achieve anything you want in this business. Work hard at whatever you are doing, have the willpower to stay the course no matter how hard things get, and try to learn something new every day!

Always keep in mind as you start out that the really successful people in the industry are those who—early in their careers—stepped forward when their chef asked for volunteers. They were always willing to try new things. They constantly stay in a learning mode—exploring new techniques and working hard to get better at their craft each and every day!

Last, but not least, never forget the importance of passion. Love what you are doing. Others will see your passion and want to hire you or better yet—work for you!

12.1 Starting a Career in Foodservice	12.2 Completing Applications Effectively	12.3 The Job Interview	12.4 Advancing in a Career	12.5 Careers in the Industry
• Skills needed for a successful career • The job search • Preparing a résumé, portfolio, and cover letter	• Job applications • College applications • Scholarships	• Preparing for the job interview • The interview • Follow up after the interview	• Health and wellness • Stress and time management • Resigning from a job • Staying educated and involved	• Entry-level jobs • A selection of careers

SECTION 12.1 STARTING A CAREER IN FOODSERVICE

Those who have had a part-time or summer job might already know the kind of work they enjoy doing. They also know that working helps them develop such essential skills as responsibility, self-confidence, decision making, problem solving, and developing initiative while they earn a paycheck. Readers who haven't had a job yet shouldn't worry. The most important first step toward a good career is taking classes in school that will help build essential skills.

Reinforce and Review

- Working helps young employees develop essential skills like responsibility, self-confidence, decision making, problem solving, and initiative.
- The most important step toward a successful career is taking classes to help build these and other essential skills.

Teaching Tips

- Relate the material in 8.3 and 8.4 to this section, as students learn to create résumés and other professional documents.

Focus and Engage

Discuss

- Based on the last year of study, how is the restaurant and foodservice industry like other industries? How is it different?
- Chapter 8 discussed building an industry career from the perspective of the manager responsible for hiring and developing employees. Chapter 12 looks at the same subject, but from the student's perspective. How do the two differ? In what ways do they overlap?
- Over the last year, students have learned a great deal about the restaurant and foodservice industry. How has this year made a foodservice career more or less attractive to students?
- Establishing a successful career in this industry takes not only many years of hard work, but the willingness to volunteer for additional learning opportunities as they arise.
- Much of the material in this chapter can be directly linked to material in Chapters 4, 7, and 8.

Section 12.1 Starting a Career in Foodservice

Introduce the Section

a. Review the skills that are needed for a successful career and how they can be attained.
b. Describe how to put together the tools needed for a successful job search as well as how to Conduct a search.
c. Discuss the objectives for the section.

Vocabulary Review

a. Direct students to the key terms.
b. Pronounce each word, and have the students repeat the pronunciation out loud.
c. Discuss the definition of each word.

Teach

Discuss

- What essential skills have students learned so far during this course? How well have they learned these skills? Do they need more practice?
- How is this class similar to or different from other types of training and professional development such as on-the-job training or group training? Students may want to review relevant sections of Chapter 8 as they discuss this question.

Discuss

- What career choices within the foodservice industry interest students and why? What are some attractive options outside this industry?
- How can moving laterally become a step ahead?
- How do communication and teamwork play roles in all career paths?
- Coworkers, employers, and guests value enthusiasm and optimism. Encourage students to suggest other attributes of valued employees.

Reinforce and Review

- People advance in their careers by mastering the skills they need for their current jobs and demonstrating the ability to take on fresh responsibilities.
- Communication and teamwork play vital roles in both an employee's professional growth and in the daily business of an establishment.
- Keeping a positive and enthusiastic outlook at work is always important, although it can be challenging when problems arise.

In-Class Activity: Value-Added

Literacy Connection, 21st-Century Skills— Reason Effectively, Make Judgments and Decisions, Work Independently

Students should identify and write down the following:

- Three ways in which they are valuable to potential employers
- Three ways in which they are valuable to their families
- Three ways in which they are valuable to their friends
- Three ways in which they are valuable to their school

Now think about how these overlap. Are students valuable to their friends in the same ways that they are valuable to their families?

Now students should identify and write down three ways in which they could become more valuable to either of these groups and consider how to act on this knowledge in both the short term and the long term. For instance, if someone wants to be more valuable as a helper at home, then a short-term goal might be to wash the dishes and clean the kitchen after dinner each night, and a long-term goal might be to take a course in babysitting to care more effectively for younger siblings.

Each student should keep this paper. In what ways can referring to it occasionally be empowering?

Study Questions

After studying Section 12.1, you should be able to answer the following questions:

- What are the skills needed by restaurant and foodservice professionals?
- What does an effective job-search plan include?
- How do you write a résumé that lists experiences, skills, and achievements?
- How do you prepare an effective cover letter?
- What is a portfolio?

Skills Needed for a Successful Career

It's never too early to begin thinking about a career. A **career** is a profession or work in a particular field, such as foodservice, that individuals choose for themselves. People advance in their careers by mastering the skills needed for their jobs and by showing that they are qualified to take on new responsibilities. Training and experience are important, but employers are also looking for certain skills that students can develop while they are still in school. Training and additional education can help motivated individuals move higher up the career ladder. A **career ladder** is a series of jobs through which people can advance to further their careers, as shown in Figure 12.1. All of these skills become more complex as individuals progress from beginner to intermediate to advanced for each stage:

- **Communication and teamwork:** The ability to communicate effectively is one of the top skills for which employers look. Communication skills include writing, speaking, reading, and listening. Understanding and following directions are also important. Employees, especially in the restaurant and foodservice industry, must be team players, doing their share of the workload. Sometimes, employees do more work if that's what it takes to get the job done.
- **Positive attitude:** Maintaining a positive attitude is a key attribute of any employee. Employers, customers, and coworkers value a person who is enthusiastic and optimistic. The challenge is keeping this attitude even when things are going wrong.

734

Vocabulary Terms

- **Career ladder:** A series of jobs through which people can advance to further their careers.

■ **Willingness to learn:** Learning new technology and new ways of doing things is important to career success. Employees who advance are the ones who are willing to learn new skills and techniques and not think that the way they know is the only way to do something. Stay flexible.

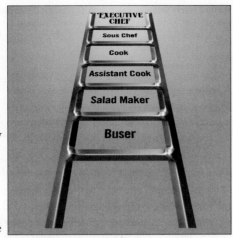

Figure 12.1: A sample career ladder starting with entry-level restaurant and foodservice positions.

■ **Technology skills:** Technology is critical to success. Computer skills are also valuable in the restaurant and foodservice industry. Most jobs today require some knowledge of computers. For example, in many restaurants, servers place orders on computers; cashiers and counter servers in quick-service operations use computerized cash registers.

■ **Math skills:** Math skills are also essential, even though computers may be used. For example, if a customer tells a server to keep 15 percent of the payment as a tip, the server needs to know how to calculate that percentage. **Back-of-the-house** positions use math, too. They count, weigh, and measure items frequently, in addition to calculating yields and converting recipes.

■ **Analyzing and problem solving:** Critical thinking and problem solving are also important skills to develop. Employers value employees who can think of fresh solutions to problems.

■ **Knife and other equipment skills:** Knowing how to use the basic tools and equipment is essential to working in a kitchen. To progress in a restaurant or foodservice career, broaden the number of techniques and processes performed, which increases versatility.

735

Discuss

• How does having the willingness and ability to master new skills make an employee stand out in the workplace? How does this relate to the earlier discussion of humility in Chapter 7?

Reinforce and Review

• Employees who advance in their careers are those who are willing to learn new skills and techniques.
• Good mathematics skills are important in every workplace, but especially in the restaurant and foodservice industry.
• The ability to think critically and to solve complex problems is highly valued by all employers.
• The mastery of basic and complex tools, such as knives, kitchen equipment, and even computers, is essential to professional development and growth.

Teaching Tips

• Humility is discussed in Chapter 7, Section 7.3.

Homework Activity: Up We Go!

Literacy Connection, 21st-Century Skills— Think Creatively, Use Systems Thinking, Create Media Products

Design a sample career ladder. It can be for any career you'd like, except executive chef. You do not have to select a career you personally want to have. There should be at least six rungs in your ladder.

Illustrate your career ladder, using a poster or other visual medium. Be able to explain how one step logically leads to the next.

Relate this to the Prior Planning Prevents Poor Performance activity in Chapter 8. Have your goals and aspirations changed at all since then? If so, in what ways?

Figure Focus
Figure 12.1: What might be the next step on this career ladder? Is there always a next step?

Discuss

- How is knowledge about food safety and about products used in the workplace related to professionalism, as discussed in Chapter 4?
- How can the activities listed on p. 736 help students to develop essential skills?
- How can early initiative, as demonstrated by willingness to learn essential employment skills while still a student, translate into actual performance? How can demonstrating this behavior give young employees more credibility in the workplace?

Reinforce and Review

- Food safety knowledge is essential to every establishment and virtually every employee in the restaurant and foodservice industry.
- Product knowledge demonstrates both credibility and consistent performance.
- All prospective employees, no matter what the industry, should make a commitment to put forth their best efforts each day.
- Students should take advantage of all learning opportunities, whether formal or informal, that will reinforce or expand their skills.

Teaching Tips

- Chapter 4, Section 4.1 discusses professionalism at length, which can be tied to most discussions in Section 12.1.

- **Food safety knowledge:** You must keep food safe, no matter what happens. Knowing how and why to keep food safe will ensure customers never get sick from the food served. Food safety knowledge is fundamental to every operation in the industry.

- **Product knowledge:** Servers who know details about menu items better meet their customers' needs. In the back of the house, this knowledge helps produce high-quality food consistently.

As individuals progress through their careers, they learn skills from the back to the front of the house. They might be involved in every step of the flow of food through the operation, from writing specifications for what food they want to buy to delivering dessert plates to a table. Successful restaurant and foodservice managers work in all areas of an operation at one time or another. They fill in for sick employees to keep an operation running smoothly.

How to Develop These Skills Now

To develop the skills necessary to succeed in the restaurant and foodservice industry, potential employees should do the following:

- Make a commitment to put forth their best efforts.
- Work part-time in the industry while in school.
- Take on challenges in school and work to learn new skills.
- Be active in school clubs and activities.
- Volunteer time in the community; i.e., help out in a local soup kitchen, nursing home, or food bank.
- Take some time to read and learn on their own.
- If they can use a computer in school, the library, or at home, they should become familiar with basic computer functions and software programs, including word processing, spreadsheets, presentation software, and the Internet.
- Take advantage of every opportunity to improve learning and work habits while still in school and working part-time. The more they practice these habits now, the farther they will be able to advance in their careers.

Consider entering into a relationship with a mentor. A **mentor** is someone who can play the role of a wise adviser. See Figure 12.2. Ideally, this person should have a higher position in the company and be willing to serve in this capacity. A mentor should be available to offer insights, coach, be a sounding board, and provide feedback on career-development plans and progress.

Along with identifying a mentor who can help with professional development, also develop a sound relationship with a supervisor. Upward and lateral communication is very important to professional development.

Figure 12.2: A mature chef mentors a new chef.

Essentials Skills
Making the Most of a Mentor

Developing a relationship with a mentor is one of the most rewarding things someone can do personally or professionally. Identify good candidates and then talk with them about their willingness to serve as a mentor and ways in which they can help in professional growth before making a final selection. Although it's wise to have a single mentor, remember that good advice can come from any direction. Someone who is not a strong mentor candidate may still be a good source of information and assistance.

Here are some ways to work with a mentor:

❶ Make regular appointments with a mentor—and keep them. Continually postponing meetings is unprofessional, and it doesn't help toward career goals.

❷ During meetings, plan to discuss previously agreed-upon topics; be focused on the meeting and be respectful of a mentor's time.

❸ Be clear about communicating with a mentor when scheduling appointments and discussing career needs. This person is doing a huge favor, so in return make it as easy as possible.

❹ Be responsible. For recommendation letters for a school, scholarship, or job, don't wait until just before the deadline to ask a mentor. Always present yourself in the best possible light.

❺ Express appreciation to the mentor in a professional way. A thank-you note is always appropriate.

Remember, you and your mentor are embarking upon what could be a life-changing path.

737

Figure Focus
Figure 12.3: How is the mature chef communicating to the younger chef?

Discuss
- How can students find mentors? Who are appropriate people to approach, and why?
- Can mentors work for different companies or even different industries than the mentees? What are some advantages and disadvantages to this?

Reinforce and Review
- Ideally, a mentor should work in your company at a higher level and should be willing to help you succeed.
- Working with a mentor is different from developing a sound relationship with a supervisor, although both are strongly encouraged.

Teaching Tips
- If your school has an adult mentoring program available to students, consider asking either the person in charge of the program or one of its volunteers to speak to the class about mentoring and its advantages.

Essential Skills:
Making the Most of a Mentor

Encourage students to discuss the following:

- How is communication central to the mentoring relationship?
- What are some appropriate ways to express appreciation to a mentor for his or her assistance?
- Why is it important to act as a mentor, especially if you have been mentored yourself?
- How can the presence of a strong mentoring program at a workplace reduce employee turnover and help to build a positive working environment?

Vocabulary Terms
- **Mentor:** Someone who can function as a wise adviser to a younger employee or colleague.

Discuss

- Encourage students to share their experiences with job searches. Where have they looked for jobs? What documents have they prepared? What factors may have made their searches successful or unsuccessful?
- Many online employment sites allow aspiring employees to post their résumés for free, although they may be required to establish a user account. Why do students think this is the case?
- How have online employment sites changed the way people search and apply for jobs?

Reinforce and Review

- People find jobs in many different ways. Word of mouth, advertisements, networking, job fairs, and local agencies are just a few options.
- Newspapers typically list employment ads alphabetically by title or category. Online sources typically require the searcher to enter a keyword, and then all ads containing that word will be displayed.
- Employers often specify the methods candidates should use to apply for a job. These should be followed explicitly, as following directions is a desirable character trait.

Homework Activity: Looking for Jobs

Literacy Connection, 21st-Century Skills— Business Literacy, Make Judgments and Decisions, Communicate Clearly

Look for local jobs available in a career path that interests you. What skills and background do employers require or desire? What do the job descriptions include? What other information do employers provide about jobs in this field?

Are you still attracted to these jobs, having read these advertisements? Why or why not?

Write a one-page paper describing your findings.

The Job Search

Students who learn how to find a job now have a head start when they're ready to work full-time. Finding and keeping a job helps develop both personal and career skills.

Job hunting can be exciting and fun. The job market is the ideal place to tell others about abilities, talents, and dreams. As the average age of people in today's workplace grows older, younger people have even more opportunities before them.

People find jobs in a wide variety of ways. Some employers recruit graduates from a particular high school. Many recruit from colleges and universities. Others print employment ads online and in local newspapers. Other sources include the following:

- Personal contacts
- School placement offices
- Employment agencies
- Community agencies
- Internet resources such as online job search engines and banks
- Networking
- Job fairs
- Youth work studies

Search job ads in online job search engines and job banks by keyword, discipline, and location. The sites are usually more current than traditional classified ads, since posters often update them immediately. Most online job sites allow job seekers to post their résumés online for free. Some sites require job seekers to complete an online résumé or questionnaire as well.

Job ads in newspapers are listed alphabetically by job title or job category. For example, a position as a buser may be in an ad under "B" for buser or an ad under "R" for restaurant. Most ads will specify how to apply for the job—in person, by mail, by phone, or by email. Sometimes restaurant and foodservice operations state a designated time for prospective employees to apply in person. Others will request a cover letter with a résumé or a direct telephone call.

Table 12.1 lists the steps for searching for a job.

Table 12.1: Steps for Searching for a Job

1.	Decide what characteristics a job should have, including the hours and days desired, as well as job responsibilities. Although finding a job that matches such a list exactly is unlikely, generally knowing the desired job characteristics will help.
2.	Figure out what areas are open to compromise. Are you willing to work part of the weekend? How late is too late to catch a ride? Think about what trade-offs can be made to accept a job.
3.	Gather and organize the information needed for applying. Compile a work history (if possible), including complete contact information for each of your previous employers. Make sure all personal contact information is at hand. Talk with people about being references and review all past training and skills.
4.	Create the documents needed for applying—a résumé, reference list, a customizable cover letter, and a portfolio.
5.	Identify the search methods. Examples include the Internet, newspapers, and friends.
6.	Choose the businesses to contact. Create a list of their addresses and contact information.
7.	Research each business chosen. Knowing as much as possible about the business makes for a better prepared interview and shows an eagerness to work for the business.
8.	Contact the businesses chosen in whatever method they've indicated. If applying in person, be sure to dress professionally and be prepared with all application documents.
9.	When a potential employer makes contact, decide on an interview time. Don't be late! Ask questions during the interview to make sure that the job meets all needs.
10.	After sending a résumé or applying, call the business once a week to ask about open positions and the status of an application (if they haven't initiated a follow-up contact). Keep searching.

Preparing a Résumé, Portfolio, and Cover Letter

Potential employees need the right tools for conducting a job search. The tools needed are a résumé, portfolio, and cover letter. Creating these tools makes applicants feel more confident. They present a clear picture of interests, abilities, and talents to a prospective employer.

An Effective Résumé

A key ingredient in a portfolio is the résumé. A **résumé** (RE-zoo-may) is a written summary of experience, skills, and achievements that relate to the job being sought. A résumé is not a life story. It is like a sales brochure that tells an employer why the applicant is the best person to hire for the job. When looking at a résumé, ask, "If I were the employer, would I hire this person?"

739

Table 12.1:
Steps for Searching for a Job

- How can thinking seriously about the first item in Table 12.1 affect all the other steps in the process?

- Why is it important to gather all relevant information before applying for a job?

- What are some good ways to research prospective employers?

- How can potential employees demonstrate professionalism during the entire job search?

Discuss

- A job interview is primarily a sales pitch. Interviewees do their best to demonstrate their skills and abilities, focusing on why they would be a valuable addition to the company. Interviewers evaluate and assess the applicants. How can young applicants sell themselves without appearing egotistical or self-important?

Reinforce and Review

- Creating the right tools for conducting a job search can help a potential employee feel more confident.
- Professional application materials give a clear idea of the applicant's interests, abilities, and talents to the prospective employer.
- A résumé is more like a sales brochure than a life story. Only relevant material should be included.

Vocabulary Terms

- **Résumé:** A written summary of experience, skills, and achievements that relate to the job being sought.

Discuss

- Why is accuracy so important on a résumé? What about truthfulness and clarity? How can a slight exaggeration result in the termination of a job offer, and why?
- How should prospective employees select their references? Who should be chosen, and why? How can prospective employees help their references give the most accurate and helpful information possible to an inquiring employer?
- What did students learn about management perspectives on résumés and other application materials that can help them as they prepare application materials of their own? Students may want to review relevant sections of Chapter 8 before discussing this question.

Vocabulary Terms

- **References:** Unrelated people who know the applicant well and can provide specific information about the applicant's character, work ability/ethic, and academic standing to a potential employer.

A résumé should be short—no more than one page—and contain only the most important information. Include relevant work experience on a résumé. If no work experience has been gained so far, concentrate on the activities that show skills and abilities and how they relate to the job. The following is a sample résumé format:

Name (first name first)

Home street address

City, State, ZIP code

Phone number where you can be reached

Email address

Objective:

Discuss the job for which the résumé is being reviewed. (Customize the objective as necessary for specific positions.)

Qualifications:

List the applicant's skills and capabilities.

Experience:

Demonstrate how these skills and capabilities impacted past jobs, volunteer efforts, or classroom experiences. List all jobs here, beginning with the most recent.

Education:

Include the applicant's high school, college status (i.e., junior, senior), and current courses

List references (on a separate page) or the phrase "References available on request."

Special Skills, Training, or Certifications:

References are unrelated people who know the applicant well and can provide information about that applicant. Specifically, the person's character, work ability/ethic, or academic standing. Some people to consider as references are teachers, previous supervisors, church leaders, and neighbors. It is considerate to ask these people first before using them as job references. Be sure to have their full names, addresses, and phone numbers when applying.

In most cases, emphasize a current job. The other work experience is important as well. As an applicant gains more work experience, he or she can eliminate less important items. An applicant who has recently graduated from high school, would state on the education line:

740

Education:

2008; Diploma, High School, Town, State

Courses:

Pre-Management and Foods

Foundations of Restaurant Management & Culinary Arts Level 1 Certificate of Recognition from the National Restaurant Association

A résumé changes as the applicant gains more experience, training, and education. Like a portfolio, developing a résumé is an ongoing process. No matter how much experience an applicant has, a résumé should be an easy-to-read outline of successes and achievements. Figure 12.3 is a completed sample résumé.

Faith Fitzpatrick
110 West 84th Street
Funtown, USA 50094
Phone: 123-456-7890
E-mail: ffitz@notmail.net

Objective

To work as a part-time server at Uptown Grille

Work Experience:

2009-present, Busperson, Blue Bird Café, Funtown, USA

- Clear tables quickly and set correctly
- **Refill water and other beverages during dinner service**
- Assist servers in serving food, as needed

Related Experience:

- Help serve food at high school café (sponsored by Foodservice Class)
- Organized junior class bake sale
- Developed new recipe for low-fat chocolate chip cookies sold at annual bake sale
- Used computer program to type recipes for class cookbook
- Volunteer kitchen worker at community Thanksgiving dinner

Related Skills and Abilities

- Strong customer service, teamwork, and interpersonal skills
- Ability to use word-processing and spreadsheet programs
- Dedicated to maintaining a clean dining area and adhering to all safety and health guidelines
- Work well with others

Education

- Senior at Funtown High School
- Currently taking food, management, and health and safety procedures classes in Foodservice school-to-career program.

References Available on Request

Figure 12.3: A sample résumé.

Essential Skills

Successful Résumé

A résumé is a selling tool. It's a chance to sell the applicant in short, powerful statements. Potential employers decide after reading the first few lines whether they will call the applicant in for an interview. How can applicants increase their chances at getting an interview? Use these basic tips to create a successful résumé:

■ Include all important information such as name, address, telephone number, and email address in case the résumé gets separated from the cover letter.

741

Discuss

- What particular skills might a restaurant employer look for when examining résumés and other application materials?
- What makes a résumé stand out? Should an applicant use graphics, uncommon papers, or other elements to attract attention, or is the applicant's experience enough to catch the employer's eye?

Reinforce and Review

- A résumé changes as the applicant gains more experience, education, and training. It is a living document that develops as the applicant develops.
- Résumés should always be straightforward, clear outlines of the applicant's accomplishments.

**Essential Skills:
Successful Résumé**

Encourage students to discuss the following:

- How can writing a clear and professional résumé impress a potential employer, even when the applicant has little experience that is relevant for the job?

- In what ways can a poorly designed résumé work against a job applicant?

- Explain the difference between active and passive language.

Figure Focus

Figure 12.3: How does a résumé reflect the applicant's background and aspirations?

What's New: Video Résumés and Blogs

Encourage students to discuss the following:

- What can submitting a video résumé to a prospective employer demonstrate about the applicant? How can it increase or decrease one's chances of getting an interview?

- Why is it important to follow basic communication rules when creating a video résumé or writing a blog? For instance, should the traditional format of "Introduction—Body—Conclusion" be maintained?

Homework Activity: Virtually Real

Literacy Connection, 21st-Century Skills—Apply Technology Effectively, Create Media Products, Communicate Clearly

Write a brief statement about yourself, describing your accomplishments and achievements and noting any particular skills or experiences. Be sure to include your name, address, and other contact information. When read aloud, this statement should be between two and three minutes in length.

Now use this script to create a video résumé, using tools available at your school's media center or local library. Dress and behave professionally so that this résumé can be a useful part of your application materials.

The class should watch each video résumé, offering constructive criticism where necessary and always focusing on how to improve the product.

Successful Résumé (continued)

- Use active language.
- Avoid using buzzwords or jargon.
- Show off accomplishments. Employers want to know what the applicant has accomplished, not what his or her responsibilities or duties were. If possible, quantify achievements with percents or dollars. Put work experience first unless just entering the job market; then showcase education first. List degrees, GPA, honors, scholarships, and accomplishments.
- Include professional references that speak about accomplishments. Grab the employer's attention!
- Leave white space and use headings and section breaks. Visual layout is important. If it looks unprofessional or cluttered, a résumé will not impress the employer.
- Keep the length of a résumé to one to two pages. The employer needs just enough information about accomplishments to make a decision about an interview.
- Edit and proofread any résumé or cover letter before sending it out.

[what's new]

Video Résumés and Blogs

The use of video résumés is an emerging trend. It's a new technique that allows a potential employer to see applicants—how they present themselves, speak, and dress. Think of video résumés as an online commercial and personal marketing tool.

Make video résumés 1 to 3 minutes in length and capture and keep the viewer's attention. This is enough time for the hiring manager to get to know applicants and to decide who will be called in for an interview. The following are some tips to creating successful video résumés:

- Make sure the audio and video quality is clean and clear.
- Dress appropriately.
- Make the background professional, not distracting.
- Speak clearly. Edit out any mistakes.
- Cover the basics: introduction, objectives, professional experience, accomplishments and skills, education, and closing summary. State why the applicant would be a good employee and what he or she can bring to the business.
- Practice several times before recording.

In today's more visual environment, job applicants need to set themselves apart from all other job seekers. So, multimedia résumés are becoming more popular. Include photographs, samples of work, videos, or even a personal Web site. Remember, résumés are tools for selling an applicant to prospective employers, so be sure to showcase skills, interest, experience, and passion for the job.

742

A Successful Portfolio

A portfolio is a collection of samples that showcase interests, talents, contributions, and studies. A portfolio displays an applicant's finest efforts and is a good self-marketing tool to show potential employers.

Make sure that portfolios are complete, neat, and well-organized. Include a cover page that gives the following:

- Full name, address, phone number
- Career objectives
- A brief description of the contents

Select samples that highlight the applicant's best talents. Each sample should be accompanied by a brief explanation of why it is important. Type information whenever possible. Include clean photocopies of letters and other important documents or certificates.

A portfolio is best displayed in a three-ring binder or folder. It's a good idea to use three-ring clear plastic sleeves to hold samples. A portfolio should be about 10 pages in length and easy to carry to interviews. A portfolio that is sloppy, too long, or too big does not make a good impression.

Start collecting materials for a portfolio while still in school. Creating a complete and accurate portfolio is an ongoing process. Think about what would impress potential employers. Ask friends and family for advice. The following is a list of items a portfolio may include:

- A list and samples of skills and abilities (such as the list of competencies learned at worksites)
- Samples of work (for example, if you decorated a cake that you're especially proud of, take a picture of it and include it as a sample; or describe how you decorated it or what inspired you)
- Examples of problems solved (at school, in the community, with friends)
- Examples demonstrating teamwork
- Examples showing leadership and responsibility
- Important experiences and what was learned from them
- Certificates of recognition and reward (the certificate received upon successful completion of this program and a high school diploma are two examples)
- Newsletters or announcements (with name or group highlighted)
- Essays, reports, and papers (those with high grades or positive teacher remarks)
- Letters of thanks

743

Discuss

- How can a portfolio provide a more nuanced portrait of a job applicant? Will a busy foodservice employer take the time to examine a portfolio as it deserves? How can portfolios be used most effectively?
- How can a high-quality portfolio help an applicant's chances of getting a job? How can a poor-quality portfolio injure an applicant?

Reinforce and Review

- A portfolio displays an applicant's finest efforts and is a good self-marketing tool.
- Materials included in a portfolio should highlight the applicant's best talents.
- Like a résumé, a portfolio is a living document that should be updated regularly as an individual grows professionally.
- When assembling a portfolio, consider the manager's perspective when determining what to include and what to omit.

Homework Activity: Showcasing Skills

Literacy Connection, 21st-Century Skills— Critical Thinking and Problem Solving, Initiative and Self-Direction, Communicate Clearly

Many employers, especially in the restaurant and foodservice industry, will ask job applicants to spend a day working in their facilities. This is commonly called a stage or trail. This allows an employer to observe the applicant's skill level as well as his or her interpersonal skills, which can help the employer decide whether the applicant would be a good member of the team.

Select an employer for whom you would like to work. Prepare a formal request to spend some time working in his or her establishment so that you can learn more about the workplace and so the employer, in turn, can learn more about you and your skills. This request can be part of your cover letter and should accompany your résumé. Be clear as to why you would like to work for this particular business.

Bring this letter to class and exchange it with another student for proofreading. You do not actually have to send the letter to the employer if you do not want to, but your letter should be professional enough that you could send it with high hopes of a response.

Vocabulary Terms

- **Portfolio:** A collection of samples that showcase interests, talents, contributions, and studies.

Discuss

- How can an effective cover letter or cover message affect an applicant's chances of getting a job?
- What did students learn about the management perspective on cover letters and other application materials that can help them as they prepare application materials of their own?
- Students may want to review relevant sections of Chapter 8 before discussing this question. How do cover letters and cover messages act as the first impressions that an employer has of a job candidate?

Reinforce and Review

- Electronic portfolios can successfully showcase a collection of work.
- Both a cover letter and a cover message highlight an applicant's strengths and confirm his or her interest in the available position.
- Cover letters should be clear and straightforward. Check spelling and grammar, and double-check the company's contact information.

Trends:
1.8 Million Jobs

Encourage students to discuss the following:

- In what capacities might most of these new employees be working? What types of jobs seem like the biggest growth areas?

- In what type of environment might most of these new employees be working? For instance, will they be working as researchers in test kitchens, as line cooks in hospitals, or as banquet servers in hotels?

- What impact might this change have on society, since an already large industry will become even larger?

In-Class Activity:
Foodservice by the Numbers

Mathematics Connection, Literacy Connection, 21st-Century Skills—Access and Evaluate Information, Reason Effectively, Work Independently

If the restaurant and foodservice industry is projected to add 1.8 million jobs during the current decade, reaching 14.8 million total jobs in 2019, how many jobs did the industry have in 2009? [13 million] What percentage increase is this? [13.8%] What is the average increase in jobs per year? [180,000]

Vocabulary Terms

- **Cover letter:** A brief letter in which an applicant introduces herself or himself to an employer.

- Résumé
- Audio or videotapes that display abilities
- Test scores
- Original recipes
- Letters of recommendation from past employers or groups. (These can be from the sponsors of a charity walk-a-thon in which you participated, or a school event, for example.)

Electronic portfolios are another great way to showcase a collection of work. Electronic portfolios can be stored on hard drives, DVDs, CDs, or uploaded to a Web site. They provide a lot of information and require minimal effort to access. To enhance an electronic portfolio, add music and graphics to make it more appealing.

[trends]

1.8 Million Jobs

The restaurant and foodservice industry is expected to add 1.8 million jobs over the next decade, with employment reaching 14.8 million by 2019.

Source: National Restaurant Association

An Eye-Catching Cover Letter

When sending a résumé to a potential employer, send a cover letter along with it. A **cover letter** is a brief letter in which an applicant introduces herself to an employer. Nowadays, more résumés are being delivered electronically. A cover letter can also mean a cover message. Both a cover letter and a cover message highlight strengths and confirm an applicant's interest in the position being offered. In a cover message, an applicant can explain her qualifications with a more personal touch. Figure 12.4 is an example of a good cover message.

Keep the cover message brief, to the point, and straightforward. Use a word processor and utilize correct grammar and punctuation. Make sure the company name, address, and person's name are all correct. Use the spelling and grammar check functions in the word processing program to ensure a quality product. Always proofread messages carefully before sending them. If possible, have someone else also proofread the cover message before doing the final version. Remember, first impressions are critical. Many employers who see a sloppy cover letter will get the feeling that an applicant's work might be sloppy, too. The following are tips for writing a cover message:

744

- **Attention:** Grab a reader's attention in the first paragraph to make sure the person continues reading. State the reason for writing the letter.

- **Interest:** Hold the reader's interest by mentioning the source of his or her name as a contact or how the job opening or company became of interest.

- **Desire:** Tell the reader what you want to do for his or her company. List qualifications and the reasons for the application.

- **Action:** End the letter by mentioning meeting in an interview.

Ms. Linda Brown
Manager
Uptown Grille
75 East Pleasant Street
Funtown, USA 50094

January 5, 2011

Dear Ms. Brown:

I am applying for the position of part-time server with the Uptown Grille that I read about in Sunday's *Anytown Daily*. This position offers a great opportunity for me to continue my career in foodservice. I am a senior at Anytown High School, where I'm enrolled in a new program that combines food preparation classes with health and safety procedures as well as business management courses. Currently, I work as a busperson at the Blue Bird Café, so I have learned some of the basics of customer service and have received food safety training.

For your review, I am enclosing a copy of my resumé that shows my qualifications. I am hard working, dependable, and honest, with a pleasant disposition and outgoing personality. My references can testify to these characteristics.

I am sure that once you have had a chance to review my resumé and meet with me, you will agree that my enthusiasm and willingness to learn will help me become an ideal server at Uptown Grille. You can reach me Monday through Friday after 3:30 p.m. or at any time on Saturday and Sunday at 123-456-7890.

I look forward to hearing from you at your earliest convenience. Thank you for your consideration.

Sincerely,

Faith Fitzpatrick
110 West 84th Street
Funtown, USA 50094
Phone: 123-456-7890
Email: ffitz@notmail.net

Figure 12.4: A sample cover message.

745

Discuss

- How do the four key tips for writing cover messages relate to the traditional model of communicating, which includes an introduction, body, and conclusion?

Reinforce and Review

- The four key tips for writing a cover message are attention, interest, desire, and action.

Teaching Tips

- The process of applying for a job is similar to the process of hiring a new employee, but there are clear differences.

Figure Focus

Figure 12.4: Does this document follow the four key tips for writing a cover message? Why or why not?

On the Job: Culinary School Career Counselor

Encourage students to discuss the following:

- Why might the number of jobs in this field be projected to grow?

- How does a career as a culinary school career counselor relate to the topic of reaching back, raised by Ron Yudd in the Professional Profile?

- Why might employees in this field have so many skills? What other attributes might be important to have?

Discuss

- In what ways has the material covered in Chapters 4, 7, and 8 helped you understand this material better?
- How is the material in this section relevant no matter what career a person may seek?

[on the job]

Culinary School Career Counselor

Ever think about a career in helping other people find careers? If so, consider a future as a culinary school career counselor. These professionals work at culinary schools. The industry is growing, and the need for culinary school career counselors to help students identify future career paths is growing, too. Working as a chef or as a restaurant manager is great, but a huge variety of other foodservice careers are out there. Some possible areas include food writing, culinary technology, and even niche farming.

Career counselors provide a number of resources to aspiring culinary students. They review résumés, identify possible career opportunities for students to research, and assign "homework" to help students identify their own strengths, weaknesses, desires, and motivations. Counselors usually have access to a large array of potential employers. They can provide recommendations for their students long after the student has graduated. Often, the school will host career fairs, which the counselors coordinate, screening potential employers and welcoming returning companies. In general, career counselors help their student-clients develop their job-search skills and pursue successful careers in the restaurant and foodservice industry.

Culinary school career counselors typically have bachelor's degrees and usually have worked in the restaurant and foodservice industry. Often, they also hold a master's degree and have received state licenses and professional certifications, such as Certified Hospitality Educator. Career counselors must have excellent communication skills and be good listeners, with the ability to inspire trust. Multitasking is critical. Students are often working to meet strict deadlines, so counselors must be highly flexible and extremely organized. To learn more, contact the American Counseling Association or the National Board for Certified Counselors.

Summary

In this section, you learned the following:

- Restaurant and foodservice professionals must have the ability to do the following things:
  - Communicate effectively with a team
  - Maintain a positive attitude
  - Have a willingness to learn
  - Learn new technology and new ways to do things
  - Perform math functions
  - Analyze and problem solve
  - Know how to use basic tools and equipment to work in a kitchen
  - Know how and why to keep food safe
  - Know details about menu items

746

- An effective job plan includes deciding what characteristics you want your job to have, figuring out where you can compromise, gathering and organizing information you need for applying, creating the documents you need for applying, identifying the search methods you want to use, choosing the business you want to contact, contacting the business you have chosen, setting an interview time, calling the business if you have not heard a response after sending your résumé.

- A résumé should be short and contain only the most important information such as your objective, qualifications, experience, education, special skills, training or certification, and references.

- A cover letter should grab the reader's attention, hold the interest of the reader, tell the reader why you want to work for that company, and end by saying that you look forward to a meeting for an interview.

- A portfolio is a collection of samples that highlight your interests, talents, contributions, and studies.

747

Summary

- Remind students to review the following:
  1. The skills needed by restaurant and foodservice professionals
  2. Effective job search plans
  3. Writing a résumé that lists your experiences, skills, and achievements
  4. Preparing an effective cover letter
  5. Use of portfolios

Section 12.1 Review Questions

1. Having a mentor can provide a wise counselor and a source of professional insight, both into the company and into the profession itself. This person can assist with professional development and guidance throughout one's career.

2. The purpose of a résumé is to sell the job applicant, explaining to the employer why this candidate is the ideal person to fill the vacant position.

3. Items that can be part of a portfolio include a list and samples of skills and abilities; samples of work; examples of problems solved; examples demonstrating teamwork; examples showing leadership and responsibility; important experiences and what was learned from them; certificates of recognition and reward; newsletters or announcements; essays, reports, and papers; letters of thanks; audio or videotapes that display abilities; test scores; original recipes; and letters of recommendation from past employers or groups.

4. The elements of a cover letter are attracting the reader's attentions, holding the reader's interest, demonstrating the applicant's desire, and calling the reader to action.

5. Students may answer this question in a variety of ways.

6. Sam can discuss his background as a kitchen manager, highlighting the skills or abilities used in that position that a field distributor should have.

7. Employers may pass over certain résumés because they are poorly organized, too long, poorly spelled or written, or omit important information. Also, even a well-written résumé can be lost in the shuffle, especially if the employer is overwhelmed with applications.

8. Students should refer to relevant information throughout the textbook, especially the material in Chapters 4, 7, and 12.

Section 12.1 Review Questions

1. Why is it important to have a mentor?

2. What is the purpose of a résumé?

3. List six items that can be part of your portfolio.

4. What are the elements of a cover letter?

5. Ron Yudd says that you should "never forget the importance of passion. Love what you are doing. Others will see your passion and want to hire you..." Assume you are applying for a job. What types of media would you use to promote yourself and why? How can you show prospective employers your passion for this work?

6. Sam, who has been a kitchen manager, hopes to find a new position as a field distributor. How should he address this change in his cover letter?

7. For what reasons might a potential employer pass over certain résumés?

8. What specific skills do you think apply to all restaurant and foodservice positions, whether they are front or back of house?

Section 12.1 Activities

1. Study Skills/Group Activity: Create Your Résumé

Create your own résumé. Work with two other students and critique one another's résumés based on the information given in this section.

2. Activity: Cover Letter

You are applying for an entry-level buser position at a popular local restaurant. Write a cover letter to accompany your application.

3. Critical Thinking: Creating Your Portfolio

Collect materials for your portfolio. What elements are missing? How should the information be arrayed? How do you think a prospective employer would respond to your portfolio? How could you make your portfolio more appealing?

749

Section 12.1 Activities

1. Students should use the sample résumé on p. 741 as a template for creating their own résumés.

2. Students should use the sample cover letter on p. 745 as a template for creating their own cover letters.

3. Students should assemble all relevant materials for their portfolios, using the list on pp. 743–744 as a guide. They should look at these documents from an employer's perspective. How would a potential employer view this portfolio?

Section 12.2
Completing Applications Effectively

Introduce the Section

a. Explain why it is important to complete applications thoroughly and accurately.
b. Identify resources that are available to help interested students select and pursue higher education.
c. Discuss the objectives for the section.

Vocabulary Review

a. Direct students to the key terms.
b. Pronounce each word, and have the students repeat the pronunciation out loud.
c. Discuss the definition of each word.

Teach

Discuss

- What essential skills are involved in correctly completing an application for a job, a school, or a scholarship? How can these skills relate to positions in the foodservice industry?
- What can an applicant learn about his or her potential employers just from reading the application form?
- How has your understanding of employment application forms changed since reading Chapter 8, Section 8.3, which discussed how to create an application form?

Reinforce and Review

- Learning to complete an application form properly is an important step in obtaining jobs and attending school.
- Successfully completing a job application indicates to the employer that the applicant can follow directions and communicate clearly.

Vocabulary Terms

- **Job application:** A standardized document that requests information about a candidate's educational and professional history, revealing important insights to an employer.

12.1 Starting a Career in Foodservice	12.2 Completing Applications Effectively	12.3 The Job Interview	12.4 Advancing in a Career	12.5 Careers in the Industry
• Skills needed for a successful career • The job search • Preparing a résumé, portfolio, and cover letter	• Job applications • College applications • Scholarships	• Preparing for the job interview • The interview • Interview questions and answers • Follow up after the interview	• Health and wellness • Stress and time management • Resigning from a job • Staying educated and involved	• Entry-level jobs • A selection of careers

SECTION 12.2 COMPLETING APPLICATIONS EFFECTIVELY

Whether applying to a college, trade school, or job, a potential employee has to complete an application form. Application forms ask basic personal information about the applicant and his or her background. Learning how to effectively complete applications will serve all applicants in both higher education and the professional world.

Study Questions

After studying Section 12.2, you should be able to answer the following questions:

- What is a job application form?
- What are the steps to choosing a college or trade school?
- What resources are available to help you choose a college or trade school?
- What is a scholarship application form?
- How can you apply for a scholarship?

Job Applications

The **job application** is important because it gives general information, and it reveals some insights about an applicant to the employer. It shows how well you—the applicant—can follow instructions, your ability to communicate, and

750

---

your employment history. Treat the application seriously and take time to fill it out carefully and completely. It is illegal for a job application to ask about marital status, height, weight, age, handicaps, race or national origin, religion, or political information. The job application form usually asks you to state your work experience and list references.

When filling out the job application, be sure to write or print clearly. It is always good practice to bring a pen when applying. Blue or black ink pens are best. Use correct grammar and punctuation and organize thoughts before writing them on the form. If responses on an application are unclear or messy, you will not make a good impression on the interviewer. Remember, if completing an application online, grammar, spelling, punctuation, and organization are equally important.

If there is something on the form that you don't understand, you should leave the space blank or write "please see me" in the space. Write "n/a" if a question is **"not applicable"** (doesn't apply). Later, you can ask the person who handed you the application to explain any questions, or you can discuss them with the interviewer.

When answering questions about money on the application, write "Open." Learn about the job before making any decisions about the salary. You might be asked to state how much money you earned on previous jobs. Be honest. Don't exaggerate.

Even if you have no work experience, you still may have qualities and skills that are needed in the workplace. List any volunteer work, baby-sitting jobs, or school or church activities that show experience, such as contributing efforts to projects.

Applicants are asked to sign their name on the application form to state that they have answered all questions and given information that is true and accurate to the best of their knowledge. An online application will also require some sort of acknowledgment. Being dishonest on a job application can be a reason for immediate termination (firing). Employers do check on educational and work background, as well as contact references.

All job applications are basically the same, so once you have completed one form, you will know what to expect on others. Table 12.2 lists some terms that are commonly found on job application forms.

751

Discuss

- What information and other materials should an applicant gather before completing an application form?
- How is it possible to impress a potential employer when completing a standardized form? Are there legitimate ways to make an application form stand out?

Reinforce and Review

- Using proper grammar, spelling, and punctuation are essential to completing an application successfully.
- Never exaggerate your background, experience, or salary history when completing an application form. This can be cause for rejection or even termination after the hire.
- Employers commonly check references and backgrounds to confirm that the applicants have told the truth.

Vocabulary Terms

- **"Not applicable":** Refers to information that does not apply to an applicant.

Table 12.2: Words Commonly Found on Job Applications

- Why are these particular words or terms used so frequently on application forms? What else do they have in common?
- What other words are often found on application forms? How are they used?

Discuss

- How do applications to enter a school differ from applications for a job? How are they similar?
- What do admissions departments hope to learn about an applicant from reading an essay?

Reinforce and Review

- College and trade school applications typically ask more personal questions than might a job application, including specific information about academic performance, and they often require one or more essays.

Vocabulary Terms

- **College/trade school application:** A standardized document completed by those wishing to attend a particular academic institution.

Table 12.2: Words Commonly Found on Job Applications

Word	Meaning
Employment	Work; a job
Personal information	Facts about self
Social Security number	Numbers assigned by the government to all people who apply; everyone who wants to work is required to have a Social Security number
Related	From the same family
Employment desired	The kind of job wanted
Position	Job; area an applicant wants to work in
Salary desired	Wage or salary the applicant will accept to do a job
Inquire	Ask
Education	School experience
Location	Where something is
Permanent address	The location of applicant's permanent home
Date graduated	The day, month, and year the applicant finished school; if still in school, the applicant can write an expected graduation date
Activities	Things an applicant does, especially for relaxation or fun
Former employers	People for whom the applicant used to work
References	People who know the applicant and will tell an employer about the applicant
Business	The kind of work a person does
Years acquainted	How long the applicant has known a particular person
Physical conditions	State of health or fitness
Injured	Hurt
Detail	A small item or piece of information
Emergency	An unexpected situation calling for fast action
Notify	To inform

College Applications

In addition to asking for name and address, **college** or **trade school applications** require education information. The application may also require that applicants state the program or course of study they are applying for and ask

752

them to complete a short essay. When writing the essay, remember that the person reviewing the application is looking for signs that you will be successful. If the essay is open-ended, write about successes and future goals. Ask parents or a teacher to review draft essays. It is always a good idea to have an essay proofread by someone who is particularly strong in grammar and composition.

[fast fact]

Did You Know...?

Many schools accept online applications that require the same type of information as traditional applications. In addition, the Common Application has become acceptable at many colleges. This is a common, standardized first-year application form for use at any member institution. Both online and print versions of its first-year and transfer applications exist and are suitable for submission to nearly 400 institutions across the country.

Source: www.commonapp.org

You will also be asked to have high school transcripts sent to the college. The admissions office at the school will look at the application and transcript to see the courses you took and your grade point average. This information helps determine whether or not you will be accepted into the program.

It is *not* illegal for college applications to ask about race, national origin, or birth date. However, you may choose not to answer these questions. Schools use this information to gather statistics about their student population and make decisions about incoming classes.

It's important to remember that the process of completing college applications has stages with strict deadlines. Applications and essays must be delivered to schools within a specified time frame. Essays take time to write. Also be aware of the time it will take for a school district to provide grades to application schools. Certain school districts have longer return times after transcripts have been requested. Keep track of deadlines and make sure there's enough time to provide all the necessary documents.

Most careers in the restaurant and foodservice industry require at least a high school diploma or the equivalent. Admission to a college or trade school also requires a high school diploma. No matter what careers are of interest, completing high school and continuing education are the first steps to a successful future.

Although not all restaurant and foodservice careers require a college education, many do. For instance, to become a professional certified chef, dietitian, nutritionist, food stylist or food scientist, marketer, home economist, manager of

753

Discuss

- Does a student's academic performance in high school always predict his or her performance in college? What other factors might be involved?
- If a student lacks high grades, why should a college, university, or trade school take a chance on accepting him or her? How can the student convince the school that he or she will do well in this new environment?
- What are some ways in which college and trade school applicants can impress an admissions department?

Reinforce and Review

- Always have someone else review an application essay. Admissions staff look for signs of current and future academic success, so misspellings and grammatical errors can be detrimental.
- Colleges may ask a number of questions forbidden to employers, such as those involving race and ethnicity. However, the applicant is not obliged to answer them.
- Virtually all colleges and universities have strict deadlines for admissions applications, so organization is critical.
- An increasing number of foodservice positions require diplomas or degrees from trade schools, colleges, or universities.

**Fast Fact:
Did You Know...?**

Encourage students do discuss the following:

- Why might using an online application process help admissions staff work more efficiently?
- What are some positive and negative aspects of using the Common Application?

**Homework Activity:
College Applications**

Literacy Connection, 21st-Century Skills—Access and Evaluate Information, Reason Effectively, Work Independently

Obtain application forms from three colleges, universities, or trade schools. Do not use the Common Application.

What elements do each of these forms have in common? How are they different?

How are these forms similar to or different from job application forms?

Describe your findings in a one-page paper, attaching each of the three application forms.

Discuss

- How is each of the questions listed on p. 754 relevant to determining which college or trade school to attend? How do you know if a school is right for you?
- What resources are available to help you answer these questions? Where can they be obtained?

Reinforce and Review

- Most people change their careers multiple times. What you major in may not bear much relation to your ultimate career.
- Apply for as much financial aid, especially in the form of grants, work-study, or scholarships, as necessary. Federal or private loans are also available, but these must be paid back with interest.
- Research desirable schools as thoroughly as possible before applying to determine whether the institution can meet your needs. Ask as many questions as you think necessary until you feel comfortable.

Teaching Tips

- Invite the school guidance or career counselor to discuss available resources.

a restaurant or property, or accountant, you will most likely need to complete additional classes and training.

Consider the following questions when deciding which college or trade school to attend:

- Does the school have a program in your chosen field that fits your needs? Does it offer the certification, associate's degree, or bachelor's degree in which you are interested?

- Is the institution regionally accredited? This will allow the credits you earn to be transferred to other regionally accredited institutions.

- If class times or schedules conflict with your other priorities, find out whether the school offers evening classes or correspondence classes through video, satellite, or Internet broadcasts.

- What are the entrance requirements? Several schools place just as much emphasis on motivation and interest in succeeding as they do on grades and test scores.

- What are the fees for applying?

- What are the application deadlines?

- Where is the school? Can you live at home or must you live on campus? Will you need your own car? If the school's main location is not convenient for you, remember that many colleges offer classes in several locations. If you are interested in visiting campuses, colleges offer tours for prospective students and their families.

- How much does it cost? What kind of financial aid is available? Are scholarships available for which you would qualify? Many colleges have private and federally funded financial-aid programs, including grants, loans, scholarships, and work-study programs. Be sure to ask about them.

- What is the reputation of the program? The reputation of the program determines the value of the degree in seeking employment.

- What is the success rate of the graduates of the school? Does the school assist former students in their job searches? Several schools actually have their own placement offices that help link graduates directly with employment opportunities.

- What other activities are available at the school? What kinds of clubs and organizations are available for you to explore your interests and develop skills? Participation in college organizations can also contribute to an impressive résumé.

754

To find the answers to these questions, begin with a high school guidance office or local library. Don't be afraid to make some phone calls. Find college application and financial aid information, as well as phone numbers, on the Internet. Finally, visit the narrowed list of colleges and universities if possible. See what they have to offer in person.

[fast fact]

Did You Know...?
Do you like researching online? Want help in learning how to tackle going to college or trade school? Try:

www.knowhow2go.org

or

www.whatsnext4me.com

Scholarships

A **scholarship** is a grant or financial aid award to a student for the purpose of attending college. A large number of available **scholarships** aren't awarded each year because no one applies. The first step in being awarded a scholarship is applying. Applicants who meet the base criteria for the scholarship should apply and let the awarding organization make the decision. They should not assume that they will not get a scholarship. Only by not applying do students guarantee that they won't get any scholarships.

To find scholarships, try the following:

- Contact the financial aid office of the school to find out what types of scholarships the school offers and how to apply for them.

- Search the Internet. Some Web sites collect and organize scholarship information. Narrow the search based on potential majors, but don't overlook scholarships that might be available to all students. Also consider searching for scholarships based on ethnicity or disability.

- Talk with a guidance counselor. Share findings and ask about any local scholarships that might be available.

Scholarship applications are similar to college applications in that they always have deadlines. Some also require applicants to answer questions or submit an essay. Add these due dates to the continuing list of application deadlines.

Some states and schools also have **financial aid** to offer students. This includes grants, educational loans, and **work study** (working as a student for the school). To qualify for financial aid at any school that receives federal funds (almost all

755

Vocabulary Terms

- **Scholarship:** A grant or financial aid awarded to a student for the purpose of attending college. These need not be repaid.
- **Financial aid:** A blanket term used to describe federal or private grants, loans, work-study programs, or other financial awards to a student for the purpose of attending college. Loans must be repaid with interest, although grants and work-study monies need not.
- **Work-study program:** A program that pays needy students to perform work on school grounds and on school affairs.

Reinforce and Review

- Visiting a college or trade school that appeals to you, if possible, is an excellent way to see first-hand how the institution might help you achieve your goals.
- All students who meet the base criteria for a scholarship should apply for it. Each year millions of dollars in scholarship monies are not awarded.
- Scholarship-granting organizations have very specific guidelines and deadlines, so organization is critical.

Homework Activity: Scholarship Options

Literacy Connection, 21st-Century Skills—Access and Evaluate Information, Reason Effectively, Communicate Clearly

Special Needs Students

Do you plan to attend a postsecondary school? What colleges, universities, or trade schools interest you, and why? What do you plan to study?

Identify a scholarship, either one tied to a specific school or one that can be used anywhere, for which you are qualified. Obtain and complete the application form as practice either for actual college applications or for employment applications.

ESOL Students

In addition to the above activity, students should give a brief presentation on the school of their choice.

Less Advanced Students

In addition to the above activity, students should write a brief essay on the school of their choice.

More Advanced Students

In addition to the above activity, students should research the organization that grants the scholarship. How much money does it award annually, and how much does it have in reserve? What is the source of its money? How long has it been in operation?

Give a brief presentation on the scholarship organization to the class.

Discuss

- Is accepting a student loan a burden or an investment opportunity? Why might someone choose to decline an offer of financial aid?

Reinforce and Review

- In most cases, students should apply for financial aid, whether or not they think they will qualify.
- Grants do not need to be repaid, whereas loans do.

Trends:
Financial Aid

Encourage students to discuss the following:

- How much education can a student get for $9,100? That is, does the average amount of financial aid given cover a year of college tuition, books, and fees?

- How much is too much to pay for a postsecondary education? Are inexpensive schools as educationally rewarding as their more prestigious colleagues?

Fast Fact:
Did You Know...?

Encourage students to discuss the following:

- How does the NRAEF contribute to leadership in the foodservice industry?

- What might judges look for when choosing award recipients?

CUSTOMIZED INSTRUCTION

Mathematics Connection, Literacy Connection, 21st-Century Skills—Access and Evaluate Information, Analyze Media, Work Independently

Less Advanced Students

The federal government, as well as many states, awards grants to students seeking higher education. These grants do not have to be repaid, unlike loans. Other grants are also available and may be based on a wide variety of factors.

Select one agency that awards grants and write a brief essay on it. Be sure to address how grants are awarded, how many types of grants are available, how many total grants are given each year, and the average amount of money given in each grant.

Vocabulary Terms

- **Free Application for Federal Student Aid (FAFSA):** An application form used by the federal government to determine the total amount of financial aid for which a student qualifies.

---

of them), the student and the student's parents will need to complete the **Free Application for Federal Student Aid (FAFSA).** Get information about the FAFSA and the deadlines for submission at www.fafsa.ed.gov. This application is used by the federal government to determine the total amount of financial aid for which an applicant qualifies. In most cases, students should automatically apply for financial aid and let the school determine whether they qualify. Remember that educational loans do have to be repaid, so students should minimize borrowing if possible.

Most people need help to pay for tuition and other expenses at colleges, trade schools, and community colleges. The Free Application for Federal Student Aid, or FAFSA, is a government form students and their parents can complete and submit to obtain federal grants or student loans at low interest rates. Grants do not need to be repaid; loans, however, must be repaid over a period of time after graduation.

[trends]

Financial Aid
In 2008–2009, 66 percent of undergraduates received some type of financial aid. The amount of aid given averaged $9,100.

Source: U.S. Department of Education, National Center for Education Statistics

[fast fact]

Did You Know...?
The National Restaurant Association Educational Foundation (NRAEF) is the leading scholarship provider for the restaurant and foodservice industry. The organization's goal is to award scholarships to motivated individuals who are committed to furthering their education and succeeding in careers in the restaurant and foodservice industry.

Scholarships are available to first-time and continuing undergraduate students who want an education and a career in the restaurant and foodservice industry. Interested students must complete an application packet, which is then evaluated by judges from across the industry. The scholarships are awarded based on merit.

For more information and to apply for an NRAEF scholarship, visit www.nraef.org.

756

CUSTOMIZED INSTRUCTION

Literacy Connection, 21st-Century Skills—Access and Evaluate Information, Communicate Clearly, Work Independently

More Advanced Students

Research three scholarships given by three distinct agencies. You may not include the scholarship you researched as part of the Scholarship Options activity on p. 755. The scholarships should be foodservice related. What are the criteria for the awards? How much is awarded annually? How many recipients are there each year, and how many have received the awards over the organization's history?

Present a brief report to the class, highlighting the main facts for each organization and including any other relevant information you choose.

Many colleges that offer foodservice-related degrees provide information to their students about unaffiliated scholarship opportunities.

Essential Skills
Completing a FAFSA

All students should complete the FAFSA even if they think they are not eligible for assistance. Here are some tips on completing and submitting the form, which is available both in hard copy and online.

❶ Gather the necessary documents. These usually include parents' most recent tax returns, as well as the student's (if employed), plus driver's license, Social Security number, and statements from any bank accounts. Other documents may be necessary, depending on personal circumstances; check the U.S. government's Web site for details.

❷ Complete the application as early in the year as possible. The FAFSA can be submitted at any time throughout the year, but January is when new funds become available for grants and loans. The earlier a student applies, the greater the chance of obtaining money. Moreover, state or school deadlines may exist for submitting a FAFSA; be sure to look into this.

❸ Students should know what schools they would like to attend, when they expect to start classes, and, possibly, what degrees they plan to pursue. Copies of the Student Aid Report will be sent to these schools (and to the student) when available.

❹ Be sure to fill out the FAFSA correctly. For questions, talk with the school's guidance counselor. Intentionally providing incorrect information can result in fines or even prison.

Don't forget to look for scholarships and grants. Thousands are available each year, and unlike loans, they don't need to be repaid. Work-study positions on campus are also available: these jobs pay students directly, so they have cash for textbooks or even the occasional movie night with friends.

Summary

In this section, you learned the following:

- A job application form gives general information, and it reveals some insights about you to the employer. When completing a job application form, write or print clearly, use correct grammar and punctuation, and organize your thoughts.

- College and trade school applications require education information. Consider the following questions before choosing a college or trade school:

  - Does the school have a program in your chosen field?

  - Is the institution regionally accredited?

  - Does the school offer evening or correspondence classes?

Essential Skills: Completing a FAFSA

Encourage students to discuss the following:

- How is the FAFSA similar to any other application form? How is it different?

- How can the FAFSA encourage college attendance?

- Why must loans be repaid, as opposed to other forms of financial aid?

Homework Activity: Really Completing a FAFSA

Mathematics Connection, Literacy Connection, 21st-Century Skills—Critical Thinking and Problem Solving, Access and Evaluate Information, Use and Manage Information

Obtain and complete a copy of the Free Application for Federal Student Aid (FAFSA), either online or in print form. You should not submit this form unless you are actually planning to apply for financial aid for the upcoming school year.

How long did this process take you? What types of information did the form include? What documents did you need to obtain from family members? Did any questions seem inappropriate or intrusive? What changes in the form would you suggest? What was your overall impression of the FAFSA?

Answer these questions in a one-page essay.

Do not submit the completed FAFSA to your instructor, and do not include any financial or otherwise sensitive material in your essay.

Summary

- Remind students to review the following:
    1. The job application form
    2. Choosing a college or trade school
    3. Resources available to help students choose a college or trade school
    4. Scholarship application forms
    5. Applying for a scholarship

- What are the entrance requirements?

- What are the fees for applying?

- What are the application deadlines?

- Where is the school?

- How much does the school cost?

- What is the reputation of the program?

- What is the success rate of the graduates of the school?

- What other activities are available at the school?

■ Consult with your high school guidance office or library before choosing a college or trade school. Visit the schools that you are interested in to see what they have to offer in person.

■ Scholarship application forms are similar to college applications. They have deadlines and ask for personal information about you and your financial situation.

■ Contact the financial aid office of the school you are interested in to find out what types of scholarships the school offers and how to apply for them. Search the Internet for scholarship opportunities. Talk with your guidance counselor and ask about local scholarship opportunities.

758

Section 12.2 Review Questions

1. What information do you need to complete a job application form?

2. List the steps you should take when applying to a college or trade school.

3. List three ways to find out about scholarship opportunities.

4. Explain the Free Application for Federal Student Aid (FASFA).

5. Although Ron Yudd had a degree in English literature, he chose to stay in the restaurant industry, which was his passion. What types of degrees more closely related to the restaurant and foodservice industry might be of interest to you? Why?

6. Suppose Sam's first interview doesn't work out. What tools and resources can he use to find a new job as a field distributor?

7. What types of financial aid are available for college or trade school education?

8. How can you determine which school offers the best program for you? How can you learn about the school environment as well as its program offerings?

759

Section 12.2 Review Questions

1. Information used to complete a job application form typically includes the applicant's name and address, employment history, educational background, references, any qualities and skills the applicant may have, and the applicant's signature.

2. To apply to a college or trade school, students should first speak with a guidance or career counselor. Then they should complete application forms and essays, provide high-school transcripts and letters of reference, and apply for financial aid.

3. Ways to learn about scholarship opportunities include asking the school's financial aid office for information, searching online and print sources, and talking with a guidance counselor.

4. The Free Application for Federal Student Aid is a government form students and their parents can complete and submit to obtain federal grants, which do not need to be repaid, and student loans, which must be repaid but at low interest rates. The application is used to determine the total amount of financial aid for which the applicant qualifies.

5. Students should identify and describe foodservice-related degrees that interest them.

6. Sam can use his networking skills, online career-building sites, print media, career centers and counselors, and word-of-mouth in searching for a new position as a field distributor.

7. Scholarships, grants, and student loans are types of financial aid available for college or trade-school education.

8. Students should consider a variety of elements when selecting a college or trade school. A guidance counselor or local library can help, as can online and print research and actual visits to the schools. Students should include components of the list on p. 754 in their answers.

Section 12.2 Activities

1. Students should think deeply about each scenario, considering why different people might choose different paths.

2. Students should be able to find numerous scholarship and financial aid opportunities online.

3. The admissions office at a local college or university will often provide opportunities for interested students to speak with current students or with recent graduates.

Section 12.2 Activities

1. Study Skills/Group Activity: Career Path

With two other students, discuss the positive and negative opportunities in each scenario.

a. Taking a full-time job after graduating from high school

b. Attending college or trade school full-time after graduating from high school

c. Working while attending college or trade school after graduating from high school

Why might some paths be better for some individuals than others?

2. Activity: Scholarships and Financial Aid

Search the Internet to find out what types of scholarships and financial aid are available to you.

3. Critical Thinking: Career Paths

Talk with some recent graduates or students at a local college or university to learn more about how they made their own decisions about career paths. What suggestions do they have?

760

12.1 Starting a Career in Foodservice	12.2 Completing Applications Effectively	12.3 The Job Interview	12.4 Advancing in a Career	12.5 Careers in the Industry
• Skills needed for a successful career	• Job applications	• Preparing for the job interview	• Health and wellness	• Entry-level jobs
• The job search	• College applications	• The interview	• Stress and time management	• A selection of careers
• Preparing a résumé, portfolio, and cover letter	• Scholarships	• Follow up after the interview	• Resigning from a job	
			• Staying educated and involved	

SECTION 12.3 THE JOB INTERVIEW

The job interview is an important hiring tool used by potential employers. Interviewers will interview many candidates to find the most suitable person for the position. Potential employees have a chance to "sell themselves" and to show the interviewer that they are the most suitable person for the position. Appearance, punctuality, and demeanor are important, as well as being fully prepared. Research the company and industry and practice answering and asking appropriate interview questions.

Study Questions

After studying Section 12.3, you should be able to answer the following questions:

■ What are the steps to an effective job interview?

■ What are the differences between closed and open-ended questions?

■ What are the follow-up steps for a job interview?

Preparing for the Job Interview

If an employer likes a cover letter and résumé, an applicant may be asked for a job interview. At the **job interview**, that applicant meets with the employer to discuss qualifications for the job. This is the applicant's opportunity to "show his or her stuff" in person to a potential employer. Do everything possible to make the interview a success.

761

Section 12.3
The Job Interview

Introduce the Section

a. Review the process of preparing for a job interview.

b. Explain how to interview successfully and follow up with the employer.

c. Discuss the objectives for the section.

Vocabulary Review

a. Direct students to the key terms.

b. Pronounce each word, and have the students repeat the pronunciation out loud.

c. Discuss the definition of each word.

Teach

Discuss

• The prospect of a job interview makes most applicants very excited and nervous. What steps can applicants take to calm down and maintain a professional demeanor? Encourage students to share techniques they use to prepare for major challenges and opportunities, such as exams or important sporting events.

• What do students think is the most important action a job applicant can take during a job interview?

Reinforce and Review

• During a job interview, potential employees work to communicate their talents and strengths to an employer in hopes of getting a job.

• Job applicants need to demonstrate to employers that they are the most qualified candidate for the job available.

Vocabulary Terms

• **Job interview:** A meeting between an employer and a potential employee to discuss the latter's qualifications for an available position.

Discuss

• How does one's personal appearance function as a form of nonverbal communication? What signals do your clothes send? Relate this to the material covered in Chapter 7, Section 7.3.

Reinforce and Review

• An applicant's physical appearance can play an important role in hiring decisions. If the person is dressed professionally, he or she is likely to work professionally.
• The key to appropriate dress for a job interview is to avoid wearing anything in excess. Let your work speak for you, not your attire.
• Punctuality is very important. It signals respect for the other person and his or her time.

Teaching Tips

• Ask students to describe the message that they want their clothing to convey.

This first impression to a potential employer will make the strongest statement about an applicant. Résumés and cover letters (cover message) will be remembered if the interviewer likes what he or she sees in the interview. The following key points will help applicants make a great first impression:

▪ **Punctuality:** The first rule of business etiquette is to arrive at the interview on time. Punctuality for the interview indicates that the applicant will be punctual on the job. Plan to arrive a bit early, in case something slows you down.

▪ **Appearance:** Applicants that look neat and clean give the impression that their work will also be neat and clean. Applicants don't have to wear expensive clothes to have a good appearance. They should wear clothes that are clean and appropriate for the job for which they are interviewing.

Figure 12.5: A man and a woman wearing appropriate interview clothes.

For example, when interviewing for a job in an office, women might wear a modest dress or pants suit and a blouse while men might wear pants with a shirt and tie. For a position at a quick-service restaurant, women might wear pants and a blouse, while men might wear pants and a polo shirt or other collared shirt. If a student is applying for a back-of-house job, he or she should wear checks and a chef coat so that the interviewer knows that the applicant is serious and has appropriate clothing. In all cases, avoid T-shirts, jeans, sleeveless or midriff tops, tennis shoes and sandals, and excessive jewelry, makeup, and strong perfume. Remember: The key is to avoid wearing anything in excess. Figure 12.5 shows job applicants dressed appropriately.

Figure Focus

Figure 12.5: What makes these clothes appropriate for job interviews? What clothing might be inappropriate?

■ **Good personal hygiene**: When applying for a position in the restaurant or foodservice industry, the most important point to remember is that applicants will be working with food and people—preparing, serving, and removing food or greeting guests in a restaurant and foodservice operation. In the restaurant and foodservice industry, cleanliness and neatness are absolutely essential. Good personal hygiene is no less important in any other job sought. Employers expect employees to be clean and neat in their appearance every day on the job, too.

■ **Positive attitude**: If applicants smile and are enthusiastic, it suggests that they will do their work with that same attitude. Remember, the ability to smile and stay calm under pressure is necessary for a successful career in any area, but particularly in foodservice. Applicants should not worry if they're a little nervous during the interview. Most interviewers will see through the nerves and determine that the applicant is a person who takes a serious attitude toward work.

■ **Good manners**: Good manners are the basis for business **etiquette** (EH-tah-kit). Saying "Please," "Thank you," and "Excuse me" all show good manners. If an applicant is considerate and thoughtful, the behavior implies that he or she will also act that way around coworkers and customers; excellent customer service is expected in the restaurant and foodservice industry.

When meeting the interviewer, applicants should smile, extend their hands, and exchange a friendly greeting. (See Figure 12.6.) Unless asked to do otherwise, applicants should always call the interviewer "Mr." or "Ms." They should wait until the interviewer invites them to sit down and then sit up straight in the chair—don't slouch or sprawl out. Avoid nervous fidgeting, such as playing with hair, drumming fingers, or tapping a pen. It's best to sit still, look alert, and pay attention to what the interviewer is saying. Practice effective listening skills. If applicants bring someone with them to the interview, they should have that person wait outside.

Remember to learn basic facts about the company before the interview. This research shows a serious interest in working for the company and in the job. Also, the potential employer may ask an applicant

Figure 12.6: When meeting the interviewer, smile and extend hands to the interviewer.

763

Figure Focus
Figure 12.6: How is this person communicating without words?

Discuss
- Candidates should pay great attention to even small details when preparing for interviews. What does this demonstrate about their work to a prospective employer?
- How does handling stress well apply to every career, including those in the restaurant and foodservice industry? What other careers might be particularly stressful and why?

Reinforce and Review
- Cleanliness and neatness are absolutely essential in the restaurant and foodservice industry.
- The ability to stay calm and smiling during pressure is necessary for a successful career in any industry.
- Every employee in the restaurant and foodservice industry is expected to provide excellent customer service at all times.
- During an interview, practice effective listening skills.
- Before an interview, research the company to learn some basic facts about the organization. This demonstrates a serious interest in the company and in the position.

Teaching Tips
- Relate the material about personal hygiene to Chapter 2.

Homework Activity: Interview Prep

Literacy Connection, 21st-Century Skills— Access and Evaluate Information, Communicate Clearly, Work Independently

Identify a company for which you'd like to work. This may be a local shop or a multinational corporation.

Research the company using whatever means are available to you. In some cases, you may even need to conduct interviews with staff members to obtain the necessary information.

Your goal is to learn enough basic material about this employer to feel comfortable interviewing there for a job. This information includes the company's products, its history, its target audience, its size, and its major competitors. What other knowledge about the company might help you prepare for your interview?

Give a brief oral presentation summing up your findings.

Vocabulary Terms
- **Etiquette:** Good manners.

Discuss

- How can interviews be learning experiences? How can applicants learn both about the company and themselves?
- In Chapter 8, interviews were addressed from an interviewer's perspective. What did students learn from that material that can help them be more confident and successful as interviewees?

Reinforce and Review

- Interviewees should know the company size and reputation, its key products and services, and the names of its competitors.
- Interviewers assess whether candidates would be suitable for the vacancy they seek to fill, both in terms of skill set and personality.
- Interviews are opportunities to learn and grow. Even the worst interview has some educational merit.
- If interviewees are unsure what to bring to an interview, they should always call ahead to ask.
- Practicing sample interviews can be a successful preparation tactic, but only if everyone involved takes the exercise seriously.

Teaching Tips

- Remind students to pursue finding a job as if that, in fact, is their job.

what he or she knows about the company. Applicants should know the company size and reputation, its key products and services, and names of its competitors. This information can be found in a school library/media center, the community library, local chambers of commerce and business associations, and often online.

Some key business publications that are helpful for finding company information include *Fortune Magazine*, *The New York Times*, *The Wall Street Journal*, *Barron's*, *Forbes*, *Dun & Bradstreet*, and the *Thomas Register*. Community newspapers are also good sources for information about local businesses. The school or community librarian can help access these services.

The Interview

Most job interviews last about an hour, depending on the job level. Most interviewers try to help applicants relax and feel comfortable. The potential employer will ask questions to get to know the applicant better and to see whether the applicant's talents would be a suitable match for the job available. The potential employer has a job position to fill and wants to hire someone capable of doing the job or learning it quickly. The interviewer also wants to know whether the applicant will fit in with the restaurant or foodservice team and the organization as a whole.

Think of the interview as a chance to visit a workplace, to learn more about an interesting job, and an opportunity to meet new people. It's important to make a good impression, but it's also important to be true to self.

Bring the following to the interview:

- Portfolio, including résumé
- Names, addresses, and phone numbers of three people as references, personal and professional
- Birth certificate or valid passport; Social Security card; driver's license or state-issued ID; green card or proof of ability to work in the United States

An applicant who is unsure about what work documents to bring should call the interviewer. A potential employer will be impressed by an applicant's preparedness and attention to detail.

Practicing interviewing skills with a friend is a good way to prepare for the real interview. A friend, family member, or teacher can play the role of the employer and ask sample interview questions. Give each question serious thought and come up with an answer that is honest and complete. Practicing before an interview will help answer questions quickly and accurately during the actual interview.

764

Although no correct or incorrect answers to interview questions are possible, some responses are more appropriate than others. The first question the interviewer may ask is, *"Why don't you tell me a little about yourself?"* The appropriate response is to talk about accomplishments, experience, and qualifications. Practice a three-minute statement that presents capabilities. Table 12.3 lists some examples of personal characteristics that applicants might use to describe themselves during an interview.

Here is an example:

"My name is Anna Johnson. I am looking for a job that will get me started in my professional foodservice career. Currently, I am a junior at Easton High School enrolled in a program that teaches both food preparation and business management skills. For the past three years, I have been a server in our school cafeteria, the Cram Café, where I also work as a kitchen helper. The chef has even used some of my original low-fat dessert recipes. I am a good team player, and I am dependable. My grades are above average, and I really enjoy working with people. My goal is to be a restaurant manager some day. That's why I thought this position as a part-time server at the Red Robin Café would be a great opportunity to move up the career ladder."

Table 12.3: Personal Characteristics

accurate	able to remain calm under pressure
communicate well	dependable
energetic	entertaining
enthusiastic	good attitude
hard worker	good computer skills
high standards	leader
like people	responsible
sense of humor	tolerant
trustworthy	willing to learn and take instructions

Interview Questions and Answers

Although interviewers might ask many different kinds of questions, they all can be categorized as closed questions or open-ended questions. **Closed questions** can be answered with a simple yes or no or with a brief, factual statement. **Open-ended questions** encourage job applicants to talk about themselves,

765

Reinforce and Review

- Some answers are more appropriate than others. Interviewees should think before answering questions.
- Brevity is important in an interview. If the interviewer wants the candidate to say more about a certain topic, he or she will ask.
- All interview questions are either open-ended or closed.

Teaching Tips

- Remind students that talking about one's activities and achievements is a sales pitch, so they should be focused and concise while demonstrating enthusiasm about the position available.

Table 12.3: Personal Characteristics

- Encourage students to pick three words from the list that describe them. How would each be discussed in a job interview?

- What personal characteristics do students believe are relevant to job performance but are not included on this list?

- Which characteristics on this list might be most appealing to a prospective employer in the restaurant and foodservice industry?

Homework Activity: Questions and Answers

Literacy Connection, 21st-Century Skills— Think Creatively, Reason Effectively, Communicate Clearly

Design three sample open-ended interview questions. These should be your own questions, so make sure they are not included in either Chapter 8 or Chapter 12. Other than that, they can address any relevant and legal employment issue.

Bring these to class and exchange with another student. How would each of you answer the other's questions?

Vocabulary Terms

- **Closed questions:** Questions that can be answered with a simple yes or no or with a brief factual statement.
- **Open-ended questions:** Questions that can be answered a number of different ways and which encourage job applicants to talk about themselves and their experiences.

Discuss

- Some interviewers like to think up unusual questions to gauge interviewees' ability to think quickly and adjust to unfamiliar situations. Why might those be important skills in the restaurant and foodservice industry? How can interviewees prepare for this type of question?

Reinforce and Review

- Closed questions provide information without going anywhere.
- Open-ended questions usually require applicants to develop in-depth responses and become actively involved in the interviewing process.

Teaching Tips

- Remind students that interviewees should always be able to make even negative information, such as an employment termination or chronically poor grades, into positive statements by focusing on what the individual learned from those experiences.

In-Class Activity: Interview-ese

Literacy Connection, 21st-Century Skills— Reason Effectively, Communicate Clearly, Make Judgments and Decisions

A number of sample interview questions are provided on pp. 766–767. Think about what the interviewer is trying to learn through each. How would you respond to each question? Write down your answers.

As a class, discuss some ways each question could be addressed, in addition to the suggestions given in the text.

---

making them feel more comfortable and giving the interviewer important information and valuable insight about the applicant.

Although **closed questions** often provide interviewers with the information they need, they don't lead anywhere. **Open-ended questions**, on the other hand, are usually thought-provoking, requiring applicants to develop in-depth responses and become actively involved in the interviewing process.

A **closed question** can be turned into an open-ended question by simply adding one or two key words, such as *what* or *how*. For example, instead of asking an applicant *"Can you work on weekends?"* a better, open-ended question might be *"What hours can you work?"* Rather than asking *"Do you like to travel?"* an interviewer can ask, *"How do you feel about traveling?"* Creating and answering interview questions are skills that must be developed. Just like any other skills, interviewing techniques improve with practice.

Following are some examples of typical interview questions:

Why do you want to work for this company? Why do you want to be a _____ in this company?

Reply: Talk about why the job or the company interests you. Avoid any reference to money.

What contributions can you make to this company?

Reply: Talk about your qualifications and skills and how they will benefit the company.

How did you hear about us?

Reply: Mention either the newspaper, Internet, a friend, a relative, or a teacher.

The next three questions are relevant if you have previous work experience:

How many jobs have you had during the past three years?

Reply: State how many jobs you've had.

What exactly did you do on your last job/current job?

Reply: Talk about your responsibilities, duties, and achievements.

Why are you leaving your present job? Why did you leave your last job?

Reply: Be honest, but don't speak ill of your previous employer or job responsibilities. Appropriate responses depend on your situation. You could say that the previous/current job allowed you to work part-time, and you're now ready to commit to full-time employment. You could also say that you are now ready to take on more responsibilities, but those opportunities were not available with

766

---

your current/previous employer. Other reasons include layoffs, reduction in work hours, or the employer was not able to accommodate your school schedule.

If we hire you, how long do you think you would be able to work here?

Reply: If you're looking at a part-time job for one semester, say so. If you're looking for full-time, permanent employment, say you hope to stay with the organization for a long time.

What are your favorite subjects in school? Why?

Reply: Name your favorite subjects and tell why.

What subject do you find most difficult?

Reply: Here is one example: "World history was my worst subject. It really bored me, and my grades showed it. But I knew a D would hurt my overall grade average, so I found a senior to tutor me in exchange for typing her term papers. By the end of the semester, I was able to pull a B." The interviewer is trying to determine your ability to persevere under less than favorable circumstances. Everyone has difficulty learning things sometimes, but a person with ambition will find a workable solution. That's what the potential employer is looking for in a good employee.

Did you participate in any school activities? Why or why not?

Reply: Name the activities. Joining school activities shows that you're a sociable person. If you had to work after school and for this reason you were not able to join any activities, say so. Be sure your answer reflects that you do work well with others.

Do you plan to continue your education?

Reply: Continuing your education is not limited to college. It can include taking additional courses in food preparation, for example, or a willingness to participate in on-the-job training. Your answer should reflect that you want to gain as much knowledge and training as possible to advance in your restaurant and foodservice career.

How many days of school or work did you miss during the last year?

Reply: While regular attendance and punctuality are extremely important in any workplace, restaurant and foodservice operators in particular depend on employees who show up for work every day and on time. Someone who is absent for several days at school or work may not be dependable on the job. If you have been absent for many days at school or work, have a reasonable explanation prepared.

767

CUSTOMIZED INSTRUCTION

Literacy Connection, 21st-Century Skills—Reason Effectively, Communicate Clearly, Work Independently

ESOL Students

Job interviews can be particularly challenging for non-native speakers of English. How does this relate to the material on barriers to communication discussed in Chapter 7? In what way could interviews create opportunities for the display of bias, prejudice, or discrimination, as discussed in Chapter 8?

Write one paragraph on how barriers to communication can complicate job interviews conducted in an interviewee's non-native language and a second paragraph on how to protect oneself against discriminatory behavior.

In-Class Activity: Practice Makes Perfect

Literacy Connection, 21st-Century Skills—Communicate Clearly, Reason Effectively, Think Creatively

What interview skills should you practice most? List three areas where you feel you need to improve. Now think of strategies for addressing each area.

For instance, if your biggest concern is nervousness, then consider checking out a book on stress relief from the library. If you're concerned about your interview appearance, consider speaking with your school's career counselor or with a department-store clerk for some advice. You should come up with at least two strategies for each area you'd like to improve.

Spend some time resolving these issues until you feel more comfortable with them.

In-Class Activity: Ask Me, Ask Me, Ask Me

Literacy Connection, 21st-Century Skills—Think Creatively, Reason Effectively, Interact Effectively with Others

Students should each write an interview question that is as strange as possible while still serving a legitimate purpose in a professional interview setting. The question should then be submitted to the teacher. The teacher will call on students randomly to answer the submitted questions.

The test is for the students answering the questions to remain calm and unflustered, even if other students are laughing at the question, and answer in the most professional and appropriate manner possible.

The goal is to demonstrate two things. First, employers can choose unusual questions to elicit certain pieces of information about an interviewee. Second, the ability to maintain grace and composure when faced with a difficult situation is a valuable characteristic in any employee.

CUSTOMIZED INSTRUCTION

Literacy Connection, 21st-Century Skills—Reason Effectively, Communicate Clearly, Solve Problems

Special Needs Students

What is the hardest question you could ever be asked in a job interview? What is the easiest? Why?

Answer both the hardest and the easiest questions. How do you think your answers would impress an interviewer?

Discuss

- What is the overall impression an interviewee should give an interviewer? How can interviewees establish and reinforce a key message about themselves and their abilities?

Reinforce and Review

- Always tell the truth during an interview, but do so in the most positive way you can.
- Employers cannot ask questions about certain subjects, such as race or gender, as doing so is illegal and discriminatory.
- Interviewees should take the opportunity to ask questions during the interview, which allows them to display self-confidence while obtaining additional pertinent information that could affect the decision of whether to accept an offered job.

Homework Activity: The Bare Minimum

Mathematics Connection, Literacy Connection, 21st-Century Skills—Use Systems Thinking, Access and Evaluate Information, Work Independently

Most entry-level foodservice employees are paid at or near the minimum wage, or the lowest amount of money most employees may legally be paid. Although federal law sets a national minimum wage, several states and even cities have established minimum wages that are higher than the federal law. On the other hand, some states allow employers to pay employees who receive tips at a rate below the minimum wage. What are the minimum wages for tipped and untipped employees in your area?

Calculate the gross annual pay, before tips, for a full-time tipped worker earning minimum wage, assuming a 40-hour workweek. Now assume that tips would constitute an additional 20 percent. Now what is the gross annual pay? What if tips were 40 percent? What if they were 100 percent?

Now calculate the gross annual pay for a full-time untipped employee earning minimum wage, assuming a 40-hour workweek.

If minimum wages for tipped and untipped workers are the same in your area, how does that affect the restaurant's finances? On the other hand, if minimum wages for tipped and untipped workers vary, how does that affect the restaurant's employees?

Other questions interviewers may ask include questions about salary, what motivates an applicant to do a good job, and whether the applicant has ever been fired from a job. For questions regarding salary on previous jobs, tell the truth. If the interviewer asks what salary an applicant is looking for in this job, the applicant should be diplomatic, saying that they have no set figure in mind, or ask the interviewer what salary is usually offered to someone with similar qualifications.

If the applicant has ever been fired from a job, they shouldn't panic. A possible reply goes something like this, "While I usually can work with everyone, this particular boss and I just weren't a good match, in spite of my efforts to work out the problems." Applicants should always remain positive about the reasons they are no longer with an employer. Avoid talking negatively about previous managers and coworkers.

The interviewer is not allowed to ask about your race, national origin, gender, religion, marital status, age, physical or mental disabilities, or sexual preference. Asking these questions is illegal and discriminatory.

Before ending the interview, the potential employer will ask whether the applicant has any questions. This is the chance for applicants to show that they have confidence in themselves and to make sure the job is a good match for personal and professional goals.

Here are some questions applicants might consider asking the interviewer:

- Is this a new position or would I be replacing someone?
- Was the person who previously had this job promoted? (This is very important for a full-time job. The object is to discover whether the company is promoting employees or whether there is a high rate of employees leaving the company because they are unhappy.)
- Could you please describe a typical workday for me?
- If you hired me, when would you expect me to start working?
- How long would it take for me to be trained for the job?
- When do you plan on filling the position? If the interviewer says a decision will be made within one or two weeks, ask whether you may call to inquire about the decision.

Avoid asking questions about salary, vacation, bonuses, or holidays. Salary is a sensitive issue. Wait for the interviewer to bring up the subject. Ask the interviewer what the standard salary is for someone with similar qualifications. It's a good idea to have a general idea of the salary range for the job before going to the interview. Find this information at a school or community library. Although applicants should not begin the discussion, they should leave the interview knowing the overall salary range

768

When the interview is ended, smile, shake the person's hand, and thank the interviewer for taking the time to explain the job. If an applicant wants the job, this is the time to say so. For example, "This would be a great opportunity for me—I hope you give my qualifications serious consideration. I know I'd work well with your restaurant and foodservice team." Even if you know you don't want the job, it is important to observe business courtesy.

[fast fact]

Did You Know...?
CNN reports that the most common interview mistakes are dressing inappropriately (51 percent), badmouthing the boss (49 percent), appearing uninterested (48 percent), arrogance (44 percent), and insufficient answers (30 percent).

Follow Up After the Interview

Before leaving, gather contact information from the interviewer and follow up on the interview. A simple thank-you note can make an applicant stand out from the crowd of job seekers. Figure 12.7 is a sample thank-you note. It's a good idea to write the thank-you note as soon as possible. This proves to the employer that the applicant really wants the job. Sending a thank-you note by email is a good idea but also send a handwritten one by regular mail.

The note should be short, confirm a desire for the job, reinforce qualifications, give a time for follow-up with a phone call, and offer to meet with the potential employer again to answer any additional questions. Ending the letter with a sentence that encourages the potential employer to call is a good marketing idea. Most people read the beginning few sentences and the last sentence before reading the body of any letter.

The follow-up phone call should be on the day promised. Here is a sample follow-up phone call:

Remind the person who you are.

"Good afternoon, Ms. Brown. This is Rose Hernandez. How are you today?"

State the reason for your call—what position you applied for.

"Ms. Brown, I'm calling to follow up on our meeting last Thursday regarding the part-time server position. It sounded like the ideal job for me."

Find out if the potential employer made a decision.

"I was wondering if you had made a decision yet."

769

Discuss

- Interviewees don't always decide to accept jobs that they are offered. Encourage students to discuss what factors might affect their decision to accept or reject a job offer.
- What message does sending a thank-you note to an interviewer convey? How can it influence a hiring decision?

Reinforce and Review

- Even if an interviewee knows at the end of an interview that he or she does not want the job, it is important to observe business courtesy.
- Before leaving an interview, make sure to obtain the interviewer's contact information.
- Thank-you notes should be professional and concise. Most people read the first few sentences and the last sentence of a letter before reading its body.

**Fast Fact:
Did You Know...?**

Encourage students to discuss the following:

- How can interviewees appear interested in the interview and what they are learning?
- Why is dressing inappropriately the most common mistake interviewees make?
- What is the difference between arrogance and self-confidence?

Teaching Tips

- The importance of observing appropriate follow-up methods should be emphasized.

Discuss

- How can newly hired employees prepare for their first day at a new job? What material in Chapter 8 might be relevant?
- How can newly hired employees practice their interpersonal communication skills with their new colleagues? What verbal and nonverbal communication can help them succeed?
- It can be difficult to communicate intended messages over the telephone, where nonverbal behavior cannot be observed. How can an applicant prepare for a follow-up call so that he or she will sound calm and professional?

If you got the job, write down the answers to the following questions:

"When would you like me to start working, and what time should I be there?"

"What should I bring with me?"

"Where should I go on my first day?"

"Who should I see?"

"I just need to coordinate my bus schedule; do you know how many hours I'll be working on my first day?"

If the employer has not made a decision, don't panic.

"I understand. Could you please tell me whether you're still considering me for the position?"

If you are a candidate:

"Are there any questions I can answer that will show you I'm really the server you're looking for?"

Ms. Linda Brown

Manager

Uptown Grille

75 East Pleasant Street

Funtown, USA 50094

January 5, 2011

Dear Ms. Brown:

Thank you for meeting with me on Thursday afternoon to explain the part-time server position at Uptown Grille. The responsibilities of the server position, along with the training and flexible hours, would give me a head start in my foodservice career. I definitely want to be a member of your team.

I'm confident that I can quickly learn the service techniques and become a productive member of your staff. My teachers have told me that I am a fast learner and I'm willing to attend your weekend training classes.

If I may, I'll call you next Thursday to see if you've made a decision and to answer any additional questions you may have. Please don't hesitate to call me at 123-456-7890 if you have any new questions in the meantime. Once again, thank you for considering me for the position.

Sincerely,

Faith Fitzpatrick

110 West 84th Street

Funtown, USA 50094

Figure 12.7: A sample thank-you note.

770

Figure Focus

Figure 12.7: How does this letter demonstrate professionalism? How does it demonstrate communication skills?

[on the job]

Advice from the Front

How can you stand out in a job interview? What should you do to impress your potential employers? We asked a few seasoned professionals in human resources departments around the industry to offer their advice on what you can do to go from a candidate to a new employee. Here's what they had to say:

- "Research the company you will interview with to identify not only what they do, but also what their challenges and growth areas are. Then you can convey how you will be part of the solution."

- "I always look for leadership qualities and to see whether the person is a fit with our company's values of service spirit, team spirit, and the spirit of progress."

  —Arie Ball, Vice President, Sourcing and Talent Acquisition, Sodexo

- "Inquire about the organization's culture and ask the interviewer why he or she enjoys working with the company. Remember: you're interviewing them as much as they're interviewing you. You want to make the best decision now so that you're not job hopping in the future."

- "Prepare a list of professional references with contact information for your prospective employer. Contact those references for permission prior to your interview so they are aware of your job search status."

  —Erika Braun, Director of Human Resources, Golden Corral Corporation

- "Always bring a smile and make eye contact. Smiles are a welcoming gesture when walking in to meet someone, like an ice breaker. Eye contact shows that you are interested in what is being said and that the interviewer has your undivided attention."

- "Make sure to dress in a style that's commensurate with the position for which you are applying. Check ahead of time about the dress code of the company you are applying to and dress accordingly."

  —Michael Santos, Vice President of Operations and Human Resources,
  Fry Cook and Cashier, Micatrotto Restaurant Group

- "Excel at your current job by being a problem solver. Demonstrate this by reducing costs, increasing sales, enhancing customer satisfaction, promoting creativity, and being innovative."

- "Discuss what you can bring to the job that no else can. What impresses me most in the best-qualified candidates is how they can bring their unique qualities to work in a way that will support the team and ultimately the company to make a difference for our customers."

  —Jerry Paulison, Senior Director, Talent Acquisition Group, Sodexo

On the Job:
Advice from the Front

Encourage students to discuss the following:

- Compare the various pieces of advice in this box. Which one statement do students think is most relevant to their own situations? Why?

- How can job applicants demonstrate leadership skills during an interview?

- How can getting to know a company's culture, through research and questioning, help an applicant decide whether he or she will accept a job?

- What elements of nonverbal communication do students think will help them be more successful during interviews?

- What do students find unique about themselves? How can that be marketable?

771

Essential Skills: Completing an I-9 Form

Encourage students to discuss the following:

- Why must I-9 forms be completed before newly hired employees may work?

- Why must employees establish their identities?

- What is the difference between documents that establish identity and documents that establish eligibility for employment?

Homework Activity: Shape-Shifting

Science Connection, Literacy Connection, 21st-Century Skills—Critical Thinking and Problem Solving, Access and Evaluate Information, Think Creatively

In 1943, psychologist Abraham Maslow proposed a "Hierarchy of Human Needs" based on his research of the human personality. He described a pyramid in which the broad base represents basic human needs like food, air, and water, referring to these as physiological needs. The pyramid then moved upward through safety needs (security, employment, health), loving and belonging needs (family, friends), esteem needs (self-esteem, confidence, respect), and self-actualization needs (creativity, spontaneity, problem-solving). Maslow posited that humans need to fulfill their physiological needs before they could begin to address the needs further up the pyramid. Once each step has been reached, individuals can begin striving toward the next. At the top, they are fully developed humans.

Research Maslow's hierarchy of needs to understand how it operates and what it addresses. Do you think he includes the correct elements at each stage of the pyramid? Does the process he describes make sense? What does self-actualization mean in this context? What are some positive and negative attributes of Maslow's schema?

Develop your own explanation for how the human personality develops and evolves, including a visual depiction of your hypothesis. What shape is your diagram? Write a one-page paper on your research and your explanation for the development of personality.

If there are no questions:

"Thanks again, Ms. Brown. I hope you'll call me if you do have any questions, and I look forward to hearing from you soon."

If you didn't get the job:

"Oh, I'm sorry to hear that. Thank you for taking the time to explain the position to me. I hope you'll think of me if you have other openings."

If an applicant did not get the job, it is acceptable to ask the person for constructive feedback on interviewing skills, or ask the interviewer what he or she could do to get more experience or training. Sometimes interviewers can refer an applicant to other jobs that would be more suitable for their abilities. Don't be afraid to ask the person. Every interview is an opportunity to sharpen communication skills and meet restaurant and foodservice professionals. It also helps applicants to determine their strengths and weaknesses and gives them the chance to do better next time.

Table 12.4 reviews the steps to be taken before an interview, during the interview, and after the interview.

Essential Skills
Completing an I-9 Form

New hires must complete an I-9 form before they will be allowed to work. This is a federal form to determine whether employees are legally eligible to work in the United States. Every employee hired after 1986 is required to fill out this document at the time of hire. For those who need assistance, a translator or preparer will be provided.

❶ Provide full name, address, date of birth, and Social Security number.

❷ Attest that you are a U.S. citizen, a noncitizen national of the United States, a lawful permanent resident, or an alien authorized to work.

❸ Sign the document. When you sign this, you are affirming that all the information you are providing is true. If you intentionally provide inaccurate information, you could be fined or imprisoned.

❹ Present documents that establish your identity and your eligibility for employment to your employer. Some documents can do both these things, such as a U.S. passport or a Permanent Resident Card. Other documents do one or the other. Your school photo I.D. card or driver's license are two items that can establish your identity. You need a Social Security card to establish your employment eligibility. After your employer examines these documents, he or she will complete and submit the rest of the form.

If you have questions about this process, talk with your guidance counselor or check the U.S. government's Web site.

772

Table 12.4: Interview Steps

Before the interview	Know the route to the job. Take a preview trip to the interview site. Consider traffic.
	If you're taking public transportation, bring enough money and allow time for delays.
	Know what materials to take.
	Review important interview questions and responses.
	Practice aloud.
	Bring a pen that writes clearly and a clean notebook.
	Write down the name, address, and telephone number of the interviewer.
	Give yourself enough time to get ready.
	Get a good night's sleep.
	Arrive at the interview 15 minutes before the appointment.
	If you are going to be late, call the interviewer.
	Good luck and relax!
During the interview	Smile, look interested, and pay attention.
	Sit with back straight; lean back in the chair.
	Practice good listening skills.
	Never say unkind or bad things about previous bosses or coworkers.
	Be an interactive participant. Avoid answering questions too quickly, which makes the answers appear to be not thought out.
	Ask questions.
	Look confident (and feel confident).
	Sell yourself! Explain how your skills and abilities make you the ideal person for the job.
After the interview	Write a brief thank-you note to the interviewer as soon as possible.
	Follow up with a phone call to the interviewer.
	Congratulate yourself on doing your best!

773

Table 12.4: Interview Steps

- Encourage students to think about why they want particular jobs. What talents will they bring to those positions?

- Why might a job not be a good fit for someone? Sometimes these are real concerns, and sometimes they are simply fears motivated by anxiety. How can people tell the difference?

Discuss

- After reading Chapter 8 and Chapter 12, which do students think was more effective at preparing them for job interviews? Why?
- Managers begin evaluating employees at job interviews. The evaluation process continues on a daily basis after that. In what ways can it be argued that the interview process never ends? Encourage students to share their thoughts.

Summary

- Remind students to review the following:
  1. Steps to an effective job interview
  2. The difference between closed and open-ended questions
  3. Follow-up steps for a job interview

Summary

In this section, you learned the following:

- The critical factors to an effective job interview include the rules below:

  - Make a good impression.

  - Be punctual.

  - Present a clean and neat appearance.

  - Have good personal hygiene.

  - Promote a positive attitude.

  - Use good manners.

  - Smile and extend your hand to greet the interviewer. Refer to the interviewer as "Mr." or "Ms."

  - Learn basic facts about the company.

- Closed questions can be answered with a yes or no or with a brief, factual statement. Open-ended questions encourage job applicants to talk about themselves, which gives the interviewer important information and insight about the applicant:

  - Be an active participant in the interview.

  - Avoid asking questions about salary, vacation, bonuses, or holidays. Wait for the interviewer to bring up the subject.

  - When the interview is ended, smile, shake the person's hand, and thank the interviewer for taking the time to explain the job to you. If you do want the job, this is the time to say so.

- After the interview, send a thank-you note. This shows the employer that you want the job. The thank-you note should be short and reinforce your qualifications. Also, make a follow-up phone call to the interviewer.

774

Section 12.3 Review Questions

1. What steps should you take prior to an interview?

2. Explain the difference between a closed question and an open-ended question.

3. List three questions that you might ask an interviewer during the interview.

4. What materials should you bring with you to an interview?

5. Ron Yudd notes that successful people "stay in a learning mode." In an interview, you want to showcase your skills and experience. You also want to show the interviewer that you are eager to learn and grow. Think of a few sentences that might convey this idea to an interviewer.

6. How has Sam benefited from having a mentor like Linda?

7. Most of us get nervous during a job interview. What can you do to prepare yourself so that you appear calm and in control?

8. What do you think you need to do to impress an interviewer?

775

Section 12.3 Review Questions

1. Before going to an interview, applicants should research the company to learn important facts about its reputation, products, and customers. They should know the route to the interview site and how long it takes to arrive there by various modes of transportation. Applicants should dress appropriately, practice their interviewing skills, and bring all necessary materials, including a pen and notebook. Finally, applicants should give themselves plenty of time to prepare, including a good night's sleep.

2. A closed question can be answered with a simple yes or no, or with a brief factual statement. An open-ended question, on the other hand, encourages the respondent to talk about himself or herself, making that person feel more comfortable and giving the interviewer important information and insights.

3. Questions to consider asking an interviewer include whether the vacant position is new, or whether the applicant would be replacing someone; whether the person who previously held the job was promoted, leaving a vacancy; what a typical workday entails; the expected start date; the length of training; and the date by which the company expects to fill the position.

4. Job applicants should bring their portfolios and résumés, contact information for their references, and proof of identity and eligibility to work in the United States.

5. Students should identify ways in which they can contribute to a company as well as continue to learn.

6. Linda has helped Sam obtain a job interview and will work with him to practice his interviewing and follow-up skills, giving Sam opportunities for professional growth and development.

7. Practicing for a job interview can calm an applicant's nerves, as can preparing for the interview as thoroughly as possible.

8. Students should identify ways in which they can impress a prospective employer.

Section 12.3 Activities

1. Student presentations should be brief and clear, giving relevant information about the speaker and how he or she can contribute to the imaginary company as well as benefit as an employee.

2. Students should write professional thank-you notes, following the example on p. 770.

3. Student answers will vary but should consider material in Chapters 4, 7, and 12 when responding.

Section 12.3 Activities

1. Study Skills/Group Activity: Interview Skills

Work with another student to practice your interview skills, using the information provided in this chapter. Develop a brief 1- to 2-minute speech describing who you are, what your experience has been, and why you want this (imaginary) job, and present this to the class.

2. Activity: Thank-You Note

Write a thank-you note to be sent after interviewing with a potential employer, using the information provided in this section.

3. Critical Thinking: Characteristics of Good Employees

You own a local restaurant and are hiring for entry-level staff. What characteristics do you expect potential employees to have? What type of person do you want to hire?

776

12.1 Starting a Career in Foodservice	12.2 Completing Applications Effectively	12.3 The Job Interview	12.4 Advancing in a Career	12.5 Careers in the Industry
• Skills needed for a successful career • The job search • Preparing a résumé, portfolio, and cover letter	• Job applications • College applications • Scholarships	• Preparing for the job interview • The interview • Follow up after the interview	• Health and wellness • Stress and time management • Resigning from a job • Staying educated and involved	• Entry-level jobs • A selection of careers

SECTION 12.4 ADVANCING IN A CAREER

Everyone wants to advance in his or her career. In order to do so, maintain a healthy and well-balanced lifestyle. Learning how to manage time and stress by prioritizing goals and tasks can lead to a successful and satisfying career. Professional development will help to refine skills and add to a knowledge base as a career advances.

Study Questions

After studying Section 12.4, you should be able to answer the following questions:

- What are the factors for maintaining health and wellness throughout a restaurant and foodservice career?

- What is the relationship between time and stress?

- What are the ways to manage time and stress?

- What are the steps for resigning from a job?

- What is the importance of professional development?

Health and Wellness

Employees of the restaurant and foodservice industry, especially those just starting out, often work long hours in physically and mentally demanding jobs. It can seem overwhelming at first and harder than first thought. But one of the best things to remember about this industry is that it will reward good efforts.

777

Section 12.4
Advancing in a Career

Introduce the Section

a. Describe ways in which students and young employees can stay healthy while pursuing professional goals.

b. Explain ways in which students and young employees can engage in professional growth and development.

c. Discuss the objectives for the section.

Vocabulary Review

a. Direct students to the key terms.

b. Pronounce each word, and have the students repeat the pronunciation out loud.

c. Discuss the definition of each word.

Teach

Discuss

- Why is balance important both in work and throughout life?

- How can working in a demanding position help employees grow and develop?

Reinforce and Review

- Professional development will help to refine skills and add to a person's knowledge base as a career advances.

- Despite the long hours and challenging work, one of the best things to remember about the restaurant and foodservice industry is that it will reward good efforts.

Discuss

- How can students protect themselves while being professionals? How can students know how much is too much to do?

Reinforce and Review

- The most important thing employees can do to ensure that they advance in the restaurant and foodservice industry is to protect and care for their bodies and minds.
- Staying healthy is the key to building skills, gaining experience, and working up the career ladder.
- Young employees should practice healthy habits, like eating properly, exercising regularly, and not smoking, drinking, or using illegal drugs.
- Finding enjoyable and interesting jobs and staying active outside the workplace are ways people can stay happy even when busy.
- Employees should take advantage of the resources offered by their employers, including saving a significant portion of their salaries.

In-Class Activity: Staying Strong

Literacy Connection, 21st-Century Skills— Think Creatively, Make Judgments and Decisions, Work Independently

Page 778 lists a number of ways that young employees can find balance and growth in their personal and professional lives.

Identify three specific activities you can do each day to live a healthy, balanced life. For instance, walking 30 minutes each day or volunteering regularly might be good choices. Keep track of how you feel each time you perform an activity on this list. After one week, write two paragraphs on the activities you have selected and how you feel after performing them.

Some of the most successful CEOs and owners in the world started as dishwashers. Some of the most famous chefs did, too.

The most important thing employees can do to ensure that they advance in the restaurant and foodservice career is to take care of body and mind. Staying healthy is the key to building skills, gaining experience, and working up the career ladder. Plan to live a healthy lifestyle:

- **Eat right:** Eating healthy helps avoid disease and maintain a high energy level.

- **Get exercise:** It helps to control weight and reduce stress. Be as active as possible. Take a longer route to work or take the stairs. Even five extra minutes of walking adds to an overall daily exercise amount.

- **Don't smoke:** Some people turn to smoking when they're exposed to stressful environments, and restaurants are famously fast-paced. Instead of lighting up, find ways to reduce stress throughout the day. Find ways to avoid stress early; continue them throughout a long and healthy career.

- **Find something else to love:** Those who continually work aggressively hard without giving themselves a break burn out. Passion for the industry often drives our ability to work continuously; however, a break from passion is also needed to simply recharge. Find an activity outside of work, such as a sports team or a hobby. It will help to have a balance between work and a personal life.

- **Don't take drugs, and, when of legal age to do so, drink alcohol responsibly:** Abusing drugs or alcohol can ruin lives, not just careers. Making legal, safe choices is the best plan for also maintaining health.

- **Take advantage of the resources offered:** Many companies provide employees or managers with programs for learning how to cope with stress. These include employee assistance programs, stress management courses, and counseling. Some companies also offer health and wellness programs, including gym memberships.

- **Have a plan for saving money:** In the first few years, focus on building skills. This will help achieve financial success later, when those skills pay off.

- **Find a job that makes you happy:** Are you happiest providing the highest level of service you can? Do you want to build kitchens or design menus? Do you want to create the latest cuisine? Pursue what you like and choose an establishment that fits your personality. Opportunities in the restaurant and foodservice industry are endless.

Homework Activity: Healthy Recipes

Science Connection, Mathematics Connection, Literacy Connection, 21st-Century Skills— Access and Evaluate Information, Initiative and Self-Direction, Reason Effectively

Poor eating habits can take a toll on one's health, which can also cause stress. Sometimes, poor eating habits are caused by lack of time, which is in turn a stress factor. Healthy eating habits, on the other hand, are an important component of a balanced lifestyle.

Design a healthy recipe that your family and friends would enjoy. The recipe should be quick and easy to produce, and should include minimal amounts of fat and sugar. It can be for a dish enjoyed at any time of the day.

Record the amounts of each ingredient that you use in the recipe. The U.S. Department of Agriculture has a database where you can learn the nutritional values for each ingredient in the dish. For each ingredient used, list the number of grams of protein, carbohydrate, and fat as well as the number of calories. Add the amounts to learn the calorie count for the dish as well as the total protein, carbohydrate, and fat grams. Why is it important to know these figures? What other nutrients does the dish include?

How long does it take to make the dish? What is the technique you use to make it? Why do you think your family and friends will like it?

[trends]

More Fruits and Veggies

The Center for Disease Control and Prevention reports that:

■ 33 percent of American adults are not eating the recommended daily two or more servings of fruits per day.

■ 27 percent of American adults are not eating the recommended daily three or more servings of vegetables per day.

■ Less than 10 percent of teens are getting enough servings of fruits and vegetables per day.

To add more fruits and vegetables to your diet, drink 100 percent fruit juice instead of soda, add vegetables such as carrots, sprouts, and cucumber to sandwiches; add vegetables to soups and casseroles; and keep a handy stash of healthy snacks, such as fruits and nuts.

Stress and Time Management

Stress is the condition or feeling that demands exceed the resources available for use. One of the key resources a person has is time, which represents what he or she can accomplish in a given period. Far too often, people feel intense daily pressures.

Many people feel that there is not enough time in the day to meet the demands on them. Most people also want a life that balances work or school and home.

Although most people can feel overwhelmed at times, tools are available to help them manage both their time and stress. Two critical areas needed for building a career are stress management and time management. The following are some stress indicators:

■ Irritability and depression

■ Headaches

■ Indigestion

■ Pain in neck and/or lower back

■ Changes in appetite or sleep patterns

Stress may be caused by factors such as time pressures, grades, getting into college, and relationships with friends, parents, and teachers. It might also be due to loss of a family member, divorce, constant changes, or failure to accept what cannot be changed. Workplace challenges, such as lack of planning or poor communication, also can contribute to stress levels.

Stress can be driven by internal or external factors, and sometimes both. Internal factors are the stress people place on themselves. External factors are the pressures

779

Encourage students to discuss the following:

- Why do students think people do not eat the recommended amounts of fruits and vegetables?

- How many fruits and vegetables does your campus foodservice operation offer each day? In your experience, how popular are these items?

- How can students in classes such as this one model appropriate eating behaviors to their friends and families?

Discuss

- What are some sources of stress in the restaurant and foodservice industry? How can professionals handle these problems?

- Have students experienced any stress indicators from the list on p. 779? How do they handle them?

Reinforce and Review

- Time, which is one of an individual's key resources, represents what he or she can accomplish in a given period.
- Far too often, people feel intense daily pressures.
- Two critical areas needed for building a career are stress management and time management.
- Stress can be caused by time pressures, relationships, change, and workplace challenges.
- Internal stress factors are the pressures people place on themselves, while external stress factors are the pressures circumstances and other people place on them.

Vocabulary Terms

- **Stress:** The condition or feeling that demands exceed the resources available for use.

Discuss

- How can changing a menu or service style in a restaurant or foodservice establishment affect stress levels, either positively or negatively?
- Which of the suggestions on p. 780 for coping with stress seem practical?

Reinforce and Review

- Stress management techniques can help people minimize the negative effects of stress on their lives.
- Time management skills help individuals waste less time on nonessential tasks and focus on important activities.
- Effective time management includes planning, goal setting, setting priorities, and delegating.

Homework Activity: Stress Diaries

Science Connection, Literacy Connection, 21st-Century Skills—Manage Goals and Time, Reason Effectively, Adapt to Change

Keep a diary for one week, identifying when you feel stressed and what you think may have caused the stress. How can you reduce sources of stress in your life? Are there any skills you could learn that might help you better manage your time?

Vocabulary Terms

- **Stress management:** A process that people use to identify what causes stress for them in the workplace as well as their personal lives, and then to apply various strategies to minimize its effects.
- **Time management:** A process through which people use tools to increase their efficiency and productivity.

that circumstances and other people place on them. For example, a manager might feel pressure to meet certain performance goals, which leads her to put unrealistic expectations on herself and her staff as to what can be accomplished during a shift.

Stress management is a process people use to identify what causes stress for them in the workplace as well as in their personal lives, and then to apply various strategies to minimize its effects.

To identify and prevent stress, ask these questions:

- Is the stress due to poor planning or scheduling?
- Are tight time lines causing the stress?
- Is the pressure due to problems with equipment or the facility?
- Is the pressure from peers or other employees?
- Is the pressure being caused by self-imposed, unrealistic expectations?
- Are personal problems interfering with work?

After determining the causes, design and implement a stress-reduction plan. Seek input on the plan from valued and trusted people. Also consider incorporating some of these suggestions for coping with and preventing stress:

- Plan and evaluate daily activities to minimize any unanticipated situations.
- Delegate some work or ask for help from other employees.
- Evaluate progress along the way and make adjustments to plans as needed.
- Set daily realistic goals for self and/or with team.
- Get regular sleep, eat healthy, avoid smoking, and get regular exercise.
- Identify and use resources that can assist you with managing stress.

Time management uses tools to increase a person's efficiency and productivity. To manage time effectively also means to know how to waste less time on noncritical, unimportant activities and avoidable problems.

The skills needed for effective time management include the following:

- **Planning:** Document what needs to happen during a certain period of time (daily, monthly, yearly).
- **Goal setting:** Always set a time line for completing a task.
- **Setting priorities:** Identify the importance of tasks and then choose their order of completion.
- **Delegating:** As a leader, assign tasks to someone else and ensure their completion.

780

Even those who have good intentions at the beginning of a day and write down the day's plan might encounter other things that can get in their way. Being aware of all the things a person does during a day can result in better planning, decision making, delegating, and goal setting in order to use time more wisely. Consider leaving a small percentage of time during the day for unexpected tasks or events. That way, an entire daily plan won't be thrown off track if a surprise happens.

[fast fact]

Did You Know...?
The average person gets one interruption every 8 minutes. Although interruptions have a purpose and a message, use strategies to limit the number of interruption, such as shutting the door, blocking off time for priorities, or have scheduled times when interruptions are acceptable.

One method that can improve the ability to plan time more effectively is to review the activities a person needs to complete on a daily or weekly basis and break these activities into smaller tasks. Divide these activities into a controllable size to organize a work schedule more effectively. What may appear to be insurmountable tasks to complete in a day can actually become easier to handle when using this approach.

Create this list of smaller tasks and then follow through and act on the daily plan. Physically crossing tasks off the list also provides a visual sense of accomplishment. Evaluating later how the plans of daily and weekly activities actually worked is an additional way to improve time management skills.

Many people find that time management tools such as a PDA or time planner or computer programs like Microsoft Outlook help them organize their time more effectively. These tools make it easier to schedule and monitor activities and appointments on a daily, weekly, and monthly basis.

Restaurant and foodservice leaders who manage stress factors and their time so that they maintain a quality of life for themselves help foster that behavior in their employees.

781

Discuss
- What are your most important responsibilities each day? What activities take the most time? How are these two areas related?

Reinforce and Review
- Being aware of all the things that a person does each day can result in better time management skills.
- Reviewing the activities that are necessary each day or week and then breaking them into smaller components is one method that can help plan time and organize work more effectively.
- Evaluating how plans of daily and weekly activities actually worked is a way to improve time-management skills.
- Restaurant and foodservice leaders who manage stress factors and their time so they maintain a quality of life for themselves help foster that behavior in their employees.

**Fast Fact:
Did You Know...?**

Encourage students to discuss the following:

- How can students handle interruptions from family and friends?
- How can people identify whether interruptions are important?

Essential Skills: Handling Self-Imposed Pressures

Encourage students to discuss the following:

- How can improper eating habits make your stress level worse and put even more pressure on your body?

- Why is exercising with another person more effective?

- How can people learn to stop procrastinating?

- Why do people put pressures on themselves? Shouldn't people know better?

Discuss

- How long is too long to stay at the same job?
- What are some reasons people resign from jobs?

Reinforce and Review

- When planning to leave a job, it is both courteous and customary to give your employer two weeks' notice in writing.

Essential Skills

Handling Self-Imposed Pressures

A lot of external pressures are placed on teenagers: family needs, school, work, friends, thinking about the future. These external pressures can create a great deal of stress if not managed appropriately. But internal factors can also cause problems as well. Here are some common self-imposed pressures with coping mechanisms for each:

❶ **Procrastination:** It's always easier to postpone completing a task until later, isn't it? But working at the last minute, or missing important deadlines, can be a big source of stress. Try making a list of everything you need to accomplish over the next week or two (be sure to leave room for family, friends, and personal time). For each item, make a reasonable guess at how long it might take you to complete the task and then add 30 minutes to your estimate. Also, list upcoming deadlines: school projects, term papers, application forms, and family events. Now you can see realistically what your obligations are and plan to manage them effectively.

❷ **Overeating and undereating:** Poor eating habits can take a serious toll on you, both physically and mentally. If you're eating the wrong foods, or not enough of the right foods, your growing body and brain aren't receiving proper nutrition, which can cause significant short- and long-term damage. Consider speaking with a registered dietician to help you determine and act upon better solutions.

❸ **Lack of exercise:** It can be hard to make time to work out, but regular physical activity is one of the most effective stress relievers known. One effective way to get moving is to enlist a friend. Having a buddy can motivate you to exercise, even on those rainy mornings when you just want to stay in bed. Scheduling a regular meeting time is important, too; otherwise, it's easy to push exercise out of your routine. You don't need a gym membership, either; just going for a walk can relieve stress. If you haven't exercised in a while, consider speaking with a health-care professional before beginning an exercise program.

❹ **Smoking, drinking, and drug use:** It's often thought that using these substances can relieve stress and tension. But nothing could be further from the truth! Smoking, drinking, and drug use all cause important physiological changes, which, by altering how your body functions, can cause both physical and mental stress. These behaviors can also become external factors; peer pressure and family concerns can create even more stress. If you are using these substances, stop. Contact a health-care professional if you need help. If you aren't using these substances, don't start.

Resigning from a Job

Most people eventually leave a job because of a better opportunity, change in school schedule, or any number of reasons. Give a current employer a two-week notice before leaving; it's standard business practice. Inform him or her in person, or write a letter of resignation. Do not resign in an email. This is a serious and formal process. Figure 12.8 is an example of a resignation letter.

Take care in writing a letter of resignation. Include the reasons for leaving, but always be polite. Avoid any negative comments, and always thank the employer for providing the opportunity. As learned when filling out a job application, prospective employers ask about work records and request references from previous employers. Showing negativity when resigning might ruin future opportunities.

Ms. Linda Brown

Manager

Uptown Grille

75 East Pleasant Street

Funtown, USA 50094

October 15, 2011

Dear Ms. Brown:

As much as I have enjoyed working as a server at the Uptown Grille, I must resign effective October 25, 2010.

I have been offered a position as assistant manager in a full-service restaurant in Anytown that will enable me to continue to pursue my long-term goals in foodservice. Working at Uptown Grille has been a wonderful training experience for me. I know I'll be more considerate of all servers in my new position.

Thank you personally for setting such a great example as a manager. I hope you'll visit me at the Grand Café at your earliest convenience.

Thank you again for giving me the opportunity to work at Uptown Grille.

Sincerely,

Faith Fitzpatrick

110 West 84th Street

Funtown, USA 50094

Figure 12.8: A sample resignation letter.

A good guide to follow throughout your working career is always to leave on a positive note. Keep long-term goals in mind and rise above any negative words and attitudes of others. Have the patience and persistence to see a career vision to its ultimate goal. Possessing excellent skills and having good education and training are only part of the equation for a successful career in the restaurant and foodservice industry; successful employees also need commitment to service, a positive attitude, and perseverance to get to the top.

Discuss
- How can leaving a job on a negative note poison all the positive work the employee had previously accomplished?
- Why is it important for people to focus on long-term goals instead of short-term concerns?

Reinforce and Review
- A letter of resignation should always include the reason an employee is leaving, but should also be polite.
- Showing negativity when resigning might ruin future opportunities.
- Keep long-term goals in mind and rise above any negative words and attitudes of others.
- Excellent skills, good education and training, commitment to service, a positive attitude, and perseverance are all essential components in achieving a successful career.

Figure Focus
Figure 12.8: What is professional about this letter?

Discuss

- Why is it important for young employees to engage themselves with other professionals?
- How can people find a role for self-development in the balance between their work and life?
- Why would someone want to earn professional certifications?

Reinforce and Review

- Part of self-development is being involved in the industry.
- Continuous improvement or professional development is essential for success in the restaurant and foodservice industry.
- Achieving certification through a professional organization is a key way to improve professionally.

Vocabulary Terms

- **Certification:** Recognition given when an individual has demonstrated a high level of skill and has met specific performance requirements by participating in a rigorous process.

Staying Educated and Involved

Part of self-development is being involved in the industry. The following opportunities will present themselves to students who are aware of what's out there:

- **Staying current with industry publications and online groups:** Examples might include:
    - The National Restaurant Association's Web site, www.restaurant.org
    - The ACF (American Culinary Federation) publication *Sizzle*
    - Restaurant news sites, such as http://www.nrn.com
    - Center for the Advancement of Foodservice Education—www.cafe meetingplace.com, or *Restaurants & Institutes*—http://www.rimag.com
- **Participating in professional organizations:** One example might be the Junior Association of the ACF.
- **Networking.**
- **Completing training and education:** One example is the Foundations of Restaurant Management & Culinary Arts Level 1 Certificate of Recognition, which acknowledges students who have successfully completed an examination based on the curriculum of this textbook.

Continuous Improvement

Continuous improvement or professional development is essential for success in restaurant or foodservice management. Achieving certifications is one key way to improve yourself professionally. **Certification** indicates that a student has demonstrated a high level of skill and has met specific performance requirements by participating in a rigorous process to become certified. Several certifications for restaurant and foodservice managers include the following:

- Foodservice Management Professional (FMP)
- ServSafe Food Protection Manager Certification
- ServSafe Alcohol Certificate
- Certified Executive Chef (CEC)
- Certified Hospitality Executive (CHE)
- Certified Food Manager (CFM)

Certifications are usually administered through professional organizations. Some organizations require that students become members to become certified

784

while others do not. Many certifications also may require work experience as a demonstration of competence in the field. Work experience counts as a part of the overall certification process.

Attending continuing education courses through either a local college or university also is essential for a manager to stay updated with the latest information in the industry. Many times, workshops are offered at conferences that provide continuing education credits as well.

Professional Organizations

Professional organization membership is one way to stay on the "cutting edge" of the hospitality and restaurant industry. Weekly and/or monthly newsletters, workshops, and conferences are just some of the benefits of belonging to a professional organization. Consider joining some of these organizations:

- National Restaurant Association (NRA). *Appendix A, Staying Connected with the National Restaurant Association Throughout Your Career*

- American Culinary Federation

- International Food Services Executive Association

- Council of Hotels, Restaurants, and Institutional Educators (CHRIE)

In addition, most national organizations have state and local chapters. Also consider joining specific state restaurant associations.

Other Resources

Other resources to consider for professional development opportunities include industry publications, such as *Nation's Restaurant News, Chain Leader, QSR Food Management*, and *Restaurant Business*. These publications provide the latest in industry information and should be part of a manager's journal and magazine reading list. The Internet also provides a wealth of information for the restaurant and foodservice professional, and a manager should keep up with a variety of Web-based resources to further continuous education.

Networking

Restaurant and foodservice managers must stay connected to the industry. Staying connected means networking with other industry professionals. The purpose of **networking** is to connect with several people to build relationships that may result in career advancement, industry updates, and knowledge or career enhancements. One method of networking is to attend trade shows and interact

785

Discuss
- How is joining a professional organization different from joining a student-based organization? How is it similar?
- How do one's professional goals help determine what one studies and reads during free time?
- How can young employees engage in professional development while still in school?

Reinforce and Review
- Continuing their educations can help managers stay abreast of industry developments.
- Regular newsletters, workshops, and conferences are some benefits of membership in professional organizations.
- A variety of print and online resources can help foodservice professionals expand their knowledge.
- Networking helps professionals stay connected to others within the industry.

Teaching Tips
- Obtain sample foodservice publications for students to examine.

Vocabulary Terms
- **Networking:** Connecting with people to build relationships that may result in career advancement, industry updates, and knowledge or career enhancements.

Discuss

- How do internal and external networking opportunities differ? How can students engage in either type of networking?

Reinforce and Review

- Networking helps professionals stay current with industry trends.
- Internal networking involves building relationships within one's business, while external networking involves building relationships with outside individuals.

What's New:
Increases in Online Professional Development Options

Encourage students to discuss the following:

- Why is online professional development increasingly popular?

- How are professional development and networking related? How does the use of online options both increase and decrease networking opportunities?

with people who are attending. Typically, a reception is held at the beginning or closing of the trade show. Other methods for networking include the following:

- Attending designated networking sessions during conventions, seminars, and conferences
- Participating in community events and sharing information about the organization
- Attending state and local restaurant association meetings and social events
- Participating in community career days, forums, charity events, and service projects
- Attending Chamber of Commerce meetings
- Volunteering as a community mentor and getting to know key community leaders
- Becoming an active member of a professional restaurant and foodservice organization
- Visiting area competitors and other businesses to establish rapport and business opportunities

Networking is also valuable because it helps keep professionals current with industry trends. Develop a network that is both internal and external. Develop outside contacts through memberships in various professional organizations and establish a contact list of peers, vendors, and government personnel.

[what's new]

Increases in Online Professional Development Options

As the restaurant and foodservice industry continues to professionalize, more and more people are taking advantage of online professional development options, such as continuing education units or hours (CEUs/CEHs), online degrees, and even social-networking sites. Organizations such as the National Restaurant Association and the Research Chefs Association often provide online resources, such as research papers and other industry reports. The American Culinary Federation offers online classes to help members prepare for certification examinations as well as CEUs for those successfully completing online quizzes. A certain number of CEUs are required to maintain certification, and quizzes are one way to earn these credits.

Online courses and degrees are available from a wide variety of accredited programs, both colleges and trade school. Online courses can be an easy way for a busy cook or chef to take classes or earn advanced degrees. Online courses allow students to do their schoolwork from home. Social-networking sites such as Facebook, Twitter, and Culinary Cartel can help link restaurant and foodservice professionals. These sites allow members to share knowledge and build relationships. In short, where once a chef was isolated in a kitchen, the rise of the Internet has facilitated the chef's ability to interact with and learn from the world and to bring knowledge back to that once confining restaurant.

786

An important factor to remember about networking relationships is that they must be a two-way street. A professional does not expect his or her network to always provide information, contacts, or opportunities. Each member must return opportunities in the network as well. For example, a professional can share his or her best practices with particular individuals in his or her network.

Another networking opportunity is to seek assistance in complex problem-solving situations. Colleagues can offer insights and perspectives on challenging situations. In this way, they are developing a stronger personal relationship that is mutually beneficial to everyone in the network. Networking also promotes important dialogue among industry professionals, which in some cases promotes changes that serve to improve the overall performance of the industry.

Many online social-networking sites, such as LinkedIn or Plaxo, focus specifically on career development. These sites help professionals connect, discuss their chosen fields, and discuss the latest industry news and trends.

Summary

In this section, you learned the following:

- To stay healthy as an industry employee, eat right, exercise, don't smoke, make the most of breaks, find a hobby, don't take drugs, drink responsibly, take advantage of the resources available, sleep, save money, and find a job that makes you happy.

- Stress is the condition or feeling that demands exceed the resources a person has. Stress management is a process that people use to identify what causes stress for personal life and then to apply various strategies to minimize its effects. Use time management tools to increase efficiency and productivity. Learning time management tools reduces stress.

- To manage time and stress, plan and evaluate daily activities, delegate work or ask for help from other employees, evaluate progress along the way, make adjustments as necessary, and set daily personal and team goals.

- To resign from a job, write a letter of resignation that includes the reasons for leaving. The letter should be positive and thank the employer for the opportunity to work at the company.

- Professional development is a continuous process of improvement. It allows a professional to stay current on industry trends, participate in professional organizations, become certified, and network.

787

Discuss

- How do networking relationships relate to communication skills? How do they relate to networking?
- How can building relationships with others in the same industry help to control stress?

Reinforce and Review

- Networking relationships must be a two-way street.
- Seeking assistance with complex problem-solving situations serves as a networking opportunity.

Teaching Tips

- Networking rarely involves just two people. It is a complex web of interactions.

Summary

- Remind students to review the following:
  1. How to maintain health and wellness throughout a restaurant and foodservice career
  2. The relationship between time and stress
  3. The ways to manage time and stress
  4. How to resign from a position
  5. Importance of professional development

Section 12.4
Review Questions

1. Steps to leading a healthy lifestyle include eating properly, getting exercise, not smoking, finding other passions outside the workplace, not abusing drugs or alcohol, taking advantage of employer-provided resources for healthy living, saving money, and finding a job that confers happiness.

2. Resigning from a job should be done in writing, giving two weeks of notice and thanking the employer for the opportunity. The reason for leaving the company should be given, but presented in polite terms. In short, always leave on a professional, positive note.

3. Stress indicators include irritability and depression, headaches, indigestion, pain in the neck and/or lower back, and changes in appetite or sleep patterns. They may be caused by time pressures, concerns about grades or future plans, relationships with others, changes or failure to accept changes, and workplace challenges.

4. The purpose of networking is to connect with other industry professionals to build relationships that may result in career advancement, industry updates, and knowledge or career enhancements.

5. Students should research these organizations through online or print sources.

6. Personal issues can cause stress, which can lead to poor performance in the workplace.

7. Students should research a certification that interests them. The examples of certifications on p. 784 and the examples of professional organizations on p. 785 may be useful.

8. Professionals, even during the earliest stages of their careers, should work to develop themselves by staying abreast of industry activity. Networking, reading industry publications, furthering one's education, participating in professional organizations, and obtaining certifications are all ways employees can keep moving forward.

Section 12.4 Review Questions

1. List five steps to having a healthy lifestyle.

2. What is an appropriate way to resign from a job?

3. List three stress indicators and their causes.

4. What is networking?

5. Ron Yudd says that you should "try to learn something new every day!" Think about a job in which you might be interested. What organization(s) offer support and professional development for that job? What activities and resources do they make available?

6. Sam had to resign from his job due to personal issues. How else can personal issues affect your working life?

7. Why do some professionals seek formal certifications? Research one certification related to the restaurant and foodservice industry, including its requirements, the number of people that have it, and what it does for you (or allows you to do). Compile all of these findings and use as a reference tool for your fellow students.

8. After you have a job, what do you need to do to keep moving forward on your career path?

788

Section 12.4 Activities

1. Study Skills/Group Activity: Stress Relief

Work with two other students to identify some ways that you and your fellow students have successfully combated stress in the past. Create a handout for your classmates describing the most effective solutions.

2. Activity: Stress-Management Plan

Stress-management plans are crucial to your professional and personal development. Create a stress-management plan to help you organize your life and goals.

3. Critical Thinking: Career Goals

What do you hope to achieve professionally? Draft your career goals and then develop a time line for accomplishing your desires.

789

Section 12.4 Activities

1. Students should work together to identify and share useful stress-relieving techniques.

2. Students should develop stress-management plans based on their current situations.

3. Students should identify at least three professional goals and develop a clear and realistic time line for achieving them.

Section 12.5
Careers in the Industry

Introduce the Section

a. Describe some common entry-level jobs in the restaurant and foodservice industry.
b. Identify some career opportunities in the hospitality industry.
c. Discuss the objectives for the section.

Vocabulary Review

a. Direct students to the key terms.
b. Pronounce each word, and have the students repeat the pronunciation out loud.
c. Discuss the definition of each word.

Teach

Discuss

- What foodservice career opportunities are the most attractive, and why?

Reinforce and Review

- The first impression guests receive when entering a foodservice establishment is that of the employee meeting them at the entrance.
- The restaurant and foodservice industry is among the nation's leading employers.

12.1 Starting a Career in Foodservice	12.2 Completing Applications Effectively	12.3 The Job Interview	12.4 Advancing in a Career	12.5 Careers in the Industry
• Skills needed for a successful career	• Job applications	• Preparing for the job interview	• Health and wellness	• Entry-level jobs
• The job search	• College applications	• The interview	• Stress and time management	• A selection of careers
• Preparing a résumé, portfolio, and cover letter	• Scholarships	• Follow up after the interview	• Resigning from a job	
			• Staying educated and involved	

SECTION 12.5 CAREERS IN THE INDUSTRY

The restaurant and foodservice industry has many career opportunities. It is among the nation's leading employers.

Study Questions

After studying Section 12.5, you should be able to answer the following questions:

- What are some of the popular entry-level jobs in the restaurant and foodservice industry?
- What are the career opportunities in the restaurant and foodservice industry?
- What are the career opportunities in the lodging industry?
- What are the career opportunities in the travel industry?
- What are the career opportunities in the tourism industry?

Entry-level Jobs

The following are brief descriptions of the responsibilities in some popular entry-level jobs in the restaurant and foodservice industry:

- **Host/hostess/cashier:** The very first impression of an operation that guests receive is from the host/hostess or employee who meets them at the entrance. If that impression is friendly, hospitable, and gracious, guests will feel relaxed and ready to enjoy themselves. In addition to greeting customers, hosts assist guests with coats or other things they wish to check; take reservations; seat customers; ask whether departing customers enjoyed their meals; thank customers for their visit; and answer customers' questions

790

---

about hours of the operation, types of credit cards accepted, and what menu items are available. In some operations, hosts act as the cashier; in others, cashiers are separate positions.

- **Server:** Servers spend more time with the guests than any other employee. The server's attitude and performance have a tremendous impact on the guest's enjoyment of the dining experience. In a full-service operation, servers greet customers; take their order; serve the order; check on customers' needs after serving the meal; and continue to provide service until customers have left the table.

- **Quick-service counter servers:** Quick-service counter servers usually have only brief contact with each customer. This means that servers have only a few moments to make a good first impression. Counter servers greet customers, take their orders, accept payment, and thank customers for their patronage. Figure 12.9 shows a quick-service counter server in action.

- **Buser:** The buser assists the server and takes care of guests' needs; his or her work makes an immediate impression on guests. The buser is primarily responsible for clearing and grooming the table.

- **Prep cooks:** Prep cooks help the more experienced cooks and chefs prepare and cook guests' orders. Often, assistant cooks prepare meals, which means to portion out food, precook it, or get it ready ahead of time, so everything is ready to assemble when guests order that menu item.

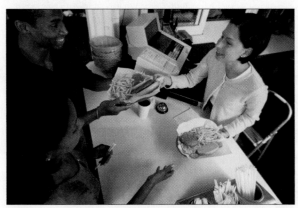

Figure 12.9: A quick-service counter server.

791

- How are quick-service counter servers similar to hosts and hostesses? What responsibilities do they share for providing guests with a good impression of the establishment?
- How are all the entry-level foodservice jobs described on pp. 790–792 related?

Reinforce and Review
- In some establishments, hosts or hostesses also act as cashiers.
- Servers spend more time with guests than any other foodservice employees and are responsible in large measure for the guests' enjoyment of the dining experience.
- Quick-service counter servers have only a brief time to make a good impression on their guests.
- Busers are primarily responsible for clearing and grooming tables.
- Prep cooks help other cooks and chefs prepare orders.

Figure Focus
Figure 12.9: What does this employee's nonverbal communication tell her guests?

Discuss

- How are all foodservice jobs and careers linked? How does communication play a role in each? What role does professionalism play?

Reinforce and Review

- The dishwasher helps determine the guests' overall impression of the establishment.

Trends:
Professionalization of the Restaurant and Foodservice Industry through Certification and Education

Encourage students to discuss the following:

- Why did the American Culinary Federation push for the professionalization of chefs?

- How has the restaurant and foodservice industry changed outwardly in the last decade?

- What is the relationship between education and professionalization? Does education have to be formal to be professional?

- **Dishwasher:** Clean, sparkling, sanitary tableware is essential to an enjoyable meal, and dishwashers see that this function is fulfilled. Although the dishwashers work in the back of the house, their work is very visible in the front of the house, helping determine the guests' overall impression of the operation. The dishwasher also keeps an eye on service areas, making certain that supplies do not run out.

[trends]

Professionalization of the Restaurant and Foodservice Industry through Certification and Education

At one time, society considered cooks and chefs to be low-skilled employees and gave them little status or respect. Carême and Escoffier helped to change that with their emphasis on training and educating their employees. Today, their names are synonymous with culinary professionalism. In 1976, the American Culinary Federation successfully lobbied to list chefs as professionals instead of service workers in the U.S. Department of Labor's Dictionary of Official Titles. Although this might seem a tiny change, the impact galvanized the entire industry. More recently, the rise of the Food Network and the explosion of interest in professional and home cooking have elevated respect for cooks and chefs to new heights.

The restaurant and foodservice industry of today continues to professionalize. Employees and employers are raising their standards each day in an effort to improve both what they produce and how consumers view it. Employers increasingly demand workers with culinary degrees, diplomas, or certificates, and interest in professional certification. Each year, new culinary programs and colleges open as more and more aspiring students enroll. Opportunities for continuing education are expanding, often at conventions and trade shows, and restaurant and foodservice professionals are increasingly working to achieve certification as experts in their fields. The industry has achieved a new level of prestige and honor as society has come to recognize the intense effort and sacrifice involved in professional cooking.

A Selection of Careers

Table 12.5 describes a selection of careers in the restaurant and foodservice, lodging, travel, and tourism industries.

Table 12.5: Careers in Restaurant and Foodservice, Lodging, Travel, and Tourism

A. Careers in Restaurant and Foodservice

Jobs in foodservice can be varied and unique. Higher-level jobs include planning menus, developing recipes, managing a restaurant and foodservice operation, writing about food, developing marketing and advertising strategies, teaching others about food and nutrition, and supplying food to restaurants.

Restaurant and Foodservice Career	Description of Responsibilities
Owner/Operators and Entrepreneurs	Owner/operators and entrepreneurs (ON-trah-prah-NOOR) own and run their own businesses. Successful entrepreneurs must dedicate themselves to their businesses. They need to be **well-organized** and **committed to working long hours** as well as have a strong general knowledge of business practices. Entrepreneurs are usually risk-takers who work well without supervision.
General managers	General managers are responsible for the **overall planning, direction, and coordinating** of the operation. They are responsible for hiring, firing, and promoting employees. They leave the day-to-day management of various functions to the managers, who report back to them.
Managers	Responsibilities of managers are often divided into categories within an operation, such as catering, beverage, kitchen, and dining room. They are responsible for **hiring and supervising** employees; **staff training; maintaining an operation** and its property; keeping food safe; keeping guests and employees safe; marketing and promoting the operation; ensuring profits; keeping costs down; purchasing and storing food; and other necessary tasks.
Assistant managers	Assistant managers are responsible for **helping the managers.** This is the usual training position for future managers.
Executive chef	The executive chef is part of an operation's management team. An executive chef **oversees the entire kitchen,** from supervising all kitchen employees to purchasing food supplies and making decisions about menu items.
Sous chefs	A sous chef is responsible for the kitchen team in the executive chef's absence and also lends his or her **cooking expertise** to overall food preparation.
Banquet chefs	Banquet chefs are responsible for catered parties, functions, and banquets. Banquet chefs **usually work in lodging operations and clubs.** They work closely with the catering department in an operation.
Pastry chefs	Pastry chefs are responsible for **pastry and baking production** in an operation. Most pastry chefs work in hotels, fine-dining restaurants, and restaurants with high volumes of customers.
Station cooks	Station cooks can be **responsible for a variety of areas within a kitchen.** The pantry or *garde manger* cook is responsible for cold food and buffet arrangements. The roast cook prepares meat, poultry, and fish. The sauce and stock cook prepares sauces and stocks. The vegetable cook prepares vegetables and soups, and the pastry cook prepares desserts and specialty baked goods.

continued

Table 12.5: Careers in Restaurant and Foodservice, Lodging, Travel, and Tourism (continued on pp. 794–797)

A. Careers in Restaurant and Foodservice (continued on p. 794)

- How are owner/operators and entrepreneurs major participants in the restaurant and foodservice industry?

- Which of the careers listed on p. 793 could be considered managerial positions? Why?

- How do executive chefs play a role in the day-to-day cooking responsibilities at a foodservice establishment?

- What do all of the careers listed on p. 793 have in common?

- What is the difference between a job and a career? For instance, cashiers are not on this list, although someone could choose to spend the majority of his or her working years as a cashier. What is the distinction?

Table 12.5 (continued)

A. Careers in Restaurant and Foodservice (continued)

- What do food writers, foodservice marketers, and food stylists have in common?

- How are food scientists related to research and development chefs? How do both of these differ from kitchen chefs?

- In what ways do accountants/controllers play significant roles in an establishment's decisions about menus, service styles, décor, and other issues that affect their guests' experiences?

- Why does demand for nutritionists and dietitians continue to grow?

Table 12.5: Careers in Restaurant and Foodservice, Lodging, Travel, and Tourism *continued*

Restaurant and Foodservice Career	Description of Responsibilities
Food writers	Food writers with strong communication skills are needed to **write books, magazine articles, and brochures,** providing consumers with information about food and related matters. Writers may also contribute their talents to the development of training and instructional materials for both restaurants and foodservice companies.
Food stylists	Food stylists **arrange food attractively** for photographs to be included in magazines and brochures and to be used by government agencies, associations, and food producers and distributors.
Foodservice marketers	Foodservice marketers are **active in sales, management, and distribution** of food products and services. An enormous variety of food items and products must be marketed and sold to foodservice operators.
Research and development chefs	Opportunities in research and development involve the **development and testing of new products** in test kitchens and laboratories. Marketing and promotion tasks also can be a part of these chefs' functions. Governments, food producers, universities, and manufacturers of kitchen appliances all need people with these interests and skills.
Food scientists	Food scientists **study the composition of food.** They develop new food products as well as new ways to process and package them. In addition, they test food for quality, purity, and safety to ensure that they meet government standards.
Nutritionists and dietitians	Dietitians are **trained in the principles of food and nutrition.** They help people make wise food choices and help develop special diets when needed. Dietitians typically work in universities, restaurants, schools, hospitals, and institutional cafeterias developing nutritious menus.
Food production and food processing	Careers in this area include everything from **running a food manufacturing and processing facility to distributing food products** to restaurants. The production of food and delivering it to consumers requires a large network of dedicated people.
Accountants/ controllers	Accountants and controllers in the restaurant and foodservice industry are knowledgeable about trends in the industry, **give financial advice, and handle payroll and financial procedures.** Smaller operations contract accounting services; larger operations, hotels, and chains hire controllers to perform these functions.
Trainers	Trainers **conduct training sessions** for groups of employees or managers. Typically, trainers work for large restaurant and foodservice companies that own many units. Training managers are responsible for ensuring that all employees and managers receive the right kind of training for their jobs.

794

Table 12.5: Careers in Restaurant and Foodservice, Lodging, Travel, and Tourism *continued*

Restaurant and Foodservice Career	Description of Responsibilities
Retail food managers	Retail food managers are increasingly finding that their jobs are like those of restaurant managers. Many stores sell foods that are ready to eat, so managers and employees must know how to prepare food, understand and apply food safety standards, and promote what they have to their customers. **This area of the industry is growing rapidly,** and many employees and managers will be needed in years to come to supply this demand.
Foodservice and hospitality educators	Many opportunities are available for foodservice and hospitality education **in many levels of education, including high school, two-year colleges, and universities.** Positions usually require at least a bachelor's degree and training in education and/or appropriate certifications. Many people work in the industry for some time and then move into educator positions.

B. Careers in Lodging

The careers in the lodging industry are typically divided into those with customer contact and those that support the running of the operation.

Lodging Career	Description of Responsibilities
General management	General managers are responsible for the **overall planning, direction, and coordinating of the operation.** They are responsible for hiring, firing, and promoting employees. They leave the day-to-day management of various functions to the managers, who report back to them.
Accounting and financial management	These managers keep track of overall profits, record sales, and **calculate costs.**
Human resources	Human resources personnel not only **recruit, select, and train** qualified applicants, but evaluate performance as well. They are also responsible for administering federal, state, and local labor laws and overseeing the operation's benefits program.
Marketing and sales	Marketing and sales are largely responsible for **generating the property's sales.** They do this by making sure that its lodging facility and services are well suited to its customers' needs.
Front office	Often described as **the "nerve center,"** the front office represents what a lodging establishment is to most guests. For this reason, it's vital that front-office employees have good people skills and know the importance of quality service.
Housekeeping	In addition to **maintaining property,** housekeeping personnel are responsible for keeping rooms guest-ready and ensuring that accommodations are clean and safe.

continued

795

Table 12.5 (continued)

A. Careers in Restaurant and Foodservice (continued)

- Retail food management opportunities, as discussed in Chapter 1, continue to increase.

- How do foodservice and hospitality educators affect the professionalization of the entire industry?

B. Careers in Lodging

- Which lodging careers involve customer contact and which support the running of the operation? In what ways can these overlap?

- Why is the front office of a lodging operation considered the "nerve center"?

- How do marketing and sales staff members help generate revenue for an operation?

Table 12.5 (continued)

B. Careers in Lodging (continued)

- What role does the food and beverage director play in guest service? How does his or her work overlap with that of the marketing and sales staff?

- How does a concierge work with the front desk to put a face on the lodging establishment?

C. Careers in Travel and Tourism: Transportation

- Do students agree that these employees should be considered members of the hospitality industry? Why or why not?

- What challenges might employment on a cruise ship present? What opportunities might it provide?

- How do travel agents and corporate travel office employees facilitate guest experiences?

- What are some foodservice opportunities in transportation?

Table 12.5: Careers in Restaurant and Foodservice, Lodging, Travel, and Tourism *continued*

Lodging Career	Description of Responsibilities
Engineering and facility maintenance	Engineers and facility maintenance workers keep the **physical building in good running order.**
Security	Depending on its size, a lodging facility may employ a number of security personnel, including a **director, watchmen, guards, and detectives.**
Food and beverage	As with the front office department, employees in food and beverage need **good people skills and a commitment to quality.** The food and beverage director oversees the kitchen, dining room, and lounge, as well as banquet rooms and room service. The director's other responsibilities include supervising and scheduling employees, monitoring product cost control, and composing menus.
Concierge	Employed by hotels, motels, and resorts, the concierge (kahn-see-AIRJE) **serves guests** by helping them buy tickets to shows and events, answering questions, booking restaurant reservations, and more.

C. Careers in Travel and Tourism: Transportation

Travel and tourism offer many options for those seeking careers in the hospitality industry, including jobs in restaurant and foodservice, lodging, human resources, accounting, marketing, and many other areas.

Transportation careers focus on all aspects and methods of traveling. Many of these companies must employ drivers, ticket agents, mechanics, engineers, managers, and other administrators.

Transportation Careers	Description
Travel agent	**Helping travelers with just about all of their arrangements,** travel agents must know how to make airline reservations, plan trips, and set itineraries, which are travel plans. They also rent cars, purchase tickets for shows and events, book cruises and train travel, make hotel reservations, and put together tours and travel packages. Travel packages combine several travel services for one set price. Travel agents are often sent on trips so they can describe the hotels at which they've stayed and the places they've visited.
Corporate travel office employees	Many companies are large enough to employ their own **in-house travel services.** Employees of these corporate travel offices take care of the arrangements for the company's employees, officers, and representatives, much like travel agents do for the public.
Airline careers	The airline industry **offers a number of jobs,** including flight attendant, reservations agent, ticket agent, pilot, mechanic, and baggage handler. Airports themselves also employ many people, such as baggage porters (skycaps), restaurant and foodservice workers, and taxi coordinators.
Trains	Both the national railway and local lines employ many people. **Conductors, engineers, and ticket agents** make up the core of this industry. Many stations also have restaurant and foodservice operations.

796

Table 12.5: Careers in Restaurant and Foodservice, Lodging, Travel, and Tourism *continued*

Transportation Careers	Description
Cruise ships	The lifestyle required of a crew member isn't for everyone, but **opportunities in cruising are varied and plentiful.** Many large cruising ships can have a thousand employees on board, from chefs to engineers to entertainers.
Charter services	**Private companies offer specific traveling arrangements** for groups or individuals. Opportunities include private aviation and bus charters, among others.
Buses, limousines, and cars	**Drivers** of all types are an important part of this segment. Car and limo services are especially popular in urban areas. Rental car companies would also be included here.

D. Careers in Travel and Tourism: Tourism

Careers in this area focus on the many ways that people spend their time and money when they're away from home.

Tourism Careers	Description
Tour guide	Some travelers choose to be part of an organized group with a leader who knows all about where the group is, where it's going, and how to get from one place to another. That leader is the tour guide. Many tour guides **lead trips that appeal to niche markets,** or groups of people having similar interests, ages, or skills, and common travel objectives.
Tourism office employees	Tourism offices are established by state and local governments and **provide information to people who are visiting** or who would like to visit an area. Many people work in and for these offices by answering questions, creating marketing and advertising campaigns, and collecting statistics on travelers.
Convention and meeting planners	Planners are needed to see to the countless arrangements and details that go into **large meetings and conventions.** Planners do everything from inviting speakers and arranging meeting rooms to hiring video producers and selecting banquet centerpieces. They may work for a company or act as an independent contractor.
Travel writers and photographers	Most newspapers and many magazines and journals carry **travel-related stories.** Journalists and professional photographers provide the words and photos for these stories. Many travel firms and tour companies also employ writers and photographers to create promotional materials.
Theme park and amusement park employees	Large theme parks can employ hundreds or sometimes thousands of people. The Disney Company, for example, has become one of the largest employers in the world, with Disney World alone employing thousands of people in **management, accounting, administrative, and entertainment positions.**
National Park Service (NPS)	**Park rangers** are probably the most famous type of employees of the NPS, but many other professionals are involved in protecting the nation's parks. They include archaeologists, firefighters, restaurant and foodservice managers, and many administrative positions.

797

Table 12.5 (continued)

C. Careers in Travel and Tourism: Transportation (continued)

- How are careers in private aviation and driving services similar? How are they different?

- Do students believe that drivers of city buses and operators of intra-city rail services should be included on this list of careers? Why or why not?

D. Careers in Travel and Tourism: Tourism

- Encourage students to relate this material to the discussion of hospitality and tourism careers in Chapter 1.

- How are travel writers linked professionally to food writers?

- How is the work of convention and meeting planners related to the work of marketing and sales staff in the lodging industry?

- How is the work of the employees of the National Park Service similar to that of theme park and amusement park employees? How is it different?

Summary

- Remind students to review the following:
  1. Popular entry-level jobs in restaurant and foodservice operations
  2. Career opportunities in restaurant and foodservice operations
  3. Career opportunities in lodging
  4. Career opportunities in travel
  5. Career opportunities in tourism

Summary

In this section, you learned the following:

- Entry-level positions in the restaurant and foodservice industry include host/hostess, server, quick-service counter servers, buser, prep cooks, and dishwashers.

- Careers in the restaurant and foodservice industry include owner, general manager, manager, assistant manager, executive chef, sous chef, banquet chef, pastry chef, station cook, food writer, food stylist, dietician/nutritionist, food production and food processing, accountant/controller, trainer, retail food manager, and foodservice education.

- The careers in the lodging industry are typically divided into those with customer contact and those that support the running of the operation.

- Travel and tourism offer many options for those seeking careers in the hospitality industry, including jobs in restaurant and foodservice, lodging, human resources, accounting, marketing, and many other areas.

- Careers in the travel and tourism area focus on the many ways that people spend their time and money when they're away from home.

Section 12.5 Review Questions

1. Give examples of entry-level positions in the restaurant and foodservice industry.

2. What are some of the higher-level jobs in the restaurant and foodservice industry?

3. Provide a brief description of the following careers in the restaurant and foodservice industry:

    a. General manager

    b. Executive chef

    c. Sous chef

    d. Retail food manager

4. Describe three careers in the travel and tourism industry.

5. Ron Yudd worked in many positions as he grew his career. Think of your current position or a job for which you may be interviewing. Can you see a career path that starts with this position? If not, what skills are you learning that will make you a valuable asset at another company?

6. Sam is looking for a distributor position. He originally started working in the kitchen and worked his way up to kitchen manager. Why would "field distributor" be an appropriate next step on his career path?

7. What are some common career paths in the hospitality industry, starting with a typical entry-level position?

8. What is the outlook for the restaurant and foodservice industry over the next decade?

799

Section 12.5 Review Questions

1. Entry-level positions in the restaurant and foodservice industry include host/hostess/cashier, server, quick-service counter server, buser, prep cook, and dishwasher.

2. Higher-level positions in the restaurant and foodservice industry include owner/operators and entrepreneurs, general managers, managers, assistant managers, executive chefs, sous chefs, banquet chefs, and pastry chefs, among others.

3. Careers in the restaurant and foodservice industry include the following positions:

    a. General managers are responsible for the overall planning, direction, and coordinating of the operation. They are responsible for hiring, firing, and promoting employees.

    b. Executive chefs oversee the entire kitchen, from supervising all kitchen employees to purchasing food supplies and making decisions about menu items.

    c. Sous chefs are responsible for the kitchen team in the executive chef's absence and lend their cooking expertise to overall food preparation.

    d. Retail food managers are responsible for preparing food, understanding and applying food safety standards, and promoting their products. Their jobs are increasingly similar to those of restaurant managers.

4. Students may describe any three careers in the travel and tourism industry, using the material on pp. 796–797.

5. Students should consider how a current or potential position can lead to a fruitful career or provide skills that will be valuable in another line of work.

6. Students should identify ways in which Sam's previous jobs and responsibilities position him for a job as field distributor. For instance, he has worked with a wide variety of ingredients during his career in the kitchen, so he is familiar with many of the items he would be working with as a distributor.

7. Students should select two or three entry-level positions and build career paths from them. For instance, a career that begins as a prep cook could end as an executive chef, a trainer, or an educator.

8. According to the National Restaurant Association, the restaurant and foodservice industry is expected to add 1.8 million jobs over the next decade, with employment reaching 14.8 million by 2019.

Section 12.5 Activities

1. Students should note a wide variety of employment options in the restaurant and foodservice industry by consulting online sources.

2. Students should select different career paths and starting points from the ones used in question seven on the previous page.

3. Students should research and report on a career that appeals to them, using the lists in section 12.5 as a starting point but not limiting themselves to this list.

Section 12.5 Activities

1. Study Skills/Group Activity: Local Career Opportunities

Look through the classified section of your local newspaper or go online to job search sites such as Monster.com or CareerBuilder.com and browse the restaurant job listings. How many different headings can you find? What are the hours? How much does the job pay?

2. Activity: Diagram

Beginning with a typical entry-level position, diagram three potential career paths, including at least three positions in each path.

3. Critical Thinking: Off the Career Path

Use the lists in this section to select a career that you've never thought of for yourself. Research that career and write a three-paragraph report on your findings.

800

Case Study Follow-Up *Moving On*

At the beginning of the chapter, we note that Sam is an excellent worker, so his mentor Linda is happy to be an active participant in his job search.

1. However, what if Sam hadn't been a good worker? What if you were mentoring an employee who didn't perform well? To what extent would you assist that person in a job search and why?

2. Sam hopes to move from a position as kitchen manager into a job as field distributor. What challenges might he face? How can he address these challenges, either neutralizing them or turning them into opportunities?

3. What obstacles could make it difficult for Sam to find a job in a new city? What resources can he use to improve his chances?

4. What new career skills will Sam need for his new position? How can he prepare for the transition?

801

Case Study Follow-Up

1. Students should consider the perils of mentoring a mediocre or poor employee and how their own reputation might be affected by this person's performance.

2. Students should think realistically about the challenges Sam may face. For instance, Sam's communication style as kitchen manager, where he primarily interacted with his employees, may need to change now that he is in a position where he will primarily interact with customers and potential customers. He could address this particular challenge by working to improve his interpersonal communication skills, either on his own or with Linda.

3. Students should identify challenges Sam will face, such as lack of contacts and lack of knowledge about the local foodservice industry, and how he can resolve them using networking, and researching.

4. Students may need to research field distributors to answer this question properly. They should identify skills that Sam may not have learned in the kitchen, such as salesmanship, and how he can obtain them.

Apply Your Learning

Budget

Students should develop a realistic budget, incorporating as much information as possible so that this can be a useful project. Encourage students to think about how their daily habits and living expenses might need to change. Students should also explore scholarship and financial aid opportunities.

The Right Job for You

Students should think deeply about their likes, dislikes, and character traits, and how these will help determine their career paths. As the process of completing this assignment continues, students may sense that their professional goals and interests have shifted, changing their opinions of various careers.

Apply Your Learning

Budget

Coming up with college or trade school tuition would be a lot easier if there weren't so many other costs. Books, fees, and living expenses can equal or even exceed tuition costs, depending on the school you choose and the area where you will live. How can you make this work?

Identify a school you would like to attend full-time and determine its total cost per year. Many schools have Web sites with estimated costs. If you will not be living on campus, research apartment rentals and food costs to estimate your living expenses.

Do you plan to work off-campus? If so, what jobs are available locally, what can you expect to earn, and how many hours each week will you be able to work if you are a full-time student?

Will you have a car, will you use public transportation, or will you ride a bicycle? What costs are associated with these options?

How much money do you and your family have saved for tuition?

What financial aid and scholarship options are available?

Now create a budget, estimating all your expenses and income for the year. Remember, you will have living expenses no matter where you live, although some areas are more expensive than others. Is this school affordable? If not, what other options do you have—other scholarships, other schools, working full-time for a year before attending school?

Be as realistic as you can on this project. If you plan to attend a school after graduating from high school, you will need to be able to perform these calculations.

The Right Job for You

What kind of career do you want to have? Do you know all the options available to you? What types of work make you happy, interest you, or repel you?

Hundreds of different careers are available in the restaurant and foodservice industry. The hard part is deciding which, if any, career is right for you. Talk with your guidance counselor about your interests and goals. Use your school or public library to research career options. Consider taking a free online personality test. This test might reveal some character traits you've undervalued and present some new paths

802

to explore. Identify some people in careers you'd like to have and, if possible, talk with them about the positive and negative aspects of their jobs.

After you have done this research, write a report on your findings. In your report, include what you have learned about yourself, how your career goals have developed and changed during this process, and what careers are more or less appealing now than when you started.

H Stress Relief

What exactly is stress? How has it played a role in human evolution and development? Some physical indicators are listed on pages 779–780, but what in your body makes those changes happen? Does "good" stress differ physiologically from "bad" stress?

Write a report explaining the science of stress, focusing on what it is, why it's important, and what it can do to your body and mind. Make an argument for why stress should or should not be a factor in our contemporary lives. What needs does it serve, if any?

Critical Thinking   The Best School for You

Pick out three colleges or trade schools that appeal to you. Research the answers to the questions listed on page 754 to help you learn more about what each school offers. What other factors would you consider in determining whether or not to attend each school? Compare the results from each school. Which seems like the best fit for you and why? Write four paragraphs, one on each school, describing the positive and negative attributes of each, and one explaining your choice.

803

Stress Relief

Students should research stress and its effects on daily life, both positive and negative. Encourage students to envision a life in which stress does not exist.

Critical Thinking   The Best School for You

Students should select and research particular schools to determine which might be the best choice for their professional goals.

Exam Prep Answers

1. A
2. B
3. A
4. D
5. A
6. B
7. B
8. D
9. A
10. D

Exam Prep Questions

1 A written summary of a candidate's experience, skills, and achievements that relate to the job being sought is called a

   A. résumé.

   B. portfolio.

   C. career plan.

   D. cover letter.

2 A collection of samples that showcases a candidate's interests, talents, contributions, and studies is known as a

   A. résumé.

   B. portfolio.

   C. cover letter.

   D. job application.

3 What type of question can be answered with a simple yes or no?

   A. Closed

   B. Categorical

   C. Open-ended

   D. Multiple-choice

4 "Where do you see yourself in five years?" is what type of question?

   A. Essay

   B. Closed

   C. Categorical

   D. Open-ended

5 The execution of processes and the use of tools that increase a person's efficiency and productivity are called _____ management.

   A. time

   B. stress

   C. career

   D. situation

6 What is the best way for an employee to inform an employer that he or she is resigning?

   A. Walk into the employer's office to say goodbye.

   B. Write a letter of resignation listing the reasons for leaving.

   C. Leave a message for the employer with a two-week notice.

   D. Write a thank-you note to the employer for the experience.

7 When a person has demonstrated a high level of skill and has met specific performance requirements, he or she receives

   A. a diploma.

   B. certification.

   C. a scholarship.

   D. a thank-you note.

⑧ What level of job includes planning menus, developing recipes, and managing a restaurant and foodservice operation?

A. Mentor

B. Apprentice

C. Entry-level

D. Higher-level

⑨ Who is responsible for the kitchen team in the executive chef's absence and also lends his or her cooking expertise to overall food preparation?

A. Sous chef

B. Station chef

C. Nutritionist

D. Banquet chef

⑩ Who is responsible for the overall planning, direction, and coordinating of a restaurant or foodservice operation?

A. Owner

B. Sous chef

C. Executive chef

D. General manager

Appendix A
Staying Connected with the National Restaurant Association throughout Your Career

The National Restaurant Association has the resources and tools to support you throughout your education and career in the restaurant and foodservice industry. Through scholarships, educational programs, industry certifications, and member benefits, the Association is your partner now and into the future.

■ **Scholarships:** The Association's philanthropic foundation, the National Restaurant Association Educational Foundation (NRAEF), offers scholarships to college students through its **NRAEF Scholarship Program**. These scholarships can help pave your way to an affordable higher education and may be applied to a culinary, restaurant management, or foodservice-related program at an accredited college or university. We encourage you to investigate the opportunities, which include access to special program scholarships for ProStart students who earn the National Certificate of Achievement, as well as ManageFirst Program° students. You may be awarded one NRAEF scholarship per calendar year—make sure you keep applying every year! The NRAEF partners with state restaurant associations to offer student scholarships. Check with your state to see if they offer additional scholarship opportunities. The NRAEF also offers professional development scholarships for educators. Visit www.nraef.org/scholarships for information.

807

■ **College education**: As you research and apply to colleges and universities to continue your industry education, look for schools offering the National Restaurant Association's **ManageFirst Program**. Just like *Foundations of Restaurant Management & Culinary Arts*, the ManageFirst Program and curriculum materials were developed with input from the restaurant and foodservice industry and academic partners. This management program teaches you practical skills needed to face real-world challenges in the industry, including interpersonal communication, ethics, accounting skills, and more. The program includes the ten topics listed below, plus ServSafe® Food Safety and ServSafe Alcohol®:

- Controlling Foodservice Costs

- Customer Service

- Food Production

- Hospitality and Restaurant Management

- Human Resources Management and Supervision

- Inventory and Purchasing

- Managerial Accounting

- Menu Marketing and Management

- Nutrition

- Restaurant Marketing

You can also earn the ManageFirst Professional® (MFP™) credential by passing five required ManageFirst exams and completing 800 work hours in the industry. Having the MFP on your resume tells employers that you have the management skills needed to succeed in the industry. To learn more about ManageFirst or to locate ManageFirst schools, visit www.managefirst. restaurant.org.

■ **Certification**: In the competitive restaurant field, industry certifications can help you stand out among a crowd of applicants.

The National Restaurant Association's **ServSafe** Food Protection Manager Certification is nationally recognized. Earning your certification tells the industry that you know food safety and the critical importance of its role—and enables you to share food safety knowledge with every other employee.

Through ServSafe Food Safety, you'll master sanitation, the flow of food through an operation, sanitary facilities, and pest management. ServSafe is the training that is learned, remembered, shared, and used. And that makes it the strongest food safety training choice for you. For more information on ServSafe, visit www.ServSafe.com.

The challenges surrounding alcohol service in restaurants have increased dramatically. To prepare you to address these challenges, the National Restaurant Association offers **ServSafe Alcohol**. As you continue to work in the industry, responsible alcohol service is an issue that will touch your business, your customers, and your community. Armed with your ServSafe Alcohol Certificate, you can make an immediate impact on an establishment. Through the program, you'll learn essential responsible alcohol service information, including alcohol laws and responsibilities, evaluating intoxication levels, dealing with difficult situations, and checking identification. Please visit www.ServSafe.com/alcohol to learn more about ServSafe Alcohol.

- **National Restaurant Association membership**: As you move into the industry, seek out careers in restaurants that are **members of the National Restaurant Association and your state restaurant association.** Encourage any operation you are part of to join the national and state organizations. During your student years, the National Restaurant Association also offers student memberships that give you access to industry research and information that can be an invaluable resource. Students in the ProStart program receive a complimentary student membership; ask your educator for details. For more information, or to join as a student member, visit www.restaurant.org.

- **Management credentials**: After you've established yourself in the industry, strive for the industry's highest management certification—the National Restaurant Association's **Foodservice Management Professional**® (FMP®). The FMP certification recognizes exceptional managers and supervisors who have achieved the highest level of knowledge, experience, and professionalism that is most valued by our industry. You become eligible to apply and sit for the FMP Exam after you've worked as a supervisor in the industry for three years. Passing the FMP Exam places you in select company; you will have joined the ranks of leading industry professionals. The FMP certification is also an impressive credential to add to your title and resume. For more information on the Foodservice Management Professional certification, visit www.managefirst.restaurant.org.

Make the National Restaurant Association your partner throughout your education and career. Take advantage of the Association's scholarship, training, certification, and membership benefits that will launch you into your career of choice. Together we will lead this industry into an even brighter future.

809

Appendix B
Handling a Foodborne-Illness Outbreak

Foodborne-illness is the greatest threat to a foodservice operation's customers. As a manager, you'll need to know what to do if some of your customers get sick. Handling a foodborne-illness outbreak involves the following three steps:

1. Preparing
2. Responding
3. Recovering

Preparing for a Foodborne-Illness Outbreak

As you know by now, the first step to preventing outbreaks is to put a food safety program in place. That program must train all staff on the policies and procedures that will keep food safe in your operation, such as personal hygiene and good cleaning and sanitizing.

But even with your best efforts, an outbreak might happen. How you respond to it can make the difference between your operation surviving or closing. Successful managers create tools that will be helpful in the event of an outbreak and that increase the chance of overcoming it.

One such tool is a foodborne-illness incident report form. This form will help you document the following critical pieces of information:

811

- When and what the customer ate at the operation

- When the customer first became ill

- Medical attention received by the customer

- Other food eaten by the customer

Get legal help when developing your form and make sure you teach staff how to fill it out the right way. Whenever a customer reports getting sick from food eaten at your operation, fill out the form. Don't wait for more than one customer to report something.

Another tool you'll need is an emergency contact list. This list should contain contact information for the local regulatory authority, testing labs, and the operation's management team.

Finally, your operation should determine who will be in charge if a foodborne-illness outbreak happens. You should also identify who will speak to the media —there should be one person to handle all of the contact with journalists.

Responding to a Foodborne-Illness Outbreak

In a foodborne-illness outbreak, you may be able to avoid a crisis by quickly responding to customer complaints. Here are some things you should consider when responding to an outbreak.

IF	Then
A customer calls to report a foodborne-illness.	• Take the complaint seriously and express concern. Do not admit or deny responsibility. • Complete the foodborne-illness incident report form. • Evaluate the complaint to determine if there are similar complaints.
There are similar customer complaints of foodborne-illness.	• Contact the operation's management team. • Identify common food items to determine the potential source of the complaint. • Contact the local regulatory authority to help with the investigation.
The suspected food is still in the operation.	• Put the suspected food somewhere away from other food. Put a label on it to prevent selling it. • If possible, get samples of the suspected food from the customer.
The suspected outbreak is caused by an ill staff member.	• Do not allow the staff member to continue to be in the operation until he or she has recovered.
The regulatory authority confirms that your operation is the source of the outbreak.	• Cooperate with the regulatory authority to resolve the crisis.
The media contacts your operation.	• Follow your communication plan. Let your spokesperson handle all communication.

Recovering from a Foodborne-Illness Outbreak

The final step in preparing for a foodborne-illness outbreak is developing procedures to recover from one. Think about what you need to do to make sure that the operation and the food are safe. This is critical for getting your operation running again. Consider the following in your recovery plan:

■ Work with the regulatory authority to resolve issues.

■ Clean and sanitize all areas of the operation so the incident does not happen again.

■ Throw out all suspected food.

■ Investigate to find the cause of the outbreak.

■ Establish new procedures or revise existing ones based on the investigation results. This can help to prevent the incident from happening again.

■ Develop a plan to reassure customers that the food served in your operation is safe.

Appendix C
Identifying Pests

Despite a foodservice manager's best efforts to prevent infestations, pests may still get into an operation. Remember, the best way to deal with pests is to work with a pest control operator (PCO). To work with a PCO effectively, you must be able to determine the type of pests you are dealing with. Record the time, date, and location of any signs of pests and report them to your PCO. Early detection means early treatment.

Cockroaches

Roaches often carry pathogens. Most live and breed in dark, warm, moist, and hard-to-clean places. You can often find them in sink and floor drains, in spaces around hot water pipes, and near motors and electrical devices in equipment. If you see a cockroach in daylight, you may have a major infestation. Generally, only the weakest roaches come out during the day. There are several types of roaches that can infest your operation. See the illustrations below.

American

German

Brown-banded

Oriental

815

If you think you have a roach problem, check for the following signs:

- **Odor.** Usually there will be a strong, oily odor.

- **Droppings.** Roach feces look like grains of black pepper.

- **Egg cases.** These are capsule-shaped. They may be brown, dark red, or black, and may appear leathery, smooth, or shiny.

Rodents

Rodents are a serious health hazard. They eat and ruin food, damage property, and spread disease. A building can be infested with both rats and mice at the same time. Rodents hide during the day and search for food at night. Like other pests, they reproduce often. Typically, they do not travel far from their nests. Mice can squeeze through a hole the size of a nickel to enter a facility, while rats can fit through half dollar-sized holes. Rats can jump 3 feet (1 meter) in the air and can even climb straight up brick walls. There are several types of rodents that can infest your operation. See the illustrations below.

Roof rat

Common house mouse

Norway rat

Here are some signs that there are rodents in the operation:

- **Gnaw marks:** Rats and mice gnaw to get at food and to wear down their teeth, which grow continuously.

- **Tracks:** Rodents tend to use the same pathways through your operation. If rodents are a problem, you may see dirt tracks along light-colored walls.

- **Droppings and urine stains:** Fresh droppings are shiny and black. See figure at right. Older droppings are gray. Rodent urine will "glow" when exposed to a black (ultraviolet) light.

- **Nests:** Rats and mice use soft materials, such as scraps of paper, cloth, hair, feathers, and grass to build their nests. The photo at right shows an example of a mouse's nest.

- **Holes:** Rats usually nest in holes located in quiet places. Nests are often found near food and water and may be found next to buildings.

Illustrations courtesy of Orkin, Inc.

Glossary

Chapter 1

aboyeur: Expediter who takes orders from servers and calls out the orders to the various production areas in the kitchen.

all-suite properties: Apartment-style facilities offered at midmarket prices. They have larger spaces that include a sitting area, often with dining space, and small kitchen or bar area, in addition to a bedroom and bath.

amenity (a-MEN-i-tee)**:** A service or product provided to guests for their convenience, either with or without an additional fee.

American Automobile Association's *AAA TourBook*®**:** The most widely recognized rating service in the United States; it uses a diamond system in judging overall quality.

back of the house: Employees who work outside the public space. Back-of-the-house positions include chefs, line cooks, pastry chefs, dishwashers, bookkeepers, storeroom clerks, purchasers, dietitians, and menu planners.

bed and breakfasts: Cater to guests looking for quaint, quiet accommodations with simple amenities. Bed and breakfasts are usually privately owned homes converted to have several guest rooms. Guests are served breakfast during a specified time in a small dining room.

café: A coffeehouse usually offering pastries and baked goods.

cafeteria: An assembly line process of serving food quickly and cheaply without the need for servers.

chain: A group of restaurants owned by the same business organization.

chef: A mark of respect and distinction that describes a professional cook who has reached the position through hard work and dedication to quality.

concessions: A branch of a foodservice operation set up and operating in a place belonging to another commercial enterprise, such as a monument, museum, or ballpark.

contract feeding: Businesses that operate foodservice for companies in the manufacturing or service industry. Contractors will manage and operate the employee dining facilities.

convention: A gathering of people, all of whom have something in common. They are often all members of a particular organization, or they may simply be individuals who share a hobby.

convention centers: Facilities specifically designed to house large-scale special events, including conventions, expositions, and trade shows.

818

economy lodging: Clean, low-priced accommodations primarily designed for traveling salespeople, senior citizens, and families with modest incomes.

epicurean (ep-ih-KUR-ee-an): A person with a refined taste for food and wine.

expositions: Large shows, open to the public, that highlight a particular type of product or service. Such shows give manufacturers and service providers a chance to display their offerings to many people at a single event.

front of the house: Employees who serve guests directly. Front-of-the-house positions include managers, assistant managers, banquet managers, dining room managers, maître d's, hosts/hostesses, cashiers, bar staff, serving staff, and busers.

full-service properties: Properties that cater to travelers in search of a wide range of conveniences. They offer larger rooms and well-trained staff and feature amenities such as swimming pools, room service, fitness centers, or services for business travelers.

gourmet: A lover of fine food and drink.

guilds: Associations of people with similar interests or professions.

haute cuisine (hote kwee-ZEEN): An elaborate and refined system of food preparation.

hospitality: The services that people use and receive when they are away from home. This includes, among other services, restaurants and hotels.

kitchen brigade system: A system that assigns certain responsibilities to kitchen staff. Developed by Georges August Escoffier.

lesche (LES-kee): Private clubs for the ancient Greeks that offered food to members.

luxury properties: Hotels that offer top-of-the-line comfort and elegance. While often defined as part of the full-service sector, luxury hotels take service and amenities to new heights of excellence.

***Michelin Guide*:** A rating system better known in Europe than the United States, but it has recently begun rating organizations in the United States and elsewhere. Restaurants are rated from one to three stars.

mid-priced facilities: These fall somewhere between the full-service and economy sectors. They are designed for travelers who want comfortable, moderately-priced accommodations. Also known as tourist-class properties.

***Mobil Travel Guides*:** A major American rating resource. The *Mobil Travel Guides* rate thousands of properties with a five-star system.

monuments: Typically either structures built to memorialize something or someone, or structures recognized for their historical significance. Examples of monuments include the Statue of Liberty, the Eiffel Tower, Mount Rushmore, and the pyramids.

pasteurization: Process of making milk safer to drink by heating it to a certain temperature to destroy harmful bacteria. Named for Louis Pasteur.

phatnai (FAAT-nay): Establishments that catered to travelers, traders, and visiting diplomats in ancient Greece.

POS system: "POS" means "point of sale" or "point of service." POS refers to the place where some sort of transaction occurs. Although POS could be a retail shop or restaurant, a POS system generally indicates a computer terminal or linked group of terminals.

Property Management System (PMS) software: This technology can serve a variety of functions by which managers and staff can improve guest experiences, such as scheduling, database maintenance, accounting, and sales.

refrigeration: Keeps food from spoiling quickly and also helps to feed larger numbers of people.

resorts: Locations that feature extensive facilities for vacationers who are looking for recreational activities and entertainment.

restorante: In 1765, a man named Boulanger began serving hot soups called *restaurers* (meaning restoratives) for their health-restoring properties. He called his café a "restorante," the origin of our modern word "restaurant."

satellite/commissary feeding: When one kitchen prepares food that is then shipped to other locations to be served.

self operators: Employees at a manufacturing or service company who are also utilized for foodservice.

trade shows: Restricted to those involved in the industry being featured. Producers or manufacturers rent space at trade shows to exhibit, advertise, and demonstrate their products or services to people interested in that specific field.

travel and tourism: The combination of all of the services that people need and will pay for when they are away from home. This includes all of the businesses that benefit from people traveling and spending their money, such as transportation or restaurants.

Zagat Survey, The: A consumer-based guide that rates restaurants on four qualities: food, décor, service, and cost.

Chapter 2

bacteria: Cause many foodborne illnesses. Some bacteria, as they grow and die, create toxins (poisons) in food. Cooking may not destroy these toxins, and people who eat them can become sick.

bimetallic stemmed thermometer: Can check temperatures from 0°F to 220°F. This makes it useful for checking both hot and cold types of food.

calibration: Regular adjustments to tools to keep them accurate.

cleaners: Chemicals that remove food, dirt, rust, stains, minerals, and other deposits.

cleaning: Removing food and other dirt from a surface.

contact time: The specific period of time during which objects being sanitized must be immersed in a solution. The contact time depends on the type of sanitizer being used.

contamination: Occurs when harmful things are present in food, making it unsafe to eat.

corrective action: Action taken to fix a problem if a critical limit hasn't been met.

critical control points (CCPs): The points in a process where identified hazard(s) can be prevented, eliminated, or reduced to safe levels.

critical limit: A requirement, such as a temperature requirement, that must be met to prevent, eliminate, or reduce a hazard.

cross-contact: The transfer of allergens from food containing an allergen to the food served to a customer.

cross-contamination: The spread of pathogens from one surface or food to another.

FAT TOM: A way to remember the six conditions pathogens need to grow: food, acidity, temperature, time, oxygen, and moisture.

first-in, first-out (FIFO) method: Rotation of food in storage to use the oldest inventory first. Many operations use the FIFO method to rotate refrigerated, frozen, and dry food during storage.

flow of food: The path that food takes in an operation. It begins when you buy the food and ends when you serve it.

food allergy: The body's negative reaction to a food protein.

food safety management system: A group of procedures and practices that work together to prevent foodborne illness.

foodborne illness: A disease transmitted to people by food.

foodborne-illness outbreak: When two or more people get the same illness after eating the same food items.

foodhandlers: This includes more than just the people who prepare food. Servers and even dishwashers are considered foodhandlers, because they either handle food directly or work with the surfaces that food will touch.

fungi: Can cause illness, but most commonly, they are responsible for spoiling food. Fungi are found in air, soil, plants, water, and some food. Mold and yeast are two examples of fungi.

handwashing: The most important part of personal hygiene.

hazard: Something with the potential to cause harm. In the preparation of food, hazards are divided into three categories: biological, chemical, and physical.

Hazard Analysis Critical Control Point (HACCP): A type of food safety management system. HACCP identifies major hazards at specific points within a food's flow through the operation.

high-risk populations: Certain groups of people who have a higher risk of getting a foodborne illness than others.

host: A person, animal, or plant on which another organism, such as a parasite, lives and feeds.

immune system: The body's defense against illness.

infrared thermometers: These thermometers, which measure the temperatures of food and equipment surfaces, do not need to touch a surface to check its temperature, so there is less chance for cross-contamination and damage to food.

821

inspection: A formal review or examination conducted to see whether an operation is following food safety laws.

integrated pest management program (IPM): A system that will prevent, control, or eliminate pest infestations in an operation.

master cleaning schedule: A schedule that contains what should be cleaned, who should clean it, when it should be cleaned, and how it should be cleaned.

mold: Molds grow under almost any condition, but especially in acidic food with little moisture. Molds often spoil food and sometimes produce toxins that can make people sick. Refrigerator and freezer temperatures may slow the growth of molds, but cold doesn't kill them.

parasites: Parasites are organisms that live on or in another organism (the host). The parasite receives nutrients from the host.

pathogens: The microorganisms that cause illness.

personal hygiene policies: These policies must address personal cleanliness, clothing, hand care, and health in order to prevent foodhandlers from contaminating food.

pest control operator (PCO): Experts at applying, storing, and disposing of pesticides who have access to the most current and safe methods for eliminating pests. They are trained to determine the best methods for eliminating specific pests and are knowledgeable about local regulations.

ready-to-eat food: Food that can be eaten without further preparation, washing, or cooking.

sanitizing: Reducing pathogens on a surface to safe levels.

TCS food: Food that is most vulnerable for pathogen growth is also referred to as food that needs time and temperature control for safety (TCS).

temperature danger zone: The temperature range between 41°F and 135°F. Pathogens grow well in food that has a temperature in this range.

thermocouples and **thermistors:** Common in restaurant and foodservice operations. They measure temperatures through a metal probe and display them digitally. The sensing area on thermocouples and thermistors is on the tip of the probe.

time-temperature abused: Food that is cooked to the wrong internal temperature, held at the wrong temperature, or cooled and reheated improperly.

viruses: The leading cause of foodborne illness. Viruses can survive refrigerator and freezer temperatures.

yeast: Can spoil food quickly. The signs of spoilage include the smell or taste of alcohol, white or pink discoloration, slime, and bubbles.

Chapter 3

accident: An unplanned, undesirable event that can cause property damage, injuries or fatalities, time lost from work, or disruptions of work.

accident investigation: Each operation needs to have forms for reporting injuries or illnesses involving both guests and employees. The investigation involves eight steps:

1. Record information as soon as possible after the event occurs, ideally within one hour. Use OSHA-required forms as well as appropriate corporate or company forms.

2. Include a description of the event, the date, and two signatures on accident report forms.

3. Collect physical evidence or take pictures at the site.

4. Interview all people involved and any witnesses.

5. Determine as clearly as possible the sequence of events, the causes and effects, and the actions taken.

6. Submit reports to OSHA, the insurance carrier, lawyer, and corporate headquarters, as appropriate. Keep copies of all reports and photographs for your files.

7. Keep all employees informed of procedures and hazards that arise from the situation.

8. If they aren't already available, post emergency phone numbers in public places.

arson: The deliberate and malicious burning of property.

automatic systems: These fire safety systems operate even when no one is in the facility and usually include a type of heat detector that releases dry or wet chemicals, carbon dioxide, or inert gases.

cardiopulmonary resuscitation (CPR) (CAR-dee-oh PULL-man-air-ee ree-SUHS-i-TAY-shun): Restores breathing and heartbeat to injured persons who show no signs of breathing or a pulse.

class A fires: Usually involve wood, paper, cloth, or cardboard and typically happen in dry-storage areas, dining areas, garbage areas, and restrooms.

class B fires: Usually involve flammable liquids and grease and typically start in kitchens and maintenance areas.

class C fires: Usually involve live electrical equipment and typically occur in motors, switches, cords, circuits, and wiring.

emergency plan: A plan designed to protect workers, guests, and property in the case of an emergency or disaster.

evacuation routes: Routes planned to give everyone at least two ways out of the building to a safe meeting place in case of emergency.

first aid: Medical treatment given to an injured person either for light injuries or until more complete treatment can be provided by emergency service or other health care providers.

flame detectors: Work by reacting to the movement of flames.

general safety audit: A safety inspection of facilities, equipment, employee practices, and management practices. The purpose of a general safety audit is to judge the level of safety in the operation.

Hazard Communication Standard (HCS): Also called Right-to-Know and HAZCOM. This safety standard requires that all employers notify their employees about chemical hazards present on the job and train employees to use these materials safely.

health hazards: Items (including chemicals) that cause short- or long-term injuries or illnesses.

heat detectors: Work by reacting to heat. Detect fires where there is no smoke. They are activated by the significant increase of temperature associated with fire.

Heimlich maneuver (HIME-lick mah-NOO-ver): Removes food or other obstacles from the airway of a choking person.

liability: The legal responsibility that one person has to another.

Material Safety Data Sheet (MSDS): A report OSHA requires from chemical manufacturers and suppliers for each hazardous chemical they sell.

near miss: An event in which property damage or injury is narrowly avoided.

Occupational Safety and Health Administration (OSHA): The federal agency that creates and enforces safety-related standards and regulations in the workplace.

OSHA Form No. 300: A summary of occupational injuries and illnesses that each operation maintains throughout the year.

physical hazards: Materials, situations, or things (including chemicals) that can cause damage to property and immediate injury.

premises: All the property around a restaurant or foodservice establishment.

safety program guidelines: Designed to meet the specific needs of the operation, these guidelines are based on existing safety practices and the insurance carrier's requirements.

smoke detectors: Work by reacting to smoke. Smoke detectors require a flow of air in order to work well and should not be used in food preparation areas.

Chapter 4

as purchased (AP): The amount of a product before it has been trimmed and cut and before being used in recipes.

baker's scale: Also called a **balance beam.** The weight of the item is placed on one end and the product is placed on the other end until the beam balances.

balance beam: Also called a **baker's scale.** The weight of the item is placed on one end and the product is placed on the other end until the beam balances.

borrowing: A technique often used when subtracting large numbers. If a digit in one column is too large to be subtracted from the digit above it, then 10 is borrowed from the column immediately to the left.

conversion chart: A list of food items showing the expected, or average, shrinkage from AP amount to EP amount.

conversion factor: Desired yield ÷ Original yield = Conversion factor, which is the number by which to multiply the ingredients.

culinarian: One who has studied and continues to study the art of cooking.

customary units: The most commonly used system of measurement in the United States is based on customary units. Some examples of these customary units are ounces, teaspoons, tablespoons, cups, pints, and gallons.

denominator: The lower portion of a fraction.

desired yield: The number of servings that are needed.

dividend: Larger numbers are divided using a combination of division and subtraction. The dividend is the number being divided and is placed inside the long division sign.

divisor: The divisor is the number by which another number (the dividend) is divided. It is placed outside the long division sign.

dry measuring cup method: Used to measure fat by packing the fat down into a cup, pressing firmly to remove air bubbles. Level off the top.

edible portion (EP): The amount left after vegetables have been trimmed and cut, and before being used in recipes.

electronic scale: A scale that measures resistance electronically.

equivalent: The same amount expressed in different ways by using different units of measure.

flavor: All the sensations produced by whatever is in the mouth, but mostly food's aroma and taste.

like fractions: Fractions in which the denominators are the same.

lowest common denominator: The smallest number that both denominators can be divided into evenly.

measurement: How much of something is being used in a recipe.

metric units: Based on multiples of 10 and includes milliliters, liters, milligrams, grams, and kilograms. The metric system is the standard system used in many parts of the world, outside of the United States.

mise en place (MEEZ ehn plahs): French for "to put in place;" the preparation and assembly of ingredients, pans, utensils, and equipment or serving pieces needed for a particular dish or service.

numerators: The upper portion of a fraction.

nutrition information: May include amounts of fat (saturated and

825

unsaturated), carbohydrates, protein, fiber, sodium, vitamins, and minerals.

percent: Part per 100. Percentages are a particularly important mathematical operation in foodservice operations.

personal responsibility: A term that indicates that a person is responsible for the choices he or she makes.

portion size: The individual amount that is served to a person.

recipe: A written record of the ingredients and preparation steps needed to make a particular dish.

respect: Having consideration for oneself and others.

sifting: A process that removes lumps from an ingredient and gives it a smoother consistency.

spring scale: A scale that measures the pressure placed on the spring.

standardized recipes: Recipes for institutional use.

step-by-step directions: How and when to combine the ingredients.

stick method: Used to measure fat that comes in $1/4$-pound sticks, such as butter or margarine. The wrapper is marked in tablespoons and in fractions of a cup.

taring: Accounting for the weight of the container in which the item is located when correctly weighing an item.

temperature, time, and equipment: Includes size and type of pans and other equipment needed, the oven temperature, cooking time, and any preheating instructions.

umami: One of the five basic tastes: salt, sour, bitter, sweet, and **umami** (or savory).

volume: The amount of space an ingredient takes up.

water displacement method: Used to measure fat by combining fat with water in a liquid measuring cup. First, do some math: subtract the amount of fat to be measured from one cup. The difference is the amount of water to pour into the measuring cup.

weight: The measurement of an item's resistance to gravity. Weight is expressed in ounces and pounds.

work section: A group of workstations using the same or similar equipment for related tasks.

workstation: A work area in the kitchen dedicated to a particular task, such as broiling or salad making.

yield: The number of servings or the amount the recipe makes.

Chapter 5

Adequate Intakes: Similar to RDAs, they also identify daily intake levels for healthy people, but AIs are typically assigned when scientists don't have enough information to set an RDA.

bain-marie (bayn mah-REE): Any type of hot-water bath meant to keep food items warm.

baker's scale: Also called a **balance scale**; this weighs dry ingredients in the bake shop area.

826

baking: Cooking food by surrounding the items with hot, dry air in the oven. As the outer layers of the food become heated, the food's natural juices turn to steam and are absorbed into the food.

balance scale/baker's scale: A balance scale weighs dry ingredients in the bake shop area.

barding: Wrapping an item (usually a naturally lean piece of meat, such as a pork tenderloin) with strips of fat before cooking to baste the meat, making it more moist.

basket method: When deep-frying an item, bread the food, place it in a basket, lower the basket and food into the hot oil, and then lift it all out with the basket when the food is done.

batter: A combination of dry and wet ingredients. It is a mixture of the primary dry ingredient (wheat flour, all-purpose flour, cornmeal, rice flour), the liquid (beer, milk, wine, water), and a binder (usually egg), which helps the mixture adhere to the product.

bench scraper: A rigid, small sheet of stainless steel with a metal blade used to scrape material off a work surface or "bench" or to cut or portion soft, semi-firm items (like bread dough or cookie dough).

bimetallic coil thermometers: A thermometer that stays in food as it cooks and provides an instant read.

blade: The cutting surface of a knife.

blanching: A moist-heat method of cooking that involves cooking in a liquid or with steam just long enough to cook the outer portion of the food.

blanquette (blahn-KETT): A white stew made traditionally from veal, chicken, or lamb, garnished with mushrooms and pearl onions, and served in a white sauce.

bolster: Located at the heel of a knife blade where the blade meets the handle.

boning knife: A 6-inch knife used to separate raw meat from the bone. The blade is thin, flexible, and shorter than the blade of a chef's knife.

bouillabaisse (boo-yuh-base): A Mediterranean fish stew combining a variety of fish and shellfish.

bowl scraper: A flexible piece of rubber or plastic used to combine ingredients in a bowl and then scrape them out again, to cut and separate dough, and to scrape extra dough and flour from wooden work tables.

braising: A cooking method in which the preparer first sears the food item in hot oil and then partially covers it in enough liquid to come halfway up the food item. Then, they cover the pot or pan tightly and finish cooking the food slowly in the oven or on the stovetop until it is tender.

braising pan: A high-sided, flat-bottomed cooking pan used to braise, stew, and brown meat. Also called a brazier or a rondeau.

brazier: A medium to large pot, more shallow than sauce pots, with straight sides and two handles for lifting. Also called a rondeau.

breading: Has the same components as batter, but they are not blended together. A standard breading would be seasoned all-purpose flour and an egg and buttermilk dip.

broiling: A rapid cooking method that uses high heat from a source located above the food.

butcher knife: Also known as a scimitar, cooks use the butcher knife to fabricate raw meat. It is available with 6- to 14-inch blades.

butt: The end of a knife handle.

butter knife: A small knife with a blunt-edge blade used to spread butter, peanut butter, and cream cheese on bread or dinner rolls.

cake pans: Baking pans with straight sides. They are available in a variety of sizes and shapes including round, rectangular, square, and specialty (such as heart-shaped).

can opener: In restaurant and foodservice kitchens, can openers are mounted onto metal utility tables because they are used to open large cans. A small handheld can opener, like those for home use, may be used in a restaurant or foodservice kitchen to open small cans of food.

carbonated beverage machine: This machine is attached to tanks that hold the premixed blends for selected soft drinks and to a tank that contains CO_2. Pressing the switch on the unit automatically mixes the blend and gas to make the completed beverage.

carryover cooking: This is what happens to food after it has been removed from the oven, when the roasted item holds a certain amount of heat that continues to cook the food.

cast-iron skillet: A heavy, thick pan made of cast iron. Use it to pan grill, pan-fry, and braise food items such as meat or vegetables.

ceramic steels: Slender ceramic rods embedded in a wooden handle. They are used both on ceramic and metal knives to hone sharpened knives.

chafing dishes: Used to keep food items hot on a buffet table. The heat source for chafers are sternos that are placed underneath the chafers filled with hot water.

channel knife: A small knife used to cut grooves lengthwise in a vegetable such as a carrot.

charbroiler: Uses gas or electricity to mimic the effects of charcoal in a grill. Food juices drip onto the heat source to create flames and smoke, which add flavor to broiled food items.

cheesecloth: A light, fine mesh gauze for straining liquids, such as stocks or custards, for bundling herbs, or for thickening yogurt.

cheese knife: A thinly shaped utensil that cooks use to cut through hard or soft-textured cheese.

chef's (French) knife: An all-purpose knife for chopping, slicing, and mincing all types of food items. Its blade is normally 8 to 14 inches long and tapers to a point at the tip.

China cap: A pierced, metal, cone-shaped strainer used to strain soups, stocks, and other liquids to remove all solid ingredients.

chinois (chin-WAH)**:** A very fine China cap made of metal mesh that strains out very small solid ingredients.

clam knife: A short, blunt-point knife used to shuck, or open, clams. Unlike the oyster knife, it has a very sharp edge.

cleaver: A heavy, rectangular knife used to chop all kinds of food, from vegetables to meat. It is also able to cut through bones.

coffee maker: A machine that automatically makes coffee.

colander (CAH-len-der): Used to drain liquid from cooked pasta and vegetables. Colanders stand on metal feet, while strainers are usually handheld.

combination cooking: A combination of both dry-heat and moist-heat cooking methods.

combi-oven: Combines a convection oven with a steamer. Using a combi-oven, cooks can work with convective steam, with convective dry hot air, or with a combination of both. These are very efficient, flexible units, but they are relatively expensive.

conduction: The transfer of heat from one item to another when the items come into direct contact with each other.

convection: The transfer of heat caused by the movement of molecules (in the air, water, or fat) from a warmer area to a cooler one.

convection oven: Has a fan that circulates heated air around the food as it cooks. This shortens cooking times and uses energy efficiently.

convection steamers: Steam is generated in a boiler and then piped to the cooking chamber, where it is vented over the food. Pressure does not build up in the unit. Rather, it is continually exhausted, which means the door may be opened at any time without danger of scalding or burning as with a pressure steamer. Cooks use convection steamers to cook large quantities of food.

conventional (standard) oven: The heat source is located on the floor of the oven. Heat rises into the cavity, or open space in the oven, which contains racks for the food to sit on as it cooks. These ovens are usually located below a range-top burner.

conveyor (con-VAY-er) **oven:** In this type of oven, a conveyor belt moves the food along a belt in one direction. It cooks with heat sources on both top and bottom.

cook's fork (kitchen fork): A fork with two long, pointed tines used to test the doneness of braised meat and vegetables, to lift items to the plate, and to steady an item being cut.

cookware: Pots and pans.

corer: A small tool used to remove the core of an apple or pear in one long, cylindrical piece.

countertop blender: Used to purée, liquefy, and blend food. The blender consists of a base that houses the motor and a removable lidded jar with a propeller-like blade in the bottom.

countertop broiler: A small broiler that sits on top of a work table. Primarily quick-service restaurants use these. The heat source is located above the food and produces an intense radiant heat.

crêpe pan (KRAYP): A shallow skillet with very short, slightly sloping sides. Used to create crêpes, a specialty pancake.

cuisson: The liquid from shallow poaching, which transfers much of the flavor of the food from the food item to the liquid. The liquid is used as a sauce base.

cutting edge: The edge located along the bottom of a knife blade between the tip and the heel. Use it for slicing, carving, and making precision cuts.

daube (DAWB): A braised dish usually made with red meat, often beef, vegetables, red wine, and seasoning. The main item is often marinated before braising.

deck oven: A deck oven is a type of conventional oven in which two to four shelves are stacked on top of each other. Cook food directly on these shelves, or decks.

deep-fat fryer: Gas and electric fryers cook food in oil at temperatures between 300°F and 400°F. Some computerized fryers lower and raise the food baskets automatically.

deep-frying: Breading- or batter-coating food, immersing (completely covering) it in hot fat, and frying it until it is done. The outside of the food item develops a crispy coating while the inside stays moist and tender.

deglazing: Process of using liquid in the bottom of a pan to dissolve the remaining bits of sautéed food.

deli knife: A knife with a serrated blade used for thick sandwiches. The most common deli knife is 8 inches.

diamond steels: Slender metal rods, or sometimes flattened rods, that are impregnated with diamond dust. They should not be used to hone ceramic knives.

Dietary Guidelines for Americans 2005: A document published jointly by the Department of Health and Human Services and the USDA. This report offers science-based advice for healthy people over the age of two about food choices to promote health and reduce risk for major chronic diseases.

Dietary Reference Intakes (DRIs): Recommended daily amounts of nutrients and energy that healthy people of a particular age range and gender should consume. They are the guides for nutrition and food selection.

digital (electric) scale: A precise scale used to measure weight. Provides a digital readout in both U.S. and metric systems.

discretionary calorie allowance: The remaining amount of calories in a food intake pattern after accounting for the calories needed from all food groups.

double boiler: A pot that has an upper pot and a lower pot. The lower pot holds boiling or simmering water that gently cooks the food in the upper pot; used it for melting chocolate or heating milk, cream, or butter.

double-basket method: When deep-frying certain food items, they need to be fully submerged in hot oil for a longer period of time in order to develop a crisp crust. In this method, place the food item in a basket, then fit another basket on top of the first. The top basket keeps the food from floating to the surface of the oil.

dough arm (hook): A mixture attachment used to mix heavy, thick dough.

espresso machine: Produces the traditional Italian coffee beverage called espresso, a concentrated coffee beverage brewed by forcing hot water under pressure through finely ground coffee.

estouffade (ess-too-FAHD): This French term refers to both the braising method and the dish itself (a beef stew made with red wine).

fillet knife: A thin, flexible blade for cutting fish fillets. It is a short knife, about 6 inches long.

fish poacher: A long, narrow, metal pan with a perforated rack that cooks use to raise or lower the fish so it doesn't break apart.

fish scaler: A small tool used to remove scales from a fish.

flat beater paddle: Used in a mixer to mix, mash, and cream soft food items.

flat ground and **tapered:** When the cutting edge of a knife has both sides of the blade taper smoothly to a narrow V-shape.

flat-top burner: Also called a French top; a flat-top burner cooks food on a thick slate of cast iron or a steel plate that covers the heat source. A flat-top burner provides even and consistent heat.

flavor: The way a food tastes, as well as its texture, appearance, doneness, and temperature.

flavoring: Something that enhances the base ingredients of a dish or can bring another flavor to the product.

float: The point when deep frying an item when the item rises to the surface of the oil and appears golden brown; this indicates doneness.

fondue pot: A pot with a heat source placed directly below the pot; use it for a food preparation process known as fondue.

food chopper: Chops vegetables, meat, and other food using a vertical rotating blade and a bowl that rotates the food under the blade. This unit is often called a buffalo chopper.

food mill: A machine that comes with several detachable parts. Cooks use it to purée food to different consistencies.

food processors: A processing machine that houses the motor separately from the bowl, blades, and lid. Food processors grind, puree, blend, crush, and knead food.

food warmer or steam table: This unit differs from the bain-marie in two ways. First, the unit is designed to hold hotel pans, either one full-size pan or multiple smaller pans per slot. Second, different types of units are designed to work with water in the holding unit, without water, or either way.

forged blade: Cutting surface of a knife made from a single piece of heated metal that is dropped into a mold and then struck with a hammer and pounded into the correct shape.

fricassée (frick-uh-SAY): A white stew, often made from veal, poultry, or small game.

funnel: Use a funnel to pour liquid from a large to a smaller container.

garnish: Enhances the food being served. A garnish should be something that will be eaten with the item, functioning as a flavor component, while visually adding to the appearance of the item.

goulash (GOO-losh): This stew originated in Hungary and is made from beef, veal, or poultry, seasoned with paprika, and usually served with potatoes or dumplings.

granton: A type of knife edge in which ovals are ground into the sides of a blade, which helps food to release easily.

grater: A small tool used to grate hard cheeses, vegetables, potatoes, and other food items.

griddle: Similar to a flat-top range, a griddle has a heat source located beneath a thick plate of metal. Cook food directly on this surface, which is usually designed with edges to contain the food and a drain to collect waste.

griddling: Cooking a food item on a hot, flat surface (known as a griddle) or in a relatively dry, heavy-bottomed fry pan or cast-iron skillet.

grilling: A very simple dry-heat method that is excellent for cooking smaller pieces of food. The food is cooked on a grill rack above the heat source.

guiding hand: When using a knife, the guiding hand is the one that is not holding the knife; it prevents slippage and helps to control the size of the cut.

handle: The part of a knife that you grip. Made with various materials including hardwoods or textured metal.

heel: The widest and thickest part of a knife blade. The heel is used to cut through large, tough, or hard food.

herbs (URBS): The leaves, stems, or flowers of an aromatic plant.

hollow-ground: When the sides of a knife blade near the edge are ground away to form a hollow, making the blade extremely sharp.

honing: The regular maintenance required to keep knives in the best shape.

honing steel: When performing knife maintenance, this steel helps remove broken pieces and realign the remaining ground edges. It looks like a short sword with a round blade.

horizontal cutter mixer (HCM): This mixer cuts, mixes, and blends food quickly with a high-speed horizontal rotating blade that is housed in a large bowl with a tight cover.

hot box: This is an insulated piece of equipment designed to hold sheet pans and hotel pans.

hotel broiler: Use this large, radiant broiler to broil large amounts of food quickly.

hotel pan: Used to hold prepared food in a steam table, hot-holding cabinet, or refrigerator. These are sometimes used for baking, roasting, or poaching meat and vegetables.

hot-holding cabinet: A heavily insulated cabinet designed to hold either hotel pans or sheet pans on racks in the interior. A thermostat controls the temperature so that the cabinet holds food at the desired temperature.

ice machine: Make ice cubes, flakes, chips, and crushed ice.

immersion blender: Also known as a hand blender, stick blender, or burr mixer. It is a long, stick-like machine that houses a motor on one end of the machine with a blade on the other end. This operates in the same manner as a countertop blender to purée and blend food, except that a cook holds it manually in a container of food, whereas a countertop blender contains the food itself.

induction burner: Generates heat by means of magnetic attraction between the cooktop and a steel or cast-iron pot or pan. The cooktop itself remains cool. Reaction time is significantly faster with the induction cooktop than with traditional burners. Do not use pans on this burner that contain copper or aluminum. They will not work.

infrared heat: Created when the heat from a source is absorbed by one material and then radiated out to the food.

kitchen shears: Strong scissors used to cut string and butcher's twine and cut grapes into small clusters.

lacto-ovo-vegetarian: Person who consumes all vegan items plus dairy products and eggs.

lacto-vegetarian: Person who consumes all vegan items plus dairy products.

ladle: Used to portion out liquids; available in various sizes measured in fluid ounces and milliliters.

larding: Inserting long, thin strips of fat into a large, naturally lean piece of meat with a special needle before cooking with the purpose of basting the meat from the inside.

lettuce knife: A plastic serrated knife designed to cut lettuce without causing the edges of the lettuce to turn brown.

mandoline: A manually operated slicer made of stainless steel with adjustable slicing blades to slice and julienne. Its

narrow, rectangular body sits on the work counter at a 45-degree angle. It is useful for slicing small quantities of fruit or vegetables, situations where a large electric slicer isn't necessary.

marinating: Soaking an item in a combination of wet and dry ingredients to provide flavor and moisture.

matelote (ma-tuh-LOAT): A special type of fish stew, usually prepared with eel.

measuring cup: Measures varying quantities of both dry goods and liquids. Measuring cups with spouts measure liquids, and those without spouts measure dry ingredients.

measuring spoon: Cooks use this item to measure small quantities of spices or liquids. The spoons measure the amounts of $1/8$ teaspoon (not all sets include this smallest size), $1/4$ teaspoon, $1/2$ teaspoon, 1 teaspoon, and 1 tablespoon.

meat grinder: A free-standing machine or an attachment for a standing mixer. Food is dropped in through a feed tube, pulled along by a metal worm, and then cut by blades as the food is forced out through the grinder plate.

meat slicer: Most have a slanted circular blade. Food either passes through the machine automatically, or a cook pushes a hopper holding the product along a carriage into the blade. The thickness of the slicer is set by increasing and decreasing the distance between the guide plate and the blade.

microwave oven: Heats food not with heat, but with microwaves of energy that cause a food's molecules to move rapidly and create heat inside the food.

mise en place (MEEZ ehn plahs): French for "to put in place." It refers to the preparation and assembly of ingredients, pans, utensils, equipment, or serving pieces needed for a particular dish or service.

mixer: Available in 5-quart, 20-quart, 60-quart, and 80-quart sizes. Used to mix and process large amounts of food with any number of specialized attachments, including paddles, wire whips, dough hooks, meat grinders, shredders, slicers, and juicers.

muffin tins: Small, round cups or molds used to make muffins, cupcakes, or other small baked goods.

MyPyramid: This food guide from the USDA, along with the Nutrition Facts Panel, serves as a tool to help people put dietary guidelines into practice. MyPyramid translates the RDAs and dietary guidelines into the kinds and amounts of food to eat each day.

navarin (nav-ah-RAHN): A stew usually prepared from mutton or lamb, with a garnish of root vegetables, onions, and peas. The name probably comes from the French word for turnips (navets), which are used as the principal garnish.

Nutrition Facts Panels: Help people select the appropriate packaged food products for their nutritional needs.

obese: A person who is overweight or has a weight that is greater than what is generally considered healthy.

offset spatula (SPACH-e-la): A small tool used to turn food items on a griddle or broiler. It has a wide, chisel-edged blade and a short handle.

open burner: A grate-style gas burner supplies direct heat by way of an open flame to the item being cooked. The heat can be easily controlled.

overportioning: When too great an amount of an item is served to guests, resulting in increased cost and lower profit from an item.

ovo-vegetarian: Person who consumes all vegan food items plus eggs.

oyster knife: A short, stubby knife with a pointed tip for shucking oysters.

pan-frying: Cooking food in an oil over less intense heat than that used for sautéing or stir-frying.

pans: Usually smaller and shallower than pots. Pans are used for general stove top cooking, especially sautéing, frying, or reducing liquids rapidly, baking, and for holding food.

par-cooking: *See* blanching.

paring knife: A small knife with a sharp blade, only 2 to 4 inches long, used to trim and pare vegetables and fruits.

parisienne (pah-REE-see-en) **scoop:** Also called a melon baller; used to cut ball shapes out of soft fruits and vegetables.

pastry bag: A bag made of canvas, plastic, or nylon which is used to pipe out frostings, creams, and puréed food. Different pastry tips create a variety of decorations.

pastry brush: A small brush used to brush egg wash, melted butter, glazes, and other liquids on items such as baked goods, raw pasta, or glazes on meat.

pastry knife (paddle): Used in a mixer to mix shortening into dough.

834

paupiettes: Thin slices of meat or fish rolled around a filling of ground meat or vegetables. Often shallow poached.

peeler: A small tool used to cut a thick layer from vegetables and fruits more efficiently than a paring knife.

pie server: A specially shaped spatula made for lifting out and serving pieces of pie.

piping tools: Include piping bags (canvas, plastic, disposable), decorative tips (metal, plastic, of varying shapes), and presses (cylinders with a handle on one end that force dough through a metal cutout).

pizza cutter: A small tool used to cut pizza and rolled-out dough.

plating: The decision about what serving vessel will be used to present the product as well as the layout of the item on the plate or in the bowl. Garnishing of the item is included in this decision.

poaching: Cooking food in liquid between 160°F and 180°F. The surface of the poaching liquid should show some motion, but no air bubbles should break the surface.

portion: The amount of an item that is served to the guest.

portion scale: Use this scale to measure recipe ingredients, from $1/4$ ounce to 1 pound to 2 pounds.

pot roasting: A common American term for braising as well as the name of a traditional dish.

pots: Available in a range of sizes based on volume; use them on the stove top for making stocks or soups, or for boiling or simmering food.

pressure steamer: Cooks food with high-temperature steam. Water is heated under pressure in a sealed compartment, allowing it to reach temperatures greater than 212°F. It's very important to release the pressure before opening the door on a pressure steamer.

radiation: Does not require physical contact between the heat source and the food being cooked. Instead, heat moves by way of microwave and infrared waves.

ragout (ra-GOO): This is a French term for stew that means "restores the appetite."

reach-in freezer: A freezer that can have one, two, or three internal compartments.

reach-in refrigerator: A refrigerator that can have one, two, or three internal compartments.

receiving table/area: Location where employees weigh, inspect, and check delivered items.

Recommended Dietary Allowances: Daily nutrient standards established by the U.S. government. They are the average daily intakes that meet the nutrient requirements of nearly all healthy individuals of a particular age and gender group.

recovery time: When deep-frying, this is the amount of time it takes oil to reheat to the correct cooking temperature once food is added. The more food items dropped in the oil at one time, the longer the recovery time.

ricer: A pierced hopper (small basket-shaped container that holds the material) through which cooked food is pressed by means of a plate on the end of a lever. The result is rice-like pieces.

ring-top burner: With a ring-top burner, cooks add or remove different-sized rings or plates to allow more or less heat to cook the food item. A ring-top burner provides direct, controllable heat. It can be either gas or electric.

rivets: On a knife, they hold the handle to the tang.

roasting: Cooks food by surrounding the items with hot, dry air in the oven. As the outer layers of the food become heated, the food's natural juices turn to steam and are absorbed into the food.

roasting pan: A shallow, rectangular pan with medium-high sides and two handles. Use it to roast and bake food items, such as meat and poultry.

rolling pin: A cylinder that cooks use to roll over pastry to flatten or shape it.

rondeau: A medium to large pot, more shallow than a sauce pot, with straight sides and two handles for lifting. Also called a brazier.

rotary oven: Has three to five circular shelves on which food cooks as the shelves move around a central rod.

rotisserie (roe-TIS-er-ee): A unit in which cooks place food on a stick, or spit, and roast it over or under a heat source. The unit may be open or enclosed like an oven. Cooks use it most often for cooking chicken, turkey, and other types of poultry.

rubber spatula: A spatula with a long handle, often called a scraper, used to fold ingredients together and scrape the sides of bowls.

salamander: A small radiant broiler usually attached to the back of a range. Use it to brown, finish, and melt food to order.

sandwich spreader: A short, stubby spatula that cooks use to spread sandwich fillings and condiments.

santoku: A general-purpose kitchen knife with a 5- to 7-inch blade length. The santoku knife is designed for a comfortable, well-balanced grip, while allowing for full blade use.

saucepan: A pan with medium height, straight sides, and a single long handle. Use it for general cooking, in particular liquid or liquid-based mixtures, on ranges.

sauce pot: Used to prepare sauces, soups, and other liquids. Sauce pots are more shallow than stock pots, with straight sides and two loop handles for lifting.

sauté (saw-TAY) **pan:** The original French sauté pan is slope-sided and made of thin metal for quick heating. It is used strictly to sauté items. In the United States, the "fry pan" is generally referred to as a sauté pan. A fry pan has curved sides and a long handle and is generally made of slightly thicker metal. It is used both to sauté and to pan-fry.

sautéing (saw-TAY-ing): This method cooks food rapidly in a small amount of fat over relatively high heat.

sautoir (saw-TWAHR): The classic *sautoir* shape is called a sauté pan in the United States. It has a wide bottom and straight sides. Some typical tasks include pan-frying, stir-frying, and shallow poaching.

scales: Employees weigh items using a scale to confirm that what was ordered matches what is delivered.

scales: The part of a knife that creates the handle.

scimitar (SIM-ah-tahr): Also known as a butcher knife; a long, curved blade used for cutting through large cuts of raw meat.

scoop: This short-handled measuring utensil scoops out soft food, such as ice cream, butter, and sour cream. These portion scoops come in various sizes.

seasoning: Something that enhances the flavor of an item without changing the primary flavor of the dish.

serrated: When a knife blade is shaped into a row of teeth that can be set very closely or widely apart.

serrated slicer: A knife with a long, thin serrated blade used to slice breads and cakes.

shallow poaching: Cooks food using a combination of steam and a liquid bath. Shallow poaching is a last-minute cooking method best suited to food that is cut into portion-sized or smaller pieces.

sharpening stone: Used to grind and hone the edges of steel tools and implements.

sheet pan: Cooks use this very shallow pan, about 1-inch deep, for just about anything from baking cookies to roasting vegetables.

shelving: Used for food storage. Shelving in storage areas should be made of stainless steel.

shocking: Immediately placing blanched food in ice water to stop carryover cooking.

sieve (SIV)**:** A small tool with a mesh screen to sift flour and other dry baking ingredients and to remove any large impurities.

simmering: Completely submerging food in a liquid that is at a constant, moderate temperature.

single-side: When the cutting edge of a knife is on just one side.

skimmer: A small tool with a larger round, flat head with holes. Use it to remove foam from stock or soup and remove solid ingredients from liquids.

slicer: A knife used for slicing cooked meat; its blade can be as long as 14 inches.

slow-roasting oven: Use this oven to roast meat at low temperatures. This helps preserve the meat's moisture, reduce shrinkage, and brown its surfaces.

smallware: Small hand tools and small equipment.

smoker: Use a smoker for smoking and slow-cooking food items. A true smoker treats food with smoke and operates at either cool or hot temperatures. Smokers generally have racks or hooks, allowing food to smoke evenly.

smoking point: The temperature at which fats and oils begin to smoke, which means that the fat has begun to break down.

sous vide: A method in which food is cooked for a long time, sometimes well over 24 hours. *Sous vide* is French for "under vacuum." Rather than placing food in a slow cooker, the sous vide method involves cooks putting food in airtight plastic bags and then placing the bags in water that is hot but well below boiling point. This cooks the food using precisely controlled heating, at the temperature at which it should be served.

speed racks: Generally made of metal and have slots into which foodhandlers can slide sheet pans. This can create shelves of various heights, depending on need.

spices: The bark, roots, seeds, buds, or berries of an aromatic plant.

spine: The top of a knife blade, which is the noncutting edge of the blade.

spoons: Cooking spoons for quantity cooking are solid, perforated, or slotted. They are made of stainless steel, and hold about 3 ounces. Solid spoons are serving spoons without holes in them. Perforated and slotted spoons have holes that allow liquid to drain while holding the solid items on the spoon.

springform pans: A two-part, spring-loaded baking pan. The bottom piece and ring are secured with a spring to hold the bottom in place. Once an item is baked, the pastry chef can release the spring to make it easy to remove the cake from the pan.

stamped blade: The cutting surface of a knife made by cutting blade-shaped pieces from sheets of milled steel.

steak knife: A curved knife used for cutting beef steaks from the loin.

steamer: Used to steam food items like vegetables and grains. It uses low or high steam pressure. A steamer often consists of a set of stacked pots. The lower pot holds boiling water. The upper pot has a perforated bottom that allows the steam to enter through and cook the food in the pot above. All types of steamers cook food items quickly in very hot (212°F) water vapor.

steaming: Cooking food by surrounding it in steam in a confined space such as a steamer basket, steam cabinet, or combi-oven. Direct contact with the steam cooks the food.

steam-jacketed kettle: Available in free-standing and tabletop versions and in a very wide range of sizes. The kettle's bottom and sides have two layers, and steam circulates between the layers, heating liquid food like soups and stews quickly and evenly.

steel: A long metal rod that is lightly grooved and magnetized. It removes the microscopic burrs that are created as a knife is used.

stewing: Cooking technique similar to braising, but the prepreparation is a little different. First, cut the main food item into bite-sized pieces and either blanch or sear them. As with braising, cook the food in oil first and then add liquid. Stewing requires more liquid than braising. Cover the food completely while it is simmering.

stir-frying: A cooking method closely related to sautéing. Food is cooked over a very high heat, generally in a wok with a little fat, and stirred quickly.

stockpot: A large pot for preparing stocks. Stockpots with spigots allow the liquid to be poured out easily without losing any of the solid ingredients.

straight spatula: A flexible, round-tipped tool used for icing cakes, spreading fillings and glazes, leveling dry ingredients when measuring, and turning pancakes and other food items.

strainer: A tool made of mesh-like material or metal with holes in it. Strainers come in different sizes and are often shaped like a bowl. Strainers are used to strain pasta, vegetables, and other larger food cooked in liquid.

swimming method: To use this method, when deep-frying an item, gently drop a breaded or batter-coated food in hot oil. It will fall to the bottom of the fryer and then swim to the surface. Once the food items reach the surface, turn them over, if necessary, so they brown on both sides.

tamis (TA mee)/**drum sieve:** A screen that stretches across a metal or wood base that is shaped like a drum. Food is forced through it, and it's used to purée very soft food items and remove solids from purées.

tandoori oven: A cylindrical or barrel-shaped oven, often made of clay, with a wood or charcoal fire inside at the base and an open top. Food can be thrust inside the oven on long metal spikes (famously, chicken), or portions of thin dough can be slapped against the inside of the oven to develop characteristic bubbling and charring. These ovens easily reach 800°–900°F.

tang: The metal that continues from a knife blade through the handle. A full tang is as long as the whole knife handle.

tea maker: Works the same as the coffee maker, but it makes tea for iced tea.

thermocouple: An accurate thermometer that measures temperature in thick or thin food instantly.

tilting fry pan: Often called a fry pan or skillet; used to grill, steam, braise, sauté, and stew many different kinds of food. Most tilting fry pans have lids that allow the unit to function as a steamer.

tip: The forward part of a knife that includes the knife point. Cooks use the tip for detailed work such as paring, trimming, and peeling.

tongs: A scissor-like utensil foodhandlers use to pick up and handle all kinds of solid food.

tourné (tour-NAY): Similar to a paring knife, but with a curved blade for cutting the curved surfaces of vegetables.

utility carts: Carts of durable injection molded shelving or heavy steel used to carry food cases to storage areas.

utility knife: An all-purpose knife used for cutting fruits, vegetables, and some meat. Its blade ranges from 6 to 8 inches long.

vegan: A person who follows the strictest diet of all and will consume no dairy, eggs, meat, poultry, fish, or anything containing an animal product or byproduct, including honey. They consume only grains, legumes, vegetables, fruit, nuts, and seeds.

vegetable peeler: Not technically a knife, but this tool has sharp edges for peeling potatoes, carrots, and other vegetables.

vegetarian: A person who consumes no meat, fish, or poultry products.

volume measures: Similar to liquid measuring cups but bigger, usually available in sizes of 1 pint, 1 quart, $1/2$ gallon, and 1 gallon.

walk-in freezer: Often called a "walk-in;" built right into the foodservice facility itself.

walk-in refrigerator: Often called a "walk-in;" built right into the foodservice facility itself.

wing whip: A heavier version of the wire whip; used in a mixer to whip, cream, and mash heavier food items.

wire whip (whisk): Small tools of different sizes and heaviness used to mix, beat, and stir food.

wire whip: Used in a mixer to beat and add air to light food items, such as egg whites and cake frosting.

wok burner: A gas burner (or propane for home use) with multiple jets, designed to cradle a rounded wok pan in extremely intense heat. The high heat of a wok burner produces the "*wok hey*," which is a particularly savory charred flavor associated with the best wok-cooked dishes.

wok: A metal pan with a rounded bottom and curved sides. The curved sides make it easy to toss or stir food. Cooks use woks especially for frying and steaming in Asian cooking.

zester: A small tool used to shred small pieces of the outer peel of citrus fruits such as oranges, lemons, and limes.

Chapter 6

aromatics: Herbs, spices, and flavorings that create a savory aroma, such as bouquet garni and sachet d'epices.

au jus (oh ZHEW): Meat served with its own juice.

béchamel (BAY-shah-MELL): A grand sauce made from milk and white roux.

beurre manié (byurr man-YAY): A thickener made of equal parts flour and soft, whole butter.

bisque (BISK): A cream soup made from puréed shellfish shells, such as lobster, shrimp, or crab.

bouillon (BOO-yon): The liquid that results from simmering meat or vegetables; also referred to as broth.

bouquet garni (boo-KAY gahr-NEE): French for "bag of herbs;" a bundle of fresh herbs, such as thyme, parsley stems, and a bay leaf tied together.

brown or **espagnole sauce** (ess-spah-NYOL): A grand sauce made from brown stock and brown roux.

brown stock: An amber liquid produced by simmering poultry, beef, veal, or game bones, after these bones have been browned.

China cap: A pierced metal cone-shaped strainer; use it to strain soups, stocks, and other liquids to remove all solid ingredients.

chinois (chin-WAH): A very fine China cap made of metal mesh that strains out very small solid ingredients.

clarified: The liquid that remains after the removal of the raft when making consommé.

clear soups: Flavored stocks, broths, and consommés.

compound butter: A mixture of raw butter and various flavoring ingredients, such as herbs, nuts, citrus zest, shallots, ginger, and vegetables.

concassé (kawn-ka-SAY): A coarsely chopped mixture. Tomato *concassé* is created by adding tomatoes, garlic, and seasonings to vegetable stock to flavor or darken the stock, but tomatoes must be strained with a cheesecloth or filter so that no seeds or skins get into the stock.

coulis: A thick, puréed sauce, such as tomato coulis.

court bouillon (court boo-YON): An aromatic vegetable broth, used for poaching fish or vegetables.

degreasing: The process of removing fat that has cooled and hardened from the surface of stock.

demi-glace (deh-mee glahs): A rich brown sauce traditionally made by combining equal parts espagnole sauce and veal stock.

foodborne pathogens: Microorganisms on food that cause illness. These need time and moisture to grow, but they won't grow when the temperature of the food is colder than 41°F or hotter than 135°F.

fumet (foo-MAY): A highly flavored stock made with fish bones; fish stock is very similar to fumet.

glace (glahs): A reduced stock with a jelly-like consistency, made from brown stock, chicken stock, or fish stock; it is sometimes referred to as "glaze."

grand sauces: Five classical sauces that are the basis for most other sauces. These are sometimes called "mother sauces."

hollandaise (HALL-en-daze): A rich, emulsified grand sauce made from butter, egg yolks, lemon juice, and cayenne pepper.

jus: A rich, lightly reduced stock used as a sauce for roasted meat.

jus-lié (ZHEW-lee-AY): A sauce made from the juices of cooked meat and brown stock.

liaison (lee-AY-zohn): A mixture of egg yolks and heavy cream, often used to finish some sauces, such as Allemande sauce.

maître d'hôtel butter (MAY-tra doe-TEL): A softened butter that is flavored with lemon juice and chopped parsley. It is often used to garnish grilled meat or fish.

mirepoix: A French word that refers to the mixture of coarsely chopped onions, carrots, and celery. This mixture provides a flavor base for stock.

oignon brûlé: A "burnt onion." Cut an onion half across its hemisphere and then char the flat part either on a flattop or in a dry (fat-free) pan.

raft: When making consommé, the raft is the floating layer of egg whites, meat and vegetable solids, and fats.

remouillage (ray-moo-LAJ): A weak stock made from bones that have already been used in another preparation, sometimes used to replace water as the liquid used in a stock; *remouillage* is the French word for "rewetting."

roux (ROO): A thickener made of equal parts cooked flour and a fat, such as clarified butter, oil, or shortening.

sachet d'épices (sah-SHAY day-PEESE): Similar to bouquet garni, except it really is a bag of herbs and spices.

salsa: A cold mixture of fresh herbs, spices, fruits, and/or vegetables.

sauce: A liquid or semisolid product that is used in preparing other food items.

saucier: A cook who specializes in making sauces.

slurry: Cornstarch mixed with a cold liquid, which can be used instead of roux.

stock: A flavorful liquid made by gently simmering bones and/or vegetables.

temper: To slowly mix a little bit of hot sauce with eggs or cream to raise the temperature slowly and prevent the mixture from cooking or curdling.

thick soups: Cream and purée soups.

tomato sauce: A grand sauce made from a stock and tomatoes (roux is optional).

vegetable stock: Usually made from mirepoix, leeks, and turnips.

velouté (veh-loo-TAY): A grand sauce made from veal, chicken, or fish stock and a white or blond roux.

white stock: A clear, pale liquid made by simmering poultry, beef, or fish bones.

wringing method: An easy way to strain sauce. In this method, place a clean cheesecloth over a bowl and pour the sauce through the cheesecloth into the bowl. The cloth is then twisted at either end to squeeze out the strained sauce. The cheesecloth catches the unwanted lumps of roux, or herbs, spices, and other seasonings.

yield: The given amount of a dish that a recipe makes.

Chapter 7

communication: The process of sending and receiving information by talk, gestures, or writing for some type of response or action.

credibility: The ability of a person to be believed.

empathy: The act of identifying with the feelings, thoughts, or attitudes of another person.

feedback: Communication that helps a person understand how well he or she has done something and how to improve.

interpersonal communication: Any two-way communication that has immediate feedback.

listening: The ability to focus closely on what another person is saying to summarize the true meaning of a message.

mission statement: Primarily serves an internal function; it describes the company's purpose and key objectives to its team and owners.

organizational communication: The numerous messages and information that convey operational procedures, policies, and announcements to a wide variety of audiences.

842

vision statement: Directed both internally and externally; it defines the company's purpose and values to employees (so they know how they are expected to behave)

and customers (so they understand why they should work with or patronize the company).

Chapter 8

action plan: A strategy of steps to carry out so that a problem does not recur.

bias: A tendency toward a particular perspective or idea based on prejudice.

child labor laws: Offer additional protections for children and youth in the workplace.

complainant: The person with a complaint, usually in regards to harassment.

cover letters and résumés: Letters that show a person's interest in a job, accompanied by an outline of their experience and education.

cross-training: When employees learn the functions of another job within the operation.

cultural tendencies: A term to describe the fact that many groups of people have common beliefs, such as religion, or share common ways of acting that produce tendencies to act in certain ways based on their beliefs and habits.

discrimination: Making a decision based on a prejudice.

diversity: The great variety of people and their backgrounds, experiences, opinions, religions, ages, talents, and abilities.

empathy: The act of showing understanding and sensitivity to someone else about a situation.

employee manual: Contains general information about employment, including company policies, rules and procedures, employee benefits, and other topics related to the company.

employee performance appraisal: A formal evaluation of a person's work performance over a specific period of time.

Equal Employment Opportunity Commission (EEOC): Enforce laws that ensure everyone, regardless of race, age, gender, religion, national origin, color, or ability/disability, gets a fair chance at any job opening.

ethics: A set of moral values that a society holds. They are typically based on the principles of honesty, integrity, and respect for others.

exempt positions: Positions not covered under the Fair Labor Standards Act (FLSA); not legally entitled to overtime pay or the minimum wage established by the FLSA.

external motivation: When personal drive comes from the desire to receive something, such as a reward or recognition for achieving results.

goals: Statements of desired results.

harassment: When slurs or other verbal or physical conduct related to a person's race, gender, gender expression, color, ethnicity, religion, sexual orientation, or disability interfere with the person's work performance or create an unhealthy work environment.

harassment-free environment: A workplace in which complaints are handled appropriately and respect for all employees is supported on an ongoing basis.

internal motivation: The personal drive to do the best work possible whether there are rewards or not.

interpersonal skills: People skills; a person who possesses good interpersonal skills can generally relate to and work well with others.

job application: A standard form filled out by anyone who wants a job in an operation; the form helps managers to get the same types of information from every interested person.

job description: A document that defines the work involved in a particular assignment or position.

mission statement: Refines the vision statement by stating the purpose of the organization to employees and customers. It should include what the organization intends to sell or provide and to whom, and sometimes the geographic region as well.

modeling: Demonstrating the behavior expected from others.

motivation: The reasons why a person takes action or behaves in a certain way.

nonexempt positions: Positions covered by the Fair Labor Standards Act (FLSA); these employees must be paid for every hour of overtime.

objective: A specific description or statement of what a manager wants to achieve.

onboarding: The process that a company uses to integrate new employees into an organization.

on-the-job training (OJT): Appropriate for teaching skills that are easily demonstrated and practiced, such as preparing menu items, operating cash registers, and using tools and equipment.

organizational goals: Goals that focus on broad statements of what the organization as a whole wants to achieve.

orientation: The process that helps new employees learn about the procedures and policies of the operation and introduces them to their coworkers.

performance appraisal form: The most effective way a manager has to rate and evaluate employee performance.

personal treatment: The ways in which managers interact with staff and the value system that governs their daily conduct.

point-of-sale (POS) systems: These systems allow servers to enter orders and prompts for other order information.

positive cross-cultural interaction: Meaningful communication among employees from diverse cultures and backgrounds.

prejudice: A general attitude toward a person, group, or organization on the basis of judgments unrelated to abilities.

problem solving: An intentional process followed in a logical sequence. Following the sequence leads to a reasonable conclusion.

problem-solving model: Used to explore all of a problem's potential causes. Each step provides input to the next until the final phase, which calls for documenting the outcome of the process.

professional development: The sum of activities a person performs to meet goals and/or to further his or her career.

professionalism: The combination of the knowledge, skills, attitudes, and behavior a person shows while performing a job. It includes interactions with other employees, vendors, and guests.

root cause: The action or situation that initiates a problem.

screening interviews: Discussions that come before a job interview. They are intended to find out whether an applicant meets the basic requirements to be considered for the job.

stereotypes: Generalizations that individuals make about particular groups that assume that all members of that group are the same.

successive interviewing: A series of interviews used as part of the screening process for a job.

team: A group of individuals with different skill and experience levels who are working to complete a task or meet a goal.

teamwork: Working as a group and using each member's strengths, so that the group can attain a higher level of success than working alone.

training: The process of acquiring the knowledge, skills and competencies necessary for a specific position or assignment.

turnover: The number of people who leave a company during a given time period.

vision statement: Describes what an organization wants to become and why it exists. Vision statements aim high and are inspiring, stimulating, and exceptional.

workplace ethics: Guiding principles that effective leaders use in setting the professional tone and behavior in their operations.

zero tolerance policy: No violation is forgiven; the offender is disciplined accordingly. The discipline goes up to and includes termination.

Chapter 9

acids: Help fruit to retain its structure (for example, lemon juice).

alkalis: Cause the cells to break down more quickly, making fruit soft (for example, baking soda).

brassica: A vegetable in the cabbage family, which is strong enough to survive the winter and often found in spring salads.

caramelization: A browning process.

compote: A sauce made by simmering dried fruits, such as apricots, currants, and raisins.

coulis: A sauce made from a purée of vegetables or fruits that can be served hot or cold.

crudités: Sticks or pieces of raw vegetables, often seasonal, usually served with a dipping sauce.

dicing: Cutting a product into cubes with a chef's knife. Normally, dicing refers to about a half-inch cube—the same size as dice.

drupes: Fruits that have a central pit enclosing a single seed.

enzymatic (en-zi-MAT-ick) **browning:** A chemical process that occurs when the oxygen in the air comes in contact with the flesh of cut fruit.

ethylene (ETH-el-leen) **gas:** A gas emitted by certain fruits (including apples, bananas, melons, and avocados) that causes fruits to ripen. It also causes ripe fruits and vegetables to spoil.

field mixes: Tender greens that can be planted in the spring for harvest a few weeks later.

fructose (FROOK-tose): A natural form of sugar responsible for the sweetness of fruits.

fruit: An organ that develops from the ovary of a flowering plant and contains one or more seeds.

fungi (FUN-ghee): *A* large group of plants ranging from single-celled organisms to giant mushrooms.

glazing: A finishing technique that gives vegetables a glossy appearance by adding a small amount of honey, sugar, or maple syrup to the vegetable to coat it and give it a sheen as the vegetable reheats.

hydroponic (hi-dro-PON-ick) **farming:** Vegetables are grown indoors year-round, under regulated temperatures and light in nutrient-enriched water.

mesclun mix: A seed blend that includes a variety of leafy lettuce and other greens.

microplane: A small handheld tool used to zest the peel of citrus fruit.

mincing: A fine chop cut made by using a chef's knife or mezzaluna. This cut is commonly used on smaller food items, such as garlic, fresh herbs, and ginger.

parboiling: Like blanching, parboiling partially cooks vegetables in boiling water.

poaching: A cooking technique in which food is cooked in simmering liquid.

polyphenol oxidase (pol-lee-feen-nole OX-ee-days) **(PPO):** An enzyme in some fruit that causes enzymatic browning to occur more quickly.

puréed (PYOO-rayed): A technique in which food is cooked until it is tender enough to purée easily by pushing it through a sieve or food mill, or using a vertical chopping machine or blender.

quality grades: The U.S. Department of Agriculture (USDA)'s rating system based on quality standards. The better the quality, the higher the quality grade assigned to it. The quality is based on a combination of size, color, shape, texture, and defects.

root vegetables: Rich in sugars, starches, vitamins, and minerals, these plants exist both above and below ground. A single root extends into the ground and provides nutrients to the leafy green part of the vegetable that is above the ground.

seed: The process of removing seeds from fruit or vegetables.

sous vide: A method in which food is cooked for a long time, sometimes well over 24 hours. Rather than placing food in a slow cooker, the sous vide method uses airtight plastic bags placed in hot water well below boiling point. Food is cooked using precisely controlled heating, at the temperature at which it should be served.

summer fruits: Berries, cherries, grapes, melons, peaches, nectarines, plums, and pears.

tempura (tem-POO-rah)**:** Japanese-style breaded and deep-fried vegetables.

tropical fruits: Named for the climatic conditions under which they are grown. None of these fruits can tolerate frost. Tropical fruits include figs, dates, kiwis, mangos, bananas, papayas, pomegranates, guava, star fruit, and passion fruit.

tuber vegetables: Includes potatoes, sweet potatoes, and yams. Tubers are enlarged, bulbous roots capable of generating a new plant. Tubers are actually fat, underground stems.

vegetable: An edible herb-like plant.

winter fruits: Apples and citrus fruits, such as oranges, grapefruits, lemons, limes, and tangerines.

Chapter 10

American service: Food is arranged on plates in the kitchen by cooks and brought directly to the guests' table by the server. The meal is complete on one plate.

appearance: Includes dress, hygiene, and behavior. Employees make a good impression on guests by presenting themselves professionally.

apprentice: A server in training.

bouillon spoon: Use for clear soups or broths. The bouillon spoon has a rounded spoon head.

bread and butter plate: This is used for more than bread and butter. Use it as a base for jams and other condiments that may easily spill.

busers: Assist with the cleaning up and resetting of tables.

butter knife: Smaller than a dinner knife and used to butter bread or cut breakfast food, fruit, and other softer food items.

cake fork: Has only three tines and is used to eat cakes, tortes, pies, and pastries.

captain: Responsible for a server area of usually 15 to 25 guests and is assisted by the front waiter or an apprentice.

chargers: Service plates that don't directly touch the food.

china: Dinnerware.

coffee spoon: Smaller than a soup or sauce spoon; used not only with coffee, tea, and hot chocolate, but also for fruit cocktails and ice cream.

comment cards: Quick surveys that customers complete noting their satisfaction with the food and service.

competitive advantage: The thing that attracts a customer to one operation over another.

customer interaction: One of the best ways in which to make a strong first impression. An initial interaction can come in many different settings, and a good customer service plan accounts for them all.

dessert forks: Often have a broader tine and can cut like a knife through a soft cake or other pastry.

dinner fork: Used to eat main courses, vegetables, and pasta.

dinner knife: Used for all entrées and main courses.

dinner plate: 10 to 12 inches across; these plates are used for all kinds of main courses and meals and as a base plate for smaller plates and bowls.

drinking glasses: Includes mugs and cups; they come in many shapes and sizes; and often are made of clear glass, plastic, or a thicker, solid ceramic.

English service: Also known as family-style dining, English service is the simplest and least expensive. In English service, bowls and platters of food are placed on the table, and a seated host or hostess places the food onto plates.

espresso spoon, or **demitasse spoon:** Much smaller than a coffee spoon and matches small espresso cups.

family-style dining: Also known as English service, the simplest and least expensive. In English service, bowls and platters of food are placed on the table, and a seated host or hostess places the food onto plates.

finger bowl: A small bowl filled with water and often a citrus fruit slice (lemon or orange), to clean the fingers after eating, especially with messier meals such as shellfish or ribs.

first impressions: An impression made within the first few seconds of meeting someone; often the strongest impression we have of a person, place, or event.

fish fork: Used only for eating fish.

fish knife: Used only to filet and cut fish.

floor manager: Person in charge of the operation during a particular shift; supervises a team of servers.

focus groups: Consist of customers that meet as a group to talk with managers about possible improvements in service or other areas.

food runners: These staffers are sometimes employed to assist with bringing food from the kitchen to the tables.

French service: This style is typically considered the most elegant, but it is very expensive. Servers present the food to guests from a tableside cart.

front waiter: Typically, this waiter has only 1 to 2 years of experience and works with the captain.

grapefruit spoon: Has jagged edges for carving into the grapefruit.

gravy boat: Has a special lip or spout to prevent spilling when pouring the sauce onto the plate.

greeter: Provides the first impression in appearance, friendliness, and attentiveness. To do this, the greeter evaluates and determines the customer's specific needs for the current visit.

guéridon (gay-ree-DAHN): A tableside cart used in French service that holds food or liquid items that will be served to guests, as well as serving dishes and other utensils the servers and guests may need.

headwaiter: Responsible for service in a particular area, such as a banquet room or dining room.

hospitality: The feeling that guests take with them from their experience with the operation. It refers to the interaction between a guest and host—the service, care, and attention.

maître d'hotel (may-tra doe-TEL): Responsible for the overall management of service.

monkey dish: A shallow bowl, often used for relishes or dipping sauces.

mugs: Made from thick glass or ceramic; used to serve hot drinks like coffee, tea, and cocoa.

mystery shoppers: Hired by an operation to visit and report on their experiences and impressions of a particular foodservice operation.

quick-service: An easy and fast way to dine; typically, it involves no servers.

Instead, guests help themselves to food set up in food bars or order at a counter.

rechaud (ray-SHOW): A warming unit in the tableside cart used in French service.

Russian service: This style is the most formal service style. All food preparation is done in the kitchen. The bowls and platters of food are then brought on a cart to guests at the table.

salad fork: Smaller than the dinner fork and used for salads, appetizers, desserts, fruit, smoked fish, and other delicate food items.

salad plate: Much smaller than a dinner plate (7 or 8 inches across). Use it for desserts and appetizers as well as salads and as a base plate for gravy and sauce boats and sundae glasses that are served with a napkin or paper doily to prevent slipping.

sauce spoon: Use with dishes served with sauce on the side.

service: Work, behavior, and actions of restaurant and foodservice employees that impact the customers' experience in their establishment.

service station: The area in which an operation keeps additional items; napkins, silverware, cups and saucers, condiments, menus, and water glasses.

serving utensils: Servers use these tools when they serve food to guests.

shell cracker: Used to crack the hard and thick shells of lobsters and crabs.

snail fork and **lobster fork:** Small, thin forks used only to eat those shellfish. Small, round **oyster fork** is served with both oysters and clams.

snail plate: Has six or twelve indentions for holding snails.

snail tongs: A specialized utensil for holding a snail shell so the snail can be removed.

soup bowl: Small and deep bowl with no flat edge, and unlike the soup plate, used only for soup. Soup bowls or cups are sometimes equipped with lids (individual tureen) or a single handle for easier service.

soup plate: Flat around the edge with a dip in the center to hold soup, pastas, and even mussels, shrimp, and clams.

soup spoon: Large spoon with an oval spoon head used for cream soups and long strands of pasta.

steak knife: A table knife with a sharp, usually serrated blade, suitable for cutting beef.

suggestive selling: Involves recommending additional or different items to a guest. It is one of the keys to the success of any retail business.

sundae or **iced tea spoon:** Has an especially long handle to dip into a deep sundae or stir large glasses of tea.

surveys: Similar to comment cards, but sometimes include more open-ended questions.

traditional service: This style reflects four main influences: American, French, English, and Russian. Each service style varies depending on the menu, theme, and décor.

tureen: A large covered bowl used to serve soup for up to eight people.

underliner plate or **charger:** A large decorative plate used underneath the plate on which food is served.

Chapter 11

al dente (ahl DAN-tay)**:** A state of doneness when pasta feels firm to the bite.

arborio (ahr-BORE-ee-oh)**:** Medium-grain rice often used in risotto.

bran: A great source of fiber and B vitamins; the tough layer surrounding the endosperm of whole grains.

colander (CAH-len-der)**:** A colander is used to drain liquid from cooked pasta and vegetables. Colanders stand on metal feet, while strainers are usually handheld.

dumplings: Small, round balls of dough often cooked in liquid; sometimes dumplings are filled with ground meat or vegetables.

en casserole: A cooking technique in which the ingredients are cooked and served in the same dish.

endosperm: The largest part of a grain and a major source of protein and carbohydrate.

gnocchi (nee-YO-key)**:** Small potato dumplings served in Italian cuisine.

grains: Grasses that grow edible seeds.

hull: The protective coating, or husk, that surrounds a whole grain.

latkes (LAHT-keys)**:** Potato pancakes.

legumes (LEG-yooms)**:** Seeds from pod-producing plants.

milling process: When the germ, bran, and hull of the grain are removed or polished.

multiple-stage technique: A cooking technique in which food is prepared using more than one cooking method before it becomes a finished dish.

pierogi (pyeh-RRAW-ghee): A Polish dumpling.

pilaf (PEEL-ahf): A technique for cooking grains in which the food preparer sautés the grain briefly in oil or butter and then simmers it in stock or water with various seasonings.

resting stage: When mixing pasta dough, this is the most important stage. If the dough is not sufficiently relaxed, it will be difficult to roll the dough into thin sheets.

risotto (rih-ZO-to): A labor-intensive Italian rice specialty made by stirring hot stock into a mixture of rice that has been sautéed in butter.

sieve (SIV): A small tool with a mesh screen to sift flour and other dry baking ingredients and to remove any large impurities.

single-stage technique: A cooking technique in which food goes directly from the raw state to the finished state by using one cooking method.

solanine (SOLE-ah-neen): A harmful, bitter-tasting substance that appears as a greenish color on potatoes that are exposed to light.

spaetzle (SPAYT-z-el): Small German dumplings, or breadlike dumplings, that are tasty in stews.

stone ground: The process in which grains are ground and broken down; the grains retain more of their nutrients because the germ, bran, and hull are left intact.

tubers: Fat, underground stems capable of growing a new plant.

whole grains: Grains that have not been milled.

Chapter 12

back of the house: Employees who work outside the public space. Back-of-the-house positions include chefs, line cooks, pastry chefs, dishwashers, bookkeepers, storeroom clerks, purchasers, dietitians, and menu planners.

career: A profession or work in a particular field, such as foodservice, that individuals choose for themselves.

career ladder: A series of jobs through which people can advance to further their careers.

certification: Indicates that a student has demonstrated a high level of skill and has met specific performance requirements by participating in a rigorous process to become certified.

closed questions: Can be answered with a simple yes or no or with a brief, factual statement.

college or **trade school applications:** These documents require education information; they may also require that applicants state the program or course of study they are applying for and ask them to complete a short essay.

concierge: Employed by hotels, motels, and resorts, the concierge serves guests by helping them buy tickets to shows and events, answering questions, booking restaurant reservations, and more.

cover letter: A brief letter in which an applicant introduces herself or himself to an employer.

etiquette (EH-tah-kit)**:** Good manners.

financial aid: Monetary help for students that includes grants, educational loans, and work study.

Free Application for Federal Student Aid (FAFSA): An application used by the federal government to determine the total amount of financial aid for which an applicant qualifies.

job application: A standard form filled out by anyone who wants a job in an operation; the form helps managers to get the same types of information from every interested person.

mentor: Someone who can play the role of a wise adviser.

networking: Connecting with several people to build relationships that may result in career advancement, industry updates, and knowledge or career enhancements.

open-ended questions: These questions encourage job applicants to talk about themselves, making them feel more comfortable and giving the interviewer important information and valuable insight about the applicant.

portfolio: A collection of samples that showcase interests, talents, contributions, and studies.

references: Unrelated people who know an applicant well and can provide information about that applicant.

résumé (RE-zoo-may)**:** A written summary of experience, skills, and achievements that relate to the job being sought.

scholarship: A grant or financial aid award to a student for the purpose of attending college.

stress: The condition or feeling that demands exceed the resources available for use.

stress management: A process people use to identify what causes stress for them in the workplace as well as in their personal lives, and then to apply various strategies to minimize the effects of that stress.

time management: Using tools to increase a person's efficiency and productivity. To manage time effectively also means to know how to waste less time on noncritical, unimportant activities and avoidable problems.

work study: Working as a student for the school to offset educational costs.

Index

856

870

Photo Credits

All photographs and images in this product are presented for educational purposes only and should not be considered actual materials or settings.

3M Touch Systems
635, 667

Vincent Cannon/**Abshier House**
14, 16-20, 23, 143, 164, 177, 236-240, 274, 303-304, 320, 354, 356-357, 437, 451, 485, 490, 493, 501, 506-507, 514, 526, 529, 531, 622, 629, 631, 633, 650, 700, 735, 741, 745

Doug Scott/**AGE Fotostock America, Inc.**
117, 148

American Automobile Association
60

Bibliotheque des Arts Decoratifs, Paris, France/**The Bridgeman Art Library**
24

Museo Correr, Venice, Italy/**The Bridgeman Art Library**
18

Cambro Manufacturing
121, 125

© Chris Gregerson/**cgstock.com**
42

Mark Richards/**Contact Press Images Inc.**
27, 33

David Graham/**CORBIS**
37, 66-67

Historical Picture Archive/**CORBIS**
20

Crowne Plaza Christchurch Hotel
47

© **Culinary Institute of America**
286, 322, 373, 375-376, 389, 393, 395, 397, 399-400, 402, 589, 600

© JULIE EGGERS/**DanitaDelimont.com**
59

© **Dorling Kindersley**
257, 277, 323, 334, 371, 380, 567, 588, 593, 596, 682, 719

Peter Anderson © **Dorling Kindersley**
305, 317

Martin Brigdale © **Dorling Kindersley**
407

Martin Cameron © **Dorling Kindersley**
286

Demetrio Carrasco © **Dorling Kindersley**
52, 56

Andy Crawford © **Dorling Kindersley**
284, 685

Philip Dowell © **Dorling Kindersley**
366-367

Stephen Hayward © **Dorling Kindersley**
660

Will Heap © **Dorling Kindersley**
286

John Heseltine © **Dorling Kindersley**
708-709, 724

Jeff Kauck © **Dorling Kindersley**
599

Dave King © **Dorling Kindersley**
21, 32, 304, 558, 565-566, 590, 596

David Murray © **Dorling Kindersley**
305, 563

David Murray and Jules Selmes © **Dorling Kindersley**
257, 297, 304-305, 314-315, 318, 385, 391, 559, 566, 587-588, 600-601, 684, 688, 698, 727

Ian O'Leary © **Dorling Kindersley**
559, 593, 601

Gary Ombler © **Dorling Kindersley**
194-195, 209, 277, 289, 567, 589

Roger Phillips © **Dorling Kindersley**
285-286, 576

William Reavell © **Dorling Kindersley**
706

Tim Ridley © **Dorling Kindersley**
251

Howard Shooter © **Dorling Kindersley**
286

Simon Smith © **Dorling Kindersley**
257, 261

Philip Wilkins © **Dorling Kindersley**
595, 606

Jerry Young © **Dorling Kindersley**
253, 305, 387, 396, 563, 587, 719

Kristen Brochmann/**Fundamental Photographs, NYC**
250

Getty Images, Inc. – Digital Vision
576

Colorblind Images/**Getty Images, Inc.**
737

Jon Feingersh/**Getty Images, Inc. – Blend Images**
410-411, 425

Hulton Archive/**Getty Images, Inc.**
24

DAVID LEAHY/**Getty Images, Inc. – Taxi**
438, 442

Rita Maas/Image Bank/**Getty Images, Inc.**
598

Ryan McVay/**Getty Images, Inc.**
170, 464, 477, 522

Skip Nall/**Getty Images, Inc. – Photodisc/Royalty Free**
662, 669, 730-731

Photodisc/**Getty Images, Inc.**
479, 535, 655-656

ALAN POWDRILL/**Getty Images, Inc. – Taxi**
170, 173

Rene Sheret/**Getty Images, Inc. – Stone Allstock**
219, 232

Robert Harbison
225

Hobart Corporation
289, 291, 294

International Apple Institute
551

istockphoto.com
44, 103, 175, 202, 207, 286, 719

Grant LeDuc
37

Library of Congress
22

Photograph by Byron, Byron Collection, **Museum of the City of New York**
23

Ron Sherman/Creative Eye/**MIRA.com**
686

Justin Guariglia/**National Geographic Image Collection**
230

Owned or licensed by the **National Restaurant Association**
Cover, 4, 38, 62, 73, 75, 79-80, 82-83, 85-86, 88, 96-100, 105-113, 114, 118, 120, 124, 128, 130, 133-134, 140-141, 143, 146-147, 149, 154, 180, 185, 197, 214, 217, 219, 270, 272, 284, 304, 338, 368, 412, 414, 430, 450, 456-457, 462, 470, 481, 485, 488, 493, 498-499, 505, 536-538, 544, 616, 639, 651, 653, 658, 663-664, 676, 705, 732, 791, 803

Mancuso, Michael/**Omni-Photo Communications, Inc.**
40, 51

OSHA – Occupational Health and Safety Administration
159

Pearson Education/PH College
281

Brady/**Pearson Education/PH College**
195, 227, 233

Richard Embery/**Pearson Education/PH College**
80, 178, 198, 252, 254, 257, 284, 304, 312, 316, 322, 324, 328-330, 332-333, 336, 343, 359, 362-363, 370, 374, 377, 381, 383, 386, 388, 408, 586-587, 589-590, 597-598, 607-608, 611-612, 679, 683, 687, 691, 706-708, 710, 717, 725, 728

Michael Heron/**Pearson Education/PH College**
191-192

Vincent P. Walter/**Pearson Education/PH College**
139, 166, 227, 284, 585

Catherine Ursillo/**Photo Researchers, Inc.**
583

Myrleen Ferguson Cate/**PhotoEdit, Inc.**
46, 619

Mary Kate Denny/**PhotoEdit, Inc.**
47

Amy Etra/**PhotoEdit, Inc.**
89

Tony Freeman/**PhotoEdit, Inc.**
9, 244, 264-265, 340

Spencer Grant/**PhotoEdit, Inc.**
445, 454

Jeff Greenberg/**PhotoEdit, Inc.**
654, 668

Michael Newman/**PhotoEdit, Inc.**
43, 416, 423, 453

Rudi Von Briel/**PhotoEdit, Inc.**
39

David Young-Wolff/**PhotoEdit, Inc.**
324, 643

Dennis Kunkel/**Phototake NYC**
81, 93

Penny Haufe/**Prentice Hall School Division**
662

Russ Lappa/**Prentice Hall School Division**
252

David A. J. Ripley
250

Shutterstock.com
2-3, 10, 19, 54-58, 64-65, 70-71, 79-80, 83, 87, 92, 102, 116, 152-153, 162, 166, 169, 172, 176, 189, 200, 203, 206, 208, 212-213, 222, 229, 252, 257, 262-263, 268-269, 274, 277-281, 289, 293-294, 300, 305, 308-311, 314, 325-326, 330, 332, 337, 340, 344, 355-356, 360-361, 384, 386, 392, 398, 403-404, 409, 422, 446, 450-451, 455, 460-461, 476, 480, 503, 508, 521, 534, 542-543, 548-553, 560-563, 566-567, 569-570, 572-574, 576-582, 594, 604-605, 613-615, 620-622, 626-627, 631, 642, 650, 655-657, 659-660, 664-665, 674-675, 679-680, 683, 685, 690, 705, 715-716, 721-724, 729, 748-749, 759-760, 762-763, 775-776, 788-789, 799-802

Accademia Gallery, Venice/Canali PhotoBank, Milan/
SuperStock
15

Traulsen & Co., Inc.
273

David J. Kamm/**U.S. Army**
45

U.S. Department of Agriculture Center for Nutrition Policy and Promotion
351, 354

U.S. Department of Health and Human Services
348

U.S. Department of Labor
160, 168

U.S. Department of State
639

U.S. Equal Employment Opportunity Commission
470-471

U.S. Travel Association; Domestic Travel Market Report, 2007 Research Report
54

Vulcan
291-294, 297, 301

White Castle Management Company
25

Wolf Appliance, Inc.
292

Jeff Zaruba/**Zaruba Photography**
428, 441

874